Antique Trader®

Antiques&
Collectibles

PRICE GUIDE 2005

20th Anniversary Edition

Edited by
Kyle Husfloen

Published by

An imprint of F+W Publications, Inc.

700 East State Street • Iola, WI 54990-0001
715-445-2214 • 888-457-2873

Our toll-free number to place an order or obtain
a free catalog is (800) 258-0929.

Library of Congress Catalog Number: 2004093883
ISBN: 0-87349-818-6

Designed by Wendy Wendt
Edited by Kyle Husfloen

Printed in United States

On the Front Cover
Rhodium brooch with clear rhinestones, glass
beads, and enameling, $245.
Golf ball Spanish red goblet, $50
Roseville Tourmaline blue two-handled bulbous
vase, $110-140

On the Back Cover
Ships cobalt blue cocktail shaker, $35
Oyster and Pearls ruby sandwich plate, $50

AT Price Guide celebrates 20th anniversary in color

This new edition of the *Antique Trader Antiques & Collectibles Price Guide 2005* marks a major anniversary. It was exactly **20** years ago that the first edition of our annual price guide arrived on the market. As if that was not reason enough to celebrate, we are also very excited to publish this new edition with all the illustrations in **full color!** In recent years we have been including in each annual price guide a special 16-page color supplement, but we have now moved to make it even more exciting and informative by adding color throughout.

It was back in 1970 that the first price guide was published by Antique Trader in the form of a quarterly magazine. This format continued to be used until the early 1990s, when it was decided to concentrate on producing this large annual edition. So it is that for 35 years Antique Trader has been at the forefront of tracking and recording collecting trends and reporting on them in our many guides.

Over the decades our staff has taken special pride in covering the widest possibly variety of collecting interests and compiling detailed price listings and illustrations that accurately reflect the world of collecting. The range of collectibles has truly exploded since 1970, so we not only work to cover all the well-established fields, but also to make sure that we add new categories as they become part of the established marketplace. Unlike some price guides, we strive to educate the reader by providing detailed listings rather than vague one-line descriptions. In most of our categories you will find such background information on pieces as their material, construction, color, pattern, maker, date of production and size. Many categories also begin with a brief introduction and, especially in the **Ceramics** and **Glass** listings, we also provide a sketch of the mark or markings that may appear on those pieces.

Dionne Quints by Madame Alexander, $850

Hand-painted Royal Worcester Plate,
$225-$275

To aid us in our efforts to provide the most accurate and up-to-date information possible we consult numerous auction and other sale results as well as working closely with many experts who you'll find listed in our "Special Contributors" section. Reviewing, editing and entering all this material in our database is demanding, but it is the best way to provide you with accurate information. As a reader consulting this, or any, price guide, however, you must keep in mind that this book should only be used *as a guide!* In the vast world of collecting there are many factors that can influence the value of a particular piece, the most important being condition and market demand. Something *rare* or *one-of-a-kind may*, therefore, not be particularly valuable if it has no great market appeal. Also, local markets vary widely around this country and the world, so it is important to also keep this in mind when buying or selling. The values we list herein most often reflect a *general retail replacement value*, in the

broadest sense. The factors mentioned above or described in our listings must be kept in mind when comparing something we list with something you may own or wish to buy.

Presented in this 2005 edition are nearly **14,000** entries highlighted by more than **5,000 color pictures.** You should find a great deal of valuable information, no matter what your collecting specialty may be as a collector, dealer, researcher or appraiser. As in our past annual guides we present our categories in alphabetical order. However, for the very large specialty fields of Ceramics, Glass and Furniture, we have the categories gathered under these headings. Then, within each section, their categories are listed alphabetically by name. As mentioned earlier, we also work to always add some new categories each year and there are several great ones included for

Decorative Moravian Box Mill, $250

2005. These include: Hawaiiana; Horse Collectibles; Matchcovers & Match Boxes; Pinball Games; Pocket Knives; View-Master and Tru-Vue Viewers & Reels; and, last but not least, Wedding Memorabilia. The experts who provided us with these listings are due a special note of thanks.

To make using this price guide as easy as possible you will also find a detailed, cross-referenced **Index** at the close of the price listings. In addition, in many cases, an additional cross-reference to other categories is included with the introduction to a category. This is all part of our effort to provide you with the most comprehensive and accurate price reference on the market. However, although our descriptions, prices and illustrations have been double-checked to ensure accuracy, neither the editors, publisher nor contributors can assume responsibility for any losses that might be incurred as a result of consulting this guide, or of typographical or other errors.

Because this reference could not be prepared without the assistance and input from many sources, we wish to express our gratitude to all the photographers, dealers, auction houses, galleries and private collectors who aided us. In addition to our "Special Contributors," we also wish to acknowledge the following for other photographs, artwork, data or permission to photograph in their shops or utilize material from their sales:

Of course, we are tremendously grateful for the support of our readership and thank everyone who uses the *Antique Trader Antiques & Collectibles Price Guide.* May our audience continue to grow for the next 20 years! Meantime, our staff will continue to work diligently to make this book an invaluable part of your reference library. If in perusing this edition you have questions about material included, feel free to write and we'll make every effort to respond personally. Happy hunting!

Kyle Husfloen, Editor

Mickey Mouse Jazz Drummer, $1,200

SPECIAL CONTRIBUTORS
Index by subject

Hull: Joan Hull
Ironstone: Bev Dieringer
Limoges: Debbie DuBay
Majolica: Michael Strawser
Mettlach: Gary Kirsner
Minton: Michael Strawser
Noritake: Tim Trapani
Old Ivory: Alma Hillman
Quimper: Sandra Bondhus
Royal Bayreuth: Mary McCaslin
Royal Copley: Tim Holthaus
R.S. Prussia: Mary McCaslin
Russel Wright Designs: Kathryn Wiese
Torquay Pottery: Judy Wucherer
Uhl Pottery: Lloyd Martin
Vernon Kilns: Pam Green
Warwick: John Rader, Sr.
Zeisel (Eva) Designs: Pat Moore
Zsolnay: Federico Santi

GLASS
Agata: Louis O. St. Aubin Jr.
Amberina: Louis O. St. Aubin Jr.
Animals: Helen and Bob Jones
Burmese: Louis O. St. Aubin Jr.
Cambridge: Helen and Bob Jones
Carnival Glass: Bruce Dooley
Central Glass Works:
Helen and Bob Jones

Crown Milano: Louis O. St. Aubin Jr.
Custard Glass: Dr. James Measell
Cut Glass: House of Brilliant Glass
Depression Glass:
Debbie and Randy Coe
Duncan & Miller: Helen and Bob Jones
Fenton: Helen and Bob Jones
Fostoria: Helen and Bob Jones
Fry: Helen and Bob Jones
Heisey: Helen and Bob Jones
Imperial: Helen and Bob Jones
McKee: Helen and Bob Jones
Milk Glass: Frank Chiarenza
Morgantown: Helen and Bob Jones
Mt. Washington: Louis O. St. Aubin Jr.
New Martinsville: Helen and Bob Jones
Paden City: Helen and Bob Jones
Pairpoint: Louis O. St. Aubin Jr.
Pattern Glass: Randall McKee; Nancy
Smith, Lamplight & Old Glass
Peach Blow: Louis O. St. Aubin Jr.
Rose Bowls: Johanna Billings
Royal Flemish: Louis O. St. Aubin Jr.
Wall Pockets: Bobbie Zucker Bryson
Wave Crest: Louis O. St. Aubin Jr.
Westmoreland: Helen and Bob Jones

Contributor directory

Ellen Bercovici
5118 Hampden Lane
Bathesda, MD 20814
(301) 652-1140
eb625@verizon.net

Johanna Billings
P.O. Box 244
Danielsville, PA 18038-0244

Sandra Bondhus
P.O. Box 100
Unionville, CT 06085
nbondhus@pol.net

James R. and Carol S. Boshears
375 W. Pecos Rd., #1033
Chandler, AZ 85225-7405
(480) 899-9757

Brown Auction Services
27 Fickett Rd.
Pownal, ME 04069
(800) 248-8114
ceb@FineToolJ.com

Bobbie Zucker Bryson
1 St. Eleanoras Lane
Tuckahoe, NY 10707
(914) 779-1405
Napkindoll@aol.com

Dana Cain
5061 S. Stuart Ct.
Littleton, CO 80123
dana.cain@att.net

Charles W. Casad
801 Tyler Ct.
Monticello, IL 61856-2246

8

Frank Chiarenza
The Frank Chiarenza Museum of Glass
39 W. Main St.
Meriden, CT 06451-4110
(203) 639-9778
chiarenzaglassmuseum@snet.net

The Clocksmith
806 El Camino Real
San Carlos, CA 94070
www.theclocksmith.com

Debbie and Randy Coe
1240 S.E. 40th Ave.
Hillsboro, OR 97123
coeran@aol.com

Les and Irene Cohen
P.O. Box 17001
Pittsburgh, PA 15235
am4ah@yahoo.com

Amphora Collectors International
10159 Nancy Dr.
Meadville, PA 16335
(814) 333-3125
www.amphoracollectors.org

Marion Cohen
14 Croyden Ct.
Albertson, NY 11507
(516) 294-0055

Kerra Davis
925 Bud St.
Blackshear, GA 31516
kbb@gate.net

Bev Dieringer
P.O. Box 536
Redding Ridge, CT 06876
dieringer1@aol.com

Del E. Domke
16142 N.E. 15th St.
Bellevue, WA 98008-2711
(425) 643-3359
delyicious@aol.com

Bruce Dooley
2571 7th Ave.
Sweetwater, NJ 08037

Debbie DuBay
Limoges Antiques Shop
20 Post Office Ave.
Andover, MA 01810
(978) 470-8773

James Elliot-Bishop
500 S. Farrell Dr., S-114
Palm Springs, CA 92264
gmcb@ix.netcom.com

Joe Fex
5061 S. Stuart St.
Littleton, CO 80123
joefex@att.net

Joan M. George
67 Stevens Ave.
Oldbridge, NJ 08856
drjgeorge@nac.net

Roselyn Gerson
12 Alnwick Rd.
Malverne, NY 11565
(516) 593-8746
compactldy@aol.com

Michael J. Goldberg
823 S.E. 25th Ave.
Portland, OR 97214
(503) 238-1977
emjaygee@inetarena.com

Cheryl Goyda
Box 137
Hopeland, PA 17533
Mzczech@aol.com

Pam Green
You Must Remember This
P.O. Box 822
Hollis, NH 03049
ymrt@aol.com
www.ymrt.com

Jeannie Greenfield
310 Parker Rd.
Stoneboro, PA 16153
(724) 376-2584
dlg3684@yahoo.com

Carl Heck
Box 8416
Aspen, CO 81612
(970) 925-8011
www.carlheck.com

Alma Hillman
362 E. Main St.
Searsport, ME 04974
oldivory@acadia.net

Tim Holthaus
CAS Collectors Association
P.O. Box 46
Madison, WI 53701-0046

House of Brilliant Glass
www.brilliantglass.com

Joan Hull
1376 Nevada S.W.
Huron, SD 57350

Hull Pottery Association
11023 Tunnel Hill N.E.
New Lexington, OH 43764

Michael Ivankovich
 Antiques & Auction Co.
P.O. Box 1536
Doylestown, PA 18901
(215) 345-6094
www.wnutting.com

Helen and Bob Jones
Berkeley Springs, WV
BGlances@aol.com

Dorothy Kamm
P.O. Box 7460
Port St. Lucie, FL 34985-7460
(772) 465-4008
dorothykamm@adelphia.let

Marty Kennedy
4711 S.W. Brentwood Rd.
Topeka, KS 66606
(785) 554-5837 or 273-4981

Gary Kirsner
Glentiques, Ltd.
1940 Augusta Terrace
P.O. Box 8807
Coral Springs, FL 33071
gkirsner@myacc.net

Vivian Kromer
11 800 Shanklin St.
Bakersfield, CA 93312
(661) 588-7768

Elyce Litts
P.O. Box 394
Morris Plains, NJ 07950
(908) 964-5055
happymemories@worldnet.att.net

Lloyd Martin
1582 Gregory Lane
Jasper, IN 47546
lmartin@psci.net

Mary McCaslin
6887 Black Oak Ct. E.
Avon, IN 46123
(317) 272-7776
maryjack@indy.rr.com

Randall McKee
(262) 657-6958

Dr. James Measell
c/o Fenton Art Glass Co.
700 Elizabeth St.
Williamstown, WV 26187
(304) 375-6122
www.fentonartglass.com

Carole Meeker
5702 Vacation Blvd.
Somerset, CA 95684

David G. Miller
1971 Blue Fox Dr.
Lansdale, PA 19446-5505
(610) 584-6127

Florence Ceramics Collectors Society
FlorenceCeramics@aol.com

Pat Moore
695 Monterey Blvd., Apt. 203
San Francisco, CA 94124
ezcclub@pacbell.net

Mark Moran
5887 Meadow Dr. S.E.
Rochester, MN 55904
(507) 288-8006

Reg G. Morris
7360 Martingale
Chesterland, OH 44026
min@modex.com

Rhona Nabi
The Silver Lady Antiques
P.O. Box 27
Foxboro, MA 02035
(781) 784-9184
silant@aol.com

John Rader, Sr.
Vice President, National Assn. of
Warwick China & Pottery Collectors
(Betty June Wymer, 28 Bachmann Dr.,
Wheeling, WV 26003, 304-232-3031);
editor, "The IOGA" Club Quarterly
Newsletter; author, *Warwick China*
(Schiffer Publishing, 2000)
780 S. Village Dr., Apt. 203
St. Petersburg, FL 33716
(727) 570-9906

Jim and Jamie Saloff
P.O. Box 339
Edinboro, PA 16412
tim.saloff@verizon.net

Louis St. Aubin Jr.
Brookside Antiques
New Bedford, MA
Brooksideartglass@aol.com

Federico Santi
The Drawing Room Antiques
152 Spring St.
Newport, RI 02840
(401) 841-5060
www.drawrm.com

R.O. Schmitt Fine Arts
P.O. Box 1941
Salem, NH 03079
(603) 893-5915

Peggy Sebek
3255 Glencairn Rd.
Shaker Heights, OH 44122
pegsebek@earthlink.net

Jeff Siptak
4013 Russellwood Dr.
Nashville, TN 37204

Nancy Smith
Lamplight and Old Glass
P.O. Box 6192
Grand Rapids, MI 49506

Paul Smith
P.O. Box 487
Harlan, IA 51537

Steve Stone
12795 W. Alameda Pkwy.
Lakewood, CO 80225
Sylvanlvr@aol.com

Michael G. Strawser Auctions
P.O. Box 332
Wolcottville, IN 46795
(260) 854-2859
www.majolicaauctions.com

Phillip Sullivan
P.O. Box 69
South Orleans, MA 0266
(508) 255-8495

Tim Trapani
7543 Northport Dr.
Boynton Beach, FL 33437

Jim Trautman
R.R. 1
Orton, Ontario, Canada L0N 7N0
trautman@sentex.net

Nora Travis
13337 E. South St.
Cerritos, CA 90701
(714) 521-9283
Travishrs@aol.com

Elaine Westover
210 Knox Hwy. 5
Abingdon, IL 61410-9332

Mike White
P.O. Box 483
Fraser, CO 80442
(970) 726-0448
mwhite483@rkymtnhi.com
http://grinder.rkymtnhi.com

Kathryn Wiese
Retrospective Modern Design
P.O. Box 1138
Kamuela, HI 97643
retrodesign@earthlink.net

Dannie Woodard
1310 S. Bowie Dr.
Weatherford, TX 76080
al1310@aol.com

Judy Wucherer
Transitions of Wales, Ltd.
P.O. Box 1441
Brookfield, WI 53045

North American Torquay Society
214 N. Ronda Rd.
McHenry, IL 60050
(815) 385-2040

Table of Contents

George III-Style Armchair,
$1,965

Rare Baker's Orange Grove
Bitters Bottle, $2,464

16" Honey-colored
Steiff Bear, $3,565

ABC PLATES
Ceramic

These children's plates were popular in the late 19th and early 20th centuries. An alphabet border was incorporated with nursery rhymes, maxims, scenes or figures in an apparent attempt to "spoon feed" a bit of knowledge at mealtime. An important reference book in this field is A Collector's Guide to ABC Plates, Mugs and Things *by Mildred L. and Joseph P. Chalala (Pridemark Press, Lancaster, Pennsylvania, 1980)*

Girl with Alphabet Book ABC Plate

ABCs, 4 3/4" d., purple transfer of small girl reading alphabet book to dog in doghouse, letters "N," "S" & "Z" reversed (ILLUS.) **$200**

"Baked Taters All Hot" ABC Plate

"Baked Taters All Hot," 7 1/8" d., blue transfer of man & woman dressed for the cold selling potatoes at a stove on the street (ILLUS.) **175**

"Base Ball Running to First Base," 6 1/4" d., from "American Sports" series, illustration of field w/several boys playing baseball, crazing, small rim flake **600**

"Canotiers - Boatmen" ABC Plate

"Canotiers - Boatmen," 6 3/4" d., blue transfer w/slight color added of two young boys dressed as sailors w/a large oar (ILLUS.) **175**

Children at Lunch ABC Plate

Children at lunch, 8 3/8" d., sepia transfer w/colors added of two children sitting at table, two more children carrying food to the table (ILLUS.) **175**

"Commander A.H. Foote" ABC Plate

"Commander A.H. Foote," 5 1/8" d., black transfer portrait, no mark (ILLUS.) **350**

"Contemplation" ABC Plate

"Contemplation," 6 5/16" d., from the "Flowers that Never Fade" series, transfer w/color added, "Lord, what is life? - Tis like a flow'r. That blossoms & is gone! We see it flourish for an hour. With all its beauty on" & related illustration of young girls looking at a flower (ILLUS.) **250**

ABC Plate from "Conundrum" Series

Conundrum, 6 1/8" d., from "Conundrum" series, "What fruit does our sketch represent?" under illustration of two figures sitting at table piled high, both waving spoons, one rubbing his stomach (ILLUS.).. **250**

ABC Plate, "The Lord's Prayer" series

"Give Us This Day Our Daily Bread," 6 1/4" d., from "The Lord's Prayer" series, blue transfer picture of old man w/a cane receiving food from children (ILLUS.).. **225**

"The Gleaners" ABC Plate

"Gleaners (The)," 5 5/8" d., illustration of woman w/bundle on her head walking across bridge w/two children (ILLUS.) **175**

"The Graces" ABC Plate

"Graces (The)," 7 1/4" d., black transfer of three girls in period dress embracing, red luster rim (ILLUS.) **300**

"Highland Dance" ABC Plate

"Highland Dance," 5 1/2" d., black transfer w/color added of several people dancing (ILLUS., previous page).................... **175**

"The Irish Jig" ABC Plate

Irish Jig (The)," 6 1/4" d., pink transfer of a girl dancing, "The Irish Jig" printed at top (ILLUS.) **200**

Kite ABC Plate

Kite, 5 1/8" d., black transfer w/colors added of three boys holding a large yellow kite (ILLUS.)... **220**

"The Nurse" ABC Plate

"Nurse (The)" 5 1/2" d., black transfer of nicely dressed woman sitting on the front lawn of a large house, two children hugging her, two black lines outlining edge of plate (ILLUS.).. **350**

Piano ABC Plate

Piano, 5 7/8" d., black transfer w/color added of girl in blue dress on tiptoes at a piano w/"The pretty child on tiptoe stands - to reach the piano with her hands" underneath, Elsmore & Forster (ILLUS.) **200**

"Playing at Lovers" ABC Plate

"Playing at Lovers," 5 1/2" d., black transfer w/colors added of a boy & a girl dressed as adults (ILLUS.) **175**

Riddle ABC Plate

Riddle, 6 1/16" d., blue transfer w/riddle "I ever live man's unrelenting foe - mighty in mischief though I'm small in size - And he at last that seems to lay me low - My food and habitation both supplies" and answer ("Worm") printed around center illustration of two girls playing a game w/hoops & sticks (ILLUS., previous page) **250**

"Rupert and Spot," multicolor image of young boy on hands & knees being watched over by a big dog in center, letters in black around image, Roman numerals up to XII & decorative border around letters **250**

Sign Language ABC Plate with Owls

Sign language, 6 1/2" d., center w/illustration of schoolmaster owl at desk, little owls in attendance, circled by illustrations of hand signs & letters, red line around rim (ILLUS.)... **300**

Woman Riding Spotted Horse Plate

Woman riding, 5 3/16" d., center illustration of woman balancing large basket on her head & riding on spotted horse (ILLUS.) **175**

ADVERTISING ITEMS

Thousands of objects made in various materials, some intended as gifts with purchases, others used for display or given away for publicity, are now being collected. Also see various other categories and Antique Trader Advertising Price Guide.

Ad for Auto-Lite Spark Plugs

Advertisement, "Auto-Lite Spark Plugs," promotion tied in to Rita Hayworth movie "You'll Never Get Rich," color photo of Hayworth in grass skirt, a spark plug in the foreground, stylized illustration of Art Deco-style movie theater in background w/marquee showing name of movie, a row of movie goers at bottom, text reads "Theatres! Look at this sensational Auto-Lite Tip-up - featuring Rita Hayworth - It's Free - It's Colorful - It's Box Office - It's One of Many Valuable Auto-Lite Tie-ins" & "Auto-Lite Dealers Offer You 100% Cooperation!" at bottom, 1941 (ILLUS.).......... **$100**

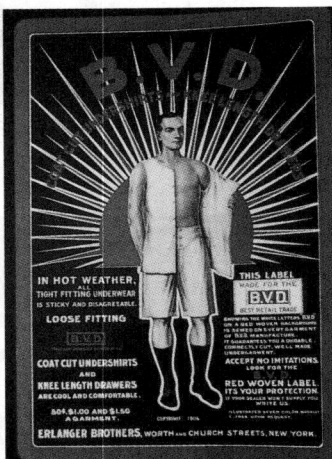

Ad for B.V.D.

Advertisement, "B.V.D.," rectangular, black w/red border & red & white sunburst taking up top half of ad in background, black & white illustration of semidressed man w/"B.V.D. - Coat Cut Undershirts and Knee Length Drawers" arched above him in red letters, other product information in white or red on either side of figure filling bottom half, 1910 (ILLUS.) 10

Advertisement, "Cream of Wheat," little boy & girl looking at grandfather clock, a smiling black waiter in background bringing tray holding bowls of cream of wheat, rectangular panel in lower right reading "Children everywhere 'watch the clock' for time to eat - Cream of Wheat - because they love it so," framed, copyright 1906, 11 x 15" 176

Ashtray, "Standard Plumbing Fixtures," porcelain, rectangular, ivory color, figural Boston bull terrier at one end, other end reading "Standard Plumbing Fixtures" on rim, 4 x 5 x 6".................................. 66

Backbar Whiskey Bottle

Backbar bottle, "Old Prentice Whisky," clear cylindrical waisted form w/a cylindrical neck, enameled in white w/the brand name, ground pontil, late 19th c., 11" h. (ILLUS.) 209

Buster Brown Helium Balloon Inflator

Balloon inflator, "Buster Brown Shoes," figural winking Buster Brown in-store display that fits over standard helium tank, one-piece molded fiberglass head w/in-

flation valve that sits atop gas cylinder & two-piece vinyl cape & sheath that slides over cylinder, sheet metal base, 24 x 24" head (ILLUS.).................................. 230

Baseball bat, "Peter's Shoes," ash, branded w/"Peter's Shoes Diamond Brand" & "Peter's Weatherbird Shoes For Boys," 33" l.................................. 144

Bean crock, "Heinz," cov., ceramic, electric variety, panel on front reads "Heinz - Oven - Baked - Beans".................................. 116

Capewell Horse Nail Calendar

Calendar, 1901, "The Capewell Horse Nail," illustration of winter scene w/two horse-drawn sleighs racing, the name dripping w/images of icicles, full pad for 1901, Gray Litho, New York, 10 x 13 1/2" (ILLUS.).................................. 546

Calendar, 1923, salesman's sample, rectangular, w/color illustration titled "The Trail Blazer" by Phillip R. Goodwin of cowboy on white horse riding past pine tree w/mountains in background, "Dealer's name here" below illustration, calendar pad for 1923 at bottom, 10 x 16 1/2" 198

1928 Calendar for Western Ammunition

Calendar, 1928, "Western Ammunition," rectangular, illustration titled "Snow Geese" by Lynn Bogue Hunt of group of geese flying in modified V formation toward sun sitting low on horizon, above "Western - World's Champion Ammunition," one calendar page for September 1928 below, w/top band (ILLUS., previous page) **523**

Maxfield Parrish 1924 Calendar Illustration for Edison Mazda

Calendar illustration, 1924, "Edison Mazda," Maxfield Parrish illustration titled "The Venetian Lamplighter," for large size 1924 Edison Mazda calendar, 15 3/4 x 25" (ILLUS. framed) **1,208**

Clock, "Abbott's Ice Cream," round white clock face w/red dots for the hours, black hands, in black scroll frame that also holds pale blue rectangular panel w/red-bordered white oval reading "Abbott's Ice Cream" in red over blue illustration of bonneted woman in long dress, grey marquee w/"Fountain Service" in white at top, 22 1/2 x 26" **264**

Clapperton's Thread Advertising Clock

Clock, "Clapperton's Thread," figure-8 style, wood w/papier-mâché bezels, Roman numerals, the upper bezel reading "Clapperton's Six Cord Spool Cotton," the lower bezel reading "Is the Best," w/pendulum & key, 18 1/2" w., 31" h. (ILLUS.) **1,035**

Clock, "Makomb Chicken," black metal square case w/white face, black Arabic numerals & hands, the center w/"Makomb" in red over red image of chicken head, Middlebury Electric Co., Macomb, Ill. **94**

Jake's Place Promotional Coin Purse

Coin purse, "Jake's Place," leather w/metal frame, one side of frame embossed w/clover leaves, horseshoe & head of a woman w/flowing hair, the other w/celluloid advertising panel reading "Compliments of Jake's Place - Wines, Liquors and Cigars - Volga, S.D.," 3 x 3" (ILLUS.)...... **121**

Cookbook, "Sleepy Eye Flour," in the shape of a loaf of bread, cover titled "Sleepy Eye Milling Co. Cookbook" & illustrated w/color bust of Sleepy Eye Chief **99**

Whiskey Counter Display

Counter display, "Black & White Scotch Whiskey," plastic, figural black Scottie & white Westie dogs sitting on black base w/edge reading "Scotch - 'Black & White' - Whiskey" in white, 1950s, 3 x 8", 10 1/2" l. (ILLUS.) **66**

Counter Display Advertising Items

Counter display, "Carborundum Sharpening Stone," rectangular holder supporting the double-sided well-used stone, holder in red w/black & white lettering reading "Step up and Sharpen Your Pocket Knife on the Genuine Carborundum Sharpening Stone," early 20th c. (ILLUS. top left with Lufkin Rules cabinet) **85**

Chalkware Figural Goose

Counter display, "Red Goose Shoes," chalkware figural goose painted red w/"Red Goose Shoes" in yellow on breast, yellow bill & feet, on green base, 11 1/2" h. (ILLUS.).. **144**

Comfy Slippers Counter Display

Counter display, "Comfy Slippers," 24" d. charger set within elaborate die-cut tin easel probably meant to hold five samples of Comfy slippers, the charger w/illustration of toddler gazing up at the Comfy logo of a sheep-drawn blue shoe, "Comfy Slippers - For Men, Women and Children" printed at bottom, 30" w., 32" h. (ILLUS.)... **1,639**

Red Goose Shoes Neon Countertop Display

![Stanley Counter Display photograph]

Stanley Counter Display

Counter display, "Red Goose Shoes," die-cut porcelain neon sign, figural goose, red w/yellow bill & feet, black base, reads "Red Goose Shoes" in white, ca. 1930s, 6 x 12", 24" h. (ILLUS., bottom previous page) **3,738**

Counter display, "Stanley Legend Power-lock," wood & composition, an upright open-front display cabinet on the right w/16 pigeonholes, a colorful half-figure of a workman on the left, reglued, 28" l., 19" h. (ILLUS., top of page) **55**

![Counter Display for Winchester Arms illustration]

Counter Display for Winchester Arms

Counter display, "Winchester Firearms," cardboard cutout gun rack, colorful dual

rack for .22 rifles or shotguns, top shows two men holding guns on either side of circular advertising area that can display one of three rounded attachments, one a Christmas wreath w/"Give a 22" inside, one w/image of a crow in the center w/"Get him with a new Winchester 22" around rim & across bottom, & one w/image of gopher in center w/"Get him with a new Winchester 22" around rim & across bottom, red & white striped gun rack w/gold oval panels reading "Winchester" in red, 1950s, 12 x 18", 20" h. (ILLUS.) **633**

Counter display, "Winchester Tools," cardboard, rectangular, easel-back type, black w/"Winchester - Tools" in orange/red above "Best Workmanship" in blue, 4 1/2 x 10" **275**

Wrigley's Chewing Gum Counter Display

Counter display, "Wrigley's Chewing Gum," tin w/gilt paint, half-cylinder base reading "Be sure its [sic] Wrigley's" around side, the die-cut marquee featuring Wrigley arrow figure w/smiling face

pointing to panel reading "WRIGLEY'S,"
6 x 13", 13" h. (ILLUS.) **2,875**
Counter display cabinet, "Lufkin Spring
Joint Rules," a long rectangular oak cabinet w/glass front over interior slots for
eight rules, back acts as storage for sale
stock, full decals, early 20th c. (ILLUS.
bottom left with Carborundum Sharpen-
ing Stone display, top, page 19) **240**

Planters Peanut Display/Container

Counter display/container, "Planters Peanuts," papier-mâché two-piece peanut,
embossed w/"Planters" in script, the end
coming off for filling w/one pound of pea-
nuts, 5 x 6", 12" l. (ILLUS.) **44**
Display bin, "McLaughlin Coffee," red metal
case w/three glass windows in front, for
storage & display of bulk coffee beans,
red marquee reading "McLaughlin - Kept-
fresh - Coffee Service," 25 x 38" **154**

Shoe Blacking Display Box

Display box, "Mason's Challenge Shoe
Blacking," wood, rectangular, inside of lid
w/color illustration of black boy & white
boy w/oversized black & red boots, the
front panel of box reading "3 doz. - No. 2
- Mason's - Challenge - Blacking,"
9 x 12", 3" h. (ILLUS.) **110**
Display cabinet, "Diamond Dyes," oak
case w/tin litho front panel illustration of
jester in king's court, two rear-hinged
doors opening on multiple dye storage
compartments, made by Wells Richard-
son & Co., ca. 1890, 10 x 20 3/4", 27" h. **863**

Dr. Daniels Veterinary Medicines Cabinet

Display cabinet, "Dr. Daniels Veterinary
Medicines," oak case w/lithographed embossed tin panel in door w/illustration of
Dr. Daniels & some of his products &
reading "Dr. Daniels Warranted Veterinary Medicines - Home Treatment for
Horses and Cattle - Dr. Daniels Famous
Dog   Remedies,"   7 1/2 x 21 1/2",
28 1/2" h. (ILLUS.) **2,588**
Door pull, "P & G Bread," brass, embossed
vertically "Ask For P & G Bread," made
by Erickson of Des Moines, Iowa, ca.
1930s, 3 x 18 1/2" **198**

Clicquot Club Door Push

Door push, "Clicquot Club," tin litho, gold
vertical panel w/black embossed figure
dressed like Eskimo & holding oversized
beverage bottle, "Clicquot Club" at top,
"Beverages" at bottom, 3 x 9" (ILLUS.) **105**

Door push, "Ridgways Coffee," metal, rect-angular, "Ridgways Coffee" printed verti-cally in red on gold ground, company logo in upper right corner, 3 1/4 x 9" **44**

Armour's Pork & Beans Fold-out Fan

Hand fan, "Armour's Pork & Beans," paper, fold-out fan decorated w/color illustra-tions of 19 whimsical caricatures, the handle reading "Armour's Pork and Beans - with or without Tomato Sauce," 12" l. w/handle, 8 1/2" d. open (ILLUS. of fan & handle) **44**

Kiss-Me Gum Folding Fan

Hand fan, "Kiss-Me Gum Co.," paper litho, fold-out fan reads "Chew 'Kiss-Me' Gum - Kiss-Me Gum Co." when open,   15" l. w/handle, 9 1/2" d. open (ILLUS.).................... **66**

Promotional Hand Mirror

Hand mirror, "Norton Mercantile Co.," cellu-loid frame w/brass handle, sepia image of little girl w/long brown hair holding flower tinted pink, banner below image reads "Norton Mercantile Co. - Norton, Kan.," 2 x 5 1/4" (ILLUS.) **209**

Dobbs Fifth Avenue Hats Hatbox

Hatbox, "Dobbs Fifth Avenue Hats," card-board, miniature size, given to customers for gift-giving as one would give a gift cer-tificate, the recipient returning it to the store to redeem for the right size hat, sides illustrated w/color scene of fancy horse-drawn carriage being driven through a snowy city street, the lid w/name of company around rim & stencil on top reading "Dobbs Fifth Avenue Hats New York" & "For" followed by space for names of recipient & gift giver, 1935 (ILLUS.)... **75**

Heinz's Raspberry Jelly Crock

Jelly crock, "Heinz's Raspberry Jelly," cov., stoneware, cylindrical, w/colorful label featuring illustration of various fruits & banners reading "Heinz's Raspberry Jelly" & "Standard Quality," lid w/wire closure, 5 1/2" d., 9" h. (ILLUS., previous page).. **288**

Jug, "I.W. Harper Whiskey," miniature size, stoneware, dark glazed top half w/ring handle, white bottom half reading "Compliments - I.W. Harper - Nelson Co. - Kentucky," 3 1/2" h. **154**

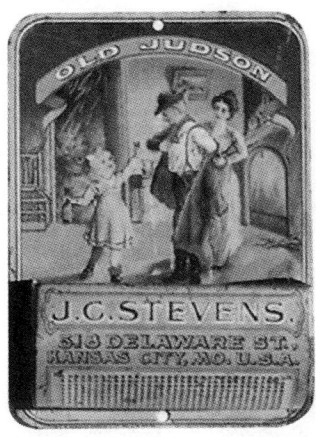

Old Judson Whiskey Match Holder/Striker

Match holder/striker, "Old Judson Whiskey," tin litho w/color illustration of cozy setting w/woman helping man off w/his coat as little girl reaches up toward him, under banner reading "Old Judson" & over pocket for holding matches that reads "J.C. Stevens - 518 Delaware St. - Kansas City, Mo. U.S.A.," w/area for striking immediately below, by Foster & Reed of Kansas City, 3 1/2 x 5" (ILLUS.) **176**

DeLaval Cream Separator Match & Toothpick Holder

Match & toothpick holder, "DeLaval Cream Separators," tin litho, form of a cream separator, panel at bottom reads "The DeLaval Separator Co." w/list of cities where it operated, in original cardboard box, box is 4 x 6 1/2", 1 1/4" h. (ILLUS. w/box) **550**

Mirror, "Stanley Tools," oval, reverse painting on glass, "This Mark Our Guarantee. Stanley Tools" in the notched logo w/a circle at the center, gold mirror around center logo, believed to be countertop advertising device, ca. 1925, 6" x 7" **750**

Rare Early Movie House Slide

Movie house slide, color-printed glass, a rectangular matted slide w/color logo & various tools & reading "Yes! We have a full line of household necessaries - and Stanley Four-Square Household Tools - C.C. Bruscke & Son," early 20th c. (ILLUS.)... **700**

Promotional Paperweight

Paperweight, "Magnesia Sectional Covering," glass w/milk glass bottom, circular, illustration of product appears beneath "Magnesia Sectional Covering" & above "Macan, Pechin & Co. - Agents - 7 S. Delaware Ave. - Philadelphia Pa.," 3" d., 3/4" h. (ILLUS.)... **66**

Victor Spring Beds Promotional Paperweight

Paperweight, "Victor Spring Beds," glass, rectangular w/rounded corners, milk glass bottom, reading "Victor Spring Beds - Noiseless, Will never sag. - Guaranteed for Five Years - McElroy-Shannon Spring Bed Mfg. Co. - Louisville - Philadelphia," made by Kyle Advertising Co. of Louisville, 2 1/2 x 4", 1" h. (ILLUS.).. **77**

"Selby B.B. Split Shot" Pin

Pinback button, "Selby," celluloid over tin, round, "SELBY" in center, "B.B." curved above & "Split Shot" curved below, litho by American Artworks, 1 1/2" d. (ILLUS.)....... **66**

"Bradshaw's Fancy" Pinback Button

Pinback button, "Sportsman's League," celluloid, round, gold-colored edge reading "Sportsman's League" in black, the center w/illustration of fishing lure in orange & grey & reading "Bradshaw's Fancy - Wet Fly for Trout," 1 1/4" d. (ILLUS.)....... **77**

Sportsman's League "Johnson" Pinback Button

Pinback button, "Sportsman's League," celluloid, round, gold-colored edge reading "Sportsman's League" in black, the center w/illustration of fishing lure in orange & grey & reading "Johnson - Wet Fly for Trout," 1 1/2" d. (ILLUS.)...................... **88**

Sportsman's League Pinback Button

Pinback button, "Sportsman's League," celluloid, round, gold-colored edge reading "Sportsman's League" in black, the center w/illustration of two men in canoe, 1 1/4" d. (ILLUS.).................................... **99**

Federal Hi-Power Shells Wall Plaque

Plaque, "Federal Hi-Power Shells," tin litho, wall hanging display, black arched-top rectangular backdrop w/embossed color image of oversized shell casing in orange & gold illustrated w/lion & reading "Federal Hi-Power Shells - For Sale Here," an open box of shells in the foreground, w/original mailing box, 11 1/2 x 28" (ILLUS., previous page) **473**

Promotional Pocket Mirror

Pocket mirror, "Hotel Raymond," celluloid back w/litho image of long-haired woman in center & "Good For 10¢ in Trade" around edge on one side, other side reading "Meet your friends - at the - Hotel Raymond" & listing proprietor & location, made by Kruver of Chicago, 2 1/4" d. (ILLUS.)... **264**

Point of sale sign, "The Simonds Saw," color-printed tin, rectangular, a large silver circular saw blade surrounding the head of a workman carrying an ax, brown wood grain background w/red & white wording, early 20th c., minor wear, 13 x 17" (ILLUS. right with Lufkin Rules display cabinet, top, page 19) **140**

Nipper Give-away from RCA

Plush toy, "RCA," figure of Nipper, the RCA mascot, white dog w/black ears, black collar w/"RCA" in red, give-away w/purchase of RCA product, 1990 (ILLUS.)................ **5**

Postcards, "DuPont Ammunition," each w/color illustration of hunting dog that won annual DuPont National Field Trial Championship, the backs w/written information on winner, w/identification card & original mailing cover, complete set of 13 from 1896 to 1910, 3 1/4 x 5 1/4", the set **925**

Howard Raspberry Preserves Crock

Preserves crock, "Howard Raspberry Preserves," stoneware, cylindrical, small wire ring handles at sides, w/colorful label featuring illustration of various fruits & banners reading "Howard Brand Raspberry Preserves," 4 1/2" d., 5" h. (ILLUS.)...... **288**

Carmen Complexion Powder Pocket Mirror

Pocket mirror, "Carmen Complexion Powder," celluloid, round, "Carmen Complexion Powder" fills top half, above oval w/color image of smiling woman w/flowing curls wearing red costume, the rim reading "Stafford Miller Co. - St. Louis, Mo.," all against a backdrop of deep red stage curtains, 1 3/4" d. (ILLUS.).................. **110**

Puzzle, "Aunt Jemima Pancake Flour," cardboard die-cut premium, color bust of black woman caricature wearing turban-style bandanna, reading "Use Aunt Jemima Pancake Flour," two rectangular blocks suspended from image w/twine, for R.T. Davis Mill Co., St. Joseph, Mo., ca. 1910-15, 3 x 5"..................................... 127

Sack & string holder, "Lion Coffee," original green paint, front w/floral decoration & "Lion - is the - King of - Coffees" **1,100**

Sample card, "Martin's Kingfisher Casting Line," rectangular cardboard w/information printed alongside short samples of fishing lines attached along left side, 1920s, 3 3/4 x 9" 55

Shinola Shoe Polish Shoe Horn

Shoe horn, "Shinola Shoe Polish," tin litho, black ground decorated w/graphics of shoe shining equipment & diagonal yellow panel reading "Shinola" in red at top & "The Wonderful Shoe Polish" in yellow at bottom, w/hanging hole, made by Chas W. Shonk Co. of Chicago, 1 3/4 x 6 3/4" (ILLUS.) 121

Stickpin, "Savage Arms Co.," brass stamped w/enamel work, image of Indian chief in profile, embossed features & feathers in headdress, orange enamel decorating headdress, above triangle section impressed w/"Savage Arms Co.," 1/2 x 2" 209

Store bin, "A & P Coffee," wood, six-sided, slant lid, red paint w/bands of Greek key design, black oval on front reads "A & P," for storing bulk coffee beans 358

Store display, "Blaul's Pancake Flour," cardboard, stand-up type, rectangular panel w/color illustration of plate of stacked pancakes & syrup dispenser on pink ground under caption "Blaul's Pancake Flour," the image of a bag of "Blaul's Pancake Flour Compound" seeming to rest against the panel 50

Store display, collar display, oak, rectangular frame w/space to display about 7 collars in each of three rows **1,210**

Store display, "Hanes - Merrichild Sleeper," composition, figural, sleepy little boy in sleeper outfit standing w/puppy at his feet, on 18" d. composition base reading "Hanes - Merrichild Sleeper," 21 1/2" h. 288

Store display, "Jell-O," cardboard, three-panel die-cut display, Maxfield Parrish illustration of royal court valet presenting molded gelatin dessert to king & queen, above illustration a banner reading "Jell-O" & below illustration a box reading "The King and Queen Might Eat Thereof and Noblemen Besides," ca. 1921, 9 1/2 x 41 1/2" (ILLUS., below)............................... **10,638**

Maxfield Parrish Jell-O Store Display

Store display, "Old Doc Brox Horehound Drops," cardboard, barrel shape, "Old Doc Brox - Candy - Horehound Drops - Double Strength" in script on front of barrel, holds 25 lbs., ca. 1936 .... **44**

Store mannequin, "Korrect-Way Display Forms," hollow-bodied type w/cast iron shoes, labeled "Korrect-Way Display Forms," 44" h. (missing broken portion of one shoe) **575**

La Touraine Coffee String Holder

String holder, "La Touraine Coffee," tin painted black, two identical sides, pouch decorated w/image of Arab, yellow text reading "La Touraine - The Perfect Coffee, Fresh Roasted, Ground to Order," mounts for spools, made by W.S. Quinby Co., Boston and Chicago, 20" w. x 17" h. (ILLUS.) **719**

Die-cut Tin Red Goose Shoes String Holder

String holder, "Red Goose Shoes," die-cut tin goose reading "Red Goose Shoes" on both sides, wire string holder hanging below display, 18" w., 26" h. (ILLUS.)............. **2,530**

Cast-iron Red Goose Shoes String Holder

String holder, "Red Goose Shoes," two-piece cast-iron figural goose painted red w/"Red Goose Shoes" embossed on wing, grey ovoid base, 15" l. (ILLUS.)........ **1,725**

B.S.A. Firearm Safetipaste Trade Card

Trade card, "B.S.A. Firearm Safetipaste," die-cut fold-out card shaped like two labeled tubes of the product, each reading "B.S.A. Firearm Safetipaste" above logo, "The No Trouble Firearm Barrel Preserver" & company information below, 2 x 5 1/4" (ILLUS.).. **44**

AUDUBON PRINTS

John James Audubon, American ornithologist and artist, is considered the finest nature artist in history. In about 1820 he conceived the idea of having a full color book published portraying every known species of American bird in its natural habitat. He spent years in the wilderness capturing their beauty in vivid color only to have great difficulty finding a publisher. In 1826 he visited England, received immediate acclaim, and selected Robert Havell as his engraver. "Birds of America," when completed, consisted of four volumes of 435 individual plates, double-elephant folio size, a combination of aquatint, etch-

ing and line engraving. W.H. Lizars of Edinburgh engraved the first ten plates of this four-volume series. These were later retouched by Havell, who produced the complete set between 1827 and early 1839. In the 1840s, another definitive work, "Viviparous Quadrupeds of North America," containing 150 plates, was published in America. Prices for Audubon's original double-elephant folio size prints are very high and beyond the means of the average collector. Subsequent editions of "Birds of America," especially the chromolithographs done by Julius Bien in New York (1859-60) and the smaller octavo (7 x 10 1/2") edition of prints done by J.T. Bowen of Philadelphia in the 1840s, are those that are most frequently offered for sale.

Anyone interested in Audubon prints needs to be aware that many photographically produced copies of the prints have been issued during this century for use on calendars or as decorative accessories, so it is best to check with a print expert before spending a large sum on an Audubon purported to be from an early edition.

Blue Yellow Back Warbler - Plate XV, hand-colored etching, engraving & aquatint by Robert Havell, Jr., London, 1827-38, 19 13/16 x 25 3/4" (slight creasing, few pale fox marks, minor soiling)............ **$1,175**
Great American Hen & Young - Plate VI, hand-colored etching & aquatint by W.H. Lizars, repaired tear, light & mat stain, scattered foxing, numerous short margin tears, 26 3/8 x 39 3/4" **32,900**

Grey Rabbit Audubon Print

Grey Rabbit - Plate XXII - hand-colored lithograph from "The Vivaparous Quadrupeds of North America," by Bowen of Philadelphia, 1845-48, matted & framed, 22 x 28" (ILLUS.) **978**
Purple Grackle - Plate VII, hand-colored, engraving & aquatint by Robert Havell, Jr., London, 1827-38, 25 5/8 x 38 5/8" (central horizontal fold, several soft creases, minor soiling, several small margin tears) **2,820**
Song Sparrow - Plate 25, hand-colored etching, engraving & aquatint by Robert Havell, Jr., London, 1827-38, 20 x 25 3/4" (scattered pale soiling, soft margin crease) **2,233**
Towee Bunting - Plate 29, hand-colored etching, engraving & aquatint by Robert Havell, Jr., London, 1827-38, 26 1/4 x 39"

(tiny abrasion on right of "No. 6," minor soiling in margins, repaired tear to lower sheet, other minor tears) **3,055**

BANKS

Original early mechanical and cast-iron still banks are in great demand with collectors. Their scarcity has caused numerous reproductions of both types and the novice collector is urged to exercise caution. The early mechanical banks are especially scarce and some versions are seldom offered for sale but, rather, are traded with fellow collectors attempting to upgrade an existing collection. Numbers after the bank name in mechanical banks refer to those in John Meyer's Handbook of Old Mechanical Banks. However, another book Penny Lane—A History of Antique Mechanical Toy Banks, by Al Davidson, provides updated information and the number from this new volume is indicated in parenthesis at the end of each mechanical bank listing.

In past years, our standard reference for cast-iron still banks was Hubert B. Whiting's book Old Iron Still Banks, but because this work is out of print and a well illustrated book, The Penny Lane Bank Book—Collecting Still Banks by Andy and Susan Moore pictures and describes numerous additional banks, we will use the Moore numbers as a reference after the name of each listing. Other newer books on still banks include Iron Safe Banks by Bob and Shirley Peirce (SBCCA publication), The Bank Book by Bill Norman (N), Coin Banks by Banthrico by James Redwine (R), and Monumental Miniatures by Madua & Weingarten (MM). We will indicate the Whiting or other book reference number, with the abbreviation noted above, in parenthesis at the end.

The still banks listed are old and in good original condition with good paint and no repair unless otherwise noted. An asterisk (*) indicates this bank has been reproduced at some time.

Mechanical

Nodding Head Alms Box Mechanical Bank

Alms Box, painted papier-maché & wood, black boy praying, slide drawer in rear of base w/lock, stamped "Germany" on bottom, ca. 1920s, minor damage at shoulder, 3 1/2 x 5 1/2", 8 1/2" h. (ILLUS.)... **$420**

"Always Did 'Spise a Mule" Bank Variation

(I) Always Did 'Spise a Mule - 4 - boy on bench facing mule, red version, rarer white plus white version known, by J. E. Stevens Co., coin trap missing, 10" w., PL 250 (ILLUS.) **800-1,000**

"Always Did 'Spise a Mule" Bank

(I) Always Did 'Spise a Mule - 5 - black jockey riding mule, PL 251 (ILLUS.) **700-1,200**

Bad Accident - 9 - man riding in cart pulled by donkey w/boy hiding behind cattail plant, J. & E. Stevens, multicolored, overpaint on driver, cart & boy, PL 20 (ILLUS., top of column)....................... **1,500-2,000**

Bad Accident Mechanical Bank

Boy Robbing Nest Mechanical Bank

Boy Robbing Bird's Nest - 20 - a.k.a. Tree Bank, multicolored, J. & E. Stevens, ca. 1906, PL 51 (ILLUS.) **9,488**

Boy Scout Camp - 21 - tent w/boy, tree w/owl & two other figures, multicolored, repair to base, PL 52 (ILLUS., below)........ **5,175**

Boy Scout Camp Mechanical Bank

Bulldog Mechanical Bank

Bull Dog Bank - 63 - seated, coin on nose, brown & red, rare white variant known, J. & E. Stevens, 1880, old paint restoration, PL 64 (ILLUS.) **1,668**

Butting Goat Mechanical Bank

Butting Goat - 116 - cast iron, when coin is placed in tray & mechanism activated, billy goat slides forward to ram coin into gold-painted tree stump, 4 3/4", PL 91 (ILLUS.) **360**

Man in Lean-to Mechanical Bank

Cabin - 33 - cabin w/man standing in doorway, red & black w/yellow walls, pivoting man kicks coin through roof, J. & E. Stevens, PL 93 (ILLUS.)............................... **2,415**

Chief Big Moon Mechanical Bank

Chief Big Moon - 42 - Indian seated in front of teepee holding fish w/flipping frog and pond, J. & E. Stevens, 1899, PL 108 (ILLUS.).. **2,185**

Darktown Battery Mechanical Bank

Darktown Battery - 56 - three black baseball figures - pitcher, catcher, & batter, multicolored, known in rarer white player version, J. & E. Stevens, ca. 1888, probable repaint of pitcher, 9 3/4", PL 146 (ILLUS.).. **1,265**

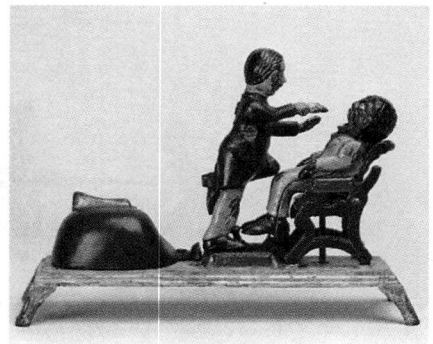

Dentist & Patient Mechanical Bank

Dentist - 57 - dentist extracting tooth from seated patient, some restoration, PL 152 (ILLUS.) **4,658**

Dinah Mechanical Bank

Dinah - 58 - bust of black woman, places coin in mouth, "Dinah" cast on back, short-sleeved yellow dress, overpaint to dress, PL153 (ILLUS.) .... **500+**

Eagle Nest Mechanical Bank

Eagle & Eaglets - 75 - bending mother eagle & rising young, w/bellows that simulate birds chirping, grey, white & yellow, green grass version known, J. & E. Stevens, ca. 1883, PL 165 (ILLUS.) **2,300**

Elephant with Howdah Bank

Elephant Howdah - "Pull Tail" - 80 - white body w/red & blue howdah, Hubley Mfg. Coo., 1930s, PL 174 (ILLUS.) **201**

Butting Goat, Old Man & Frog Bank

Goat, Frog & Old Man (Initiating 2nd Degree) - 114 - bearded old man on goat facing frog, similar action to Initiating, 1st Degree bank, black, yellow & green paint, Mechanical Novelty Works, 1880s, large areas of overpaint, PL 220 (ILLUS.) **805**

Hall's Liliput Bank

Hall's Excelsior - 118 - cast iron & wood, considered the first cast-iron mechanical bank, string-pull mechanism, building w/pop-up monkey in roof, paper "Cashier" label, multicolored, J. & E. Stevens, ca. 1869, PL 228 (ILLUS.) **316**

Hall's Liliput Bank

Hall's Liliput Bank (with Tray) - 146 - pivoting cashier & white domed building, ca. 1877, PL 230 (ILLUS.) **690**

Jonah & the Whale Mechanical Bank

Home Mechanical Bank

Home Bank (No Dormer Windows) - 124
- door w/three-paneled windows on each
side & three steps, seated man in doorway, no Dormer windows, small chip on
corner of roof, PL 243 (ILLUS.) **690**

Indian Shooting Bear Bank

Indian Shooting Bear - 129 - Indian kneeling w/rifle shooting coin into bear, ca.
1883, 10 1/2" l., PL 257
(ILLUS.) **2,000-2,500**

J.E. Stevens "Jolly Nigger Bank"

"Jolly Nigger Bank" - 132 - red shirt, moving arm, tongue & rolling eyes, J. & E.
Stevens, patented on March 14, 1882,
1880s-1930s, many variations, PL 275
(ILLUS.).. **500-1,000**

"Jolly Nigger" Mechanical Bank

"Jolly Nigger Bank" (High Hat) - 135 -
black man wearing red coat & red top hat,
eyes roll & tongue moves, John Harper &
Co., England, PL 277
(ILLUS.).. **1,000-1,200**

Jonah & the Whale - 138 - Jonah in boat w/whale in water, multicolored, Shepard Hardware, pat. July 15, 1890, pedestal base version much rarer, missing coin trap, PL 282 (ILLUS., top of previous page).. **3,565**

Leap Frog Bank - 143 - two boys play leap frog near fence & tree stump, one boy leaps over the other to hit a lever which causes the coin to fall into the tree, multicolored, Shepard Hardware, 1890, touchups to paint on boys & fence (PL 292) **1,840**

Magician Mechanical Bank

Magician Bank - 154 - magician holding top hat w/table, multicolored, J. & E. Stevens, PL 315 (ILLUS.) **4,320**

Mama Katzenjammer & Kids Bank

Mama Katzenjammer - 140 - Mama Katzenjammer wearing rose-colored dress & holding kids at her side, one dressed in blue, one in tan, when coin is dropped in bank, Mama rolls her eyes, rare, older repaint, 3 1/2", PL 317 (ILLUS.) **780**

Mule Entering Barn Bank

Mule Entering Barn - 169 - multicolored, J. & E. Stevens, marked "Pat'd. Aug. 30, 1880," paint faded, PL 342 (ILLUS.).............. **460**

Mechanical Bank with Cashier

Novelty Bank - 176 - house w/dormers & chimneys in light brown w/opening door to reveal teller, small crack above door, PL 361 (ILLUS.)... **863**

Owl Mechanical Bank

Owl (Turns Head) - 182 - grey, black & yellow paint, J. & E. Stevens, ca. 1880, PL 375 (ILLUS.).. **431**

Paddy & Pig Mechanical Bank

Paddy & His Pig - 185 - Irish figure holding pig in his lap, multicolored, J. & E. Stevens, ca. 1885, PL 376 (ILLUS.) **1,323**

Professor Pug Frog's Bicycle Feat

Professor Pug Frog's Great Bicycle Feat - 201- Mother Goose reading w/frog riding bicycle & clown holding large basket, multicolored, J. & E. Stevens, ca. 1886, small repair & paint touchup, PL 400 (ILLUS.) **4,485**

"The Robot" Mechanical Bank

(The) Robot (Aluminum), figure of black-painted mail carrier robot standing in front of red-painted building reading "The Robot" above door, when coin is placed in right hand of robot & mechanism is activated, the hand comes forward & deposits the coin in slot on door, rare, Starkie's, England, early 20th c., PL 416 (ILLUS.).. **4,600**

Punch & Judy Mechanical Bank

"Punch & Judy Bank" - 203 - figures in theater setting, embossed name on front, multicolored, Shepard Hardware, ca. 1884, catch not working, PL 404 (ILLUS.).. **1,150**

Santa Claus Mechanical Bank

Santa Claus - 214 - Santa drops coin down chimney, red, white & gold paint, Shepard Hardware, ca. 1889, heavy paint wear to face, overall fair paint, PL 428 (ILLUS.).. **500-1,000**

Speaking Dog Mechanical Bank

Speaking Dog - 69 - seated girl w/large dog, rectangular coin trap, multicolored, J. & E. Stevens, ca. 1885, lever to activate bank not working, PL 447 (ILLUS.).... **1,035**

Stump Speaker Mechanical Bank

Stump Speaker - 222 standing Black figure w/carpetbag, w/moving arm & opening mouth & carpetbag, multicolored, Shepard Hardware, ca. 1896, top & areas of base repainted, minor in-painting on figure, PL 453 (ILLUS.) **800-1,200**

Tammany Mechanical Bank

Tammany Bank (Little Fat Man) - 224 - seated figure representing William "Boss" Tweed, moving head & arm, various color variations, J. & E. Stevens, pat. Dec. 23, 1873, repaint to face, erratic nodding action, PL 455 (ILLUS.)..................... **213**

Tank & Cannon Mechanical Bank

Tank & Cannon, Starkie's, Burnley, Lancaster, England, ca. 1919, repair to base, PL 456 (ILLUS.)................................ **575**

Teddy & the Bear Mechanical Bank

Teddy and the Bear - 226 - Teddy Roosevelt shoots the bull's-eye, raises his head & the bear pops out of the brown tree, green base, J. & E. Stevens, ca. 1907, repairs to both feet, PL 459 (ILLUS.).. **460**

"Thrifty Tom's Jigger Bank"

Thrifty Tom's Jigger Bank, windup tin, caricature of black man in gaudy outfit stands on rectangular base lithographed w/images of coins & beehive & reading "Thrifty Tom's Jigger Bank" the base serving as bank, when key is wound, figure dances, w/original box, Strauss Corporation, box is split at one corner, PL 468 (ILLUS.)... **4,025**

Trick Dog Mechanical Bank

Trick Dog Bank (solid base) - 72 - clown w/hoop, barrel & dog, dog jumps through the clown's hoop, modern w/one-piece solid base, w/original paint & key, Hubley, ca. 1925-40, 8 3/4" w., PL 482 (ILLUS.) **2,128**

Trick Pony Mechanical Bank

Trick Pony - 196 - pony lowers head to deposit the coin in the trough trap door which opens & closes to receive the coin, red, brown, black & yellow paint, Shepard Hardware, coin trap missing, PL 484 (ILLUS.) **805**

Uncle Remus Mechanical Bank

Uncle Remus - 230 - cast iron, figure holding chicken in doorway of chicken coop w/policeman holding stick outside, Kyser & Rex Co. or Mechanical Novelty Works, if in near mint condition, PL 492 (ILLUS.).. **3,500-4,500**

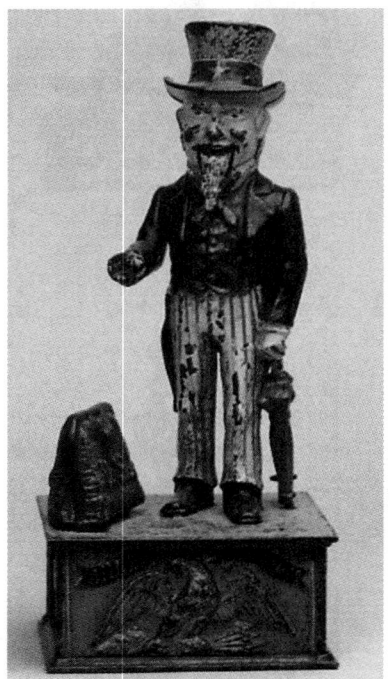

Uncle Sam Mechanical Bank

Uncle Sam w/Satchel & Umbrella - 231 - coin is dropped into open satchel, w/moving hand & mouth, red, white, blue & gold, Shepard Hardware, PL 493 (ILLUS.) **1,668**

William Tell Mechanical Bank

William Tell - 237 - figure firing rifle at boy w/apple on head, into the tower & strikes the bell, multicolored, J. & E. Stevens, ca. 1896, PL 565 (ILLUS.).......... **1,093**

Still

Black Man with Suitcase Bank

Black man w/suitcase, cast iron, kneeling figure wearing red coat, white shirt, black tie & white brimmed hat, his arms crossed in front of him & leaning on a suitcase, original paint fair, 7 3/4" h. (ILLUS.) **201**

"Globe Savings Fund" House Bank

Building - "Globe Savings Fund" - 1199 cast iron w/red, gold, brown & silver paint, house w/arched door w/combination lock flanked by two arched panels on either side, the bottom two containing scroll decoration, the top two w/figures carrying vessels on their heads, the roof adorned w/figures of mythical beasts, "Globe Savings Fund - 1888" at top, 5 1/2" w., 7" h. (ILLUS.) **1,800**

Cast-iron "State Bank" Still Bank

Building - State Bank - 1078 - cast iron, w/cupola dormer windows & locking door, "STATE BANK" embossed at front under eaves, Kenton Mfg. Co., ca. 1900, 5 1/2 x 7 x 8" h. (ILLUS.) **1,380**

Buster Brown & Tige Bank

Buster Brown & Tige - 241 - figural Buster standing next to seated Tige, red & gold paint, 5" h. (ILLUS.) **127**

Dolphin Still Bank

Dolphin - 33 - cast iron w/gold paint, boy in boat w/"Dolphin" on side, Grey Iron Casting Co.(?), 1900(?), 4 1/2" h. (ILLUS.) **460**

Elephant on Wheels Still Bank

Elephant on Wheels - 446 - cast iron w/gold wash, circus elephant w/howdah standing on base w/red-spoked wheels, original paint, 4" h. (ILLUS.) **201**

Army/Navy Double Bank

Safe - Army/Navy Bank, cast iron w/burnished copper highlights, double bank w/double combination doors at front each w/a figure, decorated w/Civil War era motifs, top marked "Army Bank" on one side w/picture of soldiers w/caisson & "Navy Bank" on other w/picture of ship, Kenton, 6 x 6 1/2" (ILLUS.) **1,064**

"Burglar Proof House Safe" Bank

Safe - "Burglar Proof House Safe," nickel-plated cast iron, double key entry, "Burglar Proof House Safe" in circular panel on door, J.E. Stevens, 6" h. (ILLUS.) **230**

"Imperial Safe Deposit" Bank

Safe - "Imperial Safe Deposit," cast iron & tin w/black paint & gold highlights, combination lock, "IMPERIAL SAFE DEPOSIT" & leaf decoration in gold on door, 5 1/2 x 8 1/2" (ILLUS.) **345**

"Security Safe Deposit" Bank

Safe - "Security Safe Deposit," cast iron w/gold & copper paint, decorated w/ornate casting & lion heads w/ring handles on either side, "Security Safe Deposit" embossed on the door, fitted interior w/three wooden rabbit-jointed drawers, 6 x 8" (ILLUS.) **575**

"Transvaal Money Box" Still Bank

"Transvaal Money Box" - 78 - pipe-smoking fat man wearing green top hat & coat, "Transvaal Money Box" inscribed in gold on front of hat, original paint, John Harper, England, late 19th c., 5 3/4" h. (ILLUS.) **259**

BARBERIANA

A wide variety of antiques related to the tonso-rial arts have been highly collectible for many years, especially 19th- and early-20th-century shaving mugs and barber bottles and, more recently, razors. We are now combining these closely related categories under one heading for easier reference. A selection of other varied pieces relating to barbering will also be found below.

Barber Bottles

Blue Bottle with Gold Florals

Cobalt blue, footed flaring bell-shaped body tapering to a tall cylindrical neck, decorated w/gold stylized Art Nouveau florals, ca. 1900, 8 1/4" h. (ILLUS.).............. **$246**

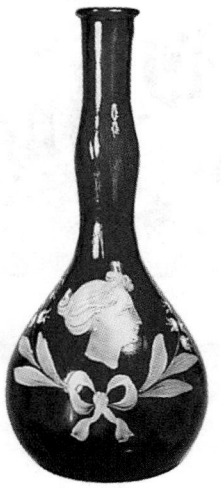

Blue Bottle with Enameled Portrait

Cobalt blue, ovoid tapering to a lady's leg neck, mold-blown Coin Spot patt., exteri-or enameled in white w/a profile bust por-trait of a lady above a bow & wreath design, ca. 1900, 8 1/2" h. (ILLUS.) **420**

Rare Iridescent Barber Bottle

Iridescent, spherical body molded around the bottom w/swirled lobes, the tall cylin-drical neck in bluish green iridescence shading to overall cranberry oil spotting around the lower body, polished lip, rare, early 20th c., 7" h. (ILLUS.)............................. **840**

Pair of Mary Gregory Barber Bottles

Mary Gregory, cobalt blue bulbous body ta-pering to a lady's leg neck, one decorat-ed in brownish white enamel w/the figure of a running girl w/tennis racket, the oth-er w/a figure of a boy w/a tennis racket, rolled lips, ca. 1900, 7 7/8" h., facing pair (ILLUS.)... **364**

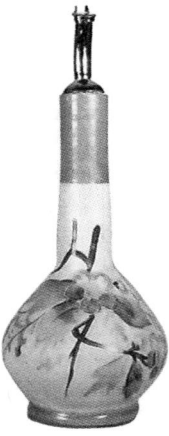

Barber Bottle with Colorful Flowers

Milk glass, footed squatty bulbous body tapering to a tall cylindrical neck w/metal dispensing spout, the frosted ground h.p. w/large colorful stylized flowering branches, ca. 1900, 7" h. (ILLUS.)................ **101**

Rare Personalized Barber Bottle

Milk glass, tapering cylindrical ringed body w/a tall ringed neck fitted w/the original metal screw-on dispenser cap, the wide center band h.p. w/a colorful scene of a woodpecker on a branch w/flowers & berries, gold line trim, panel below the scene inscribed "Christiena Noeckel - Florida Water," marked on the smooth base "W.T. & Co.," ca. 1900, 10 1/8" h. (ILLUS.)... **1,064**

Blue & White Spatter Barber Bottle

Spatter, blue & white spatter cased in clear, slightly tapering cylindrical body w/molded rings around the base & shoulder w/a tall cylindrical neck, tooled mouth, ca. 1900, 12 1/4" h. (ILLUS.)................................. **146**

Mugs

General

Floral-decorated Shaving Mug

Florals, the body w/a pink background decorated w/green leaves & white blossoms, a wide wrapped banner decorated w/the name of the owner, base stamped "Will & Fink 818 Market Street San Francisco," ca. 1900, 3 7/8" h. (ILLUS.)................................ **78**

Occupational

Rare Chauffeur Occupational Mug

Chauffeur, decorated in color w/a scene of
an early open auto w/a uniformed driver,
name in gold around the top & gold band
around the base, ca. 1919, 3 7/8" h.
(ILLUS.) **950**

Sportsman Occupational Shaving Mug

Sportsman, decorated in color w/a scene of
a standing sportsman in a woodland setting aiming his rifle, his hunting dog in
front of him, name in gold around the top,
gold band around the base, ca. 1900,
3 5/8" h. (ILLUS.) **101**

Miscellaneous

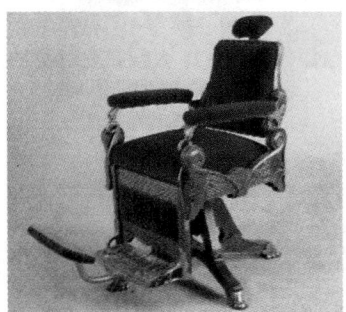

Nice Victorian Barber Chair

Barber chair, carved oak frame reupholstered in burgundy fabric, adjustable foot
& neck rest w/nickel-plate trim, brass lion
paw feet, patent-dated 1891, one repair
to the frame, 48" h. (ILLUS.) **1,035**

Colorful Electric Barber Pole

Barber pole, electric floor model, porcelainized metal, a cylindrical green lower base
below a swirled red & white striped section below a cream section topped by a
clear cylinder enclosing a rotating red,
white & blue cylinder, the top fitted w/a
milk glass globe, a green angled mounting bar at the top, early 20th c., few touchups & minor break in cast-iron globe
vase, overall 77" h. (ILLUS.) **2,243**

Rare Electric Leaded Glass Barber Pole

Barber pole, electric floor model, porcelainized metal & leaded glass, a tall hexagonal lime green porcelain on cast iron base supporting the cylindrical red & white swirled leaded glass pole framed by six nickel-plated rods, the porcelain top cap mounted w/a milk glass globe, by Koken, early 20th c., a few paint chips, overall 86" h. (ILLUS., previous page) **3,105**

Early Painted Wood Barber Pole

Barber pole, wooden floor model, a multifaceted cylindrical base section w/red, white & blue painted stripes supporting the tall multi-faceted & slightly tapering post painted w/red, white & blue swirled stripes below a small striped top section w/a red cap topped by a painted silver ball finial, probably an older repaint, late 19th c., overall 83" h. (ILLUS.) **1,668**

Rare Decorated Shaving Paper Vase

Shaving paper vase, mold-blown milk glass, a flaring base below the wide ovoid body tapering to a ringed widely flaring neck, h.p. w/a central scene of cherubs framed by a green wreath w/pink blossoms, pink leafy stems around the sides, white shaded to yellow background, American, ca. 1900, 7 3/4" h. (ILLUS.) **952**

BLACK AMERICANA

Over the past decade or so, this field of collecting has rapidly grown. Today almost anything that relates to Black culture or illustrates Black Americana is considered a desirable collectible. Although many representations of African-Americans, especially on 19th- and early-20th-century advertising pieces and housewares, were cruel stereotypes, even these are collected as poignant reminders of how far American society has come since the dawning of the Civil Rights movement, and how far we still have to go. Other pieces related to this category will be found from time to time in such categories as Advertising Items, Banks, Character Collectibles, Kitchenwares, Signs and Signboards, Toys and several others. For a complete overview of this subject see Antique Trader Black Americana Price Guide, 2nd Edition.

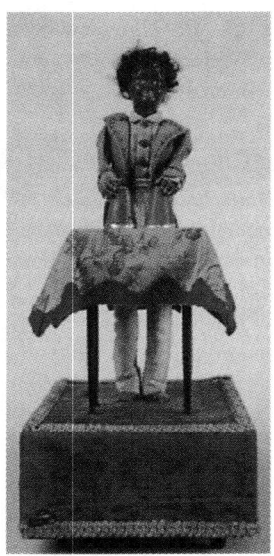

Copy of Vintage Automaton

Automaton, Black magician, musical-type, of newer vintage, styled after the original French piece by Lambert or Vichy, the black magician stands behind a small table & when activated turns his head & lifts the cones in his hands, something different appears under cones each time, 18" h. (ILLUS.) **$1,495**

Rare Folk Art Electric Automaton Scene

Automaton, carved & painted wood, electrical vignette scene, on a rectangular base fitted w/a long drawer, the painted scenic backdrop gallery on the top surrounding a scene w/several black characters, some playing music & dancing, also a man feeding chickens, a woman spanking her child as well as Amos & Andy in their taxi & a primitive-looking Mickey Mouse, in the background a rolling linen banner reading "Have You Lost Your Dog?," ca. 1930s, some characters w/cracks & paint flaking, background w/flaking & foxing, 14 x 28", 18" h. (ILLUS.) **4,680**

Black Boy Figural Candy Holder

Rare Figural Majolica Black Girl Bell

Bell, majolica, figural, a standing black child w/one hand to her face, wearing a long pink dress, white apron & blue cap, late 19th - early 20th c., 8 1/4" h (ILLUS.)......... **1,150**

Candy holder, figural papier-maché, grotesque caricature of a standing black boy wearing a blue jacket, white shirt, red bow tie & pants, exaggerated lips & bare feet, opening in top of head, bright colors, ca. 1900, 3 1/2" w., 5 1/2" h. (ILLUS.) **130**

Black Jockey Hitching Post

Hitching post, cast iron, figural standing black jockey on a square pedestal base, colorful old repaint, some rust, late 19th - early 20th c., 38" h. (ILLUS.) **500-1,000**

Figural Black Boy Inkwell

Inkwell, cast bronze, an oblong tray cast at one end w/the full-relief head of a black boy wearing a hat, hinged to show the original porcelain well, the lower portion of the tray showing his shirt & a leafy branch, numbered on bottom "4507," late 19th - early 20th c., 3 x 6", 2 1/2" h. (ILLUS.) **253**

Sign, automated, lithographed paper, half-length figure of a black farmer wearing a blue checkered shirt & worn overalls & a brown rain hat, identical to version for Momenta but w/no advertising, winding the key causes the facial features to move, in original black wood frame, late 19th - early 20th c., small water stain on left ear, some flaking to white background, working, overall 21 x 26" (ILLUS., below) **3,450**

Rare Automated Black Farmer Sign

Sign, folk art painted wood type, "The Leroy Minstrels" in red across the pedimented top, painted w/a primitive landscape scene centered by a large figure of a black man playing a banjo, apparently on early Masonite w/a stretcher structure in back, from New York State, early 20th c., repair to hand at top of banjo, hinge plate marks on the side, 35 x 40" (ILLUS., below) **3,450**

Primitive Painted Minstrel Show Sign

"Picaninny Freeze" Ice Cream Sign

Sign, "Picaninny Freeze," rectangular cardboard printed in color w/a dark green background w/large yellow moon, grotesque caricature of a black child holding a slice of watermelon, yellow, black, white & red wording reads "Eat Seeds 'n All! - Picaninny Freeze - 5¢ - A Pal For Your Palate," Henlers Ice Cream logo in corner, early 20th c., bright colors, unused condition, 11 x 14" (ILLUS.) **578**

Japanese Kobe Folk Art Toy

Toy, animated folk art-type, a rectangular base fitted w/a half-length animated black man who cuts watermelon, tips his head & opens his mouth while lifting a watermelon slice, Kobe, Japan, early

20th c., excellent condition, 3 1/2" h. (ILLUS.) **259**

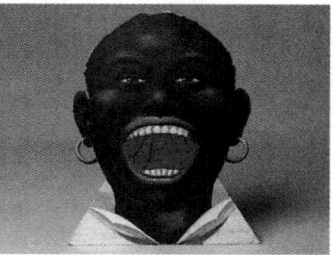

Early Black Man Beanbag Game

Toy, beanbag target game, lithographed die-cut cardboard, the head of a black man w/his mouth wide open to catch beanbags or wooden balls, ca. 1880s, splits at corners of mouth, very good condition, 13" h. (ILLUS.) **230**

Toy, clockwork, black boy orange seller, animated black youth sits on a cart & pushes it in an erratic movement, all-original w/no repairs or repaint, original paint & clothing w/slight soiling & one pant leg detached, w/original box w/illustrated label, Martin, early 20th c., 7" l. (ILLUS, bottom of page) **1,080**

Black Man & Donkey Pull Toy

Toy, pull-type, wood & pressboard, a black figure w/a top hat holds the tail of a kicking donkey, figure leans forward & donkey's ears move, Toy Tinkers, Evanston, Illinois, early 20th c., excellent condition, 10 1/2" l. (ILLUS.) **201**

Early Clockwork Orange Seller Toy

Black Boy & Dog Windup Toy

Toy, windup celluloid, "Pete," crying black boy holding a slice of watermelon while a shaking dog bites his backside, cloth clothing, Japan, 1930s, very good condition, working, 6" h. (ILLUS.) **460**

"Alabama Coon Jigger" Toy & Box

Toy, windup tin, "Alabama Coon Jigger," colorfully lithographed figure of a jointed black man above a rectangular platform base, w/original color-illustrated box w/original instructions & one spare rod, partial side flap missing, near mint, Lehmann, 1930s, 10" h. (ILLUS.) **1,080**

Strauss Windup Black Porter Toy

Toy, windup tin, black porter dressed in red pushes a green trunk that dog lurches out of, Strauss, 1930s, very good condition, 6" h. (ILLUS.) **600**

Ham & Sam Windup Tin Toy

Toy, windup tin, "Ham and Sam," an upright piano w/seated player & another standing man playing the banjo, Strauss, copyright 1921, all-original & working, 7 1/2" h. (ILLUS.) **460**

Marx "Hey-Hey Chicken Snatcher" Toy

Toy, windup tin, "Hey-Hey The Chicken Snatcher," grotesque figure of a black man w/a chicken in one hand, a small dog nipping at his backside, face moves showing different expressions, Louis Marx, copyright 1926, all-original & working, 8 1/2" h. (ILLUS.) **1,200**

Japanese Louis Armstrong Toy

Toy, windup tin, "Louis Armstrong Trumpet Player," the figure balances on one foot & kicks up leg, tips hat & blows a trumpet sound via an interior bellows, T.N., Japan, 1950s, excellent working condition, 10 1/2" h. (ILLUS.) **259**

BOTTLES

Bitters

(Numbers with some listings below refer to those used in Carlyn Ring's For Bitters Only.*)*

Baker's Orange Grove Bitters Bottle

Baker's - Orange Grove - Bitters, square w/rope twist corners, applied sloping collar mouth, smooth base, ca. 1865-75, golden yellow w/amber tone, 9 1/2" h. (ILLUS. front & back)..................................... **$784**

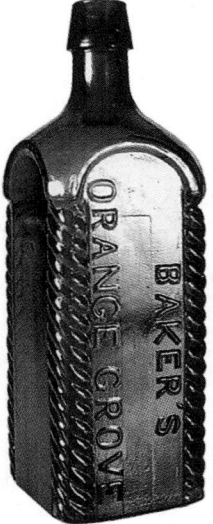

Rare Baker's Orange Grove Bitters Bottle

Baker's - Orange Grove - Bitters, square w/rope twist corners, applied sloping col-

lar mouth, smooth base, ca. 1865-75, medium pinkish puce, 9 1/2" h. (ILLUS.).. **2,464**

Flask-shaped Bitters Bottle

Bitter [over horseshoe design] Trade Mark (within horseshoe) Witch, flask shape, smooth base, applied double collar mouth, medium yellowish amber, ca. 1870-80, faint inside haze, 8 1/8" h. (ILLUS.).. **364**

Brown's Celebrated Indian Herb Bitters Bottles

Brown's Celebrated Indian Herb Bitters Patented 1867, figural Indian maiden, rolled lip, medium amber, 12 1/4" h. (ILLUS. left w/lighter Indian Herb Bitters bottle, previous page) 660

Brown's Celebrated Indian Herb Bitters Patented 1868, figural Indian maiden, string of glass extending from calf of leg to reverse, golden amber, 12 1/4" h. (ILLUS. right w/darker Indian Herb Bitters bottle, previous page) 880

Bryant's Stomach Bitters Bottle

Bryant's Stomach - Bitters, octagonal w/lady's leg neck w/applied sloping double collar mouth, ca. 1865-75, medium olive green, 12 1/4" h. (ILLUS.) **2,800**

M.G. Landsburg & Professor Byrne Bitters

Byrne (Professor Geo J.) New York - The Great Universal Compound Stomach Bitters Patented 1870, square shape w/applied top, assorted embossed letters & symbols, golden amber (ILLUS. right w/Landsburg Bitters bottle) **2,640**

Carter's - Liver Bitters Bottle

Carter's - Liver Bitters - C.M. Co. New York, oval, rounded shoulder, smooth base, tooled mouth, ca. 1890-1900, amber, 8 1/4" h. (ILLUS. front & back) **448**

Dingen's Napoleon Cocktail Bitters Bottle

Dingen's - Napoleon Cocktail Bitters - Dingen Brothers - Buffalo N.Y., banjo shape on pedestal, w/lady's leg neck, iron pontil, applied sloping collar mouth, smoky clear, ca. 1865-75, 10 1/8" h. (ILLUS.)... **6,160**

Dr. Petzold's Genuine German Bitters Bottle

Dr. Petzold's Genuine German Bitters IN-CPT. 1862, oval, 20-rib, smooth base, applied mouth, medium amber shading to a more yellow amber, ca. 1875-85, some light content stain, 10 1/4" h. (ILLUS.) **213**

Log Cabin Bitters Bottle in Yellow Amber

Drake's (S T) - 1860 - Plantation - X - Bitters - Patented - 1862, cabin-shaped, six-log, smooth base, applied mouth, ca. 1862-70, yellow amber, 9 7/8" h., D-108 (ILLUS.)... **952**

Dr Soule's - Hop - Bitters Bottle

Dr Soule's - Hop - Bitters - 1872, square, semi-cabin, w/embossed decoration of hop berries & leaves, smooth base, applied sloping double collar mouth, yellow olive, ca. 1872-80, light outside dullness, 9 3/4" h. (ILLUS.) **504**

Log Cabin Bitters Bottle in Strawberry Puce

Drake's (S T) - 1860 - Plantation - X - Bitters - Patented - 1862, cabin-shaped, six-log, smooth base, applied sloping collar mouth, ca. 1862-70, deep strawberry puce, 10" h., D-108 (ILLUS.) **336**

Figural Fish Bitters Bottle

Fish (The) Bitters - W.H. Ware - Patented 1866, figural fish, smooth base, applied mouth, ca. 1866-70, amber, 11 1/4" h. (ILLUS.).. **308**

Fish (The) Bitters - W.H. Ware - Patented 1866, figural fish w/embossed scales, fins, gills & eyes, applied lip, reddish-chocolate amber, 11 1/2" h. (ILLUS. left w/Dr. Fisch's Bitters bottle) **264**

Yellow Log Cabin Bitters Bottle

Drake's (S T) - 1860 - Plantation - X - Bitters - Patented - 1862, cabin-shaped, six-log, smooth base, applied sloping collar mouth, ca. 1862-70, yellow w/strong olive tone, 9 7/8" h., D-108 (ILLUS.)........... **1,904**

Dr. Fisch's Bitters & The Fish Bitters Bottles

Fisch's (Dr.) Bitters - W.H. Ware - Patented 1866, figural fish w/embossed scales, fins, gills & eyes, amber, 11 3/4" h. (ILLUS. right w/The Fish Bitters bottle) **264**

The Fish Bitters Bottle in Yellow Green

Fish (The) Bitters - W.H. Ware - Patented 1866, figural fish w/embossed scales, fins, gills & eyes, "W.H. Ware Patent 1866" on base, brilliant yellow-green, 11 3/8" h. (ILLUS.)....................................... **1,540**

German Hop Bitters Bottle

German - Hop - Bitters - 1880 - Dr C. D. Warner's - Reading, Mich, square, semi-cabin, smooth base, applied sloping double collar mouth, ca. 1880-85, medium amber, 9 7/8" h. (ILLUS. front & back) **448**

Greeley's Bourbon Bitters Bottle in Olive Green

Greeley's Bourbon Bitters, barrel-shaped, ten rings above & below center band, applied mouth, smooth base, ca. 1855-70, medium olive green w/yellow tone, 9 1/8" h. (ILLUS.)... **4,200**

Greeley's Bourbon Bitters Bottle

Greeley's Bourbon Bitters, barrel-shaped, ten rings above & below center band, applied mouth, smooth base, ca. 1860-75, deep strawberry puce, 9 1/4" h. (ILLUS.) **728**

Greeley's Bourbon Bitters Bottle

Greeley's Bourbon Bitters, round ribbed barrel shape, applied top, smooth base, mossy green, 9 3/8" h. (ILLUS.)................. **4,180**

Hertrichs Bitter Bottle from Germany

Hertrichs Bitter Arztlichempfohlen, ovoid body, long neck w/bulge at shoulder & tooled mouth, smooth pedestal base w/"1900," medium olive green, Germany, ca. 1880-1900, 5 3/8" h. (ILLUS.) **616**

John W. Steele's Niagara Star Bitters Bottle

John W. Steele's Niagara [five-pointed star] Bitters - John W. Steele's Niagara Star Bitters, square, semi-cabin, embossed w/design of flying bird under thirteen stars, a five-pointed star on each of three roof panels, smooth base, applied mouth, w/98 percent original label, medium amber, ca. 1865-75, wear to label, open bubble located on one shoulder corner, 10 1/4" h. (ILLUS. of two views) **1,568**

Jackson's Aromatic Bitters Bottle

Jackson's Aromatic - Life - Bitters, rectangular, smooth base, applied sloping collar mouth, crude glass full of seed bubbles, one of few known examples, deep olive green, ca. 1855-1870, 8 7/8" h. (ILLUS.) **6,160**

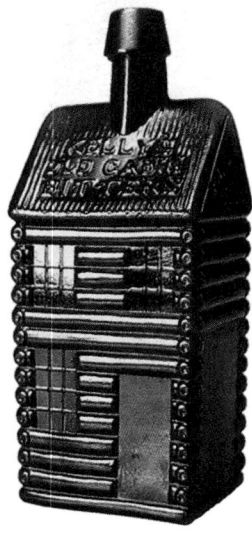

Kelly's Old Cabin Bitters Bottle

Kelly's - Old Cabin - Bitters - Patented 1863, rectangular, log cabin form, smooth base, applied sloping collar mouth, medium reddish amber, ca. 1863-70, 9 1/8" h. (ILLUS.) **3,080**

Barrel-shaped Bitters Bottles

Keystone Bitters, ribbed barrel shape, applied top, medium to light amber, 9 3/4" h. (ILLUS. left w/Wormser Bros. bottle)... **880**

Kimball's Jaundice Bitters Bottle

Kimball's - Jaundice - Bitters - Troy, NH, rectangular, iron pontil, applied sloping collar mouth, yellow amber w/olive tone, lighter than most, somewhat different shade, ca. 1840-60, 7" h. (ILLUS.) **1,344**

Landsburg (M.G.) Chicago - [reverse w/"Bitters" peened out for label], square shape w/applied top & smooth base, emblem of eagle on front panel, thirteen stars on shoulder, "1876" on side panel, other assorted symbols include

sunray, cannonballs, crossed swords, mace & cannon, golden-orange amber, 11"h. (ILLUS. page 48 left w/Byrne Bitters bottle).. **1,980**

National Bitters, figural ear of corn w/undecorated oval panel amid embossed kernels & husk, applied top, light amber (ILLUS. center w/other National Bitters bottles)... **413**

Ears of Corn National Bitters Bottles

National Bitters, figural ear of corn w/undecorated oval panel amid embossed kernels & husk, applied top, medium amber (ILLUS. left w/other National Bitters bottles)... **413**

National Bitters Bottle with No Lip

National Bitters, figural ear of corn w/undecorated oval panel amid embossed kernels & husk, base reads "Pat Applied For," no applied lip, medium apricot-amber, very rare (ILLUS., previous page) **990**

National Bitters, figural ear of corn w/undecorated oval panel amid embossed kernels & husk, applied top, greenish yellow citron, believed to be one of less than five of this color to exist (ILLUS. previous pageright w/other National Bitters bottles) **8,250**

Nibol Kidney and Liver Bitters Bottle

Nibol Kidney and Liver Bitters - The Best Tonic Laxative & Blood Purifier, square, smooth base, tooled lip, w/98 percent original front & back labels & contents, medium amber, 9 1/2" h. (ILLUS. of two sides)....................................... **728**

Old Homestead Wild Cherry Bitters - Patent, square, log cabin form, smooth base, applied mouth, medium amber, ca. 1865-75, light inside haze, 9 5/8" h. (ILLUS.)... **308**

Old Sachem Bitters and Wigwam Tonic Bottle

Old Sachem Bitters and Wigwam Tonic, barrel-shaped, ten-rib, pontil scarred base, applied mouth, deep bluish aqua w/patch of olive in area of embossing, ca. 1855-70, 10 1/4" h. (ILLUS.)....................... **5,040**

Old Homestead Wild Cherry Bitters Bottle

Prickly Ash Bitters Bottle, Two Views

Prickly Ash Bitters, square, smooth base, ABM lip, w/99 percent original label on three sides & contents, made by Meyer Brothers Drug. Co., St. Louis, Missouri, medium amber, ca. 1910-15, 9 1/4" h. (ILLUS. of two sides, previous page) **258**

Bust of Washington Bitters Bottle

Simon's Centennial Bitters - Trademark, bust of George Washington on pedestal, applied top, reddish amber, lighter color on arms, 9 3/4" h. (ILLUS.) **3,300**

Solomon's Strengthening & Invigorating Bitters

Solomon's Strengthening & Invigorating Bitters - Savannah Georgia, square, smooth base, applied sloping collar mouth, deep cobalt blue, ca. 1875-85, professionally cleaned, 9 3/4" h. (ILLUS.) **1,344**

Suffolk Bitters - Philbrook & Tucker Boston, figural pig, smooth base, applied double collar mouth, medium amber shading to more yellow in feet, ca. 1865-75, 10 1/8" l. (ILLUS., below) **1,064**

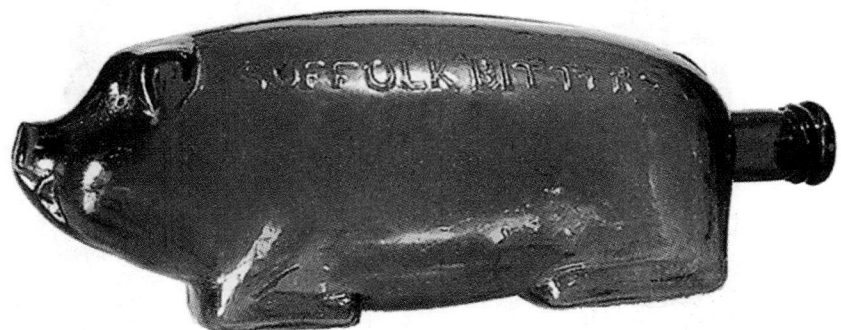

Suffolk Bitters Pig-form Bottle

Amber Pineapple Bitters Bottle

W. & Co. - N.Y., round pineapple form, diamond-shaped label panel interrupting diamond diaper, open pontil, applied double collar mouth, amber, ca. 1865-75, some faint inside stain, 8 1/2" h. (ILLUS.)...... **532**

Octagonal Bitters Bottle in Amber

Thads. Waterman - Warsaw - Stomach Bitters, octagonal, smooth base, applied sloping double collar mouth, many seed bubbles, medium golden amber, ca. 1865-75, 10 1/2" h. (ILLUS.)........................ **3,920**

W & Co - N.Y. Bitters Bottle in Rare Color

W & Co - N.Y., round pineapple form, diamond-shaped label panel interrupting diamond diaper, iron pontil, applied double collar mouth, medium olive yellow, ca. 1865-75, some faint inside stain (ILLUS.)... **4,200**

Wormser Bros San Francisco, ribbed barrel shape, applied top, golden amber (ILLUS. page. 53 right w/Keystone bottle)... **3,300**

Turner Brothers Barrel-shaped Bitters Bottle

Turner Brothers New York, ribbed barrel shape, smooth base, applied mouth, deep yellow w/olive tone, ca. 1855-70, pinhead size flake off top edge of lip, 10" h. (ILLUS.).. **1,008**

Figurals

Figural Fish Bottle in Painted Clear Glass

Fish, clear glass w/embossed scales, fins, gills & eyes, w/80 percent original blue, grey & white paint, ground lip w/original screw-on cap, "PAT APLD. FOR" on smooth base, ca. 1890-1910, 8 3/4" l. (ILLUS.)... **246**

"Big Bill" Figural Bottle

"Big Bill," stout man in three-piece suit, top hat, standing on square smooth base, tooled lip (similar to figure pictured on label of Big Bill's Best Bitters bottles), medium amber, ca. 1890-1910, 11 5/8" h. (ILLUS.) **784**

Mint Green Milk Glass Log Cabin Bottle

Log cabin, milk glass, smooth base, ground lip w/original metal neck band, mint green, Europe, extremely rare in form & color, ca. 1880-1900, 10" h. (ILLUS.)............. **448**

Egyptian Pharaoh Figural Bottle

Egyptian Pharaoh seated on throne, black milk glass w/traces of original paint, smooth base, sheared & ground lip, "DEP" embossed on rear indented panel edge, very rare, probably France, ca. 1890-1920, 13 1/8" h. (ILLUS.) **896**

Figural Oyster Bottle

Oyster, closed shell, aqua w/99 percent original grey brown paint, smooth base, ground lip, original metal screw-on cap, ca. 1890-1910, 6" h. (ILLUS.) **179**

Clear Glass Santa Claus Bottle

Santa Claus, clear glass, standing figure w/arms joined in front, on rounded rectangular smooth base, tooled mouth, embossed "M.C. Husted" on side near base, America, ca. 1890-1910, 11" h. (ILLUS.) **213**

Shoe with Protruding Toe Bottle

Shoe, lace-up shoe w/toe protruding from hole in front, ground lip w/original screw-on cap at ankle, "PAT. APL. 00" on smooth base, black amethyst w/original flesh-color paint on toe, ca. 1890-1910, 3 3/4" h. (ILLUS.) **258**

Historical Octopus Flask

Octopus draped over silver dollar, milk glass, smooth base, ground lip w/original screw-on cap, 90 percent original gold & red paint, date of "1901" embossed near base (referring to Frank Norris novel "The Octopus," this represents the organized power of the many-armed railroads & their far-reaching capacity for harm to the financial welfare of the farmers in the early 1900s), America, 4 1/2" h. (ILLUS.)........ **1,112**

Flasks

Flasks are listed according to the numbers provided in American Bottles & Flasks and Their Ancestry *by* Helen McKearin *and* Kenneth M. Wilson.

Green "General Washington" Flask

GI-14 - Washington bust below "General Washington" - American eagle w/shield w/seven bars on breast, head turned to right, "E Pluribus Unum" in semicircle above, vertically ribbed edges, w/"Adams & Jefferson July 4. A.D. 1776" & "Kensington Glassworks Philadelphia," pontil scarred base, sheared & tooled lip, emerald green, pt. (ILLUS.)................................. **5,880**

GI-37 - Washington bust below "The Father of His Country" - Taylor bust below "Gen. Taylor Never Surrenders" & "Dyottville Glass Works Philada.," smooth edges, applied double collar mouth, smooth base, yellow w/amber tone center shading to clear yellow in sides, , surface bubble has been filled in & made to appear normal, qt. (ILLUS.)..................................... **3,080**

Washington Flask in Blue Green

Washington Flask in Desirable Color

GI-24 - Washington bust facing left w/"Washington" above, "Bridgeton New Jersey" & bust of Taylor, pontil scarred base, sheared & tooled lip, seed bubbles throughout, medium blue green, pt. (ILLUS.) **1,456**

GI-38 - Washington bust below "The Father of His Country" - Taylor bust below "Gen. Taylor Never Surrenders" & "Dyottville Glass Works Philada.," smooth base, sheared lip, blue-green approaching teal, pt. (ILLUS.) **560**

Washington Flask in Rare Color

"New Jersey Bridgeton" Flask

GI-111 - "New Jersey Bridgeton" w/bust of Kossuth & sailing boat, pontil scarred base, sheared & tooled lip, aquamarine, pt. (ILLUS., previous page) 672

Two Columbia Flasks

GI-117 - bust of Columbia with Liberty cap w/"Kensington" inscribed below - American eagle w/"Union Co." inscribed below, single broad vertical rib, sheared lip & pontil, pale aqua (ILLUS. right w/other Columbia flask) 825

Columbia Flask in Bluish Aqua

GI-121 - bust of Columbia & American eagle w/"B.&W." in script below, vertically ribbed edges, open pontil, sheared & tooled lip, bluish aqua, pt. (ILLUS.) 504

GI-121 - bust of Columbia with Liberty cap - American eagle w/"B & W" in script below, vertically ribbed edges, sheared lip & pontil, pale green-aqua (ILLUS. left w/other Columbia flask) 413

Eagle Flask in Cobalt Blue

GII-24 - American eagle facing left w/ribbon above head w/ribbing, two arched rows of four-point stars at top, arrows & olive branch in talons above bottom oval frame enclosing an elongated eight-point star - large conventionalized floral medallion above an oval frame enclosing an elongated eight-point star, horizontally corrugated edges, sheared & tooled lip, pontil scarred base, cobalt blue, chip in lip professionally repaired, pt. (ILLUS.) 2,128

Eagle Flask in Rare Orange Amber

GII-24 - American eagle facing left w/ribbon above head w/ribbing, two arched rows of four-point stars at top, arrows & olive branch in talons above bottom oval frame enclosing an elongated eight-point star - large conventionalized floral medallion above an oval frame enclosing an elongated eight-point star, horizontally corrugated edges, sheared & tooled lip, pontil scarred base, orange amber, pt. (ILLUS.) .. **5,320**

"Liberty" Flask in Rare Deep Amber

GII-60 - American eagle facing left in oval medallion, "Liberty" in scroll above beaded medallion around leafy oak tree, sheared & tooled lip, pontil scarred base, deep amber, 1/2 pt. (ILLUS.) **3,080**

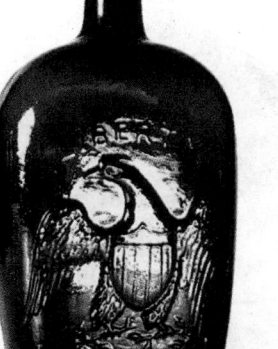

Quart "Liberty" Flask in Amber

GII-61 - American eagle facing left under "Liberty," inscribed in four lines, "Willington - Glass Co. - West Willington - Conn.," smooth base, applied double collar mouth, many seed bubbles & swirl lines, amber w/no trace of green, qt. (ILLUS.) **896**

"New London Glass Works" Flask

GII-67 - American eagle standing on laurel wreath below nine five-pointed stars - large anchor w/"New London" in banner above & "Glass Works" in banner below, smooth base, applied double collar mouth, smooth base, orange amber, very minor open shoulder bubble, 1/2 pt. (ILLUS.) **1,680**

Eagle Flask in Scarce Emerald Green

GII-106 - American eagle facing left above oval panel obverse & reverse, w/"Pittsburgh PA" in oval on obverse, narrow vertical rib on edges, smooth base, applied mouth, emerald green, pt. (ILLUS., previous page) **672**

cal palm motif, edges w/horizontal beading, pontil scarred base, inward rolled lip, aqua, 1/2 pt. (ILLUS.) **5,600**

GIII-2 - Cornucopia w/produce obverse & reverse, vertically ribbed edges, sheared tooled lip & pontil, aqua, 1/2 pt. **132**

Cornucopia/Pinwheel Flask

GIII-1 - Cornucopia w/produce surrounded by oval beaded panel - Large circular beaded medallion enclosing star-shaped design w/six ribbed points & small eight-petaled rosette center, above symmetri-

Olive Green Cornucopia/Urn Flask

GIII-4 - Cornucopia w/produce - Urn w/produce, vertically ribbed edges, pontil scarred base, sheared & tooled lip, deep olive green w/no trace of amber, pt. (ILLUS.) **101**

Double Cornucopia Flasks

GIII-4 - Cornucopia w/produce - Urn w/produce, vertically ribbed edges, plain lip, pontil, olive, pt. (ILLUS. left w/emerald green double cornucopia flask, bottom previous page) **110**

GIII-7 - Cornucopia w/produce - Urn w/produce, vertically ribbed edges, sheared lip w/pontil, light to medium olive green, 1/2 pt. **132**

GIII-17 - Cornucopia w/produce - Urn w/produce, vertically ribbed edges, applied top w/plain lip, pontil, emerald green, pt. (ILLUS. right w/olive double cornucopia flask, page 62)............................ **880**

Blue Green Cornucopia/Urn Flask

GIII-17 - Cornucopia w/produce - Urn, pontil scarred base, applied double collar mouth, medium blue green, pt. (ILLUS.)....... **616**

Emerald Green Cornucopia/Urn Flask

GIII-17 - Cornucopia w/produce - Urn, pontil scarred base, tooled mouth, Lancaster, New York Glassworks, deep emerald green, pt. (ILLUS.)... **1,064**

Masonic Arch Flask in Blue Green

GIV-1a - Masonic arch - American eagle w/ribbon above "I P" in oval, pontil scarred base, sheared & tooled lip, medium blue green, pt. (ILLUS.) **364**

Masonic Arch Flask in Yellow Olive

GIV-8a - Masonic arch - American eagle above oval containing pinwheel, pontil scarred base, sheared & tooled lip, deep yellow olive, extremely rare mold in un-listed color, possibly unique, two minor sliver-type chips off one rib, pt. (ILLUS., previous page) **2,800**

Masonic Arch Flask in Blue Green

GIV-14 - Masonic arch, pillars & pavement w/Masonic emblems inside the arch - American eagle above oval frame w/elongated eight-pointed star, plain rim, vertically ribbed sides, pontil scarred base, sheared & tooled lip, medium blue green, 1/2 pt. (ILLUS.) **1,792**

Seeing Eye Flask in Yellow Amber

GIV-43 - Seeing Eye over "A.D." - Star & arm w/"G.R.J.A.," open pontil, sheared & tooled lip, yellow amber, pt. (ILLUS.) **448**

"Success to the Railroad" Flask

GV-4 - "Success to the Railroad" around embossed horse pulling cart, reverse identically embossed, pontil scarred base, sheared & tooled lip, yellowish ol-ive amber, pt. (ILLUS.) **672**

Pint Railroad Flask in Olive Green

GV-7 - Embossed horse pulling cart, re-verse identically embossed, smooth base, applied collar mouth, thought to have been blown at Mt. Vernon, New

York Glassworks, one of the rarer flasks
in the railroad group, olive green, pt.
(ILLUS., previous page).................................. **896**

Sunburst Flask in Yellow Olive

GVIII-5a - Sunburst w/twenty-four rounded
rays obverse & reverse, horizontal corrugated edges, pontil scarred base,
sheared & tooled lip, yellow olive, pt.
(ILLUS.).. **4,200**

"Corn for the World" Flask

GVI-4 - "Baltimore" below monument - "Corn
for the World" in semicircle above ear of
corn, smooth edges, smooth base, applied double collar mouth, yellow w/olive
tone, 1/4" open bubble near base, qt.
(ILLUS.)... **2,128**

E.G. Booz & Bininger's Flasks

GVII-3 - Cabin shape w/beveled roof ends,
applied top, smooth base, one end inscribed "E.G. Booz's Old Cabin Whiskey," other end "120 Walnut St Philadelphia," roof over obverse inscribed "E.G.
Booz's Old Cabin Whiskey," reverse roof
"1840," medium amber (ILLUS. left
w/Bininger's Regulator flask) **2,640**

*Extremely Rare Emerald Green
Sunburst Flask*

GVIII-14a - Sunburst centered by ring w/a
dot in middle, horizontal corrugated edges, pontil scarred base, sheared & tooled
lip, extremely rare color, emerald
green, 1/2 pt. (ILLUS.) **4,760**

Scroll Flask in Medium Cobalt Blue

GIX-2 - Scroll w/two six-point stars obverse & reverse, vertical medial rib, long neck, pontil scarred base, sheared & tooled lip, medium cobalt blue, qt. (ILLUS.)................. **3,080**

Corset-waist Scroll Flask

GIX-45 - Scroll, corset-waist style, elaborate scroll decoration forming acanthus leaves w/four-petal flower at top & diamond at center obverse & reverse, vertical medial ribs, pontil scarred base, sheared & tooled lip, deep aqua, pt. (ILLUS.).. **840**

Scroll Flask in Golden Amber

GIX-10 - Scroll w/two eight-point stars obverse & reverse, applied collar, iron pontil, golden amber, pt. (ILLUS.)...................... **1,650**

"Zanesville Ohio" Flask in Aqua

GX-14 - "Murdock" in semicircle - "& Cassel" in two straight lines, beneath rectangular band of heavy diagonal ribbing & below that a wider band of heavy vertical ribs extending to the base - "Zanesville" in semicircle & "Ohio" in straight line, below ribbing similar to obverse, vertically ribbed edges w/narrow medial rib, pontil scarred base, sheared & tooled lip, greenish aqua, pt. (ILLUS., previous page).. **1,904**

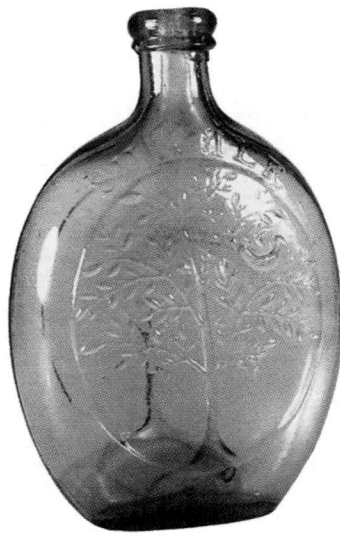

Summer/Winter Flask with Unusual Coloration

GX-15 - "Summer" over tree in circle - "Winter" over tree in circle, smooth base, applied double collar mouth, yellowish topaz w/subtle puce striations, pt. (ILLUS.).. **3,640**

Summer/Winter Tree Flask with Extremely Rare Deep Coloration

GX-19 - Summer tree - Winter tree, smooth base, double collar mouth, dark amber, qt. (ILLUS.) **2,240**

Rare Amber "For Pike's Peak" Flask

GXI-22 - "For Pike's Peak" above prospector w/tools standing on oblong frame - American eagle, smooth base, applied ringed mouth, amber, pt. (ILLUS.).............. **3,920**

"For Pike's Peak" Flask in Deep Aqua

GXI-46 - "For Pike's Peak" above prospector w/tools & cane - Hunter shooting deer, smooth base, applied ringed lip, deep aqua, milky stain inside base, minor shoulder scratches, qt. (ILLUS.) **336**

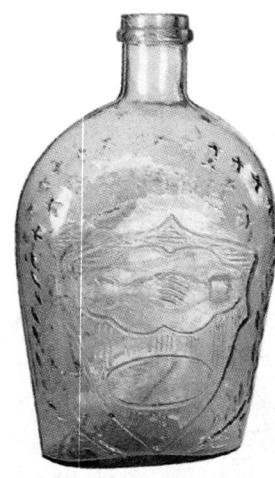

Extremely Rare Light Cobalt Blue Flask with Clasped Hands Design

GXII-37 - Clasped hands above oval all inside shield w/"Union" above shield, reverse similar, smooth base, applied ringed mouth, light cobalt blue, only two known examples known in this color, qt. (ILLUS.)... **2,352**

Clasped Hands Flask in Olive Yellow

GXII-7 - Clasped hands above oval, all inside large shield under "Union" - American eagle w/banner & "No. 2," smooth base, applied ringed mouth, olive yellow, shallow flake off side near mold seam, qt. (ILLUS.)... **1,456**

Hunter/Fisherman Calabash Flask

GXIII-4 - Hunter facing left wearing flat-top stovepipe hat, short coat & full trousers, game bag hanging at left side, firing gun at two birds flying upward at left, large puff of smoke from muzzle, two dogs running to left toward section of rail fence - Fisherman standing on shore near large rock, wearing round-top stovepipe hat, V-neck jacket, full trousers, fishing rod held in left hand w/end resting on ground, right hand holding large fish, creel below left arm, mill w/bushes & tree in left back-

Clasped Hands Flask in Orange Amber

GXII-13 - Clasped hands in shield under "Union" & over "L.F. & Co." - American eagle w/banner & "Pittsburgh, Pa.," smooth base, applied ring mouth, orange amber, qt. (ILLUS.).. **672**

ground, calabash, edges w/wide flutes, iron pontil, applied mouth, orange amber, 9 1/4" h. (ILLUS., previous page).................. **420**

"Dr. Taylor's Olive Branch Bitters" Flask

GXIII-4 - Hunter facing left wearing flat-top stovepipe hat, short coat & full trousers, game bag hanging at left side, firing gun at two birds flying upward at left, large puff of smoke from muzzle, two dogs running to left toward section of rail fence, "Dr. Taylor's Olive Branch Bitters" painted in gold - Fisherman standing on shore near large rock, wearing round-top stovepipe hat, V-neck jacket, full trousers, fishing rod held in left hand w/end resting on ground, right hand holding large fish, creel below left arm, mill w/bushes & tree in left background, calabash, edges w/wide flutes, iron pontil, applied mouth, salmon puce, 9 1/4" h. (ILLUS.) **1,680**

"Baltimore Glassworks" Flask

GXIII-49 - Anchor w/fork-ended pennants inscribed "Baltimore" & "Glassworks" - Sheaf of grain w/rake & pitchfork crossed behind sheaf, smooth edges, smooth base, applied mouth, yellow olive, 1/2 pt. (ILLUS.)... **3,080**

Yellow Olive "Spring Garden" Flask

GXIII-59 - Anchor w/fork-ended pennants inscribed "Spring Garden" & "Glass Works" - Cabin w/pebbly ground, smooth base, open pontil, applied double collar, yellow olive, pt. (ILLUS.).. **5,600**

GXIII-87 - Clock dial shape, "Bininger's" embossed above Roman numerals, "Regulator" beneath, "19 Broad St - New York" around perimeter, hands pointing to 11 o'clock, smooth base, medium amber, pt. (ILLUS. , page 65, right w/E.G. Booz's Old Cabin Whiskey flask) **468**

Early 19th Century Nailsea Flask

Nailsea, ovoid lobed shape, yellow amber w/white loop pattern, pontil scarred base, tooled mouth, England, ca. 1820-50, 5 3/8" h. (ILLUS., previous page) **308**

Nailsea Teardrop Flask

Nailsea, teardrop shape, cranberry red glass w/overall white & pink loop pattern, pontil scarred base, tooled mouth w/original threaded neck collar & fancy screw-on lid, England or America, ca. 1860-80, 7 1/8" h. (ILLUS.) **336**

36-Rib Pitkin Flask in Golden Amber

Pitkin, thirty-six ribs swirled to the left, open pontil, sheared & tooled lip, blown in the German half-post method, golden amber, America, ca. 1815, 6" h. (ILLUS.) **1,008**

Inks

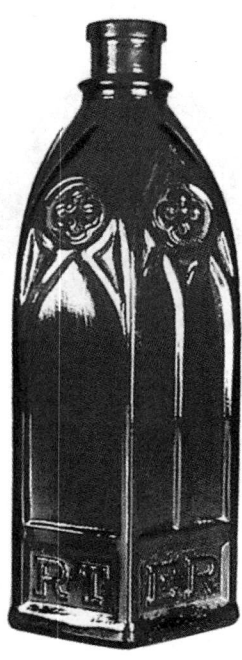

Carter's Ink Bottle in Cobalt

Cathedral, medium electric cobalt blue, master size, six Gothic arch panels embossed at the bottom "CA - RT - ER - CA - RT - ER," ABM lip, smooth base marked "Carter's," ca. 1925-35, 9 7/8" h. (ILLUS.) **112**

Cone & Squatty Inks

Cone, blue, rolled lip, open pontil, minor interior haze (ILLUS. left w/squatty ink) **770**

"Hover" Ink Bottle in Medium Blue Green

Cylindrical, medium blue green, "Hover
Phila.," master size, open pontil, applied
mouth w/tooled pour spout, ca. 1840-60,
9 1/4" h. (ILLUS.) **560**

Squatty, teal, embossed "A.M. Bertinguiot,"
long ground lip, 2 1/2" h. (ILLUS., previ-
ous page right w/cone ink) **303**

Clear Teakettle Ink

Teakettle, clear, ground lip, minor stain,
3 1/4" h. (ILLUS.) **88**

Deep Amber Turtle Ink

Turtle-form, deep amber, "J & I E M,"
smooth base, tooled mouth, ca. 1875-85,
1 3/4" h. (ILLUS.) **392**

Very Rare Gallon-size Ink Bottle

Twelve-sided w/central neck, deep cobalt
blue, gallon size, central neck, iron pontil, applied mouth, "Harrison's Columbian
Ink" embossed on sides & shoulder, one
of only five or six known to exist, ca.
1845-60, 11 1/3" h. (ILLUS.) **30,240**

Umbrella Ink with Label

Umbrella-type (8-panel cone shape), apricot-amber, rolled lip, open tubular pontil,
95 percent intact label reads "Sheppard -
Allen's Writing Fluid Manufactured at Al-
bany NY," 2 3/4" h. (ILLUS.) **550**

Deep Olive Green Umbrella Ink

Three Umbrella Inks

Umbrella-type (8-panel cone shape), deep olive green, short neck w/rolled lip, open pontil, ca. 1840-60, slight outside dullness, tiny open bubble near base, 2 1/2" h. (ILLUS., previous page)................. **258**

Umbrella-type (8-panel cone shape), light orange, Stoddard-type, sheared lip, pontil, 2 3/8" h. (ILLUS. left w/other umbrella inks, top of page) **330**

Umbrella-type (8-panel cone shape), olive green, sheared lip, pontil, 2 1/2" h. (ILLUS. right w/other umbrella inks) **242**

Umbrella-type (8-panel cone shape), red amber, Stoddard-type, sheared lip, pontil (ILLUS. center w/other umbrella inks)........... **275**

Medicines

Dr. Birmingham's Antibillious Blood Purifier

Birmingham's (Dr.) - Antibillious - Blood Purifier, paneled cylinder, smooth base, applied square collar mouth, medium teal blue, ca. 1865-75, 8 5/8" h. (ILLUS.).......... **1,344**

Yellow Olive Green Umbrella Ink

Umbrella-type (8-panel cone shape), yellow olive green, short neck w/tooled mouth, smooth base, w/97 percent original label reading "Unoco Fast Black Writing Ink," ca. 1870-85, 2 3/4" h. (ILLUS.) **532**

Brinckerhoffs Health Restorative Bottle

Brinckerhoffs (C.) - Health Restorative - New York - Price One Dollar, rectangular w/beveled corners, applied sloping collared mouth, sticky ball type pontil, olive w/some yellow, 7" h. (ILLUS.) **1,540**

Duffy's Tower Mint Cure Bottle

Duffy's Tower Mint Cure, tower form embossed w/stones, windows & doors, smooth base, applied mouth, embossed w/image of castle & "Trade Mark Est 1842," yellowish amber, ca. 1875-85, slight bruise in lip where chip has been partially polished out, 9" h. (ILLUS.) **616**

Clouds Cordial Bottle in Rare Yellow Olive

Clouds Cordial, rectangular form w/paneled tapering sides, smooth base, applied mouth, medium yellow olive, ca. 1870-85, 10 1/2" h. (ILLUS.) **840**

Fisher's Seaweed Extract Bottle

Fisher's Seaweed Extract Manx Shrub - [design of shrub] - Registered Company Ulverston - Quarrie's Patent, triangular form w/bulged neck, tooled lip, smooth base, yellow green, England, ca. 1890-1910, 5 1/4" h. (ILLUS.).......................... **616**

Doct. Harrison's Tonic Chalybeate Bottle

Harrison's (Doct.) - Tonic - Chalybeate,
rectangular w/sloping shoulder, smooth
base, applied mouth, medium emerald
green, ca. 1865-75, 9" h. (ILLUS.)............... **952**

Unlisted Cure Bottle in Aqua

**Johnston's (Dr. S.I.) Compound Extract -
Still - Ingia - King of the Blood Purifi-
ers - [design of standing lion] - 1862 -
The Great Cure for Blood Impurities -
New York,** round, smooth base, tooled
lip, unlisted, aqua, ca. 1875-85, 5 5/8" h.
(ILLUS.)... **1,120**

Jacob's Cholera & Dysentery Cordial Bottle

Jacob's - Cholera & - Dysentery - Cordial,
square shape w/applied mouth, open
pontil, number of seed bubbles,
aqua, ca. 1840-60, 6 3/4" h. (ILLUS.)............ **134**

*Mrs. E. Kidder Dysentery Cordial
Balsam Bottle*

Kidder (Mrs. E.) Dysentery Cordial Balsam, cylindrical w/rounded shoulder, applied top, open pontil, light green, 8 1/4" h. (ILLUS.) **2,090**

Miner's Damiana and Celery Compound Bottle

Miner's Damiana and Celery Compound [above image of woman standing amid boxes] - For the Cure of All Nervous Diseases Manufactured by H.C. Miner New York, rectangular w/sloping shoulder, smooth base, tooled mouth, one of only two known to exist, medium amber, ca. 1885-95, 8 3/4" h. (ILLUS.) **7,280**

Peuser & Kadish Druggists Bottle

Peuser & Kadish Druggists Chicago, cylindrical w/sloping shoulder, smooth base, tooled lip, rare in size & form, medium teal blue, ca. 1875-1890, 7 1/2" h. (ILLUS.) **504**

Rohrer's Expectoral + Wild Cherry Tonic Bottle

Rohrer's Expectoral + Wild Cherry Tonic Lancaster, Pa., tapering rectangular form w/rounded corners decorated w/rope twist design, smooth base, applied mouth, yellow w/amber tone, ca. 1865-75, 10 3/8" h. (ILLUS.) **504**

Swaim's - Panacea Bottle in Olive Green

Swaim's - Panacea - Philada, cylindrical w/rounded shoulder & paneled sides, pontil scarred base, applied mouth, deep olive green in base shading to lighter color in shoulder area, ca. 1840-60, 7 5/8" h. (ILLUS., previous page).................. **672**

lar mouth, deep apple green, ca. 1840-60, 8 1/8" h. (ILLUS.) **728**

U.S.A. Hosp. Dept. Bottle in Emerald Green

U.S.A. Hosp. Dept., cylindrical w/rounded shoulder, smooth base, applied mouth, blown in four-piece mold, emerald green, ca. 1860-75, shallow chip off side of lip, 6" h. (ILLUS.)... **560**

Warner's Safe Bitters Rochester NY, flask shape, slug-plated embossing of safe, "A & DHC" on base, amber (ILLUS. right w/other Warner's bottles) **770**

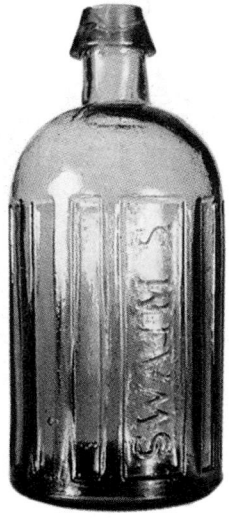

Swaim's - Panacea Bottle in Apple Green

Swaim's - Panacea - Philada, cylindrical w/rounded shoulder & paneled sides, pontil scarred base, applied sloping col-

Three Warner's Medicine Bottles

Warner's Safe Diabetes Cure Bottle

Warner's Safe Diabetes Cure Rochester, N.Y., smooth base, applied mouth, embossed image of safe, amber, ca. 1880-95, 9 1/2" h. (ILLUS.) 213

Warner's Safe Kidney & Liver Cure, flask shape, embossed w/image of safe, "57" on base, tooled blob top, original cork, golden (ILLUS., previous page, center w/other Warner's bottles) 66

Warner's Safe Kidney & Liver Remedy Rochester, N.Y., flask shape, embossed w/image of safe, tooled blob top, amber (ILLUS., previous page, left w/other Warner's bottles)... 55

Pine Tree Tar Cordial Bottle

Wishart's (L.Q.C.) - Trade [image of pine tree] Mark - Pine Tree Tar Cordial Phila., rectangular w/rounded shoulder, smooth base, tooled lip, deep blue-green, ca. 1880-1890, faint inside content haze, 10 1/8" h. (ILLUS.) 728

Amber Clock Face Flask

Clock face, embossed w/clock face w/Roman numerals & "Bininger's Regulator - 19 Broad St. - New York," open pontil, applied double collar mouth, amber, America, ca. 1855-70, spotty outside stains, 5 3/4" h. (ILLUS.) 420

Mineral Waters, Sodas & Sarsaparillas

Bay City, Ghirardelli & Casey Bottles

Bay City Soda Works, cylindrical w/sloping shoulder, medium cobalt blue, star decoration (ILLUS. center w/Ghirardelli & Owen Casey bottles).. 253

Mineral Water Bottle in Electric Cobalt Blue

Boardman (John) - Mineral Waters - New York, eight-sided shape, electric cobalt blue, applied blob mouth, iron pontil, ca. 1840-60, faint inside haze, 7 1/4" h. (ILLUS.) **616**

Coca-Cola Bottle in Tobacco Amber

Coca-Cola Registered Scranton, Pa. C.G.Co., cylindrical w/tooled crown top, medium tobacco amber, "490" on smooth base, ca. 1900-1915, 7 7/8" h. (ILLUS.) **78**

Three Western Soda Bottles

Bremenkampf & Regli Eureka Nev., cylindrical w/sloping shoulder, light aqua, applied top (ILLUS. left w/Morrill & Wright bottles) **154**

Casey (Owen) Eagle Soda Works - Sac City, cylindrical w/sloping shoulder, medium cobalt blue (ILLUS., previous page, right w/Ghirardelli & Bay City bottles) **110**

A.R. Cox Bottle in Deep Blue Green

Cox (A.R.) Norristown, cylindrical form w/long neck, deep blue green, applied double collar mouth, iron pontil, ca. 1840-60, 7 1/8" h. (ILLUS.) **179**

Crystal Palace Soda Water Bottle

Crystal Palace - Premium - Soda Water - W. Eagle - New York - "Union Glass Works Phila." [beneath image of Crystal Palace], cylindrical w/sloping neck, medium blue green, applied blob mouth, iron pontil, ca. 1840-60, 7 1/8" h. (ILLUS. of both sides) **896**

J.C. Davison Bottle in Teal Blue

Davison (J.C.) Chester, Pa., squat cylindrical form w/long neck, medium teal blue,

applied mouth w/original lightning-type closure, smooth base, ca. 1870-80, 7 1/8" h. (ILLUS.).. **179**

Mineral Water Bottle in Deep Cobalt

Dearborn (J. & A.) - New York - Mineral Waters, eight-sided shape, deep cobalt blue, applied blob mouth, iron pontil, ca. 1840-60, 7" h. (ILLUS.)................................... **392**

Very Rare J. Dowdall - Avondale - Bottle

Dowdall (J.) - Avondale - The - Excelsior, eight-sided shape, blue green, iron pontil, applied blob mouth, extremely rare, ca. 1840-60, minor scratching, 7 3/8" h. (ILLUS.).. **3,920**

Dowdall Bottle in Deep Cobalt

Dowdall (J.) [in slug plate] - Union Glass Works Phila. - Superior - Mineral Water, cylindrical shape w/panels at base, deep cobalt blue, iron pontil, applied blob mouth, rare, ca. 1840-60, 7 3/8" h. (ILLUS.) **2,128**

Excelsior & B.R. Lippincott Bottles

Excelsior (The) Water, eight-sided, green, applied top, iron pontil, 1850s-60s (ILLUS. right w/Lippincott bottle)................... **413**

Ghirardelli's Branch Oakland, cylindrical w/sloping shoulder, light cobalt blue (ILLUS. page 77, left w/Bay City & Owen Casey bottles) **220**

Rare Koka Nola Bottle

Esposito (J.) 812 & 814 Trade Mark Koka Nola Washington Ave Philada, cylindrical shape, light straw yellow hutch, smooth base, tooled mouth, "JE" monogram, ca. 1890-1910, faint rainbow-type bruise on inside of lip, rare copycat of Coca-Cola bottle, 7 3/4" h. (ILLUS.) **246**

Hard-to-find Brooklyn Soda Water Bottle

Hamilton [in slug plate] - & Church - Excelsior - Mineral Water - Brooklyn, eight-sided shape, medium teal green, applied mouth, iron pontil, ca. 1840-60, ice pick bruise inside edge of lip, minor ground imperfections, 7 1/4" h. (ILLUS.) **896**

H. Kneble's, M.R. Sacrimento, & Neyman & Drake Bottles

Kneble's (H.) Mineral Water 458 Fourth St NY, eight-sided, emerald green, applied top, iron pontil (ILLUS. left w/Sacrimento & Neyman & Drake bottles) **440**

(ILLUS., previous page, left w/Excelsior bottle) **1,540**

Morrill (G.P.), cylindrical w/sloping shoulder, bluish teal (ILLUS., page 78, center w/Bremenkampf & Wright bottles) **523**

Wm. W. Lappeus Bottle in Cobalt

Lappeus (Wm. W.) - Premium - Soda or - Mineral - Waters - Albany, N.Y., ten-sided shape, deep cobalt blue, iron pontil, applied blob mouth, ca. 1840-60, 7 1/4" h. (ILLUS.) **840**

Lippincott (B.R.) & Co Stockton, cylindrical w/ten panels arranged horizontally around base, medium cobalt, iron pontil

Rare Soda Bottle in Blue Green

Neyman & Drake Mok Hill Union Glass Works - Philadelphia, cylindrical shape w/sloping shoulders, medium blue green, applied blob-type mouth, iron pontil, one of only five examples known, ca. 1850, 7 1/2" h. (ILLUS.) **1,456**

Neyman & Drake Mok Hill Union Glass-works Philad.a, cylindrical w/sloping shoulder, teal, applied top & pontil (ILLUS., previous page, center w/Kneble & Sacrimento bottles)...................................... **1,500**

J. Townsend's Bottle in Blue Green

Old Dr - J. Townsend's - Sarsaparilla - New York, rectangular w/beveled sides, blue green or teal, iron pontil, applied sloping collar mouth, ca. 1845-60, tiny flake off shoulder edge on label panel, 9 5/8" h. (ILLUS.) **784**

Poland Mineral Springs Water Bottle

Poland Water - Ricker (H.) & Sons Proprietors Poland Mineral Springs Water,

figural man w/long beard, monogram on reverse, applied top, smooth base, golden amber, 10 3/4" h. (ILLUS.)......................... **990**

Sarsaparilla Bottle in Rare Teal Blue Color

Rose's (Dr J.S.) - Sarsaparilla - Philadelphia, rectangular w/beveled sides, teal blue, iron pontil, applied sloping collar mouth, extremely rare in this color, ca. 1845-60, light outside scratching, 9 1/4" h. (ILLUS.)...................................... **7,280**

Sacrimento (M.R.) - Union Glassworks Phila., cylindrical w/sloping shoulder, teal, very sloppy applied top, examples also known w/"Sacramento" spelling (ILLUS., previous page, right w/Kneble & Neyman & Drake bottles)... **2,200**

Torpedo Soda Water Bottle in Stand

Torpedo soda water, deep emerald green, in silver-plate three-prong stand on pedestal, applied mouth, smooth base, probably from Baltimore Glass District, ca. 1855-70, 7 3/4" h. (ILLUS., previous page) **784**

Wright (W.S.) - Pacific Glassworks, cylindrical w/sloping shoulder, teal blue, base embossed "1861-69" (ILLUS. page 78, right w/Bremenkampf & Morrill bottles) **468**

Pickle Bottles & Jars

Aqua Barrel-form Pickle Jar

Aqua, barrel shape, six-rib, half-gallon size, iron pontil, rolled lip, ca. 1855-65, 10 5/8" h. (ILLUS.) **532**

Medium Blue Green Cathedral Pickle Jar

Medium blue green, four-sided cathedral-type w/Gothic windows below rare clamshell design, applied mouth, smooth base, ca. 1860-70, 13 3/8" h. (ILLUS.) **1,008**

Rich Blue Green Cathedral Pickle Jar

Rich blue green, four-sided cathedral-type w/Gothic windows, applied ring mouth, smooth base, ca. 1860-70, 14 1/8" h. (ILLUS.) **1,120**

Yellow Olive Pickle Jar

Yellow olive, cylindrical w/side neck & tooled mouth, smooth base, embossed w/"Skilton, Foote & Co's Bunker Hill Pickles Trade Mark" & image of monument, ca. 1880-95, light overall inside stain, 7 5/8" h. (ILLUS.) **45**

Poisons

Coffin-shaped & George Bathurst Poison Bottles

Cobalt blue, coffin shape w/tooled top, hobnail-type decoration, 3 1/2" h. (ILLUS. left w/Bathurst Poison bottle) **99**

Cobalt blue, front panel embossed w/diamond lattice design & "George Bathurst Poison," tooled top, extremely rare, 4 1/2" h. (ILLUS. right w/coffin-shaped poison bottle) **110**

Cobalt Poison in Lattice & Diamond Design

Deep cobalt blue, Lattice & Diamond design full of seed bubbles, tooled mouth, "U.S.P.H.S." on smooth base, gallon size, ca. 1890-1910, 13 1/4" h. (ILLUS.).... **3,360**

Whiskey & Other Spirits

Owl Drug Company Triangular Bottle

Cobalt blue, triangular form, "Poison - The Owl Drug Co" embossed on front w/image of owl on mortar & pestle, smooth base, tooled mouth, ca. 1890-1915, 8" h. (ILLUS.) **472**

Rare Pint Beer Bottle in Moss Green

Beer, "Bay View Brewing Co Seattle Wash.," "NOT TO BE SOLD" on reverse, cylindrical, moss green, pt. (ILLUS.) **303**

Dallas Brewery Beer Bottle

Beer, "Dallas Brewery - Malt Wein - Dallas, Texas," smooth base, tooled mouth, medium amber, ca. 1890-1900, 8 1/4" h. (ILLUS.) **78**

"Frey & Co" Beer Bottle

Beer, "Property of Frey & Co San Rafael," cylindrical, w/original stopper, medium amber (ILLUS.) **55**

Grace Bros. Beer Bottle

Beer, "Grace Bros. Brewing Co Santa Rosa Cal" embossed around monogram, cylindrical, w/original stopper, amber (ILLUS.) **55**

Raspiller Brewing Beer Bottle

Beer, "Raspiller Brewing Co West Berkeley," cylindrical, tooled top w/embossed bird, amber (ILLUS.) **55**

Phoenix & AAA Old Valley Bottles

Bourbon, "Phoenix Old Bourbon," w/embossed eagle, flask shape, brilliant golden, 1/2 pt. (ILLUS. right w/AAA Old Valley Whiskey bottle)...................................... **935**

Taylor & Co. Whiskey Bottles

Whiskey, "Thos. Taylor & Co. Importers Virginia, N.," cylindrical w/long neck, applied top, deep reddish chocolate, 1874-80, fifth (ILLUS. left w/other Taylor & Co. bottle) **4,620**

Whiskey, "Thos. Taylor & Co. Importers Virginia, N.," cylindrical w/long neck, applied top, golden amber, sixth, very rare in this size (ILLUS. right w/other Taylor & Co. bottle)... **12,650**

Royal Champion Gin Bottle

Gin, case gin form, "Royal - T.M.W. - Champion," smooth base, applied mouth, blue-green, ca. 1870-80, 8 7/8" h. (ILLUS.) **102**

Whiskey, "AAA Old Valley Whiskey," w/embossed cross, flask shape, single roll collar, reddish amber (ILLUS. left w/Phoenix Old Bourbon bottle) **935**

Cobalt V. Squarza Spirits Bottle

Whiskey (?), "V. Squarza," cylindrical w/long neck & tapering shoulder, applied top, cobalt blue, ca. 1863 (ILLUS., previous page) **8,800**

BOXES

Band box, cov., oval, covered w/wallpaper w/floral drapery motifs in blues, greens & browns, America, mid-19th c., 14 3/4" h. (tears, separations, fading) **$940**

Band box, cov., oval, covered w/wallpaper w/large eagle motif w/trees in the background, green, white & brown on blue field, America, mid-19th c., 14 x 17", 12" h. (wear, losses, fading) **353**

Band box, oval, covered w/wallpaper in "Castle Garden" patt. in green, yellow & brown on blue field, America, mid-19th c., 17 x 19 1/4", 13 1/2" h. (lid missing, wear, fading) **470**

Bentwood, cov., oval, pine top & bottom w/old worn salmon paint on bottom, three swallow tails on base & one on lid, all w/copper tacks, Shaker-made, 11" **440**

Bentwood box, cov., oval, rich old dry blue paint w/copper tack construction, three swallow tails on base & one on lid, Shaker-made, 9 x 11 7/8", 4 1/4" h. (some tacks around the bottom edge missing) **770**

Candle box, cov., walnut w/original dark brown surface, dovetailed construction, sliding lid w/chamfered edges, 4 3/4 x 12", 4 1/2" h. **248**

Candle box, hanging-type, pine, rectangular shape w/keyhole-shaped crest, wooden pegs, rosehead nails, several later square-cut nails, 5 1/4 x 13 1/4", 11 1/4" h. w/crest (refinished, small piece restored on lower corner) **303**

Inlaid box, cov., mahogany, rectangular w/molded top & base, raised center panel on lid inlaid w/12-point patera, the front, back & sides outlined w/stringing, the interior lid fitted w/mirror in a tiger maple frame, interior lined in green velvet, America, 19th c., 7 x 11 1/8", 4 1/2" h. (minor scratches) **323**

Knife box, curly maple, canted sides w/unusual cut joints & a turned, pegged handle, pine bottom attached w/various nails, old refinishing, 9 x 13", 5 1/2" h. **715**

Snuff box, cov., oblong form, the lid w/h.p. scene of man rocking a baby in a cradle, a woman in bed, surrounded by a dog, cat & wood stove w/kettle, w/gilt border on black lacquered ground, England, early 19th c., 1 7/8 x 4 1/2", 1 1/4" h. **2,233**

Storage box, cov., curly maple, dovetailed construction, slide lid w/beveled edges, poplar bottom board, worn reddish stain, 5 1/2 x 9", 2 1/4" h. (old split) **523**

Storage box, cov., curly maple, wire nail construction, brass hinges, round wooden keyhole escutcheon, old refinishing has fine alligatoring on outside, 8 3/4 x 13", 4" h. (surface scratches, later reinforcing block nailed inside) **138**

Storage box, cov., oblong shape covered in wallpaper w/various floral patterns, the lid centered w/figure by a manor, 19th c., 9 x 11 1/8", 6 3/8" h. **235**

Storage box, cov., bentwood, oval Shaker-type, the four-finger lapped box in bittersweet wash w/paper label attached to interior of lid inscribed "Jennet Angus. Watervliet, 1832," Watervliet, New York, 5 1/2 x 10 1/2 x 7 1/2" **7,050**

Storage box, cov., pine, dome-top, wire hinges, iron handles & latch, dovetailed joinery, America, 19th c., 11 x 19 3/4", 8 7/8" h. (minor cracks) **999**

Polychrome Box with Sliding Lid

Storage box, cov., pine, dovetailed construction, polychrome rectangular form w/sliding lid, the lid decorated w/red, white & blue diamond pattern basket filled w/strawberries, surrounded by grapes, leaves, flourishes & scrolls within a striped border, the box w/central shell design on three sides w/similar scrolling, leafy vines & geometric star devices in red, white, blue, gold & salmon colors on black ground, America, early 19th c., repair to lid, 4 x 8 x 12" (ILLUS.) **1,880**

Storage box, cov., pine, dovetailed construction & scalloped trim, red base w/dark slate blue on lid & dark red over alligatored black on trim, "E.J.C. Concord, Mass." in yellow on front & "CO" in nails on the lid, stained interior, 8 1/4 x 12 1/4", 5 1/4" h. (damage to one hinge) **413**

Storage box, cov., pine, dovetailed corners, raised lid w/reeding, old decoration of red compote of tulips & other flowers on two sides, additional large flower & initials "A.P.S. Ar 1816" on the end, red, black & white decoration on blue/green ground, 9 x 17", 7 1/2" h. (small holes, some later screws added underneath) **523**

Storage box, cov., pine, grain painted, rectangular, lid w/brass ring pull, America, 19th c., 6 1/2 x 10 1/2", 3 1/8" h. (small loss on one corner) **235**

Storage box, cov., pine, grain painted, rectangular w/fitted lift-off lid, America, 19th c., 11 1/2 x 14", 9 1/2" h. **1,880**

Storage box, cov., pine & maple, oval, probably Shaker, w/two fingers facing left, maple sides, pine lid & bottom, mid-19th c., 2 x 6 1/8" **323**

Storage box, cov., pine, rabbeted joints &
wire cut nails, flat peaked lid, original
mustard paint overpainted w/red & then
comb-grained in wavy lines, zigzags & diamonds, lid has no red, 11 1/2 x 21 1/8",
10 1/4" h. **440**
Storage box, cov., pine, rectangular, sliding
lid, painted decoration of eagle & foliage
outlined in black w/gilt highlights on burnt
orange ground, America, 19th c., 5 x 9",
3 1/2" h. **705**
Storage box, cov., pine, w/old grain decora-
tion in black over a red ground, dovetailed case & lid, wrought-iron handles on
either end, external hasp lock, square
nails in bottom, 15 x 30", 14" h. (minor
edge wear) **303**
Storage box, cov., poplar, dovetailed con-
struction, step-down molding around
base & cove molding around lid, square
cut   nails,   original   green   paint,
10 x 16 1/2", 8" h. (wear to lid &
edges) **523**

Rare Early Decorated Storage Box

Storage box, painted & decorated pine,
shallow rectangular form w/hinged top,
black ground w/gold banding, the top
painted w/a large angel wearing a gown
& a flowing red sash, holding an olive
branch in one hand & a trumpet in the
other issuing a green banner inscribed in
gold "Peace Unto - All Women," lid interi-
or fitted w/a mirror within a mahogany veneer frame, American, early 19th c.,
wear,   imperfections,   6 7/8 x 10 7/8",
3 1/2" h. (ILLUS.) **7,050**

BREWERIANA

*Beer is still popular in this country, but the
number of breweries has greatly diminished.
More than 1,900 breweries were in operation in
the 1870s, but we find fewer than 40 major breweries supply the demands of the country a century
later, although microbreweries have recently
sprung up across the country.*

*Advertising items used to promote various
breweries, especially those issued prior to Prohibi-
tion, now attract an ever growing number of collectors. The breweriana items listed are a
sampling of the many items available.Also see
Antique Trader Advertising Price Guide.*

Blatz Brewing Company Figural Clock

Clock, "Blatz Brewing Company," oak, figural half-beer keg on three-legged stand,
oak face w/applied brass Arabic numerals & "Blatz" in script just above center,
includes key & pendulum, 10 x 17 1/2",
23" h. (ILLUS.) **$259**

Pabst Blue Ribbon Beer Door Push

Door push, "Pabst Blue Ribbon Beer," rectangular embossed tin in yellow, red &
dark blue, ca. 1930s, 4 x 9" (ILLUS.) **66**

Jacob Ruppert's Lager Beer Mug

Mug, "Jacob Ruppert's Lager Beer," glass w/reverse-painted glass label advertisement reading "Jac. Ruppert's Lager Beer - Centennial - Prize Medal" around coat of arms-type illustration, reverse of glass label bearing paper label reading "J.T. Murphy & Co., Manufacturers Decorated Glassware, 72 Murray Street, NY," reverse glass label w/crack, line of lifting running through middle, 10" h. (ILLUS.) **1,725**

Rare Bay View Brewery Sign

Sign, "Bay View Brewery," paper, rectangular, color illustration of man & woman on the banks of a stream w/dog & fishing paraphernalia & drinking beer, "Compliments Bay View Brewery, Baltimore" in blue lettering at top, ca. 1880s-90s, very rare, possibly unique, some restoration, 17 1/2 x 22" (ILLUS. framed) **3,163**

Blatz Brewing Company Sign

Sign, "Blatz Brewing Company," tin litho, color illustration of table holding Private Stock- & Wiener-labeled brands of beer in bottles & poured in glass, reflecting in ornately framed mirror on table behind them, on red ground w/rich purple drapery at left, by Beach Co. of Coshocton, Ohio, self-framed, ca. 1890-1900, 1"

scratch to image, frame scratched & dinged, 22 1/4 x 28 1/4" (ILLUS.).............. **1,680**

Emmerling's Grossvader Beer Sign

Sign, "Emmerling's Grossvader Beer," tin litho, color illustration of grey-haired Old World couple seated at table that holds bottles of beer & a plate of sausages, the couple smiling at each other & holding steins, on black ground, upper right corner reading "Emmerling's" in red & "Grossvader German Lager Beer" in white, text at bottom reading "Das Schmeckt Gut," by Kaufmann & Strauss Co., New York, ca. 1913, small nail holes at each corner, slight bending, surface haze, random surface blemishes, 19 1/2 x 27 1/2" (ILLUS.)................................ **540**

Sign, "Genesee Lager Beer," reverse on glass, color illustration of plant in mostly gold paint, "Genesee Brewing Co. Lager Beer" in lower left corner, "Rochester, N.Y." in lower right, in old original frame, 24 x 34" without frame (areas of flaking) **2,013**

Two-sided Illuminated Beer Sign

Sign, "Gilt Edge Beer," glass in metal casing, round, two sided w/reverse painting on each side, jade green w/gold & red stylized lettering reading "Gilt Edge - Best - Ruhstaller - Beer - Lager," electrical wiring illuminates from inside, made by Bacharach & Co., San Francisco, rare, 18" d. (ILLUS.) **5,500**

Kamm & Schellinger Brewing Sign

Sign, "Kamm & Schellinger Brewing Company," paper, colorful illustration of maned lion climbing atop blue globe, "The Kamm & Schellinger" in bold yellow lettering above it & "Brewing Company - Challenge the World" emblazoned on the globe in red, the globe & a bottle of beer positioned on top of barrel against brilliant blue & yellow ground, by Gugler, in old frame, ca. 1890-1900, two small tears at top, small scuffs & stains, 23 x 32" without frame (ILLUS.) 840

Tap knob, Bakelite w/enamel insert, Hamm's Beer, Hamm Brewing Co., St. Paul, Minnesota, 1940s (overall wear & small scratches) 128

Tap knob, Bakelite w/enamel insert, Hensler's Beer, Hensler Brewing Co., Newark, New Jersey, 1950s (wear overall, cracks around insert) 29

Tap knob, Bakelite w/enamel insert, KDK Cream Ale, Hornell Brewing Co., Hornell, New York, 1940s (some wear & small scratches) 69

Tap knob, Bakelite w/enamel insert, Lion Beer, Lion Brewing Co., New York, New York, 1940s (chip in rim of knob, scratches on insert) 31

Tap knob, Bakelite w/enamel insert, Michelob Beer, Anheuser-Busch Brewing Co., St. Louis, Missouri, 1940s (wear, small chips to rim) 60

Tap knob, Bakelite w/enamel insert, Mule Head Ale, Wehle Brewing Co., West Haven, Connecticut, 1940s (light wear) 92

Tap knob, Bakelite w/enamel insert, Neuweiler Beer, Neuweiler Brewing Co., Allentown, Pennsylvania, 1940s (scratches on insert) 35

Tap knob, Bakelite w/enamel insert, Otterstedt's Birch Beer, brewery name & location not listed, 1940s (missing enamel, wear, scratches, etc.) 30

Tap knob, Bakelite w/enamel insert, Pickwick Ale, Haffenreffer Brewing Co., Boston, Massachusetts, 1950s (wear to knob) 29

Tap knob, Bakelite w/enamel insert, Pon Beer, Feigenspan Brewing Co., Newark, New Jersey, 1940s (wear to knob, nicks & scuffs in insert) 34

Tap knob, Bakelite w/enamel insert, Rheingold Beer, United States Brewing Co., Chicago, Illinois, 1940s (a few scratches, insert turned) 36

Tap knob, Bakelite w/enamel insert, Ruppert Beer, J. Ruppert Brewing Co., New York, New York, 1940s (overall wear & light scuffs) 52

Tap knob, Bakelite w/enamel insert, Silver Label Beer, Lancaster Brewing Co., Lancaster, Ohio, 1940s (wear) 47

Tap knob, Bakelite w/enamel insert, Stanton Lager, Stanton Brewing Co., Troy, New York (wear, some staining to insert) 40

Tap knob, Bakelite w/enamel insert, Stegmaier Beer, Stegmaier Brewing Co., Wilkes-Barre, Pennsylvania, 1940s (1/8" chip in edge of insert) 25

Tap knob, Bakelite w/enamel insert, Stegmaier Beer, Stegmaier Brewing Co., Wilkes-Barre, Pennsylvania, 1950s (pliers marks on stem) 26

Tap knob, Bakelite w/enamel insert, Supreme Beer, South Bethlehem Brewing Co., South Bethlehem, Pennsylvania, 1940s (light wear, nick in edge of knob) 70

Tap knob, Bakelite w/enamel insert, Tam O Shanter Beer, American Brewing Co., Rochester, New York, 1940s (overall wear, small pits in insert) 54

Tap knob, Bakelite w/printed aluminum insert, Columbia Beer, Columbia Brewing Co., Shenandoah, Pennsylvania, 1940s (large scuff in rear of knob) 65

Tap knob, Bakelite, w/printed brass insert, Liebert & Obert, Philadelphia, Pennsylvania, 1940s (wear to insert) 60

Tap knob, Bakelite w/printed enamel insert, Erlanger Beer, Erlanger Brewing Co., Philadelphia, Pennsylvania, 1940s (wear to knob) 65

Tap knob, Bakelite w/printed metal insert, Plymouth Beer, Plymouth Brewing Co., Plymouth, Wisconsin, 1940s (overall wear) 44

Tap knob, Bakelite w/printed metal insert, Poc Beer, Pilsener Brewing Co., Cleveland, Ohio, 1940s (small spots on insert, wear) 100

Tap knob, chrome ball w/enamel insert, (Star) Pilsener Special, Star Union Co., Peru, Illinois (overall light scratches to knob & insert, a few small dings around rim of insert in chrome) 155

Tap knob, chrome w/copper insert, Braumeister Beer, Michigan Brewing Co., Grand Rapids, Michigan, 1940s (slightly bent insert, a few nicks on knob) 76

Tap knob, chrome w/enamel insert, Gettelman Rathskeller Brew, Gettelman Brewing Co., Milwaukee, Wisconsin, 1930s (a few tiny spots) 105

CANDLESTICKS & CANDLEHOLDERS

Early European Brass Candlestick

Candlestick, brass, a ring-turned socket above a turned knob & wide drip pan raised on a knob- and ring-turned shaft on a domed ringed base, hole in side of socket for candle removal, Europe, 17th c., 8 1/2" h. (ILLUS.)...................................... **$518**
Candlestick, brass, baluster-form shaft w/mid-drip pan above a stepped triangular base, probably Spain, 17th c., 9" h. (wear, pitting, dents)..................................... **460**
Candlesticks, brass, Arts & Crafts style, square pedestal form, green patination, marked "B & H - 201," early 20th c., 9 3/4" h., pr. **115**
Candlesticks, brass, Federal style, slightly domed round foot tapering to a knob at the bottom of the cylindrical stem w/flat flared rim, beaded detail, push-up knob at the side, first half 19th c., 7" h., pr. (some battering)............................. **248**

French Neoclassical Candlesticks

Candlesticks, brass, Neoclassical taste w/a wide round raised foot w/a gadrooned rim & rayed center supporting a gently flaring shaft w/a gadrooned shoulder band below the socket, w/detachable bobeches, France, Restauration period, first quarter 19th c., 10" h., pr. (ILLUS.)........ **690**

Queen Anne-Style Brass Candlesticks

Candlesticks, brass, Queen Anne-style, an oblong octagonal base supporting a baluster- and ring-turned standard w/a cylindrical socket, side hole in socket for removing candle, probably England, 18th c., split in one stick, 8" h., pr. (ILLUS.).......... **403**
Candlesticks, brass, thin square base centered by a slender tapering shaft to a disk knob below the cylindrical socket w/flattened rim, original push-ups, early, 9 1/2" h., pr. (one w/two minor splits, wear)... **440**

Brass-washed Roycroft Candlesticks

Candlesticks, brass-washed copper, Arts & Crafts style, hand-hammered, round base supporting a cylindrical stem below a dished drip pan & cylindrical socket, Roycrofters orb & cross mark, minor wear, early 20th c., 6 3/4" h., pr. (ILLUS.)...... **489**

Karl Kipp Copper Candlesticks

Candlesticks, copper, hand-hammered Arts & Crafts style, a rectangular foot w/riveted double stems form the shaft below a bobeche & socket, Princess patt., stamped initials of Karl Kipp, good original patina, early 20th c., 8" h., pr. (ILLUS., previous page)................................ **1,093**

Early European Pewter Candlesticks

Candlesticks, pewter, wide domed & dished footed base centered by a ring- and knob-turned stem below the cylindrical socket, Europe, probably 17th - 18th c., 7" h., pr. (ILLUS.)...................................... **1,495**

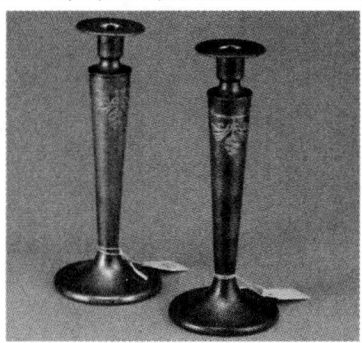

Silver Crest Silver Plated Candlesticks

Candlesticks, silver plate, round foot tapering to a slightly flaring cylindrical shaft below the socket w/a wide flattened rim, band of stylized pine cone silver overlay near the top, overall acid-etched silver finish, Silver Crest mark of Smith Metal Arts Co., Buffalo, New York, ca. 1920s, minor dent to one bobeche & minor dent to rim of other, 9 3/4" h., pr. (ILLUS.) **230**

Jarvie Copper Chamberstick

Chamberstick, copper, Arts & Crafts style, shallow dished base w/an arched riveted strap handle from the rim to the cylindrical center socket, stamped Jarvie mark, some cleaning to patina, early 20th c., 5 3/4" d., 3" h. (ILLUS.)..................................... **633**

Decorated Copper Chamberstick

Chamberstick, copper, Arts & Crafts style, three-sided base w/cutout feet, scrolled strap handle, bobeche w/upturned sides, the base decorated w/stylized flowers in green, red & black, stamp marked for Buffalo Art Craft Shop, 4 1/2" (ILLUS.) **489**

Arts & Crafts Copper Chamberstick

Chamberstick, copper, hand-hammered Arts & Crafts style, trumpet-form base w/riveted angular handle, cupped socket, medium patina, either Onondaga or Benedict, recent mark on base, early 20th c., 6 1/2" h. (ILLUS.).............................. **345**

Scottish Arts & Crafts Copper Sconce

Wall sconce, copper, Arts & Crafts style, a tall rectangular backplate embossed w/large stylized trees, a narrow projecting tray at the bottom centered by a candle socket, natural patina, Scotland, early 20th c., small tear at base, unmarked, 8 1/2 x 14 1/4" (ILLUS.) **345**

Early Tin Wall Candle Sconce

Wall sconce, tin, a wide round dished reflector w/a radiating crimped design, the base w/a curved flat arm supporting the candle socket, America, early 19th c., minor wear & corrosion spots, 14 1/2" h. (ILLUS.) **499**

CANDY CONTAINERS

*Indicates the container might not have held candy originally.

+Indicates this container might also be found as a reproduction.

‡Indicates this container was also made as a bank.

All containers are clear glass unless otherwise indicated. Any candy container that retains the original paint is very desirable; readers should follow descriptions carefully, realizing that an identical candy container that lacks the original paint will be less valuable.

Airplane, "Liberty Motor," clear glass, all original tin, metal wheels, original tin prop spinner & propeller **$1,500**
Airplane, "Spirit of St. Louis," blue glass, all original tin, top wing painted **375**
Airplane, "Spirit of St. Louis," green glass, all original tin **620**
Airplane, "Spirit of St. Louis," pink glass, all original tin **510**
"Amos and Andy," open car, original closure, great paint **540**

1970s Auto Candy Container

Automobile, 1929 model touring car, indented windows, embossed "FP 1929" under grill, black plastic cap at rear, ca. 1970s, 2 x 4 7/8" (ILLUS.) **15**

Beau Brummel Candy Container

Beau Brummel, standing man w/a handlebar mustache, dressed as a dandy wearing boater hat & suit w/vest & holding a cane, painted on eyes & mustache, Erte Company, New Jersey, ca. 1930s, 3 3/4" h. (ILLUS.) **60**
Boat, "Submarine F 6," all original **450**
Cannons, several designs of World War I-style cannons, some sit flat, others came w/moveable metal wheels, depending on design, each **380-600**

Hound Puppy Candy Container

Dog, Hound Puppy, seated clear dog w/threads at top for metal cap, ca.1940s, 3 1/2" h. (ILLUS. without metal cap) **20**
Felix the Cat, standing on round base, clear painted black except around eyes & mouth, ca. 1930s, 4 1/2" h. **125**

Fire Engine, clear, Victory Glass Co., 1940s, 2" l. **25**

Ice truck, 1920s vintage vehicle w/tin top & wheels, clear body, marked on base "West Glass Co., Grapeville, Pa.," ca. 1920s, 4 1/2" l. **685**

Papier-maché Jack O' Lantern

Jack O' Lantern, papier-maché, painted orange, paper insert eyes & smiling mouth, wire bail handle, made in Germany, ca. 1920s (ILLUS.) **90**

Jackie Coogan, original closure, excellent paint **1,300**

Jeep & Driver Candy Container

Jeep, clear, modeled w/a soldier driver, marked "Willys Jeep" on both sides, by J.H. Millstein Co., 1940s, 4 1/2" l. (ILLUS.) **45**

Lantern Candy Container

Lantern, clear w/molded cage bands & silvered metal top & base, wire bail handle, Victory Glass Co., 3 1/2" h. (ILLUS.) **25**

Phonograph with Glass Horn, original tin closure, good paint, 3 3/4" h. **200**

Rabbit w/Basket On Arm, embossed "1 oz. AVOR" & "USA," original closure, good paint, Victory Glass Co., 1920s, 4 3/8" h. **50**

Refrigerator, clear one-piece design w/motor on the top, tin snap closure in base, Victory Glass Co., 1930s **1,350**

Rocking Horse w/Clown Rider, aqua blue, original closure, 95% paint **250**

Glass Sailboat with Separate Sail

Sailboat, clear, separate fiber sail on wire mast, cardboard closure in base, sail 4" h., overall 6" l. (ILLUS.) **30**

Three Plastic Santas for Candy

Santa Claus, hard plastic in red, white & black, produced in various poses, some w/sacks on backs, some on sleds, some on skis, etc., produced by Rosbro Plastic Company, Providence, Rhode Island, late 1940s - early 1950s, 5 1/4" h., each (ILLUS. of three variations) **20**

Hard Plastic Snowman Container

Snowman, hard plastic, Frosty the Snowman style w/black top hat, eyes & buttons
& a red scarf, made by Rosbro Plastics of
Providence, Rhode Island, late 1940s -
early 1950s, 5 1/4" h. (ILLUS.) **18**

Early "Spark Plug" Candy Container

"Spark Plug," clear w/original painted orange blanket, red snap-on closure,
marked on bottom "Copyright 1923. King
Feature Syndicate Inc.," 4 1/4" l. (ILLUS.) **115**

Plastic Statue of Liberty Containers

Statue of Liberty, plastic, issued to com-
memorate the 100th Anniversary of the
Statue of Liberty in 1986, made in red,
white or blue, by Topps of Duryea, Penn-
sylvania, 4 3/4" h., each (ILLUS. of three) **7**

Tank, clear w/dark paint, World War II model w/figure of driver looking out of turret,
marked "USA" on each side, base
marked "Victory Glass - Toy Division,"
4 1/4" l. **35**
Toonerville Depot Line, original closure,
good paint, 3 1/2" h. **725**

CANS & CONTAINERS

Early Calumet Baking Powder Can

Baking powder, "Calumet Double-Action
Baking Powder," cylindrical can w/fitted
lid & paper label, dark red background
w/black & gold wording & center image of
a Native American chief, early 20th c., no
label on metal lid, 3" d., 5 1/2" h. (ILLUS.) **$26**

Columbia Biscuit Tin

Biscuit, "Columbia Biscuit Co.," cov., tin,
rectangular, bright red ground w/yellow
scroll design in upper corners & center
circular panel w/color illustration of Columbia figure & "Columbia Biscuit Co."
under arching blue banner reading "Columbia Biscuit Co." & over blue banner
reading "Family Goods," "St. Louis" at
bottom, about 8 x 10", 7" h. (ILLUS.) **460**

Colorful English Biscuit Tin

Biscuit, "Keen Robinson & Co., Ltd., London," squared form w/projecting rounded corners & curved sides, each side printed in color w/a different scene & large color florals at each corner, scenes titled "The Dog and the Shadow," "The Shepherd's Boy," "The Old Man and His Sons," & "The Dog in the Manger," early 20th c., 6 3/4" w., 6" h. (ILLUS.) **99**

Bouillon Cube Container

Bouillon cubes, cov., cylindrical, the front w/lithograph illustration of waiter holding tray w/steaming cup over "Henri" in red & "Bouillon Cubes" in scallop-edged black panel, red lid, holds five cubes, by L.C. Co., 1" d., 3 1/2" h. (ILLUS.) **44**

ZED Cigarette Rolling Paper Tin

Cigarette rolling paper, "ZED," small square stamped tin w/pale green ground & silver trim, some paper still inside, early 20th c., 1 1/2 x 1 3/4" (ILLUS.) **35**

Mohican Cinnamon Pure Spice Tin

Cinnamon, cov., 2-oz. container, rectangular, both sides w/black panel on red ground w/lithographed bust of Indian in headdress under "Mohican" in red, bottom reading "Pure Spices" in yellow, edge of lid reading "Cinnamon," 1 1/4 x 2 1/4", 3 3/4" h. (ILLUS.) **55**

Container for Arrow Brand Cloves

Cloves, rectangular, 2-oz. container, green ground w/yellow label reading "Arrow [picture of arrow] Brand - Pure - Cloves - Van Loan & Company" & address in New York City, 1920 (ILLUS.) **25**

Schepp's Cocoanut Container

Coconut, "Schepp's Cocoanut," cov., tin litho, cylindrical w/tapering shoulder, red ground w/illustration of children playing, black decorative borders, 19th c., 5" h. (ILLUS.) **196**

Holleb's One-pound Coffee Can

Coffee, "Holleb's Supreme Coffee," 1 lb. can, cylindrical w/keywind lid, black ground w/wording in white, red & gold, color image of cup & saucer w/white flowers, ca. 1930s, 5" d., 4" h. (ILLUS.) **99**

Kaffee Hag Coffee Can

Coffee, "Kellogg's Kaffee Hag Coffee," 1 lb. can, cylindrical w/keywind lid, white background w/orange & black wording & orange ring, some rim wear, ca. 1930s, 5" d., 4" h. (ILLUS.) **59**

Puritas Coffee Half-pound Can

Coffee, "Puritas Pure Delicious Coffee," 1/2 lb. can, short cylindrical shape w/pry-off lid, red background w/white & gold wording & gold & black image of a classical woman holding up a wreath, dated 1922, 4" d., 2 3/4" h. (ILLUS.) **121**

Swell Blend One-pound Coffee Can

Coffee, "Swell Blend Coffee," 1 lb. can, short cylindrical shape w/keywind lid, pale blue ground w/dark blue panel w/gold trim & white wording around an oval panel in shades of blue showing a steamship, ca. 1930s, 5" d., 3 1/2" h. (ILLUS.) **132**

Hodgsons Cough Drops Container

Cough drops, cov., tin litho, low square shape w/inset glass panels in top, front & sides, red, gold & black trim on natural ground, the rounded corners reading "Sole Makers - The Hodgsons," 7" sq. (ILLUS.) **69**

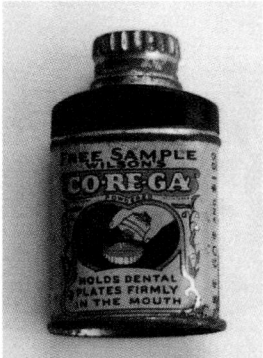

Wilson's CO-RE-GA Dental Powders Container

Dental adhesive, cov., cylindrical, black, red & yellow, w/front illustration of hand applying product to false teeth under words "Free Sample - Wilson's - CO-RE-GA - Powders" & over "Holds dental plates firmly in the mouth," gilt leafy border, 1910, 2" h. (ILLUS.) **25**

Engine grease, "Pennzoil Supreme Quality Safe Lubrication," 1 lb. can, cylindrical w/pry-off lid, black background w/large yellow, red & black oval logo above narrow yellow panel & more wording, no contents, ca. 1930s, 4 1/2" h. (minor nicks, dings & wear) **44**

Early Power-lube Lubricant Can

Engine grease, "Power-lube Lubricant," 1 lb. can, cylindrical w/pry-off lid, yellow background w/dark blue panel w/yellow wording & yellow & blue stalking tiger, ca. 1930s, back rough w/paint loss & fading, front w/dings, rubs & scratches, rust spots on bottom rim, no contents (ILLUS.) **187**

Gun powder, "DuPont 30 Calibre Smokeless Rifle Powder," 1 lb. can, black cylindrical shape w/ribbed horizontal bands, round paper label on the top in black & white centered by a spread-winged American eagle & crossed flags, late 19th - early 20th c. (minor alligatoring) **66**

Hall's Cannonite Sporting Powder

Gun powder, "Hall's Safety Smokeless Cannonite Sporting Powder - London," 1 lb. can, upright cylindrical shape w/wide low-domed shoulder w/small central neck, black w/a large diamond-shaped paper label in red & white w/white & black wording, England, late 19th - early 20th c., 4 1/4" d., 6 1/2" h. (ILLUS.) **88**

Hercules Black Sporting Powder

Gun powder, "Hercules Powder - Black Sporting," 1 lb. can, upright rectangular shape w/small screw cap on top, paper label w/red ground w/large black & white image of Hercules against a white triangle, black & white bands w/red & black wording, ca. 1940, 1 1/2 x 3 3/4", 6" h. (ILLUS.) **77**

Household oil, "Shell Handy Oil," 3 1/2 oz. oiler can, upright oval shape w/a metal cap & straight tall spout, yellow background w/red wording above images of an auto, lawn mower & sewing machine, Shell logo at bottom, no contents, ca. 1940 (overall rust spots, scratches w/ding dents at centers) **231**

Household oil, "Signal Products Household Oil," 4 oz. oiler can, cylindrical w/center cap & spout neck, red & yellow background w/round black & white logo & black & red wording, partial contents, ca. 1950s (minor scattered nicks & scratches) **88**

Choice Lard Bucket

Lard, "Choice Leaf Lard," tin, cylindrical bucket w/tab handles, lithographed label on front showing bucket of piglets in center & "Choice Leaf Lard - Kettle Rendered," no lid, 14" h. (ILLUS.) **92**

Licorice Lozenges Container

Licorice lozenges, cov., rectangular, w/arched glass inset panel on front side flanked by two oval decorative panels w/"LICORICE" & "LOZENGES" reading vertically in ornate stylized script, stencil painted label, 19th c., 7" h. (ILLUS.) **29**

Motor oil, "Mobiloil Arctic," 1 qt. can, cylindrical w/white background & red Pegasus logo over blue brand name, red band around bottom, full contents, ca. 1950s (minor scattered nicks, scratches & wear) **105**

Early Oilzum Motor Oil Can

Motor oil, "Oilzum Motor Oil," 1 qt. can, cylindrical w/red ground & dark blue bands at top & base w/dark blue front panel below the head of a rajah & wording in red & white, ca. 1930s, empty w/new top & bottom, seam resoldered, minor rust spots on back, scratch & rust on front (ILLUS.) **275**

Large Old Dutch Lubricant Can

Motor oil, "Old Dutch Lubricant," 5 qt. can, large cylindrical shape w/top spout neck & wire bail handle w/wooden grip, blue & black background w/black & white scene of large Dutch windmill on the upper half & white wording below, ca. 1930s, overall rust spots & wear (ILLUS.) **231**

Para-Field 2-Gallon Motor Oil Can

Motor oil, "Para-Field 100% Pure Paraffin Base Motor Oil," 2 gal. can, upright rectangular shape w/screw cap & top strap handle, yellow background w/sketch of early wooden oil derrick & red & black wording, no contents, ca. 1930s, minor scattered nicks & scratches (ILLUS.) **385**

Motor oil, "Penn Seal 100% Pennsylvania Motor Oil," 1 qt. can, orange & dark green ground w/green & white wording, top punched, no contents, late 1930s (few small nicks & dings) **83**

Rare Early Texaco Oil Can

Motor oil, "Texaco Motor Oil - Heavy," 1/2 gal. can, tall slender cylindrical shape w/tall angled "easy-pour" spout top, green ground w/white panel & black wording above the red, white, black & green Texaco star logo, ca. 1930s, no contents, nicks, flecks & overall scratches, 5" h. (ILLUS.) **633**

Motor oil, "Veedol 100% Pennsylvania Supreme Quality Motor Oil," 1 qt. can, black background w/white & orange diamond logo & white & orange wording, top punched, no contents, late 1930s (scattered rim dings, dents & nicks) **33**

Shampoo Container

Shampoo, cov., circular, the lid w/illustration of woman w/flowing hair & "Mary T. Goldman's Shampoo - Write for Booklet and Free Advice to Mary T. Goldman, St. Paul, Minn.," 1900, 2" d. (ILLUS.) **75**

Small Bruton Scotch Snuff Tin

Snuff, "Bruton Scotch Snuff," cylindrical w/a white background printed in black & red, pry-off lid, 1 3/4" d., 2 3/8" h. (ILLUS.) **8**

Talcum powder, "Mennen's Violet Talcum Toilet Powder," shaker can, upright flattened oval shape w/short neck & cap, cream ground decorated overall w/colorful violets, a rectangular pale blue front panel w/picture of Mr. Mennen & wording in dark red, dated 1910, 2 1/2" w., 4 1/2" h. (slight wear) **121**

Unusual Palm Olive Talcum Can

Talcum powder, "Palm Olive Talcum - Rose Egyptian," flattened flaring & arched shape w/gold shaker cap, dark green sides w/embossed gold label & pink & green roses, ca. 1919, 1 1/4 x 3 3/4", 3 1/2" h. (ILLUS.) **149**

Colorful Talcum Powder Container

Talcum powder, "Rawleigh's Pan-Jang Talcum Powder," cov., tin litho, flattened cylindrical shape w/short neck & cap, colorful gold, green, pink & yellow illustration on both sides of smiling Japanese woman in kimono looking out window at gold long-tailed birds in flowering cherry tree in foreground, "Rawleigh's Pan-Jang Talcum Powder" in gold at top, cherry blossom decoration on shoulder, 1 1/2 x 3", 5" h. (ILLUS.) **121**

Ocean Blend Tea Container

Tea, "Ocean Blend Tea," 5-lb. container, tin litho, rectangular, bright red ground w/scene of luxury ocean liner on front & "Ocean Blend" at top over banner reading "Indian & Ceylon," "The Ocean Blend Tea Co." at the bottom & in dark blue ovals on the sides, includes partial contents, 8 1/2" h. (ILLUS.) **92**

Mayo' s Tobacco Roly-Poly Dutchman

Tobacco, "Mayo' s Tobacco," roly-poly figure of smiling Dutchman in wide belt & red bandana & holding long-stemmed pipe, w/tax stamp, by Tin Deco, 6" d., 6 1/2" h. (ILLUS.) **460**

Tobacco, "Squadron Leader Mixture Tobacco," flat rectangular tin w/rounded corners, colorful lid w/thin red border band around blue sky & color image of World War I biplane in battle, wording in white, red & black, Samuel Gawith & Co., early 20th c., 3 1/4 x 4 1/4" **99**

Tuxedo Tobacco Gold & Green Canister

Tobacco, "Tuxedo Tobacco" 1 lb. canister, slightly domed fitted lid, green & gold printed front panel centered by a scene of a young man wearing a tuxedo, the background in green & gold stripes, some wear, 4" d., 5 3/4" h. (ILLUS.) **55**

Early Twin Oaks Tobacco Pocket Tin

Tobacco, "Twin Oaks" pocket tin, hinged curved flap top, red acorn logo & wording in gold & red, worn gold vine & silvered ground, early 20th c., 3 1/2" w., 4" h. (ILLUS.) **65**

Scarce Victorian Tooth Powder Can

Tooth powder, "Sozodont Powder," low rectangular can w/serpentine sides & indented lid, sepia background printed w/black wording & the image of a young Victorian man brushing his teeth, second half 19th c., 2 x 2 3/4", 7/8" h. (ILLUS.)......... **165**

Typewriter Ribbon Container

Typewriter ribbon, "Columbia Typewriter Ribbon," circular, the lid w/Art Deco-style line drawing of twin girls labeled "Clean" & "Good," geometric border, orange ground, 1920s, 2 1/2" d. (ILLUS.) **15**

CAT COLLECTIBLES

Art Print, Morris, by Charles Frace, 16 x 20", signed, 1976 (ILLUS., bottom of page) **$150-200**
Board game, Pink Panther, Warren, ca. 1977... **20-40**

Sylvester Bank on Fish Crate

Character bank, vinyl, Sylvester on fish crate, 11 1/2", Dankin, 1969 (ILLUS.)........ **20-40**

Morris Art Print by Charles Frace

Kliban Cat Christmas Cards

Christmas cards, Kliban Cat, "Bah, humbug!" boxed set (ILLUS.) **8-12**

Katnip Hand Puppet

Hand puppet, Katnip from Terrytoon's Herman & Katnip, cloth w/soft vinyl head, Gund, ca. 1960 (ILLUS.) **15-40**
Hand puppet, "Linus the Lionhearted," talking-type, Mattel, ca. 1965, 14" **40-90**

Esso Tiger Key Chain

Key chain, Esso tiger, painted rubber w/metal ring, ca. 1960, 1 1/4" h. (ILLUS.) **15-20**

Figural Ceramic Kitten Lamp

Garfield Hand-held Massager

Lamp, ceramic, figural kitten, pink & blue, unmarked, ca. 1930-40, figure 6 3/4" tall (ILLUS., previous page)................................ **25-45**

Lunch box, Pink Panther, vinyl, Aladdin, ca. 1980.. **65-95**

Lunch kit, "Linus the Lionhearted," vinyl w/metal bottle, Aladdin, ca. 1965 .... **400-600**

Massager, Garfield, hand-held, Pollenex, in original box (ILLUS., bottom previous page)... **15-25**

Black Panther Model Kit

Model kit, Black Panther, Endangered Species, Revell, ca. 1974, 7 x 9" box (ILLUS.) **40-60**

Aurora Saber Tooth Tiger Model Kit

Model kit, Saber Tooth Tiger from Prehistoric Scenes Snap Together All Plastic Custom Builder Kits, plastic, in box, Aurora, 1971 (ILLUS.) **30-40**

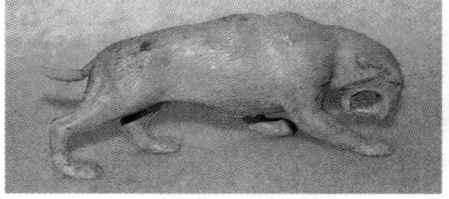

Model of Tiger (Smilodon)

Model of Saber Tooth Tiger (Smilodon), light green plastic, Marx, ca. 1950s, 3" l. (ILLUS.).. **10-15**

"Three Lives of Thomasina" Disney Movie Poster

Movie poster, "Three Lives of Thomasina," insert type, Disney, ca. 1964 (ILLUS.).. **15-25**

MGM Lion Mug

Mug, ceramic, MGM lion, black w/MGM logo (ILLUS.) **5-10**

Kliban Cat Mug

Mug, Kliban cat, Sigma Taste Setter, ca. 1970 (ILLUS.)................................... **5-10**

Beatrix Potter's Music Box

Music box, ceramic, Beatrix Potter's Miss Moppet chases mouse, by Schmid, 1980, 6" h. (ILLUS.)................................... **20-35**

Music box, Pink Panther, Christmas Limited Edition, Royal Orleans, 1982, 1983, 1984, each **50-100**

Music box, Pink Panther, plush figure w/"Think Pink" shirt, Mighty Star, 25" **18-28**

Paint-by-number Picture of Kittens

Paint-by-number picture, two kittens w/daisies, 16 x 12" (ILLUS.) **10-15**

Pinback button, w/MGM lion photo & "On World Tour, The Greatest Star of the Screen," ca. 1930s.. **15-25**

Plush Rabbit Fur Kitten

Plush toy, kitten, covered in pink rabbit fur w/felt ears, ca. 1960, 11" l. (ILLUS.)........... **14-22**

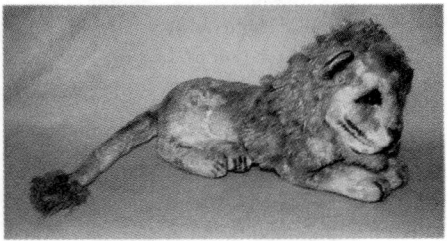

Plush Toy Mohair Lion

Plush toy, mohair lion, ca. 1950s, 22" l. (ILLUS.).. **20-30**

Mohair Plush Toy

Plush toy, tiger, mohair, ca. 1950, 4 1/2" l. (ILLUS.)... **8-15**

Plush toy, "Linus the Lionhearted," cereal mail-away, ca. 1960s................................. **50-100**

Puppet, Pink Panther, plush, ca. 1980-1990s, 11"....................................... **12-20**

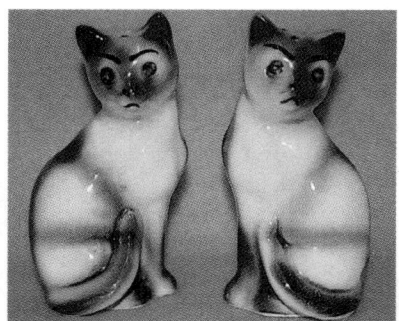

Siamese Cat Salt & Pepper Shakers

Salt & pepper shakers, ceramic, Siamese cats w/rhinestone eyes, ca. 1950, 3 3/4" h., pr. (ILLUS.) **12-18**

Kitten Sitting Up Squeak Toy

Squeak toy, kitten sitting up, pink, unmarked, 1950s, 8" (ILLUS.)......................... **12-20**

"Morris for President - 1988" T-shirt

T-shirt, "Morris for President - 1988" w/photo in center (ILLUS.) **10-15**
Tapestry, crouching leopard, fringed, ca. 1940, 40" l. (ILLUS., top next page) **50-75**
Tapestry, kittens on fence, 39" (ILLUS., middle next page) **15-25**

Telephone, Garfield, eyes open when handset is lifted, Tyco, 1982 (ILLUS., bottom next page) **15-25**
Thermos, Pink Panther, plastic, for vinyl kit, Aladdin, ca. 1980... **15-35**

Morris Canvas Tote Bag

Tote bag, Morris, white canvas, w"Purr if You're a Morris Fan" and "I'm Morris, 9-Lives is My Bag" (ILLUS.) **12-20**

Vinyl Plaid Cat

Toy, cat, vinyl, plaid, ca. 1940, 6" (ILLUS.)...... **8-12**

Tom Wind-up Walker

Crouching Leopard Tapestry

Kittens on Fence Tapestry

Garfield Telephone

Top Cat TV-Tinykins Characters

Toy, Tom of Tom and Jerry wind-up walker, plastic, Japan, ca. 1960, 4" h. (ILLUS., on page 106) **20-30**

Toy, Top Cat and Benny ramp walker, plastic, Marx, ca. 1960 .... **40-70**

Toys, hard plastic figures of various characters from Top Cat TV-Tinykins, Marx, ca. 1960, 1 1/2", each (ILLUS. of six, top of page).. **10-20**

TV lamp, ceramic, cat w/bow, black & white, Maddux of California, ca. 1950, 6 1/2" l. (ILLUS.).. **40-65**

Chartreuse Green Panther on Log

TV lamp, ceramic, panther on log, chartreuse green, ca. 1950, 7 3/4 x 11" (ILLUS.).. **25-45**

TV lamp, panthers on rocky base, ceramic, black, ca. 1950, 12 x 8 1/2" (ILLUS., bottom of page) **40-75**

View-Master, Top Cat, 3-reel packet, #B513 or BB513 .... **12-20**

Figural Cat with Bow TV Lamp

TV Lamp With Two Panthers

Born Free Movie Lobby Card

Big Cats

Comic book, "A Tiger Walks," Disney, photo cover, Gold Key #10117-406, ca. 1964 .... **10-40**
Movie lobby card, "Born Free," 1966 (ILLUS., top of page)..................................... **8-12**

Movie Born Free Lobby Card

Movie lobby card, "Born Free," 1966 (ILLUS.).. **8-12**
Movie poster, "Born Free," one-sheet, ca. 1966, 27 x 41" **35-50**
Movie poster, "Charlie the Lonesome Cougar," one-sheet, 1967.................................... **20-35**
Movie poster, "Clarence the Cross-Eyed Lion," 1965 (ILLUS., next column) **25-35**
Movie poster, "Living Free," one-sheet, ca. 1972, 27 x 41" **15-25**
Playset, "Clarence the Cross-Eyed Lion" from Daktari TV show, 110 pcs., Marx, ca. 1967 .... **300-500**
Playset, "Clarence the Cross-Eyed Lion" from Daktari TV show, 140 pcs., Marx, ca. 1967 .... **400-650**

Movie Poster "Clarence, the Cross-eyed Lion"

Record, "Born Free," LP, Andy Williams, ca. 1960.. **3-5**
Record, "Living Free," LP, book inside, 33 1/3 rpm, Disneyland Records, 1972.......... **10-16**
Sheet music, "Born Free," by John Barry & Don Black, ca. 1966.. **4-8**

Books & Magazines

"Charlie, The Lonesome Cougar" Paperback

Book, "Charlie, The Lonesome Cougar," Disney, Scholastic paperback, TX 1159, photo cover, ca. 1967 (ILLUS.) **1-3**

Book, "Clarence the Cross-Eyed Lion," from Daktari TV show, by Jess Shelton, w/photos, Ace paperback, ca. 1966 .... **3-6**

"The Cat and the Captain" Book

Book, "The Cat and the Captain," by Elizabeth Coatsworth, illustrated, Macmillan, ca. 1929 (ILLUS.) **8-18**

"Clarence the Cross-Eyed Lion" Book

Book, "Judy and the Kitten," from Daktari TV show, w/Clarence the Cross-Eyed Lion on the cover, Whitman Tell-A-Tale, ca. 1969 (ILLUS.).................................... **3-6**

"The Morris Approach" Book

Book, "The Morris Approach," by Barbara Burn, 1st ed., William & Morrow, 1980 (ILLUS.).. **8-12**

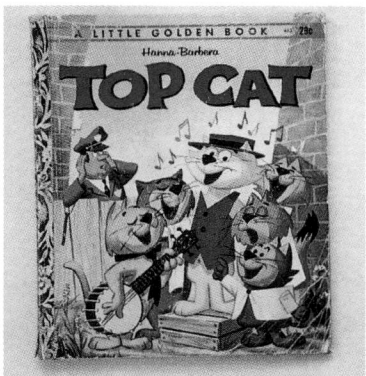

"Top Cat" Little Golden Book #453

Book, "Top Cat," Little Golden Book #453, ca. 1962 (ILLUS.) **9-18**

"Top Cat Tales" Book

Book, "Top Cat Tales," Whitman, ca. 1960 (ILLUS.) **7-15**

Comic book, "Linus the Lionhearted," one issue produced, Gold Key, ca. 1965 .... **10-50**

TV Guide Cover Featuring Clarence the Cross-Eyed Lion

Magazine, TV Guide, w/Clarence the Cross-Eyed Lion from Daktari TV show on cover, August 6, 1966 (ILLUS.) **8-12**

Figural Items

Air Freshener and Cotton Dispenser

Air freshener/cotton dispenser, ceramic, ca. 1930, 3" h. (ILLUS.) **10-15**

Air Freshener and Cotton Dispenser Set

Air freshener/cotton dispenser, ceramic, ca. 1930, 3" h., the set (ILLUS.) **10-15**

Figural Cat Wicker Basket

Basket, wicker, figural cat, painted white w/button eyes, nose, 21" h. (ILLUS.) **35-55**

Cat and Bird House Figural Bottle

Bottle, ceramic, figural cat & flickering bird house, Drioli, Italy, ca. 1950, 5" h. (ILLUS.) **35-60**

Figural Cat Ceramic Cookie Jar

Cookie jar, cov., green ceramic figural cat in outfit, Doranne of California, 12" h. (ILLUS.) **25-35**

Model of Angry Kitten

Model of angry kitten, ceramic, black & white , Japan, ca. 1950, 3" h. (ILLUS.) **10-15**

Shangri-La Souvenir Cat Figurine

Model of cat, painted plaster w/rhinestone eyes, Shangri-La souvenir, 3" h. (ILLUS.).. **15-20**

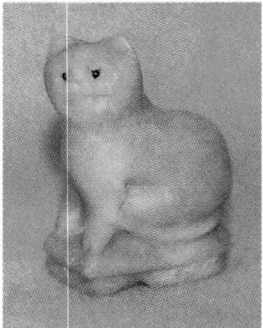

Hand-carved Soapstone Cat Figurine

Model of cat, soapstone, hand-carved, 1 1/2" h. (ILLUS.) **8-14**

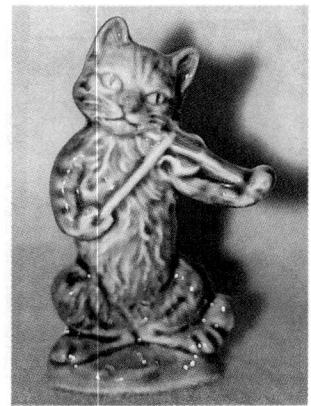

Cat and the Fiddle Ceramic Figurine

Model of Cat and the Fiddle, ceramic, Wade, Large Nursery Favorites series, 1972-1981, 3" h. (ILLUS.) **25-40**

Pewter Cat Figurine

Model of cat w/arched back, pewter, Franklin Mint Curio Cats, ca. 1988, 2 3/4" h. (ILLUS.) **5-10**

Cat with Butterfly Figurine

Model of cat w/butterfly, bone china, brown, marked "150," ca. 1950, 2 1/4" h. (ILLUS.) **10-18**

Ceramic Figurine Cat With Flute

Model of cat w/flute, ceramic, "1346," 2 1/4" h. (ILLUS.) **8-14**

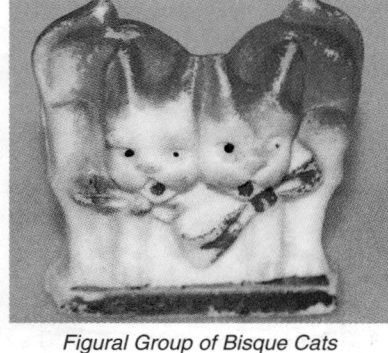

Figural Group of Bisque Cats

Model of cats, bisque, two cats wearing bows, on blue base, Japan, 1 3/4" h. (ILLUS.) **35-55**

Mod Design Model of Cats

Model of cats, plaster, cat attached w/chains to two kittens, mod design, ca. 1960-70 (ILLUS.) **8-12**

Franklin Mint Curio Cat

Model of Egyptian cat, black metal, Franklin Mint Curio Cats, ca. 1988, 2 3/4" h. (ILLUS.) **15-20**

Kitten and Child on Pillow Figurine

Model of kitten & child on pillow, ceramic, Josef Originals, 2 x 2 1/2" h. (ILLUS.) **25-45**

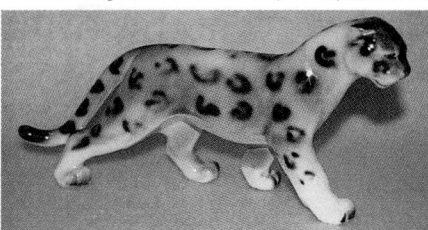

Leopard Figurine

Model of leopard, ceramic, w/clover mark, Japan, 5 1/2" l. (ILLUS.) **8-12**

Lion Chalkware Figure

Model of lion w/ball, chalkware, gold/green paint, on rectangular molded base, 1940s-50s, 8", (ILLUS.) **20-35**

Miniature Ceramic Lioness Figurine

Model of lioness, ceramic, miniature size, 1 x 2" (ILLUS.) **4-8**

Figural White Longhaired Cat

Model of longhaired cat, bone china, white, 5 1/2" h. (ILLUS.) **8-12**

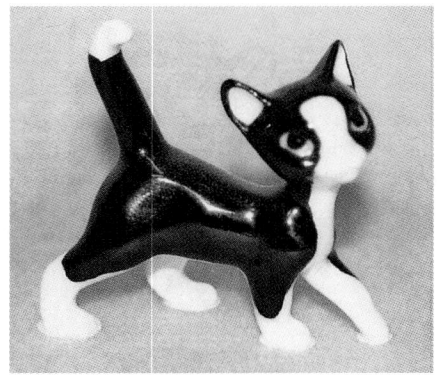

Papa Cat Figurine

Model of Papa Cat, ceramic, miniature size, by Hagen Renaker, 1995, 1 3/4" h. (ILLUS.) **4-6**

Carnival Chalkware Model of Lion

Model of roaring lion, chalkware, carnival-type, w/pink glitter, ca. 1940-50s, 8 x 12 1/2" (ILLUS.).. **35-50**

Wood Carved Cat

Model of sitting cat, wood carving w/brass decorations & copper ears, unmarked, 5" h. (ILLUS.)... **10-20**

Vinyl Model of Sylvester

Model of Sylvester, articulated vinyl, Dankin, 1960, 8 1/2" (ILLUS.)...................... **15-30**

Ceramic Tiger Figurine

Model of tiger, ceramic, w/clover mark, Japan, 5 1/2" l. (ILLUS.) **8-12**

Ceramic Tiger Figurine

Model of tiger, terra cotta, painted black & gold, by Wales, Japan, 12" l. (ILLUS.)....... **10-20**

Kittens with Red Bows Figurines

Models of kittens, ceramic, black & white w/red bows, Royal Copley, 8" h., each (ILLUS. of two)... **65-85**
Planter, ceramic, panther, black, McCoy, ca. 1950, 15 1/2" l. (ILLUS, below.) **30-50**

Figural Black Panther Planter

Figural Cat Show Trophy

Trophy for cat show, brass & wood, model of seated cat, 1961, 6" h. (ILLUS.)............. **15-25**

CERAMICS

Abingdon

From about 1934 until 1950, Abingdon Pottery Company, Abingdon, Illinois, manufactured decorative pottery, mainly cookie jars, flowerpots and vases. Decorated with various glazes, these items are becoming popular with collectors who are especially attracted to Abingdon's novelty cookie jars.

Also see Antique Trader Pottery & Porcelain Ceramics Price Guide, 4th Edition.

Abingdon Mark

Ashtray, New Mode, round, divided in half by ridge to hold cigarettes, rectangular base, pink, No. 456, 1939-48, 5 3/4" d. (ILLUS. left, below).. **30**

Ashtray, round, white, No. 334 (ILLUS. right, w/New Mode ashtray, below) **20**

Cactus Book Ends/Planters

Book ends/planters, model of cactus, No. 374, 1936-8, 7" h., pr. (ILLUS.) **125**

Bowl, 9 x 14" rectangular, turquoise, Han patt., No. 523, 1940 (ILLUS., below)............... **40**

Abingdon Ashtrays

Abingdon Han Bowl

Abingdon Shell Candleholder

Candleholder, double, Shell line, green, No. 505, 1940-49, 4" h., pr. (ILLUS.).............. **25**

Bamboo Candleholders & Console Plate

Candleholders, Bamboo patt., No. 716, pr. (ILLUS. left & right w/console plate) **30**
Candleholders, Sunburst, in the form of three ribbed connected semicircles, rose, No. 447, 1938, 8" l., pr. (ILLUS. right & left w/window box, bottom of page) **60**
Console plate, Bamboo patt., No. 715, 10 1/2" d. (ILLUS. above w/candleholders) **125**

Abingdon Choo Choo Cookie Jar

Cookie jar, Choo Choo, No. 651D, 1948-50, 7 1/2" h. (ILLUS.) **225**

Fat Boy Cookie Jar

Cookie jar, Fat Boy, No. 495, 1940-46, 8 1/4" h. (ILLUS.)..................................... **500-700**
Cookie jar, Hippo, No. 549, plain & decorated, 8" h.. **350-550**
Cookie jar, Little Girl, No. 693, 9 1/2" h. **225**
Cookie jar, Miss Muffet, No. 662D, 11" h. **350**
Cookie jar, Money Bag, No. 588D, 7 1/2" h......... **40**

Sunburst Candleholders & Window Box

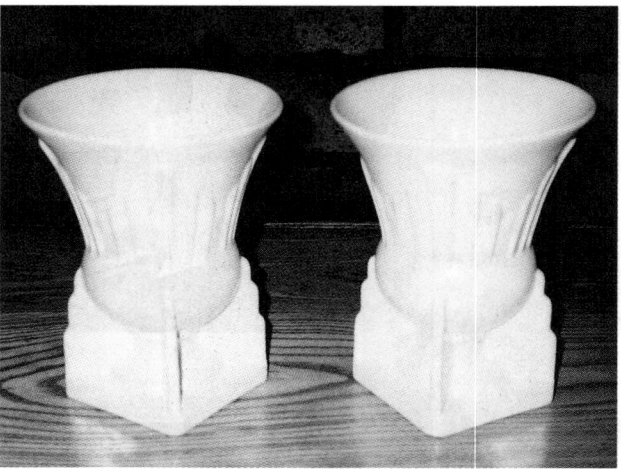

Abingdon Capri Vases

Pineapple Cookie Jar

Cookie jar, Pineapple, No. 664, 1949-50,
   10 1/2" h. (ILLUS.) **200**
Cookie jar, Witch, No. 692, 11 1/2" h. **1,000**
Model of penguin, black, wearing top hat,
   No. 573, 5" h. (ILLUS., next column) **50**
Model of penguin, white, 3" h. **25**
Model of swan, No. 661, 3 3/4" h. **150**
Vase, 4 1/2" h., No. C1, whatnot type **100**
Vase, 5" h., No. B1, whatnot type **100**
Vase, 5" h., white floral decoration on blue
   ground, small handles, No. 567D, 1942-
   46 (ILLUS. page 120, right w/window box
   No. 570D) **40**

Abingdon Penguin Figurines

Vase, 5 3/4" h., Capri, urn form w/quatrefoil
   bases, white, No. 351, 1935-37, each
   (ILLUS. of two, top of page) **125**

Figural Blackamoor Vase

Vase, 7 1/2" h. figure of Blackamoor, No.
497D (ILLUS.) **150**

Fern Leaf Pattern Vase

Vase, 8 1/2" h., No. 424, Fern Leaf patt.,
medium size (ILLUS.) **100**

Abingdon Athenian Vase

Vase, 9" h., Athenian, white, No. 315, made
in 1934-36 & 1947 (ILLUS.) **60**

Abingdon Laced Cuff Vase

Vase, 10" h., Laced Cuff, side handles,
white, No. 446, 1938-39 (ILLUS.) **60**

Lung Pattern Vase

Vase, 11" h., Lung patt., No. 302 (ILLUS.) **225**
Wall pocket, figural Dutch girl, No. 490,
10" h. **150**

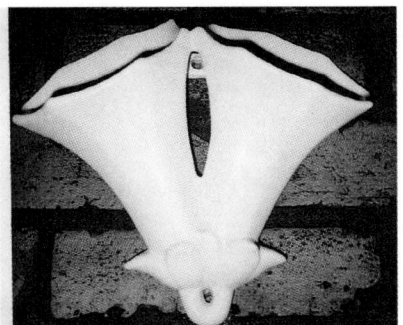

Double Trumpet Wall Pocket

Abingdon Window Box & Vase

Wall pocket, Morning Glory, double trumpet
form, No. 375, 1936-40, 6 1/2" h.
(ILLUS., bottom previous page) **45-55**

Window box, oblong, scalloped rim, white
floral decoration on blue ground, No.
570D, 1942-46, 10" l. (ILLUS. left w/vase
No. 567D, top of page) **35**

Window box, Sunburst, in the form of three
connected ribbed semicircles, rose, No.
448, 1938-39, 9" l. (ILLUS. page 117,
center w/Sunburst candleholders) **80**

American Painted Porcelain

*During the late Victorian era American arti-
sans produced thousands of hand-painted porcelain items, including tableware, dresser sets,
desk sets, and bric-a-brac. These pieces of porcelain were imported and usually bear the marks
of foreign factories and countries. To learn more
about identification, evaluation, history and
appraisal, the following books and newsletter by
Dorothy Kamm are recommended:* American
Painted Porcelain: Collector's Identification &
Value Guide, Comprehensive Guide to American Painted Porcelain, *and* Dorothy Kamm's
Porcelain Collector's Companion.

Bowl, 6" d., 4" h., deep rounded form on a
pedestal base, decorated w/conventional
butterfly design in tan luster & burnished
gold outlined in black, burnished gold rim
& foot, signed "E.T. LOW, Dec. 1909,"
marked w/wreath "O. & E.G., Royal, Aus-
tria" (ILLUS., next column) **$60**

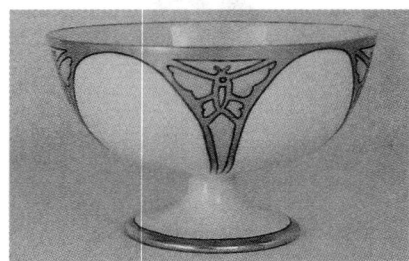

Butterfly Design Pedestal Base Bowl

Double-handled Cake Plate

Cake plate, 7" d., individual, paneled edges
w/double handles, decorated w/central
conventional floral bouquet in pastel col-

Burnished Gold Celery Dish

ors, light yellow brown rim, signed "IFP" & marked w/a shield, "Schumann, Bavaria," ca. 1910-1930 (ILLUS.) **20**

Celery dish, oblong shape w/rounded ends, decorated w/conventional border design in apple green & burnished gold outlined in black, burnished gold border, signed "L. Amundson" & marked "J.P.L., Limoges, France," ca. 1891-1932, 12 1/2" l. x 5 3/4" h. (ILLUS., bottom previous page) **60**

Coffeepot with Enamel Decoration

Coffeepot, cov., tall urn-form on a pedestal on a square foot, high angled handle & long slender spout, the cover w/burnished gold urn-shaped finial, on a burnished gold square applied base, the body decorated w/conventional design in ivory & pink enamel, outlined in raised paste covered w/burnished gold, ivory & pale pink ground, marked "CAC, BELLEEK," 1889-1906 (ILLUS.) **600**

Monogram Cracker and Cheese Dish

Cracker & cheese dish, round tiered form, decorated w/conventional border design of primrose, light yellow ground, w/burnished gold fancy monogram, borders & trim, signed "E.S.P., I.M.P.," & marked "T & V, Limoges, France," ca. 1891-1907, 9 3/8" d. (ILLUS.) **125**

Demitasse Cup & Saucer

Demitasse cup and saucer, cylindrical cup w/gold twig handle, decorated w/sprigs of forget-me-nots, light blue cup interior, burnished gold rims & twig handle, signed "HJK," ca. 1890-1910 (ILLUS.) **40**

Dessert set: 7 1/2" d. plate & rounded cup w/saucer; plate decorated w/forget-me-not clusters on multicolored grounds, w/opal luster on cup interior, burnished gold rims & handle, various manufacturers, ca. 1925-1930, the set (ILLUS., below) **40**

Forget-Me-Not-decorated Dessert Set

Polychrome Three Piece Dresser Set

Dresser set: two 6 1/4" h. candlesticks, 5 1/4" x 3 1/2" pin tray; decorated w/clusters of pink & white roses & greenery, connected by leafy vines, on pastel polychrome grounds, w/burnished gold rims & detail, signed "J. Christopher," pin tray marked w/crown & double-headed bird, "MZ, Austria," ca. 1884-1909, the set (ILLUS.) **150**

Plate with Clusters of Pink Roses

Small Plate with Yellow Blossoms

Plate, 6" d., bread & butter, white ground h.p. w/a large cluster of small yellow blossoms on delicate green leafy stems, burnished gold border on feathered edge, artist initials, marked "CFH/CDM," ca. 1882-90 (ILLUS.) **25**

Plate, 8 1/2" d., decorated on rim w/clusters of pink roses & leaves, apple green edging, burnished gold rim & decorative trim, ca. 1914-1917, marked "Haviland, France" (ILLUS., next column) **50**

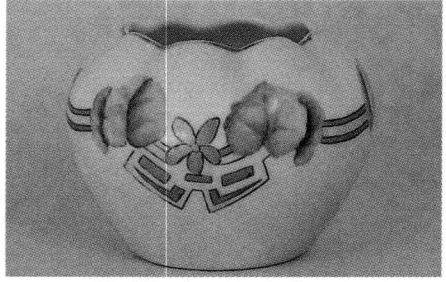

Rose Bowl with Violets and Leaves

Rose bowl, squatty ovoid form w/incurved, ruffled rim, decorated w/band of conventional-style violets & bands in burnished gold, w/naturalistic leaves, on pale yellow & lavender ground, marked w/wreath, "O. & E.G., Royal, Austria," ca. 1898-1918, 2 7/8" h. (ILLUS.) **30**

Salt & Pepper Shakers with Violets

Salt & pepper shakers, squatty base tapering to tall sides, h.p. creamy ground decorated w/purple violets & green leaves, gold cap paint, initialed by artist, ca. 1900-20, 2 3/8" h., pr. (ILLUS.) **40**

Burnished Gold Stickpin Holder

Stickpin holder, octagonal w/nine holes in the top, covered w/burnished gold, marked "LaSeynie, Limoges, PP, France," ca. 1903-1917, 2 1/4" h. (ILLUS.)............................ **45**

Sugar Shaker with Floral Design

Sugar shaker, cylindrical shape on foot, decorated w/conventional floral design in enamel & burnished gold outlined in black, ivory ground, w/burnished gold top, marked "H C Royal, Bavaria," ca. 1905-1920, 4 5/8" (ILLUS.) **75**

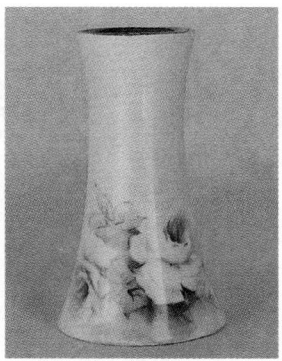

Porcelain Talcum Powder Shaker

Talcum powder shaker, upright waisted shape, decorated w/pink roses & leaves on pastel ground, burnished gold top, marked w/wreath, "O. & E.G., Royal," Austria, ca. 1898-1918, 4 1/4" h. (ILLUS.).. **85**

Toothpick Holder with Pink Roses

Toothpick holder, short waisted cylindrical form, decorated w/pink roses & leaves on light yellow ground, w/burnished gold border & rim, ca. 1910-1920, 2 1/4" h. (ILLUS.).. **30**

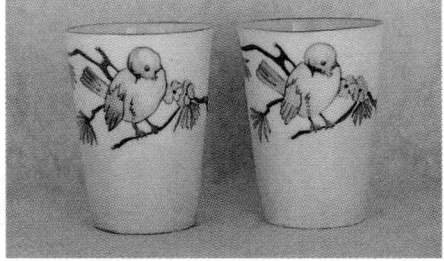

Tumblers with Bluebirds

Tumblers, tapering cylindrical shape, decorated in conventional Japanesque design of bluebirds on flowering branches on pale yellow & blue ground, w/burnished gold rims, signed "Merry man," marked "Victoria, Austria," ca. 1904-1915, 3 3/4", pr. (ILLUS.).. **30**

Two-handled Vase with Violets

Vase, 4 3/4" h., two-handled, decorated w/violets & leaves on multicolored ground, white enamel highlights, burnished gold rim, signed "France," ca. 1880-1900 (ILLUS.)... **45**

Amphora-Teplitz

In the late 19th and early 20th centuries numerous potteries operated in the vicinity of Teplitz in the Bohemian region of what was Austria but is now the Czech Republic. They included Amphora, RStK, Stellmacher, Ernst Wahliss, Paul Dachsel, Imperial and lesser-known potteries such as Johanne Maresh, Julius Dressler, Bernard Bloch and Heliosine.

The number of collectors in this category is growing while availability of better or rarer pieces is shrinking. Consequently, prices for all pieces are appreciating, while those for better and/or rarer pieces, including restored rare pieces, are soaring.

The price ranges presented here are retail. They presume mint or near mint condition or, in the case of very rare damaged pieces, proper restoration. They reflect such variables as rarity, design, quality of glaze, size and the intangible "in-vogue factor." They are the prices that knowledgeable sellers will charge and knowledgeable collectors will pay.

Amphora - Teplitz Marks

Indian Heads Amphora Humidor

Humidor, cov., figural, a massive Native American theme composed of three Indian heads w/high-glazed pink & green feathered headdresses, "jeweled" & draping beaded necklaces on two, a draping necklace of animal teeth on the third, high-glaze green & cobalt blue finial handle on a decorative mixed glazed top, basic color of Campina brown w/much contrasting high-glaze in green, pink, brown & blue, rare, impressed ovals w/"Amphora" & "Austria," a crown & "Imperial - Amphora - Turn" in a circle & "S-1633-46," 10 1/2" h. (ILLUS.) **$2,500-3,500**

Vase, 7 1/2" h., a playful expression of Amphora w/a pink snake draped around the body of the bulbous vase & extending to the top where its delicate tongue protrudes, a subtle leaf design extends around the bottom, the pink color of the snake distinguishes this piece from more drab versions, impressed in ovals "Amphora" & "Austria," & "4114 - 52"...... **1,500-1,800**

Vase, 7 3/4" h., round bulbous shape, decorated w/a profile of a young girl w/long flowing brownish hair full of numerous multicolored high-glazed flowers w/gold touches, all surrounded by a brownish tan forest scene, finely executed, impressed "Amphora - 663," overglaze red mark "RStK - Turn - Teplitz - Made in Austria" **2,000-2,200**

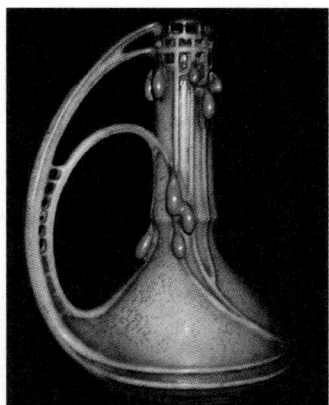

Abstract Paul Dachsel Vase

Vase, 9 7/8" h., a Paul Dachsel abstract design w/a reticulated geometric top & a reticulated handle within a reticulated handle sweeping in an arc from the top to the bottom w/abstract tendrils extending around the bottom of the body & back of the handles, several high-glazed green pods resembling teardrops of various sizes hang from the abstract handle, vines & a center funnel, the top rim & top of handle finished in gold, rare, stamped over glaze w/intertwined "PD - Turn - Teplitz" (ILLUS.) **4,000-4,500**

Vase, 10" h., a Paul Dachsel abstract architectural style w/a geometric design consisting of a rounded bottom from which four handles begin flush & extend to the top of the rim where they flare open, each handle suggests an abstract candelabrum w/charcoal flames rising from each, finished in iridescent gunmetal grey w/charcoal black sheen touches, gold wash on top, modern in all respects even though produced in the 1904-10 period, rare form, stamped over glaze w/intertwined "PD - Turn - Teplitz," impressed "1049" **4,500-5,500**

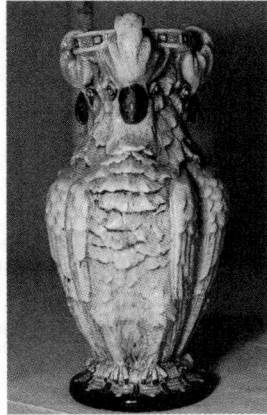

Amphora Figural Cockatoo Vase

Vase, 12" h., figural, three standing cockatoos, fully feathered, extend around the body of the vase, their plumes rising over the rim, very detailed w/glossy glaze, subtle color mix of blues, greens & tans w/brown streaks, semi-rare, impressed "Amphora" & "Austria" in ovals, a crown & Imperial circle & "11986 - 56" (ILLUS.) **2,000-2,500**

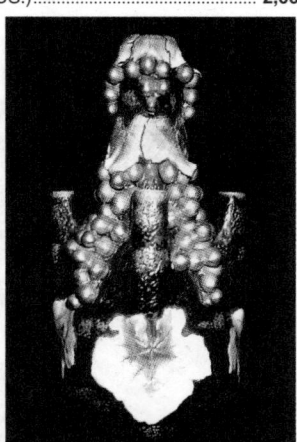

Amphora Vase with Golden Grapes

Vase, 15 1/2" h., cascades of golden grapes stream down on all sides between four funnel necks, the central funnel projecting skyward, this funnel design suggests Paul Dachsel, especially desirable because the piece is viewable from any angle, metallic purplish glaze w/metallic gold highlights containing numerous little gold circles, marked "Amphora" & "Austria" in ovals, a crown & "3680" (ILLUS.) **1,500-2,000**

Rare Reticulated Amphora Vase

Vase, 17 1/2" h., an important reticulated piece composed of a basket-like vase within a vase elaborately entwined w/swooping gold handles joined in the middle, numerous varied colored "jewels" around the sides, viewed through the reticulation a high-glazed blue swirly design w/gold highlights is seen, the exterior w/a metallic bluish green w/gold wash & gold highlights, high-glazed gold rim, only one known so far, impressed "Amphora" & "Austria" in ovals, a crown & "3791-45" (ILLUS.)........................ **12,000-14,000**

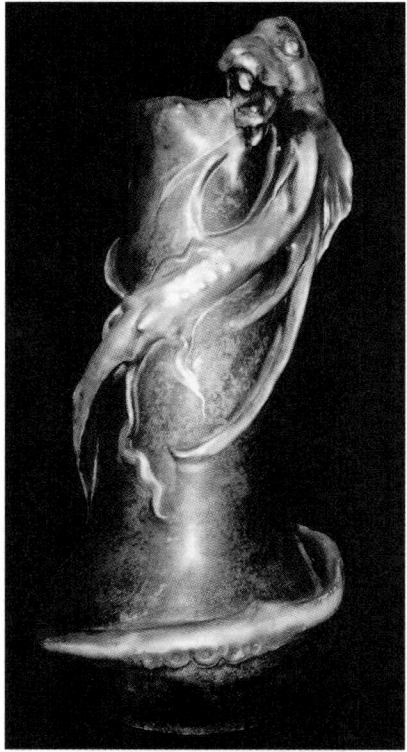

Amphora Vase with Coiling Beast

Vase, 18 1/4" h., a fantasy piece w/a coiling beast not really a dragon, snake or octopus but w/characteristics of each, finished in a golden color w/gold highlights, the head extends above the top, the body entwines down around the sides, mottled metallic purplish blue background, impressed "Amphora" & "Austria" in ovals, a crown & "4539-50," values vary w/the glaze (ILLUS.) .... **4,000 -4,500**

Vase, 20" h., footed tall wide cylindrical body w/squatty bulbous base & closed-in rim, mottled mauve glaze w/relief-molded dragon figure in yellow, tan & gilt glaze conforming entirely around body & rim, minor restorations to chips, impressed "AMPHORA" in a lozenge, a crown & "4548 50".. **6,000-6,500**

Somber, Eerie Dragon Vase

Vase, 22" h., figural, a somber swampy-green dragon encircles the tall body several times, its wings spread like a cobra's hood, leering down hungrily at a frog restrained by his tail at the base, this piece can be found finished in other colors including red & tan, impressed "Amphora" & "Austria" in ovals, a crown & "4536 - 6" (ILLUS.)... **5,500-6,000**

Belleek

Belleek china has been made in Ireland's County Fermanagh for many years. It is exceedingly thin porcelain. Several marks were used, including a hound and harp (1865-1880), and a hound, harp and castle (1863-1891). A printed hound, harp and castle with the words "Co. Fermanagh Ireland" constitutes the mark from 1891. Belleek-type china also was made in the United States last century by several firms, including Ceramic Art Company, Colombian Art Pottery, Lenox Inc., Ott & Brewer and Willets Manufacturing Co.

American Belleek
Marks:

American Art China Works - R&E, 1891-95

AAC (superimposed), 1891-95

American Belleek Company - Company name, banner & globe

Ceramic Art Company - CAC palette, 1889-1906

Colombian Art Pottery - CAP, 1893-1902

Cook Pottery - Three feathers w/"CHC," 1894-1904

Coxon Belleek Pottery - "Coxon Belleek" in a shield, 1926-1930

Gordon Belleek - "Gordon Belleek," 1920-28

Knowles, Taylor & Knowles - "Lotusware" in a circle w/a crown, 1891-96

Lenox China - Palette mark, 1906-1924

Ott & Brewer - crown & shield, 1883-1893

Perlee - "P" in a wreath, 1925-1930

Willets Manufacturing Company - Serpent mark, 1880-1909

Cook Pottery - Three feathers w/"CHC

Baskets and Bowls

Lenox, fernery, h.p. violets on a bowl-shaped base on shell gilded feet, artist palette mark, 7" d., 6" h. **$500**
Ott and Brewer, tazza, hand-decorated w/twig feet & gilt paste ferns, crown, sword & O.B. mark, 8" d. **900**
Willets, bowl, 6 1/4" d., 5" h., handled, h.p. apple blossoms, leaves & twigs accented w/heavy gold, artist-signed "ES James," serpent mark **650**

Ruffled Rim Bowl with Gold Accents

Willets, bowl, 7" d., 3" h., ovoid form h.p. w/decoration of roses, heavy gold accents on ruffled rim, foot & two applied handles, serpent mark (ILLUS.) **625**

Cups and Saucers

Ceramic Art Company Cabinet Cup

Ceramic Art Company, cabinet cup, no saucer, delicately enameled fretwork on footed base, CAC palette mark, 3 3/4" h. (ILLUS.) **75**
Ceramic Art Company, demitasse cup & saucer, decorated w/scenes of elves & pixies inspired by illustrator Palmer Cox, CAC palette mark, saucer 4" d. **750**
Lenox, bouillon cup & saucer, cream-colored body w/gold banding around top of cup & saucer, palette mark, saucer 6" d. **125**

Art Deco Silver Overlay Cup, Saucer

Lenox, demitasse cup & saucer, cov., sterling silver overlay of Art Deco design w/orange & green enameling, silver overlay around rim of cup & octagonal saucer, palette mark, 4 1/2" w. saucer (ILLUS.) **125**
Lenox, demitasse cup & saucer, filigree sterling silver overlay on two sides of the cup & around the rim of the cup & saucer, palette mark, saucer 1 1/2" d. **125**
Morgan, demitasse cup & saucer, w/heavy gold embossed rims & handle, footed cup, 2 3/4" d. x 1 7/8" h. cup **125**
Willets, bouillon cup & saucer, h.p. flowers w/gold trim, serpent mark, saucer 5 1/2" d. **350**

Pink Luster Bouillon Cup & Saucer

Willets, bouillon cup & saucer, "Tridacna" body patt., pink luster finish interior, cream color exterior w/gold trim & double handles, serpent mark, 3 1/2" d. cup, 5 1/4" d. saucer (ILLUS.) **250**

Willets, demitasse cup & saucer, fluted white body w/purple monogram "W," outlined in gold w/gold-flecked purple dragon-shaped handle, serpent mark, saucer 4" d. 110

Mugs

Ceramic Art Company, h.p. chrysanthemums & leaves, artist-signed in gold "A.B. Wood," CAC palette mark, 5 1/2" h. 225

Ceramic Art Company, h.p. design of grapes of various colors & grapevines, accented w/heavy gold on a pink pastel body, artist-signed "KR" & dated 1904, CAC palette mark, 6" h. 350

Mug with Blackberries

Ceramic Art Company, ovoid form w/h.p. blackberries & foliage on pastel pink ground, CAC palette mark, 5" h. (ILLUS.) 325

Ceramic Art Company, portrait-type, h.p. "Colonial Drinkers," artist-signed by Fred Little, CAC palette mark, 5" h. 325

Ceramic Art Company, portrait-type, h.p. portrait of an old man w/a stein seated at a table, artist-signed "E.D. Westphal," CAC palette mark, 5 3/4" h. 300

Lenox, h.p. heavy enameled flowers in the Art Deco style, artist-signed "HRM," palette mark, 7" h. 150

Lenox, h.p. w/intense green leaves & berries on a rust & brown ground, palette mark, 5" h. 175

Rust Mug with Grape Decoration

Willets, cylindrical shape flaring at base, decorated w/h.p. grapes & foliage on a rust ground, serpent mark, 5 1/2" h. (ILLUS.) 175

Willets, h.p. blackberries & foliage on a pastel ground, serpent mark, 4 1/2" h. 125

Orange Mug with Currants

Willets, ovoid form, h.p. orange currants & green leaves on orange ground, serpent mark, 5" h. (ILLUS.) 125

Mug with Handpainted Cherries

Willets, slightly tapering cylindrical form w/panel at base w/raised design, decorated w/cherries, h.p. & marked "D'Arcy's Hand Painted," serpent mark, 5 1/2" h. (ILLUS.) 190

Pitchers, Creamers and Ewers

Ceramic Art Company, creamer, footed swan-form, gold highlights, artist-signed "ES," dated "1903," CAC palette mark, 3 1/2" h. 225

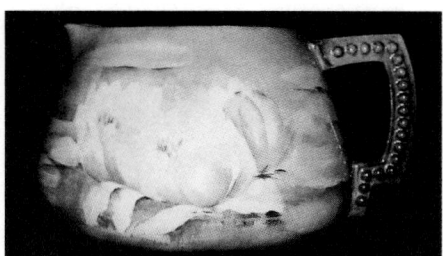

Water Lily Cider Pitcher

Lenox, cider pitcher, h.p. overall w/water lilies & leaves, artist-signed, 6 1/2" h., palette mark (ILLUS.) 750

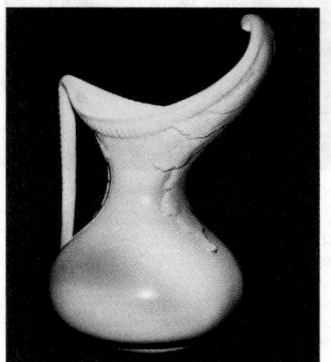

American Belleek Ewer

Lenox, ewer, cream-colored body w/design of flowing colors in yellow, green & mauve, 5 1/2" h., 3 1/2" d., palette mark (ILLUS.) 295

Lenox, pitcher, 14" h., tankard-type, h.p. grapes, leaves & vines, embossed handle trimmed in gold, palette mark 725

Ott and Brewer, ewer, shaped form w/raised gold paste stylized leaf decoration on a matte ground, cactus-shaped handle, crown & sword mark, 8" h., 7 1/2" d. 1,500

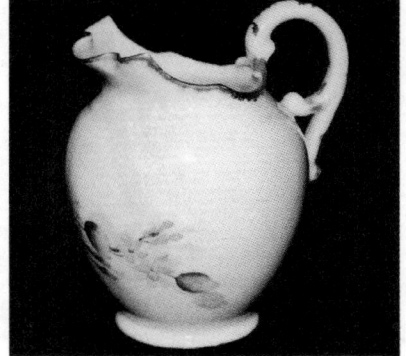

Willets Creamer

Willets, creamer, thin porcelain w/arched, ruffled spout & forked handle, delicate h.p. pink blossoms & green leaves, 3 1/2" h., 3" d. (ILLUS.) 125

Willets, pitcher, 7" h., jug-shaped, h.p. large poppies w/soft gold-accented foliage & handle, artist-signed "A.B. Julia," dated "1910," serpent mark 250

Plates and Platters

Lenox, plate, 7 1/2" d., cream-colored w/sterling silver overlay of festoons of ribbons, silver around outer rim, palette mark 40

Lenox, plate, 8" d., h.p. w/a few flowers, palette mark 50

Morgan, plate, 10 5/8" d., Orient, Deco-style h.p. enamel decoration 150

Ott and Brewer, plate, 8 1/2" d., scalloped rim w/h.p. ferns in pink, dark green, mauve & light green, crown & sword mark 125

Vases

Vase with Jonquil Decoration

Ceramic Art Company, 8 1/4" h., cylindrical body tapering to small 4 1/2" top opening, h.p. w/large yellow jonquils & leaves all around, on a pale blue ground, some gold highlights, CAC palette mark (ILLUS.) 975

Ceramic Art Company, 10 1/2" h., ovoid body w/narrow waisted neck opening to flaring rim, h.p. w/large pink roses on a lavender ground, high glaze, CAC palette mark 800

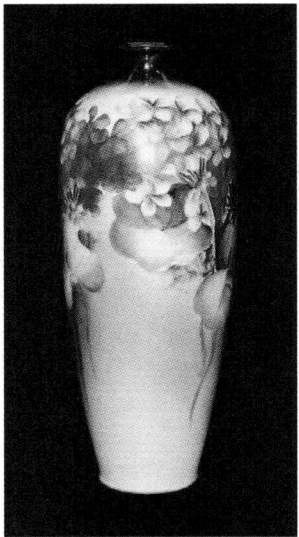

Artist-signed Vase with Flowers

Ceramic Art Company, 13" h., ovoid body w/short narrow neck & flaring rim, decorated w/h.p. orange flowers & green leaves on pale green & cream ground, artist-signed, CAC palette mark (ILLUS.) **900**

Ceramic Art Company, 17" h., w/h.p. wisteria decoration, artist-signed, CAC palette mark **1,400**

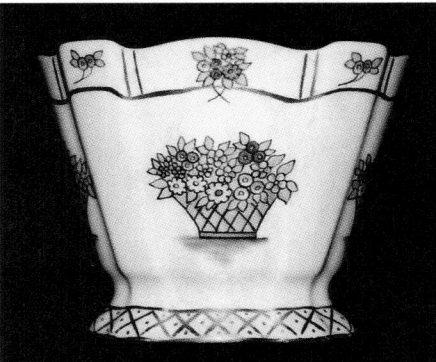

Basket-style Lenox Vase

Lenox, basket-style, w/scalloped rim & foot, h.p. w/Deco-style baskets of flowers & gold highlights on white ground, palette mark (ILLUS.) **175**

Lenox, 8" h., 5" d., bulbous body, h.p. floral decoration in mint condition, palette mark..... **510**

Lenox, 10 1/4" h., ovoid body tapering to short, wide, flared neck, h.p. decoration of open roses, leaves & petals on mauve matte ground, palette mark **550**

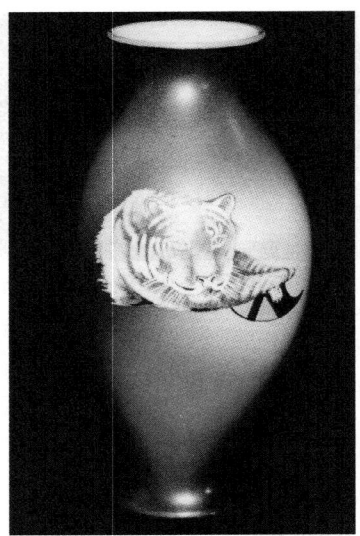

Willets Vase with a Tiger

Willets, 9" h., 4" d., baluster-form w/flared foot & rim, dark green ground decorated w/a h.p. tiger on one side, serpent mark (ILLUS.)... **900**

Willets, 10" h., bulbous form w/all over floral decoration, artist-signed, dated 1905, serpent mark **1,200**

Willets, 10" h., 3" d., cylindrical, h.p. design of three Japanese women in kimonos on a pale green ground, serpent mark **450**

Willets, 10" h., 8" d., bulbous body w/a short pinched neck & fluted rim, h.p. overall w/large pastel roses & foliage, serpent mark **500**

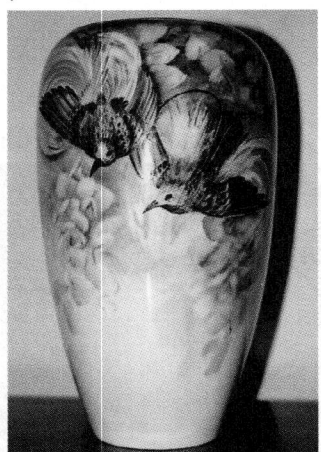

Willets Vase with Birds & Wisteria

Willets, 10 1/2" h., 6" d., ovoid form w/h.p. decoration of birds & wisteria, serpent mark (ILLUS.).. **900**

Willets, 10 1/2" h., 6" d., h.p. Pickard decoration of a full-length Art Nouveau woman
w/flowing hair & gown on a pink lustre
ground, serpent mark.................................. **1,600**
Willets, 11" h., h.p. chrysanthemums ac-
cented w/gold on white ground, serpent
mark... **665**
Willets, 15 1/2" h., 3" d., h.p. large flowers,
artist-signed "J. Brauer," serpent mark....... **1,200**
Willets, 15 1/2" h., 4" d., cylindrical w/flared
bottom & flared scalloped top, h.p. completely w/pink & red roses on a soft pastel
pink ground, serpent mark **1,200**

Miscellaneous

Ceramic Art Company, loving cup, h.p. images of grapes & foliage, gilded rim, base
& handles, topped w/figural children's
heads, serpent mark, 8 1/4" h., 6 1/4" d. ... **2,000**
Knowles, Taylor & Knowles Lotus Ware
rose bowl, 5" d., 6" h., "Columbia," raised
cameo-style flowers w/gold branching or-
namentation... **760**
Knowles, Taylor & Knowles Lotus Ware
rose bowl, 7" d., 7 1/2" h., cov., h.p. ornately patterned pierced cover & han-
dles, applied gilded roses & "jewels"......... **2,500**

Lenox Teapot with Roses Decoration

Lenox, teapot, cov., pedestal base on
square foot, boat-shaped body w/angled
handle, h.p. sprays of pink & white roses
w/green leaves, gold band trim, palette
mark, 10" l., 8" h. (ILLUS.) **450**
Lenox, toothpick holder, h.p. ravens sitting
on pine branches, straight sides, palette
mark, 2 1/4" h. **150**

Three-handled Loving Cup

Willets, loving cup, three-handled ovoid
form on pedestal base, decorated w/h.p.
chrysanthemums & foliage in teal on
white ground, serpent mark, 5 1/2" d.,
8" h. (ILLUS.)... **200**

Willets Sherbet in Holder

Willets, sherbet, porcelain insert in sterling
silver reticulated holder w/pedestal base,
serpent mark, 3 1/2" d., 3 3/4" h.
(ILLUS.).. **125**

Irish Belleek

Basket Ware

Basket, Henshall's Twig Basket, large size,
D120-1.. **2,600**
Basket, round, center arched handle, flat-
tened rim w/applied colored blossoms,
flat rod, D1274-1 .... **5,000**
Basket, Sydenham Twig Basket, large size,
D108-1.. **4,400**
Brooch, flowered (D1525-II) **400**
Frame, photo or mirror, oblong w/two oval
picture openings, ornately applied
w/flowers overall, D66-II............................... **6,200**
Jewel stand, Woven Flowered Jewel
Stand, D1575-II.. **1,200**

Comports & Centerpieces

Centerpiece, Bird Nest Stump Vase,
w/eggs in nest, D57-II................................... **3,200**
Comport, Boy on Swan Comport, beetle
flys on base, D33-I **8,000**

Earthenware

Chamber Pot with Gladstone

Chamber pot, printed portrait of William
Gladstone on the inside bottom, D2082-I
(ILLUS.).. **1,600**
Mug, cylindrical, scenic transfer-printed
decoration (D858-II) **360**
Serving dish, open, oval, embossed end
handles, pedestal base, D915-II **400**

Figurines

Bust of Clytie, low pedestal base, D14-II **2,200**
Candleholder, figure of a sleeping shep-
herd & his dog on the rounded base, ring
handle, green tint & gilt trim, D1603-I........ **4,000**
Figure of Affection, fully-decorated,
D1134-I **3,400**
Figure of Erin, standing figure by well, D1-I **10,000**
Figure of Leprechaun, painted, D1142-IV **350**
Figure of Leprechaun, painted, D1142-V **250**
Figure of Leprechaun, undecorated,
D1142-III **450**
Figure of Meditation, fully-decorated,
D20-I **3,400**
Models of Polar Bears, standing & resting,
pottery, No. 550 & 551, the pair **340**
Paperweight, model of frog on oval lily pad,
painted, D1526-I **1,600**

Tea Ware - Common Patterns (Harp, Shamrock, Limpet, Hexagon, Neptune, Shamrock & Tridacna)

Harp Shamrock butter plate, D1356-III **200**
Hexagon breakfast set: small teapot, open
sugar & creamer, two plates & two cups
& saucers, h.p. floral decoration, no tray,
D396-II.. **2,600**
Neptune creamer & open sugar bowl,
green tint, pr. (D416-II & D417-II) **400**
Neptune teacup & saucer, green tint,
D414-II **240**
Neptune tray, green tint (D418-II) **1,200**
Shamrock egg cup, footed (D389-II) **120**
Shamrock muffin dish, cov. (D388-II)............. **680**
Shamrock pitcher, milk, jug-form
(D390-II) **320**
Shamrock salt tub, large size (D1564-II)......... **120**
Shamrock teacup & saucer, tall shape,
lavender decoration, D375-II **300**
Shamrock teakettle, cov., large size,
D386-III.. **540**
Shamrock teapot, cov., medium size,
D247-VI **440**
Tridacna sugar bowl, open, gilt-trimmed,
large size, D472-I... **440**

Tea Ware - Desirable Patterns (Echinus, Limpet (footed), Grass, Hexagon, Holly, Mask, New Shell & Shell)

Echinus cup & saucer, egg shell, crested
(D358-I) **500**
Echinus mustache cup & saucer (D664-I)..... **660**
Echinus teacup & saucer (D645-I).................. **400**
Echinus teapot, cov., pink tint w/gold trim,
small size (D659-I)... **900**
Echinus tray, pink tint w/gold trim (D649-I)... **1,800**

Grass Teapot Kettle & Tray

Grass creamer & covered sugar bowl,
middle size, D746-I & D748-I, pr.................... **800**
Grass mustache cup & saucer (D739-I)......... **620**
Grass tea trivet, rounded footed form
(D1405-I).. **1,000**
Grass teacup & saucer, decorated, D732-
I, each **260**
Grass teakettle, cov., large size, D751-I
(ILLUS. at right with the set) **1,000**
Grass teapot, cov., small size, D750-I
(ILLUS. left with set)...................................... **800**
Grass tray, round, D736-I (ILLUS. with
set) **2,000**

Tea Ware - Rare Patterns (Aberdeen, Blarney, Celtic (low & tall), Cone, Erne, Fan, Institute, Ivy, Lily (high & low), Scroll, Sydney, Thistle & Thorn)

Celtic fruit dish, round, D1512-II................... **1,200**
Celtic plate, 5" d., low shape, painted
(D1453-III).. **220**
Celtic teacup & saucer, low shape, painted
(D1456-III & D1457-III) **400**
Institute plate, 6" d., pink tint (D724-I)............ **160**
Institute sugar bowl, cov., decorated,
D728-I... **600**
Institute teacup & saucer, pink tint (D722-
I) **300**
Thorn creamer & open sugar bowl, small
size (D760-I & D761-I), pr.............................. **1,000**
Thorn mug, cylindrical, D217-II....................... **160**
Thorn plate, turquoise & gilt decoration,
D35-I... **460**
Thorn teacup & saucer, decorated (D758-
I) **460**
Thorn tray, oval, decorated (D762-I)............. **2,600**

Vases & Spills

Aberdeen vases, left & right, flowered, me-
dium size (D58-II), pr. **1,600**
Celtic Vase-J, D1199-III, each **460**
Clam Shell & Griffin vase, pink tint,
D140-I... **2,200**
Daisy spill, D178-III.. **220**
Flowerpot, ovoid shape w/pierced rim,
D2006-III **340**
Frog vase, model of frog w/head up &
mouth open, large size, D181-II.................. **1,000**
Ivy Stump spill (D147-I)................................... **420**
Nautilus on Coral vase, pink tint (D131-I)........ **980**
Rathmore flowerpot, bulbous w/flaring
scalloped rim & applied flowers, D43-II **2,200**
Rock spill, middle size (D162-III)....................... **280**
Round Tower vase, model of tower w/harp
& hound at the base, 929-VII **460**
Seahorse and Shell flower holder, rectan-
gular base, D129-I.. **1,200**
Shamrock spill, D191-III **220**
Shamrock Tree Stump spill, D1224-III **240**

Bisque

Bisque is biscuit china, fired a single time but not glazed. Some bisque is decorated with colors. Most abundant from the Victorian era are figures and groups, but other pieces, from busts to vases, were made by numerous potteries in the United States and abroad. Reproductions have been produced for many years, so care must be taken when seeking antique originals.

Figural Bisque Candlesticks

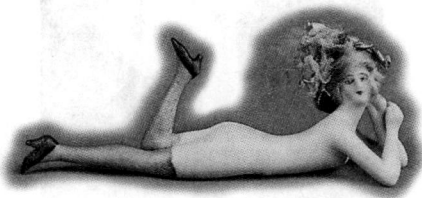

Reclining Bisque Bathing Beauty

Bathing beauty figure, nude lady reclining on stomach w/head raised resting on her arms, legs w/painted-on stocking & shoes, original blonde mohair wig w/flowered hat, marked "1740 2/0 B," early 20th c., 4 1/2" l. (ILLUS.) **$400-500**

Bathing beauty figure, seated nude lady wearing lavender high heels & strumming a lute, real wig & turban, marked "Bavaria - 2739 B," early 20th c., 5" l. (ILLUS., bottom of page) **625-675**

Candlesticks, figural, two-light, an ornate scroll-molded tan base & shaft supporting lift-off serpentine arms ending in sockets, one base w/a figure of a lady wearing a dark blue & white outfit, the other w/a facing man in a blue & white outfit, each 6" w., 8 1/2" h., pr. (ILLUS., next column) **275-300**

Figure Group of Young Couple

Figure group, a young man & woman in 18th c. attire walking & holding a large umbrella, pastel coloring, late 19th c., 6" h. (ILLUS.) **140-150**

Rare Bisque Bathing Beauty with Lute

Bisque Dutch Girl Figure

Figure of a Dutch girl, seated pose w/hands on her knees, wearing a white bonnet over light brown hair, tinted face & arms, blue dress w/white bodice & trim on sleeves & at waist, unmarked Heubach, 3 1/2 x 5", 6 1/2" h. (ILLUS.) **200-225**

Lovely Bisque Baby in Highchair

Figure of baby in highchair, delicate baby wearing a blue-tinted bonnet, pink lace collar & white gown, in a tan-colored wicker highchair, marked w/sunburst trademark of Gebruder Heubach, Germany, late 19th - early 20th c., 8" h. (ILLUS.) **275-325**

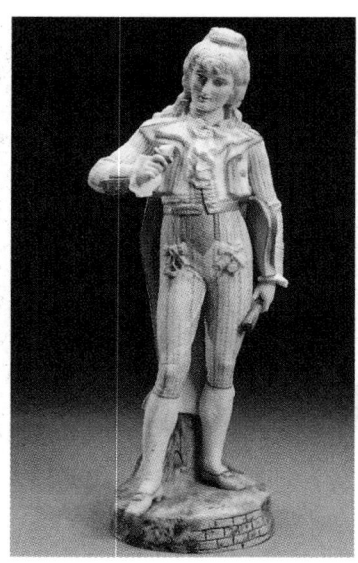

Tall Bisque Figure of Gentleman

Figure of gentleman, young man in gold-trimmed pastel-colored outfit w/white ruffled shirt, holding rose in one hand, on round base modeled to resemble stones or bricks of a courtyard, marked w/blue diamond "R," 20 1/2" h. (ILLUS.) **104**

Bisque Girl & Boy Figures in Armchairs

Figures, a young girl in a late Victorian outfit w/a light & dark green dress & matching large hat molded in a large tan & green armchair, a matching young boy in fancy green suit & hat also in a large armchair, gold trim, late 19th c., 6 1/4" h., pr. (ILLUS.) **140-150**

Bisque Figures of Man & Woman

Figures of man & woman, wearing buff-colored outfits & draping cloaks, h.p. features, each on molded cylindrical base, unmarked, 20 1/2" h., pr. (ILLUS.) **978**

Bisque Figures of Young Tennis Players

Figures of tennis players, the girl wearing aqua pleated skirt & cream colored blouse w/gold sash belt, white hat w/short aqua brim, holding racket in one hand & ball in the other, the boy wearing aqua knee breeches & matching shirt w/cream colored neckerchief, white hat w/short aqua brim, also holding racket & ball, each on base formed to resemble green grass of playing field, h.p. features, unmarked, Heubach, Germany, 15" h., pr. (ILLUS.) **748**

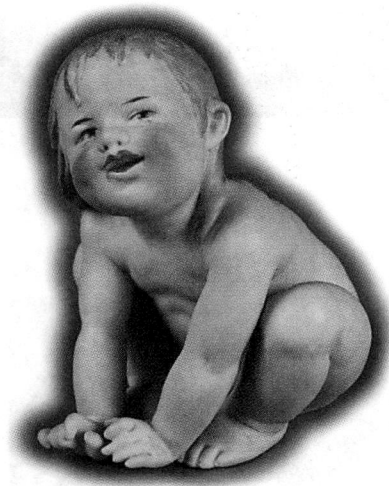

Fine Heubach Bisque Piano Baby

Piano baby, nude baby seated & leaning forward on his arms, tilted head w/blond-painted hair, blue intaglio eyes, molded red lips & pink cheeks, marked w/sunburst trademark of Gebruder Heubach, late 19th - early 20th c., 6" h. (ILLUS.) **325-400**

Blue & White Pottery

The category of blue and white or blue and grey pottery includes a wide variety of pottery, earthenware and stoneware items widely produced in this country in the late 19th century right through the 1930s. Originally marketed as inexpensive wares, most pieces featured a white or grey body molded with a fruit, flower or geometric design and then trimmed with bands or splashes of blue to highlight the molded pattern. Pitchers, butter crocks and salt boxes are among the numerous items produced, but other kitchenwares and chamber sets are also found. Values vary depending on the rarity of the embossed pattern and the depth of color of the blue trim; the darker the blue, the better. Some entries refer to several different books on Blue and White Pottery. These books are: Blue & White Stoneware, Pottery & Crockery by Edith Harbin (1977, Collector Books, Paducah, KY); Stoneware in the Blue and White by M.H. Alexander (1993 reprint, Image Graphics, Inc., Paducah, KY); and Blue & White Stoneware by Kathryn McNerney (1995, Collector Books, Paducah, KY).

Peacock Berry Bowl & Custard Cup

Bowl, 4 1/2" d., 2 1/4" h., berry, embossed
Peacock patt., Brush-McCoy Pottery Co.,
(ILLUS. left, top of page) **$325**
Bowl, 4 1/2" to 14" d., embossed Pineapple
patt., ten sizes, Brush-McCoy Pottery
Co., price ranges **174**

GrapeWare Pattern Bowls

Bowl, 8" d., embossed GrapeWare patt.,
Brush-McCoy Pottery Co. (ILLUS.)............... **225**
Bowl, 9 1/2" d., 4 1/2" h., embossed Ga-
droon Arches or Petal Panels patt................ **175**
Bowl, 10" d., embossed GrapeWare patt. **275**
Bowl, 10 1/2" d., 5 1/2" h., embossed Dia-
mond Point patt.. **170**
Bowls, nesting-type, embossed Scallop
patt., 6" d., 3 1/2" h., 8" d., 3 1/2" h.,

9 1/2" d., 5" h., depending on size,
each.. **85-125**

Bow Tie Blue-banded Brush Vase

Brush vase, embossed Bow Tie (Our Luci-
le) patt., w/narrow blue bands, Brush-Mc-
Coy Pottery Co., 5 1/2" h. (ILLUS.) **225**

Advertising & Daisy Pattern Butter Crocks

Dragonfly & Flower Butter Crocks

Butter crock, cov., advertising "Compliments of J. Mueller," Western Stoneware Co., 4 1/4" h. (ILLUS. left w/Daisy patt. crock, bottom of previous page).................... 295

Butter crock, cov., embossed Apricot patt., A.E. Hull Pottery Co., 7" d., 4" h.................... 250

Butter crock, cov., embossed Cow and Fence patt., 7 1/4" d., 5" h............................. 525

Butter crock, cov., embossed Daisy and Trellis patt., 6 1/2" d., 4 1/2" h. 225

Butter crock, cov., embossed Daisy and Trellis patt., 6" d., 4" h................................... 175

Butter crock, cov., embossed Daisy patt., Red Wing Pottery Co., 3 1/2" h. (ILLUS. right with advertising butter crock, previous page) 395

Butter crock, cov., embossed Diffused Blue with Block Bands patt., 7 1/2" d., 5 1/2" h. 225

Butter crock, cov., embossed Dragonfly and Flower patt., found in at least three sizes, Logan Pottery Co., large, 8" d., 5" h. (ILLUS. right, top of page)..................... 345

Butter crock, cov., embossed Dragonfly and Flower patt., smallest size, Logan Pottery Co., rare (ILLUS. left, top of page)... 500

Canister, cov., embossed GrapeWare patt., various contents, Brush-McCoy Pottery Co., 6" h., each 400-800

Canister, cov., embossed Robinson Barrel patt., Robinson Clay Products Co. 275

Printed Dutch Scene Sugar Canister

Canister, cov., stenciled Dutch Scene patt., "Sugar," Brush-McCoy Pottery Co., 5 1/2 to 6" h. (ILLUS.) 450-650

Canister, cov., stenciled Snowflake patt., various contents, A.E. Hull Pottery Co., 5 3/4" d., 6 1/2" h., each......................... 235-300

Embossed Flying Bird Casserole

Casserole, cov., embossed Flying Bird patt., A.E. Hull Pottery Co., 9 1/2" d. (ILLUS., top of page)....................................... **600**

Chamber pot, cov., embossed Peacock patt., Brush-McCoy Pottery Co., 11" d., 6" h. **1,250**

Chamber pot, cov., stenciled Wildflower patt., Brush-McCoy Pottery Co., 11" d., 6" h. **250**

Coffeepot, cov., Diffused Blue patt., oval design, w/bottom plate, 11" h. (ILLUS. left with embossed Bull's-Eye pot, bottom of page, no bottom plate) **2,700**

Coffeepot, cov., embossed Bull's-Eye patt., w/bottom plate (ILLUS. right, no bottom plate, bottom of page) **3,250**

Bull's-Eye & Diffused Blue Coffeepots

Stenciled Wildflower Ewers

Rare Flying Bird Cookie Jar

Cookie jar, cov., embossed Flying Bird patt., A.E. Hull Pottery Co., 6 3/4" d., 9" h. (ILLUS.)... **1,250**

Cuspidor, embossed Sunflowers patt., 9 3/4" d., 9" h.. **200**

Custard cup, embossed Peacock patt., Brush-McCoy Pottery Co., 2 7/8" h. (ILLUS. page 136, right w/berry bowl) **545**

Ewer, stenciled Wildflower patt., pear-shaped, Brush-McCoy Pottery Co., 6 1/2" h. (ILLUS. left, top of page) **225**

Ewer, stenciled Wildflower patt., pear-shaped, Brush-McCoy Pottery Co., 8 1/2" h. (ILLUS. center, top of page) **295**

Ewer, stenciled Wildflower patt., pear-shaped, Brush-McCoy Pottery Co., 10 1/2" h. (ILLUS. right, top of page).............. **325**

Ewer & basin set, embossed Willow (Basketweave & Morning Glory) patt., Brush-McCoy Pottery Co., basin 15" d., 4 1/2" h., ewer, 9" d., 13" h., pr. **675**

Ewer & basin set, stenciled Wildflower patt., stenciled designs inside the ewer & the basin, basin 15" d., ewer 11" h., Brush-McCoy Pottery Co., pr. (ILLUS., below).. **650**

Wildflower Ewer & Basin Set

Three Miniature Advertising Jugs

Tulip Pattern Jardiniere & Pedestal

Mixing bowl, embossed Flying Bird. patt.,
A.E. Hull Pottery Co., 8" d............................... 340
Mixing bowl, embossed Flying Bird. patt.,
A.E. Hull Pottery Co., 6" d............................... 225
Mixing bowl, embossed Flying Bird. patt.,
A.E. Hull Pottery Co., 7" d............................... 295
Mug, embossed Bow Tie patt. w/Rose de-
cal, Brush-McCoy Pottery Co.,
3 3/4" h... 100

Printed Dutch Scene Mug

Jardiniere & pedestal base, embossed Tulip patt., made by Nelson McCoy Sanitary
Stoneware Co., Burley-Winter Pottery Co.
& A.E. Hull Pottery Co., jardiniere 6" h.,
pedestal 7" h., the set (ILLUS.)..................... **1,500**
Jug, miniature, Diffused Blue w/advertising
in gold letters, each (ILLUS. of three, top
of page) **325**

Mug, stenciled Dutch Scene mug, boy on
one side, girl on the other, J.W. McCoy
Pottery & Brush-McCoy Pottery Co.,
4 1/4" h. (ILLUS.).. **275**
Pitcher, embossed Bands & Rivets patt.,
side-pour, molded bands, no advertising,
Western Stoneware, several sizes,
each **400**

Western Side-Pour Pitchers

Pitcher, embossed Bands & Rivets patt., side-pour, molded bands, w/advertising, Western Stoneware, depending on size, each (ILLUS. of two, top of page) **400-1,200**

Pitcher, 10" h., embossed Beaded Rose patt., large, A.E. Hull Pottery Co. **425**

Pitcher, 6 1/4" h., 6 3/4" d., embossed Capt. John Smith and Pocahontas patt., A.E. Hull Pottery Co. (ILLUS. bottom right, below) **325**

Capt. John Smith, Castle and Shield Pitchers

Chrysanthemum Pitchers & Salt Box

Pitcher, 4 1/2" h., embossed Castle patt., A.E. Hull Pottery Co. 225

Pitcher, 6" h., embossed Castle patt., A.E. Hull Pottery Co. 275

Pitcher, 8" h., embossed Castle patt., A.E. Hull Pottery Co. (ILLUS. bottom left w/Capt. John Smith pitcher, previous page).. 325

Pitcher, 8" h., embossed Chrysanthemum patt., White Hall Sewer Pipe & Stoneware Co. (ILLUS. right, top of page).............. 225

Pitcher, 9 1/2" h., embossed Chrysanthemum patt., White Hall Sewer Pipe & Stoneware Co. (ILLUS. left, top of page)..... 275

Pitcher, 9" h., 6" d., embossed Flying Bird patt., A.E. Hull Pottery Co. (ILLUS.).............. 725

Pitcher, 9 1/2" h., embossed Grape Leaf Band patt. 250

Pitcher, 7" h., embossed Grape Leaf Band patt. 165

Lovebird Pattern Pitcher

Pitcher, 8 1/2" h., 5 1/2" d., embossed Lovebird patt., A.E. Hull Pottery Co. (ILLUS.)... 500

Pitcher, 8 1/2" h., 6" d., embossed Shield patt. (ILLUS. top center w/Capt. John Smith pitcher, previous page)........................ 475

Embossed Flying Bird Pitcher

Bulbous Wildflower Pitcher

Pitcher, 10 3/4" h., stenciled Wildflower patt., bulbous body, Brush-McCoy Pottery Co. (ILLUS.) **425**

Salt box, cov., embossed Butterfly patt., Nelson McCoy Sanitary Stoneware Co., 5 3/4" d., 5 3/4" h. **275**

Salt box, cov., embossed Chrysanthemum patt., White Hall Sewer Pipe & Stoneware Co., 4 1/4" h. (ILLUS. front w/pitchers, previous page) **210**

Salt box, cov., hanging-type, stenciled Wildflower patt., hinged wooden cover, Brush-McCoy Pottery Co., 6" d., 4 1/2" h. **170**

Wildflower Advertising Salt Crock

Salt box, open, hanging-type, stenciled Wildflower patt., printed advertising "Your Credit Is Good - Freed Furniture & Carpet Co.," Brush-McCoy Pottery Co., 6" d., 4 1/2" h. (ILLUS.) **550**

Slop jar, cov., embossed Beaded Rose patt., A.E. Hull Pottery Co., 8 1/2" h. **350**

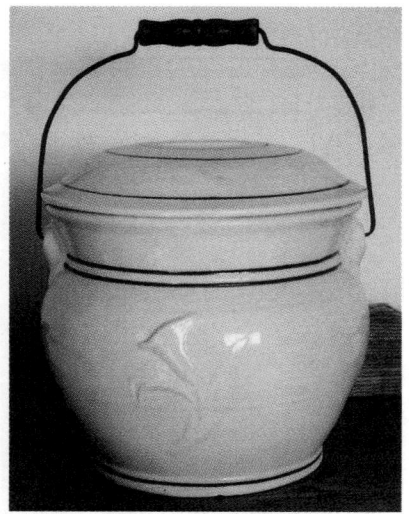

Red Wing Lily Pattern Slop Jar

Slop jar, cov., embossed Lily patt., Red Wing Pottery Co. (ILLUS.) **250-300**

Soap dish, cov., embossed Beaded Rose patt., A.E. Hull Pottery Co., 7" h.................... **500**

Tobacco jar, cov., embossed Berry Scrolls patt., Western Stoneware Co., 5" d., 6 1/2" h. **300**

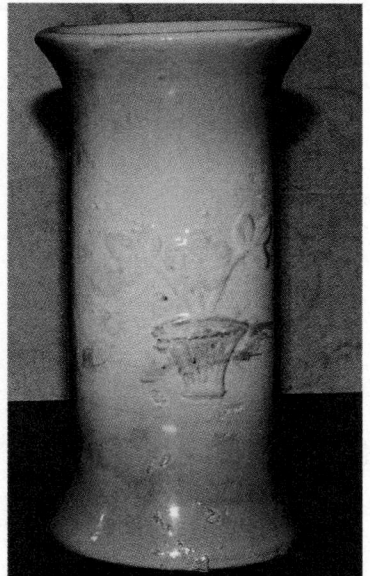

Wicker Basket and Bouquet Vase

Vase, 11" h., embossed Wicker Basket and Bouquet patt. (ILLUS.).................................... **300**

Water cooler, cov., embossed Polar Bear patt., w/spigot, Uhl Pottery Co., 6 gal............ **850**

Water cooler, cov., embossed Polar Bear
patt., w/spigot, Uhl Pottery Co., 8 gal. **975**

Wildflower Water Cooler and Base

Water cooler, cov., stenciled Wildflower
patt., w/spigot & base, 3 gal. (ILLUS.) **4,000**

Buffalo Pottery

Incorporated in 1901 as a wholly-owned subsidiary of the Larkin Soap Company, founded by
John D. Larkin of Buffalo, New York, in 1875, the
Buffalo Pottery was a manufactory built to produce premium wares to be included with purchases of Larkin's chief product, soap.

In October 1903, the first kiln was fired and
Buffalo Pottery became the only pottery in the
world run entirely by electricity. In 1904 Larkin
offered its first premium produced by the pottery.
This concept of using premiums caused sales to
skyrocket and, in 1905, the first Blue Willow pattern pottery made in the United States was introduced as a premium.

The Buffalo Pottery administrative building,
built in 1904 to house 1,800 clerical workers, was
the creation of a 32-year-old architect, Frank
Lloyd Wright. The building was demolished in
1953, but many critics considered it to be Wright's
masterpiece.

By 1910 annual soap production peaked and
the number of premiums offered in the catalogs
exceeded 600. By 1915 this number had grown to
1,500. The first catalog of premiums was issued
in 1893 and continued to appear through the late
1930s.

John D. Larkin died in 1926, and during the
Great Depression the firm suffered severe losses,
going into bankruptcy in 1940. After World War
II the pottery resumed production under new
management, but its vitreous wares were generally limited to mass-produced china for the insti-
tutional market.

Among the pottery lines produced during Buffalo's heyday were Gaudy Willow, Deldare, Abino
Ware, historical and commemorative plates and
unique handpainted jugs and pitchers. In the
1920s and 1930s the firm concentrated on personalized wares for commercial clients including
hotels, clubs, railroads and restaurants.

In 1983 Oneida Silversmiths bought the pottery, an ironic twist since, years before, Oneida
silver had been featured in Larkin catalogs. The
pottery has now ceased all domestic production of
ceramics. - Phillip M. Sullivan.

Buffalo Pottery Mark

Abino Ware (1911-1913)

Matchbox holder w/ashtray **$1,600**
Pitcher, 10 1/2" h., tankard-type **1,900**

Blue Willow Pattern (1905-1916)

Chop plate, scalloped edge, 11" d. **250**
Oyster tureen, notched cover **550**
Pitcher, jug-type, "Hall Boy," 6 1/2 oz., 3
pts. **300**
Pitcher, jug-type, "Chicago," 4 1/2 pts **400**
Sauceboat w/attached stand, oval, dou-
ble-handled, 1 pt. **400**
Teapot, cov., individual size, 12 oz. **300**

Deldare Ware (1908-1909, 1923-1925)

*Note: "Fallowfield Hunt" and "Ye Olden Days"
scenes are similarly priced for the equivalent
pieces in this line.*

Candleholder, shield-back style, "Ye Olden
Days" scene, 7" h. .... **1,800+**
Dresser tray, rectangular, "Dancing Ye
Minuet" scene, 9 x 12" **750**
Humidor, cov., octagonal, 7" h. **1,200**

Very Rare Deldare Jardiniere & Base

Jardiniere & garden seat pedestal base,
"Ye Lion Inn" scenes on jardiniere, two
"Ye Olden Days" scenes on base, 1908,
jardiniere 9" h., base 13 1/2" h., the set
(ILLUS.) **12,000**
Plate, 6 1/4" d., salesman's sample .... **2,200+**
Relish dish, oblong, 6 1/2 x 12" **500**
Salad bowl, 12" d., 5" h. **500**
Vase, 9" h., tall waisted cylindrical form, "Ye
Olden Days" scene **1,400**

Emerald Deldare (1911)

Very Rare Emerald Deldare Pitcher

Pitcher, 8 3/4" h., octagonal, angled handle, color scene of "Dr. Syntax Setting
Out to the Lakes," signed by M. Gerhardt,
dated 1911 (ILLUS.) **18,000-19,000**
Plaque, round, "Friday," scene of monks at
a long table eating fish on Friday, 12" d... **1,900+**

Plate, 8 1/4" d., stylized floral & geometric
decoration **750**

Gaudy Willow (1905-1916)

*Note: Pieces dated 1905 and marked "First Old
Willow Ware Manufactured in America" are
worth double the prices shown here. This line is
generally priced five times higher than the Blue
Willow line.*

Large Display of Gaudy Willow Pottery

Boston egg cup, 7 oz. **350**
Cake plate, double-handled, 10 1/4" d. **500**
Gravy/sauceboat, 14 1/2 oz. **400**
Plate, dinner, 10 1/2" d. **275**
Saucer, 6 1/2" d. **50**
Teacup, 10 oz. **175**

Jugs and Pitchers (1906-1909)

Jug, "Mason," brown/beige colors, 1907,
8 1/2" h. .... **1,000+**
Pitcher, "Chrysanthemum," dark green,
1908, 7 1/2" h. **500**
Pitcher, "Cinderella," jug-type, ca. 1907,
marked w/Buffalo transfer logo & date,
"Cinderella" & "1328," 6" h. **700**
Pitcher, "John Paul Jones," blue & white,
1908, 8 3/4" h. .... **1,000+**
Pitcher, "New Bedford Whaler - The Niger,"
bluish green, 1907, 6" h. **850**
Pitcher, "Robin Hood," multicolored, 1906,
8 1/4" h. **575**
Pitcher, "Sailor" patt., waisted-tankard
form, decorated in blues w/the heads of
two seamen above scenes of sailing
ships, opposite side w/a lighthouse &
rocky coastline, 1906, 9 1/4" h. **1,000-1,100**

Plates - Commemorative (1906-1912)

Gen. A.P. Stewart Chapter, United Daughters of the Confederacy, No. 81, Richmond, Virginia, blue & white, 1907, 10 1/2" d. 300

Improved Order of the Redman, green border w/multicolored design, 7 1/2" d. 175

New Bedford, Massachusetts, blue & white, 1908, 10 1/2" d. 175

Richest Hill in the World, Butte, Montana, deep bluish green, 7 1/2" d. 150

Plates - Historical - Blue or Green (1905-1910)

Capitol Building, Washington, D.C., 10" d. 75

Independence Hall, Philadelphia, 10" d. 75

Niagara Falls, 10" d. 75

Miscellaneous Pieces

First Buffalo China Christmas Plate

Christmas Plate, 1950, first of a series of annual plates ending in 1962, 9 1/2" d. (ILLUS.) 65

Feeding dish, child's, alphabet border, color or center scene of Dolly Dingle children signed by Grace Drayton 175

Gravy boat, Seneca patt., 8 1/2" l. 45

Rare York Pattern Pitcher

Pitcher, York patt., white body w/blue & red flowers, 1910, rare, 7 1/2" h. (ILLUS.) 650

Plate, 6 3/8" d., bread & butter, made for the New York, New Haven & Hartford Railroad, ca. 1935 (ILLUS. right, bottom of page) 75

Plate, 8 3/8" d., luncheon, made for the New York, New Haven & Hartford Railroad, ca. 1935 (ILLUS. center with other railroad plates, bottom of page) 125

Plate, 9" d., Multifleure patt., Buffalo China 300

Plate, 9 1/2" d., dinner, Roycroft Inn service...... 300

Plate, 9 3/4" d., dinner, made for the New York, New Haven & Hartford Railroad, ca. 1935 (ILLUS. left with other railroad plates, bottom of page) 150

Plate, 10 1/4" d., dinner, Bangor patt., eagle backstamp, 1906 600

NY, NH & H Railroad Plates

Plate, 10 1/2" d., Stuyvesant Hotel service, green & gold 250

Plate, 10 3/4" d., Pere Marquette Hotel service, Ye Olde Ivory 300

Plate, George Washington portrait, gold-embossed border band, made for the Chesapeake & Ohio Railroad, 1932, 11" d.. 750

Portland vase, reproduced in 1946, 8" h....... 1,000

Tom & Jerry set: punch bowl & 12 cups; Colorido Ware, the set 1,000

Carlton Ware

The Staffordshire firm of Wiltshaw & Robinson, Stoke-on-Trent, operated the Carlton Works from about 1890 until 1958, producing both earthenwares and porcelain. Specializing in decorative items like vases and teapots, it became well known for its lustre-finished wares, often decorated in the Oriental taste. The trademark Carlton Ware was incorporated into its printed mark. Since 1958, a new company, Carlton Ware Ltd., has operated the Carlton Works at Stoke.

Harebell Pattern Carlton Posy Bowl

Bowl, 9" d., 3 1/2" h., posy-type, Harebell patt., a wide angled rim around a small cylindrical well, blue background painted w/pink bellflowers & other yellow & purple flowers & green, yellow, black & gold leaves (ILLUS.) **$400-425**

Bowl, 7 1/8 x 12 1/4", 3 1/4" h., long oval form w/scalloped sides & squared end handles, Art Deco style decoration w/a large stylized tree in blue w/green leaves & red blossoms, shaded pale yellow to black ground & lustred brick red end handles, ca. 1930s (ILLUS., bottom of page) **300-350**

Bowl & Jar from Garniture set

Garniture set: two cov. jars & large bowl, "Kang Hsi" patt., each w/a dark blue ground decorated w/elaborate gold & light blue Chinese landscapes w/temples, bowl 8 3/4" d., 4" h., jars 4 1/2" d., 9 1/4" h., set of 3 (ILLUS. of part) **950**

Long Oval Carlton Ware Bowl

Carlton Ware Tobacco Humidor

Humidor, cov., spherical body w/wide, short cylindrical neck, dark orange background w/a large black reserve painted w/colorful birds & leafy trees & grasses, gold trim, flat brass cover w/disk finial, 4 1/2" d., 4 1/4" h. (ILLUS.) **300-350**

Carlton Rouge Royale Pitcher

Pitcher, 6 3/4" h., 5" d., Rouge Royale line, flaring gold foot below the ovoid body decorated w/an iridescent deep red ground w/a large flying bird & trees & branches in the background, overall gold trim & squared gold handle, mother-of-pearl interior (ILLUS.) **500-550**

Carlton Ware Potpourri Jar

Potpourri jar, cov., wide ovoid body w/a fitted domed cover, yellow ground decorated w/a large cartouche-form black reserve painted in color w/a Chinese landscape w/temples, trees & figures, heavy gold trim, smaller scene on reverse & on the cover, 7 1/2" d., 9 3/4" h. (ILLUS.) **400-450**

Carlton Ware Persian Pattern Vase

Vase, cov., 6 5/8" h., 3 1/4" d., footed ovoid body w/a wide, low pagoda-form cover, Persian patt., dark blue ground decorated in color w/an Islamic landscape w/figures in the foreground & a mosque in the distance, gold trim (ILLUS.) **300-350**

Carlton Temple Jar-form Vase

Vase, cov., 8 3/4" h., 3 1/2" d., temple-jar form, the body background in sponged blue painted w/a large black & white tree w/large pink blossoms & green leaves, gold trim, domed cover w/figural gold foo dog finial (ILLUS.) **350-375**

Carlton Persian Vase with Landscape

Vase, 10 1/2" h., 4 3/4" d., Persian patt.,
footed ovoid body w/a narrow shoulder to
the short flared neck, dark blue ground
decorated in color w/a continuous Islamic
landscape w/a garden pavilion & figures
surrounded by trees, flowers, birds & an-
imals, gold trim (ILLUS.) **350-400**

Ceramic Arts Studio of Madison

*During its 15 years of operation, Ceramic Arts
Studio of Madison, Wisconsin, was one of the
nation's largest producers of figurines, shakers
and other decorative wares. Its originality and
high production standards make its wares highly
collectible works of art. In 1940, the artistic talent
of Lawrence Rabbitt merged with the business
acumen of Reuben Sand to start Ceramic Arts
Studio. Their partnership was successful. Rabbitt
remained artist in residence and the Studio produced hand-thrown bowls, pots and vases explor-
ing the potential of Wisconsin clay. After
Rabbitt's departure in 1942, a serendipitous meeting between Sand and Betty Harrington brought
her artistic talents to the Studio. Under her artistic direction, the focus was changed to finely
sculpted decorative wares, including figurines of
people, animals and fantasy figures. Metal Art
accessories to complement the ceramic pieces were
assembled at the Studio under the direction of
Zona Liberace (stepmother to the famous pianist),
who also functioned as the Studio's decorating
director.*

*From 1942 to 1948, the Studio's business flour-
ished while imports from Europe and the Far
East were suspended as a result of World War II.
Annual production of 500,000 pieces and employ-
ment of 100 people were typical for these years.
Harrington, although not the only designer on
staff, is credited with the creation of the vast
majority of the 800+ pieces put into production.
This level of output and quality helped to solidify*

*the Studio's reputation as one of the most original
and enduring ceramic producers in America.*

*The popularity of the Studio's work drew many
poor quality imitations and outright copies. After
World War II, lower-priced decorative imports
began to flood the market, forcing the Studio's
eventual close in 1955. Attempts to continue the
enterprise in Japan resulted in products bearing
the name Ceramic Arts Studio - Japan and/or
Mahana Imports. Some of the original molds
were taken there and many of the models were
produced with little or no design change, but with
wide variations in quality. The ink stamp on
these Japanese Studio wares is in red or blue and
the clay color is bright white. In contrast, the
semicircle mark, Ceramic Arts Studio, Madison,
WI is always in black and the clay is ivory and
heavier. But since only one out of four Madison
Ceramic Arts Studio works were ink-stamped,
other clues to authenticity are the decoration and
clarity of the glaze.*

Ceramic Arts Studio Marks

Adam & Eve (one-piece), 12" h. .. **Too rare-price**

African Man Mask Vase

African Man vase, stylized mask on ringed
base, dark brown, 8" h. (ILLUS.).......... **$125-150**
African Woman vase, 8" h. 125-150
Ancient Cat, 4 1/2" h..................................... 80-100
Aphrodite, 7" h... 250-350

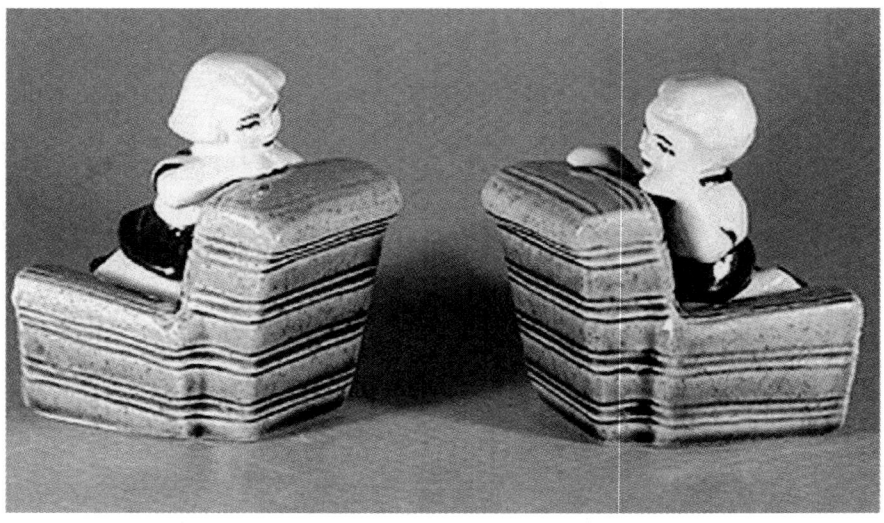

Boy & Girl in Armchairs

Baby Mermaid, diving, 2 1/2" h. **150-175**
Barbershop Quartet mug, 3 1/2" h. **650-750**

ing chair, 1" to 1 1/2" h., each set
(ILLUS., top of page) **60-80**
Cupid, 5" h. **275-500**
Dawn, 6 1/2" h. **175-200**
Drum Girl bank, 4 1/2" h. **220-250**
Egyptian Man, 9 1/2" h. **700-750**

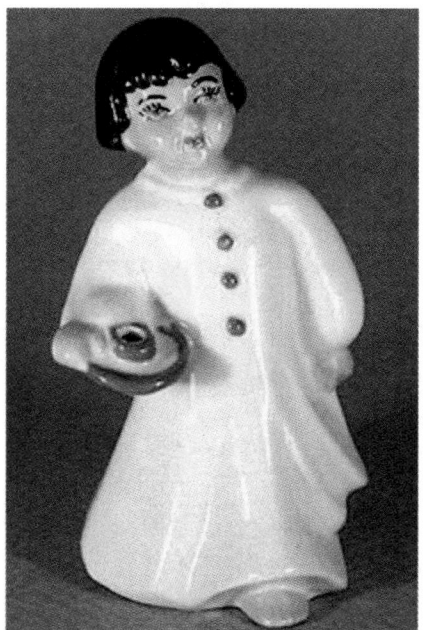

Bedtime Girl

Bedtime Girl, 4 3/4" h. (ILLUS.) **75-95**
Blythe, 6 1/2" h. **150-175**
Boy with Puppy, shelf-sitter, 4 1/4" h. **75-100**
Butch Boxer, 3" l. **60-80**
Children in Chairs, boy looking over back
  of one armchair, girl looking over match-

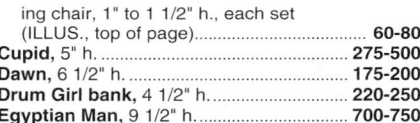

Rare Egyptian Woman Figure

Egyptian Woman, 9 1/2" h. (ILLUS.) **700-750**
Fire Man, 11 1/4" h. **200-250**
Flute Girl, 4 1/2" h. **140-160**
French Horn Man, 6 1/2" h. **500-600**
Gleeful Imp, sitting, 3 1/2" h. **500-550**
Gremlin, sitting, 2" h. **250-300**

Lion & Lioness Figures

Rare Guitar Man Figure

Jack Be Nimble Wall Plaque

Guitar Man, stylized seated figure, grey
   glaze, 6 1/2" h. (ILLUS.) **500-600**
Happy Imp, lying, 3 1/2" h. **500-550**
Harem Girl, reclining, 6" l............................. **100-125**
Harlequin Girl with Mask, 8 1/2" h. **900-950**
Honey or Sonny Spaniel bank, 5 3/4" h.,
   each **300-350**
Honey Spaniel, 5 3/4" h............................... **200-225**
Jack Be Nimble wall plaque, 5" h.
   (ILLUS., next column) **400-450**
Joey, baby kangaroo, 2 1/2" h. **70-90**
Kangaroo Mother, 4 3/4" h............................... **60-80**
King's Jester Lutist Woman, 12" h.......... **100-200**
Lion, 7 1/4" l. (ILLUS. left, top of page) **170-190**
Lioness, 5 1/2" l. (ILLUS. right with
   lion, top of page) **170-190**
Madonna with Bible, 9 1/2" h.................... **325-350**

Mary Contrary Wall Plaque

Tembino & Tembo Elephants

Mary Contrary wall plaque, 5" h.
(ILLUS., previous page)........................... 160-180
Mermaid on Rock, 4" h. 150-175
Modern Doe, reclining, 3 3/4" h................. 100-125
Modern Fawn, 2" h...................................... 75-100
Mother Seal on Rock, 5" h. 500-600

Mr. Blankety Blank Bank

Mr. Blankety Blank bank, 4 1/2" h.
(ILLUS.).. 120-140
Nineteenth (19th) Century Man,
6 3/4" h.. 250-300
Nineteenth (19th) Century Woman,
6 1/2" h.. 250-300

Paisley Pig Figure

Paisley Pig, 5 1/2" l., 3" h. (ILLUS.)........... 325-375
Pensive, 6" h. 150-175
Sad Imp with Spear, 5" h........................... 500-550
Seal Mother, 6" l. 400-450
Seal Pup, 3" l... 350-400
See No Evil candleholder, 5" h................... 80-100
Sonny Spaniel, 5 3/4" h. 200-225
Speak No Evil candleholder, 5" h. 80-100
Square Dance Boy, 6 1/2" h. 100-125
Square Dance Girl, 6 1/2" h. 100-125
St. Agnes with Lamb, 6" h. 260-285
Summer Sally, Four Seasons group,
3 1/2" h.. 100-130
Swan Lake Man, 7" h................................. 900-950
Tembino Elephant, realistic, trunk down,
2 1/2" h. (ILLUS. right, top of page)........ 160-190
Tembo Elephant, realistic, trunk up,
6 1/2" h. (ILLUS. left with Tembino, top of
page) 185-225
Thunder Stallion, 5 3/4" h. 150-175
Tortoise with Cane, 2 1/4" h. 120-140
Violin Lady, 8 1/2" h. 500-600
White Willy, ball down, 4 1/2" h. 240-270

White Winnie, sleeping, 5 1/2" l. **240-270**
White Woody, 3 1/4" h. **240-270**

Cowan

R. Guy Cowan opened his first pottery studio in 1912 in Lakewood, Ohio. The pottery operated almost continuously, with the exception of a break during the First World War, at various locations in the Cleveland area until it was forced to close in 1931 due to financial difficulties.

Many of this century's finest artists began with Cowan and its associate, the Cleveland School of Art. This fine art pottery, particularly the designer pieces, are highly sought after by collectors.

Many people are unaware that it was due to R. Guy Cowan's perseverance and tireless work that art pottery is today considered an art form and found in many art museums.

Cowan Mark

Ashtray, center relief-molded unicorn decoration, caramel glaze, designed by Waylande Gregory, w/footed foliate metal stand, Shape No. 925, 3/4 x 5 1/2" **$90**
Ashtray, three-section base w/figural leaping gazelle & foliage on edge, Oriental Red glaze, designed by Waylande Gregory, 5 3/4" h. (ILLUS. lower right with horse book end & boy & girl book ends, below) **350**
Book ends, figural, model of a fish, Oriental Red glaze, Shape No. 863, 4 5/8" h., pr. **750**
Book ends, figural, a nude kneeling boy & nude kneeling girl, each on oblong bases, creamy white glaze, designed by Frank N. Wilcox, Shape No. 519, Marks 8 & 9, ca. 1925, 6 1/2" h., pr. (ILLUS. with Cowan ashtray & kicking horse book end, bottom of page) **550**

Elephant Book Ends & Paperweights

Book ends, figural, modeled as a large rounded stylized elephant w/trunk curved under, standing on a stepped rectangular base, overall Oriental Red glaze, designed by Margaret Postgate, Shape No. E-2, 7 1/4" h., pr. (ILLUS. top center & lower left) **2,000**

Cowan Book Ends & Ashtray

Book ends, model of a stylized horse, back legs raised in kicking position, black, designed by Waylande Gregory, Shape No. E-1, 9" h., pr. (ILLUS. of one, with ashtray & boy & girl book ends, bottom of previous page) **2,500**

Book ends, figural, a little girl standing wearing a sunbonnet & full ruffled dress, on a thick rectangular base, ivory semi-matte glaze, Shape No. 521, impressed mark & "Z," ca. 1925, 4" w., 7 1/4" h., pr....... **550**

Cowan Bowl & Vases

Bowl, 5 1/4" d., individual, green & black, designed by Arthur E. Baggs (ILLUS. right) **3,000**

Bowl, 2 1/2 x 9 1/4", Egyptian blue glaze, designed by R.G. Cowan, Shape No. B-12 .... **75**

Bowl, 2 1/4 x 10 1/4", blue pearl finish **140**

Bowl, 3 x 9 1/4 x 12 1/4", copper crystal glaze, Shape No. B-785-A **150**

Bowl, 2 3/4 x 11 1/2 x 15", Oriental Red glaze, designed by Waylande Gregory, Shape No. B-4.. **200**

Cowan Bust

Bust of a woman, close-cut hair in ringlets, original sculpture by Jose Martin, terra cotta, 13 1/2" h. (ILLUS.) **6,200**

Candleholder, flaring base w/flattened rim, black & silver, Shape No. 870, 1 1/2" h. **50**

Cowan Figural Nude Candlestick

Candlestick, figural, seminude female standing before figural branches on round base w/flared foot, one arm across her body & the other raised overhead, shaded tan & green glaze, designed by R.G. Cowan, Shape No. 744-R, 12 1/2" h. (ILLUS.)...................................... **1,000**

Candlestick/bud vase, tapering cylindrical shape w/flared foot & rim, rainbow blue finish, Shape 530-A, 7 1/2" h........................... **50**

Candlesticks, figural sea horse w/flared base, green, Shape No. 716, 4 3/8" h., pr. **60**

Cowan Candlesticks & Vase

Candlesticks, model of a marlin on wave-form base, verde green, designed by Waylande Gregory, 8" h., pr. (ILLUS. right, previous page) **1,300**

Charger, "Polo" plate, incised scene w/polo players & flowers under a blazing sun, covered in a rare glossy brown & cafe-au-lait glaze, designed by Victor Schreckengost, mark Nos. 8 & 9, Shape No. X-48, impressed "V.S. - Cowan," 11 1/4" d. (grinding chips to retaining ring)................ **900**

Cigarette holder, w/wave design, Oriental Red glaze, designed by Waylande Gregory, Shape No. 927-J, 3 1/4" **100**

Cigarette/matchholder, flared foot w/relief-molded sea horse decoration, orange glaze, Shape No. 72, 3 1/2" h.......................... **40**

Comport, footed, square, green & white glaze, Shape No. 951, 4 1/2" sq., 2 1/4" h. **40**

Console bowl, footed, flaring fluted sides, white glaze exterior, blue glaze interior, Shape No. 713-A, 3 1/2 x 7 1/4 x 10 1/2" **90**

Desk set, w/paper clip dish, Oriental Red glaze, Shape PB-1, 2 1/2 x 5 1/2", the set..... **125**

Cowan Figurines & Flower Frog

Figurine, "Spanish Dancer," female, white, designed by Elizabeth Anderson, Shape No. 793, 8 1/2" h. (ILLUS. right).................... **900**

Figurine, "Spanish Dancer," male, white, designed by Elizabeth Anderson, Shape No. 793, 8 3/4" h. (ILLUS. left) **900**

Figurines, "Spanish Dancer," male & female figures h.p. in polychrome glazes, the male mark No. 9, Shape No. 794-D, 8 1/4" h. & the female mark No. 8, Shape No. 793-D, 8 1/2" h., designed by Elizabeth Anderson, impressed marks, pr. **2,400**

Flower frog, model of an artichoke, light green, Shape No. 775, 3" h. **90**

Flower frog, fluted flower-form base centered by relief-molded stalk & leaves supporting the figure of a female nude standing w/one leg bent, knee raised, leaning backward w/one arm raised overhead & the other resting on a curved leaf, ivory glaze, designed by R.G. Cowan, Shape

No. F-812-X, 10 1/2" h. (ILLUS. center with Spanish Dancers)..................................... **900**

Flower frog, figural nude w/long flowing scarf, ivory, designed by R.G. Cowan, Shape No. 687, 11 3/4" h.......................... **1,000**

Flower frog, figural, "Triumphant," figure of a standing seminude Art Deco woman w/one leg raised, leaning back w/one arm raised above her head & the other on her hip, a clinging drapery around her lower body, standing on a round incurved leaf cluster base, overall Original Ivory glaze, stamped mark, 4 1/2" w., 15" h. **2,200**

Ginger jar, cov., orange lustre, Shape No. 583, 10" h. **500**

Lamp, candlestick-form, a disk foot & spiral-twist standard w/a flaring molded socket fitted w/an electric bulb socket, overall marigold lustre glaze, impressed mark, 11" h. **90**

Lamp, girl w/deer decoration, ivory, 18" h. **450**

Bird on Wave Model

Model of bird on wave, Egyptian blue, designed by Alexander Blazys, Shape No. 749-A, 12" h. (ILLUS.) **1,500**

Paperweight, figural, modeled as a large rounded stylized elephant w/trunk curved under, standing on a stepped rectangular base, ivory glaze, designed by Margaret Postgate, Shape No. D-3, 4 3/4" h. (ILLUS. lower center with elephant book ends, page 153)........................ **400**

Paperweight, figural, modeled as a large rounded stylized elephant w/trunk curved under, standing on a stepped rectangular base, blue glaze, designed by Margaret Postgate, Shape No. D-3, 4 3/4" h. (ILLUS. lower right with elephant book ends, page 153) **450**

Paperweight, figural, modeled as a large rounded stylized elephant w/trunk curved under, standing on a stepped rectangular base, overall Oriental Red glaze, designed by Margaret Postgate, Shape No. D-3, 4 3/4" h. (ILLUS. top right with elephant book ends, page 153) **500**

Plaque, seascape decoration, designed by Thelma Frazier Winter, 11 1/2" d. **900**

Plaque, terradatol, designed by Alexander Blazys, Egyptian blue, Shape No. 739, 15 1/2" **1,000**

Strawberry jar w/saucer, Oriental Red glaze, designed by R.G. Cowan, Shape No. SJ-1, mark No. 8, 7 1/2" h., 2 pcs.......... **350**

Urn, classical form w/trumpet foot supporting a wide bulbous ribbed body w/a wide short cylindrical neck flanked by loop handles, overall Peacock blue glaze, stamped mark, 8" d., 9 1/2" h. **100**

Vase, 3 1/4" h., footed, baluster-form, Feu Rouge glaze, Shape No. 533........................ **100**

Vase, 4 1/4" h., mottled green, Shape No. V-54 .... **75**

Vase, 5 1/4" h., Lakeware, melon-lobed shape **90**

Vase, 5 1/2" h., footed wide semi-ovoid body w/flaring rim, dark bluish green, Shape 575-A, mark No. 4............................... **50**

Vase, 6 1/2" h., spherical body w/flaring cylindrical neck flanked by scroll handles, Egyptian blue, designed by Viktor Schreckengost, Shape No. V-99 (ILLUS. center w/bowl, page 154) **650**

Vase, bud, 7" h., blue lustre glaze **75**

Vase, 7 1/2" h., baluster-form w/trumpet-form neck, blue rainbow lustre, Shape No. 631 .... **90**

Vase, 5 1/4 x 7 3/4", flared tulip-shaped body, squared feet, blue.................................. **80**

Vase, 8" h., bulbous body tapering to cylindrical neck w/flaring rim, verde green, Shape No. V-932 .... **180**

Vase, 8" h., bulbous body tapering to cylindrical neck w/flaring rim, Feu Rouge (red) glaze, Shape No. V-932 .... **550**

Vase, 10 1/2" h., footed bulbous ovoid body, Star patt., decorated w/relief-mold-

ed foliage, orange glaze, designed by Waylande Gregory, Shape V-32, mark No. 8 & 9 (ILLUS. left w/bowl, page 154) **600**

Vase, 11 3/4" h., wine & yellow glaze, Shape No. V-15 .... **500**

Vase, 13" h., swelled cylindrical body w/a narrow shoulder to the short cylindrical wide neck covered in a lustered grey & yellow dripping glaze, mark No. 7, Shape No. 552, stamped ink mark............................ **825**

Vase, 13 1/2" h., baluster-form body w/flaring rim, light blue glaze, Shape No. 563 (ILLUS. left w/marlin candlesticks, page 154).. **275**

Czechoslovakian

Czechoslovakia did not exist until the end of World War I in 1918. The country was put together with parts of Austria, Bohemia and Hungary as a reward for the help of the Czechs and the Slovaks in winning the war. In 1993 Czechoslovakia split and became two countries: the Czech Republic and the Slovak Republic. Items are highly collectible because the country was in existence only 75 years. For a more thorough study of the subject, refer to the following books: Made in Czechoslovakia Books 1 and 2 by Ruth A. Forsythe; Czechoslovakian Glass & Collectibles Books I and II by Dale & Dian Barta and Helen M. Rose and Czechoslovakian Perfume Bottles and Boudoir Accessories by Jacquelyne Y. Jones North.

Bell, w/original pottery heart clapper, geometric patt. on black ground, J. Mrazek, Peasant Art Industries, 4 1/4" h. (ILLUS. front row, left w/various J. Mrazek pieces, bottom of page)... **$150**

Biscuit jar, w/rattan handle, decorated w/orange flower, 7" h. **125**

Book ends, in the form of Indian heads, pr....... **125**

Cache pot, decorated w/cherries, 4 1/2" h. **65**

Cigarette box, white, w/horse finial, 4" h. **150**

Various J. Mrazek Pieces

Console bowl, footed, lilac, purple & green, Eichwald, 6" h.. **150**

Creamer, decorated w/orange cherries, 4 1/2" h. **55**

Creamer, w/handle in the form of a cat, white iridescent, 4" h. **65**

Flower frog, round, w/airbrushed roses around middle.. **150**

Humidor, cov., ovoid shape, geometric patt. on light green sponge ground, knobbed lid, J. Mrazek, Peasant Art Industries, 7 1/2" h. (ILLUS. previous page, back row, right w/various J. Mrazek pieces).......... **375**

Model of bulldog, white w/brown & black splotches, 7" h... **135**

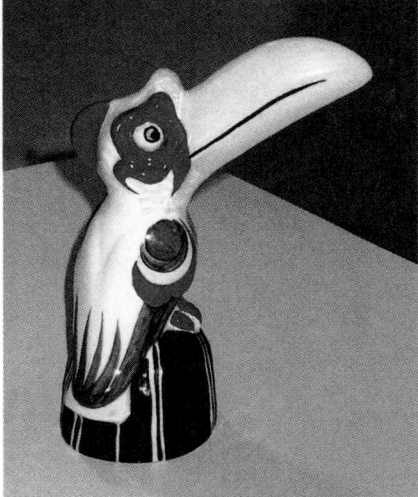

Model of Toucan

Model of toucan, bird w/large yellow beak perches on black base, white body w/green, blue, yellow & red detail, 8" h. (ILLUS.)... **750**

Mug, "Monte Carlo" patt., 1/2 liter........................ **40**

Hand-painted Pitcher

Pitcher, bulbous form w/short circular base, C-scroll handle, h.p. w/decoration of large flower on front & back w/green leaves as accents, "BATNA," Ditmar-Urbach (ILLUS.)... **350**

Pitcher, 1-liter, bulbous body w/flaring cylindrical neck, short base & S-scroll applied handle, h.p. decoration of orange, blue & black ellipses, green leaves & orange trim, LOSTRO (ILLUS. second from right w/other pitcher & vases, bottom of page)...... **150**

Pitcher, 1-liter, cov., ovoid body w/cylindrical neck, short base & C-scroll applied handle, h.p. overall floral decoration (ILLUS. second from left w/other pitcher & vases, bottom of page) **125**

Pitcher, 4" h., spherical form, geometric design on yellow sponge ground, J. Mrazek, Peasant Art Industries (ILLUS. front row, center w/various J. Mrazek pieces, bottom page 156).. **175**

Pitcher, 6" h., figural, in the form of a girl holding flowers, orange & white, Erphila **85**

Czechoslovakian Pitchers & Vases

Cat Pitcher

Pitcher, 8" h., figural, in the form of a seated cat w/head turned to side, tail forms handle, one ear forms spout, cream w/red & black accents, imported by Eberling & Reuss (Erphila) (ILLUS.) 950

Pitcher, cover & underplate, 9" h., decorated on front w/orange flower w/green leaves, 3 pcs. 150

Plate, 6 1/2" h., geometric patt. on orange sponge ground, J. Mrazek, Peasant Art Industries (ILLUS. back row, center w/various J. Mrazek pieces, page 156)........... 55

Plate, 9 1/2" d., white w/border decorated w/images of lobster, crab & shrimp................. 45

Plate, 12" d., cheese & crackers, white w/green airbrushed lines in several places, center w/figural multicolored rooster & holes for toothpicks.................................... 125

Salt & pepper shakers, "Monte Carlo" patt., pr. 30

Toby, Mr. Bumble, Erphila, 3 1/4" h. 45

Vase, 4 1/2" h., cylindrical form, geometric design on light green sponge ground, J. Mrazek, Peasant Art Industries, 7 1/2" h. (ILLUS. front row, right w/various J. Mrazek pieces, page 156)............................ 110

Vase, 7" h., fan-shaped, w/multicolored h.p. slip decoration 195

Vase, 7" h., segmented ovoid form w/flaring rim & base, h.p. overall floral decoration (ILLUS. previous page far right w/other vase & pitchers) 175

Vase, 7 1/2" h., waisted cylindrical form, geometric patt. on orange sponge ground, J. Mrazek, Peasant Art Industries (ILLUS. back row, left w/various J. Mrazek pieces, page 156)............................ 275

Vase, 8" h., bulbous form w/short flared neck, short circular base, two side loop handles, airbrushed in purple & red (ILLUS. previous page far left w/other vase & pitchers) 150

Vase, 8" h., two-handled, brown & yellow w/image of cottage on front............................. 55

Vase, 8" h., white matte finish w/decoration of woman's head at base 175

Wall pocket, decorated w/orange flower, 7" h. 65

Doulton & Royal Doulton

Doulton & Co., Ltd., was founded in Lambeth, London, in about 1858. It was operated there until 1956 and often incorporated the words "Doulton" and "Lambeth" in its marks. Pinder, Bourne & Co., Burslem was purchased by the Doultons in 1878 and in 1882 became Doulton & Co., Ltd. It added porcelain to its earthenware production in 1884. The "Royal Doulton" mark has been used since 1902 by this factory, which is still in operation. Character jugs and figurines are commanding great attention from collectors at the present time.

John Doulton, the founder, was born in 1793. He became an apprentice at the age of 12 to a potter in south London. Five years later he was employed in another small pottery near Lambeth. His two sons, John and Henry, subsequently joined their father in 1830 in a partnership he had formed with the name of Doulton & Watts. Watts retired in 1864 and the partnership was dissolved. Henry formed a new company that traded as Doulton & Co.

In the early 1870s the proprietor of the Pinder Bourne Co., located in Burslem, Staffordshire, offered Henry a partnership. The Pinder Bourne Co. was purchased by Henry in 1878 and became part of Doulton & Co. in 1882.

With the passage of time the demand for the Lambeth industrial and decorative stoneware declined whereas demand for the Burslem manufactured and decorated bone china wares increased.

Doulton & Co. was incorporated as a limited liability company in 1899. In 1901 the company was allowed to use the word "Royal" on its trademarks by Royal Charter. The well known "lion on crown" logo came into use in 1902. In 2000 the logo was changed on the company's advertising literature to one showing a more stylized lion's head in profile.

Today Royal Doulton is one of the world's leading manufacturers and distributors of premium grade ceramic tabletop wares and collectibles. The Doulton Group comprises Minton, Royal Albert, Caithness Glass, Holland Studio Craft and Royal Doulton. Royal Crown Derby was part of the group from 1971 until 2000 when it became an independent company. These companies market collectibles using their own brand names.

Royal Doulton Mark

Animals & Birds

Bird, Bullfinch, blue & pale blue feathers, red breast, HN 2551, 1941-46, 5 1/2" h........... 80

Cat, Persian Cat, seated, black & white, HN 999, 1930-85, 5" h.. 115

Dog, Airedale Terrier, Ch. "Cotsford Top-sail," standing, dark brown & black, light brown underbody, HN 1024, 1931-68, 4" h. **275**

Dog, Alsatian, "Benign of Picardy," dark brown, HN 1117, 1937-68, 4 1/2" **250**

Dog, Boxer, Champion "Warlord of Maze-laine," golden brown coat w/white bib, HN 2643, 1952-85, 6 1/2" h. **145**

Dog, Bull Terrier, K 14, lying, white, 1940-59, 1 1/4 x 2 3/4" **325**

Dog, Bulldog, HN 1044, brown & white, 1931-68, 3 1/4" h. **250**

Dog, Bulldog Puppy, K 2, seated, tan w/brown patches, 1931-77, 2" **85**

Dog, character dog yawning, white w/brown patches over ears & eyes, black patches on back, HN 1099, 1934-85, 4" h. **75**

Dog, Chow (Shibu Ino), K 15, golden, 1940-77, 2 1/2" **135**

Dog, Cocker Spaniel, Ch. "Lucky Star of Ware," black coat w/grey markings, HN 1021, 1931-68, 3 1/2" h. **195**

Dog, Cocker Spaniel w/pheasant, seated, white coat w/black markings, HN 1137, 1937-66, 6 1/2 x 7 3/4" **375**

Dog, Collie, Ch. "Ashstead Applause," dark & light brown coat, white chest, shoulder & feet, HN 1057, 1931-60, 7 1/2" h. **750**

Dog, Dalmatian, "Goworth Victor," white w/black spots, black ears, HN 1113, 1937-85, 5 1/2" **225**

Dog, Doberman Pinscher, Ch. "Rancho Do-be's Storm," black w/brown feet & chin, HN 2645, 1955-85, 6 1/4" **165**

Dog, Dog of Fo, Flambé, RDICC, Model 2957, 1981, 5 1/4" h. **215**

Dog, English Setter, Ch. "Maesydd Mus-tard," off-white coat w/black highlights, HN 1051, 1931-68, 4" h. **215**

Dog, Fox Terrier, K 8, seated, white w/brown & black patches, 1931-77, 2 1/2" **90**

Dog, Foxhound, K 7, seated, white w/brown & black patches, 1931-77, 2 1/2" **110**

Dog, French Poodle, HN 2631, white w/pink, grey & black markings, 1952-85, 5 1/4" h. **195**

Dog, Great Dane, "Rebeller of Ouborough," light brown, HN 2562, 191-52, 4 1/2" **725**

Dog, Greyhound, standing, golden brown w/dark brown markings, cream chest & feet, HN 1065, 1931-55, 8 1/2" h. **1,150**

Dog, Irish Setter, Ch. "Pat O'Moy," HN 1056, 1931-68, 6" l., 4" h. **225**

Dog, Labrador, "Bumblikite of Mansergh," black, HN 2667, 1967-85, 5 1/4" **145**

Golden Labrador

Dog, Labrador, standing, golden, DA 145, 1990-present, 5" h. (ILLUS.) **55**

Dog, Pekinese, Ch. "Biddee of Ifield," gold-en w/black highlights, HN 1012, 1931-85, 3" **95**

Dog, Rough-haired Terrier, Ch. "Crackley Startler," white w/black & brown mark-ings, HN 1014, 1931-85, 3 3/4" h. **125**

Dog, Scottish Terrier, Ch. "Albourne Arthur," black, HN 1015, 1931-60, 5" **315**

Dog, Sealyham, Ch. "Scotia Stylist," white, HN 1031, 1931-55, 4" **425**

Dog, Springer Spaniel, "Dry Toast," white coat w/brown markings, HN 2517, 1938-55, 3 3/4" **175**

Dog, Springer Spaniel, white w/black mark-ings, HN 1078, 1932-68, 3" **150**

Dog, St. Bernard, lying, brown & cream, K 19, 1940-77, 1 1/2 x 2 1/2" **105**

Dogs, Terrier Puppies in a Basket, three white puppies w/light & dark brown mark-ings, brown basket, HN 2588, 1941-85, 3" h. **105**

Duck, Drake, standing, green, brown & white, HN 807, 1923-77, 2 1/2" h. **105**

Elephant, trunk in salute, grey w/black, HN 2644, 1952-85, 4 1/4" **175**

Horse, Punch Peon, Chestnut Shire, bay w/white markings on legs, HN 2623, 1950-60, 7 1/2" h. **750**

Horses, Chestnut Mare and Foal, chestnut mare w/white stockings, fawn-colored foal w/white stockings, HN 2522, 1938-60, 6 1/2" h. **695**

Kitten, licking hind paw, brown & white, HN 2580, 2 1/4" **75**

Kitten, on hind legs, light brown & black on white, HN 2582, 1941-85, 2 3/4" **75**

Kitten, sleeping, brown & white, HN 2581, 1941-85, 1 1/2" **75**

Monkey, Langur Monkey, long-haired brown & white coat, HN 2657, 1960-69, 4 1/2" h. **255**

Penguin, grey & white w/black tips, K 22, 1940-68, 1 3/4" **195**

Shetland Pony

Pony, Shetland Pony (woolly Shetland mare), glossy brown, DA 47, 1989 to present, 5 3/4" (ILLUS.) **45**

Tiger, crouching, brown w/dark brown stripes, HN 225, 1920-36, 2 x 9 1/2" **575**

Beatrix Potter

The John Beswick factory in Longton, Stoke on Trent, celebrated its 100th anniversary in 1994. Originally, it produced earthenware household items and decorative ornaments. With the passage of time, the product line became more diverse and the decorations more ornate and attractive. Moreover, small domestic, farmyard and wild animal figurines were added to the product lines. Beswick was a family-owned and family-run pottery. As the owners neared retirement, they realized there were no next of kin to carry on the business. They sold the company to Royal Doulton in 1969.

Beatrix Potter is known the world over. Generations of children since the early 1900s have been fascinated by the antics of her coterie of small animals in her series of illustrated children's "Tales of Peter Rabbit and Friends." These storybook characters have been produced as small china figurines since the 1920s, but it was not until 1947 that Beswick gained copyright approval from the Frederick Warne Co., the Peter Rabbit book publisher, to manufacture and market them. Upon acquisition of the manufacturing rights, Royal Doulton continued to promote and sell the Beatrix Potter figures using the Beswick trademark until 1989, when it switched to a "Royal Albert" underprint. Royal Albert was another of its famous product lines and had greater brand recognition in the United States. The backstamp change was not well received by the global collector community. Within a decade, the Beswick backstamp was reintroduced and used on the Beatrix Potter figurines until the end of 2002, when the Warne license expired. The old Beswick factory was closed.

All the Beatrix Potter figurines were assigned a "P" or production model number. Although these "P" numbers do not appear on the figures themselves, they are used extensively by collectors to uniquely identify a particular figure.

Many varieties of backstamp exist. They indicate a period of manufacture and influence secondary market values. The basic types of backstamp are shown. If collectible subtypes exist, a range of market values is given for the basic type. Many special backstamps were used in the 1990s to promote sales. These details are outside the scope of this compendium.

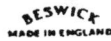

Basic Beatrix Potter Backstamps

Amiable Guinea Pig, P2061, tan jacket, brown line backstamp, 1967-83 .... **$350**

Amiable Guinea Pig Figure

Amiable Guinea Pig, P2061, tan jacket, gold circle or oval backstamp, 1967-83 (ILLUS.).. **700**

Anna Maria, P1851, brown line backstamp, 1963-83 .... **225**

Anna Maria Figure

Anna Maria, P1851, gold circle/oval backstamp, 1963-83 (ILLUS.).................................... **500**

Benjamin Bunny Sat on a Bank

Benjamin Bunny Sat on a Bank, P2803, head down, brown jacket, brown line backstamp, 1983-85 (ILLUS.)......................... **105**
Cecily Parsley, P1941, brown line backstamp, 1965-93 .... **125**
Cecily Parsley, P1941, crown backstamp, 1965-93 .... **50**

Cecily Parsley Figure

Cecily Parsley, P1941, gold circle/oval backstamp, 1965-93 (ILLUS.)........................ **300**
Hunca Munca, P1198, Beswick Made in England backstamp, 1951-2000 .... **35**
Hunca Munca, P1198, brown line backstamp, 1951-2000 .... **75**

Hunca Munca Figure

Hunca Munca, P1198, crown backstamp, 1951-2000 (ILLUS.).. **45**
Hunca Munca, P1198, gold circle/oval backstamp, 1951-2000 .... **350**
Hunca Munca, P1198, John Beswick script backstamp, 1951-2000 .... **165**

Jemima Puddle-Duck

Jemima Puddle-Duck, P1092, yellow scarf clip, Beswick Made in England backstamp, 1948-2002 (ILLUS.) **35**
Jemima Puddle-Duck, P1092, yellow scarf clip, brown line backstamp, 1948-2002 .... **80**
Jemima Puddle-Duck, P1092, yellow scarf clip, crown backstamp, 1948-2002 .... **50**
Jemima Puddle-Duck, P1092, yellow scarf clip, gold circle/oval backstamp, 1948-2002 .... **250**
Jemima Puddle-Duck, P1092, yellow scarf clip, John Beswick script backstamp, 1948-2002 .... **145**
Mr. Alderman Ptolemy, P2424, brown line backstamp, 1973-97 .... **175**

Mr. Alderman Ptolemy

Mr. Alderman Ptolemy, P2424, crown backstamp, 1973-97 (ILLUS.) **65**

Mr. Benjamin Bunny & Peter Rabbit

Mr. Benjamin Bunny & Peter Rabbit,
P2509, brown line backstamp, 1975-95
(ILLUS.) **195**
Mr. Benjamin Bunny & Peter Rabbit,
P2509, crown backstamp, 1975-95 .... **95**
Mrs. Rabbit & Peter, P3646, Beswick Made
in England backstamp, 1997-2002 .... **60**

Mrs. Rabbit & Peter

Mrs. Rabbit & Peter, P3646, crown backs-
tamp, 1997-2002 (ILLUS.) **55**

Mrs. Tittlemouse

Mrs. Tittlemouse, P4015, Beswick Made in
England backstamp, 2000-2002 (ILLUS.) **50**
Old Mr. Brown, P1796, brown owl, brown
line backstamp, 1963-99 .... **75**

Old Mr. Brown Figure

Old Mr. Brown, P1796, brown owl, gold cir-
cle/oval backstamp, 1963-99 (ILLUS.) **200**

Peter Ate a Radish

Peter Ate a Radish, P3533, crown backs-
tamp, 1995-98 (ILLUS.) **35**

Peter with Daffodils

Peter with Daffodils, P3597, Beswick Made in England backstamp, 1996-99 (ILLUS.) 45
Peter with Daffodils, P3597, crown backstamp, 1996-99 40

Sir Isaac Newton

Sir Isaac Newton, P2425, brown line backstamp, 1973-84 (ILLUS.) 450

Susan Figure

Susan, P2716, brown line backstamp, 1983-89 (ILLUS.) 300
Susan, P2716, crown backstamp, 1983-89 250
Tailor of Gloucester, P1108, Beswick Made in England backstamp, 1949-2002 35
Tailor of Gloucester, P1108, brown line backstamp, 1949-2002 65
Tailor of Gloucester, P1108, crown backstamp, 1949-2002 35

Tailor of Gloucester, P1108, gold circle backstamp, 1949-2002 325
Tailor of Gloucester, P1108, gold oval backstamp, 1949-2 200

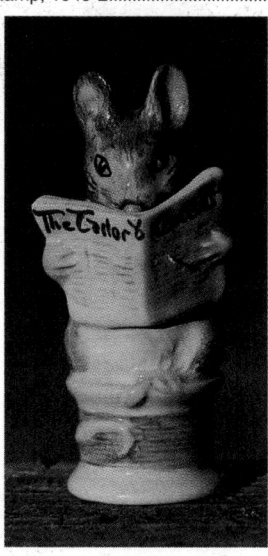

Tailor of Gloucester

Tailor of Gloucester, P1108, John Beswick script backstamp, 1949-2002 (ILLUS.) 100

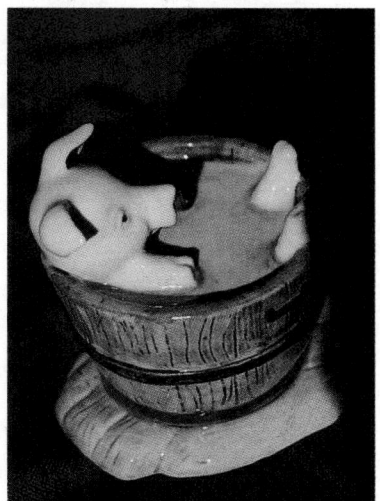

Yock-Yock in the Tub

Yock-Yock in the Tub, P3946, Beswick Made in England backstamp, 2000-02 (ILLUS.) 60

Bunnykins Figurines

Ace, DB 42, white & blue, 1986-89 250
Astro, DB 20, white, red & blue, 1983-88 155

Bunnykins Australian Digger

Australian Digger, DB 248, brown, yellow webbing, edition limited to 2001 (ILLUS.)..... **125**

Basket Ball Players, DB 208, limited edition of 2,500, the set (sold only in set of 5)..... **625**

Bedtime, DB 55, blue & white striped pajamas, 1987-98 .... **40**

Billie Bunnykins Cooling Off, DB 3, burgundy, yellow & greenish grey, 1972-87....... **185**

Boy Skater, second variation, DB 187, blue jacket, white trousers, red boots, 1998, limited edition of 2,500............................. **55**

Business Man, DB 203, 1999, limited edition of 5,000.. **85**

Cheerleader, DB 142, second variation, yellow, 1994, limited edition of 1,000 .... **225**

Cymbals, DB 88, blue coat, 1990, limited edition of 250.. **525**

Doctor, DB 181, white lab coat & shirt, dark blue trousers, black shoes, white & blue striped tie, 1998-2000 .... **45**

Dollie Bunnykins Playtime, DB 80, white & yellow, 1988, by Strawbridge & Clothier, limited edition of 250 .... **225**

Double Bass Player, DB 185, green & yellow striped trousers, 1999, limited edition of 2,500 .... **125**

Lawyer, DB 214, black robe, white wig, 2000, RDICC exclusive..................................... **60**

Magician, DB 126, black suit, yellow shirt, yellow table cloth, 1992, limited edition of 1,500.. **375**

Mary, Mary, Quite Contrary, DB 247, pink, 2002 .... **55**

Morris Dancer, DB 204, multicolored, 1999, limited edition of 2,000...................................... **45**

Mountie, Sergeant, DB 136, red coat w/yellow stripes on sleeve, blue & brown, 1993, limited edition of 250 .... **1,500**

Mr. Bunnybeat Strumming, Music Box, DB 38, pink, white, yellow, 1987-89 .... **355**

Mrs. Bunnykins Clean Sweep, DB 6, blue & white, 1972-91... **75**

New Baby, DB 158, blue dress w/white trim, white cradle, pink pillow, yellow blanket, 1995-99.. **45**

Rainy Day Bunnykins

Rainy Day, DB 147, yellow coat & hat, blue trousers, black boots, 1994-97 (ILLUS.).......... **40**

Santa Bunnykins Happy Christmas

Santa, DB 17, red, white & brown, 1981-96 (ILLUS.)... **45**

Scotsman (The), DB 180, dark blue jacket & hat, red & yellow kilt, white shirt, sporran & socks, black shoes, 1998, limited edition of 2,500 .... **185**

Soccer Player, DB 123, dark blue & white, 1991, limited edition of 250 .... **650**

Stopwatch, DB 253, green & yellow, produced only in 2002 .... **55**

Storytime, DB 9, white dress w/blue design & pink dress, 1972-97 .... **45**

Sweetheart, DB 130, yellow sweater, blue trousers, red heart, 1992-97 .... **50**

Tyrolean Dancer, DB 246, black & white, 2001 .... **60**

Waltzing Matilda, DB 236, yellow, red jacket, brown hat, 2001, limited edition of 2,001 .... **225**

Character Jugs

Anne Boleyn

Anne Boleyn, large, D 6644, 7 1/4" h. (ILLUS.) **85**

Antony & Cleopatra, large, D 6728, 7 1/4" h. **95**

Aramis, miniature, D 6508, 2 1/2" h. **45**

'Ard of 'Earing

'Ard of 'Earing, large, D 6588, 7 1/2" h. (ILLUS.) **1,250**

'Arriet

'Arriet, large, D 6208, 6 1/2" h. (ILLUS.) **65**

'Arry, tiny, D 6255, 1 1/2" h. **150**

Athos, small, D 6452, 3 3/4" h. **50**

Bacchus

Bacchus, large, D 6499, 7" h. (ILLUS.) **60**

Baseball Player, small, D 6878, 4 1/4" h. **115**

Beefeater

Beefeater, large, D 6206, 6 1/2" h. (ILLUS.)..... **125**
Ben Franklin, small, D 6695, 4" h. **90**
Bootmaker, small, D 6579, 4" h. **65**
Buzfuz, small, D 5838, 4" h. **55**
Capt. Ahab, large, D 6500, 7" h. **90**

Capt. Henry Morgan

Capt. Henry Morgan, large, 6 3/4" h.
(ILLUS.) **115**

Capt Hook

Capt Hook, large, D 6597, 7 1/4" h.
(ILLUS.) **500**
Cardinal (The), small, D 6033, 3 1/2" h. **60**

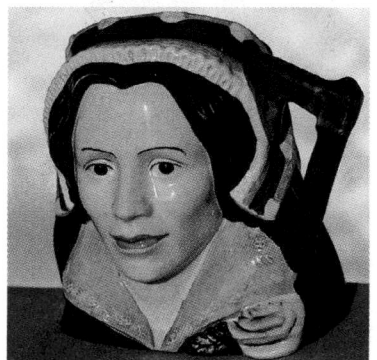

Catherine Howard

Catherine Howard, large, D 6645, 7" h.
(ILLUS.) **115**

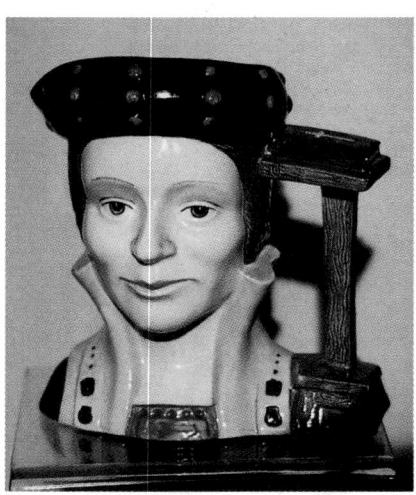

Catherine Parr

Catherine Parr, large, D 6664, 6 3/4" h.
(ILLUS.) **220**
Cavalier (The), small, D 6173, 3 1/4" h. **50**
Cliff Cornell, large, variation 2, dark blue
suit, red tie w/cream polka dots, 9" h. **250**
Clown w/red hair (The), large, D 5610,
7 1/2" h. **2,750**

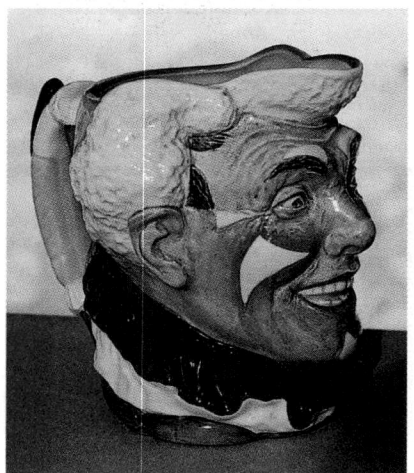

Clown with White Hair

Clown w/white hair (The), large, D 6322,
7 1/2" h. (ILLUS.) **1,000**
Collector (The), large, D 6796, 7" h. **165**
Davy Crockett & Santa Anna, large, D
6729, 7" h. **150**
Dick Turpin, pistol handle, small, D 5618,
3 1/2" h. **35**
Dick Whittington, large, D 6375, 6 1/2" h. **350**

Don Quixote

Don Quixote, large, D 6455, 7 1/4" h.
(ILLUS.) **60**
Falconer (The), small, D 6540, 3 3/4" h. **50**

Falstaff

Falstaff, large, D 6287, 6" h. (ILLUS.) **65**

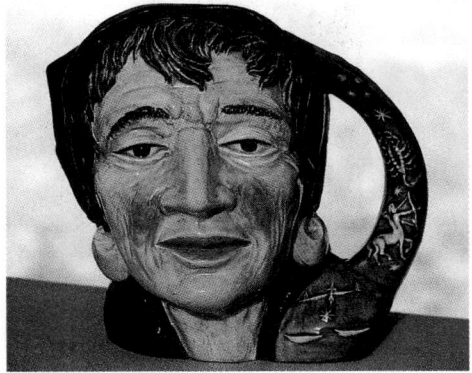

The Fortune Teller

Fortune Teller (The), large, D 6497,
6 3/4" h. (ILLUS.) **550**
Friar Tuck, large, D 6321, 7" h. **450**
Gaoler, small, D 6577, 3 3/4" h. **55**

The Gardener

Gardener (The), large, D 6630, 7 3/4" h.
(ILLUS) **115**
Genie, large, D 6892, 7" h. **175**
George Washington, large, D 6669,
7 1/2" h. **145**

Gladiator

Gladiator, large, D 6650, 7 3/4" h.
(ILLUS.) **600**
Granny, large, D 5521, 6 1/4" h. **55**

Groucho Marx

Groucho Marx, large, D 6710, 7" h.
(ILLUS.) **155**

Gulliver

Gulliver, large, D 6560, 7 1/2" h. (ILLUS.) **700**
Gunsmith, small, D 6580, 3 1/2" h. **80**
Happy John "A," large, D 6031, 8 1/2" h. **85**

Henry VIII

Henry VIII, large, D 6642, 6 1/2" h.
(ILLUS.) **105**

Jane Seymour

Jane Seymour, large, D 6646, 7 1/4" h.
(ILLUS.) **100**
Jester, seated, medium, D 6910, 5" h. **145**
Jockey, large, D 6625, 7 3/4" h. **150**

Johnny Appleseed

Johnny Appleseed, large, D 6372, 6" h.
(ILLUS.) **325**
Juggler (The), large, D 6835, 6 1/2" h. **125**
Leprechaun, large, D 6847, 7 1/2" h. **125**

Louis Armstrong

Louis Armstrong, large, D 6707, 7 1/2" h.
(ILLUS.) **185**

Lumberjack

Lumberjack, large, D 6610, 7 1/4" h.
(ILLUS.) **90**

Mad Hatter

Mad Hatter, large, D 6598, 7 1/4" h.
(ILLUS.) **165**
Mark Twain, small, D 6694, 4" h. **65**

Merlin

Merlin, large, D 6529, 7 1/4" h. (ILLUS.) **85**

Night Watchman

Night Watchman, large, D 6569, 7" h.
(ILLUS.) **130**
North American Indian, small, D 6614,
4 1/4" h. **45**
Old Salt, large, D 6551, 7 1/2" h. **125**
Pied Piper, large, D 6403, 7" h. **75**
Punch & Judy Man, large, D 6590, 7" h. **675**
Queen Victoria, small, D 6913, 3 1/2" h. **165**

The Ringmaster

Ringmaster (The), large, D 6863, 7 1/2" h.
(ILLUS.) **150**

Rip Van Winkle

Rip Van Winkle, large, D 6438, 6 1/2" h.
(ILLUS.) **115**

Robin Hood

Robin Hood, 2nd version, large, D 6527,
7 1/2" h. (ILLUS. left).. **65**
Robin Hood, 2nd version, small, D 6234,
3 1/4" h. (ILLUS. right) **55**

Robinson Crusoe

Robinson Crusoe, large, D 6532, 7 1/2" h.
(ILLUS.) **140**

St. George

St. George, large, D 6618, 7 1/2" h.
(ILLUS.)... **175**
Town Crier, large, D 6530, 7" h. **175**

Shakespeare

William Shakespeare, large, D 6689,
7 3/4" h. (ILLUS.).. **125**
Winston Churchill, style 1, large, D 6907,
Union Jack & bulldog handle, 7" h................. **325**

Yachtsman

Santa Claus w/Doll & Drum Handle

Santa Claus, doll & drum handle, large, D
6668, 7 1/2" h. (ILLUS.) **145**

Yachtsman, large, D 6626, 8" h. (ILLUS.) 145

Figurines

Abdullah, HN 2104, multicolored, 1953-62 425
Afternoon Tea, HN 1747, pink & blue, 1935-82 475
Anna, HN 2802, purple & white, Kate Greenaway Series, 1976-82 225
Anne Boleyn, HN 3232, red & grey, 1990, limited edition of 9,500 550
Artful Dodger, M 55, black & brown, Dickens Miniatures Series, 1932-83 75
Ascot, HN 2356, green dress w/yellow shawl, 1968-95 200

The Auctioneer

Auctioneer (The), HN 2988, black, grey & brown, 1986, R.D.I.C.C. Series (ILLUS.) 195
Babie, HN 1679, green dress, 1935-92 70
Ballerina, HN 2116, lavender, 1953-73 425
Balloon Seller (The), HN 583, green shawl, cream dress, 1923-49 950
Basket Weaver (The), HN 2245, pale blue & yellow, 1959-62 450
Beachcomber, HN 2487, matte, purple & grey, 1973-76 215
Blacksmith of Williamsburg, HN 2240, white shirt, brown hat, 1960-83 225
Bluebeard, HN 2105, purple, green & brown, 1953-92 450
Bo Peep, HN 1811, orange dress, green hat, 1937-95 115
Bride (The), HN 2166, pale pink dress, 1956-76 175
Bridesmaid (The Little), M 12, multicolor gown, 1932-45 425
Broken Lance (The), HN 2041, blue, red & yellow, 1949-75 450
Bunny's Bedtime, HN 3370, pale blue, pink ribbon, 1991, RDICC Series, limited edition of 9,500 175
Captain Cook, HN 2889, black & cream, 1980-84 425

Carpet Seller (The), HN 1464 (hand open), green & orange, 1929-? 275
Cavalier, HN 2716, brown & green, 1976-82 265
Centurian, HN 2726, grey & purple, 1982-84 225
Chief (The), HN 2892, gold, 1979-88 225
China Repairer, HN 2943, blue, white & tan, 1983-88 205
Christmas Morn, HN 1992, red & white, 1947-96 175

Christmas Parcels

Christmas Parcels, HN 2851, black, 1978-82 (ILLUS.) 225
Coachman, HN 2282, purple, grey & blue, 1963-71 575
Country Lass (A), HN 1991A, blue, brown & white, 1975-81 210
Curly Locks, HN 2049, pink flowered dress, 1949-53 225
Daffy Down Dilly, HN 1712, green dress, 1935-75 375
David Copperfield, M 88, black & tan, Dickens Miniatures Series, 1949-83 65
Duchess of York (The), HN 3086, cream, 1986, limited edition of 1,500 750
Duke of Edinburgh (The), HN 2386, black & gold, 1981, limited edition of 1,500 425
Easter Day, HN 1976, white dress, blue flowers, 1945-51 650
Embroidering, HN 2855, grey dress, 1980-90 275
Ermine Coat (The), HN 1981, white & red, 1945-67 365
Eventide, HN 2814, blue, white, red, yellow & green, 1977-91 275
Fagin, M 49, brown, 1932-83 65
Fair Lady, HN 2193, green, 1963-96 125
Fair Maiden, HN 2211, green dress, yellow sleeves, 1967-94 80
Falstaff, HN 3236, brown, yellow & lavender, 1989-90 50
Farmer's Wife, HN 2069, red, green & brown, 1951-55 250

First Prize, HN 3911, white shirt, brown jodhpurs, black hat, dark blue coat, 1997-99 135

Flirtation, HN 3071, pale blue, 1985-95 215

Foaming Quart (The), HN 2162, brown, 1955-92 125

French Peasant, HN 2075, brown & green, 1951-55 575

Friar Tuck, HN 2143, brown, 1954-65 595

Frodo, HN 2912, black & white, Middle Earth Series, 1980-84 175

Gamekeeper (The), HN 2879, green, black & tan, 1984-92 250

Gandalf, HN 2911, green & white, Middle Earth Series, 1980-84 275

Geisha (The), HN 3229, Flambé, RDICC, 1989 315

Genie (The), HN 2989, blue, 1983-90 185

Gimli, HN 2922, brown & blue, Middle Earth Series, 1981-84 235

Golfer, HN 2992, blue, white & pale brown, 1988-91 275

Good King Wenceslas, HN 2118, brown & purple, 1953-76 275

Graduate (The), HN 3017, male, black & grey, 1984-92 215

Gypsy Dance, HN 2230, lavender dress, 1959-71 275

Happy Anniversary, HN 3097, style one, purple & white, 1987-93 205

Harlequin, HN 2186, blue, 1957-69 425

The Huntsman

Huntsman (The), HN 2492, grey coat, cream pants, black hat & boots, 1974-79 (ILLUS.) 325

Ibrahim, HN 2095, brown & yellow, 1952-55 625

Jersey Milkmaid (The), HN 2057, blue, white & red, 1950-59 325

Jester (A), HN 2016, pink, purple & orange, 1949-97 325

Joker (The), HN 2252, white, 1990-92 250

Judge (The), HN 2443, red & white, 1972-76 250

La Sylphide, HN 2138, white dress, 1954-65 475

Lady of the Georgian Period (A), HN 41, gold & blue, 1914-38 3,000

Little Boy Blue, HN 2062, blue, 1950-73 175

Mary, Mary, HN 2044, pink, Nursery Rhymes Series, 1949-73 225

Masque, HN 2554, hand holds wand of mask, blue, 1973-82 315

Mayor (The), HN 2280, red & white, 1963-71 275

News vendor, HN 2891, gold & grey, 1986, limited edition of 2,500 225

Newsboy, HN 2244, green, brown & blue, 1959-65 425

Old King Cole, HN 2217, brown, yellow & white, 1963-67 625

Oliver Twist, M 89, black & tan, Dickens Miniatures Series, 1949-83 65

Omar Khayyam, HN 2247, brown, 1965-83 195

Orange Lady (The), HN 1953, light green dress, green shawl, 1940-75 315

Parisian, HN 2445, blue & grey, matte glaze,1972-75 150

Pied Piper (The), HN 2102, brown cloak, grey hat & boots, 1953-76 275

Polka (The), HN 2156, pale pink dress, 1955-69 295

Puppetmaker, HN 2253, green, brown & red, 1962-73 475

Queen Anne, HN 3141, green, red & white, 1989, Queens of the Realm Series, limited edition of 500 400

Queen Elizabeth I, HN 3099, red & gold, 1987, Queens of the Realm Series, limited edition of 5,000 650

Sailor's Holiday, HN 2442, apricot jacket, 1972-79 295

Salome, HN 3267, red, blue, lavender & green, 1990, limited edition of 1,000 950

Schoolmarm, HN 2223, 1958-81 275

The Shepherd

Shepherd (The), HN 1975, light brown, 1945-75 (ILLUS.) **205**
Sir Edward, HN 2370, red & grey, 1979, limited edition of 500 .... **550**
Skater (The), HN 3439, red, 1992-97 .... **250**

Sleeping Beauty

Sleeping Beauty, HN 3079, green, 1987-89 (ILLUS.) **225**
Southern Belle, HN 2229, red & cream, 1958-97 .... **350**
St. George, HN 2051, 1950-85 .... **475**
Stop Press, HN 2683, brown, blue & white, 1977-81 .... **175**
Teatime, HN 2255, 1972-95 .... **250**
This Little Pig, HN 1793, red robe, 1936-95 .... **85**
Tiny Tim, HN 539, black, brown & blue, 1922-32 .... **75**
Town Crier, HN 2119, 1953-76 .... **275**
Toymaker (The), HN 2250, brown & red, 1959-73 .... **425**
Tumbler, HN 3183, pink & yellow, 1989-91 ...... **225**
Uriah Heep, HN 554, black jacket & trousers, 1923-39 .... **525**
Victorian Lady (A), HN 728, red skirt, purple shawl, 1925-52 .... **495**
Wizard (The), HN 2877, blue w/black & white hat, 1979 to present **295**
Writing, HN 3049, flowered yellow dress, 1986, limited edition of 750, Gentle Arts Series **1,150**

Miscellaneous

Bowl, 8" d., The Gleaners series **185**
Bowl, 8 1/2" h., Gallent Fishers series **200**
Bowl, 8 7/8" d., 3 3/4" h., wide shallow rounded form, interior w/transfer-printed polychrome fox hunt scenes, green vintage border w/gilt trim, early 20th c. **125**
Bowl, 9" d., 4 1/8" h., Coaching Days series, street scenes **125**
Cabinet plates, 10 1/4" d., each w/a different English garden view within a narrow acid-etched gilt border, transfer-printed & painted by J. Price, ca. 1928, artist-signed, green printed lion, crown & circle mark, impressed year letters, painted pattern numbers "H3587," set of 12 .... **2,750**
Candlestick, "Old Moreton" series, low flaring round foot & slightly swelled cylindrical shaft below widely flaring flattened socket rim, color transfer of 16th c. gentleman titled "Old Moreton," impressed "7277," 6 3/8" h. **80**
Charger, Shakespeare Series, scene from "A Midsummer Night's Dream," 12 5/8" d. **65**

Royal Doulton Charger

Charger, central scene of a lady riding horse sidesaddle w/hound racing alongside, in yellow, brown, green, black & white, border band of dark green stylized grapevine, marked "George Morland #1784," 14" d. (ILLUS.) **125**
Chocolate set: 8" h. cov. chocolate pot, 6 1/2" h. cov. water pot, creamer, sugar bowl & eight cups & saucers; bone china, each enamel decorated w/relief-molded fox in various poses, crop-form handles, 20th c., England, the set **650**
Chop plate, round w/flanged rim, "Old Moreton" series, black transfer-printed design decorated in polychrome, a large center interior scene titled "Queen Elizabeth at Old Moreton 1589," early 20th c., 12 3/4" d. **85**
Cracker jar, cov., Gallant Fisher, Isaac Walton Ware, signed "NOKE" **175**
Dish, round w/flattened fluted rim w/gold edging around a floral band, center scene of romantic couples in a landscape, transfer-printed blue on white, late 19th c., 5 1/2" d. **45**
Dish, oval, Old English scene "The Gleaners," 9 x 11 1/4, 2 1/8" h. **55**
Ewers, Carrara ware, bulbous body w/a tan ground decorated w/life-sized pink wild roses w/enameled white highlights, gold molded leaf & florals, grey rim & ornate handle, marked "Doulton Carrara Lambeth," 11 1/2" h., pr. **375**
Fish plates, 10" d., each transfer-printed in blue & white w/a different fish, late 19th c., set of 12 .... **400**
Humidor, cov., mottled brown leaves on a mottled light brown ground w/light blue to white sponge pattern, green band on lid & shoulder, metal finial & tongue on lid, "Patent No. 194168," has mark "Royal Doulton England" & #8846, 6" h. **100**
Humidor, cov., Sung Ware, flambé glaze, figural elephant finial, artist-initialed **2,400**
Jar, cov., Rouge Flambé, footed squatty bulbous body w/a wide low-domed cover, scattered black splotches on crimson red ground, by Noke, fully stamped, 3 1/4" d., 2 3/4" h. **358**

Lamp base, slender ovoid ceramic body w/a tapering neck supporting electric lamp fittings, base decorated w/daffodils in greens, blue, white & yellow, fine brass round base mount w/a ring on the backs of four tiny figural turtles resting on a round disk on small ball feet, early 20th c., overall 28 1/2" h. (minor damage to body) 325

Loving cup, stoneware, cylindrical body w/low tapering base & wide short flaring rim, the wide tooled central band in band w/enameled floral designs in white & green flanked by thin brown stripes, three applied ear-form loop handles, handles, top & base in blue, marked "Doulton Lambeth," 6 1/8" h. 275

Loving cup, stoneware, three-handled cylindrical form w/a sterling silver rim band, a dark brown glaze band below the rim, most of the body w/a tan glaze, molded around the sides w/three white relief groups of bicycle riders, each titled either "Path," "Military," or "Road," late 19th c., base incised "8238," 5 1/2" h. 275

Mug, stoneware, tall slender & slightly tapering sides w/a sterling silver rim band, the upper third w/a dark brown glaze, the lower section w/a tan glaze, the upper band molded in relief w/a large scrolling ribbon band reading "Speed Wheel," the lower sides w/three white relief groups of bicycle racers each titled either "Path," "Military," or "Road," base incised "1957," late 19th c., 6" h. 275

Pitcher, jug-form, Kingsware, "Memories" design w/twelve faces shown, ca. 1920........ 600

Pitcher, Juliet, scene from Shakespeare's Romeo & Juliet... 150

Pitcher, 5 1/2" h., brightly colored rose design on a salmon pink background, angled handle, mottling on the collar & base rim, gold trim, Doulton, Burslem, artist-signed 150

Pitcher, 5 1/2" h., Jackdaw of Rheims scene 150

Pitcher, 5 1/2" h., stoneware, bulbous form, the tan ground incised w/playful cats, the shoulder & neck glazed w/cobalt blue strap work, decorated by Hannah Barlow, impressed Doulton Lambeth mark, late 19th c. 750

Pitcher, jug-form, 8 3/4" h., Lambethware style & color, Doulton Archives series, blue tracery on tan body, limited edition of 100, 2002 (ILLUS.) **1,000**

Pitcher, 9" h., stoneware, bulbous ovoid body tapering to a cylindrical neck w/pinched spout, C-form handle, the upper half w/a dark brown glaze over a tan glaze on the lower half, lower half applied w/white relief designs including a windmill, dogs chasing deer, men drinking, etc., Model No. 6859, Doulton, Lambeth mark, late 19th c. 125

Pitcher, 9 1/4" h., Shakespeare character series, standing portrait of Sir John Falstaff, tall waisted cylindrical form w/high arched spout, printed around the bottom border "A Tapster is a Good Trade," early 20th c. 150

![Hannah Barlow Lambethware Pitcher]

Hannah Barlow Lambethware Pitcher

Pitcher, 11" h., Hannah Barlow Doulton Lambethware, design of hounds chasing fox, 1875, vertical hairline crack (ILLUS.).. **1,250**

Pitcher, 11" h., Poplars at Sunset patt. 175

Lambethware-style Limited-edition Jug

Limited Edition Planter

Planter, ovoid form w/flat rim, short foot, decorated w/design of ferns or oak leaves on tan ground, Lambethware style & colors, Doulton Archives series, limited edition of 100, 2002 (ILLUS.) **800**

"Robin Hood" Series Plate

Plate, 7 1/2" sq., "Robin Hood" series (Friar Tuck Joins Robin Hood), natural-colored scene of Robin Hood & Friar Tuck standing & talking under large tree (ILLUS.) **85**
Plate, 9 1/8" d., Peony patt., dark blue floral center w/rectangular panels around the border, trimmed w/reddish rust & beige, ca. 1900 .... **65**
Plate, 9 1/2" d., Gallant Fishers series, Izaac Walton Ware, signed "NOKE" **75**
Plate, 10" d., rack-type, Mr. Micawber **75**
Plate, 10" d., rack-type, Old Jarvey **75**
Plate, 10" d., rack-type, The Parson **75**
Plate, 10 1/4" d., Bradley Golfers, "All Fools Are Not Knaves...," **150**
Plate, 10 1/4" d., Old English scenes, "The Gleaners" **65**
Plate, 10 1/4" d., "The Gypsies" **65**
Plate, 10 1/2" d., blue transfer w/center portrait of Shakespeare, border w/twelve characters from his plays **75**
Plate, 10 1/2" d., blue transfer w/central portrait of Dickens, border w/eleven of the Doulton characters used on various wares, unmarked **75**
Plate, 10 1/2" d., overall decoration of Aesthetic Movement florals in green & blue, marked w/lion & crown, "Royal Doulton, England, Cyprus" **75**
Plate, 10 1/2" d., rack-type, The Mayor **75**
Plate, 10 1/2" d., rack-type, The Squire **75**
Plate, 10 3/4" d., blue transfer w/Burns portrait in center, border shows characters such as Tam-O-Shanter, Highland Mary & others **75**
Plates, 10 1/4" d., series-type, color transfer-printed scenes on a tan speckled ground, one titled "The Battle," the other "The Press Gang," pr. **150**
Plates, 9" d., each h.p. w/different type of game bird including ducks, pheasant & quail, gold encrusted rims, artist signed "S. Wilson," purple stamped label w/impressed "Doulton," set of 6 .... **425**

Plates, dessert, 8 3/4" d., raised gilt enamel scrolls, floral & diapered cartouches, on a pale blue ground, ca. 1920, set of 15 .... **1,300**
Plates, 7 5/8" sq., creamware, transfer-decorated scenes, ca. 1900, set of 6 .... **110**
Plates, 8" d., Coaching Days series, includes three scenes, "Boarding the Coach," "The Journey" & "Farewell," polychrome transfer decoration, early 20th c., set of 12 .... **413**
Plates, 9" d., slightly dished w/scalloped rim, gilt-trimmed rim w/polychrome leafy vines bordering brown enameled Shakespearean sites, retailed by Theodore B. Starr, New York City, Doulton, Burslem, late 19th c., set of 12 .... **450**
Plates, 10 1/4" d., each w/a central rosette, the border elaborately gilded & enameled in the Art Nouveau style w/displaying peacocks, spade ornaments & trailing berried branches, the outer paneled blue border gilded w/beaded flowers, dated 1902, retailed by Tiffany & Co., New York, set of 4 .... **1,500**
Platter, 17 1/2" l., oval, Imari patt., ca. 1860s **1,000**

Doulton Stoneware Soap Dish

Soap dish, stoneware, oblong w/large brown & lavender flying insect molded along one side of the dark blue glazed dish, impressed markings on base for Wright's Coal Tar Soap, 4 1/4 x 5 3/4", 1 1/2" h. (ILLUS.) **150**
Teapot, cov., Nightwatchman scene **125**
Teapot, cov., Queen Elizabeth at Moreton Hall series **125**

Babes in the Wood Tray

Tray, oblong, flattened diamond shape w/rounded corners, Babes in the Wood series, center design of woman followed by girl holding woman's cloak, 13 1/2" l. (ILLUS.) 1,000

Tureens, cov., earthernware sauce tureens, "Raby" patt., w/cobalt floral motif & gilt accents, each w/small matching ladle, ca. 1900, 6" h., 8 3/4" l., pr. 225

Tyg (three-handled drinking vessel), waisted cylindrical shape decorated w/applied figures & animals in relief, Sheffield silver rim band marked "Maypin and Webb," Doulton, Lambeth, late 19th - early 20th c., 4 3/4" d., 6 1/2" h. 175

Lovely Royal Doulton Covered Urn

Urn, cov., tall slender ovoid body raised on a ribbed & gadrooned gold & Kelly green pedestal base w/square foot & flanked by long gold full-length handles, tapering to a ringed & ribbed cylindrical neck w/flaring rim fitted w/a high Gothic spire-form cover, finely h.p. w/a colorful scene of highland cattle against a purplish mountain backdrop, glossy glaze, artist-signed by S. Kelsall, small professional repair to handle & pedestal, ca. 1910, 32" h. (ILLUS.) 2,500

Doulton Lambeth Stoneware Vase

Vase, 5 1/4" h., 3 1/8" d., stoneware, footed ovoid body w/short tapering neck, grey ground w/an incised design of pointed panels framing stylized leafy scrolls in brown, green & light blue, artist-signed by Arthur Beeve, Doulton, Lambeth (ILLUS.) 175

Vase, 5 3/4" h., 3 3/4" d., baluster-form w/short flaring neck, slip-decorated in color w/celadon green fish & kelp on a dark brown ground, stamped "Doulton-Lambeth - 1883 - GTH - WP (?) - 593" 350

Royal Doulton "Babes in Woods" Seriesware Vases

Vase, 6" h., "Babes in Woods" Seriesware, bulbous base, short slightly bulbous neck w/flat rim, decorated w/blue & white scene of young woman at snowy gate, printed green mark, early 20th c. (ILLUS. front row, left w/other Seriesware vases, bottom previous page) **431**

Vase, 6" h., 3" d., Sung Ware, footed simple ovoid body tapering to a small trumpet neck, bright red & blue Flambé glaze, marked "Royal Doulton - Flambé - Sung - Noke"... **250**

Vase, 6 1/2" h., "Babes in Woods" Seriesware, ovoid form tapering to ring foot & flaring rim, decorated w/blue & white scene of woman w/basket at snowy gate, printed green mark, early 20th c. (ILLUS. previous page, front row, right w/other Seriesware vases) **633**

Vase, 6 1/2" h., "Babes in Woods" Seriesware, tapering rectangular arched shape w/rounded edges, gilt flat rim & foot, gilt angular handles, decorated w/blue & white winter scene of woman carrying basket, printed green mark, early 20th c. (ILLUS. previous page, front row, center w/other Seriesware vases) **690**

Vase, 7" h., "Babes in Woods" Seriesware, cylindrical shape w/slightly flaring rim, ruffled foot & small gilt angled handles near base, decorated w/blue & white scene of bonneted woman & child holding basket, printed green mark, early 20th c. (ILLUS. previous page, back row, right w/other Seriesware vases) **748**

Doulton Rouge Flambé Vase

Vase, 7" h., 4 1/4" d., Rouge Flambé, footed ovoid body w/the wide shoulder tapering to a small, short rolled neck, black silhouetted desert landscape against the crimson red ground, shallow scratch, stamped "ROYAL DOULTON - FLAMBÉ - MADE IN ENGLAND" (ILLUS.) **250**

Vase, 7 3/4" h., Art Deco style baluster-form decorated w/alternating vertical green & black panels, horizontal black & white panels on shoulder, impressed "Royal

Doulton Lambeth England," "8190" w/"S" in black slip, artist's monogram incised in bottom **400**

Vase, 8 1/2" h., "Babes in Woods" Seriesware, ovoid form w/short slender cylindrical neck w/slightly flaring rim, decorated w/blue & white scene of little girl carrying basket, printed green mark, early 20th c. (ILLUS. previous page, back row, second from right w/other Seriesware vases).. **431**

Vase, 9 5/8" h., Rouge Flambé, small footring under a spherical body tapering to a short stick neck, red "flambé" glaze w/veined design **175**

Vase, 10 3/4" h., Kingsware, cylindrical w/raised scene of Dr. Johnson in a tavern scene, verse on the back **300**

Vase, 11" h., baluster form, the shoulder tapering to a tall wide cylindrical neck w/flat rim, the center w/sgraffito continuous scene depicting eight deer in blue, black or brown, by Hannah Barlow, the dark brown neck & shoulder decorated w/raised scrolled designs in gold & swags of white beads, beaded bands flanking the center scene, the dark brown base w/raised gold lines, impressed "Doulton - Lambeth - England" & incised artist's initials.. **1,250**

Vase, 11 1/4" h., tall slender baluster-form w/flaring domed foot & waisted short widely flaring neck, the neck & foot in cobalt w/lacy gilt decoration, the body w/a creamy ground decorated w/scattered clusters of colorful flowers, Doulton-Burslem mark & incised "Lambeth - Doulton - Faience L6339," ca. 1882 .... **225**

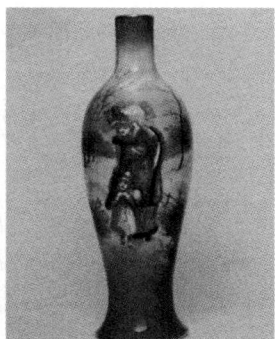

Babes in the Wood Baluster-form Vase

Vase, 11 1/2" h., tall slender baluster-form w/cylindrical neck & flat rim, Babes in the Wood series, design of woman sheltering child in wintry landscape (ILLUS.) **750**

Vase, 17" h., "Babes in Woods" Seriesware, slightly ovoid cylindrical body w/ring foot & rim, decorated w/blue & white scene of woman looking back at child, who is holding the train of her cloak, printed green mark, early 20th c. (ILLUS. previous page, back row, center w/other Seriesware vases)... **1,380**

Vases, 13 1/4" h., "Babes in Woods" Seriesware, tapering ovoid body, tapering
shoulder, ruffled foot, short flaring cylindrical neck, slender gilt handles, decorated w/blue & white winter scene of young
woman & child walking along path, printed green mark, early 20th c., pr. (ILLUS.
of both page 176 back row, far left w/oth-
er Seriesware vases) **2,070**
Wash bowl & pitcher set, deep rounded
wide bowl & tall slightly tapering tankard-
form pitcher w/gently arched rim & angled handle, blue, white & gold-trimmed
Art Nouveau-style "Aubrey" patt., ca.
1910, bowl 16" d., pitcher 13 1/2" h., the
set.. **450**
Wash bowl & pitcher set, Royal Mail se-
ries, early English coaching scenes
around the sides of each, four in polychrome, early 20th c., bowl 11 7/8" d.,
pitcher 7 3/8" h., pr. **225**
Whiskey jug w/figural stopper, "King-
sware," bulbous ovoid body w/a loop
shoulder handle, the body in overall dark
brown, the stopper in the shape of a stout
18th c. man wearing a tricorn hat & paint-
ed in polychrome, 8 1/4" h. **135**

Florence Ceramics

*Some of the finest figurines and artwares were
produced between 1940 and 1962 by the Florence
Ceramics Company of Pasadena, California. Florence Ward began working with ceramics following the death of her son, Jack, in 1939.*

*Mrs. Ward had not worked with clay before her
involvement with classes at the Pasadena Hobby
School. After study and firsthand experience, she
began production in her garage, using a kiln
located outside the garage to conform with city
regulations. The years 1942-44 were considered
her "garage" period.*

*In 1944 Florence Ceramics moved to a small
plant in Pasadena, employing fifty-four employees and receiving orders of $250,000 per year. In
1948 it was again necessary to move to a larger
facility in the area with the most up-to-date
equipment. The number of employees increased to
more than 100. Within five years Florence Ceramics was considered one of the finest producers of
semi-porcelain figurines and artwares.*

*Florence created a wide range of items includ-
ing figurines, lamps, picture frames, planters and
models of animals and birds. It was her extensive
line of women in beautiful gowns and gentlemen
in fine clothes that gave her the most pleasure
and was the foundation of her business. Two of
her most popular lines of figurines were inspired
by the famous 1860 Godey's Ladies' Book and by
famous artists from the Old Master group. In the
mid-1950s two bird lines were produced for several years. One of the bird lines was designed by
Don Winton and the other was a line of contemporary sculpted bird and animal figures designed
by the well-known sculptor Betty Davenport Ford.*

*There were several unsuccessful contemporary
artware lines produced for a short time. The*

*Driftware line consisted of modern freeform bowls
and accessories. The Floraline is a rococo line
with overglazed decoration. The Gourmet Pottery,
a division of Florence Ceramics Company, produced accessory serving pieces under the name of
Scandia and Sierra.*

*Florence products were manufactured in the
traditional porcelain process with a second firing
at a higher temperature after the glaze had been
applied. Many pieces had overglaze paint decoration and clay ruffles, roses and lace dipped in slip
prior to the third firing.*

Florence Marks

Figures

"Amber," brown hair, pink ruffled long
dress & large bonnet, right arm bent &
holding a pink parasol at right shoulder,
left arm extended w/fingers touching her
dress, articulated fingers, 9 1/4" h. **$425-475**
"Amelia," Godey lady, 8 1/4" h. **175-225**

Florence "Angel," Downcast Eyes

"Angel," downcast eyes, yellow hair, arms
bent across upper body, part of angel's
wings showing, white robe w/gold
trimmed rope sash, cuffs & collar, gold &
brown ribbon sticker, 7" h. (ILLUS.).......... **50-75**
"Anita," standing w/right arm bent, palm extended near waist, left arm almost
straight down at side, gold brocade long
dress w/short sleeves & fitted waist, artic-
ulated fingers, 15" h. **1,500-2,000**

Early "Annabelle" Florence Piece

"Annabelle," woman standing wearing a large dished hat & long flaring coat w/ruffled collar over a long striped dress, arms extended w/articulated hands, bird perched on her right hand (ILLUS.) **450-500**

"Ballet," 7" h. **225-250**

"Barbara," girl standing wearing a large picture hat & long dress w/puffed sleeves, holding a basket of flowers, 6" h. **75-100**

Rare Birthday Girl Figure

"Birthday Girl," standing w/her arms bent & hands close together, wearing a long flaring aqua gown, 9 3/4" h. (ILLUS.) **750-825**

"Blynkyn," young girl standing in long pink nightgown, holding a doll at her side, 5" h. **150-200**

"Bride," porcelain veil, 8 1/2" h. **1,000-1,250**

"Butch," boy w/hands in pockets, 5" h. **100-125**

"Camille," figure of standing woman wearing white dress trimmed in gold, shawl over both arms, triangular hat w/applied pink rose, ribbon tied to right side of neck, articulated hands, no lace, 8 1/2" h. **125-150**

"Charles," man standing & wearing 18th c. attire w/a long cape, 8" h. **150-175**

"Charmaine," woman holding a parasol, wearing ruffled long dress, large hat w/flowers, w/articulated hands, 8 1/2" h. **250-350**

"Chinese girl," standing wearing a flaring jacket applied w/roses & long flaring pants, 7 3/4" h. **100-125**

Florence "Cleopatra" Figure

"Cleopatra," exotic figure in flowing blended blue robes, standing on square base, 12" h. (ILLUS.) **1,200-1,250**

"Colleen," woman standing w/head slightly turned to left, right hand behind back & left arm to the front w/articulated hand, long wind-blown dress w/white collar, bonnet w/ribbon tied under chin, 8" h. **150-200**

Florence Figure of "Darleen"

"Darleen," standing w/head tilted, brown hair w/curls & roses at neck, long dress w/white underskirt, white lace trim on bodice & extending to bottom of dress, right arm bent & holding an open parasol at right shoulder, left arm at waist, articulated fingers, 8 1/4" h. (ILLUS.) **600-650**

"Dear Ruth," lady on bench, 7 1/2" h. **1,500-1,750**

"Denise," off-the-shoulder white dress w/gold trim extending down the dress front, violet overskirt, brown hair w/roses, both arms bent at waist w/right hand holding a closed fan, articulated fingers, 10" h. **500-650**

Rare Variation of "Elizabeth"

"Elizabeth," woman in 18th c. costume w/a wide flaring aqua gown w/half-sleeves & a lace-trimmed bodice, long curls down her neck, seated on a white settee, rare

white settee variation, 7" w., 8 1/4" h. (ILLUS.) **1,200-1,400**

"Eve," woman standing wearing a long slightly flaring gown, one hand holding up the front hem to expose lace-trimmed petticoat, other hand at shoulder, lace-trimmed collar & cuffs on half-sleeves, 8 1/2" h. **200-225**

Variation of "Fair Lady" Figure

"Fair Lady," woman in Gay Nineties gown standing on scrolled base decorated w/a small basket of strewn flowers across the front, royal red dress w/ornate white lace collar, upswept brown hair w/roses, arms away from body w/articulated fingers, 11 1/2" h. (ILLUS.) **1,750-2,000**

Rare "Georgia" in Brocade Gown

"Georgia," woman standing wearing a long wide real brocade fabric gown, her hands lifting sides of gown at the front, 12" h. (ILLUS.) **1,500-2,000**

Florence "Karen" Figure

"Karen," woman in late Victorian costume, wearing a narrow-waisted fur-trimmed half-length coat over a widely flaring gown, small fur-trimmed hat, w/arms away from body, articulated fingers, 8 1/2" h. (ILLUS.) **1,250-1,500**

"Lady Diana" with Plain Cuffs

"Lady Diana," woman stepping forward w/her arms away from her body, wearing flowers in her piled hair & a low-cut narrow lilac gown w/a flaring lacy collar, tight waist & overgown pulled into a bustle, the half-length sleeves w/plain cuffs, 10" h. (ILLUS.) **500-575**

"Leading Man," man standing w/right leg in front of left, royal red knee britches, white stockings w/gold-trimmed shoes, knee-length coat w/lacy jabot at neck, left arm

bent at elbow & raised upward, left arm extended outward holding a scroll, black hair, 10 1/4" h. **300-350**

Florence "Linda Lou" Figure

"Linda Lou," girl standing wearing a long full green dress w/peplum & long sleeves, holding a bouquet of flowers to her cheek, a high-fronted bonnet on her head, 7 3/4" h. (ILLUS.) **100-125**

"Marc Antony," Roman warrior wearing helmet, breastplate, white short garment & long flowing cape, one sandaled leg resting on a rectangular block on a square base, 13" h. **750-1,000**

"Marie Antoinette," woman in ornate 18th c. gown, her hair piled high & trimmed w/flowers, high lace collar & wide rounded gown w/center flower-trimmed drapes opening over tiered lace panels, arms in front, one holding a closed fan, smaller skirt style, 10" h. **225-250**

Florence "Marilyn" Figure

"Marilyn," woman standing wearing 18th-c. moss green gown w/half-length sleeves w/lace cuffs & large balloon gathers at the waist above the long flaring gown, carrying a basket over one arm, 8 1/2" h. (ILLUS.) **350-400**

"Mary," woman seated in balloon-back armchair, wearing a large picture hat, gown w/lace jabot & long sleeves, her hands in lap & on chair arm, 7 1/2" h. .. **600-625**

"Reggie," boy standing wearing Victorian outfit, Eton jacket & vest & long pants, scrolls at the side bottom, 7" h. **225-250**

"Rhett," man standing in front of low wood fence, right hand on vest, left hand in pocket, white ruffled shirt trimmed in color, flaring frock coat, 9" h. **175-200**

"Sally," woman wearing Victorian outfit, high rounded bonnet tied w/bow, simple ruffled collar & long-sleeved coat over wide swirled & ruffled gown, both hands at sides, 6 3/4" h. **125-150**

"Scarlett," Godey lady, wearing royal red dress & bonnet, right hand holding a muff near face, left hand holding handbag, articulated hands showing, 8 3/4" h. **250-300**

"Story Hour," seated mother & girl, woman reading book held in left hand, wearing rose dress w/lace at neck, roses in her hair, & girl w/blonde hair w/right arm on bench, wearing ruffled lace short-sleeved white dress w/blue & pink trim, no little boy, 8" l., 6 3/4" h. **800-850**

"Susan/Susann," woman standing in simple off-the-shoulder Victorian gown, hair pulled back w/long side curls & cluster of flowers, one hand holding up side of dress, other arm holding basket of flowers to her side, 9" h. **300-350**

"Tess," woman standing wearing long dress w/lace ruffle at neckline, large picture hat, arms away w/one hand holding edge of skirt up over shoe, 7 1/4" h. **250-300**

"Virginia" Figure with No Lace

"Virginia," woman standing wearing a wide picture hat & off-the-shoulder gown, variation w/no lace at collar or sleeves, long flaring & tiered rose red gown, 9" h. (ILLUS.) **900-1,000**

"Wynkin," boy toddler wearing long blue pajamas & holding a Teddy bear, 5 1/2" h. **150-200**

"Yvonne," woman standing wearing Victorian outfit, small ribbon-trimmed bonnet, long-sleeved jacket w/peplum over long wide dress, articulated hands w/one arm out & other one holding a small ribbon-trimmed box, 8 3/4" h. **275-300**

Other Items

Bust, "American Lady," heavy lace trim, 7 3/4" h. **350-400**

Bust, "Gigi," 10" h. **175-200**

Bust, "Modern Girl," 9 1/2" h. **100-125**

Bust, "Shen," Chinese woman w/wide upright scrolling headdress, scroll-trimmed jacket, 7 1/2" h. **175-200**

Flower holder, "Beth," woman standing in a dirndl-style dress & holding up one corner of her long apron, holder at the back, 7 1/2" h. **50-75**

Flower holder, "Chinese Boy," holder at the back, 7 3/4 .... **40-50**

Flower holder, "Chinese Child/Girl," bamboo-form holder at side, 7" h. **100-125**

Flower holder, "Jerry," young man standing in white suit trimmed in blue, pink tie, holding a white bass fiddle trimmed w/gold, 7 3/4" h. **175-200**

Flower holder, "Molly," standing girl wearing long gown w/short ruffled sleeves at shoulder, standing beside a large cylinder vase embossed w/leafy boughs, 6 1/2" h. **35-40**

Flower holder, "Sally," girl standing wearing long-sleeved long dress swirled to the side, hands to her side, one hand holding large picture hat, holder at the back, 6" h... **35-40**

Head vase, "Fern," girl wearing wide lightly ruffled hat & dress w/small ruffled collar & wide ruffles at the shoulders, 7" h. **125-150**

TV lamp, "Dear Ruth," 9" h. **800-1,000**

Flow Blue

Flow Blue ironstone and semi-porcelain was manufactured mainly in England during the second half of the 19th century. The early ironstone was produced by many of the well known English potters and was either transfer-printed or hand-painted (brush stroke). The bulk of the ware was exported to the United States or Canada.

The "flow" or running quality of the cobalt blue designs was the result of introducing certain chemicals into the kiln during the final firing. Some patterns are so "flown" that it is difficult to ascertain the design. The transfers were of several types: Asian, Scenic, Marble or Floral.

The earliest Flow Blue ironstone patterns were produced during the period between about 1840 and 1860. After the Civil War Flow Blue went out of style for some years but was again manufactured and exported to the United States beginning about the 1880s and continuing through the turn of the century. These later Flow Blue designs are on a semi-porcelain body rather than heavier ironstone and the designs are mainly florals. Also see Antique Trader Pottery & Porcelain Ceramics Price Guide, 3rd Edition.

Adams (Wood & Son, ca. 1907)

Vegetable dish, open, oval, 7 x 12" **$95**

Agra (Ridgways, ca. 1891)

Sardine dish, cov., w/attached underplate,
   fish finial on lid, 6 1/2 x 7 3/4", 4 1/2" h. 575

Agra (W.H. Grindley & Co., ca. 1891)

Plate, luncheon, 9" d. 90
Plate, dinner, 10" d. 100
Tea cup & saucer, cup 3 1/2" h., saucer
   6" d. 100

Albemarle (Alfred Meakin Ltd., ca. 1891)

Plate, dinner, 10" d. 80

Albion (Brown-Westhead, Moore & Co., ca. 1882)

Strawberry bowl w/undertray, reticulated,
   footed, bowl 10" d., 3 1/2" h., undertray
   10" d. 500

Alhambra (Alfred Meakin, Ltd., ca. 1891)

Alhambra Dinner Plate

Plate, dinner, 10" d. (ILLUS.) 85

Althea (Villeroy & Boch, German, ca. 1860-70)

Fish platter w/"split" drainer, very rare,
   9 x 21" (ILLUS., bottom of page) **1,500**

Amerillia (Podmore Walker & Co., ca. 1834-1859)

Plate, 7 1/2" d. 70
Plate, 8 1/2" d. 75
Plate, 10 1/2" d. 160
Platter, 16" 600

Amerillia Teapot

Teapot, cov., oval body style (ILLUS.) **800**

Amoy (Davenport, ca. 1844)

Coffeepot, cov., large 1,395
Creamer, 6" 295
Creamer, 6 1/2" h. 300
Cup & saucer, handled 195
Cup & saucer, handleless 125
Gravy boat 395
Pitcher, 7 1/2" h. 725

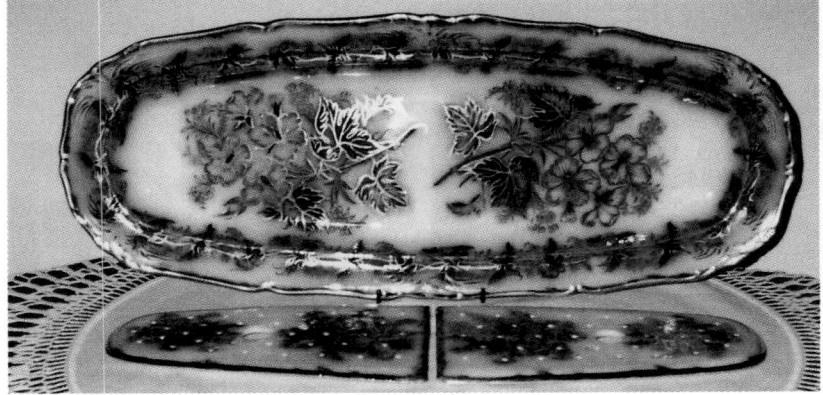

Very Rare Althea Fish Platter with Drainer

Amoy Water Pitcher

Pitcher, water, 12" h., rare body style
(ILLUS.) **1,500**
Plate, 7 1/2" d.. **75**
Plate, 8 1/2" d.. **85**
Plate, 9" w. **143**
Plate, 9 1/2" d.. **120**
Plate, 10 1/2" d. **165**
Platter, 12" l. **250**
Platter, 16" l. **450**
Platter, 18" l. **650**
Platter, 20" l. **2,000**

Amoy Potato Bowl

Potato bowl, 12 1/4" d. (ILLUS.) **350**
Soup plate w/flanged rim 10" d. **200**
Sugar bowl, cov. **375**
Teapot, cov. **675**
Vegetable bowl, open, 8" l. **595**
Vegetable bowl, open, 10" l. **795**

Amoy Waste Bowl

Waste bowl, "double bulge" (ILLUS.) **325**

ANEMONE (Minton & Co., ca. 1860)

Plate, 8 1/2" d.. **95**
Plate, 9 1/2" d.. **125**

Platter, 14", oval.. **400**
Razor box, cov., 3 x 8"..................................... **295**

Anemone Covered Vegetable Bowl

Vegetable bowl, cov., footed (ILLUS.)............. **400**

Arabesque (T.J. and J. Mayer, ca. 1845)

Creamer **495**
Creamer, Classic Gothic style, 6" h. **500**
Plate, 7 1/2" d. **150**
Plate, 10 1/2" d. **195**
Soup plate w/flanged rim, 10" d. **185**
Sugar bowl, cov., Classic Gothic style.............. **595**
Teapot, cov., Classic Gothic style **800**

Asiatic Pheasants (John Meir & Sons, ca. 1865)

Butter dish w/insert **495**
Butter pat **60**

Asiatic Pheasants (Thomas Hughes, ca. 1895)

Vegetable dish, cov., round, 10" d. **250**

Aster & Grapeshot (Joseph Clementson, ca. 1840) - Brush-stroke

Creamer, six-sided Gothic, 5 1/2" h. **375**
Pitcher, 11" h... **575**
Sugar bowl, cov., six-sided Gothic,
6 1/2" h.. **450**
Teapot, cov., six-sided Gothic, 9" h. **725**

Astral (W.H. Grindley & Co., ca. 1891)

Cake plate, w/tab handles, 9 x 9 1/2"............... **225**
Compote, w/pedestal, 9 1/2" d., 4 1/2" h. **300**
Egg cup, 3 3/4" h... **175**
Platter, 16" l... **450**

ATHENS (Charles Meigh, ca. 1840)

Cup & saucer, handleless................................. **225**
Gravy boat **350**
Plate, 7 1/2" d. **95**
Plate, 10 1/2" d. **125**

Athens Punch Cup

Punch cup (ILLUS.)............................... 145
**Tazza/pedestal   comport,   9 1/2" d.,
3 3/4" h.** 325

Birds and Bloom (George Jones & Sons, ca. 1885)

Birds and Bloom Cache Pot

Cache pot, 7" h. (ILLUS.) 325

Bisley (W.H. Grindley & Co., ca. 1900)

Cake plate, w/tab handles, 9 3/4" handle to
handle... 175
Platter, 18" l. 375
Waste bowl, 5" d., 3" h. 150

Blue Bell (William Ridgway & Co., ca. 1834-1854)

Dessert tray, leaf shape, one open handle,
impressed "Opaque Granite China,"
12" l.. 350
Vegetable dish, cov., 10 1/4 x 12", 6" h........... 650

Blue Diamond (Wheeling and La Belle Potteries, American, ca. 1896)

Charger, 13" d. 325
Creamer & cov. sugar, creamer 4" h., sug-
ar 4 1/2" h. 425

Blue Diamond Iced Beverage Jug

Lemonade/iced beverage jug, cov., pewter lid, 9" h. (ILLUS.)........................ 475

Bryonia (Paul Utzshneider & Co., German, ca. 1891)

Berry set: 9" master bowl & twelve 5" d. individual bowls; the set..................... 575
Teapot, cov. 400

Buccleuch (maker unknown, ca. 1845)

Fruit compote, reticulated 475
Tea set: 9" h. cov. teapot, 6" h. cov. sugar,
5 1/2" h. creamer; the set................. 900

Burgee (maker unknown, ca. 1860)

Soup tureen on pedestal, cov., 14" w.,
13" h. 650

Calendar Plate #2 (Sterling China Co., American, 1915)

Plate, 9" d. 75

Campion (W.H. Grindley & Co., ca. 1891)

Toothbrush vase, 6" h. 175

Celtic (W.H. Grindley & Co., ca. 1897)

Celtic Bone Dish

Bone dish, crescent shape, 7" w. (ILLUS.) 75
Creamer, 6 1/2" h.................................. 175
Platter, 18" l. 525

Chapoo (John Wedge Wood, ca. 1850)

Plate, luncheon, 9 3/4" 150
Teapot, cov., 9 1/2" h. 850

Chatsworth (Keeling & Co., ca. 1896) (This pattern is a deep slate blue.)

Plate, dinner, 10" d. 85

Chen-Si (John Maddock, ca. 1842-1855)

Chen-Si Twelve-sided Plate

Plate, 9" d., twelve-sided (ILLUS.)...................... 150
Relish, mitten, 8" w. 250

China (Petrus Regout Co., Maastricht, Holland, ca. 1850-1880)

China Waste Bowl

Waste bowl, 5" d., 3" h. (ILLUS.) 150

Chusan (J. Clementson, ca. 1840)

Creamer, 6" h... 250
Plate, 7 1/2" d... 125
Plate, 9 1/2" d... 145

Platter, 13" l. 300
Platter, 14" l. 350
Vegetable bowl, open, 8" l................................. 200

Ciris (Wood & Baggaley, ca. 1875)

Cake plate, reticulated, 9" d............................... 300

Claremont (Johnson Bros., ca. 1891)

Gravy boat w/underplate, 8 1/2" l. 165

Clematis (Wm. Davenport, ca. 1835-1869)

Fish platter, 11 x 23 1/2" (ILLUS., middle of
   page) 800

Coburg (John Edwards, ca. 1860)

Cup & saucer, handleless.................................. 150
Plate, 8 1/2" d. 135
Plate, 10 1/2" d. 155
Platter, 16" 300
Teapot, cov. 1,025
Vegetable bowl, open, 10" l. 300

Corea (Wedgwood & Co., ca. 1900)

Meat well platter, cov., 8 1/2 x 11 1/2"
   w/cover (ILLUS., bottom of page)................. 575

Clematis Fish Platter

Corea Meat Well Platter

Corean (Podmore, Walker & Co., ca. 1834-1859)

Teapot, cov., cock's comb handle, 10" h. 575

Countess (W.H. Grindley & Co., ca. 1891)

Creamer, 4 1/2" h. 125
Sugar, cov., 5" h. 225
Teapot, cov., 6 1/2" h. 375

Country Scenes (F. Wood & Son, ca. 1891)

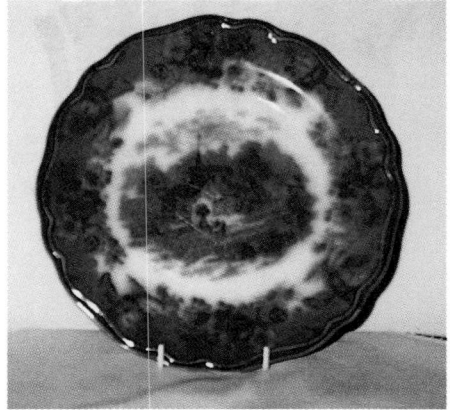

Country Scenes Plate

Plate, 10" d. (ILLUS.) 100

Cows (Wedgwood & Co., Ltd., ca. 1906)

Plate, 10" d. 150

Dainty (John Maddock & Son, ca. 1896)

Platter, 12" l. 175

Del Monte (Johnson Bros., ca. 1900)

Bowl, berry, 5" d. 40
Plate, 10" d. 90

Duchess (W.H. Grindley & Co., ca. 1891)

Butter pat, 3" d. 35
Demitasse cup & saucer, cup 2 1/2" h.,
    saucer 5" d. 125
Pitcher, 8" h. (ILLUS. left w/tureen & vege-
    table dish, bottom of page) 275
Platter, 16" l. 375
Soup plate w/flanged rim, luncheon, 9" d. 85
Soup tureen, cov., round, w/ladle & under-
    plate (ILLUS. center w/pitcher & vegeta-
    ble dish, bottom of page) 750
Vegetable dish, cov., round, hard-to-find
    small size (ILLUS. right w/pitcher & tu-
    reen, bottom of page) 300

Fairy Villas I (William Adams & Sons, ca. 1891)

Butter dish, cov. 275
Creamer, 4 1/2" h. 165
Teapot, cov., 6 1/2" h. 650

Florida (W.H. Grindley & Co., ca. 1891)

Bone dish, crescent shape, 8" l. 75

Duchess Pitcher, Covered Soup Tureen & Covered Vegetable

Harley (W.H. Grindley & Co., ca. 1891)

Harley Toothbrush Vase

Toothbrush vase, 5 1/2" h. (ILLUS.)............... **165**
Wash set: pitcher, bowl, cov. slop jar, cov.
chamber pot, cov. soap dish, shaving
mug, water pitcher, toothbrush vase; the
set... **3,000**

Ivy (maker unknown, ca. 1840-1850) - brush-stroke

Ivy Pitcher

Pitcher, 8" h., molded relief (ILLUS.)................. **325**

La Belle (Wheeling Pottery Co., American, ca. 1893-1900)

La Belle Biscuit Jar or Tea Caddy

Biscuit jar/tea caddy, cov., 6" d., 7 1/2" h.
(ILLUS.).. **400**
Chocolate pot, cov., 7 1/2" h............................. **750**
Creamer & cov. sugar bowl, sugar 5" h.,
creamer 4" h., pr. (ILLUS. left & right
w/tray, bottom of page)................................. **425**
Demitasse cup & saucer, 2 1/2" h................... **175**
Gravy/sauce boat, two-handled **375**
Tray, rectangular, 8 x 10 1/2" (ILLUS. rear
w/sugar bowl & creamer, bottom of page)...... **300**

La Belle Sugar Bowl, Creamer & Tray

Marble (maker unknown, ca. 1860-1880)

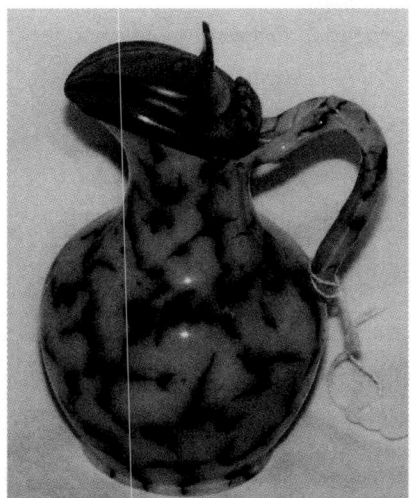

Marble Syrup Pitcher

Syrup pitcher, 5" h. (ILLUS.) 400

Neopolitan (Johnson Bros., ca. 1900)

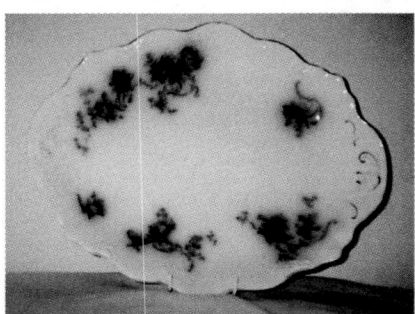

Neopolitan Platter

Platter, 16" l. (ILLUS.) 325
Soup tureen, cov. 350

OSBORNE (Ridgways, ca. 1905)

Osborne Teapot

Teapot, cov., 7 1/2" h., 10" w. from spout to
handle (ILLUS.) 400

Patagonia (Brown-Westhead, Moore & Co., registry mark September 12, 1878)

Patagonia Dinner Plate

Plate, dinner, 10 1/4" d. (ILLUS.) 125

Rose (W.H. Grindley & Co., ca. 1893)

Plate, 9" d. 80

Rose Pattern Platter

Platter, 16" l. (ILLUS.) 325
Rim soup, flanged edge, 9" d. 75

Scroll (Wm. Davenport, ca. 1830)

Scroll Meat Well & Tree Platter

Platter, 22" l., w/meat well (ILLUS.) **750**

Teutonic (Brown-Westhead, Moore & Co. - Cauldon, ca. 1868)

Teutonic Platter

Platter, 20" l. (ILLUS.) **500**

Watteau (New Wharf Pottery & Co., ca. 1891)

Pitcher, 6 1/2" h.. **225**
Plate, 10" d... **100**
Waste bowl, 5" d... **125**

Waverly (W.H. Grindley & Co., ca. 1891)

Waverly Platter

Platter, 14" l. (ILLUS.) **300**

Wheel (maker unknown, possibly Wm. Adams & Co., ca. 1850s) - brush-stroke

Wheel Pattern Soup Bowl

Rim soup bowl, flanged edge, 9" d. (ILLUS.)... **125**

Yeddo (G.L. Ashworth & Bros., ca. 1870)

Cake stand, 9" d., 4" h...................................... **350**

Franciscan Ware

A product of Gladding, McBean & Company of Lincoln, California, Franciscan Ware was one of a number of lines produced by that firm over its long history. Products made at the Lincoln Plant were Architectural Terra Cotta, Terra Cotta Tiles, and Garden Ware. In 1923, Gladding, McBean purchased the Tropico Pottery in Glendale, California. At this location Gladding, McBean began producing dinnerware. Franciscan Ware was introduced in 1934 beginning with the colorful dinnerware pattern of El Patio. Coronado, a swirled pattern offered in satin and gloss glazes, was introduced in 1935. Gladding, McBean also introduced Art Ware in 1934 as Tropico Art Ware; later, after the acquisition of the Catalina Clay Products company on Catalina Island in 1937, the line was marketed as Catalina Art Ware as well as Franciscan Art Ware. In 1940, Gladding, McBean introduced the handpainted dinnerware line Apple and in 1941 Desert Rose. Desert Rose has the distinction of being one of the most popular patterns ever produced in dinnerware history. In 1942, Gladding, McBean introduced the first of many lines of fine china. Art Ware was discontinued in 1942. In the 1950s, Franciscan introduced three very popular patterns on the Eclipse shape designed by George James: Starburst, Oasis, and Duet. In 1962, Gladding, McBean merged with the International Lock Pipe and Joint Co. to form the company Interpace. Fine china was discontinued in 1977. In 1979, Interpace's Glendale Franciscan Ware Division was purchased by Wedgwood, Ltd. Finally, in October of 1984, the Glendale Franciscan Ware Plant was closed and all dinnerware operations were moved to England. All Franciscan dinnerware patterns produced prior to 1984, except for Apple, Desert Rose and Fresh Fruit, were discontinued. Fresh Fruit was discontinued in 1989. Wedgwood continues to manufacture Desert Rose and Apple, adding new pieces each year. In 2001, Wedgwood, Ltd. reintroduced Franciscan Ivy.

For Oasis and Duet, use prices for Starburst, less 20 percent. For Strawberry Fair and Fresh Fruit, use prices for Desert Rose. Café Royal and Meadow Rose prices are about 20 percent less than Desert Rose. Bountiful and Strawberry Time are 20 percent higher than Desert Rose. For Small Fruit, use prices for Poppy. For Fine China patterns, use prices for Arden except for Mariposa, which is 20 percent more. The prices for Desert Rose, Ivy, Fresh Fruit, and Apple are for pre-1984 "Made in USA" items. Desert Rose, Ivy and Apple that are marked "Made in England" are 70 percent less than "Made in USA" items. "Made in England" Fresh Fruit is 20 percent lower than "Made in USA" Fresh Fruit.

Ashtray, Apple patt., 4 1/2 x 9" oval **$95**
Ashtray, Desert Rose patt., square **125**
Ashtray, individual, California Poppy patt........... **65**

El Patio Coffee Server

Westwood Coffee & Tea Service

Coronado Demitasse Pieces

Coffeepot, cov., demitasse, Coronado Table Ware, coral satin glaze (ILLUS. rear, w/demitasse pieces, top of page) 95
Compote, open, Apple patt., 8" d., 4" h............. 75
Compote, open, Meadow Rose patt., 8" d., 4" h... 85
Cookie jar, cov., Apple patt. 245
Creamer, Apple patt. 21
Creamer, individual, Desert Rose patt., 3 1/2" h. 65
Creamer, Desert Rose patt., 4 1/4" h. 28
Creamer & cov. sugar bowl, Apple patt., pr. 55
Creamer & cov. sugar bowl, Desert Rose patt., pr. 55
Creamer & cov. sugar bowl, Ivy patt., pr. 90
Creamer & cov. sugar bowl, October patt., pr. 45
Creamer & open sugar bowl, Tiempo patt., lime green, pr. 25
Creamer & open sugar bowl, individual, El Patio Nuevo patt., orange, pr. 50
Cup & saucer, Apple patt., jumbo size.............. 78
Cup & saucer, California Poppy patt.................. 35
Cup & saucer, demitasse, Coronado, various colors, each set (ILLUS. top of page of variety of colors w/demitasse coffeepot) 22-28
Cup & saucer, El Patio tableware, glossy yellow glaze 6
Cup & saucer, October patt................................ 16
Cup & saucer, tall, Desert Rose patt................. 55
Cup & saucer, Twilight Rose patt. 26
Cup & saucer, demitasse, Desert Rose patt. 42
Cup & saucer, demitasse, El Patio tableware, Mexican blue glossy glaze 20
Dinner service: 6 each dinner plates, soup plates, berry bowls, cups & saucers, 3 salad plates, one each open sugar bowl, creamer, oval platter & vegetable bowl; Coronado patt., matte coral, the set 135
Egg cup, Desert Rose patt., 2 3/4" d., 3 3/4" h. 36
Egg cup, Twilight Rose patt., 2 3/4" d., 3 3/4" h. 350
Ginger jar, cov., Apple patt. 395
Goblet, footed, Desert Rose patt., 6 1/2" h...... 225
Goblet, Picnic patt., 6 1/2" h.............................. 20

Gravy boat, California Poppy patt. 95
Gravy boat, Tiempo patt., lime green................ 20
Gravy boat w/attached undertray, Desert Rose patt. 42
Hurricane lamp, Desert Rose patt. 325
Jam jar, cov., Desert Rose patt.......................... 95
Mixing bowl, Apple patt., 6" d. 75
Mixing bowl, Apple patt., 7 1/2" d. 95
Mixing bowl, Apple patt., 9" d 125
Mixing bowl set, Apple patt., 3 pcs.................. 350
Mug, Apple patt., 7 oz. 28
Mug, Apple patt., 10 oz. 120
Mug, Desert Rose patt., 10 oz. 125
Mug, Apple patt., 17 oz., rare........................... 110
Napkin ring, Desert Rose patt. 45
Pepper mill, Starburst patt................................ 165
Pickle/relish boat, Desert Rose patt., interior decoration, 4 1/2 x 11"........................... 350
Pitcher, milk, 6 1/4" h., Apple patt., 1 qt. 90
Pitcher, milk, 8 1/2" h., Daisy patt....................... 50
Pitcher, water, 8 3/4" h., Apple patt., 2 qt......... 125
Pitcher, water, 8 3/4" h., Desert Rose patt., 2 1/2 qt. 95
Pitcher w/ice lip, El Patio tableware, golden glow glossy glaze, 2 1/2 qt. 65
Plate, bread & butter, Arden patt............................ 6
Plate, luncheon, Arden patt................................. 12
Plate, bread & butter, 6 1/4" d., California Poppy patt. 15
Plate, bread & butter, 6 1/2" d., Desert Rose patt. 6
Plate, bread & butter, 6 1/2" d., October patt. 8
Plate, coupe dessert, 7 1/4" d., Meadow Rose patt. 29
Plate, coupe dessert, 7 1/2" d., Desert Rose patt. 65
Plate, salad, 8" d., California Poppy patt............. 45
Plate, snack, 8" sq., Desert Rose patt. 125
Plate, side salad, 4 1/2 x 8", Desert Rose patt., crescent-shaped 35
Plate, side salad, 4 1/2 x 8, Meadow Rose patt., crescent-shaped 29
Plate, salad, 8 1/2" d., Desert Rose patt. 13
Plate, salad, 8 1/2" d., Ivy patt. 28
Plate, salad, 8 1/2" d., October patt. 16
Plate, salad, 8 1/2" d., Wildflower patt................ 95
Plate, child's, 7 1/4 x 9", divided, Apple patt....... 145
Plate, luncheon, 9 1/2" d., Apple patt. 19

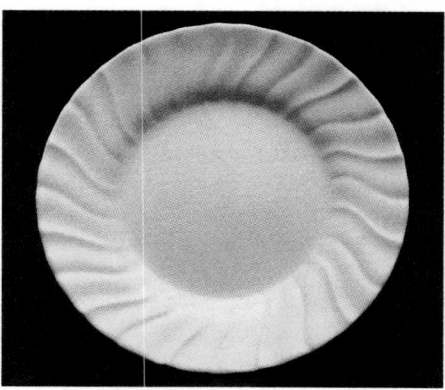

Coronado Table Ware Plate

Plate, luncheon, 9 1/2" d., Coronado Table
Ware, coral satin glaze (ILLUS.) 10
Plate, luncheon, 9 1/2" d., Desert Rose patt. 22
Plate, coupe, party w/cup well, 10 1/2" d.,
Desert Rose patt.. 160

Dessert Rose Dinner Plate

Plate, dinner, 10 1/2" d., Desert Rose patt.
(ILLUS.).. 23
Plate, T.V. w/cup well, 8 x 13 1/2", Ivy patt. 125
Plate, T.V. w/cup well, 14" l., Desert Rose
patt. 125
Plate, chop, 11 1/2" d., Desert Rose patt. 52
Plate, chop, 12" d., California Poppy patt......... 125
Plate, chop, 14" d., Apple patt............................... 95
Plate, chop, 14" d., Ivy patt................................ 155
Plate, coupe, steak,11" l., Apple patt. 125
Plate, dinner, 10 1/4" d., Ivy patt........................ 32
Plate, dinner, 10 1/2" d., Coronado Table
Ware, coral satin glaze 10
Plate, dinner, 10 1/2" d., Meadow Rose
patt. 26
Plate, dinner, 10 1/2" d., Wildflower patt. 65
Plate, grill or buffet, 11" d., Desert Rose
patt. 75
Platter, 11" l., oval, Arden patt. 45
Platter, 8 1/2 x 12" oval, Cafe Royal patt. 32
Platter, 12 3/4" l., Desert Rose patt. 38
Platter, 14" l., Apple patt. 55
Platter, 14" l., Meadow Rose patt....................... 36

Platter, 14" l. oval, Wildflower patt. 425
Platter, 19" l., oval, Apple patt. 225
Platter, 19" l., turkey-size, Desert Rose
patt., ... 225
Relish dish, Ivy patt., 4 1/2 x 10 1/2" 65
Relish dish, three-part, oval, Desert Rose
patt., 12" l. 67
Salt & pepper shakers, Arden patt., pr. 18
Salt & pepper shakers, October patt., pr........... 35
Salt & pepper shakers, California Poppy
patt., 2 3/4" h., pr.. 55
Salt & pepper shakers, Strawberry Time
patt., 3" h., pr.. 45
Salt & pepper shakers, Desert Rose patt.,
6 1/4" h., pr. 55
Salt shaker & pepper mill, Daisy patt., pr........ 95
Salt shaker & pepper mill, Meadow Rose
patt., 6" h., pr.. 145
Serving bowl, Desert Rose patt., aka Long
& Narrow, 7 3/4 x 15 1/2", 2 1/4 " h. 350
Sherbet, Desert Rose patt., footed, 4" d.,
2 1/2" h... 24
Sherbet, Coronado Table Ware, ivory glaze....... 12
Soup bowl, rimmed, Desert Rose patt................ 35
Soup plate w/flanged rim, Apple patt.,
8 1/2" d. 28
Soup tureen, cov., Desert Rose patt................. 525
Sugar bowl, cov., Coronado Table Ware,
glossy coral glaze 14
Sugar bowl, cov., Ivy patt. 35
Sugar bowl, cov., Strawberry Time patt. 30
Sugar bowl, open, individual size, Desert
Rose patt. 75
Syrup pitcher, Apple patt., 1 pt., 6 1/4" h........... 82
Tea canister, cov., Desert Rose patt................. 225
Tea tile, Apple patt., 6" sq. 45
Teapot, cov., Apple patt., 6 3/4" h..................... 125
Teapot, cov., Ivy patt., green rim band,
5 1/2" h. 225
Thimble, Desert Rose patt., 1" h........................ 55
Tidbit tray, two-tier, Desert Rose patt................. 95
Toast cover, Desert Rose patt., 5 1/2" d.,
3" h.. 145
Trivet, Apple patt., 6" d. 245
Tumbler, El Patio tableware, coral glaze 28
Tumbler, El Patio tableware, redwood
glossy glaze 28
Tumbler, Apple patt., juice, 6 oz., 3 1/4" h. 30
Tumbler, Ivy patt., 10 oz., 5" h........................... 55
Tumbler, California Poppy patt., water, 10
oz., 5 1/4" h. 125
Tumbler, Wildflower patt., water, 10 oz.,
5 1/2" h. 250
Tureen, cov., flat-bottomed, Desert Rose
patt., 8" d., 5" h. 425
Vase, bud, 6" h., Desert Rose patt. 95
Vegetable bowl, divided, Apple patt.,
7 x 10 3/4"... 42
Vegetable bowl, divided, Desert Rose patt.,
7 x 10 3/4"... 55
Vegetable bowl, open, oval, Arden patt.,
large... 45
Vegetable bowl, open, oval, Daisy patt.,
6 3/4 x 13 3/4", 2 1/4" h. 38
Vegetable bowl, open, round, Apple patt.,
7 3/4" d... 35

Vegetable bowl, open, round, California
Poppy patt., 9" d. **125**
Vegetable bowl, open, round, Ivy patt.,
8 1/4" d. **47**

Fulper Pottery

*The Fulper Pottery was founded in Fleming-
ton, New Jersey, in 1805 and operated until 1935,
although operations were curtailed in 1929 when
its main plant was destroyed by fire. The name
was changed in 1929 to Stangl Pottery, which
continued in operation until July of 1978, when
Pfaltzgraff, a division of Susquehanna Broadcasting Company of York, Pennsylvania, purchased the assets of the Stangl Pottery, including
the name.*

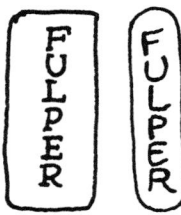

Fulper Marks

Center bowl, "Effigy Bowl," a round disk
base supporting a cluster of four stylized
ancient squatting figures supporting a
wide shallow bowl w/rolled sides, frothy
ivory over matte mustard yellow glaze,
ink racetrack mark, 10 1/2" d., 6 1/2" h. **$978**

Fulper Pottery Copper Dust Jug

Jug, bulbous ovoid body w/a wide shoulder
centered by a short cylindrical neck, a
high arched handle from base of neck to
edge of shoulder, Copper Dust Crystalline glaze, small in-the-making grinding
chip on base, incised racetrack mark,
7 3/4" d., overall 11 1/2" h. (ILLUS.).......... **2,760**

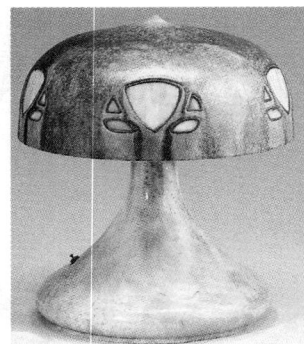

Fine Fulper Pottery Table Lamp

Lamp, table model, a wide pottery mushroom-shaped shade w/a fine Leopard
Skin Crystalline glaze, the border pierced
w/clusters of small openings centered by
a large triangular opening, all inset
w/leaded slag glass pieces, on a widely
flaring matching pottery pedestal base,
original sockets & switch, hairline in a ceramic bridge between the two pieces of
slag glass, rectangular ink mark on both
pieces, shade 15 1/4" d., overall
18 1/2" h. (ILLUS.)..................................... **10,925**
Lamp, table model, wide mushroom-
shaped pottery shade w/a brown, celadon green & blue glaze, pierced around
the border w/heart-shaped & geometric
openings inset w/green & amber slag
glass, on a widely flaring pottery pedestal
base w/a Cucumber Green matte glaze,
both parts w/a rectangular ink mark,
shade 17" d., overall 21 1/2" h. **17,250**
Urn, bulbous ovoid form tapering to a wide
short cylindrical neck w/thick rim, horizontal loop handles at the shoulder, hammered texture under a Leopard Skin
crystalline glaze, ink racetrack mark,
11 1/2" d., 12 1/4" h. (small abraded area
on one handle)... **2,185**

Fulper Corseted Vase with Fine Glaze

Vase, 7 1/2" h., 4" d., corseted cylindrical
body, dripping frothy ivory, blue & mahogany flambé glaze, rectangular ink
mark (ILLUS.)... **1,035**

Vase, 8" h., 4" d., bottle-form, bulbous ovoid body tapering to a tall stick neck wrapped w/a stylized salamander, green & blue flambé glaze, rectangular ink mark **748**

Vase, 8" h., 5 1/2" d., a small pedestal foot below the very wide bulbous body tapering sharply to a shoulder molded w/three small, short cylindrical necks centered by a larger cylindrical neck, mahogany, ivory & turquoise flambé semi-matte glaze, incised racetrack mark **805**

Vase, 8" h., 6" d., footed squatty wide body tapering sharply to a cylindrical neck w/flared rim, overall Mirror Black crystalline flambé glaze, incised racetrack mark..... **575**

Vase, 8" h., 8" d., wide bulbous ovoid body w/the shoulder centered by a short cylindrical neck, a frothy gunmetal & blue flambé glaze over a Famille Rose ground, raised racetrack mark **1,093**

Vase, 9 1/2" h., 6" d., bulbous baluster-form body w/a short trumpet neck, mirrored Cat's-eye flambé glaze, ink racetrack mark **633**

Fulper Vase with Cat's-eye Glaze

Vase, 11 1/2" h., 9" d., footed baluster-form body w/flaring rim, molded w/vertical low ribs forming panels up the sides, fine mirrored Cat's-eye flambé glaze, raised racetrack mark (ILLUS.) **4,025**

Fulper "Cattail" Pattern Vase

Vase, 12 3/4" h., 4 3/4" d., "Cattail" patt., tall cylindrical form molded overall w/cattails, Leopard Skin crystalline glaze, minor burst bubble at rim, rectangular ink mark (ILLUS.).. **4,025**

Geisha Girl Wares

Geisha Girl Porcelain features scenes of Japanese women in colorful kimonos along with the flora and architecture of old Japan. Although bearing an Oriental motif, the wares were produced for sale in the West and are primarily found in Occidental dinnerware and decorative forms. Geisha Girl Porcelain was primarily an offshoot of the fine Kutani hand-painted porcelains. Less expensive production methods, e.g. stenciling as a foundation for hand painting, enabled the company to sell to a larger target market. Geisha ware was sold in five-and-dime stores and used as marketing premiums in addition to being sold through distributors and in high-end department stores. Among the hundreds of patterns and producers, quality can vary greatly. Advanced collectors favor those examples that are well executed, with detailed and careful painting and gilding. Beware, however, of overly ornate and gilded items, which are often indicative of modern day reproductions that combine Kutani and Satsuma styling on ware with fake Nippon marks.

Collectors tips: Geisha Girl Porcelain is found in a variety of border colors, the most common being shades of red-orange. Other border colors include shades of blue and green as well as multicolors and patterns. Geisha ware was sold in sets as well as open stock; actual sets will share the same pattern, border color and border embellishments. Cocoa sets were not sold with sugars and creamers. Teacups and saucers, 7" lunch plates, powder jars and hair receivers are among the most common forms found. Despite being destined for the Western market, where an even number of accessory items is considered standard, many Japanese sets were produced with five accessory pieces, e.g. individual nut bowls, cups and saucers. Therefore, sets may be found with either five or six accessory pieces. Due to the proliferation of Geisha ware manufacturers, Geisha ware can bear a wide variety of makers' marks. Many examples, however, are unmarked. With perhaps the exception of Nippon collectors, Geisha collectors do not currently place much focus or value on particular marks. Reference: Litts, E. The Collector's Encyclopedia of Geisha Girl Porcelain, Collector Books, 1988 (out of print).

Bowl, 4 1/2" d., 1 1/4" h., rice, Garden Party patt., multicolor border...................................... **$15**

Geisha Girl Trinket Box

Box, cov., trinket, Temple B patt., butterfly-shaped, red-orange border, marked "Japan," 2 3/4 x 2 x 1 1/4" (ILLUS.) 25

Butter pat, Lantern Processional patt., red-orange border w/gold lacing 15

Celery set (child's): master plus six salts; Flower Gathering A patt., pine green border w/white dots 45

Chocolate pot, Parasol C patt., red border w/gold buds, marked "Japan," 9 1/2" h. 45

Cup & saucer, child's demitasse, Torii patt., gold border, marked "Made in Japan" 15

Cup & saucer, tea, four decorative reserves including Meeting & Parasol patts., ornate all-over design 25

Dish, Fan F patt., footed sherbet, red-orange border 35

Geisha Girl Dresser Tray

Dresser tray, rectangular, Blind Man's Bluff patt., designs in floral medallions on cobalt blue ground, 11 1/2 x 8" (ILLUS.) 85

Geisha Girl Hanging Match Holder

Match holder, Temple B patt., hanging type, red-orange border, unusual divided style, 3 5/8 x 5" (ILLUS.) 65

Small Geisha Girl Pitcher

Pitcher, 4 5/8" h., 7" spout to handle, Gardening patt., ornately molded bottom, swirl fluted body, gold striations & buds over red-orange border, signed in Japanese "Made in Japan by Kato" (ILLUS.) 55

Plate, 8 1/2" d., Child Reaching for Butterfly patt., red-orange border 15

Geisha Girl Music Recital B Plate

Plate, 8 1/2" h., Music Recital B patt., cobalt blue border w/gold lacing (ILLUS.) 35

Geisha Girl Ring Tree

Ring tree, Temple B patt., red-orange border w/interior gold lacing, signed "Kutani," 2 3/4" h., 3 1/2" d. (ILLUS.) 30

Sugar & creamer, Chinese Coin patt., signed "Terazawa" 45

Geisha Girl Carp Sugar Shaker

Sugar shaker, Carp patt., red-orange border, floriate foot w/gold lacing, gold line around neck, gold star on top (ILLUS.) 65

Teapot, cov., Battledore patt., apple green border 35

Teapot, cov., Dragonboat patt., red & cobalt blue border w/gold lacing, swirl ribbed body 40

Geisha Girl Serving Tray

Tray, dual-handled, Parasol G patt., gold embellished red-orange border w/ornate interior framing, signed in Japanese "Nagoya Mukomatsu sei," 10 x 13 1/4" (ILLUS.) 80

Gonder

Lawton Gonder founded Gonder Ceramic Arts in Zanesville, Ohio, in 1941 and it continued in operation until 1957.

The firm produced a higher priced and better quality of commercial art potteries than many firms of the time and employed Jamie Matchet and Chester Kirk, both of whom were outstanding ceramic designers. Several special glazes were developed during the company's history and Gonder even duplicated some museum pieces of Chinese ceramic. In 1955 the firm converted to the production of tile due to increased foreign competition. By 1957 its years of finest production were over.

Increase price ranges as indicated for the following glaze colors: red flambé - 50 percent, antique gold crackle - 70 percent, turquoise Chinese crackle - 40 per cent, white Chinese crackle - 30 per cent.

Gonder Frappe Lamp Base

Lamp base, Frappe, Catalog #2067, no mark, Rutile Green w/Green Overlay glaze, 15 3/4" h. (ILLUS.) **$50-75**

Rose Lady Head Lamp or Figurine

Lamp base, Rose Lady Head, no mark, Light Blue glaze, Mold #588, can be used as figurine, 12 1/4" h. (ILLUS.) **150-175**

Planter, basket shape w/overhead handle, Mold H-39, 7 x 8" **10-20**

Planter, figural Madonna, Mold E-303 & R-303, 4 x 6" **10-20**

Planter, figural nude w/deer, Mold No. 593, 9 1/2 x 14" **250-300**

Planter, figure of Gay 90s man w/basket, no mold number, 13 1/4" h. **150-175**

Planter, model of swan, Mold No. J-31, 8 1/2" h. **30-45**

Planter, model of wishing well, 6 1/2 x 9 1/4" **100-125**

Tankard, Mold No. M-9, 14" h. **60-80**

Vase, 6" h., fan shape w/relief-molded scroll design, Mold No. H-82 .... **25-35**

Vase, 6" h., footed, bulbous lobed base w/flaring square top, Mold E-71 .... **20-35**

Vase, 6" h., footed, squatty bulbous base, cylindrical neck w/flared rim, applied leaf decoration, Mold E-68.............................. **15-30**

Vase, 6" h., waisted twisted form, Mold E-64 .... **10-20**

Vase, 5 x 6 1/4", rectangular, Mold No. 709 .... **10-25**

Vase, 9" h., tieback drape design, Mold No. 605 & H-605 .... **50-75**

Vase, 9 1/4" h., fan shape, Mold No. H-601 .... **35-50**

Vase, 9 1/4" h., footed leaf form w/open circle in center, Mold No. H-603 .... **35-50**

Vase, 8 x 11 1/2", leaf swirl design, Mold No. 596.. **50-75**

Vase, 11 3/4" h., swallow design, Mold K-25 .... **150-200**

Gonder Seashell Vase

Vase, 13 3/8" h., Seashell Ewer with Starfish, marked "508 Gonder U.S.A." in script, Chinese Turquoise Crackle glaze (ILLUS.).. **95-120**

Grueby

Some fine art pottery was produced by the Grueby Faience and Tile Company, established in Boston in 1891. Choice pieces were created with molded designs on a semi-porcelain body. The ware is marked and often bears the initials of the decorators. The pottery closed in 1907.

GRUEBY

Grueby Pottery Mark

Jardiniere, wide bulbous body w/a wide low rolled flat rim, molded around the lower body w/three rows of curled leaves issuing slender stems topped by nine light blue five-petaled flowers around the shoulder, fine oatmealed matte green background glaze, stamped "Grueby Faience - 174 - EG," 9" d., 7 1/2" h. **$18,400**

Tile, square, decorated in cuenca w/a brown, tan & cream turtle below a garland of heart-shaped green leaves against a dark brown ground, marked "AS" on the back, 6" sq.............................. **10,350**

Rare Grueby Tile with Oak Tree

Tile, square, decorated in cuenca w/a large oak tree against a blue sky w/puffy white clouds, numbered 28 on the back, 6" sq. (ILLUS.) **12,650**

Rare Blue-glazed Grueby Vase

Vase, 5 1/2" h., 3 3/4" d., ovoid body swelling to a six-lobed rim, full-length tooled & applied leaves alternating w/narrow green buds against an overall fine oatmealed blue glaze, circular pottery mark (ILLUS.)... **17,250**

Wide Squatty Grueby Vase

Vase, 6 1/4" h., 6 3/4" d., wide squatty bulbous shape tapering to a short rolled neck, crisply decorated w/a band of long, wide pointed leaves around the sides alternating w/yellow buds below the neck, fine leathery matte green glaze, circular pottery mark & "MS" (ILLUS.)................... **13,800**

Vase, 6 3/4" h., 4 1/4" d., squatty bulbous base tapering to a tall cylindrical neck, six tooled panels around the sides & base, leathery pale blue glaze, stamped "Grueby Faience - 78?".. **1,840**

Vase, 7 1/2" h., 4 1/2" d., ovoid body tapering to a short cylindrical neck, decorated w/tooled & applied tall oval leaves w/curled tips alternating w/buds at the rim, good dark matte green glaze, circular pottery mark... **3,450**

Rare Grueby Vase with Daffodils

Vase, 12" h., 7 3/4" d., footed large ovoid body w/a wide flat mouth, crisply tooled & applied w/clusters of yellow daffodils & green leaves, overall fine pulled leathery matte green glaze, restoration to drilled holes in base, small kiln kiss near base, signed by Wilhelmina Post and dated 5/27/06 (ILLUS.).................................... **26,450**

Wall hanging, model of a ram's head w/curled-under horns, overall matte green glaze, 6" w., 5 1/2" h. **1,380**

Hall China

Founded in 1903 in East Liverpool, Ohio, this still-operating company at first produced mostly utilitarian wares. It was in 1911 that Robert T. Hall, son of the company founder, developed a special single-fire, lead-free glaze that proved to be strong, hard and nonporous. In the 1920s the firm became well known for its extensive line of teapots (still a major product), and in 1932 it introduced kitchenwares, followed by dinnerwares in 1936 and refrigerator wares in 1938.

The imaginative designs and wide range of glaze colors and decal decorations have led to the growing appeal of Hall wares with collectors, especially people who like Art Deco and Art Moderne design. One of the firm's most famous patterns was the "Autumn Leaf" line, produced as premiums for the Jewel Tea Company. For listings of this ware see "Jewel Tea Autumn Leaf."

Helpful books on Hall include The Collector's Guide to Hall China *by Margaret & Kenn Whitmyer, and* Superior Quality Hall China - A Guide for Collectors *by Harvey Duke (An ELO Book, 1977).*

 HALL CHINA

MADE IN U.S.A.

Hall Marks

Ashtray w/match holder, closed sides, No. 618 1/2, cobalt... **$20**

Baker, French Fluted shape, Silhouette patt. **30**

Five Band Batter Bowl

Batter bowl, Five Band shape, Chinese Red (ILLUS.) **95**

Bean pot, cov., New England shape, No. 4, Blue Blossom patt. **225**

Bean pot, cov., New England shape, No. 4, Shaggy Tulip patt. **275**

Bean pot, cov., New England shape, No. 488 patt. **275**

Pert Shape Bean Pot

Bean pot, cov., Pert shape, Chinese Red (ILLUS.).. **100**

Bowl, 6" d., Medallion shape, Silhouette patt. **23**

Bowl, 6" d., Radiance shape, Yellow Rose patt. **20**

Bowl, 7" d., Medallion shape, Silhouette patt. **25**

Bowl, 7 1/2" d., straight-sided, Rose White patt. **18**

Bowl, 8 3/4" d., Five Band shape, Cactus patt. **45**

Bowl, 9" d., salad, Rose Parade patt. **44**

Bowl, 9" d., salad, Silhouette patt. **25**

Butter dish, cov., Crocus patt., Zephyr shape, 1 lb. **1,200**

Canister, cov., Radiance shape, Chinese Red **200**

Casserole with Chrome Base

Casserole, cov., Art Deco w/chrome reticulated handled base (ILLUS.)............................. **75**

Casserole, cov., Medallion shape, Silhouette patt. **60**

Casserole, cov., Radiance shape, Crocus patt. **65**

Casserole, cov., round, No. 76, Wild Poppy
patt., 10 1/2" d. 75
Casserole, cov., tab-handled, Rose Parade
patt. 42

Casserole with Inverted Pie Dish Lid

Casserole w/inverted pie dish lid, Radi-
ance shape, No. 488, 6 1/2" d., 4" h.
(ILLUS.) 60
Coffeepot, cov., Drip-O-Later, Duse shape 50

Hall Coffeepots

Coffeepot, cov., Drip-O-Lator, Jerry shape
(ILLUS. left)... 50
Coffeepot, cov., drip-type, all-china, Jordan
shape, Morning Glory patt. 275
Coffeepot, cov., electric percolator, Game
Birds (Ducks & Pheasants) patt. 85

Crocus Pattern Coffeepot

Coffeepot, cov., Terrace shape, Crocus
patt. (ILLUS.) 80
Coffeepot, cov., Tricolator, Coffee Queen,
Chinese Red... 55
Coffeepot, cov., Tricolator, Ritz shape, Chi-
nese Red (ILLUS. right w/Jerry Drip-O-
Lator) 135

Cookie jar, cov., Five Band shape, Blue
Blossom patt. 330

Meadow Flower Cookie Jar

Cookie jar, cov., Five Band shape, Meadow
Flower patt. (ILLUS.).. 325

Flareware Cookie Jar

Cookie jar, cov., Flareware (ILLUS.)................... 65
Cookie jar, cov., Owl, brown glaze.................... 120
Cookie jar, cov., Sundial shape, Blue Blos-
som patt. 400
Cookie jar, cov., Zeisel, Gold Dot design 95
Creamer, Medallion shape, Silhouette patt. 18

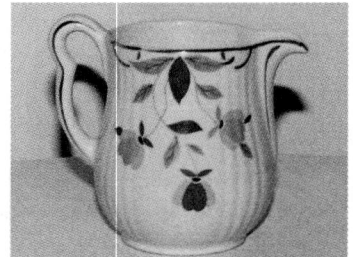

Creamer in Autumn Leaf Pattern

Creamer, Radiance shape, Autumn Leaf
patt. (ILLUS.) **45**
Creamer, Sundial shape, Chinese Red, 4
oz. **45**
Custard, straight-sided, Rose Parade patt. **32**
Custard cup, Radiance shape, Serenade
patt. **20**
Custard cup, Thick Rim shape, Meadow
Flower patt. **35**
Drip jar, cov., Thick Rim shape, Royal Rose
patt. **25**
Gravy boat, Red Poppy patt. **125**

Humidor with Walnut Lid

Humidor, cov., Indian Decal, walnut lid
(ILLUS.) **55**
Leftover, cov., rectangular, Blue Bouquet
patt. **100**

Zephyr Shape Leftover

Leftover, cov., Zephyr shape, Chinese Red
(ILLUS.) **110**
Mixing bowl, Thick Rim shape, Royal Rose
patt., 8 1/2" d. **30**
Mug, flagon shape, Monk patt. **45**

Hall Commemorative Mug

Mug, Irish coffee, footed, commemorative,
"Hall China Convention 2000" (ILLUS.) **40**
Mug, Tom & Jerry, Red Dot patt. **15**
Pitcher, ball shape, Autumn Leaf patt.,
1978, w/box (ILLUS., bottom of page) **65**
Pitcher, ball shape, No. 3, Delphinium blue **35**
Pitcher, ball shape, Royal Rose patt. **95**
Pitcher, jug-type, Doughnut shape, cobalt
blue **75**

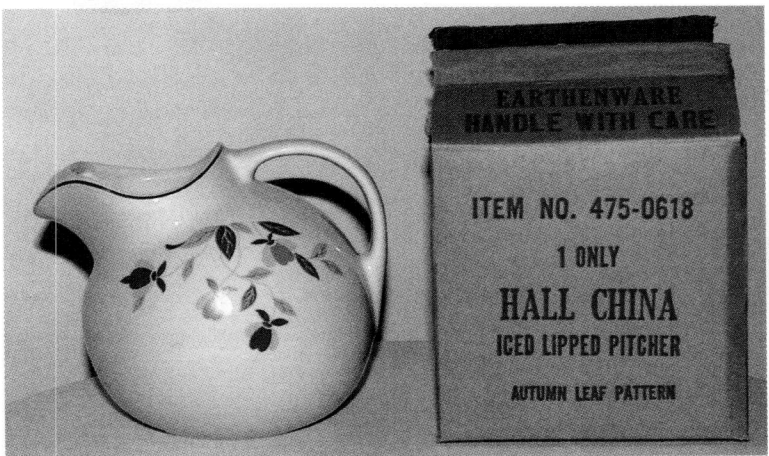

Autumn Leaf Pitcher with Box

Pert Pitchers in Various Sizes

Pitcher, jug-type, Loop-handle, Blue Blossom patt. **195**
Pitcher, jug-type, Medallion line, No. 3, Silhouette patt. **45**
Pitcher, jug-type, Nora, yellow **25**
Pitcher, jug-type, Radiance shape, No. 5, Wildfire patt. **45**
Pitcher, Rose White patt., large **35**
Pitchers, Pert shape, Chinese Red, three sizes (ILLUS. of three, top of page) **35-55**
Plate, dinner, 9" d., Silhouette patt. **15**
Platter, 11 1/4" l., oval, Springtime patt. **20**
Pretzel jar, cov., Crocus patt. **225**
Punch set: punch bowl & 10 punch cups; Old Crow, punch bowl reads "May YOU always - have an eagle in your pocket ...a turkey on your table - and Old Crow in your glass," the set **175**
Salt & pepper shakers, Five Band shape, Blue Blossom patt., pr. **75**
Salt & pepper shakers, handled, Royal Rose patt., pr. **34**
Salt & pepper shakers, Novelty Radiance shape, Orange Poppy patt., pr. **95**

Pert Salt & Pepper Shakers

Salt & pepper shakers, Pert shape, Chinese Red, pr. (ILLUS.) **35**

Adele Shape Teapot

Teapot, cov., Adele shape, Art Deco style, olive green (ILLUS.) **200**
Teapot, cov., Airflow shape, cobalt blue w/gold trim, 6-cup **100**
Teapot, cov., Aladdin shape, Crocus patt. **1,950**
Teapot, cov., Aladdin shape, round opening, Cadet blue w/gold trim **75**
Teapot, cov., Aladdin shape, yellow w/gold trim, w/infuser **65**
Teapot, cov., Albany shape, mahogany w/gold trim, 6-cup **75**
Teapot, cov., Automobile shape, turquoise w/platinum **750**

Birdcage Teapot

Teapot, cov., Birdcage shape, yellow, "Gold
Special" decoration (ILLUS.)......................... **500**

Blue Garden Teapot

Teapot, cov., Blue Garden patt., morning
set (ILLUS.).. **350**
Teapot, cov., Boston shape, canary yellow,
2-cup **45**
Teapot, cov., Boston shape, Chinese Red **150**
Teapot, cov., Boston shape, Crocus patt.......... **225**
Teapot, cov., Cleveland shape, turquoise
w/gold decoration... **75**
Teapot, cov., Coverlet shape, white w/gold
cover, 6-cup **40**
Teapot, cov., Cube shape, turquoise, 2-cup..... **140**

Orange Poppy Doughnut Shape Teapot

Teapot, cov., Doughnut shape, Orange
Poppy patt. (ILLUS.) **450**
Teapot, cov., Football shape, commemora-
tive, "Hall 200 Haul, East Liverpool, Ohio" **125**
Teapot, cov., French shape, Chinese Red &
white, 2-cup **125**
Teapot, cov., Manhattan shape, Chinese
Red, 8-cup **500**
Teapot, cov., Manhattan shape, side han-
dle, cobalt blue, 2-cup...................................... **95**
Teapot, cov., McCormick shape, turquoise **50**
Teapot, cov., Medallion shape, Crocus patt........ **85**
Teapot, cov., Medallion shape, Silhouette
patt... **70**
Teapot, cov., Melody shape, Chinese Red........ **305**
Teapot, cov., Melody shape, Orange Poppy
patt... **370**
Teapot, cov., Pert shape, Chinese Red, 4-
cup **80**
Teapot, cov., Pert shape, Chinese Red &
white, 2-cup **80**

Philadelphia Shape Teapot

Teapot, cov., Philadelphia shape, Chinese
Red (ILLUS.) **250**
Teapot, cov., Radiance shape, Acacia patt....... **225**
Teapot, cov., Rhythm shape, cobalt blue........... **180**

Rutherford Ribbed Teapot

Teapot, cov., Rutherford shape, ribbed,
Chinese Red (ILLUS.)...................................... **250**
Teapot, cov., Streamline shape, Chinese
Red **150**

Fantasy Teapot

Teapot, cov., Streamline shape, Fantasy patt. (ILLUS.) 400
Teapot, cov., Streamline shape, Orange Poppy patt. 350
Teapot, cov., Sundial shape, ivory w/gold decoration 95
Teapot, cov., Surfside shape, cadet blue 175
Teapot, cov., Surfside shape, canary yellow 185
Teapot, cov., Windshield shape, Gamebird patt. 250
Teapot, cov., Windshield shape, turquoise w/gold decoration 68
Twin-Tea set: cov. teapot, cov. hot water pot & matching divided tray; Pansy patt. 225
Vase, bud, Trumpet, No. 631, Chinese Red 35
Vase, bud, No. 641, canary yellow 10

Zephyr Shape Water Bottle

Water bottle, cov., refrigerator ware line, Zephyr shape, Chinese Red (ILLUS.) 350
Water server, Plaza shape, Chinese Red 135
Water server w/hinged cover, Westinghouse refrigerator ware, Hercules shape, cobalt blue 110

Haviland

Haviland porcelain was originated by Americans in Limoges, France, shortly before the mid-19th century and continues in production. Some Haviland was made by Theodore Haviland in the United States during the last World War. Numerous other factories also made china in Limoges. Also see LIMOGES.

H&Cᵒ

Haviland Marks

Baker, oblong open bowl shape, unglazed bottom, Schleiger 33, Blank 19 .... $75
Beaner, open, oval, Schleiger 876, 3 1/2 x 5" 45
Bone dish, Schleiger 72, decorated w/roses & green flowers 30
Bouillon cup & saucer, Drop Rose patt., Schleiger 55C, pale pink 125
Bouillon cups & saucers, No. 72 patt., Blank No. 22, ten sets 550
Bowl, 9 1/2" d., soup, cobalt & gold w/floral center, Theodore Haviland 125
Bowl, 8 3/8 x 10 3/8", 3 1/2" h., Christmas Rose patt., Blank No. 418 650
Butter dish, cov., No. 133 patt. 145
Butter pat, Schleiger 271A, decorated w/blue flowers & pink roses, 3" 25
Cake plate, handled, 87C patt., Blank No. 2, 10 1/2" d. 125
Cake plate, handled, No. 72 patt., Blank No. 22 175
Candleholders, Swirl patt., decorated w/dainty roses, pr. 135
Celery tray, Schleiger 150, Harrison Rose, decorated w/small pink roses, 12" l. 125
Celery tray, Blank No. 305, titled "Her Majesty," 13" l. 125
Cheese dish w/underplate, CFH/GDM, straight sides, high dome w/flat top, small hole in top near handle, decorated w/blue flowers & gold trim 295
Chocolate pot, Autumn Leaf patt., 9" h. 325
Chocolate set: cov. pot & eight cups & saucers; decorated w/pink & blue flowers w/green stems, Blank No. 1, the set 468
Coffee set: cov. coffeepot, creamer, sugar bowl & twelve cups & saucers; Ranson blank No. 1, the set 523
Coffeepot, cov., Old Wedding Ring patt., white w/gold trim, Old H & Co 225
Coffeepot, cov., Schleiger 98, Cloverleaf, 9" h. 325
Comport, divided, shell-shaped, white w/green trim, full-bodied red lobster at center, non-factory decor of red, green & black 550
Comport, round, English, shaped like regular pedestal comport without pedestal, Schleiger 56 variation, decorated w/lavender flowers, 9" d. 125
Cracker jar, cov., floral decoration, cobalt, gold & blue bells, 1900 & decorator's marks 450
Cream soup w/underplate, Schleiger 31, Ranson blank, decorated w/pink roses, 5" d. bowl, 2 pcs. 55
Creamer, Moss Rose patt., gold trim, 5 1/2" h. 50
Creamer & open sugar, Ranson blank, Drop Rose patt., w/very ornate gold trim, pr. 695

Creamer & sugar bowl, Mont Mery
patt., ca. 1953, pr.. 125
Cup & saucer, demitasse, Arcadia, bird
patt. 45
Cup & saucer, breakfast, Moss Rose patt.
w/gold trim.. 45
Cup & saucer, demitasse, Papillon Butterfly
patt., floral by Pallandre.................................... 75
Cup & saucer, Moss Rose patt., "Haviland
& Co. - Limoges - France," pr......................... 40

Meadow Visitors Cup & Saucer

Cups & saucers, Papillon butterfly handles
w/Meadow Visitors decoration, six sets
(ILLUS. of one set) 900
Cuspidor, Moss Rose patt, smooth blank,
8" d., 3 1/4" h... 248
Dessert set: 9 x 15" oblong tray w/twelve 7"
square matching plates; centers decorated w/Meadow Visitors patt. & bordered in
rich cobalt blue w/gold trim, commis-
sioned for Mrs. Wm. A. Wilson, 13 pcs...... **2,300**
Egg cup, footed, No. 69 patt. on blank No. 1...... 65
Egg cups, footed, No. 72 patt., Blank No.
22, pr.. 190

Plate from Fish Set

Fish set: 22" l. oval platter & twelve
8 1/2" d. plates; each piece w/a different
fish in the center, the border in two
shades of green design w/gold trim, h.p.
scenes by L. Martin, mark of Theodore
Haviland, 13 pcs. (ILLUS. of plate)............. **2,750**
Gravy boat, No. 761 95
Gravy boat w/attached underplate,
Schleiger 46, Ranson blank, decorated
w/pink & blue flowers 125
Honey dish, 4" d., bowl-form, Schleiger 33,
decorated w/white flowers, pink shading........ 25
Jam jar w/underplate, cov., Christmas
Rose patt.. 795

Match box, gold trim, 1882 & decorator's
marks.. 175
Oyster plates, four-well, all white w/relief-
molded scrolled design, 7 1/2" d., pr............. 250
Oyster scoop, oyster-shaped,
CFH/GDM, h.p., 1 3/4 x 2 1/5" 65
Pancake server, decorated w/yellow flowers w/pale green stems, smooth blank,
1892 & decorator marks.................................. 154
Pin box, cov., oblong, ornate scrolled base
& rim, loop finial on h.p. floral decorated
lid, marked "H & Co. L. France," 4" l. 175
Pitcher, syrup-type, Schleiger 144, decorated w/pink roses & green scrolls 145

Pitcher with Anchor in Relief

Pitcher, 7" h., milk-type, tankard style w/ta-
pering cylindrical white body w/a large relief-molded anchor under the heavy ropetwist loop handle, bright gold trim, old
Haviland & Co. mark (ILLUS.)......................... 125
Plate, dinner, Rosalinde patt. 35
Plate, ice cream, 5" l., leaf-shaped w/han-
dle, cobalt & gold... 125
Plate, bread & butter, 6 1/2" d., Schleiger
340, decorated w/pink roses & blue
scrolls 28
Plate, 8 1/2" d., cobalt & gold Pallandre
patt. 175

Plate with Draped Pink Roses

Plate, luncheon, 8 1/2" d., smooth edge, design on border of draped pink roses, Schleiger 152, Theodore Haviland (ILLUS.) 28

Plate, dinner, 9 1/2" d., Schleiger 29-K, decorated w/pink flowers & gold trim 40

Plate, 9 3/4" d., portrait of woman in forest scene, artist-signed, Blank No. 116 125

Plate, 10 1/2" d., service, Blank 20, white w/gold trim 45

Plate, chop, 12" d., Schleiger 233, The Norma, decorated w/small pink & yellow flowers 125

Platter, 16" l., rectangular, Marseilles, Schleiger 9 125

Platter, 14 x 20", Ranson blank No. 1 275

Punch bowl, Baltimore Rose patt. 2,000

Ramekins & underplates, Ranson Blank No. 1, set of 12 540

Salad plate, bean-shaped, variation of Schleiger 1190, decorated w/orange flowers & gold trim, 4 1/2 x 9" 95

Salt, Schleiger 31, decorated w/pink roses & gold trim, 2 x 1" 65

Sauce tureen w/attached undertray, cov., oval, Schleiger 619, green design w/gold trim, Theodore Haviland 125

Serving bowl, Schleiger 235B, 12" d., 2" h. 195

Multifloral Serving Dish

Serving dish, quatrefoil form, Multifloral patt., Old H & Co, 9" sq., 2" h. (ILLUS.) 125

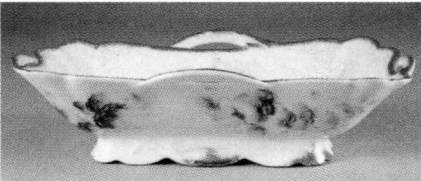

Haviland Serving Dish with Poppies

Serving dish, scalloped rectangular form w/a scalloped foot ring below the flaring side w/low open side handles, decorated w/pale yellowish green to dark green poppies & pale pink shadows, gold trim, variation of Schleiger No. 665, Haviland & Co. mark, 8 x 10" (ILLUS.) 175

Serving plate, blue & burgundy Art Deco decoration, black ground, "Haviland & Co. - Limoges - France," 10 1/2" d. 95

Sipper dishes, Meadow Visitors patt., smooth blank, 4 3/4" d., set of 8 176

Sorbet, footed, w/gold embossed trim, Schleiger 276 65

Soup plate w/flanged rim, No. 761 35

Soup tureen, round, Ranson blank, Schleiger 29M, decorated w/tiny blue flowers 350

Tea caddy, cov., Ranson blank 275

Tea set: small cov. teapot, creamer & sugar bowl, six cups & saucers; No. 19 patt., 15 pcs. 650

Tea & toast tray & cup, No. 482 patt., Blank No. 208, pr. 275

Butterfly-handled Cup and Saucer

Teacup & saucer, cup w/tapering cylindrical bowl & figural butterfly handle, h.p. grey band design on rim & border, Haviland & Co. (ILLUS.) 125

Teapot, cov., Henri II blank w/gold & silver decoration (inner rim restored) 250

Vases, 15" h., Terra Cotta, brown w/white water lily & large green leaves in relief, Haviland & Co, pr. 4,500

Vegetable dish, cov., Marseille patt., Blank No. 9, 9 1/2" l. 145

Wash pitcher, Moss Rose patt. w/gold trim, smooth blank, 12" h. 350

Hull

In 1905 Addis E. Hull purchased the Acme Pottery Company in Crooksville, Ohio. In 1917 the A.E. Hull Pottery Company began to make a line of art pottery for florists and gift shops. The company also made novelties, kitchenware and stoneware.

Hull's Little Red Riding Hood kitchenware was manufactured between 1943 and 1957 and is a favorite of collectors, as are the beautiful matte glaze vases it produced.

In 1950 the factory was destroyed by a flood and fire, but by 1952 it was back in production. Hull added its newer glossy glazed pottery plus pieces sold in flower shops under the names Regal and Floraline. Hull's brown dinnerware lines achieved great popularity and were the main lines being produced prior to the plant's closing in 1986.

References on Hull Pottery include: Hull, The Heavenly Pottery, 7th Edition, 2001 and Hull, The Heavenly Pottery Shirt Pocket Price Guide, 4th Edition, 1999, by Joan Hull. Also The Dinnerwares Lines by Barbara Loveless Click-Burke (Collector Books 1993) and Robert's Ultimate Encyclopedia of Hull Pottery by Brenda Roberts (Walsworth Publishing Co., 1992). -- Joan Hull, Advisor.

Hull Marks

Ashtray, Ebb Tide patt., E8 .... **$225**
Ashtray, Continental patt., No. A1, 8" 50
Ashtray, Parchment & Pine patt., No. S-14,
14" l. 175
Bank, figural Corky Pig, pink, white & blue,
5" 225
Basket, hanging-type, Woodland Matte
patt., cream & blue 575
Basket, Wildflower patt., fan-shaped, scal-
loped rim, handle, pink & blue, matte
glaze, 12 1/2" h., 16 1/2" w. 375
Basket, Blossom Flite patt., No. T2, 6" h. 65
Basket, Sueno Tulip patt., No. 102-33-6",
6" h. 350
Basket, Sun Glow patt., No. 84, 6 1/2" h. 75
Basket, Blossom Flite patt., No. T4,
8 1/2" h. 125
Basket, Woodland Matte patt., fan-shaped
w/center handle, pink & green, glossy,
W9-8 3/4", 8 3/4" h. 175
Basket, Poppy patt., No. 601, 9" h. 800
Book ends, Orchid patt., No. 316, 7" h., pr. .. 1,200
Bowl, 6 1/2" d., low, Poppy patt., No. 602 295

Hull Mixing Bowl

Bowl, 8" d., 4 1/2" h., House 'N Garden line,
pour spout, Mirror Brown glaze w/ivory
foam trim, marked "8 Lip Oven Proof
U.S.A." (ILLUS.) 18
Bowl, fruit, 9 1/2" d., Tokay patt., No. 7 175
Bowl, fruit, 10 1/2" d., Butterfly patt., No.
B16 150
Candleholders, Butterfly patt., No. B22,
2 1/2" h., pr. 85
Candleholders, Woodland Matte patt., pink
ground, No. W30, 3 1/2" h., pr. 105
Candleholders, Dogwood patt., No. 512,
4" h., pr. 160
Candleholders, Serenade patt., No. S16,
6 1/2" h., pr. 105
Candy dish, Continental patt., C62,
8 1/4" h. 45
Candy dish, cov., Tokay patt., No. 9C,
8 1/2" h. 100
Canister, cov., Little Red Riding Hood patt.,
"Salt" 1,250
Casserole, oval w/figural duck cover,
House 'N Garden line, Mirror Brown, 2 pt. 95
Console bowl, Magnolia Gloss patt., No. H-
23, 13" l. 95
Console bowl, Royal Woodland patt., No.
W29, 13" l. 75

Cookie jar, cov., Barefoot Boy 450
Cookie jar, cov., figural Ginger Bread Man,
grey Flint Ridge line, 1980s, 12" h. 425
Cookie jar, cov., Gingerbread Man, brown 390
Cookie jar, cov., Little Red Riding Hood,
closed basket **300-1,000**
Cornucopia-vase, Parchment & Pine patt.,
No. S-2-5, 7 3/4" h. 65
Cornucopia-vase, Water Lily patt., pink
w/gold, L7-6 1/2", 6 1/2" h. 95
Cornucopia-vase, Wildflower patt., pink,
yellow & green, No. W7, 7 1/2" 95
Cornucopia-vase, Parchment and Pine
patt., No. S-2, 7 3/4" h. 65
Cornucopia-vase, Magnolia Gloss patt.,
No. H-10-8 1/2, 8 1/2" h. 75
Creamer, Bow-Knot patt., turquoise & blue,
No. B-21-4", 4" h. 175
Creamer, Rosella patt., No. R-3, 5 1/2" h. 50
Creamer, Royal Woodland patt., No. W28 25
Creamer & open sugar bowl, Open Rose
(Camellia) patt., pink & blue, No. 111-5"
& No. 112-5", 5" l., pr. 200
Ewer, Bow-Knot patt., No. B-1-51/2,
5 1/2" h. 195
Ewer, Open Rose (Camellia) patt., No. 128,
4 3/4" h. 95
Ewer, Rosella patt., No. R-9, 6 1/2" h. 75
Ewer, Woodland Gloss patt., No. W6-6 1/2",
6 1/2" h. 70
Ewer, Dogwood patt., No. 505-6 1/2",
8 1/2" h. 275
Ewer, Woodland Gloss patt., No. W24-
13 1/2", 13 1/2" h. 225
Flower dish, Butterfly patt., No. B7,
6 3/4 x 9 3/4" 50
Flowerpot & saucer, Calla Lily patt., No.
592, 6" h. 125
Flowerpot w/attached saucer, Water Lily
patt., pink ground, No. L-25-5 1/4",
5 1/4" h. 175
Fruit bowl, Serenade patt., No. S15-7",
7" h. 130
Honey jug, Blossom Flite patt., No. T1, 6" h. 55
Jardiniere, Dogwood patt., No. 514, 4" h. 110
Lamp base, Rosella patt., No. 63-4", 4" h. 300
Lamp base, Orchid patt., No. 303, 10" h. 600
Lavabo & base, Butterfly patt., Nos. B24 &
B25, cream & blue, overall 16" h., 2 pcs. 160
Mustard jar & spoon, Little Red Riding
Hood patt., 2 pcs. 500

Early Utility Ware Pitcher

Pitcher, 4 1/2" h., Early Utility ware, vertical ribs from base to bottom of handle, white thin horizontal line, wider dark brown line & a second thin white line directly below shoulder, marked "107 - H" in a circle & "36" below it (ILLUS.) 78

Pitcher, 7 1/2" h., Sun Glow patt., No. 55 85

Pitcher, 8 1/2" h., Blossom Flite patt., No. T3 125

Planter, bust of the Madonna w/child, pink semi-glaze, impressed Hull "USA 26," No. 26, 7" h. 45

Planter, model of two Siamese cats, No. 63, 5 3/4" l. 85

Planter, model of a parrot pulling a flower blossom-form cart, Novelty line, No. 60, 9 1/2" l., 6" h. 50

Rose bowl, Iris patt., No. 412-7", 7" l. 175

Salt & pepper shakers, Floral patt., No. 44, 3 1/2" h., pr. 25

Serving tray, three-part w/butterfly handle, Butterfly patt., gold-trimmed scalloped rim, B23, 11 1/2" l. 200

Sugar bowl, cov., Blossom Flite patt., No. T16 45

Tea set: cov. teapot, creamer & cov. sugar bowl; Bow-Knot patt., 3 pcs. 850

Tea set: cov. teapot No. S-11, cov. sugar bowl No. S-13 & creamer No. S-12; Parchment and Pine patt., 3 pcs. 250

Teapot, cov., Serenade patt., No. S17, 5" h., 6-cup 195

Teapot, cov., Mardi Gras/Granada patt., No. 33, 5 1/2" h. 200

Teapot, cov., Wildflower patt., No. 72, 8" h. 1,200

Tray, Mirror Brown patt., 10 x 10" 75

Vase, 5" h., Bow-Knot patt., No. B-2-5, shaded pink to blue matte finish 175

Vase, 5 1/2" h., Water Lily patt., No. L-2-5 1/2" 75

Vase, 6 1/2" h., Water Lily patt., No. L6-6 1/2" 95

Vase, 6 1/2" h., Wild Flower patt., No. W-5-6 1/2 85

Vase, bud, 6 1/2" h., Serenade patt., No. S1-6 1/2" 55

Vase, 6 1/2" h., Sueno Tulip patt., blue & pink, 106-33-6 125

Vase, bud, 6 3/4" h., Orchid patt., No. 306 175

Vase, 8 1/2" h., Orchid patt., No. 309-8 1/2, handled, pink & yellow flowers on shaded blue ground 195

Vase, 8 1/2" h., Woodland Matte patt., pink ground, No. W16-8 1/2" 185

Vase, 9" h., Mardi Gras/Granada patt., No. 48-9" 55

Vase, 9" h., Morning Glory patt., No. 215-9" 55

Vase, 10" h., Calla Lily patt., No. 520-33 350

Vase, 15" h., Magnolia patt., 16-15", pink & green 500

Wall pocket, Woodland Gloss patt., conch shell shape, No. W13-7 1/2", 7 1/2" l. 95

Wall pocket, Bow-Knot patt., model of a whisk broom, No. B27-8", 8" h. 285

Wall pocket, Bow-Knot patt. 300

Window box, Parchment & Pine patt., No. S-5, 10 1/2" l. 95

Hummel Figurines & Collectibles

The Goebel Company of Oeslau, Germany, first produced these porcelain figurines in 1934, having obtained the rights to adapt the beautiful pastel sketches of children by Sister Maria Innocentia (Berta) Hummel. Every design by the Goebel artisans was approved by the nun until her death in 1946. Although not antique, these figurines with the "M.I. Hummel" signature, especially those bearing the Goebel Company factory mark used from 1934 and into the early 1940s, are being sought by collectors, although interest may have peaked some years ago. A good reference is Luckey's Hummel Figurines & Plates, Identification and Value Guide by Carl F. Luckey (Krause Publications). Trademarks:TMK 1 - Crown - 1934-1950TMK 2 - Full Bee - 1940-1959; TMK 3 - Stylized Bee - 1958-1972; TMK 4 - Three Line Mark - 1964-1972; TMK 5 - Last Bee - 1970-1980; TMK 6 - Missing Bee - 1979-1991; TMK 7 - Hummel Mark - 1991-1999; TMK 8 - Goebel Bee - 2000-

Early Hummel Marks

A Stitch in Time, #255, 6 3/4" h., Trademark 3 .... $550-800

A Stitch in Time

A Stitch in Time, #255, 6 3/4" h., Trademark 6 (ILLUS.) 300

Accordion boy, #185, 5 1/2" h., Trademark 2 425

Adoration, #23/I, 6 1/4" h., Trademark 2 ... 600-800

Angel at Prayer font, #91/A, 4 3/4" h., Trademark 2 200-260

Angel Duet, #261, 5" h., Trademark 5 270

Angel Serenade, #214D (angel standing), color decoration, part of Nativity set, 3" h., Trademark 2 125-145

Angel Serenade with lamb, #83, 5 1/2" h, Trademark 5 240

Angel with Lute candleholder, #III/38/I, 2 1/2" h., Trademark 2 250-300

Apple Tree Boy, #142/3/0, 4" h., Trademark 2 .... **300-350**
Apple Tree Boy, #142, 6" h., Trademark 2 .... **600-700**
Apple Tree Girl, #141/3/0, 4 1/4" h., Trademark 6 .... **150**
Apple Tree Girl table lamp, #229, 7 1/2" h., Trademark 2 .... **900-1,000**
Auf Wiedersehen, #153/0, 5 3/4" h., Trademark 6 .... **255**
Ba-Bee Ring plaque, #30/B, boy, 5" d., Trademark 2 .... **350-450**
Baker, #128, 4 3/4" h., Trademark 5 .... **245**
Band Leader, #129, 4 1/4", Trademark 2 .... **425**
Barnyard Hero, #195, 4" h., Trademark 5 .... **200**
Be Patient, #197/2/0, 4 1/4" h., Trademark 2 .... **400-500**
Begging His Share, #9, 5 1/2" h., Trademark 1 .... **750-900**
Bird Watcher, #300, 5" h., Trademark 5 .... **255**
Birthday Serenade, #218/2/0, 4" h., Trademark 6 .... **185**
Blessed Event, #333, 5 1/2" h., Trademark 6 .... **365**
Book Worm, #3/III, 9 1/2" h., Trademark 3 .... **1,600-1,800**
Botanist (The), #351, 4 1/4" h., Trademark 6 .... **200**
Boy with Toothache, #217, 5 1/2" h., Trademark 6 .... **225**
Call to Glory (Fahnentager), #739/I, 5 3/4" h., first issue 1994, three flags included **265**
Carnival, #328, 5 3/4" h., Trademark 6 .... **235**
Celestial Musician, #188, 7" h., Trademark 2 .... **850-1,100**
Chef, Hello, #124/0, 6" h., Trademark 6 .... **240**
Chick Girl, #57/0, 3 1/2" h., Trademark 2 .... **310-375**
Chick Girl candy dish, #III/57, 5 1/4" h., Trademark 2 .... **580-650**
Chimney Sweep, #12/1, 6 1/2" h., Trademark 2 .... **475**
Christmas Song, #343, 6 1/2" h., Trademark 6 .... **240**
Close Harmony, #336, 5 1/2" h., Trademark 5 .... **365-395**
Coffee Break, #409, 4 1/4" h., 1984, exclusive special edition No. 8 for Members of the Goebel Collectors' Club **300**
Coquettes, #179, 5" h., Trademark 6 .... **325**
Crossroads, #331, 6 3/4" h., Trademark 2 .... **4,000-5,000**
Daddy's Girl, #371, 4 3/4" h.,Trademark 6 ...... **250**
Doctor, #127, 4 3/4" h., Trademark 2 .... **300-350**
Doll Bath, #319, 5 1/4" h., Trademark 3 .... **750-1,000**
Easter Greetings, #378, 5" h., Trademark 5 ..... **245**
Evening Prayer (Abengebet), #495, 4" h., first issue 1992 .... **110**
Fair Measure, #345, 6" h., Trademark 5 .... **365**
Favorite Pet, #361, 4 1/2" h., Trademark 6 ...... **320**
Feeding Time, #199/0, 4 1/4" h., Trademark 3 .... **300-350**

Feeding Time, #199, 5 3/4" h., Trademark 2 .... **525-625**
Festival Harmony, #173/0, 8", Trademark 6 .... **355**
Flitting Butterfly plaque, #139, 2 1/2 x 2 1/2", Trademark 1 .... **350-550**
Flower Madonna, #10/I, white, 9 1/2" h., Trademark 1 .... **500-600**
Flower Vender, #381, 5 1/4" h., Trademark 6 .... **275**
For Father, #87, 5 1/2" h., Trademark 2 .... **400-530**
For Mother, #257, 5 1/4" h., Trademark 6 .... **225**

Forest Shrine

Forest Shrine, #183, 9" h., Trademark 6 (ILLUS.) **625**
Friends, #136/1, 5 3/8" h., Trademark 6 .... **225**
Gift from a Friend (Aus Nachbars Garten), #485, 5 1/4" h., exclusive edition 1991/92 M.I. Hummel Club, original box **275**
Globe Trotter, #79, 5" h., Trademark 1 ..... **500-750**
Going to Grandma's, #52/0, 4 3/4" h., Trademark 1 .... **750-1,000**
Goose Girl, #47/3/0, 4 1/4" h., Trademark 6 ...... **185**
Goose Girl, #47/II, 7 1/2" h., Trademark 2 .... **700-900**
Happy Traveler, #109/0, 5" h., Trademark 2 .... **275-350**
Hear Ye, Hear Ye, #15/0, 5" h., Trademark 5 .... **225**
Heavenly Protection, #88, 9 1/4" h., Trademark 2 .... **1,300-1,600**
I'm Carefree, #633, 4 3/4" h., signature on back, first issue 1994 .... **875**
Joyful, #53, 4" h., Trademark 1 .... **350-450**
Jubilee, #416, 6 1/4" h., 1980, 50 years, M.I. Hummel Figurines 1935-1985, "The Love Lives On" **475**
Just Resting table lamp, #II/112, 7 1/2" h., Trademark 3 .... **375-525**
Knit One, Purl One, #432, 3" h., Trademark 5 .... **130**
Latest News, #184, inscribed "Munchener Presse," 5 1/4" h., Trademark 3 .... **425-500**
Little Bookkeeper, #306, 4 3/4" h., Trademark 4 .... **425**
Little Drummer, #240, 4 1/4" h., Trademark 3 .... **245-260**
Little Fiddler, #2/0, 6" h., Trademark 3 ...... **350-400**

Little Goat Herder, #200/I, 5 1/2" h, Trademark 5.. 275
Little Nurse, #376, 4" h., Trademark 6............. 270
Little Pharmacist, #322, 6" h., Trademark 6.. 265
Little Sleeper, #171/4/0, 3" h., Trademark 6..... 115
Madonna plaque, #48/II, 4 3/4 x 6", Trademark 2... 375-525
Make a Wish (Die Pusteblume), #475, 4 1/2" h., Trademark 6 225
Max & Moritz, #123, 5 1/4" h., Trademark 5..... 265
Merry Wanderer, #11/2/0, 4 1/4" h., Trademark 1.. 450-550
Mischief Maker, #342, 5" h., Trademark 5...... 345
Mother's Helper, #133, 5" h., Trademark 4...... 275
On Holiday, #350, 4 1/4" h., Trademark 6........ 165
Out of Danger, #56/B, 6 1/2" h., Trademark 6.. 335
Photographer (The), #178, 4 3/4" h., Trademark 5 345-370
Pigtails, #2052, 3 1/4" h., M.I. Hummel Club Membership Year, 1999/2000, original box 75
Postman, #119, 5" h., Trademark 3................. 300
Puppy Love, #1, 5" h., Trademark 6................. 325
Ride into Christmas, #396, 5 3/4" h., Trademark 4 2,000-2,500

Saint George

Saint George, #55, 6 3/4" h., Trademark 6 (ILLUS.).. 350
School Girls, #177, 9 1/2" h., Trademark 2.. 3,000-4,000
Sensitive Hunter, #6, 4 3/4" h., Trademark 1.. 850-1,000
Serenade, #85/0, 4 3/4" h., Trademark 3.......... 200
She Loves Me, She Loves Me Not!, #174, 4 1/4" h., Trademark 6 225
Shining Light, #358, 2 3/4" h., Trademark 5 100
Sing Along (Auf los geht's los), #433, 4 1/2" h., Trademark 6 315
Sister, #98/2/0, 4 3/4" h., Trademark 6 155
Sleep Tight (Schlaf gut), #424, 4 3/4" h., Trademark 6.. 240
Soloist, #135, 4 3/4" h., Trademark 2............... 325
Sound of the Trumpet, #457, 3" h., Trademark 6.. 110

Spring Dance, #353/0, 5 1/2" h., Trademark 6 365

Star Gazer

Star Gazer, #132, 4 3/4" h., Trademark 3 (ILLUS.).. 350
Storybook Time (Marchenstude), #458, 5" h., First Issue 1992............................. 445
Street Singer, #131, 5 1/2" h., Trademark 3..... 325
Supreme Protection, #364, 9 1/4" h., 1984, "1909-1984, In Celebration of the 75th Anniversary of the Birth of Sister M.I. Hummel" 375
Sweet Greetings, #352, 4 1/4" h., Trademark 6 200
Telling Her Secret, #196/0, 5 1/4" h., Trademark 5 365
To Market, #49/3/0, 4" h., Trademark 1 500-650
To Market, 6 1/4" h., Trademark 1 1,400-1,700
Trumpet Boy, #97, 4 3/4" h., Trademark 6 145
Two Hands, One Treat (Rechts oder links?), #493, 4" h., 1991-99, M.I. Hummel Club... 125
Umbrella Boy, #152, 8" h., Trademark 2 2,400-2,900
Umbrella Girl, #152/B, 8" h., Trademark 2 2,200-2,700
Valentine Gift, #387, 5 3/4" h., 1972, exclusive special edition No. 1 for members of the Goebel Collectors' Club 575
Village Boy, #51/3/0, 4" h., Trademark 1 .. 350-450
Visiting an Invalid, #382, 5" h., Trademark 4 1,000-1,500
Volunteers, #50/0, 5 1/2" h., Trademark 3 455-480
Waiter, #154/0, 6" h., Trademark 2 375-475
Wash Day, #321, 5 3/4" h., Trademark 3 750-1,000
Wayside Devotion, #28/III, 8 3/4" h., Trademark 2................................... 1,000-1,200
We Congratulate, #220/2/0, 4" h., Trademark 2 475-575
What Now?, #422, 5 3/4" h., 1983, exclusive special edition No. 7 for members of the Goebel Collectors' Club 375
Whitsuntide, #163, 6 1/2" h., Trademark 6....... 325
Whitsuntide, #163, 7 1/4" h., Trademark 1 1,000-1,200
Worship, #84, 5" h., Trademark 1 475-625

Ironstone

The first successful ironstone was patented in 1813 by C.J. Mason in England. The body contains iron slag incorporated with the clay. Other potters imitated Mason's ware, and today much

*hard, thick ware is lumped under the term iron-
stone. Earlier it was called by various names,
including graniteware. Both plain white and decorated wares were made throughout the 19th century. Tea Leaf Lustre ironstone was made by
several firms.*

General

Gaudy Ironstone Footed Bowl

Bowl, 7 1/2" d., 4" h., wide bowl on deep
flaring base, gaudy Amherst Japan patt.,
large orange flowers & vining green
leaves on a white ground w/cobalt blue &
gold trim, England, 19th c. (ILLUS.) **$175-225**

Cabinet plates, each w/a scrolling gilt floral
border w/alternating cartouches of birds
& flowers, centered by a coat-of-arms,
Ashworth, England, ca. 1875, set of 8
(normal surface scratches) **365**

Dessert service: 10 5/8" l. shaped dish,
5 3/4" h. open compote, four 10" l. leaf-
shaped dishes & fourteen 9 1/4" d.
plates; Imari-style designs w/shaped
edges & deep green borders, Mason's,
mid-19th c., the set **3,680**

Mug, Gothic patt., all-white, ca. 1840s,
James Edwards **120-130**

Pitcher, 9 3/4" h., footed wide squatty bulbous body molded w/wide ribs & tapering
to a wide mouth w/arched spout, high
arched C-scroll handle, transfer decoration of birds in flowering trees & foliage
w/polychrome enamel, mark of Ashworth
Brow., England, ca. 1890 .... **303**

Plate, 8" d., twelve-sided, "gaudy" Bittersweet patt. w/underglaze flow blue &
copper luster, impressed "Real Iron-
stone" (light stains) **83**

Plate, 8 1/2" d., "gaudy" decoration, vintage
grape vine design painted in underglaze-
blue, black, ochre & two shades of green
(wear, crazing) **110**

Plate, 8 3/4" w., "gaudy" Strawberry patt.,
paneled shape w/underglaze-blue
trimmed w/red, pink, green & copper lus-
tre, impressed mark, mid-19th c. **138**

Plate, 9 1/2" d., Bordered Hyacinth/Lily
shape, all-white, ca. 1860, W. & E. Corn... **50-65**

Plate, 9 5/8" d., "gaudy" Blackberry patt.,
underglaze-blue & black trimmed w/red,
yellow & copper lustre, impressed "E.
Walley - Niagara Shape," 1850s **193**

Plate, 10 1/4" d., twelve-sided "gaudy" style
w/strawberries, pink flowers & under-
glaze flow blue leaves................................... **248**

Plates, 8 1/2" d., decorated w/floral motif in
blue & rust, marked "Ashworth Brothers
Hanley," England, ca. 1890, set of 9 .... **134**

Plates, 10 1/2" d., scalloped flanged rim,
overall Imari-style transfer decoration in
polychrome trimmed w/gold, mid-19th c.,
pr. **303**

Platter, 13 1/2" l., octagonal, "gaudy"
Strawberry patt., underglaze-blue w/red,
pink & green enamel & luster trim, wear,
stains & some enamel flaking........................ **770**

Platter, 11 3/8 x 14 1/8", rectangular, romantic transfer scene of a lakeside cabin
w/boaters, marked "Cat, Albion" & "Turn-
bull, Stepney," light blue, mid-19th c. **121**

Platter, rectangular, 16" l., Rolling Star
shape, all-white, James Edwards **90-100**

Platter, 18 1/2" l., Indiana patt., ca. 1880,
Wedgwood... **196**

Platter, 21 1/4" l., oval w/flanged rim, the
center transfer-printed w/a large landscape scene of a dog holding a stick on
the bank of a river w/figures rowing a
boat, the river flanked by trees & a country house in the distance, wide floral border, blue & white, back w/printed mark of
a ribbon-tied banner inscribed "British
Views," mid-19th c.................................... **1,265**

Platters, 8 1/4 x 10 1/2" & 10 1/2 x 13 1/4",
oval, each decorated w/a scrolling gilt floral border w/alternating cartouches of
birds & flowers, centered by a coat-of-
arms, Ashworth, England, ca. 1875, pr.
(normal surface scratches) **300**

Relish dish, 1851 Shell shape, all-
white, ca. 1851, T. & R. Boote.................. **90-100**

Relish dish, plain, oval w/two tab handles,
all-white, ca. 1870s, Wood, Son & Co. **20-30**

Sauce tureen, cov., oblong form, decorated
in color w/the Japanese Garden patt.,
molded butterfly handles & finial, En-
gland, 19th c., 5 3/4" h.................................. **173**

Soap box, cover & liner, President shape,
all-white, John Edwards, 3 pcs............... **120-130**

Soup plate, flanged paneled rim, Paradise
patt., purple floral transfer design w/poly-
chrome trim, mid-19th c., 10 1/2" w.................. **83**

Soup tureen, cover, ladle & underplate,
Stafford shape, all-white, ca. 1854, S. Al-
cock & Co., 4 pcs. **750-800**

Teapot, cov., "gaudy" strawberry design,
paneled body w/a domed cover w/blos-
som finial, decorated w/blue flowers, red
& green strawberries & gilt trim, ca. 1850,
9 3/4" h. (nick) **2,300**

Teapot, cov., tall tapering paneled form
w/angled handle & inset high domed cover w/floret finial, "gaudy" Strawberry patt.
w/large blossoms highlighted w/flowing
blue & copper lustre, mid-19th c., 9" h.
(minor flake on spout, reglued finial) **1,375**

Wash bowl & pitcher, "Tudor" patt., transfer-printed overall w/stylized floral medallions, branches & berries in lilac on an
ivory ground, William Brownfield & Sons,

1871-91, bowl 15" d., overall 10" h., 2 pcs...... **287**

Tea Leaf Ironstone

Bacon rasher, rectangular, Alfred Meakin......... **25**
Bacon rasher, rectangular, Alfred Meakin (very slight wear).. **35**
Baker, rectangular, Victory patt., Edwards, 7 x 9".. **50**
Boston egg cup, Alfred Meakin (mild crazing).. **250**
Bowl, 10" d., melon-ribbed shape, Grindley (moderate wear)....................................... **65**
Brush vase, Cable patt., Anthony Shaw.......... **125**
Butter dish, cover & drainer, Chelsea patt., Alfred Meakin, the set (drain hole roughness).. **170**
Butter dish, cover & drainer, Peerless (Feather) patt., Edwards (chip under base)... **125**
Butter dish, cover & insert, Fish Hook patt., Alfred Meakin **110**
Butter dish, cover & insert, Iona patt., gold motif, Bishop & Stonier, 3 pcs. **70**
Cake plate, Basketweave patt., Anthony Shaw (small under rim chip) **500**

Meakin Brocade Pattern Cake Plate

Cake plate, Brocade patt., Alfred Meakin (ILLUS.).. **155**
Cake plate, Bullet variant patt., Anthony Shaw.. **325**
Cake plate, Chelsea patt., Alfred Meakin.......... **190**
Cake plate, Fishhook patt., Alfred Meakin **45**
Cake plate, Maidenhair Fern patt., Wilkinson... **300**
Cake plate, squared shape w/angled handles, Red Cliff, ca. 1960s **40**
Cake stand, low footed, square w/angled rim handles, Red Cliff, ca. 1970.......................... **40**
Chamber pot, cov., Cable patt., Anthony Shaw... **170**
Chamber pot, cov., Crewel patt., Alfred Meakin (potting flaw, small lid flake).............. **375**
Chamber pot, cov., Lily of the Valley patt., Anthony Shaw... **600**
Coffeepot, cov., Bamboo patt., Alfred Meakin.. **100**

Adams Empress Pattern Coffeepot

Coffeepot, cov., Empress patt., Micratex by Adams, ca. 1960 (ILLUS.).............................. **270**
Coffeepot, cov., Square Ridged patt., Red Cliff, ca. 1960s **40**
Compote, open, Peerless (Feather) patt., Edwards (mild crazing, tiny chip under rim)... **525**
Compote, open, scalloped bowl, pedestal base, Wilkinson (minor pit marks)................... **325**
Compote, open, square top, Iona patt., Powell & Bishop, gold lustre **110**
Creamer, Bamboo patt., Alfred Meakin, 5" h.. **80**
Creamer, Basketweave patt., Anthony Shaw.. **325**
Creamer, Cable patt., Anthony Shaw **130**
Creamer, Cable patt., Anthony Shaw, 5" h......... **90**
Creamer, Chelsea patt., Alfred Meakin, 5" h. (slight rim lustre wear)........................... **120**
Creamer, Fig Cousin patt., Davenport, pink lustre trim, 5 3/8" h. (mild crazing)................. **525**
Creamer, Ginger Jar Round patt., Elsmore & Forster (some wear, tiny rim flakes).......... **185**
Creamer, Iona patt., Powell & Bishop, gold lustre (mild wear).. **85**
Creamer, LeNoir mark, gold motif, Homer Laughlin, ca. 1930s-40s................................ **130**
Creamer, Lily of the Valley patt., Anthony Shaw, 6 1/2" h.. **350**
Creamer, plain round shape, Alfred Meakin...... **110**
Creamer, Square Ridged patt., Red Cliff, ca. 1970, 5" h.. **60**
Creamer & cov. sugar bowl, Simple Square patt., beaded handle, East End Pottery, the pair (slight fading) **80**
Cup & saucer, handled, Basketweave patt., Anthony Shaw.. **90**
Cup & saucer, handled, Chelsea patt., Alfred Meakin (slight crazing).............................. **60**
Cup & saucer, handled, Lily of the Valley patt., Anthony Shaw, the set.......................... **55**
Cup, saucer & plate, child's, East End Pottery, the group (mild lustre wear)................... **250**

Anthony Shaw Tea Leaf Cuspidor

Cuspidor, mask handles, Anthony Shaw (ILLUS.).. 500
Demitasse cup & saucer, Empress patt., Micratex by Adams, ca. 1960s 35
Donut stand, high stand, squared scalloped rim, Square Ridged patt., Mellor Taylor.. 500
Doughnut stand, square, Red Cliff, ca. 1970.. 85
Egg cup, Empress patt., Micratex by Adams, ca. 1960.. 170
Gravy boat, Basketweave patt., Anthony Shaw.. 265
Gravy boat, Chinese patt., Anthony Shaw 140
Gravy boat, Lily of the Valley patt., Anthony Shaw... 220
Gravy boat, Pagoda patt., T. Burgess.............. 110
Gravy boat, Squared Ridged patt., Wedgwood 25
Gravy boat w/fixed undertray, Empress patt., Micratex by Adams, ca. 1960 160
Mug, cylindrical, Ruth Sayers decoration, ca. 1980s...................................... 80
Mug, Lily-of-the-Valley patt., Anthony Shaw..... 155
Mug, Maidenhair Fern patt., Wilkinson (professional rim repair).. 425
Pancake dish, cov., round, Empress patt., Micratex by Adams, ca. 1960 250
Pickle dish, Maidenhair Fern patt., Wilkinson (very minor spotting)................................ 120

Edge Malkin Polonaise Pitcher

Pitcher, 6" h., Polonaise patt., Edge Malkin, some wear, professional repair (ILLUS.)......... 80

Meakin Bamboo Tea Leaf Pitcher

Pitcher, 7" h., Bamboo patt., Alfred Meakin (ILLUS.).. 170
Pitcher, 7 1/2" h., Basketweave patt., Anthony Shaw.. 275
Pitcher, 7 1/2" h., Chinese patt. Anthony Shaw... 325
Pitcher, 7 3/4" h., Bamboo patt., Alfred Meakin... 110
Pitcher, 8" h., Cable patt., Anthony Shaw (circle of light discoloration) 210
Pitcher, 8" h., Iona patt., gold motif, Powell & Bishop... 60
Pitcher, 8" h., Simple Square patt., Burgess...... 275
Pitcher, 8 1/2" h., Bamboo patt., Alfred Meakin` 250
Pitcher, 8 5/8" h., lustre band trim, Grape Octagon shape, Livesley & Powell 85

Shaw Chinese Pattern Pitcher

Pitcher, 8 3/4" h., Chinese patt., Anthony Shaw, tiny base rim nick (ILLUS.)................... 310

Davenport Rondeau Pattern Pitcher

Pitcher, 9 1/2 h., Rondeau patt., lustre band at neck, Davenport (ILLUS.) 300
Pitcher, 10" h., water-type, Chelsea patt., Johnson Bros., 3 1/2 qt. 425
Pitcher, hot water-type, Cable patt., Furnival 900
Platter, 9 x 12", oval, Hanging Leaves patt., Anthony Shaw (lustre wear) 50
Platter, 12 x 17" oval, Brocade patt., Alfred Meakin (minor scratches) 70
Relish dish, mitten-shaped, Gentle Square patt., T. Furnival 165
Relish dish, mitten-shaped, Grenade patt., Burgess 425
Relish dish, oval, Cable patt., Anthony Shaw 90
Relish dish, Square Ridged (Hearts) patt., Mellor Taylor (underglaze potting flaw) 225
Sauce dish, Lily of the Valley patt., Anthony Shaw 30
Sauce tray, rectangular, Red Cliff, ca. 1970 35
Sauce tureen, cover & undertray, Cable patt., Anthony Shaw, 3 pcs. 125
Sauce tureen, cover, undertray & ladle, Lion's Head patt., Mellor Taylor, the set 250
Sauce tureen, cover, undertray & ladle, Victory patt., Edwards, the set (chip inside rim) 350
Shaving mug, Chinese patt., Anthony Shaw 120
Shaving mug, Gentle Square patt., rounded shape, T. Furnival 1,600
Shaving mug, Niagara Fan patt., Anthony Shaw 750
Soap dish, slab-type, Grindley (mild wear) 180
Soup plate, Wedgwood & Co., 9" d. 25
Soup tureen, cover, ladle & undertray, Square Ridged patt., Red Cliff, ca. 1970, the set 175
Soup tureen, cover & undertray, Cable patt., T. Furnival, the set 325
Soup tureen, cover, undertray & ladle, Square Ridged patt., Red Cliff, ca. 1970, the set 170
Spoon holder, oblong horizontal form w/loop end handles, decorated by Cumbow, ca. 1950s 170
Sugar bowl, cov., Bamboo patt., Alfred Meakin 50

Basketweave Sugar Bowl

Sugar bowl, cov., Basketweave patt., Anthony Shaw, minor inner rim nicks (ILLUS.) 160

Johnson Bros. Chelsea Sugar Bowl

Sugar bowl, cov., Chelsea patt., Johnson Bros., medium crazing (ILLUS.) 50
Sugar bowl, cov., child's, East End Pottery (mild wear) 180

Fish Hook Sugar Bowl by Meakin

Sugar bowl, cov., Fish Hook patt., Alfred Meakin (ILLUS.) 55

Sugar bowl, cov., Square Ridged patt., Red Cliff, ca. 1970 40

Tea set: cov. coffeepot, cov. sugar bowl & creamer; Gothic patt., decorated by Cumbow for the Henry Ford Museum, ca. 1950s, the set 185

Tea set: cov. teapot, cov. sugar bowl & creamer; Chinese patt., Red Cliff, ca. 1970, 3 pcs. 500

Teapot, cov., Cable patt., Cochrane, gold lustre band 50

Toothbrush holder, Bamboo patt., cylindrical w/scalloped top, Alfred Meakin (slight wear) 130

Toothbrush holder, Chelsea patt., ovoid shape, Alfred Meakin (professional rim repair) 325

Toothbrush holder, cylindrical w/flared mouth, Chelsea patt., Powell & Bishop, gold lustre 200

Tray, rectangular, Peerless (Feather) patt., Edwards, 6 5/8 x 8" 90

Vegetable dish, cov., Chelsea patt., Alfred Meakin 100

Vegetable dish, cov., Simple Square patt., Wedgwood (tiny finial chip) 70

Vegetable dish, cov., Square Ridged (Hearts) patt., Mellor Taylor 90

Vegetable dish, cov., Square Ridged patt., Mellor, Taylor & Co., 12" l. 70

Vegetable dish, cov., Sunburst patt., Wilkinson 60

Wash bowl, Peerless (Feather) patt., Edwards 300

Wash bowl & pitcher set, Cable patt., Anthony Shaw, 2 pcs. 325

Daisy 'n Chain Pitcher & Bowl Set

Wash bowl & pitcher set, Daisy 'n Chain patt., Wilkinson, mild discoloration & crazing, the set (ILLUS.) 245

Wash bowl & pitcher set, Square Ridged patt., Wedgwood & Co., pr. (small hairline in pitcher lip) 225

Davenport Fig Cousin Wash Pitcher

Wash pitcher, Fig Cousin patt., Davenport, pink lustre trim, professional handle repair (ILLUS.) 270

Wash pitcher, Maidenhair Fern patt., Wilkinson, 9 1/2" h. 950

Waste bowl, child's, East End Pottery 350

Waste bowl, Ginger Jar Round patt., Elsmore & Forster 60

Waste bowl, Lily of the Valley patt., Anthony Shaw 220

Waste jar, cov., Cable patt., Anthony Shaw (professional repair on lid) 5,600

Hawthorn Master Waster Jar

Waste jar & insert, Hawthorn patt., Wilkinson, professional top edge repair (ILLUS.) 600

Meakin Panelled Waste Jar

Waste jar & insert, twelve-paneled shape, Alfred Meakin, glaze crack, slight interior discoloration (ILLUS.) **1,200**

Tea Leaf Variants

Brush box, cov., Morning Glory patt., Portland shape, Elsmore & Forster **2,100**

Brush box, cov., oblong, Lily of the Valley shape, lustre band trim, Anthony Shaw (rim roughness) **500**

Brush box, cov., oblong, New York shape, lustre band trim, Clementson **425**

Butter dish, cover & insert, Pinwheel patt., Gothic shape, unmarked **1,400**

Cake plate, copper lustre & cobalt blue trim, Lafayette shape, J. Clementson (slight handle roughness) **650**

Cake plate, Quartered Rose shape, plumes & pinstripes trim, J. Furnival **300**

Chamber pot, cov., New York shape, lustre band trim, Clementson **300**

Coffeepot, cov., lustre scallop decoration, Wrapped Sydenham shape, E. Walley **500**

Cinquefoil - Panelled Grape Creamer

Creamer, Cinquefoil patt., Panelled Grape shape, J. Furnival (ILLUS.) **450**

Creamer, Gothic shape, lustre band trim, Red Cliff, ca. 1970... **30**

Creamer, green Reverse Teaberry patt., Elsmore & Forster (minor professional repair)... **350**

Creamer, lustre band trim, Gothic shape, Livesley Powell & Co. (minor wear)............... **110**

Creamer, Pinwheel patt., Gothic III shape........ **250**

Creamer, Teaberry patt., New York shape, Clementson (rim flake) **400**

Cup, handled, child's, Teaberry patt., Prairie shape, Clementson (small rim flake)............. **175**

Cup, handleless, Morning Glory patt., Ceres shape, Elsmore & Forster **130**

Cup & saucer, handled, Ceres shape, lustre trim, Elsmore & Forster, the set.................. **50**

Cup & saucer, handled, child's, Teaberry patt., Clementson Bros. (slight crazing on cup)... **350**

Cup & saucer, handleless, lustre trim, Ceres shape, Elsmore & Forster..................... **55**

Cup & saucer, handleless, Pinwheel patt., Ring 'o Hearts patt. (fine crazing) **70**

Egg cup, Cloverleaf patt. in gold lustre **35**

Gravy boat, lustre band trim, Grand Loop shape, J. Clementson..................................... **350**

Lustre-trimmed Hen on Nest Dish

Hen on nest covered dish, lustre trim, American (ILLUS.)... **160**

Rare Teaberry Prairie Shape Mug

Mug, Teaberry patt., Prairie shape, Clementson, small bull's-eye inside, some rim wear (ILLUS.)... **800**

Pitcher, 7" h., Pinwheel patt., Gothic shape (slight rim roughness, small handle chip)...... **150**

Pitcher, 9 1/2" h., rounded shape, Teaberry
patt., Clementson (spiders on bottom) 200
Pitcher, 8" h., Teaberry patt., Full Panelled
Gothic shape (stress crack at lower han-
dle end) 225
Pitcher, 9" h., New York shape, lustre band
trim, Clementson 300
Pitcher, 9" h., Teaberry patt., Full Panelled
Gothic shape 300
Pitcher, 9 1/2" h., Teaberry patt., Chinese
shape, J. Clementson 800
Pitcher, 9 1/2" h., Teaberry patt., New York
shape, Clementson (some slight wear) 375
Plate, 10" w., Thistle & Berry patt., Gothic
shape, E. Walley 100
Platter, 9 x 11 3/4", lustre band trim, Grape
Octagon shape, E. Walley 45
Platter, 14 x 20", rectangular, Pre-Teaf Leaf
design, E. Walley (edge wear) 240
Relish dish, leaf-shaped, Columbia shape,
lustre trim, Livesley & Powell 200
Relish dish, mitten-shape, lustre trim,
Ceres shape, Elsmore & Forster (tiny flea
bite) 240
Relish dish, mitten-shape, Teaberry patt.,
Elegance shape, Clementson Bros. 625

Tobacco Leaf - Fanfare Soap Dish

Soap dish, cover & drainer, Tobacco Leaf
patt., Fanfare shape, Elsmore & Forster,
light crazing, the set (ILLUS.) 550
Sugar bowl, cov., Cinquefoil patt., Panelled
Grape shape, J. Furnival 175

Ceres Lustre-trimmed Sugar Bowl

Sugar bowl, cov., copper lustre trim, Ceres
shape, Elsmore & Forster (ILLUS.) 250
Sugar bowl, cov., Teaberry patt., Elegance
shape, Clementson 275

Cinquefoil - Panelled Grape Teapot

Teapot, cov., Cinquefoil patt., Panelled
Grape shape, J. Furnival (ILLUS.) 275
Teapot, cov., Morning Glory patt., Portland
shape, Elsmore & Forster 200
Teapot, cov., Pomegranate patt., Niagara
shape, E. Walley (professional lid edge
repair) 200

Reverse Teaberry - Portland Teapot

Teapot, cov., Reverse Teaberry patt., Portland shape, Elsmore & Forster (ILLUS.) 375
Teapot, cov., Teaberry patt., New York
shape, Clementson (small inside rim
chip) 225

Vegetable dish, cov., Gothic (octagonal) shape, lustre band trim **100**

Wash bowl & pitcher set, Gothic shape, lustre band trim, E. Walley, the set (small blemish at top of handle) **325**

New York Shape Wash Bowl & Pitcher

Wash bowl & pitcher set, New York shape, lustre band trim, Clementson, minor wear, hairline in bowl, the set (ILLUS.) **250**

Waste bowl, lustre band & dot trim, Laurel Wreath patt., Elsmore & Forster.................... **375**

Tobacco Leaf - Fanfare Waste Bowl

Waste bowl, Tobacco Leaf patt., Fanfare shape, Elsmore & Forster (ILLUS.)............... **205**

Water pitcher, lustre band trim, Grape Octagon shape, Livesley Powell & Co., 11" h. **250**

Limoges

Limoges is the generic name for hard paste porcelain that was produced in one of the Limoges factories in the Limoges region of France during the 19th and 20th centuries. There are more than 400 different factory identification marks, the Haviland factory marks being some of the most familiar. Dinnerware was commonly decorated by the transfer method and then exported to the United States.

Decorative pieces were hand painted by a factory artist or were imported to the United States as blank pieces of porcelain. At the turn of the 20th century, thousands of undecorated Limoges blanks poured into the United States, where any of the more than 25,000 American porcelain painters decorated them. Today hand-painted decorative pieces are considered fine art. Limoges is not to be confused with American Limoges. (The series on collecting Limoges by Debby DeBay, Living With Limoges, Antique Limoges at Home and Collecting Limoges Boxes to Vases are excellent reference books.)

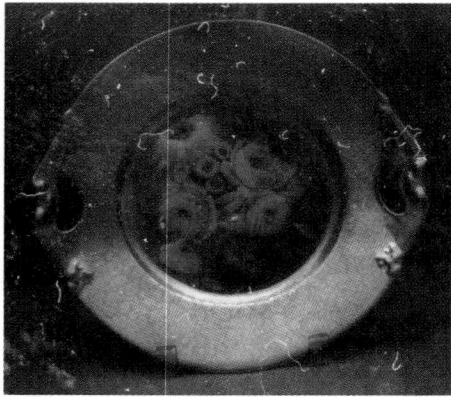

Limoges Cake Plate

Cake plate, h.p. in the Pickard factory, underglaze factory mark "B&C France," 11 1/2" d. (ILLUS.)... **$600**

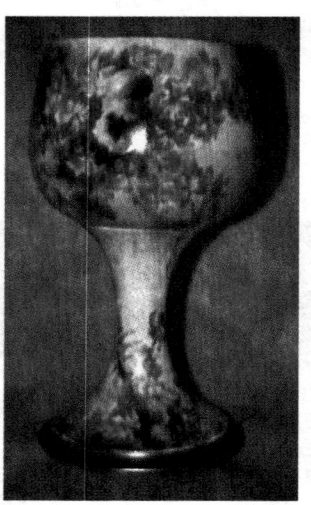

Limoges Chalice

Chalice, h.p. violets, underglaze factory mark "J.P.L. France" (Jean Pouyat), 10 1/2" h. (ILLUS.)... **700**

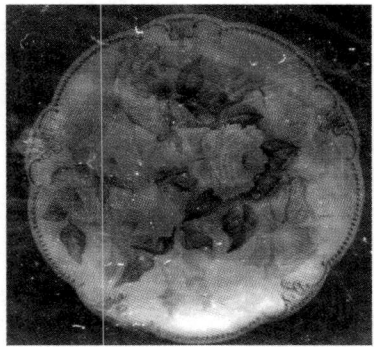

Limoges Charger with Roses

Charger, h.p. all over w/light roses, underglaze factory mark in green "AK [over] D
France," 15" d. (ILLUS.)................................ **1,000**

Limoges Chocolate Set

Chocolate set: 10 1/2" pot, six cups &
saucers; h.p. & signed by factory artist
"Magne," underglaze factory mark in
green "T&V Limoges France," decorating
factory mark "All Over Hand Painted" in
red banner, the set (ILLUS.)....................... **3,500**

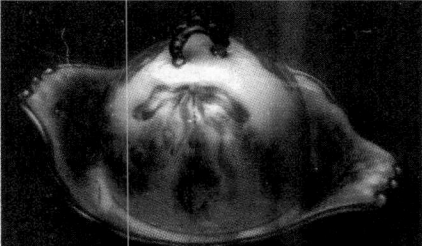

Limoges Domed Cheese Dish

Cheese dish, cov., rare domed style, h.p.,
underglaze factory mark in green "J.P.L
France," 7" h. (ILLUS.)................................... **400**

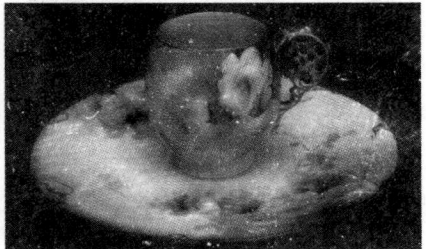

Large Limoges Cup & Saucer

Cup & saucer, tea/toast, underglaze factory
mark in green "T&V Limoges," 9" d.
(ILLUS.).. **200**

Large Dinner Set of Limoges China

Dinner service: composed of 39 dinner plates, 22 salad plates, six soup plates, a footed compote, a
low footed compote, a two-handled cov. sugar tureen on stand, four two-handled elliptical relish
dishes, two low footed round pastry stands, two nested circular platters, two nested oval platters, a
large footed round bowl, a cov. handled vegetable tureen, a cov. handled soup tureen, a double-
lipped gravy boat on stand & a creamer; in the "Meadow Flowers" patt., retailed by P. Cellerin, Paris,
late 19th c., 88 pcs. (ILLUS., above).. **633**

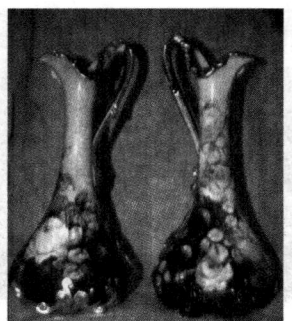

Rare Pair of Limoges Ewers

Ewers, h.p. by unknown amateur artist, underglaze factory mark in green "W.G.&Co.," rare pair, 15 1/4" h., pr. (ILLUS.).. **2,500**

Limoges Ice Cream Set

Ice cream set: serving dish & 12 individual dishes in original presentation case; cobalt & gold, two Haviland marks, ca. 1888-1896, the set (ILLUS.)........................ **3,500**

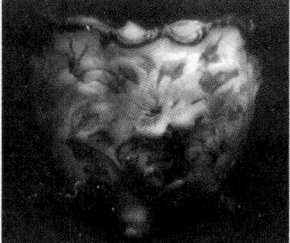

Limoges Jardiniere, 1897

Jardiniere, footed, h.p. & artist signed "H.E. Page," dated 1897, underglaze factory mark in green "Limoges France" w/an-

chor (probably A. Lanternier), 10" h. (ILLUS.).. **3,000**

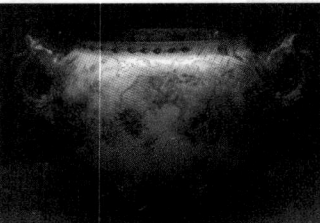

Limoges Jardiniere with Cherubs

Jardiniere, footed, ornate handles, cherub decoration, underglaze factory mark in green "D&Co." (R. Délinieres), 11" h. (ILLUS.).. **3,000**

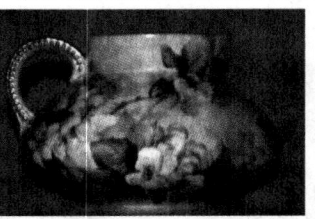

Small Limoges Cider Pitcher

Pitcher, cider, 7" h., h.p. by amateur artist "E. Miler," underglaze factory mark in green "J.P.L. France" (ILLUS.) **600**

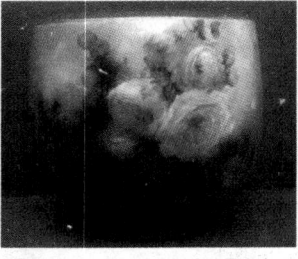

Limoges Planter with Roses

Planter, no base, h.p. roses, underglaze factory mark in green "W.G.&Co.," 14" h. (ILLUS.).. **2,500**

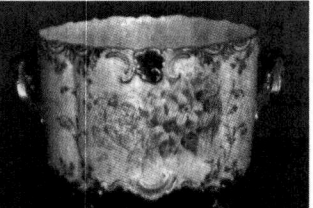

Unusual Limoges Planter

Planter, tall, unusual blank, underglaze factory mark in green "D&Co.," 9 x 9 1/2" (ILLUS.).. **2,000**

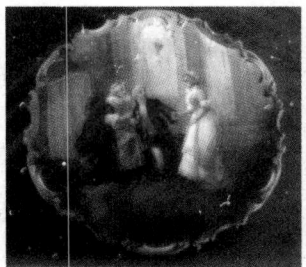

Limoges Hanging Plaque

Plaque, underglaze factory mark in green "Limoges France," overglaze decorating mark in red "Limoges France," artist signed "Dubois," pierced factory holes in back for hanging, 14" d. (ILLUS.) **2,500**

Limoges Plates

Plates, red & gold, underglaze factory mark in green "GDA," overglaze decorating mark in red "GDA" (Gérard Dufraisseix and Abbot), set of 12 (ILLUS. of four) **3,000**

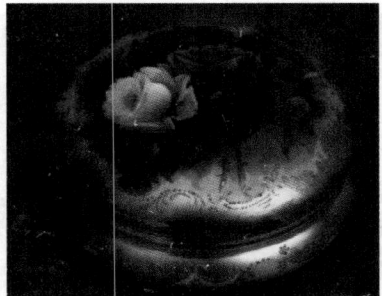

Limoges Powder Jar

Powder jar, cov., h.p. roses w/heavy gold, underglaze mark in green "T&V," 5 1/2 x 6 1/2" (ILLUS.) **550**

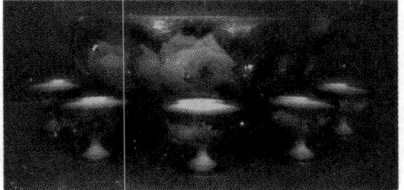

Limoges Punch Set

Punch set: bowl, 18" tray, cups; factory-decorated h.p. roses & heavy gilt, all factory artist signed "Aubin," underglaze factory mark in green "T&V Limoges France," factory decorating mark in grey "L.R.L.," the set (ILLUS.) **6,500**

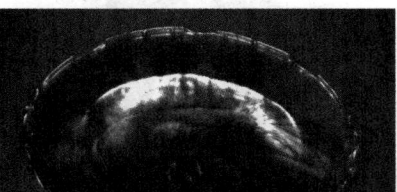

Limoges Seafood Serving Platter

Seafood set: platter, 14 1/2" gravy boat, plates; h.p. w/image of lobster & signed by factory artist "Dubois," "Limoges France" mark w/star, Flambeau studio decorating mark, rare, the set (ILLUS. of platter) **4,000**

Artist-signed Limoges Tea Set

Tea set: cov. teapot, cov. sugar, creamer, tray; unusual pot on pedestal w/roses, artist signed "C. Wynn" & dated 1901, the set (ILLUS.) **1,000**

Large Painting on Porcelain

Tile, h.p. porcelain, artist signed "Ann" & dated 1898, underglaze factory mark in green "T&V Limoges, France," 14 x 17" (ILLUS.) **2,500**

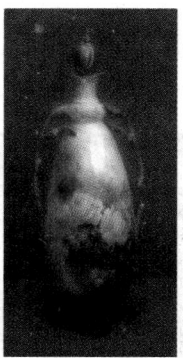

Limoges Urn with Stopper

Urn, w/original stopper, blank w/split handles, h.p., underglaze factory mark in green "W.G.&Co., Limoges, France," 14" h. (ILLUS.)... **2,000**

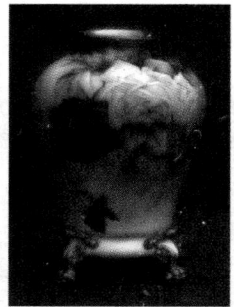

Limoges Vase with Separate Base

Vase, 12 1/2" h., w/separate original base, underglaze factory mark in green "J.P.L.," unusual (ILLUS.)............................ **2,500**

Limoges Vase with Image of Woman

Vase, 14" h., one of a pair h.p. in a factory in Chicago w/image of woman known to be a factory model in the early 20th c., underglaze mark in green "J.P.L. France," each (ILLUS.) **3,500**

Vases, 27" h., gently tapering cylindrical form w/thin flared rim, decorated w/a continuous hand-painted woodland scene w/lake & heron, on a round turned ebonized wood base, late 19th c., pr. (slight losses to paint).. **460**

Majolica

Majolica, a tin-enameled glazed pottery, has been produced for centuries. It originally took its name from the island of Majorca, a source of figuline (potter's clay). Subsequently it was widely produced in England, Europe and the United States. Etruscan majolica, now avidly sought, was made by Griffen, Smith & Hill, Phoenixville, Pa., in the last quarter of the 19th century. Most majolica advertised today is 19th or 20th century. Once scorned by most collectors, interest in this colorful ware so popular during the Victorian era has now revived and prices have risen dramatically in the past few years. Also see MINTON.

Etruscan

Butter pat, Begonia Leaf on Wicker patt. (minor rim nick) **$110**
Butter pat, Shell & Seaweed patt. w/seaweed.. **193**
Cake plate, Napkin patt., pink & white napkin on yellow ground w/cobalt blue border (handle repaired) **330**
Cake stand, Maple Leaves patt., white ground **138**
Cake stand, Morning Glory patt., rare cobalt blue morning glories, 8" d., 4" h. **385**
Cake stand, Morning Glory patt., yellow morning glories, 8" d., 4" h. **275**

Rare Etruscan Cheese Dish

Cheese dish, cov., Lily, Fern & Floral patt., high domed cover w/large green leaves & yellow blossoms w/a bud finial on a white ground, wide base flange w/further leaves, very minor hairline in cover, 11 1/4" d., 6" h. (ILLUS.) **1,925**
Cup & saucer, Shell & Seaweed patt. **220**
Mug, Oak Leaf & Acorn patt.............................. **121**
Mug, Water Lily patt.. **121**
Plate, 8" d., Bamboo patt.................................. **220**
Plate, 9" d., Classical Dog patt. **275**
Plate, 9" d., Maple Leaves patt., pink ground, great color... **303**

Platter, Geranium patt., large leaf w/twig handles.. **220**

Sauce dishes, shell-shaped, natural colors, pr. **358**

Syrup pitcher w/hinged pewter cap, Rose patt., w/butterfly spout.................................... **138**

Syrup pitcher w/hinged pewter cap, Sunflower patt., white ground **440**

General

Basket, Bird, Fan & Floral patt., oblong shape pinched in at the center & joined by an arched handle, pinks & greens w/cobalt blue trim, 11" l., 8" h. **413**

Box, cov., round, pale turquoise ground molded w/flying birds in dark green flanking a central brown twig handle, Joseph Holdcroft, England, 4 1/2" d. **715**

Bread tray, oblong, Napkin patt., woven napkin design in center in brown & yellow, yellow rope border band, rim embossed "Eat Thy Bread With Thankfulness," 15" l. **413**

Bread tray, oval, Begonia Leaf patt. w/mottled cobalt blue, green, pink & yellow leaves in center, brown border embossed "Eat Thy Bread With Thankfulness," 13" l. **303**

Cake stand, round w/low pedestal, Bird in Flight patt., large brown bird on a pale blue pebbled ground, pink blossoms around rim, Joseph Holdcroft, England, 9 1/2" d. **220**

Centerpiece, figural, a large wide shallow bowl w/green interior & wide rolled rim molded by a band of blue shells, raised on a leaf-cast pedestal supported by two winged cupids resting on a shell-molded round base, Hugo Lonitz & Co., Germany, late 19th c., 16" w., 20" h. (various professional repairs to high points)............. **2,475**

Large Thos. Forester Cheese Dish

Cheese dish, cov., high domed cover w/branch handle, molded overall w/birds, flowers, leaves & branches in white, yellow, brown & green, flanged rim on base, Thomas Forester & Sons, England, late 19th c., professional repair on base, 11" h. (ILLUS.).. **2,200**

Cheese dish, cov., wide cylindrical cover w/flat top, Pansy patt., yellow blossoms on green leafy vines around the sides

against a cobalt blue ground, George Jones, England, late 19th c., base 10 1/4" d., overall 7 1/2" h............................ **5,500**

Compote, open, 9" d., low pedestal, Floral & Pinwheel patt., deep red blossoms & brown stems on cream & pale green ground, Samuel Lear, England, late 19th c... **248**

Unique Elephant Majolica Dish

Dish, cov., figural, a model of a large grey elephant walking & carrying a black trainer & large brown & white howdah on its back, Hugo Lonitz & Co., Germany, late 19th c., 10" l., 9" h. (ILLUS.) **935**

Egg server, rounded basket-form frame decorated w/red blossoms & green leaves on a cream ground around the sides, holds six egg cups, S. Fielding & Co., England, late 19th c. (professional repair to base of egg cups) **468**

George Jones Game Dish

Game dish, cov., deep oval form, the base molded w/upright green leaves & ferns on a brown ground, yellow rope band around rim centered by a dead game bird in brown & yellow on green ferns on a brown ground, George Jones, England, 11" l. (ILLUS.).. **1,100**

Humidor, cov., figural, model of a large fat green frog wearing a red smoking jacket, Europe, late 19th c., 6 1/2" h. **468**

Jam pot, cov., cylindrical, Strawberry patt., molded green leaves & red berries around the sides, berry finial, Brownfield & Son, England, late 19th c. **143**

Rare George Jones Jardiniere

Jardiniere, footed bell-form bowl w/flared yellow rim, the sides in turquoise blue molded w/water lilies, cattails & a bird in shades of green, white, brown & black, George Jones, England, late 19th c., professional hairline repair, 17" d., 15 1/2" h. (ILLUS.).. **6,050**

Mug, Bird in Flight & Water Lily patt., green leaves w/brown & yellow bird on a cobalt blue ground, high relief, 4 1/4" h. **358**

Nut Serving Tray with Squirrel

Nut serving tray, wide, shallow, rounded tray w/large green leaves & brown twigs on a turquoise ground, a figural brown squirrel w/nut seated at the rim, George Jones, England, late 19th c., repair to tail, 10 1/2" w. (ILLUS.) **1,100**

Paperweight, slab-type, rectangular, relief-molded brown owl on branch against a pale green ground, Mayer, late 19th c. **138**

Pitcher, 6" h., Fish on Waves with Shell patt. **275**

Colorful Majolica Pitcher with Parrot

Pitcher, 6 1/2" h., 4" d., slightly tapering cylindrical body w/angled handle, molded w/narrow bands flanking a parrot-like bird on leafy branches, in mottled shades of brown, green, yellow & pink, late 19th c. (ILLUS.)...................................... **175-225**

Pitcher, 6 3/4" h., Stork in March patt., brown & white bird on pale blue ground w/cobalt blue rim & base bands, angled branch handle, George Jones, England.... **2,200**

Pitcher, 8 1/2" h., Ram patt., lavender top, great color... **303**

Pitcher, 9" h., Bird's Nest patt., branch handle, probably American-made (minor hairline) **440**

Pitcher w/hinged pewter cover, 9 1/2" h., Dogwood patt., mottled brown & green ground **385**

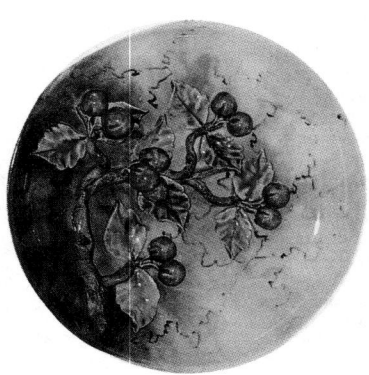

French Majolica Plaque with Cherries

Plaque, round, molded & applied in full-relief w/red cherries, green leaves & brown branches on a shaded brown to pale blue ground, France, late 19th c., 12 3/8" d. (ILLUS.).. **225-275**

Plate, 7 3/4" d., Strawberry patt., large green leaves w/pink blossoms & berries on a brown ground **154**

Plate, 8 3/4" d., Bellflower patt., pink & white blossoms & green leaves on a cobalt blue ground.. **248**

Plate, 9" d., Pineapple patt., George Jones, England, late 19th c. (very minor rim glaze nick)... **605**

Platter, 13" l., oval, molded flowers & berries on a pale blue ground around the sides, pink ribbon border & bow handles, mottled dark green center, George Jones, England (hairline) **1,980**

Salt dip, figural, large green & pink shell supported atop a green dolphin on an oval foot, 4 3/4" h.. **374**

Sauce dish, Strawberry patt., round, w/scalloped rim molded w/pink blossoms, green leaves on turquoise ground in sides, George Jones, England, 5" d.......... **440**

Strawberry server, Napkin & Strawberry patt., oblong, shallow dish molded w/a creamy napkin & green strawberry leaves, inset at each end, one holding the small pink w/green leaves creamer, the other the matching open sugar, George Jones, England, 15" l., the set **1,430**

Strawberry spoon, green w/pink blossom in bowl & on handle, George Jones, England, 7 1/2" l. **605**

Sweet meat dish, figural, modeled as a young girl seated on the side of a rowboat, a fishing net draped along the side, Europe, 19th c., 9" l., 7" h. **385**

Syrup pitcher w/hinged pewter cover, Floral & Basket patt., great color, 4 3/4" h. **385**

Tea set: cov. teapot, open sugar & creamer, water server, milk pitcher, tray & two cups & saucers; embossed stylized Oriental design of pink blossoms & green leaves among brown angular lines on a cream ground, brown bamboo-form handles, Brownhills Pottery Co., England, late 19th c., the set **440**

Teapot, cov., spherical body w/large applied green leaves & white blossoms on a cobalt blue ground, brown branch spout, figural brown monkey handle, George Jones, England, 9 1/4" l., 6" h. (repair to head of monkey, rim of cover & spout) **1,925**

Tray, rectangular w/rounded corners, Leaf patt., molded oak leaf & acorn end handles, mottled dark green, pink & yellow w/cobalt blue accents, 10" l. **303**

Very Rare Bear Umbrella Stand

Umbrella stand, figural, a model of a large standing brown bear snarling & holding a large wooden log bar, molded leafy branches forming the square rockwork base, Brownfield & Son, England, late 19th c., very rare, professional repair to oak leaves & feet, 34" h. (ILLUS.) **11,000**

Vase, 7" h., baluster-form body w/flaring rim, angled branch handles, brown ground molded w/large pink morning glory blossoms & green leafy vines, Brownfield & Son, England, late 19th c. **303**

Wall pockets, Palissy Ware, molded as brown branches of green oak leaves & acorns, each w/a model of a lizard on the front, Thomas Sergent, 12" l., pr. (one w/professional repair to rim, other w/repair to lizard's head) **2,530**

Mettlach

Ceramics with the name Mettlach were produced by Villeroy & Boch and other potteries in the Mettlach area of Germany. Villeroy and Boch's finest years of production are thought to be from about 1890 to 1910. Also see STEINS.

Mettlach Mark

Cracker jar, cov., wide, squatty, bulbous body w/a silver plate rim, flat cover w/turned finial & swing handle, mosaic decoration of narrow geometric bands in shades of dark blue, tan, brown & white above a wider base band w/stylized flowering branches, tan ground, No. 1332, 5" d. **$575**

Flowerpot, a narrow footring below the wide cylindrical body w/a slightly flared rim, the sides divided into panels etched w/color scenes of Cavaliers drinking, white lappet band around the rim, No. 2170, 6" h. **374**

Jardiniere, Art Nouveau design, low narrow oblong form w/rounded tapering sides raised on low brackets, the flat rim w/stepped ends, decorated w/an etched design of panels formed by brown lattice & bars against a tan ground w/clusters of green buds, No. 2980, 14" l., 5" h. **460**

Unique Mettlach Garniture Set

Mantel garniture: clock in urn & pair of matching side urns; the large baluster-form central urn w/a mosaic design of stylized floral & leaf panels in alternating cream w/green & tan & rust red w/tan, brown & green, the flared neck w/tan ground & floral swags, raised on a high gilt-metal plinth w/a scroll-cast footed base, gilt-metal serpent-form shoulder handles & a scalloped metal rim band & gadrooned domed cover w/leaf bud finial, a clock set into one side within a brass bezel, the matching shorter urns w/similar gilt-metal details, shorter urns 15 1/2", tallest urn 19" h., the set (ILLUS., above).. **3,565**

Plaque, Art Nouveau design, a large etched bust portrait of an Art Nouveau woman on the left sniffing large tan roses on dark green leafy stems, tan border band decorated w/dark green & rust red leaf devices, No. 2544, pierced to hang, 20" d. (ILLUS.).. **863**

Phanolith Plaque with Figures

Plaque, phanolith, a dark green ground decorated in white relief w/three seminude classical water nymphs & flying birds, No. 7043, pierced to hang, 21" d. (ILLUS.) **719**

Plaques, etched designs, each centered by a bust portrait of a Renaissance woman wearing a large feathered hat, in natural tones & dark blue, dark pink & white

Mettlach Woman & Roses Plaque

against a pale blue ground, the wide border band w/overall stylized scrolling leaves in brown, tan & blue on a dark blue ground, No. 1424 & 1425, pierced to hang, 15 1/2" d., facing pr. **1,035**

Tobacco jar, cov., barrel-shaped, an etched design w/repeating pairs of large herringbone panels in dark blue & dark red separated by horizontal & vertical white bands w/"Tabac" in black, four alternate white panels etched w/an outlined figure of a man smoking a pipe above another panel w/a dark blue, dark red & dotted black checkerboard design w/another white band w/"Tabac," domed cover w/checkerboard panels & white knob, very rare, No. 4504, 6 1/2" h. **719**

Mettlach Vase with Poppies

Vase, 7" h., bulbous ovoid body tapering to a bulbed neck w/narrow scalloped rim, a dark blue ground etched overall w/an Art Nouveau design w/clusters of large deep pink poppy blossoms & a narrow pale blue ribbon band, tiny pink leaf designs scattered around the sides & neck, No. 2434 (ILLUS.). **460**

Vase, 7" h., mosaic decoration on a brick red ground, a funnel foot w/dark blue band & leaf tips below the wide ovoid body decorated w/bands of tiny florets flanking the wide center band w/vertical almond-form devices w/scroll leaves in dark blue & stylized four-petal designs in tan & slate blue, short flaring neck w/band of tiny beads, No. 1573 .... **311**

Vase, 9" h., bulbous ovoid form w/a dark blue ground decorated in mosaic w/scattered pink & pale blue three-petal blossoms & tiny blue bead blossoms, a brick red neck band decorated w/a band of applied dark blue beads, No. 2868 .... **288**

Vase, 13 1/2" h., tall cylindrical body raised on small scroll legs, Oriental landscape scene, a dark brown matte ground molded in relief w/pairs of geese in white, brown & greyish blue on brown rockwork, tall golden brown bamboo stocks behind them & pale blue water in front of them, No. 1515 (one leg repaired) **719**

Vase, 16 1/2" h., Art Nouveau design, baluster-form body tapering to a tall cylindrical neck w/flared rim, slender serpentine handles from rim to shoulder, decorated

w/a glossy moss green glaze w/dark green handles & base bands, the neck & shoulder molded in low relief w/suspended fuchsia blossoms, No. 2731 .... **891**

Vases, 10" h., a low, round foot supporting a tall, squared body w/a short flaring neck, each side w/a large oblong mosaic panel filled w/arabesque entwined scrolls in white, light blue, green & gold w/a maroon almond-form central reserve, dark blue borders, No. 2032, pr. **1,093**

Minton

The Minton factory in England was established by Thomas Minton in 1793. The factory made earthenware, especially the blue-printed variety, and Thomas Minton is sometimes credited with the invention of the blue "Willow" pattern. For a time majolica and tiles were also an important part of production, but bone china soon became the principal ware. Mintons, Ltd., continues in operation today. Also see MAJOLICA.

Minton Marks

Bowl, majolica, deep, rounded, molded & ribbed yellow basketweave exterior w/a band of wide overlapping green leaves around the rim, turquoise interior, shape No. 582, date code for 1865, mint **$495**

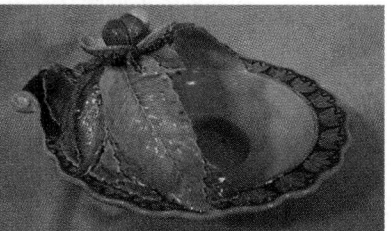

Unusual Minton Chestnut Server

Chestnut server, majolica, shell-form dish w/scalloped flanged rim molded w/green leaves on brown, large arching green & pink leaves & figural chestnut cover half the turquoise blue bowl, shape No. 494, date code for 1862, 9 1/2" w. (ILLUS.)....... **1,540**

Ewer, majolica, monumental piece, large figural handle of a mermaid w/braided hair & fish scale vest & tail reaching down & entwining w/the horns of a bold relief satyr's head, the large wide curved spout above a neck molded in a ruffled pink shell & green leaf design above the bulbous lower portion, which features a full-figure putto at the rim opposite the handle, large green garland bands divide the lower body into panels molded in white relief w/a classical woman & putti against a tan ground, short swirled brown pedestal on the round foot w/a yellow shell-molded edge band, date code for 1871, shape No. 1290, mint, overall 16" w., 21" h. **55,000**

Minton Majolica Garden Seat

Garden seat, majolica, large ovoid form w/a flaring, lightly ruffled top, cobalt blue w/a large turquoise blue ribbon & bow around the neck above a large suspended branch of pink & white flowers & green leaves, shape No. 2367, date code for 1881, 17" h. (ILLUS.) **2,750**

Humidor, cov., majolica, figural, a cylindrical tall coil of yellow rope forming the body, a large seated figure of a sailor drinking from a mug on the flat top, shape No. 716, 9" h. **2,200**

Jardiniere, majolica, large bulbous urn top w/a flaring cobalt blue neck, the turquoise sides molded w/two large bold-relief lion masks supporting green swags molded w/colorful fruit, nuts & wheat, floral rosettes w/pink ribbons & bows alternate w/the lion masks, on a pedestal molded w/green leaves above the round tur-

quoise foot w/a golden brown lappet band, date code for 1869, 15" d., 14 1/2" h. **3,300**

Salt dip, master size, majolica, model of a small tapering cylindrical basket in yellow w/a large square tab at one rim, turquoise interior, date code for 1872, 5" h. **193**

Salt dip, master size, majolica, oblong four-lobed form w/pink interior & cobalt blue exterior on a green foot, date code for 1862, 5" l., 2 1/2" h. **330**

Toby jugs, majolica, figural Barrister & Lady, stocky figures in colorful 18th c. attire, great detail, 11 1/2" h., pr. (minor professional rim repair) **2,750**

Nippon

"Nippon" is a term used to describe a wide range of porcelain wares produced in Japan from the late 19th century until about 1921. It was in 1891 that the United States implemented the McKinley Tariff Act, which required that all wares exported to the United States carry a marking indicating their country of origin. The Japanese chose to use "Nippon," their name for Japan. In 1921 the import laws were revised and the words "Made in" had to be added to the markings. Japan was also required to replace the "Nippon" with the English name "Japan" on all wares sent to the United States.

Many Japanese factories produced Nippon porcelain, much of it hand-painted with ornate floral or landscape decoration and heavy gold decoration, applied beading and slip-trailed designs referred to as "moriage." We indicate the specific marking used on a piece, when known, at the end of each listing. Be aware that a number of Nippon markings have been reproduced and used on new porcelain wares.

Important reference books on Nippon include: The Collector's Encyclopedia of Nippon Porcelain, Series One through Three, by Joan F. Van Patten (Collector Books, Paducah, Kentucky) and The Wonderful World of Nippon Porcelain, 1891-1921 by Kathy Wojciechowski (Schiffer Publishing, Ltd., Atglen, Pennsylvania).

Hand Painted Nippon Pieces

Various Nippon Ceramic Pieces

Bowl, squatty round body on short feet, slightly lobed flat rim, ornate C-scroll side handles, h.p. floral design in pale pinks & greens, w/moriage scrolling decoration on handles, feet, around base & at intervals on body, blue maple leaf mark, 7 1/2" d. (ILLUS. front row, far right w/other h.p. Nippon pieces, bottom previous page) **$115**

Bowl, 8 1/2" d., three-handled, decorated w/a scene of a sailing ship w/palm trees & ruins on the shore, green "M" in wreath mark **144**

Bowl, 10" d., low sides, three-footed, decorated w/large open roses, blue maple leaf mark **56**

Box, cov., squatty round form on footring, decorated around sides & rim of lid w/h.p. floral design in blue & pink, w/transfer portrait in center of lid, 4 1/2" d. (ILLUS. front row, second from right w/various Nippon pieces, top of page) **104**

Chocolate set: cov. pot & six cups & saucers; an Art Deco-style mold copied from R.S. Prussia wares, painted w/open roses, green "I&E" wreath mark, pot 8" h., the set **280**

Condensed milk container, cylindrical, decorated w/gilt scrolls & florals, green "M" in wreath mark, 5 1/2" h. **67**

Dresser tray & tumbler, h.p. Egyptian scene w/enameled rim, 2 pcs. **112**

Hand Painted Nippon Humidor

Nippon Scenic Chamberstick

Chamberstick, saucer-form base decorated w/scene of house by lake w/trees & mountains, natural colors, green "M" in wreath mark, 4 1/4" d., 2" h. (ILLUS.) .. **100-125**

Humidor, cov., cylindrical form, moriage decorated w/h.p. scene of white owl on branch, distant mountains in background, in browns & buffs, blue maple leaf mark, 6" h. (ILLUS.) **3,565**

Humidor, cov., squared form, decorated w/four scenic panels of sailboats, green "M" in wreath mark, 4 1/2" h............ 308

Mug, h.p. landscape scene w/embossed rim & handle w/raised enameling, green "M" in wreath mark, 5 1/2" h.................. 112

Nappy, souvenir, trefoil shape w/ornate gilt scroll decoration & h.p. pink roses framing scene of U.S. Capitol in center, gilt scroll ring handle at side, green maple leaf mark, rare, 6 1/2" w. (ILLUS. previous page front row, center w/various Nippon pieces) 115

Nut tray, molded in relief w/beechnuts painted in natural colors, green "M" in wreath mark, 8" l................................. 78

Pitcher, tankard, 13" h., tapering cylindrical form, slightly scalloped rim w/high arched spout, C-scroll handle, decorated w/h.p. pink roses, pale green leaves & gilt ferns on gilt-decorated cobalt ground (ILLUS. front row, far left w/other h.p. Nippon pieces, page 228) 460

Pitcher, tankard, 13 1/2" h., cylindrical shape on short squatty bulbous base, flaring to scalloped rim w/arched spout, D-form handle, decorated w/h.p. pink floral design in oval gilt medallion, w/gilt scrolling & bead decoration overall on body of pale aqua, cream, cobalt & deep reddish brown (ILLUS. back row, far right w/other h.p. Nippon pieces, page 228) 374

Plaque, oval, decorated w/scene of sailboat docked at waterside cottage h.p. in pastel shades, the rim w/border of stylized floral & leaf design, 10" l. (ILLUS. page 228 front row, center w/other h.p. Nippon pieces)... 316

Plaque, round, decorated w/relief molded scene of a squirrel w/nut set against background of trees & water in pastel shades of green, yellow & blue, 10 3/4" d. (ILLUS. back row, left w/various Nippon pieces, page 229)...................... 719

Tankard, cylindrical, finely painted gold-decorated rim & base, applied scroll handle, blue maple leaf mark, 13" h. (minor gold loss)... 345

Vase, 8 1/4" h., slightly waisted cylindrical form, w/h.p. scene of ships at sail in still waters against pastel ground & sky, decorated w/bands of scrolled moriage lace, enameled jewels & iridescent abalone applications, blue "M" in wreath mark........... 431

Vase, 8 1/2" h., slightly waisted cylindrical form, the body decorated w/h.p. pastoral scene & gilt floral designs, the shoulder w/horizontal panel h.p. w/pink & yellow enameled blossoms against deeper rose ground & gilt borders (ILLUS. back row, right w/various Nippon pieces, page 229)..... 230

Vase, 9" h., Art Deco form w/"coralene" decoration of lotus leaves & flowers, marked in magenta "KinRan - U.S. Patent Feb. 9, 1909" (minor loss to beading)....................... 661

Vase, 9 1/4" h., slightly ovoid form on footring, tapering shoulder w/cylindrical neck w/slightly flaring rim, the body decorated w/h.p. scene of lone traveler in pastoral setting, the shoulder & rim decorated w/stylized floral & geometric designs, two raised enamel handles (ILLUS. previous page front row, second from left w/various Nippon pieces).. 86

Vase, 9 1/2" h., tall six-sided form w/bamboo-style handles, the body w/panels of h.p. pastoral scenes against cobalt ground decorated w/ornate gilt scroll designs overall, indistinguishable mark (ILLUS. front row, second from right w/other h.p. Nippon pieces, page 228)......... 345

Vase, 10" h., baluster form, disk foot, cylindrical neck w/short flaring rim, decorated w/h.p. scene of palm trees on island w/ships at sea and mountains in the distance, the neck decorated w/band of scrolling floral enamel designs, green "M" in wreath mark (ILLUS. front row, far right w/various Nippon pieces, page 229).............. 173

Vase, 10 1/4" h., tapering cylindrical form on footring, w/ruffled flaring rim, the body decorated w/raised brickwork design in deep greens, rectangular panels around sides decorated w/h.p. scenes in pastel colors, narrow panels of moriage extending from top of body to rim at intervals (ILLUS. front row, far left w/various Nippon pieces, page 229)................................... 201

Vase with Ornate Gilt Decoration

Vase, 10 1/4" h., 5" d., baluster-form body raised on a scalloped flaring foot & tapering to a flaring pointed lobed rim, long slender S-scroll handles up the sides, decorated overall w/heavy gold stylized leaves & berries on vines, blue maple leaf mark (ILLUS.)....................................... 175

Vase, 12" h., ovoid form w/short neck & flaring ruffled rim, slightly scalloped base, open scroll handles holding ring bases, w/h.p. decoration of pink & rose flowers & green leaves against pastel ground decorated w/raised enameled gilt scroll designs, blue maple leaf mark (ILLUS. back row, center w/other h.p. Nippon pieces, page 228).. 2,530

Vase, 13" h., 7" d., finely painted landscape w/heavy etched gold decoration of flowers & striped band, probably studio decorated, green "M" in wreath mark..................... 489

Vase, 16" h., cylindrical form w/ring neck, overall decoration of h.p. flowers in shades of pink, green leaves & gilt raised leafy scrolls on dark green ground (ILLUS. back row, far left w/other h.p. Nippon pieces, page 228).............................. 460

Wall plaque, h.p. scene of palm trees & sailboats, pierced for hanging........................ **101**

Hand Painted Nippon Wine Jug

Wine jug, cov., bulbous base tapering to short neck & flared rim, decorated w/h.p. scene of owl on branch against blue sky w/white clouds, this decoration extending to lid, applied moriage decorated C-form handle, in asymmetrical woven split bamboo basket frame, green "M" in wreath mark, 8" h. (ILLUS.)..................................... **1,150**

Noritake

Noritake china, still in production in Japan, has been exported in large quantities to this country since early in the last century. Although the Noritake Company first registered in 1904, it did not use "Noritake" as part of its backstamp until 1918. Interest in Noritake has escalated as collectors now seek out pieces made between the "Nippon" era and World War II (1921-41). The Azalea pattern is also popular with collectors.

Noritake Mark

Ashtray, figural toucan, 3 1/4" h., 4 1/2" w..... **$530**
Ashtray, horse shoe-shaped **137**

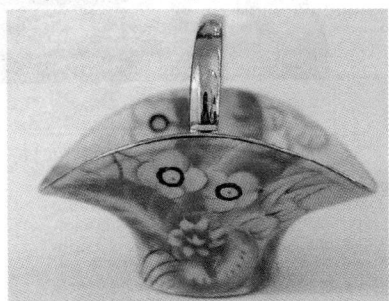

Peach Floral Motif Basket

Basket, short form w/extremely flaring sides, decorated inside & out in/floral motif in peach, pearl grey & black, silvered rim & center handle, 4 1/2" d., 6 1/2" h. (ILLUS.)... **188**
Berry set: master bowl & 6 sauce dishes; decal & h.p. purple orchids, green leaves & pods decoration on green ground, 7 pcs. **70**
Bowl, 6" h., Gemini-type **2,689**
Box, cov., in the form of a clown, 3 5/8" d., 5 1/2" h... **3,150**
Box, cov., in the form of an elephant on base, the howdah on its back making up the elaborate floral decorated box, beveled lid & knob, 2 1/4 x 5 1/8", 6 1/2" h...... **1,850**

Noritake Breakfast Set

Calendar Holder with Figural Rabbit

Breakfast set: cov. teapot, teacup, sugar, creamer, tray; tray w/ruffled sides & four depressions to hold teapot, cup & creamer, all w/yellow C-form handles & decorated w/pastoral scene of woman in ruffled yellow dress & wide brimmed yellow bonnet standing under tree & holding flowers, the cylindrical sugar w/scene of tree & flowers, all w/gilt line trim at rims, tray 8 1/2 x 10 1/2", the set (ILLUS., bottom of previous page) **293**

Calendar holder, narrow rectangular base w/an upright oblong holder at one end & a flattened figural rabbit at the other end, iridized orange & green w/stylized purple & blue blossoms, 5 1/4" l., 2" h. (ILLUS., top of page) **720**

Candlesticks, decorated w/an Art Deco lady, 7 1/2" h., pr... **1,775**

Chip & dip, cov., round, the attached plate & dip container & lid decorated w/blue ribbons around their rims, the plate & lid w/red, orange, pink, lavender & yellow flowers, the lid's handle in the form of a seated/kneeling black-haired woman in blue, overall 4 1/2" h., plate 9 1/2" d. (ILLUS., bottom of page) **945**

Covered Chip & Dip Server

Noritake Chocolate Pot

Chocolate pot, cov., decorated w/figure of black-haired girl in purple knee-length dress w/wide skirt, the hem decorated w/red flowers, a matching sash flowing out at each side, yellow-trimmed white petticoats showing where dress appears to be billowing in breeze, the waist decorated w/yellow & red flowers, a large green floppy-brimmed hat w/floral trim obscuring one eye, one hand reaching up toward hanging flowers in yellow, red & caramel w/green leaves, a purple bird flying by, all on caramel ground, the lid w/handle in the form of a perched bird in red, blue, brown, green & yellow, C-scroll side handle, 9" h. (ILLUS.) **650**

Figural Swan Cigarette Holder

Cigarette holder, footed, figural swan, orange lustre w/black neck & head, black outlining on wing feathers & tail, 3" w., 4 1/2" h. (ILLUS.) **156**

Condiment set in the form of three buildings of various sizes on 6 7/8" l. tray **367**

Creamer & Sugar Set

Creamer & sugar, the sugar container a round shallow form w/gilt scroll side handles, slight depression in center to hold creamer, the creamer a cylindrical form w/angled gilt trimmed handle & slightly arched spout, both pieces decorated in alternating black & white panels, the black w/white & gilt oval designs, the white w/stylized floral designs in deep red/orange, black & white, both pieces w/gilt trim, 5 1/2" d., the set (ILLUS.) **153**

Pierrot Covered Dish

Dish, cov., caramel colored bowl & lid, the lid w/embossed daisy-like flowers, the handle in the form of a seated black-haired masked Pierrot-type figure dressed in pearl-grey, black & white w/caramel ruff, holding one leg up to chest, 7" h., 7 1/8" d. (ILLUS.) **2,890**

Figurine, Arnold Palmer, 10" h. **168**

Humidor, cov., model of an owl w/head as cover, lustre finish, 7" h. **960**

Noritake Jam Server

Jam server, cov., three-legged round container on disk base, the lid w/opening just big enough for handle of serving spoon, in pink, deep orange & black w/green leaf decorations, orange knob handle on lid, white spoon, 4 1/4" w., 5 1/4" h., the set (ILLUS.) **203**

Decorated Noritake Jug

Jug, slender ovoid form w/cut-out handle at top & short cylindrical spout set in body at an angle, the top a deep cyan w/black line trim, the rest of the body a deep red ground decorated w/scene of an 18th-c. woman w/powdered hair & wearing a blue off-the-shoulder top & full white skirt holding a songbird on one outstretched finger, the birdcage open in front of her, all against a background of shade trees & arbor vitae, the foreground w/yellow roses, 3 1/2 x 4 1/4", 7 1/2" h. (ILLUS.) **325**
Lemon dish, center handle, Art Deco decoration **95**
Lemon dish, floral decoration, 6 1/2" d. **33**
Nut bowl, tri-lobed bowl w/figural squirrel seated at side eating nut, 7 1/2" w. **147**
Perfume nightlight, figural woman, 9 3/4" h. **3,785**
Pin tray, in the form of a reclining clown, 4 1/2" l. **960**

Pin Tray with Dog Decoration

Pin tray, round, mauve tray decorated w/applied image of seated dog in caramel & black, 2" h., 2 3/5" d. (ILLUS.) **65**

Noritake Plate

Plate, 6 1/4" d., caramel ground w/figure of woman wearing elaborate powdered coiffure or wig bedecked w/yellow, deep pink, mauve & apricot flowers w/green leaves & black ribbons, dressed in blue sleeveless gown w/full skirt trimmed in yellow, one hand fingering green bead necklace, the other holding a black mask (ILLUS.) **740**

Covered Potpourri Pot

Potpourri pot, cov., ovoid form, the flat lid white w/black line trim & black & white knob handle, the body decorated w/figure of Oriental woman in deep red kimono holding green flower-decorated fan in one hand, a sprig of cherry blossoms in the other, standing beneath branches of cherry trees in bloom, all against a caramel ground, 4" d., 5" h. (ILLUS.) **395**

Noritake Powder Box

Powder box, cov., round, in the form of a woman in full-skirted off-the-shoulder dress in coral-pink decorated w/light pink roses & green leaves, the bottom of the skirt making up the powder container, the top of the skirt the lid, the handle formed by the figure of a fan-holding woman w/powdered hair & a beauty mark, 3 1/2" d., 6 1/4" h. (ILLUS.) **875**

Noritake Powder Puff Box

Powder puff box, cov., round, the lid decorated w/figure of woman sitting w/back to viewer, wearing dark green & cream-colored dress w/full skirt, dark green bodice, festooned w/lavender ribbons at waist & shoulders & pink & yellow flowers decorating skirt, two dark curls escaping from back of the yellow & green flower-bedecked bonnet that hides her face, all on caramel ground, 1 3/4" h., 4 1/4" d. (ILLUS.) **420**

Powder Puff Box with Bird Lid

Powder puff box, cov., squat circular shape, pale mauve w/black line trim, the cover w/caramel top upon which perches a blue, red, yellow & black bird, 1" h., 4" d. (ILLUS.) **434**
Salt & pepper shakers, in the form of lady heads, 1 1/8" w., 2 3/4" h., pr. **475**

Noritake Sandwich Serving Plate

Sandwich serving plate, round, w/gilt angular handle in middle, the plate decorated w/scene of pink-clad figures on rolling green ground gathering red fruit from large tree, a line of shrubs in the background, all against a pink & green ground, 9 1/2" d. (ILLUS.) **385**
Talcum powder shaker, in the form of an owl, 5 1/2" h. **375**

Noritake Tea Set

Tea set: cov. teapot, creamer, cov. sugar, tray; the teapot, creamer & sugar w/ gold angled loop handles, the 6 x 11" tray w/tab side handles, all in vivid deep orange w/gold & black trim, decorated w/desert scene of robed, turbaned figure against backdrop of palm trees & a tower, the set (ILLUS.) **395**

Tea strainer & underplate, floral decoration, 2 pcs. **107**

Trinket dish, decorated w/image of nude by pond, 6 1/2 x 7 1/4", 3 1/4" h. **920**

Vase, 6" h., trumpet form w/wavy black-trimmed rim & flared base, the ringed body decorated w/green & white checked sash & rose-like flowers in shades of pink & yellow, all on a caramel ground (ILLUS.) **171**

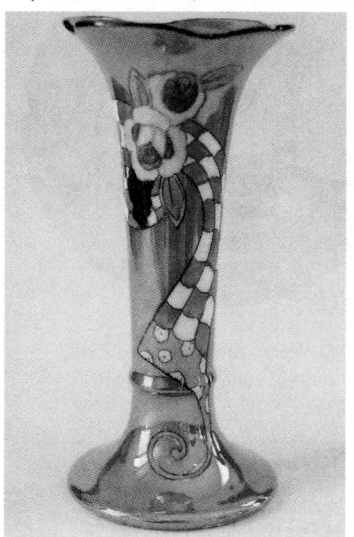

Noritake Trumpet-form Vase

Noritake U-form Double Vase

Vase, 6 7/8" h., U-form double vase, the two receptacles joined by double bars, the top one serving as roost for tropical bird in vivid orange, dark blue, green, yellow & pink, the double vases in pale mauve decorated w/deep orange & yellow/gold flowers & green leaves, the scalloped rims w/gilt trim, flared base (ILLUS.) **261**

Handled Vase

Vase, 8" h., squatty form w/tapering shoulder & high pointed arch handle at top, caramel ground w/black trim on handle & short pink neck, the body decorated w/figure of young woman in powdered hair adorned w/a single red rose, wearing black full-skirted gown trimmed w/red roses, one hand holding a decorative fan (ILLUS.) **615**

Vase, 8 1/4" h., decorated w/image of "muscle man" **178**

Noritake Vase with Unusual Handles

Vase, 8 1/4" h., ovoid shape tapering out to scalloped rim, C-scroll handles, the bottoms of which are applied to the top of

vase, w/the tops of the handles unconnected to vase, pale mauve disk base, the body decorated w/ornate flower in deep red, grape, yellow, pink & blue/grey colors & black dots, green leaves, against caramel ground w/pale mauve & brown trim (ILLUS.) **156**

Wall pocket, figural bird, 2 5/8 x 4 5/8", 8 1/4" h. **515**

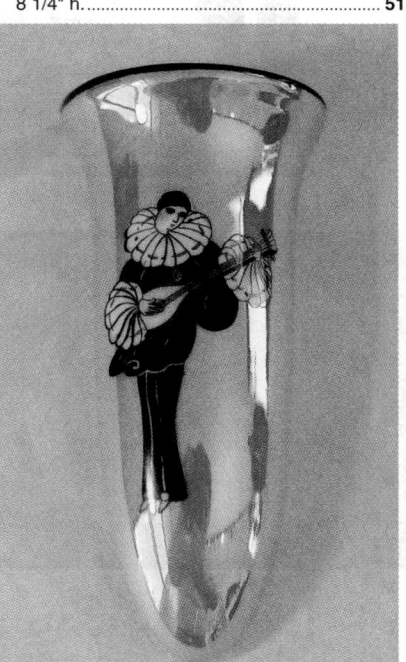

Noritake Wall Pocket

Wall pocket, trumpet form in caramel w/black rim, decorated w/figure of lute-playing musician dress in black w/extravagant white & red ruff & cuffs, 2 7/8" w. x 6" h. (ILLUS.) **505**

Old Ivory

Old Ivory china was produced in Silesia, Germany, in the late 1800s and takes its name from the soft white background coloring. A wide range of table pieces was made with the various patterns, usually identified by a number rather than a name.

The following prices are averages for Old Ivory at this time. Rare patterns will command higher prices, and there is some variance in prices geographically. These prices are also based on the item being perfect. Cups are measured across the top opening.

Berry set: 9 1/2" master bowl & six small berries; No. 12 Clairon blank, the set **$350**

Bowl, 6" d., cereal, No. 76 Louis XVI blank **95**

Bowl, 9" d., No. 200 Deco blank **100**

Bowl, 10" d., No. 10 Clairon blank **200**

No. U15 Florette Sugar & Creamer

No. 204 Deco Cake Plate

Cake plate, w/open handles, No. 204 Deco
  blank, 10" d. (ILLUS.).................................... **300**
Celery dish, No. 12 Clairon blank, 11 1/2" l...... **200**
Charger, No. 8 Clairon blank, 13 1/2" d. **385**
Chocolate pot, No. 118 Empire blank, rare,
  9 1/2" h. **600**
Chocolate set, No. 200 Deco blank, 7 pcs....... **600**
Cracker jar, No. 120 Clairon blank, rare,
  8 1/2" h. **650**
Creamer & cov. sugar bowl, No. 4 Elysee
  blank, 4" h., pr. **300**

Creamer & cov. sugar bowl, No. U15 Florette blank, 4" h., pr. (ILLUS., top of
  page) **250**
Creamer & cov. sugar bowl, No. 16 Deco
  blank variant, 6" h., pr. **400**

No. 4 Elysee Chocolate Cup & Saucer

Cup & saucer, chocolate, No. 4 Elysee
  blank, 2 1/2" d. (ILLUS.) **250**
Cup & saucer, No. 15 Clairon blank,
  3 1/2" d... **65**
Cup & saucer, bouillon, No. 27 Alice blank,
  rare, 3 1/2" d... **450**

No. 15 Clairon Demitasse Set

Cup & saucer, No. 114 Clairon blank, very rare, 3 1/2" d. 400
Demitasse pot, No. 16 Clairon blank, 7 1/2" h. 500
Demitasse set: 7 1/2" pot & 4 cups & saucers; No. 15 Clairon blank (ILLUS., bottom previous page) 900
Dresser tray, No. 122 Clairon blank, 11 1/2" l. 285
Mayonnaise set: dish & underplate; No. 84 Empire blank, 6 1/2", the set 265
Mustard pot, cov., No. 200 Deco blank, 3 3/4" h. 450
Olive dish, No. 17 Clairon blank, 6 1/2" l. 400
Pickle dish, No. 84 Empire blank, 8 1/2" l. 85
Plate, 9 1/2" d., No. U30 Alice blank 100
Plate, 8 1/2" d., luncheon, No. 73 Clairon blank 100
Plate, 10" d., No. 16 Clairon blank, open-handled 100

Rare No. 99 Empire Plate

Plate, 7 1/2" d., No. 99 Empire blank, rare (ILLUS.) 400
Plate, 7 3/4" d., No. 84 Empire blank 65
Plate, 9 1/2" d., tab handle, No. U16 Florette blank 350
Plate, 8 1/2" d., luncheon, No. 76 Louis XVI blank 150
Platter, 13 1/2" l., No. 75 Alice blank 400
Porringer, No. 39 Empire blank, very rare, 6 1/4" h. 900
Spoon rest, No. 200 Deco blank, 8 3/4" l. 250

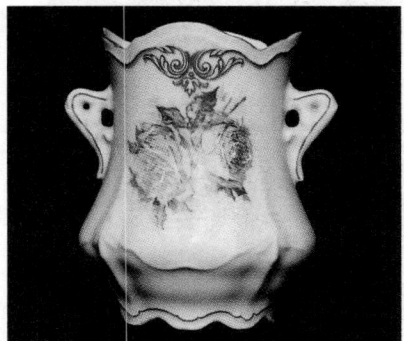

No. 29 Carmen Spooner

Spooner, No. 29 Carmen blank, 4" h. (ILLUS.) 400
Teapot, cov., No. 204 Deco blank, 5 1/2" h. 700
Toothpick holder, No. 121 Quadrille blank, 2 1/4" h. 325
Vegetable dish, cov., No. 16 Clairon blank, 10 1/2" l. 1,500
Vegetable dish, cov., No. 75 Rivoli blank, 10 1/2" l. 1,500

Quimper

This French earthenware pottery has been made in France since the end of the 17th century and is still in production today. Because the colorful decoration on this ware, predominantly of Breton peasant figures, is all hand-painted and each piece is unique, it has become increasingly popular with collectors in recent years. Most pieces offered today date from about the mid-19th century to the present. Modern potteries continue to operate today, with contemporary examples available in gift shops.

The standard reference in this field is Quimper Pottery A French Folk Art Faience *by Sandra V. Bondhus (privately printed, 1981).*

Quimper Marks

Basket, exterior w/raised basketweave design, interior w/image of peasant woman w/flower sprays, "HB Quimper - x364," 8 1/4 x 7", 6" h., mint **$350**
Book ends, Modern Movement-style girl toddlers hold onto brown sponged wall as they attempt their first steps, both wearing white caps & navy dresses, one w/yellow checked apron, one w/pink checked apron, "HenRiot Quimper 136" & artist "J.E. Sevellec," 5 1/2" h., excellent, pr. 450
Charger, w/image of woman in profile holding flower, framed by flower garland band, "HR" mark only, early, 11" d. (slight wear on outer edge) 100
Cigarette holder/ashtray, figural, yellow-glazed Modern Movement form of woman wearing turquoise polka dotted blouse & red striped apron & holding double baskets w/holes on top for cigarettes, molded indentation on base forming ashtray, "HB Quimper 605," 8 1/2" h., mint 325

Coffee set: 9 1/4" h. cov. coffeepot, creamer & cov. sugar; each decorated w/different Breton musician & very richly ornamented "Rouenesque" border, "HB Quimper 15," excellent, the set (ILLUS., top next page) **525**

Divided Dish

Dish, divided, double bagpipe shape, "decor riche" patt., bow & twisted knot handles, each division featuring peasant couple standing beneath sprigs of Breton wildflowers, 13 1/2" l., 11" w., excellent (ILLUS.) **600**

Doll chamber pot, decorated w/floral band on outside & eye painted on bottom of interior, "HenRiot Quimper 115," 2 1/2" l. from lip to handle tip, mint **35**

Doll plate, red & blue striped pinwheel geometric patt., "HenRiot Quimper France 115," 1 3/4" d., mint (glaze skips).................... **45**

Egg cup, figural, in the form of a yellow-sponged chick w/blue feathers, w/attached 3 1/2" d. underdish, "HB Quimper," mint **75**

Figure group, Modern Movement-style dancing couple posed so woman's flaring skirt shows off decorative trim on hem, "HenRiot Quimper 78" & artist "R. Micheau-Vernez," 12 1/2" h., mint **450**

Figure of St. Anne w/child Mary, "HenRiot Quimper France 127," 5 1/2" h., mint **55**

Figure of woman w/cane, Modern Movement-style figure of elderly woman in polka dotted blue shawl & green & orange striped apron leaning on cane, artist "L.H. Nicot" embossed on base, "Henriot Quimper 136," 8" h., mint **325**

Inkwell, cov., in the form of a Breton hat, w/original inset & lid w/acorn finial, scene on lid of seated woman w/basket of eggs at her side, "HenRiot Quimper France 72," 5 1/2" w., mint (ILLUS. left, w/plate, middle next page)..................................... **175**

Jardiniere, cradle shape on four tiny feet, double knobs at four upper corners, w/scene of peasant couple executed in the "demi-fantasie" style, back panel displaying full-blown red & yellow rose set in flower branch, "HR Quimper," 7 1/4" l., mint (ILLUS., bottom next page).................... **800**

Jardiniere, octagonal shape w/country French geometric patt., blue sponged ropetwist handles, unsigned, 19th c., excellent, 12" l. (ILLUS., bottom of page)......... **200**

Scalloped-rim Jardiniere

Jardiniere, oval w/scalloped rim, footed, flat ring handles, "decor riche" patt., image of seated musician on front, "HB Quimper 128," 9" l., mint (ILLUS.) **325**

Knife rests, tricorner shape, each decorated w/images of peasant figure & flower branches, HB Quimper "xo" mark, excellent overall, 3" l., six pcs.................................. **100**

Jardiniere with Ropetwist Handles

Coffee Set with Music Theme

Quimper Inkwell & Plate

Cradle-shaped Jardiniere

Quimper Liquor Set

Liquor set: 7" d. tray, 6" h. cov. decanter & four 1" h. handleless cups; figure of traditional peasant woman adorning decanter, a bold daisy patt. covering the tray, each cup w/flower spray on front, "HenRiot Quimper France 75," mint (ILLUS., top of page) **150**

Model of swan, figure of seated peasant lad holding pipe is depicted on swan's breast, "HenRiot Quimper France 89," 4" h., 4 3/4" l., mint **120**

Pitcher, 2 1/2" h., child-size, decorated w/image of Breton man & flowers, "Made in France 12" beneath handle, "HenRiot," mint **65**

Pitcher, 6" h., decorated w/scene of Breton man & flowers, concentric bands of yellow & blue on border, "HenRiot Quimper France 115," mint **35**

Plate, 6" d., w/pie crust rim, center shows woman standing in profile w/one hand tucked into apron pocket, flower garland border w/blue sponged edges, "HenRiot Quimper France 72," mint (ILLUS. right, w/inkwell, middle previous page) **100**

Plate, 9" d., yellow glaze w/row of French houses w/a fountain in front & trees on either side of homes, clouds in sky, "HB Quimper France 176," mint **75**

Plate in "Botanique" Pattern

Plate, 9 1/2" d., First Period Porquier Beau, "Botanique" patt., decorated w/spray of yellow narcissus & snail, signed w/intersecting "PB" mark in blue, mint (ILLUS.) ... **1,150**

Pair of Matched Plates

Platter with Courting Scene

Plates, 7 1/2" d., pale blue sponged ruffled rims, center display of seated peasant man on one, seated peasant woman on other, "HB" mark only, 19th c., mint, pr. (ILLUS., bottom previous page) 300

Platter, 12" l., 8 1/2" w., oval, "decor riche" patt., center showing courting scene of young Breton couple seated beneath canopy of trees, "HB Quimper," excellent (ILLUS., top of page)...................................... 550

Oval Platter with Peasant Couple

Platter, 14 1/2" l., 11" w., oval, scene of peasant couple & "a la touche" flower garland band, "HB" mark only, 19th c., mint (ILLUS.) 175

Porringer, traditional decoration of peasant woman & flowers, blue sponged tab handles, "HenRiot Quimper France," 5 1/2" handle to handle, mint.................................. 25

Salt, pepper & mustard set, "Ivoire Corbeille" patt. "menagere," acorn-shaped mustard pot w/figural twig handle & tiny acorn on lid & bust portrait of young peasant girl on the side, salt & pepper are attached open compartments w/twig feet, "HenRiot Quimper," 5 1/2" l., 5" h., mint........ 125

Tobacco jar, cov., figural, Modern Movement style, in the form of a Bretonne woman w/Quimper coif & "embroidery" detailing on blouse & sleeves, the top lifting off at elbow level, by Andre Galland, "HenRiot Quimper A.G. 161," 7" h., mint 300

Tray with Ropetwist Handles

Tray, yellow glaze w/multicolor ropetwist handles, center featuring a pitcher-toting woman wearing the headdress of Cherbourg flanked by floral designs, HenRiot made-on-commission example, signed only "Cherbourg," 12 x 8", mint (ILLUS.) 175

Tureen w/attached underplate, cov., oval shape, the lid decorated w/image of peasant woman w/flower sprays & seashell finial, sides adorned w/garlands of flowers, "HenRiot Quimper France 101," 6" l., 4" h., excellent 200

Vase, 7 1/2" h., 9" w., Modern Movement style, bust portrait of Breton man framed in triangular cartouche on front, the reverse w/stone church w/trees & grassy slope, "Quimper" in blue on base, artist "P. Fouillen" signature beside figure of the man, mint 300

"Decor Riche" Double Vase

Vase, 9" h., donut shape divided at top center w/separate openings on each side of division, four short outcurved feet, "decor riche" patt., decorated w/cartouches featuring woman holding basket & man playing flute flanking one w/view of the city of Quimper reflected in the Odet River, reverse side decorated w/multicolor flower garland, dragon-like side handles, mint (ILLUS.) 2,000

Vases, 6" h., matched pair, bagpipe shape, "Demi-fantasie" patt., decorated w/images of man playing horn & woman holding distaff of flax, "HR Quimper," excellent, pr. 375

Redware

Red earthenware pottery was made in the American colonies from the late 1600s. Bowls, crocks and all types of utilitarian wares were turned out in great abundance to supplement the pewter and handmade treenware. The ready availability of the clay, the same used in making bricks and roof tiles, accounted for the vast production. The lead-glazed redware retained its reddish color, although a variety of colors could be obtained by adding various metals to the glaze. Interesting effects occurred accidentally through unsuspected impurities in the clay or uneven temperatures in the firing kiln, which sometimes resulted in streaks or mottled splotches.

Redware pottery was seldom marked by the maker.

Crock, bulbous ovoid form w/flat flaring rim, eared handles & incised lines, glaze w/dark brown daubs in vertical rows around the sides, 19th c., 8 5/8" h. (edge chips, hairline) $660

Maine Redware Jar with Cover

Jar, cov., ovoid body tapering to a dish rim supporting the flat cover w/knob finial, orange & green splotchy glaze, probably John Safford, Maine, 19th c., incised on base "203," 5 1/2" h. (ILLUS.) 240

Jar, cylindrical w/narrow angled shoulder to flaring rim, black brush marks starting at shoulder & running downward, incised rings around top & center, glaze stopping short of base, 19th c., 8 1/2" h. (edge chips) 281

Jug, ovoid body tapering to a small cylindrical neck, applied strap handle, reddish glaze w/green highlights, three incised shoulder rings, probably John Safford, Maine, 19th c., 6" h. 575

Jug, ovoid body tapering to a short cylindrical banded neck, remnants of applied handle, dark brown & green glaze, branded across the front by the maker, John M. Safford, Maine, 19th c., 7" h. 805

Early Maine Redware Jug

Jug, ovoid body tapering sharply to a small neck w/molded rim & applied strap handle, nice red & green speckled glaze, Norcross-type shape, Maine, 19th c., some chips & hairline, 8 1/2" h. (ILLUS.)... 1,035

Model of a lion, seated hollow-molded animal w/open front legs, on a thin rectangular base, black mica glaze w/painted red mouth & yellow eyes, base painted yellow & orange, 19th c., 6 3/4 x 11", 14" h. (few chips, tail handmade replacement).... 1,210

Stew pot, cov., ovoid body tapering to a flared rim, applied side strap handle, inset flat cover w/ringed knob finial, brownish red glaze, five incised shoulder lines, bottom incised "703," cover impressed "John Safford 2d - 703," shoulder also incised w/maker's mark, Maine, 19th c., 7" h. (chip to rim, some bottom roughness).. 1,600

Rookwood

Considered America's foremost art pottery, the Rookwood Pottery Company was established in Cincinnati, Ohio, in 1880 by Mrs. Maria Nichols Longworth Storer. To accurately record its development, each piece carried the Rookwood insignia or mark, was dated, and, if individually decorated, was usually signed by the artist. The pottery remained in Cincinnati until 1959, when it was sold to Herschede Hall Clock Company and moved to Starkville, Mississippi, where it continued in operation until 1967.

A private company is now producing a limited variety of pieces using original Rookwood molds.

Rookwood Mark

Ewer, short squatty bulbous body tapering to a flared & pinched rim, small loop shoulder handle, Standard glaze, decorated w/yellow & brown pansies on a mottled tan & green ground, fine overall crazing, 1892, Harriet Straefer, 3 3/4" h. **$345**

Humidor Decorated by Maria Nichols

Humidor, cov., Limoges-style decoration, round foot below the four-sided rounded body w/a flattened domed cover, painted w/an overall design of spiders & bats on a mottled tan, rust, blue & white ground, glaze bubble under outer lid, 1882, Maria Longworth Nichols, 6" w., 6" h. (ILLUS.)... **2,185**

Early Standard Glaze Humidor

Humidor, cov., wide slightly tapering cylindrical form w/a low cupped rim around the inset flattened cover w/a button finial, Standard glaze, decorated around the sides w/orange nicotiana blossoms & green leaves against a shaded gold to moss green ground, hairline inside cover, 1893, Bruce Horsfall, 6" d., 6 1/4" h. (ILLUS.)............ **575**

Plaque, rectangular, Vellum glaze, a verdant landscape w/a large meadow in the foreground & a small river & trees in the distance, shades of green, grey, blue & white, original wide flat oak frame, 1915, Kate Van Horn, 8 3/4 x 11" (ILLUS., below) **6,325**

Fine Meadow Landscape Plaque

Platter, 6 x 10 1/4", oblong undulating organic shaped w/a low upright edge, Standard glaze, decorated w/leafy strawberry vines on a light green ground, uncrazed, 1892, Edward Abel **805**

Trivet, round, embossed w/a large bird among bare branches, matte light yellow glaze on an ivory ground, 1929, 5 1/2" d. **403**

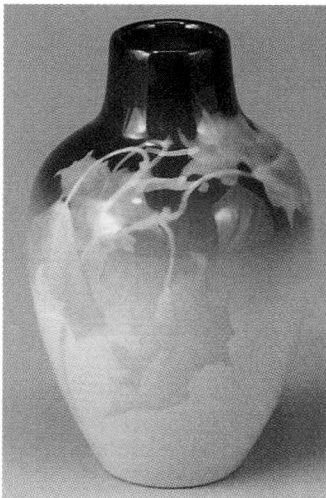

Lovely Iris Glaze Vase with Leaves

Vase, 6 1/2" h., 3 3/4" d., ovoid body tapering to a short cylindrical neck, Iris glaze, decorated w/yellowish amber maple leaves against a dark grey shaded to pale yellow ground, overall crazing, No. 1905E, 1903, Irene Bishop (ILLUS.) **1,725**

Sea Green Glazed Vase with Flowers

Vase, 6 3/4" h., 5" d., ovoid body tapering to a wide flat mouth flanked by small loop handles, Sea Green glaze, decorated w/large brown & cream flowers on dark

green stems against a dark blue to green ground, No. 604D, 1902, Sallie Toohey (ILLUS.) **3,738**

Vase, 7" h., slightly swelled cylindrical form tapering to a short flared neck, Standard glaze, decorated w/yellow narcissus against a dark brown to green to yellow ground, a few scratches, 1894, Lenore Asbury **546**

Vase, 7" h., 3" d., slightly swelled cylindrical form w/a narrow shoulder tapering to a short rolled neck, Green Vellum glaze, stylized scenic w/a bird's-eye view of an arid landscape w/a cobalt blue river, No. 904E, 1911, Sara Sax................................ **6,900**

Elegant Scenic Vellum Rookwood Vase

Vase, 7 1/2" h., 3 1/2" d., cylindrical w/incurved flat wide mouth, Vellum glaze, scenic design elegantly painted w/flying Canada geese above stalks of bamboo against a dark blue to cream to green ground, no crazing, 1911, No. 952E, Kataro Shirayamadani (ILLUS.) **8,625**

Vase, 7 1/2" h., 4" d., footed swelling cylindrical body w/a wide closed rim, Wax Matte glaze, decorated around the upper body w/a wreath of blue dogwood blossoms & green leaves against a shaded purple to blue butterfat ground, No. 1779, 1925, Margaret McDonald **1,495**

Vase, 8 1/4" h., 3 3/4" d., slightly waisted cylindrical form w/a flat rim, Standard glaze, decorated w/large yellow tulips & green leaves against a shaded black to green to orange ground, No. 950D, 1905, Caroline Steinle **748**

Vase, 8 1/2" h., 3 3/4" d., slightly tapering ovoid form w/a small flat mouth, Vellum glaze, a scenic design w/a large leafy tree beside a pond w/trees in the distance, in shades of greens, creams & peach, very light crazing, 1916, No. 2033E, Elizabeth McDermott..................... **4,600**

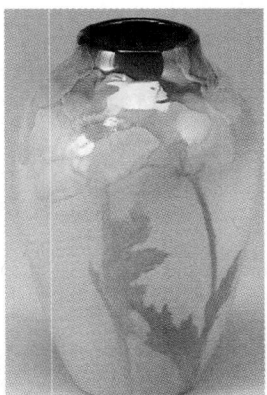

Rare Iris Glaze Vase with Poppies

Vase, 9 1/2" h., 6" d., simple ovoid body tapering to a flat rim, Iris glaze, decorated
w/large mauve poppies w/yellow centers
on pale green leafy stems against a
shaded mauve to pale yellowish green
ground, Pan American Exposition paper
label, No. 900B, 1900, O.G. Reed
(ILLUS.).. 9,775
Vase, 10" h., 3 1/4" h., footed slender baluster-form body w/a widely flaring trumpet
rim, Jewel Porcelain, decorated w/long
green leafy vines of orange trumpet flowers against a light yellow ground, 1923,
No. 2545C, Sara Sax 3,335
Vase, 10 1/2" h., 4 1/4" d., slightly swelled
cylindrical form w/a flat closed rim,
Carved Matte glaze, deeply modeled
around the top w/oak branches & acorns
in green, brown & burgundy on a brown
butterfat ground, No. 951C, 1905, Rose
Fechheimer.. 3,220
Vase, 10 1/2" h., 5 1/2" d., ovoid body ta-
pering to a wide flat mouth, Incised Matte
glaze, molded around the shoulder
w/bright red fruit & green & purple leaves
on a shaded deep purple to umber butterfat ground, No. 943C, 1918, Elizabeth
Lincoln 3,450

Jewel Porcelain Vase with Magnolias

Vase, 11" h., 7 1/2" d., footed cylindrical
form w/a rounded base & shoulder centered by a flat mouth, Jewel Porcelain,
decorated w/smeary branches of large
pink & grey magnolia blossoms on an
ivory ground, No. 2581, 1923, William
Hentschel (ILLUS.)...................................... 4,025
Vase, 11 3/4" h., 5" d., slightly swelling cylindrical body w/a wide flat mouth, Incised
Matte glaze, decorated w/a stylized pattern around the shoulder in red & turquoise over a purple butterfat ground,
No. 2039C, 1915, William Hentschel 3,450

Roseville

Roseville Pottery Company operated in Zanes-
ville, Ohio, from 1898 to 1954, having been in
business for six years prior to that in Muskingum
County, Ohio. Art wares similar to those of Owens
and Weller Potteries were produced. Items listed
here are by patterns or lines.

Roseville Mark

Apple Blossom (1948)

White apple blossoms in relief on blue, green or
pink ground; brown tree branch handles.

Basket w/overhead handle, blue ground,
No. 309-8", 8" h. $288
Candlesticks, green ground, No. 351-2",
2" h., pr.. 58
Wall pocket, conical w/overhead handle,
green ground, No. 366-8", 8" h. 230

Baneda (1933)

Band of embossed pods, blossoms and leaves
on green or raspberry pink ground.

Vase, 4" h., footed bulbous body w/incurved
flat rim, flat shoulder handles, raspberry
pink ground, No. 587-4"................................ 288

Small & Large Baneda Vases

Vase, 5" h., footed, pear-shaped w/small loop handles near rim, green ground, No. 601-5" (ILLUS. left, previous page) **345**

Vase, 7" h., footed swelled cylindrical body tapering to a short, wide cylindrical neck flanked by small down-curved loop handles, raspberry pink ground, No. 590-7" **460**

Vase, 7" h., footed wide cylindrical body tapering to short wide cylindrical neck, small loop handles, raspberry pink ground, No. 592-7" **350-450**

Vase, 9" h., cylindrical w/short collared neck, handles rising from shoulder to beneath rim, green ground, No. 594-9" (ILLUS. right previous page with small vase) **1,150**

Vase, 12" h., expanding cylinder w/small rim handles, green ground, No. 599-12"....... **575**

Bittersweet (1940)

Orange bittersweet pods and green leaves on a grey blending to rose, yellow with terra cotta, rose with green or solid green bark-textured ground; brown branch handles.

Basket w/pointed overhead handle, asymmetrical scalloped rim, grey ground, No. 808-6", 6" h... **115**

Book ends, handles, grey ground, No. 859, 5 1/2" h., pr. **144**

Ewer, grey ground, No. 816-8", 8" h. **173**

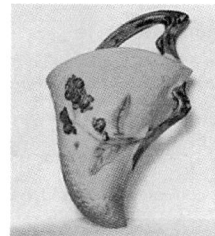

Yellow Bittersweet Wall Pocket

Wall pocket, curving conical form w/overhead handle continuing to one side, yel-

low ground, No. 866-7", 7 1/2" h. (ILLUS.)... **288**

Blackberry (1933)

Band of relief clusters of blackberries with vines and ivory leaves accented in green and terra cotta on a green textured ground.

Candleholders, tapering domed base below a tall socket flanked by small open handles, No. 1086, 4 1/2" h., pr. (ILLUS. bottom left, bottom of page)............................ **748**

Console bowl, rectangular w/small handles, No. 228-10", 3 1/2 x 13" (ILLUS. top with candleholders, bottom of page) **460**

Vase, 4" h., two-handled, bulbous, No. 567-4" **500**

Vase, 5" h., loop handles at midsection, bulbous base tapering to wide cylindrical neck, No. 570-5" (ILLUS. bottom right with candleholders, bottom of page) **748**

Vase, 6" h., wide flaring lower body w/a wide slightly tapering upper body flanked by small loop handles at the rim, No. 572-6" **431**

Vase, 6" h., globular w/tiny rim handles, No. 574-6".. **690**

Vase, 8" h., handles at mid-section, slightly globular base & wide neck, No. 575-8" (bruise on one handle).................................... **500**

Bleeding Heart (1938)

Pink blossoms and green leaves on shaded blue, green or pink ground.

Jardiniere, green ground, No. 651-6", 6" h. **150-250**

Vase, 5" h., footed trumpet-form w/angled side handles, pink ground, No. 962-5".......... **144**

Bushberry (1948)

Berries and leaves on blue, green or russet bark-textured ground; brown or green branch handles.

Basket w/asymmetrical overhead handle, blue ground, No. 370-8", 8 1/2" h. **259**

Blackberry Candleholders & Other Pieces

Ewer, cut-out rim, green ground, No. 3-15",
15" h.. **690**
Vase, 14 1/2" h., tall ovoid body w/an up-
ward pointed handle at one side & a
small downward pointed handle on the
other side, blue ground, No. 39-14".............. **460**
Vases, bud, 7 1/2" h., cylindrical body,
asymmetrical base handles, russet
ground, No. 152-7", pr. **374**
Wall pocket, high-low handles, blue
ground, No. 1291-8", 8" h. **431**

Carnelian I (1915-27)

*Matte smooth glaze with a combination of two
colors or two shades of the same color with the
darker dripping over the lighter tone. Generally
in colors of blue, pink and green.*

Bowl, 9" d., 3" h., two-handled, canted
sides, pink & grey, No. 164-7"...................... **104**
Ewer, footed bulbous ovoid body w/a short
neck & wide arched spout, long loop han-
dle, pink & grey, No. 1312-10", 10" h. **259**
Plate, footed wide flattened round shape,
green, 158-12", 12 1/2" d. **300-400**
Vase, double bud, 5" h., gate-form, olive
green & blue-green, No. 56-5"...................... **115**
Vase, 7" h., double gourd-form w/wide neck
& flaring rim, ornate pointed & scrolled
handles from mid-section of base to be-
low rim, light & dark green, No. 310-7" **144**

Carnelian II (1915-31)

*Intermingled colors, some with a drip effect,
giving a textured surface appearance. Colors similar to Carnelian I.*

Candleholders, angular pyramidal base
flanked by low open handles, rectangular
socket, mottled pink & purple, No. 1064-
3", 3 1/2" h., pr. **173**
Wall pocket, widely flaring peaked rim
above a ringed neck & bullet-form base,
straight handles from bottom of rim to the
sides, mottled pink & purple, No. 1253-
8", 8" l. **374**

Cherry Blossom (1933)

*Sprigs of cherry blossoms, green leaves and
twigs with pink fence against a combed blue-
green ground or creamy ivory fence against a
terra cotta ground shading to dark brown.*

Cherry Blossom Flowerpot

Flowerpot, footed wide slightly flaring cylindrical shape w/small loop handles at the
rim, terra cotta ground, No. 239-5", 5" h.
(ILLUS.)... **288**

Experimental Cherry Blossom Lamp

Lamp, footed spherical vase body w/a short
neck flanked by small loop handles, a low
domed cap at the top for wiring, shaded
yellowish green, experimental, repaired
chip on base, No. 625-8", 9" h. (ILLUS.) **863**
Vase, 4 1/4" h., wide squatty bulbous form
w/a wide tapering shoulder centered by a
small rolled mouth flanked by tiny loop
handles, terra cotta ground, No. 617-
3 1/2" **230**
Vase, 5" h., two-handled, slightly ovoid, pink
& blue ground, No. 619-5"............................. **403**
Vase, 15" h., floor-type, bulbous ovoid
w/wide molded mouth, small loop shoulder handles, terra cotta to brown ground,
No. 628-15" (bruise to base rim)............... **1,495**

Three Blue Clemana Vases

Clemana (1934)

Stylized blossoms with embossed latticework and basketweave on blue, green or tan ground.

Vase, 6" h., footed spherical body w/a wide flat mouth flanked by small angled tab handles, blue ground, small flakes on handles, No. 280-6" (ILLUS. center with other Clemana vases, bottom previous page)... **201**

Vase, 6" h., swelled cylindrical body w/a small flat mouth, small angled handles at the shoulders, tan ground, No. 749-6" **230**

Vase, 6 1/2" h., footed gently flaring cylindrical body w/a wide flat rim, small angled shoulder handles, green ground, No. 750-6" **374**

Vase, 7 1/2" h., ovoid body tapering to a short cylindrical neck, small pointed shoulder handles, tan ground, No. 752-7" **173**

Vase, 8 1/2" h., trumpet foot below the wide gently flaring cylindrical body flanked by small pointed handles near the base, blue ground, No. 753-8" (ILLUS. left with spherical vase, bottom of previous page)..... **230**

Vase, 10" h., footed slightly swelled cylindrical body w/a short wide neck, small pointed shoulder handles, blue ground, No. 757-10" (ILLUS. right with spherical vase, bottom of previous page)..................... **259**

Clematis (1944)

Clematis blossoms and heart-shaped green leaves against a vertically textured ground, white blossoms on blue, rose-pink blossoms on green and ivory blossoms on golden brown.

Large Blue Clematis Basket

Basket w/high overhead handle, pedestal base, blue ground, No. 389-10", 10" h. (ILLUS.)... **150-200**

Vase, 12 1/2" h., tall gently swelled cylindrical body w/a flat mouth, open angled handles hear the rim, blue ground, No. 112-12".. **201**

Vase, 15" h., footed tall waisted cylindrical form w/flaring rim flanked by long pierced pointed handles, blue ground, No. 114-15" (minor base chip).............................. **250-350**

Columbine (1940s)

Columbine blossoms and foliage on shaded ground, yellow blossoms on blue, pink blossoms on pink shaded to green, and blue blossoms on tan shaded to green.

Basket, elaborate handle rising from mid-section, tan ground, No. 365-7", 7" h. **115**

Basket, asymmetrical overhead handle, blue ground, No. 367-10", 10" h. **288**

Jardiniere, squatty body w/small handles at shoulder, tan ground, No. 655-4", 4" h. **115**

Vase, 7" h., footed tall waisted form w/fanned rim, pointed angled handles at the lower body, tan ground, No. 16-7" **115**

Dahlrose (1924-28)

Band of ivory daisy-like blossoms and green leaves against a mottled tan ground.

Candleholders, angular handles rising from low slightly domed base, No. 1069-3", 3" h., pr.. **288**

Center bowl, 11" l., footed oval squatty bulbous body tapering to a wide flared rim, angular end handles from rim to shoulder, No. 180-8" (ILLUS. center with chamberstick & jardiniere, bottom page)....... **288**

Chamberstick, domed oval base w/an off-center swelled cylindrical stem flanked by asymmetrical loop handles, 7 1/2" h. (ILLUS. right with other Dahlrose pieces, bottom page) **316**

Jardiniere, bulbous slightly squatty body w/a molded rim & tiny rim handles, No. 614-7", 7" d., 4" h. (ILLUS. left with other Dahlrose pieces, bottom page) **230**

Dahlrose Chamberstick, Center Bowl & Jardiniere

Planter, tall upright rectangular form w/small angled handles at the top ends, 6 x 8".. **403**

Vase, triple bud, 6" h., a domed round base w/a swelled cylindrical central shaft joined by floral panels to outcurved squared side holders, No. 76-6" **250-300**

Vase, 6" h., cylindrical form w/small pointed handles at the shoulder, No. 363-6".............. **104**

Vase, 8" h., footed bulbous lower body w/a slightly tapering upper half below the molded incurved mouth, angled handles from the rim to the shoulder, No. 367-8"... **201**

Vase, 12" h., footed wide ovoid body w/wide flaring rim, angled handles from shoulder to rim, No. 370-12" **690**

Dawn (1937)

Incised spidery flowers on green ground with blue-violet tinted blossoms, pink or yellow ground with blue-green blossoms, all with yellow centers.

Rose bowl, squatty spherical body w/tab handles at sides, square base, yellow ground, No. 316-6", 6" d................................. **230**

Vase, 6" h., semi-ovoid form, tab handles at rim, square foot, pink ground, No. 827-6"..... **230**

Vase, 8" h., slender cylinder w/tab handles below rim, square foot, pink ground, No. 828-8" **230**

Dogwood I - Smooth (1916-19)

White dogwood blossoms & black branches against a smooth green ground.

Basket, wide bulbous body w/a heavy arched branch handle across the top w/forked ends, 6" h... **288**

Basket, low widely flaring body w/incurved rim, a high arched & pointed handle from rim to rim, w/flower frog, 7" h. **230**

Basket, ovoid body w/an arched & forked handle across the top, 9" h. **316**

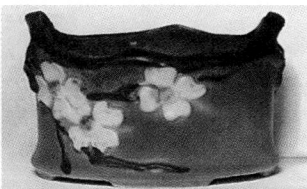

Dogwood I Planter Tub

Planter tub, oval w/upright sides, small branch handles at rim ends, 4 x 7" (ILLUS.)... **259**

Vase, 8" h., ovoid body tapering to wide cylindrical neck, No. 135-8" **230**

Dogwood II - Textured (1926)

White dogwood blossoms and brown branches against a textured green ground.

Bowl, 9" d., wide flattened squatty form w/heavy molded rim, No. 150-9"..................... **115**

Falline (1933)

Curving panels topped by a semi-scallop separated by vertical pea pod decorations; blended backgrounds of tan shading to green and blue or tan shading to darker brown.

Vase, 6" h., footed, cylindrical, w/large loop handles from midsection to rim, tan shading to brown, No. 642-6" (ILLUS. right with other Falline vases, bottom of page)...... **633**

Vase, 6" h., globular body w/a narrow swelled shoulder below the wide short cylindrical neck, C-scroll handles from the neck to the top of the body, green "pods" on a light shaded to dark brown ground, No. 644-6" (ILLUS. center with other Falline vases, bottom of page).............. **690**

Vase, 9" h., two large handles rising from midsection to neck, horizontally ribbed lower section, tan shading to blue & green, No. 652-9" (ILLUS. left with other Falline vases, bottom of page)................... **1,840**

Three Fine Roseville Falline Vases

Ferella Bowl and Two Vases

Vase, 14" h., tall cylindrical body w/a flat mouth flanked by small loop handles, tan shading to green & blue, No. 654-13 1/2".. **2,990**

Rare Tall Falline Vase

Vase, 15" h., tall ovoid body w/stepped cylindrical neck flanked by curved handles, No. 655-15" (ILLUS.) **4,025**

Ferella (1931)

Impressed shell design alternating with small cut-outs at top and base; mottled brown or turquoise and red glaze.

Bowl, 8" d., sharply canted sides, low foot, turquoise & red glaze, No. 211-8" (ILLUS. center with smaller vases, top of page) **1,035**

Vase, 4" h., angular handles, short narrow neck, mottled brown glaze, No. 497-4" (ILLUS. left with Ferella bowl, top of page) **500**

Vase, 4" h., angular handles, short narrow neck, turquoise & red glaze, No. 497-4" (ILLUS. right with Ferella bowl, top of page) **546**

Ferella Mottled Brown Vases

Vase, 6" h., handles rising from shoulder of compressed globular base to beneath the rim of the long tapering neck, mottled brown glaze, No. 502-6" (ILLUS. left with other brown vases, bottom previous page).. **550-750**

Vase, 6" h., bulbous base w/canted shoulder flanked by small angular handles, wide cylindrical neck, mottled brown glaze, No. 505-6" (ILLUS. right with other brown vases, bottom previous page) **550-750**

Vase, 9" h., flaring lower body w/an angled mid-shoulder tapering to the tall flared neck, long handles from the upper neck to the shoulders, mottled brown glaze, No. 510-9" (ILLUS. center with other brown vases, bottom previous page)........ **$1,250-1,500**

Foxglove (1940s)

Sprays of pink and white blossoms embossed against a shaded dark blue, green or pink matte-finish ground.

Basket w/circular overhead handle, footed conical body w/widely flaring rim, pink ground, No. 374-10", 10" h. **230**

Ewer, wide squatty body w/a wide shoulder centered by a short split neck w/long angled spout & pointed loop handle, pink ground, No. 4-6 1/2", 6 1/2" h. **200-250**

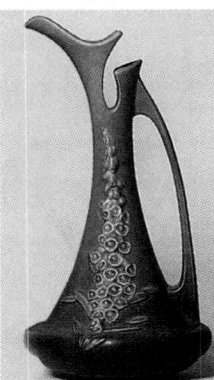

Very Tall Pink Foxglove Ewer

Ewer, wide squatty base w/a very tall tapering body w/a split neck & high arched spout, long handle from rim to top of base, pink ground, No. 6-15", 15" h. (ILLUS.) **500**

Foxglove 7" Pink Vase

Vase, 7" h., semi-ovoid w/long slender angled side handles, pink ground, No. 45-7" (ILLUS.)... **230**

Vase, 8 1/2" h., fan-shaped, handles rising from disk base to midsection, green & pink ground, No. 47-8".............................. **200-250**

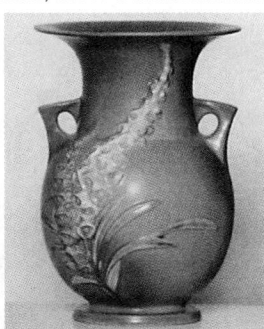

Tall Green & Pink Foxglove Vase

Vase, 9" h., footed spherical body tapering to wide cylindrical neck w/flaring rim, small angled shoulder handles, green & pink ground No. 50-9" (ILLUS.)............... **225-275**

Freesia (1945)

Trumpet-shaped blossoms and long slender green leaves against wavy impressed lines, white and lavender blossoms on blended green, white and yellow blossoms on shaded blue, or terra cotta and brown.

Cookie jar, cov., bulbous ovoid body w/angled shoulder handles, slightly domed lid w/knob finial, green ground, No. 4-8", 8" h.. **546**

Ewer, footed squatty body w/a wide shoulder tapering to a short split neck w/high arched spout, loop handle from rim to shoulder, terra cotta ground, No. 19-6", 6" h... **104**

Ewer, disk foot & ringed base below the tall ovoid body w/a short split neck w/long arched spout & pointed loop handle, terra cotta ground, No. 21-15", 15" h...................... **460**

One of a Pair of Blue Freesia Lamps

Lamps, pierced brass base supporting the tall ovoid body tapering to a trumpet neck, angled loop shoulder handles, blue ground, No. 127-12", 12" h., pr. (ILLUS. of one) **546**

Tea set: cov. teapot, creamer & open sugar bowl, green ground, No. 6, 3 pcs. **546**

Very Rare Experimental Freesia Vase

Vase, experimental, swelled cylindrical body w/a wide flat mouth, curved loop handles at the upper sides, pastel shaded blue to yellow ground w/pink blossoms (ILLUS.) **4,600**

Fuchsia (1939)

Coral pink fuchsia blossoms and green leaves against a background of blue shading to yellow, green shading to terra cotta, or terra cotta shading to gold.

Basket, footed inverted bell-form body w/overhead handle, terra cotta ground, No. 351-10", 10" h. **374**

Basket w/flower frog, a short pedestal foot supporting a wide squatty half-round body w/small half-round tabs on two sides of the incurved rim, a high round handle joining the two other edges, green ground, No. 350-8", 8" h. **325-350**

Console bowl, footed low oblong boat-shaped form w/under-rim end loop han-

dles, blue ground, No. 353-14", 15 1/2" l. .... **200 - 225**

Ewer, footed rounded lower body w/a wide shoulder tapering to a tall neck w/a high upright spout & long handle from rim to shoulder, terra cotta ground, No. 902-10", 10" h. **316**

Ewer, footed rounded lower body w/a wide shoulder tapering to a tall neck w/a high upright spout & long handle from rim to shoulder, blue ground, No. 902-10", 10" h. **345**

Jardiniere, footed spherical body w/short wide neck flanked by small angled handles, terra cotta ground, No. 645-3", 3" h. **81**

Vase, 7" h., bulbous base tapering to flaring rim, large loop handles from shoulder to below rim, terra cotta ground, No. 895-7" **230**

Vase, 9" h., footed cylindrical form w/wide flaring rim & large C-form handles, terra cotta ground, No. 900-9" **259**

Vase, 9" h., footed cylindrical form w/wide flaring rim & large C-form handles, green ground, No. 900-9" **288**

Wall pocket, two-handled bullet shape w/fanned rim, terra cotta ground, No. 1282-8", 8 1/2" h. **345**

Futura (1928)

Varied line with shapes ranging from Art Deco geometrics to futuristic. Matte glaze is typical although an occasional piece may be high gloss.

Bowl, 4" h., square inverted pyramidal bowl supported between four open buttress legs on a square base, yellow speckled w/green matte glaze, No. 189-4-6" **1,265**

Candleholders, shaped square base rising to square candle nozzle, relief-molded stylized green vine & foliage on sandy beige ground, No. 1073-4", 4" h., pr. **460**

Console bowl, cut-out base, sharply canted sides w/embossed stylized floral design, No. 196-5-6 1/2" , 12" l., 5" h. **748**

Vase, 6" h., 3 1/2" d., cylindrical body swelling to wider bands at the top & base, long pierced angled handles down the sides, apricot w/green bands & handles, No. 381-6" **403**

Vase, 6" h., upright squared buttressed form, terra cotta & gold, No. 423-6", paper label **500-600**

Three Futura Blue-Green Vases

Vase, 7" h., spherical top w/large pointed dark blue & green leaves curving up the sides, resting on a gently sloped rectangular foot, shaded blue & green blue ground, No. 387-7" (ILLUS. center with other blue-green vases, bottom previous page).. **1,093**

Vase, 8" h., upright rectangular form on rectangular foot, stepped neck, long square handles, grey & pink ground, No. 386-8" **748**

Vase, 10" h., compressed globular base supporting long flaring squared neck, elongated triangular design on each side, blue & green, No. 392-10" (ILLUS. left with spherical blue-green vase, bottom previous page) **800-1,000**

Vase, 10" h., footed tall tapering ringed body w/a short flaring neck, shaded bluish green glossy glaze, No. 434-10" (ILLUS. right with spherical blue-green vase, bottom previous page) **2,760**

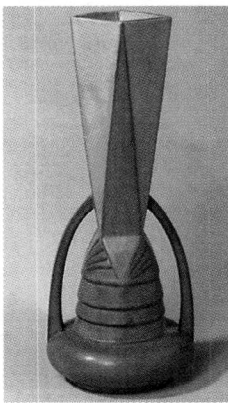

Rare Tall Futura Vase

Vase, 14" h., 5 1/2" d., two large handles at lower half, squat stacked base & faceted squared neck, matte glaze in three shades of brown, No. 411-14" (ILLUS.) **4,312**

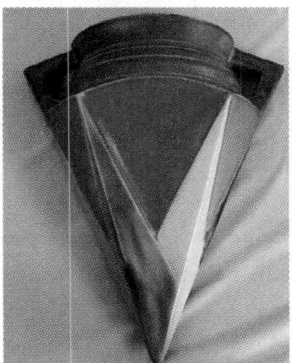

Colorful Futura Wall Pocket

Wall pocket, canted sides, angular rim handles, geometric design in blue, yellow, green & lavender on brown ground, No. 1261-8", 6" w., 8 1/4" h. (ILLUS.)............ **400-600**

Gardenia (1940s)

Large white gardenia blossoms and green leaves over a textured impressed band on a shaded green, grey or tan ground.

Large Green Gardenia Basket

Basket, widely flaring fan-shaped body w/high circular arched handle enclosing the body, green ground, No. 609-10", 10" h. (ILLUS.) **175**

Book ends, green ground, No. 659, 5 1/2" h., pr.. **200-250**

Ewer, footed ovoid body tapering to a tall slender neck w/upright arched spout, loop handle from neck to shoulder, grey ground, No. 617-10", 10" h. **175-200**

Jardiniere & pedestal base, grey ground, No. 605-8", 24 1/2" h., 2 pcs........................... **920**

Jonquil (1931)

White jonquil blossoms and green leaves in relief against textured tan ground, green lining.

Jardiniere, bulbous form w/wide flat mouth flanked by tiny loop handles, No. 621-7", 7" d... **316**

Jardiniere & pedestal, jardiniere No. 621-10" & pedestal No. 621-18-10", overall 29" h. **1,725**

Strawberry jar, flaring cylindrical form w/wide central vase flanked on opposing sides by small tapering vases, opposing pair of handles down the other two sides, on a saucer base, No. 96-7", 7 1/4" h. **633**

Rare Jonquil Strawberry Jar & Plate

Three Jonquil Vases

Strawberry jar & underplate, the wide ovoid body w/flat rim pierced around the top w/four wide projecting openings alternating w/clusters of flowers, separate underplate, No. 97-6", 2 pcs. (ILLUS., previous page) **3,105**

Vase, 4" h., bulbous spherical form, downturned loop handles from rim to shoulder, No. 524-4" (ILLUS. center with other Jonquil vases, top of page) **230**

Vase, 5 1/2" h., spherical w/a wide flat rim flanked by small pointed loop handles, No. 542-5 1/2" (ILLUS. left with other Jonquil vases, top of page) .... **300 - 400**

Vase, 6 1/2" h., wide bulbous body tapering to flat rim, C-form handles, No. 543-6 1/2" **403**

Vase, 9 1/2" h., bulbous base tapering slightly to wide cylindrical neck, loop handles at midsection, No. 544-9" (ILLUS. right with other Jonquil vases) **805**

Laurel (1934)

Laurel branch and berries in low relief with reeded panels at the sides. Glazed in deep yellow, green shading to cream or terra cotta.

Bowl, 6" d., squatty bulbous body w/incurved rim & angled shoulder handles, terra cotta ground, No. 250-6 1/4" **345**

Laurel Terra Cotta Vase

Vase, 6" h., cylindrical w/stepped rounded shoulder flanked by low curved shoulder handles, terra cotta ground, No. 668-6" (ILLUS.) **230**

Vase, 6" h., tapering cylinder w/wide mouth, closed angular handles at shoulder, green ground, No. 667-6" **259**

Vase, 7 1/4" h., tapering cylinder w/pierced angular handles at midsection, green ground, No. 671-7 1/4" **316**

Luffa (1934)

Relief-molded ivy leaves and blossoms on shaded brown or green wavy horizontal ridges.

Spherical Luffa Jardiniere

Jardiniere, brown ground, spherical w/a wide flat mouth flanked by tiny angled handles, brown ground, No. 631-7", 7" (ILLUS.) **201**

Vase, 6" h., tapering cylindrical body w/angled handles from shoulder to rim, green ground, No. 683-6" **230**

Vase, 6" h., tapering cylindrical body w/angled handles from shoulder to rim, brown ground, No. 683-6" **230**

Vase, 7" h., ovoid body w/small angled handles from shoulder to rim, brown ground, No. 685-7" **258**

Vase, 8" h., footed widely swelling ovoid body w/a wide shoulder to the short cylindrical neck flanked by low angled handles, brown ground, No. 689-8" **345**

Vase, 8 1/2" h., ovoid body tapering slightly to a low cylindrical neck flanked by small angled handles, green ground, No. 687-8" **258**

Luffa Brown Wall Pocket

Wall pocket, long ovoid form w/arched & flaring rim flanked by tiny angled handles, brown ground, No. 1272-8", 8" h. (ILLUS.) **575**

Magnolia (1943)

Large white blossoms with rose centers and black stems in relief against a blue, green or tan textured ground.

Ashtray, two-handled, low bowl form, tan ground, No. 28, 7" d., 2" h. **46**
Basket w/ornate overhead handle, blue ground, No. 383-7" **230**

Experimental Blue Magnolia Vase

Vase, experimental, bulbous nearly spherical body w/small loop handles on shoulder, shaded light blue ground w/white blossoms & brown branches (ILLUS.) **4,025**

Large Tan Magnolia Vase

Vase, 14" h., footed tall ovoid body w/angled shoulder handles, tan ground, No. 97-14" (ILLUS.) **374**

Ming Tree (1949)

High gloss glaze in mint green, turquoise, or white is decorated with Ming branch; handles are formed from gnarled branches.

Basket w/overhead branch handle, ruffled rim, white ground, No. 509-12", 13" h. **201**

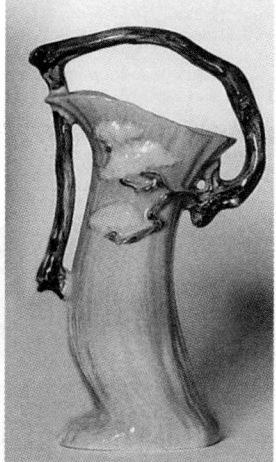

Tall Curved Ming Tree Basket

Basket w/overhead branch handle, curved body w/asymmetrical rim, green ground, No. 510-14", 14 1/2" (ILLUS.) ... **200-225**
Ewer, white ground, No. 516-10", 10" h. ... **100-150**
Vase, 6 1/2" h., single branch handle, white ground, No. 572-6" **50-100**
Wall pocket, overhead branch handle, blue ground, No. 566-8", 8 1/2" h. **173**

Three Morning Glory Vases

Morning Glory (1935)

Delicately colored blossoms and twining vines in white or green with blue.

Vase, 7" h., footed flattened fanned shape w/angular handles at the bottom, white ground, No. 120-7" (ILLUS. right with other Morning Glory vases, top of page) **374**

Vase, 8 1/2" h., trumpet-shaped handles at base, green ground, No. 726-8" **633**

Vase, 8 1/2" h., trumpet-shaped handles at base, white ground, No. 726-8" (ILLUS. left with other Morning Glory vases, top of page) **600-800**

Vase, 10" h., bulbous base tapering to wide molded rim, two-handled, white ground, No. 730-10" (ILLUS. center with other Morning Glory vases, top of page) **700-900**

Moss (1930s)

Green moss hanging over brown branch with green leaves; backgrounds are pink, ivory or tan shading to blue.

Bowl-vase, spherical body w/a wide flat mouth, small angular handles rising from base to mid-section, ivory, No. 290-6", 6" h. (ILLUS. left with console bowl and vase, bottom of page) **345**

Console bowl, oval w/shaped rim & angled end handles, pink shading to green ground, No. 293-10", 10 1/2" l., 3" h. (ILLUS. center with Moss bowl-vase and vase, bottom of page) **259**

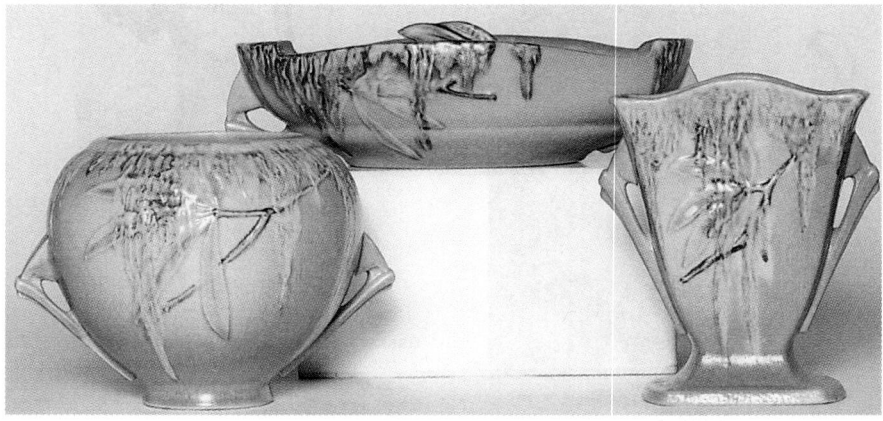

Moss Bowl-Vase, Console Bowl & Vase

Rare Moss Jardiniere & Pedestal

Jardiniere & pedestal base, tan to blue ground, No. 635-10", 29" h., 2 pcs. (ILLUS.) **3,738**

Vase, 6" h., footed flaring lower body below cylindrical sides, large open angular handles, pink & green ground, No. 774-6" **201**

Vase, 7" h., flattened fan shape w/angular handles down the side, blue ground, partial foil label, No. 778-7" (ILLUS. previous page right with Moss bowl-vase and console bowl) **200-250**

Panel (Rosecraft Panel 1920)

Background colors are dark green or dark brown; decorations embossed within the recessed panels are of natural or stylized floral arrangements or female nudes.

Bowl, 9" d., wide flat bottom w/low incurved sides, pink & light green floral panels on a dark green ground, marked **125-200**

Vase, 6" h., fan-shaped body w/wide disk foot, female nudes in panels, orange on dark brown ground **431**

Rosecraft Panel Fan Vase with Nudes

Vase, 8" h., flattened fan-shaped bowl on a short knob pedestal on flaring round foot, nudes in panels, orange on a dark brown ground (ILLUS.) **700-800**

Rosecraft Panel Floral Window Box

Window box, long narrow rectangular shape w/three panels on each long side, swirling flower & leaf design, light green on dark green ground, 6 x 12" (ILLUS.) **460**

Peony (1942)

Floral arrangement of white or dark yellow blossoms with green leaves on textured, shaded backgrounds in yellow with mixed green and brown, pink with blue, and solid green.

Basket, hanging-type, bulbous wide body w/a wide flat molded rim flanked by small loop handles, yellow blossoms on mixed green & brown ground, No. 467-5" **150-250**

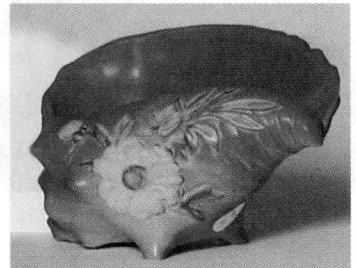

Peony Conch Shell

Model of a conch shell, pale yellow blossom on pink shaded to blue ground, No. 436, 9 1/2" w. (ILLUS.) **173**

Wall pocket, bullet-shaped w/widely flaring deeply ruffled rim, two side handles, white blossoms on green ground, No. 1293-8", 8" **230**

Pine Cone (1935 & 1953)

Realistic embossed brown pine cones and green pine needles on shaded blue, brown or green ground. (Pink is extremely rare.)

Ashtray, blue ground, No. 25............................. **201**

Basket, w/overhead branch handle, asymmetrical fanned & pleated body, blue ground, No. 408-6", 6" h.................................. **374**

Basket, long boat-shaped body w/long arched overhead branch handle, raised on short peg feet, 12" l. **201**

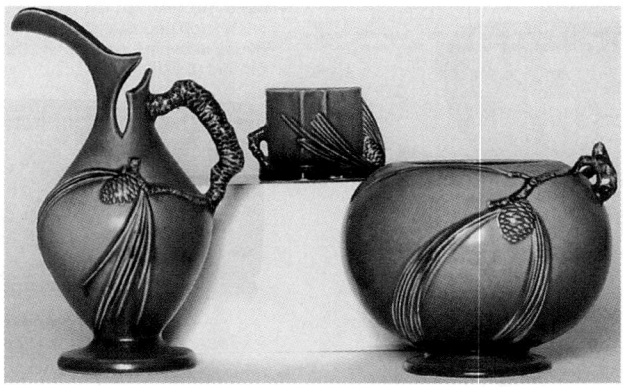

Brown Pine Cone Ewer, Match Holder & Vase

Ewer, footed ovoid body tapering to a split neck w/a high arched spout, branch handle, brown ground, No. 909-10", 10" h. (ILLUS. left with match holder and vase)...... **805**

Flowerpot & saucer, brown ground, No. 633-5", 5" h. **316**

Large Blue Pine Cone Jardiniere

Jardiniere, blue ground, 632-10", 10" h. (ILLUS.)... **900-1,200**

Match holder, upright oval form, brown ground, No. 498, 3" h. (ILLUS. center with ewer and vase, top of page).................. **288**

Pitcher, 10 1/2" h., upright curved & fanned body w/long branch & sprig handle from rim to base, green ground, No. 485-10" (ILLUS.)... **460**

Pitcher w/ice lip, 8" h., footed wide spherical body w/curved rim & squared spout, brown ground, No. 1321................................. **460**

Vase, 6" h., 6 1/2" d., footed spherical body w/closed rim, small branch handle at one side of rim, brown ground, No. 261-6", 6" d. (ILLUS. right with ewer and match holder, top of page)................................. **300-325**

Vase, bud, 7" h., green ground, No. 112-7"....... **173**

Vase, 7" h., two-handled, footed wide cylinder, brown ground, No. 704-7" **230**

Vase, 8" h., pillow-type, wide flattened bulbous body w/asymmetrical branch handles, green ground, No. 114-8" (ground flake on base).. **374**

Vase, 10" h., footed expanding cylinder, brown ground, No. 709-10"..................... **400-500**

Vase, 12" h., corseted form w/asymmetric branch handles, brown ground, No. 712-12".. **431**

Tall Fanned Pine Cone Pitcher

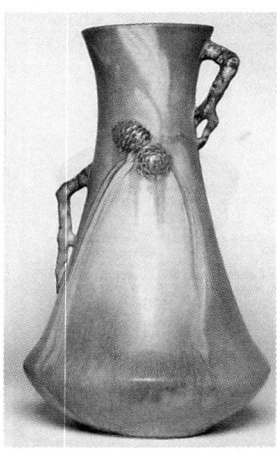

Tall Green Pine Cone Vase

Vase, 12" h., corseted form w/asymmetric branch handles, green ground, No. 712-12" (ILLUS.) **431**

Wall pocket, bucket-shaped, green ground, No. 1283-9", 9" h.. .... **850-950**

Wall shelf, brown ground, No. 1-5 x 8", 5" w., 8" h. **374**

Poppy (1930s)

Shaded backgrounds of blue or pink with decoration of poppy flower and green leaves.

Ewer, footed gently flaring cylindrical body w/a cut-out lip w/arched spout, C-form handle, pink ground, No. 876-10", 10" h. **450-550**

Ewer, very tall slender ovoid body w/a split neck & high arched spout, C-scroll handle, pink ground, foil label, No. 880-18", 18" h. **550-650**

Vase, 10" h., two-handled, semi-ovoid, cut-out rim, pink ground, No. 875-10" **300-400**

Tall Grey Poppy Vase

Vase, 15" h., footed squatty lower body tapering to tall cylindrical sides w/a flared rim, small C-scroll lower shoulder handles, grey ground, No. 878-15" (ILLUS.) **450-550**

Silhouette (1950)

Recessed area silhouettes nature study or female nudes. Colors are rose, turquoise, tan and white with turquoise.

Basket, flaring cylinder w/pointed overhead handle, florals, turquoise blue, No. 708-6", 6" h. **173**

Brown Silhouette Basket with Florals

Basket, curved rim & asymmetrical handle, florals, brown ground, No. 710-10", 10" h. (ILLUS.) **259**

Vase, 7" h., fan-shaped, nude woman, brown ground, No. 783-7" **230**

Sunflower (1930)

Tall stems support yellow sunflowers whose blooms form a repetitive band. Textured background shades from tan to dark green at base.

Bowl, 7 1/2" d., wide squatty form w/wide flat rim, No. 208-5" (ILLUS. right with Sunflower vases, bottom of page) **805**

Console bowl, elongated low diamond form w/loop end handles, 12 1/2" l., 3" h. **920**

Urn-vase, nearly spherical w/closed rim flanked by tiny rim handles, 4" h. (ILLUS. left with Sunflower bowl and vase, bottom of page) **575**

Sunflower Bowl and Vases

Roseville Sunflower Vase

Vase, 5" h., swelled cylindrical body w/long side handles & flat rim (ILLUS.)...................... 575
Vase, 9" h., bulbous base w/wide cylindrical neck, small loop handles, No. 493-9" (ILLUS. previous page center with bowl and urn-vase) 1,495

Rare Sunflower Wall Pocket

Wall pocket, bucket-form w/pierced double-arch top handle, No. 1265-7", 7" h. (ILLUS.) 1,380

Tuscany (1928)

Marble-like finish most often found in a shiny pink, sometimes in matte grey, more rarely in a dull turquoise. Suggestion of leaves and berries, usually at the base of handles, are the only decorations.

Flower arranger vase, flaring oval foot w/ringed stem supporting a flattened urn-form body w/loop handles on the shoulder pierced w/holes, mottled pink ground, No. 69-5", 5 1/2" h. 81
Lamp, table model, upright flat three-sided vase No. 343-7" fitted on a squared gilt-metal base, pink, overall 9" h................. 150-200
Vase, 4" h., footed widely flaring trumpet-form w/open handles from under rim to the foot, grey, No. 67-4"..................................... 92
Vase, 5" h., footed wide squatty bulbous body tapering sharply to a flat mouth, loop handles from rim to shoulder, grey, No. 341-5" 144

Three-sided Tuscany Vase

Vase, 7" h., upright flat three-sided shape, two-handled, pink, No. 343-7" (ILLUS.)......... 173
Wall pocket, conical w/wide ringed rim, loop handles at sides, pink, No. 1254-7", 7" h.. 201
Wall pocket, long open handles, rounded rim, mottled pink glaze, paper label, No. 1255-8", 8" h. 230

Water Lily (1943)

Water lily and pad in various color combinations: tan to brown with yellow lily, blue with white lily, pink to green with pink lily.

Basket, trumpet-shaped w/widely flaring rim, high arched & pointed handle across the top & under the rims, pink to green ground, No. 380-8", 8" h........................ 150-200
Basket, conch shell-shaped w/high arched handle, tan shaded to brown ground, No. 381-10", 10" h. 288
Console set: 14" l. bowl w/large pointed end handles, shaped sides, & pr. of 2" h. candleholders, pink shading to green ground, bowl No. 444-14", 14" l., candleholders No. 1154-2", the set 288
Cookie jar, cov., angular handles, pink shading to green ground, No. 1-8", 8" h. 403
Ewer, squatty flared bottom tapering to a tall split neck w/high arched spout & high pointed loop handle, tan to brown ground, No. 10-6", 6" h. 115

Wincraft (1948)

Revived shapes from older lines such as Pine Cone, Bushberry, Cremona, Primrose and others. Vases with animal motifs, contemporary shapes in high gloss of blue, tan, lime and green.

Tea set: cov. teapot, creamer & sugar bowl; white floral decoration in relief on glossy tan ground, No. 271, 3 pcs. 201
Vase, 7" h., square, paneled sides w/swirled Art Deco style design in relief on glossy yellow and tan ground, No. 274-7" 100-200

Wisteria Bowl and Vases

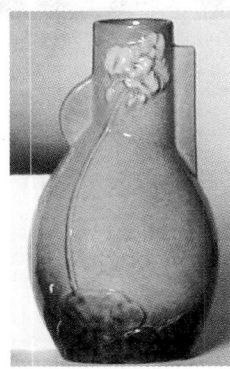

Tall Tan Wincraft Vase

Vase, 10" h., ovoid base & long cylindrical neck w/wedge-shaped closed handle on one side & long closed column-form handle on the other, shaded tan ground, No. 284-10" (ILLUS., left column) **150-200**

Wall pocket, rectangular box-like holder w/horizontal ribbing & ivy leaves as rim handle, glossy light green ground, No. 266-4", 8 1/2" h. 173

Wisteria (1933)

Lavender wisteria blossoms and green vines against a roughly textured brown shading to deep blue ground or brown shading to yellow and green; rarely found in only brown.

Bowl & flower frog, 6 1/2" d., 3" h., sharply flaring low rounded sides w/a closed rim, brown ground (ILLUS. center with bowl-vase and vase, top of page) 374

Squatty and Tall Wisteria Vases

Bowl-vase, bulbous spherical form tapering to a small flat mouth flanked by tiny shoulder handles, brown shading to yellow & green ground, No. 632-5", 5" h. (ILLUS. right with bowl and vase, top of previous page) **450-500**

Vase, 4" h., squatty, angular handles on sharply canted shoulder, brown ground, No. 629-4" **345**

Vase, 6 1/2" h., globular w/small flat mouth & tiny angular shoulder handles, brown to blue ground, No. 637-6 1/2" (ILLUS. left with tall vase, bottom of previous page)..... **1,035**

Vase, 8" h., pear-shaped body w/short cylindrical neck & tiny angled shoulder handles, brown shading to yellow & green ground, No. 636-8" (ILLUS. left with bowl and bowl-vase, top previous page) **633**

Vase, 8" h., 6 1/2" d., wide tapering cylindrical body w/small angled handles flanking the flat rim, brown ground, No. 633-8" **575**

Vase, 10" h., cylindrical body w/closed rim, angled shoulder handles, brown to blue ground, No. 639-10" (ILLUS. right with squatty vase, bottom previous page) **2,300**

Rare Tall Wisteria Vase

Vase, 15" h., bottle-shaped w/angular handles at shoulder, blue ground, No. 641-15" (ILLUS.) **2,530**

Zephyr Lily (1946)

Tall lilies and slender leaves adorn swirl-textured backgrounds of Bermuda Blue, Evergreen and Sienna Tan.

Basket, footed flaring rectangular body w/upcurved rim & long asymmetrical handle, green ground, No. 394-8", 8" h. **173**

Basket, footed cylindrical body flaring slightly to an ornate cut rim w/low wide overhead handle, blue ground, No. 395-10", 10" h. **230**

Tray, leaf-shaped, terra cotta ground, No. 477-12", 14 1/2" l. **115**

Cup & saucer, demitasse, footed, figural

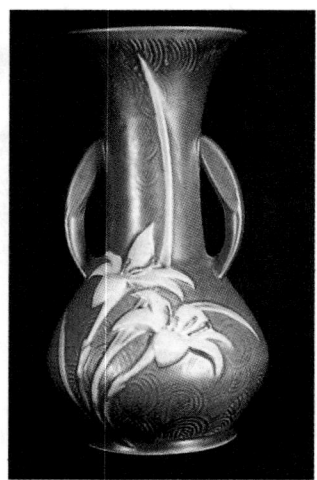

Tall Terra Cotta Zephyr Lily Vase

Vase, 10" h., bulbous base tapering to a tall trumpet neck, low curved handles at center of the sides, terra cotta ground, No. 137-10" (ILLUS.) **150-200**

Royal Bayreuth

Good china in numerous patterns and designs has been made at the Royal Bayreuth factory in Tettau, Germany since 1794. Listings below are by the company's lines, plus miscellaneous pieces. Interest in this china remains at a peak and prices continue to rise. Pieces listed carry the company's blue mark except where noted otherwise.

Among the important reference books in this field are Royal Bayreuth - A Collectors' Guide and Royal Bayreuth - A Collectors' Guide - Book II by Mary McCaslin (see Special Contributors list).

Royal Bayreuth Mark

Devil & Cards

Ashtray, two cards.................................... **$275-300**
Creamer, figural red devil, 3 1/2" h. **300-350**
Plate, 6" d. **400-500**
Salt shaker **150-175**
Sugar bowl, cov. **350-400**

Mother-of-Pearl

Compote, open, decorated w/roses, pearlized finish, small **50**
Creamer, Murex Shell patt., spiky form........ **75-100**
Spiky Shell patt., pearlized finish **125-150**

Hatpin holder, figural poppy mold, pearlized white finish...................................... **550-600**
Pitcher, milk, boot-shaped, figural Spiky Shell patt., pearlized finish, 5 1/2" h. **325-375**
Toothpick holder, Murex Shell patt. **110-125**

Rose Tapestry

Basket, two-color roses, 3" h. **300-350**
Cake plate, pierced gold handles, three-color roses, 10 1/2" d. **500-600**

Rare Rose Tapestry Centerpiece Bowl

Centerpiece bowl, a large squatty bulbous lobed body decorated w/roses & a scene of a garden wall above deep red dot & blue bands around the lower body & pedestal base, mounted w/an ornate gilt-brass pierced rim w/winged putti masks, scrolled dolphin handles & on a pierced, domed scroll base, 18 1/2" w., 13 1/2" h. (ILLUS.) **978**
Chocolate set: cov. chocolate pot w/four matching cups & saucers, three-color roses, 9 pcs. **2,200-2,600**
Creamer & cov. sugar bowl, two-color roses, pr. **500-550**
Hatpin holder, small red roses at top & base, large yellow roses on body, reticulated base, gold trim, 4 1/2" h............... **450-500**
Humidor, cov., three-color roses, 7" h...... **600-650**
Model of a Victorian woman's high-heeled shoe, three-color roses.............. **400-450**
Pitcher, 5" h., wide cylindrical body tapering slightly toward rim, three-color roses, 24 oz.. **350-400**
Tray, rectangular, with short rim, three-color roses, 11 1/2 x 8" **500-600**

Tomato Items

Tomato creamer, cov., large **150-200**
Tomato plate, 5 1/2" d., ring-handled, figural lettuce leaf w/molded yellow flowers **30-35**
Tomato plate, 7" d., ring-handled, figural lettuce leaf w/molded yellow flowers **40**
Tomato salt & pepper shakers, pr. **125-150**

Miscellaneous

Ashtray, figural lobster................................. **125-150**
Ashtray, scenic decoration of Dutch woman w/basket, 5 1/2" d. **50-75**
Basket, miniature, scene w/cows, unmarked **70**
Basket, handled, boy & donkey decoration, artist-signed, 5 3/4" h. **150-175**
Bell, peacock decoration, 2 1/2" d., 3" h............ **300**

Bowl, 5 3/4" d., nursery rhyme scene w/Jack & Jill.. **125-175**

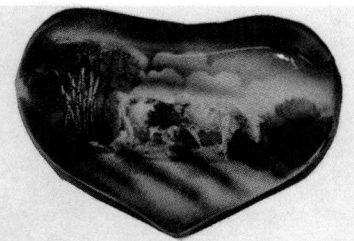

Royal Bayreuth Heart-shaped Box

Box, cov., heart-shaped, decorated w/scene of two brown & white cows & trees in pasture, green & yellow background, unmarked, 2 x 3 1/4", 1 1/2" h. (ILLUS.).. **75-100**
Creamer, figural black cat **200-300**
Creamer, figural duck.................................... **250-300**
Creamer, figural fish head, grey **250**
Creamer, figural grape cluster, light green **125**
Creamer, figural monkey, green................. **500-550**
Creamer, figural oak leaf, white w/orchid highlights.. **250-300**
Creamer, figural snake............................. **750-1,000**
Creamer, figural watermelon....................... **300-350**
Creamer, "Huntsman," scene of hunter & dogs, small flying bird on flared rim, 4" h.. **100-125**
Creamer, pasture scene w/cows & trees, 3 1/4" h. **75-100**
Creamer, crowing rooster & hen decoration, 4 1/4" h. **125-175**
Creamer & cov. sugar bowl, figural rooster, pr. **300-350**
Creamer & open sugar bowl, figural poppy, white satin finish, pr. **500-550**
Gravy boat w/attached liner, decorated w/multicolored floral sprays, gadrooned border, gold trim, cream ground......................... **60**
Hair receiver, cov., three-footed, scene of dog beside hunter shooting ducks......... **250-300**
Match holder w/striker, decorated water scene w/brown "Shadow Trees" & boats on orange & gold ground, unmarked, 3 1/4" d., 2 1/2" h. **75-100**
Model of a man's shoe, black oxford **250-300**
Pitcher, 3 1/2" h., scenic decoration of Arab on horse **75-100**

Pitcher with Musicians Scene

Tray with Girl & Geese Scene

Pitcher, 3 1/2" h., 2 1/4" d., scene of musicians, one playing bass & one w/mandolin, unmarked (ILLUS.)..................... **65**
Pitcher, squatty, 5" h., 5" d., decorated w/hunting scene....................................... **100-125**
Pitcher, 7 1/2" h., w/orange, cream & green bands, applied handle........................... **150-200**
Pitcher, milk, figural oak leaf...................... **500-600**
Pitcher, milk, Goose Girl decoration.......... **150-175**
Pitcher, milk, 5 1/2" h., figural fish head.... **300-400**
Pitcher, water, 6" h., figural apple............. **600-700**

Figural Sunflower Pitcher

Pitcher, water, 6 1/2" h., figural sunflower (ILLUS.).. **4,000-4,500**
Pitcher, water, 7 3/4" h., 6" d., figural lobster, red shaded to orange w/green handle... **450-550**
Plate, 8 1/2" d., scene of man fishing................ **135**
Plate, 9 1/2" d., "tapestry," landscape scene w/deer by a river...................................... **250-300**
Toothpick holder, decorated w/scene of girl w/two chickens.................................... **150-200**
Toothpick holder, three-handled, harvest scene decoration **150-200**
Toothpick holder, two-handled, four-footed, scene of horsemen, unmarked.......... **75-125**
Tray, decorated w/scene of girl w/geese, molded rim w/gold trim, 9 x 12 1/4" (ILLUS., top of page)............................... **400-450**

Tray, "tapestry," scene of train on bridge over raging river, 7 3/4 x 11"................... **700-800**
Tureen, figural, in the form of a rose on short petal feet, 6" w., 2 3/4" h. **450-550**

Miniature Royal Bayreuth Spouted Vase

Vase, miniature, 3" h., 3 1/2" d., spherical body w/two flaring spouts at the top centered by a small loop handle, Cavalier Musicians decoration (ILLUS.) **75-125**
Vase, 3 1/2" h., Cavalier Musicians decoration **75-125**
Vase, 4" h., ovoid body w/a tiny, short flaring neck, "tapestry," scene of two cows, one black & one tan **425-475**
Vase, bud, 4 3/4" h., "tapestry," rounded body w/a thin tall neck, Lady & Prince scenic decoration **150-200**
Vase, 5" h., "tapestry," decoration of cockfight against scenic ground..................... **135-175**
Vase, 6" h., "tapestry," decorated w/a scene of an elk & three hounds in a river......... **425-475**
Vase, 8" h., colorful "tapestry" portrait of girl & pony on blue ground **375-425**
Vase, 11 1/2" h., polar bear scene **900-1,100**
Vases, 2 1/2" h., decorated w/sunset scene of a ship, pr.. **100-150**

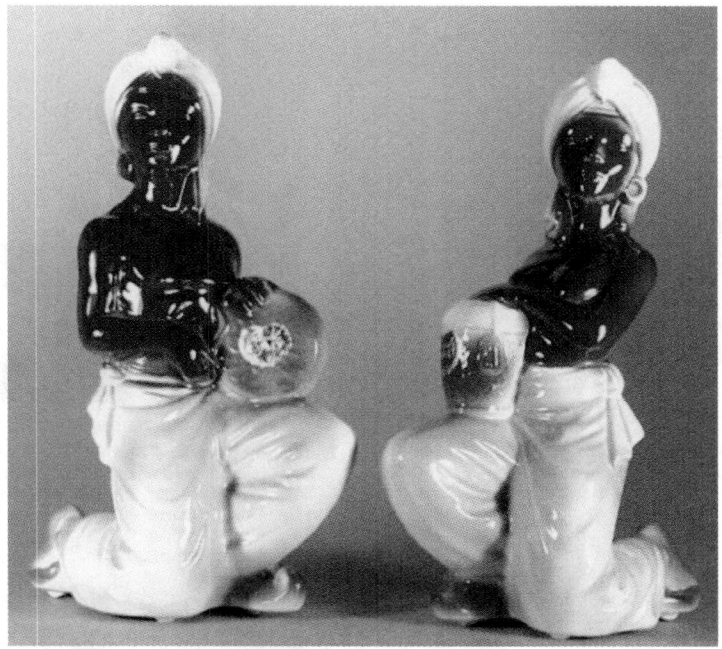

Blackamoor Man & Woman Figures

Royal Copley

Royal Copley was a trade name used by the Spaulding China Company of Sebring, Ohio, during the 1940s and 1950s for a variety of ceramic figurines, planters and other decorative pieces. Similar pieces were also produced under the trade name "Royal Windsor" as well as the Spaulding China mark.

The Spaulding China Company stopped producing in 1957, but for the next two years other potteries finished production of its outstanding orders. Today these originally inexpensive wares are developing a dedicated collector following.

Figurines

Blackamoor Man & Blackamoor Woman, kneeling, 8 1/2" h., pr. (ILLUS., top of page)... **$80-100**
Cocker Spaniel, 6 1/4" h. **30-35**
Dog, 6 1/2" h. **25-30**
Hen & Rooster, large, Royal Copley mark, 7" & 8" h., pr. **80-110**
Hen & Rooster, small, Royal Copley mark, 6" & 6 1/2" h., pr.................................... **80-90**
Mallard Duck, 7" h... **35-40**
Parrots, 8" h.. **30-40**

Planters

Spaniel Pup with Collar Figurine

Spaniel Pup with Collar, 6" h. (ILLUS.)........ **35-40**
Swallows on Double Stump, 7 1/2" h., pr. **100-120**
Titmouse, 8" h... **20-30**

Large Kneeling Angel Planter

Angel, large, kneeling, blue robe, 8" h.
(ILLUS.) **60-75**
Apple and Finch, 6 1/2" h. **40-50**
Bare Shoulder Lady head vase, 6" h. **60-70**
Blackamoor Prince head vase, 8" h. **30-40**

Royal Copley Clown Planter

Clown, 8 1/4" h. (ILLUS.) **100-125**
Deer & Doe, 7 1/2" h. **15-20**

Dog in Picnic Basket Planter

Dog in Picnic Basket, 7 3/4" h. (ILLUS.) **80-90**
Dog with Suitcase (Skip), 7" h. **40-45**
Dogwood, small, 4 1/2" h. **20-25**

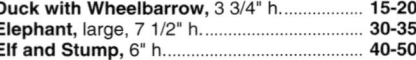

Duck with Wheelbarrow, 3 3/4" h. **15-20**
Elephant, large, 7 1/2" h. **30-35**
Elf and Stump, 6" h. **40-50**

Fancy Finch on Tree Stump Planter

Fancy Finch on Tree Stump, red, white &
black bird perched on brown leafy branch
beside white planter, 7 1/2" h. (ILLUS.) **80-90**
**Girl Leaning on Barrel & Boy Leaning on
Barrel,** 6 1/4" h., pr. **40-50**
Goldfinch on Stump, 6 1/2" h. **40-50**

Horse Head with Mane Planter

Horse Head with Flying Mane, 8" h.
(ILLUS.) **30-50**
Kitten in Picnic Basket, 8" h. **60-70**

Kitten on Cowboy Boot Planter

Kitten on Cowboy Boot, 7 1/2" h. (ILLUS.).. **55-60**

Mallard Drake, sitting, 5 1/4" h. 40-45
Mallard Duck on Stump, 8" h. 30-40
Nuthatch, 5 1/2" h. 25-30

Palomino Horse Head Planter
Palomino Horse Head, 6 1/4" h. (ILLUS.)..... 40-50
Poodle with Bow, posing, 5 1/4" h. 70-80

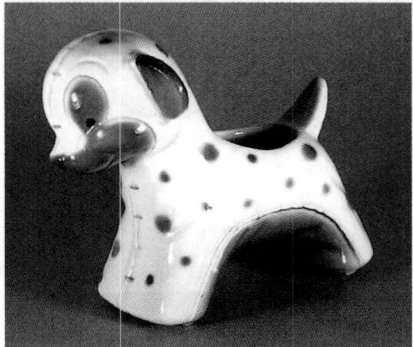

Stuffed Animal Dog Planter
Stuffed Animal Dog, white & brown,
  5 1/2" h. (ILLUS.) 60-70

Stuffed Animal Rooster Planter
Stuffed Animal Rooster, pale green &
  white, 6" h. (ILLUS.) 70-80

Teddy Bear, 6 1/4" h. 30-40
Teddy Bear in Picnic Basket, 8" h. 70-90
Teddy Bear with Mandolin, 6 3/4" h. 50-75
Wide Brim Hat Boy & Wide Brim Hat Girl,
  7 1/4" h., pr. 90-100
Wren on Tree Stump, 6 1/4" h....................... 40-50

Miscellaneous

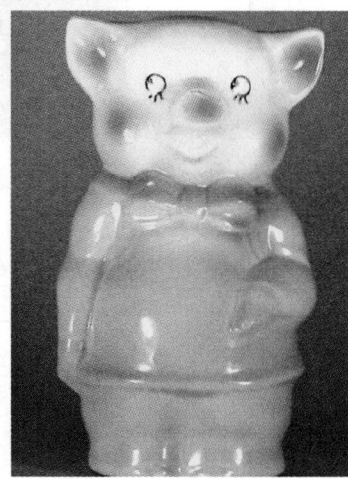

Bow Tie Pig Bank
Bank, Bow Tie Pig, standing, wearing green
  bow tie & blue outfit, 6 1/4" h. (ILLUS.)...... 75-85

Barber Pole Blade Bank
Blade bank, model of a barber pole in red &
  white w/"Blades" on the side, 6 1/4" h.
  (ILLUS.)... 70-80
Smoking set, models of ducks, 3" & 4" h., 3
  pcs. 60-75

Happy Anniversary Vase

Vase, 6" h., upright rectangular form w/flaring serpentine rim, dark blue centered by a large white panel decorated w/wedding bells & bluebirds & "Happy Anniversary" in gold (ILLUS.) **50-60**

Vase, 7" h., Carol's Corsage............................ **25-35**

Vase, 7 1/4" h., Flying Bird, open center **45-50**

Vases, 8 1/4" h., cornucopia-shaped w/decal decoration, pr. **50-60**

Wall pocket, Salt Box, 5 1/2" h........................ **60-70**

Wall pocket, Straw Hat, large, 7" h................ **75-85**

Royal Dux

This factory in Bohemia was noted for the figural porcelain wares in the Art Nouveau style it exported around the turn of the 20th century. Other notable figural pieces were produced through the 1930s. The factory was nationalized after World War II.

Royal Dux Marks

Two Shepherds Resting at Rock

Figure group, two shepherds, the man sitting on rock w/legs crossed & about to blow into primitive pipe, the woman standing next to him holding crook, polychrome decoration in shades of buff, applied pink triangle mark, early 20th c., 21 1/2" h. (ILLUS.).................................... **$1,035**

Young Woman Embracing Young Man

Figure group, young hunter wearing primitive tunic & sandals, carrying quiver & laden w/dead fowl embraces young barefoot woman, polychrome decoration in olive greens & buffs, applied pink triangle mark, first half 20th c., 22" h. (ILLUS.)....... **1,150**

Figure of Boy on Donkey

Figure of boy on donkey, the boy wearing apricot trousers & matching brimmed hat & pale olive shirt, bare feet, sitting astride saddled white donkey, both looking to side, applied pink triangle mark, first half 20th c., 14 1/4" h. (ILLUS., previous page)..... **518**

Figure of Woman Reading Book

Figure of woman, sitting on rock-form base & reading book, wearing off-the-shoulder reddish brown top & draping long olive green skirt, applied pink triangle mark, first half 20th c., 19" h. (ILLUS.) **1,093**

Woman with Water Jars

Figure of woman, w/h.p. features, wearing turban-style headdress & olive green tunic w/sleeves rolled up above elbows,

holding water jar in each hand, a mug hanging from her sash belt, on base decorated w/leaves, applied pink triangle mark, first half 20th c., 23" h. (ILLUS.).......... **920**

Pair of Royal Dux Shepherds

Figures of shepherds, the young woman standing w/lamb, the young man w/goat, each w/h.p. features & wearing apricot & pale olive green clothes, each on paneled base, applied pink triangle mark, first half 20th c., 20 1/2" h., pr. (ILLUS.) **1,725**

Royal Dux Shepherds

Figures of shepherds, w/h.p. features, the young woman wearing apricot dress & pale olive turban-style headdress, holding kid in her arms, w/two other kids at her feet, the young man wearing short apricot tunic w/sheepskin & green hat, holding panpipe as if about to play, two lambs at his feet, each on oval base, applied pink triangle mark, mid-20th c., 17" h., pr. (ILLUS.).. **1,955**

Figures of Water Carriers

Figures of water carriers, the young man wearing apricot turban-style headdress & pale olive tunic belted w/apricot sash, holding large handled earthenware jar in both hands as if pouring contents out, the young woman wearing a pale pink veil-type headdress & pale olive gown w/apricot sash, holding handle of earthenware jar on ground at her feet, each on oval base w/pale pink floral trim, applied pink triangle mark, early 20th c., 20" h., pr. (ILLUS.).. **1,265**

Pair of Figures Carrying Baskets

Figures of woman & man, the woman wearing mid-calf-length apricot dress &

pale olive short-sleeved blouse, the man wearing apricot trousers & matching brimmed hat & pale olive long-sleeved shirt, each w/one hand on hip, the other steadying a large empty basket on shoulder, each on oval base, applied pink triangle marks, first half 20th c., 16" h., pr. (ILLUS.)... **805**

Figures of Women in Classical Dress

Figures of women, wearing classical dress in shades of olive green & pale pink & peach, one posed as if playing cymbals, the other arching back as if dancing, holding hem of gown out in dramatic pose, each on oval bases trimmed w/scroll design, applied pink triangle mark, early 20th c., some minor professional repair, 22" h., pr. (ILLUS.) **1,610**

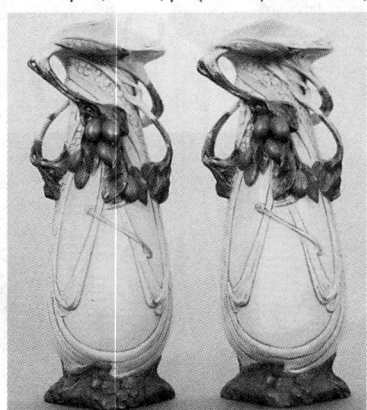

Royal Dux Vases with Vines & Fruit

Vases, 19" h., Art Nouveau style, tall ovoid body on a squared foot, molded in bold relief w/undulating foliage & fruit, the ivory ground highlighted w/dark gold, pink triangle mark, early 20th c., bases drilled for lamp adaptation, pr. (ILLUS.)................ **1,380**

Various Royal Worcester Pieces

Royal Worcester

This porcelain has been made by the Royal Worcester Porcelain Co. at Worcester, England, from 1862 to the present. Royal Worcester is distinguished from wares made at Worcester between 1751 and 1862, which are referred to only as Worcester by collectors.

Royal Worcester Marks

Candlesticks, figural seated boy & girl w/h.p. features, each dressed in pale peach & white, leaning against tree trunk forms that make up candlesticks, printed marks, late 19th c., 9" h., pr. (ILLUS. back row, left w/other Royal Worcester pieces, top of page).. **$690**

Cracker jar, cov., ovoid melon-lobed body & disk lid decorated w/h.p. florals in pastel shades on ivory ground, gilt trim, the lid w/gilt handle, printed purple mark, late 19th c., 7 1/2" h. (ILLUS. front row, second from left w/other Royal Worcester pieces, top of page).. **288**

Cracker jar, cov., spherical melon-lobed body w/flattened cover & gold branch handle, cream ground painted w/flowering vines in shades of deep rose, pink, brown & green, all trimmed w/gold, ca. 1889, 6 1/2" d., 7" h. (ILLUS., next column).. **325**

Fine Royal Worcester Cracker Jar

Ewer, bulbous form bisected w/gilt horizontal band, short gilt ring foot, long slender neck w/gilt ring at base & gilt trim at rim, arched spout, applied gilt C-scroll handle w/embossed scroll designs, h.p. floral decoration in pale pinks & greens on ivory ground, marked "Royal Worcester," late 19th c., 10" h. (ILLUS. front row, far right w/other Royal Worcester pieces, top of page)... **431**

Jug, bulbous shape tapering to flared scalloped rim w/arched spout, applied gilt ribbed angular handle, applied figural salamander & gilt band at neck on cream-colored embossed basketweave ground, marked "Royal Worcester," late 19th c., 5 1/2" h. (ILLUS. front row, second from right w/other Royal Worcester pieces, top of page).. **345**

Fine Royal Worcester Dinner Plates

Hand-painted Royal Worcester Plate

Plate, 10 3/4" d., h.p. English village scene w/road & trees in the foreground, artist-signed, dated 1953 (ILLUS.).................. **225-275**

Plates, 10 1/2" d., dinner, a broad salmon pink border w/swags of two-color gold featuring antique vases, white center, ca. 1900, set of 12 (ILLUS., top of page)......... **1,380**

Urn, cov., spherical shape w/long cylindrical neck, figural bronze serpent handles, flared foot, reticulated rim & applied embossed foliage, h.p. features, marked w/purple "Royal Worcester" crown & "1168," 19th c., 15" h. (ILLUS. front row, far left w/other Royal Worcester pieces, top of previous page) **1,955**

Vase, 12" h., bulbous form on short tapered gilt foot w/rickrack design, slender fluted gilt neck below gilt reticulated everted rim, small ring scroll gilt handles, the body w/h.p. floral decoration in pinks & green on ivory ground, marked "Royal Worcester," late 19th c. (ILLUS. back row, right w/other Royal Worcester pieces, top of previous page)............................... **633**

R.S. Prussia & Related Wares

Ornately decorated china marked "R.S. Prussia" and "R.S. Germany" continues to grow in popularity. According to the Third Series of Mary Frank Gaston's Encyclopedia of R.S. Prussia (Collector Books, Paducah, Kentucky), these marks were used by the Reinhold Schlegelmilch porcelain factories located in Suhl in the Germanic regions known as "Prussia" prior to World War I, and in Tillowitz, Silesia, which became part of Poland after World War II. Other marks sought by collectors include "R.S. Suhl," "R.S." steeple or church marks, and "R.S. Poland."

The Suhl factory was founded by Reinhold Schlegelmilch in 1869 and closed in 1917. The Tillowitz factory was established in 1895 by Erhard Schlegelmilch, Reinhold's son. This china customarily bears the phrase "R.S. Germany" and "R.S. Tillowitz." The Tillowitz factory closed in 1945, but it was reopened for a few years under Polish administration.

Prices are high and collectors should beware of the forgeries that sometimes find their way onto the market. Mold names and numbers are taken from Mary Frank Gaston's books on R.S. Prussia.

The "Prussia" and "R.S. Suhl" marks have been reproduced, so buy with care. Later copies of these marks are well done, but quality of porcelain is inferior to the production in the 1890-1920 era.

Collectors are also interested in the porcelain products made by the Erdmann Schlegelmilch factory. This factory was founded by three brothers in Suhl in 1861. They named the factory in honor of their father, Erdmann Schlegelmilch. A variety of marks incorporating the "E.S." initials were used. The factory closed circa 1935. The Erdmann Schlegelmilch factory was an earlier and entirely separate business from the Reinhold Schlegelmilch factory. The two were not related to each other.

R.S. Germany Chocolate Sets

R.S. Prussia & Related Marks

R.S. Germany

Bowl, 8" h., handled, decorated w/scene of two colorful parrots, green highlights... **$275-325**

Bowl, 10 1/2", handled, Lebrun portrait, Tiffany finish, artist's palette, paintbrush **1,800-2,000**

Chocolate set: cov. 10" pot & six cups & saucers; Art Deco-style mold, transfer decoration of pink roses on ivory ground w/etched gilt trim, marked "R.S. Germany," early 20th c., the set (ILLUS. second from left w/other R.S. Germany chocolate sets, top of page) **800-1200**

Chocolate set: cov. 10" pot & six cups & saucers; slightly ovoid Art Deco mold, transfer decorated w/delicate pink roses on white ground w/gilt accents, marked "R.S. Germany," early 20th c., the set (ILLUS. second from right w/other R.S. Germany chocolate sets, top of page) **316**

Chocolate set: cov. 9 1/2" pot & six cups & saucers; graceful tapering shape w/C-scroll handle, transfer decoration of delicate floral bouquets on white ground, printed "R.S. Wreath" mark, early 20th c., the set (ILLUS. center w/other R.S. Germany chocolate sets, top of page) **374**

Chocolate set: cov. 9 1/2" pot & six cups & saucers; w/floral transfer decoration in white, pale green & pale aqua on white satin ground, blue "R.S. Germany" mark, early 20th c., the set (ILLUS. far right w/other R.S. Germany chocolate sets, top of page) **374**

Chocolate set: cov. 9" pot & six cups & saucers; eight-panel mold, transfer decoration of pink roses on white satin ground, green "R.S. Germany" mark, early 20th c., the set (ILLUS. far left w/other R.S. Germany chocolate sets, top of page) **316**

Coffeepot, cov., demitasse, Ribbon & Jewel mold, rose garland decoration............. **400-450**

R.S. Germany Cup & Saucer

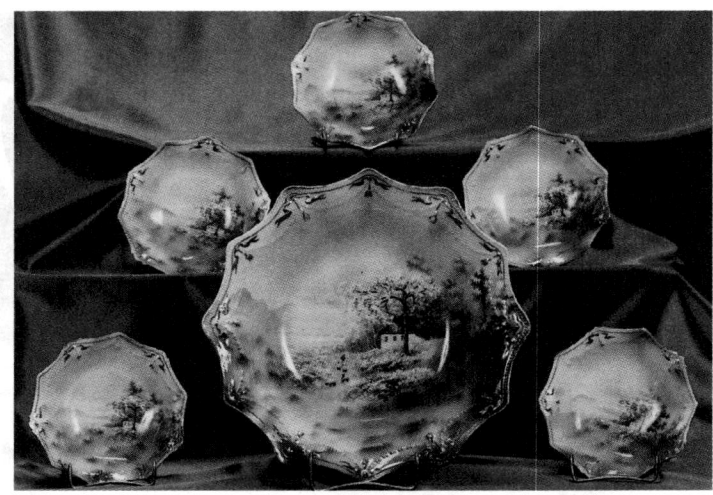

Sheepherder Prussia Berry Set

Cup & saucer, decorated w/blue, black & white bands on beige lustre ground, cup w/center silhouette of Art Deco woman in blue dancing w/blue scarf, cup 3 1/2" d., 2 1/4" h., saucer 5 3/4" d. (ILLUS.) **100-150**

Gravy boat w/underplate, poppy decoration **75-100**

Pitcher, 9" h., Mold 343, floral decoration w/overall gilt tracery on cobalt blue (red castle mark) **700-800**

Plate, 8" d., decorated w/scene of colorful parrots, gold rim **250-300**

Toothpick holder, two-handled, decorated w/roses & gold trim, artist-signed............. **75-125**

R.S. Prussia

Berry set: 11" d. master bowl & five 4" d. sauce dishes; Mold 155, each decorated w/a Sheepherder landscape scene w/cottage & flowering trees & shrubs, the set (ILLUS., top of page) **1,250-1,650**

Bowl, 7" d., decorated w/roses, satin finish... **150-200**

Bowl, 10" d., floral decoration in black & gold **150-175**

Bowl, 10" d., Iris mold, Spring Season portrait decoration **2,400-2,600**

Bowl, 10" d., Mold 85, Summer Season portrait w/mill scene in background (ILLUS.).. **2,200-2,600**

Bowl, 10 1/4" d., Mold 251, apple blossom decoration, satin finish............................. **250-300**

Bowl, 10 1/2" d., decorated w/pink roses & carnations on white shaded to peach ground, iridescent Tiffany finish **595**

Bowl, 10 1/2" d., handled, four-lobed, decorated w/Art Nouveau relief-molded scrolls & colorful sprays on shaded green ground **200-250**

Bowl, 10 1/2" d., Mold 101, Tiffany finish around rim, orchid & cream trim on molded border blossoms, central bouquet of pink, yellow & white roses w/green leaves **250-300**

Bowl, 10 1/2" d., Point & Clover mold (Mold 82), decorated w/forget-me-nots & roses, satin finish, artist-signed........................ **300-350**

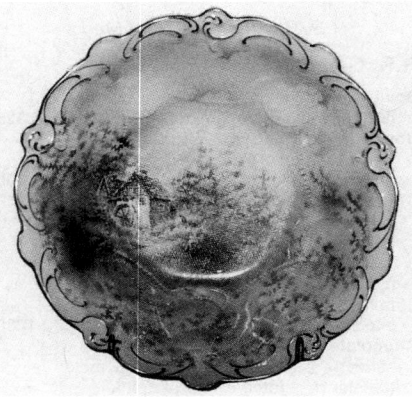

Rare "Tapestry" Bowl

Bowl, 10 3/4" d., Mold 217, "tapestry" center mill scene, gilt scroll border (ILLUS.)... **1,100-1,400**

Summer Season Portrait Bowl

Bowl, 11" d., Mold 155, Sheepherder scene decoration in shades of green w/gold & pink............ **350-400**

Man in the Mountain Prussia Bowl

Bowl, 11" d., Mold 304, gilt scroll border, overall color scene of the Man in the Mountain (ILLUS.) **550-600**

Bread tray, Mold 428, wide oval form w/low flared sides w/a narrow flanged rim, pierced end rim handles, decorated w/a large cluster of roses in peach, pink & green, traces of gold edging, 9 x 12 1/2" **175-225**

Cake Plate with Dice Players

Cake plate, Ribbon & Jewel mold (Mold 18), open-handled, heavy gold border around florals framing the keyhole scene of Dice Players, 9" d. (ILLUS.) **1,000-1,200**

Cake plate, open-handled, Fleur-de-Lis mold, Spring Season portrait, 9 3/4" d. **1,300-1,600**

Cake plate, open-handled, Mold 259, decorated w/pink & yellow roses, pearl button finish, 10" d. **350-400**

Cake plate, open-handled, Medallion mold, center Flora portrait, Tiffany finish w/four cupid medallions, unmarked, 10 1/2" d. **900-1,000**

Cake plate, open-handled, Carnation mold (Mold 28), dark pink roses against teal & green w/gold trim, 11" d. **250-300**

Cake plate, Hidden Image mold, light blue highlights, 11 1/2" d. **450-500**

Cake plate, open-handled, Mold 330, decorated w/snapdragons on pastel ground, artist-signed, 11 1/2" d. **350-375**

Cake plate, Bow-tie mold, pink & gold **500-600**

Celery dish, Carnation mold, carnations & pink roses decoration on white shaded to peach ground, iridescent Tiffany finish, 9" l. **375**

Celery dish, Mold 25, oblong, pearlized finish w/Surreal Dogwood blossoms w/gold trim, 6 x 12 1/4" **75-125**

Celery tray, Ribbon & Jewel mold (Mold 18), pink roses & white snowball blossoms within a wide cobalt blue border w/gilt trim, 12" l. **250-300**

Celery tray, open-handled, decorated w/soft pink & white flower center w/lily-of-the-valley, embossed edge of ferns & pastel colors w/gold highlights, 12 1/2" l. **200-250**

Centerpiece bowl, Carnation mold, decorated w/pink & yellow roses, 15 1/2" d. **2,300-2,600**

Chocolate pot, cov., Carnation mold (Mold 526), pink background & pink roses w/gold-trimmed leaves & blossoms & ornate gold handle, 12" h. **400-500**

Chocolate pot, cov., Ribbon & Jewel mold (Mold 645), Dice Players scene, jeweled trim, 11" h. **2,000-2,300**

Chocolate pot, cov., Hidden Image mold, image on both sides, light green, 9 3/4" h. **1,000-1,100**

Chocolate pot, cov., Swag & Tassel mold, decorated w/scene of sheepherder & swallows... **900-1,000**

Chocolate set: 10" h. cov. chocolate pot & four cups & saucers; Mold 729, pansy decoration w/gold trim, the set **900-975**

Chocolate set: tankard-style cov. pot & six cups & saucers; Mold 510, laurel chain decoration, the set **1,000-1,300**

Coffeepot, cov., Mold 517, raised floral designs as part of border, unmarked......... **250-300**

Cracker jar, cov., Mold 634, molded feet, surreal dogwood blossoms decoration on pearlized lustre finish, 8" d., 6 1/2" h. **250-300**

Cracker jar, cov., decorated w/hanging basket of flowers, satin finish, 6 x 9 1/2" **325-375**

Cracker jar, cov., Lebrun portrait decoration, no hat, satin finish..................... **1,500-2,000**

Creamer & cov. sugar bowl, Mold 505, pink & yellow roses, pr. **125-175**

Creamer & cov. sugar bowl, satin finish, Tiffany trim, pr..................................... **175-200**

Dessert set: 9 1/2" d. cake plate & six 7" d. individual plates; Carnation mold, decorated w/carnations, pink & white roses, iridescent Tiffany finish on pale green, the set **995**

Dresser tray, decorated w/mill scene, shaded green ground, 7 x 11"................... **350-450**

Ferner, six vertical ribs, scalloped, decorated w/lilies-of-the-valley on shaded pastel ground, artist-signed, 3 7/8 x 8 1/4" **200-250**

Match holder w/striker, floral decoration. **100-125**
Mug, Lily mold, Lebrun portrait decoration
(no hat) **200-250**
Mustache cup, Mold 502 .... **250-300**
Mustard pot, cov., Mold 521, pink rose dec-
oration, satin finish............................... **150-200**
Nut dish, Carnation mold (Mold 28), floral
decoration w/pearlized finish **200-250**

Unique Bird of Paradise Pitcher

Pitcher, tankard, 12 1/4" h., Mold 569, very
rare Bird of Paradise decoration w/shad-
ed gold & light green in the lower half,
white above, gold trim, only one known
(ILLUS.).. **17,000-20,000**

Carnation Mold Pitcher with Roses

Pitcher, tankard, 13" h., Carnation mold
(Mold 526), decorated w/clusters of dark
pink & creamy white roses w/a shaded
dark green ground & pale green molded
blossoms (ILLUS.)............................ **1,000-1,200**
Pitcher, lemonade, 6" h., Mold 501, relief-
molded turquoise blue on white w/pink
Surreal blossoms & fans around scal-
loped top & base, unmarked.................. **250-300**

Pitcher, tankard, 11" h., Carnation Mold,
overall decoration of pink poppies & carnations, white ground, iridescent Tiffany
finish **1,100**
Pitcher, tankard, 13" h., decorated w/pop-
pies **600-650**
Pitcher, tankard, 13 1/4" h., Stippled Floral
mold (Mold 525), roses decoration, un-
marked **625-675**
Pitcher, water, 8 3/4" h., Carnation mold.......... **660**
Plate, 7" d., Fleur-de-Lis mold, Summer
Season portrait decoration..................... **450-500**
Plate, 7 1/2" d., Carnation mold, decorated
w/pink roses, pink ground, unmarked........... **175**
Plate, 7 3/4" d., Medallion mold (Mold 14),
Snowbird decoration, landscape scenes
in medallions, black rim band.......... **1,800-2,200**
Plate, 8 1/2" d., Medallion mold (Mold 14),
Reflecting Lilies patt. **125-150**
Plate, 8 1/2" d., Mold 261, Ostrich decora-
tion **2,000-2,500**
Plate, 8 1/2" d., Mold 300, beaded gold
band around the lobed rim, Old Mill
Scene decoration in center against a
shaded dark green to yellow & blue
ground **150-200**
Plate, 9" d., Mold 343, spring figural scenic
decoration in keyhole medallion, iridescent Tiffany purple finish at base of figure, gold finish around portrait decoration
w/small pink roses........................... **1,800-2,100**
Plate, 11" d., decorated w/carnations &
roses w/gold trim, white shading to peach
ground, iridescent Tiffany finish (slight
gold wear).. **250**

Rare Madame Recamier Plate

Plate, 12" d., Lily mold (Mold 29), Madame
Recamier portrait, dark blue Tiffany
bronze finish in border panels
(ILLUS.)... **3,000-4,000**
Relish dish, Fleur-de-Lis mold, basket of
flowers decoration w/shadow flowers,
8" l. **100-125**
Relish dish, Icicle mold, scene of swans on
lake **450-500**
Shaving mug, Hidden Image mold, floral
decoration... **175-225**
Syrup pitcher, Mold 512, dogwood & pine
decoration.. **175**
Tea set: child's, cov. teapot & four cups &
saucers; decorated w/roses, the set....... **650-700**

Tea set: cov. teapot, creamer & cov. sugar bowl; mill & castle scene, shaded brown ground, 3 pcs... **900-1,000**
Tea strainer, floral decoration.................... **200-250**
Toothpick holder, Stippled Floral mold (Mold 23), white floral decoration........... **150-175**
Toothpick holder, urn-shaped, floral decoration, molded star mark......................... **150-175**
Tray, rectangular, pierced handles, Mold 404, decorated w/pink & white roses, Tiffany border w/gold clover leaves........... **250-300**
Vase, 4 1/2" h., Mold 910, decorated w/pink roses, satin finish w/iridescent Tiffany finish around base...................................... **250-275**
Vase, 6 1/4" h., castle scene decoration, brown tones w/jewels............................. **450-500**
Vase, 6 1/4" h., decorated w/mill scene, brown w/jewels.. **450-500**

R.S. Prussia Ovoid Vase w/Parrots

Vase, two-handled, tall, slender, ovoid body w/colorful scene of two parrots, shaded brown foliage, unmarked (ILLUS.) ... **1,800-2,000**

Rare Melon Eaters Vases

Vases, 11 3/4" h., Mold 901, footed, slightly tapering cylindrical bodies w/high, flaring, cupped, deeply fluted necks w/jewels, beading & jewels around the shoulders & feet, ornate scrolled gilt handles, Melon Eaters decoration against shaded dark green ground, each (ILLUS. of pair)... **1,600-2,000**

Other Marks

Bowl, 10" d., shallow w/very ornate, large Flora portrait, front pose past waist, floral garland, veiling, four different cameo portraits of Flora, wide Tiffany border, lavish gold (E.S. Prov. Saxe)...................... **1,100-1,300**
Chocolate pot, cov., lemon yellow ground w/Art Deco decoration & gold trim (R.S. Tillowitz - Silesia)... **150**
Fernery, pedestal base, decorated w/pink & white roses, mother-of-pearl finish (R.S. Poland)... **450**
Plate, 7" d., scene of girl w/rose, trimmed w/gold flowers, beading & a burgundy border **100-125**
Plate, 8" d., peafowl decoration (R.S. Tillowitz - Silesia).................................... **150-200**
Relish dish, woman's portrait w/shadow flowers & vine border on green ground, 8" l. (E.S. Germany Royal Saxe) **100-125**
Serving dish, center-handled, decorated w/lavender & pink roses, gold trim, 11" d. (R.S. Poland)... **500-550**
Vase, miniature, 3 1/2" h., cylindrical body w/a rounded shoulder tapering to a tiny rolled neck, decorated w/a colored scene of crowned cranes (R.S. Poland)........... **375-425**
Vase, 7" h., footed urn form w/scrolled handles, decorated w/scene of two geese, R.S. Poland **1,500-1,800**
Vase, 9" h., 3" d., tall, slender, ovoid body tapering to a tall, slender trumpet neck, a wide band around the body decorated w/a colored scene of The Melon Eaters between narrow gold & white bands, the neck & lower body in deep rose decorated w/gilt leaf sprigs (R.S. Suhl) **800-1,000**
Vase, 9 1/2" h., portrait of "Lady with Swallows," gold beading, turquoise on white ground (Prov. Saxe - E.S. Germany) **500-550**
Vase, 13 1/2" h., portrait of "Lady with Swallows," gold beaded frame, green pearl lustre finish w/gold trim (Prov. Saxe - E.S. Germany) **600-650**

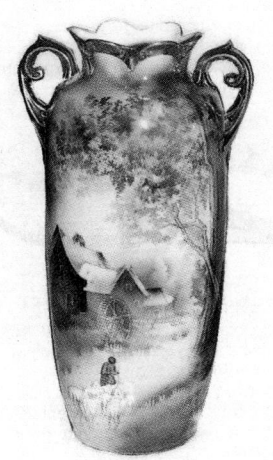

R.S. Poland Landscape Vase

Vases, 10" h., gently swelled body tapering to narrow rounded shoulders & a short, flaring, scalloped neck, ornate C-scroll gilt shoulder handles, gold neck band, the body decorated w/a colored scene of a sheepherder leading his flock toward a mill in the background, trees overhead, the second identical except w/a cottage scene, R.S. Poland, pr. (ILLUS. of one) **1,350-1,400**

Russel Wright Designs

The innovative dinnerwares designed by Russel Wright and produced by various companies beginning in the late 1930s were an immediate success with a society that was turning to a more casual and informal lifestyle. His designs, with their flowing lines and unconventional shapes, were produced in many different colors, which allowed a hostess to arrange creative tables.

Although not antique, these designs, which we list below by line and manufacturer, are highly collectible. In addition to dinnerwares, Wright was also known as a trendsetter in the design of furniture, glassware, lamps, fabric and a multitude of other household goods.

Russel Wright Marks

American Modern (Steubenville Pottery Co.)

Baker, granite grey, small	$25
Bowl, child's, chartreuse	100
Bowl, fruit, lug handle, glacier blue	40
Bowl, salad, white	165
Butter dish, cov., granite grey	255
Carafe, granite grey (no stopper)	200
Casserole, cov., stick handle, black chutney	40

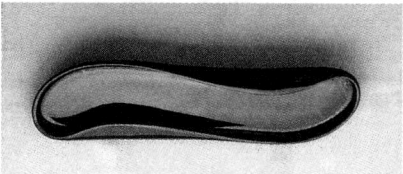

Black Chutney Celery Tray

Celery tray, black chutney, 13" l. (ILLUS.)	30
Coaster, white...	30
Coffee cup cover, coral...................................	175
Coffeepot, cov., cedar green	275
Coffeepot, cov., demitasse, chartreuse	120
Coffeepot, cov., demitasse, granite grey	120
Creamer, white	35
Cup & saucer, coffee, seafoam blue	27
Cup & saucer, demitasse, chartreuse	30
Hostess plate, chartreuse	75

American Modern Hostess Set

Hostess plate & cup, white, pr. (ILLUS.)	175
Ice box jar, cov., coral...................................	225
Mug (tumbler), cedar green............................	100
Pickle dish, white	45
Pitcher, cov., water, white	500+
Pitcher, water, 12" h., granite grey	100
Plate, bread & butter, 6 1/4" d., coral	6
Plate, salad, 8" d., white	25
Plate, dinner, 10" d., granite grey	20
Plate, chop, 13" sq., seafoam blue..................	50
Plate, child's, seafoam blue...........................	75
Platter, 13 3/4" l., oblong, white	65
Ramekin, cov., individual, granite grey	188
Relish dish, divided, raffia handle, white.........	300
Relish rosette, granite grey............................	200
Salad fork & spoon, coral, pr..........................	150
Sauceboat, bean brown	75
Shaker, single, chartreuse	8
Stack server, cov., chartreuse	250
Sugar bowl, cov., chartreuse..........................	15
Teapot, cov., cedar green................................	150
Tumbler, child's, cedar green	140
Vegetable bowl, cov., cedar green, 12" l.	75
Vegetable dish, open, divided, black chutney	110
Vegetable dish, open, oval, cantaloupe, 10" l..	75

Casual China (Iroquois China Co.)

Bowl, 5 1/2" d., fruit, ice blue, 9 1/2 oz...............	15
Bowl, 10" d., salad, pink sherbet, 52 oz.............	40
Butter dish, cov., white, 1/2 lb.	150
Carafe, cov., charcoal	350
Casserole, cov., lettuce green, 8" d., 2 qt.	75
Casserole, deep tureen, white..........................	260
Coffeepot, cov., oyster grey (ILLUS. right, top of next page)...	225
Coffeepot, cov., demitasse, avocado yellow...	135
Cover for 4 qt. casserole, oyster grey	45
Cover for vegetable bowl, open/divided	35
Creamer, family-style, oyster grey (ILLUS. left w/coffeepot & pitcher, top next page)	55
Creamer, stacking-type, ice blue........................	20
Cup & saucer, tea, charcoal	25
Cup & saucer, demitasse, pink sherbet.............	175
Gravy, redesigned w/cover which becomes stand, ripe apricot...	185

Casual Creamer, Pitcher & Coffeepot

Gravy bowl, 5 1/4", 12 oz. 40
Gravy stand, oyster grey 70
Gravy w/attached stand, nutmeg brown.......... 125
Gumbo soup bowl, charcoal, 21 oz. 50
Hostess set: plate w/well & matching cup;
   sugar white, 2 pcs. 90
Mug, restyled, aqua 225
Mug, sugar white, 13 oz. **175-200**
Pitcher, cov., charcoal, 1 1/2 qt. 200
Pitcher, nutmeg brown...................................... 200
Pitcher, redesigned, ripe apricot (ILLUS.
   center with creamer & coffeepot, above) 200
Plate, salad, 7 1/2" d. 15
Plate, dinner, 10" d., oyster grey 25
Plate, chop, 13 7/8" d., parsley green 65
Platter, 12 3/4" oval, brick red 90
Platter, 14 1/2" oval, sugar white 45
Salt & pepper shakers, stacking-type,
   parsley green, pr. 60
Salt shaker, single, redesigned .... **200+**
Soup, 11 1/2 oz. 30
Sugar, redesigned, aqua..................................... 150
Sugar, stacking-type, pink sherbet 15
Teapot, cov., restyled, aqua .... **3,000+**
Tumbler, water, Pinch patt., ruby red, Impe-
   rial Glass Co., 11 oz. .... **125+**
Vegetable dish, open, cantaloupe, 8 1/8",
   36 oz. 60
Vegetable dish, open or divided (casse-
   role), 10", sugar white 60

Sèvres & Sèvres-Style

*Some of the most desirable porcelain ever pro-
duced was made at the Sèvres factory, originally
established at Vincennes, France, and trans-
ferred, through permission of Madame de Pompadour, to Sèvres as the Royal Manufactory about
the middle of the 18th century. King Louis XV
took sole responsibility for the works in 1759,
when production of hard paste wares began.
Between 1850 and 1900, many biscuit and soft-
paste pieces were made again. Fine early pieces
are scarce and high-priced. Many of those available today are late productions. The various
Sèvres marks have been copied, and pieces listed
as "Sèvres-Style" are similar to actual Sèvres
wares but not necessarily from that factory. Three
of the many Sèvres marks are illustrated here.*

Sèvres marks

Bowl, 9 1/4" d., a footring below the wide
flaring rounded & lobed sides, white
ground painted on the exterior w/three
different musical trophies alternating
w/three gilt sprigs of fruiting vine below a
blue foliate scroll border, the interior w/a
colorful garland of flowers, second half
18th c. **$3,000**

Fine Sèvres-Style Centerpiece Bowl

Artist-signed Sèvres Garniture Set

Centerpiece bowl, in the Louis XVI taste, a celeste blue wide border w/gilt floral sprig band around the center painted w/a colorful scene of 18th c. peasant figures, mounted in a gilt-brass framework w/scroll handles & scroll feet joined by floral swags, pseudo-Sevres interlaced Ls mark on base, late 19th c., 16 1/2" w., 6" h. (ILLUS., bottom previous page) **690**

Cup & saucer, footed slightly swelled cylindrical cup & deep dished saucer, the cup decorated en grisaille w/a reserve of a cupid reclining on clouds & holding a vine of grapes, surrounded by gilt edging on a trelliswork & bird's-eye decorated ground, the saucer w/a similar design w/two reserves of marshal trophies flanking a central scrolling foliate medallion, Sèvres mark & date code for 1770, cup 3 1/8" h., the set **3,600**

Garniture set: centerpiece & a pair of cov. vases; the vases w/ovoid bodies w/flaring necks ending in flattened dome lids w/pinecone finials, on slender ringed flaring pedestals on gilt bronze rectangular plinths w/bracket feet, the necks w/pierced gilt decorative band joined to gilt scroll handles mounted to shoulders, the body decorated w/h.p. romantic scenes in pastel shades on emerald green ground framed in raised gilt scroll & bead design, the wide bowl-form centerpiece w/matching pierced gilt rim & handles attached at rim & scrolling to base of bowl, bowl w/matching decoration & raised on a matching pedestal base, artist signed "Poylet," lids marked "Chateau de Longpre" w/"S" in diamond & "France," ca. 1900, centerpiece 17" w., vases 18" h., the set (ILLUS., top of page) **3,450**

Pitcher w/hinged cover, 5 1/8" h., a silvergilt footring supporting the bulbous body tapering to a cylindrical neck w/a rim spout, large loop handle, the cover attached w/later silver-gilt French mounts, white ground painted around the neck & cover w/garlands of flowers suspended from a gilt foliate & laurel wreath border & narrow claret-ground band at the rim, Sèvres mark & date code for 1760 .... **1,800**

Salt dips, triple, three slightly flaring cylindrical cups forming three lobes joined across the top w/a triple-loop handle, white ground, molded gilt-trimmed ribbons topped by a bow knop on the handle, the sides painted near the rim w/thin gold & green leaf bands, Sèvres mark & date code for 1778, 3 1/2" h., pr. **960**

Serving dish, cover & underplate, deep round base w/D-form loop side handles, white ground finely painted overall w/bowknotted festoons of colorful flowers, foliate-entwined handles, cover w/twig finial, Sèvres mark & date code for 1760, underplate 8 1/4" d., the set **2,700**

Serving dish, cover & undertray, deep round bowl-form w/side loop handles, low domed cover w/gilt-trimmed scroll handle, Bleu Celeste ground painted en grisaille w/panels of cherubs among clouds & marshal trophies reserved within a gilt-edged berried laurel wreath border on the blue white-dotted ground, Sèvres mark & date code for 1770, oval undertray 7 1/8" l., the set **10,200**

Staffordshire Figures

Small figures and groups made of pottery were produced by the majority of the Staffordshire, England potters in the 19th century and were used as mantel decorations or "chimney ornaments," as they were sometimes called. Pairs of dogs were favorites and were turned out by the carload, and 19th-century pieces are still available. Well-painted reproductions also abound, and collectors are urged to exercise caution before investing.

Staffordshire Hens on Nests

Chimney vase, figural, model of a boy kneeling at the right & wearing a pink & green outfit, feeding a white & gold swan to the left, tree trunk vase at back center, decorated in pink, orange & yellow coleslaw, 19th c., 5 1/8" h. **495**

Chimney vase, figural, model of a family of three white swans w/gilt trim, tree trunk vase at back w/orange interior & light blue coleslaw foliage, 19th c., 5" h. **275**

Chimney vases, figural, one w/a standing sheep in white w/sanded coat & long tail & other w/standing matching ram, each standing in front of a tree trunk vase w/coleslaw foliage, oval bases painted red, yellow & green, mid-19th c., 5 1/8" h., facing pair (repair, minor edge damage) **303**

Equestrian group, a young boy wearing a bright red skirted outfit standing in front of a white horse upon which is seated a young girl in a white dress & hat, said to represent Prince Albert & Princess Victoria, children of Queen Victorian, mid-19th c., 12 3/4" h. **316**

Hen on nest, bisque hen trimmed w/grey w/red comb & wattle on amber glazed basketweave base, late 19th c., 9" l. (ILLUS. top right w/other hens on nests, top of page) **748**

Hen on nest, bisque hen trimmed w/grey w/red wattle on custard glazed basketweave base, mid to late 19th c., 11" l. (ILLUS. top left w/other hens on nests, top of page, top of page) **748**

Hen on nest, h.p. grey hen w/darker grey trim & black w/red comb & wattle on yellow gold glazed basketweave base, 19th c., 9" l. (ILLUS. bottom left w/other hens on nests, top of page) **748**

Hen on nest, hen h.p. in shades of browns & greys, w/red comb & wattle on amber gold glazed basketweave base, 19th c.,

9" l. (ILLUS. bottom right w/other hens on nests, top of page) **978**

Stoneware

Stoneware is essentially a vitreous pottery, impervious to water even in its unglazed state, that has been produced by potteries all over the world for centuries. Utilitarian wares such as crocks, jugs, churns and the like were the most common productions in the numerous potteries that sprang into existence in the United States during the 19th century. These items were often enhanced by the application of a cobalt blue oxide decoration. In addition to the coarse, primarily salt-glazed stonewares, there are other categories of stoneware known by such special names as basalt, jasper and others.

Churn with Paddletail Bird & Flowers

Butter churn, slightly ovoid body w/a molded rim & eared handles, slip-quilled cobalt blue large paddletail bird perched on a long flowering stem, fine shading & detail, impressed mark of N.A. White & Son, Utica, New York, chip at front & right ear professionally repaired, tight short hairline from rim on back, ca. 1870, 3 gal., 15" h. (ILLUS.).. **$9,900**

Churn with Less Detailed Bird & Flower

Butter churn, slightly ovoid body w/a molded rim & eared handles, slip-quilled cobalt blue large paddletail bird perched on a long flowering stem, impressed mark of N.A. White & Son, Utica, New York, chip at leaf ear professionally restored, ca. 1870, 3 gal., 16" h. (ILLUS.) **2,420**

Cream Pot with Bold Blue Flowers

Cream pot, ovoid form w/a molded rim & eared handles, slip-quilled large cobalt blue blossoms on leafy stems below the number "3," impressed mark of T. Harrington, Lyons, New York, washed in blue, ca. 1850, 3 gal., 12" h. (ILLUS.).. **2,200**

Advertising Crock with Large Hen

Crock, advertising-type, cylindrical w/molded rim & eared handles, slip-quilled cobalt blue large hen pecking at corn, impressed advertising for Cornells & Mumford, Providence, Rhode Island, above a "2", unsigned Norton of Bennington pieces, ca. 1865, 2 gal., 9 1/2" h. (ILLUS.) **3,300**

Unique Crock with a Camel Scene

Crock, wide cylindrical form w/molded rim & eared handles, cobalt-blue slip-quilled decoration of a standing camel w/palm trees & a pyramid in the distance, impressed mark of Wm. A. Macquoid & Co., Little Wst. 12th St., New York, New York, small rim chip on front, tight full-length hairline on back, ca. 1870, 1 1/2 gal., 10" h. (ILLUS.) **12,650**

Boldly Decorated John Bell Crock

Crock, cov., ovoid w/eared handles & a wide molded rim, heavy brushed cobalt blue bands of leafy flowering vines around the sides & on the cover, also blue-slip date "1874" under each handle, impressed mark of John Bell, Waynesboro, Pennsylvania, tightly glued hairline behind right handle, small piece reglued, ca. 1874, 4 gal., 13" h. (ILLUS.) **11,550**

Two-Gallon Jar with Large Flower

Jar, cylindrical tapering to a short upright rim & eared handles, slip-quilled cobalt blue large stylized flower & leaves w/a number "2" beside them, impressed mark of F. Stetzenmeyer & G. Goetzman, Rochester, New York, washed in blue, very tight line through bottom, surface chip at base of right handle, ca. 1857, 2 gal., 11" h. (ILLUS.)...................................... **1,430**

Crock with Very Rare Decoration

Crock, cylindrical w/eared handles & molded rim, slip-quilled cobalt blue extremely detailed scene of a large reclining stag & fence in the foreground & a large house & tree in the distance, impressed mark of J. & E. Norton, Bennington, Vermont, & a "5," minor surface chipping to rim interior, very tight minor hairline in left handle, ca. 1855, 5 gal., 13" h. (ILLUS.) **23,650**

Jug with a Large Stylized Flower

Jug, ovoid body tapering to a small molded mouth, slip-quilled cobalt blue large eight-petalled flower blossom w/fine shading & the number "2" above it, impressed mark of N. Clark & Co., Rochester, New York, washed in blue, couple of minor stack marks, ca. 1850, 2 gal., 14 1/2" h. (ILLUS.)... **3,520**

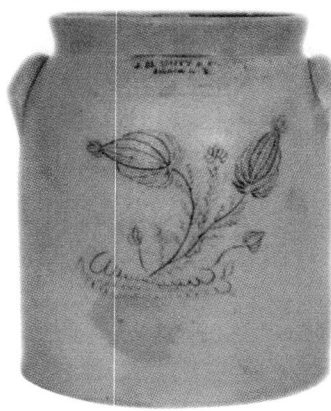

Rare Early "Brandy" Keg

Keg, barrel-shaped, molded pairs of horizontal bands trimmed in cobalt blue, top band hand-incised "BRANDY" trimmed in blue, the center band incised w/a scene of a rowboat & oars trimmed in blue, impressed mark of Tyler & Dillon, Albany, New York, chip on left to edge, hairline across from chip, short-lived pottery, ca. 1825, 2 gal., 13 1/2" h. (ILLUS.)................ **5,500**

Preserve Jar with Nice Incised Flowers

Preserve jar, cylindrical tapering slightly to an upright rim & eared handles, finely incised design of large double pod-like flowers on leafy stems washed w/cobalt blue, impressed mark of J.M. Mott & Co., Ithaca, New York, washed w/blue, minor staining, ca. 1855, 2 gal., 11" h. (ILLUS.).. **3,630**

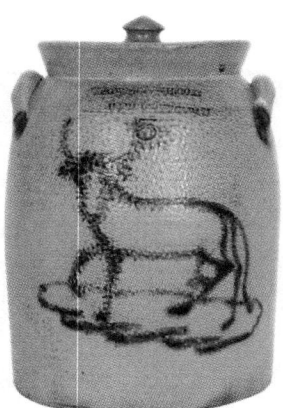

Rare Fish-decorated Preserve Jar

Preserve jar, tapering cylindrical form w/molded rim & eared handles, slip-quilled cobalt blue swimming fish, impressed mark of H.M. Whitman, Havana, New York, trimmed in blue, w/original hand-wrought iron lid, ca. 1860, 1 gal., 9" h. (ILLUS.).. **7,425**

Preserve Jar with Rare Long Horn Cow

Preserve jar, cov., tapering cylindrical form w/eared handles & short flared rim w/inset cover, slip-quilled cobalt blue scene of a Texas Long Horn steer, impressed mark of Cowden & Wilcox, Harrisburg, Pennsylvania, & a "3," overglazed in the making, ca. 1870, 3 gal., 12 1/2" h. (ILLUS.).. **14,300**

Bennington Preserve Jar with Stag

Preserve jar, cylindrical tapering body w/a molded rim & eared handles, slip-quilled cobalt blue elaborate scene of a large reclining stag w/fences & fir trees, impressed mark of J. & E. Norton, Bennington, Vermont, washed in blue, surface wear at rim interior, few glaze flakes, ca. 1855, 4 gal., 14 1/2" h. (ILLUS.)................. **9,350**

Water Cooler with a Plump Bird

Water cooler, wide ovoid body w/bung hole at bottom front, eared handles, short cylindrical neck w/molded rim, slip-quilled cobalt blue large plump bird perched on a scrolled branch, fine detail, impressed mark of O.L. & A.K. Ballard, Burlington, Vermont, couple of very tight hairlines from rim, few glaze spiders & flakes, professional restoration to chip at bung hole, ca. 1870, 6 gal., 15" h. (ILLUS.) **2,640**

Tiffany Pottery

In 1902 Louis C. Tiffany expanded Tiffany Studios to include ceramics, enamels, gold, silver and gemstones. Tiffany pottery was usually molded rather than wheel-thrown, but it was carefully finished by hand. A limited amount was produced until about 1914. It is scarce.

Tiffany Pottery Mark

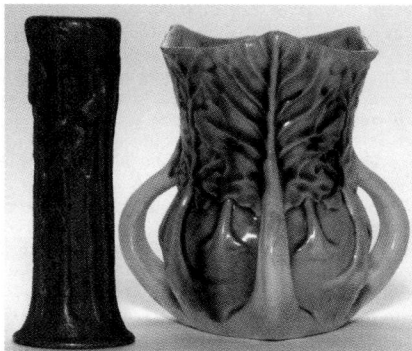

Tiffany Favrile Vases

Vase, 6 3/4" h., Favrile bronze pottery type, cylindrical shape w/molded flowers & stems in relief, signed on bottom "LCT" conjoined & "BP197" w/"L," ca. 1910-14 (ILLUS. left w/Tiffany Favrile plant-form vase)... **$2,358**

Vase, 6 3/4" h., Favrile, plant form, bulbous base w/three handles forming stems of leaves that form neck of vase, glazed in cream, shades of green & black, signed on base "Tiffany Favrile Pottery P1014" & "LCT" conjoined w/"L," ca. 1910 (ILLUS. right w/Tiffany Favrile bronze pottery vase)... **8,913**

Torquay Pottery

In the second half of the 19th century several art potteries were established in the South Devon region of England to take advantage of a belt of fine red clay there. The coastal town of Torquay gives its name to this range of wares, which often featured incised sgraffito decoration or colorful country-style decoration with mottos.

The most notable potteries operating in the Torquay area were the Watcombe Pottery, The Torquay Terra-cotta Company and the Aller Vale Art Pottery, which merged with Watcombe Pottery in 1901 and continued production until 1962. Other firms whose wares are collectible include Longpark Pottery and The Devonmoor Art Pottery.

Early wares feature unglazed terra cotta items in the Victorian taste including classical busts, statuary and vases and some painted and glazed wares including examples with a celeste blue interior or highlights. In addition to sgraffito designs, other decorations included flowers, Barbotine glazes, Devon pixies framed in leafy scrolls and grotesque figures of cats, dogs and other fanciful animals, produced in the 1890s.

The dozen or so potteries flourishing in the region at the turn of the 20th century introduced their most popular product, Motto Wares, which became the bread and butter line of the local industry. The most popular patterns in this line included Cottage, Black and Colored Cockerels and Scandy, based on Scandinavian rosemaling designs. Most of the mottoes were written in English, with a few in Welsh. On early examples the sayings were often in Devonian dialect. These Motto Wares were sold for years at area seaside resorts and other tourist areas, with some pieces exported to Australia, Canada and, to a lesser extent, the United States. In addition to standard size teawares and novelties, some miniatures and even oversized pieces were offered.

Production at the potteries stopped during World War II, and some of the plants were destroyed in enemy raids. The Watcombe Pottery became Royal Watcombe after the war, and Longpark also started up again but produced simpler patterns. The Dartmouth Pottery, started in 1947, produced cottages similar to those made at Watcombe and also developed a line of figural animals, banks and novelty jugs. The Babbacombe Pottery (1950-59) and St. Marychurch Pottery (ca. 1962-69) were the last two firms to turn out Motto Wares, but these later designs were painted on and the pieces were lighter in color, with less detailing.

Many books on the various potteries are available, and information can be obtained from the products manager of the North American Torquay Society.

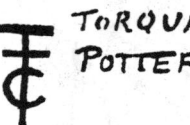

Torquay Pottery Marks

Cockerel Pattern

Curling iron tile, Black Cockerel patt., Motto Ware, "O list to me ye ladies fair - and when ye wish to curl your hair - For the safety of your domicile - Pray place your lamp upon this tile," Longpark Torquay mark, scarce, ca. 1903-09, 5 x 7 1/4" **$198**

Hot water pot, cov., Black Cockerel patt., Motto Ware, "Good Morning - Life is a struggle Not a race - A wise man keeps an even pace," Aller Vale mark, ca. 1902-24, overall 7 1/4" h. **176**

Mug, miniature, Colored Cockerel patt., Motto Ware, "If you can't fly - climb," Longpark Torquay impressed mark, scarce, ca. 1910, 1 5/8" h. **95**

Vase, 5 3/4" h., Black Cockerel patt., four spouts, Motto Ware, "May you never find a mouse in your cupboard with tears in its eyes," desirable motto, Longpark Torquay early mark, ca. 1904-18 .... **279**

Cottage Pattern

Bowl, 4" d., 3 1/2" h., four-handled, Motto Ware, in Devon dialect, "Come an' zee us in the zummer," Crown Dorset Pottery, ca. 1915 .... **134**

Coffeepot, cov., long spout, Motto Ware, "Gude things be scarce take care of me," Watcombe Torquay mark, ca. 1925-35, 7" h. **151**

Molded Cottageware Pieces

Creamer, miniature, Motto Ware, "Isle of Wight - Fresh from the cow," Royal Watcombe circle mark, ca. 1950, 1 3/4" h............. 41

Cup & saucer, Molded Cottageware, details in relief w/sponged details in rose, green & yellow, Torquay Pottery Co., ca. 1918-24, scarce, saucer 5 1/4" d., cup 3" h., the set (ILLUS. left & right, bottom previous page) 63

Dog bowl, Motto Ware, "Love Me - Love My Dog," lovely calligraphy & "Tintern," Longpark Torquay, England mark, ca. 1930s, 5 5/8" w. 175

Humidor, cov., Motto Ware, "When work is done the pipe don't shun," painted Watcombe mark, ca. 1901-20, overall 5 1/4" h. 165

Pin dish, round, Motto Ware, "I'll take care ov the pins," Longpark Torquay, ca. 1918-30, 3 1/8" d. 45

Cottage Motto Ware Pitcher

Pitcher, 5 1/4" h., 4" d., Motto Ware, wide ovoid body tapering to a flat rim w/spout, brown loop handle, inscribed "If you can't be easy, Be as easy as you can" (ILLUS.) **110-120**

Plate, 6 3/4" d., Molded Cottageware, cottage scene w/thatched roof, sponged design of flowers & trees w/windows & door slip-lined, Torquay Pottery Co. impressed mark, scarce, ca. 1908-15 (ILLUS. previous page center with cups & saucers).. 82

Shaving mug, Motto Ware, "A hair on the head is worth two on the chin," Watcombe Torquay, England mark, ca. 1925-35 (tiny sealed hairline) 151

Teapot, cov., Molded Cottageware, colorful sponge-decorated design, large & heavy, Torquay Pottery Co. mark, ca. 1905-20, overall 9 1/4" l., 6 3/4" h................................. 152

Toast rack, four large tines, Motto Ware, "Crisp Toast" on front, "Truro" on short side, Watcombe Torquay, England impressed mark, ca. 1930, 5 1/4" l. 178

Scandy Pattern

Dresser tray, oval, Motto Ware, "A place for everything and everything in its place," Watcombe Torquay mark, ca. 1920s, 7 3/8 x 12".. 176

Hot water-coffeepot, cov., Motto Ware, "May we be kind but not in words alone," many details, Aller Vale, ca. 1891-1910, overall 5" h. 108

Inkwell, Motto Ware, "Don't forget the dear ones far away," Watcombe mark, ca. 1920s, 2" h. 61

Match holder, Motto Ware, Devon dialect, "No place on earth so plaizes me - as this wan Babbacombe By-the-zay," Longpark Torquay mark, ca. 1903-09, 3 1/4" h............. 100

Pitcher, 4 1/2" h., Motto Ware, "Another little drink won't do us any harm," Lemon & Crute Pottery, ca. 1920 (rim roughness, spout rub)... 53

Plate, 5" d., Motto Ware, "Carry a vision in your heart," Watcombe Torquay impressed mark, ca. 1930................................. 59

Puzzle jug, Motto Ware, "Within this jug there is good liquor - Fit for Parson or for Vicar. But how to drink and not to spill - will try the utmost of your skill," Longpark, ca. 1920, 4 1/4" h. 125

Teapot, cov., Motto Ware, "Ye may get better cheer but no' wi' Better heart," Aller Vale mark, ca. 1891-1910, 6 3/4" l., 3 3/4" h. 120

Other Patterns

Torquay Pixie Design Ashtray

Ashtray, Motto Ware, long rectangular shape w/cigarette rests in each corner, creamer ground molded in the center w/an elfin figure in colorful clothes, inscribed "Lucky Devon Pixie," 3 x 5" (ILLUS.).. **60-70**

Basket, Art Nouveau swags, braided black handle, Barton Pottery, ca. 1922-38, overall 5" h.. 135

Large Cockington Forge Bowl

Bowl, 12" d., Cockington Forge patt., round shallow form w/h.p. scene of the forge, inscribed at rim "Cockington Forge - Torquay," Devon Tors Pottery, ca. 1925-30 (ILLUS., previous page) 335

Candlesticks, Primrose patt., Motto Ware, "Many are called but few get up" on one, the other w/"Be the day weary or be the day long - At last it ringeth to Evensong," H.M. Exeter Pottery mark, ca. 1920, 7" h., pr. 125

Curling iron tile, Forget-me-not patt., Motto Ware, "O list to me ye ladies fair - And when Ye wish to curl your hair - For the safety of this domicile - Pray place your lamps upon this tile," Watcombe Torquay impressed   mark,   ca.   1920s, 5 1/2 x 7 3/4" 140

Humidor, cov., C3 Pattern, Motto Ware, "Help yersel tae a pipe o' bacca," early Scandy-type pattern, Watcombe mark, ca. 1910-20, overall 5" h. 88

Mug, commemorative, "Coronation of Queen Elizabeth - June 2, 1953," no mark, Sandygate Pottery, 2 3/4" h. 50

Sailboat Commemorative Mug

Mug, Sailboat patt., commemorative, "Barbara - Peace Celebrations - Bath - 1919," black sailboat w/rosy sunset background, Torquay Pottery Co. mark, 3 3/4" h. (ILLUS.) 122

Pitcher, 2 7/8" h., jug-form, Passion Flower patt., Motto Ware, green ground w/motto in a band between the flowers, "May all the hours be winged with joy," H.M. Exeter Pottery, ca. 1930 71

Pitcher, 4 3/4" h., Pixie patt., three pixies in relief amid a colorful leafy scroll design, "Pixy fine - Pixy gay," scarce, impressed Aller Vale mark, ca. 1891-1910 350

Scent bottle, Gardenia patt., black curled handle, Motto Ware, "A thing of beauty is a joy Forever - Gardenia Eau de Cologne - Toogoods - London - England," pink gardenia on blue ground, brass crown-form stopper, Watcombe, ca. 1930s, 5" h. 151

Scent bottle, Lavender patt., "Hill's English Lavender," marked "Genuine Devon Pottery - Made in England," still sealed, ca. 1930s, 2 1/2" h. 50

Scent bottle, Violets patt., curved lavender handle & motto "May the hinges of friendship Never go rusty," gold crown-form stopper, "Made in England" stamped mark, Watcombe, 1930s, 4" h. 119

Toby jug, inscribed "Peter Gurney from Widecombe Fair," Royal Torquay mark, ca. 1924-30, 2 3/4" h. 80

Toby jug, inscribed "Jan Stewer from Widecombe Fair," Royal Torquay, ca. 1924-30, 5 1/4" h. 132

Vase, 4 1/2" h., D1 Scroll patt., colorful leafy scrolls & geometric designs on a blue ground, scarce, Aller Vale, ca. 1890s 146

Vase, 6 1/4" h., Moonlight Cottages patt., faience, two cottages on a blue ground, impressed   Bovey   mark,   very unusual, ca. 1930 203

Rare Cavalier Pattern Vase

Vase, 7 1/2" h., Cavalier patt., faience, two handles, large ovoid form w/wide flat mouth, decorated w/portrait of a Cavalier standing in a landscape, rare subject, Mosanic Pottery mark, Crown Dorset, rare, ca. 1910 (ILLUS.) 395

Vase, 8" h., Persian patt., three handles, six colorful Persian flowers on a cream ground,   very   early   pattern, Watcombe, ca. 1890s-1910 210

Uhl Pottery

Original production of utilitarian wares began at Evansville, Indiana, in the 1850s and consisted mostly of jugs, jars, crocks and pieces for food preparation and preservation. In 1909, production was moved to Huntingburg, Indiana, where a more extensive variety of items was eventually produced including many novelty and advertising items that have become highly collect-

ible. *Following labor difficulties, the Uhl Pottery closed in 1944.*

Unless it is marked or stamped, Uhl is difficult to identify except by someone with considerable experience. Marked pieces can have several styles of ink stamps and/or an incised number under glaze on the bottom. These numbers are die-cut and impressed in the glazed bottom. Some original molds were acquired by other potteries. Some production exists and should not be considered as Uhl. These may have numbers inscribed by hand with a stylus and are usually not glazed on the bottom.

Many examples have no mark or stamp and may not be bottom-glazed. This is especially true of many of the miniature pieces. If a piece has a "Meier's Wine" paper label, it was probably made by Uhl.

While many color variations exist, there are about nine basic colors: blue, white, black, rose or pink, yellow, teal, purple, pumpkin and browns/tans. Blue, pink, teal and purple are currently the most sought after colors. Animal planters, vases, liquor/wine containers, pitchers, mugs, banks, kitchenware, bakeware, gardenware and custom-made advertising pieces exist.

Similar pieces by other manufacturers do exist. When placed side by side, a seasoned collector can recognize an authentic example of Uhl Pottery.

A Variety of Uhl Marks

Ashtray, brown, American Legion emblem **$105**
Ashtray, round, black, unmarked 25
Bank, figural, medium-size grinning pig, white, painted circus theme, unmarked 400
Bean pot, brown/tan, side handles, marked..... 120
Bowl, 5" d., picket fence.. 40
Bowl, 8" d., blue, marked "Boonville Implement Company" 90
Bowl, 8" d., luncheon, green, unmarked 50
Canteen, miniature, blue, Meier Wine paper label 30
Churn, 3-gal., white, acorn mark 90
Cookie jar, miniature, blue, unmarked 178
Creamer & sugar, cov., robin's-egg blue, both w/hand-turned mark 475
Funnel, brown, unmarked..................................... 22
Jar, 2-gal., white, acorn mark............................. 40
Jar, 3-gal., white, acorn mark............................. 50

Miscellaneous Uhl Containers

Jar, blue & white (ILLUS. middle row left w/Uhl containers).. 55
Jar, cov. (ILLUS. top row right w/miscellaneous Uhl containers)................................... 75
Jug, 3-oz., miniature Egyptian, rose, marked #6.. 25
Jug, 5-gal., brown/white, acorn mark................. 60
Jug, blue Egyptian, marked #133....................... 35
Jug, brown/white, "1939 Merry Christmas," marked 200
Jug, in the form of a football, large size, brown, unmarked.. 240
Jug, in the form of a football, small size, brown, unmarked.. 35

Various Uhl Mugs & Jugs

Jug, miniature, "Canadian Apple Blossom," 3 3/8" h. (ILLUS. bottom left w/various Uhl mugs & jugs) 90
Jug, miniature prunella, black, unmarked........... 25
Jug, miniature, "Pure Corn, Souvenir Lincoln Birthplace, Kentucky," 3" h. (ILLUS. bottom right w/various Uhl mugs & jugs)...... 225
Jug, "Season's Greetings, 1940-1941, Henderson, Kentucky," 6 5/8" h. (ILLUS. top row previous page w/various Uhl mugs & jugs) 175

Match holder, marked Uhl, 2 1/4" h. (ILLUS. previous page bottom row right w/miscellaneous Uhl containers).................... 120

Model of shoe, miniature woman's slipper, blue, marked... 75

Model of shoe, miniature woman's slipper, purple, marked 100

Model of shoes, tied baby shoes, pink, both marked, pr.. 180

Mug, barrel-shaped, blue & white, marked "Dillsboro Sanitarium" 300

Mug, Chicco Beverage Co." (ILLUS. middle row left w/various Uhl mugs & jugs, previous page) 90

Mug, "Chicco Beverage, Norristown" (ILLUS. middle row right w/various Uhl mugs & jugs, previous page) 90

Orange blossom jar, #118 (ILLUS. prevous page top row left w/miscellaneous Uhl containers).. 85

Orange jar (ILLUS. middle previous page row right w/miscellaneous Uhl containers)... 85

Pepper shaker, light blue, unmarked 30

Pitcher, barrel-shaped, brown, marked............. 40

Pitcher, bulbous grape, blue, #183 60

Pitcher, globe-shaped, light blue, unmarked... 28

Pitcher, ice water, yellow, unmarked................. 50

Pitcher, miniature, teal green, marked #28 95

Plaque, Lincoln 550

Salt & pepper shakers, pink, unmarked 77

Uhl Sand Jar

Sand jar, basketweave design, brushed green or ivory, used to snuff cigarettes, Item #530, 20" h., 10 1/2" d. (ILLUS.) ... **200-300**

Stein, 3-oz., miniature, teal green, marked....... 140

Syrup pitcher, cov., blue, marked 180

Thieves jar, miniature, black, #138..................... 83

Uhl Garden Urn

Urn, garden, Roman style, Old Ivory, two pieces, 19 x 12" (ILLUS.) 175

Vase, blue, marked #158 74

Vase, plum, marked #156..................................... 75

Vase, 3 5/8" h., marked "American Legion Huntingburg Post 221" on bottom (ILLUS. previous page bottom row left w/miscellaneous Uhl containers) 225

Water cooler, 3-gal., cov., white, acorn mark... 160

Water cooler, 6-gal., blue & white, w/embossed polar bears...................................... 1,500

Van Briggle

The Van Briggle Pottery was established by Artus Van Briggle, who formerly worked for Rookwood Pottery, in Colorado Springs, Colorado, at the turn of the century. He died in 1904, but the pottery was carried on by his widow and others. From 1900 until 1920, the pieces were dated. It remains in production today, specializing in Art Pottery.

Early Van Briggle Pottery Mark

Bowl, 8 3/4" d., 2 3/4" h., low incurved sides molded in relief w/four dragonflies, deep mulberry matte glaze, ca. 1920s................ **$345**

Bowl-vase, wide low squatty form w/a wide shoulder tapering to a wide flat mouth, molded overall w/large swirled pointed leaves, dark green matte glaze w/buff clay showing through, dated 1903, Shape No. 145, 4 1/2" d., 2" h..................... 2,185

Bowl-vase, footed spherical body w/a wide flat mouth, embossed around the shoulder w/large heart-shaped leaves, fine leathery green & cobalt blue matte glaze, ca. 1908-11, 4 1/2" d., 4" h. 2,415

Vase, 3 3/4" h., 4" d., squatty nearly spherical smooth form, green & raspberry matte glaze, dated 1903, Shape No. E209 575

Vase, miniature, 4 1/4" h., 3" d., ovoid body tapering to a flat mouth, molded around & down the sides w/poppy pods on long stems, rare cobalt blue & yellow striated matte glaze, dated 1902, Shape No. 24.... 4,140

Vase, 5" h., 4 1/4" d., bulbous ovoid body w/a wide flat mouth, molded around the top & down the sides w/Jugenstil-style irises, rare dark bluish-green leathery matte glaze, dated 1906, Shape No. 443.. 2,185

Vase, 5 1/4" h., 5 3/4" d., wide squatty bulbous form w/a flat mouth, molded around the lower body w/stylized blossoms & leaves, mustard yellow matte glaze, ca. 1908-11, Shape No. 643 1,035

Vase, 6" h., 3 1/2" d., cylindrical lower half & a bulbous upper half w/a closed rim, molded around the top w/crocus blossoms, the stems curving down the sides, mustard yellow matte glaze, dated 1903, Shape No. 195 .... **2,415**

Vase, 6 1/2" h., 3 1/4" d., copper-clad, cylindrical lower body w/the top molded w/large stylized blossoms, the rim flanked by small loop handles, original patina, ca. 1908-11, Shape No. 521 .... **2,875**

Yellow "Dos Cabezas" Vase

Vase, 7 1/2" h., 4 3/4" d., "Dos Cabezas," ovoid body molded around the top w/two Art Nouveau maidens, unusual mustard yellow matte glaze, small flat chip in one fold, ca. 1908-11 (ILLUS.) **6,900**

Vase, 7 1/2" h., 6 1/4" d., bulbous ovoid body tapering to a wide short neck, embossed cornflowers & stems around the sides forming a ribbed effect, thick curdled brown matte glaze, dated 1907 .... **2,415**

Vase, 8" h., 3 1/2" d., simple tall ovoid body w/a tiny mouth flanked by small loop handles, overall blackish-green leathery matte glaze, dated 1903, Shape No. 192 .... **1,610**

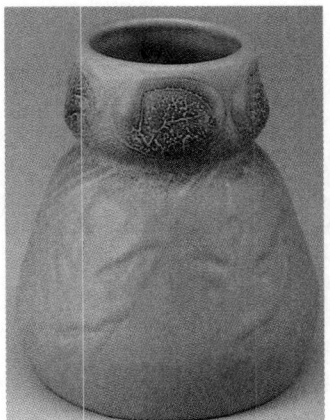

Green Dandelion Van Briggle Vase

Vase, 8 1/2" h., 7 1/2" d., tapering bulbous body w/a wide cupped rim w/a flat mouth, molded w/dandelion blossoms glazed in red w/leafy stems around the sides all on a chartreuse matte ground, dated 1904, Shape No. 137 (ILLUS.) **6,325**

Rare Van Briggle Green Poppy Vase

Vase, 9 3/4" h., 8" d., bulbous ovoid body tapering to a flat mouth, molded overall w/poppy blossoms on leafy stems, mottled red & sheer chartreuse matte glaze w/buff clay showing, dated 1903, Shape No. 143 (ILLUS.) **12,650**

Vase, 10 1/4" h., 4 1/2" d., swelled cylindrical form w/a short shoulder tapering to a low cylindrical neck, molded up around the sides w/curving poppy pods & leaves, sheer frothy lime green matte glaze w/tan clay showing through, dated 1903, Shape No. 173 .... **4,600**

Fine Tall Blue Van Briggle Vase

Vase, 13 1/2" h., 5" d., a low swelled base below the slightly tapering cylindrical sides w/a small flat mouth, crisply molded w/tall irises & leaves, periwinkle blue leathery matte glaze, buff clay showing through, dated 1903, Shape No. 133 (ILLUS.) **10,350**

Vase, 15" h., 10" d., large ovoid body tapering to a small flared neck, overall frothy matte green glaze, dated 1905, Shape No. 978 .... **2,645**

Vernon Kilns

The story of Vernon Kilns Pottery begins with the purchase by Mr. Faye Bennison of the Poxon China Company (Vernon Potteries) in July 1931. The Poxon family had run the pottery for a number of years in Vernon, California, but with the founding of Vernon Kilns, the product lines were greatly expanded.

Many innovative dinnerware lines and patterns were introduced during the 1930s, including designs by such noted American artists as Rockwell Kent and Don Blanding. In the early 1940s items were designed to tie in with Walt Disney's animated features "Fantasia" and "Dumbo." Various commemorative plates, including the popular "Bits" series, were also produced over a long period of time. Vernon Kilns was taken over by Metlox Potteries in 1958 and completely ceased production in 1960.

Vernon Kilns Mark

"Bits" Series

Plate, 8 1/2" d., Bits of the California Missions Series, San Rafael Archangel **$40**
Plate, 8 1/2" d., Bits of the Old West Series, The Fleecing **40**

Cities Series - 10 1/2" d.

Plate, "Atlanta, Georgia," maroon **20**
Plate, "Augusta, Maine," blue **20**

Dinnerwares

Bowl, fruit, Native California patt. **8-10**
Bowl, 8 1/2" d., soup, Bel Air patt. **15-20**
Bowl, Homespun patt. 1 pt. **30-35**
Butter dish, cov., Tam O'Shanter patt. **35-40**
Butter pat, individual, Organdie patt., 2 1/2" d. **40-45**
Casserole, cov., chicken pot pie, Gingham patt. **35-40**
Casserole, cov., individual, Organdie patt., 4" d. **30-35**
Casserole, cov., Vernon's 1860s patt. **75**
Coffee server w/stopper, carafe form, Tam O'Shanter patt. **45-55**
Coffeepot, Ultra California patt. **80-100**

Creamer, Ultra patt. **15**
Cup & saucer, after-dinner size, Monterey patt. **40-45**

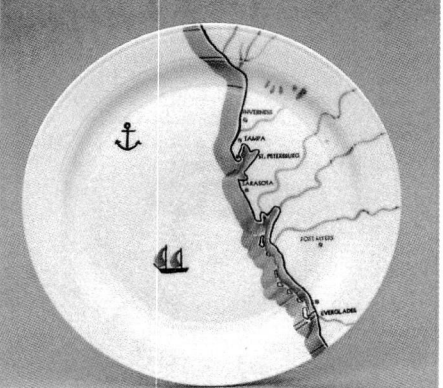

Organdie Flowerpot & Saucer

Flowerpot & saucer, Organdie patt., 4" d. (ILLUS.) **45-50**
Gravy boat, Native California patt. **35**
Muffin cover, Early California patt., red, cover only **125-150**
Mug, Homespun patt., 9 oz. **35-40**
Pitcher, jug-form, bulb bottom, Tam O'Shanter patt., 1 pt. **25-30**
Pitcher, Streamline shape, Gingham patt., 2 qt. **50-75**
Plate, 6 1/2" d., bread & butter, Gingham patt. **5**
Plate, 7 1/2" d., salad, Tweed patt. **8-10**

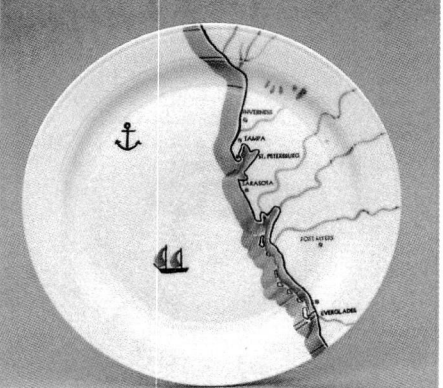

Coastline Series Florida Plate

Plate, 9 1/2" d., Coastline series, Florida patt., Turnbull design (ILLUS.) **100-125**
Plate, 9 1/2" d., Native American series, Going to Town patt., Turnbull design **35-45**
Plate, 10 1/2" d., Casa California Hermosa patt., Turnbull design **25-30**
Plate, 10 1/2" d., Iris patt., Harry Bird design **50**
Plate, chop, 12" d., Organdie patt. **25-30**
Plate, 17" d., chop-type, Early California patt. **30-50**

Platter, 14" l., oval, Native California patt. **30-35**
Relish dish, single leaf shape, Monterey
   patt., 12" l **35-45**
Salt & pepper shakers, Native California
   patt., pr. **20**

Trumpet Flower Saucer

Saucer, Trumpet Flower patt., Harry Bird
   design (ILLUS.) **8-10**
Teacup & saucer, colossal size, Homespun
   patt., 15" d. saucer, 4 qt. **250-275**
Teacup & saucer, Ultra patt. **10**
Teapot, cov., Santa Barbara patt. **65-80**
Tidbit, two-tier w/wooden handle, Home-
   spun patt. **30-35**
Tumbler, Homespun patt. **35**

Disney "Fantasia" & Other Items

Bowl, 6" d., chowder, Nutcracker patt. **50**
Bowl, 8" l., No. 134, decorated figural bird **75-85**
Plate, 17" d., chop, Fantasia patt. .... **600+**
Vase, 4 1/2" h., Pine Cone patt., No. 5, ivory **85-105**

Don Blanding Dinnerwares

Creamer, demitasse size, Hawaiian Flow-
   ers patt., blue **50**
Platter, 16 1/2", Lei Lani patt. **200-250**
Sugar bowl, cov., Hawaiian Flowers patt.,
   blue **75-85**

Rockwell Kent Designs

Creamer, regular, "Our America" series,
   houseboaters, brown **50-75**
Cup & saucer, Salamina patt. **45-55**
Plate, 6 1/2" d., Salamina patt. **40**
Plate, 17" d., chop, Salamina patt. **400-500**

States Map Series - 10 1/2" d.

Plate, Connecticut **20**

States Picture Series - 10 1/2" d.

Plate, Alaska, blue **25**
Plate, Vermont, blue **18-20**

Miscellaneous Commemoratives

Ashtray, Vermont... **20-25**
Plate, 8 1/2" d., Memento Plate of factory **75**
Plate, 10 1/2" d., General MacArthur, brown **20**
Plate, 10 1/2" d., Knott's Berry Farm, Cali-
   fornia... **35**

Plate, 10 1/2" d., Old Man of the Mountain,
   New Hampshire **25**

1952 Postmasters Convention Plate

Plate, Postmasters Convention, showing
   buildings in Boston, border reading "Souvenir of the 48th National Convention of
   the National Association of Postmasters
   of the United States - Boston, Massachusetts, October 12-16, 1952," multicolor
   (ILLUS.)... **30-35**
Plates, 8 1/2" d., Cocktail Hour series,
   brown transfer, complete set of 8 .... **400-600**

Warwick

Numerous collectors have turned their atten-
tion to the productions of the Warwick China
Manufacturing Company that operated in Wheel-
ing, West Virginia, from 1887 until 1951. Prime
interest seems to lie in items produced before 1911
that were decorated with decal portraits of beauti-
ful women, monks and Native Americans. Frater-
nal Order items, as well as floral and fruit
decorated items, are also popular with collectors.

Warwick Mark

Warwick Flow Blue Fern Dish

Fern dish, Pansy decor patt. in Flow Blue, gold trim & highlights, marked "Warwick China" in black, ca. 1896, 4 3/4" h., 7 1/2" d. (ILLUS.) 475

Pitcher, 6 1/2" h., lemonade shape, brown shaded to brown ground, color floral decoration, No. A-27 100

Pitcher, 7" h., Tokio #2, overall white ground, color bird decoration, D-1 185

Pitcher, 10 1/4" h., monk decoration 165

Vase, 4" h., Parisian shape, overall charcoal ground, color nude portrait signed "Carreno," No. C-1 400

Violet Vase with Beechnut

Vase, 4" h., Violet shape, brown shading to tan ground, color beechnut decoration, matte finish, M-2 (ILLUS.) 110

Vase, 4" h., Violet shape, overall charcoal ground, color floral decoration, C-6 130

Warwick Violet Style Vase

Vase, 4" h., Violet style, brown & tan w/poppies, marked w/IOGA knight's helmet, decor code A-6 in red, scarce, ca. 1904 (ILLUS.) 110

Vase, 4 1/2" h., Dainty shape, brown shaded to brown ground, colored floral decoration, No. A-27 145

Vase, 6" h., Narcis #3 shape, brown shaded to brown ground, decorated w/a fisherman wearing a yellow slicker, No. A-35 165

Vase, 6 3/4" h., Narcis #2 shape, overall red ground, color portrait of Princess Potaka, No. E-1 220

Vase, 7" h., Albany shape, tan shading to tan ground, color nut decoration, matte finish, M-64 200

Vase, 7 1/4" h., Cuba shape, brown shading to brown ground, color pine cone decoration, A-64 260

Vase, 7 1/2" h., Verbena #2 shape, brown shaded to brown ground, adult portrait of Madame Lebrun, No. A-17 220

Vase, 8" h., Carol shape, green shaded to green ground, red rose decoration, No. F-2 255

Vase, 8" h., Carol shape, overall pink ground decorated w/a "Gibson Girl" type decoration w/portrait of a woman wearing a boa, No. H-1 300

Vase, 8 1/4" h., Narcis #1 shape, overall white ground w/color bird decoration, No. D-1 190

Vase, 8 1/4" h., Victoria shape, overall red ground w/red poinsettia decoration, No. E-2 190

Vase, 9" h., Flower shape, green shaded to green ground, portrait of a young woman w/flowing red hair, No. M-1 200

Warwick Verbena Style Vase

Vase, 9" h., Verbena #1 style, grey w/pink poppies & pink & white daisies, rim trimmed in gold, marked w/IOGA knight's helmet, decor code C-6 in red, ca. 1906 (ILLUS.) 160

Vase, 9 1/4" h., brown shaded to brown ground, floral decoration, No. A-23 160

Vase, 9 1/4" h., Windsor shape, brown shaded to brown ground, acorn decoration, No. A-67 290

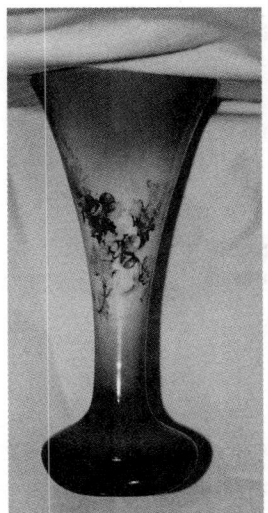

Penn Vase with Acorn Decoration

Vase, 9 1/2" h., Penn shape, brown shaded to brown ground, acorn decoration, No. A-64 (ILLUS.) **195**

Vase, 10" h., Royal #2 shape, brown shaded to brown ground, floral decoration, No. A-27 .... **295**

Vase, 10" h., Virginia shape, overall pink ground, "Gibson Girl" type decoration w/portrait of a young woman w/a flower in her hair, No. H-1 .... **300**

Warwick Bouquet #2 Style Vase

Vase, 10 1/4" h., Bouquet #2 style in pink w/red, pink & white roses, marked

w/IOGA knight's helmet in green, decor code H-4, ca. 1908 (ILLUS.) **190**

Vase, 10 1/4" h., Orchid shape, overall red ground, poinsettia decoration, No. E-2 .... **210**

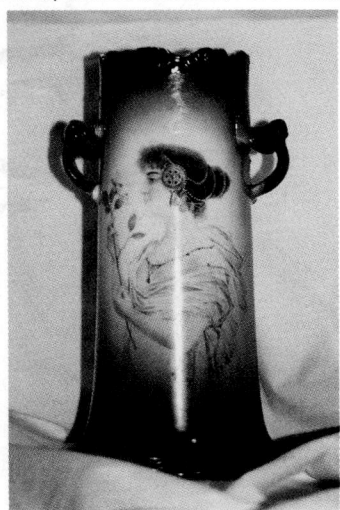

Warwick Bouquet #2 Portrait Vase

Vase, 10 1/2" h., Bouquet #2 shape, brown shaded to brown ground, portrait of a young woman w/dark hair holding a branch w/white flowers, No. A-17 (ILLUS.) **225**

Vase, 11 1/2" h., Senator #3 shape, brown shading to brown ground, color floral decoration, A-6 .... **165**

Bouquet Style Vase with Orchid

Vase, 11 3/4" h., Bouquet #1 style, brown & cream w/orchid in shades of pink, marked w/IOGA knight's helmet in green, decor code A-14, ca. 1904 (ILLUS.) **150**

Warwick Restaurant Soup Bowls

Bowl, 5" d., white w/bands, star emblem
w/"Bethlehem Chapter No. 14 O.E.S.".............. **15**
Butter pat, white w/"The Brass Rail" logo, 3"........ **20**

Warwick Commercial Creamer

Creamer, white w/green tree & bands &
"Camp Lone Tree," marked w/Warwick
knight's helmet, ca. 1937, 4 1/4" h.
(ILLUS.).. **21**
Cup, white w/"Johnny's" logo **25**
Cup & saucer, brown wave decoration,
Santone finish **25**
Cup & saucer, white w/"Duckwall's" logo **40**
Cup & saucer, white w/"Liggett's" logo **20**

Egyptian Shape Vase with Flowers

Vase, 11 3/4" h., Egyptian shape, brown
shaded to brown ground, red floral deco-
ration, No. A-27 (ILLUS.)................................. **245**
Vase, 12" h., Helene shape, color portrait of
woman w/large hat, matte finish, M-1........... **255**
Vase, 12 1/2" h., Alexandria shape, brown
shaded to brown ground w/color floral
decoration, No. A-40 .... **275**
Vase, 15" h., Senator #1 shape, green
shading to green ground, color acorn
decoration, matte finish, M-4 .... **200**
Vase, 15 1/2" h., Chrysanthemum #1
shape, overall red ground w/a Madame
Lebrun child portrait, No. E-1......................... **180**

Commercial China

Bowl, 4 1/4 x 10 1/4" oval, white ironstone
w/green band, "Osiris" emblem **20**
Bowl, 3 3/4" d., soup, double-handled,
white w/black & orange decorative band
below rim & on handles, marked w/War-
wick knight's helmet in green, ca. 1940s,
each (ILLUS. of six, top of page)........................ **6**

Warwick "Duckwall's" Mustard Jar

Mustard jar, cov., white w/"Duckwall's" logo
(ILLUS.) **28**
Plate, 6 1/4" d., white w/one green band,
double headed eagle emblem w/"AASR
32" & "Valley of Wheeling" **24**

4H Plate by Warwick

Plate, 7 1/4" d., white w/4H camp w/stream
& trees in green, two green bands inside
rim, marked w/Warwick knight's helmet in
green, scarce, ca. 1944 (ILLUS.) **20**
Plate, 9" d., white w/"Hotel Anthony" logo **18**
Plate, 9" d., white w/black & red bands, "Masonic Temple of Austin" emblem **18**
Plate, 10" d., white w/"compliments of Dine
Furniture Company" **40**

"Oakley's" Oval Vegetable Dish

Vegetable dish, individual, oval, white
w/"Oakley's" logo (ILLUS.) **25**

Dinnerwares

Cup & saucer, Pattern No. 9572, Silver
Poppy decoration **10**
Cup & saucer, Pattern No. B-9551 .... **20**
Gravy boat w/underplate, Pattern No. B-
9289 .... **30**
Pitcher, 8" h., milk-type, white ground w/flo-
ral decoration of blue forget-me-nots **35**
Plate, 6 1/2" d., bread & butter, Pattern No.
D-9351, platinum bands **20**
Plate, 9" d., Pattern AB-9231 .... **8**
Plate, 9" d., Pattern No. C-9295, Bird of Par-
adise decoration w/two birds **12**
Plate, 10" d., Pattern No. 2098, Venetian
Rose decoration **10**
Vegetable bowl, cov., Pattern No. 2001 .... **40**

Willow Wares

This pseudo-Chinese pattern has been used by numerous firms throughout the years. The original design is attributed to Thomas Minton about 1780, and Thomas Turner is believed to have first produced the ware during his tenure at the Caughley works. The blue underglaze transfer print pattern has never been out of production since that time. An Oriental landscape incorporating a bridge, pagoda, trees, figures and birds supposedly tells the story of lovers fleeing a cruel father who wished to prevent their marriage. The gods, having pity on them, changed them into birds, enabling them to fly away and seek their happiness together.

Blue

Bowl, 12 1/4" d., serving-type w/beaded rim
(small flake on table ring) **$50**
Bowls, 8", 9 1/4" & 10 1/2" l., rectangular,
stacking-type, Ridgways, set of 3 .... **325**
Butter dish, drain & cover, Ridgways, 3
pcs. **225**
Cracker jar, cov., cylindrical w/slightly
domed cover w/button finial & woven
wicker bail handle, Noritake, Japan, ca.
1945-52, 7 3/4" d., 7 1/2" h. (heavily
crazed, crack on cover, crack to base
rim) **173**

Copeland-Spode Willow Platter

Platter, 11 x 14 1/2", oblong w/canted corners, Copeland-Spode, late 19th - early
20th c., some gilt edge wear & knife
marks (ILLUS.) **345**
Platter, 12 x 15 1/4", oval, dark blue, mark
of Wedgwood & Co., England, ca. 1900 .... **403**
Platter, 14 1/4 x 17 3/4", oval, light blue,
banner mark of Podmore, Walker & Co.,
England, late 19th c., minor glaze
flaws, ca. 1900 (ILLUS. right, top next
page) **144**
Platter, 13 3/4 x 18", oval w/scalloped cor-
ners, dark blue, mark of Wedgwood &
Co., England, ca. 1900, minor glaze
flaws (ILLUS. left with Podmore, Walker
platter, top next page) **316**
Platter, 14 1/4 x 18", oblong, unmarked,
probably England, late 19th c. (two small
glaze flaws) **173**
Platter, 20 1/2" l., oval, English arrow & cir-
cle mark, late 19th - early 20th c **468**
Trivet, scalloped foot, Moriyama, very rare,
6" **225**

Two Large Blue Willow Platters

Other Colors

Plate, dinner, pink.. **10**
Platter, 12 1/2 x 15 3/4", oblong w/canted
corners, brown, impressed mark for J. &
G. Meakin, England, second half 19th c...... **110**

Zsolnay

This pottery was made in Pecs, Hungary, in a factory founded in 1862 by Vilmos Zsolnay. Utilitarian earthenware was originally produced, but by the turn of the 20th century ornamental Art Nouveau-style wares with bright colors and lustre decoration were produced; these wares are especially sought today. Currently Zsolnay pieces are being made in a new factory.

Zsolnay Marks

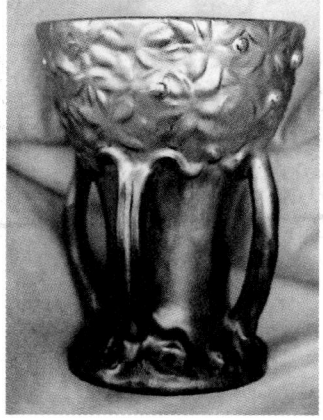

Zsolnay Chalice

Chalice, organic form w/applied handles curving out connecting base to bowl, multi eosin glazes, printed Zsolnay Factory mark, incised form number 5668, ca. 1900, 6" h. (ILLUS.) **$1,500-2,000**

Zsolnay Polychrome Charger

Charger, cream ground w/enameled polychrome flowers & leaves in the Iznik style copying designs from the 18th c., printed factory mark & incised form number 470, ca. 1875, 14 1/5" d. (ILLUS.) **750-900**

Zsolnay Jardiniere

Jardiniere, realistic polychrome decoration of thistles & leaves, majolica glaze, incised Zsolnay Factory mark & form number 5454, ca. 1899, 18" h. (ILLUS.) **5,000-7,000**

Zsolnay Hungarian-style Jug

Jug, on circular base, C-scroll handle, typical Hungarian folkloric form w/cream ground & enameled polychrome flower & leaf decoration, incised Zsolnay Factory mark, incised form number 1157, ca. 1883, 11 1/2" h. (ILLUS.)........................ **550-650**

Zsolnay Miniature Pitcher

Pitcher, 4 1/2" h., miniature form, squatty footed base tapering to long cylindrical body, flared rim, handle formed by woman peering into the pitcher, exceptional eosin glazes, round raised Zsolnay Factory mark, incised form number 5956, ca. 1900 (ILLUS.).................................... **2,250-2,750**

Pitcher, 12 3/4" h., crackled glaze, red color, modern design by Gabriella Törzsök, printed Zsolnay Factory mark, ca. 1959... **300-500**

High-relief Zsolnay Pitcher

Pitcher, 15 1/2" h., tapering tankard style w/C-scroll handle, overall high-relief decoration of oak leaves, acorns & large beetles, pale green eosin glaze, incised Zsolnay Factory mark & form number 4115, ca. 1893 (ILLUS.) **4,500-5,500**

Zsolnay Puzzle Jug

Puzzle jug, shriveled yellow glaze w/applied stylized flowers & bird figure attached to C-scroll handle, based on 17th-c. designs, pierced neck & flowers, stepped circular base, incised factory mark & form number 547, ca. 1875, 9 1/2" h. (ILLUS.)...................................... **550-750**

Zsolnay Tile

Tile, square, decorated w/flowers & leaves, green & gold eosin glazes, unmarked, unusual & rare, ca. 1900, 5" sq. (ILLUS.) **1,250-1,500**

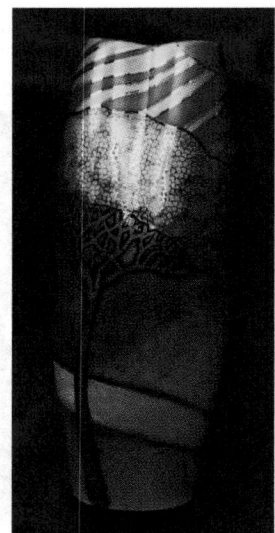

Zsolnay Vase with Sun & Trees

Vase, 8 1/2" h., slightly ovoid cylindrical shape, decorated w/idyllic view of trees, sun & road, metallic eosin glazes, round raised Zsolnay Factory mark, incised form number 6011, ca. 1906 (ILLUS.) **12,500-15,000**

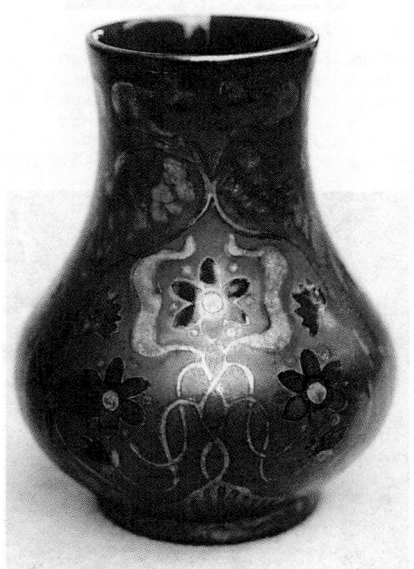

Miniature Footed Zsolnay Vase

Vase, miniature, 4 3/4" h., footed form w/ovoid body tapering to narrower neck, decorated w/Hungarian folkloric designs in metallic blue eosin glaze, incised Zsolnay Factory mark, ca. 1906 (ILLUS.) **750-1,000**

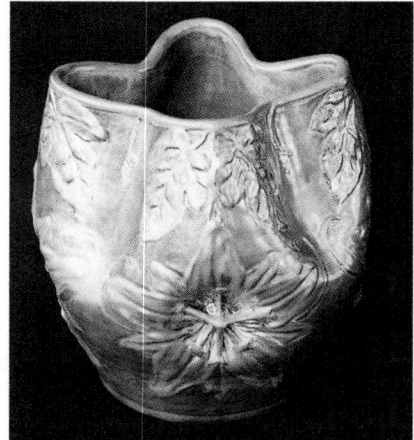

Zsolnay Vase with Metallic Glaze

Vase, 10 1/2" h., freeform body w/quatrefoil opening, decorated w/relief & applied leaves & lilies, highly metallic silver/blue eosin glaze, printed Zsolnay Factory mark, incised form number 5424, ca. 1900 (ILLUS.) **10,000-12,500**

Zsolnay Owl Vase

Vase, 11" h., figural, consists of three realistic owls in high relief, green/gold metallic eosin glaze, round raised Zsolnay Factory mark, incised form number 5236, ca. 1898 (ILLUS.) **6,500-8,500**

Zsolnay Vase with Swirled Banding

Vase, 12" h., cylindrical footed body tapering to narrow neck w/highly stylized fluted lip, raised banding in swirl pattern around body & neck, soft green/blue eosin glaze, incised Zsolnay Factory mark, incised form number 4626, ca. 1897 (ILLUS.) **2,500-3,500**

Zsolnay Vase with Swirl Base

Vase, 12 1/4" h., swirl pattern ovoid base, long, slightly tapering cylindrical neck, scalloped rim, cream ground w/enameled painted flowers & leaves, gilt decoration, printed Zsolnay Factory mark, incised form number 3088, ca. 1885 (ILLUS.) **400-600**

CHARACTER COLLECTIBLES

Numerous objects made in the likeness of or named after comic strip and comic book personalities or characters abounded from the 1920s to the present. Scores of these are now being eagerly collected and prices still vary widely. Also see DIS-NEY COLLECTIBLES and TOYS and "ANTIQUE TRADER TOY PRICE GUIDE."

Amos & Andy Candy Container

Amos & Andy candy container, glass, Amos in grey driving "Fresh Air Taxi" & Andy in back wearing red suit & brown derby, the car w/embossed yellow spoked wheels, left side marked "Avor. 1 Oz.," right side marked "Victory Glass Co.," Jeannette, PA," traces of original paint remaining, ca. 1928, missing closure, 4 1/4" l. (ILLUS.) **$360**

Amos & Andy Fresh Air Taxi Toy

Amos & Andy toy, windup tin, Amos driving red "Fresh Air Taxi" & Andy in back wearing blue suit & brown derby, the car w/red-spoked wheels, back door reading "Amos 'n' Andy," w/original box, somewhat distressed & missing end flaps, Marx (ILLUS.) 960

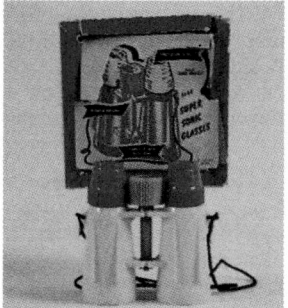

Buck Rogers "Super Sonic Glasses"

Buck Rogers binoculars, hard plastic, 3x40 strength, bright yellow, red & green, w/original "Super Sonic Glasses" box showing Buck peering at space rockets & faraway planets, Norton-Honer Mfg. Co., copyright 1963, box has separated, 5 1/2" l. (ILLUS.) 115

Buck Rogers Chemical Laboratory

Buck Rogers chemistry set, includes graphic miniature cardboard cans hold-

ing various chemicals, test tubes w/corks, instruction manual & instruments, in original box w/brightly colored illustration of Buck & friends in the laboratory under "Buck Rogers 25th Century Chemical Laboratory," Gropper Mfg. Co., box w/some wear, 8 x 12" (ILLUS.) 1,320

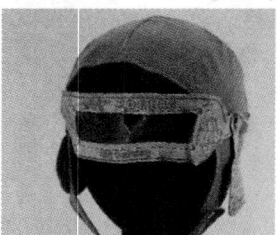

Buck Rogers Helmet

Buck Rogers helmet, suede-like cloth helmet w/rear reflector button, suspended ear flaps, button chin strap & celluloid goggles, Daisy, split in goggles, 7" w. (ILLUS.) 259

Buck Rogers Pocket Watch

Buck Rogers pocket watch, gold tone metal, round frame w/white face illustrated w/color figures of Buck & Wilma, black Arabic numerals & lightning bolt copper hands & smaller sweep second hand, Cyclops character engraved on rear, in original box w/colorful graphics of characters, ships & ray gun & marked "J. Dille Co.," prewar, slight tarnishing on hands, box 2 3/4 x 3" (ILLUS.) 1,800

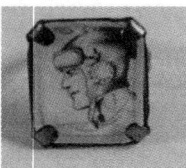

Buck Rogers Ring

Buck Rogers ring, novelty/premium, the square face illustrated w/black & white bust of helmeted Buck in profile, 3/4" sq. (ILLUS.) 240

Buck Rogers Roller Skates

Buck Rogers roller skates, nickel-plated metal w/leather straps, futuristic streamlined design, reflector at rear of each, original key, rare, Marx, copyright 1935, dark oxidation to area of plating, rear reflectors replaced, 11" l. (ILLUS.) **2,013**

Buck Rogers Windup Toy

Buck Rogers toy, windup tin, rocket w/Buck Rogers at helm, in bright orange, green & black, "Buck Rogers Rocket Police Patrol" emblazoned on side, Marx, 12" l. (ILLUS.).. **420**

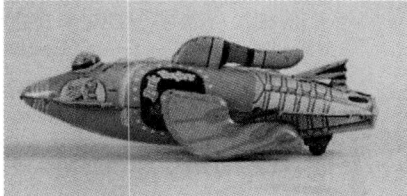

Buck Rogers Mechanical Space Ship

Buck Rogers toy, windup tin, space ship w/brightly colored decoration & streamlined design, when activated makes space noise & sparks, made for Daisy Mfg. Co. by Marx, copyright 1927, 12" l. (ILLUS.).. **300**

Buck Rogers Walkie-Talkie Set

Buck Rogers walkie-talkie set, includes two walkie-talkies, connecting wire, secret decoder & original certificate, w/original box graphically illustrated on interior w/Buck on TV screen, Remco Inc. 8 1/2 x 13" box (ILLUS.).................................. **230**

Buck Rogers Water Pistol

Buck Rogers water pistol, pressed steel, yellow w/bright orange lightning bolt graphics, "Buck Rogers Liquid Helium Water Pistol" on barrel, Daisy Co., 7 1/2" l. (ILLUS.).. **300**

Felix the Cat Candy Container

Felix the Cat candy container, glass, smiling cat standing next to paneled barrel reading "Felix," the barrel notched to accommodate snap-on closure, bottom marked "Copyright 1922-24 by Pat. Sullivan/Pat. applied for," no paint remaining, missing closure, 3 1/2" l., 3 1/2" h. (ILLUS.)... **431**

Felix the Cat Toy

Felix the Cat toy, fully jointed black & white cat w/leather ears & "Felix" printed across chest, copyright Pat Sullivan, Schoenhut, 4" h. (ILLUS.) **115**

Humphrey Mobile Windup Toy

Humphrey Mobile toy, windup tin, three-wheeled conveyance rolls forward in circular motion, w/driver Humphrey pushing pedals, waving arm & tipping hat, bright red w/yellow accents, Humphrey in green trousers, red vest & black coat, "Humphrey Mobile" printed across front of vehicle, copyright Ham Fisher, Wyandotte, 7 1/2" h. (ILLUS.) **259**

Windup Dogpatch Band Toy

Li'l Abner Dogpatch Band toy, windup tin, Daisy Mae sitting playing upright piano, Mammy standing on piano conducting, Pappy sitting at side playing drum, Li'l Abner standing at other side, bright yellow, red, green & black, copyright 1945 King Features Syndicate, Unique Art, 9 1/2" h. (ILLUS.) **546**

Marx Merry Makers Windup Toy

Marx Merry Makers toy, windup tin, upright piano w/marquee reading "Marx Merry Makers," a mouse sitting playing, one standing atop it conducting, one sitting beside it playing a drum & one standing on other side, black, white & red, Marx, 1930s, 9 1/2" h. (ILLUS.) **518**

Peanuts advertising sign, color-printed cardboard, a long rectangular form w/advertising for The Hartford Times newspaper, shows a line of cartoon characters including Charlie Brown, Lucy & Snoopy as well as Nancy & Dennis the Menace, dark green background, 1950s, 21 x 43 1/2" (ILLUS., bottom of page) **555**

Rare Early Peanuts Advertising Sign

Peanuts Band Banks Figures

Peanuts bank set, ceramic, each bank in the form of a Peanuts character holding a musical instrument, includes Charlie Brown, Lucy, Schroeder, Snoopy & Linus, United Features Syndicate markings, the set (ILLUS.) **300-350**

Popeye & Olive Oyl Windup Toy

Popeye & Olive Oyl toy, windup tin, rooftop base holds Popeye dancing jig & Olive sitting on box of dynamite & playing accordion, Marx, 1930s, mechanism sluggish, 9 1/2" h. (ILLUS.) **575**

Rare Battery-operated Popeye Toy

Popeye toy, battery-operated, white uniformed figure of Popeye sits atop over-sized green spinach can, arms wave, pipe lights up & figure blows smoke when activated, in original box labeled "Smoking Popeye" w/color illustration of Popeye on spinach can & smaller figure of Swee' Pea against background of ocean w/liner in distance, very rare due to limited distribution, Linemar, 1950s, 9" h. (ILLUS.).. **4,140**

Popeye in Barrel Windup Toy

Popeye toy, windup tin, figure of Popeye in barrel reading "Popeye" across front, figure waddles & nods head, copyright 1932 King Features Syndicate, Chein, 7" h. (ILLUS.) 420

Popeye with Parrots Windup Toy

Popeye toy, windup tin, lithographed figure of Popeye holds cages of parrots at either side, figure walks while cages roll when activated, Chein, one replaced wheel, 8 1/2" h. (ILLUS.) 270

Popeye on Roller Skates Toy

Popeye toy, windup tin, lithographed figure of Popeye on roller skates delivering can of spinach, in original box, Linemar, 6" h. (ILLUS.) **1,080**

Popeye Punching Bag Toy

Popeye toy, windup tin, lithographed figure of Popeye w/celluloid floor model punching bag, Popeye in blue pants & hat, black shirt, red boxing gloves & yellow shoes, on green rectangular base, Chein, 7 1/2" h. (ILLUS.) 900

Porky Pig with Umbrella Windup

Porky Pig toy, windup tin, lithographed figure of Porky holding umbrella, when activated, figure vibrates in circles & umbrella spins, Marx, copyright 1939 by Leon Schlesinger, 8" h. (ILLUS.) 374

Roosevelt Bears Tin Pail

Roosevelt Bears pail, tin, tapering cylindrical shape w/wire handle, gold anodized rims on red ground decorated w/illustrations of Teddy Roosevelt riding on back of bear & bears playing drums & trumpet & toting a flag, rare, handle probable replacement, 4 1/2" d., 3 1/4" h. (ILLUS.) **1,208**

Smokey the Bear Ceramic Bank

Smokey the Bear bank, ceramic, model of a seated Smokey holding a shovel, painted in brown, yellow & blue, made by Norcrest (ILLUS.) **175-200**

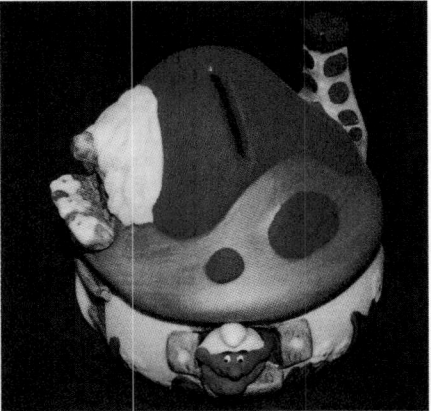

Ceramic Smurf House Bank

Smurf bank, ceramic, model of a Smurf house painted red, tan, white & blue, by Wallace Berry, 1982 (ILLUS.) **75-100**

Toonerville Trolley Candy Container

Toonerville Trolley candy container, glass, modeled on the tin windup top, w/driver & "Toonerville" on both sides & "7 Depot Line" below windows, red tin slide closure, traces of red paint remaining, marked "© 1922 by Fontaine Fox" on bottom (ILLUS.) **374**

Toonerville Trolley Toy

Toonerville Trolley toy, windup tin, trolley rolls forward in eccentric motion w/animated conductor, "Toonerville" along edge of top, "Trolley" printed under windows, comes w/boxtop w/faded label, copyright 1922 by Fontaine Fox, Germany, 7" h. (ILLUS.) **660**

Wimpy Windup Toy

Wimpy toy, windup, celluloid, hand-painted, figure from Popeye cartoon waddles forward & sways torso, swings cane & nods head when wound, Star trademark, pre-war Japan, 7 1/2" h. (ILLUS.) **360**

CHRISTMAS COLLECTIBLES

Hallmark Ornaments

1973 Angel, yarn.. $21
1973 Betsey Clark glass ball, 1st in series 95
1973 Mr. Santa, yarn.. 25
1974 Norman Rockwell glass ball 46
1974 Raggedy Ann & Andy glass balls, set of 4 75
1974 Soldier, yarn 10
1975 Adorable Raggedy Ann 95
1975 Currier & Ives satin ball................................ 15
1975 Marty Links glass ball.................................... 8

Hallmark Raggedy Ann Ornament

1975 Hallmark Santa Ornament

"Happy Holidays" House Ornament

Rocking Horse Ornament

1981 Rocking Horse, 1st in series, dated
(ILLUS.)... 400
1981 Rooftop Deliveries, 3rd in "Here
Comes Santa" series.. 275
1981 St. Nicholas, tin... 23
1982 Cowboy Snowman 35
1982 Jingling Teddy 15
1982 Jogging Santa 20
1982 Locomotive, tin, 1st in series.................. 425

Old Fashioned Christmas Glass Ball

1982 Old Fashioned glass ball, decorated
w/scene of children putting up Christmas
decorations (ILLUS.) 25
1982 Peeking Elf 20
1982 Santa & Reindeer 30
1982 Spirit of Christmas (The) 85
1982 Teacher glass ball...................................... 5
1983 Angel Messenger 37
1983 Heart, acrylic... 25
1983 Old Fashioned Santa 42
1983 Skiing Fox 12
1984 "12 Days of Christmas" Partridge,
1st in series.. 75
1984 Katybeth, porcelain 10
1984 Muffin 15
1984 Polar Bear Drummer 10

Santa's Deliveries Ornament

1984 Santa's Deliveries, Santa at wheel of
truck loaded w/Christmas trees, 6th in
"Here Comes Santa" series (ILLUS.) 55

1984 Sister Bell 12
1984 Uncle Sam, pressed tin.............................. 20

Victorian Dollhouse Ornament

1984 Victorian Dollhouse, 1st in "Nostalgic
House" series (ILLUS.).................................... 100
1985 Ice Skating Owl 8
1985 Kit the Shepherd 13
1985 Rainbow Brite & Friends glass ball.......... 10
1985 Spirit of Santa Claus (The) 55
1985 Sugarplum Cottage, lighted...................... 15
1986 Dasher, 1st in "Reindeer" series................ 55
1986 Old Fashioned Santa 30
1986 Paddington Bear 20
1986 Soccer Beaver 13
1987 Icy Treat 9
1987 Jack Frosting 25
1987 Let It Snow 12
1987 Wee Chimney Sweep 10

Buttercup Angel Ornament

1988 Buttercup, 1st in "Mary's Angels" se-
ries (ILLUS.) 21
1988 Filled With Fudge 15
1988 Purrfect Snuggle 12
1988 Son 20
1988 Wonderful Santacycle (The) 22
1989 Baby's First Christmas 35

Claus & Co. Railroad Series

Frosty Friends 1989 Ornament

Barbie Ornament

1995 Peanuts Ornaments

1999 Best Pals Ornament

Miscellaneous

Feather tree, brown tape-wrapped trunk w/green feather needles & red composition berries, original white painted dovetailed base, 49 1/2" h. **413**

House Beautiful 1938 Christmas Issue

Magazine, "House Beautiful," December 1938, colorful cover showing a large Christmas tree & presents, excellent condition (ILLUS.) **10**

Paper Christmas Tree & Nativity Set

Nativity set, lithographed paper, large multi-branched tree w/numerous angels, candles, toys, etc. for decorating it, figures of Holy Family mounted to set up at base of tree, w/original box illustrated w/color picture of family gathered around a table on which the tree & Nativity scene are set, box reads "Weihnachtsfreud" & "Joies de Noel" & "Christmas Joys," box 10 x 15" (ILLUS.) **4,700**

Early Mechanical Santa Claus Figure

Rare Early Santa Pull Toy

Pull toy, lithographed paper on wood, Santa's sleigh pulled by two reindeer, Santa dressed in blue, possibly by Bliss, late 19th c., minor edge wear, 12" l. (ILLUS.)... **1,265**

Santa Claus figure, mechanical, a standing figure of Santa dressed in red & white coat w/black pants & boots, face w/glass eyes & a long cotton beard, the head on a pendulum-like device attached to a clockwork mechanism in the stomach, early 20th c., slight costume soiling & wear on boots, non-working, 34" h. (ILLUS., next column) **960**

Tree Light in Rare Teardrop Pattern

Tree light, glass, cylindrical, tooled flared lip, pontil scarred base, overall teardrop pattern, ice blue, very rare, probably England, ca. 1860-1880, 2 7/8" h. (ILLUS., previous page)................................... **448**

Christmas Light with Diamond Pattern

Tree light, glass, ovoid, sheared lip, smooth base, overall diamond pattern, deep teal green w/heavy greyish puce coloration mixed throughout, England, ca. 1880-1900, lip w/bruise & flakes, 3 3/4" h. (ILLUS.)... **179**

CLOCKS

ALSO SEE Antique Trader Clocks Price Guide *(Krause Publications)*

Late German Bracket Clock

Bracket clock, Linden, Germany, mahogany case w/a domed top & metal loop handle, the square glass front w/molding over a dial w/Roman numerals & applied gilded spandrels, stepped bottom molded on flat tab feet, eight-day time & triple chime movement, ca. 1940s, 7 1/2 x 11", 14 1/2" h. (ILLUS.)... **$350**

Seth Thomas Modern Bracket Clock

Bracket clock, Thomas (Seth) Clock Co., Thomaston, Connecticut, walnut case w/a domed top & brass loop handle, brass & enamel dial w/Roman numerals, based on an 18th c. English design, eight-day time & strike movement w/floating balance, ca. 1950s, 3 3/4 x 7 1/2", 10 1/2" h. (ILLUS.).................. **180**

Early Swiss Calendar Desk Clock

Calendar desk clock, DuBois & Fils, Switzerland, tall silver case w/round top dial section w/notched rim & topped by spread-winged eagle finial, a white porcelain time dial w/Arabic numerals framed by a/polychrome scene at top showing a man holding dog & looking toward draped columns, two subsidiary dials for date & days of the week, raised on a flattened waisted support w/a bulbous lower body w/applied flower decoration, all supported by two figural satyrs standing on a rectangular stepped base w/bands of notched decoration & leaf & bead trim, keywind calendar movement, chain fusée movement w/monometallic balance just visible behind the fancy gilt cock that fits in dial, both dial & movement signed, replaced crystal, ca. 1830, 7" h. (ILLUS.)... **1,960**

Rare Ithaca Calendar Shelf Clock

Calendar shelf or mantel clock, Ithaca Calendar Clock Co., Ithaca, New York, upright walnut case w/ebonized trim, the top section w/an arched & pierced leaf-carved crest above columns flanking the round bezel & paper dial w/Roman numerals, the slightly stepped-out deep lower case enclosing a large glass calendar dial exposing the crystal gridiron pendulum & date roles, molded base, eight-day time & strike movement, second half 19th c., 20 1/4" h. (ILLUS.)........................... **3,600**

Crystal regulator, Boston Clock Co., Boston, Massachusetts, upright brass case w/glass sides & front enclosing the large dial w/Arabic numerals in the porcelain outer ring around a relief-cast cast-brass dial center, tandem wind eight-day time & strike movement, 10 1/4" h. (crack in side glass) **563**

Decorative Crystal Regulator Clock

Crystal regulator, gold-painted cast-spelter upright case w/an arched top w/five flower basket finials, an egg-and-dart cornice over a scroll-cast panel above the long beveled glass door & sides, porcelain dial w/Arabic numerals & decorated w/flower swags, glass tube pendulum, rectangular platform base cast w/a scroll & floret band on flat tab feet, eight-day time & strike movement, early 20th c., 5 3/4 x 8 3/8", 15" h. (ILLUS.).. **600-650**

American Cuckoo Co. Wall Clock

Cuckoo wall clock, American Cuckoo Clock Co., Philadelphia, Pennsylvania, fumed oak Neo-Gothic Arts & Crafts case, stepped flat top above Gothic arched & flat pilasters flanking the cuckoo door & brass dial w/Arabic numerals, eight-day weight-driven movement, time & strike, oak pendulum bob in a wheel design, tall obelisk-shaped iron weights, early 20th c., 5 1/4 x 9 1/4", 12 3/4" h. plus chain & weights (ILLUS. disassembled)... **200-250**

Cast-brass French Inkstand-Clock

Desk clock, clock-inkstand combination, cast-brass, Rococo style, the small clock w/a round dial w/Roman numerals framed by ornate pierced scrolls in an upright case above a rectangular inkstand w/ornate scroll trim & fitted w/two inkwells w/domed covers, on small peg feet, 30-hour movement, probably French, late 19th - early 20th c., 6 x 10 1/2", 8 1/8" h. (ILLUS.) **180-200**

Haddon Electric Motion Clock

Novelty shelf or mantel clock, Haddon Clock Co., electric motion clock, "Home Sweet Home," model of a house in plastic & composition, a square large window over the dial on the left, a window on the right w/a scene of an old woman in a rocker, when plugged in woman rocks & fire shimmers, 20th c., 3 1/2 x 12 1/4", 7 3/8" h. (ILLUS.) **185**

Novelty shelf or mantel clock, Mastercrafter electric motion clock, the brown plastic case designed to resemble an open stage w/railing showing a boy & girl who sit on moving swings, the large round top centering a steel dial w/Arabic numerals & a sweep seconds hand, ca. 1950s, 5 x 7 1/4", 10 3/4" h. (ILLUS. left, bottom of page) **180**

Novelty shelf or mantel clock, Mastercrafter electric motion clock, the brown plastic case w/an opening showing a girl sitting on a moving swing, large rounded top enclosing a steel dial w/Arabic numerals, ca. 1950s, 3 x 7 1/4", 10 3/4" h. (ILLUS. center, bottom of page) **165**

Novelty shelf or mantel clock, Mastercrafter electric motion clock, the tall copper-colored plastic case w/molded green & brown fir trees flanking an opening w/a painted waterfall scene that shimmers when plugged in, ca. 1950s, 5 x 7 1/4", 10 3/4" h. (ILLUS. right, bottom of page) **125**

Novelty shelf or mantel clock, New Haven Clock Co., New Haven, Connecticut, a fancy cast metal gilt & bronzed figural case w/a cherub atop the round dial frame enclosed w/leaf branches all on a wheeled base pulled by two oxen, dial w/Roman numerals, 6 3/4" h. (missing chain to oxen) **371**

Novelty shelf or mantel clock, Welch (E.N.) Mfg. Co., Bristol, Connecticut, "Little Grip" model, bronzed metal model of a small suitcase w/clock dial w/Roman numerals inset on the side, original handle, 3" w. **394**

Novelty wall clock, figural Oswald Scottie carved wood case w/revolving eyes telling the time, label under base, Germany, early 20th c., 5 3/4" h. **366**

Paperweight clock, Ansonia Clock Co., Ansonia, Connecticut, square clear diamond-cut case enclosing the round dial w/Arabic numerals, made for H.D. Phelps, 3" w. **135**

Plato calendar clock, Ever Ready Fitch Clock Co., upright gilt-brass French-style case w/ornate loop top handle, reeded columns down the sides & a wide floral-cast band along the base, two stacks of white turning pages w/numbers indicating the date, 4 7/8" h. **214**

Shelf or mantel clock, Ansonia Clock Co., Ansonia, Connecticut, gilt-metal, seated figure of a 17th c. writer or poet beside the upright ornately scroll-cast case surrounding the porcelain dial w/Arabic numerals, long ornate scrolling base on scroll feet, eight-day movement, time & strike, case repainted, ca. 1890, 7 x 14 1/4"., 11 1/4" h. **600-700**

Three Mastercrafter Motion Clocks

Shelf or mantel clock, Ansonia Clock Co., Ansonia, Connecticut, miniature Royal Bonn china case "Granite" model, arched & scrolled top & waisted sides on scroll feet, small brass bezel enclosing the dial w/Roman numerals, overall floral decoration, late 19th c., 6 1/2" h. **214**

Ornate Figural Ansonia Clock

Shelf or mantel clock, Ansonia Clock Co., Ansonia, Connecticut, "Opera" model cast-metal case, the tapering rectangular base w/sawtooth apron & cast-metal scroll feet supporting a large cast-metal figure of a seated classical woman on an elaborate stool & holding a wreath w/a lyre at the side, the ornate upright cast-metal clock case to one side enclosing a brass bezel around the porcelain face w/Roman numerals, eight-day movement, time & strike, open escapement, minor surface wear, ca. 1885-95, 8 x 21", 16 1/4" h. (ILLUS.).............................. **800-1,000**

Shelf or mantel clock, Ansonia Clock Co., Ansonia, Connecticut, ornate Royal Bonn china "La Lomme" model case, wide serpentine top & wide scroll-case serpentine sides on a low footed case, overall floral decoration around the large brass bezel & dial w/Roman numerals, time & strike movement, 11" h....................... **647**

Fine China Clock & Ansonia Works

Shelf or mantel clock, Ansonia Clock Co., Ansonia, Connecticut, ornate Royal Bonn "La Mine" model china case, the tall upright arched case w/waisted sides molded at the top w/a central shell flanked by long open scrolls w/further scrolls down the sides & across the base w/incurved scroll feet, painted a deep magenta at the top w/pale yellow in the center shading to dark green at the base, decorated on the front w/large h.p. white & magenta blossoms & green leaves, the large brass bezel around the porcelain dial, Arabic numerals, open escapement, eight-day movement, time & strike, ca. 1900, 6 1/4 x 11", 13 1/2" h. (ILLUS.).. **1,000-1,200**

Quality Ansonia Victorian Clock

Shelf or mantel clock, Ansonia Clock Co., Ansonia, Connecticut, Victorian walnut Renaissance Revival style case w/a high scroll-carved crest centered by a classical head over the arched, molded cornice w/urn-form finials above an arched glass door w/gilt stencil decoration of cupids & ferns, white dial w/Roman numerals, the door flanked by tall narrow angled mirrors backing gilt-metal standing cupid figures, base w/curved, molded sides flanking a front panel w/gilt-metal scroll boss, eight-day movement, time & strike, third-quarter 19th c., 5 1/2 x 16 1/2", 24 1/4" h. (ILLUS.) **750-800**

Ansonia-Royal Bonn China Clock

Shelf or mantel clock, Ansonia Clock Co., New York, New York, "La Charny" model, Royal Bonn china case, the upright arched case molded at the top w/a grotesque mask & scrolls continuing down the sides flanked at each corner by a stylized figure of a seated griffin, the borders in gold & brown shaded to golden yellow & green & decorated w/large red & yellow iris-like flowers, brass door & bezel around the porcelain dial w/Roman numerals, eight-day movement, time & strike, ca. 1900, 5 1/2 x 11 1/4", 11 3/4" h. (ILLUS.) **700-800**

Figural Cast-Spelter German Clock

Shelf or mantel clock, cast spelter, figural case, a large spread-winged eagle atop a rockwork base enclosing a round brass bezel & small dial w/Arabic numerals, Germany, late 19th - early 20th c., 6 x 8 3/4", 13 1/2" h. (ILLUS.) **250-300**

Early Rosewood Beehive Clock

Shelf or mantel clock, Brewster & Ingrahams, Bristol, Connecticut, Kirk's patent movement, beehive form rosewood case w/molded frame & round molding around the round white signed dial w/black Roman numerals, the lower pane reverse-painted w/an image of Ballston Springs, eight-day time & strike rack & snail movement w/original brass springs, age cracks to dial paint, key escutcheon repaired, pendulum a later Seth Thomas type, hands are old but incorrect for this model, ca. 1845, 19" h. (ILLUS.) **560**

Shelf or mantel clock, Brewster & Ingrahams, Bristol, Connecticut, steeple-type, mahogany veneer case w/a pointed crest flanked by pointed finials above half-round columns flanking the two-pane glazed door, the short pointed upper pane over the painted metal dial w/Roman numerals, the tall rectangular lower pane frosted & etched w/flowers & leaves in a vase, flat base, Kirk patent backplate, eight-day movement, good label inside, mid-19th c., 19 1/2" h. **703**

Forestville Mfg. Co. Shelf Clock

Shelf or mantel clock, Forestville Mfg. Co., Bristol, Connecticut, tall upright "column & cornice" case in crotch-grained mahogany veneer, a deep ogee molded blocked cornice over tall half-round columns w/ringed capitals & bases flanking a two-pane door, the upper pane over the polychrome wooden dial w/spandrels, black

Roman numerals, open escapement & marked "Forestvill [sic], Manufacturing Co. - Bristol, CT. U.S.A.," the lower pane w/an original Wm. B. Fenn monochromatic silver-colored decoration of a vase w/floral stems, bottom ogee-front block feet flank another glass pane w/an original Wm. B. Fenn monochromatic silver-colored decoration of a bird on limb, good label, hand-colored lithograph of Saturday night scene on backboard, time & strike movement, ca. 1850, 34" h. (ILLUS.) **1,456**

Ornate French Gilt-bronze Clock

Shelf or mantel clock, French Victorian Renaissance Revival-style, gilt-bronze case w/a large swag-draped urn finial on the upright case topped w/ornate scrolls & grape clusters above the round gilt-trimmed enameled dial w/Roman numerals flanked by caryatids, the blocked rectangular base w/leafy scrolls & grapes flanking the case & decorated w/scroll bands & florets, pinwheel movement, third quarter 19th c. (ILLUS.) **5,200**

Wm. Gilbert Acheron Model Clock

Shelf or mantel clock, Gilbert (Wm. L.) Clock Co., Winsted, Connecticut, "Acheron" model, walnut case w/fan-carved crest & line-incised scrolls above the arched molded glazed door opening to a dial w/Roman numerals, the lower door w/original silver stenciled leaves, flowers & a checkerboard design, deep flared platform base, paper label inside, late 19th c., 4 1/2 x 13", 19 1/4" h. (ILLUS.).. **200-250**

Gilbert Eastlake Style Clock

Shelf or mantel clock, Gilbert (Wm. L.) Clock Co., Winsted, Connecticut, walnut kitchen-style case, Victorian Eastlake design, the sawtooth-cut central cornice flanked by tall corner blocks w/knob finials above reeded sides flanking the tall glazed door w/ornate silver stenciled arches below the dial w/Roman numerals, brass pendulum w/applied grape leaves, molded & blocked base w/line-incised decoration, original varnish, eight-day movement, time & strike, ca. 1885, 4 x 12 1/4", 21 1/4" h. (ILLUS.) **450-550**

Fine Ingraham Temple-style Clock

Shelf or mantel clock, Ingraham Company, Bristol, Connecticut, temple-style, black enamel over wood, the long, high rectangular case w/applied stamped metal columns & cast-metal paw feet, metal lion head mask end handles, top panels on the front inset w/slag glass framed by metal simulating curtained windows, eight-day movement, time &

strike, ca. 1900, 5 1/2 x 20", 10 7/8" h.
(ILLUS.) **300-400**

Jennings Art Nouveau Metal Clock

Shelf or mantel clock, Jennings Bros. Mfg.
Co., Bridgeport, Connecticut, gilt spelter,
the tall Art Nouveau design case bulbous
at the top & tapering down to a wide serpentine foot, openwork leaves & cherries
at the top & down the front w/loop side
handles, the round dial w/Arabic
numerals, ca. 1900, 4 3/4 x 5 1/4", 12" h.
(ILLUS.) **200**

Lux Miniature Celluloid Clock

Shelf or mantel clock, Lux Clock Mfg. Co.,
Waterbury, Connecticut, miniature
domed celluloid case, dial w/Arabic numerals, flat molded base, early 20th c.,
2 1/4 x 6 1/4", 3 1/4" h. (ILLUS.) **40**
Shelf or mantel clock, miniature, cast gun
metal upright case w/Art Nouveau-style
serpentine sides & the front set w/rhine-
stones around the small round porcelain
dial w/Roman numerals, early 20th c.,
2 1/2" h. **39**

Unusual Victorian Neo-Gothic Clock

Shelf or mantel clock, New Haven Clock
Co., New Haven, Connecticut (attributed), Victorian Neo-Gothic style walnut
case, a steeply pointed top w/Gothic
scroll cutout border & trefoil finial flanked
by sunburst side finials on thin blocks
over roundels & shaped side panels w/in-
cised scrolls, the tall steeply pointed door
w/heavy molding around the glass decorated w/a fancy gilt stencil border band
w/Oriental motifs, the dial w/a brass bezel & Roman numerals printed w/patent
date "Feb. 11, 1879," brass pendulum
w/unique inset compensating needle indicator, deep rectangular platform base
w/incised scrolls, original finish, eight-
day movement, time & strike,
4 3/4 x 14 5/8", 22 1/4" h. (ILLUS.) **350-400**

Seth Thomas Classical Revival Clock

Shelf or mantel clock, Thomas (Seth) Clock Co., Plymouth, Connecticut, Classical Revival tall case, mahogany veneer, the deep ogee cornice w/blocked corners above a pair of gilt columns flanking the two-pane door, the large upper pane over the worn painted metal dial w/Roman numerals, clear lower pane, the lower section w/ogee corner blocks flanking a panel w/a small round pendulum window, eight-day movement, time & strike, some veneer damage, last quarter 19th c., 4 1/2 x 8 1/2", 16" h. (ILLUS.).......... **225**

Thomas Late Classical Shelf Clock

Shelf or mantel clock, Thomas (Seth) Clock Co., Plymouth, Connecticut, Classical-style ogee rosewood veneer case, the front w/rounded molding around the two-pane long door w/rounded molding, the upper pane over the painted metal dial w/Roman numerals, the lower pane showing the pendulum & works, eight-day movement, time, strike & alarm, face wear, ca. 1880, 4 x 10 3/4", 16 1/2" h. (ILLUS.)...................................... **200-250**

Thomas Domed Mahogany Clock

Shelf or mantel clock, Thomas (Seth) Clock Co., Plymouth, Connecticut, mahogany, the angled domed case top above a conforming glazed door opening to a dial w/Roman numerals above a brass & silvered metal pendulum w/inset brass star, rectangular stepped base, paper label inside, eight-day movement, time & strike, 1850-80, 4 3/4 x 10 3/8", 16" h. (ILLUS.) **150**

Thomas Rosewood Cottage Clock

Shelf or mantel clock, Thomas (Seth) Clock Co., Plymouth, Connecticut, round-topped rosewood veneer case, the front forms a door w/a molded ring around the dial w/Roman numerals, eight-day movement, time & strike, ca. 1865, 4 x 8 3/8", 12 1/4" h. (ILLUS.).............. **200**

Seth Thomas Ogee Case Clock

Shelf or mantel clock, Thomas (Seth) ogee-case clock, mahogany veneer w/tall two-part door, the upper section over the dial w/Roman numerals, a clear lower pane showing the printed label inside, time-and-strike movement, ca. 1850-70 (ILLUS.) **175**

Waterbury "Steeple" Clock

Shelf or mantel clock, Waterbury Clock Co., Waterbury, Connecticut, mahogany veneer "steeple" clock, pointed top flanked by turned tapering finials above a pointed two-pane glazed door, the top pane over the dial w/Roman numerals, the replaced pane w/a frosty & etched leafy vine design, half-round columns down the sides, stepped base, one finial replaced, eight-day movement, strike & alarm, ca. 1860-80, 4 3/8 x 11 1/4", 19 1/4" h. (ILLUS.) **250-300**

Waterbury Round-top Clock

Shelf or mantel clock, Waterbury Clock Co., Waterbury, Connecticut, round-top walnut case, an arched top molding continuing to tapering gilt spear points at the front flanking the tall glazed door w/gilt scroll decoration & opening to the replaced dial face w/Roman numerals, rectangular molded base, eight-day

movement, strike & alarm, adjustable mercury pendulum, late 19th c., 4 3/4 x 11 1/4", 17 1/4" h. (ILLUS.) **200-300**

Welch, Spring & Co. Classical Clock

Shelf or mantel clock, Welch, Spring & Co., Forestville, Connecticut, Classical Revival rosewood veneer case, the paneled arched top above conforming molding framing a round molding around the dial w/Roman numerals & two roundels over a trapezoidal glass panel showing the pendulum, rectangular base w/ogee border, label inside, ca. 1880, 5 x 11 1/4", 16 1/4" h. (ILLUS.) **200-250**

Atkins Cottage Clock with Alarm

Wall clock, Atkins Clock Co., Bristol, Connecticut, rosewood veneer cottage-style, arched paneled top over a conforming door w/two glass panes, upper pane over the original painted dial w/Roman numerals, lower pane w/original gilt-stenciled rose & wreath decor, interior label coming loose, 30-hour movement, time & alarm, ca. 1865, 10 1/4" h. (ILLUS.) **252**

Very Ornate Black Forest Wall Clock

Wall clock, Black Forest-type, ornate carved walnut case w/a large carved crest of a spread-winged eagle attacking a mountain goat, the wide sides of the rounded case finely carved w/evergreen trees & roots entwining around the round black glass dial w/white Roman numerals, two further carved goats at the bottom of the case, eight-day movement, Germany, late 19th - early 20th c., dial possibly replaced, overall 47" h. (ILLUS.) **3,600**

English Drop Octagon Wall Clock

Wall clock, drop octagon-style, brass-inlaid mahogany veneer, the large octagonal top frame enclosing a large brass bezel around the dial w/Roman numerals, the short rectangular drop case flanked by carved reed & cattail brackets & decorated w/inlaid brass lines around a narrow glazed shaped window showing the brass pendulum bob, eight-day time-only movement, England, ca. 1900-10, 16 x 26" (ILLUS.) **950-1,150**

French Picture Frame Wall Clock

Wall clock, Dugas, Paris, France, picture frame style, square molded wood frame

enclosing a brass-inlaid & enameled panel w/a round opening over the glass dial w/Roman numerals, dial signed "Dugas à Paris," eight-day spring-wound time & strike movement w/silk thread pendulum, ca. 1870s, 19 1/2" sq. (ILLUS.) **800-1,000**

Vienna-style Carved Wall Clock

Wall clock, Hamburg American Clock Co., Vienna-style dark stained softwood case, a gilt cast-metal spread-winged eagle finial on the high central crest w/a dentil band & applied carved swag flanked by corner blocks w/turned finials, heavy half-round ring-turned spindles flank the tall two-pane front, the upper pane over the square brass dial w/brass spandrels & an applied Roman numeral chapter ring, the lower pane showing the pendulum & brass bob, spring-wound eight-day time & strike on a rod movement, ca. 1910, 13" w., 36" h. (ILLUS.) **850-950**

Junghans Wall Box Clock with Trim

Wall clock, Junghans, Germany, mahogany-finished hardwood box-style, arched pediment w/applied brass classical wreath & swags above top corner blocks w/similar brass trim flanking the two-pane glass front, the top pane over the celluloid dial w/Arabic numerals, the lower long pane w/slender brass wire overlay showing the pendulum & large brass bob, half-round base apron w/applied brass wreath, eight-day time & strike movement, ca. 1920, 12" w., 33" h. (ILLUS.) **900-1,000**

Kroeber Neo-Gothic Wall Clock

Wall clock, Kroeber (Frederick J.) Clock Co., New York, New York, Model No. 46, Victorian Neo-Gothic style walnut case, the pointed pediment w/blossom finial flanked by matching corner finials above shaped sides w/applied half-round bobbins flanking the rounded tall glass door opening to the dial w/Roman numerals & pendulum w/large brass bob, deep base drop w/Gothic-style curved bracket trim, eight-day movement, time & strike, original finish, ca. 1890, 4 3/4 x 9 1/2", 33 1/2" h. (ILLUS.) **800-1,000**

Mauthe Clock Co. Berliner Clock

Wall clock, Mauthe Clock Co., Germany, Berliner style, walnut & softwood case, a cast-metal spread-winged eagle finial atop the high stepped pediment w/shell carving flanked by corner blocks w/urn-turned finials over the stepped flat cornice above boldly ring-and-baluster-turned half-columns flanking the dial panel w/leaf carvings in each corner around the wide brass bezel enclosing the celluloid chapter ring w/Arabic numerals centered by an embossed brass Art Nouveau floral center disk, turned drop finials at the front base corners backed by a large, long scroll-cut board behind the free-hanging ornate floral-stamped pendulum bob, eight-hour time & strike movement w/hour & half hour gong strike, ca. 1895-1910, 15" w., 36" h. (ILLUS.) **1,200-1,500**

Novelty German Landscape Clock

Wall clock, novelty movement, hand-carved landscape w/a waterwheel & stream, trees & an onion-dome church w/the clock dial set in the tower, framed, eight-day seven-jewel movement, string on reverse runs from waterwheel to clock & is wound by turning the wheel, Germany, ca. 1950s, 15 x 31" (ILLUS., bottom previous page) **300**

Picture Frame Wall Clock

Wall clock, picture frame-style, oblong un-dulating heavy outer molding around a mother-of-pearl inner border enclosing the brass bezel & glass dial w/Roman nu-merals, eight-day time & strike move-ment, France, ca. 1900, 16 x 20" (ILLUS.) **900-1,100**

Sessions Mission Oak Wall Clock

Wall clock, Sessions Clock Co., Bristol, Connecticut, miniature "Aztec" model Mission Oak case, a square molded frame enclosing the square wood dial face w/applied brass Arabic numerals, the free-hanging pendulum w/brass bob backed by a lattice framework, eight-day time & strike movement, ca. 1915-20, 10" w., 19" h. (ILLUS.) **500-600**

Anglo-American Short-drop Clock

Wall clock, short-drop style, walnut burl ve-neer case, the large round molded top enclosing the brass bezel & painted dial w/Roman numerals, the short drop case flanked by pierce-carved grapevine brackets, centered by a small rectangular glass pane showing the brass pendulum bob, short curved base drop, Anglo-American, eight-day spring-wound time & strike movement, ca. 1870s, 15" w., 28" h. (ILLUS.) **1,100-1,500**

Seth Thomas "World" Wall Clock

Wall clock, Thomas (Seth) Clock Co., Ply-mouth, Connecticut, "World" model, oak case w/a large octagonal top framing the brass bezel enclosing the dial w/Roman numerals & sweep seconds hand, the long pointed drop base enclosing a point-ed glass door over the pendulum w/a brass bob, double spring 15-day move-ment w/Graham dead beat escapement, ca. 1905-15, 17" w., 32" h. (ILLUS.) **1,500-1,750**

French Clock with Weather Station

Wall clock, walnut case w/a top gallery w/turned bobbins & urn-form corner fini-als above a narrow flared cornice above the case w/turned & reeded colonettes flanking a round molding enclosing the dial w/enameled plaques w/black Roman numerals, the tapering lower case carved w/ornate leaf scrolls at the sides flanking a small rectangular thermometer over a round brass bezel enclosing a barometer dial, eight-day German time & strike movement, France, ca. 1900, 16" w., 35" h. (ILLUS.).................................... **1,900-2,200**

Fine Classical Revival Wall Clock

Wall clock, Waterbury Clock Co., Waterbury, Connecticut, Classical Revival style rosewood veneer case, the flat stepped cornice over an ogee panel flanked by end blocks above half-round maple columns w/gilt capitals & bases flanking the two-pane door, the large upper pane over the painted tin face w/Roman numerals & green-stenciled leaves, the lower door pane reverse-painted w/a bluebird in a gilt ring surrounded by flowers on a tan ground, deep blocked ogee base, open escapement, paper label in side, ca. 1890, 4 3/8 x 14 3/4", 24 3/4" h. (ILLUS.)... **600-700**

Waterbury "Galesburg" Model Clock

Wall clock, Waterbury Clock Co., Waterbury, Connecticut, "Galesburg" model, long oak case, the molded arched crest centered by a block w/turned urn finial flanked by turned corner finials, short reeded columns & turned drops flank the

top sides above the tall arched & glazed door, a wood molding encloses the brass bezel & original paper dial w/Roman numerals, the long lower pane shows the pendulum & large brass bob, short reeded columns & finials flank the bottom of the door, a long stepped & tapering base drop w/a turned finial, two drop finials at the bottom case corners, original finish, late 19th - early 20th c., eight-day time & strike movement w/half-hour gong strike, 52" h. (ILLUS.) **1,069**

Welch Short Drop Octagonal Clock

Wall clock, Welch (E.N.) Mfg. Co., Bristol, Connecticut, octagonal drop wall case, original dark varnish finish, the stepped octagonal top w/a large brass bezel enclosing the dial w/Roman numerals, sweep seconds hands & an outer day-of-the-month band, the short pointed drop case w/a small glass door w/gilt trim, eight-day movement, time, strike & calendar, open escapement, minor wear on face, ca. 1890, 4 1/2 x 17", 22" h. (ILLUS.)... **350-400**

Ansonia "Regulator A" Wall Clock

Wall regulator clock, Ansonia Clock Co., Ansonia, Connecticut, "Regulator A" model, walnut veneer case w/a large octagonal top section w/molded black ring around the brass bezel enclosing the paper dial w/Roman numerals & an outer calendar date ring w/Arabic numerals, the long drop case w/a pointed bottom w/conforming molding framing the glazed door printed w/"Regulator A," pendulum w/large brass bob, eight-day time & strike movement, ca. 1900-10, 17" w., 32" h. (ILLUS.) **900-1,000**

Ingraham Western Union Regulator

Wall regulator clock, Ingraham & Co., Bristol, Connecticut, "Western Union" model, long oak case w/a flat rectangular top w/a wide cornice lightly carved & centered by a fan device above the flat case molding enclosing the tall, wide two-pane glazed door, the upper pane w/black corners centered by the large brass bezel & dial w/Roman numerals, the lower pane w/a gilt Greek key border band & the word "Regulator" over the pendulum & large brass bob, short base brackets flank the scroll-cut & carved drop backboard, late 19th - early 20th c., 37" h. (ILLUS.) **338**

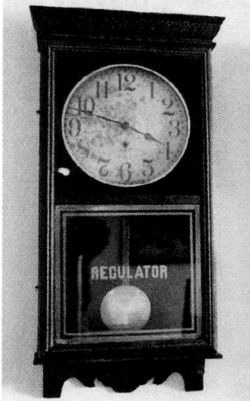

Nice Sessions Oak Wall Regulator

Wall regulator clock, Sessions Clock Co., Bristol, Connecticut, oak case w/wide flaring flat cornice above the large two-pane door, the top pane reverse-painted in black w/a gold ring over the paper dial w/Arabic numerals, the lower pane banded in gold & printed "Regulator," showing the pendulum w/brass bob, molded base above cutout side scallops & a scroll-cut backboard w/stamped designs, eight-day movement, time-only, original finish, foxing on paper dial, ca. 1900, 5 1/8 x 17 3/4", 36" h. (ILLUS.) **700-800**

Thomas "No. 2" Wall Regulator

Wall regulator clock, Thomas (Seth) Clock Co., Plymouth, Connecticut, "No. 2" model, tall oak case w/a large molded round top enclosing the brass bezel & painted dial w/Roman numerals & sweep seconds hand, the long rectangular drop base w/a tall rectangular molding enclosing a glass pane over the cylindrical brass weight & large brass pendulum bob, ca. 1890-1900, 17" w., 36" h. (ILLUS.) **1,800-2,000**

COCA-COLA ITEMS

Coca-Cola promotion has been achieved through the issuance of scores of small objects through the years. These, together with trays, signs and other articles bearing the name of this soft drink, are now sought by many collectors. The major reference in this field is Petretti's Coca-Cola Collectibles Price Guide, 11th Edition, by Allan Petretti (Antique Trader Books). An asterisk (*) indicates a piece which has been reproduced.

Coca-Cola Calendar for 1921

Calendar, 1921, roll-down type, color illustration of young woman wearing dark blue & white outfit & hat sitting in garden setting amid pink & yellow flowers & holding glass of Coke, metal band at top, portion of calendar pad for November at bottom, framed, 16 1/2 x 36" (ILLUS.) **$900**

Calendar, 1937, lithograph, color illustration of a straw-hatted boy striding along carrying a fishing rod over his shoulder in one hand & bottles of Coke in the other, calendar page for March 1937 attached below, the Coke logo at top of calendar page, signed on lower right by N.C. Wyeth, original metal band & hanger at top, 16 1/2 x 29 1/2" **518**

Coca-Cola Perpetual Calendar

Calendar, perpetual type, metal frame w/red button at top reading "Drink Coca-Cola in Bottles" in white lettering, the lower portion white w/gold trim, panel reading "Have a Coke" in red above paper calendar pages, the top showing date of Friday, March 27, 1953, 8 w. x 19" h. (ILLUS.) **431**

Coca-Cola Clock Counter Sign

Clock counter sign, light-up type, brass colored metal, square clock w/white face & dark green number panel w/gold Arabic numerals, attached at side to panel reading "Drink Coca-Cola" in white lettering on red ground, all on base w/white front edge reading "Have a Coke" in green lettering, a Price Makers decal on back, 19 1/2" l., 8 1/2" h. (ILLUS.) **840**

Coca-Cola Cooler with Advertising

Cooler, rectangular, red embossed tin advertising panels on all four sides, legs that have been cut down just above lower case storage rack, metal tag reads "The Coca-Cola Company Cooler Patented March 4, 1930. Mfg. by Glascock Bros. Mfg. Co. Muncie, IN," no top, 23 1/2 x 31 1/2", 31 3/4" h. (ILLUS.).............. **374**

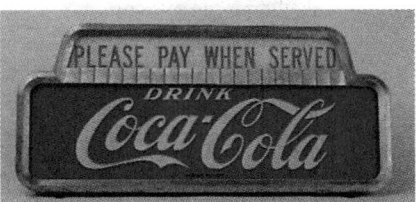

Coca-Cola Light-up Counter Sign

Counter sign, light-up type, aluminum frame holding rectangular panel reading "Drink Coca-Cola" in white lettering on red ground, marquee at top reading "Please Pay When Served" in green lettering on white, back marked "Price Bros. Chicago and New York," rare, 19" w., 9" h. (ILLUS.)... **575**

Rare Light-up Counter Sign

Counter sign, light-up type, brass colored frame, square panel w/silver textured ball in reverse & "Pause and Refresh" bisecting ball in gold lettering on dark green ground, attached at side to panel reading "Drink Coca-Cola in Bottles" in white lettering on red ground, all on base w/white front edge reading "Have a Coke" in green lettering, Price Manufacturing label on rear, rare, 19 1/2" l., 9" h. (ILLUS., above).. **1,840**

Coca-Cola Light-up Sign

Counter sign, light-up type, metal frame, square panel w/textured glass dial reading "Pause" in yellow, attached at side to panel reading "Drink Coca-Cola in Bottles" in white lettering on red ground, all on base w/white front edge reading "Please Pay When Served" in green lettering, ca. 1950, corrosion to housing, glass dial cracked, not operational, 20" l., 9" h. (ILLUS., at left)...................................... **431**

Counter sign, light-up waterfall type, brass colored frame, square panel w/waterfall effect reading "Pause and Refresh" in gold on black ground w/green top & bottom borders, attached at side to panel reading "Drink Coca-Cola" in white lettering on red ground, all on base w/white front edge reading "Please Pay When Served" in green lettering, Price Manufacturing label on rear, rare, 19 1/2" l., 9" h. (ILLUS., bottom of page)................... **1,898**

Waterfall Effect Counter Sign

Coca-Cola Salesman's Sample Cooler

"Drink Coca-Cola" Counter Sign

Counter sign, reverse printed transfer on glass in wooden base, rectangular, reads "Drink Coca-Cola" in white lettering on bright red ground, the rear w/original paper decal reading "Price Bros. The Sign of Quality Chicago, NY," the wooden base w/attached white panel reading "Coke" in red, 5 x 12" (ILLUS.) **460**

Salesman's sample cooler, open-front version, red w/"Drink Coca-Cola" in white on front, comes w/carrying case, ring binder pages on inside of lid labeled "A Business Builder," & Cellotex insulation insert, 1939, paint touchups, exterior has been clear-coated, 7 1/4 x 12 1/4", 10 1/4" h. (ILLUS., top of page).................. **3,220**

Sign, aluminum die-cut sign spelling out "Drink Coca-Cola In Bottles," to be used on soda cooler, stamped "Trademark Registered," marked on reverse "Brown Manufacturing Co. Newport News, VA Made In USA," 17" l., 7" h. **345**

Sign, enamel die-cut sign spelling out "Drink Coca-Cola" in white w/black trim, marked "Trademark Reg. U.S. Pat. Off.," about 18" l., 5 1/2" h... **926**

Sign, porcelain, rectangular w/scroll crest, green w/pale yellow trim & "Fountain Service" in pale yellow at top above red panel reading "Drink Coca-Cola - Delicious and Refreshing" in white lettering, by Tennessee Enamel Mfg. Co., Nashville, ca. 1934, slight bend at bottom, a few perimeter porcelain chips, 46 x 60" (ILLUS.) **1,200**

Wooden Scroll Coca-Cola Sign

Sign, wood, scroll sign spelling out "Drink Coca-Cola" in red atop fluted base, tail of first "C" marked "Trade Mark, Reg. U.S. Pat. Off.," by Kay of Austria Displays Inc., New York, 1930s, 6 3/4 x 20 1/4" (ILLUS.)... **1,380**

Coca-Cola Thermometer

Thermometer, enameled tin litho, red button at top reads "Drink Coca-Cola in Bottles" in white lettering, thermometer flanked by black geometrical line decora-

Coca-Cola Porcelain Fountain Service Sign

tion, bottom w/more line decoration & reading "Quality Refreshment" in red, all on white ground, 9 1/2" h. (ILLUS.) **230**

Round Coca-Cola Thermometer

Thermometer, round, red center w/gold outline of Coke bottle & "Drink Coca-Cola" in white lettering, surrounded by green border w/black degree marks & numerals, black hand for indicating temperature, marked at bottom "Pam Clock Co. Mt. Vernon, New York 48," 12" d. (ILLUS.) **518**

1916 Coca-Cola Advertising Tray

Tray, 1916, serving, rounded rectangular shape, center w/color illustration of young woman wearing wide-brimmed hat & cream-colored dress seated under a tree near pink cut roses while holding a glass of Coke & looking back over her shoulder at viewer, "Drink Coca-Cola" in light blue letters at top, decorated gilt rim, edge wear, 8 1/2 x 19" (ILLUS.) **220**

1922 Coca-Cola Serving Tray

Tray, 1922, serving, tin litho, rounded rectangular shape, center panel w/close-up color illustration of dark-haired young woman wearing peach dress & wide-brimmed hat w/pale blue ribbon holding flared glass of Coke & looking back over her shoulder toward viewer, "Coca-Cola" at top of gilt-trimmed dark border w/rolled rim, mottled finish, light surface pitting, paint chips to rolled rim, 10 1/2 x 13 1/2" (ILLUS.) **460**

1937 Coca-Cola Serving Tray

Tray, 1937, serving, tin litho, rounded rectangular shape, center panel w/color illustration of fair-haired young woman wearing bathing suit running on beach toward viewer & holding a bottle of Coke in each hand, a cape-like cover-up flowing behind her, the gilt-trimmed rim w/"Drink Coca-Cola" in yellow lettering on red ground at both top & bottom, American Art Works, 10 1/2 x 13 1/4" (ILLUS.) **237**

1939 Coca-Cola Serving Tray

Tray, 1939, serving, tin litho, rounded rect-angular shape, center panel w/color illus-tration of young woman wearing white bathing suit & sandals sitting on towel on red-striped diving board & holding bottle of Coke, a rectangular red panel at top reading "Drink Coca-Cola - Delicious and Refreshing" in grey lettering, red rim w/silver-grey trim, 10 1/2 x 13 1/2" (ILLUS.)... **259**

1941 Coca-Cola Serving Tray

Tray, 1941, serving, tin litho, rounded rect-angular shape, center panel w/color illus-tration of young woman wearing babush-ka, short red skirt & white ice skates sitting on a log at rink's edge against wooded backdrop & holding bottle of Coke, the gilt-trimmed red rim w/"Drink Coca-Cola" in yellow lettering at both top & bottom, American Art Works, 10 1/2 x 13 1/4" (ILLUS.).............................. **237**

1942 Coca-Cola Serving Tray

Tray, 1942, serving, tin litho, rounded rect-angular shape, center panel w/color illus-tration of two young women, one seated in convertible car, the other standing alongside, both holding bottles of Coke, "Drink Coca-Cola" in grey lettering on red rim w/silver-grey trim, 10 1/2 x 13 1/2" (ILLUS.)... **403**

Coca-Cola Vending Machine

Vending machine, Vendorlator VMC Model No. 44, w/original red & white paint, "Drink Coca-Cola" in raised red letters at top of front, "Have a Coke" on the sides, zinc-lined door, w/original paper instruc-tions in interior of door, some scrapes & pitting to paint, 15 x 15 1/2", 58" h. (ILLUS.)... **2,013**

Rare Coca-Cola Whirligig

Whirligig, enamel, consisting of four Coca-Cola button signs in red, white & green reading "Drink Coca-Cola," "Sign of Good Taste," etc., on stand w/arched rectangular base, very rare, about 13 1/2" h. (ILLUS.)... **1,725**

COMPACTS & VANITY CASES

A lady's powder compact is a small portable cosmetic make-up box that contains powder, a mirror and puff. Eventually, the more elaborate compact, the "vanity case," evolved, containing a mirror, puffs and compartments for powder, rouge and/or lipstick. Compacts made prior to the 1960s when women opted for the "au natural" look are considered vintage. These vintage compacts were made in a variety of shapes, sizes, combinations, styles and in every conceivable natural or man-made material. Figural, enamel, premium, commemorative, patriotic, Art Deco and souvenir compacts were designed as a reflection of the times and are very desirable. The vintage compacts that are multipurpose, combined with another accessory—the compact/watch, compact/music box, compact/fan, compact/purse, compact/perfumer, compact/lighter, compact/cane, compact/hatpin—are but a few of the combination compacts that are not only sought after by the compact collector but also appeal to collectors of the secondary accessory.

Today vintage compacts and vanity cases are very desirable collectibles. There are compacts and vanities to suit every taste and purse. The "old" compacts are the "new" collectibles. Compacts have come into their own as collectibles. They are listed as a separate category in price guides, sold in prestigious auction houses, displayed in museums, and several books and many articles on the collectible compact have been written. There is also a newsletter, Powder Puff, written by and for compact collectors. The beauty and intricate workmanship of the vintage compacts make them works of fantasy and art in miniature.

For additional information on the history and values of compacts and vanity cases, readers should consult Vintage and Vogue Ladies' Compacts by Roselyn Gerson, Collector Books.

Bakelite Compact with Carrying Cord

Bakelite compact, round, the lid decorated w/center rose surrounded by rhinestones on brown ground, interior holds mirror & powder compartment, w/silken carrying cord & large tassel (ILLUS.)........................ **$350**

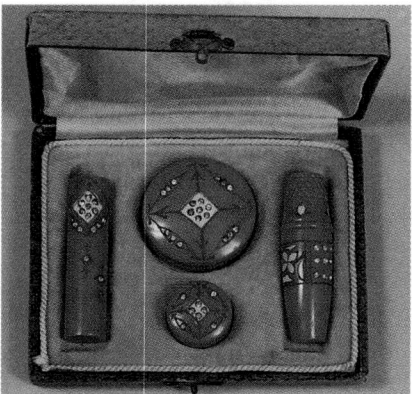

Bakelite Compact/Sewing Kit

Bakelite compact/sewing kit, coral, green & white case containing wells for powder & rouge pots, perfume & sewing containers, the rouge pot w/mirror & puff, the perfume bottle in Bakelite tube, the sewing tube containing needles, thread & pins, the lid doubling as thimble, all w/green & white engraved decoration enhanced w/rhinestones (ILLUS.) **325**

Black compact, round, designed to resemble a record, complete w/grooves & red center label which reads "Melody, J.D. Creation," interior reveals beveled mirror, puff & powder well; also available w/blue, green or cream-colored center labels; made for the international market; available in the U.S. under the Columbia Records name label **450**

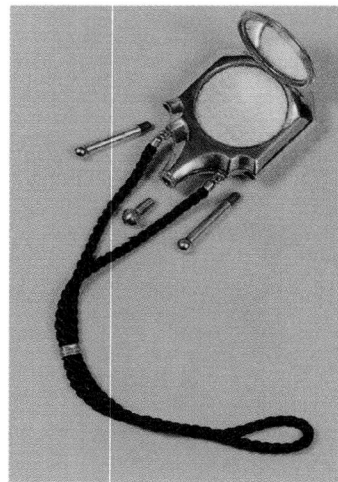

Powder, Rouge & Perfume Compact on Cord

Brass compact, two-sided model on black silk braid cord, one side opening to powder compartment, the other side holding rouge compartment, both lids w/mirror inside, two pull-out rouge sticks on either side of cord, a center lid between the cord attachments unscrewing to reveal perfume compartment (ILLUS., previous page).. 120

Brushed goldtone compact, round, the lid decorated w/hands in high relief playing a piano, Pilcher.. 550

Brushed goldtone compact, round, the lid decorated w/polished goldtone stars, attached to black silk carrying wrist cuff, the reverse of cuff w/snap-shut mini-pocket for money, complete w/black tassel, interior of compact holding mirror & powder well 225

Brushed goldtone compact, round, the lid set w/round mobe pearl framed by pronged, faceted turquoise stones, twist closure, Germaine Monteil 45

Brushed goldtone compact, square, decorated w/dancing legs in high relief, further enhanced w/black enamel legs & skirt, Volupte... 550

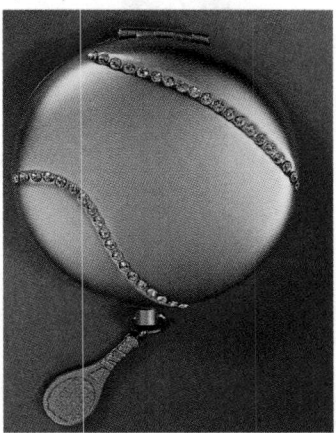

"Tennis Ball" Compact

Brushed goldtone compact, "Tennis Ball" compact, lid decorated w/crystal seams & tennis racket charm, Estee Lauder (ILLUS.)... 75

Brushed goldtone royal commemorative compact, round, the lid decorated w/picture of Prince Charles & Princess Diana, "H.R.M. The Prince Charles - Lady Diana Spencer, 1981" printed around edge of picture, very rare, Kigu................................... 550

Brushed silvertone compact, round, "Odyssey" compact, lid beautifully decorated w/pastel-colored crystals, interior reveals mirror, puff & pressed powder well, Nieman Marcus exclusive, Debbie J. Palmer....... 65

Celluloid compact, round, black, the lid decorated w/h.p. Art Deco-style woman's face, hand-engraved, Antonin of France 300

Celluloid compact, round, the lid decorated w/painted three-dimensional face of Pierrot, the interior holding mirror & puff, Austria (ILLUS., top next column) 400

Celluloid Compact with Pierrot Lid

Cork, goldtone & enamel compact, round, goldtone metal lid decorated w/blue & orange abstract enamel design, rare............... 125

"Crystelle" compact/pillbox, model of butterfly, black, blue & silver design on lid, compartments in wings, both containing mirrors, one compartment holding puff & powder, the other for holding pills, Wadsworth... 350

Enamel compact, square, shocking pink w/logo in white on lid, interior holds mirror, puff & signed powder well, Schiaparelli 150

Enamel & silvertone compact/dress clip, round, black, the lid centered w/white profile silhouette of woman's face, the interior holding metal mirror & perforated rotating powder well 225

Enamel tandem compact, octagon-shaped green powder & rouge compacts w/matching lipstick attached by two goldtone chains, the lids decorated w/pink roses 800

Enamel vanity case, the blue case painted w/windmill scene on lid, interior holding powder sifter & rouge compartment, w/wrist carrying chain w/key, D.F.B. Co. 150

Fabric compact, black, designed to resemble bellows, the lid decorated w/gold design highlighted w/orange & gunmetal beads, Houpalix, France 550

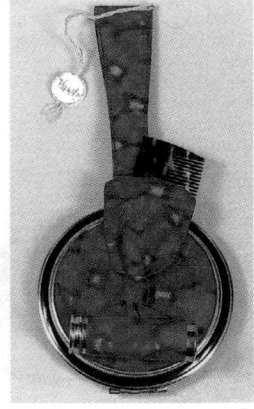

Fabric-covered Compact

Fabric-covered goldtone & enamel compact, round shape w/carrying strap, black enamel & goldtone rim, red floral fabric covering front & back & forming carrying strap, the interior w/powder well, the front lid w/sleeve for lipstick & pocket for comb behind decorative bow, Vanity (ILLUS.) **175**

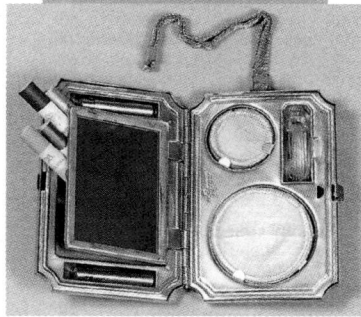

Two Views of Gold-plated Mini Carryall

Gold plate carryall, textured polished goldtone lid decorated w/bands of black enamel flanking cartouche of black enamel, the gilded interior w/powder & rouge compartments & well for mini-perfume bottle, the center mirror flanked by two lipstick tubes, a cigarette compartment behind mirror, mesh carrying chain, Dermey (ILLUS. open & closed) **450**

Jockey Cap Compact

Goldtone compact, model of jockey's cap, polished gold w/black visor & red plastic bow, the interior w/mirror & puff (ILLUS.) **450**

Goldtone compact, round, designed to resemble tambourine, the lid decorated w/incised birds & disk w/logo, w/moveable rings on rim, the interior containing mirror, powder compartment & puff, Lucien Lelong **325**

Goldtone compact, round, the lid decorated w/goldtone, silvertone & bronze neoclassical high-relief profile disks.................... **175**

Goldtone compact, round, the lid decorated w/picture of the Beatles, unmarked, rare.. **475**

Goldtone Compact/Bracelet

Goldtone compact/bracelet, round compact decorated w/multicolored stones on bubble link chain, interior holding mirror & puff (ILLUS.) **450**

Goldtone "Dial a Date" compact, round, the lid decorated w/sunburst & tiny raised balls & featuring dial that sets month & day, the interior containing framed mirror, puff & powder well, Zell **175**

Karess Enamel-decorated Compact

Coty Domino Compact

Goldtone & enamel compact, round, the lid decorated w/profile of woman's face, a rose & a star on dark blue & black background, goldtone decorations over the top & around rim, silvertone bottom, Karess (ILLUS., previous page)........................ **150**

"Vanity-Bank" with Enamel Highlights

Goldtone & enamel compact/bank, square case w/textured goldtone hinged lid highlighted w/blue enamel acorns & incised oak leaves, "The Broadway National Bank of Paterson" imprinted on dime bank, reverse reads "A.R. Martine Co., Inc. 2 Wall Street, New York," interior holds mirror, bank & powder compartment, Lucille Buhl "Vanity-Bank" (ILLUS.).. **225**

Goldtone & enamel domino compact, rectangular hinged goldtone case, the lid decorated in black & white enamel to re-semble dice or domino, interior holds mirror, powder & rouge compartments & puffs, Coty "Come Eleven" (ILLUS., top of page)... **250**

Goldtone mini compact, designed to re-semble fan, the lid decorated w/yellow, pink, silvertone & goldtone flowers, pearl twist lock, the interior holding mirror & powder well... **50**

Goldtone mini compact, model of chair w/cabriole legs, lid decorated w/coin, in-terior holding beveled mirror, puff & sifter, signed "Robert Original"........................ **450**

Goldtone two-sided vanity, lids & rims decorated w/filigree overlay enhanced w/cabochon & faceted blue & green col-ored stones, one side opening to reveal mirror & powder well, the other holding pocket w/pull-string powder puff, w/black tassel & carrying cord, Trinity Plate......... **550**

Goldtone vanity case, designed to resem-ble large matchbook complete w/black striker & two applied matches w/red tips, interior holding beveled mirror, compart-ment for lipstick, powder well & extra compartment, Wadsworth...................... **550**

Goldtone vanity set: compact, lipstick & carrying case; the square compact w/model of large poodle applied to lid & holding puff marked "Original by Robert," the lipstick in the form of a fire hydrant, its top decorated w/a clear rhinestone, the carrying case of black moire w/red lining imprinted w/"Original by Robert," 3 pcs. **550**

Ivorene lipstick tube holder/walking cane, brown wood shaft w/metal ferrule protector at end, the cap of the cane painted w/image of cat's head, unscrews to reveal well for removable lipstick tube... **450**

Lilly Dache Vanity Set

Ivorene vanity set: goldtone lipstick tube, round plastic compact in hatbox presentation box & rectangular hinged rouge case; w/carved decorations of figures on a swing applied to lipstick & on lids of compact & rouge case, the lids also w/foliage decoration around rims & imprinted initials "L.D.," interior of compact w/mirror & powder compartment, Lilly Dache "Loving Touch," the set (ILLUS.) **300**

Leather compact, oval shape resembling football, brown, Elgin American **125**

Lucite compact, scalloped rim, slot behind interior mirror allows photo to be inserted to show through lid, ca. 1940s, Ziegfeld Creation **120**

Lucite photo compact, the lid w/space for photo to be inserted through sliding mirror in interior so that it can be viewed on outside of lid, Abarbanel Original **120**

Metal cosmetic applicators, three bullet-shaped white metal applicators for powder, lotion & perfume, w/red flannel carrying case, Lady Acme Applicators for Cosmetics **125**

Plastic compact, coral & green, the lid decorated w/image of Bodhisattva in lotus blossom, the interior holding mirror & powder well, w/carrying cord & tassel **450**

Plastic composition compact, round, the lid decorated w/white daisies & girl w/blonde bouffant hair on blue ground, Revlon "Love Pat" **125**

Polished goldtone compact, the lid decorated w/crown set w/five red stones & image of woman sitting on chair, banner beneath reading "Queen for a Day," interior holding mirror & powder compartment, Elgin American **250**

Silvertone compact, designed to resemble apple w/goldtone stem & leaves, interior containing mirror, sifter & puff, rare, Napier **550**

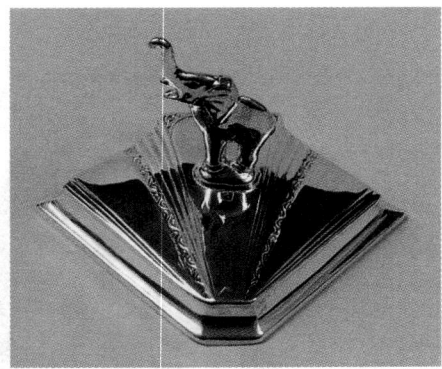

Art Deco Dresser Vanity

Silvertone dresser vanity, triangular Art Deco form, the lid decorated w/model of elephant w/raised trunk, the interior holding fitted wells for powder, rouge & lipsticks, W.B. Manufacturing Co., ca. 1930 (ILLUS.) **175**

Combination Compact & Bridge Indicator

Silvertone & enamel combination compact & bridge indicator, round shape w/enameled blue & white lid, the reverse w/center dial w/raised numbers 1-6 & spinning selector displaying heart, diamond, spade, club or NT (no trump) in black or red enamel, interior holds mirror & powder well, H.W.K. Co. (ILLUS. front & back) **425**

Silvertone & enamel vanity, the lid decorated w/colorful enamel scene of Robin Hood in Sherwood Forest, the interior containing mirror, two lipstick tubes, powder & rouge compartments, w/link chain for carrying, J.M. Fisher 550

Silvertone vanity, mini bolster-shaped engine-turned case, the bottom cap containing rouge compartment & puff & w/mirror on outside, the upper compartment containing puff & powder well, wrist chain attached to top lid, Winnie Winkle, ca. 1920s 550

Sterling & red enamel compact/watch, side-by-side combination holding cards, one side containing powder compartment, puff & mirror, the other side holding watch, w/pull-out lipstick, Germany 650

Compact/Fan Shown from Rear & Open

Tortoiseshell compact/fan, round compact w/mirror on outside of lid forms center of three-blade tortoiseshell fan & opens to reveal powder compartment &

puff, the fan activated by pressure on plunger, La Brise, England (ILLUS. of rear & opened, left) 375

DECOYS

Decoys have been used for years to lure flying water fowl into target range. They have been made of carved and turned wood, papier-mâché, canvas and metal. Some are in the category of outstanding folk art and command high prices.

Ben Schmidt Canada Goose

Canada goose, Ben Schmidt, Detroit, Michigan, good feather carving detail, hollowed out from underside, detachable head w/small metal plate at neck seam, original paint, crack in tail, second quarter 20th c. (ILLUS.) $5,500

Canada goose, Marcel Dufour, Verdun, Quebec, Canada, swimming position, head turned slightly, original paint, shot marks (ILLUS. right, bottom of page) 1,100

Canada goose, silhouette type, w/swivel base on underside, original paint, South Shore Massachusetts 495

Canada goose, Sinclair Wynne, Kinogie Lake, Ontario, Canada, roothead style, made in traditional burn & scrape method of Cree Indians... 2,805

Canvasback drake, attributed to Floyd Crooks, Tom Run, Michigan, "Bobtail" style, second quarter 20th c. 770

Canvasback drake, attributed to Sam Barnes, Havre de Grace, Maryland, original paint, first quarter 20th c. 1,540

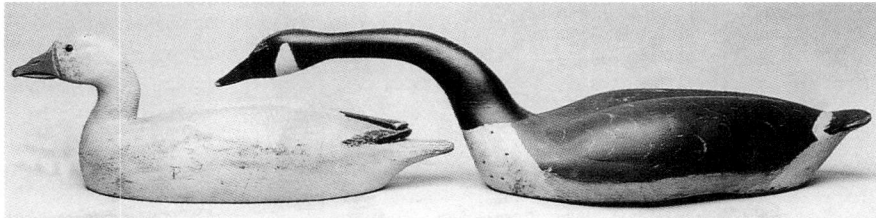

Snow Goose & Canada Goose

Ed Phillips Redhead & Canvasback

Canvasback drake, Ed Phillips, Cambridge, Maryland, original paint in black w/white midsection, red neck & head, grey bill, early second quarter 20th c. (ILLUS. top w/Ed Phillips redhead drake)..   **2,475**

Canvasback drake, Elmer Crowell, East Harwich, Massachusetts, relief wing tip carving, fluted tail, head turned very slightly, Crowell's rectangular stamp & signature on underside, original paint, round weight inserted inside for use as doorstop **14,300**

Canvasback drake, Frank Resop, Berlin, Wisconsin, oversize, w/original scalloped paint around breast, good bill delineation & incised "V" carved wing detail, first quarter 20th c. **2,530**

Very Rare Lee Dudley Canvasback

Canvasback drake, Lee Dudley, Knott's Island, North Carolina, humpback "classic" style w/"V" wing carving, original paint w/some overpaint removed, branded "ELM" for E.L. Mayer, vice president of Morse Point Gunning Club & Pocahontas Fowling Club, very rare, professional repair to bill, ca. 1900 (ILLUS.) **25,300**

Ward Brothers Canvasback Drake

Canvasback drake, Ward Brothers, Crisfield, Maryland, 1932-36 model, original paint (ILLUS.) **10,450**

Canvasback drake & hen, Frank DeRoevan, Walpole Island, Ontario, Canada, used at St. Anne's Duck Club, original paint, pr. **1,210**

Canvasback drake & hen, Ralph Reghi, Mount Clemens, Michigan, old repaint, second quarter 20th c., pr. **1,265**

Canvasback hen, Mason Decoy Factory, Detroit, Michigan, Standard grade, original paint, first quarter 20th c. (neck filler replaced, small crack in underside) **825**

Canvasback hen, Mason Decoy Factory, original paint, first quarter 20th c. **880**

Canvasback hen, Thomas Chambers, Toronto, Ontario, Canada, hollow long body model, branded "GEO. M. HENDRIE" of the St. Clair Flats Shooting Company, dry original paint, first quarter 20th c. **9,075**

Canvasback hen & drake, Ken Anger, Dunnville, Ontario, Canada, original paint, pr. (ILLUS., bottom of page) **4,620**

Fish spearing decoy, Leroy Howell, Hinkley, Minnesota, natural w/wood burned scales & wooden tail, first to second quarter 20th c., 7" l. **1,815**

Fish spearing decoy, Leroy Howell, Hinkley, Minnesota, red & white, wooden tail, first to second quarter 20th c., 9 1/2" l. **1,100**

Fish spearing decoy, Leroy Howell, Hinkley, Minnesota, two-tone red color, glass eyes, first to second quarter 20th c., 10 3/4" l. **1,540**

Fish spearing decoy, Leroy Howell, Hinkley, Minnesota, unusual green blended w/white, first to second quarter 20th c., 7" l. **1,925**

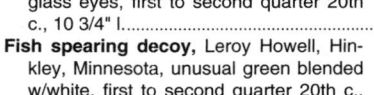

Canvasback Pair

Early Goldeneye Drake & Hen

Goldeneye drake, Ward Brothers, Crisfield, Maryland, "Fat Jaw" model, head turned approximately 20 degrees & lifted slightly, dry original paint w/alligatored surface, old replaced glass eyes, ca. 1918 (ILLUS. left)... **28,600**

Goldeneye hen, Ward Brothers, Crisfield, Maryland, "Fat Jaw" model, old replaced glass eyes, only traces of paint remain, nail added to top of head, ca. 1918 (ILLUS. right w/goldeneye drake) **7,700**

Long Island Standing Gull

Gull, standing position, relief wing carving w/crossed wing tips, old black overpaint removed to show original paint, Long Island, New York, ca. 1900 (ILLUS.) **12,650**

Mallard drake, Hays Decoy Factory, Jefferson City, Michigan, original paint, second quarter 20th c. **605**

Mallard drake, painted & carved by I. Miller of Monroe, Michigan, head carved by E. Kelly, glass eyes, rare, 14" l., 7 1/2" h. (missing keel) **990**

Mallard drake, Robert Elliston, Bureau, Illinois, original combed & feathered paint, original Elliston weight, last quarter 19th c. (professional repair to bill)........................ **2,640**

Merganser, maker unknown, believed to be from Long Island, paint completely worn away, leaving mellowed natural surface, third to fourth quarter 19th c. **550**

Red-breasted Merganser Drake

Merganser drake, George Huey, Friendship, Maine, large red-breasted body w/slightly turned inlet head attached to body w/small wooden dowel, carved eyes, "G R HUEY" carved in underside, original paint, second quarter 20th c., professional repair to bill (ILLUS.) **11,275**

Merganser drake, Mason Decoy Factory, Detroit, Michigan, Challenge grade, repainted by Elmer Crowell (filled crack in underside, small chip missing from neck filler).. **4,840**

Miniature canvasback drake, by Elmer Crowell, East Harwich, Massachusetts, feeding position, on semicircular base, original paint, Crowell's signature & rectangular stamp on underside (repair to bill chip).. **2,035**

Miniature greenwing teal drake, by Elmer Crowell, East Harwich, Massachusetts, on semicircular base, original paint, Crowell's rectangular stamp on underside **1,320**

Miniature merganser drake, by Elmer Crowell, East Harwich, Massachusetts, on semicircular base, original paint, Crowell's rectangular stamp on underside, 6 1/4" l...................... **1,870**

Miniature pintail drake, by Elmer Crowell, East Harwich, Massachusetts, on semicircular base, original paint, Crowell's rectangular stamp on underside **1,870**

Miniature pintails, by Ben Schmidt, Detroit, Michigan, 1/3 size, pr. (tiny tail chip missing from hen) **1,320**

Miniature redheads, by Ben Schmidt, Detroit, Michigan, 1/4 size, pr.......................... **1,045**

Pair of Old Squaw by Gus Wilson

Old squaw, Gus Wilson, South Portland, Maine, w/characteristic carved eyes & raised shoulder & wings, dry original paint, swivel heads, rare, second quarter 20th c., pr. (ILLUS.)..................................... **5,500**

Early Mason Factory Pintail Drake

Pintail drake, Mason Factory, Detroit, Michigan, hollow body, original paint w/crazed & crackled surface, original feathering still visible, thin crack in tail secured from bottom w/two small nails, first quarter 20th c. (ILLUS.) **9,900**

Pintails, Larry Zalesky, Vallejo, California, layered, carved primaries, original paint, ca. 1950, pr. **1,045**

Redhead drake, Ed Phillips, Cambridge, Maryland, dry original paint in black w/white midsection, red neck & head, white bill, early second quarter 20th c. (ILLUS. page 340, bottom w/Ed Phillips canvasback drake) **2,420**

Redhead drake, Thomas Chambers, Toronto, Ontario, Canada, hollow body, original paint, branded "THOS. CHAMBERS MAKER" & "P.H.D." for St. Clair Flats Shooting Company member Paul H. Deming, last quarter 19th - first quarter 20th c. **5,060**

Snow goose, Marcel Dufour, Verdun, Quebec, Canada, carved crossed wing tips & fluted tail, original paint (ILLUS. page 339, left w/Canada goose) **770**

Lake Chautauqua Trout Decoy

Trout, metal fins & tail, original paint, Lake Chautauqua, New York, 6 1/4" l. (ILLUS.).. **2,420**

DISNEY COLLECTIBLES

Scores of objects ranging from watches to dolls have been created showing Walt Disney's copyrighted animated cartoon characters, and an increasing number of collectors now are seeking these, made primarily by licensed manufacturers. ALSO SEE Antique Trader Toy Price Guide.

Disney characters Disneykins set, molded plastic, cardboard & paper, "See and Play" set, long rectangular molded base w/houses, rocks & a center island holding a large clear plastic model of a castle, Louis Marx & Co., made in Hong Kong, w/original worn & mended box, no figures, ca. 1960s, box 8 3/4 x 12 1/4" **$402**

Donald Duck Toy Walker & Box

Donald Duck toy, windup tin, Donald Duck walker, by Schuco, original colorful box w/one inside flap missing, ca. 1950s, 6" h. (ILLUS.).. **480**

Donald the Drummer Windup Toy

Donald Duck toy, windup tin, Donald the Drummer, Donald sways back & forth & nods & drums, Line-Mar, Japan, 6" h. (ILLUS.).. **210**

Donald Duck & Goofy Duet Toy

Donald Duck & Goofy toy, windup tin, Donald & Goofy Duet, large Goofy standing on a large drum w/a small Donald on a drum in front of him, 1946, Marx, Goofy missing one arm, replaced ears, 10 1/4" h. (ILLUS.)... **201**

Elmer Elephant figurine, bisque, movable trunk, w/doctor's kit and cane, 1930s, Borgefelt, 4 1/2" h. 850

Fantasia figurines, ceramic, Three Elephants, Vernon Kilns, about 6" h. 991

Fantasia figurines, ceramic, Three Unicorns, #13 (Gray), #13 (Black) & #15, Vernon Kilns, 5-6" h. 506

Fantasia figurines, china, Nubian Centaurettes w/zebra bodies, Vernon Kilns, 1940-41, Nos. 23 & 24, 8" h., pr. 1,360

Fantasia serving set: Mushroom Bowl #120 & Hop Low salt & pepper shakers; ceramic, the rectangular mushroom bowl w/raised h.p. mushroom figures decorating the sides, 7 x 12", 2" h.; the brown salt & pepper shakers in the form of Hop Low 805

Key-wind Ferdinand Toy

Ferdinand the Bull toy, key-wind tin, walking Ferdinand w/fabric flowers in his mouth, marked "Japan - Walt Disney Productions," 1938, all original w/box, 5 1/2" l., 4" h. (ILLUS.) 360

Ferdinand & Matador Windup Toy

Ferdinand the Bull toy, windup tin, Ferdinand & the matador, each figure on a platform joined by a wheeled base, Louis Marx & Co., 1938, working, 7" l. (ILLUS.)..... 240

Mickey Mouse alarm clock, w/luminous hands, Ingersoll, 1947, near mint w/box . 450-500

Rare Mickey Mouse Souvenir Bank

Mickey Mouse bank, cast pot metal, a standing pie-eyed Mickey w/his arms spread beside a spherical bank marked "Delaware Water Gap," on a thin rectangular base, base marked "Germany," original paint & miniature padlock on the bank, 1930s, base 3 1/4" l., Mickey 3 1/2" h. (ILLUS.).. 1,553

Mickey Mouse book, "Mickey Mouse Alphabet," linen-like, Whitman, No. 889, 1938 165-185

Mickey Mouse book, "Mickey Mouse and Mother Goose," Whitman, No. 411, 1937 165-175

Mickey Mouse book, "Mickey Mouse and Tanglefoot," Wee Little Books, Disney Enterprises, 1930s 60

Mickey Mouse book, "Mickey Mouse in Ye Olden Days," pop-up type, Blue Ribbon Books, 1934, excellent condition 275-300

Mickey Mouse book, "Mickey Mouse's Misfortune," Wee Little Book, 1934 45-55

Mickey Mouse book, "Mickey Mouse's Summer Vacation," Whitman, No. 801, 1948 80-100

Mickey Mouse book, "Mickey Sees the USA," w/color pictures, published by Heath, 1944 60-80

Mickey Mouse book, "School Days in Disneyville," published by Heath, 1939 60

Mickey Mouse book, "The Story of Mickey Mouse and the Smugglers," Big Big Books, No. 4062, 1935 80-100

Mickey Mouse brush set, two brushes w/rectangular black-painted wood handles w/silvered metal trim, silver, red & black figure of Mickey on the handle, The Hughes-Autograf Brush Company, New York, New York, 1930s, in original box 325-375

Mickey Mouse figure, bisque, holding a sword, wearing helmet, part of a military set, Japan, 1930s, 3 1/2" h. 80-100

Mickey Mouse figure, bisque, w/slouch hat & walking cane, marked "Made in Japan," 1930s, 4 1/4" h. 140

Rare Mickey Celluloid Nodder Figure

Mickey Mouse figure, celluloid nodder, flattened standing figure of Mickey w/a nodding head, holding a square banjo, on a blue round base, excellent original paint

& rare paper label reading "Mickey Mouse Copt. 1928, 1930 by Walter E. Disney," made in Japan, 7" h. (ILLUS.) **805**

Mickey Mouse game, "Mickey Mouse Target," round enameled steel target w/large color figure of Mickey in the center, red heavy cardboard box, Marks Bros., Boston, 1930s, 10 1/2" d., complete w/box **625-650**

Mickey Mouse paint box, lithographed tin, Transogram, 1952 .... **65-85**

Early Mickey Pencil Sharpener

Mickey Mouse pencil sharpener, celluloid, rounded upright figure of Mickey w/sharpener in the base, 1930s, original paint, slight rim damage at back, 3" h. (ILLUS.) **98**

Mickey Mouse record album, "Mickey and the Beanstalk, " 78 rpm, Capitol Records **65-85**

Mickey Mouse tea set: cov. teapot, cov. sugar, creamer & six cups & saucers; porcelain lusterware decorated w/transfer images of Mickey & Minnie playing hockey, skating, flying in airplanes, etc., w/additional hand painting, original box covered w/images showing other activities, copyright Walt Disney Enterprises, Japan, 1930s, box measures 10 x 12" (one chip), the set **540**

Mickey Mouse toy, pull-type, "Mickey Mouse Drummer," Fisher-Price No. 476, 1941 .... **300**

Mickey Mouse toy, pull-type, "Mickey Mouse Drummer," Fisher-Price No. 795, pie-eyed Mickey plays cymbal & drum, 1937 .... **700**

Mickey Mouse Jazz Drummer

Mickey Mouse toy, windup tin, "Jazz Drummer," plunger causes a lithographed two-dimensional Mickey to play the drum, by Nifty, Germany, ca. 1931, 6 3/4" h., good working condition (ILLUS.) **2,100**

Mickey Mouse Ferris Wheel Toy

Mickey Mouse toy, windup tin, Mickey Mouse Ferris Wheel, colorful printing w/the head of Mickey at the side of the base, other Disney characters on the baskets, by Chein, mechanism replaced, other restoration, 17" h. (ILLUS.) **230**

Rare Mickey Mouse & Pluto Windup Toy

Rare Early Pluto Pull Toy

Mickey Mouse & Donald Duck coloring book, "Mickey Mouse, Donald Duck and All Their Pals," Whitman, No. 887, 1937, uncolored **100-125**

Mickey Mouse & Pluto toy, windup tin & celluloid, celluloid figure of Mickey standing on two-wheeled platform joined by a wire to a larger wheeled platform w/a figure of Pluto running, Japan, 1930s, original paint, missing string reins, working, overall 8" l. (ILLUS., bottom previous page).. **2,990**

Minnie Mouse Knitter Toy

Minnie Mouse toy, windup tin, "Minnie Mouse Knitter," Minnie sitting in rocking chair knitting, colorful, Line Mar, Japan, 1950s, mechanism works but skips, 6 1/2" h. (ILLUS.) **288**

Pluto toy, pull-type w/bell, lithographed paper on wood figure of a racing Pluto pulling a four-wheeled platform w/bell, three small lithographed cardboard figures of Mickey Mouse are detached from the platform & one is missing, early 1930s, overall 20 1/2" l. (ILLUS., top of page) **1,898**

Pluto toy, windup tin, "Drum Major," seated Pluto holding a horn, cane & bell, Line Mar, Japan, replaced ears, 5 1/2" h. (ILLUS. next column) **201**

Pluto Drum Major Windup Toy

Silly Symphony card game, "Snap Cards," color picture of a running Mickey Mouse on the box, different Disney character on each card, Chad Valley, England, 1930s, w/original box **125-175**

Snow White Candy Container Set

Snow White & the Seven Dwarfs candy containers, hand-painted papier-mâché, many w/original tags marked "© W.D.P. Container made in Germany," four w/fixed heads, 1930s, large 5 1/2" h., the set (ILLUS.) **180**

Snow White & Dwarfs Doll Set

Snow White & the Seven Dwarfs dolls, Snow White in stockinet w/painted features, black mohair wig & wearing a velvet & silk dress w/the hem silk screened w/images of the Dwarfs, made by Ideal, the seven Dwarfs in jointed composition w/molded shoes & felt outfits & hats w/their names, made by Knickerbocker, 1930s, Dwarfs 9" h., Snow White 15 1/2" h., the set (ILLUS., previous page).. **1,610**

Set of Snow White Lawn Ornaments

Snow White & the Seven Dwarfs lawn ornaments, cast cement, small airbrushed & hand-painted figures of each Dwarf & a reclining Snow White, minor chipping & fading, Doc missing right arm, break in right elbow of Snow white, largest 9 1/4" h., the set (ILLUS.)............................... **230**

DOLLS
Also see: STEIFF TOYS & DOLLS.

A.M. Bisque Socket Head Toddler

A.M. (Armand Marseille) bisque socket head toddler, marked "1894 - A.M. 3/0 DEP," set blue eyes, single-stroke brows, open mouth w/four upper teeth, original blonde mohair wig, jointed wood & composition body, wearing all original outfit of light blue lace-trimmed print dress, lace-trimmed bonnet, underclothing, black cotton socks w/garters attached to chemise, original handmade shoes, minor repair on neck socket, 11" (ILLUS.)............ **$400**

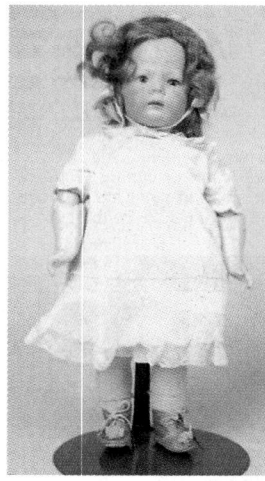

A.M. "Fany" Girl

A.M. bisque head "Fany" girl, marked "AM Fany 231," blue sleep eyes, closed mouth, blonde mohair wig, composition ball-jointed child's body w/straight wrists, wearing white dress, white bonnet w/blue ribbon, socks & shoes, pinkie missing on right hand, 15 1/2" (ILLUS.) **5,175**

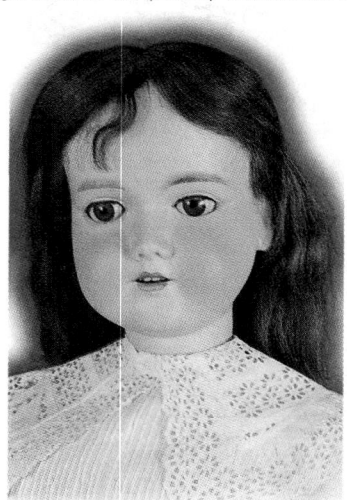

Large Armand Marseille Girl

A.M. bisque socket head girl, marked "A. 18 M." on back of head, bisque socket head w/blue sleep eyes, molded & feathered brows, painted lashes, open mouth w/four upper teeth, long brown h.h. (human hair) wig, jointed wood & composition body, wearing antique child's dress w/eyelet trim & many tucks, underclothing, knit socks, black leather shoes, missing real lashes, some repair on body, minor cracks in finish, 39" (ILLUS.)................ **1,200**

Pair of Googlies in Ethnic Costumes

A.M. Googlies, marked "Germany - 323 - A. 11/0 M." on back of heads, bisque socket heads w/blue sleep side-glancing eyes, single-stroke brows, painted lashes, closed smiling mouths, original blond mohair wigs, crude five-piece bodies w/unfinished carton torsos, molded & painted socks & shoes, wearing ethnic-type costumes, the boy in black pants, red wool vest front w/gold buttons, black velvet jacket w/red embroidery & black silk top hat, the girl in black dress w/blue embroidered apron w/yarn flower decorations, black neck scarf, original underclothing, replaced bow in hair, 7", pr. (ILLUS.) **1,800**

Dionne Quints by Madame Alexander

Alexander (Madame) Dionne Quintuplets, marked "Dionne - Alexander" on heads, "Alexander" on backs, composition heads w/painted brown eyes to side, single-stroke brows, painted upper lashes, closed mouths, molded & painted hair, composition baby bodies, all wearing white flannel diapers & short white baby dresses, all in one wood & wicker cradle w/pink flannel blanket, some crazing, 7 1/2", the set (ILLUS.)............................. **850**

Madame Alexander Jacqueline

Alexander (Madame) Jacqueline, marked "Alexander - 19©61" on head, "'Jacqueline' - by Madame Alexander" on tag on seam of slip, vinyl head w/brown sleep eyes w/blue shadow, real lashes, feathered brows, closed mouth, pierced ears, rooted hair, hard plastic body jointed at hips & knees, vinyl arms w/jointed elbows, adult figure, high heel feet, wearing original white satin gown w/matching cape, taffeta slip & panties, stockings, high heeled shoes, "diamond" bracelet & ring, pearl necklace, purse & earrings w/pearls & "diamond," some stains, one pearl missing from right earring, 21" (ILLUS.)... **450**

Alexander (Madame) McGuffey Ana, marked "Princess Elizabeth - Alexander Doll Co." on head, "'McGuffey Ana' - Madame Alexander, N.Y. U.S.A. - Reg. No. 350, 781" on dress tag, composition head w/brown sleep eyes w/real lashes, single-stroke brows, open mouth w/four upper teeth, original h.h. wig, five-piece composition child body, wearing original red plaid dress, white organdy pinafore, original underwear combination, socks & red two-snap shoes, 16" (missing hat, small tears in pinafore) **375**

Alexander (Madame) Special Girl, marked "Madame - Alexander - New York U.S.A." on dress tag, composition head on composition shoulder plate, blue sleep eyes w/real lashes, feathered brows, closed mouth, original h.h. wig in original set, cloth torso w/composition arms & legs, wearing original pale blue taffeta dress w/lace & ribbon trim, attached blue panties, original socks & center-snap shoes, 23" (part of sole of left shoe missing) **750**

Averill (Georgene) "Bonnie Babe," marked "Copr. by - Georgene Averill - 1105/3652 - Germany," solid dome bisque flange head w/blue sleep eyes, softly blushed brows, open mouth w/two lower teeth & molded tongue, cloth body w/rubber hands, wearing antique lace-trimmed baby dress, matching slip, undershirt, diaper, long socks & booties, 13" (rubber hands have hardened & curled).. **575**

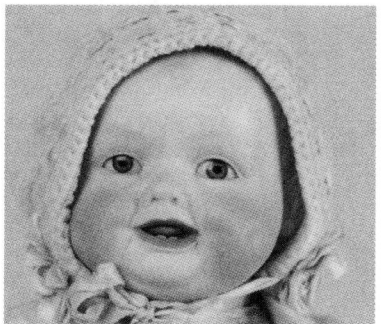

Georgene Averill "Bonnie Babe"

Averill (Georgene) "Bonnie Babe" doll, marked "Copr. by Georgene Averill 7005/365 2/0, Germany," bisque head w/painted hair, blue glass eyes, open smiling mouth w/tongue & two bottom teeth, five-piece cloth body w/swivel arms & legs, composition arms, 13" (ILLUS.)......... **518**

Large Babyland Rag

Babyland Rag, unmarked, cloth head w/flat face, h.p. features, blushed cheeks, strip of human hair sewn across forehead at bonnet line for bangs, cloth body stitch jointed at shoulders, elbows, hips & knees, stitched fingers, wearing antique, possibly original faded blue dress w/lace-trimmed bodice, matching bonnet, antique underclothing, pale blue cotton socks, black leather doll shoes w/buckles, hole on outside of left foot, 1 1/2" split on seam of torso, fingers missing some stitches, 30" (ILLUS.) **1,850**

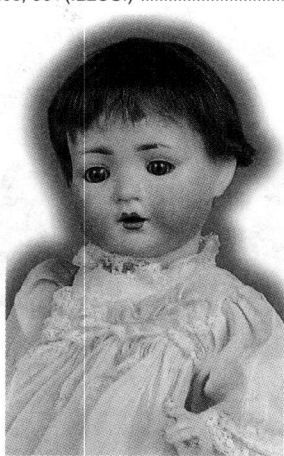

Bahr & Proschild Baby

Bahr & Proschild bisque socket head baby, marked "678 - 7 - BP [in heart] - Made in - Germany" on back of head, stamped "Made in Germany" in red on lower back, blue sleep eyes, feathered brows, painted lashes, open mouth w/two upper teeth, antique mohair wig, composition bent limb baby body, wearing pale pink baby dress, new underclothing, socks & shoes, missing tip of left little finger, 15" (ILLUS.).. **275**

Barrois (E.) Poupee Peau bisque socket head lady, marked "E 4 B" on shoulder plate, illegible oval stamp on front of torso, blue paperweight eyes, multi-stroke brows, closed mouth w/accented lips & accent line between lips, pierced ears, original mohair wig, kid fashion-type body w/gussets at elbows, hips & knees, individually stitched & wired fingers, wearing short dress of iridescent green taffeta w/iridescent mauve taffeta lower sleeves & mauve trim, antique underclothing, black stockings & possibly original brown high button boots, dark green velvet hat, 18" (body has assumed squatty position from sawdust settling in gussets, mend at knee gussets)...................... **1,800**

Bergmann (C.M.) bisque socket head girl, blue glass sleep eyes, open mouth w/teeth, replacement blonde wig w/long bangs, ball jointed composition body, wearing antique red dress & original shoes, replaced socks, 22" **345**

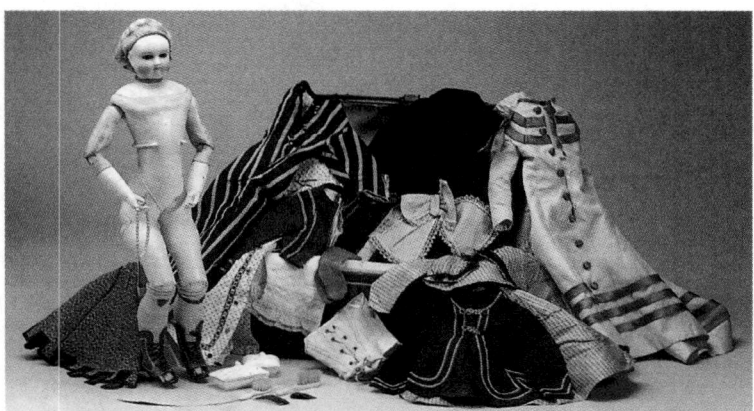

Early French Lady Doll with Wardrobe

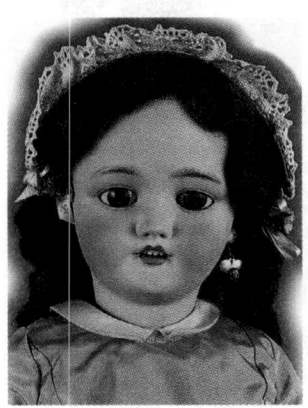

C.M. Bergmann Bisque Socket Head Girl

Bergmann (C.M.) bisque socket head girl, marked "C.M. Bergmann - Simon & Halbig - 13 1/2" on back of head, blue sleep eyes, molded & feathered brows, painted lashes, open mouth w/four upper teeth, pierced ears, original h.h. brunette wig, jointed wood & composition body, wearing pale green taffeta dress, lace bonnet, antique underclothing, socks & center-snap leatherette shoes, repair at neck socket of body, 29" (ILLUS.) **500**

Bisque head lady w/wardrobe, unmarked, dark blue stationary eyes, closed mouth, cup & saucer neck, original light blonde braided mohair wig, kid body w/ball-jointed knees, bisque lower arms, 18", w/red leatherette trunk w/tray & variety of clothing including cream-colored dress w/green trim, black silk jacket, black & grey striped silk princess dress, pink cotton skirt, purple wool bodice w/black & white trim, skirts, jacket, undergarments, rubberized overshoes, hair accessories & jewelry, original high button leather boots, France, ca. 1870 (ILLUS., top of page).. **9,400**

White Bisque Shoulder Head Lady

Bisque shoulder head lady, unmarked, white bisque w/blue glass eyes, closed mouth, pierced ears, elaborate molded cafe au lait hair w/molded flower decoration, new cloth body, wearing purple velvet dress, drop earrings & necklace, evidence of repair on shoulder plate, redressed, 21" (ILLUS.).................................... **201**

Lady Doll Attributed to Alexandre Dehors

Bisque socket head lady, body stamped "Rohmer," attributed to Alexandre Dehors, heart-shaped face w/blue stationary eyes, feathered brows, smiling closed mouth, double chin, pierced ears, original ash blonde mohair wig, shoulder plate w/molded bosom, kid body, wearing old gold silk taffeta gown w/train, France, ca. 1870s, small chip to front of shoulder plate, small finger of right hand broken, left ring finger broken, middle finger cracked, sides of body restitched, 18" (ILLUS., previous page)............................ **15,275**

Bru Girl Flanked by Jumeau Dolls

Bru bisque head girl, marked w/impressed "3" at crown, shoes marked w/"B" in script in oval & "2," brown paperweight eyes, open closed mouth w/painted upper & lower teeth, blonde skin wig, fully articulated wooden baby body w/mortise & tenon joints, wearing white cotton undergarments, pink silk satin & faille dress, ribbon festooned straw hat & cream leather ankle-strap shoes, France, ca. 1880, 19" (ILLUS. center w/Jumeau dolls) **18,800**

Bru bisque socket head girl, impressed "Bru Jne 1" mark, brown paperweight eyes, closed mouth w/tongue tip, pierced ears, blonde wig, bisque shoulder plate w/molded bosom & scalloped kid trim, full kid body w/bisque lower arms, wearing original deep maroon silk dress w/brocaded anemone pattern, matching hat, small maroon silk & lace-trimmed parasol, red net stockings & brown leather shoes marked "BRU JNE" in oval, ca. 1880, some wear to clothing, 11 1/4" (ILLUS., top next column)......................... **24,675**

Celluloid socket head lady, large blue paperweight eyes, closed smiling mouth, blonde mohair wig, celluloid shoulder plate, kid body w/ungusseted legs, white kid arms, wearing brown silk faille dress

w/red plaid trim, one boot, France, ca. 1880, 17"....................................... **1,410**

Bru Girl in Original Maroon Dress

Chase (Martha) cloth doll, molded & painted features & hair, blue eyes, blonde hair w/heavy brushstrokes, blonde brows, closed mouth, applied ears, blushing to ears & cheeks, stitched joints at elbows & knees, painted arms & legs, wearing cotton chemise, early 20th c., 8 3/4" (minimal paint wear, some soiling on face)........ **8,225**

Chase stockinette baby, painted blue eyes, painted blonde sculpted hair, sateen body w/stamp at hip, original paper label sewn to rear of body, 16"....................... **690**

China Head Man with Unusual Side-parted Hair

China head man, unmarked, painted blue eyes w/molded lids, single-stroke brows, closed mouth, molded & painted curly side-parted hair, new cloth body w/china lower arms, green leather boots, re-dressed in white shirt, black pants, gold jacket w/dark velvet collar & silk tie in antique fabrics, 21" (ILLUS.) **1,500**

"Currier & Ives"-style China Shoulder Head Doll

China shoulder head lady, so-called "Currier & Ives" style, marked "5" on back of shoulder plate, stamped "Made - in - Germany" on left front of torso, painted blue eyes, single-stroke brows, closed mouth, molded black hair w/short wavy bangs & long curls worn behind ears & falling to shoulders, pink cloth body w/china lower arms & lower legs, molded black boots w/blue tassels, wearing old red & black plaid dress w/white lace bodice, underclothing, repair to left ankle, 17" (ILLUS.) **500**

Early Pressed China Shoulder Head Lady

China shoulder head lady, marked in red inside shoulder plate, pressed china shoulder head w/painted blue eyes, single-stroke brows, closed mouth, molded black hair showing under molded hat trimmed in yellow, white & green feathers & molded red decoration, cloth body jointed at shoulders, hips & knees, no indication of hands, fingers or toes, wearing antique white skirt, gathered top, chemise, half slip & pantalets, cotton socks & leather shoes, 1 1/2" hairline through left back sew hole, light soil, 19" (ILLUS.)...... **15,000**

China shoulder head lady, unmarked, painted blue eyes w/red accent lines, outlined irises, single-stroke brows, closed mouth w/accent line between lips, pierced ears, molded & painted black hair w/curls at bangs, brush strokes at temples, long curls across back of head, cloth body w/china lower arms & lower legs, wearing purple satin dress w/ecru lace overlay, underclothing, 20" (new body w/new china lower arms & legs) **1,500**

"Dean's Patent Tru-to-Life" rag doll, fabric tag on leg & paper label from dress reading "I am British from the top of my head to the tips of my toes," molded face, blue painted eyes, smiling mouth, blonde mohair wig, stuffed body w/painted pink & white chemise & black lacy stockings, white cotton slip, England, early 20th c., 14" (some soil overall) **323**

China Shoulder Head Dolley Madison

Dolley Madison china shoulder head lady, unmarked, painted blue eyes, brown single-stroke brows, closed mouth, heavily rouged cheeks, pierced ears, molded & painted blonde hair w/molded blue ribbon & bow, cloth body w/leather lower arms, striped lower legs w/leather boots, wearing black velvet two-piece outfit w/lace trim, antique underclothing, torso re-covered, arms replaced, right boot patched & repaired, leather on left boot deteriorating, 24" (ILLUS.) **725**

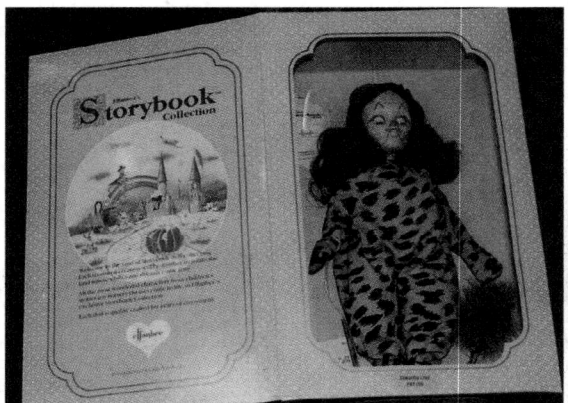

Effanbee Cowardly Lion Doll Set

Dressel composition socket head girl, "Holz Masse" winged mark on shoulder plate, brown glass eyes, open closed mouth w/two painted teeth & suggestion of tongue, pierced ears, composition shoulder plate, kid body, bisque lower arms, wearing aqua wool challis dress w/feather stitching, dotted Swiss blouse, Germany, late 19th c., 17" **823**

Effanbee Cowardly Lion doll, vinyl, from the Effanbee Storybook Collection, posable heads w/sleep eyes, mint in box (ILLUS., top of page) **25**

Effanbee "Grumpy Cowboy," marked "Effanbee - Dolls - Walk * Talk * Sleep" on back of shoulder plate, composition shoulder head, painted blue eyes to side, single-stroke brows, closed pouty mouth, molded & painted hair, cloth body w/composition arms & feet, wearing rare cowboy outfit of plaid shirt, gold pants, green bandana, imitation leather chaps & holster complete w/gun, replaced felt hat, 11" **475**

Effanbee "Patsy Ruth," marked "Effanbee - Patsy Ruth" on head, "Effanbee - Durable - Dolls" on tag on dress & on metal heart bracelet, composition head w/brown sleep eyes w/real lashes, feathered brows, closed "rosebud" mouth, original h.h. wig, five-piece composition body wearing original peach silk dress, matching romper, socks & leatherette T-strap shoes, eyes cloudy, dress very fragile & deteriorating on bodice, 26" (ILLUS., right) **800**

Fashion bisque head man, brown stationary glass eyes, closed mouth, molded & painted brown mustache & small goatee, replaced skin wig, ungusseted kid body, wearing early black wool suit & flocked beige top hat w/leather trim, w/hat box, France, ca. 1870s, 17 1/2" (light kiln dirt on bridge of nose, light line at ear hole) **8,813**

Frozen Alice parian doll, blue painted eyes, blonde molded hair w/black hair band, arms slightly outstretched, molded purple lustre boots & red-decorated white socks on legs w/generous fat rolls, Germany, ca. 1865, 4 5/8" **823**

Effanbee "Patsy Ruth" Doll

Frozen Charlie, china, pink tint, blue painted eyes, smiling mouth, short black hair w/brush strokes around face, arms outstretched, clenched fists, bare feet, w/small shallow paper-lined dome-top trunk, Germany, ca. 1860, 5" h. (restored at elbow) **1,058**

Frozen Charlotte, china, pink lustre, blue painted eyes, golden brown center-part hair w/short curls, arms outstretched, bare feet, wearing cotton print dress, Germany, ca. 1850s, 3 3/8" **558**

Francois Gaultier Poupee Peau

Gutta Percha, Papier-mâché & Metal Head Dolls

Gaultier (Francois) bisque Poupee Peau, marked "4" on back of head, "F.G." on left shoulder, bisque socket head on bisque shoulder plate, blue paperweight eyes, heavy feathered brows, painted lashes, closed mouth, pierced ears, replaced mohair wig, kid body w/gussets at elbows, hips & knees, individually stitched fingers, redressed in pale green plaid two-piece outfit of antique fabric, antique underclothing, new socks & lace boots, floral headpiece, small repair at each earring hole (ILLUS.).. **1,400**

Grand Kabuki Theatre Tamabasura doll, composition/gofun doll, narrow pupil-less black eyes, open mouth, short wig, articulation at neck, shoulders, elbows, wrists, hips, knees & ankles, pelvic piece swivels, cloth at upper arm, wearing partial paper wrap, housed in original segmented 8 x 17" box w/paper label, includes five extra wigs for various Kabuki theatre roles, set of colorful priest robes, Samurai warrior outfit w/accessories, two Samurai unmarried lady kimono, one gold striped, one grey, Japan, early 19th c., 12 1/4" (fine crazing)............................... **2,703**

Greiner papier-mâché head lady, stamped "PATENT HEAD" on back of shoulder plate, painted features, dark brown eyes, smiling mouth w/row of molded painted teeth, dark center-part hair w/curls behind exposed ears, pierced ears, cloth body, one lower arm (detached), America, ca. 1850s, 25" **999**

Gutta percha head lady, painted features, black pupil-less eyes, lower lashes angling outward, upper lashes angling toward center of face, slightly smiling closed mouth, molded dark hair falling into curls behind exposed ears onto shoulder plate, suggestion of wire at lower edge as on mystery linen head dolls, cloth body, kid arms w/separate fingers, wearing red wool princess-line dress w/pleated hem & black buttons down back, early kid slippers, probably America, ca. 1840s, breaks to hands, 18 1/2" (ILLUS. front right w/papier-mâché & metal head dolls) **2,350**

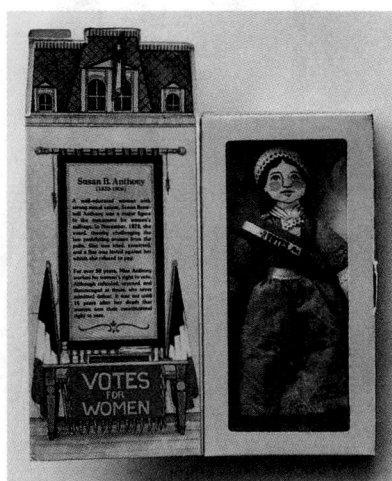

Susan B. Anthony Cloth Doll

Hallmark Susan B. Anthony doll, stuffed cloth, wearing a long blue dress & a red, white & blue sash reading "Votes," house-form box cover includes the story of Susan B. Anthony, sold in Hallmark stores, 1979, in original box, doll 6 1/2" h. (ILLUS.)... **7**

Handwerck (Heinrich) bisque socket head girl, marked "Heinrich Handwerck - Simon & Halbig - Germany" & "W," brown sleep eyes w/remnants of real lashes, feathered brows, open mouth w/four upper teeth, pierced ears, synthetic wig, jointed wood & composition body w/straight wrists, wearing original traditional Scottish plaid outfit, original socks, replaced shoes, 15".. **240**

Handwerck (Heinrich) bisque socket head girl, marked "Germany - Heinrich - Handwerck - Halbig - 4 1/2" on head, "Heinrich Handwerck - Germany - 4 1/2" stamped on left hip, "4 1/2 - HH" in heart on shoes, brown sleep eyes w/real lashes, molded & feathered brows, open mouth w/accented lips & four upper teeth, pierced ears, original h.h. wig, jointed wood & composition body, wearing possibly original white lace-trimmed dress, underclothing, white cotton socks, Handwerck shoes, 25" (touchup to neck socket & right side seam of torso, sole of left shoe damaged so "Handwerck" mark is missing)... **450**

Heinrich Handwerck 32 1/2" Girl

Handwerck (Heinrich) bisque socket head girl, marked "Germany - Heinrich - Handwerck - Simon & Halbig - 7" on head, "Heinrich Handwerck - Germany - 7" stamped in red on back, blue sleep eyes, molded & feathered brows, open mouth w/accented lips & four upper teeth, pierced ears, original brown h.h. wig, jointed wood & composition Handwerck body, wearing antique white

child's dress, antique underclothing, cotton socks, black patent leather shoes, left knee ball replaced, 32 1/2" (ILLUS.) **1,025**

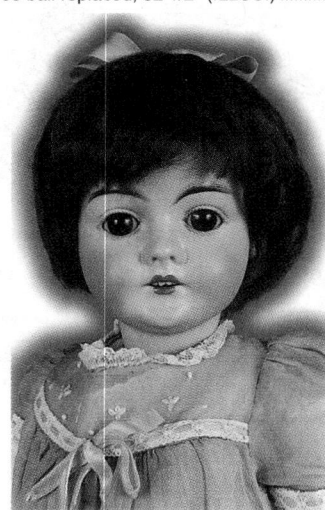

Karl Hartman Brown-eyed Girl

Hartman (Karl) bisque socket head girl, marked "28.5 - K/0" inside large "H" on back of head, brown sleep eyes, heavy feathered brows, painted lashes, open mouth w/four upper teeth, replaced mohair wig, jointed wood & composition body, wearing blue lace-trimmed organdy dress, underclothing, socks & replaced shoes, small chips, size of body may be slightly large for head, 22 1/2" (ILLUS.).. **200**

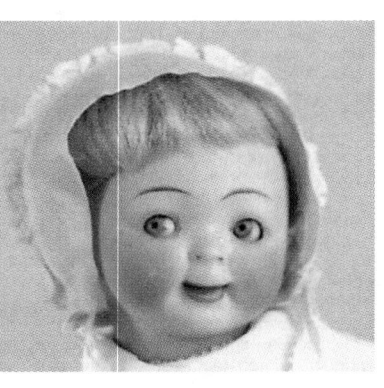

Hertel & Schwab Googlie

Hertel & Schwab bisque head googlie, marked "165/4," blue set googlie eyes, single-stroke brows, open closed smiling mouth, pink cheeks, replacement blonde wig, jointed composition baby body, wearing older baby clothes & bonnet, comes w/remainder of original wig, small hairline to rear of head, 13" (ILLUS.)......... **1,783**

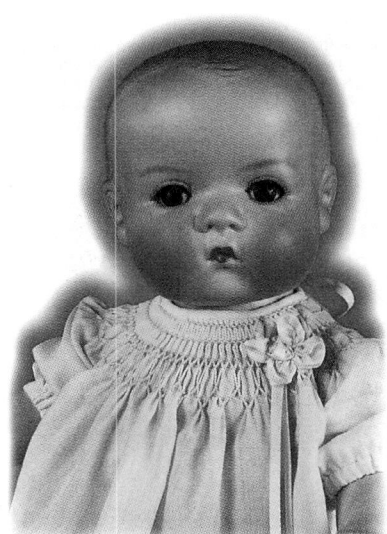

Hertel, Schwab & Co. "Patsy" Baby

Hertel, Schwab & Co. "Patsy" baby, no visible marks, solid dome bisque head w/brown sleep eyes w/real lashes, soft brows that match molded & painted baby-type hair, closed "rosebud" mouth, five-piece composition toddler body, wearing baby-style smocked dress, matching panties, socks & shoes, body repainted, 18" (ILLUS.) **1,400**

Ernst Heubach Bisque Girl

Heubach (Ernst) bisque socket head girl, marked "Heubach Koppelsdorf - 417 8/0 - Germany" on back of head, blue sleep eyes to side, feathered brows, tiny painted upper lashes, open mouth w/two up-

per teeth, antique mohair wig, five-piece composition body w/unfinished torso, wearing blue blouse w/white dots, matching bonnet, white pinafore, underclothing, original socks & leatherette shoes w/pompoms, 12" (ILLUS.) **975**

Heubach (Gebruder) bisque socket head baby, marked "8420" at crown, "5 - Heubach [in square] - 41 - Germany" on neck, "Made in Germany" stamped in red at top of back, blue sleep eyes, multi-stroke brows, closed mouth, mohair wig, composition bent-limb baby body, wearing blue checked romper w/white bodice, matching cap, socks & old leatherette baby shoes, 13" (missing tips of left little finger & right thumb) **925**

Gebruder Heubach Twin Boy & Girl

Heubach (Gebruder) twins, marked "1 - Germany - 72 Heubach [in square] 46 - 16" on backs of heads, bisque socket heads w/blue sleep eyes, single stroke brows, painted lashes, closed pouty mouths, original mohair wigs, jointed wood & composition bodies w/jointed wrists, wearing completely original factory outfits, the boy in two-piece wool outfit of short pants & belted tunic-style top w/silk-covered buttons, felt cap w/tassel, original socks & shoes, the girl in blue wool drop-waist dress w/silk-covered buttons, straw hat w/pompom trim, factory underclothing, socks & shoes, minor cracks & hairlines, wooden upper arms & legs split & glued on each, 11", pr. (ILLUS.).. **2,650**

Huret bisque head lady, blue lined paperweight eyes, closed mouth, pierced ears, bulbous socket neck, blonde mohair wig over cork pate, fully articulated wooden body w/metal hands & joints, wearing large straw hat, carrying early valentine, ca. 1880, 18" (ear chip, wax holding one earring on)............................... **27,025**

Huret Character Dolls

Huret bisque socket head character girl, impressed "MA" & "HURET" on head, dark blue stationary glass eyes, closed mouth, pink cheeks, long blonde wig, composition & wood child body, wearing ribbed aqua silk dress & bonnet, France, late 19th - early 20th c., paint flaking on hands, tiny chip at neck hole, 16" (ILLUS. right w/Huret character lady)...................... **7,638**

Huret bisque socket head character lady, blue painted eyes, open closed smiling mouth, dark blonde h.h. wig w/snood, articulated wood body w/metal hands, wearing plaid dress, bonnet, France, late 19th - early 20th c., two mold lines on each side of head, 17 1/2" (ILLUS. left w/Huret character girl)................................. **3,525**

Ideal 11" Shirley Temple Doll

Ideal Shirley Temple, marked "11 - Shirley Temple" on head, "Shirley Temple - 11" on back, "Genuine - Shirley Temple - Doll - Registered - [illegible]!" on dress tag, composition head w/blue sleep eyes w/real lashes, feathered brows, open mouth w/six teeth, original mohair wig,

five-piece composition child body wearing original red & white organdy coin dot dress from movie "Stand Up and Cheer," underwear combination, rayon socks, center-snap leatherette shoes, tiny crack over left eye, minor crazing, socks replaced, 11" (ILLUS.).. **575**

Ideal 15" "Toni"

Ideal "Toni," marked "P-91 - Ideal Doll - Made in U.S.A." on head, "Ideal Doll - P-91" on back, "Genuine Toni Doll - with nylon wig - Made by Ideal Novelty & Toy Co." on dress tag, hard plastic head w/blue sleep eyes w/real lashes, single-stroke brows, closed mouth, original wig, five-piece hard plastic body wearing tagged red & yellow pique dress w/embroidery, attached half slip w/matching panties, socks, original red center-snap shoes, hair repinned & w/net, 15" (ILLUS.).. **235**

Jenny Lind China Shoulder Head Doll

Jenny Lind china head lady, marked "6" on front edge of shoulder plate, china shoulder head w/painted blue eyes, single-stroke brows, closed mouth, molded & painted black hair w/full rolls on sides flowing back to bun, cloth body jointed at shoulders, hips & knees, leather lower arms, red & white striped lower legs w/leather boots, wearing antique two-piece outfit & antique underclothing, some rubs & flaking, torso re-covered, lower arms replaced, lower legs reattached, boots worn, 19 1/2" (ILLUS.) **1,050**

Jumeau 1st Series Portrait Doll

Jumeau bisque head 1st series portrait doll, marked "2/0" on head, hazel almond-shaped eyes, feathered brows, closed mouth, pierced ears, honey-colored replacement wig, repainted original eight ball jointed body, newer replacement clothes, 14 1/2" (ILLUS.) **8,625**

Jumeau bisque head girl, marked w/impressed backwards/forwards "C" on head, stamped in blue "Jumeau Medaille d'Or Paris," shoes marked "MG," blue paperweight eyes, open closed mouth, original ash blonde skin wig over cork pate, fully articulated eight-ball composition & wood body, wearing white batiste dress w/pierced & embroidered lace, straw hat w/blue silk ribbons & pompoms, red socks & black leather shoes, France, ca. 1870s, lower arms repainted, 14" (ILLUS. right w/Bru & Jumeau dolls, page 350) **5,581**

Jumeau "Long Face" Girl

Jumeau bisque head "long face" girl, blue paperweight eyes, feathered brows,

closed mouth, blonde wig, composition body, wearing fancy ivory colored dress, buff-colored shoes marked "12" & socks, comes w/pale blue bonnet, blue silk dress w/ivory cape & bonnet, parasol, wire rimmed hat & white shoes marked "12," plaster has been added to eyes, slight repair to body at neck, 26" (ILLUS.) **13,225**

Jumeau bisque head portrait doll, marked w/impressed "1" on head, stamped "Jumeau Medaille d'Or Paris" on back in original paint, dark blue stationary glass eyes, closed mouth, original blonde skin wig, fully articulated composition body, wearing white cotton undergarments, original pale moss green silk dress w/ruching & lace trim, original socks & leather shoes, France, ca. 1878, 10 3/4" (ILLUS. left w/Bru & Jumeau dolls, page 350).. **14,100**

Jumeau Bisque Head Portrait Lady

Jumeau bisque socket head portrait lady, large blue paperweight eyes, feathered brows, closed mouth, large applied ears, slightly double chin, brown wig, fully articulated wooden body, wearing aubergine silk satin dress & ribbon-trimmed peaked hat, brown leather shoes marked "Jumeau," model associated w/Jumeau production for 1876 exhibition, 27" (ILLUS.).. **22,325**

K [star] R (Kammer & Reinhardt) bisque socket head baby, marked "K [star] R - Simon & Halbig - 126 - 36," blue flirty sleep eyes w/tin lids, feathered brows, open mouth w/two upper teeth, original mohair wig, composition baby body, wearing blue baby romper, crocheted blue & white tam, socks & leatherette baby shoes, 15" **235**

K [star] R Character Girl

K [star] R (Kammer & Reinhardt) bisque socket head character girl, marked "K [star] R - 114 - 23," painted blue eyes, single-stroke brows, closed pouty mouth, mohair wig in coiled braids, five-piece composition body w/molded & painted white socks & brown two-strap shoes, wearing original factory chemise trimmed w/red embroidery, 8 1/2" (ILLUS.) **1,175**

K [star] R (Kammer & Reinhardt) bisque socket head girl, marked "Simon & Halbig - K [star] R - 46," blue flirty eyes w/tin lids, molded & feathered brows, open mouth w/four upper teeth, pierced ears, replaced h.h. wig, jointed wood & composition KR body, wearing pink embroidered low-waisted dress w/underclothing, socks & black leatherette shoes, 17 1/2" **700**

K [star] R (Kammer & Reinhardt) solid dome bisque socket head boy, marked "Germany - Simon & Halbig - K [star] R - 36 - 127n," blue sleep eyes, feathered brows, open mouth w/two upper teeth, molded & brush-stroked hair, jointed wood & composition teenage body w/diagonal hip joints & high knee joints, torso cut for crier, wearing antique white shirt, black wool pants & formal jacket, red ribbon tie, replaced socks & shoes, 19" (crier absent or non-working, lower arms repainted, hands replaced, left hand badly cracked, left toes damaged, body not typical of type normally seen on this head)........ **725**

18" Kamkins Doll

Kamkins doll w/wardrobe, unmarked, oil painted cloth swivel head w/painted blue eyes, single-stroke brows, closed mouth, original mohair wig, cloth body tab jointed at shoulders, stitch jointed at hips, stitched fingers & separate thumb, wearing original organdy dress w/flower print trim along bottom, matching teddy w/flower print trim, orange wool coat w/black curly mohair collar, matching hat w/black ribbon reading "US Navy," replaced rayon socks, original brown leather shoes w/button strap, 18"; comes w/extra original Kamkins orange, gold, black & white striped dress w/orange trim, matching teddy & orange hat, white pique dress w/pleated print skirt, matching print coat & hat, red mohair jacket w/beige trim & matching hat, extra pair of shoes, knit sweater, skirt & matching hat, flannel pajamas, black felt buckle boots, some paint missing from face, rust stains on back from non-working crier (ILLUS. of doll without coat & hat) **5,700**

Small Kestner All-bisque Child

Kestner (J.D.) all-bisque child, marked "3/0" on back of head & below neck opening of body, swivel head w/blue sleep eyes, feathered brows, painted lashes, open mouth w/two square upper teeth, original mohair wig, body jointed at shoulders & hips, black boots w/blue tassels, wearing off-white dress w/embroidered decoration, probably child-made, large chip at top of left hip, small chip on left toes touched up, 5" (ILLUS.)........................ **1,300**

Kestner (J.D.) bisque shoulder head girl, marked "154 dep. 5," brown sleep eyes, feathered brows, open mouth w/four molded upper teeth, original h.h. wig over plaster pate, kid body w/bisque lower arms, gussets at elbows, pin joints at hips & knees, wearing possibly original dress w/embroidered design, underclothing, socks & shoes, 15" (repair at right shoulder) **375**

Kestner Bisque Socket Head Girl

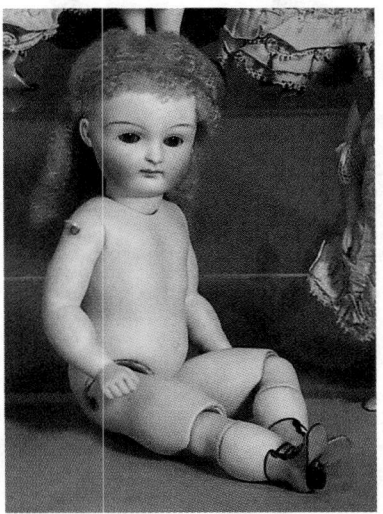

Kestner Bisque Socket Head Girl

Kestner (J. D.) bisque socket head girl, impressed "111" on upper torso & back of upper legs, brown sleep eyes, closed mouth, rosy cheeks, original blonde curly mohair wig w/blue hair ribbon, kid-lined swivel neck, peg-jointed limbs, the right hand molded in closed fist, left hand open, wearing molded pink high-heeled boots w/four straps, green banded ribbed stockings w/lacy imprint at top, ca. 1880, 8 1/2" (ILLUS.)... **8,225**

Kestner (J.D.) bisque socket head girl, marked "(?) made in - Germany 0 - 143," brown sleep eyes, feathered brows, open mouth w/four upper teeth, original auburn mohair wig, composition Kestner body w/straight arms, jointed at shoulders, hips & knees, wearing possibly original white dress trimmed w/tucks & lace, original underclothing, white cotton socks, white leather shoes, lace-trimmed bon-

net, arms have been restrung w/elastic through composition at shoulders, 8 3/4" (ILLUS.)... **825**

Kestner (J.D.) bisque socket head girl, marked "8," brown sleep eyes, feathered brows, closed mouth w/accented lips & white space between lips, original blonde mohair wig on plaster pate, early jointed composition body w/jointed wrists, separate balls at shoulders & hips, wearing original maroon wool & velvet dress, factory chemise trimmed w/pleats, lace & maroon trim, original maroon socks & leather shoes, 13" (sole of right foot missing)... **2,500**

Kestner (J.D.) bisque socket head girl, marked "K. made in Germany. 14 - 171 - 5" on head, "Germany - 5" stamped in red on back, brown sleep eyes, molded & feathered brows, open mouth w/accented lips & four upper teeth, mohair wig, jointed wood & composition Kestner body, redressed in beige French-style outfit of dress & matching bonnet, antique underclothing, new stockings & shoes, 24 1/2" (missing real lashes, repair at right hip socket & on right ring finger)... **550**

Kestner (J.D.) bisque socket head "Hilda" baby, marked "F. made in Germany 10. - 245 - J.D.K. - © - Hilda - Ges. Gesch. N. 1070," brown sleep eyes, feathered brows, open mouth w/accented lips & two upper teeth, original mohair wig on original plaster pate, composition bent-limb Kestner baby body, wearing lace-trimmed antique baby dress, slips & diaper, 12".. **1,025**

Kestner (J.D.) solid dome bisque socket head "Baby Jean," marked "E - J.D.K. - made in 13. Germany," blue sleep eyes, feathered brows, open mouth w/accented lips, two upper teeth & spring tongue, lightly molded & brush-stroked hair, composition Kestner baby body, wearing white smocked baby dress, underclothing, blue socks, 18" (eyes don't work because head is packed, left first finger tip repaired) **800**

Kestner 10" Kewpie

Kestner Kewpie, marked "Ges. gesch. - O'Neill. J.D.K. - 10" on back of head, solid dome bisque socket head w/topknot, oversized brown glass eyes set to side, dash brows, painted lashes, closed smiling mouth, five-piece chubby composition body w/"starfish" hands, wearing old white underwear w/crocheted trim, peach organdy dress w/new blue silk ribbon trim, front of torso & bottom of left foot repainted, touchups to both heels, right shoulder, left fingers, toes worn, 10" (ILLUS.) **4,600**

Kley & Hahn bisque socket head toddler, marked "K & H [in banner] - 548 - 15 - Germany" on head, "Germany" stamped in black on right shoulder, blue sleep eyes w/real lashes & painted lashes, feathered brows, open closed laughing mouth w/molded tongue, molded dimples, replaced blonde curly mohair wig w/"tails," heavy jointed composition body w/diagonal hip joints, jointed at shoulders, elbows, wrists, hips & knees, wearing antique white clothing w/red cross-stitch embroidery, antique underclothing, big red taffeta bow in hair & red fabric boots, 22" (touchup on front & back of left thigh & left heel, general aging/soil) **3,800**

Kley & Hahn bisque socket head "Walkure," marked "5 1/2 - Walkure - Germany - 15" on head, "80" stamped in red on bottom of both feet, blue sleep eyes w/real lashes, painted upper & lower lashes, molded & feathered brows, open mouth w/four upper teeth, pierced ears, h.h. wig, jointed wood & composi-

tion body, redressed in ecru & blue outfit w/matching tam, underclothing, socks & old leather shoes w/pompoms, 31" (tiny scratch on cheek, repainted right upper arm & upper torso, worn finish on lower arms & lower legs) **550**

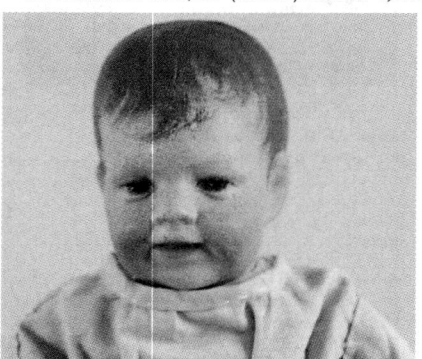

Kling Bisque Shoulder Head Lady

Kling bisque shoulder head lady, marked "144-9" on back of shoulder plate, painted blue eyes, single-stroke brown brows, closed mouth, pierced ears, elaborate molded blonde hair w/black comb, molded lace collar w/decorative trim, cloth body jointed at shoulders, hips & knees, leather lower arms, printed lower legs, leather boots, redressed in gown of antique fabric, antique underclothing, repairs on leather arms, edges of boots & toe of left boot worn, 24" (ILLUS.) **1,100**

Rare Smiling "Schlenkerchen" by Kathe Kruse

Kruse (Kathe) "Schlenkerchen" baby, cloth head w/painted features & hair, brown eyes, smiling open closed mouth, brown hair, wearing period clothing, rare smiling model, 13" (ILLUS.) **7,475**

Kuhnlenz (Gebruder) bisque socket head girl, marked "34 - 16" on head, brown head, set brown eyes, single-stroke brows, open mouth w/four upper teeth, light brown mohair over original black mohair on original pate, fully jointed wood & composition brown body, wearing possibly original white dress, original underclothing, crocheted hat, no socks or shoes, 7 1/4" (original eyes have been set w/no rocker, several areas of lightened color on torso & legs) **700**

Largo Scarecrow Doll in Box

Largo Scarecrow doll, stuffed cloth, from The Wizard of Oz series, mint in original box (ILLUS.) **30**

Lenci "400 D" Girl

Lenci "400 D" girl, illegible mark on bottom of right foot, marked "Lenci Turin - (Italy) - Di E. Scavini - Made in Italy - 400/D - Pat. Sept. 8-1921 - Pat. N. 142433 - Bte S.G.D.G. X87395 - Brevetto 501-178" on paper tag, pressed felt swivel head w/painted brown eyes to side, single-stroke brows, painted upper lashes, closed mouth, applied ears, original long

mohair wig, cloth torso w/felt arms & legs, individually stitched fingers w/middle fingers together, stitched & tinted toes, wearing light green felt dress, original underclothing, silk stockings to hips, black leather shoes, blue-green felt cape-coat & matching hat, some soil & fading, 16" (ILLUS.) **850**

Lenci Socket Head Girl

Lenci Series 110 felt socket head girl, marked "Lenci" on bottom of left foot, painted features of brown side-glancing eyes, pouty closed mouth, blonde wig, wearing peach dress w/applied felt flowers & matching pink & yellow wide-brimmed hat & pink shoes, Italy, ca. 1930s, head loose in socket, small moth hole to shoe, 23" (ILLUS.) **805**

Lerch and Klag papier-mâché shoulder head girl, w/seldom found Lerch and Klag label, dark blue painted eyes, closed mouth, molded blonde hair worn back from face in molded hair band, cloth body, wearing cream-colored printed floral dress, flat brown leather boots, Philadelphia, Pennsylvania, ca. 1860s, 16 1/2" **2,115**

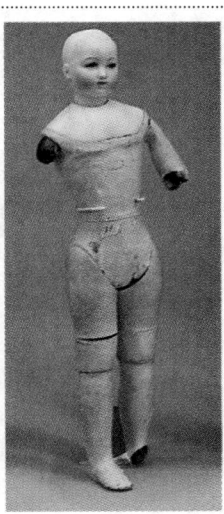

Alexandre Leverd Character Lady

Leverd (Alexandre) bisque socket head character lady, impressed "SGDG" on head, torso stamped "E. Leverd Cie PARIS Brevete S.G.D.G.," narrow dark blue glass eyes, open closed mouth, deeply sculpted facial modeling, recessed hairline area for application of wig as patented in 1869, bisque shoulder plate, jointed body of kid over gutta percha, France, ca. 1870, missing right arm, left forearm & left foot, small damage to joints, 19" (ILLUS.) **10,575**

Loews Dorothy & Toto Doll Set

Loews Dorothy & Toto dolls, vinyl, from The Wizard of Oz series, Dorothy w/long brown hair, wearing a blue checked jumper & white blouse, by Turner Entertainment, ca. 1988, in original box (ILLUS.) **12**

Large French "Mascotte" Doll

"Mascotte" bisque head girl, marked "Mascotte" & "Bebe Mascotte Paris" on body, amber paperweight eyes, closed mouth, possibly original brown h.h. wig on cork pate, ball-jointed body, wearing antique shoes, replacement clothing, France, minor wear to fingertips & joints, 29" (ILLUS.) **2,645**

Metal shoulder head milliner's model, molded head w/painted blue eyes, single-stroke brows, closed mouth, black wavy hair worn in bun, kid body w/long slender wooden limbs, orange painted slippers, mid-19th c., missing left arm, 15 1/2" (ILLUS. front left w/papier-mâché & gutta percha head dolls, page 353) **2,233**

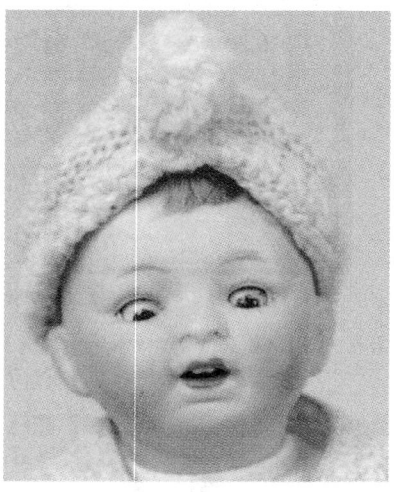

Japanese Bisque Head Baby

Morimora Bros. bisque head baby, marked w/two parts of "Morimora Bros." emblem & "Japan" & "3," brown sleep eyes, open mouth w/two upper teeth, five-piece composition bent-leg body, skull cut for voice box, which is present but not working, 11" (ILLUS.) **144**

Papier-mâché head lady, brown painted eyes, feathered brows, closed mouth, unusual molded head w/three tufted curls in front of exposed ears, braided bun at back, kid body w/wooden lower limbs, yellow painted slippers, wearing white cotton dress, Germany, ca. 1810, wear & age discoloration to finish, dress heavily melting at sleeves & skirt, 33" (ILLUS. at rear w/metal head & gutta percha head dolls, page 353) **4,406**

Papier-mâché shoulder head milliner's model, unmarked, painted blue eyes, single-stroke brows, closed mouth, molded & painted hair w/long side curls to shoulders, braided bun in back, kid body w/wooden lower arms & legs, painted or-

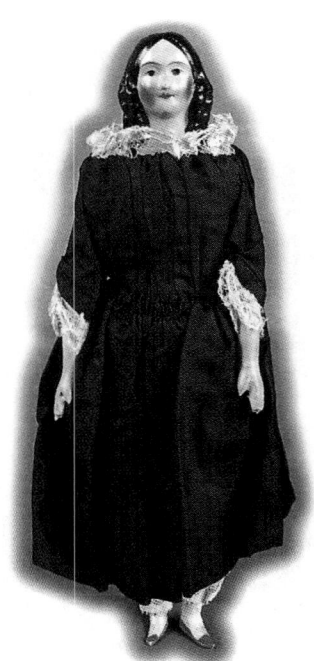

Papier-mâché Milliner's Model

ange shoes, wearing original black silk dress w/lace trim, original underclothing, 8 1/4" (ILLUS.).. **500**

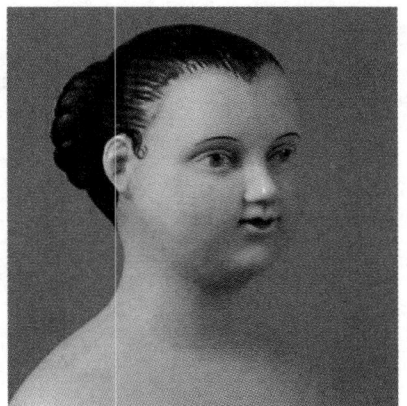

Parian Lady with Widow's Peak

Parian shoulder head lady, pressed parian-type bisque w/blue painted eyes, closed smiling mouth, brown molded hair pulled back into a bun w/defined widow's peak, wispy tendrils at ears, cloth body, Germany, ca. 1850, 15 1/2" (ILLUS.) **5,288**
Parian shoulder head lady, marked "6" on front of body at edge of shoulder plate, painted blue eyes, single-stroke brows,

closed mouth, pierced ears, molded & painted curly blonde hair w/two black ribbons, molded curls in back, cloth body w/leather lower arms, blue cloth boots as feet, redressed w/antique fabric, antique underclothing, 21 1/2" (replaced cloth on upper arms, blue cloth boots are worn so that fabric underneath shows).................... **1,450**

Norwegian Celluloid Dolls in Ethnic Costumes

Petterssen (Ronnaug) Norwegian ethnic dolls, marked "Made in Norway - Vare-Marke - Ronnaug Petterssen" on paper tags on clothing, celluloid socket heads w/painted blue eyes, single-stroke brows, closed mouths, original h.h. blond wigs, five-piece celluloid bodies, wearing original wool & felt Norwegian ethnic costumes, the girl in red felt skirt, white cotton blouse w/lace trim, black felt jacket, red felt bodice w/gold decorative pins & beading, red felt ribbons w/embroidery, underclothing, black stockings & black felt shoes, a gold crown w/red felt backing on her head, the boy in white cotton shirt w/gold decorative pin at neck, black wool pants w/embroidery, red wool jacket edged in green w/decorative buttons, black felt top hat, white stockings & black felt shoes, some small moth holes on girl's skirt, girl's right cuff missing, 17", pr. (ILLUS.)... **1,000**
Poured wax head child, blue glass stationary eyes, inset lashes, closed mouth, long blonde wavy mohair wig w/bangs, deeply modeled shoulder plate, original cloth body, poured wax lower limbs, wearing layers of white undergarments, white embroidered & lace-trimmed lawn dress, red leather heeled boots, England, ca. 1880, small shrinkage line at back of shoulder plate, 21"...................... **1,116**
Poured wax should head girl, body w/purple stamp of Mrs. Peck's London, inset

blue glass eyes w/heavy lids, feathered brows, closed mouth, long brown h.h. wig, cloth body, long wax limbs from above elbows & knees, wearing old white undergarments & cream-colored wool flannel dress w/lace trim, England, ca. 1870, 25" **2,350**

"Queen Anne" Wooden Doll

"Queen Anne" wooden doll, painted features, black pupil-less eyes, stylized line & dot brows, dots for lashes, closed mouth, carved ears, nailed-on woven dark brown h.h. wig, wooden upper arms & upper legs, carved hands & feet, wearing cream-colored silk flowered Watteau-style gown of period fabric w/coral-colored stomacher, long silk stockings, silk slippers from dress fabric, England, ca. 1780, 17 1/2" (ILLUS.) **5,875**

S.F.B.J. bisque socket head toddler, marked "S.F.B.J. - 236 - Paris - -10-" on head, "10 - S.F.B.J." on both shoe soles, blue sleep eyes w/real lashes, painted lower lashes, feathered brows, open closed mouth w/two upper teeth, original h.h. wig, jointed wood & composition body w/joints at shoulders, elbows, wrists, diagonal hip joints, & knees, wearing original wool sailor suit w/matching hat, cotton ribbed socks, unmatched white leather shoes, 20" (1 1/4" hairline on head, some flaking, wear at joints) **550**

S.F.B.J. (Société Francaise de Fabrication de Bebes et Jouets) bisque socket head boy, marked "S.F.B.J. - 226 - Paris - 6" on back of head, solid dome head w/blue "jewel" eyes, single-stroke brows, painted lashes, open closed mouth, molded hair, jointed wood & composition French body, redressed in light blue velvet lace-trimmed boy's outfit w/matching hat, black cotton socks, black leather shoes, 19" (roughness around neck opening, flocking missing from hair, hands repainted, touchup to chips in bisque on head) **1,500**

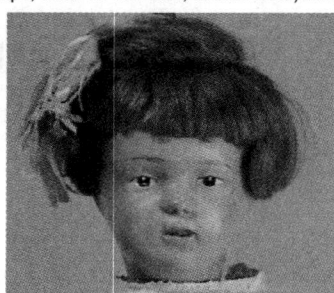

French Schmitt Baby

Schmitt wax over papier-mâché socket head baby, Schmitt shield stamp on bottom, pale blue paperweight eyes, closed mouth, fully articulated eight-ball composition body, France, late 19th c., extensive repainting, 14" (ILLUS.) **705**

Schoenau & Hoffmeister bisque socket head girl, marked "2/0 - S PB [in star] H - 1909 - 2/0 x - Germany" on back of head, blue sleep eyes w/real lashes & painted lashes, single-stroke brows, open mouth w/four upper teeth, original mohair wig, jointed wood & composition body, wearing original Dutch outfit of black wool, flowered accent pieces, lace cap, wool striped skirt, striped slip, pants, black socks & wooden shoes, 16" (clothing aged w/some wear, deterioration in flowered fabric) **195**

Schoenhut 16/102 wooden socket head girl, no marks visible, blue intaglio eyes, closed mouth, carved hair in braids w/blue bow in back, wooden body spring jointed at shoulders, elbows, wrists, hips, knees & ankles, redressed in copy of original sailor dress, knit union suit, black cotton socks, old cloth shoes, 16" (rub on nose, cheeks, most of color worn off hair & lips, wear on hair bow, overall wear) **850**

Schoenhut Character Girl

Schoenhut character girl, all painted wood, brown eyes, closed mouth, original ash brown wig, jointed body, wearing original shoes & older replacement clothing, some crazing on face, 15" (ILLUS.) **1,035**

Schoenhut composition head baby, marked "Schoenhut - Toys - Made in - U.S.A." on label on back, painted blue eyes, lightly molded & single-stroke brows, closed mouth, molded & painted hair, five-piece composition body w/bent right arm, wearing pale pink dotted Swiss dress, panties, replaced socks & shoes, 12" (stringing elastic glued into top of legs, chipped left first finger) **1,300**

Scottish bisque boy, unmarked, tinted bisque shoulder head, painted blue eyes, single-stroke brows, closed mouth, molded & painted blond hair, cloth body w/bisque lower arms & lower legs w/molded socks & shoes, wearing original traditional Scottish plaid outfit, 15" (repair on left upper leg & bottom of torso above leg, feet repaired) **225**

Simon & Halbig bisque socket head girl, marked "S. 11 H. - 939," blue sleep eyes, heavy feathered brows, open mouth w/six upper teeth, pierced ears, original mohair wig, jointed composition body w/straight wrists, separate balls at shoulders, elbows, hips & knees, wearing possibly original brown & black checked silk taffeta dress, original underclothing, black socks & high button boots, straw hat w/flower & ribbon trim, 17 1/2" **2,700**

Simon & Halbig bisque socket head Oriental lady, marked "1129 - S&H - DEP - 0 - Germany," set brown eyes, feathered brows, open mouth w/four upper teeth, pierced ears, original black mohair wig w/original queue, five-piece composition body w/molded & painted socks & shoes, wearing original red crepe kimono, 9" (ILLUS.) **1,275**

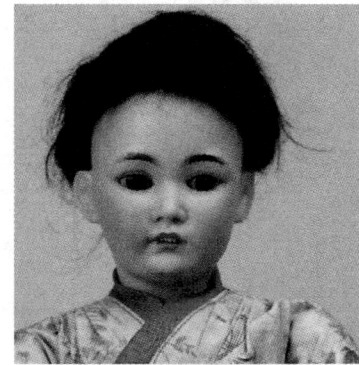

Simon & Halbig Oriental Child

Simon & Halbig Oriental bisque head child, marked "S & H 1329," brown sleep eyes, feathered brows, open mouth w/teeth, black wig, ball jointed composition body, wearing original kimono, 18" (ILLUS.) **1,380**

Simon & Halbig Oriental Lady

Steiner Bisque Head Girl

Steiner bisque head girl, marked "Fre A 17 Steiner," blue paperweight eyes, closed mouth, replacement brunette wig w/long curls, straight-wristed body, body repainted, later clothing, 24" (ILLUS.) **2,013**

A. Thullier 30" Girl

Thullier (A.) bisque head girl, marked "A. 14 T" on head, large blue paperweight eyes, feathered brows, closed mouth w/protruding upper lip, light brown h.h. wig, original jointed composition body, wearing antique blue mariner's outfit of pleated skirt & sailor-style top & hat & antique shoes marked "Bebe Jumeau 12," body repainted, 30" (ILLUS.) **21,275**

Walker (Izannah) cloth doll, molded & painted features & hair, large brown shaded eyes, closed mouth, two corkscrew curls in front of ears, cloth body, unpainted limbs, separately stitched thumb, bare undelineated feet, wearing cotton dress & apron, prototype for Walker dolls of 1860s-70s, Central Falls, Rhode Island, mid-19th c., 27 1/2" (breaks & damage at neck) **8,813**

Wax shoulder head shell woman with dog, painted features, shell eyes, cotton wool wig, wearing fabric hat & long draped dress totally covered in tiny brown seeds or shells w/white apron covered in petal-shaped slivers of mother-of-pearl, holding small shell-covered spaniel-type dog, on shell-covered base housed in oblong footed 12"-h. wooden-based tapered glass dome, Europe, early 19th c., one shell eye missing from woman, 7" **1,528**

Wooden carved lady, brown painted eyes, lash dots, single-stroke brows, rosy cheeks, pierced ears, painted black tendrils around face, remains of wig cap, fully articulated wooden body jointed at shoulders, elbows, hips & knees, painted bust, lower arms & legs, red slippers, wearing original chemise & corset

w/gauze lace & light blue silk ribbon trim, Germany, ca. 1820, 11 1/2" (earrings missing, left thumb chipped) **2,233**

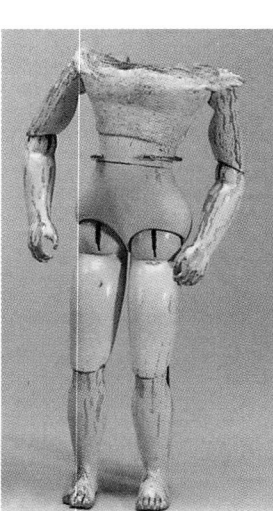

Wooden Lady with Jointed Body

Wooden lady body, articulated body jointed at shoulders, hips, elbows & knees w/flat swivel at waist, cupped hands, probably Jumeau, ca. 1870s, 4" w. at shoulders, 13" h. for 17-18" doll (ILLUS.) **3,995**

FIRE FIGHTING COLLECTIBLES

American fire fighting "antiques" are considered those items over 100 years old that were directly related to fire fighting, whereas fire fighting "collectibles" are items less than a century old. Pieces from both eras are very sought-after today.

Foreign-made fire fighting antiques and collectibles have a marketplace of their own and, for the most part, are not as expensive and in demand as similar American pieces.

Early Leather Fire Bucket

Bucket, painted leather, swelled cylindrical form w/a leather handle across the top, dark green paint decorated w/a mustard yellow & black banner reading "E.S. Towle," America, early 19th c., handle loose, 13 1/4" h. (ILLUS.) **$660**

Fire Fighting Chemical Glass Container

Fire chemical container, barrel-shaped amber glass container w/a short cylindrical neck, embossed "Hazelton's High Pressure Chemical Fire Keg," tooled mouth, smooth base, ca. 1900, 1 gal., 10 7/8" h. (ILLUS.) **213**

Rare German Glass Fire Grenade

Fire grenade, reddish amber glass, cylindrical 14-sided body w/a domed top w/small neck, panels embossed "Deutsche - Loschgranate - Eberthardt," also "Gesetzlich - Geschutzt" on the smooth base, very rare, German, ca. 1900, 8" h. (ILLUS.) **580**

Rare Green Glass Fire Grenade

Fire grenade, spherical green glass ribbed ball w/a cylindrical neck, oval panel embossed "Harkness - Fire - Extinguisher," crude, American, ca. 1880, 6 1/8" h. (ILLUS.) **616**

Early Cast-Iron Fire Mark

Fire mark, cast iron, oval, cast w/a raised tree, used by the Mutual Assurance Co. of Philadelphia, ca. 1810, rust, no paint, 8 1/4 x 12 1/4" (ILLUS.) **300**

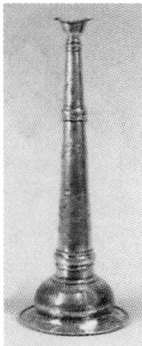

Rare Presentation Fire Trumpet

Fire trumpet, presentation-type, silver plate, engraved around the sides w/a fire pumper, hat w/eagle crest, trumpet, ax & bucket, the flaring rim w/flower decoration, monogrammed, late 19th - early 20th c., 23" l. (ILLUS.) **1,725**

Rare Firehouse Alarm Indicator

Firehouse automatic alarm indicator gong, wall-mounted master unit used in a fire station, connected by telegraph to various city call boxes, in a fine late Victorian carved oak case w/a broken-scroll pediment, the front w/three glass panes, the upper pane shows a three-roll number, the middle & bottom panes show the brass works, patent information on an interior brass plaque, by The Gamewell Fire Alarm Telegraph Company, New York, New York, w/large brass key, late 19th c., case 18 1/2 x 32" (ILLUS.)........... **13,225**

Decorative Fireman's Parade Helmet

Fireman's parade helmet, brass w/a fireman's seal at the front w/decorative crossed axes on the visor, a black hair band attached to the decorative crest, now mounted on a base, 19th c., 21" h. (ILLUS.).. **300**

Early Wooden Fireman Parade Ax

Parade ax, carved & painted wood, model of a fireman's ax w/a natural wood handle & the head painted in red, silver & green, several old repairs, American, 19th c., overall 43 1/2" l. (ILLUS.)................................ **460**

FIREARMS

Blunderbuss, flintlock, barrel w/widely flared bell-shaped muzzle, chased designs near the breech & decorative silver overlay, walnut stock covered w/fine wire inlay w/traces of gold wash, engraved wrought-iron hardware, Europe, 17th - 18th c., barrel 14 1/2" l., overall 27 1/2" l. (areas of wire inlay missing) **$1,650**

Carbine, Burnside Fourth Model .54 caliber percussion, round barrel, overall dark surface on stock & barrel w/clear inspector's mark & signature on breech, Serial No. 19046, barrel 21" l................................ **1,210**

Carbine, Cosmopolitan Arms Co. .52 caliber percussion model, round barrel, walnut stock, overall browned surface on metal w/bold marking & 1853 date, Serial No. 1070, barrel 19" l. (few old scrapes on stock) **1,980**

Carbine, Gallager's Patent percussion model, round barrel w/overall mottled brown surface, walnut stock w/iron patch box, Serial No. 15541, barrel 22" l................ **990**

Carbine, Hall-North Model 1843 .52 caliber percussion-type, unusual rifled barrel, walnut stock, overall good patina & stampings, barrel 21" l. (stock w/usual dents & scrapes)....................................... **1,375**

Carbine, Joslyn Model 1864 .52 caliber rimfire, old browned metal surface, stock w/good patina, crisp inspector's marking, Serial No. 9969, barrel 22" l........................ **1,485**

Carbine, Merrill (J.H.) .54 caliber percussion model, round barrel, brass hardware including cap box, iron saddle ring, stock w/old dark finish, barrel 20" l., overall 37" l. (hairlines in stock at wrist).................... **990**

Carbine, Merrill (J.H.) percussion model, first type w/brass hardware, faint stampings on lock & Serial No. 2272 behind hammer, walnut stock w/good patina, overall 37" l. (hairline in stock at wrist & age crack near buttplate) **990**

Carbine, Sharps Model 1853 slanting breech model .52 caliber percussion-style w/round barrel, brass patch box, butt plate & barrel band, retains the long sling ring slide bar of the 1852 model, old dark finish on wood stock, Serial No. 15723, barrel 21 1/2" l. (missing rear sight, areas of pitting) **1,870**

Carbine, Sharps percussion New Model 1863, round barrel, bold stampings & faint inspector's marks on stock, Serial No. C27301, barrel 22" l., overall 39" l....... **2,310**

Carbine, Smith .50 caliber percussion model, octagonal to round barrel, original bluing, crisp inspector's markings & case coloring on frame, Serial No. 19522, barrel 21 1/2" l. **2,365**

Carbine, Smith Patent .50 caliber percussion model, round barrel, faint inspector's mark on walnut stock, Serial No. 13487, barrel 21 1/2" l. (metal carefully cleaned) .. **1,128**

Carbine, Springfield Armory Model 1873 trap door .45-70 caliber, walnut stock retains part of inspector's cartouche, barrel w/old blued finish, Serial No. 1282, barrel 22" l., overall 41 1/4" l. (splits near saddle ring, mainspring weak) **770**

Carbine, Starr Arms .54 caliber percussion model, round barrel, worn walnut stock w/good patina & brass overlay on one side, initials "J.W." carved on the other side, brass barrel band & buttplate, barrel 20" l. (stock chips) **1,128**

Carbine, Winchester Model 1873 .44 caliber, originally an early first model rifle w/barrel shortened, walnut butt stock & forearm w/a nickel silver inlay on one side of the butt stock & an open inlay on the other which is open to the chamber for cleaning rod, retains engraved oval thumb piece on the dust cover, Serial No. 4352, barrel 19 1/4" l. **1,100**

Long rifle, percussion-type w/curly maple stock w/old mellow brown surface & a raised carved molding along the ramrod channel, brass hardware including a finely engraved patch box & shaped floor plate, engraved eagle cheek piece in addition to the fourteen other mother-of-pearl, silver & nickel silver inlays, octagonal barrel, Kentucky-type, barrel 41 3/4" l., overall 56 1/2" l. (barrel lightly pitted, couple inlays replaced, one missing) **1,100**

Musket, Harpers Ferry Model 1816 percussion conversion type III, round barrel w/three bands, lock retains the eagle stamp w/signature & 1837 date, faint inspector's marks on stock w/some crudely carved initials, barrel 42" l. **1,265**

Musket, Harpers Ferry percussion model w/bayonet, lock w/the eagle stamp & dated 1843, walnut stock w/faint inspector's marks, iron hardware, overall fair condition w/old finish, barrel 42" l. (some pitting on buttplate) **1,293**

Musket, U.S. Model 1816 flintlock .69 caliber model, round barrel, lock signed "N. Starr, Midltn. Conn. 1831" & has small star behind the date, bold inspector's marking on barrel & stock, overall good patina & condition, barrel 42" l. **1,925**

Musket, U.S. Model 1861 percussion model w/bayonet, lock stamped "U.S. Trenton" w/an eagle & "1864," overall dull nickel plating to metal w/good stampings, barrel dated 1863, walnut stock w/"N.J." stamp opposite the lock, barrel 40" l. **1,320**

Musket, U.S. Model 1861 percussion model w/bayonet, three-band type marked "U.S. Bridesburg" w/an eagle & "1862" on lock, light grey surface on metal, walnut stock w/inspector's marks, barrel 40" l., overall 56 3/4" l. (minor metal pitting, minor dings on stock) **1,375**

Musket, Virginia Manufactory flintlock model, good dark patina to walnut stock & the metal w/old brown finish, lock marked w/the block & script signature beneath the double-throated hammer & w/"Richmond 1811" near the tail, round barrel w/three bands w/band springs mounted behind, early carved initials on buttstock & behind side plate, barrel 44" l. (old age splits along barrel channel) **4,950**

Pistol, Aston (H.) & Co. percussion model, brass hardware, lock w/1851 date & sharp signature, good as-found condition, 14 1/2" l. (minor age hairlines in stock near lock bolt) **578**

Pistol, Model 1836 flintlock, mark of R. Johnson, inspector's mark & 1838 date, wooden grips, overall good condition, 14" l. (old chip above lock, replaced rammer) **1,045**

Pistol, North (S.) Model 1816 flintlock .54 caliber model w/stand, walnut stock w/old dark finish & inspector's stamps, earlier signature w/eagle stamp on lock, w/20th c. handmade cherry stand (glued split just ahead of lock) **990**

Pistol, Palmetto Armory .54 caliber percussion model, round barrel, clear stampings on lock plate include "Columbia S.C." & "1854 - V.P." & palmetto tree stamp on barrel w/"Wm. Glaze & Co.," brass hardware w/small "H" inspector's stamp on the back strap & guard, wood grip, overall good condition, 14 1/2" l. (minor wear behind lock bolt, later ramrod) **1,540**

Pistol, Waters (A.) percussion model, early conversion from flintlock w/brass spacer, clear eagle head stamp, signature & 1838 stamp, barrel stamped "J.H.," barrel 8 1/2" l., overall 14" l. **550**

Revolver, Colt 1849 .31 caliber pocket model, faint roll engraved cylinder scene, all serial numbers match, Serial No. 263733, barrel 5" l. **660**

Revolver, Colt 1862 .36 caliber Police model, fluted cylinder & brass hardware, walnut grips, old rebluing, Serial No. 25572, barrel 5 3/8" l. (grips damaged) **715**

Revolver, Colt Bisley single-action Army model 38 W.C.f. caliber, overall mellow grey finish to metal w/the original hard rubber grips that include the rampant Colt logo, single line signature w/the Hartford address on the barrel, patent dates & Colt stamp on the frame, all matching except the loading gate, Serial Nos. 245314, barrel 5 1/2" l. **1,045**

Revolver, Savage Revolving Firearms Co. .36 caliber Navy percussion model, octagonal barrel, six-shot cylinder, walnut grips w/traces of inspector's cartouche, overall worn brown finish on metal, barrel 7 1/8" l., overall 14 1/2" l. (loading lever, latch & a couple of screws replaced) **605**

Revolver, Starr Arms .44 caliber Army percussion model, round barrel, retains areas of original bluing & bold inspector's mark on either side of the walnut grips,

Serial No. 15378, barrel 6" l. (trigger spring needs work) **1,100**

Revolver, Starr Arms percussion model, overall browned finish on metal, walnut grips w/old plug in base, clear stampings, Serial No. 53064 .... **825**

Rifle, Colt percussion model, crisp inspector's marks on walnut stock & barrel, bolster w/old eagle mark & lock dated 1864 w/a good signature, barrel 40" l. (couple of very old minor dents on stock & tight hairline behind the lock) **770**

Rifle, Marlin, Ballard #9 Union Hill .32-40 caliber model, browned octagonal to round barrel, stamped signature & patent date on the frame, select grade checkered stock, worn nickel plating on butt plate, Serial No. 29099, fine condition, barrel 28" l. **2,475**

Rifle, Sharps New Model 1859 .52 caliber percussion-type, full stock w/three barrel bands & an iron patch box, clear signature & stampings, Serial No. 39833, overall good condition w/some shallow chips near lock & hairline above, barrel 30" l. **3,300**

Rifle, Spencer .52 caliber Army repeating model, round barrel w/three barrel bands & lug-type front sight for bayonet, military inspector's marks on the stock, metal light grey w/areas of dark brown on the barrel, Civil War era, Serial No. 7925, barrel 30" l. **2,420**

Rifle, Whitney-Remington-style rolling block #2 sporting model, .22 caliber, tapered octagonal barrel w/adjustable open sights, stamped signature on the tang, dark patina on walnut stock, Serial No. 71458, barrel 26" l., overall 41 1/2" l. **385**

FRATERNAL ORDER COLLECTIBLES

Ashtray and Cigarette Box

Masonic ashtray & cigarette box, composition plastic w/glass insert, brown, Masonic emblem & tools embossed on box cover, pipe rest in center, 9 1/2" l. x 4 3/4" w. (ILLUS.) **$12-15**

Masonic clock pendulum, metal w/gold finish, compass & square design, letters "HTWSNTKS" in circle in center, 4" l. (ILLUS., top next column) **55-75**

Masonic Clock Pendulum

Masonic columns, carved & painted wood, each tall slender ribbed column topped w/scrolled leaves supporting a crown-form device, raised on a tall square plinth base, dark gold paint w/polychrome trim, America, late 19th - early 20th c., 17 3/4" w., 98 1/2" h., pr. (minor imperfections) **1,380**

Masonic Delegate Medal

Masonic delegate medal, white metal on red, white & blue ribbon, the Masonic emblem in top arch, circular medal depending from bottom w/image of building & "39th Annual Convention, Sept. 4-5, 1911, Albany, NY" (ILLUS.) **8-12**

Match Safe with Brass Masonic Emblem

Masonic match safe, cast brass, Masonic emblem on top, square marked "Friendship, Love, Truth," 4" w. x 8" l., (ILLUS.).. **20-25**

Masonic Delegate Ribbon

Masonic delegate ribbon, 27th Annual Convention, Washington, DC, The National League of Masonic Clubs, George Washington Masonic National Memorial, May 11-14, 1932, w/images of Memorial building & Masonic emblem, 6 3/4" l. x 1 1/4" w. (ILLUS.)................... **125-150**

Embossed Masonic Medal

Masonic medal, white metal w/red, white & blue ribbon, Masonic symbol & "Massachusetts" embossed in metal at top, a heart embossed w/"51st Annual Session, National Council, Sept. 8-14, 1896, Worcester, Mass." hanging at bottom (ILLUS.)... **8-12**

Crewel Masonic Emblem

Masonic emblem, crewel on canvas, Masonic "G" in compass & square, sewn in gold & blue thread, 16 1/2 x 20 1/2" (ILLUS.) **25-30**

Masonic Medal/Ribbon

Masonic medal w/ribbon, goldtone & fabric, the top bar w/"Jr. O.U.A.M." in scroll border, from which depends a circular piece w/shield above embossed eagle, the bottom w/the Masonic logo, all three pieces linked together over small U.S. flag (ILLUS.) **15-20**

Masonic Picture Frame

Masonic picture frame, brass, square & compass design, 8 1/2" w. x 10 1/2" h. (ILLUS.) **30-40**

"Masonry" Gilded Pot Metal Plaque

Masonic plaque, gilded pot metal, "Masonry" embossed in blue w/motto & Masonic tools & emblem, marked "1925 C.J.T.," 6 7/8" h. x 11 5/8" l. (ILLUS.) **15-18**

"Centennial 1861-1961" Plate

Masonic plate, white ceramic w/cobalt blue border & gold trim, "Centennial, 1861-1961, Grand Lodge, A.F. & A.M. of Colorado," marked "Syracuse China U.S.A.," 11 1/4" d. (ILLUS.) **30-35**

Masonic Seat Cover

Masonic seat cover, hand-hooked yarn, round, gold Masonic "G" in compass & square sewn in shades of gold & grey on dark blue ground, 6" d. (ILLUS.) **35-45**

Masonic Sign

Masonic sign, wood, shield shape w/several applied carved wooden Masonic symbols including the All-Seeing Eye, sun, moon, stars, large center "G," pillars & more, w/gilt highlights on blue field w/red & white stripes below, molded gilt frame, America, 19th c., 28 3/4 x 34" (ILLUS.)...... **3,055**

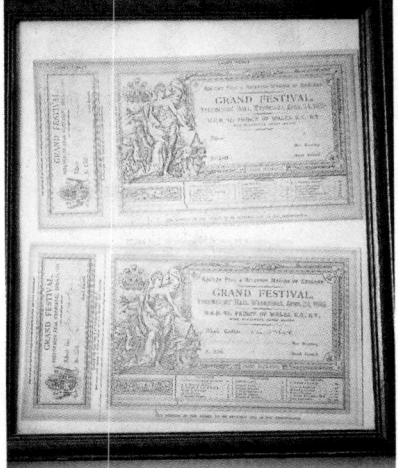

English Grand Festival Tickets

Masonic tickets, one each man's & woman's admission, English Grand Festival of Prince of Wales, April 24, 1889, framed, 15 3/4" w. x 18 3/4" l. (ILLUS.)...... **25-35**

"Mason" Tobacco Tin with Ashtray Cover

Masonic tobacco tin, "Mason" brand, round, blue w/red & white writing, "Rock City Tobacco Co., Ltd., Quebec," cover is ashtray, 5 3/8 d. x 2 3/4" h. (ILLUS.) **30-40**

"Master Mason" Tobacco Tin

Masonic tobacco tin, "Master Mason" brand, square, red & white, "Rock City Tobacco Co., Ltd., Quebec, Net 3 lbs.," 6 1/2" x 7 1/4", 2 3/4 h. (ILLUS.) **40-50**

"What Is A Mason?" Glass Tray

Masonic tray, rectangular w/rounded corners, blue glass w/gold writing & trim, "What Is A Mason?," features images of altar pillars, Masonic symbols & tools, 5 1/4 x 8 1/4", 3 1/4" h. (ILLUS.) **10-15**

Masonic Emblem Trivet

Masonic Wristwatch

Masonic trivet, cast bronze, Masonic emblem w/loop handle, 6 3/4" l. (ILLUS., previous page) **12-15**

Masonic wristwatch, triangular face w/images of tools of the Masonic order around sides of face, the Masonic emblem at top attaching face to leather band, 17 jewels, Waltham (ILLUS., bottom previous page) **400-500**

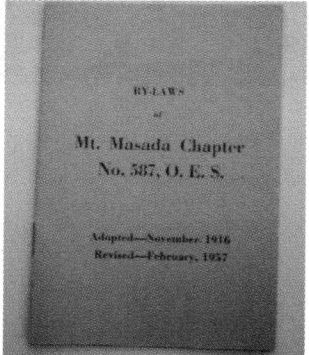

O.E.S. By-Laws Manual

Order of the Eastern Star manual, "By-Laws of Mt. Masada Chapter No. 587, O.E.S. - Adopted November 1916 - Revised February 1957" on front cover (ILLUS.) **6-8**

Order of the Eastern Star ring, platinum w/enamel overlay, Eastern Star emblem.. **110-150**

Order of the Eastern Star salt & pepper shakers, ceramic, white w/the four-color OES emblems, base marked "Made in Japan KF103," 3 1/4" h., pr. **6-8**

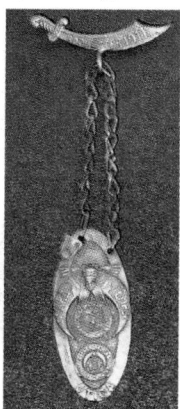

Shriner Pin

Shriner pin, white metal, scimitar embossed w/"Rochester 1911" holds chain from which depends oval medal embossed w/"Ziyara Temple, Utica, N.Y." & various images, made by "Whitehead & Hoag Co., Newark, N.J.," 7 1/8" l. (ILLUS.) **15-18**

Shriner Brass Wall Hanging

Shriner wall hanging, brass, Shriner symbol, 11 1/2" w. (ILLUS.) **25-35**

Wood Framed Shriner Wall Hanging

Shriner wall hanging, Shrine emblem mounted on a board at the top w/a running baby Shriner wearing his first fez at the bottom, wood framed, 3" w., 10" h. (ILLUS.).. **20-25**

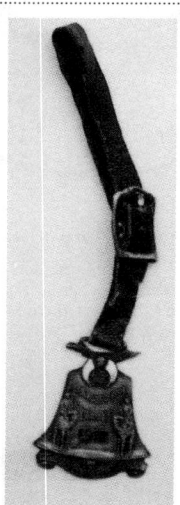

Shriner Watch Fob

Shriner watch fob, metal bell-shaped fob embossed w/"Palestine Temple, Providence, R.I., 1913" & various symbols hangs from leather strap w/buckle, 1 3/8" (ILLUS.) **20-25**

FURNITURE

Furniture made in the United States during the 18th and 19th centuries is coveted by collectors. American antique furniture has a European background, primarily English, since the influence of the Continent usually found its way to America by way of England. If the style did not originate in England, it came to America by way of England. For this reason, some American furniture styles carry the name of an English monarch or an English designer. However, we must realize that, until recently, little research has been conducted and even less published on the Spanish and French influences in the area of the California missions and New Orleans.

After the American revolution, cabinetmakers in the United States shunned the prevailing styles in England and chose to bring the French styles of Napoleon's Empire to the United States and we have the uniquely named "American Empire" (Classical) style of furniture in a country that never had an emperor.

During the Victorian period, quality furniture began to be mass-produced in this country with its rapidly growing population. So much walnut furniture was manufactured, the vast supply of walnut was virtually depleted and it was of necessity that oak furniture became fashionable as the 19th century drew to a close.

For our purposes, the general guidelines for dating will be: Pilgrim Century - 1620-85 William & Mary - 1685-1720 Queen Anne - 1720-50 Chippendale - 1750-85 Federal - 1785-1820 Hepplewhite - 1785-1820 Sheraton - 1800-20 American Empire (Classical) - 1815-40 Victorian - 1840-1900 Early Victorian - 1840-50 Gothic Revival - 1840-90 Rococo (Louis XV) - 1845-70 Renaissance - 1860-85 Louis XVI - 1865-75 Eastlake - 1870-95 Jacobean & Turkish Revival - 1870-95 Aesthetic Movement - 1880-1900 Art Nouveau - 1890-1918 Turn-of-the-Century - 1895-1910 Mission (Arts & Crafts movement) - 1900-15 Art Deco - 1925-40

All furniture included in this listing is American unless otherwise noted.

Bedroom Suites

Renaissance-Style: bed, chest-of-drawers, cheval mirror, two-door armoire, pair of nightstands; burled elm & walnut, the large armoire w/a widely flaring stepped cornice w/blocked ends over a dentil-carved band above a frieze band w/lion mask carved blocks at the sides & a scroll-carved center panel flanked by narrow burl panels, all above the tall burl-paneled doors flanked by side pilasters carved w/angel heads, fruit clusters & scallops, blocked & stepped base on

Renaissance-Style Armoire

carved grotesque mask front feet, the other pieces w/matching details, Italy, ca. 1900, bed 74 x 87", 71" h., armoire 31 x 80", 91" h., the set (ILLUS. of armoire) **$4,830**

Eastlake Washstand from Set

Victorian Eastlake substyle: half-tester double bed, two-door armoire, chest-of-drawers & washstand; walnut & burl walnut, each w/a high stepped crestrail carved w/scrolls & flanked by tapering block corner finials above a narrow dentil

& block band, the washstand w/a large rectangular mirror swiveling between uprights above the rectangular red marble top w/a high splashback over a case w/two long narrow burl-paneled drawers slightly stepped-out above a pair of burl-paneled cupboard doors, molded base on casters, bed 62 x 74", 92 1/2" h., washstand 18 x 32 1/4", 78 1/2" h., the set (ILLUS. of washstand)......................... **4,370**

Renaissance Revival Tall Bed

Victorian Renaissance Revival substyle: bed & chest of drawers; walnut & burl walnut, the bed w/a tall headboard w/a palmette & leafy scroll crest flanked by scrolled ears above an arched molding w/roundel above a tall rectangular burl panel flanked by half-round ring-turned columns & bars flanked by lower arched burl panels & short blocked & baluster-turned side stiles, the low footboard w/a raised & arched center crest over long burl panels & ring-turned rails, the chest of drawers w/similar carving & a tall arched mirror above a drop-well case w/white marble tops, ca. 1875, bed 68 x 85", 106" h., the pair (ILLUS. of bed).. **12,650**

Victorian Renaissance Revival substyle: bed, chest of drawers & washstand; walnut & burl walnut, the bed & chest w/a tall back topped by an ornately carved arched pediment centered by a carved winged angel head over raised burl panels above large scrolls at the top corners, the chest w/a very tall rectangular mirror between narrow stiles w/raised burl panels & candle shelves above a drop-well top w/three sections w/faux black marble painted tops, pairs of small paneled drawers w/large drop pulls flank the center well all above a long concave-front drawer w/matching pulls over a concave deep molded base, similar set attributed to Thomas Brooks, Brooklyn, New York, ca. 1875, washstand marble top re-

Renaissance Revival Tall Chest

placed, bed 65 x 84", 95 1/2" h., chest-of-drawers 24 x 57 1/2", 95" h., the set (ILLUS. of chest of drawers)....................... **8,050**

Ornately Carved Renaissance Chest

Victorian Renaissance Revival substyle:
high-backed double bed & chest of drawers; walnut & burl walnut, the headboard w/a very high arched crest topped by a full-figure carved cupid w/quiver flanked by small dolphins above carved scrolls all above a large arched burl panel flanked by detailed urn corner finials above three molded arched panels, the low footboard w/an arched crestrail over three arched burl panels flanked by rounded corners w/burl panels, the chest of drawers w/a matching finial & crestrail over a tall arched mirror flanked by scroll-carved sides w/burl panels & candle shelves over the drop-well top w/white marble, the rectangular raised side section w/chamfered corners above a conforming case w/a stack of three burl-paneled drawers at each side flanking the low center section w/a concave front over a conforming long burl-paneled drawer, original pulls, refinished, ca. 1870, bed 58 x 78", 9' h., 2 pcs. (ILLUS. of chest, previous page) **25,000**

Victorian Rococo substyle: high-backed double bed & chest of drawers; carved mahogany, the chest of drawers w/a very high superstructure topped by a Prince-of-Wales plumes carved finial over a broken-arched pediment w/scroll-pierced panels above wide pierced scroll-carved sections supporting two half-round shelves on each side & flanking a tall arched swiveling mirror, the rectangular white marble top w/a serpentine front & outset chamfered corners above a conforming case w/four long bow-front drawers w/ornate scroll-carved panels & pulls, molded bow-front apron; the bed headboard w/a pierced & scroll-carved finial on the wide arched & molded crestrail

Fine Mitchell & Rammelsberg Chest

above a wide arched flame veneer panel flanked by heavy side posts w/large urn-form finials, low footboard w/raised scroll-carved corners & arched center crest above a cartouche-carved roundel, deep side rails, by Mitchell & Rammelsburg Co., Cincinnati, Ohio, ca. 1850-60, bed 62 x 80", overall 9' h., pr. (ILLUS. of chest & bed, bottom of page) **10,000**

Victorian Rococo substyle: high-backed double bed & chest of drawers; carved rosewood, the bed headboard w/a high pierced arched crest elaborately carved w/scrolling leafy vines w/an exotic bird

Ornate Rosewood Bed & Chest

perched at each side over the arched & stepped crestrail above the three-panel backboard w/further scroll carving flanked by block-and-column-carved stiles w/urn-form finials, the lower arched footboard w/ornate scroll carving centered by a large oval knob above two arched panels, curved low corner boards; the chest w/a tall superstructure w/ornately pierced-carved twining branches w/an exotic bird on each side & resting on tall square plinths w/round candle shelves all enclosing a tall oblong swiveling mirror, the rectangular white marble top w/a serpentine front above a conforming case w/ three long drawers w/scroll-carved pulls flanked by canted front corners w/further carved scrolls, low serpentine apron, Mitchell & Rammelsberg Co., Cincinnati, Ohio, ca. 1855, original finish, bed 64 x 82", 8' 6" h., pr. (ILLUS., top of previous page)................. **20,000**

Beds

Classical low-poster bed, mahogany, the gently arched headboard w/scroll-cut end flanked by ornate baluster-turned & leaf-carved sections topped by acorn finials, matching foot posts joined by a wide rail, bulbous tapering ovoid legs, brass bolt covers, probably original finish, ca. 1840, 40 x 74", 42" h. (ILLUS., next column).. **800**

Classical "sleigh" bed, mahogany, double-size, the even upright S-scroll head-

Classical Bed with Ornate Posts

and footboards joined by shaped side rails on flat rounded feet, ca. 1830-40, 57 1/2 x 75", 41 1/2" h. (ILLUS., bottom of page)... **1,160**

American Classical Double Sleigh Bed

Classical Bed with Ornate Tall Posts

Classical tall-poster bed, mahogany, the arched & scroll-carved headboard over two large rectangular flame veneer panels flanked by tall knob-, ring- and acanthus leaf-carved tall posts w/knob finials, matching foot posts, short baluster-turned legs, original brass bolt covers, original dark finish, ca. 1835, 58 x 80", 7' h. (ILLUS.) **5,500**

Classical Revival Mahogany Bed

Classical Revival tall-poster bed, mahogany, each post w/ring-turned segments alternating w/reeded segments & carved pineapple designs, the narrow cut-out headboard w/a carved crest bar w/rosette ends, on pineapple- and paw-carved legs, late 19th c., 52 x 79", 96" h. (ILLUS.) **3,680**

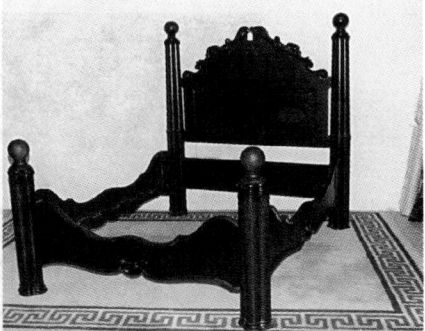

Classical Transitional Bed

Classical-Rococo transitional tall-poster bed, mahogany, the high arched headboard w/ornate carved scrolls flanked by tall posts formed by a cluster of four columns topped w/a ball finial, shorter matching foot posts, serpentine scroll-trimmed siderails & footrails, possibly original finish, ca. 1845, 66 x 84", 6' h. (ILLUS.) **4,500**

Colonial Revival Canopy Bed

Colonial Revival tall-poster canopy bed, mahogany w/stenciled decoration, the rectangular cove-molded canopy frame raised on tall baluster-, ring- and rod-turned posts, a high scroll-cut arched headboard w/carved center shell above an arched stenciled panel, wide side rails & foot rail w/carved scrolls & beaded base band, on short Spanish feet, original dark finish, full-sized, ca. 1920s, 60 x 80", 6' 8" h. (ILLUS.) **1,500**

Country-style "low-poster" twin bed, walnut, matching solid head- and footboards peaked at the center & flanked by turned knob finials, on baluster- and ring-turned legs w/peg feet, pegged construction, old finish, Zoar, Ohio, 19th c., 39" w., 30" h. **495**

French Empire-Style Bed

Empire-Style bed, ormolu-mounted mahogany, the high flat-topped headboard w/a rounded crestrail fitted w/a small figural ormolu boss over an arched panel w/corner bosses flanked by free-standing side columns w/ormolu capitals, the matching lower footboard trimmed w/ormolu bar mounts & a large wreath, on short, square tapering legs, France, ca. 1900, 59 1/2 x 81", 4' 4" h. (ILLUS., above)... **1,265**

French Louis Philippe Bed

Louis Philippe bed, mahogany, the even headboards & footboards w/arched scroll-carved crests above plain panels flanked by paneled stiles w/turned button finials, deep shaped siderails, heavy tapering ring- and knob-turned legs, France, mid-19th c., 40 1/2 x 74", 39" h. (ILLUS.).. **805**

Fine Federal Revival Twin Bed

Federal Revival tall-poster twin-sized canopy beds, mahogany, a rectangular molded canopy rail above tall baluster ring-turned & leaf-carved posts w/pineapple finials, the headboard carved across the top w/a spread-winged eagle, the similar footboard w/shell & scroll carving, tall tapering baluster-turned legs on knob feet, original finish, ca. 1920s, 48 x 76", 8' h., pr. (ILLUS. of one).............. **5,000**

Ornate Chinese Rosewood Bed

Rococo Carved Rosewood Bed

Oriental canopy bed, rosewood, the rectangular canopy top pierce-carved w/rectangular panels & raised on six slender tapering posts above the platform base enclosed by a three-quarters gallery pierce-carved w/squares & quatrefoils, raised on high incurved blocked legs, the top w/overall subtle low-relief carved foliage sprays, China, late 19th c., 59 x 87", 94" h. (ILLUS., previous page) **3,450**

Victorian Rococo bed, carved rosewood, the high headboard w/a tall broken-arch crest composed of ornate carved scrolls & pierced scroll panels centered by a turned urn finial, the arched crestrail above a simple paneled board flanked by matching turned urn corner finials, the lower arched footboard w/matching turned finials, wide sideboards, probably New York City, ca. 1855, original finish, 60 x 80", 6' h. (ILLUS., top of page) **2,800**

Simple Victorian Rococo Bed

Victorian Rococo bed, chestnut & walnut, the high headboard w/an arched, stepped crestrail topped by a scroll-carved cartouche finial above a central scroll-carved cartouche over an oval raised band, blocked top corners w/knob-turned finials, the matching low footboard w/curved leg panels, refinished, ca. 1860, 58 x 78", 5' h. (ILLUS.) **950**

Early Rococo Tall-poster Bed

Victorian Rococo tall-poster bed, mahogany, the high arched & scroll-carved headboard centered by a shell-carved crest & flanked by tall tapering octagonal posts, wide serpentine side & foot rails, matching tall tapering octagonal foot posts, mid-19th c., missing canopy tester, 66 x 90", 8' 5" h. (ILLUS.) **5,060**

Early Charles II English Bench

Benches

Early Ohio Bucket Bench

Bucket (or water) bench, country-style, painted pine, a narrow rectangular top shelf atop wide board upright ends w/bootjack feet & chamfered at the top over two open dovetailed medial shelves, original deep red paint, attributed to Ohio, mid-19th c., good patina, minor age splits & wear, 13 x 43", 41 1/2" h. (ILLUS.) **2,760**

Bucket (or water) bench, painted poplar, a rectangular top shelf w/a low three-quarters gallery w/rounded front corners flanked by one-board sides & above an open lower shelf, angled bootjack cutouts on sides, square nail construction, old grey over earlier black paint, 19th c., 10 1/4 x 37", 31" h. (age splits, some later nails) **358**

Charles II bench, oak, long narrow rectangular seat cushion on a conforming frame raised on six block- and knob-turned legs joined by barley-twist turned rails, last quarter 17th c. or later, England, 22 x 60", 18 1/2" h. (ILLUS., top of page) **2,070**

Country-style bench, painted pine, long narrow rectangular seat w/cut corners on finely shaped cutout & notched board legs w/arched bracket braces w/chamfered edges, old dark red paint & traces of old brown underneath, square nails in the scrubbed seat, 19th c., 8 5/8 x 46", 19" h. **798**

Leather-working bench, painted pine, a rectangular board seat w/two hand holes on board legs w/bootjack cutouts & angled braces, one end of the top fitted w/a wide vise adjusted w/a large cast-iron wing nut, old dark red & black paint, stamped "W.H. Snook," 19th c., 9 3/4 x 26", 29 3/4" h. (wear) **110**

Louis XV-Style bench, carved fruitwood, the long, narrow, rectangular upholstered seat cushion decorated w/gros & petit point designs of birds & animals in Aubusson-style cartouche, the apron w/carved frieze of shell & acanthus leaf decoration, cabriole legs w/shell-carved knees & scrolled feet, base missing original stretcher, France, late 19th c., 15 x 39", 22" h. **1,045**

Mammy's bench (rocking settee w/removable cradle rail on seat), painted & decorated wood, a long flat crestrail above twelve simple turned spindles flanked by tapering stiles & S-scroll arms over a spindle & ring-turned canted arm support, the long shaped plank seat fitted w/removable baby guard rail w/eight spindles, heavy baluster-, knob- and ring-turned front legs joined by a long flat stretcher & inset into rockers, old dark red over black graining w/gold & yellow line detail, first half 19th c., 27 1/2 x 46 1/2", 28" h. (glued split in one stretcher, other one loose at back leg) **1,265**

English William IV Long Bench

Wicker Photographer's Bench

Photographer's bench, wicker, the ornate stepped back w/an arched band of tight scrolls above panels of tight woven wicker & bobbins beside a lower section of slender strands & bobbins, a high rolled arm at one end composed of rows of bobbins, oblong wooden seat, ring- and scroll-trimmed front apron, slender wrapped legs, natural finish, ca. 1880 (ILLUS.) **825-850**

Regency-Style Window Bench

Regency-Style window bench, giltwood, long slender U-shaped outswept rails enclosing upholstered arms & seat, raised on tapering reeded & leaf-carved turned legs, England, ca.1900, 19 x 43", 35" h. (ILLUS.) **1,725**

William IV bench, mahogany, rectangular padded & upholstered top raised on heavily reeded short legs raised on brass caps & casters, England, mid-19th c., 24 x 54", 15" h. (ILLUS., top of page) **1,380**

Bookcases

Fine American Classical Bookcase

Classical bookcase, mahogany, the peaked pediment w/a thin edge ribbon molding above a tall case w/a pair of tall arched glazed doors opening to six adjustable wooden shelves, a slightly projecting base w/a pair of drawers raised on simple bracket feet, old finish, probably Boston, ca. 1840-50, 14 x 47 1/4", 7' 3" h. (ILLUS.) **3,910**

Regency Marble-topped Bookcase

George III-Style English Bookcase

Regency-Style Bookcase

w/matching doors, conforming plinth base, England, first quarter 19th c., 17 x 72 1/2", 37" h. (ILLUS., top of page) **5,750**

George III-Style bookcase, mahogany, the rectangular top w/a narrow flaring & stepped cornice above a pair of tall geometrically glazed doors opening to four adjustable wooden shelves, flat plinth base, England, late 19th - early 20th c., 18 x 51", 6' 10" h. (ILLUS.)........................... **2,990**

Regency breakfront-style bookcase, rosewood, the long rectangular white marble top w/a stepped-out center section w/two doors set w/diamond lattice metal grills flanked by large scroll blocks at the top, the set-back end sections

Regency-Style bookcase, mahogany, rectangular top w/a widely flaring stepped cornice w/a dentil band above a pair of tall diamond-paned glazed doors opening to five adjustable wooden shelves, molded base on ogee bracket feet, ebonized trim, England, Edwardian period, ca. 1905, 19 x 50", 6' 3" h. (ILLUS.).. **1,955**

Extraordinary Aesthetic Movement Bookcase

Victorian Aesthetic Movement break-front-style bookcase, walnut, amboyna & ebonized wood, the long rectangular top w/a stepped-out center section over a pair of tall arched glazed doors opening to wooden shelves, the top glass pane in stained amber green glass in a leaded frame, all above a wide mid-molding over a pair of four-panel cupboard doors, the set-back side sections w/pairs of similar doors above matching pairs of doors in the base, on eight small knob feet, ebonized trim, attributed to Gillow, probably designed by Bruce Talbot, England, third quarter 19th c., 20 1/4 x 120", 7' 4" h. (ILLUS., top of page).................................. **13,800**

Victorian Baroque Revival bookcase, oak, the long rectangular top w/projecting block ends, a wide flaring leaf-carved cornice over a frieze band carved w/scrolling leafy vines flanked by florette side blocks over a pair of tall arched glazed doors opening to wooden shelves, side columns boldly carved w/fruits & leaves above the coved carved apron matching the top cornice, refinished, ca. 1880s, 21 x 54", 6' 8" h. (ILLUS. left) **3,500**

High-crested Golden Oak Bookcase

Victorian Golden Oak bookcase, oak, a high, deeply scalloped & scroll-carved back crest on the rectangular top, a pair of tall glazed doors w/serpentine scroll-

Boldly Carved Baroque Bookcase

carved top borders, a wide serpentine base on block feet, adjustable shelves, original finish, ca. 1900, 16 x 42", 5' 8" h. (ILLUS., previous page) **1,750**

Renaissance Breakfront Bookcase

Victorian Renaissance Revival break-front-style bookcase, walnut, a tall stepped-out central cabinet w/a broken-scroll crest carved w/flowering vines centered by a shell over a wide frieze band over a pair of tall flat reeded pilasters flanking a pair of tall glazed doors over a single paneled cupboard door, the short side cabinets w/scroll-carved crestrails above tall narrow glazed doors over a drawer at the base, conforming molded apron, adjustable wooden shelves, original hardware, refinished, ca. 1875, 21 x 72", 8' h. (ILLUS.) **5,500**

Very Large Renaissance Bookcase

Victorian Renaissance Revival break-front-style bookcase, walnut & burl walnut, the tall stepped-out central section w/a high arched pierced scroll-carved crest over a flaring blocked crest rail over a tall arched glazed door w/raised burl panels at the top & flanked by blocked & leaf-carved designs, the lower side cabinets w/a carved scroll above the flaring cornice over matching narrower glazed doors; the stepped-out lower case w/a pair of raised-panel arched center doors w/wide matching doors at each side, deep molded base, original finish, ca. 1875, 24 x 84", 10' 3" h. (ILLUS.) **10,000**

English William IV Bookcase

William IV bookcase, mahogany, two-part construction: the upper section w/a rectangular top w/a deep, flaring round-cornered cornice above a conforming case w/a pair of tall glazed doors opening to four wooden shelves; the stepped-out lower section w/a pair of drawers above a pair of arched-panel cupboard doors, on a plinth base, England, mid-19th c., 18 1/2 x 53 1/2", 7' 5" h. (ILLUS.) **2,530**

Bureaux Plat

Louis XV-Style bureau plat, ormolu-mounted hardwood, the rectangular top w/serpentine sides decorated w/elaborate inlay surrounding the writing surface, the serpentine floral-inlaid apron fitted w/three hand-dovetailed drawers, the cabriole legs w/elaborate female head ormolu mounts, traces of original gilding, France, early 20th c., separations & chips to veneer, 31 x 63", 32" h. **1,980**

Fine Louis XV-Style Bureau Plat

Louis XV-Style bureau plat, ormolu-mounted kingwood, the rectangular top w/rounded corners fitted w/an ormolu border band enclosing the rectangular writing surface w/old gilt-tooled black leather, the shaped apron on one side fitted w/three drawers w/ornate ormolu pulls & mounts, large ormolu mask mounts at the knee of each cabriole leg ending in ormolu sabots, in the manner of Charles Cressent, France, late 19th c., 31 x 54 1/2", 29" h. (ILLUS., top of page).. **4,140**

Louis XVI-Style bureau plat, ormolu-mounted mahogany, the rectangular top w/a brass-bound border enclosing a yellow leather writing surface, one apron fitted w/pairs of small drawers w/ormolu mounts flanking a single center drawer over the kneehole opening, the corner blocks fitted w/ormolu swag drops, on tapering reeded legs w/ormolu mounts & ending in brass foot caps, France, early 20th c., 30 x 60 1/2", 30" h. (ILLUS., bottom of page) **920**

Louis XVI-Style Bureau Plat

Cabinets

Old Oriental Apothecary Cabinet

Apothecary cabinet, painted & decorated wood, a nearly square top w/molded edges above a tall case w/three rows of nine small square drawers, decorated overall in old reddish brown paint w/dark mustard yellow drawer panels w/Oriental characters on each, drawers w/small ring pulls, probably China, 19th c., later background, 23 1/2 x 26", 5' 6 1/2" h. (ILLUS.)..... **805**

Simple Colonial Revival Cabinet

China cabinet, Colonial Revival, mahogany, a flat plain wide crest board above the half-round D-form top over a conforming case w/two curved glass panels, one forming a hinged door opening to a mirror-backed interior w/two glass shelves, molded half-round apron on three simple curved legs w/scroll-carved corner brackets & ending in paw feet, ca. 1910, refinished, 16 x 24", 5' 6" h. (ILLUS.)............... **1,200**

China cabinet, early 20th c., oak, the half-round top w/a flat center section above a conforming case w/a tall flat glazed center door flanked by curved glass sides, four wooden shelves, molded base on blocky claw-and-ball feet, 16 x 37", 5' 7" h... **920**

Large Renaissance-Style Cabinet

China cabinet, Renaissance-Style, fumed oak, the large rectangular top w/a widely flaring dentil-carved cornice over a wide blocked frieze band centered by a long panel carved w/an urn issuing leafy vines above a pair of tall 12-pane glazed doors flanked by boldly carved caryatids atop carved pilasters, the deep base w/a carved band over a plain band all raised on scroll-carved feet, Flanders, ca. 1900, 24 x 59 1/2", 6' 1" h. (ILLUS.)..................... **1,380**

China cabinet, Rococo Revival style, mahogany, arched serpentine center crestrail w/a carved cartouche flanked by ornate carved scroll bands above a pair of arched glazed doors open to a mirrored back & fixed shelves above three long serpentine-front drawers, each side w/a shorter cabinet w/serpentine short cornice over a narrow conforming glass door & ends backed by a mirror above paneled front & sides; serpentine scroll-carved apron raised on four front cabriole

Large French Rococo China Cabinet

legs w/scroll feet, original finish, France, early 20th c., 22 x 72", 7' h. (ILLUS.).......... **1,800**

Mirrored Crest on Oak Cabinet

China cabinet, Victorian Golden Oak style, the high arched back crestrail w/a shell finial over a shaped oblong beveled mirror flanked by tiny shelves on the half-round top w/flattened center section over the flat tall glass door trimmed w/ornate scrolls, curved glass sides, four wood shelves w/mirrored back in upper half, on simple squared cabriole legs, refinished, ca. 1900, 18 x 48", 6' 3" h. (ILLUS.)... **2,000**

Heavily Carved Oak Cabinet

China cabinet, Victorian Golden Oak style, the wide half-round top w/a wide flattened center section w/a large arched & scroll-carved crest above a conforming frieze band ornately carved w/scrolls, the curved glass center door flanked by dividers, boldly carved blocks & bands of leaf carving resting on heavy blocks over large paw feet, curved glass sides, mirrored interior w/four wooden shelves, refinished, ca. 1890s, 22 x 48", 6' h. (ILLUS.)... **3,500**

Rococo China Cabinet with Mirror

China cabinet, Victorian Rococo substyle, mahogany, two-part construction: the upper section w/a very tall pointed pierced scroll-carved crest & urn-form finials above the arched cornice over a wide single door centered by a large round mirror & flanked by chamfered corners w/scroll-carved drops; the stepped-out lower section w/a rectangular top w/serpentine edges overhanging a case w/a long drawer over a pair of cupboard doors w/large oval veneered panels, chamfered front corners w/scroll-carved drops, projecting rounded base corners on squatty bulbous front feet, 18 x 40", 7' 10" h. (ILLUS.)... **3,000**

Unusual Tall Oak Dentil Cabinet

Two-piece Corner Cupboard

China corner cabinet, Rococo-style, mahogany, two-piece dovetailed construction: the top section w/molded cornice & five garniture platforms above two domed doors, each w/18 panes of glass w/through muntins & pull-out platform & two shelves w/shaped fronts; the base section w/two domed doors, each w/12 panes of glass w/through muntins, partially replaced bracket feet, possibly Dutch, late 18th or early 19th c., 20 x 40", 82" h. (ILLUS.)... **4,840**

Dentil cabinet, Victorian Golden Oak style, the top w/a narrow rectangular shelf & three-quarters arched gallery w/scroll-carved trim above a top section w/a stack of seven small drawers at the left, two small cupboard doors in the center & a rectangular beveled-mirror door on the right, all above a mid-section w/a stack of five long graduated drawers beside a tall flat cupboard door, the bottom section w/a pair of paneled cupboard doors, raised on ogee bracket feet on casters, ca. 1900 (ILLUS., top next column)... **3,600**

Finely Carved Chinese Cabinet

Display cabinet, Oriental-style, rosewood, the tall case w/a stepped Chinese pagoda-style top w/an ornately pierce-carved top crest above a stepped roof w/outswept pierce-carved corners, a glazed door at the front & glass sides all trimmed along the top w/pierced fretwork, the lower front w/a single two-panel door w/bold tree carving in each panel, an ornately carved serpentine apron raised on claw feet, China, late 19th c., 33 1/2 x 46", 8' 4 1/2" h. (ILLUS.) **7,188**

Victorian Bamboo Display Cabinet

Display cabinet, Victorian bamboo-style, the superstructure w/a bamboo framework w/short spindles & frames enclosing two rectangular lacquered panels above the rectangular cabinet w/a pair of tall glazed cupboard doors, bamboo front stiles continuing to outswept front legs, Anglo-Indian, late 19th c., 11 x 23 1/2", 5' h. (ILLUS.) **805**

Renaissance Revival Music Cabinet

Music cabinet, Victorian Renaissance Revival substyle, walnut & burl walnut, the rectangular top above a single door w/a raised molding panel w/roundels & carved musical instruments on the burl ground over a narrow long drawer, ring- and rod-turned quarter-round columns at each side, raised on tapering turned & blocked legs joined by a shaped medial shelf, on pointed knob feet on casters, ca. 1870s, 19 3/4 x 31", 43" h. (ILLUS.) **633**

Side cabinet, Neoclassical, mahogany, rectangular Susini marble top w/elaborate multicolored composition inlay, black & pale salmon rocaille border, central rectangular panel w/two classical figures, signed below "Clemente Susini F. en Firenze 1797," flanked by two side panels w/neoclassical scroll & foliate decoration w/putti; the ormolu-mounted cabinet w/ebonized surface & cast gilt bronze mounts, two doors each w/oval panel w/figures similar to those in marble top & scrolled spandrels, ormolu rocaille frieze, molded base w/bracket feet, back w/paper label reading "Preaubert...S M. Madgar Re (??)," possibly a marriage, extensive losses to veneer & molding, one spandrel missing from one door, cabinet in poor condition, Italy, 18th c., 21 x 43 1/2", 39 1/2" h. **8,800**

Extraordinary Renaissance Cabinet

Side cabinet, Victorian Renaissance Revival substyle, marquetry-inlaid & bronze-mounted rosewood, the large case w/a central shell-carved crest over a marquetry-inlaid panel, the projecting central cupboard door w/a panel framed by marquetry banding & centered by a bronze figural plaque among gilt incising & foliate carving, flanked by niches w/arched mirrors & supported by fluted columns, the mirror fronted by a display shelf, the base edged in Greek key marquetry, the back of the cabinet marked in heavy ink "Elbio 4565," attributed to Pottier & Stymus, New York City, ca. 1875, 20 x 61", 5' 1" h. (ILLUS.) **16,100**

Ornate Renaissance Side Cabinet

Side cabinet, Victorian Renaissance Revival substyle, walnut & burl walnut, the high back crest w/a horizontal spindle between blocks w/pointed finials above carved side scrolls flanking a small rectangular veneer panel over a raised rectangular platform on the rectangular top w/rounded sides, the conforming case w/a narrow drawer slightly projecting above a single door w/an arched molding over an arched burl panel & flanked by half-round tapering columns, incurved side panels on a conforming base molding on low block feet, refinished, ca. 1875, 21 x 44", overall 5' h. (ILLUS.).......... **2,500**

Ornately Carved Burmese Cabinet

Side cabinet, Victorian Rococo substyle, carved hardwood, the very high serpentine backsplash pierce-carved overall w/birds among intertwined leaves & vines, the rectangular top w/a bowed center section above a case w/a pair of tall doors centered by narrow rectangular pierce-carved panels flanking a bowed central door w/a similar panel, the doors separated by boldly fruit-carved pilasters,

deep scalloped & pierce-carved aprons & carved front feet, Burma, mid- to late 19th c., 15 x 48 1/2", overall 4' 3 1/2" h. (ILLUS.).. **1,610**

Spool cabinet, oak, a rectangular top above a case of six long narrow drawers each w/an inset glass panel in gold & black, blocked stiles & flat molded base, wording on panels reads "Clark's - George A. Clark - Sole Agent - O.N.T. - White. - Fast Black" (ILLUS. below, bottom w/Chadwick's spool cabinet)............... **1,100**

Chadwick's & Clark's Spool Cabinets

Spool cabinet, oak, a rectangular top above a stack of four narrow drawers w/small black wood knobs & each w/an inset glass panel w/silver lettering, panels read "Six Cord - Spool - Chadwick's Cotton," scroll-cut corners & flat molded base, slight paint damage, late 19th c. (ILLUS. above, top w/Clark's spool cabinet).. **650**

Oriental Decorated Lacquer Cabinet

Storage cabinet, inlaid & decorated lacquer, a rectangular top above a pair of tall flush doors w/ornate scroll-cut brass hardware, the stiles & door borders in black w/red & green Oriental designs & the recessed door centers w/red ground inlaid & applied w/a continuous scene of vases w/flowers & writing accessories in soapstone, a deep lower drawer w/similar decoration, the recessed side panels w/further soapstone decoration of large vases & tall flowers, scalloped aprons & short block feet, shelved interior, Oriental, probably China, ca. 1920-40, 20 x 26", 4' h. (ILLUS., previous page) **400**

Painted Louis XV-Style Vitrine

Vitrine cabinet, Louis XV-Style, the half-round top w/a low three-quarters pierced brass gallery above a tall door w/a long glazed panel above a bowed lower section centered by an oval reserve painted in the Vernis Martin style, matching sides w/painted panels, raised on slender square splayed legs ending in brass caps, accented overall w/ormolu mounts & millwork, France, late 19th c., 29 1/2" w., 5' 7" h. (ILLUS.)........................ **1,840**

Fine Louis-XVI-Style Vitrine

Vitrine cabinet, Louis-XVI-Style, gilt-bronze mounted marquetry, the rectangular marble top bordered by a gilt-bronze band above a frieze band w/a narrow floral & bird marquetry panel flanked by diamond lattice marquetry all above a tall glazed door opening to three glass shelves & bordered by diamond-lattice marquetry, the rounded front stiles w/ormolu mount, marquetry floral panels & diamond lattice, narrow glazed side panels, the serpentine apron topped by a gilt-bronze band & fitted in the center &

French Art Deco Club Chairs

on the rounded front corners w/gilt-bronze mounts, by Charles Guillaume Diehl, Paris, France, late 19th c., the lock w/his stamped mark, 15 x 30", 4' 3" h. (ILLUS., previous page) **2,185**

Chairs

Art Deco club chairs, leather & mahogany, the rectangular russet leather back above deep squared arms & a deep cushion seat, on short wooden block feet, France, ca. 1930, 30" h., pr. (ILLUS., bottom previous page) **1,955**

Unusual Art Nouveau Side Chair

Art Nouveau side chair, giltwood, the asymmetrical back composed of ornate scrolls enclosing a long fan-shaped caned panel above the wide caned seat, slender cabriole front legs w/scroll-carved knees & seatrail, Europe, late 19th c., 35" h. (ILLUS.) **575**

Italian Baroque-Style Armchair

Baroque-Style armchair, oak, the wide arched & scroll-carved crestrail flanked by scroll-carved ears above the rectan-

gular leather-upholstered back panel raised above the leather seat & flanked by open shaped arms, square legs w/a wide arched & ornate scroll-carved front stretcher & small carved side stretchers, Italian, possibly Tuscan, late 19th c., 47" h. (ILLUS.) **518**

Chippendale Country-style Side Chair

Chippendale country-style side chair, mahogany, openwork splat, scrolled crestrail & ears, drop-in seat w/later upholstery, original glue blocks & handwrought nails, America, probably Virginia, late 18th c., damage & repair to top of crestrail, 37" h. (ILLUS.) **1,760**

Decorated Chippendale Side Chair

Chippendale country-style side chair, painted mahogany, the serpentine crestrail, outswept stiles & pierced vasiform splat all painted w/a finely alligatored design of green & yellow vining w/red flowers on a black ground, paper rush seat, square legs w/molded edges, late 18th c. w/later paint, 36" h. (ILLUS.) **518**

Chippendale Revival Dining Chairs with Pierced Splats

Chippendale Revival dining chairs, mahogany, an ox-yoke crestrail w/ears above slightly canted stiles flanking a pierced scroll-carved vasiform splat, wide upholstered seat, cabriole front legs w/leaf-carved knees & ending in ball-and-claw feet, original finish, new upholstery, ca. 1900, 38" h., set of 6 (ILLUS., top of page).................................. **15,000**

Chippendale-Style chairs: two armchairs & two side chairs; mahogany, openwork splats & carved crestrails, square front legs w/chamfered interior corners & stretcher bases, upholstered shaped seats, late 19th or early 20th c., wear, scratches & minor chips, 40" h., set of 4 (ILLUS., bottom of page)............................ **1,430**

Set of Chippendale-Style Chairs

Chippendale-Style Lolling Chair

Chippendale-Style "lolling" armchair, mahogany, the tall upholstered rectangular back flanked by shaped open arms w/incurved arm supports above the wide upholstered seat, square reeded legs joined by H-stretchers, early 20th c., 42" h. (ILLUS.)... **316**

American Chippendale-Style Chair

Chippendale-Style side chairs, mahogany, the serpentine carved crest above a pierced Gothic style splat over the upholstered slip seat, a shell-carved front seatrail raised on cabriole legs w/scroll-carved knees & ending in claw-and-ball feet, one w/loose joints, other w/small glued crest split, early 20th c., 39 3/4" h., pr. (ILLUS. of one)... **460**

English Chippendale-Style Chair

Chippendale-Style side chair, mahogany, the serpentine crestrail above an ornately pierced splat above the wide upholstered seat, square legs joined by an H-stretcher, England, late 19th c., 37 1/4" h. (ILLUS.)... **173**

Chippendale-Style Chair from Set

Chippendale-Style side chairs, mahogany, the serpentine crest w/carved scrolls above the ornate pierced & scroll-carved splat, upholstered slip seat, plain seatrail on heavy cabriole front legs ending in claw-and-ball feet, old finish, early 20th c., 37 1/4" h., set of four (ILLUS. of one)... **1,265**

Chippendale-Style Wing Chair

Chippendale-Style wing chairs, mahogany, tan upholstery w/woven gold colored outdoor scenes including couples dancing, rolled arms w/serpentine wings, molded front legs, stretcher base, early 20th c., light edge wear & stains, seats 18" h., overall 43" h., pr. (ILLUS. of one) **920**

Classical country style side chairs, curly maple, two arched back slats, scrolled finials, seat frames graduating into rear stiles, saber legs, one back leg w/pegged restoration, seats 17 1/2" h., overall 32 3/4" h., pr. (ILLUS. of one, top next column) **460**

Classical side chair, mahogany, the flat shaped acanthus-carved crestrail above a boss & leaf-carved lower rail, backswept molded stiles flanking the upholstered slip seat, front saber legs w/finely carved hairy ankle & paw feet, America, probably New York, old refinishing, repair

to one rear post & one front foot, 34 1/2" h. **1,650**

Curly Maple Country Side Chair

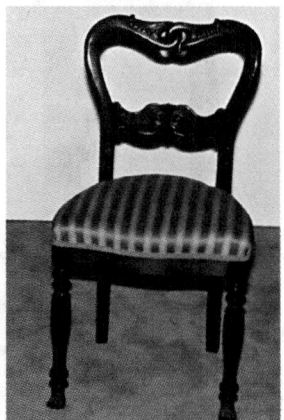

One of a Pair of Transitional Chairs

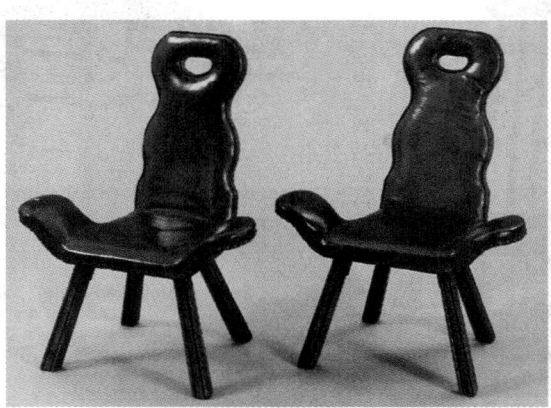

Unusual English Cock-fighting Chairs

Classical-Victorian transitional side chairs, mahogany, open balloon-back w/a pierced scroll-carved crestrail & scroll-carved lower rail above the wide overupholstered seat, serpentine seatrail over baluster-and-ring-turned front legs on small paw feet, refinished, later upholstery, ca. 1840s, 32" h., pr. (ILLUS. of one, previous page) **600**

Cock-fighting chairs, mahogany, tall, narrow, oblong & serpentine leather-upholstered back w/pierced hand hole above the leather-upholstered seat w/outswept low sides, raised on canted square molded legs, England, early 20th c., 32" h., pr. (ILLUS., bottom of previous page) **3,450**

Early American Shaker Highchair

Early American country-style highchair, birch, the tall turned canted back legs forming the back stiles w/small knob finials & flanking three arched slats above simple rod arms joining the canted front legs, woven splint seat, traces of red stain, from the Alfred, Maine, Shaker colony, 19th c., 37" h. (ILLUS.) **1,725**

Early Country-style Rocker

Early American country-style rocking chair w/arms, pine & maple, a stepped oblong crestrail above four tall simple spindles flanked by twisted serpentine stiles, simple rod arms on baluster-and-ring-turned arm supports over the S-roll seat, canted baluster-turned legs joined by stretchers, carpet-cutter rockers, old refinish, ca. 1840, 44" h. (ILLUS.) **300**

Early American country-style side chair, hardwood, two splats w/canted corners between unusual shaped back stiles shaped to a point, damaged original oak split seat, ring-turned legs w/flared feet, probably black paint w/traces of gold highlights, 19th c., scuffs, paint chips, surface wear, seat in poor condition, 30" h. **99**

Early American "ladder-back" armchair, maple & hickory, the tall back w/four arched slats flanked by simple turned stiles w/pointed knob finials above the shaped open arms on baluster-turned arm supports continuing to simple turned legs, woven splint seat, simple turned double stretchers on front & sides of base, mellow refinishing, late 18th - early 19th c., Pennsylvania, 42 3/4" h. **220**

Mace-made Ladder-back Chair

Early American-Style "ladder-back" chair, walnut & hickory, five arched splats, ice cream cone finials, corn-shuck seat, double stretchers, peg feet, Shadrick Mace, North Carolina, 1930s-1950s, scattered chips & flakes, 46" h. (ILLUS.) **358**

Fine French Empire-Style Armchairs

Empire-Style armchairs, mahogany, a square upholstered back w/a back-scrolled frame w/ormolu mounts above padded open arms ending in ormolu eagle head handrests above incurved arm supports, the wide overupholstered seat on a narrow seatrail, shaped tapering squared front legs ending in ormolu paws, France, mid-19th c., 40" h., pr. (ILLUS.) **4,830**

Early Ohio Decorated Side Chair

Federal country-style "fancy" side chair, painted & decorated, the wide slightly curved crestrail over a lower rail & three short arrow slats all between the back-swept tapering stiles, shaped plank seat on ring-turned tapering legs joined by slender turned stretchers, original mustard yellow paint w/black & green foliate decoration on the back rails, branded mark under seat for S. Saiter of Marion County, Ohio, ca. 1840-50, 36" h. (ILLUS.) **863**

Federal country-style rocking chair w/arms, painted & decorated, the tall back w/a notch-cornered crestrail over a similar flat rail above four tall arrow-slats all flanked by tapering styles, flat arms above canted turned spindles, oblong shaped seat on bamboo-turned canted legs on rockers & joined by a turned front stretcher, original black over red graining w/yellow border detail, dark green flowers w/black centers on the crestrail, old John Gordon Gallery label, first-half 19th c., 42 3/4" h. **633**

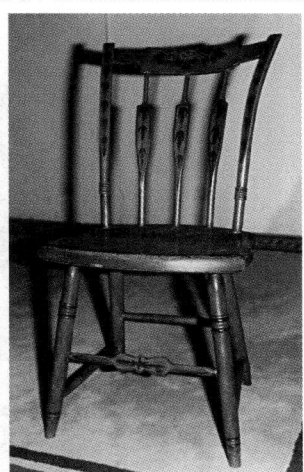

Decorated Federal Side Chair

Federal country-style side chair, painted & decorated pine & maple, a flat gently curved crestrail tapering at each end between tapering curved stiles flanking three arrow slats, wide plank seat over canted simple ring-turned front legs joined by a shaped stretcher, original painted & stenciled decoration w/roses & leaves on the crestrail & bands of leaves down the slats & stiles, ca. 1830, 32" h. (ILLUS., previous page)...................................... **200**

Federal country-style side chairs, curly maple, a wide, narrow & curved crestrail atop tapering stiles joined by a center slat above the rush seat, ring-, knob- and baluster-turned front legs joined by a turned front stretcher, old mellow varnished finish, first half 19th c., 33" h., pr. **275**

One of Two Federal "Fancy" Chairs

Federal "fancy" side chairs, painted & decorated, a rectangular crestrail fitted on stiles joined by three slender lower rails above the balloon-form woven rush seat, tapering ring- and rod-turned front legs joined by simple turned stretchers, original black on red paint simulating rosewood, the crestrail w/gold & red shell & acanthus leaf decoration, further gilt trim, probably New York state, ca. 1820, 33" h., pr. (ILLUS. of one) **546**

George III-Style Armchair

George III-Style armchairs, mahogany, the domed backrail above a pierced wheel-form splat, shaped open arms on incurved arm supports above the padded seat, square paneled tapering legs ending in spade feet & joined by an H-stretcher, England, late 19th c., 38" h., pr. (ILLUS. of one).. **1,955**

Georgian-Style Wingchairs

Georgian-Style wingchairs, upholstered mahogany, the high back & shaped back wings tufted & padded w/leather upholstery continuing to the outscrolled arms above the cushion seat & apron, molded square legs joined by an H-stretcher, England, Edwardian period, ca. 1905, 47" h., pr. (ILLUS., bottom previous page) **4,830**

French Louis XV Armchair

Louis XV fauteuil (open-arm armchair), fruitwood, the squared upholstered back w/molded serpentine framing raised above the wide upholstered seat & flanked by padded molded arms w/incurved arm supports, the serpentine seatrail centered by a carved blossom, cabriole front legs w/floral-carved knees & ending in scrolled toes, France, mid-18th c., 32" h. (ILLUS.) **1,610**

Louis XV-Style Bergere Armchair

Louis XV-Style bergeres (closed-arm armchairs), giltwood, the tall upholstered back w/a gently arched crestrail continuing around the shaped upholstered wings that taper to the padded closed arms, wide cushion seat, molded

serpentine seatrail centered by carved florals & continuing into short front cabriole legs w/floral-carved knees & ending in scrolled toes, France, late 19th c., 44" h., pr. (ILLUS. of one) **2,990**

Louis XV-Style Fauteuil Armchair

Louis XV-Style fauteuil (open-arm armchair), giltwood, the wide caned back w/an arched crestrail centered by a pierce-carved scroll crest, scroll-carved stiles above the padded, molded open arms above the wide cushion seat, molded serpentine seatrail centered by a scroll-carved reserve & continuing to cabriole legs w/shell-carved knees & ending in scrolled toes, France, late 19th c., 43" h. (ILLUS.) **1,265**

Fine Louis XVI-Style Wingchair

Louis XVI-Style bergere avec orielles (wingchair), polychromed wood, the tall upholstered back w/an arched leaf-carved crestrail centered by a floral crest & continuing around the incurved upholstered back wings down to the low padded closed arms flanking the wide cushion seat, the seatrail carved w/leaf bands flanking a floral-carved reserve above the turned tapering fluted legs ending in peg feet, France, first half 19th c., 46 1/4" h. (ILLUS.)... **4,830**

Classic Eames-Designed Armchair

Louis XVI-Style Fauteuils

Louis XVI-Style fauteuils (open-arm armchairs), giltwood, the peaked & curved crestrail w/bellflower decoration & artichoke finials above the squared upholstered back, padded open arms on urn-shaped arm supports, cushion seat above turned beechwood legs, old cotton upholstery, label for "Flint & Horner," early 20th c., upholstery faded & soiled, 37" h., pr. (ILLUS.)....................................... **2,090**

Modern style Eames armchair & ottoman, laminated wood & leather, the high wide back w/a padded black leather curved upper panel above a lower panel flanked by rolled upholstered arms & wide upholstered seat, all within a laminated wood framework, raised & swiveling on a metal pedestal supported on a star-shaped metal base, produced by Herman Miller & w/original paper label, mid-20th c., worn original leather, armchair 32" h., 2 pcs. (ILLUS. of chair only)... **1,265**

Moravian closed-stool chair, walnut & poplar, the high rectangular back w/vertical slats above two arms w/scrolled ends & chamfered arm supports, the lift-seat above a deep apron, mortise-and-tenon construction, front, side & back w/frame-&-panel construction, sliding panel on back, Salem, North Carolina, 1810-40, old refinishing, 19 3/4 x 22 1/4", 43 3/4" h.. **1,430**

Elaborate Moroccan Armchairs

Moroccan armchairs, inlaid & marquetry fruitwood, the stepped & blocked crestrail w/ornate mother-of-pearl & marquetry inlay above the low angular inlaid arms & a paneled & inlaid central back panel flanked by turned spindles & side panels, wide tapering ornately inlaid seat raised on deep arched & ornately inlaid base panels between the square line-incised legs ending in turned disk feet, Morocco, late 19th c., 33 1/2" h., pr. (ILLUS., bottom previous page).. **920**

Fine Baltic Neoclassical Armchair

Neoclassical armchairs, birch, the long gently curved rectangular tiger-grained crestrail raised on a squared frame enclosing a pierced & ebonized scroll-carved splat, turned rounded arms above the upholstered seat, flat seatrail raised on baluster- and ring-turned front legs ending in button feet, Baltic region, mid-19th c., 36" h., pr. (ILLUS. of one)............. **2,070**

Nutting "Comb-back" Armchair

Nutting-signed "comb-back" Windsor armchair, mixed woods w/golden brown finish, the slender serpentine crestrail w/curled ears raised on nine slender spindles continuing through the U-form

mid-rail that forms the flat arms w/scrolled hand grips on canted, baluster-turned arm supports, wide shaped saddle seat, canted bold baluster- and ring-turned legs joined by a swelled H-stretcher, branded Wallace Nutting signature beneath seat, seat 18" h., overall 44" h. (ILLUS.) **1,955**

Chinese Dragon-armed Armchair

Oriental armchair, carved rosewood, the arched back ornately pierce-carved w/entwined dragon bodies & scrolls continuing into the arms formed by the dragon body & ending in dragon heads & raised on ornately carved arm supports, the wide seat w/a serpentine molded seatrail w/a pierced scroll carving & continuing into the heavy cabriole front legs ending in scroll feet, China, ca. 1900, 36" h. (ILLUS.) **863**

Chinese Dragon-Carved Armchair

Oriental armchair, carved teakwood, the high arched crestrail pierce-carved w/a pair of facing dragons among clouds above the wide solid back panel carved w/a large coiling dragon, the open arms ending in dragon heads holding pearls on reeded incurved arm supports, the wide seat w/a serpentine molded front above a pierce-carved seatrail over the cabriole front legs w/large winged bats carved at the knees & ending in scroll feet, old reddish brown finish, China, late 19th - early 20th c., 44 1/2" h. (ILLUS.)............................ **575**

Ornate Inlaid Persian Side Chair

Persian side chair, carved & inlaid hardwood, the tall rectangular back formed by a series of interlocking spindles & balls & framed by mother-of-pearl-inlaid stiles w/urn-form finials, the upholstered seat above a similarly formed apron between square inlaid legs ending in pad feet, an inscription under the seat in an archaic Persian dialect, late 19th c., 41" h. (ILLUS.)... **805**

Queen Anne side chair, Santo Domingo mahogany, the ox-yoke crestrail w/shaped ears centered by a carved shell above the scroll-carved vasiform splat, trapezoidal slip seat on cabriole front legs w/shaped returns & ending in raised pad feet, old dark finish, attributed to the Philadelphia area, 18th c., 38 1/4" h. (replaced corner blocks)............. **3,300**

Queen Anne side chair, walnut, serpentine crestrail w/flared ears above the vasiform splat, the slip seat w/faded blue & white floral upholstery, cabriole front legs w/trifid feet & scalloped returns, the molded seat frame mortised through the rear stiles, "Hannah Jarrett Spencer" painted inside seat frame in old white, attributed to Philadelphia, 18th c., overall 38" h. **5,175**

Queen Anne-Style Side Chair

Queen Anne-Style side chairs, mahogany, the ox-yoke crestrail above a tall vasiform splat, the upholstered slip seat in a plain seatrail raised on cabriole front legs ending in pad feet, glued split at top of one leg, America, early 20th c., 41" h., pr. (ILLUS. of one)... **173**

Fine Decorated Regency Armchair

Regency armchair, painted & decorated wood, the flat crestrail w/a pair of white-painted incised panels flanking a lion mask boss, the lower pierced rail also centered by a lion mask boss, serpentine back stiles & scrolled open arms raised on turned tapering post supports above the wide caned seat, flat fluted & gilt-trimmed seatrail, square tapering & slightly outswept fluted front legs, overall rosewood graining & white trim, England, first quarter 19th c., 36" h. (ILLUS.)............ **1,495**

Rococo-Style side chairs, painted wood, upholstered shaped back & seat, serpentine seatrail over cabriole front legs, old grey-green paint, Italy, probably early 20th c., chips & losses to paint, several frames loose, upholstery w/stains & losses, 38" h., set of 7....................................... **2,420**

Rustic Folk Art Twig Chair

Rustic style folk art twig chair, rectangular back formed by crossed bent twigs, single-twig low arms slope to front legs, cross-stretcher base, chip-carved surface w/green paint, Blowing Rock, North Carolina, or East Tennessee, early 20th c., paint w/losses & chips, 47" h. (ILLUS.)..... **770**

Shaker Ladder-back Side Chair

Shaker "ladder-back" side chair, birch, three arched slats between turned stiles w/oval finials above the woven rush seat, slender legs & posts w/wooden tilters on back feet, double stretchers on front & sides, attributed to Enfield, New Hampshire, seat 18" h., overall 41" h. (ILLUS.) .. **2,070**

Fussy Aesthetic Movement Chair

Victorian Aesthetic Movement side chair, Louis XV inspiration, giltwood, the wide ornately scroll-carved & pierced crestrail w/a small inset marquetry panel above an upholstered D-form back panel over a pierced scroll-carved & spindled panel, the wide over-upholstered spring seat above a shaped seatrail centered by another small marquetry panel, on scroll-carved front cabriole legs ending in peg feet, England or America, late 19th c., 32" h. (ILLUS.) **546**

Victorian Baroque Revival side chairs, oak, the high rectangular upholstered back raised above the wide spring cushion upholstered seat w/a molded seatrail centered by a scroll-carved front drop, raised on ring- and rod-turned legs joined by an H-stretcher w/scroll-carved trim, Italy, mid-19th c., 38 1/2" h., set of 4 (ILLUS., below).. **1,725**

Italian Baroque Revival Side Chairs

Nicely Carved Renaissance Revival Dining Chairs

upholstery, ca. 1870s, 36" h., set of 4
(ILLUS., top of page).................................... **800**

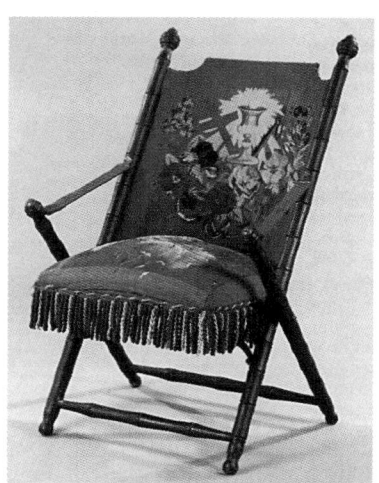

Unique Hunzinger Folding Chair

Victorian "patent" folding armchair, walnut, the needlepoint upholstered back & seat featuring ecclesiastical designs of a communion chalice & flowers, fitted on a folding bamboo-turned frame w/large knob finials & bamboo-turned stretchers, incised stamp mark & label of George Hunzinger, New York City, ca. 1880, 37" h. (ILLUS.)... **1,035**

Victorian Renaissance Revival dining chairs, walnut, an arched & ornately scroll-carved crestrail centered by a shell above a pierced leaf-sprig-carved & lunette-carved splat above a lower arched rail, molded straight stiles above the over-upholstered seat, line-incised seatrail above tapering ring-turned legs w/peg feet, original finish, old vinyl

Rare Branch-carved Hall Chair

Victorian Renaissance Revival hall chair, carved walnut, the tall pierced back ornately carved w/a pointed palmette crest above entwined leafy oak branches w/large acorns, above the flat trapezoidal seat w/molded edges above a curved apron carved w/crossed oak leaves & acorns, raised on ring- and rod-turned reeded legs w/knob feet, by Mitchell and Rammelsberg of Cincinnati, Ohio, 18 x 20", 4' h. (ILLUS.) **5,000**

Child's Renaissance Revival Chair

Victorian Renaissance Revival substyle child's armchair, gilt-incised & ebonized walnut, the arched crestrail centered by a raised platform & demi-lune crest & w/roundel-set ears above a pierced urn-form splat, the squared open arms on trumpet-turned arm supports above the wide upholstered seat, the gently curved seatrail w/a center drop & cross-incised corner blocks above the trumpet-turned front legs w/peg feet, America, ca. 1875, 26 1/2" h. (ILLUS.) **633**

Fabulous Belter "Fountain Elms" Pattern Armchair

Victorian Rococo armchair, carved & laminated rosewood, the high balloon back centered by an upholstered oval panel surrounded by an ornately pierce-carved frame, the arched scroll crestrail topped by a high floral-carved crest & continuing into the scroll- and leaf-carved serpentine sides above the shaped open arms w/incurved arm supports, a serpentine front seatrail centered by a carved floral cluster, demi-cabriole front legs w/floral-carved knees, "Fountain Elms" pattern by John H. Belter, New York City, ca. 1855, arm restorations & edge chips, 43" h. (ILLUS.) **10,925**

Rococo Armchair Attributed to Roux

Victorian Rococo armchair, carved rosewood, the large oval back w/an ornate pierce-carved scroll crestrail continuing to form the oval molding enclosing the upholstered back panel, padded serpentine open arms on incurved scroll-carved arm supports flanking the wide upholstered seat w/a serpentine fruit-and-leaf-carved seatrail above demi-cabriole front legs on casters, attributed to Alexander Roux, New York City, ca. 1860, refinished, new upholstery, 45" h. (ILLUS.) **2,500**

Victorian Rococo armchair, rosewood, high rounded back rail w/a pierced scroll-carved crest over the tufted upholstered back flanked by closed upholstered arms w/incurved arm supports, serpentine apron above demi-cabriole front legs on casters, ca. 1860 .... **476**

Unusual Victorian Rococo Armchair

Belter Victorian Rococo Armchair & Side Chair

Victorian Rococo "barrel-back" armchair, mahogany, the simple molded & scroll-carved arched crestrail above the tufted upholstered back continuing down to form the low upholstered arms flanking the upholstered spring seat, molded serpentine seatrail, molded demi-cabriole front legs, ca. 1860-70, 38" h. (ILLUS., previous page) **2,530**

Victorian Rococo chairs, laminated rosewood, arched crestrail w/elaborately carved fruit & flower crest above the shaped upholstered back w/green velvet upholstery, shaped upholstered seat w/serpentine seatrail carved w/further florals, on cabriole front legs on brass casters; the armchair probably "Rosalie" patt., w/shield-shape back, scrolled arms, probably original casters & surface, 40" h.; the side chair w/double-scrolled supports, probably original surface, 37" h., John Henry Belter, New York City, ca. 1850s, small chips & losses to carving, pr. (ILLUS., top of page) **3,520**

balloon back w/an oblong tufted upholstered panel enclosed by a molded frame, the armchair w/padded open arms on incurved arm supports, both w/wide upholstered spring seats on molded serpentine seatrails continuing into demi-cabriole front legs ending in casters, ca. 1870, armchair 40" h., pr. (ILLUS.)................ **518**

Belter Carved Rosewood Side Chair

Victorian Rococo side chair, carved & laminated rosewood, the tall back framework composed of large carved C-scrolls enclosing pierce-carved grapevines & w/a carved floral crest all centered by a small round upholstered panel, the deep over-upholstered spring seat on a serpentine seatrail w/floral carving & cabriole front legs w/floral-carved knees, on casters, original finish, reupholstered, John Henry Belter, ca. 1855, 40" h. (ILLUS.).. **3,800**

Victorian Rococo Parlor Chairs

Victorian Rococo parlor chairs, walnut, an armchair & side chair, each w/a wide

Ornately Carved Rococo Side Chairs

Victorian Rococo side chairs, carved & laminated rosewood, a tall back w/an ornate pierced & scroll-carved framework w/a pair of cornucopia forming the crest above the tall rounded & serpentine-sided upholstered back panel, rounded upholstered seat w/an ornately carved serpentine seatrail & carved S-scroll front legs on casters, new red upholstery, attributed to John H. Belter, New York City, ca. 1855, 38" h. pr. (ILLUS., top of page).. **5,520**

stered panel below the high arched & pierced crestrail carved w/scrolls & floral clusters & raised on baluster- and ring-turned free-standing back stiles above a scalloped lower back raise, S-scroll skirt guards flanking the wide round upholstered seat & conforming seatrail carved w/scrolls & raised on ring-turned tapering front legs on casters, ca. 1870, 40 3/4" h., pr. (ILLUS. of one)......................... **920**

Victorian Rococo Slipper Chair

Victorian Rococo slipper chairs, carved walnut, the tall back w/an oblong uphol-

English William IV Hall Chair

William IV hall chairs, mahogany, the tall back w/a fanned & fluted crest above large S-scrolls framing the back panel centered by a large rosette, the solid trapezoidal seat above ring-turned tapering front legs w/disk feet, England, second quarter 19th c., 35" h., pr. (ILLUS. of one, previous page)...................................... **2,990**

William & Mary side chairs, maple, yoked & carved crestrails above vasiform splats, molded stiles over the rush seats, front skirts w/cutouts, front block & knob-turned legs, front stretcher w/bulbous turning, marked for "3" & "9" of larger set, probably America, first half 18th c., old refinishing, traces of old red paint, one leg w/repaired split, one seat w/original rail w/rose-head nails, 40 x 19 x 17", pr..... **2,530**

Windsor "Comb-back" Rocker

Windsor "continuous-arm" armchair, a narrow arched crestrail curving down to form slender arms all above 11 turned spindles, canted baluster- and ring-turned arm supports, shaped saddle seat on canted baluster- and ring-turned legs joined by a swelled H-stretcher, old dry black paint, late 18th c., 38 1/4" h. (glued splits in arms) **550**

Windsor "Birdcage" Side Chair

Windsor "birdcage" side chairs, hardwood w/old mustard paint, seven-spindle back, shield-shape seats w/incised detail around spindles & fronts, bamboo turned legs & rungs, glued split in seat of one chair, another w/wear, seats 17" h., overall 33 1/4" h., set of 4 (ILLUS. of one) **1,955**

Windsor "braced bow-back" side chair, painted, the wide bowed crestrail over seven swelled spindles & w/two canted braces behind, above a shaped saddle seat on canted baluster- and ring-turned legs joined by a swelled H-stretcher, old black paint w/evidence of earlier colors, late 18th - early 19th c., 36 1/2" h. (restored split in seat) **495**

Windsor "comb-back" rocker, hardwood w/old dark refinishing, curved crestrail over seven spindles continuing through the U-form mid-rail & continuing to form scrolled arms over two spindles & a canted baluster-turned arm support, "D"-shape seat w/incised edging, canted baluster- and ring-turned legs joined by a swelled H-stretcher & mortised into shaped rockers, attributed to Philadelphia, Pennsylvania, arms missing bottoms of knuckle scrolls, replaced crest, restorations, seat 14" h., overall 37" h. (ILLUS., top of next column) **863**

George III English Windsor Chair

Windsor "fan-back" armchair, elm & maple, the tall back w/a serpentine crestrail above an upper vasiform splat flanked by three spindles on each side over a U-form medial rail forming the flat arms & raised on another splat & spindles w/five spindles under each arm & an incurved arm support, wide shaped seat on canted rear legs & cabriole front legs ending in pad feet, joined by a turned H-stretcher, England, ca. 1800, 42" h. (ILLUS.)............. **1,725**

Windsor "fan-back" side chair, painted, thin serpentine crestrail over seven spindles flanked by canted baluster- and ring-turned stiles over a shaped saddle seat, canted baluster- and rod-turned legs joined by a swelled H-stretcher, worn green repaint over earlier red, late 18 - early 19th c., 35" h. (old restoration) **550**

Nicely Decorated Windsor Rocker

Windsor tall-backed rocking chair w/arms, painted & decorated, the wide rectangular crestrail raised on seven slender turned spindles flanked by turned stiles, serpentine arms over two turned spindles & a canted turned arm support, wide shaped plank seat raised on bamboo-turned canted legs joined by box stretchers & mortised into rockers, original yellow paint w/gold & black line edging & fruit & scrolls in dark green & gold on the crestrail, walnut arms w/old brown finish, stamped mark under seat appears to read "E.R. Norman," New England, ca. 1830, 46 1/2" h. (ILLUS.)............................. **1,265**

Chests & Chests of Drawers

Adam Revival chest of drawers, brass-mounted & polychromed satinwood, the rectangular yellow & brown marble top w/a narrow stepped-out front section above a conforming case w/four long, graduated drawers, the front decorated overall w/continuous polychrome leafy vines & floral garlands, the third drawer centered by an oval reserve w/a black ground painted w/a shaded gold neoclassical figural scene, black banding w/further neoclassical designs framing the case, molded base raised on turned disk & peg feet, in the 18th c. style of Robert Adam, England, ca. 1900, 23 x 51", 36" h. (ILLUS., bottom of page) **4,025**

Fine Adam Revival Style Chest

Chinese Pine Altar Chest

Altar chest, Oriental, pine, the long narrow plain top above a case w/a row of paneled & lotus-carved drawers above a row of four plain panels, heavy square legs w/long carved front brackets, scroll-cut long brackets down the sides of the case, China, late 19th c., 17 1/2 x 76 1/2", 33" h. (ILLUS., top of page) **1,035**

Baroque vergueno, rectangular top above a dovetailed cabinet w/iron mounts, fitted w/three drawers flanking a central door opening to three drawers & above a single bottom drawer, the drawers ornately decorated w/bone-inlaid stars w/spiral columns, the door front w/architectural spiral columns w/scrolled pediment, compressed bun feet, Spain, probably 17th c., separations, repairs, inlay losses, missing one lock set, 21 x 34", 13" h. **5,720**

Blanket chest, Chippendale country-style, pine w/old blue paint & faded bittersweet trim, single-board molded top w/iron strap hinges over dovetailed case w/covered till, molded base w/shaped bracket feet, restorations, 20 1/2 x 49 1/2", 26" h. (ILLUS., bottom of page) **1,150**

Pine Blanket Chest with Old Blue Paint

Early American Country Blanket Chest

Blanket chest, early American country-style, pine w/old blue paint, single board scalloped ends, the lid w/molded edge, the interior w/unusual till w/reeded lid & dovetailed drawer below, New England, end battens of lid have screws added, lock escutcheon missing, edge wear, chip, 17 x 48", 24" h. (ILLUS., above) **1,495**

Blanket chest, Federal, walnut, the top w/applied molding, the interior w/lidded till & dovetailed drawer, top of front inlaid w/extensive tassel, vine, turnip & teardrop designs, sides w/shaped skirt & barberpole inlay, original French feet w/shaped skirt w/extensive fan, barberpole & tassel inlay, original glue blocks, Tennessee, first quarter 19th c., lid hinges repaired, some veneer losses, old refinishing, scattered scratches & dents, feet w/repaired tips, 17 3/4 x 38", 20 1/2" h. (ILLUS., bottom of page).......... **46,200**

Federal Walnut Blanket Chest

Fine Soap Hollow Blanket Chest

Blanket chest, painted & decorated poplar, pine & chestnut, the rectangular top lifting above a well w/a lidded till, a pair of molded drawers at the bottom, molded base on simple bracket feet, original black over red painted spiral decoration, strong gold-stenciled initials "N.H." on the front w/a ghost image of the date "1904," black-painted detail on feet & moldings, floral decals on case & drawers, nailed drawers w/white porcelain pulls, Soap Hollow type, attributed to the Sala Brothers of Pennsylvania, 20 3/4 x 48", 25" h. (ILLUS.)... **7,475**

Early Mustard Yellow Blanket Chest

Blanket chest, painted poplar, the rectangular top w/a molded edge opening to a well w/a covered till, a dovetailed case w/narrow base molding & turned bun feet, old dark mustard yellow paint, mid-19th c., 18 x 38", 22" h. (ILLUS.)................... **460**

Cellaret (wine chest) on stand, Federal, inlaid cherry, compartmentalized dovetailed top, lid & front w/string & star or floral inlay, base w/dovetailed drawer above tapered legs w/descending bellflower inlay & extensive single & double string inlay, original brass hinges, probably Piedmont, North Carolina, early 19th c., missing original lock, brass pulls replaced, old refinishing, some fading, 12 1/2 x 13", 16" h. (ILLUS., top next column)... **15,400**

Chippendale chest of drawers, cherry, rectangular two-board top w/molded edges above the dovetailed case w/four long graduated drawers flanked by quarterround corner columns above a base molding on ogee bracket feet, original

dark reddish brown finish & old thin coat of wax, attributed to Lebanon County, Pennsylvania, late 19th c., 22 1/2 x 44", 37" h. (minor glued splits in feet, replaced simple bail pulls).. **7,700**

Federal Cherry Cellaret on Stand

Maple & Birch Chippendale Chest

Chippendale chest of drawers, maple & birch, rectangular one-board top above a case of four long graduated beaded drawers w/replaced batwing brasses & escutcheons, molded base on ogee bracket feet, refinished, feet & base moldings old replacements, one baseboard missing, initialed inside "H.T.," late 18th - early 19th c., 20 1/2 x 40 3/4", 35 1/2" h. (ILLUS.).. **1,093**

Fine Chippendale Chest-on-Chest

Chippendale chest-on-chest, curly maple, two-part dovetailed construction: the upper section w/cove molded cornice above five graduated drawers; the bottom section w/three drawers; all w/beaded trim & original brass pulls, molded waist & base, high bracket feet w/scalloped returns, a couple splits to foot facings w/section of one back facing missing, 37 1/2 x 20", 6' 5" h. (ILLUS.) **23,000**

Chippendale country-style blanket chest, painted pine, rectangular top w/molded edges opening to a well w/till & iron strap hinges, dovetailed case w/a row of two larger flanking a small drawer across the bottom, molded base on scroll-cut bracket feet, original blue paint w/later black on base molding & feet, late 18th - early 19th c., 23 1/4 x 52", 27" h. (replaced bail pulls, restorations w/replacements & paint touch-up) **1,210**

Dark Mahogany Classical Chest

Classical chest of drawers, mahogany & mahogany veneer, the rectangular top above a case w/a long top drawer w/an inset arch projecting over three long deep drawers w/original pressed glass pulls flanked by ring-turned & leaf-carved half-columns, raised on heavy carved front paw feet, top w/old refinishing, remainder w/original dark finish, age split in top, ca. 1840, 21 1/4 x 47", 49" h. (ILLUS.) **460**

Classical Country-style Butler's Chest

Classical country-style butler's chest of drawers, curly maple, central pull-out top drawer w/eight dovetailed graduated & cockbeaded drawers, central prospect door w/two drawers behind, six cubbyholes, three long drawers flanked by beaded pilasters, turned & reeded legs, bottom of fall-front pull-out drawer w/chalk inscription, possibly initials, faint pencil inscription on back of top graduated drawer, Tennessee, early 19th c., old refinishing, some separation to top, 46 x 43 x 23" (ILLUS.) **2,310**

Coffer chest, Louis XIV Provincial, carved oak, long rectangular hinged top opening to a well, the case front heavily carved w/bands of shallow geometric designs & scrolls, heavy stile legs, back of plank construction, restorations, France, late 17th c., 22 x 67 1/2", 27 1/2" h. (ILLUS., top next page) **1,725**

Early American country-style blanket chest, painted & decorated poplar & pine, the rectangular hinged top w/molded edges opening to a well & till, dovetailed cast w/a mid-molding over a pair of bottom drawers, narrow base molding raised on turned bulbous double-knob feet, original reddish brown flame graining w/black, brown & mustard yellow on the drawer fronts, wrought-iron strap hinges, first half 19th c., 22 3/4 x 50", 28 1/2" h. (old replaced bail drawer pulls & front lock escutcheon, insect damage on back & bottom, one foot w/glued repair) **825**

Provincial Louis XIV Coffer Chest

Late Federal "Bow-front" Chest

Federal "bow-front" chest of drawers, mahogany & mahogany veneer, the rectangular top w/a bowed front & ovolu projecting corners above a conforming case w/four long graduated drawers w/replaced batwing brasses, ring- and spiral-turned columns down the side, scalloped apron, raised on baluster- and ring-turned legs w/peg feet, originally had a small case on top w/bonnet drawers, New England, ca. 1820, 19 x 40", 39 1/2" h. (ILLUS.).. **920**

Fine Federal Butler's Chest

Federal butler's chest of drawers, mahogany & cherry, the rectangular top above a row of three narrow drawers over a deep drawer w/fold-down front forming a writing surface & enclosing small compartments above three long graduated drawers, batwing brasses, molded base on incurved bracket feet, late 18th c., 20 3/4 x 48", 46" h. (ILLUS.)...................... **4,370**

Rare Federal Chest of Drawers

Federal chest of drawers, bow-front chest w/light wood corner inlay, four graduated dovetailed & cockbeaded drawers w/string & oval inlay, fancy book-matched walnut veneer drawer facings, top drawer w/compartments & ratchet for lift-up dressing mirror w/single-line inlay, inlaid pointed oval escutcheons, skirt w/light inlay & demi-lune fan apron, shaped French feet, includes box of parts, mostly interior compartment sections & supports, Tennessee, 1800-1819, repairs, veneer chips, stains, minor separations, base missing original glue blocks, one rear glue block replaced, most of missing inlay on front present but not attached, 23 3/4 x 44", 39 1/2" h. (ILLUS.) **33,000**

Cherry Federal Chest of Drawers

Federal chest of drawers, cherry, four dovetailed drawers w/beaded edges, line inlay & original oval brasses w/embossed plow designs, ring-turned legs w/raised beaded panels on ends, Kentucky, bolt missing from one brass, 21 1/2 x 42 1/2", 41 1/2" h. (ILLUS.) **3,105**

Fine Federal Cherry Chest-on-Chest

Federal chest-on-chest, cherry, two-part construction: the upper section w/a rect-angular top w/a coved cornice above a row of three small drawers above a stack of four long graduated drawers flanked by quarter-round reeded columns; the lower section w/a mid-molding above a case w/three long graduated drawers, original oval brasses, molded base on tall French feet, old refinish, glued splits on foot facings, late 18th - early 19th c., 22 x 40 1/2", 6' 2 1/4" h. (ILLUS.) **13,513**

Inlaid Cherry Chest of Drawers

Federal country-style chest of drawers, cherry, double-line inlaid top over four graduated dovetailed & cockbeaded drawers w/double-string inlay, chamfered corners w/line inlay, shaped feet & skirt, chalk inscription inside at bottom of proper right side reads "Amos Downey (?)," interior bottom of top drawer w/painting of three figures including woman w/curly black hair, Kentucky, feet & skirt probably replacements, separation, splits & old paint, two backboards missing, repair to runners, replaced brass pulls, locks missing, old refinishing, 19 1/2 x 39", 39 1/2" h. (ILLUS.) **2,970**

Southern Federal Walnut Chest

Federal country-style chest of drawers, walnut, the rectangular top w/light-wood corner inlay, the case w/two over three dovetailed drawers w/triple dark & light string inlay, original brass pulls & inlaid kite escutcheons, shaped skirt w/French feet, yellow pine vertical backboards w/cut nails, original glue blocks for skirt & feet, American South, patches to foot, refinished, 21 1/2 x 42", 39 1/2" h. (ILLUS.) **990**

Federal "Swell-front" Chest

Federal "swell-front" chest of drawers, mahogany & cherry veneer, rectangular top over four graduated dovetailed & cockbeaded drawers w/brass pulls, prob-

ably original, w/inlaid diamond escutcheons, the top drawer w/compartments, original skirt w/cherry veneer, feet facings w/V joints, horizontal backboards, Kentucky, scratches, small dents, one escutcheon off but present, replaced glue blocks & rear returns, old refinishing, 22 x 39 5/8", 38 1/2" h. (ILLUS.) **15,400**

Federal tall chest of drawers, cherry, rectangular top above a row of three dovetailed & cockbeaded drawers, the central drawer w/interior compartments w/two interior drawers, a stack of four long graduated drawers below, oval brass pulls, frame-and-panel sides, fluted pilasters down the front sides, spiral-turned legs, horizontal backboards, America, second quarter 19th c., old refinishing, separations, traces of old white paint, drawer runners rebuilt, replaced pulls, top backboards replaced, repair & restorations, 21 x 45", 4' 6" h. **2,530**

George III Chest-on-Chest

George III chest-on-chest, mahogany, two-part construction: the upper section w/a flaring stepped cornice above a pair of drawers over a stack of three long graduated drawers; the lower section w/a mid-molding over three long graduated drawers, molded base w/scroll-cut bracket feet, batwing brasses, England, ca. 1800, 21 x 44", 5' 8 1/2" h. (ILLUS.) **1,610**

Georgian-Style chest of drawers, mahogany, rectangular molded top over four long graduated dovetailed & cockbeaded drawers w/ornate brass pulls & escutcheons, molded base w/straight bracket feet, England, 19th c., large crack in top, feet replaced, missing four pulls, chips, scratches, old refinishing, 23 x 47", 41" h. **715**

Early English Jacobean Revival Chest of Drawers

Jacobean Revival chest of drawers, black-lacquered & decorated wood, the rectangular top w/brass corner caps above a case w/a pair of drawers over two small drawers flanking a deep square drawer over a small drawer, all above a pair of bottom drawers, heavy bun feet, decorated overall w/polychrome Oriental figures & landscapes, small ring pulls, England, first quarter 19th c., 19 1/2 x 40 1/4", 33" h. (ILLUS., above) **4,140**

ers, serpentine scroll-carved apron on cabriole legs w/raised scroll feet, extensive overall scroll & floral carving, ornate brass pulls, back w/three panels, France, 18th c., losses & repairs to decoration on top drawer, rebuilding & repairs, 21 1/2 x 39 1/2", 34" h. **7,700**

Early New England Mule Chest

Mule chest (box chest w/one or more drawers below a storage compartment), Chippendale country-style, painted pine, a rectangular one-board top w/molded edges & wrought-iron staple hinges opening to a deep well w/an old large brass batwing escutcheon at the top front above a long dovetailed base drawer w/replaced wood knob pulls, molded base on shaped bracket feet, rosehead nail construction, old reddish brown paint, split in one front foot, interior lid lock & drawer escutcheon missing, New England, 18th c., 19 1/2 x 42 3/4", 33 1/4" h. (ILLUS.)...................................... **2,530**

French Louis Philippe Chest

Louis Philippe chest of drawers, walnut & burl walnut, the rectangular charcoal marble top overhanging a case w/canted front corners & a paneled long frieze drawer over three long drawers, deep molded base on low block feet, wreath-form ring pulls & pierced brass keyhole escutcheons, France, second quarter 19th c., 22 x 49 1/2", 39 1/2" h. (ILLUS.) ... **3,450**

Louis XV chest of drawers, walnut, rectangular molded & shaped top above a case w/two conforming long dovetailed draw-

Early Pine Two-drawer Mule Chest

Country Chippendale Mule Chest

Mule chest (box chest w/one or more drawers below a storage compartment), Chippendale country-style, painted pine, the rectangular top w/molded edges opening to a deep well faced by two false drawer fronts, two long drawers below, molded base on scroll-carved bracket feet, old replaced batwing brasses & keyhole escutcheons, restorations to top, feet ended out, hand-painted inscription on back reads "R. Hathaway, Hudson, Mich.," old reddish brown finish, attributed to New England, late 18th - early 19th c., 18 1/2 x 40 3/4", 42 1/4" h. (ILLUS.) **1,610**

Mule chest (box chest w/one or more drawers below a storage compartment), country-style, painted pine, the rectangular one-board top w/molded

edges opening to a deep well above two long dovetailed drawers w/old wooden pulls, single-board sides w/bootjack legs & a base molding, rosehead nail construction, old dark red paint, New England, small molding around upper front missing sections, edge chips to feet & top, 18th c., 17 1/2 x 38", 38 1/2" h. (ILLUS.) **1,035**

Neoclassical chests of drawers, walnut & walnut veneer, a rectangular top over a case w/a long overhanging drawer above three long graduated drawers flanked by engaged columns w/carved giltwood caryatid capitals & acanthus leaf bases, on square tapering feet, the frieze drawer fitted as a secretary drawer, Austria, first quarter 19th c., 23 1/2 x 48 1/4", 39" h., pr. (ILLUS., bottom of page) **10,063**

Fine Pair of Austrian Neoclassical Chests of Drawers

Tall Chinese Chest-on-Chest

Oriental chest-on-chest, pine, three-part construction: the top section w/a rectangular top w/flaring stepped cornice above a pair of large raised-panel doors beside a small raised panel door over a small drawer; the center & lower sections each w/two long drawers, deep molded flat base, original door brasses & simple pail drawer pulls, China, first half 20th c., 19 x 47", 5' 7" h. (ILLUS.) **690**

Queen Anne Chest-on-Frame

Queen Anne chest-on-frame, walnut, two-part construction: the upper section w/a rectangular top w/a coved corner over a row of three small drawers above a pair of drawers & a stack of three long drawers, old replaced batwing brasses; the lower section w/a mid-molding over a deep scalloped apron on cabriole legs ending in pad feet, old refinishing, base a well done replacement, 18th c., 24 1/2 x 46 1/2", 4' 11" h. (ILLUS.) **2,300**

Veneered Queen Anne-Style Chest

Queen Anne-Style chest of drawers, walnut & burl walnut, the rectangular top w/molded edges above a row of three small drawers over three long graduated drawers, deep molded base on short ogee bracket feet, pierced batwing brasses & keyhole escutcheons, partially composed of antique elements, England, late 19th - early 20th c., 21 1/2 x 39 1/2", 35" h. (ILLUS.) **1,265**

Italian Rococo-Style Chest

Rococo-Style chest of drawers, pine, shaped top over three dovetailed drawers w/brass pulls & mounted w/side runners, vertically bowed front, shaped skirt, curved feet, Italy, 19th or 20th c., drawers rebuilt, replaced pulls, old black paint, repairs to runners, new supports under top, 34 x 40 x 21" (ILLUS.) **2,750**

Chippendale Style Spice Chest

Spice chest, Chippendale style, cherry & walnut, cove molded top over single raised paneled door & ten interior dovetailed drawers w/old brass pulls, molded base w/shaped bracket feet, inscription on drawer reads "Presented to Margaret Worthington by her mother May 20th, 1836 it being the property formerly of her great grandmother Anne Strode," restorations w/replacements, wood refinished, comes w/book Thomas Worthington by Alfred Byron Sears, 11 3/4 x 19 1/4", 23 3/4" h. (ILLUS.).. **7,475**

Sugar chest, walnut, single-board top w/iron butt hinges above two equal interior compartments, dovetailed case & drawer, base w/finely ring-turned legs w/knob feet, America, first half 19th c., old refinishing, battens possibly later, two locks missing, chips, top slightly warped, 20 x 31", 37" h... **3,520**

Cherry Sugar or Blanket Chest

Sugar or blanket chest, cherry, breadboard lift top over open compartment w/dovetailed drawer below, frame-and-panel construction, turned feet, two locks, probably Kentucky, first half 19th c., old refinishing, 26 1/2 x 34 x 18 1/2" (ILLUS.)... **2,750**

Child's Eastlake Chest of Drawers

Victorian Eastlake substyle child's chest of drawers, birch, the tall superstructure w/a pierced serpentine crestrail above a panel w/stylized floral & roundel incised designs above a long swiveling rectangular beveled mirror all flanked by blocks & line-incised stiles above the rectangular top w/molded edges, the case w/three long graduated drawers w/line-incised leaf spring & stamped brass pulls, original wooden casters, refinished, ca. 1890, 14 x 26", 4' 8" h. (ILLUS.)................................. **600**

Chest with Swan-head Brackets

Victorian Rococo chest of drawers, mahogany & mahogany veneer, a large oval beveled mirror w/a scroll-carved crest swiveling between an ornately scroll-carved wishbone bracket terminating in carved swans' heads, between two small handkerchief drawers on the rectangular top w/rounded front corners above a case w/a pair of large plain drawers w/beaded edge molding slightly projecting above three long drawers w/scroll-carved ends, beaded band above the scroll-carved apron w/bracket feet, turned wood pulls, old refinish, ca. 1860, 21 x 38", overall 6' h. (ILLUS.)...................... **850**

Unique Rococo Chest with Shelves

Victorian Rococo chest of drawers, walnut & feather-grained walnut veneer, the superstructure w/a high arched molded frame w/floral- and scroll-carved crest enclosing a large arched mirror flanked by small arched side panels below small half-round candleshelves & resting on very thin handkerchief drawers on the half-round top w/a wide flat central section, the flat center over three long paneled feather-grained drawers w/scroll-carved pulls flanked by scroll-carved pilasters, quarter-round side sections w/a curved veneer panel above two open rounded shelves w/pierced scroll-cut back brackets, deep conforming molded base, Philadelphia, ca. 1855, refinished, 18 x 44", overall 7' 2" h. (ILLUS.)............... **3,500**

Victorian Rococo "wig" chest of drawers, rosewood, the tall superstructure centered by a period oblong mirror in a molded frame raised between two tall narrow cupboards w/Gothic arch panels in the doors & joined at the top by a pair of scrolls w/anthemion carving, the cupboard bases w/small drawers w/cyma-

Unusual Victorian "Wig" Chest

curve fronts, all resting on the rectangular top above a pair of projecting ogee-front drawers above two long drawers, serpentine scroll-carved apron & bracket feet on casters, original pulls, attributed to the New Orleans warerooms of William & James McCracken, ca. 1850, 22 x 47", overall 7' 4" h. (ILLUS.)................................ **2,070**

William & Mary-Style Inlaid Chest

William & Mary-Style chest of drawers, inlaid walnut, the rectangular banded & quarter-veneered top above a case w/a pair of banded inlay drawers over three long graduated drawers w/pairs of rectangular banded inlay panels, the bottom drawer centered by a recessed sunburst inlay, molded base w/concave center raised on bun feet, partially composed of antique elements w/later veneers, England, late 19th - early 20th c., 21 x 38", 37" h. (ILLUS.) **2,185**

Cupboards

Classical Cherry Corner Cupboard

Corner cupboard, Classical style, cherry, two-piece construction: the upper section w/a flaring flat cornice w/blocked ends above a large 12-pane glazed cupboard door w/arched top panes opening to three shelves & flanked by half-round ring- and rod-turned colonnettes; the lower section w/a projecting mid-molding above a row of three round-fronted drawers over a pair of paneled cupboard doors flanked by half-round ring- and rod-turned colonnettes, flat base raised on knob- and ring-turned feet, old mellow refinishing, well done plugs on lower doors filling pull holes, small pieced repair on one backboard, first half 19th c., 27 x 40 3/4", 7' 1 3/4" h. (ILLUS.) **4,025**

Corner cupboard, country-style, walnut, one-piece construction, cove molded cornice over a pair of tall paneled doors above a dovetailed drawer at the waist, two shorter paneled doors below, molded bracket base, six interior shelves, square nail construction w/flat back, old replaced brass pull & latches, cornice w/pieced restorations, part of foot facings are old replacements,   18 1/2 x 48 1/4",   6' 10 1/2" h. (ILLUS., top of column) **2,185**

Country-style Corner Cupboard

Southern Pine Corner Cupboard

Corner cupboard, early American country-style, Southern yellow pine, one-piece construction, the top w/a stepped flaring cornice above a pair of tall 8-pane glazed cupboard doors opening to three shelves & flanked by beveled front sides, a mid-molding above a pair of paneled cupboard doors also flanked by beveled sides, flat molded base, old brown refinishing, areas of insect damage to base w/pieced repairs, top doors sized down in past, backboards renailed, first half 19th c., 23 1/4 x 45 1/2", 6' 5 1/2" h. (ILLUS.).. **2,070**

Federal Pine Corner Cupboard

Corner cupboard, Federal country style, yellow pine, one-piece construction, the molded cornice above a pair of two-panel doors opening to shelves, a medial molding joined to vertical molding at edges, the base w/a pair of paneled doors, molded base w/original bracket feet & four interior "H" hinges, vertical backboards w/original cut nails, original iron latch, probably Georgia, early 19th c., old refinishing, losses & separations to cornice, four replaced brass butt hinges, wear to feet, 29 x 51, 7' 7" h. (ILLUS.) **6,380**

Corner cupboard, Federal country-style, pine, one-piece construction, the top w/a very deep flaring & stepped cornice w/a thin dentil band above raised angled molding surrounding a large 9-pane glazed door opening to two scalloped shelves above a mid-molding above a pair of two-panel cupboard doors, molded base & shaped apron on short ogee bracket feet, old dark varnished finish, rosehead nail construction w/some re-nailing, hinges & back foot replaced, pads added to front feet, early 19th c., 27 x 50", 6' 9" h. (ILLUS., top of next column).. **4,485**

Large Early Pine Corner Cupboard

Country Federal Corner Cupboard

Corner cupboard, Federal country-style, pine & poplar, one-piece construction, the top w/a deep coved cornice above a pair of 6-pane glazed cupboard doors opening to two shelves above a row of three drawers over a pair of paneled cupboard doors, serpentine apron & shaped bracket feet, refinished w/brown wash, old replaced brass pull, first half 19th c., 19 x 53 1/2", 7' 4" h. (ILLUS.) **2,300**

Virginia Pine Corner Cupboard

Corner cupboard, Federal country-style, yellow pine, one-piece construction, the top w/a deep stepped cornice w/dentil-carved band above a pair of tall 4-pane glazed cupboard doors opening to three shelves above a single narrow drawer over a pair of short square raised-panel doors, moided base on scroll-cut bracket feet, rose head nails in back, old refinishing, old restorations & replacements, sized down in the past, Virginia, late 18th - early 19th c., 26 x 46", 6' 8" h. (ILLUS.)...................................... **1,955**

Corner cupboard, Georgian style, pine, two-piece construction: the top w/a deep flaring stepped cornice centered by a flaring center block above an arch-molded frieze band w/flat keystone over the arched open compartment w/three shaped shelves & barrel back flanked by molded pilasters; the lower section w/a blocked mid-molding above a pair of raised panel cupboard doors w/"H" hinges flanked by flat pilasters, blocked molded flat base, refinished, originally built-in, shelves removed from base, some molding replacements, England, late 18th c., 24 1/2 x 47 3/4", 7' 5 1/2" h. (ILLUS.)......... **1,725**

English Georgian Pine Corner Cupboard

Shaker-style Hanging Cupboard

Hanging cupboard, cherry, a flat rectangular top above the dovetailed case w/a pair of tall 4-pane glazed cupboard doors opening to three shelves, attributed to the Enfield Shaker community, 19th c., 9 x 24", 31 1/2" h. (ILLUS.) **1,380**

Hanging cupboard, cherry, a rectangular top w/a narrow molded cornice above a single large door w/four panes of glass & molded mullions opening to a bluish-green painted interior w/two adjustable shelves, thin base molding, refinished, attributed to Zoar, Ohio, 19th c., 9 x 19", 27" h. (top of door altered at one time) **1,430**

Early Ohio Hanging Cupboard

Hanging cupboard, walnut, a narrow rectangular top fronted by a tall rectangular paneled door w/a high double-arch top flanked by arch-topped side stiles, two interior shelves, flat base, old finish, Ohio, 19th c., 9 1/2 x 14 1/2", 23" h. (ILLUS.) **1,265**

One-piece Painted Jelly Cupboard

Jelly cupboard, painted pine, the rectangular top w/a molded cornice above a single tall beaded board door w/old brass ring pull opening to four shelves & flanked by wide front sides, low shaped bracket feet, old pale green paint, back half of top w/earlier grey, chips on base, rear foot replaced, 19th c., 19 1/2 x 42", 4' 5" h. (ILLUS.) **518**

Shaker-attributed Jelly Cupboard

Jelly cupboard, poplar, the rectangular top w/a low three-quarters gallery above two long narrow drawers w/small wood knobs above a pair of tall paneled cupboard doors opening to three shelves w/wooden knobs, original red wash, attributed to the Mt. Lebanon Shaker community, one back leg replaced, 20 1/4 x 49", 5' 1/4" h. (ILLUS.) **1,953**

Tall Cherry & Walnut Cupboard

Jelly cupboard, walnut & cherry, the thick rectangular top above a single tall two-panel cupboard door w/wooden thumb latch & small steel lock escutcheon, opening to four later shelves, flat apron on curved bracket feet, old finish, pegs removed from interior, one rear foot w/break, cornice replaced, 19th c., 12 1/2 x 33", 5' 7" h. (ILLUS.) **1,035**

Early Southern Pine Linen Press

Linen press, early American country-style, painted pine, the rectangular top above a pair of tall raised-panel cupboard doors opening to three shelves above two long, deep drawers w/simple bail pulls, shaped bracket feet, cleaned down to old green paint, old replaced brasses, probably Southern, first half 19th c., 19 1/4 x 40", 5' 3/4" h. (ILLUS.) **1,438**

English George III Linen Press

Linen press, George III style, mahogany, two-part construction: the upper section w/a rectangular top w/a deep flaring & stepped cornice over a thin frieze molding above a pair of large paneled cupboard doors opening to a shelved interior; the lower section w/a mid-molding over a pair of drawers over two long graduated drawers all w/oval brasses, flat apron & scroll-cut bracket feet, England, late 18th c., 22 x 52", 7 1/2" h. (ILLUS.) **2,530**

Dutch Rococo Linen Press

Linen press, Rococo style, mahogany, two-part construction: the upper section w/a deep broken-scroll dentil-carved pediment centered by a large garland-carved finial above projecting blocked front corners w/fluted Corinthian pilasters flanking a pair of tall arched & paneled cupboard doors w/carved corner rosettes opening to a shelved interior; the lower bombé-form section w/two stacks of three drawers w/pierced butterfly brasses, molded serpentine apron on squatty ball-and-claw front feet, Holland, late 18th c., 25 x 73", 8' 5 1/2" h. (ILLUS.) **6,900**

Pie safe, ash or chestnut, mortise-and-tenon construction, rectangular top w/a molded cornice above two frame-and-panel doors, each door w/four hand-punched tins w/circular & floral decoration, vertical tongue-and-groove backboards w/cut nails, found in Blountville, Tennessee, later red paint on front & molding, sides w/old peeling brown paint, tins w/scattered rust, 17 1/2 x 52", 73 1/2" h. (ILLUS., top next page) **2,090**

Early Eight-tin Pie Safe

Hardwood Country Pie Safe

Pie safe, hardwood, rectangular top above a pair of drawers w/wooden knobs over a pair of three-panel doors fitted w/replaced punched-tin panels decorated w/circle, star & quatrefoil designs, three matching tins in each side, flat apron, square stile legs, late 19th c. (ILLUS.) **310**

Tennessee Six-tin Pie Safe

Pie safe, hardwood, the rectangular top w/a shaped back panel above two tall paneled doors, each w/three punched tins w/heart & circle decoration, doors w/pegged construction, square tapering stile legs, horizontal backboards w/original cut nails, Carter County, Tennessee, old brown paint w/losses, tins w/scattered rust, 16 x 40", 59" h. (ILLUS.) **1,320**

Late Oak & Hardwood Pie Safe

Pie safe, oak & hardwoods, a thin rectangular top above a pair of tall doors fitted w/replaced pierced-tin panels w/a star design above a narrow long bottom drawer w/a stamped leafy scroll design, straight stile legs, late 19th c. (ILLUS.) **350**

Pie Safe from Tennessee

Walnut Pie Safe from Virginia

Pie safe, walnut & poplar, rectangular top above a row of three dovetailed drawers above two doors each w/two large punched-tin panels w/circular centers flanked by two candlesticks w/tulips in upper corners, chamfered horizontal backboards, turned feet, Sullivan County, Tennessee, refinished, several patches, minor surface flaws & scratches, 18 1/2 x 55 1/4", 47" h. (ILLUS.) **9,350**

Pie safe, walnut, the rectangular top over two drawers w/nailed construction above a pair of doors, each w/two punched-tin panels w/eagle designs, Scott County, Virginia, probably mid-19th c., old refinishing w/scratches & losses, replaced glass pulls, 18 x 43", 45" h. (ILLUS., top next column) **2,420**

Side cupboard, Baroque style, rectangular molded top w/dentil-carved molding above a row of three paneled drawers w/wooden knobs, a central door below w/inlaid star design flanked by two panels w/geometric light & dark wood inlay, the base w/multiple cove bed moldings & bracket feet, original rosehead nails throughout, probably Italy, 18th c., repairs to drawer bottoms, separations & losses throughout, 13 x 30", 33" h. **4,620**

Side cupboards, Regency-Style, mahogany, the rectangular top w/projecting block ends above a conforming case w/a pair of large paneled doors flanked by tapering pilasters topped by a carved maiden head & resting on a paw foot upon projecting base blocks, England, late 19th - early 20th c., 18 1/2 x 44 1/2", 36" h., pr. (ILLUS., bottom of page) **2,300**

English Regency-Style Cupboards

Step-back wall cupboard, Chippendale country-style, cherry, two-part construction: the upper section w/a rectangular top w/a widely flaring & deep stepped cornice above a pair of 6-pane glazed doors on brass H-hinges flanking a center stack of three fixed panes over a deep pie shelf w/shaped projecting sides; the lower section w/a stepped-out rectangular top over a row of four beaded drawers w/turned wood pulls above a pair of square paneled cupboard doors w/brass H-hinges, molded base on shaped bracket feet, Ohio or Pennsylvania, mellow refinishing, late 18th - early 19th c., base 21 x 61", overall 92 1/4" h. (two panes missing, few minor pieced repairs or replacements, glued foot breaks) **19,800**

Child's Step-back Wall Cupboard

Step-back wall cupboard, country-style, child's, walnut, the top w/two glass doors above four dovetailed drawers w/wooden pulls in bottom section, molded front edge, four applied turned feet, cut nails, found in Kentucky, late 19th or early 20th c., minor surface flaws, missing one glass pane, 11 x 26", 44" h. (ILLUS.) **1,100**

"Jackson Press" Wall Cupboard

Step-back wall cupboard, country "Jackson press" style, cherry, two-part construction: the upper section w/a cove-molded cornice above two 8-pane glazed doors opening to three shelves above two dovetailed drawers; the lower section w/a pair of dovetailed drawers above two double-panel doors, baluster-turned legs, original wooden pulls, horizontal frame-&-panel backboards, old refinishing, minor surface scratches & flaws, 21 x 43", 7' 11" h. (ILLUS.) **3,520**

Tennessee Wall Cupboard

Step-back wall cupboard, country-style, maple, two-part construction: a rectangular top w/a molded cornice above a pair of six-pane glazed cupboard doors opening to two shelves; the stepped-out lower section w/a long drawer w/carved wood pulls above two astragal-molded doors flanked by split columns, horizontal backboards w/cut nails, made by Reverend Robert Hicks, Jonesboro, Tennessee, 1880-90, old refinishing, top w/old red stain, glass panes & interior molding possibly replaced, missing lock, 19 3/4 x 48 1/2", 7' 1" h. (ILLUS.) **1,320**

Walnut Step-back Wall Cupboard

Step-back wall cupboard, country-style, walnut, one-piece construction, the rectangular top over a pair of two-panel doors, sides w/reverse-chamfered panels, the stepped-out lower section w/single nailed long drawer above a pair of two-panel doors, slightly tapered bracket feet, vertical backboards w/original cut nails, probably Georgia, mid-19th c., old refinishing, some rodent chew, separations, scratched, 20 x 21", 6' 1/2" h. (ILLUS.) **1,540**

French Provincial Wall Cupboard

Step-back wall cupboard, Louis XV-Style Provincial type, pine, two-part construc-

tion: the upper section w/a high arched, molded & scroll-carved crestrail over a conforming frieze band carved w/narrow panels centered by a roundel above a pair of two-pane glazed cupboard doors w/an ornate scroll-carved & molded framing, paneled sides; the lower section w/a pair of paneled doors w/carved scroll designs, serpentine apron over short cabriole front legs w/peg feet, France, late 19th c., 19 1/2 x 52", 7' 8 1/2" h. (ILLUS.).. **2,300**

Rare Ohio Step-back Wall Cupboard

Step-back wall cupboard, painted poplar, two-piece construction: the upper section w/a rectangular top w/a deep flaring molded cornice above a pair of raised panel doors w/wooden knobs opening to three shelves over a high open pie shelf; the stepped-out lower section w/a pair of dovetailed drawers w/wooden knobs over a pair of raised panel cupboard doors opening to two shelves, flat apron & curved bracket feet, old red paint, painted interiors, Ohio, mid-19th c., 20 1/2 x 49", 7' 1" h. (ILLUS.)................... **10,063**

Step-back wall hutch cupboard, Louis XV-Style Provincial type, oak, two-part construction: the upper section w/a high arched crestrail ornately carved w/floral garlands & scallops flanking a large shell-carved crest above a narrow scroll-carved frieze band over a tall arched glazed central door framed by lappet carving & ornate pierced scrolling over the glass, shorter matching glazed doors at each side & at the front corners, all above a row of short concave scroll-carved drawers; the lower section w/fancy mid-molding over a case w/a stepped-out center section w/three carved draw-

Ornate French Provincial Cupboard

ers over three conforming cupboard doors each ornately carved w/arched shell-carved molding enclosing delicate inner molding, conforming deep molded base on four heavy carved paw feet, France, late 19th c., 26 x 79", 8' 10" h. (ILLUS.) **4,600**

Italian Baroque Wall Cupboard

Wall cupboard, Baroque style, walnut, a rectangular molded top above two small square drawers centered by a longer paneled drawer all w/nailed construction, over a single paneled door w/a central carved florette flanked by narrow side panels, molded base on scroll-cut brack-

et feet, Italy, probably 18th c., extensive worm damage, later bracket feet, separations & losses, 13 x 27 1/2", 34 1/4" h. (ILLUS.) **3,960**

Vinegar Grained Wall Cupboard

Wall cupboard, country-style, cherry & walnut, the rectangular dark brown top w/a molded cornice over a single raised-panel door w/green vinegar grained panels, opening to five interior shelves, original red over orange vinegar graining, Ohio, chips along back of top, 11 1/2 x 34 3/4", 4' 2 1/2" h. (ILLUS.) **8,050**

Wall cupboard, country-style, walnut, dovetailed construction, swan's-neck pediment w/pinched center over two frame-and-panel doors, the interior w/20 small dovetailed drawers, a large dovetailed & divided drawer below, tongue-and-groove vertical backboards w/cut nails, original surface, traces of old yellow or green paint in interior dividers, probably missing two small drawers, no evidence of having had feet, missing one piece of molding beside drawer, old scratches & scuffs, missing one drawer pull, America, early 19th c., 14 x 35", 46" h. **1,045**

Wall cupboard, Gothic Revival style, oak, one-piece construction, the rectangular top w/a flaring molded cornice above a pair of tall ornate Gothic arch-carved doors centered by small shields & flanked by carved figures of knights atop spiral-twist columns, the doors centered by a Gothic arch-carved narrow panel w/fancy iron lock plate, a mid-molding w/blocked corners above a tall lower recess topped by a pierce-carved Gothic arch & quatrefoil cornice & flanked by plain columns, the back carved w/three

Gothic Revival Wall Cupboard

linen-fold panels, slightly arched apron between block front feet, France, late 19th c., 21 1/4 x 38 3/4", 4' 10 1/4" h. (ILLUS.) **920**

Italian Neoclassical Cupboard

Wall cupboard, Neoclassical style, painted & giltwood, the rectangular top w/a deep flaring dentil-carved cornice centered by a large gilt urn finial on a platform flanked by pierced scrolls, the case w/two tall paneled doors each painted w/a long ribbon swag w/trophies, a wide flaring gilt leaf-carved base molding on projecting gilt scroll-carved feet, Italy, late 18th c., 8 1/2 x 29", 42" h. (ILLUS.) **1,840**

Chinese Red Lacquered Cupboard

Wall cupboard, Oriental, lacquered & decorated, the rectangular top above a pair of tall flat cupboard doors w/a large fitted round brass latch, opening to an interior fitted w/two shelves & two drawers w/a bin below, a deep apron w/a carved Greek key design, short square stile legs, decorated overall in old red lacquer w/gold & black Oriental river scenes, flying bats & flowers, black-painted sides, putty restoration, feet ended out, China, 19th c., 21 x 45 1/4", 6' 1/2" h. (ILLUS.) **920**

Desks

Art Nouveau desk & chair, walnut, the desk w/a low superstructure w/an undulating pierced crestrail over two shaped side drawers & a central shelf raised above the rectangular quarter-veneered top w/serpentine molded edges above an apron fitted w/two side drawers flanking the kneehole opening & a center drawer, rounded bottom on lower drawers continues into the cabriole legs ending in peg feet, w/a matching balloon-back side chair, Europe, late 19th c., desk 32 x 55 1/2", 42" h., the set (ILLUS., top next page) **2,070**

Art Nouveau Walnut Desk & Chairs

Fine Biedermeier Ash Desk

Biedermeier desk, ash, in the Gothic taste, the modified kidney-shaped top banded & w/an inlaid leather writing surface above a conforming quatrefoil inlaid frieze fitted w/a single drawer, raised on two paneled bow-front cupboards w/inlaid arches flanking a central recessed cupboard door, raised on plinth bases, Europe, early 19th c., 24 x 44", 31 1/2" h. (ILLUS.) **3,680**

Chippendale country-style slant-front desk, inlaid birch, dovetailed construction, the narrow rectangular top above a hinged slant front w/mitered corners opening to an interior w/eight drawers & six cubbyholes flanking prospect door w/single drawer, the lower case w/three graduated drawers w/oval pulls, Virginia, late 18th - early 19th c., two front feet ended out 3", front skirt & foot facings replaced, 2" of side facings replaced, brasses replaced, slant front faded, 22 x 42", 4' 1" h. (ILLUS., next column) **2,310**

Chippendale Country-style Desk

Rare "Oxbow-front" Boston Desk

Chippendale "oxbow-front" slant-front desk, mahogany, a narrow rectangular top above a hinged slant lid centered by a large carved fan & opening to an interior fitted w/drawers & pigeonholes, the double-swelled "oxbow-front" case w/four long graduated drawers w/batwing brasses & keyhole escutcheons, a molded base w/central drop & short cabriole legs w/carved returns ending in claw-and-ball feet, Boston, late 18th c., 23 x 42 1/2", 44" h. (ILLUS., previous page).. **15,525**

Chippendale Slant-front Desk

Chippendale slant-front desk, mahogany, a narrow rectangular top above a wide hinged slant front opening to an unusual interior w/a total of twenty dovetailed drawers, also pigeonholes & a hinged center door w/tombstone panel & additional hidden compartments & shelves, the lower case w/four long graduated beaded drawers w/old replaced batwing brasses, molded base on ogee bracket feet, refinished, feet expertly replaced, some other minor restorations, late 18th c., 24 x 43 1/2", 31 1/2" h. (ILLUS.)........... **3,450**

Chippendale-Style partner's desk, mahogany, the shaped rectangular top w/three inset leather sections, the two large pedestals carved w/large lion mask corner pilasters & carved swag & wreath designs, opening to reveal folio compartments below shallow drawers, a central drawer above the kneehole opening, facsimile of the renowned Thomas Chippendale model from Nostell Priory, England, late 19th - early 20th c., 39 x 72", 32 1/4" h. (ILLUS., bottom of page)........... **6,900**

Colonial Revival partner's desk, mahogany, the wide rectangular top w/molded edges above a case fitted on each side w/a scroll-carved central drawer over the arched kneehole opening flanked on one side by a large square cupboard door carved w/ornate scrolls centering a cartouche & on the other side by two scroll-carved small drawers, large lion heads carved at each corner above large wingform brackets over the cabriole legs w/leaf-carved knees & large paw feet, ornately scroll-carved side panels, attributed to Horner of New York City, original dark finish, ca. 1880s, 30 x 60", 30" h. (ILLUS., top next page) **7,500**

Copy of Famous Chippendale Partner's Desk

Ornate Colonial Revival Partner's Desk

Carved Colonial Revival Slant-front Desk

Colonial Revival slant-front desk, mahogany, an arched & scroll-carved crestrail flanked by brass rail ends on the narrow rectangular top over the wide hinged slant front boldly carved w/rounded panels of leafy scrolls above a case w/three long graduated drawers w/ornate stamped brass pulls, narrow rounded apron above leaf-carved ogee bracket feet, old refinish, ca. 1890s, 22 x 38", 42" h. (ILLUS.)................................. **1,000**

Country-style desk, walnut, a set-back top section w/central prospect door flanked by four drawers on the rectangular lift top opening to 20 interior compartments & a case w/two drawers above single long drawer, ring-turned tapering legs, frame-and-panel sides w/mortise joints, original turned wooden pulls, backs w/chamfered horizontal panels w/deep oxidation, cut nails, 19th c., 25 1/2 x 27 1/2", 39" h......... **3,960**

Country-style Plantation Desk

Country-style plantation desk, yellow pine, two-part construction: the top fitted w/a three-quarters gallery above two paneled doors opening to an interior w/14 compartments & two drawers; the lower section w/a slant front opening to a well, tapered ring-turned legs, drawers w/original leather pulls, cut nails throughout, old refinishing, possibly a marriage, top & bottom w/traces of old green paint, some rebuilding, Southern U.S., 19th c., 24 x 37", 5' 4" h. (ILLUS.)............................ **1,100**

English George III Kneehole Desk

Walnut Two-part Plantation Desk

Federal country-style plantation desk, walnut, two-part construction: the upper section w/a rectangular top w/a wide coved cornice above a pair of tall 6-pane glazed doors opening to two shelves above two shallow drawers w/turned wood knobs; the projecting lower section w/a pair of drawers w/turned wood knobs, raised on ring- and baluster-turned tapering legs ending in peg feet, old finish, age splits, mid-19th c., 23 1/2 x 46 1/2", overall 6' 2" h. (ILLUS.)... **1,840**

George III kneehole desk, mahogany, the rectangular top w/molded edges above a long fold-down drawer opening to reveal a writing surface supported by corner pilasters that extend w/the drawer, a central kneehole w/a recessed cupboard flanked by two ranks of four small drawers each, simple brass bail pulls, molded base w/pairs of arched bracket feet, England, ca. 1800, 24 1/2 x 42", 33" h. (ILLUS.).. **3,450**

Jacobean-Style pedestal desk, oak, the rectangular top w/an inset leather writing surface above a frieze fitted w/three drawers each w/pairs of raised-molding panels, a long center drawer above the kneehole opening, each side pedestal composed of three double-paneled drawers, brass teardrop pulls & brass keyhole escutcheons, molded bases on large bun feet, England, ca. 1900, 29 1/2 x 52", 31" h. (ILLUS., bottom of page) **1,265**

English Jacobean-Style Oak Pedestal Desk

Delicate Louis XVI-Style Desk

Louis XVI-Style lady's writing desk, rosewood, the top w/a two-tiered open gallery w/shelves w/a delicate pierced-scroll crest & slender turned supports, the highly figured hinged slant front opening to an inset felt-work surface & small compartments, the apron w/a narrow full-width crossbanded drawer, raised on slender tapering foliate-carved & fluted legs ending in peg feet, restored original finish, New York City, ca. 1870, 18 1/2 x 30 1/2", overall 4' 5 1/4" h. (ILLUS.) **2,760**

Ornately Carved Chinese Desk

Oriental writing desk, stained rosewood, the superstructure w/an ornately pierce-carved crestrail above two projecting compartments, one fitted w/three small carved drawers & the other w/a carved paneled door, backed by a delicate pierce-carved panel above a short carved panel, the projecting writing surface over a pair of elaborately carved drawers, raised on cabriole legs w/carved bats at the knees & ornately pierce-carved returns, ending in claw-and-ball feet, China, ca. 1900, 25 x 38 1/2", 46 1/2" h. (ILLUS.) **1,150**

Aesthetic Style Partner's Desk

Victorian Aesthetic Movement partner's desk, cherry, the rectangular top w/inset leather writing surface & gadroon-carved edges above matching case arrangements, each side w/a long narrow central drawer over the kneehole opening fitted w/an inner arcaded shelf & flanked on each side by one small working drawer & one false drawer each above a square cabinet door carved in relief w/the tools of various professions, tapering ring-turned legs joined by heavy square stretchers, metal casters, original finish, ca. 1880s, 30 x 60", 30" h. (ILLUS., bottom previous page) **3,500**

Victorian Elizabethan Revival Desk

Victorian Elizabethan Revival lady's desk, mahogany, two-part construction: the top supporting a recessed pair of two-over-two shallow drawers w/the shelf above supported by S-scroll brackets

above a low pierced back gallery; the lower section w/a felt-lined projecting writing surface over a pair of drawers supported by a trestle base w/spiral-twist supports & cross stretcher, mid-19th c. (ILLUS.) **805**

Jacobean Revival Oak Desk

Victorian Jacobean Revival desk, oak, the rectangular top w/deep molded edges inset in the middle w/leather, raised on a cabinet w/ornately carved leafy scroll sides, the front w/a long central paneled & carved drawer flanked by large arched recesses, raised on four heavy vase-turned posts on large block feet joined by end stretchers & a thick arched-ended cross stretcher, on casters, refinished, ca. 1900, 26 x 54", 30" h. (ILLUS.) **1,500**

William IV writing desk, mahogany, the rectangular top w/rounded corners inset w/a gilt-tooled leather writing surface, the apron fitted w/three drawers w/wooden knobs, raised on knob-turned & reeded tapering legs ending in trumpet feet on brass casters, England, second quarter 19th c., 37 x 60", 30" h. (ILLUS., bottom of page) **4,600**

English William IV Mahogany Writing Desk

Dry Sinks

Painted & Decorated Poplar Dry Sink

Rare Dated Ohio Dry Sink

Painted & decorated poplar, the long arched splashback above a long well above a case w/a pair of large paneled cupboard doors above simple bracket feet, old dark brown graining over an amber-colored ground, evidence of earlier red, interior w/two shelves painted light green, wear, door latch missing, 19th c., 17 3/4 x 45", 36" h. (ILLUS.) **575**

Painted pine & poplar, a long rectangular shallow well w/a half-round backsplash toward one end, the base w/two large paneled doors opening to two shelves, gently serpentine apron & low bracket feet, old worn blue over earlier red paint, mid-19th c., 19 1/2 x 45", 32" h. (restorations, backboards renailed, few door pegs replaced) **1,430**

Painted pine & poplar, a narrow rectangular shelf atop the raised backboard flanked by shaped sides on the long well above a pair of drawers w/turned wood knobs over a pair of paneled cupboard doors opening to two shelves, simple bracket feet, old yellow paint over earlier colors, signed in pencil in one drawer "Thos. Underwood, Clark Co. Ohio, August 10, 1881," 18 x 42", 41" h. (ILLUS.) **4,025**

Garden & Lawn

Cast iron unless otherwise noted.

Armchairs, rounded back curving down to all all pierced w/ornate fern leaves & berries, rectangular geometrically-pierced seat, base pierced side panels ending in canted legs, painted white, cast mark "Glen," 19th c., 32 3/4" h. pr. (one w/minor welded back repair) **935**

Carved Marble Garden Bench

Bench, carved marble, the back w/shaped & scrolled pediment above frieze w/elaborate relief-carved scrolls & dragons, arm supports scrolled w/extensive leaf & petal carving, cable borders on seat, 19th c., stains, minor chips & discoloration, marble w/some irregularities & fissures, central pediment w/large chip, 20 x 80", 46" h. (ILLUS., bottom previous page)..... **15,400**

Swan-form Garden Bench

Bench, cast iron & wood, cast-iron ends in the form of swans, their necks serving as bench arms, seat & back formed by single boards, old white & orange paint w/repainting, 19th c., scattered rust, boards probably later replacements, 28 x 72", 38" h. (ILLUS.)............................... **4,840**

French Garden Bench

Bench, cast iron & wood, cast-iron frame decorated w/scrolls & lion heads, canted legs ending in paw feet, curved beaded wooden slat seat & back, traces of old green paint, France, 19th c., 29 x 57", 35" h. (ILLUS.) **825**

Unusual Set of Garden Furniture

Chair & table set: two side chairs & a matching table; a pair of folding metal side chairs w/tall rectangular patterned backs & matching square seats, the table w/a rectangular top over a narrow Greek key apron raised on slender metal cross-style folding legs, worn golden yellow paint, 19th c., chairs 31" h., the set (ILLUS.).. **1,150**

Plant stand, cast iron & marble, round marble top on cast-iron tripod legs w/angels at tops in relief, platform stretcher below, old white paint, Europe, 19th c., scattered rust, marble w/stains & discoloration, 24" d., 30" h. **1,430**

Plant stand, composed of two long cast-iron slat shelves tiered on scrolled iron supports & straight rear legs, old oxidized surface, late 19th c., 14 1/2 x 66 1/2", 19" h. (ILLUS., bottom of page) **1,035**

Plant stand, openwork round top above tripod legs w/female heads in relief, platform stretcher below, hoof feet, old green paint, England or Europe, 19th c., scattered light rust, 24" d., 28" h. **550**

Long Victorian Iron Plant Stand

Plant stand, polished slate circular top, a tall slender pedestal on a tripod base w/scrolled legs w/hoof feet, England or Europe, late 19th c., possibly missing decorative chains, top probably later, 16" d., 30" h. **550**

Renaissance Design Victorian Garden Settee

Settee, Renaissance Revival style, the long pierced back centered by a wide arched fanned panel framing a large trefoil & flanked by lower square panels, the shaped tapering arms w/pierced lacy designs, iron slat seat w/pierced scroll apron, curved saber-form legs, painted white, second half 19th c., 23 x 46 1/2", 37 1/2" h. (ILLUS.) **546**

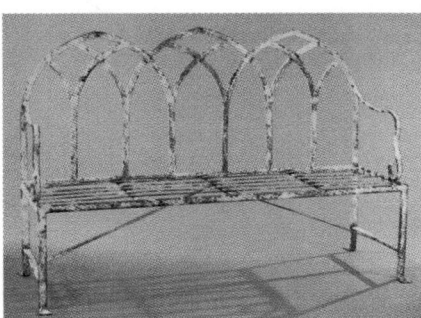

English "Strawberry Hill" Settee

Settee, "Strawberry Hill" type, wrought-iron design w/the back composed of three overlapping Gothic arches, undulating open-end arms over the iron slat seat, on straight legs w/long angled braces, rusted white-painted surface, England, 19th c., 57 1/2" l., 41 1/2" h. (ILLUS.) **1,265**

Settee, the arched serpentine back composed of pierced scrolling oak leaf & acorn vines flanked by straight arms w/bands of ivy & berry or acorns & oak leaves & terminating in a figural dog head, the wooden slat seat above an oak leaf branch apron, raised on cabriole legs ending in paw feet, painted white, second half 19th c., 32 x 59", 37 1/2" h. (ILLUS., top of column) **920**

Oak Leaf & Acorn Pattern Settee

Victorian-style Cast-iron Settee

Settee, the high arched & pieced back w/a flower-filled urn crest over scrolls centered by a female head above a band of large interlocking ovals, flared scroll arms above the circle-pierced seat, cabriole legs w/scroll feet, 19th c., multiple coats of old green & white paint, scattered rust, 2 1/2" piece on back broken but present, 19 x 46", 42" h. (ILLUS.) **1,100**

Settee, the scroll-carved serpentine crestrail above a back pierced w/rows of small arches, stepped scroll-carved arms above the scroll-pierced seat w/a shallow scroll-carved apron, scrolled cabriole legs, America or England, second half 19th c., old black paint w/scattered rust, 20 x 47", 35" h. **990**

Chinese Decorated Lacquer Stools

Stools, lacquer, barrel-shaped, a round seat above curved square supports each w/a central ring & joined at the base by flat shaped stretchers, a red & black ground decorated overall w/Oriental garden scenes & scrolling lotus designs, China, late 19th c., 12" d., 14" h., pr. (ILLUS.) **546**

Figural Bronze & Granite Table

Table, the demi-lune granite top supported by two bronze young mermaids w/entwined tails, Europe, 19th c., 20 x 39 1/2", 29" h. (ILLUS.) **3,450**

Hall Racks & Trees

Elaborate Cast-iron Hall Tree

Hall tree, cast iron, elaborate Renaissance-style decoration of grapes, vines, full-figured putti in center, grotesque head below, female head above, seven hat/coat hooks w/lion's head above, base w/removable cast-iron shell-form basin below

spiral bar flanked by two openwork sides, scattered light rust & black paint, ca. 1875, 12 x 32", 6' 6" h. (ILLUS.) **3,960**

Ornately Spindled Oak Hall Tree

Hall tree, Victorian Golden Oak style, oak, a large serpentine scroll-carved crestrail on the flaring cornice above a dentil-carved band & a turned spindle rail above a large square beveled mirror flanked by side panels w/a shell carving over three tall slender spindles above another turned spindle rail over a row of five vasiform scroll-carved splats, mounted w/six cast-brass hooks, open shaped arms flanking the rectangular seat over a single long drawer w/stamped brass pulls, turned tapering front legs w/knob feet joined to square back legs w/square stretchers, a side base half-round rail for the wooden drip pan, upper support arm missing, refinished, ca. 1890s, 16 x 44", 7' 10" h. (ILLUS.) **2,400**

Oak Hall Tree with Oval Mirror

Hall tree, Victorian Golden Oak style, oak, the wide oval top frame w/a high arched & scroll-carved crest & four cast-brass coat hooks enclosing a large oval beveled mirror above a wide shaped back panel centered by a V-form leafy scroll-carved panel above the flat serpentine arms on S-form flat arm supports flanking the lift seat over a deep apron w/scalloped base, flat S-scroll front legs, refinished, ca. 1900, 18 x 30", 7' h. (ILLUS.) **1,400**

Oak Hall Tree with Diamond Mirror

Hall tree, Victorian Golden Oak style, quarter-sawn oak, a large flat diamond-shaped frame enclosing a beveled mirror below a high arched scroll-carved crest, supported on flat pointed stiles w/carved ovals at the peaks, a serpentine mid-rail above a pierced & scroll-trimmed lower splat, rounded open arms above the lift seat above a scalloped apron, ca. 1890s, refinished, 18 x 24", 6' 10" h. (ILLUS.) **1,250**

Hall tree, Victorian Golden Oak style, quarter-sawn oak, a large wide top w/an arched molded crestrail centered by scroll-carved crest flanked by scroll-carved corner finials above rounded side columns flanking the wide flat panels enclosing the arched & shaped rectangular beveled mirror w/a bottom section of arched carved scrolls, mounted w/four ornate cast-metal double coat hooks, a rectangular top above a deep long drawer w/stamped brass pulls raised on spiral-turned spindles above a rectangular pull-out bench on flat arched front legs w/scroll-carved trim & supported on square tapering frame legs, the back of the framework w/flattened scroll-carved

Oak Hall Tree with Pull-out Bench

legs w/paw feet, ca. 1890s, refinished, 30 x 34", 7' h. (ILLUS.) **1,600**

Rare Gothic Revival Hall Tree

Hall tree, Victorian Gothic Revival style, mahogany, the tall paneled back topped by a projecting trefoil-pierced hood surmounted by crockets & over a curved panel above a central Gothic arch beveled mirror flanked by Gothic arch-carved panels above a central lift-top bench seat flanked by open arms & further Gothic arch-carved panels, fitted overall w/curved metal coat hooks & angled metal brackets to support umbrellas, probably England, late 19th c., 18 x 46", 8' 4" h. (ILLUS.).. **1,380**

Very Large Renaissance Hall Tree

Hall tree, Victorian Renaissance Revival style, walnut & burl walnut, the high broken-scroll crestrail centered by a large projecting crest w/carved scrolls & leaves above raised burl panels & roundels over a narrow molding over the tall rectangular mirror w/rounded top flanked by narrow burl panels & slender ring-turned freestanding side columns mounted w/turned wood pegs above C-form side support loops centered by a narrow vertical burl panel over a wide rectangular white marble shelf above a narrow burl panel drawer raised on scroll-carved supports flanked by arched base brackets over round base rings enclosing the cast-metal drip pans, ca. 1870s, refinished, 20 x 50", 8' 2" h. (ILLUS.)............................ **3,500**

Hall tree, Victorian Renaissance Revival style, walnut & burl walnut, the wide arched molded crestrail w/a pierced & scroll-carved crest above narrow raised burl panels over a deep flaring & stepped cornice above the tall rectangular mirror w/notched top corners, shaped scroll-carved sides w/narrow raised burl panels fitted w/six coat pegs, C-form side brackets above the white marble top w/concave side & notched front above a long burl-paneled drawer flanked by round

Arch-topped Renaissance Hall Tree

iron drip pans on the deep platform base, refinished, ca. 1870s, 16 x 48", 8' 2" h. (ILLUS.).. **3,600**

Highboys & Lowboys

Highboys

Cherry "Bonnet-top" Highboy

Queen Anne "bonnet-top" highboy, cherry, two-part construction: the top section w/swan's-neck pediment w/three urn finials above a row of three drawers, the center one fan-carved, above four long graduated lipped & dovetailed drawers; the base w/a long narrow drawer above a row of three drawers, the center one fan-carved, a scalloped skirt above cabriole legs ending in pad feet, original batwing brass pulls & keyhole escutcheons, horizontal backboards, original hand-wrought nails, America, 18th c., old refinishing, feet & legs repaired w/possible replacements, one finial w/repaired tip, 22 x 38 1/2", 6' 1/2" h. (ILLUS.)................... **9,350**

Rare American Queen Anne Highboy

Queen Anne "bonnet-top" highboy, walnut, two-part construction: the upper section w/a broken-scroll crest centered by an urn & flame finial w/matching corner finials above a pair of small drawers flanking a deep fan-carved drawer above a stack of three long graduated drawers; the lower section w/a mid-molding above a long drawer over a row of three drawers, the center one fan-carved, the scalloped apron fitted w/two long acorn drops, cabriole legs ending in pad feet, glued splits & pieced restoration, later finials, 18th c., 22 x 42", 7' 4 1/4" h. (ILLUS.).. **14,375**

Queen Anne "bonnet-top" highboy, walnut & walnut flame veneer, mortised, two-part construction: the upper section w/a broken-scroll pediment centered by an urn- and spiral-turned finial on a platform w/matching corner finials above a frieze centered by a deep shell-carved drawer over a pair of banded drawers over three long graduated drawers; the lower section w/a mid-molding over a long narrow banded drawer above a row of three drawers over a serpentine apron cen-

Veneered Queen Anne Highboy

tered by a carved shell, finely shaped cabriole legs ending in pad feet, America, 18th c., mellow refinishing & thin coat of old varnish, replaced brasses, lower shell an old addition, backboards of upper case are replacements, pieced restorations to case & old alterations to aprons & bonnet, 20 1/2 x 42", 7' h. (ILLUS.) **17,250**

Queen Anne "Flat-top" Highboy

Queen Anne "flat-top" highboy, maple w/fancy crotch-figure walnut drawer fronts, dovetailed, two-part construction: the rectangular top w/a cove-molded cornice above two drawers over three long, graduated dovetailed & band-inlaid drawers; the lower section w/a long narrow drawer above a row of three band-inlaid drawers, the scalloped apron above cabriole legs ending in pad feet, original brass pulls & escutcheons, original iron locks throughout, chamfered & lap-jointed vertical backboards, Boston area, 1730-60, backboards w/some added nails, several drawer runners flipped, old refinishing, 23 x 40", 5' 7" h. (ILLUS.) **16,500**

Lowboys

Queen Anne Fruitwood Lowboy

Queen Anne lowboy, fruitwood, the rectangular top w/molded edges overhanging a case w/a shallow drawer flanked by deep drawers all above the deeply arched apron, on straight cabriole legs ending in pad feet, Europe, mid-18th c., 21 x 34", 27 1/2" h. (ILLUS.) **2,530**

Love Seats, Sofas & Settees

Louis XVI-Style Caned & Polychromed Daybed

Daybed, Louis XVI-Style, polychromed wood & cane, the matching headboards & footboards w/rolled crestrails above wide caned panels flanked by baluster-turned columns on blocks above the baluster-turned legs, joined by molded side rails, France, early 20th c., 34 x 80", 34" h. (ILLUS.) **920**

Rare Louis XV Beechwood Duchesse

Duchesse, Louis XV style, carved beechwood, one end w/an arched upholstered back enclosed by a serpentine carved frame flanked by padded open arms & raised above the very long upholstered seat w/a molded serpentine seatrail, raised on six cabriole legs ending in peg feet, signed "H. Amand" (Henri Amand, master in 1749), France, mid-18th c., 64" l., 35" h. (ILLUS.) **2,530**

Fine American Classical Mahogany Meridienne

Meridienne, Classical style, rosewood-banded mahogany, an upright upholstered end w/heavy S-scroll uprights above the long rectangular upholstered

Handsome Biedermeier Blonde Fruitwood Settee

seat on the deep crotch-veneered apron w/rosewood crossbanding, raised on heavy tapering squared & carved feet on casters, first quarter 19th c., 23 x 48", 26" h. (ILLUS., previous page) **2,530**

Settee, Biedermeier style, blonde fruitwood, a long narrow crestrail flanked by even outscrolled arms all above upholstered panels over slender pierced diamond-form stretchers, the long upholstered seat on square tapering & slightly splayed legs, Europe, second quarter 19th c., 28 x 81", 34" h. (ILLUS., bottom of previous page) **3,220**

Attractive English George III-Style Settee

Settee, George III-Style, mahogany, triple-chairback style, the crestrail composed of three turned bars above three sets of rails flanking narrow horizontal diamonds over smaller vertical diamond lattice-pierced panels, the curved back stiles joined to serpentine open arms on baluster-turned arm supports flanking the long upholstered seat, three baluster- and ring-turned front legs ending in peg feet, England, late 19th c., 24 x 54", 37" h. (ILLUS.) **690**

Settee, Louis XVI-Style, gilt gesso, the flat crestrail w/wreath & blossom decoration continuing down to form the padded open arms flanking the upholstered back panel, acanthus leaf & scroll arm supports, upholstered seat, France, early 20th c.,

upholstery badly damaged, chips & separations, 26 x 41", 57" l. **1,320**

Chinese Carved Softwood Settee

Settee, Oriental, carved softwood, the long back centered by a raised carved crest w/scrolled ends enclosing a narrow carved panel above a row of three carved rectangular panels flanked by solid carved-panel arms, the deep seat above a deep apron fitted w/a row of three drawers above two small drawers flanking two larger drawers, square stile legs w/horse-hoof feet, China, 19th c., 23 x 43 1/2", 39" h. (ILLUS.) **690**

Settle, country-style, oak, the back composed of four paneled frames, shaped arms w/scrolled ends on turned arm supports & corner legs, long upholstered seat on a box-stretcher base w/heavy block corner legs, old mellow finish, probably England, late 17th - early 18th c., later upholstery, replaced frame under seat, other minor supports added, surface w/chips, scratches, wear & separations, made originally for rope webbing, 26 x 40", 72" l. **2,750**

Sofa, Baroque style, the long flat upholstered crestrail & back flanked by downswept upholstered arms flanking the cushion seat, cross-stretcher base w/eight serpentine & scrolled legs & stretchers, 18th c. verdure tapestry upholstery adapted to sofa using borders &

Chippendale-Style Upholstered Sofa

American Classical Carved Mahogany Sofa

figures of trees & birds, back panel w/two large birds in woodland setting, cushion w/matching borders, Dutch or German, 18th c., extensive losses, separation & repairs to tapestry, fading, pest damage, 34 x 45", 78" l. **5,500**

Sofa, Chippendale style, mahogany, the long arched camel back above out-scrolled arms above the over-upholstered seat, on square tapered front legs w/spade feet, front legs w/diamond inlay w/shield-shaped tops, England or America, probably early 19th c., upholstery badly torn, 30 x 37", 72" l. **2,310**

Sofa, Chippendale-Style, the long arched & upholstered camel back flanked by out-scrolled upholstered arms above the long over-upholstered seat, raised on four square bead-trimmed front legs joined by serpentine box stretchers, England, late 19th c., the base w/several loose joints, side stretchers repaired, upholstery from several sources w/scattered losses & worn areas, 39 x 40", 8' 1" l. (ILLUS., bottom previous page)...................................... **4,400**

Sofa, Classical, mahogany & mahogany veneer, a raised flat central crestrail flanked by scrolling leaf-carved rails above the low upholstered back flanked by rolled upholstered arms w/bolsters supported by leaf-carved scroll supports, the long upholstered seat on a narrow rounded seatrail centered by a leaf-carved reserve & raised on carved cornucopia legs ending in paw feet, old red velvet upholstery, ca. 1830, 23 x 95", 36" h. (ILLUS., top of page)................................... **1,955**

Sofa, Classical style, mahogany & mahogany veneer, a long flat & slightly rolled crestrail w/scroll-carved end brackets above the upholstered back flanked by deep scrolled arms w/scroll supports continuing down into the seat rail, raised on carved paw feet w/scroll-carved & pierced feather returns, attributed to Anthony Quervelle, Philadelphia, ca. 1820-30, missing toes on left rear foot, 85" l........ **3,600**

Classical Transitional Style Sofa

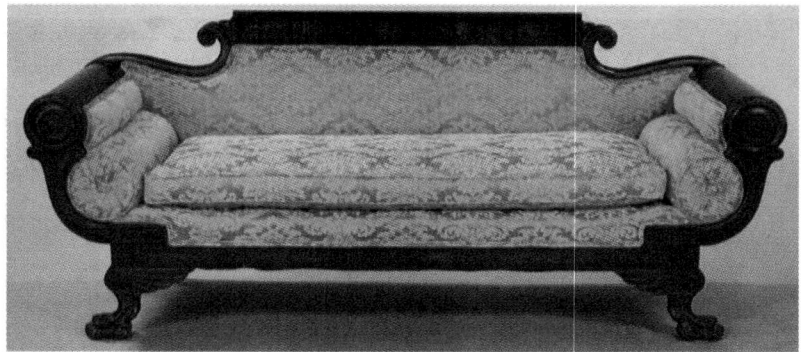

Late Victorian Classical Revival Sofa

English Knole-style Upholstered Sofa

Sofa, Classical Transitional style, mahogany, the triple-serpentine crestrail centered by three leaf-and-fruit-carved crests above the low upholstered back, heavy outscrolled arms w/scroll-carved supports on scroll-carved blocks flanking the deep ogee seatrail, on scroll-carved front feet, original finish, ca. 1850, 28 x 80", 34" h. (ILLUS., previous page) **800**

Sofa, Classical Revival style, mahogany, a flat central back crestrail flanked by long S-scroll rails above the long upholstered back flanked by cylindrical arms on forked curved front arm supports flanking bolsters & a long cushion seat, the flat molded seatrail raised on carved winged-paw front legs, America, late 19th c., 27 x 78", 33" h. (ILLUS., bottom of previous page) **1,265**

Sofa, Louis XVI-Style, hardwood w/carved & gilt decoration, the long rounded crestrail & arms w/ribbon, scroll & acanthus leaf decoration, padded open arms w/incurved arm supports above the over-upholstered seat on a narrow carved seatrail, on tapered & fluted front legs, France, probably early 20th c., traces of old gilt & white paint, upholstery worn & soiled, missing cushion, 32 x 38", 75" l. **825**

Sofa, Victorian Knole-type, upholstered, the high flat back upholstered w/three pads flanked by high flat upholstered arms all topped by large pairs of bamboo-turned corner finials, a three-cushion seat over a deep upholstered fringe-trimmed apron, England, late 19th c., 31 x 67", 35" h. (ILLUS., top of page) **2,530**

Sofa, Victorian Rococo style, carved & laminated rosewood, finely carved crestrail w/scrolls topped by floral-carved crests above the upholstered back, crestrail continuing down to form closed arms

Belter Victorian Rococo Sofa

w/incurved arm supports, the long upholstered seat w/serpentine seatrail centered by carved florals, demi-cabriole front legs on casters, probably "Rosalie" patt., John H. Belter, New York City, ca. 1855, one rear leg repaired, 34 x 42", 5' 2" l. (ILLUS.) **3,740**

Sofa, Victorian Rococo style, carved & laminated rosewood, the high serpentine crestrail pierce-carved overall w/leafy scrolls & grape clusters & centered by a high flower- and shell-carved crest, the crestrail curving down around the high tufted upholstered back to the closed rolled arms w/incurved arm supports, a long upholstered seat w/serpentine molded seatrail centered by a scroll-carved cluster, on demi-cabriole legs on casters, the "Hawkins" pattern by J. & J.W. Meeks, New York City, ca. 1855, 40 x 65", 50" h. (ILLUS., top next page) **10,925**

Rare Meeks "Hawkins" Pattern Rosewood Sofa

Meeks "Henry Ford" Pattern Sofa

Sofa, Victorian Rococo style, carved & laminated rosewood, the ornate arched & pierce-carved crestrail centered by a pointed rose crest over gadrooned bands & open scrolls continuing to curved pierce-carved corners continuing down & flanking the high tufted upholstered back, closed arms w/incurved carved arm supports continuing to the serpentine finger-carved seatrail & demi-cabriole front legs on casters, "Henry Ford" patt. attributed to J. & J.W. Meeks, ca. 1855 (ILLUS.)..... **13,200**

Sofa, Victorian Rococo style, carved & laminated rosewood, the very long serpentine crest topped by a very ornate high pierced & carved crestrail, the highest central arch w/an ornate flower-carved crest above a long C-scroll & fruit-and-leaf carving, continuous S- and C-scrolls across the top w/high flower-carved crests at each end & continuing down & around to the half-length upholstered arms w/incurved arm supports, the long serpentine-front seat w/conforming seatrail carved w/ornate leafy scrolls & a central flower cluster, demi-cabriole front legs on casters, attributed to John H. Belter, New York City, similar to the "Tu-

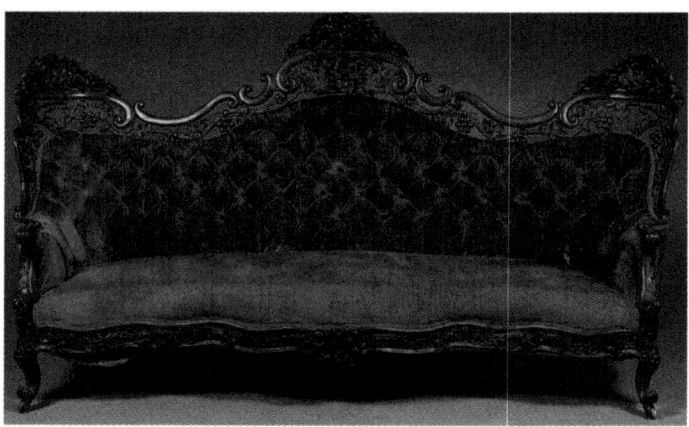

Fabulous Belter Rococo Sofa

thill King" patt., ca. 1855, 30 x 89 1/2", 4'
1 1/2" h. (ILLUS., bottom previous
page)... **49,450**

Triple-back Rosewood Rococo Sofa

Sofa, Victorian Rococo style, carved rosewood, triple-back style, a large oblong upholstered center section w/an arched rose-
carved crest & scroll-carved side brackets
to the flanking oval upholstered sections
w/smaller rose-carved crests, padded
open arms on incurved arm supports, long
serpentine seat above a deep conforming
seatrail carved w/leafy scrolls, on demi-cabriole front legs, original dark finish, later
upholstery, ca. 1860, 26 x 66", 42" h.
(ILLUS.) **2,500**

Sofa, Victorian Rococo style, carved rosewood, triple-back style, the high curved
end sections w/boldly carved C- and S-
scrolls topped by large carved cornucopias, the rails continuing to the arched lower center section w/C-scroll & fruit-carved
crest all above the tufted upholstered
back, closed half-arms w/incurved arm
supports flanking the long serpentine-
fronted seat w/a conforming seatrail
carved w/scrolls & a central fruit cluster,
demi-cabriole front legs on casters, attributed to John H. Belter, New York
City, ca. 1855, related to "Cornucopia"
patt., 31 x 72", 41 1/2" h. (ILLUS., bottom
of page) **20,125**

Sofa, Victorian Rococo style, walnut, triple-
back style, a large upholstered central
oval medallion within a molded frame
topped by a fruit-and-scroll-carved crest &

Rococo Triple-back Walnut Sofa

flanked by matching waisted balloon-form
upholstered panels w/further fruit-and-
scroll-carved crests, open padded arms
on incurved arm supports, the long dou-
ble-serpentine seat w/a conforming seatrail, raised on demi-cabriole front legs
on casters, refinished, ca. 1860, 30 x 72",
38" h. (ILLUS.)   .. **1,800**

Country-style Wagon Seat

Wagon seat, country-style, hardwood w/old
mustard paint over an earlier red, two-
part back w/double arched slats, tapered
round legs w/large round post at center
between the two old woven splint seats
w/grey paint, turned arms, wafer finials,
19th c., old gesso filler in some areas,
6 x 33 1/2", 29" h. (ILLUS.) **431**

Rococo Sofa with Carved Cornucopias

Mirrors

Dutch Baroque-Style Wall Mirror

Baroque-Style wall mirror, ebonized wood & cut glass, the wide rectangular frame composed of delicately pierce-carved corner squares & small center rails above mirrored panels & joined by a carved inner border framing the beveled mirror plate, Holland, late 19th c., 27 x 30 1/2" (ILLUS.) **546**

Mahogany Veneer Wall Mirror

Chippendale-Style wall mirror, dark & light mahogany veneer w/string inlay border, the arched scroll-carved crestrail centered by a pierced circle w/applied bird, arched scroll-carved base drop, England, probably 19th c., old refinishing, one scroll at side bottom replaced, separations & veneer losses, 37" h. (ILLUS.)...... **605**

American Chippendale Wall Mirror

Chippendale wall mirror, mahogany & mahogany veneer, the high domed & scroll-carved crest w/incurved ears above a rectangular molding enclosing the mirror plate, an ornate scroll-carved bottom drop crest, a short ear tip replaced, minor veneer restorations, mellow refinishing, 18th c., 22 x 44 1/2" (ILLUS.) **2,760**

Chippendale-Style Scrolled Mirror

Chippendale-Style wall mirror, mahogany, the high arched & boldly scroll-carved crestrail centered by an oval cut-out w/a gilt feather cluster, a rectangular molding around the mirror plate, a boldly scroll-carved bottom drop crest, America or England, late 19th c., 18 x 30 1/4" (ILLUS.)....... **230**

Classical Mirror-on-Stand

Classical mirror-on-stand, mahogany & mahogany veneer, a long horizontal wide rectangular frame enclosing a mirror & tilting between tall tapering spiral-twist carved uprights w/tiny carved pineapple finials, supported on a trestle base w/reeded outswept legs ending in paw feet joined by a spiral-twist stretcher centered by a leaf-carved block, possibly from the workshop of Duncan Phyfe, New York City, ca. 1820, 35" l., 30 1/2" h. (ILLUS.) **920**

Large Gilt Plaster Classical Mirror

Classical wall mirror, molded gilt plaster, a large rectangular frame molded in each corner w/a large fleur-de-lis joined along the sides by half-round molded columns enclosing a three-part mirror, original finish, mirrors resilvered, ca. 1830s, 20 x 44" (ILLUS.) **1,800**

Labeled American Federal Mirror

Federal wall mirror, mahogany veneer, the flat coved crestrail w/blocked ends above a rectangular reverse-painted glass panel brightly decorated w/a landscape scene of children playing, the sides mounted w/slender half-rounded reeded colonettes supported on lower corner blocks, original mirror plate, original paper label on the back reads "Thomas Natt & Son, Looking Glass Manufacturers, Print sellers...Philadelphia," worn silvering on mirror, slight flaking on top panel, ca. 1820, 21 x 40 1/4" (ILLUS.) **1,955**

20th Century Federal-Style Mirror

Federal-Style wall mirror, gilt gesso, a round molded frame set w/small spherules & topped by ornate pierced scrolls centered by a large spread-winged eagle, a leaf-carved base drop, first half 20th c., minor gesso damage, 24 x 41" (ILLUS.) **920**

Early George II Wall Mirror

George II wall mirror, walnut, the wide arched crestrail cut w/small notches above the arched & molded frame enclosing the conforming mirror plate, England, first quarter 18th c., 17 x 37" (ILLUS.) **633**

Louis XV-Style Overmantel Mirror

Louis XV-Style overmantel mirror, giltwood, the tall arched rectangular egg-

and-dart-carved frame topped by ornate pierced scrolls & a large shell crest, beveled mirror plate, France, late 19th c., 36 1/2" w., 5' 1 1/2" h. (ILLUS.) **1,725**

Fancy Louis XV-Style Wall Mirror

Louis XV-Style wall mirror, carved giltwood, the rectangular frame decorated around the sides & bottom w/ornate pierced scrolls, the top crestrail centered by a large scroll-carved cartouche crest, France, late 19th c., 37 x 66" (ILLUS.) **1,150**

Louis XVI-Style Rectangular Mirror

Louis XVI-Style wall mirror, giltwood, the rectangular wide coved frame decorated at each corner w/bands of delicate flowers & leaves w/a central floral cluster at

each side, France, third quarter 19th c.,
30 x 38" (ILLUS.) **633**

Napoleon III Overmantel Mirror

Napoleon III overmantel mirror, giltwood,
a deep molded rectangular frame
w/rounded top corners, France, third
quarter 19th c., 37 1/4 x 70" (ILLUS.)......... **1,150**

Italian Neoclassical Cheval Mirror

Neoclassical cheval mirror, walnut, surmounted by a gilded and pierced palmetto crest flanked by gilt urn-form finials,
the large rectangular mirror enclosed by
a floral-, urn- and griffin-inlaid frame &
supported on each side by two columns

also inlaid, raised on arched inlaid base
supports, Italy, late 18th c., 45" w., 7'
1" h. (ILLUS.).. **6,900**

Neoclassical Wall Mirror

Neoclassical wall mirror, carved wood &
gesso frame, openwork wreath pediment
w/descending bellflowers above rectangular mirror w/leaf & berry decoration at
base, original gilding, hand-planed mahogany backboard, Europe, 18th or 19th
c., gilding w/several restored corners &
leaves, small replaced parts, cracks &
separations to gesso, 17 x 32" (ILLUS.)........ **605**

Fancy Neoclassical-Style Pier Mirror

Neoclassical-Style pier mirror, gilt gesso,
the tall rectangular frame topped by an
ornate pierced crest centered by a pine-

apple & leaf finial over a large oval plaque embossed w/the figure of a classical woman, flanked by standing winged griffins, the molded crestrail w/a leaf band, openwork leafy swags across the top of the tall rectangular mirror flanked by side rails w/tall urns above caryatids & squared pilasters down the sides, deep molded base rail w/ornate scrolls, original finish, late 19th c., 30 x 66" (ILLUS.).... **2,500**

Queen Anne Wall Mirror

Queen Anne wall mirror, mahogany veneer, low arched & scroll-carved crestrail above the tall rectangular mirror within raised molded liner, flat bottom molding, backboards appear to be original, probably England, 18th c., old refinishing, veneer restoration, small veneer chip, 15 1/2 x 27 1/4" (ILLUS.)................................ **374**

Pair of Queen Anne-Style Mirrors

Queen Anne-Style wall mirrors, in the Chinese style, top panels w/raised & painted decoration of figures in exterior landscapes, base w/gilt bellflower decoration on red ground, probably England, late 18th or early 19th c., losses to silvering, back w/additional battens for support, painted surface w/extensive losses & separations, 20 x 56", pr. (ILLUS.) **14,300**

Italian Rococo-Style Wall Mirror

Rococo-Style wall mirrors, giltwood, the inner molded oval frame enclosed w/a wide border of serpentine pierce-carved leafy scrolls & blossoms w/a large shell-carved top crest & small shell-carved bottom drop crest, beveled oval mirror, Italy, 19th c., 35" w., 4' 11" h., pr. (ILLUS. of one)... **2,530**

Fancy Engraved Venetian Mirror

Venetian wall mirror, engraved glass, the high arched & pierced crestrail decorated w/delicate engraved scrolls & blossoms, the wide arched glass frame w/further delicate engraving enclosing the conforming mirror plate, Italy, 19th c., 28 1/2 x 55 1/2" (ILLUS.) **1,610**

Ornate Baroque Revival Mirror

Victorian Baroque Revival wall mirror, carved mahogany, wide rectangular frame ornately carved w/overal leafy scrolls & birds, the top crest centered by a large relief-carved cherub head w/wings, attributed to Horner of New York City, original finish, ca. 1880s, 32 x 42" (ILLUS.) **2,400**

Renaissance Revival Pier Mirror

American Beaux Arts Mirror

Victorian Beaux Arts style mirror, carved giltwood, a wide flat frame w/a narrow outer molded band of leaves & vines, the inner frame w/a molded pebbled finish, a thin inner beaded band around the mirror, late 19th c., 39 3/4 x 50" (ILLUS.)........... **460**

Victorian Renaissance Revival pier mirror, gilt-incised & ebony-trimmed walnut burl, the narrow coved crestrail w/blocked corners above the very tall slightly arched mirror plate flanked by narrow sides carved w/gilt-incised panels w/burl, the base w/a rectangular panel centered by a raised burl panel above a small rounded projecting shelf & flanked by blocked corners w/further burl, ca. 1875, 37" w., 9' 4" h. (ILLUS., top of column)... **1,265**

Ornate Gilt Oval Mirror

Victorian Renaissance Revival wall mirror, gilt gesso, oval beveled mirror in ornate frame, the pediment w/the figure of an angel & oval coat of arms flanked by scrolls over wreath swags, sides mounted w/gilt composition full-figured images of American Indians, one w/club, one w/bow & arrow, extensive vine, descending bellflower & grape decoration throughout, America, late 19th c., restoration to base, scattered repairs & regilding, angel possibly missing sword, 55 x 58" (ILLUS.) **4,620**

Rare American Overmantel Mirror

Victorian Rococo style overmantel mirror, carved giltwood, the large arched frame molded w/a narrow band of small cabochons, the crestrail further decorated w/leafy scrolls centered by a leaf crest, delicate pierced scrolls at the bottom corners, second half 19th c., 68" w., 8' 4" h. (ILLUS.)... **10,925**

Very Tall Rococo Pier Mirror

Victorian Rococo style pier mirror, giltwood, a very tall narrow rectangular mirror w/an arched top below the high arched & scroll-carved crestrail w/center

scroll cartouche & incurved corners, tall narrow gadroon-molded sides above the half-round serpentine white marble bottom shelf on a conforming base of pierced leafy scrolls & scroll front feet, surface now painted w/gold paint, mid-19th c., 16 x 45", 10' 7" h. (ILLUS.)........... **1,495**

Victorian Rococo Walnut Mirror

Victorian Rococo style wall mirror, walnut, a molded oval frame topped by a high arched pierced crest w/leafy scrolls, original dark finish, mid-19th c., 22 x 42" (ILLUS.).. **400**

Victorian English Japanned Mirror

Victorian wall mirror, japanned wood, the rectangular flattened frame w/coved corners decorated overall w/a black japanned ground highlighted w/gilt Chinese pavilion designs, long beveled mirror, England, ca. 1900, 20 x 34" (ILLUS.)... **690**

Parlor Suites

Louis XVI-Style Settee from Suite

Louis XVI-Style: settee & four side chairs; painted beechwood, the settee w/a long oval upholstered back panel within a narrow molded frame flanked by padded open arms & raised above the long upholstered seat, a narrow bowed seatrail ending in blocks above turned tapering & fluted front legs, France, ca. 1900, each piece 34 1/2" h., the set (ILLUS. of settee, above).. **3,450**

Victorian Renaissance Revival: sofa & two side chairs; walnut & burl walnut, the sofa w/a long gently curved tufted upholstery back centered by a gently arched central crestrail w/a peaked finial over an oval medallion carved in the image of a female face over narrow burl panels & urn-form corner finials, closed upholstered half-arms w/arm supports carved as female heads, serpentine seatrail trimmed w/oval burl panels, on tapering disk-and-baluster-turned front legs on casters, the matching chairs w/similar carved crests & incurved back stiles, refinished, newer upholstery, ca. 1870s, attributed to John Jelliff, Newark, New Jersey, sofa 70" l., the set (ILLUS., bottom of page)... **2,500**

Renaissance Revival Suite with Carved Heads

Top Quality Renaissance Revival Suite

Victorian Renaissance Revival: walnut; sofa, armchair & two side chairs, the sofa w/a long tufted upholstery back within a rectangular frame w/rounded top corners, the crestrail centered by a scroll-and-ribbon-carved crest, open padded arms on incurved arm supports, long oblong upholstered seat w/a carved apron raised on turned trumpet front legs on casters, the chairs w/matching frames, refinished, new brocade upholstery, attributed to Alexander Roux, New York City, ca. 1870, sofa 70" l., the set (ILLUS., above) **6,000**

Victorian Rococo: sofa, armchair & two side chairs; carved rosewood, the sofa w/an oval medallion w/tufted upholstery in the center below a floral-carved crest & curved crestrails continuing down to form the closed half-arms w/incurved arm supports, long serpentine seat w/a serpentine floral-carved seatrail on four demi-cabriole front legs on casters, the matching chairs w/shaped balloon backs, possibly original needlepoint upholstery, ca. 1865, original finish, sofa 72" l., the set (ILLUS., below) **3,000**

Restrained Rosewood Rococo Suite

Rococo Sofa from Rare Baudouine Set

Victorian Rococo: sofa, armchair & two side chairs; pierce-carved rosewood, the triple-back sofa w/tall upholstered balloon-shaped end backs enclosed by wide very ornate serpentine arched frames w/pierce-carved scrolls & a top crest carved in the form of a female face, the lower arched upholstered center back section w/a similar carved crestrail & arched crest, padded open arms w/incurved arm supports, the long upholstered seat w/a serpentine scroll-carved seatrail on demi-cabriole legs, the chairs w/balloon backs w/frames matching the end sections of the sofa, Charles Baudouine, New York City, ca. 1855, sofa 80" l., the set (ILLUS. of sofa, above) **30,000**

Armchairs from "Hawkins" Suite

Victorian Rococo: sofa, two armchairs & two side chairs; carved & laminated rosewood, each piece w/an ornate wide pierce-carved back frame composed of grapevines w/an arched & peaked scroll-carved crest, open padded arms w/incurved arm supports above the serpentine seats w/serpentine carved seatrails on demi-cabriole legs on casters, "Hawk-

ins" patt. by Meeks of New York City, ca. 1855, old refinish, sofa 65" l. (ILLUS. of armchairs)... **33,000**

Victorian Rococo style: sofa & two side chairs; carved & laminated rosewood, sofa w/a serpentine crestrail w/pierced carving consisting of scrollwork, leaves & grape clusters, the center section surmounted by a gadrooned molding centering a floral-carved cartouche, all above the upholstered back flanked by closed molded & outward scrolling arms w/incurved arm supports, serpentine seatrail carved w/scrolled cartouches, demi-cabriole front legs on casters, matching armchairs, attributed to J. & J. W. Meeks, New York City, ca. 1859, sofa 74" l., the set **7,638**

Screens

Victorian Tole Bathing Screen

Bathing screen, painted tole, a large upright convex rectangular panel w/rounded top corners raised on arched bar legs w/a center drop bar, the black ground painted in images of large stems of golden lilies & green leafy stems, England, late 19th c., 25" w., 4' 2 1/2" h. (ILLUS., previous page) **431**

arched scroll-cast crestrail topped by a loop handle, the scroll-cast upright sides joined by a scrolled bottom rail & raised on flaring arched legs, the mesh screen centered by an applied gilt-brass mount showing a young seated girl flanked by scrolls, France, late 19th c., 29 x 30 1/2" (ILLUS.).. **1,495**

Ornate Carved Rococo Firescreen

French Louis Philippe Firescreen

Firescreen, Louis Philippe style, mahogany, a large rectangular tapestry panel within a molded square w/a gently arched crestrail carved w/a gadroon band & arched, pierced & scroll-carved crest, raised on outswept leaf-carved legs ending in paw feet on casters, France, mid-19th c., 25 x 42 1/2" (ILLUS.) **1,035**

Firescreen, Victorian Rococo style, carved walnut, a plain flattened rectangular frame w/a high arched & scroll-carved crest rail centered by a pair of facing figural putti flanking a central shield, a serpentine & scroll-carved rail at the bottom, supported between slender ring-, rod- and knob-turned columns w/urn finials raised on arched & scroll-carved trestle feet, Philadelphia, mid-19th c., original finish, missing textile panel, 14 x 28", 42" h. (ILLUS.) **2,200**

Louis XV-Style Brass Firescreen

Firescreen, Louis XV-Style, gilt-brass & wire mesh, the ornate brass frame w/an

Painted Louis XVI-Style Screen

Folding screen, three-fold, Louis XVI-Style, parcel-gilt & polychrome beechwood, the three arched panels painted w/a colorful continuous landscape scene w/romantic figures in 18th c. costume, France, late 19th c., 74 1/2" w., 5' 7 1/2" h. (ILLUS., previous page)............... **2,760**

Screen with Romantic Scene

Folding screen, three-fold, Rococo-Style, the three tall arched panels painted w/a continuous colorful Italian landscape featuring figures & a large ruined Roman arch, England, early 20th c., 5' 7 1/2" h. (ILLUS.).. **1,093**

Georgian Pole Screen with Sampler

Pole screen, Georgian style, painted wood, a small square wood frame enclosing an alphabet sampler signed "Mary Nowne, Her work finished in the twelfth (sic) year of her age. 1827," also w/fruit, butterflies, dogs & a verse, raised on a tall slender tapering & ring-turned pole above a tripod base w/a turned center drop & splayed cabriole legs ending in scroll feet, overall black paint, small holes in sampler, England, overall 4' 5 1/4" h. (ILLUS.).. **748**

Georgian-Style Pole Screen

Pole screen, Georgian-Style, mahogany, oval wooden screen w/painted bouquet, on tapered pole w/urn finial, turned pedestal above three spider legs, England, probably 19th c., grime & wear to painted surface, 52" h. (ILLUS.).................................... **935**

English Needlepoint Pole Screen

Pole screen, Victorian Rococo style, European walnut, rectangular scrolled frame holds needlepoint panel of spaniel lying on a pillow, small brass urn-shaped finial on top, spiral column on three scrolled cabriole legs decorated w/raised carved fruit, England, restorations to column & one leg, 4' 10" h. (ILLUS.) **1,265**

Secretaries

Chippendale Secretary-Bookcase

Chippendale secretary-bookcase, walnut, two-part construction: the top w/two doors, each w/four chamfered panels, horizontal backboards; the base w/twelve stepped interior drawers below eight cubbyholes flanking prospect door, over four lipped & graduated dovetailed drawers, original dovetailed bracket feet & base w/vertical backboards & original rosehead nails, found in Georgia, replaced brass pulls & hinges, cornice missing one piece of molding, one door detached w/splintered hinge mounts, old refinishing, patches, separations & repair throughout, 24 x 39", 7' 4" h. (ILLUS.) **4,840**

Rare Southern Federal Secretary

Federal secretary-bookcase, cherry, curly maple & mahogany veneer, two-part construction: the upper section w/a broken-scroll crest w/star-inlaid terminals & three turned urn finials above a coved cornice over a pair of tall Gothic arch-paneled cupboard doors opening to three adjustable shelves; the stepped-out lower section w/a fall-front oval-paneled drawer w/oval brasses opening to an interior fitted w/eight pigeonholes, eight small drawers w/bold curly maple facings & a center door w/variegated star inlay opening to hidden compartments, the lower case w/a pair of cupboard doors paneled to form a single large Gothic arch & flanked by small vertical panels w/a Gothic arch over a quatrefoil, short ring-turned legs w/peg feet, replaced backboard & finials, some pieced repairs, possibly from Kentucky, early 19th c., 22 3/4 x 44", overall 8' 9" h. (ILLUS.) **7,188**

Connecticut Federal Secretary

Federal secretary-bookcase, cherry, two-part construction: the upper section w/a narrow upright cornice divided by three reeded blocks w/brass urn finials above a narrow molding above a pair of paneled cupboard doors w/wooden knobs opening to eleven shelves above a flat fold-down writing surface opening to two rows of small drawers above a row of pigeonholes; the projecting lower section w/three long reverse-graduated beaded drawers w/round brass pulls flanked by reeded stiles above the ring- and baluster-turned legs w/knob feet, minor restorations, wooden pulls replaced, attributed to Connecticut, late 18th - early 19th c., 20 1/2 x 42", overall 6' 6 3/4" h. (ILLUS.)... **3,450**

Federal secretary-bookcase, mahogany & mahogany veneer, two-part construction: the upper section w/a rectangular top & narrow coved cornice above a pair of raised-panel doors opening to two shelves above a pair of drawers w/wooden knobs; the lower section w/a mid-molding above a fold-out writing surface above a long projecting drawer above two inset long drawers flanked by baluster- and ring-turned columns, flat apron w/blocked ends raised on ring- and baluster-turned legs w/peg feet, old finish, support pulls replaced, early 19th c., 20 x 38", 5' 1 1/4" h. (ILLUS., top next column)... **1,955**

Federal-Style secretary-bookcase, inlaid mahogany, two-part construction: cornice w/urn finials & eagle pediment above three arched doors each side; the

Federal Mahogany Secretary

base w/three dovetailed & cockbeaded drawers w/brass pulls, French feet, probably Centennial, supports for fall board missing knobs, veneer chips & losses, surface worn w/scuffs & scratches, 19 x 37", 6' 3" h... **1,540**

Queen Anne-Style Secretary

Queen Anne-Style secretary-bookcase, walnut, two-part construction: the upper section w/a double-arch deep molded cornice above a pair of tall arched mirrored cupboard doors; the lower section w/a mid-molding above a hinged slant front opening to a leather-lined writing surface, storage well & various drawers & pigeonholes over a false drawer & another molded band above three long graduated lower drawers, batwing brasses & keyhole escutcheons, molded base on bun feet, England, mid-18th century & later, 24 1/2 x 36", 7' h. (ILLUS., bottom previous page) **6,613**

Unique Aesthetic Secretary

Victorian Aesthetic Movement secretary-bookcase, walnut, unusual side-by-side design, the top w/a three-section low back rail w/line-incised scrolls separated by upright narrow blocks each fronted by a low open arched bracket on the long rectangular top w/a wide deeply bowed center section above a conforming case, narrow decorative bands above the lower case centered by the wide & tall bowed center section w/a pair of sliding tambour doors opening to reveal a desk w/storage compartments above the kneehole opening, the flat side sections each w/a tall glazed door opening to shelves above a stepped-out scroll-incised drawer, paneled sides, ca. 1885, refinished, 24 x 54", 6' h. (ILLUS.) **2,400**

Victorian Golden Oak secretary-book-case, oak, side-by-side-style, the rectangular top w/a high front crestrail w/pointed & rounded corner ears featuring panels of ornate stamped scrolling, a center block of three half-round knobs, the left side of the case w/a tall glazed door opening to wood shelves beside an open compartment backed by a mirror above a drawer w/stamped brass pulls

Oak Secretary with Stamped Panels

over a square fold-down writing surface decorated w/a tapering balloon panel w/stamped scrolls above another drawer w/brass pulls, the lower case w/a pair of long rectangular cupboard doors decorated w/matching tapering balloon-shaped panels w/stamped scrolls, molded base w/bracket feet, original hardware, refinished, ca. 1900, 16 x 40", 6' h. (ILLUS.) **1,200**

Fancy Light & Dark Oak Secretary

Victorian Golden Oak secretary-book-case, quarter-sawn oak, side-by-side-style, a high arched crestrail trimmed w/a band of dark-stained scrolls above a narrow open shelf over the two-section cabinet, the left side w/a dark-stained top bracket beside a long narrow rectangular shelf below a long half-round beveled mirror & above a tall flat glazed door trimmed w/dark-stained banding & opening to wooden shelves, the right side w/a pair of large dark-stained scrolls flanking a recessed oval panel w/dark-stained scrolls beside a vertical narrow quarter-round beveled mirror above a rectangular shelf above a flat hinged fall front w/a large stamped scroll-decorated & stained panel above two drawers w/pierced brass pulls above a bottom cupboard door stamped w/a long dark-stained C-scroll panel, serpentine apron & C-form bracket feet, refinished, ca. 1900, 16 x 40", 6' 3" h. (ILLUS., previous page) .. **2,500**

Oak Secretary with Classical Details

Victorian Golden Oak secretary-book-case, quarter-sawn oak, side-by-side-style w/Classical Revival detailing, the long serpentine crestrail w/applied scrolls & a central shell above a long rectangular shelf w/an ogee apron raised on tall round columns running all the way down the sides & flanking the two-part case, a long narrow rectangular beveled mirror below the top shelf & above the case, the left side w/a tall curved glass door opening to wooden shelves, the right side w/a short rectangular leaded glass door w/a fleur-de-lis design above the wide fall front opening to a fitted interior above a stack of three long drawers w/pierced

brass pulls, raised on heavy C-scroll front feet, refinished, ca. 1900, 18 x 42", 5' 8" h. (ILLUS.)................................. **1,800**

Cherry "Cylinder-front" Secretary

Victorian Renaissance Revival "cylinder-front" secretary-bookcase, cherry & burl walnut, two-part construction: the upper section w/a gently arched & notch-cut plain crestrail on dentil-carved cornice above a pair of tall glazed doors w/angled tops trimmed w/raised triangular panels & surrounded by narrow raised panels, w/cast-iron latch opening to shelves; the lower section w/a two-panel cylinder front opening to a pull-out writing surface & fitted interior above a wide mid-molding over a pair of cupboard doors w/raised rectangular burl panels & bordered by narrow burl panels, paneled sides, flat molded base on thin square gadrooned feet, old refinish, ca. 1875, 22 x 42", 7' 8" h. (ILLUS.)........................... **2,000**

Victorian Rococo secretary, walnut & burl walnut, a large square upright shallow case w/beaded molding framing a large mirror on the drop-down front panel opening to create a writing surface w/an inset tooled leather top & fitted w/small drawers & pigeonholes, an ornate pierce-carved apron across the case bottom, raised on a trestle base w/beaded & in-curved uprights above heavy angled shoe feet joined by a pair of long baluster- and ring-turned stretchers, ca. 1860, 16 x 26", 4' 2" h. (ILLUS., top next page) **1,955**

Unusual Rococo Walnut Secretary

Austrian Rococo Secretary-Bookcase

Victorian Rococo secretary-bookcase,
carved mahogany, two-part construction:

the upper section w/a high arched cre-strail ornately pierce-carved w/scrolls & flowers flanked by turned urn finials above the arching frieze over a pair of arched cupboard doors inset w/large mirrors framed w/scroll molding & scroll-carved corner brackets; the stepped-out lower section w/a gadrooned edge above a fall-front long drawer opening to a writing surface flanked by low spindled gallery rails & exposing four rock maple small drawers above a pair of large paneled cupboard doors w/scroll-carved molding flanked by scroll-carved corner blocks, deep molded base w/outset rounded corners & an ornate serpentine scroll-carved apron, on flat bun feet, probably Austria, mid-19th c., 20 x 43", 6' 5" h. (ILLUS.)..................................... **5,520**

Shelves

Decorated Apothecary Shelves

Apothecary shelves, walnut & pine, dovetailed case at top w/twelve dovetailed drawers w/old brass pulls, a shelf at base, single-board end panels w/scalloped bases & re-shaped arched top & heart cutouts, late black over red sponged decoration, 10 1/2 x 39", 37" h. (ILLUS.).. **1,725**

Floor shelves, oak, elaborate corner posts having scalloped bracket bases & applied floral vining w/open twist columns at centers, relief carved urn finials on front, shell & grape finials on back, three shelves w/carved center aprons, old refinishing, Europe, one center apron missing, one back finial chipped, 23 1/2 x 67 1/2", 5' 10" h. (ILLUS., top next page)..................................... **1,725**

Elaborate Carved Floor Shelves

Wall corner shelves, hardwood w/red marble tops, approximately 2"-thick red marble top w/astragal molding, dovetailed & carved Greek key frieze, two scrolled legs w/paw feet centering on ball, probably Europe, 18th c., missing one marble top, feet w/repairs & restorations, other losses to frieze, repairs, separations, scattered worm damage, 16 x 22", 30" h., pr..................................... **1,650**

Unique Man-Head Folk Art Shelf

Wall shelf, carved wood, a wide rectangular shelf w/rounded front corners & an arch-carved border supported atop the large carved stylized head of a man w/curly hair & a heavy mustache, the large eyes painted white, original black paint, re-

paired splits in shelf, 19th c., 9 x 10 7/8", 8" h. plus hangers (ILLUS.)............................ **978**

English Chinoiserie Wall Shelf

Wall shelf, lacquered & parcel-gilt wood, folding-type, the large oblong backboard w/a fancy scroll-cut border, fitted w/a half-round shelf on a swing-out brace support, the backboard in black lacquer decorated overall in color w/various Chinese figures, England, second quarter 19th c., 5 1/2 x 9 3/4", 14 1/4" h. (ILLUS.)..... **690**

Early Painted Whale-end Shelves

Wall shelves, early American country-style, painted pine, whale-end style, a narrow rectangular top shelf above tapering rounded & scroll-cut sides flanking three narrow graduated shelves joined by a back slat, original black & red decoration & old varnishing, attributed to New England, early 19th c., minor wear, 8 1/4 x 32 7/8", 39 1/2" h. (ILLUS.)............. **1,840**

Maple Whale-end Wall Shelves

Wall shelves, maple, whale-end style, three narrow graduated open shelves between serpentine shaped sides, old brown wash, 19th c., nails of various ages & some empty nail holes, minor chips, 26" w., 25 3/4" h. (ILLUS.)................... **345**

Poplar Four-Shelf Wall Unit

Wall shelves, poplar, a three-arch crestrail above a narrow top shelf above three graduated open shelves fitted into the scalloped sides, old refinishing, square nail construction, 19th c., 27 1/2" w., 44 3/4" h. (ILLUS.)... **546**

Sideboards

Fine Calamander Art Deco Sideboard

Art Deco sideboard, calamander, the rectangular top w/a slightly bowed front inset w/marble above a case fitted w/two wide cabinet doors opening to a fitted bar, joined by stepped side supports above a plinth base, probably France, ca. 1930s, 21 x 65 1/2", 42 3/4" h. (ILLUS.) **6,325**

Classical Country-style Sideboard

Classical country-style sideboard, cherry, shaped top w/four conforming central dovetailed drawers flanked by two drawers w/chamfered fronts above two paneled doors, double split-spindle columns on front, turned feet, inlaid diamond escutcheons, back w/frame-&-panel construction w/cut nails, possibly Catawba Valley, North Carolina, missing locks, old refinishing w/surface chips, scattered old repairs, separations, losses, possibly missing splash panel, 24 x 48", 48" h. (ILLUS., above) **4,840**

Classical server, mahogany w/marble top, mottled salmon & ivory marble top, conforming base w/plum pudding mahogany frieze w/brass trim above tapered circular columns & ball feet, America, 19th c., small chips & separations to Ionic capitals, old refinishing, minor chips & losses to surface, missing one piece of molding under marble at one side, missing piece of brass molding under frieze proper right side, 22 1/2 x 46 1/2", 36" h. **2,860**

Large Classical Mahogany Sideboard

Classical sideboard, cherry w/mahogany veneer, the stepped flat upright crest board divided by four flat blocks above the rectangular top above a case w/a long bevel-edged drawer flanked by smaller bevel-edged drawers projecting above a pair of central paneled doors flanked by single paneled doors, all separated by a set of four heavy turned & leaf-carved columns on the plinth base raised on four heavy scroll-carved paw feet, old pressed glass drawer pulls, ca. 1840, 23 x 72", 4' 5 1/2" h. (ILLUS., next column) **1,725**

New York Classical Mahogany Sideboard

Federal Sideboard in Cherry

Classical sideboard, mahogany & mahogany veneer, a high broken-scroll backboard centered by a large block & urn finial & w/small urn finials on each end above the rectangular top fitted w/spindled end galleries above slide-out work shelves, the main case w/a long central drawer flanked by shorter drawers above a central pair of paneled cupboard doors flanked by single paneled doors, the drawers & doors separated by reeded pilasters, raised on tapering ring- and rod-turned legs w/peg feet, New York City, ca. 1820s, 25 1/4 x 66 1/4", 5' 4" h. (ILLUS., bottom previous page) **5,175**

Federal sideboard, cherry, rounded central section w/two conforming drawers above bay w/two doors, flanked by small drawers above cellaret drawer flanked by reeded pilasters & two swell-front drawers w/conforming doors below, dovetailed & cockbeaded drawers, six tapered & reeded legs, frame-and-panel sides, drawer faces w/fancy cherry veneer & mahogany banding, swell-front doors & drawers of stacked-block construction, old, possibly original uneven finish, brass pulls possibly original, Tennessee or Kentucky, early 19th c., some drawer surfaces replaned, possibly missing splash panel, most locks replaced, cellaret drawers missing interior dividers, several minor scratches, veneer losses & separations throughout, 25 x 44", 6' 5" h. (ILLUS., top of page)................................. **15,400**

Federal sideboard, inlaid mahogany, the rectangular serpentine top w/a bowed central section above a conforming case w/concave drawers over concave cupboard doors w/oval band & marquetry inlay flanking the long bowed line-inlaid drawer projecting over a pair of flat doors w/circle inlay, on four square tapering line-inlaid front legs, ca. 1800, 27 3/4 x 63", 39 1/4" h. (ILLUS., below)..... **4,370**

Fine Inlaid Mahogany Federal Sideboard

English Jacobean-Style Server

Jacobean-Style server, carved oak, a high peaked backboard centered by a large carved rosette above the rectangular top over an apron carved w/a band of arched leaves & supported on heavy turned front supports above two more open shelves each w/a carved apron & flanked by two heavy turned supports, short heavy cylinder & disk front legs, old dark finish, England, 19th c., reconstruction & pieced repair, 16 x 46", 4' 4" h. (ILLUS.)................ **1,150**

Jacobean-Style Oak Sideboard

Jacobean-Style sideboard, oak, the rectangular top above a case w/a pair of deep drawers each carved w/pairs of squared panels & flanked by knob-turned half-spindles, a molded apron raised on baluster- and ring-turned front legs joined to the square back legs w/box stretchers, partially composed of antique elements, England, 19th c., 21 x 52 1/2", 34" h. (ILLUS.) **1,150**

Louis XV-Style Provincial sideboard, pearwood, the rectangular top w/molded edges above a case w/a pair of long scroll-carved drawers w/long pierced-

Dated Louis XV-Style Sideboard

brass mounts centering a carved sunburst above a pair of long cupboard doors w/arched & scroll-carved panels & long pierced-brass hardware flanking a central caduceus-carved panel, the serpentine scroll-carved apron centered by a carved wreath enclosing the date "1831," on short scroll-carved front legs, France, 22 1/2 x 53 1/2", 37 1/2" h. (ILLUS.)... **3,450**

Renaissance Revival Sideboard

Renaissance Revival sideboard, walnut, three-part construction, the top w/beveled mirror glass at the back of the pie shelf & inside the top; the middle section w/relief-carved arched center crest w/glass interior shelf; the base w/grey, brown & white marble top, flat front w/bowed ends, two doors w/relief carving on raised panels w/two dovetailed drawers above, short turned wafer feet, Europe, 21 x 59 1/2", 6' 7 1/2" h. (ILLUS.)... **1,265**

Ornate Baroque-Style Sideboard

Victorian Baroque Revival sideboard, carved oak, two-part construction: the upper section w/a rectangular blocked top fitted w/a high arched & scrolling pierce-carved crest w/a central cartouche flanked by small turned corner finials above the deep flaring cornice w/a scroll-carved frieze band over a pair of tall cupboard doors w/rounded panels w/raised molding enclosing ornately carved game trophies flanked by pierce-carved scrolling brackets & two small shelves above a recessed paneled compartment flanked by ornately carved brackets; the lower section w/a wide rectangular top w/a molded edge over a pair of narrow paneled drawers carved w/grapevines above a pair of paneled cupboard doors w/raised molding enclosing finely carved clusters of fruits, three slender turned columns resting on projecting blocks separate & flank the doors, on compressed bun feet, refinished, Europe, late 19th c., 24 x 60", 9' h. (ILLUS.)................................ **5,500**

Victorian Baroque Revival sideboard, oak, a tall splashback w/an ornately carved crestrail w/a basket of fruit flanked by reclining dragons all above a plain recessed panel, raised block corners over carved lion masks, the long rectangular top w/blocked corners above a case w/a row of three drawers carved w/leafy scrolls & each separated by a block carved w/a stylized blossom head all above a row of three large doors w/oval carved panels, the central door w/a large scrolled cartouche framed by leafy scrolls & the matching outer doors carved w/large urns of fruit over scrolls, the central door flanked by vertical herringbone-

Very Ornate Victorian Baroque Sideboard

carved blocks above the blocked apron, each outside edge w/a large barley twist-carved column, raised on bulbous squatty feet, ca. 1890, American-made, refinished, 26 x 76", 5' h. (ILLUS.).................... **3,500**

Decorative Golden Oak Server

Victorian Golden Oak server, quartersawn oak, a shaped beveled mirror within a pierced & scroll-carved frame above the rectangular top over a pair of drawers above a pair of long rectangular leaded glass doors, a long scroll-carved drawer across the bottom, on tall slender squared legs on casters, original hardware, refinished, ca. 1895, 18 x 40", 4' 6" h. (ILLUS.)................................ **1,750**

Victorian Golden Oak sideboard, a high rectangular beveled mirror w/a wide flat frame & top scroll-carved center crest enclosing a long beveled mirror, the rectangular top w/molded edges over a pair of flat cupboard doors w/arched tops flanking a long bowed central geometrically

Golden Oak Sideboard with Mirror

glazed cupboard door above a long drawer at the bottom w/scroll-carved trim & scalloped apron, squared outswept front legs w/paw feet, original brasses & dark finish, ca. 1910, 20 x 48", 5' h. (ILLUS.) **1,600**

Victorian Renaissance Revival server, walnut & burl walnut, the superstructure w/a peaked pediment centered by a large fleur-de-lis finial & small raised burl panels above a flaring molding above a wide panel w/incurved sides centered by a large round raised burl panel w/a carved sunburst & shaped raised burl panels

Handsome Renaissance Server

over a long narrow rectangular shelf w/rounded corners & flanked by small turned finials, the shelf supported on high pierced & scroll-cut brackets flanking a wide panel centered by a raised oval banding enclosing burl veneer, all atop the rectangular white marble top w/rounded front corners over a conforming case, the case w/a pair of drawers w/oval burl panels above a pair of cupboard doors w/large oval sunken panels w/burl veneer, deep molded flat base on casters, original finish, ca. 1875, 20 x 42", 7' 4" h. (ILLUS.) **2,600**

Elaborate Renaissance Sideboard

Victorian Renaissance Revival sideboard, carved oak, the tall superstructure w/a high arched & ornately scroll-carved crestrail centered by a large carved realistic stag head above a long half-round shelf supported on baluster-turned supports on a lower open shelf w/a closed paneled back flanked by pierced scrolls, the lower shelf supported by large projecting brackets w/fruit carving resting on the long white marble top & flanked by further pierced scrolls at the sides, the lower case w/a pair of paneled drawers w/fruit- and nut-carved pulls above a pair of arched panel doors centered by large relief-carved clusters of dead game, the beveled front corners trimmed w/carved scrolls, on a plinth base, related in style to an Alexander Roux example, ca. 1870, 23 1/2 x 59", 7' 6" h. (ILLUS.) **4,140**

Victorian Renaissance Revival sideboard, walnut, burl & figured walnut, the tall superstructure topped by a high broken-scroll pediment w/an arched crest on the center section above a full-relief

Sideboard with Head of Robin Hood

Extra Wide Renaissance Sideboard

carved bust of Robin Hood above a wide rectangular shelf w/rounded corners supported on scroll-cut brackets above a molded narrow rectangular panel w/figured walnut & a long narrow shaped raised burl panel over another slightly longer shelf on brackets above a larger figured walnut panel w/a large raised burl panel all flanked by scroll-cut side brackets, a half-round grey marble top w/a flattened front section above a conforming case w/a long narrow center drawer w/narrow raised burl panels flanked by curved matching swing-out trays at the sides all above three large paneled doors each centered by a large carved cartouche, deep molded base band on wafer feet, refinished, 1870s, 22 x 60", 8' 5" h. (ILLUS.) **7,500**

Victorian Renaissance Revival sideboard, walnut & burl walnut, massive size, the tall & wide superstructure w/a high arched central section w/a long pierced crest centered by a carved palmette & scrolls above further carved scrolls & an arched molding, the matching broken-scroll side crest above tall & wide carved & burl-veneered side panels w/large half-round candle shelves flanking the large arched mirror which rests above narrow burl-paneled drawers on the long rectangular white marble top w/blocked corners & projecting center section, a conforming case w/a large stepped-out center paneled door w/burl veneer & a carved oblong medallion flanked by blocked side pilasters, each

side section w/a paneled drawer over a smaller cupboard door w/burl veneer & a large raised diamond-shaped panel, blocked pilasters at the outside corners, wide blocked flat base band, original dark finish, ca. 1875, 24 x 68", 8' 6" h. (ILLUS.)... **6,500**

Finely Carved Rococo Sideboard

Victorian Rococo sideboard, chestnut, the tall superstructure w/an arched & stepped crestrail over a panel centered by a large relief-carved cluster of fruits & nuts above two long narrow tiered half-round open shelves supported by scrolling uprights w/fruit carving, the shaped outside edges carved in bold C-scroll & fruit decoration, all resting on a half-round white marble top w/a flat projecting center section above a conforming case w/a pair of paneled central drawers flanked by curved end drawers, two flat paneled front doors w/carved fruit clusters & corner roundels w/plain curved & paneled end doors, conforming molded flat base, attributed to Alexander Roux, New York City, ca. 1855-60, original finish, 22 x 70", 6' 2" h. (ILLUS.)..................... **5,500**

Outstanding Fruit-carved Rococo Sideboard

Victorian Rococo sideboard, figured walnut, the high superstructure w/an arched pediment w/a large scroll finial flanked by delicate pierced scrolls over a panel w/shaped raised panels flanking a circle of carved fruit above a long narrow shelf w/rounded corners supported w/turned & reeded spindles on another long shelf backed by a long narrow shaped mirror flanked by incurved scroll-carved sides & raised on scroll-cut brackets flanking another matching mirror & flanked at each side by asymmetrical recessed burl panels & ornate pierced C-scrolls at the outer edges, on a long half-round white marble top w/a flattened center section, the conforming case w/a pair of paneled drawers flanked by curved swing-out side storage trays above four large cupboard doors, the center two w/flat fronts w/arched panels centering oval banding enclosing a large relief-carved cluster of fruit, the curved side doors w/similar molding but centered by large scroll-carved cartouch-

es, flat molded base, original polished finish, marked by Mitchell and Rammelsberg Co., Cincinnati, Ohio, ca. 1855, 22 x 66", 8' 6" h. (ILLUS.)......................... **10,000**

Rococo Sideboard with Oval Mirror

Victorian Rococo sideboard, walnut & burl walnut, the tall, wide superstructure w/a large arched & molded pediment centered by a fruit-carved finial over a wide smooth panel topped by a pendent carved fruit cluster, scroll-carved flaring sides down to a long narrow open shelf w/a serpentine front supported on slender turned spindles resting on small half-round side shelves on scroll-cut brackets all backed by pairs of carved scrolls centering a long oval mirror, the rectangular white marble top above a conforming case w/a pair of paneled drawers w/scroll-carved pulls over three cupboard doors each w/a large recessed oval burl panel framed at each corner by small triangular raised burl panels, deep molded flat base on casters, refinished, ca. 1860, 22 x 54", 7' 8" h. (ILLUS.)........................... **3,500**

Stands

Baker's stand, wrought iron & brass, composed of a tall rectangular back made up of narrow horizontal bars & topped by three scrolled crests, fitted w/three open half-round wire shelves w/brass band fronts & supported in the center by ornate scrolling iron brackets w/a vertical bar w/brass finial projecting at the front center, Europe, 19th c., 18 x 47 1/2", 6' 4" h. (ILLUS., top next page) **978**

Iron & Brass Baker's Stand

Decoupage-decorated Candlestand

Candlestand, Chippendale country style, hardwood w/old dark surface, oval top decorated w/ornate cutouts & birds, on turned column pedestal on snake feet, decorated w/decoupage strips on the feet & up the column to resemble fluting & around the top, late 18th - early 19th c. w/later decoration,   15 x 20 3/4", 26 1/4" h. (ILLUS.) **3,220**

Octagonal Burlwood Candlestand

Candlestand, country-style, burlwood, octagonal top on four legs, the top w/inlaid frieze, the tapered legs ending in pad feet & shaped returns, probably Italian, 19th c., missing original slide-out tray for candle, 25 1/2" h. (ILLUS.) **1,650**

Candlestand, Federal country-style, cherry, nearly square one-board top w/applied beaded edge molding raised on an urn- and baluster-turn pedestal on a tripod base w/arched spider legs, original dark finish, early 19th c., 16" w., 28" h. (minor edge chips, hairline in edge molding) **3,410**

Federal Country Candlestand

Candlestand, Federal country-style tilt-top type, birch, rectangular top w/beveled corners raised & tilting above an urn-turned pedestal on a tripod base w/spider legs, late 18th - early 19th c., traces of old red wash on base, pieced restorations to block & peg, 14 x 20", 26 1/2" h. (ILLUS.)..... **690**

Lobed-top Federal Candlestand

Candlestand, Federal country-style tilt-top type, cherry & curly maple, the oblong four-lobed top tilting above an urn-turned pedestal on a tripod base w/spider legs, old thin red wash, late 18th - early 19th c., 17 1/2 x 21", 27 1/2" h. (ILLUS.) **374**

Early Primitive Candlestand

Candlestand, primitive country-style, ash, hickory & cherry, the thin round cherry top raised on a heavy turned pedestal w/a ring-turned center raised on four simple turned canted legs, late 18th - early 19th c., rose head nails in top w/an age split, one leg damaged, 16 3/4" d., 22" h. (ILLUS.) **575**

Two-shelf Walnut Candlestand

Candlestand, Victorian novelty type, walnut, circular top on pedestal above six-sided shelf w/petal-carved border above three heavily carved tapered square legs w/lion's head designs, iron mechanism adjusts height, England, mid-19th c., separations in top two pieces, 18 x 19", 31 to 50" h. (ILLUS.) **715**

Federal Style Mahogany Canterbury

Canterbury (music stand), Federal, mahogany, two compartments w/vertical slats, openwork hand hole, turned legs w/original brass cuffs & casters, dovetailed drawer, original surface, England or America, early 19th c., minor chips to one leg, minor surface scratches & abrasions, 13 x 18", 23" h. (ILLUS.) **1,650**

Painted and Inlaid Louis XVI Revival Nightstands

Victorian Rosewood Canterbury

Canterbury (music stand), Victorian, rosewood, a flat rectangular top frame w/two slats raised on rows of slender tapering ring-turned spindles above a rectangular top over a single drawer w/small wooden knobs, raised on short bobbin-turned legs, England, mid-19th c., 16 x 22", 17 1/2" h. (ILLUS.) **1,150**

Simple Louis XV Revival Stands

Nightstands, Louis XV Revival style, walnut & burl walnut, the rectangular tan marble top w/serpentine sides above a bombe-shaped case w/a long drawer over a pair of cabinet doors, outset corners continuing down to form outswept legs, cast-brass mounts at the top corners & at the feet, overall banded veneering, original finish, ca. 1920s, 14 x 20", 28" h., pr. (ILLUS.) **750**

Nightstands, Louis XVI Revival style, inlaid mahogany, rectangular white marble top w/gently rounded ends above a conforming case w/two drawers w/patterned veneering & a delicate floral-inlaid rectangular band overlapping both drawers, the gently curved side panels w/matching inlay, a white-painted molding w/scroll-carved center drop raised on four white-painted round tapering stop-fluted legs all w/gilt trim, silvered metal teardrop drawer pulls, original finish, ca. 1920s, 16 x 20", 28" h., pr. (ILLUS., top of page)...... **650**

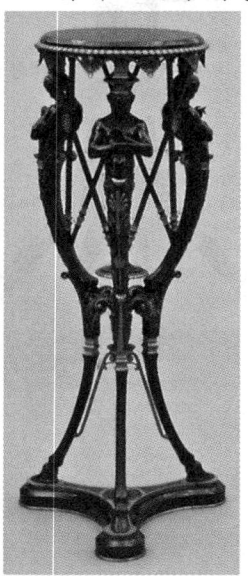

Neo-Grecque Metal Parlor Stand

Parlor stand, bronze-patinated & parcel-gilt metal, a round polished black slate top above a tripod base w/three serpentine legs composed of figural Neo-Grecque-style monopoedal classical termes highlighted w/gilt trim & resting on a tripart base, France, third quarter 19th c., 42" h. (ILLUS., previous page)............................. **4,830**

Parlor stand, Renaissance Revival style, carved oak, tapered form, dovetailed case for top portion, egg-&-leaf base molding, decorated w/carved panels w/ribbons & trophies of agriculture, England or Europe, separations & losses to carving, finish removed, 11 x 13", 4' 4" h... **1,650**

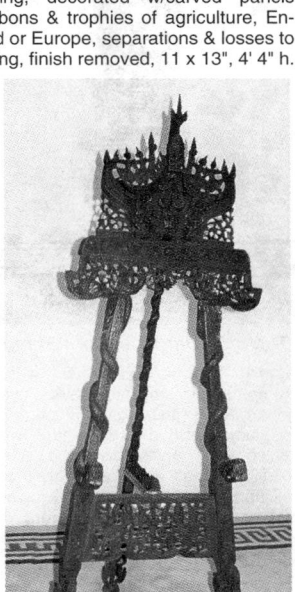

Ornate Anglo-Indian Picture Stand

Picture stand, easel-type, Anglo-Indian, carved mahogany, the top panel ornately pierce-carved w/bands of tiny figures & scrolls centering an ornately relief-carved three-prong panel, raised on three canted legs carved at the top w/entwined snakes ending in projecting small brackets, joined at the front by a wide pierce-carved stretcher above lower legs carved w/stylized dragons, original finish, India, ca. 1890, 28" w., 6' 6" h. (ILLUS.).... **2,500**

Picture stand, Victorian Renaissance Revival substyle, easel-type, gilt-incised & ebonized-accented walnut, the tall tapering front frame topped by a large carved palmette finial above an arched panel w/rosettes flanking a central gilt classical Minerva head above three slats above the lower panel w/a hinged arched folio rack decorated w/a large black scroll-trimmed cartouche, a curved & pierced

Renaissance Revival Picture Stand

front apron on scrolled front legs, a plain fold-out rear support rack, ca. 1875, 28 1/2" w., 6' 1/2" h. (ILLUS.) **2,530**

Unusual Classical Revival Stand

Plant stand, Classical Revival style, mahogany & mahogany veneer, a thin square top raised on a block & ring-turned short pedestal atop a square tapering tall pedestal w/brass spearhead mounts at the top, raised on a square pyramidal base w/a narrow ropetwist-carved edge band, on four carved paw feet, refinished, ca. 1900, 14" w., 34" h. (ILLUS.).. **400**

Carved Chinese Plant Stand

Plant stand, Oriental, carved hardwood, the round dished top above a scroll-pierced apron raised on three lion head-carved cabriole legs ending in paw feet & joined by a pierced lower shelf, China, late 19th - early 20th c., 16" d., 40" h. (ILLUS.).... **200-400**

Baroque Plant Stand with Lion Head

Plant stand, Victorian Baroque style, carved mahogany, a square top on a square tapering platform resting on the head of a figural roaring lion atop a large carved scroll pedestal tapering to a square base resting on a square platform w/square wafer feet, refinished, late 19th c., 14" w., 36" h. (ILLUS.) **850**

Tapering Baroque Plant Stand

Plant stand, Victorian Baroque style, carved mahogany, small square top w/a gadrooned edge raised on a cluster of carved plumes above a large tapering square column carved on each side w/scroll-filled panels above a square medial rail above the square flaring lower pedestal w/panels carved w/an urn & flowering vines, square tapering base molding, late 19th c., old refinish, 14" w., 38" h. (ILLUS.) **750**

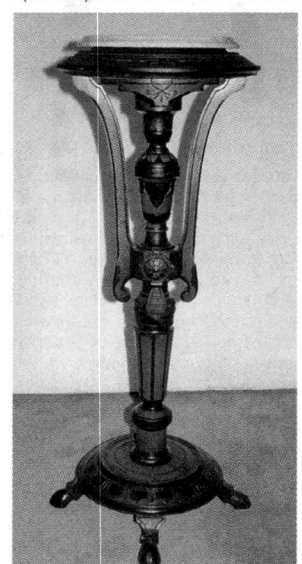

Slender Carved Renaissance Stand

Nice Federal Veneered Sewing Stand

Plant stand, Victorian Renaissance Revival style, walnut w/ebonized trim, a round white marble top above a widely flaring carved rim band w/two stepped & incised drops raised on a ring-and-urn-turned central column flanked by two long slender curved flat brackets joining a central rosette-carved knob above a paneled knob & a tall tapering paneled & ring-turned lower pedestal resting on the tapering disk base w/a band of small ebonized blocks all raised on outswept hoof feet, original finish, ca., 1870s, 14" d., 36" h. (ILLUS., bottom previous page) **900**

Fine Classical Sewing Stand

Sewing stand, Classical style, mahogany & mahogany veneer, the rectangular top w/gadrooned edge lifting to a shallow well above an apron w/an upper ogee band w/false drawer front above a flat lower band w/a narrow working drawer, a pierced scroll-carved apron, raised on a trestle-style base w/end supports composed of two pairs of molded S-scrolls joined by a slender baluster- and-ring-turned stretcher, original finish, ca. 1840, 14 x 20", 30" h. (ILLUS.)................................. **900**

Sewing stand, Federal style, mahogany & mahogany veneer, the rectangular top above a deep frame w/a pull-out work surface at one end above two long drawers w/fine crotch-grain veneering & round brass pulls raised on spiraling acanthus leaf-carved supports over the wide rectangular lower shelf w/a serpentine front, raised on small turned knob feet on original brass casters, refinished, ca. 1820s, 16 x 20" closed, 30" h. (ILLUS. open, top of page) **850**

Shaving stand, Victorian Renaissance Revival style, walnut & burl walnut, an arched rectangular mirror swiveling in a fancy framework w/a pediment centered by peaked scroll-carved crest w/roundel flanked by pointed corner finials above veneer-paneled sides, the rectangular white marble top over a single burled drawer over a scalloped narrow apron, raised on a ring-turned pedestal above a central post flanked by blocked & carved outswept legs, refinished, ca. 1870s, 16 x 18", 5' 4" h. (ILLUS., top next page) **1,800**

Shaving Stand in Renaissance Style

Fancy Eastlake Shaving Stand

Shaving stand, Victorian Eastlake style, walnut & burl walnut, the tall superstruc-

ture w/an arched & bobbin-pierced crestrail flanked by corner blocks w/pointed finials above bamboo-turned uprights flanking the tall swiveling rectangular mirror above another bobbin-pierced rail, the rectangular pink marble top above a single narrow burl-veneered drawer w/a rectangular brass pull flanked by corner blocks over drop finials flanking a scalloped narrow apron, the side of the case fitted w/a small drawer, raised on turned front spindles & flat back stiles above a lower shelf w/a bobbin-turned gallery over a small rectangular door w/a recessed burl panel, arched front legs, original finish, ca. 1880s, 16 x 18", 6' h. (ILLUS.)..**3,200**

Simple Golden Oak Shaving Stand

Shaving stand, Victorian Golden Oak style, quarter-sawn oak, a rectangular beveled mirror in a narrow frame w/a scroll-carved crest swiveling between slender scrolled uprights over the rectangular top over two plain doors, raised on four slender square tapering legs joined by a lower shelf, original finish, ca. 1900, 14 x 16", 5' 6" h. (ILLUS.)...............................**750**

Country-style Stand of Mixed Woods

Side stand, country-style, painted mixed woods, rectangular top, tapered splayed legs w/conforming paneled door above deep front apron, probably French, late 19th c., old yellow & white paint, separations, chips, several loose parts, scattered worm damage, 19 x 20," 28" h. (ILLUS.) **770**

Simple Classical Country Washstand

Washstand, Classical country-style, cherry, a rectangular top above a single drawer w/wooden knob, raised on tall S-scroll front supports & plain square back legs, lower platform shelf w/concave front, C-scroll front feet, ca. 1850, refinished, 14 x 18", 30" h. (ILLUS.) **275**

Washstand, country-style, pine & poplar, dovetailed construction, three-quarters gallery w/scrolled ends on rectangular top, the case w/single drawer over paneled door, turned front feet, old, possibly original surface, ca. 1840-50, various scuffs, cracks, separations, the drawer w/loose bottom, each side w/mount, possibly for rack or towel rod, 18 x 28", 38" h. **770**

French Directoire Washstand

Washstand, French Directoire style, fruitwood, the rectangular top inset w/three ovoid wooden compartments above a paneled apron raised on paneled tapering legs joined by two open lower shelves, on brass caps w/casters, France, first quarter 19th c., 21 1/2" l., 30 1/2" h. (ILLUS.) **920**

Classical Marquetry Washstand

Washstand, Victorian Classical style, mahogany & marquetry, the rectangular top w/a tall scroll-cut backsplash & out-scrolled sides decorated w/ornate floral & scroll marquetry, the case w/a long drawer w/further decorative marquetry & pierced brass pulls above a pair of urn-inlaid cupboard doors, further marquetry on the sides, raised on carved paw front feet, England, ca. 1850, 19 x 32", 40" h. (ILLUS.) 863

Painted Country-style Washstand

Washstand, Victorian country-style, painted pine or butternut, an arched splashback on the rectangular top over three long dovetailed drawers w/small wooden knobs, shallow scalloped apron, original worn white paint, ca. 1870, 15 x 24", 36" h. (ILLUS.) 300

Oak Washstand with Shaped Sides

Washstand, Victorian Golden Oak style, a towel bar supported by simple S-scroll uprights above the rectangular top w/a

bowed front above a long bowed drawer over a stack of two drawers beside a paneled cupboard door, serpentine side rails ending in scroll-carved feet on casters, original finish, ca. 1900, 16 x 34", 46" h. (ILLUS.) 500

Serpentine-fronted Oak Washstand

Washstand, Victorian Golden Oak style, quarter-sawn oak, a long towel bar supported by tall S-scroll uprights w/scrolled ends above the rectangular top w/a serpentine front above a conforming long drawer projecting over two flat cupboard doors, serpentine apron & simple cabriole front legs on casters, original hardware, refinished, ca. 1900, 19 x 30", 4' 2" h. (ILLUS.) 450

Fancy Renaissance Washstand

Washstand, Victorian Renaissance Revival style, walnut & burl walnut, the fancy broken-scroll backsplash centered by an arched, pierced & scroll-carved crest over a roundel & small raised burl panels flanked by side panels w/further burl panels all flanked by short side brackets, the rectangular white marble top w/rounded front corners above a case w/a long drawer centered by an arched scroll-carved burl panel flanked by small burl panels w/pulls, carved knobs at the angled front corners above a pair of arch-paneled cupboard doors centered by carved scrolled cartouches & flanked by angled front corners carved w/tapering bead bands, deep flat base w/rounded corners, refinished, ca. 1870s, 18 x 32", 38" h. (ILLUS.)... **1,500**

Mahogany Rococo Washstand

Washstand, Victorian Rococo style, mahogany & mahogany veneer, the low serpentine white marble galleried splashback on the rectangular white marble top w/a serpentine front, a long serpentine drawer flanked by angled corners w/turned half-round drops above a pair of paneled concave doors flanked by angled corners w/half-round turned drops, serpentine scroll-cut apron & bracket feet, refinished, ca. 1850s, 18 x 32", 34" h. (ILLUS.)... **1,100**

Two-drawer Stand in Mahogany

Classical two-drawer stand, mahogany, two dovetailed drawers, platform-stretcher base, tapered & turned legs w/turnip feet, pencil inscription on base reads "Jan 1906 Rep. & refinished by Louis Lavoner (?) Oswego, NY," replaced brass pulls, drawer interiors painted yellow, losses & repairs to veneer, top w/repaired separations, feet w/several chips, replaced brass casters, 16 x 22", 28" h. (ILLUS.)... **770**

Federal Veneered One-drawer Stand

Federal country-style one-drawer stand, birch, cherry & bird's-eye maple & mahogany veneer, the nearly square top slightly overhanging the apron w/a single bird's-eye maple-veneered drawer w/original round brass pulls, on ring- and rod-turned reeded legs ending in tall tapering peg feet, ca. 1820-30, one-board birch top reset w/slight warp, 17 1/2 x 18", 25 3/4" h. (ILLUS.).................... **633**

Federal Country-style Maple Stand

Federal country-style one-drawer stand, curly maple, nearly square top above an apron w/a single drawer w/wooden knob, raised on square tapering legs on tapering reeded square peg feet, old mellow refinishing, two-board top reset w/braces added, ca. 1830-40, 18 x 18 3/4", 27 3/4" h. (ILLUS.)... **805**

Painted Federal Country Stand

Federal country-style one-drawer stand, painted pine & maple, the rectangular top overhanging an apron w/a single drawer w/two turned wood knobs, on turned legs ending in swelled peg feet, ca. 1840, old mustard yellow paint, pieced restoration to drawer front, minor splits in top, 19 3/4 x 20" (ILLUS.)....................................... **546**

Federal Two-drawer Stand

Federal country-style two-drawer stand, poplar, curly maple & cherry, the nearly square one-board poplar top overhang-

ing an apron w/two curved-front drawers w/old pressed glass pulls, on square tapering legs, ca. 1850, 21 x 22", 30" h.. (ILLUS.).. **575**

Inlaid Mahogany One-drawer Stand

Federal one-drawer stand, inlaid mahogany, rectangular top w/rounded corners & band of double string inlay, tapered legs w/extensive string & elliptical inlay below bird's-eye maple panels, dovetailed drawer w/three interior compartments, original oval brass pulls, original glue blocks on back skirt, American South, missing side glue blocks, which have been replaced w/small iron cleats, drawer runners flipped, top w/old separation, possibly as made, scattered old stains, 18 1/4 x 26 1/4", 28 5/8" h. (ILLUS.).. **46,200**

Federal one-drawer stand, inlaid walnut, nearly square two-board top above an apron w/a single drawer w/an inlaid escutcheon & flanked at the sides by figured maple inlay panels, square tapering legs, old dark surface, first half 19th c., 16 1/16 x 17 7/8", 29" h. (top an old restoration)... **715**

Stools

Chippendale-Style stool, mahogany, muslin-covered seat, elaborately carved cabriole legs, ball-&-claw feet w/notched talons, England, probably 19th c., oval skirt w/multiple tack wounds, laminate reinforcement behind legs, old muslin covering stained, 19 x 27", 18" h. **1,870**

George II-Style stools, mahogany, a rectangular upholstered top & apron raised on cabriole legs w/shell-carved knees & ending in lion paw feet, England, late 19th c., 17 1/2 x 25 1/2", 18" h., pr. (ILLUS., top of next page)............................... **748**

George II-Style Mahogany Stools

George III-Style Hoof-footed Stool

George III-Style stool, mahogany, the rectangular upholstered seat on a shell- and scroll-carved serpentine seatrail on cabriole legs w/scroll-carved knees ending in hoof feet & joined by a curved H-stretcher, England, mid-19th c., 25 1/4 x 29 1/4", 19 1/4" h. (ILLUS.) **1,840**

Georgian-Style Stools

Georgian-Style stools, carved mahogany, the rectangular padded & upholstered top within a gadrooned molding above the curved ornately leaf-carved serpentine apron, raised on cabriole legs ending in dolphin mask feet, England, late 19th c., 17 x 24", 21" h., pr. (ILLUS.) **748**

Louis XV-Style stool, carved rosewood, rectangular, carved frieze w/openwork shell & scroll decoration, short cabriole legs, scroll feet, upholstered seat, Europe, late 19th c., minor repairs to wood, scuffs & scratches, old worn upholstery,

minor losses & chips to carving, 17 x 24 x 16" **1,210**

English Regency Gout Stool

Regency gout stool, mahogany, an upholstered & rolled top over scrolled sides carved w/honeysuckle vines, on bulbous knob feet, England, early 19th c., 12 3/4 x 18", 10 1/2" h. (ILLUS.) **1,610**

English Gothic Revival Stool

Victorian Gothic Revival stools, oak, a rectangular top above a line-incised apron raised on molded square legs w/carved quatrefoil corner brackets, England, mid-19th c., 13 1/2 x 18", 18" h., pr. (ILLUS. of one)... **805**

William IV Scroll-carved Stool

William IV stool, mahogany & leather, rectangular w/a high S-scroll frame, sides carved w/a large rosette & leafy scroll ending in fan-carved corners, on low bev- eled block feet, England, first half 19th c., 20 1/2 x 35 1/2", 20" h. (ILLUS.) **748**

Tables

Art Deco cocktail table, glass-topped rosewood, the rectangular glass top w/rounded corners raised on two faux ivory & brass-tipped Islamic crescents set upon the ends of H-form rosewood plinth base, France, ca. 1930, 23 x 48", 20" h. (ILLUS., middle of page) **1,093**

Baroque-Style guard room table, oak, the long rectangular planked top raised on heavy serpentine end supports joined by stretchers & w/long slender scrolled iron brackets under the top, Spain, ca. 1900, 39 x 87", 29 1/2" h. (ILLUS., bottom of page) **2,760**

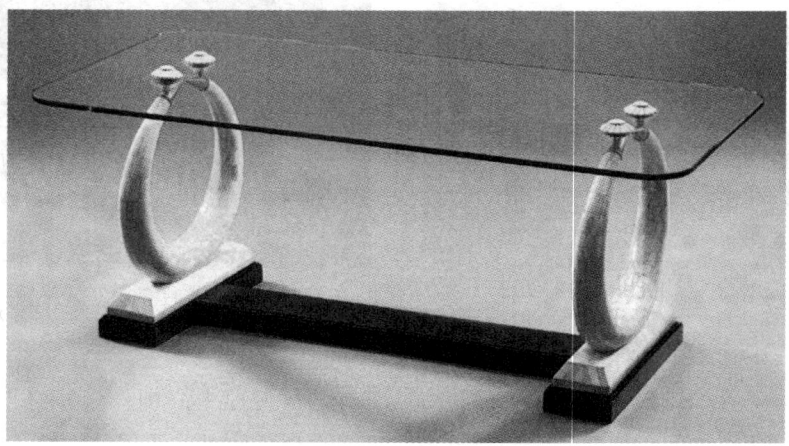

Art Deco Glass & Wood Cocktail Table

Spanish Oak Guard Room Table

Fine Austrian Bentwood Table

Bentwood center table, the oval top supported on a central cluster of four curved & outswept continuous bentwood scrolls for the legs & trimmed w/further smaller scrolls, dark finish, Austria, possibly Thonet, late 19th c., 34 x 50 1/2", 30" h. (ILLUS.) **5,520**

Biedermeier Blond Side Table

Biedermeier side tables, blond wood, a round top raised on a round upper column joined by an ebonized ring to a paneled lower column w/another ebonized ring, resting on a tripartite base, Europe, first half 19th c., 20" d., 28" h., pr. (ILLUS. of one) **1,610**

Biedermeier-style Breakfast Table

Biedermeier-Style drop-leaf breakfast table, figured maple veneer, rectangular top w/dovetailed drawer on one side w/raised front, false front on opposite side, thick round column on platform base w/carved paw feet, Europe, 20th c., some reconstruction, 28 x 33" w. plus 9" leaves, 29 3/4" h. (ILLUS.) **978**

Chippendale dining table, mahogany, the rectangular top flanked by deep rectangular drop leaves, an arched apron supported on swing-out cabriole legs w/claw-and-ball feet, New York state, late 18th c., open 48 1/4 x 57", 28 3/4" h. (ILLUS. closed, below) **4,600**

Fine Chippendale Mahogany Dining Table

Chippendale Tea Table

Chippendale tea table, mahogany, carved Chippendale borders, "birdcage" & tilt-top mechanism, spiral-carved urn pedestal w/flower-carved band at base, three legs w/fine acanthus-carved knees w/ball-and-claw feet w/articulated talons, original iron spider & brass latch, England or America, 18th c., top w/several patches, battens probably reset, old refinishing, 33 1/8 x 34 1/8", 28 " h. (ILLUS.) **10,450**

Chippendale Revival Carved Table

Chippendale Revival tea table, mahogany & mahogany veneer, the large scalloped round top w/carved shells along the border tilting above a turned pedestal on a tripod base w/three outstretched cabriole legs w/leaf-carved knees & ending in pad

feet, original dark finish, ca. 1920s, 24" d., closed 4' h. (ILLUS.) **700**

Chippendale-Style Coffee Table

Chippendale-Style coffee table, mahogany & mahogany veneer, the rectangular mirrored tray top w/low scalloped upright sides & cut-out hand holes resting in a molded frame above square legs w/block feet & Chinese-style lattice corner brackets, old finish, early 20th c., 19 x 30", 19 1/2" h. (ILLUS.) **1,208**

Chippendale-Style Dressing Table

Chippendale-Style dressing table, mahogany & yellow pine, frieze drawer above three dovetailed drawers, central drawer w/carved fan, cabriole legs w/ball-and-claw feet, some cut nails on drawer runners, composed of parts from various pieces of furniture, probably late 19th c., small drawer is reduced, refinishing, scratches & minor separations, 19 x 27", 39" h. (ILLUS.) **1,540**

Classical breakfast table, mahogany, rectangular top flanked by wide drop leaves w/rounded corners, raised on carved columns above the trestle base w/circular cross-stretcher & tapered columns, acanthus-carved saber legs, paw feet, original brass casters & iron hinges, hinges marked "JG," ca. 1820, 24 x 39", opens to 51", 29" h. **4,620**

Classical Two-Pedestal Dining Table

Fine Classical Card Table

Classical card table, mahogany, rectangular fold-over top w/rounded corners, on a scroll-tipped apron raised on a heavy ring- and acanthus-carved center post above four arched & splayed legs w/acanthus-carved knees & ending in brass hairy-paw foot caps on casters, probably made in Boston, ca. 1830, 37 1/2 x 38", 30" h. (ILLUS.) **1,955**

Classical dining table, mahogany & mahogany veneer, two-pedestal extension-type, each wide half-round top section w/a wide inside drop leaf, the deep apron w/a turned drop at each corner, each pedestal w/a bulbous acanthus leaf-carved post raised on four outswept leaf-carved legs ending in large paw feet on casters, original finish, replaced casters, ca. 1830s, open 54 x 100", 30" h. (ILLUS. open, top of page) **4,500**

Classical games table, mahogany & mahogany veneer, the rectangular fold-over top w/rounded corners opening to a conforming top over a flat ogee front apron, raised on a flat flared center support atop

Game Table with Unusual Base

a large flattened oval disk resting at the center of a resting platform base w/arched shoe feet, probably Boston, ca. 1840, original dark finish, 16 x 32", 30" h. (ILLUS.) **500**

Late Classical Games Table

Classical games table, mahogany & mahogany veneer, the rectangular fold-over top w/rounded corners opening to a matching top over a deep crotch-grain veneered apron w/a scroll-carved border, raised on a a flattened scrolled support w/a cut-out center enclosing a scroll-carved finial, resting on a long quadripartite platform base w/outswept scroll feet, original finish, ca. 1850, 18 x 38", 30" h. (ILLUS.) **750**

Fine Classical Pier Table

Classical pier table, mahogany & mahogany veneer, the rectangular white marble top w/canted front corners above a conforming deep ogee apron, supported at the front by long heavy S-scrolls & at the back by a framed rectangular mirror all joined by a half-round lower platform on projecting C-scroll front legs, ca. 1830-40, 21 x 41", 37 1/2" h. (ILLUS.) **2,530**

Rare Classical Pier Table/Vitrine

Classical pier table with vitrine, ormolu-mounted mahogany & mahogany veneer, the rectangular white marble top above an apron mounted in the center w/a long pierced scrolling ormolu mount w/smaller mounts at the front corners & at the sides, the front raised on tall columns w/ormolu capitals & bases that

flank a pair of large glazed cabinet doors, glazed side panels, on a thick plinth base, first quarter 19th c., 17 x 39 3/4", 35 3/4" h. (ILLUS.) **2,070**

One-drawer Classical Work Table

Classical work table, mahogany & mahogany veneer, a rectangular top slightly overhanging an apron w/a single drawer w/a wooden pull, raised on four ring- and knob-turned legs centered by spiral-carved sections, raised on casters, original finish, ca. 1830, 16 x 20", 30" h, (ILLUS.) **450**

Classical Serpentine Work Table

Classical work table, mahogany & mahogany veneer, rectangular top w/a serpentine front above a conforming case w/two drawers w/original cut glass pulls, raised on a flattened lyre-form support on a serpentine-sided rectangular platform w/outswept serpentine legs, refinished, ca. 1840, 16 x 24", 30" h, (ILLUS.) **400**

Lyre-based Classical Work Table

Classical work table, mahogany & mahogany veneer, the rectangular top above a case w/two ogee-fronted drawers raised on a heavy scroll-carved lyre pedestal atop a stepped rectangular platform w/ogee bracket feet on casters, ca. 1830, 22" l., 28 1/2" h. (ILLUS.) **863**

Classical-Rococo Transitional Center Table

Classical-Rococo transitional center table, rosewood, the rectangular white marble-inset top w/serpentine sides w/a gadrooned border above a serpentine apron carved at the center of each side w/leaf & blossom clusters, raised on heavy S-scroll legs w/leaf-carved knees & forming a trestle base w/an arched, shell-carved cross-stretcher, ca. 1850, 25 3/4 x 42 1/2", 29 1/4" h. (ILLUS.) **1,265**

Classical-Style Breakfast Table

Classical-Style breakfast table, mahogany, the rectangular top flanked by deep drop leaves w/notched rounded corners, the apron w/a round-fronted drawer at each end, raised on a heavy acanthus-carved pedestal on a quadripartite platform on outswept heavy carved paw feet on casters, late 19th c., open 38 x 52 1/2", 29" h. (ILLUS. closed) **863**

Classical-Style dining table, mahogany, extension-type, the round top w/a scroll-carved border band raised on a large ring-turned split pedestal w/a bulbous reeded lower section issuing heavy acanthus-carved shaped legs ending in large paw feet, late 19th c., w/four leaves, closed 54" d., 29 1/4" h. (ILLUS. extended, below) **3,220**

Fine Classical-Style Mahogany Dining Table with Leaves

Fine Classical-Style Dressing Table

Classical-Style dressing table, mahogany, a large horizontal oval mirror swiveling between long outswept dolphin-carved supports above the rectangular top above a case w/a pair of round-fronted drawers flanking a leaf-carved panel over a long round-fronted drawer above a gadroon-carved apron band, the case supported by four S-scroll carved dolphin supports joining a rectangular serpentine-sided platform raised on outswept dolphin-carved legs, late 19th c., 20 3/4 x 27", overall 5' 6 1/2" h. (ILLUS.).. **2,300**

Small Colonial Revival Table

Colonial Revival dining table, cherry, a long narrow rectangular top flanked by wide half-round drop leaves, raised on two baluster-, ring- and knob-turned pedestals above outswept cabriole legs w/pad feet joined by a turned medial stretcher, on casters, possibly English, late 19th- early 20th c., refinished, open 32 x 48", 30" h, (ILLUS. closed) **400**

Country-style dining table, mahogany & marquetry, the rectangular top w/ornate floral marquetry flanked by wide rectangular drop leaves w/further marquetry in an urn & vining flower design, the apron & square legs w/further marquetry vines, on casters, Holland, third quarter 19th c., open 48 x 63", 29 1/2" h. (ILLUS. closed, bottom of page).. **2,760**

Ornate Dutch Marquetry Dining Table

Early American Walnut Work Table

Early American country-style work table,
walnut, the large rectangular three-board
top widely overhanging the deep apron
w/two deep drawers w/wooden pulls,
raised on three turned & tapering legs
ending in knob-and-peg feet, old finish,
early 19th c., reconstruction to base &
drawers, 33 x 60", 30" h. (ILLUS.) **1,725**

Finely Inlaid Federal Card Table

French Empire-Style Center Table

Empire-Style center table, mahogany, the
round top above a paneled ormolu-
mounted apron raised on turned & tapering legs joined by a lower shelf w/con-
cave sides, on short splayed feet,
France, ca. 1900, 33" d., 29 1/2" h.
(ILLUS.) **1,610**

Federal card table, inlaid mahogany, the
hinged half-round top w/pointed front corners & delicate chain-inlaid edge lifting
above a matching top over a conforming
apron w/line-inlaid panels centering a
light-colored rectangular panel enclosing
an oval, a band of chain inlay along the

bottom edge, raised on knob-turned &
spiraled acanthus leaf-carved legs on
casters, old refinish, ca. 1820s, 19 x 38",
30" h. (ILLUS.) **1,500**

Rare Federal Mahogany Game Table

Federal card table, mahogany & mahogany veneer, the rectangular fold-over top w/angled cornersnforming figured mahogany veneer apron w/an applied ebony band replacing original lines of brass inlay, raised on four turned legs w/reed-carved cylindrical sections over spiral-carved egg-shaped sections, on a veneered plinth w/concave sides, supports on four rabbit-like outswept legs w/an acanthus leaf-carved knee, the paw feet on brass casters, possible from the workshop of Duncan Phyfe, New York City, early 19th c., 18 x 36", 29 3/4" h, (ILLUS., bottom of previous page) **10,063**

Curly Maple Dressing Table

Federal country-style dressing table, curly maple, rectangular top w/serpentine three-quarters gallery over a single long drawer, turned tapering legs w/peg feet, some family history written inside drawer, ca. 1850, feet have been ended out, gallery is old replacement, 17 x 34 1/2", 34 3/4" h. (ILLUS.) **1,495**

Cherry Pembroke Table

Federal Pembroke table, cherry, rounded leaves, tapered legs, dovetailed drawer,

hand-wrought nails, probably original brass pull, pivoting drop-leaf supports, original glue blocks, possibly Virginia, early 19th c., top reset w/some new screws, old refinishing, some insect damage, 1/2" hole, 21 x 34", opens to 43", 29" h. (ILLUS.) **1,430**

American Federal Pembroke Table

Federal Pembroke table, mahogany, the rectangular top flanked by shaped half-round drop leaves above an apron w/a drawer w/a replaced brass pull at one end, raised on turned reeded legs ending in peg feet on casters, refinished, one foot ended out, first quarter 19th c., 20 3/4 x 32" plus 10 3/8" w. leaves, 27 3/4" h. (ILLUS.) **1,380**

Federal serving table, mahogany & mahogany veneer, a rectangular top above a deep case w/two long crotch grain-veneered drawers w/rosette & ring pulls, raised on ring- and rod-turned supports above a medial shelf w/a serpentine front, on baluster-turned legs on brass casters, appears to have original hardware, probably New York City, 1810-20, 18 x 34 1/2", 34 1/2" h. **8,255**

Rare New York Classical Sofa Table

Federal sofa table, mahogany & mahogany veneer, the long rectangular top above an apron w/a pair of drawers flanked by half-round drop leaves, raised on a square center pedestal carved w/a band of acanthus leaves & resting on a quadri-partite platform supported by outswept acanthus leaf-carved legs ending in brass paws on casters, attributed to New York City, ca. 1820, 21 x 30 1/2" plus 11" leaves, 29" h. (ILLUS., previous page) **18,400**

Federal One-drawer Work Table

Federal work table, mahogany & mahogany veneer, square top over a thin pull-out writing shelf above a drawer w/two brass knobs, acanthus leaf carving at each corner above similarly carved supports on a square medial shelf, slender ring-turned & leaf-carved legs on original brass casters, original finish, early 19th c., 18" w., 30" h. (ILLUS.) **650**

Nice Federal-Style Card Table

Federal-Style card table, inlaid mahogany, the half-round serpentine fold-over top above a conforming apron inlaid at the front center by an oval enclosing an American eagle, beaded edge inlay, on square tapering legs w/bellflower inlay on the front legs, early 20th c., open 35 1/2 x 36 1/2", 29 1/2" h. (ILLUS. closed) **1,093**

George III Mahogany Dining Table

George III dining table, mahogany, the rectangular top flanked by wide rectangular top leaves, on square tapering legs, England, early 19th c., open 53 x 67", 27" h. (ILLUS. closed) **575**

Ornate George III-Style Center Table

George III-Style center table, polychromed & gilded wood, the rectangular top inset w/a specimen multicolored marble top above an apron w/a gilt Greek key band above serpentine scroll-carved edges centered by a large shell carving, the cabriole legs topped by carved gilt eagle heads above scroll-carved knees & ending in claw-and-ball feet, England, 19th c., 23 1/2 x 51 1/2", 33 1/2" h. (ILLUS.) **1,840**

George III-Style dining table, mahogany, extension-type, rounded top raised on two turned pedestals on tripod bases w/cabriole legs ending in pad feet, w/original Kittinger paper label, w/one 24" w. leaf, 20th c., 48 x 92" open, 28 1/2" h. (ILLUS. open, top next page) **1,725**

Labeled Kittinger George III-Style Dining Table

George III-Style Dumbwaiter

George III-Style dumbwaiter, mahogany, two graduated scalloped piecrust shelves joined by an urn-turned post & raised on a turned pedestal above a tripod base w/acanthus-carved knees ending in leaf-carved pad feet, England, ca. 1900, 23 1/2" d., 28" h. (ILLUS.) **374**

Gothic Revival library table, carved rosewood, the rectangular top inset w/variegated white marble over a wide apron w/a band of quatrefoil cutouts, raised on angled naturalistic animal legs w/scrolled hair at the top & ending in cloven hoof feet, mid-19th c., 25 1/4 x 43 1/2", 28" h. (ILLUS., top next page)............................ **16,675**

Harvest table, birch, long narrow rectangular top flanked by long drop leaves w/rounded corners, ring-turned legs on tapering ball feet, refinished w/traces of old red stain, found in Vermont, 19th c., 17 3/4 x 66" plus 10 1/4" drop leaves (top reset w/center brace added)...................... **2,860**

Painted Poplar Hutch Table/Chair

Hutch (or chair) table, poplar w/old green paint over earlier brown, two-board top w/old dark scrubbed surface, single-board tapered ends w/high arched cutouts at base, square nail & mortised construction, late 18th - early 19th c., top is warped, 31 x 40", 28 3/4" h. (ILLUS.)......... **1,150**

Louis XVI-Style console table, painted oak, demi-lune mottled & streaked grey marble top on conforming reeded apron w/cove-molded upper edge, supported by reeded, tapered & fluted legs, beaded cross-stretcher base, Europe, 19th c., hand-planed surfaces w/later white paint, marble w/stains, paint & tape residue, several small chips, 18 x 36", 35 1/2" h...................................... **2,200**

Rare Gothic Revival Library Table

Louis XVI-Style Shelved Side Table

Louis XVI-Style side table, giltwood, the oval top inset w/cream & rose marble above a ribbon-carved apron supported on six turned & fluted legs joined by two large oval caned lower shelves, on peg feet, France, mid-19th c., 19 x 31", 31" h. (ILLUS.) **1,495**

Louis XVI-Style Round Side Table

Louis XVI-Style side table, giltwood, the round top inset w/white marble framed by a molded edge on the fluted apron w/florette blocks above the fluted turned & tapering legs joined by a cross-stretcher, France, ca. 1900, 21" d., 24" h. (ILLUS.)....... **863**

Extremely Ornate Napoleon III Rococo Parlor Center Table

Napoleon III parlor center table, Rococo-style, gilt-brass-mounted ebonized fruit-wood & marquetry, the rectangular serpentine-sided top decorated overall w/very ornate floral scrolling marquetry above the deep serpentine apron w/ormolu-banded marquetry panels centered by large ormolu mount of a putto carrying a lute, the cabriole legs mounted w/large ormolu caryatids at the knees & fitted w/brass feet, France, third quarter 19th c., 30 x 49 1/2", 30 1/2" h. (ILLUS.)........... **4,370**

Neoclassical console tables, poly-chromed wood, the long demi-lune top w/carved palmetto banding decorated in the center w/a colorful landscape medallion flanked by mermaids & a variety of colorful swag & putti designs, all on a cream background, the narrow matching apron raised on four square tapering legs w/similar decoration & ending in tapering square peg feet, Italy, early 19th c., 58" l., 34" h., pr. (ILLUS., bottom of page)........... **5,290**

Louis XVI-Style Small Side Table

Louis XVI-Style side table, mahogany, the oval top inset w/white onyx bordered by a low pierced brass gallery above the paneled apron w/a brass-bound drawer & side panels raised on square supports to the kidney-shaped lower shelf on square simple cabriole legs, France, late 19th c., 19" w., 31" h. (ILLUS.) **1,093**

Ornately Decorated Italian Neoclassical Console Tables

Two Chinese Carved Side Tables

Oriental side table, carved rosewood, the round top w/beaded border centered by inset red marble, the scalloped apron pierce-carved w/leafy florals, on cabriole legs w/carved knees ending in paw feet, China, late 19th c., 21 1/2" d., 19" h. (ILLUS. left w/Oriental rosewood side table, top of page)..................................... **250-350**

Oriental side table, carved rosewood, the rounded top w/a beaded edge inset w/red marble, the deep scalloped apron pierce-carved w/leafy florals, raised on short cabriole legs w/carved knees & paw feet, China, late 19th c., 12" d., 13 1/2" h. (ILLUS. right w/Oriental rosewood side table, top of page)............... **150-300**

Queen Anne Country Tavern Table

Queen Anne country-style tavern table, maple w/old dark brown paint over earlier red, one-board rectangular top w/worn molded edge, dovetailed drawer w/original turned wooden pull, turned legs w/beaded stretchers & aprons, top edge

has early patched knot hole, 17 1/2 x 27 3/4", 26" h. (ILLUS.).............. **21,850**

Queen Anne work table, walnut, one-drawer two-board top, tapered legs w/pad feet, ornate brass pull possibly original, possibly by Johannes Crouse, 18th c., rebuilt dovetailed drawer, drawer runners replaced, old refinishing, top w/stains & separations, 28 x 37 1/2 x 26".................... **3,960**

English Queen Anne-Style Table

Queen Anne-Style dining table, mahogany, narrow rectangular top w/rounded ends flanked by wide half-round drop leaves above an apron w/slender ring-turned blocked legs & swing-out support legs joined by simple stretchers, on small pad feet, dark finish, England, early 20th c., small pieced restorations under top near hinges, 18 1/4 x 40" plus 19 3/4" w. leaves, 29 1/2" h. (ILLUS.).............................. **863**

Queen Anne-Style games table, red-lacquered wood, the fold-over shaped top w/a polychromed & gilt scene in the chinoiserie style, opening to a baize-lined interior, the back gatelegs supporting the open top, raised on heavily turned & pan-

Queen Anne-Style Games Table

eled tapering legs joined by a shaped box stretcher & ending in bun feet, the whole w/chinoiserie gilt trim, England, third quarter 19th c., open 13 1/2 x 31 1/2", 30 1/2" h. (ILLUS. open) **3,680**

Fine Regency Rosewood Sofa Table

Regency sofa table, rosewood, the long rectangular top flanked by half-round banded inlay drop leaves, the long apron fitted in the front w/two long banded inlay drawers w/round brass pulls, the back w/two false drawers, raised on a tiered turned pedestal above a quadripartite platform w/incurved sides resting on four outswept legs ending in brass leaf-cast caps on casters, England, first quarter 19th c., 27 1/4 x 36 1/4, 57 1/2" l. open, 29 1/2" h. (ILLUS. closed) **1,840**

Rococo Revival side table, carved mahogany, the round top over a shaped apron carved w/pairs of scrolls, raised on bulbous turned knobs atop S-scroll legs carved at the top w/an acanthus leaf & ending in a scroll foot raised on a bun, joined by a scrolled & arched cross stretcher centered by a turned urn finial,

Rococo Revival Scroll-carved Table

refinished, late 19th c., 24" d., 30" h. (ILLUS.)... **450**

Inlaid Italian Rococo-Style Table

Rococo-Style games table, mahogany & marquetry, the rectangular fold-over top w/large projecting rounded corners, decorated w/an elaborate inlay of putti & scrolling designs, opening to a similarly inlaid interior, the ornately inlaid apron fitted w/one drawer, on inlaid cabriole legs ending in square feet, the drawer w/paper label for Giovannia Bacci - Oggetti D'arte - Anticui E. Moderni - Via della Vigna Nuova St. - Firenze, Italy, mid-19th c., 33 1/2" l., 29" h. (ILLUS.) **2,760**

Victorian Aesthetic Movement parlor table, mahogany, the square top inset w/tiles forming a border band around a cluster of stylized blossoms all framed by a low brass edge gallery & a narrow brass band along the outer edges, raised on four canted ring-turned & reeded ta-

Victorian Aesthetic Parlor Table

Baroque Revival Oak Dining Table

pering legs w/brass bands near the top & supports on brass claw feet w/glass balls, joined by a lower square shelf w/a brass gallery, probably England, ca. 1900, original finish, 20" w., 32" h. (ILLUS.) **600**

Victorian Baroque Revival dining table, carved oak, extension-type, the round top over a lappet-carved apron, a fixed center support w/a cluster of four reeded columns w/a cross stretcher, four traveling legs at the corners, each carved in full-relief as winged griffins on block bases, ca. 1890, refinished, w/extra leaves, 60" d. closed, 30" h. (ILLUS. extended) **7,500**

Victorian Baroque Revival dining table, carved oak, extension-type, the wide square top w/a lappet-carved apron, raised on a large spiral-carved center post & four corner posts resting on the heads of carved full-figure reclining lions on the cross-form base w/carved paw feet, ca. 1890, w/six leaves, sold refinished, 60" w., 30" h. (ILLUS. with the leaves stacked on top, below) **4,500**

Baroque Dining Table with Lions on the Base

Labeled Oak Horner Dining Table

Victorian Baroque Revival dining table, quarter-sawn oak, extension-type, the round top w/a gadroon-carved apron, raised on four heavy cabriole legs each topped by a carved lion head & ending in a paw foot on a caster, a central split column w/a leaf-carved band, refinished, original label of the Horner Furniture Co., New York City, w/five leaves, refinished, ca. 1890, 58" d., 30" h. (ILLUS.)......................... **4,000**

Victorian Baroque Revival dining table, quarter-sawn oak, extension-type, the round top w/a gadrooned edge over the plain apron, raised on a massive center column w/a gadrooned disk over a paneled post issuing outswept legs, each leg carved w/a large head of a roaring lion & ending in a large paw foot, original dark finish, w/five leaves, ca. 1895, 54" d., 30" h. (ILLUS. with the leaves on the top, below).. **3,500**

Baroque Dining Table with Carved Lion Heads & Paw Feet

Victorian Baroque Revival library table, carved mahogany, partner's-type, wide rectangular top w/a wide scroll-carved border band over a deep rounded apron carved overall w/scrolls & fitted on each side w/a long drawer, raised on four large full-figure seated winged griffins at the corners on projecting platforms extending from a serpentine central shelf stretcher, on four thin bun feet, attributed to the Horner Furniture Co., New York City, late 19th c., 30 x 48", 30" h. (ILLUS., bottom of page)............................. **4,500**

Horner-style Carved Mahogany Library Table

Baroque Table with Masks

Victorian Baroque Revival library table, carved oak, the rectangular top covered overall w/ornate floral scrolls above a deep floral scroll-carved apron w/a relief-carved female mask at each corner above a turned drop, on a trestle-form base w/three columns at each end carved w/spiraling vines & raised on wide platforms carved at each end w/a figural sphinx, a heavy flat base stretcher centered by another carved column, fumed oak finish, late 19th c., 26 x 48", 30" h. (ILLUS.) **1,400**

Victorian Baroque Revival library table, oak, the rectangular top w/an oval center panel framed by ornately carved scrolls & scallop-carved edge, the deep apron carved w/large scrolls flanking a gro-

tesque mask between leaf-carved corner blocks, raised on four large full-figure seated winged griffins at each corner resting on projecting platforms joined to a flat center stretcher centered by a baluster- and knob-turned column w/carved leaves, late 19th c. (ILLUS., bottom of page) **2,800**

Oak Baroque Drop-leaf Parlor Table

Victorian Baroque Revival parlor table, quarter-sawn oak, a narrow rectangular top w/rounded ends flanked by wide half-round drop leaves, raised on a heavy fluted column above four outswept heavy scroll-carved feet, old refinish, ca. 1895, 36 x 46" open, 30" h. (ILLUS. closed)` **950**

Library Table with Grotesque Masks & Griffins

Fine Eastlake Walnut Dining Table

Victorian Eastlake style dining table, walnut, extension-type, the square top w/rounded corners above a deep apron w/leaf-incised blocks supported on a heavy squared center pedestal flanked by wide flat pierce-carved panels w/a diamond motif resting on platforms joining the four corner legs, each ring- and bulbous knob-turned leg resting on a stepped block foot, original finish, w/six leaves, ca. 1880s, closed 48" w., 30" h. (ILLUS.) **3,000**

Simple Golden Oak Dining Table

Victorian Golden Oak dining table, quarter-sawn oak, extension-type, round top w/plain apron raised on a heavy octagonal split pedestal resting on a cross-form base w/C-scroll feet on casters, refinished, w/four leaves, ca. 1900, 60" d., 30" h. (ILLUS.) **1,200**

Fine Column-based Golden Oak Dining Table

Victorian Golden Oak dining table, quarter-sawn oak, extension-type, round top w/scallop-incised rim above an apron w/angled blocks above a cluster of five large reeded columns on a platform base w/scroll-carved feet, w/six leaves, refinished, ca. 1895, 60" d., 30" h. (ILLUS.) **4,200**

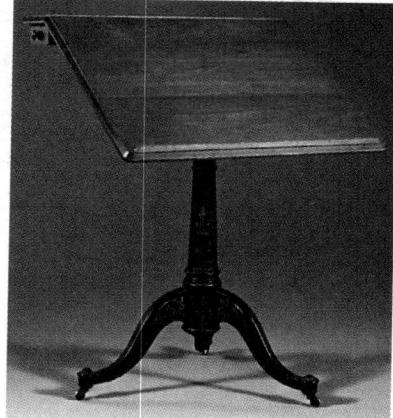

Victorian Patented Folding Table

Victorian novelty side table, walnut & cast iron, the large walnut top w/a narrow edge over a pair of tiny drawers w/wide hinged drop leaf pivoting & telescoping above the tapering columnar cast-iron pedestal on a tripod base w/flat cabriole legs ending in knob feet on casters, base w/stenciled classical decoration, marked w/a stenciled label reading "Designed and manufactured at the Washburn Machine Shop connected with the Institute of Industrial Science Worcester, Mass...Patented Nov. 19, 1872," 26 x 29", 31" h. (ILLUS.) **1,150**

Fine Renaissance Dining Table

Victorian Renaissance Revival dining table, walnut & burl walnut, extension-type, round top above a deep apron w/narrow burl bands separated by small roundels, raised on a heavy squared split pedestal on a cross-form platform base fitted w/large scroll-carved legs w/ebonized trim, refinished, ca. 1870s, w/four leaves, 48" d., 30" h. (ILLUS.) **2,500**

Victorian Renaissance Revival library table, walnut & burl walnut, the rectangular top w/wide rounded ends & inset center panel above a deep conforming apron w/large corner blocks w/turned drops, a long drawer centered by a bold oblong scroll-carved burl & roundel keyhole escutcheon, raised on a trestle-style base, w/pairs of square burl posts flanking large urn-turned supports raised on angled squared legs w/scroll feet on casters, a scroll-ended slender stretcher centered by a squatty bulbous turned finial, ca. 1875, 31 x 55", 30" h. **1,610**

Walnut Renaissance Library Table

Victorian Renaissance Revival library table, walnut, rectangular top w/chamfered corners above a conforming apron w/each side centered by a scroll-carved block cartouche, a long drawer on one side, raised block angled corners w/turned drops, raised on a trestle-style base w/a central ring-, knob- and rod-turned post flanked by flat legs w/scroll-carved brackets all raised on a slightly arched shoe base, joined by a long ring- and rod-turned stretcher w/an urn-turned finial, ca. 1875, refinished, 24 x 42", 30" h. (ILLUS.) **1,600**

Rosewood Renaissance Parlor Table

Victorian Renaissance Revival parlor table, rosewood, a round white marble top above a conforming apron carved w/four scroll cartouches & supported on four long upturned carved arms issuing from the central gadroon- and scroll-carved post raised on four scroll-carved projecting cabriole legs ending on scroll feet on casters, refinished, ca. 1875, 32" d., 30" h. (ILLUS.) **2,500**

Walnut Renaissance Parlor Table

Victorian Renaissance Revival parlor table, walnut, the oblong white marble top w/notched corners above a molded apron w/spearpoint-carved drops raised on four S-scroll incurved supports ending in turned finials & joined to a center post w/a slender ring-turned pedestal, all raised on four outswept shaped & molded legs on casters, refinished, ca. 1875, 20 x 32", 30" h. (ILLUS.) **750**

Victorian Rococo Dressing Table

Carved Rosewood Rococo "Turtle-top" Parlor Table

Victorian Rococo dressing table, rosewood, the rectangular top w/a raised central section w/coved borders, the hinged top opening to a compartment w/mirror above two drawers, a large shell- and scroll-carved drop at the front apron, raised on four incurved serpentine legs joined by a serpentine cross-stretcher centered by a small oval shelf, attributed to John H. Belter, New York City, ca. 1855, refinished, restorations to legs & stretchers, 16 x 21", 31 1/4" h. (ILLUS.) **863**

finish, ca. 1850s, 20 x 40", 30" h. (ILLUS.).. **1,800**

Victorian Rococo parlor table, carved rosewood, a white marble "turtle top" above a conforming apron carved in the center of each side w/a large scroll cluster, the blocked corners above heavy S-scroll legs w/leaf-carved knees & raised on casters, C-scroll-carved cross stretcher centered by a squatty ribbed urn finial, original finish, ca. 1860, 26 x 48", 30" h. (ILLUS., top of page).................................. **2,500**

Fine "Turtle-top" Rosewood Table

Victorian Rococo parlor table, carved rosewood, a white marble "turtle top" above a conforming apron carved w/large floral & scroll clusters & a border of heavy scrolls, raised on heavy cabriole legs w/fruit- and scroll-carved knees & ending in scrolled leaf feet on casters, joined by a serpentine cross stretcher centered by a gadrooned urn finial, original finish, ca. 1850s, 24 x 44", 30" h. (ILLUS.)... **3,600**

Fine Rosewood Rococo Games Table

Victorian Rococo games table, rosewood, the rectangular serpentine-sided lift top opening to felt lining & a matching felt-lined top over the serpentine scalloped deep apron centered by a flute & blossom-carved mount & scroll- and flower-carved knees on the cabriole legs, one rear legs swings out for support, original

Outstanding Meeks Rococo Parlor Table with a Basket of Flowers

Victorian Rococo parlor table, carved rosewood, a white marble "turtle top" above a conforming apron ornately pierce-carved w/scrolls centering a floral cluster, raised on S-scroll legs w/the knees carved w/large floral clusters, scroll feet on casters, joined by a scroll-carved serpentine cross stretcher centered by a large carved basket of flowers & smaller disk drop finial, by J. & J.W. Meeks of New York City, old refinish, ca. 1855, approximately 25 x 48", 30" h. (ILLUS., above) **18,000**

carved floral cluster, raised on tapering S-scroll legs w/leaf-carved knees & scroll feet on casters, joined by a slender serpentine cross stretcher centered by a carved basket of flowers, signed by Doe and Hazelton, Boston, Massachusetts, original top & casters, old refinish, ca. 1860, 24 x 44", 30" h. (ILLUS.) **2,500**

Fine Pierce-carved Parlor Table

Victorian Rococo parlor table, rosewood, the oblong white marble top w/notched corners above a conforming deep apron pierce-carved w/long narrow bands of scrolls over scroll-carved drops, raised on forked scroll supports joining tall C-scroll supports above a serpentine cross stretcher centered by a low carved reeded dome, on squatty disk feet, refinished, ca. 1850, 24 x 44", 30" h. (ILLUS.) **3,600**

Signed Rococo Mahogany Table

Victorian Rococo parlor table, mahogany, a tan marble "turtle top" above a conforming apron w/each side centered by a

Decorated Papier-Mâché Table

English Lacquered Side Table

Victorian Rococo side table, black lacquered papier-mâché, the scalloped oval top w/exotic painted scene of a camel & ruins tilting above a baluster- and ring-turned pedestal, the domed rounded & fluted base on small web feet, England, ca. 1870, 22 x 26", 27" h. (ILLUS.)...................... **1,035**

Victorian side table, black lacquer, composed of three open rectangular shelves w/chamfered corners, each w/a low scrolled gallery on slender turned supports, decorated overall w/Oriental scenes in black highlighted w/gilt, on eight short splayed feet, England, mid-19th c., 18 x 27", 33 1/2" h. (ILLUS., next column)...................... **2,990**

William IV side tables, mahogany, a rectangular top above an apron fitted w/two drawers w/turned wooden knobs, raised on heavy baluster- and knob-turned reeded legs ending in brass caps on casters, England, second quarter 19th c., 20 x 40", 30" h., pr. (ILLUS., bottom of page)...................... **5,750**

William & Mary dining table, oak, mortise-&-tenon construction, rectangular top w/rounded ends flanked by half-round drop leaves above two swing-out legs, baluster-, knob- & block-turned legs joined by heavy square stretchers, original feet & iron hinges, probably English, 18th c., softness & worm damage at ends of feet, drop leaves w/separations w/added supports below, 9 1/2 x 24", opens to 26 1/2", 19" h.................... **3,960**

Fine Pair of William IV Mahogany Side Tables

Wardrobes & Armoires

Fine French Provincial Armoire

Armoire, French Provincial, painted & lacquered wood, the rectangular top w/a widely flaring stepped cornice above a pair of tall three-panel doors w/heavy molded edges & fitted w/long iron hinges, three-paneled sides, a widely flaring stepped base molding on heavy bun feet, decorated overall in cream lacquer decorated w/gilt chinoiserie scenes of figures in landscapes, France, ca. 1800, 27 1/2 x 65 1/4", 7' 7 1/4" h. (ILLUS.)....... **12,650**

French Henri IV-Style Armoire

Armoire, Henri IV-Style, oak, the rectangular top widely overhanging a dentil-carved cornice above a leafy scroll-carved frieze band above a molding & a pair of tall three-panel doors, the two

larger panels carved w/scroll borders & the smaller central panel carved w/a scrolled cartouche, two-part reeded side pilasters above the carved apron band, on wide rectangular block feet, France, late 19th c., 26 1/2 x 69 1/4", 7' 10 3/4" h. (ILLUS.)... **1,265**

Fancy Burled Victorian Armoire

Armoire, late Victorian, walnut & Circassian walnut veneer, the high serpentine crestrail carved w/bold leafy scrolls at the top & rounded ends w/further carved leafy band in the frieze above a pair of tall paneled cupboard doors featuring fancy burl veneer & flanked by burl veneer side bands, the base w/a pair of raised panel burled drawers w/pierced brass pulls, deep molded base, demountable, refinished, ca. 1875-95, 20 x 48", 8' h. (ILLUS.)... **2,400**

Louis XV-Style Inlaid Armoire

Armoire, Louis XV-Style Provincial type, fruitwood, the rectangular top w/beveled front corners on the coved cornice above a paneled frieze band centered by a star-inlaid roundel over a pair of tall three-paneled doors w/long pierced brass latches, three-panel sides, serpentine carved apron on short scrolled legs w/up-turned toes, France, late 19th c., 24 1/2 x 56", 7' 1" h. (ILLUS.) **2,185**

French Provincial Paneled Armoire

Armoire, Louis XV-Style Provincial type, fruitwood, the rectangular top w/a flat-tened widely flaring cornice above a pair of three-paneled doors, the top panel w/an arched top & the middle panel w/a raised diamond design, flat apron & short stile block feet, France, mid-19th c., 22 x 51", 6' 11" h. (ILLUS.) **2,300**

Rare Mallard Rosewood Armoire

Armoire, Victorian Rococo style, rosewood, the rectangular top w/a wide arched cre-strail w/an egg-and-dart border topped by a high arched & ornately pierce-carved crest centered by a flower-filled urn, the arched & beaded-border frieze panel over a large door w/beaded border molding framing a large rectangular mir-ror, the door flanked by beveled front cor-ners w/carved half-round top & base drops, the molded base fitted w/a long paneled drawer above an egg-and-dart-carved band & flat apron on flattened bun feet, attributed to the New Orleans ware-rooms of Prudent Mallard, ca. 1850s, 24 1/2 x 57", 9' 5" h. (ILLUS.) **19,500**

Fine George III-Style Wardrobe

Wardrobe, George III-Style, mahogany, the rectangular top w/narrow cornice w/dentil band & bowed front above a conforming case w/a pair of large two-panel doors opening to shelves & hanging rods, mold-ed base on splayed bracket feet, En-gland, early 20th c., 21 x 46", 6' 10" h. (ILLUS.) **2,070**

Wardrobe, Victorian Eastlake country-style, walnut, the rectangular top w/a flaring stepped cornice above frieze band carved w/roundels & incised leafy bands above a pair of tall paneled doors cen-tered by a large rosette & incised leafy scrolls & blossoms, a pair of paneled drawers w/brass pulls at the bottom, flat molded base w/cutout apron & bracket feet, refinished, ca. 1885, 18 x 48", 7' 2" h. (ILLUS., top next page) **2,400**

Country Eastlake Walnut Wardrobe

Crested Golden Oak Wardrobe

Wardrobe, Victorian Golden Oak style, oak, demountable, a high scroll-cut & scroll-carved crestrail above the flaring cornice above a pair of tall doors w/recessed panels w/rounded corners, a mid-molding over the long line-incised bottom drawer, paneled sides, original brasses, original finish, ca. 1900, 20 x 48", 7' 10" h. (ILLUS.).. **2,000**

Country Renaissance Wardrobe

Wardrobe, Victorian Renaissance Revival country-style, butternut, one-piece construction, the rectangular top w/an arched & notch-cut crestrail centered by a walnut fruit cluster above the flaring cornice over a pair of tall doors w/arched molded panels, a pair of drawers w/small wood knobs at the bottom above the notch-cut apron w/bracket feet, possibly Norwegian-American influence, Midwest, ca. 1870s, refinished, 20 x 50", 7' 4" h. (ILLUS.) **1,500**

High-crested Walnut Wardrobe

Wardrobe, Victorian Renaissance Revival style, walnut, demountable, the rectangular top w/a high arched crestrail w/molding flanking a large scroll- and leaf-carved center crest, rounded stepped ears at the rounded top corners above a pair of wide paneled doors w/carved scrolls across the top, open interior, flat base w/cut-down bracket feet, original finish, ca. 1875, 21 x 56", 8' h. (ILLUS., previous page) **1,500**

Scroll-carved Rococo Wardrobe

Wardrobe, Victorian Rococo style, walnut & burl walnut, demountable, rectangular top w/an arched molded cornice fitted w/a high arched & pierced scroll-carved crestrail above a scroll-carved frieze band above a molding over a pair of tall arched doors w/burl panels above a molding over a pair of drawers w/a raised oval banding enclosing fan-carved pulls & a carved keyhole escutcheon, deep molded base, refinished, ca. 1860, 20 x 60", 7' 6" h. (ILLUS.) **3,200**

Whatnots & Etageres

Etagere, Oriental, carved rosewood, the peaked top decorated w/an ornate scroll-carved crestrail above the molded cornice w/turned corner finials & edged along the bottom w/further pierce-carved borders, supported on four slender carved supports to the top mirror-backed open shelves w/a pierce-carved gallery above five slender supports all framed by narrow pierced borders & centered by a

Elaborate East Asian Etagere

small open shelf & backed by another mirror, all on four additional carved supports w/pierced upper borders atop the bottom shelf backed by a mirror, the flaring carved apron w/a low pierced gallery & base band, raised on carved paw feet, East Asia, early 20th c., 17 x 39", 5' 10 1/2" h. (ILLUS.) **1,150**

Extraordinary Belter Victorian Rococo Rosewood Etagere

Etagere, Victorian Rococo style, carved & pierced rosewood, two-part construction: the tall upper section w/a high arched & ornately pierce-carved crest decorated w/grapevines centering a large magnolia blossom above the tall arched central mirror flanked by three half-round graduated shelves each w/ornate scroll-carved brackets; the lower section w/a long white marble top w/serpentine sides & small rounded projections above a conforming case w/serpentine scroll-carved drawer over a mirrored cupboard door flanked by concave apron panels over an open shelf above the plinth base, each side shelf supported by baluster- or columnar-turned supports & backed by a mirror, the serpentine apron w/a scroll-carved cluster in the center panel, attributed to John H. Belter, New York City, ca. 1855, 16 1/2 x 59", 8' 2" h. (ILLUS., previous page) **52,900**

Putto & Dolphins Garden Fountain

Large English Cast-Stone Planter

Planter, cast-stone, wide shallow urn-form w/a wide angled rim, squatty gadrooned bowl & short pedestal base, England, 19th c., 26" d., 15" h. (ILLUS.)........................ **863**

William IV Mahogany Whatnot

Whatnot, William IV, mahogany, the rectangular top w/a low three-quarters gallery raised on slender ring-turned supports over three more open shelves w/matching turned supports, raised on trumpet-turned feet, England, second quarter 19th c., 16 1/4 x 23 1/2", 5' 10" h. (ILLUS.).. **1,955**

GARDEN FOUNTAINS & ORNAMENTS

Fountain, cast iron, Victorian-style, the top w/a figure of a standing putto holding a shell that issues the water, seated atop a wide shallow fluted basin raised on a fluted pedestal flanked by three figural dolphins on a trilobed fluted platform base, painted white, 26" d., 47" h. (ILLUS.) **$748**

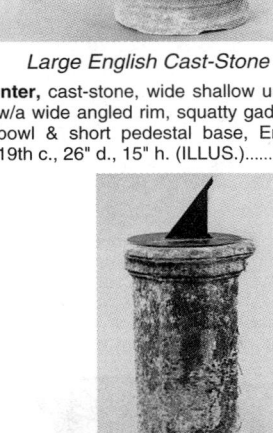

English Sundial on Pedestal

Sundial, the dark patinated metal dial raised atop a weathered octagonal limestone pedestal base, England, second quarter 19th c., base 20" w., overall 4' 6 1/4" h. (ILLUS.)... **5,060**

Neoclassical Cast-Iron Garden Urn

Urn, cast iron, the bulbous lobed & fluted vasiform body w/a center band of lion masks below the high rolled rim, raised on a short pedestal w/banded dome foot, dark patina & some rust, 19th c., 21" d., 29" h. (ILLUS.).. **1,035**

English White-Painted Garden Urn

Urns, cast iron, a wide shallow rounded & gadrooned bowl w/a flaring annulated & egg-and-dart rim, raised on a waisted & fluted pedestal on a square stepped base, old white paint, England, 19th c., 38 1/2" d., 39" h., pr. (ILLUS. of one) **1,495**

Black Cast-Iron Garden Urns

Urns, cast iron, large campana-form w/a rolled egg-and-dart rim above the fluted sides & gadrooned bottom raised on a fluted flaring pedestal above the square stepped base, black paint, England, early 20th c., 23 1/2" d., 35" h., pr. (ILLUS.)....... **1,610**

GLASS

Agata

Agata was patented by Joseph Locke of the New England Glass Company in 1887. The application of mineral stain left a mottled effect on the surface of the article. It was applied chiefly to the Wild Rose (Peach Blow) line but sometimes was applied as a border on a pale opaque green. In production for a short time, it is scarce. Items listed below are of the Wild Rose line unless otherwise noted.

Bowl, 5 1/2" d., 2 3/4" h., upright deeply ruffled sides... **$950**

Green Opaque Creamer

Creamer, Green Opaque, wide tapering ovoid body w/pinched spout, applied handle, 4 1/2" h. (ILLUS.)................. **1,000-1,250**

Squatty Agata Creamer

Creamer, squatty bulbous body w/wide cylindrical short neck, applied handle, 3 3/4" h. (ILLUS.).............................. **1,750-2,200**

Rare Agata Pitcher

Pitcher, 7" h., bulbous ovoid body tapering
to a squared slightly flaring neck, applied
handle, fine overall oil spotting (ILLUS.).... **6,325**
Spooner, deeply ruffled lavender rim,
4 1/2" h. **1,800-2,400**
Tumbler, exceptionally strong color & mot-
tling, polished pontil.................................... **1,050**
Tumbler, Green Opaque, strong decoration..... **600**

Green Opaque Vase

Vase, 6 1/4" h., Green Opaque, ovoid body
tapering to a flaring rim, minor wear
(ILLUS.)... **575**

Amberina

*Amberina was developed in the late 1880s by
the New England Glass Company and a pressed
version was made by Hobbs, Brockunier & Company (under license from the former). A similar*

*ware, called Rose Amber, was made by the Mt.
Washington Glass Works. Amberina-Rose Amber
shades from amber to deep red or fuchsia and cut
and plated (lined with creamy white) examples
were also made. The Libbey Glass Company
briefly revived blown Amberina, using modern
shapes, in 1917.*

Amberina Label

Bowl, 3 3/4" d., 2 3/4" h., cylindrical body
w/a deeply ruffled fuchsia rim **$325**

Rare Small Plated Amberina Bowl

Bowl, 4 1/2" d., 3 1/2" h., Plate Amberina,
deep squatty round tapering sides below
the flaring flat rim (ILLUS.).......................... **4,600**
Bowl, 5 3/4" d., 3 3/4" h., squatty bulbous
body w/swirled molded ribbing below the
deeply ruffled & crimped rim **135**
Bowl, 7 1/8" sq., 2 1/8" h., pressed Daisy &
Button patt. **375**

Rare Plate Amberina Bowl

Bowl, 7 1/2" d., Plated Amberina, low rolled
sides w/five crimps (ILLUS.) **7,188**
Bowl, 10" w., oblong diamond shape,
pressed Daisy & Button patt., Gillinder &
Sons.. **400**
Butter dish, cov., round blown cover in In-
verted Thumbprint patt., pressed Daisy &
Button underplate **275-350**
Butter pat, square, pressed Daisy & Button
patt. **125**

Celery vase, Diamond Quilted patt., New England Glass Co., 6 1/2" h........................... **375**

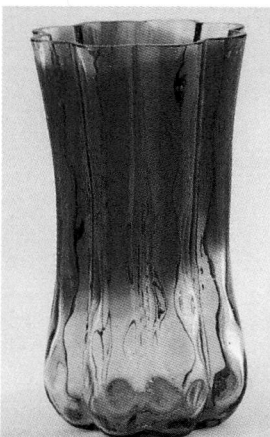

Amberina Ribbed Celery Vase

Celery vase, ribbed & waisted cylindrical form in the Diamond Optic patt., ca. 1880s, 6 3/4" h. (ILLUS.)........................ **175-225**

Creamer, spherical swirled pattern-molded body w/a wide cylindrical neck w/pinched spout, applied angled amber handle w/end curl, 3 1/2" d., 5" h. **175**

Cruet w/original facet-cut stopper, flat-bottomed domed shape tapering to a small neck w/pinched spout, applied amber handle, swirled optic rib design, 4" d., 9" h. **225-250**

Rare Plated Amberina Cruet

Cruet w/original stopper, Plated Amberina, bulbous body tapering to a cylindrical neck w/tricorner rim, applied amber handle, facet-cut amber stopper, 6 3/4" h. (ILLUS.)... **3,968**

Cruet w/original stopper, spherical body in Inverted Thumbprint patt., slender cylindrical neck w/a tricorner mouth, applied amber handle, amber bubble stopper, 3 1/2" d., 6" h. **250-275**

Finger bowl, square, Hobnail patt., Mt. Washington Glass Co. **225**

Goblet, rose to amber coloring, optic ribbed design, 3 3/8" d., 6 1/8" h. **125**

Lantern, hall-type, kerosene, the large teardrop-form shade w/an Inverted Thumbprint design, brass fittings at the top & bottom, 6 3/4" d, 12 1/2" h. **500-750**

Mug, barrel-shaped swirled optic-ribbed body on an applied disk foot, amber twisted rope handle w/end curl, heavily decorated w/gold flowers & leaves, 2 3/4" d., 4 5/8" h. **150**

Pitcher, Plated Amberina, bulbous ovoid body tapering to a tricorner mouth, applied ruby handle, creamy white lining..... **10,000**

Pitcher, 6" h., cylindrical body in a diamond optic design, tapering slightly at the shoulder below the widely flaring & tightly crimped neck, smooth applied amber handle, New England Glass Co. **750-950**

Pitcher, 9 1/8" h., 5 1/4" d., tapering ovoid body w/a wide cylindrical neck & pinched spout, applied angled amber handle, swirled optic rib design **200-250**

Diamond Quilted Amberina Pitcher

Pitcher, 9 1/2" h., tankard-type, Diamond Quilted patt., tapering cylindrical body w/a pinched spout & applied amber handle, New England Glass Co. (ILLUS.)... **750-1,000**

Salt shaker w/original two-piece lid, Baby Thumbprint patt., bulging dual mold-blown body, 2 1/2" h. **235**

Tumbler, Inverted Thumbprint patt., flat bottom, 2 3/4" d., 3 3/4" h. **65**

Large Group of Amberina Vases

Vase, bulbous base tapering to a tricorner neck trimmed w/a band of amber rigaree, deep color **750-950**

Rare Pressed Amberina Stork Vase

Vase, pressed upright square form, Stork patt., designed by Joseph Locke, New England Glass Co. (ILLUS.)............. **2,000-2,800**

Vase, 5" h., jack-in-the-pulpit type, wide squatty flat-bottomed body w/optic ribbing below the widely flaring upturned neck, circular trademark on base for Libbey Amberina (ILLUS. bottom row, center, top of page) **690**

Vase, 6" h., lily-form, deep fuchsia shading to amber (ILLUS. bottom row, far right) **345**

Vase, 7" h., jack-in-the-pulpit type, scarlet rim shading to amber (ILLUS. bottom row, second from left, top of page) **288**

Vase, 7" h., jack-in-the-pulpit type, squatty bulbous base w/tall flaring neck, fuchsia shaded to amber, souvenir inscription "World's Fair 1893" (ILLUS. bottom row, fourth from left, top of page) **345**

Vase, 7 1/4" h., lily-form, fuchsia shading to amber, three small bubbles (ILLUS. bottom row, third from right, top of page) **144**

Vase, 8" h., an ovoid optic ribbed body w/a widely flaring flattened rim raised on a disk & knob stem & round foot, signed w/the Libbey trademark, ca. 1917 (ILLUS. bottom row, second from right, top of page) **1,035**

Vase, 9" h., optic ribbed ovoid body tapering to a widely flaring ruffled rim, signed w/round Libbey trademark, ca. 1917 (ILLUS. second from left, top row, top of page) **2,990**

Vase, 10" h., jack-in-the-pulpit type, vermilion shading to amber (ILLUS. bottom row, third from left, top of page) **288**

Vase, 10 3/4" h., lily-type, disc foot below the knop & disk stem supporting the tall optic ribbed body w/a deeply ruffled rim, signed w/Libbey circular mark, ca. 1917 (ILLUS. top row, far right, top of page) **3,048**

Vase, 10 3/4" h., lily-type, tall flaring optic ribbed body w/a ruffled rim, signed w/circular Libbey mark (ILLUS. top row, far left, top of page) **575**

Vase, 11 1/4" h., jack-in-the-pulpit type, crimson shading to amber (ILLUS. bottom row, far left, top of page) **288**

Vase, 12" h., lily-type, tall flaring optic ribbed body w/rolled rim (ILLUS. top row, second from right, top of page) **403**

Rare Tall Libbey Amberina Vase

Vase, 12 1/2" h., flora-form, a round foot below a hollow stem knop supporting the tall slender optic ribbed body w/a widely flaring deeply ruffled rim, signed by Libbey, ca. 1917 (ILLUS.) **1,800-2,400**

Animals

Americans evidently like to collect glass animals. For the past sixty years, American glass manufacturers have turned out a wide variety of animals to please the buying public. Some were produced for long periods and some were later reproduced by other companies, while others were made for only a short period of time and are rare. We have not included late productions in our listings and have attempted to date the productions where possible. Evelyn Zemel's book, American Glass Animals A to Z, *will be helpful to the novice collector. Another helpful book is* Glass Animals of the Depression Era *by Lee Garmon and Dick Spencer Collector Books, 1993.*

Asiatic pheasant, clear, Heisey Glass Co., 7 1/2" l., 10 1/2" h. **$465**
Bird, scolding, jade, Imperial Glass Co., Cathay Line mold **100**
Boxer dog, lying down, clear, American Glass Co., 3 7/8" h. **60**
Cat, grotesque style, black satin, U.S. Glass Co., 6 1/2" h. **175**
Chanticleer (rooster), clear, Fostoria Glass Co., 10 1/4" h. **275**
Deer, standing, clear, Fostoria Glass Co., 1 x 2" base, 41/2" h. **35**
Dragon swan, pale blue, Paden City Glass Co., 9 3/4" l., 6 1/2" h. **600**
Egret, Imperial Glass Co. Cathay Line, marked "Virginia B Evans" in script, clear satin, 9" h. **300**
Elephant, cov. dish, Co-operative Flint Glass, clear, 7" h., 13" l. **295**

Elephant w/long trunk extended (Mama), clear, Heisey Glass Co., 1944-55, 6 1/2" l., 4" h. **550**
Fawn, w/flower floater & sockets for three candles, citron green, Tiffin Glass Co., ca. late 1940s, 14 1/2" l., fawn 10" h., ... **250**
Fighting rooster, clear, Heisey Glass Co., 1940-46, 7 1/2" h. **165**
Fish, on wave base, Tiffin Glass, clear, 9" l. **300**
Frog, covered dish, green, 1969, Erskine Glass Co. **150**
Goldfish, vertical form, Fostoria Glass, clear, 3 1/2" h. **125**
Goose, wings down, clear, A.H. Heisey & Co., 1947-55, 4 1/2" l., 4 1/2" h. (small bubble in neck) **565**
Goose, wings half up, clear w/Charleton roses decoration, A.H. Heisey & Co., 1947-55, 5 1/2" l., 5" h. **125**
Goose (The Fat Goose), clear & frosted, Duncan & Miller Glass Co., 6" l., 6 1/2" h. **395**
Hen, clear, A.H. Heisey & Co., 1948-49, 2 3/4 x 2 1/2" base, 4 1/2" h. **550**
Heron, No. 30, Duncan & Miller, clear, 7" h. **100**
Horse, pony, balking, clear, A.H. Heisey & Co., 1941-45, 3 1/2" h. **275**
Horse book end, clear, New Martinsville Glass Co., 8" h. **95**
Mama bear, clear, No. 488, New Martinsville Glass Co., 6" l., 4" h. **145**
Mama pig, w/three nursing piglets attached on each side, clear, No. 1, limited edition of approximately 200, New Martinsville Glass Co., 6" l., 3" h. **950**
Owl, book end, Fostoria Glass, clear, 7 1/2" h. **230**
Papa bear, clear, No. 489, New Martinsville Glass Co., 6 1/2" l., 4" h. **200**
Penguin, amber, No. 1319, 1960s, Viking Glass Co., 7" h. **35**
Pheasant, tail up, Tiffin Glass, No. 6042-1, Twilight, 17" l. **850**
Polar bear, clear, Fostoria Glass Co., 4 5/8" h. **80**
Police dog (German Shepherd), clear, No. 733, New Martinsville Glass Co., 5" h. **75**
Porpoise on wave, clear, No. 766, New Martinsville Glass Co., 6" h. **145**
Rabbit, bunnies, clear, ears up, ears back or ears lying down, New Martinsville Glass Mfg. Co., 1" each **75**

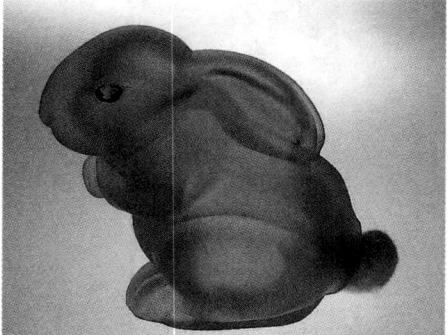

Paden City Rabbit Cotton Dispenser

Rabbit cotton dispenser, ears back, Paden City Glass, hollow pink satin, painted eyes, 5" h. (ILLUS.) 175

Rooster (Chanticleer), pale blue, Paden City Glass Co., 9 1/2" h. 275

Rooster with crooked tail, clear, No. 668, New Martinsville Glass Co., 8" h. 85

Scottie dog book ends, Cambridge Glass Co., 6 1/2" h., pr. 250

Sea horse, book end, Fostoria Glass, clear, 8" h. 200

Squirrel on curved log, clear, No. 677, Paden City Glass Co., 5 1/2" h. 60

Swordfish, blue opalescent, Duncan & Miller Glass Co., 5" h. 500

Tiger, paperweight, black opaque, Imperial Glass Co. (Heisey mold), 1982-83, 8"l., 22/3" h. 125

Wolfhound, clear, No. 716, New Martinsville Glass Co., 7" h. 90

Woodchuck, caramel slag, Imperial Glass Co., 4" h. 60

Appliquéd

Simply stated, this is an art glass form with applied decoration. Sometimes master glass craftsmen applied stems or branches to an art glass object and then added molded glass flowers or fruit specimens to these branches or stems. At other times a button of molten glass was daubed on the object and a tool pressed over it to form a prunt in the form of a raspberry, rosette or other shape. Always the work of a skilled glassmaker, applied decoration can be found on both cased (two-layer) and single layer glass. The English firm of Stevens and Williams was renowned for the appliquéd glass they produced.

Spherical Enameled Appliquéd Vase

Vase, 4 3/4" h., 3 3/4" d., spherical clear body tapering to a short flared mouth trimmed in gold, the sides enameled overall w/delicate blue & white flowers & butterflies w/gold trim, three rigaree bands down the sides continuing to form claw feet (ILLUS.) $200-225

Vase, 11 1/4" h., 7" d., bulbous tapering pale lavender body w/an applied blue pointed scalloped rim, bands of blue rigaree down the sides alternating w/applied inverted dolphins up the sides & forming feet, late 19th c. (ILLUS.) 400-425

Appliquéd Vase with Dolphin Feet

Vase, 12 1/2" h., 6 1/2" d., ovoid dark blue body tapering to a flaring rim w/an applied clear band, applied down the sides w/three long spiny rigaree bands alternating w/panels enameled in color w/wide ribbons & pink & white flowers, raised on applied pointed clear feet 325-350

Vases with Appliquéd Salamanders

Vases, 9" h., a footring below a spreading base on the tall cylindrical optic ribbed body, applied clear rigaree around the rim & large clear salamander crawling up the side, late 19th c., pr. (ILLUS.) 259

Rare Appliquéd & Overshot Vases

Vases, 13" h., stick-type, shaded Rubina Verde cylinder w/overshot decoration & an applied band of lime green icicling near the top & another band forming the base, ca. 1880s, pr. (ILLUS.)............ **1,000-1,500**

Art Glass Baskets

Popular novelties in the late Victorian era, these ornate baskets of glass were usually hand-crafted of free-blown or mold-blown glass. They were made in a wide spectrum of colors and shapes. Pieces were highlighted with tall applied handles and often applied feet; however, fancier ones might also carry additional appliquéd trim.

Rare Bluerina Art Glass Basket

Bluerina, round foot below the widely flaring, flattened Hobnail patt. rim w/two sides pulled up, tall applied clear twisted thorn handle, 9 1/2" h. (ILLUS.).................. **$633**

Cased, footed oblong body pinched in on two sides, high pointed applied clear handle form side to side, pale yellow exterior enameled w/pink & white daisies, gold leaves & branches, white lining, 5 1/2 x 7 1/4", 8" h. **200-225**

Mosaic, squatty bulbous body tapering to a widely flaring ruffled rim, high arched applied amber handle, in French "tigre" or mosaic glass in swirled cream & goldstone, cranberry lining, 5" d., 7 1/2" h. . **175-200**

Opaque custard, tapering ovoid body of opaque custard w/incurved ruffled rim, applied amber handle & leaves, two applied spatter flowers, 7 3/4" h. **160**

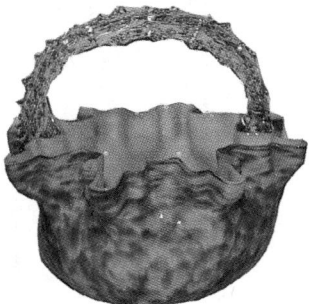

Yellow & Pink Spatter Basket

Spatter, rounded body w/flaring crimped rim pulled into points, arched applied clear thorn handle, yellow & pink spatter, white lining, 6" d., 6" h. (ILLUS.)...................... **165-185**

Spatter, rounded body w/upright crimped & scalloped rim, high arched applied clear thorn handle, the exterior in swirled colors of aqua, beige & white, white lining, 5" d., overall 7 1/2" h.............................. **165-185**

Baccarat

Baccarat glass has been made by Cristalleries de Baccarat, France, since 1765. The firm has produced various glassware of excellent quality as well as paperweights. Baccarat's Rose Tiente is often referred to as Baccarat's Amberina.

Box w/hinged cover, square crystal, the cover encrusted w/a sulfide portrait medallion of Louis Philippe of France, the body cut w/overall spiral gadroons, the ormolu mounts w/cast stiff leaftips, mid-19th c., 5 1/8" h.. **$7,475**

Rose Tiente Swirl Baccarat Pitcher

Pitcher, 9 1/4" h., 6 3/4" d., Rose Tiente Swirl patt., spherical body tapering to a cylindrical neck w/pinched spout, applied clear handle (ILLUS.).............................. **300-325**

Baccarat Zipper Pattern Wine Bottle

Large Group of Blown Three Mold Pieces

Wine bottle w/original stopper, Zipper patt. in Rose Tiente, spherical body tapering to a tall paneled neck w/flared rim, matching Zipper ball stopper, 5" d., 10" h. (ILLUS.) **165-185**

Blown Three Mold

This type of glass was entirely or partially blown in a mold and was popular from about 1820 to 1840. The object was formed and the decoration impressed upon it by blowing the glass into a metal mold, usually of three—but sometimes more—sections hinged together. Mold-blown glass actually dates back to ancient times. Recent research reveals that certain geometric patterns were reproduced in the 1920s; some new pieces, usually sold through museum gift shops, are still available. Collectors are urged to read all recent information available. Reference numbers are from George L. and Helen McKearin's book, American Glass.

Pieces are clear unless otherwise noted.

Bowl, 5 1/2" d., 1 7/8" h., geometric, wide flat bottom w/shallow upright folded sides, Boston & Sandwich Glass Co., ca. 1825-35, GII-1 (ILLUS. far left with group of pieces, top of page) **$264**

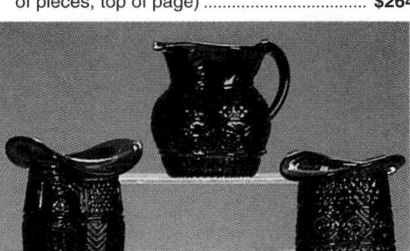

Three Small Pieces of Blue Blown Three Mold Glass

Creamer, geometric, short bulbous body w/flaring spout, applied strap handle, cobalt blue, Boston & Sandwich Glass Co., ca. 1825-35, 2 1/4" d., 3" h., GIII-23 (ILLUS. center)... **4,113**

Decanter, cylindrical body w/beveled edges, the lower body w/vertical ribs, the upper body w/crisscross diamond design, shoulders tapering to narrow neck w/flared rim, neck ground to accept a stopper, pontil scarred base, apple

Decanter in Apple Green

green, Keene, New Hampshire, ca. 1815-35, 7" h., GII-28 (ILLUS.) **3,360**

Rare Blue Baroque Design Decanter

Decanter w/stopper, Baroque design, tapering cylindrical body w/molded scrolling shells & ribs, dark blue, Boston & Sandwich Glass Co., ca. 1825-35, end of bubble stopper chipped, 11 1/2" h., GV-9 (ILLUS.).. **5,581**

Three Blown Three Mold Decanters

Decanter w/stopper, geometric, wide short cylindrical body w/a wide ribbed shoulder tapering to a ringed neck, pressed wheel stopper, possibly Midwestern, 1/2 pt., overall 6 1/2" h., GIII-11 (ILLUS. center with pair of decanters)................................. **1,045**

Decanters w/stoppers, geometric, barrel-shaped w/wide diamond bands above & below a ribbed central band, tapering to a flaring mouth w/a pinched pouring lip, pressed wheel stopper, pint, overall 8 1/2" h., GII-7, pr. (ILLUS. right & left with half-pint decanter) **248**

Dish, geometric, wide shallow flat-bottomed form w/upright folded sides, Boston & Sandwich Glass Co., ca. 1825-35, 4 1/4" d., 1 1/4" h., GIII-23 (ILLUS. previous page far right with large group of pieces)... **118**

Flip glass, geometric, tall tapering cylindrical form, folded rim, amethystine tint, 4 1/2" h., GII-18 (potstone w/star crack) **110**

Flip glass, ribbed tapering cylindrical form, etched rim has crosshatched ovals, 6 1/8" h. (GI-6).. **330**

Flip glass, tapering cylindrical form, beaded decoration, slight amethyst tint, 5 3/4" h., GII-19 (some pot stones & rim flakes).......... **330**

Flip glass, tapering cylindrical form, rim w/etched flourishes, 6 1/8" h. (GI-6) **358**

Lemonade mug, geometric, barrel-shaped w/an applied handle, Boston & Sandwich Glass Co., ca. 1825-35, rim chip, small crack, 2 3/8" d., 2 7/8" h., GII-19 (ILLUS. previous page second from right with large group of pieces) **206**

Model of a hat, geometric, cylindrical w/a rolled & folded rim, Boston & Sandwich Glass Co., ca. 1825-35, 2" h., clear, GIII-7 (ILLUS. previous page second from left with large group of pieces)........................... **118**

Model of a top hat, geometric, gently tapering cylindrical form w/rolled folded rim, cobalt blue, Boston & Sandwich Glass Co., ca. 1825-35, 2 5/8" d., 2 1/4" h., GIII-23 (ILLUS. previous page, right with blue pieces) **499**

Model of a top hat, geometric, gently tapering cylindrical form w/rolled folded rim, cobalt blue, Boston & Sandwich Glass Co., ca. 1825-35, 2 3/4" d., 2 5/8" h.,

GIII-25 (ILLUS. previous page, left with blue pieces)... **764**

Pitcher, 4 5/8" h., 3 1/4" d., ribbed, ovoid body tapering to a flared rim w/a pinched spout, applied strap handle, cobalt blue, Boston & Sandwich Glass Co., ca. 1825-35, GI-29 .... **2,585**

Tumbler, geometric, cylindrical, Boston & Sandwich Glass Co., ca. 1825-35, 2 3/8" d., 2 5/8" h., GIII-8 (ILLUS. previous page third from left with large group of pieces) **235**

Tumbler, geometric, cylindrical, ca. 1825-35, 2 1/4" d., 2 3/4" h., GII-20 variant (ILLUS. previous page third from right with large group of pieces)...................... **176**

Bohemian

Numerous types of glass were made in the once-independent country of Bohemia and fine colored, cut and engraved glass was turned out. Flashed and other inexpensive wares also were made; many of these, including amber- and ruby-shaded glass, were exported to the United States during the 19th and 20th centuries. One favorite pattern in the late 19th and early 20th centuries was Deer & Castle. Another was Deer and Pine Tree.

Bowl, 7" d., 3 1/4" h., wide squatty form w/incurved sides w/a ruffled rim, irides-cent green decorated w/overall random violet threading, supported on a three-footed embossed gilt-metal frame, Pall-me-Konig factory, ca. 1900 (ILLUS. bottom row, far right with bowls & cracker jar, top next page) **$345**

Carafe, cut-overlay, footed tapering bottle-form, cobalt blue ornately cut to white cut to clear & decorated overall w/colorful floral reserves & gold foliate scrolls, late 19th c., 12 1/2" h. **1,495**

Carafe, footed ovoid panel-cut body w/a wide shoulder band below the cylindrical neck, deep ruby decorated overall w/a continuous grapevine design in gold, late 19th c., 13" h... **201**

Center bowl, wide low squatty form w/incurved sides & ruffled rim, iridescent green w/overall random violet threading, fitted in a frame w/two arched composite deer antler handles, end cap missing from one handle, Pallme-Konig factory, ca. 1900, 8" d., 5" h. (ILLUS. bottom row, far left with bowls, top next page) **288**

Cracker jar w/plated metal cover, rim & bail handle, barrel-shaped, iridescent green decorated w/undulating & looping red & white marquetry flowers, Pallme-Konig factory, ca. 1900, 6" h. (ILLUS. top row, far left with bowls, top next page)......... **259**

Goblets, cut overlay, cup-shaped bowl on a low spreading foot, the white overlay cut to purple edged in clear, each decorated w/a center h.p. roundel depicting courting couples in early 19th c. costume, trimmed w/painted floral sprays, mid-19th c., 5 1/4" h., pr. **288**

Bohemian Bowls, Cracker Jar, Lamp & Vases

Lamp, kerosene table-type, the onion-form font in green iridescent glass w/random violet threading, on a tall cast-metal pedestal base decorated w/owls, Pallme-Konig factory, ca. 1900, 7 1/2" h. (ILLUS., center with bowls, top of page) **575**

Scent bottle, ovoid body tapering to a short ringed neck w/flattened rim, peridot green cut overall & ornately enameled w/colorful foliate scrolls, beaded festoons & clusters of flowerheads, stopper missing, late 19th c., 6" h. **104**

Smelling salts bottle w/stopper, cased & cut, short slightly tapering hexagonal form w/wide base & shoulder bands, short neck w/flattened rim & wide panel-cut & peaked stopper, ruby cut to clear, late 19th c., 5" h. **201**

Sweetmeat dish, squatty wide round body in iridescent green w/overall random violet threading, fitted w/a silvered metal rim & bail handle, cover missing, Pallme-Konig factory, ca. 1900, 5" d. (ILLUS. bottom row, second from right with bowls, top of page) **115**

Vase, 4 1/4" h., wide squatty bulbous form tapering to a wide rolled undulating rim, clear iridescence decorated w/overall random white threading (ILLUS. top row, second from left with bowls, top of page) **201**

Vase, 6" h., a cushion foot & short stem supporting the wide bulbous shouldered body w/a deeply ruffled & rolled rim, white opal & amber decorated w/overall random red threading, Pallme-Konig factory, ca. 1920 (ILLUS. top row, second from right with bowls, top of page) **259**

A Grouping of Bohemian Vases

Vase, 6" h., ringed pedestal base w/small urn-shaped vase, pink cased in white w/an overall pulled green Aventurine decoration, Rindskopf factory, ca. 1900 (ILLUS. top row, far left with other vases, bottom previous page) **173**

Vase, 6 1/2" h., "Grenada" type, a wide cushion base tapering to twisted sides below the ovoid top, shaded deep purple to yellowish green iridescent ground applied w/a green serpent wrapped down the sides, Rindskopf factory, ca. 1900 (ILLUS. bottom row, far left with other vases, bottom previous page) **431**

Vase, 8" h., "Grenada" type, pedestal base supporting a bulbous cupped bowl w/deeply folded rim in an Inverted Thumbprint patt., iridescent deep purple shading to greenish yellow, Rindskopf factory, ca. 1900 (ILLUS. top row, far right with other vases, bottom previous page).. **403**

Vase, 8" h., pedestal base supporting a bulbous cupped bowl w/deeply folded rim, iridescent purple decorated w/iridescent blue swags, Rindskopf factory, ca. 1900 (ILLUS. top row, second from left with other vases, bottom previous page) **345**

Vase, 8" h., wide squatty bulbous base w/pinched-in sides tapering to wide cylindrical sides w/a triple rolled-in rim, iridescent pink decorated w/overall green Aventurine in draped loops, roughness to one rim point, Rindskopf factory, ca. 1900 (ILLUS. bottom row, second from right, bottom previous page) **345**

Vase, 8 1/2" h., "Grenada" type, tall waisted cylindrical body w/swelled shoulder & short flared flat mouth, Inverted Thumbprint patt., overall iridescent deep maroon, Rindskopf factory, ca. 1900 (ILLUS. bottom row, second from left with other vases, bottom previous page) **259**

Vase, 9" h., a wide short squatty & tapering base centered by a tall tapering cylindrical neck, iridescent green decorated overall w/random violet threading, Pallme-Konig factory, ca. 1900 (ILLUS. top row, far right with bowls, top previous page).. **259**

Vase, 10 1/4" h., "Grenada" type, wide flaring cushion base tapering to a tall twisted body below the swelled top, applied w/a snake around the sides, iridescent shaded deep reddish purple to greenish amber, Rindskopf factory, ca. 1900 (ILLUS. bottom row, far right with other vases, bottom previous page) **575**

Vase, 11" h., ovoid body tapering to a tall neck w/in-body twist below the widely flaring flattened rim pulled into three lobes w/curled-in tips, iridescent red w/a blue & white variegated pulled decoration, Rindskopf factory, ca. 1900, drilled (ILLUS. top row, second from right, bottom previous page)....................................... **144**

Bride's Baskets & Bowls

These berry or fruit bowls were popular late Victorian wedding gifts, hence the name. They were produced in a variety of quality art glasswares and sometimes were fitted in ornate silver plate holders.

Cased Apricot Bride's Bowl

Cased bowl, apricot shaded to white satin interior, ruffled & crimped rim, enameled band of white spearpoints around the interior joined by delicate yellow enameled webbing, white exterior, 10" d., 3" h. (ILLUS.).. **$225-250**

Decorated Blue Cased Bride's Bowl

Cased bowl, deep blue satin interior w/flaring fluted sides pinched-in at one side & tightly crimped, enameled w/swags of small white blossoms w/yellow leaves, small pink buds & green leaves, applied clear edging, white exterior enameled w/a yellow & white bug, 10 1/2" d., 4" h. (ILLUS.).. **275-300**

Cased bowl, purple shaded to white satin interior, enameled along one side w/dainty purple flowers on long stems & delicate foliage around the opposite edge, white exterior, 10 3/4" d., 3 1/2" h. **200-225**

Satin glass, deep round bowl w/molded lobes around the lower half & a flaring, crimped & ruffled rim, shaded pink mother-of-pearl satin Herringbone patt. cased in yellow, the exterior h.p. w/large fern-

Ornate Satin Glass Bride's Bowl

Unusual Burmese Cracker Jar

Cracker jar w/brass rim, cover & bail handle, footed cylindrical form, unusual form, Thomas Webb & Son (ILLUS.)... **800-1,000**

like leaves & flowers, raised on an ornate silver plate stand w/loops, leaf sprigs & floral swags above the domed round foot, stand marked by the Meriden Britannia Co., ca. 1880s, 11" d. (ILLUS.).................... **1,840**

Burmese

Burmese is a single-layer glass that shades from pink to pale yellow. It was patented by Frederick S. Shirley and made by the Mt. Washington Glass Co. A license to produce the glass in England was granted to Thomas Webb & Sons, which called its articles Queen's Burmese. Gundersen Burmese was made briefly about the middle of the 20th century, and the Pairpoint Company is making limited quantities at the present time.

Bowl, 9 1/2" d., 2 3/4" h., footed wide shallow form w/an upright crimped rim, probably Mt. Washington (ILLUS., bottom of page).. **$175-225**

Lovely Decorated Burmese Cruet

Burmese Crimped Bowl

Cruet w/original stopper, squatty melon-ribbed body tapering to an arched spout, pointed ribbed hollow stopper & applied yellow handle, decorated w/delicate flower & leaf sprigs, ca. 1885 (ILLUS., previous page) **2,500-3,000**

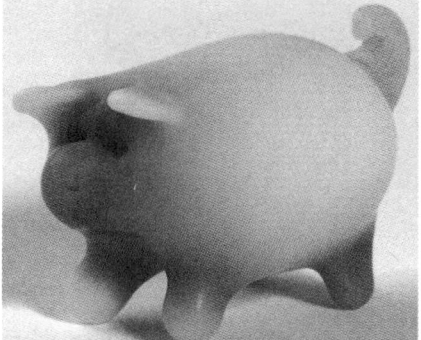

Burmese Miniature Model of a Pig

Model of a pig, good detail, satin finish, 1 1/8" l. (ILLUS.) **460**

Burmese Hobnail Pattern Pitcher

Pitcher, 7" h., mold-blown Hobnail patt., tapering cylindrical body w/applied yellow handle, satin finish (ILLUS.) **2,500-3,000**

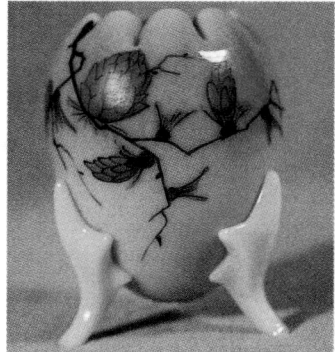

Decorated Burmese Rose Bowl

Rose bowl, eight-crimp rim, egg-shaped, raised on three applied yellow peg feet, glossy finished h.p. w/pinecones, rare (ILLUS.).. **650-750**

Burmese Toothpick Holder

Toothpick holder, squatty bulbous base tapering to a wide squared neck, decorated w/pansies, satin finish (ILLUS.).............. **650-850**
Tumbler, satin finish, ground pontil, 3 1/2" h.. **60**
Vase, 4 3/4" h., ovoid body on disk foot, incurved pinched rim, ground pontil.................... **90**

Bird-decorated Burmese Vase

Vase, 7" h., double gourd-form w/spherical bottom & tall stick neck, h.p. w/flying black birds, satin finish (ILLUS) **1,500-2,000**
Vase, 9 1/2" h., footed gently swelled cylindrical body w/a narrow shoulder tapering to the low cylindrical neck, h.p. ivy deco-

Ivy-decorated Queen's Burmese Vase

ration, Queen's Burmese, signed
(ILLUS.) **1,000-1,500**

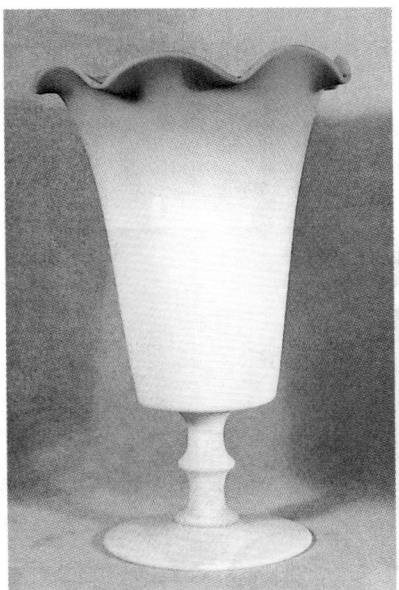

Pairpoint Burmese Chalice Vase

Vase, 11" h., chalice-form, ringed pedestal
base below the tall flaring cylindrical body
w/a ruffled rim, satin finish, Pairpoint
Corp., ca. 1920s (ILLUS.) **600-800**

Rare Large Decorated Burmese Vase

Vase, 16" h., tall ovoid body tapering to a
short cylindrical neck, upright gold loop
shoulder handles, finely painted w/a detailed "Garden of Allah" scene w/Arabs,
camels & pyramids, retouched where
one handle attached to body (ILLUS.) **7,188**

Cambridge

*The Cambridge Glass Company was founded
in Ohio in 1901. Numerous pieces are now sought,
especially those designed by Arthur J. Bennett,
including Crown Tuscan. Other productions
included crystal animals, "Black Amethyst,"
"blanc opaque," and other types of colored glass.
The firm was finally closed in 1954. It should not
be confused with the New England Glass Co.,
Cambridge, Massachusetts.*

NEAR CUT

Cambridge Marks

Etched Rose Point Pattern

Ashtray, round, Crystal, 4 1/2" d. **$65**
Basket, No. 3500/52, applied handle, Crys-
tal, 6" d. **325**
Bowl, fruit, 5" d., shallow, Crystal **75**
Bowl, 11" d., No. 3400/45, square, four-
footed, crimped, Crystal **124**
Bowl, 12" l., No. 340/160, oblong, four-foot-
ed, crimped, Crystal **100**
Brandy, No. 3106, plain stem, Crystal, 3/4
oz. **150**
Butter dish, cov., round, open handles,
Crystal, 5 1/2" **200**

Candleholders, calla lily shape, Crystal,
6 1/2" h., pr. 275
Candleholders, three-light, keyhole stem,
Crystal, 7" h., pr. 220
Candlestick, two-light, No. 3400, keyhole
stem, Crystal, 6" 59
Candy dish, cov., No. 3500/57, three-han-
dle, three part, Crystal................................... 125
Celery tray, No. 3500, Crystal, 11 1/2" l. 75
Champagne, No. 3121, Crystal, 6 1/2" h. 35

Rose Point Cocktail and Sherbet

Cocktail, No. 3500, Crystal, 3 oz. (ILLUS.
right with sherbet) 40
Cocktail shaker, cov., No. 98, Crystal
w/chrome lid, 46 oz. 175
Compote, No. 3400/14, wafer stem, Crys-
tal, 7 1/2" h.. 120
Cordial, No. 3500, Crystal, 5" h. 82
Creamer & open sugar, Gadroon blank,
Crystal, 2 1/2" h., pr.. 70
Cruet w/stopper, tilt ball stopper, Crystal,
4 1/2" h. 165
Cup & saucer, No. 3900, footed, Crystal 45

Decanter w/stopper, No. 1320, cordial,
Crystal, 9 oz. 550
Finger bowl w/liner, blown No. 3500, Crys-
tal, 2 pcs... 140
Goblet, Pristine blank, three-wafer stem,
Crystal, 11 oz. 50
Honey dish, cov., Gadroon blank No.
3500/139, Crystal 495
Lamp globe, hurricane-type, Crystal, 6" h........ 190
Mayonnaise bowl, ladle & underplate, No.
3400, Crystal, the set.................................... 100
Nut dish, four-footed, tab handled, Crystal,
2 3/4" d.. 85
Pitcher, 8" h., No. 3400, w/ice lip, Doulton-
style, Crystal... 400
Plate, 6" d., No. 3400/60, Crystal 22
Plate, 8 1/2" d., No. 3500, Crystal 27
Plate, 10 1/4" d., No. 3400, Crystal.................... 175
Relish, No. 3900/125, three-part, gold en-
crusted Crystal, 9" 85
Relish dish, two-part, No. 3400/1093, oval,
center handle, Crystal.................................... 120
Sherbet, No. 3500, Crystal, tall, 7 oz.
(ILLUS. left with cocktail)................................ 30
Tumbler, flat, No. 3400, Crystal, 4" h. 85
Tumbler, iced tea, No. 3121, Crystal,
7 1/2" h.. 50
Tumbler, No. 497, sham bottom, Crystal, 9
oz. 70
Vase, 5" h., No. 6004, footed, one-ball
stem, Crystal 70
Vase, 8" h., No. 797, flip shape, Crystal............. 165
Vase, 12" h., No. 1234, footed, keyhole
stem, crimped, Crystal.................................... 195
Wine, No. 3121, Crystal, 5 7/8" h. 80

Miscellaneous Patterns

Almond dish, individual, etched Cleo patt.,
Dianthus Pink, 2 1/2" 85
Ashtray, pressed Caprice patt., round,
Crystal, 4" d.. 10
Ashtray, triangular, pressed Caprice patt.,
No. 206, Moonlight Blue.................................. 25
Basket, footed, two-handled, etched Diane
patt., Crystal, 6" h... 38

Cambridge Amethyst Beverage Set

Beverage set: footed ball pitcher & four footed half-round tumblers; deep amethyst, Crystal ball stopper on jug, jug 6 oz., the set (ILLUS., bottom previous page)... **150-200**

Bonbon, footed, two handled, etched Candlelight patt., Crystal, 7"..................................... 42

Bottle w/stopper, salad dressing, etched Rosalie patt., footed, Dianthus Pink 245

Bowl, almond, footed, Decagon line, No. 611, Amber 12

Bowl, cream soup, Decagon line, Dianthus Pink.. 26

Bowl, nut, No. 3400/71, etched Apple Blossom patt., yellow 65

Bowl, fruit, 5 1/2" d., etched Rosalie patt., Dianthus Pink 26

Bowl, 8 1/2" d.., etched Diane patt., Tally-Ho line, three-part, Crystal 175

Bowl, 9" d., four-footed, pressed Caprice patt., deep oval, Moonlight Blue.................... 150

Bowl, 9" d., 3" h., round flaring bowl on a low standard, Azurite, ca. 1922 65

Bowl, 10", etched Wildflower patt., No. 3900/54, four-footed, Crystal 55

Bowl, 10 1/2" d., pressed Caprice patt., No. 53, four-footed, Moonlight Blue 130

Bowl, 11 1/2" d., footed, etched Chantilly patt., No. 3900/28, Crystal 85

Bowl, 12" d., Decagon line, No. 842, Willow Blue 35

Bowl, 12" d., etched Chantilly patt., Martha line blank, four-footed, Crystal......................... 90

Bowl, 12" d., pressed Caprice patt., crimped, four-footed, Dianthus Pink............... 95

Bowl, 12 1/2" d., No. 61, crimped rim, footed, Caprice patt., Moonlight Blue (ILLUS. w/other Caprice pieces, next column) 165

Bowl, 13 1/2" d., cupped gardenia, Caprice patt., No. 82, Moonlight Blue 250

Caprice Moonlight Pieces

Butter dish, cov., etched Diane patt., open handles, Crystal... 195

Butter dish, cov., etched Wildflower patt., No. 3400/52, tab handles, Crystal 195

Cake salver, etched Elaine patt., No. 170, Crystal, 13" d.. 210

Candleholder, Martha Washington line, Ebony (black), 4" h.. 35

Candleholders, No. 3121, etched Portia patt., w/bobeches & prisms, Crystal, 7 1/2" h., pr. 275

Candleholders, pressed Alpine Caprice patt., No. 72, two-light, Moonlight Blue, 6" h., pr. (ILLUS., bottom of page)................. 225

Candlestick, three-light, Cambridge Arms patt., Crystal, 5 1/4" h. 75

Caprice Two-light Candleholders

Console Set & Flower Frog in Pink

Candlestick, two-light, etched Wildflower patt., No. 647, keyhole stem, Crystal 55

Candlesticks, etched Wildflower patt., No. 3900/68, bell-footed, Crystal, 4 1/2" h., pr. 130

Candlesticks, figural dolphin stem, domed base, Crystal, 8 1/4" h., pr. 175

Candlesticks, one-light, etched Apple Blossom patt., keyhole stem, Topaz, 5" h., pr. 65

Candlesticks, two-light, pressed Caprice patt., No. 69, w/bobeches & prisms, Moonlight Blue, pr. 700

Candlesticks, one-light, pressed Caprice patt., No. 67, Moonlight Blue, 2 1/2" h., pr. 95

Candlesticks, one-light, Corinth (No. 3900) line, Crystal, 5" h., pr. 50

Candlesticks, one-light, pressed Caprice patt., No. 70, shell foot w/prism, Moonlight Blue, 7 1/2" h., pr. 160

Candy box, cov., etched Chantilly patt., footed, fancy stem, Crystal, 5 1/2" h. 170

Candy dish, cov., Decagon line, No. 864, Ebony 95

Candy dish, cov., three-footed, pressed Caprice patt., No. 165, Crystal, 6 1/4" d. 75

Celery dish, etched Chantilly patt., No. P246, oval, Crystal, 11" l. 40

Center bowl, Gadroon (No. 3400) line, footed, scalloped rim, ram's head handles, Amber, 9" d. 135

Champagne, Decagon line, Amethyst 22

Champagne, etched Wildflower patt., No 3121, Crystal 24

Cheese stand, pressed Caprice patt., Moonlight Blue 350

Cigarette box, cov., footed, etched Gloria patt., gold encrusted Crown Tuscan 220

Claret, pressed Caprice patt., Moonlight Blue, No. 5, 4 1/2 oz., 5" h. 175

Claret, Statuesque line, Carmen (bright red) bowl, clear Nude Lady stem, 7 5/8" h. 275

Coaster, pressed Caprice patt., No. 13, Dianthus Pink 45

Cocktail, engraved Lynbrook patt., Crystal 10

Cocktail, etched Portia patt., No. 3121, Crystal, 3 oz. 30

Cocktail, pressed Tally-Ho line, Cobalt blue 44

Cocktail, Statuesque line, Mandarin Gold bowl, clear Nude Lady stem 100

Cocktail, Statuesque (No. 3011) line, Emerald (light green) bowl, clear Nude Lady stem, 4 1/2 oz., 6 1/2" h. 135

Cocktail, Line No. 3121, Crystal, 3 oz. 15

Cocktail shaker, cov., etched Rosalie patt., chrome lid, Dianthus Pink, 12" h. 250

Compote, cheese, etched Imperial Hunt patt., green, 3" h., 5" w. 68

Compote, No. 3400/14, etched Apple Blossom patt., Dianthus Pink, 7" w., 7 1/2" h. ... 90

Compote, open, etched Elaine patt., No. 3500/36, Crystal, 6" h. 59

Compote, open, blown, Statuesque line, Cobalt, clear Nude Lady stem, 7" h. 425

Console set: 11 1/2" flared bowl & pair of 3 1/2" h. one-light candleholders; Decagon patt. etched Cleo patt., Dianthus Pink, the set (ILLUS. w/flower frog, top of page) 220

Cordial, blown Caprice patt., No. 300, Moonlight Blue, 1 oz. 165

Cordial, etched Diane patt., Topaz 175

Cordial, etched Portia patt., No. 3130, Crystal, 1 oz. 75

Cordial, Line 1341, mushroom-style, Amber 10

Cordial, Line No. 3500, Carmen (bright red) 90

Cordial, No. 1066, Royal blue 45

Cordial, pressed Tally-Ho line, Forest Green, 5" h. 40

Cordial, etched Wildflower patt., Crystal, 1 oz. 70

Cordial Set in Harlequin Colors

Cordial set: No. 1327, low foot, 1 oz., Harlequin colors of Amethyst, La Rosa, Forest Green, Gold Krystol, Moonlight Blue, Pistachio, Mocha & Tahoe Blue; set of 8 (ILLUS., top of page) **175**

Creamer & open sugar, etched Chantilly patt., Martha blank, Crystal w/sterling base, 3" h., pr. (ILLUS., bottom of page) **48**

Creamer & open sugar, pressed Caprice patt., Moonlight Blue, 5 oz., pr. (ILLUS. w/other Caprice pieces, on page 535) **58**

Creamer, sugar bowl & cover, individual, etched Wildflower patt., No. 3900/40, Crystal, pr.. **70**

Crown Tuscan bowl, 10 1/2 x 11 1/2", oblong body raised on four small tab feet, the widely flared rim deeply ruffled, the interior & exterior decorated w/an ornate scrolling gold floral design, marked **165**

Crown Tuscan cigarette box, cov. **75**

Crown Tuscan plate, 8" d., pressed Shell patt... **35**

Crown Tuscan urn, cov., 8" h. **150**

Cruet w/original stopper & metal holder, No. 3400 line, oil, Emerald.............................. **40**

Cup & saucer, Decagon line, Willow Blue, pr. **16**

Cup & saucer, etched Apple Blossom patt., Crystal **25**

Cup & saucer, etched Imperial Hunt patt., footed, Dianthus Pink, pr.............................. **65**

Cup & saucer, pressed Caprice patt., Midnight Blue.. **55**

Cup & saucer, pressed Cascade patt., Crystal **22**

Decanter w/stopper, etched Portia patt., No. 1321, Crystal, 28 oz...................................... **325**

Figural flower frog/holder, "Draped Lady," Crystal, 13" h. **195**

Figural flower frog/holder, Draped Lady, Peach-blo pink, 8 1/2" h. (ILLUS. w/Decagon console set, top previous page) **250**

Figure flower frog/holder, "Bashful Charlotte," Emerald, 13" h. **295**

Finger bowl, blown, etched Apple Blossom patt., No. 3130, Crystal.................................... **60**

Goblet, blown Tally Ho patt., Carmen w/Crystal stem, 10 oz. **55**

Goblet, etched Candlelight patt., Crystal, 6 1/4" h. **58**

Goblet, etched Elaine patt., water, Crystal **35**

Goblet, etched Imperial Hunt patt., plain stem, Dianthus Pink, 9 oz., 7" h. **65**

Martha Sugar & Creamer with Chantilly Etching

Goblet, Statuesque line, banquet-size, Emerald bowl, clear Nude Lady stem, 10" h. 375
Goblet, water, Decagon line, Royal Blue 45
Goblet, water, Gadroon (No. 3500 line), Royal Blue, 8 3/8" h. 65
Goblet, water, pressed Caprice patt., Moonlight Blue, No. 200, 9 oz. 60
Goblet, water, pressed Cascade patt., Crystal, 5 1/2" h. 18
Ice bucket, cov., Amethyst body in Farberware metal holder 200
Ice bucket, etched Chantilly patt., Martha blank, Crystal.. 189
Ice tub, etched Chantilly patt., No. P671, tab handle, Crystal, 4 3/4" h........................ 175
Lamp, table model, etched Diane patt., gold-encrusted, slender ovoid body, metal fittings, Carmen, 14 1/2" h. 750
Martini jug, etched Chantilly patt., No. P100, Crystal w/metal base 375
Mayonnaise bowl, pedestal base, divided, pressed Caprice patt., No. 10, Moonlight Blue, 6" 125
Mayonnaise dish, Decagon line, No. 873, handled, Willow Blue.. 35

Crown Tuscan Swan

Model of a swan, Crown Tuscan, 3" h. (ILLUS.) 45
Model of a swan, Emerald, No. 1040, 3" l......... 50
Mug, Mt. Vernon line, stein-type, No. 84, Amber, 14 oz. 38
Nut dish, low, divided, pressed Caprice patt., Moonlight Blue, No. 94, 2 1/2" d. 52
Oyster cocktail, blown Caprice patt., No. 300, Crystal... 22
Parfait, blown Caprice patt., No. 300, Dianthus Pink, 5 oz... 220
Pickle dish, pressed Caprice patt., No. 102, tab handles, Moonlight Blue, 9"....................... 65
Pitcher, Caprice patt., ball-shaped, Moonlight Blue, 80 oz. 575
Pitcher, cov., etched Imperial Hunt patt., flat, ringed at bottom, Dianthus Pink, 23 oz... 350
Pitcher, etched Apple Blossom patt., ball-shaped, Crystal, 80 oz. 250
Pitcher, etched Elaine patt., No. 3400/141, Doulton jug-form, w/ice lip, Crystal, 80 oz.. 350
Pitcher, etched Wildflower patt., No. 3400/38, ball-shaped, Crystal........................ 265

Pitcher, pressed Caprice patt., Moonlight Blue, 32 oz.. 500
Pitcher, etched Chantilly patt., Crystal w/metal base, 20 oz.. 300
Plate, 6 1/2" d., bread & butter, etched Portia patt., Crystal.. 12
Plate, 7" d., etched Cleo patt., Dianthus Pink 16
Plate, 7" d., pressed Caprice patt., Crystal......... 15
Plate, 7 1/2" d., etched Elaine patt., No. 3400/176, Crystal 12
Plate, 8" d., No. 739 line, Mandarin Gold............. 11
Plate, 8 1/4" d., low, footed, Decagon line, Dianthus Pink.. 15
Plate, 8 1/2" d., etched Apple Blossom patt., Amber 16
Plate, 8 1/2" d., low, footed, pressed Caprice patt., No. 131, Moonlight Blue 35
Plate, 10 1/2" d., dinner, etched Imperial Hunt patt., green.. 95
Plate, 10 1/2" d., dinner, etched Portia patt., Crystal 95
Plate, 14" d., Alpine Caprice patt., four-footed, Moonlight Blue.. 145
Plate, 14" d., four-footed, pressed Caprice patt., Moonlight Blue, No. 28 110
Platter, 12" l., etched Rosalie patt., green 185
Punch set: footed bowl & 12 handled mugs; Tally Ho patt., Carmen, the set 1,100
Relish dish, etched Diane patt., two-part, center handle, Crystal, 6" l............................... 85
Relish dish, etched Elaine patt., No. 3500/71, center handle, three-part, Crystal, 7 1/2" d. 125

Mt. Vernon Relish Dish

Relish dish, Mt. Vernon line, oblong, five-part, Royal Blue, 12" l. (ILLUS.)...................... 125
Relish dish, Mt. Vernon line, three-part, three open handles, Royal blue, 8" d. 55
Relish dish, pressed Caprice patt., divided, diamond shape, Crystal, 6" l............................ 35
Relish dish, etched Chantilly patt., oval, Crystal, 8 1/4" l.. 34
Relish dish, No. 3400 line, two-part, two-handled, Crystal, 8 3/4" l. 30
Relish dish, pressed Caprice patt., three-part, three tab handles, No. 124, Crystal, 8" l. 25

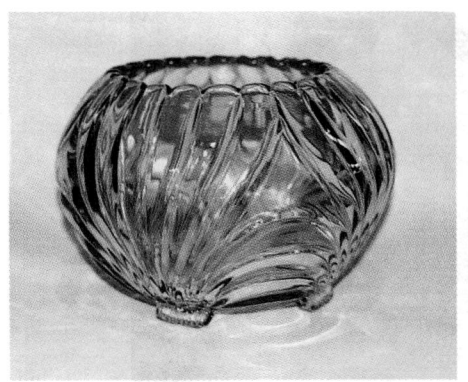

Caprice Rose Bowl

Rose bowl, pressed Caprice patt., Moonlight Blue, 6" d. (ILLUS.) 220
Salt dip, No. 3400 line, Amethyst 15
Salt & pepper shakers w/glass tops, etched Gloria patt., tall, Mandarin Gold, pr. 120
Salt shaker w/original top, etched Apple Blossom patt., Moonlight Blue 130
Salt shaker w/original top, pressed Caprice patt., flat, Moonlight Blue, No. 96, 2 3/4" h. 50
Sherbet, blown Caprice patt., No. 301, Crystal, 5 3/4" h. 20
Sherbet, Decagon line, Willow Blue, low 22
Sherbet, etched Chantilly patt., No. 3779, Crystal, tall 25
Sherbet, pressed Caprice patt., Crystal #200, 5 3/4" h. 25
Sherbet, blown Caprice patt., No. 300, Moonlight Blue, 6 oz. 40
Sherbet, blown Caprice patt., No. 300, tall, Crystal, 6 oz. 22
Sherbet, etched Wildflower patt., tall, Crystal, 6 oz. 24
Sugar sifter w/lid, etched Cleo patt., footed, Moonlight Blue, 6 3/4" h. 1,500
Tray, No. 870, etched Rosalie patt., keyhole center handle, green, 10 3/4" l. 62
Tray, oval, pressed Caprice patt., Crystal, 9" l. 26
Tumbler, blown Caprice patt., footed, No. 184, Moonlight Blue, 12 oz. 60
Tumbler, blown Caprice patt., footed, No. 300, Moonlight Blue, 12 oz. 65
Tumbler, blown Caprice patt., footed, No. 300, Moonlight Blue, 5 oz. 50
Tumbler, blown Caprice patt., juice, footed, No. 300, Crystal, 5 oz. 24
Tumbler, Caprice patt., flat, No. 310, Moonlight Blue, 5 oz. 90
Tumbler, Decagon line, footed, green, 12 oz. 30
Tumbler, Decagon line, juice, Royal Blue 25
Tumbler, etched Apple Blossom patt., footed, No. 3135, Crystal, 12 oz. 25
Tumbler, etched Apple Blossom patt., No. 3130, Crystal, 3 oz. 20
Tumbler, etched Apple Blossom patt., whiskey, footed, green, 2 oz. 85

Tumbler, etched Cleo patt., Amber, 8 oz. 30
Tumbler, etched Elaine patt., iced tea, No. 3500, flat, Crystal, 12 oz. 48
Tumbler, pressed Caprice patt., footed, No. 11, Moonlight Blue, 5 oz. (ILLUS. w/other Caprice pieces, page 535) 55
Tumbler, pressed Caprice patt., iced tea, No. 15, flat, Moonlight Blue, 12 oz. 115
Tumbler, pressed Cascade patt., footed, Crystal, 12 oz., 5 1/8" h. 15
Tumbler, Square Line, juice, footed, Crystal, 5 oz. 15
Vase, 4 1/2" h., Amethyst body in Farberware metal holder 165
Vase, 5 1/2" h., pressed Caprice patt., plain top, Moonlight Blue 189
Vase, 6" h., etched Apple Blossom patt., No. 1308, Emerald 150
Vase, bud, 6" h., also used for bitters bottle, blown Caprice patt., No. 254, Moonlight Blue 450
Vase, 8" h., bulbous-shaped, No. 1431, Cobalt blue 165
Vase, 8 1/2" h., ball-shaped, pressed Caprice patt., No. 239, three ring, Moonlight Blue 450
Vase, 10" h., etched Gloria patt., No. 1242, Crystal 160
Vase, bud, 10" h., etched Wildflower patt., No. 1528, Crystal 135
Vase, bud, Statuesque line, Amber, clear Nude Lady stem 775
Water set: Doulton-style 80 oz. pitcher & five flat tumblers; No. 3400, Cobalt (dark blue), the set 325
Water set: pitcher & six tumblers; Inverted Thistle patt., green w/gold trim, the set 325
Whimsey, top hat, Tally Ho patt., Royal Blue, 10" h. 270
Wine, blown Caprice patt., No. 300, Crystal, 4 1/2" h. 44
Wine, blown Tally-Ho line, No. 1420, Crystal, 4 1/2" h. 30
Wine, Line No. 3121, Crystal, 2 1/2 oz. 20

Carnival

Earlier called Taffeta glass, the Carnival glass now being collected was introduced early in the 20th century. Its producers gave it an iridescence that attempted to imitate that of some Tiffany glass. Collectors will find available books by leading authorities Donald E. Moore, Sherman Hand, Marion T. Hartung, Rose M. Presznick, and Bill Edwards.

Acorn Burrs (Northwood)

Bowl, 10" d., master berry, green $325
Bowl, 10" d., master berry, marigold 150
Bowl, 10" d., master berry, purple 275
Pitcher, water, green 575
Pitcher, water, marigold 450
Pitcher, water, purple 450
Punch cup, green 45
Punch cup, marigold 30
Punch cup, purple 40
Punch set: bowl, base & 6 cups; green, 8 pcs. 2,000
Punch set: bowl, base & 6 cups; purple, 8 pcs. 1,200

Acorn Burrs White Punch Set

Punch set: bowl, base & 6 cups; white, 8
  pcs. (ILLUS., above) **6,000**
Sauce dish, green 35
Sauce dish, marigold 25
Sauce dish, purple 35
Tumbler, green 60
Tumbler, marigold 35
Tumbler, purple 55

Beaded Cable (Northwood)

Candy dish, green 55
Candy dish, marigold 55
Candy dish, purple 35
Rose bowl, aqua opalescent 350
Rose bowl, blue 300
Rose bowl, green 200
Rose bowl, marigold 125
Rose bowl, purple 125
Rose bowl, white 450

Big Fish Bowl (Millersburg)

Green, round, scalloped rim, 8" d., 2 1/4" h. .. **1,050**

Butterfly & Berry (Fenton)

Bowl, 8" to 9" d., blue, master berry, four-
  footed 275
Bowl, 8" to 9" d., green, master berry, four-
  footed 350
Bowl, 8" to 9" d., marigold, master berry,
  four-footed 95
Pitcher, water, blue 400
Pitcher, water, marigold 225
Sauce dish, blue 50
Sauce dish, green 95
Sauce dish, marigold 20
Tumbler, blue 40
Tumbler, marigold 25

Butterfly & Fern (Fenton)

Tumbler, blue 45-60
Tumbler, green 60

Cosmos & Cane (U.S. Glass Co.)

Tumbler, marigold 60-110

Dahlia (Dugan or Diamond Glass Co.)

Tumbler, purple 110-150

Dandelion (Northwood)

Tumbler, marigold 35-80

Diamond Lace (Imperial)

Tumbler, purple 50-75

Diamond Point Columns

Vase, 7" to 10" h., aqua opalescent 900
Vase, 7" to 10" h., blue 300
Vase, 7" to 10" h., green 125
Vase, 7" to 10" h., green, squatty 150
Vase, 7" to 10" h., ice blue 500
Vase, 7" to 10" h., ice green 550
Vase, 7" to 10" h., ice green, squatty 750
Vase, 7" to 10" h., purple 100
Vase, 7" to 10" h., white 275
Vase, 7" to 10", marigold 75
Vase, 7 1/2" h., white 165-275

Dragon & Lotus (Fenton)

Bowl, 7" to 9" d., green, three-footed 100
Bowl, 7" to 9" d., marigold, three-footed 60
Bowl, 7" to 9" d., peach opalescent, three-
  footed 350
Bowl, 8" to 9" d., blue, collared base 125
Bowl, 8" to 9" d., green, collared base 250
Bowl, 8" to 9" d., marigold, collared base 75
Bowl, vaseline 225
Bowl, 8" to 10" d., red, ruffled 1,700

Good Luck (Northwood)

Bowl, 8" to 9" d., blue, ruffled 425

Bowl, 8" to 9" d., green, ruffled 350
Bowl, 8" to 9" d., ice blue, ruffled................... 2,350

Marigold Good Luck Bowl

Bowl, 8" to 9" d., marigold, ruffled (ILLUS.) 225
Bowl, 8" to 9" d., purple, ruffled 275
Bowl, 8" to 9" d., blue, piecrust rim 575
Bowl, 8" to 9" d., marigold, piecrust rim............. 275
Plate, 9" d., blue 2,800
Plate, 9" d., marigold.. 375
Plate, 9" d., purple 475
Plate, 9" d., white... 5,300

Grape & Cable (Northwood)

Bowl, 8" to 9" d., piecrust rim, green................. 125
Bowl, 8" to 9" d., piecrust rim, marigold.............. 60
Bowl, 8" to 9" d., piecrust rim, purple................ 100
Bowl, 8" to 9" d., piecrust rim, stippled, blue..... 300
Bowl, 8" to 9" d., piecrust rim, stippled, ice
  blue 1,200
Bowl, 8" to 9" d., piecrust rim, stippled, ice
  green... 2,200
Bowl, 8" to 9" d., piecrust rim, stippled,
  marigold... 175

Bowl, 8" to 9" d., ruffled, green............................. 75
Bowl, 8" to 9" d., ruffled, marigold........................ 50
Bowl, 8" to 9" d., ruffled rim, purple 75
Candle lamp shade, marigold............................ 350
Candle lamp shade, purple................................ 350
Candlestick, green.. 150
Candlestick, marigold... 100
Candlestick, purple... 110
Cologne bottle w/stopper, marigold 150
Cologne bottle w/stopper, purple 175
Dresser tray, green... 425
Dresser tray, marigold.. 225
Dresser tray, purple.. 300
Hatpin holder, green... 400
Hatpin holder, marigold 275
Hatpin holder, purple.. 325
Pitcher, water, 8 1/4" h., green.......................... 375
Pitcher, water, 8 1/4" h., marigold..................... 175
Pitcher, water, 8 1/4" h., purple......................... 325
Plate, 9" d., green 300
Plate, 9" d., marigold 125
Plate, 9" d., purple.. 150
Plate, 9" d., stippled, green 550
Powder jar, cov., green....................................... 350
Powder jar, cov., marigold 125
Powder jar, cov., purple 175
Punch cup, green.. 45
Punch cup, marigold.. 25
Punch cup, purple.. 30
Punch cup, white... 75
Punch set: 11" bowl, base & 6 cups; blue,
  stippled, 8 pcs... 1,000
Punch set: 11" bowl, base & 6 cups; ice
  green, 8 pcs... 10,500
Punch set: 11" bowl, base & 6 cups; mari-
  gold, 8 pcs.. 425
Punch set: 11" bowl, base & 6 cups; mari-
  gold, stippled, 8 pcs. 600
Punch set: 11" bowl, base & 6 cups; purple,
  8 pcs. 550
Punch set: 11" bowl, base & 6 cups; white,
  8 pcs.. 4,500
Punch set: 14" bowl, base & 6 cups; green,
  8 pcs.. 1,500
Punch set: 14" bowl, base & 6 cups; mari-
  gold, 8 pcs. 750

Grape & Cable Punch Set

Punch set: 14" bowl, base & 6 cups; purple,
8 pcs. (ILLUS., bottom previous page)......... 900
Punch set, master: 17" bowl, base & 6
cups; blue, 8 pcs.. 7,000
Punch set, master: 17" bowl, base & 6
cups; purple, 8 pcs. 4,000
Punch set, master: 17" bowl, base & 6
cups; white, 8 pcs. 5,500
Table set: cov. sugar bowl, creamer, cov.
butter dish & spooner; marigold, 4 pcs. 350
Table set: cov. sugar bowl, creamer, cov.
butter dish & spooner; purple, 4 pcs.............. 450
Tumbler, green... 65
Tumbler, marigold.. 35
Tumbler, purple.. 45

Holly, Holly Berries & Carnival Holly (Fenton)

Bowl, 8" to 9" d., ruffled, blue.............................. 95
Bowl, 8" to 9" d., ruffled, green......................... 125

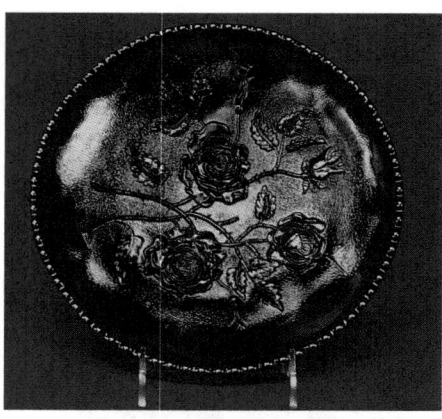

Lustre Rose Purple Fernery

Fernery, purple (ILLUS.)................................... 400
Pitcher, water, purple...................................... 1,300
Plate, 9" d., green 175
Plate, 9" d., purple... 1,500
Plate, 9" d., marigold 85
Rose bowl, marigold 75
Rose bowl, purple 750
Table set: cov. sugar bowl, creamer,
spooner & cov. butter dish; marigold, 4
pcs. 200
Table set, purple, 4 pcs. 900
Tumbler, purple.. 95

Orange Tree (Fenton)

Bowl, 9" to 10" d. , master berry, ruffled,
footed, blue.. 200
Bowl, 9" to 10", master berry, ruffled, foot-
ed, marigold... 125
Bowl, 10" d., fruit or orange, blue...................... 325
Bowl, 10" d., fruit or orange, green.................... 600
Bowl, 10" d., fruit or orange, marigold............... 125

Holly Marigold Bowl

Bowl, 8" to 9" d., ruffled, marigold (ILLUS.) 45
Bowl, 8" to 9" d., ruffled, purple 110
Bowl, 8" to 9" d., ruffled, red............................ 1,500
Plate, 9" to 10" d., blue..................................... 300
Plate, 9" to 10" d., green 600
Plate, 9" to 10" d., marigold 225
Plate, 9" to 10" d., purple 400
Plate, 9" to 10" d., white 200
Plate, iridescent green, ... 8,500

Imperial Grape (Imperial)

Pitcher, water, green... 175
Pitcher, water, marigold....................................... 85
Pitcher, water, purple 550
Punch bowl & base, marigold............................ 150
Punch bowl & base, purple 2,000
Punch cup, marigold 15
Punch cup, purple 45
Tumbler, marigold.. 20
Tumbler, purple... 65

Lustre Rose (Imperial)

Bowl, 8" to 9" d., ruffled, amber......................... 50
Bowl, 8" to 9" d., ruffled, marigold...................... 35
Bowl, 11" to 12" d., fruit, footed, green............. 250
Bowl, 11" to 12" d., fruit, footed, marigold........ 95
Bowl, 11" to 12" d., fruit, footed, purple............ 850
Fernery, marigold.. 45

Rare Orange Tree Ice Cream Bowl

Rare Peacock at the Fountain Bowl

Bowl, ice cream shape, red (ILLUS., previ-
ous page) 2,750
Pitcher, water, blue 450
Pitcher, water, marigold 250
Punch cup, blue 30
Punch cup, marigold 20
Punch set: bowl, base & 6 cups; blue, 8
pcs. 500
Punch set: bowl, base & 6 cups; marigold,
8 pcs. 275
Punch set: bowl, base & 6 cups; white, 8
pcs. 650
Rose bowl, blue 150
Rose bowl, marigold 95
Rose bowl, red 700
Rose bowl, white 225
Sauce dish, footed, blue 50
Sauce dish, footed, marigold 30
Table set: creamer, spooner, cov. butter,
cov. sugar bowl; blue, 4 pcs. 750
Table set, marigold, 4 pcs. 375
Tumbler, blue 60
Tumbler, marigold 40

Peacock at the Fountain (Northwood)

Bowl, orange or fruit, three-footed, aqua 800
Bowl, orange or fruit, three-footed, aqua
opalescent (ILLUS., top of page) 10,500
Bowl, orange or fruit, three-footed, blue 1,100
Bowl, orange or fruit, three-footed, green 5,000
Bowl, orange or fruit, three-footed,
marigold 350
Bowl, 9" d., master berry, blue 450
Bowl, 9" d., master berry, green 375
Bowl, 9" d., master berry, ice blue 600
Bowl, 9" d., master berry, ice green 700
Bowl, 9" d., master berry, marigold 200
Bowl, 9" d., master berry, purple 325
Bowl, 9" d., master berry, white 500
Butter dish, cov., marigold 325
Butter dish, cov., purple 400
Butter dish, cov., white 550
Compote, aqua opalescent 4,250
Compote, blue 1,750

Compote, green 9,500
Compote, ice blue 1,250
Compote, ice green 1,500
Compote, marigold 650
Compote, purple 1,100
Compote, white 450
Creamer, marigold 80
Creamer, purple 95
Pitcher, water, blue 600
Pitcher, water, marigold 350
Pitcher, water, purple 500
Punch set: bowl, base & 6 cups; ice blue, 8
pcs. 8,500
Punch set: bowl, base & 6 cups; purple, 8
pcs. 1,800
Punch set: bowl, base & 6 cups; white, 8
pcs. 7,500
Sauce dish, blue 75
Sauce dish, marigold 35
Sauce dish, purple 55
Table set: creamer, spooner, cov. butter
dish, cov. sugar bowl; purple, 4 pcs. 750
Table set: creamer, spooner, cov. butter
dish, cov. sugar bowl; blue, 4 pcs. 1,200
Table set: creamer, spooner, cov. butter
dish, cov. sugar bowl; ice blue, 4 pcs. 2,200
Table set: creamer, spooner, cov. butter
dish, cov. sugar bowl; marigold, 4 pcs. 600
Tumbler, blue 85
Tumbler, marigold 45
Tumbler, purple 55
Tumbler, white 175

Springtime (Northwood)

Tumbler, marigold 60-65
Tumbler, purple 70-95

Stag & Holly (Fenton)

Bowl, 8" to 9" d., spatula-footed, blue 175
Bowl, 8" to 9" d., spatula-footed, marigold 75
Bowl, 9" to 13" d., ball-footed, blue 350
Bowl, 9" to 13" d., ball-footed, green 800
Bowl, 9" to 13" d., ball-footed, marigold 150

Stork & Rushes (Dugan or Diamond Glass Works)

Tumbler, blue **45-60**
Tumbler, blue, beaded version (exterior
   flake) 25
Tumbler, pale blue... 50

Thin Rib Vase (Fenton & Northwood)

Blue, Fenton, 8" to" h... 75
Blue, Northwood, 8" to 10" h............................. 125
Green, Fenton, 8" to 10" h. 125
Green, Northwood, 8" to 10" h. 85
Marigold, Fenton, 8" to 10" h............................. 30
Marigold, Northwood, 8" to 10" h. 45

Three Fruits (Northwood)

Bowl, 9" d., footed, green 225
Bowl, 9" d., footed, marigold 65
Bowl, 9" d., footed, purple 150
Bowl, 9" d., footed, stippled, aqua opales-
   cent 800
Bowl, 9" d., footed, stippled, purple 200
Bowl, 9" d., footed, stippled, white 550
Bowl, 9" d., piecrust rim, green.......................... 150
Bowl, 9" d., piecrust rim, marigold...................... 95
Bowl, 9" d., piecrust rim, purple 125
Bowl, 9" d., piecrust rim, stippled, blue............. 500
Bowl, 9" d., ruffled, green 150
Bowl, 9" d., ruffled, marigold 75
Bowl, 9" d., ruffled, purple................................. 95

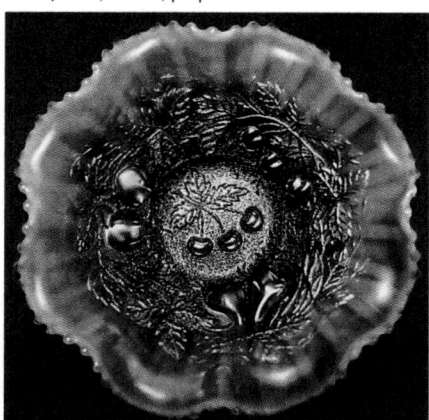

Three Fruits Aqua Opalescent Bowl

Bowl, 9" d., ruffled, stippled, aqua opales-
   cent (ILLUS.) **1,100**
Bowl, 9" d., ruffled, stippled, blue, ... 450
Bowl, 9" d., ruffled, stippled, green 750
Bowl, 9" d., ruffled, stippled, marigold............... 200
Bowl, 9" d., ruffled, stippled, white.................... 450
Plate, 9" d., green 250
Plate, 9" d., marigold 175
Plate, 9" d., purple... 200
Plate, 9" d., stippled, blue................................ 1,200
Plate, 9" d., stippled, marigold 375
Plate, 9" d., stippled, purple............................... 600

Trout & Fly (Millersburg)

Bowl, ruffled, green 650
Bowl, ruffled, marigold 450
Bowl, ruffled, purple.. 575
Bowl, square, green 950
Bowl, square, marigold 650
Bowl, square, purple 950

Water Lily & Cattails

Tumbler, marigold **40-55**
Wine, marigold... 60

Central Glass Works

From the 1890s until its closing in 1939, the Central Glass Works of Wheeling, West Virginia, produced colorless and colored handmade glass in all the styles then popular. Decorations from etchings with acid to hand-painted enamels were used.

The popular "Depression" era colors of black, pink, green, light blue, ruby red and others were all produced. Two of its 1920s etchings are still familiar today, one named for the then President of the United States and the other for the Governor of West Virginia - these are the Harding and Morgan patterns.

From high end Art glass to mass-produced plain barware tumblers, Central was a major glass producer throughout the period.

Ash receiver, cov., Frances patt., pink,
   6" d... **$135**
Bowl, finger, Morgan etching, pink....................... 68
Bowl, 5 1/2" sq., No. 1450, flat rim, black
   (ILLUS. w/cup & saucer & plate, bottom
   of page).. 24
Bowl, 13" l., Morgan etching, handled,
   green 275

No. 1450 Pieces in Black

Clear Chippendale Candlestick

Candlestick, Chippendale patt., three-handled, clear, 8 1/2" h. (ILLUS.) **75**
Candlesticks, Morgan etching, one-light, wafer stem, pink, 3" h., pr............................... **175**
Champagne, Balda etching, orchid, 4 3/4" h. **35**
Cheese & cracker set: 10 1/2" d. plate w/indent & 2 3/4" h. compote; Morgan etching, pink, the set **165**
Compote, 5" d., 6 1/2" h., Morgan etching, pink... **90**
Cordial, Harding etching, clear, 1 oz. **65**
Creamer & open sugar, Frances patt., green, pr... **80**
Cup & saucer, Morgan etching, pink, pr. **250**
Cup & saucer, No. 1450, square form, black, pr. (ILLUS. at right w/other No. 1450 pieces, previous page)........................... **26**
Decanter w/stopper, Balda etching, flat, orchid... **550**

Balda Etching Plate & Goblet

Goblet, Balda etching, water, pink (ILLUS. right w/Balda plate) **55**
Goblet, Lotus Butterfly etching, water, yellow... **75**
Ice tub, Harding etching, oblong shape, two handles, pink.. **450**
Mayonnaise bowl & liner, Morgan etching, pink **130**
Pitcher, water, Frances patt., footed, green...... **245**
Plate, 7" w., Balda etching, octagonal shape, pink (ILLUS. left w/Balda goblet) **24**
Plate, 8 1/2" d., Morgan etching, green............... **55**
Plate, 8 1/2" sq., No. 1450, black (ILLUS. w/other No. 1450 pieces, previous page)........ **15**
Powder jar, cov., Frances patt., moonstone, 6" d... **85**
Salt & pepper shakers, Morgan etching, footed, green w/chrome lids, pr...................... **175**
Tumbler, Morgan etching, cone shape, footed, green, 12 oz. **65**
Vase, 7 1/2" h., Harding etching, footed spherical bowl, amber................................... **165**
Vase, 10" h., Morgan etching, footed bud vase, black w/gold encrusted etching **325**

Coralene

Coralene is a method of decorating glass, usually satin glass, with the use of beaded-type decoration customarily applied to the glass with the use of enamels, which were melted. Coralene decoration has been faked with the use of glue.

Basket, cased shaded pink satin glass w/a white interior, the deep rounded bowl w/a widely flaring ruffled & crimped rim, raised on applied amber wishbone feet & w/an applied arched handle, the sides decorated overall w/amber "seaweed" coralene beading, late 19th c., 9" h............ **$978**
Tumbler, cranberry satin w/yellow "seaweed" coralene beaded decoration **140**

Decorated Small Coralene Vase

Vase, 3 1/2" h., 2 1/4" d., ovoid body tapering to a cupped neck, honey amber decorated overall w/branches & a four-petal design in coralene beads in yellow, green, red & blue, late 19th c. (ILLUS.).. **135-150**
Vase, 7" h., round cushion foot below a flattened oval body tapering to a slender neck w/a tricorner ruffled & crimped rim,

shaded pink mother-of-pearl Herring-bone patt. satin glass decorated w/large stylized daisy-like blossoms & leaves in yellow, green, blue & brown coralene beading, late 19th c. **345**

Vase, 8" h., a tapering cylindrical body w/a trumpet neck, cased blue satin glass decorated overall w/yellow coralene "seaweed" beading, late 19th c. **259**

Shaded Pink Satin Coralene Vase

Vase, 8 1/4" h., tapering cylindrical shaded pink satin body w/a flat trumpet-form neck, decorated w/gold "seaweed" coralene beading, late 19th c. (ILLUS.) **173**

Cranberry

Gold was added to glass batches to give this glass its color on reheating. It has been made by numerous glasshouses for years and is currently being reproduced. Both blown and molded articles were produced. A less expensive type of cranberry was made with the substitution of copper for gold.

Bell, large cranberry bell w/tall applied clear handle, possibly English, late 19th c., 10 1/2" h. (ILLUS., next column) **$275-325**

Large Victorian Cranberry Bell

Compote, open, 4 1/2" d., 3 1/2" h., wide shallow bowl w/flat rim raised on a short stem & round domed foot, overall decoration of small white, gold & black flowers w/gold leaves, bands & swags, late 19th c. **165-185**

Decanter w/original facet-cut stopper, ovoid body w/pinched-in sides below a slender cylindrical neck w/pinched spout, raised on an applied clear round foot & short stem, clear applied stopper, decorated w/gold leaves & delicate flowers & stems, late 19th c., 4 1/2" d., 12 1/4" h. **235-250**

Decanter w/original stopper, bell-shaped body tapering to a ringed shoulder & cylindrical neck w/flattened rim, decorated w/wheel-engraved flowers, raised on an applied clear waffle foot, clear flat-topped bubble stopper, 4" d., 11 1/4" h. **175-200**

A Variety of Cranberry Glass Pieces

Decanter w/original stopper, bulbous ovoid body tapering to a cylindrical neck w/flared rim, clear pointed bubble stopper, applied clear angled handle, ornate gold enameling of cherry blossoms on branches, Bohemia, early 20th c., 10" h. (ILLUS. bottom row, second from right, bottom previous page) **100-200**

Dresser bottles w/original stoppers, footed wide tapering cylindrical body w/the shoulder centered by a ringed cylindrical neck w/flared rim, cut cased cranberry knob stoppers, ornately enameled w/white floral bouquets, marked "Czechoslovakia," chip to one rim, ca. 1920, 4 1/2" h., pr. (ILLUS. bottom row, second from left, bottom previous page) **86**

Ewer, tall sharply tapering body w/a cylindrical neck w/a long pulled spout, the neck & spout w/white threaded decoration, on a clear round applied foot, long arched applied clear handle w/rigaree trim, 3 1/4" d., 10 1/2" h. **245-265**

Jar, cov., wide ovoid body tapering to a wide cylindrical neck w/a fitted domed cover w/a clear knop finial, enameled w/large yellow-centered white blossoms, early 20th c., 9 1/2" h. (ILLUS. top row, far right, bottom previous page) **144**

Lamp, kerosene table-model, a large squatty bulbous optic ribbed cranberry font raised on four applied clear figural winged fish w/curled tails forming the feet, decorated w/white enamel & gold florals, w/early burner, clear floral acid-etched period shade & clear chimney, England, late 19th c., small fitted chips on shade, overall 13 1/2" h. (ILLUS. bottom row, far left, bottom previous page) **500-750**

Pitcher, 6" h., ovoid Inverted Thumbprint patt. body tapering to a wide cylindrical neck w/pinched spout, applied clear handle, white enameled Mary Gregory-style decoration of a young girl standing in a garden, early 20th c. (ILLUS. bottom row, far right, bottom previous page) **201**

Pitcher, 7 3/4" h., 6" d., spherical body w/wide optic ribbing tapering to a wide cylindrical neck w/pinched spout, applied clear angled handle **135-150**

Cranberry Rose Bowl with Applique

Rose bowl, shaded optic-ribbed bowl w/eight-crimped rim, applied on the side w/clear branch decoration, 4 1/2" d., 3 1/2" h. (ILLUS.) **125-150**

Spooner, Inverted Thumbprint patt., eight-rib form, 5" h. (minor rim flakes) **50**

Ornately Enameled Cranberry Vase

Vase, 8" h., 3 1/2" d., footed tapering ovoid body w/a short cylindrical neck, decorated w/large enameled blossom-form white reserve w/a worn scene framed w/gold-trim maroon scallops & flanked by leafy branches w/large blue, white & yellow blossoms, late 19th c. (ILLUS.) **175-200**

Vase, 8 1/4" h., footed bulbous tapering optic ribbed body w/a cylindrical neck, applied w/two angled clear branch-form handles, decorated w/large colorful leaves & flowers, Bohemia, ca. 1900 (ILLUS. bottom row, center, previous page) **288**

Vases, 11" h., large footed bulbous ovoid body w/a narrow shoulder to a deep, wide cylindrical neck applied around the rim w/clear icicle decoration, raised on applied clear forked & pointed feet, elaborately enameled w/bold stylized flowers & geometric designs, probably Bohemia, ca. 1900, pr. (ILLUS. top row, center, previous page) **604**

Wine decanter w/clear hollow stopper, tall ovoid optic ribbed body tapering to a tall cylindrical neck w/a knop at the base & a tricorner rim, clear round applied foot & crimped applied handle, clear cylindrical stopper w/flat top, slight rubbing on sides, 3" d., 12 1/2" h. **165-185**

Wine glass, half-round cranberry bowl raised on a plain clear stem & round foot, 3 1/4" d., 4 3/4" h. **55**

Crown Milano

This glass, produced by Mt. Washington Glass Company late in the 19th century, is opal glass decorated by painting and enameling. It appears identical to a ware termed Albertine, also made by Mt. Washington.

Printed Crown Milano Mark

Melon-lobed Crown Milano Creamer

Creamer, bulbous melon-lobed body w/an attached silver plate rim, spout & handle, creamy ground h.p. w/flowers & leaves in tan, rose & green, signed (ILLUS.) ... **$750-1,000**

Fine Crown Milano Syrup Pitcher

Syrup pitcher w/original silver plate rim, domed cover & handle, bulbous melon-lobed body, creamy ground h.p. w/clusters of tan, rose & green flowers w/pale yellow shadow flowers, rare (ILLUS.) **1,500-2,000**

Vase, 5 3/4" h., squatty bulbous body tapering to a short ribbed flaring & scalloped neck, creamy ground h.p. w/red poppies, blue & green leaves & delicate gold roundels (ILLUS., next column) **2,000-2,500**

Small Crown Milano Vase

Crown Milano Vase with Flowers

Vase, 9" h., footed ovoid body tapering to a ringed neck & deep cupped rim, white ground decorated overall w/shadow flowers in light green & mauve, h.p. w/large stylized mauve, purple, white & green flowers outlined in gold (ILLUS.) **2,703**

Crown Milano Vase with Acorns

Vase, 10 1/2" h., footed bulbous spherical paneled form w/a small cylindrical neck flanked by applied gold ribbed snail-form handles, creamy ground h.p. w/large gold & tan acorns & oak leaves (ILLUS., previous page) **2,500-3,000**

Crown Milano Medallions Vase

Vase, 12" h., tall ovoid melon-ribbed body tapering to a slender twisted stick neck, small ribbed gold loop shoulder handles, h.p. w/medallions of gold dragons surrounded by gold flower, leaves & stems w/raised gold outlines, creamy ground (ILLUS.) **2,588**

Crown Milano Vase with Fancy Gold

Vase, 12 1/2" h., footed wide squatty round lower body tapering to a very tall swelled stick neck, creamy ground h.p. w/an overall ornate gold floral decoration, signed (ILLUS.) **1,200-1,500**

Cup Plates

Produced in numerous patterns beginning over 170 years ago, these little plates were designed to hold a cup while the tea or coffee was allowed to cool in a saucer. Cup plates were also made of ceramics. Where numbers are listed below, they refer to numbers assigned to these plates in the book American Glass Cup Plates *by Ruth Webb Lee and James H. Rose. Plates are of clear glass unless otherwise noted. A number of cup plates have been reproduced.*

L & R-141, round w/twenty bull's-eye scallops w/a single point between, starburst in center on a waffle ground, Midwestern, scarce, clear, 3 1/8" d. (slight tipping, a small shallow spall) **$44**

Rare Floral Sprig Cup Plate

L & R-148A, round w/thirty bull's-eye scallops, large flower sprig in the center, Midwestern, very rare, soft blue, 3" d. (ILLUS.) **1,210**

L & R-15, round w/sunburst in center, small fans around the rim, clear w/greenish tint, two shallow edge chips, rare **44**

L & R-216 round w/tiny rim scallops, cross in center surrounded by four fleur-de-lis devices & a narrow band of vesicas, outer band of small bull's-eyes, Midwestern, Fort Pitt Glass Works, medium blue, several rim chips, 3 3/8" d. (ILLUS. second from right with blue cup plates, top next page) **1,410**

Very Rare Green Floral Cup Plate

Four Blue Cup Plates

L & R-227, round w/seventy-two even scallops, large flower blossom in center, leaf & blossom border, Philadelphia area, extremely rare, bright deep green, loss of two scallops, 3 3/8" d. (ILLUS., bottom previous page) **7,150**

L & R-251, round w/sixty-three even scallops, the center w/a small star centering a scrolling cross design, the border w/plume designs alternating w/flaring small block panels, Midwestern, extremely rare, clear, 3 13/16" d. (partial loss of two scallops) **330**

L & R-36, round w/seventeen even scallops, eight-point star & florettes in center, shell devices around border, clear (few very tiny flakes) **66**

L & R-38, round w/seventeen even scallops, eight-point star & florettes in center, shell devices around border, bright amethyst (chip on reverse of one scallop, small edge flake & rim spalls) **2,200**

Rare Blue Heart Cup Plate

L & R-425, Hearts, round w/nine large scallops w/hearts between, quatrefoil of four hearts in the center, small diamonds in inner band, unrecorded, chip on large scallop, 3 3/8" d. (ILLUS.) **3,850**

L & R-440-B, Valentine patt., round w/twenty larger scallops w/two smaller between, overlapping hearts w/arrows in the center, lyre border, scarce, bright deep blue, 3 1/2" d. **303**

L & R-561A, octagonal w/seven small scallops between corners, center w/bust of George Washington w/a tilted head against a sunburst ground, laurel wreath outer band & small scrolls in the rim, Midwestern, clear w/pronounced smoky striations, extremely rare, 3 7/16" w. (three scallops & two corners tipped) **2,640**

L & R-565B, Henry Clay, round w/tiny rim scallops, center bust portrait of Clay below his name, inner band of scrolls, outer border of leaf branches flanking cartouches, sapphire blue, several rim flakes, 3 1/2" d. (ILLUS. far right with blue cup plates, above) **235**

L & R-571, Queen Victoria, round w/fifty-nine even scallops, bust portrait of the young queen in the center below her name, crown & floral wreath border band, clear, 3 15/16" d. **55**

L & R-582, Jenny Lind, round w/fifty-six even scallops, bust portrait of the singer in the center surrounded by a narrow band of stars, wide outer border w/her name in uppercase letters separated by one flower & leaf panel & one scroll panel, electric blue, 3 3/4" d. (several scallops lightly tipped) **1,980**

L & R-610A, round w/scallop alternating w/double tiny scallops, small image of sailing ship in the center surrounded by a floral vine band, scroll & star border, dark blue, several small rim chips, 3 5/8" d. (ILLUS. second from left with blue cup plates, above) **294**

L & R-677A, Eagle, scalloped rim, spread-winged American eagle looking right in the center w/an arch of stars above, palmette & rosette rim, medium blue, rim chips, 3 1/4" d. (ILLUS. far left with blue cup plates, top of page) **441**

L & R-677B, American Eagle, round w/48 egg-and-dart scallops, center w/spread-winged eagle facing right, leaftip & florette border band, clear, Midwestern, 3 5/16" d. **55**

L & R-68, round w/eighteen even scallops, large basket of flowers in the center, leaftip border, clear w/a hint of cloudiness, extremely rare, 3 11/16" d. (only two tiny rim flakes) **5,225**

L & R-99, round, band of acorns & oak leaves in the center, lyre devices around the rim, Philadelphia area, clear, 3 1/4" d. (two tiny rim spalls) **22**

L & R-99, round, band of acorns & oak leaves in the center, lyre devices around the rim, Philadelphia area, bright deep amethyst, 3 1/4" d. (small flake on table ring) **1,870**

Custard

"Custard glass," as collectors call it today, came on the American scene in the 1890s, more than a decade after similar colors were made in Europe and England. The Sowerby firm of Gateshead-on-Tyne, England had marketed its patented "Queen's Ivory Ware" quite successfully in the late 1870s and early 1880s.

There were many glass tableware factories operating in Pennsylvania and Ohio in the 1890s and early 1900s, and the competition among them was keen. Each company sought to capture the public's favor with distinctive colors and, often, hand-painted decoration. That is when "Custard glass" appeared on the American scene.

The opaque yellow color of this glass varies from a rich, vivid yellow to a lustrous light yellow. Regardless of intensity, the hue was originally called "ivory" by several glass manufacturers then who also used superlative sounding terms such as "Ivorina Verde" and "Carnelian." Most Custard glass contains uranium, so it will "glow" under a black light.

The most important producer of Custard glass was certainly Harry Northwood, who first made it at his plants in Indiana, Pennsylvania, in the late 1890s and, later, in his Wheeling, West Virginia, factory. Northwood marked some of his most famous patterns, but much early Custard is unmarked. Other key manufacturers include the Heisey Glass Co., Newark, Ohio; the Jefferson Glass Co., Steubenville, Ohio; the Tarentum Glass Co., Tarentum, Pennsylvania; and the Fenton Art Glass Co., Williamstown, West Virginia.

Custard glass fanciers are particular about condition and generally insist on pristine quality decorations free from fading or wear. Souvenir Custard pieces with events, places and dates on them usually bring the best prices in the areas commemorated on them rather than from the specialist collector. Also, collectors who specialize in pieces such as cruets, syrups or salt and pepper shakers will often pay higher prices for these pieces than would a Custard collector.

Key reference sources include William Heacock's Custard Glass from A to Z, *published in 1976 but not out of print, and the book* Harry Northwood: The Early Years, *available from Glass Press.* Heisey's Custard *is discussed in Shirley Dunbar's* Heisey Glass: The Early Years *(Krause Publications, 2000), and Coudersport's production is well-documented in Tulla Majot's book* Coudersport's Glass 1900-1904 *(Glass Press, 1999). The recently formed Custard Glass Society holds a yearly convention and maintains a web site: www.homestead.com / custardsociety.*

- James Measell.

Argonaut Shell or original name, Nautilus (Northwood at Indiana, Pa., ca. 1899)

This pattern, with pieces in the shapes of shells, was originally marketed as "Nautilus." Pieces usually feature gold accents and also green on some pieces. Look for the Northwood script signature molded on the base of most pieces.

NOTE: Reproductions of this pattern were marketed by the L.G. Wright Glass Co. of New Martinsville, West Virginia, beginning in 1969-70. The Wright pieces were made from new molds, and the Custard color is pale and rather unattractive. Some of these bear a fraudulent Northwood "N-in-a-Circle" trademark and the "N" may be altered to look like a wobbly "W."

Bowl, master berry or fruit, 10 1/2" l, 5" h... **$250-300**
Butter dish, cov. **450-500**
Compote, jelly, 5" d., 5" h......................... **175-225**
Creamer **200-225**
Cruet w/original stopper **750-850**
Pitcher, water **700-800**
Salt & pepper shakers w/original tops, pr.. **750-850**
Sauce dish **75-90**
Spooner **200**
Sugar bowl, cov.. **275-300**
Toothpick holder **325-350**
Tumbler **125**

Beaded Circle (Northwood at Indiana, Pa., ca. late 1890s)

Beautifully decorated with a spray of blue and white flowers and bright gold accents, this pattern is scarce and will fetch top dollar from avid collectors.

Bowl, master berry or fruit......................... **300-325**

Beaded Circle Butter Dish

Butter dish, cov. (ILLUS.) **500**
Compote, jelly **300**
Creamer **200**
Cruet w/original stopper **1,200**

Pitcher, water 800
Salt & pepper shakers w/original tops,
 pr. 700-750
Sauce dish 120
Spooner 200
Sugar bowl, cov. 275
Tumbler polychrome & gilt decoration.............. 175

Cane Insert (Tarentum, ca. 1899)

Decorated with heavy gold, this imitation cut glass pattern is not easy to find, but Custard glass collectors don't seem to have great enthusiasm for it.

Bowl, master berry.. 100
Butter dish, cov. 145
Creamer 110
Pitcher 165
Sauce dish 40
Spooner 100
Sugar bowl, cov.. 125
Tumbler 40

Carnelian or Everglades (Northwood at Wheeling, ca. 1903-04)

Decorated with dark green and gold accents, this is a popular, sought-after pattern. Items are not marked with the Northwood trademark.

Bowl, master berry or fruit, footed 225
Butter dish, cov. 550
Creamer 400
Cruet w/original stopper 1,500
Pitcher, water 1,250
Salt & pepper shakers w/original tops, pr...... 800
Sauce dish 145
Spooner 425
Sugar bowl, cov. 400
Tumbler 125

Cherry & Scale or Fentonia Fruit (Fenton, ca. 1914-15)

These pieces should have a rust-colored stain that is called "nutmeg" by collectors.

Bowl, master berry or fruit 150
Butter dish, cov. 200
Creamer 80
Pitcher, water 250
Sauce dish 60
Spooner 75
Sugar bowl, cov. 100
Tumbler 50

Diamond Maple Leaf or Maple Leaf (Dugan, ca. 1907)

The gold or silver decoration is so extensive on these pieces that it resembles filigree. Some pieces may have the Dugan "D-in-Diamond" trademark.

Butter dish, cov. 425-500
Creamer 175-225
Spooner 160-200
Sugar bowl, cov. 225-250

Diamond with Peg (Jefferson)

Often found with souvenir designations, these pieces are typically decorated with a lush red rose motif. Some pieces will have Jefferson's "Krys-tol"

mark, but it will take sharp eyes to detect this faint mark.

Bowl, master berry or fruit.................................. 125
Butter dish, cov. 225
Creamer 145
Mug, rose decoration..................................... 55-75
Napkin ring 250-300
Pitchers, various sizes................................. 90-225
Salt & pepper shakers w/original tops,
 pr.. 100-125
Sauce dish 35-65
Spooner 150-175
Sugar bowl, cov. 180-200
Toothpick holder 60-90
Tumbler 60-75

Double Loop (Northwood at Wheeling)

These pieces are hard to find, but only the real die-hard collectors know how scarce they are! Decorated with nutmeg stain, they may have the Northwood "N-in-a-Circle" mark.

Creamer 125
Sugar bowl, open, footed.................................... 125

Everglades - See Carnelian Pattern

Fan (Dugan at Indiana, Pa., ca. 1907)

This pattern, which features heavy gold on the feet and rims as well as the finials of covered pieces, is sometimes found with the Dugan "D-in-Diamond" mark.

Bowl, master berry or fruit........................... 225-275
Butter dish, cov. 325-375
Creamer 175-225
Pitcher, water 700-750
Sauce dish 75-95
Spooner 175-225
Sugar bowl, cov.. 250-300
Tumbler 125-145

Fentonia Fruit - see Cherry & Scale

Fluted Scrolls with Flower Band - See Klondyke pattern

Geneva (Northwood and McKee)

This pattern was designed by Harry Northwood and first made at his plant in Indiana, Pennsylvania, about 1899. Northwood Geneva pieces are a nice ivory color and are decorated with bright gold and green accents. The McKee pieces, which date from about 1901, from its Jeannette, Pennsylvania, factory, are lighter in color and are decorated in red and green. In today's market one sees the McKee pieces far more often than their Northwood counterparts; nonetheless, collectors do not seem to differentiate between the two.

Bowl, master berry, four-footed, 11" oval 85
Bowl, master berry or fruit, 8 1/2" d., three-
 footed.. 110
Butter dish, cov. 225
Compote, jelly 100-125
Creamer 125-135
Cruet w/original stopper 550
Pitcher, water 300-350
Salt & pepper shakers w/original tops,
 pr.. 300-325

Sauce dish, oval 45-50
Sauce dish, round 50
Spooner 125-150
Sugar bowl, cov. 175
Syrup pitcher w/original top 600-650
Toothpick holder, decorated........................... 350
Tumbler 60-85

Georgia, Georgia Gem or Little Gem (Tarentum, ca. 1900)

This is a rather plain pattern, but original pieces in pristine condition will have attractive gilding. Pieces decorated with a floral motif are hard to come by.

Bowl, master berry or fruit, w/gold............. 160-175
Butter dish, cov., w/gold............................. 175-200
Creamer, breakfast size, w/gold 60-75
Creamer, w/gold... 80-100
Cruet w/original stopper, w/gold 145-175
Hair receiver, cov., w/gold 175-225
Pitcher, water, w/gold.................................... 175-250
Powder jar, cov., w/gold 175
Salt & pepper shakers w/original tops,
    w/gold, pr. 125
Sauce dish, w/gold 45-55
Spooner, w/gold... 90-110
Sugar bowl, cov., w/gold 90-125
Sugar bowl, open, breakfast size, w/gold...... 60-80
Tumbler, w/gold 60-90

Grape Arbor (Northwood at Wheeling, ca. 1913-15)

This pattern is extraordinarily hard to find, and the pieces readily bring top prices.

Pitcher, blue stain 1,400-1,500
Pitcher, pink stain 1,200-1,400
Tumbler, blue stain....................................... 175-225
Tumbler, pink stain 175-200

Grape & Cable, Northwood Grape, or Grape & Thumbprint (Northwood at Wheeling, ca. 1913-15)

Most pieces have a rust-colored stain called "nutmeg" by collectors; pieces with applied stain (blue, green or pink) are quite scarce.

Banana boat 225
Bowl, master berry....................................... 150-195

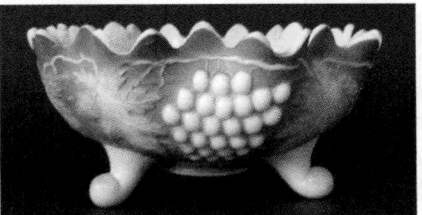

Rare Berry Bowl with Blue Stain

Bowl, master berry, blue stain (ILLUS.) 450-550
Butter dish, cov. 225-275
Cologne bottle w/original stopper 450-600
Cracker jar, cov., two-handled 475
Creamer 100-145
Creamer, breakfast size............................. 100-125
Dresser tray 350-400

Fernery, footed, 7 1/2" d., 4 1/2" h............. 325-400
Hatpin holder 450-550
Hatpin holder, blue stain........................... 775-800

Grape & Cable Humidor w/Pink

Humidor, cov. 350-400
Humidor, cov., pink stain (ILLUS.) 800
Nappy, two-handled.. 75-90
Orange bowl, crimped rim 200-225
Orange bowl, crimped rim, pink stain 425-450
Pin tray 150-185
Plate, crimped... 75-95
Plate, 8" d., flat 85-100
Punch bowl & base, 2 pcs. 900-1,000
Punch cup 75-90
Sauce dish, footed 50-65
Spooner 100-125
Sugar bowl, cov.. 165-225
Sugar bowl, open, breakfast size 100-125
Sugar bowl, open, breakfast size 100-125

Grape & Gothic Arches (Northwood at Wheeling, ca. 1913-15)

Most pieces are lightly iridized and decorated with heavy gold; pieces with applied stain (blue, green or pink) are quite rare.

Bowl, master berry or fruit 225-250
Butter dish, cov. 225
Creamer 125
Goblet, nutmeg stain 60-75
Goblet, nutmeg stain, crimped rim................. 65-85
Pitcher, water 300-375
Sauce dish 100-145
Spooner 145-175
Sugar bowl, cov.. 160-200
Tumbler 75-100
Tumbler, blue stain... 225

Intaglio (Northwood at Indiana, Pa., ca. 1899)

Although usually decorated with green & gold accents, blue & gold are sometimes seen and are always more desirable to collectors.

Bowl, master berry, footed 185
Butter dish, cov. 275
Compote, jelly 120-135
Creamer 160-175
Cruet w/original stopper 550

Intaglio Custard Pitcher

Pitcher, water (ILLUS.) 450-500
Salt & pepper shakers w/original tops,
    pr. 150-175
Sauce dish, footed.. 50-65
Spooner 150-175
Sugar bowl, cov. 225
Tumbler 80-100

Inverted Fan & Feather (Northwood at Indiana, Pa., ca. 1900)

This pattern is decorated with heavy gold plus pink on the scrollwork. Two pieces (covered sugar bowl and toothpick holder) have been reproduced by Summit Art Glass; these are not marked, but may be signed by the decorator, "Lisa V."

Butter dish, cov. 425-450
Compote, jelly 500-550
Creamer 175-200
Cruet w/original stopper 900-1,000
Punch bowl, footed 3,500-3,800
Punch cup 250-300
Salt & pepper shakers w/original tops, pr. 725
Sauce dish 75-90
Spooner 175

Inverted Fan & Feather Sugar Bowl

Sugar bowl, cov. (ILLUS.).......................... 275-300
Toothpick holder 600-700
Tumbler 125-150

Ivorina Verde - see Winged Scroll

Jackson - See Klondyke pattern

Klondyke, Jackson or Fluted Scrolls with Flower Band (Northwood at Indiana, Pa., ca. 1899)

The red and gold decoration on this pattern is subject to fading and wear.

Bowl, master berry.. 125
Butter dish, cov. 175
Creamer 75-90
Cruet w/original stopper 250-275
Pitcher, water, footed.. 225
Salt & pepper shakers w/original tops,
    pr. 150-175
Sauce dish 45-55
Spooner 60-80
Sugar bowl, cov.. 90-100
Tumbler 60-70

Louis XV (Northwood)

Bowl, master berry w/gold.......................... 175-190
Butter dish, cov. 175
Creamer 100-125
Cruet w/original stopper 300-350
Pitcher, water 200-225
Salt & pepper shakers w/original lids,
    pr. 325-375
Sauce dish, berry or fruit............................... 50-75
Spooner 90-120
Sugar bowl, cov. 125-175
Tumbler 60-70

Maple Leaf (Northwood at Indiana, Pa., ca. 1899)

The attractive green and gold decoration and the relative scarcity of these items combine to produce top prices.

Bowl, master berry or fruit................................. 325
Butter dish, cov. 300-350
Compote, jelly, footed................................. 350-500
Creamer 175-200
Cruet w/original stopper 2,000-2,500
Pitcher, water 450-550
Salt & pepper shakers w/original tops,
    pr. 700-800
Sauce dish 70-90
Spooner 145-175
Sugar bowl, cov.. 200-225
Tumbler 100-125

Optic or Rose or Tiny Optic (Jefferson, ca. 1911-12)

This is a plain pattern, but the painted floral decoration (pink and red roses with green leaves) and gold trim make these pieces quite attractive.

Bowl, master berry or fruit.......................... 125-150
Butter dish, cov. 225-300
Creamer 160-195
Pitcher, water 450-500
Sauce dish 45-60
Spooner 90-125

Sugar bowl, cov. 125-175
Tumbler 75-90

Pagoda or Chrysanthemum Sprig (Northwood at Indiana, Pa., ca. 1899)

Decorated with gold, green and pink, this is probably the most popular and best known Custard glass pattern. Most items will have the Northwood script mark on the bottom. Pieces are common enough in the marketplace that collectors should insist on top-quality, original decorations and beware of restored pieces.

In addition to the typical Ivory items, this pattern can also be found in an opaque blue that was originally called "Turquoise." The appellation "blue custard" was in use by the 1960s and seems to have persisted. It is also listed as "Chrysanthemum Sprig, Blue."

Bowl, master berry or fruit, 10 1/2" oval 275
Butter dish, cov. 375-425
Celery vase 1,600-2,200
Compote, jelly.. 145-175
Creamer 155-175

Pagoda Cruet and Other Pieces

Cruet w/original stopper (ILLUS. center with other pieces)..................................... 350-450
Pitcher, water 550-650
Salt & pepper shakers w/original tops, pr. (ILLUS. left and right with cruet)............. 250-300
Sauce dish 75-90
Spooner 150-175
Sugar bowl, cov. 200-275
Toothpick holder 325-375
Tray, round, footed (ILLUS. center with cruet).. 450-500
Tumbler 80-125

Ribbed Drape (Jefferson, ca. 1912)

Originally Jefferson's No. 250 line, these pieces are nicely decorated with red roses and some green leaves.

Bowl, master berry...................................... 150-165
Butter dish, cov. 250-275
Compote, jelly.. 185-210
Creamer 110-135
Cruet w/original stopper 375-425
Pitcher, water 450-525
Salt & pepper shakers w/original tops, pr. 350
Sauce dish 45-60
Spooner 110-145

Sugar bowl, cov. 175-200
Toothpick holder 165-195
Tumbler 75-90

Ring Band (Heisey, ca. 1897)

An early Heisey pattern, these pieces vary widely in color intensity, so it may be hard to build a matched set for a collection. Usually decorated with red flowers and gold, the gold seems to be quite subject to wear. Pieces with good heavy gold are hard to find. Some pieces will have the Heisey "H-in-Diamond" trademark.

Bowl, master berry or fruit, decorated 225-250
Butter dish, cov. 225-275
Celery Vase 325-350
Compote, jelly 175-225
Creamer 125-165
Cruet w/original stopper 275-300
Custard cup 60-75
Pitcher, water 325-375
Salt & pepper shakers w/original tops, pr. 125
Sauce dish 60-80
Spooner 110-150
Sugar bowl, cov. 135-185
Syrup pitcher w/original top 350-450
Tray 200-250
Tumbler 65-80

Tiny Thumbprint (Tarentum, ca. 1910-11)

Pieces of this scarce pattern feature bright red floral decoration and a bit of green foliage.

Bowl, master berry or fruit 225
Butter dish, cov. 275
Creamer 155
Cruet w/original stopper 900
Salt & pepper shakers w/original tops, pr. 200
Sauce dish 75
Spooner 150
Sugar bowl, cov. 200

Victoria (Tarentum, ca. 1900)

Items can be found plain or with gold decoration, but the real prize pieces have violet and reddish orange floral motifs.

Bowl, master berry or fruit, floral decoration...... 225
Butter dish, cov., floral decoration 300
Celery vase, gold decoration..................... 145-175
Creamer, floral decoration................................. 185
Pitcher, water, floral decoration 325
Salt & pepper shakers w/original tops, floral decoration, pr. 300-350
Sauce dish, plain 75
Spooner, floral decoration................................. 175
Sugar bowl, cov., floral decoration.................... 275
Tumbler, plain 65

Wild Bouquet (Northwood at Indiana, Pa., ca. 1899)

A graceful pattern with beautiful floral decoration and gold trim, this is one of the most popular Northwood Custard lines.

Pitcher, water 800-950
Salt & pepper shakers w/original tops, pr. 800-900
Sugar bowl, cov.. 400-450

Winged Scroll (Heisey, ca. 1898-1902)

This pattern is a well-known Heisey product originally designated No. 1280, but it does not have the "H-in-Diamond" Heisey mark that was introduced in 1905. Nonetheless, a complete collection of Winged Scroll decorated with heavy gold trim is an impressive site.

Bowl, master berry	150-175
Butter dish, cov.	225-250
Cake stand	375-400
Celery vase	300-325
Cigarette holder, cylindrical	190-210
Cologne bottle w/original clear stopper	250
Compote, open, high standard	400
Creamer	145-165
Cruet w/original stopper	250-325
Cup & saucer	160-185
Humidor, cov.	175-195
Match holder	175-200
Nappy, various edge crimps	65-80
Pitcher, water	300-325
Pitcher, water, tankard	350-375
Salt & pepper shakers w/original tops, pr.	250
Sauce dish, 4 1/2" d.	50-65
Spooner	160
Sugar bowl, cov.	165
Syrup jug w/original metal hinged lid	325-350
Toothpick holder	110-125
Tray	155-175
Trinket box, cov.	95
Tumbler	110
Vase, swung-type, various sizes	70-95

Miscellaneous Patterns

Heart With Thumbprint (Tarentum, ca. 1900)

This is a scarce pattern, and it has a stylized floral decoration on the heart area.

Lamps, kerosene-type, various sizes 325-500

Peacock and Urn (Northwood at Wheeling, WV, ca. 1913-15)

Decorated with a rust-colored stain called "nutmeg" by collectors, these pieces are typically marked with the Northwood "N-in-a-Circle" mark.

Peacock and Urn Ice Cream Bowl

Ice cream bowl, master w/nutmeg stain, 9 3/4" d. (ILLUS.) 300-375
Sauce dish 38

Peacocks on the Fence (Northwood at Wheeling, WV, ca. 1913-15)

These are very rare items, much sought after by a small group of Carnival glass collectors who enjoy unusual Northwood items.

Bowl, 8" d., ruffled rim, iridescent w/gold trim 2,500

Ribbed Thumbprint (Jefferson, ca. 1912)

These novelty pieces almost always have souvenir inscriptions and may also be decorated with roses.

Creamer	60-75
Creamer, individual size	50-65
Mug	45-65
Sugar, open, individual	45-60
Toothpick holder	60-80
Tumbler	55-75

Sowerby's Patented Queen's Ivory Ware (Made in England, ca. 1870s-80s)

Look for a lozenge-shaped registry mark impressed on these pieces. There are many toothpick holder-sized novelty pieces as well as spooners and spill holders.

Creamer, individual or child's 100-125
Sugar, open, individual or child's 100-125

Trailing Vine or Endless Vine (Bastow, ca. 1903-04)

Decorated with gold, this pattern is among the few documented products from the short-lived Bastow Glass Co. of Coudersport, Pennsylvania.

Bowl, master berry or fruit 225
Butter dish, cov. 450
Creamer 175

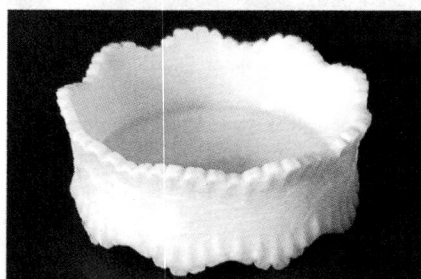

Trailing Vine Sauce Dish

Sauce dish (ILLUS.) 90
Spooner 150
Sugar bowl, cov. 250

Vermont or Honeycomb with Flower Rim (U.S. Glass, ca. 1899-1900)

Decorated with a simple floral design, these pieces also have blue or green accents on the rims and feet (occasionally, red accents are seen). The Custard color is quite light and might even be mistaken for milk glass at first glance.

Bowl, master berry 145-175
Butter dish, cov., ... 200-260

Candlestick, finger-type 50-65
Card tray w/handles, various sizes............ 90-155
Creamer 85-110
Pickle tray 65-85
Pitcher, water 250-325
Salt & pepper shakers w/original tops,
    pr. 160-185
Sauce dish 55-75
Spooner 85-110
Sugar bowl, cov. 125-160
Toothpick holder 100-135
Tumbler 60-95
Vase 85-100
Waste bowl or large sauce dish 95-125

Wild Bouquet (Northwood at Indiana, Pa., ca. 1899)

Bowl, master berry 275
Butter dish, cov. 950-1,000
Creamer 225-275
Cruet w/original stopper 1,000-1,200
Sauce dish 90-100

Decorated Wild Bouquet Spooner

Spooner (ILLUS.).. 200-300
Toothpick holder 850
Tumbler 125-175

Miscellaneous Pieces

Poinsettia Lattice Northwood Bowl

Bowl, Poinsettia Lattice patt., ruffled rim,
    Northwood (ILLUS.).. 90

Iridized Northwood Custard Bowl

Bowl, shallow w/paneled sides, iridized fin-
    ish w/black edge trim, Northwood
    (ILLUS.)... 250

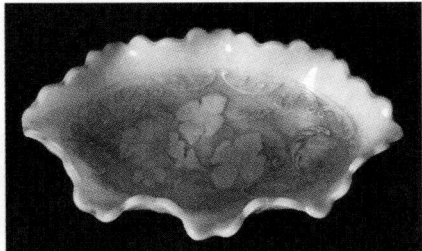

Northwood Poppy Pickle Dish

Pickle dish, oval, Poppy patt., Northwood
    (ILLUS.)... 100

Cut

Cut glass most eagerly sought by collectors is American glass produced during the so-called "Brilliant Period" from 1880 to about 1915. Pieces listed below are by type of article in alphabetical order.

Hawkes, Hoare, Libbey and Straus Marks

Baskets

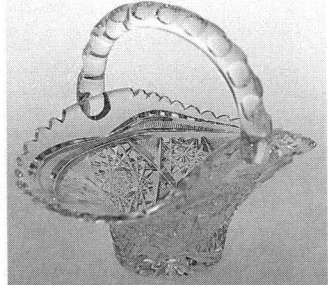

Well-cut Bonbon Basket

Bonbon, short round base w/flaring scal-
    loped rim, two sides turned up & notched

handle, decorated w/large & small hob-
stars (ILLUS.) **$425**

Exceptional Bonbon Basket

Bonbon, short round base w/flaring serrated rim, two sides turned up & annealed
double-notched handle, decorated
w/hobstars & fans, possibly Pairpoint,
4 x 6 1/4", 5" h. (ILLUS.) **480**

Libbey No. 53 Bonbon Basket

Libbey-signed bonbon, No. 53 patt. on No.
761 blank, short round base w/flaring serrated rim, two sides turned up & annealed triple-notched handle in flattened
arch shape, bottom w/16-point hobstar,
sides decorated w/hobstars, fans, crosscut diamonds & panels, signed "Libbey"
w/saber, 4 x 6 1/4", 5 1/4" h. (ILLUS.) **495**

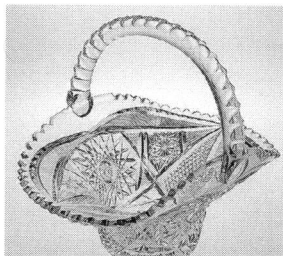

Basket with Geometric Cutting

w/cut-all-over geometric pattern, short
round base w/flaring scalloped rim, two
sides turned up & annealed double-
notched handle, decorated w/large &
small alternating hobstars & crosscut diamond design, 7 1/4 x 9 3/4", 9" h.
(ILLUS.) **775**

Bottles

Meriden Presentation Water Bottle

Water, Meriden presentation bottle w/bul-
bous base tapering to slender cylindrical
neck, sterling silver top w/flared rim, decorated w/four suspended 24-point hobstars whose center hobs are cut w/dou-
ble-miter cane, the hobstars alternating
w/vesicas filled w/hob-diamond hexad &
crosshatched bow ties, the bottom w/a
large suspended 24-point hobstar, silver
top marked "sterling" w/Wilcox trademark
of intertwined "WSW," 1904, 6 1/4" d.,
7 3/4" h. (ILLUS.) **575**

Bowls

Unusual-shaped Blown-out Bowl

Blown-out type, unusual shape formed by
six scalloped-edge lobes decorated
w/16-point hobstars alternating w/panels
of nine un-notched miter cuts, each as-
cending to a point on the rim, the bottom
decorated w/a 16-point hobstar, 7" wide
at its widest point, 2" h. (ILLUS.) **695**

Huge T.B. Clark Bowl

Clark (T.B.), round shape w/slightly flaring sides, scalloped rim w/serrated edge, decorated w/fans, hobstars, and various diamond designs, a 32-point hobstar on the bottom, 14 1/2" d., 8" h. (ILLUS.) **1,650**

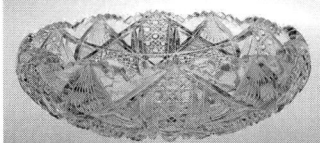

T.B. Clark & Co. Adonis Bowl

Clark (T.B.) & Co., Adonis patt., low round form w/rolled-in scalloped rim w/serrated edges, decorated w/checkerboard designs alternating w/fans, 9" d., 2 3/4" h. (ILLUS.) **325**

Cut-all-over Bowl of Unusual Shape

Cut-all-over bowl of unusual shape, flared rim w/scalloped edge, deeply cut w/all-over design dominated by hobstars, 10 x 11", 3" h. (ILLUS.) **895**

Massive Dorflinger Salad Bowl

Dorflinger salad bowl, Essex patt., 10 1/4" d., 4 1/4" h. (ILLUS.) **795**

Elmira No. 51 Pattern Bowl

Elmira Cut Glass Co., No. 51 patt., very minor tooth & pattern chips, 10" d., 2 5/8" h. (ILLUS.) **375**

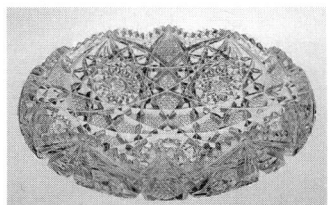

Seneca Pattern Bowl

Empire Cut Glass Co., Seneca patt., 3 1/2 x 10" (ILLUS.) **825**

Deep Seneca Pattern Bowl

Empire Cut Glass Co., Seneca patt. (ILLUS.) **625**

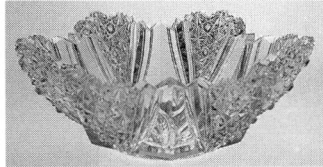

Hawkes Blown Out-type Bowl

Hawkes, blown-out type, widely flaring sides decorated w/Russian cut design in V-shaped panels alternating w/undecorated inverted-V panels, 10" d., 3 3/4" h. (ILLUS.) **1,975**

Bowl with Unusual Hexad Vesicas

Hexad motif, round shape w/scalloped rim w/serrated edge, decorated in standard hobnail hexad (six sets of parallel intersecting lines) motif plus larger hexad motif of small 6-point stars on each button, the two types of hexad appearing in the vesicas between the large 24-point hobstars, 9" d., 3 3/4" h. (ILLUS.) **495**

Small Deeply Cut Hobstar Bowl

Hobstars, low round shape, the sides deeply cut w/hobstars of various sizes & cane, 5" d., 1 2/3" h. (ILLUS.).................................. 165

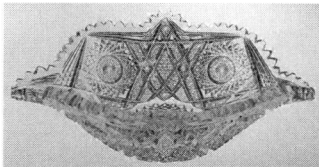

J. Hoare Napoleon's Hat Bowl

Napoleon's hat, J. Hoare & Co., w/scalloped rim, decorated w/hobstars & crosscut diamonds in geometric patterns, 8 3/4 x 13", 4" h. (ILLUS.)............................ 1,575

Bowl with Swirl Design

Swirled Hobstars & Fans, round shape, scalloped rim w/notched edge, decorated w/hobstars, fans & crosscut diamonds in swirl design, 8" d. (ILLUS.)............................. 495

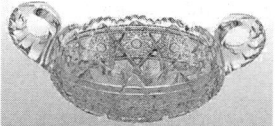

Rare Rex Pattern Handled Bowl

Tuthill, Rex patt., low oval shape w/side loop handles, scalloped rim w/serrated edge, bowl decorated w/chain of hobstars & fans, very rare, large crack down one side, 3 x 7" (ILLUS.) 200

Tuthill-signed Engraved Bowl

Tuthill-signed, round shape, decorated w/six panels around circumference, three displaying 10-point hobstars & fans alternating w/three of engraved flowers (possibly Tuthill's Primrose patt.), 7" d., 3" h. (ILLUS.).. 425

Tuthill Bowl with Geometric Cutting

Tuthill-signed, round shape w/scalloped rim w/notched edge, decorated w/geometric cutting consisting of four 24-point hobstars, four 20-point hobstars, 5- and 7-rayed fans, clear & crosshatched bow ties & four hobnail-filled kites, 8" d., 3 1/4" h. (ILLUS.) 425

Boxes

Glove Box with Hinged Lid

Glove box, rectangular, w/metal rims on body & lid, the body w/slightly bulbous sides decorated w/diamond design, the hinged lid decorated w/hobstars & beaded vesicas, attributed to Empire Glass Co. (ILLUS.) 1,525

Tall Powder Box with Hinged Lid

Powder box, tall bulbous form w/hinged lid, the body decorated w/24 concave, elongated cuts around circumference, the lid covered w/an elaborate 8-point hobstar formed w/double miters & flashed w/7-rayed fans, metal collar has been resilvered (ILLUS.)... **550**

Butter Dishes & Tubs,

Butter Cover & Underplate

Covered dish, domed cover & underplate w/dam, both decorated w/hobstars & fans, the plate w/serrated edge, the lid w/faceted knob handle, rare (ILLUS.)............ **430**

Candlesticks & Candleholders

Libbey Plain Flute Candlestick

Libbey, Plain Flute patt., signed "Libbey" w/saber mark, 10" h., pr. (ILLUS. of one....... **750**

Russian-cut Candlestick

Russian-cut, 6"-d. domed base decorated w/fans & groups of hobstars in vesicas, 6-sided fluted stem w/round ball at base, 10 1/2" h. (ILLUS.).. **795**

Short Sinclaire-signed Candleholders

Sinclaire-signed, low form, short stems w/circular bases & collars, the collars w/floral design around outside rims, amber, pr. (ILLUS. of two) **225**

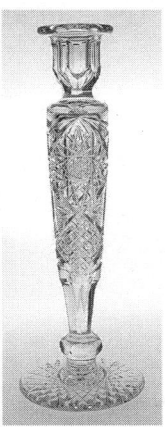

Tall Hobstar Candlestick

Tall candlestick, 5"-d. base decorated w/24-point hobstar, teardrop stem decorated w/hobstars, crosscut diamonds & fans, beveled neck w/flared rim, 14 1/4" h. (ILLUS.)...................................... **1,175**

Champagnes, Cordials & Wines

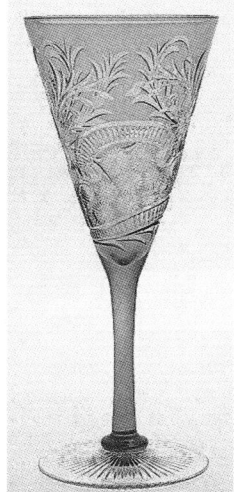

Apricot to Clear Wine Glass

Wine glass, apricot cut to clear stem & bowl, the color becoming lighter toward the top as the glass thickness decreases, the 2 3/4"-d. bowl decorated w/rock crystal cutting in leaf design, the clear foot w/a 48-point rayed star, 7" h. (ILLUS.) **475**

Wine Glass with Honeycomb Stem

Wine glass, cranberry cut to clear bowl w/clear honeycomb stem, the 2 7/16"-d. bowl decorated w/a band of 8-miter pyramidal stars topped w/9-rayed fans & separated w/kite-shaped diamonds, the stem cut in St. Louis diamond, the base w/a 32-point rayed star, 4 1/4" h. (ILLUS.) **395**

Wine glass, cranberry cut to clear bowl w/horizontal bands of decoration, the lower portion of the clear stem decorated w/inverted teardrop design conforming to shape of the stem itself, the circular base

Cranberry Wines with Clear Stems

w/24-point rayed star, 2 1/4" d. bowls, 5" h., each (ILLUS. of two) **395**

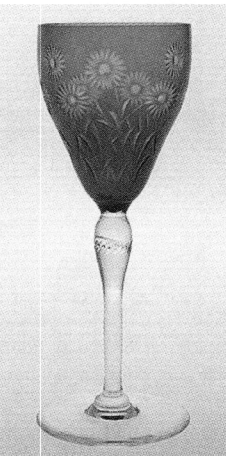

Dorflinger No. 1216 Wine Glasses

Wine glass, Dorflinger, No. 1216 patt., emerald cut to clear bowl w/clear stem (ILLUS.) **375**

Compotes

Elmira No. 100 Compote

Elmira Cut Glass Co., No. 100 patt., 1906-
1910, 9" h. (ILLUS.).. **875**

Elmira No. 33 Compote

Elmira Cut Glass Co., No. 33 patt., 1906-
1910, 9" h. (ILLUS.).. **195**

Elmira No. 67 8" Compote

Elmira Cut Glass Co., No. 67 patt., 1906-
1910, 8" h. (ILLUS.).. **595**

Elmira No. 67 9" Compote

Elmira Cut Glass Co., No. 67 patt., 1906-
1910, 9" h. (ILLUS.).. **895**

Hawkes-signed Footed Compote

Hawkes-signed, cov., footed, disk base
w/rayed design, short knobbed stem,
short squat body decorated w/panel of alternating Xs & bull's eyes, rayed collar,
lid tapering to flattened faceted knob
(ILLUS.)... **775**

Tall Handled Compote

Hobstars, disk base w/hobstar design,
straight multisided stem, shallow bowl
decorated w/hobstars & ferns, notched
rim, loop side handles, 11" h. (ILLUS.) **895**

Tazza-style Compote

Tazza-style, footed, widely flaring form,
scalloped rim w/serrated edge, round
base w/24-point hobstar, bowl decorated
w/alternating kite-shaped panels of hobstars & Russian cut design, 8 3/4" d.,
7 1/2" h. (ILLUS.).. **675**

Creamers & Sugar Bowls

Notched-handle Cream & Sugar Set

Creamer & sugar bowl w/notched handles, slightly waisted shapes deeply cut w/hobstars, C-form handles, pr. (ILLUS.) **225**

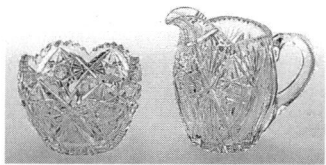

T.J. Hawkes Sugar Bowl & Creamer

Hawkes (T.J.), the sugar w/scalloped rim & serrated edge, the creamer w/C-form handle, both decorated w/hobstars, pr. (ILLUS.) **345**

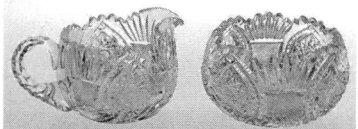

Ramona Creamer & Sugar Bowl

Pairpoint, Ramona patt., pr. (ILLUS.)................ **395**

Decanters

Decanter with Hobstar Design

Decanter w/hobstar design, ovoid body w/cylindrical neck w/spout, faceted flattened ball stopper, C-form notched handle, the body decorated w/hobstars & fans (ILLUS.) **375**

Decanter with Notched Prism Design

Decanter w/notched prism design, 18 deeply cut vertical notched miters, w/16-point rayed star on base, faceted ball stopper, 9" h. (ILLUS.) **350**

Fine Cut Flashed Green Decanter

Flashed, baluster-form body tapering to a panel-cut neck w/arched spout, bulbous flashed & cut stopper & applied facet-cut clear handle, cut overall w/flowers, stems & leaves cut from green to clear, overall 15" h. (ILLUS.) **2,588**

Color to Clear Flashed Decanter

Flashed, ovoid base tapering to long slender neck w/flared lip, purplish to clear, the body w/horizontal band of crosscut diamonds in panels, w/pattern matched stopper, the bottom w/deeply cut 32-point rayed star, 15" h. (ILLUS.).................... **925**

Hawkes Devonshire Decanter

Hawkes (T.G.) & Co., Devonshire patt., both decanter & stopper marked "No. 11," 15" h. (ILLUS.)... **850**

Tall Wine Decanter

Wine decanter, tall form tapering to waisted paneled neck, the body w/horizontal bands of cut decoration, the base decorated w/a 32-point rayed star w/tips of varied length, the stopper in the form of an elongated inverted faceted cone, 16 1/2" h. (ILLUS.)... **675**

Dishes, Miscellaneous

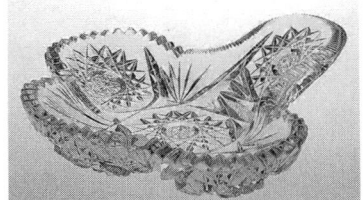

Blown-out Thumb Dish

Blown-out thumb dish, three blown-out compartments, serrated rim, decorated w/five 16-point hobstars, 6 3/4 x 6 3/4", 1 1/4" h. at blown-out areas, 2" h. at handle (ILLUS.) **275**

Cheese Dome with Underplate

Cheese dome with underplate, domed cover w/faceted knob handle, the underplate w/scalloped rim w/notched edge, both decorated w/design of parallel notched miters, hobstars, fans, radiants & bow ties of cross-hatching, underplate 9 1/4" d., dome 6 1/8" d., together 6 3/4" h. (ILLUS.).. **975**

Ice Tubs

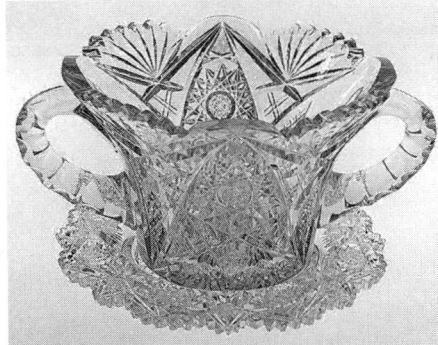

Crescent Ice Tub & Underplate

Blackmer, Crescent patt. ice tub, w/underplate (ILLUS.).. **1,450**

Jars

Champagne Cooler/Ice Tub

Champagne cooler, tapering cylindrical form decorated w/fans & hobstars, 8 3/4" d., 8" h. (ILLUS.)................................. **975**

Waldorf Ice Tub

Empire Cut Glass Co., Waldorf patt. ice tub, 4 3/4" d., 3 3/4" h. (ILLUS.) **475**

Rookwood Pattern Ice Tub

Hoare (J.) & Co., Rookwood patt. ice tub, 7 1/2" d., 5 1/2" h. (ILLUS.) **650**

Larrissa Pattern Ice Tub

Unger Bros., Larrissa patt. ice tub, 6" d., 3 1/2" h., 5+" h. including handles (ILLUS.)... **550**

Dorflinger Marlboro Cigar Jar

Cigar jar, Dorflinger, Marlboro patt., 6" d., 9 1/4" to top of stopper (ILLUS.) **1,650**

Humidor with Elaborate Stopper

Humidor, cylindrical body decoration w/fans & other designs, the ovoid stopper decorated w/24-point hobstar that covers the top & extends over the edge & half-way down sides & inside of which is a 24-point flat star w/a central pyramidal star, 4 1/2" d., 7 1/2" h. (ILLUS.)............................. **695**

Presentation Jar with Sterling Lid

Presentation jar, cov., cylindrical form decorated in pattern similar to Ribbon Star, sterling silver repousse lid by Gorham, lid w/Gorham mark followed by "sterling-D-3897," a sideways M & an indistinguishable mark, also bears information that "JEEBI" won the annual regatta at the Knickerbocker Yacht Club in 1903, 5 3/8" d., 6" h. (ILLUS.) **1,775**

Lamps

Virginia Pattern Boudoir Lamp

Boudoir lamp, Egginton (O.F.), Virginia patt. w/6 1/2"-d. peaked mushroom shade, 13" h. (ILLUS.) **1,350**

Table Lamp with Geometric Pattern

Table lamp, 12" d. mushroom dome from which 40 notched prisms hang, two horizontal bulbs, flared base, overall cut geometric pattern, rewired & resilvered, new set of notched prisms, 22" h. (ILLUS.) **4,950**

Miscellaneous

Celery tray, footed, scalloped rim, decorated w/deeply cut 24-point hobstars on the compound curves of each end, the

4 7/8"-d. base w/deeply cut 24-point fanned star, 6 x 11 3/4", 7" h. (ILLUS.) **1,875**

Footed Celery Tray

Footed Celery Vase

Celery vase, footed, waisted form, decorated w/hobstars, flat stars, fans, crosshatching & cane, the base w/a 24-point hobstar, 4 3/4" d., 9 1/2" h. (ILLUS.) **650**

Straus Finger Bowl & Underplate

Finger bowl & underplate, Straus, bowl & plate both w/scalloped rim w/notched edges, decorated w/stars, hobstars & crosscut diamonds, pr. (ILLUS.) **400**

Elmira No. 33 Flower Center

Flower center, Elmira Cut Glass Co., No. 33 patt., 9" d., 8" h. (ILLUS.) **1,100**

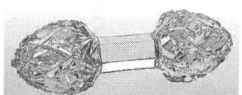

Hawkes No. 1 Pattern Knife Rest

Knife rest, Hawkes, No. 1 patt., 5" l. (ILLUS.) **375**

Three-handled Loving Cup

Loving cup, three-handled waisted form, the sides decorated w/convex columns & double-notched miters, the bottom w/a 24-point hobstar, triple-notched handles, sterling silver repousse rim stamped w/ the symbol of Redlich & Co. of New York City & "sterling 204," 5 3/4" d., 6 5/8" h. (ILLUS.) **2,250**

Meriden Sugar Shaker

Sugar shaker, Meriden, the body w/overall cut design, the metal lid w/shaker holes in the form of stars & circles (ILLUS.) **450**

Meriden Sugar Sifter

Sugar sifter, Meriden, blown body w/overall cut design, fluoresces apple green, the sterling silver repousse press-on lid marked "sterling" & signed "WSW" (Wilcox Silverplate Co. Factory N of the International Silver Co.), top ring also marked "Sterling WSW," 4 3/4" h. (ILLUS.) **495**

Perfumes & Colognes

Elmira No. 33 Pattern Perfume

Elmira Cut Glass Co. perfume, No. 33 patt., 4" d., 6 3/8" h. (ILLUS.) **450**

Libbey Corona Pattern Cologne

Libbey-signed cologne, Corona patt., signed "Libbey" w/saber mark, 4 1/2" d., 6 1/2" h. (ILLUS.) **475**

Pitchers & Jugs

Barrel-shaped Jug-form Pitcher

Barrel-shaped pitcher, jug-form, top rim descends from high arched spout in series of scallops toward C-form handle, body decorated w/large octagons running on a bias, narrow vertical & horizontal columns of alternating 5-sided lozenges & radiants separating octagons from areas of cane, additional diagonally cut miters running through areas of cane, 16-point flashed hobstar on bottom, 8 1/2" h. (ILLUS.) **595**

Dorflinger Champagne Pitcher

Dorflinger champagne pitcher, tankard-type, No. 50 patt. (ILLUS.) **895**

Dorflinger Persian Pattern Pitcher

Dorflinger pitcher, Persian patt. (ILLUS.) **495**

Elmira Fancy-cut Pitcher

Elmira pitcher, cylindrical form slightly tapering out to shoulder, triple-notched C-form handle, high arched spout, decorated w/fans & cross-hatching above horizontal step cutting, vertical parallel miter cuts at bottom, very fine miters cutting above deep miters that outline hobstars, a 24-point hobstar on bottom, 11" h. (ILLUS.) **875**

Elmira No. 100 Wine Jug

Elmira wine jug, No. 100 patt., 4-pint size (ILLUS.) **850**

Rare Amethyst Cut to Clear Pitcher

Flashed pitcher, footed squatty bulbous base tapering to a tall cylindrical body in amethyst cut to clear w/an intricate designs of swirling scrolls, flowers & leaves, applied clear handle w/three half-sunburst designs at the base & notched zipper cuts on the sides, the rim fitted w/a cylindrical sterling silver band w/spout marked by J.E. Caldwell & Co., heat check where top of handles attaches to the body, overall 14 1/4" h. (ILLUS.) **6,325**

Fancy Tall Hobstar Pitcher

Hobstar pitcher, tall ovoid form tapering out slightly to shoulder, high arched spout, annealed handle decorated w/series of parallel miters cut at 45-degree angle to handle's vertical axis, body cut all over w/hobstars, fans & cane vesicas, an 8-point hobstar on bottom, 11" h. (ILLUS.).. **525**

Meriden Glass & Silver Claret Jug

Meriden claret jug, cylindrical body slightly flaring at base, decorated w/vertical flutes, strawberry diamonds & fans, a triple C-form handle, silver collar marked "Sterling WSW" (Wilcox Silver Plate Co.) & inscribed "Presented to Brother Meyer Rosenthal, Treasurer in commemoration of his 70th birthday by Amity Lodge No. 92 IOF of I, December 14, 1904," 13" h. (ILLUS.).. **1,550**

Pitcher, cylindrical shape w/notched rim & notched C-form handle, decorated w/design of large hobstars, bow ties of hobnails, bow ties of cross-hatching, fans & a 20-point hobstar on the bottom, 8 1/2" h. (ILLUS., next column) **275**

Pitcher with Large Hobstars

Fan & Star-cut Pitcher

Pitcher, jug-form, ovoid shape w/flared three-sided scalloped rim, large notched C-form handle, body decorated w/fans & stars, a 24-point rayed star on base, 5 3/4" d., 7 1/2" h. (ILLUS.) **495**

Straus Water Pitcher

Straus water pitcher, cylindrical form w/notched handle & rim, body decorated w/cane panels, stars & strawberry diamonds, 4 3/8" d., 8" h. (ILLUS.) **395**

Plates

T.B. Hawkes Signed Plate
10" d., Hawkes (T.B.)-signed, scalloped edge w/adjoining circular miter framing six deeply cut 8-pointed hobstars separated by opposing fans (ILLUS.) **695**

Plate with Unusual Pattern
10" d., scalloped rim w/notched edge, decorated w/six large 16-point hobstars w/varied length tips contained within hexagon w/unequal sides, smaller hobstars within large hobstars have split points, clear button hobstars contained within 4-sided kite have two extended tails, minor vesicas have small bow ties w/fans above split field of nail diamonds in a kite-shaped vesica, the hobstar above these bow ties has unusually extended points that meet double-miters just below rim's highest tooth (ILLUS.).......... **425**

Libbey Loretta Pattern Plate
12" d., Libbey-signed, Loretta patt. (ILLUS.)..... **375**

Libbey Plate in Melrose Pattern
12" w., Libbey, Melrose patt., ca. 1906 (ILLUS.).. **695**

Libbey Plate in Ellsmere Pattern
7" d., Libbey-signed, Ellsmere patt. (ILLUS.).. **775**

Signed Libbey Colonna Plate
7" w., Libbey-signed, Colonna patt., ca. 1904 (ILLUS.).. **245**

Square Plate with Complex Design

7" **w.**, square w/scalloped edge, decorated w/four vesicas radiating from central point to each of the far corners, w/curved major miters outside the square bottom & straight major miters inside the bottom square, the bottom square divided into squares, triangles, four-sided kites & another four-sided geometric figure (ILLUS.) **295**

Hobstar Scallop-edged Plate

8" **d.**, w/notched scalloped edges, decorated w/ten 16-point hobstars in teardrop-shaped miter outline surrounded by flashed miters, the 24-point central hobstar also surrounded by some flashed miter cuts, the hobstar w/8-point radiants in hobstar points & crosshatching infills between outside of points (ILLUS.) **395**

Parsche Footed Cake Plate

Parsche cake plate, Propeller patt., footed (ILLUS.) **875**

Punch bowls

One-piece Punch Bowl

One-piece punch bowl, notched scalloped rim, sides decorated w/8-pointed hobstars & crosscut diamonds, bottom w/large hobstar, 6" h., 12" d. (ILLUS.) **795**

Two-piece Punch Bowl

Two-piece punch bowl, bowl on stand flaring out at bottom, both w/scalloped, notched edge, decorated w/very large 32-point hobstars separated by vesicas filled w/two double-miter 8-point hobstars separated by clear bow ties w/triple-miter outlines, the peg w/a 16-point hobstar, 13" h., 14" d. (ILLUS.) **2,475**

Punch cups

Dorflinger Handled Lemonade Cup

Dorflinger lemonade cup, No. 20 patt., handled, 3" h., 2 1/4" d. (ILLUS.) **80**

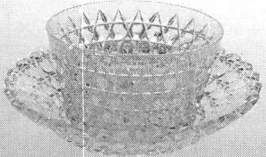

Roman Punch Glass & Plate

Dorflinger Roman punch glass & plate, Hob Diamond patt., w/4 1/2" d. plate, cup 1 3/4" h., 3 1/8" d., pr. (ILLUS.) **195**

Russian-cut Punch Glass & Plate

Roman punch glass & plate, Russian cut decoration, w/notched edge on plate & cup, pr. (ILLUS.).. 295

Rose Bowls

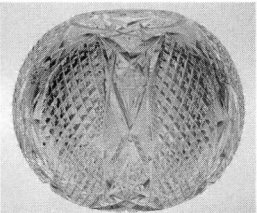

Beautifully Crafted Rose Bowl

Cane & diamonds, sides decorated w/cane & strawberry diamonds, the bottom w/a 36-point rayed star w/varied length tips, 5 1/2" h., 7" d. (ILLUS.)................................... 595

Egginton Creswick Rose Bowl

Egginton (O.F.), Creswick patt., 5 3/4" h., 7" d. (ILLUS.)... 725

Rose Bowl with Deep All-over Cutting

Hobstar, bottom decorated w/24-point hobstar within six points filled w/fine diamond, the sides w/hobstars & strawberry diamonds, 6" h., 7 1/4" d. (ILLUS.) 775

Salt & Peppers

Marlboro Pattern Master Salt

Master salt dip, Hawkes or Dorflinger, Marlboro patt. (ILLUS.) 245

Trays

Hoare Marquise Pattern Bread Tray

Bread tray, J. Hoare, Marquise patt. (ILLUS.).. 525

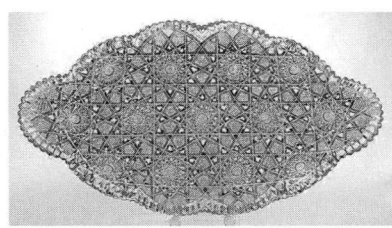

Empire Seneca Ice Cream Tray

Empire ice cream tray, Seneca patt., 18" l. (ILLUS.).. 1,775

Empire Atlantic Pattern Tray

Empire round tray, Atlantic patt., 14" d. (ILLUS.).. 995

Champion Pattern Ice Cream Tray

Hoare (J.)-signed ice cream tray, Champion patt., ca. 1896, 10 3/8 x 17" (ILLUS.) ... 1,295

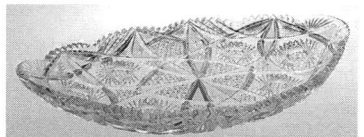

Long Ice Cream Tray

Ice cream tray, scalloped notched rim, decorated w/cane, vesicas, hobstars & fans, 18" l. (ILLUS.) **1,295**

Libbey-signed Jelly Tray

Libbey-signed jelly tray, No. 269 Corinthian patt., 5 1/2 x 8" (ILLUS.) **350**

Tray/Underplate with Persian Band

Round tray or underplate, w/1 1/4" w. band cut in rare Persian patt., scalloped rim, center w/64 rays cut through to the outside of the bottom, 12" d. (ILLUS.) **695**

Vases

Vase with Fans, Stars & Flutes

Baluster vase, 9 1/2" h., baluster-form body w/scalloped rim, decorated w/fans, stars, & vertical flutes (ILLUS.) **375**

Ornately Cut Bud Vase

Bud vase, 4 1/2" h., cylindrical shape flaring slightly out at base, notched rim, decorated w/fans, strawberry diamonds, cane & hobstars, the base w/a 16-point rayed star (ILLUS.) **75**

Cylindrical Hobstars Vase

Cylindrical vase, 12" h., notched rim, decorated w/hobstars, strawberry diamonds, & three columns of 1 1/2" d. punties, 4 1/2" d. (ILLUS.) **295**

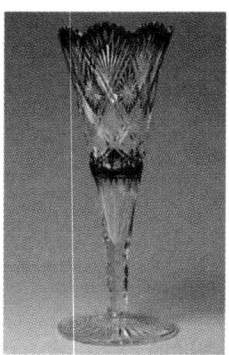

Large Red Cut to Clear Vase

Flashed vase, 18" h., red cut to clear, trumpet-form cut w/diamonds, starbursts & fans (ILLUS.) **2,300**

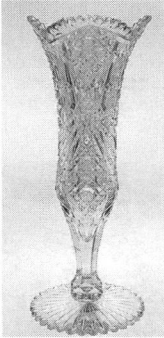

Miter-cut Footed Vase

Footed vase, 14" h., w/5" d. flared rim made up of four notched scallops, the scalloped base w/32-point rayed star topped by faceted knob leading into six notched flutes extended above vase's interior bottom point, decorated w/notched miters cut on a bias (ILLUS.) **650**

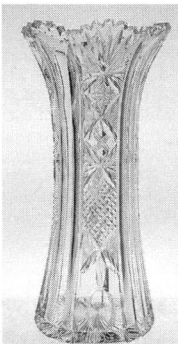

Libbey No. 225 Pattern Vase

Libbey vase, 12" h., No. 225 patt. (ILLUS.) **625**

Pinwheel Shouldered Vase

Shouldered vase, 12" h., cylindrical form tapering out slightly at shoulder, the neck w/horizontal step cutting, the flaring rim w/deep scallops, decorated w/three large pinwheels & six 16-point hobstars, the various motifs separated by notched miters, the base featuring a 24-point rayed star (ILLUS.) **795**

Fancy-cut Tall Vase

Tall vase, 14" h., cylindrical shape tapering out at shoulder, neck w/step cutting, scalloped rim slightly tapered out, the body decorated w/cane vesicas, fans, hobstars & strawberry diamonds, the 3 1/2" d. base w/hobstar (ILLUS.).............. **1,475**

Hobstar Trumpet Vase

Trumpet vase, 18" h., w/9" d. scalloped notched rim, 7" d. base w/24-point hobstar, body decorated w/8-point hobstars w/crosshatched buttons (ILLUS.)................ **1,850**

Vase with Overall Decoration

Waisted vase, 11" h., bulbous base & flaring scalloped notched rim, w/overall cut decoration of ferns, cane vesicas, strawberry diamonds & fans (ILLUS.) **875**

Czechoslovakian

The country of Czechoslovakia, including the glassmaking region of Bohemia, was not founded as an independent republic until after the close of World War I in 1918. The new country soon developed a large export industry, including a wide range of brightly colored and hand-painted glasswares such as vases, tablewares and perfume bottles. Fine quality cut crystal or Bohemian-type etched wares were also produced for the American market. Some Bohemian glass carries faint acid-etched markings on the base.

With the recent breakup of Czechoslovakia into two republics, the wares produced between World War I and II should gain added collector appeal.

Bowl, 7" d., deep bulbous tapering body w/closed rim in the Inverted Thumbprint patt., pale blue w/applied yellow rigaree bands & prunts (ILLUS. bottom row, far right, bottom of page)..................................... **$81**

Box, cov., spherical optic ribbed body w/a rounded matching pyramidal cover, green w/tooled cobalt blue dots, 5 3/4" h. (ILLUS. bottom row, fourth from left w/bowl & vases, bottom of page)..................... **81**

Signed Czech Cameo Vase

Cameo vase, 10 1/4" h., 10" d., footed bulbous ovoid body w/a short rolled neck, pearl overlaid w/orange & brown & etched w/large orange flowers & brown leaves, signed in cameo "Leopal," ca. 1920s (ILLUS.)... **1,438**

Compote, open, 7" d., widely flaring low black pedestal base below the deep widely flaring orange bowl w/an applied black rim band (ILLUS. top row, far left w/bowl & vases)... **58**

Czechoslovakian Bowl, Vases & Other Pieces

Czech Malachite Glass Dresser Set & Vases

Compote, cov., 8" h., a tall trumpet base supporting the deep optic ribbed bowl w/a fitted shallow swirled rib pagoda cover w/a pointed knob finial, light pink decorated w/random cobalt blue threading (ILLUS. top row, far right w/bowl & vases)....... **92**

Dresser set: round hand mirror, oval 11" l. hair brush & 6 1/4" l. clothes brush; Malachite glass inserts, each piece w/a gilt-metal frame, the long handles w/delicate pierced scrolling designs, Malachite w/a pressed putti design, Schlevogt factory, ca. 1935, the set (ILLUS. with vases, top of page)... **891**

Jar, cov., egg-shaped yellow body, the domed top w/a clear knob finial, raised on four applied black wishbone feet, embossed-over paper label, 6 3/4" h. (ILLUS., previous page, bottom row, second from right w/bowl & vases, top of page)... **81**

Vase, 4 1/2" h., flat-bottomed ovoid body tapering to a wide cupped rim, orange w/pulled-up purple spikes from the bottom, marked (ILLUS. bottom row, second from left w/bowl & vases, previous page)....... **86**

Gold Iridescent Czech Vase

Vase, 5 1/4" h., 7 1/2" d., footed squatty bulbous body w/a wide shoulder tapering to a wide flat rim w/a deeply rolled-out flaring rim, overall gold iridescence w/flashes of purple, blue & green, signed (ILLUS.)... **300**

Vase, 6 3/4" h., footed wide ovoid body w/a wide cupped flat rim, mottled purple & blue w/an overshot finish (ILLUS., previous page, top row, second from left w/bowl & vases)... **104**

Vase, 6 3/4" h., wide ovoid flat-bottomed body w/a wide short flaring neck, crystal decorated w/wavy lemon yellow bands (ILLUS. bottom row, third from left w/bowl & vases, previous page)............................... **40-80**

Vase, 8 3/4" h., slightly swelled cylindrical body w/a short flaring rim, red decorated around the bottom w/pulled-up amethyst spikes (ILLUS. top row, second from right w/bowl & vases, previous page)................. **40-80**

Vase, 12 1/2" h., tall waisted cylindrical form, lemon yellow enameled overall w/small black stylized florals separated by thin black stripes, oval stamped mark for Loetz, ca. 1920s (ILLUS. bottom row, far left w/bowl & vases, previous page)......... **150**

Vases, 9 1/2" h., large ovoid body tapering to a short cylindrical neck, Malachite glass, mold-blown in an ornate paneled design w/raised panels featuring Grecian woman alternating w/ribbed sunken panels, Schlevogt factory, ca. 1935, pr. (ILLUS. with dresser set, top of page).......... **920**

D'Argental

Glass known by this name is so-called after its producer, who fashioned fine cameo pieces in St. Louis, France in the late 19th century and up to 1918.

D'Argental Mark

Cameo vase, 9" h., wide tapering cylindrical lower body w/a wide angled shoulder to a bulbed neck w/flat rim, pink overlaid in various shades of green & etched w/a forested lake scene w/deer, geese flying overhead, signed in cameo, ca. 1920 .... **$1,380**

Cameo vase, 12" h., ovoid body tapering to a slender stick neck, amber overlaid in crimson & etched w/a Venetian harbor scene w/gondolas & sailing ships, signed in cameo, ca. 1910 .... **1,150**

Cameo vase, 13" h., gently flaring cylindrical form w/rounded shoulder tapering to a short cylindrical neck, amber overlaid in crimson & etched w/a landscape of towering trees in the foreground silhouetted against a tree-lined lake & mountains in the background, signed in cameo, ca. 1900 .... **1,265**

Cameo vase, 17" h., tapering swollen cylindrical body w/a flared short vertical mouth, citron overlaid w/deep crimson & etched w/a forested lake scene of tall trees in the foreground & hills in the distance, signed in cameo, ca. 1910 (ILLUS., top of next column) **4,025**

Tall D'Argental Cameo Vase

Daum Nancy

This fine glass, much of it cameo, was made by Auguste and Antonin Daum, who founded a factory in 1875 in Nancy, France. Most of their cameo and enameled glass was made from the 1890s into the early 20th century.

Daum Nancy Marks

Fine Daum Cameo Ceiling Fixture

Unusual Daum Cameo Bowl

Cameo bowl, 5 1/2" w., squared shallow form in frosted clear overlaid w/reddish brown & cut w/large oak leaves, applied w/three brightly colored cabochon insets, signed (ILLUS.) **$1,725**

Cameo ceiling fixture, a wide mushroom-shaped inverted shade in shaded grey to yellow ground overlaid in deep amethyst & cut w/a wide border of stylized flowers & leaves, signed, suspended from gilt-metal chains & ceiling plate, ca. 1900, shade 16" d. (ILLUS., bottom previous page)... **8,913**

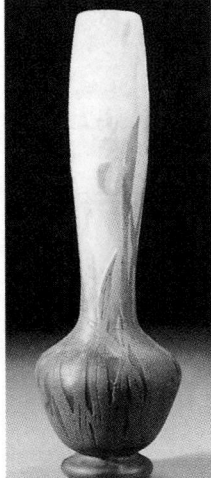

Daum Cameo Vase with Daffodil

Cameo vase, 8 3/4" h., a small cushion foot below the bulbous tapering lower body centered by a tall swelled cylindrical neck, greyish blue & yellow mottled overlaid in vitrified green & orange & cut w/tall leafy stems supporting a white padded wheel-carved daffodil, signed in intaglio, ca. 1900 (ILLUS.)........................... **3,910**

Cameo vase, 9" h., thick cushion foot below the ovoid body w/a wide flat mouth, dark green & red overlaid on the shaded rose to yellow to mottled maroon ground &

cameo-cut w/leafy branches & red cherries suspended from the rim **5,300-5,500**

Cameo vase, 9 1/2" h., cushion foot below the tall slender waisted body w/a flared rim, pale green-tinted opalescent carved w/a design of trailing clematis blossoms set against a grey textured ground w/rich red overtones, engraved signature, ca. 1910... **2,530**

Cameo vase, 10 1/2" h., round cushion foot supporting the ovoid body w/a wide cylindrical neck, mottled & shaded dark blue to green to pink body etched & enameled w/blue bachelor button blossoms & green leafy stems **3,200**

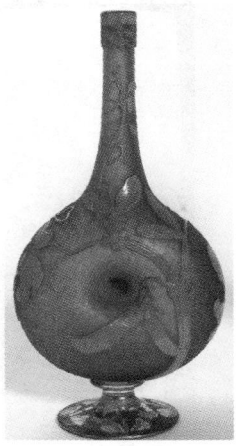

Rare Early Daum Cameo Vase

Cameo vase, 13" h., disk foot & short stem supporting the flattened round body tapering to a tall stick neck, frosted pink overlaid w/opalescent white & carved w/undulating leaves, stems, flowers & sweet pea pods in pale green outlined in gold, gold-lettered mark, pre-1900 (ILLUS.).. **7,475**

Tall Daum Cameo Vase

Daum Cruet, Tumbler & Vase

Cameo vase, 13" h., footed tall waisted cylindrical body w/a closed flat rim, amber overlaid w/orange & dark green & etched w/a continuous forested lake scene w/large fir trees in the foreground, signed in cameo (ILLUS., previous page) **1,840**

Cameo vase, 19 1/2" h., tall trumpet-form body w/flaring base, mottled dark yellow & red glass overlaid & carved w/vitrified green stemmed flowers cascading from the rim in a random pattern, signed in cameo **2,300**

Cruet w/original stopper, spherical body w/a cylindrical neck & pinched spout, applied strap handle & flattened disk stopper, mottled yellow & orange etched & enameled w/red poppies on gold-trimmed green leafy stems, signed in gold enamel, ca. 1900, 6 1/2" h. (ILLUS. center with tumbler & vase, top of page) **4,600**

Tumbler, swelled cylindrical body in dark amethyst & mottled frosted clear, etched & enameled w/purple & red fuchsia blossoms on green leafy stems, signed in cameo, ca. 1900, 4 3/4" h. (ILLUS. left with cruet, top of page) **1,265**

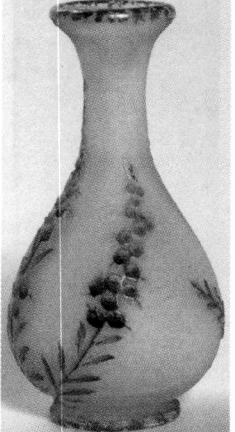

Miniature Daum Enameled Vase

Vase, 2 1/8" h., miniature, footed ovoid body tapering to a flaring neck, frosted opalescent ground etched w/sprigs of leaves & berries enameled in green, deep maroon & lavender, gilt trim on sprigs, rim & base, signed (ILLUS.) **1,093**

Daum Vases with Enameled Landscapes

Vase, 3 3/4" h., miniature, upright rectangular shape, grey & mottled purple etched & enameled w/red & purple fuchsia blossoms on green leafy stems trimmed in gold, signed in cameo (ILLUS. right with cruet, top previous page) **1,265**

Vase, 4 1/4" h., squatty ovoid pillow-form body in mottled orange & yellow, etched & enameled w/a continuous winter landscape in shades of brown, black & white, signed in black enamel, ca. 1900 (ILLUS. bottom row, center, top of page) **4,025**

Vase, 4 1/2" h., upright rectangular form, blue & grey mottled etched & enameled w/a continuous summer lakeside landscape in greens, yellows & browns, signed in black enamel, ca. 1900 (ILLUS.) **2,070**

Daum Vase Decorated with Berries

Vase, 4 1/2" h., upright rectangular form, grey internally decorated w/amethyst & yellow mottling, etched & enameled w/green leafy stems w/reddish orange berries, signed in cameo, ca. 1900 (ILLUS.) **2,300**

Summer Lakeside Scene on Daum Vase

Small Daum Vase with Violets

Vase, 4 3/4" h., slightly swelled cylindrical form w/a flat rim, mottled mustard yellow etched & enameled w/wild violets & leaves, signed (ILLUS.) **1,783**

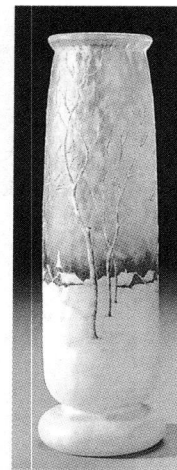

Daum Vase with Winter Village Scene

Vase, 8 1/4" h., a cushion foot below the slightly swelled cylindrical body w/a flared flat rim, mottled grey, blue & amber etched & enameled w/a continuous winter village landscape w/snow-covered trees, homes, churches & windmills, signed in black enamel, ca. 1910 (ILLUS.).. **6,325**

Daum Vase with Autumn Landscape

Vase, 6" h., a cushion foot supporting a flaring cylindrical body w/a narrow angled shoulder to the flat mouth, mottled grey & blue etched & enameled w/a continuous lakeside landscape w/yellow & red leafy trees in the foreground, signed in black enamel, ca. 1900 (ILLUS.) **3,565**

Vase, 7 1/2" h., ovoid body tapering to a wide, flat mouth, mottled orange & yellow ground etched & enameled w/a continuous winter landscape of barren trees in shades of brown, black & white signed in enamel (ILLUS. bottom row, right w/other enameled vases, previous page) **4,140**

Daum Lorrain Decorated Vase

Vase, 10" h., cushion foot tapering to a tall swelled & flaring body, yellow w/orange russet mottling, etched & enameled in color w/a crocosmia arising from leafy green stems, signed on the base in script "Lorrain," 1927-32 (ILLUS.)............................. **374**

Vase, 12 1/4" h., a cushion foot supporting a swelled trumpet-form body w/a flat rim, green mottled w/green & blue & etched &

De Latte Dresser Set

enameled w/a continuous landscape of green leafy trees in a flowering meadow w/an amethyst forest in the background, signed in green enamel (ILLUS. bottom row, far left w/other enameled vases, page 581) **3,450**

Vase, 13 3/4" h., flat-sided cylindrical form, mottled yellow & orange etched & enameled w/a continuous winter landscape of barren trees in shades of brown, black & white, signed in black enamel, ca. 1900, rim slightly ground (ILLUS. back row, center w/other enameled vases, page 581) **4,830**

De Latte

Andre de Latte of Nancy, France, produced a range of opaque and cameo glass after 1921. His company also produced light fixtures, but his cameo wares are most collectible today.

De Latte Marks

Cameo vase, 14" h., a wide cushion foot below the tall flaring body tapering to a short neck w/swelled rim, grey mottled w/amethyst & white & overlaid in purplish red & etched w/four stems of foxgloves, signed in cameo "À De Latte - Nancy," ca. 1920 (ILLUS., next column) **$920**

Dresser set: three bottles w/stoppers, soap dish, cov. powder box, barrel-shaped tumbler, open bowl & atomizer; each in mottled dark yellow & blue, all signed, the set (ILLUS., top of page) **690**

De Latte Cameo Vase with Foxgloves

Depression

The phrase "Depression Glass" is used by collectors to denote a specific kind of transparent glass produced primarily as tablewares, in crystal, amber, blue, green, pink, milky-white, etc., during the late 1920s and 1930s when this country was in the midst of a financial depression. Made to sell inexpensively, it was turned out by such producers as Jeannette, Hocking, Westmoreland, Indiana and other glass companies. We compile prices on all the major Depression Glass patterns. Collectors should consult Depression Glass references for information on those patterns and pieces that have been reproduced.

Green Block Optic Pieces

American Sweetheart, MacBeth - Evans Glass Co., 1930-38 (Process-etched)

Bowl, 3 3/4" d., berry, pink................................. $92
Bowl, 4 1/2" d., cream soup, Monax................. 120
Bowl, 4 1/2" d., cream soup, pink....................... 95
Bowl, 6" d., cereal, Cremax.............................. 18
Bowl, 6" d., cereal, Monax............................... 16
Bowl, 6" d., cereal, Monax "smoke" w/black edge... 30
Bowl, 6" d., cereal, pink.................................... 22
Bowl, 9" d., berry, Cremax................................ 45
Bowl, 9" d., berry, Monax................................. 75
Bowl, 9" d., berry, pink..................................... 60
Bowl, 9 1/2" d., soup w/flanged rim, Monax 85
Bowl, 9 1/2" d., soup w/flanged rim, pink........... 95
Bowl, 11" oval vegetable, Monax 85
Bowl, 11" oval vegetable, pink........................... 75
Console bowl, blue, 18" d............................... 1,350
Console bowl, Monax, 18" d. 475
Console bowl, ruby red, 18" d...................... 1,250
Creamer, footed, blue...................................... 185
Creamer, footed, Monax 14
Creamer, footed, pink....................................... 20
Creamer, footed, ruby red 165
Cup, blue 150
Cup, Monax 10
Cup, pink 20
Cup, ruby red 120
Lamp shade, Cremax 450
Lamp shade, Monax 495
Pitcher, 7 1/2" h., 60 oz., jug-type, pink 1,100
Pitcher, 8" h., 80 oz., pink 850
Plate, 6" d., bread & butter, Monax 6
Plate, 6" d., bread & butter, pink.......................... 8
Plate, 8" d., salad, blue.................................... 125
Plate, 8" d., salad, Monax 10
Plate, 8" d., salad, pink.................................... 14
Plate, 8" d., salad, ruby red 115
Plate, 9" d., luncheon, Monax 12
Plate, 9 3/4" d., dinner, Monax.......................... 26
Plate, 9 3/4" d., dinner, pink.............................. 40
Plate, 10 1/4" d., dinner, Monax......................... 28
Plate, 11" d., chop, Monax 18
Plate, 12" d., salver, blue 260
Plate, 12" d., salver, Monax 20
Plate, 12" d., salver, pink.................................. 28
Plate, 12" d., salver, ruby red 215
Plate, 15 1/2" d., w/center handle, blue............. 450
Plate, 15 1/2" d., w/center handle, Monax......... 250
Plate, 15 1/2" d., w/center handle, ruby red...... 425
Platter, 13" oval, Monax.................................... 65
Platter, 13" oval, pink.. 70

Salt & pepper shakers, footed, Monax, pr. 450
Salt & pepper shakers, footed, pink, pr. 650
Saucer, blue... 35
Saucer, Monax 3
Saucer, pink... 4
Saucer, ruby red 30
Sherbet, footed, pink, 3 3/4" h. 26
Sherbet, footed, Monax, 4 1/4" h. 20
Sherbet, footed, pink, 4 1/4" h. 24
Sherbet, metal holder, clear............................... 6
Sugar bowl, cov., Monax (only) 475
Sugar bowl, open, blue 185
Sugar bowl, open, Cremax................................ 14
Sugar bowl, open, Monax................................. 14
Sugar bowl, open, pink..................................... 20
Sugar bowl, open, ruby red 165
Tidbit server, three-tier, 8" d., 12" d. & 15 1/2" d., blue 775
Tidbit server, three-tier, 8" d., 12" d. & 15 1/2" d., Monax 275
Tidbit server, three-tier, 8" d., 12" d. & 15 1/2" d., ruby red....................................... 750
Tidbit server, two-tier, 8" d. & 12" d., Monax.. 45
Tidbit server, two-tier, 8" d. & 12" d., pink 50
Tidbit server, two-tier, 8" d. & 12" d., ruby red.. 325
Tumbler, pink, 3 1/2" h., 5 oz........................... 125
Tumbler, pink, 4 1/4" h., 9 oz............................. 78
Tumbler, pink, 4 3/4" h., 10 oz......................... 145

Block or Block Optic, Hocking Glass Co., 1919-33 (Press-mold)

Bowl, 4 1/4" d., berry, green 10
Bowl, 4 1/4" d., berry, pink 12
Bowl, 4 1/2" d., berry, green 30
Bowl, 5 1/4" d., cereal, green............................ 18
Bowl, 5 1/4" d., cereal, pink.............................. 35
Bowl, 7 1/4" d., salad, green............................ 175
Bowl, 7 1/4" d., salad, pink.............................. 185
Bowl, 8 1/2" d., large berry, green 32
Bowl, 8 1/2" d., large berry, pink 35
Butter dish, cov., rectangular, blue, 3 x 5"........ 475
Butter dish, cov., rectangular, clear, 3 x 5"........ 95
Butter dish, cov., rectangular, green, 3 x 5"........ 85
Butter dish, cov., rectangular, green clambroth, 3 x 5" 275
Candlesticks, amber, 1 3/4" h., pr...................... 75
Candlesticks, green, 1 3/4" h., pr..................... 125
Candlesticks, pink, 1 3/4" h., pr......................... 95
Candy jar, cov., green, 2 1/4" h........................ 65
Candy jar, cov., pink, 2 1/4" h. 65

Candy jar, cov., yellow, 2 1/4" h. 70
Candy jar, cov., green, 6 1/4" h. (ILLUS. far
    left with other Block Optic pieces, top of
    previous page) 62
Candy jar, cov., pink, 6 1/4" h. 128
Compote, 4" d., cone-shaped, green 75
Compote, 4" d., cone-shaped, pink 85
Console bowl, rolled edge, green,
    11 3/4" d. 120
Console bowl, rolled edge, pink, 11 3/4" d. 143
Creamer, various styles, green (ILLUS. far
    right with other pieces, previous page) 12
Creamer, various styles, pink 14
Creamer, various styles, yellow 16
Cup, various styles, green 6
Cup, various styles, pink 8
Cup, various styles, yellow 10
Goblet, wine, pink, 3 1/2" h. 475
Goblet, cocktail, clear, 4" h. 6
Goblet, cocktail, green, 4" h. 40
Goblet, cocktail, pink, 4" h. 45
Goblet, wine, clear, 4 1/2" h. 8
Goblet, wine, green, 4 1/2" h. 40
Goblet, wine, pink, 4 1/2" h. 45
Goblet, clear, 5 3/4" h., 9 oz. 10
Goblet, green, 5 3/4" h., 9 oz. 28
Goblet, pink, 5 3/4" h., 9 oz. 35
Goblet, clear, 7 1/4" h., 9 oz. 25
Goblet, green, 7 1/4" h., 9 oz. 19
Goblet, pink, 7 1/4" h., 9 oz. 27
Goblet, yellow, 7 1/4" h., 9 oz. 35
Ice bucket, w/metal bail handle, clear 24
Ice bucket, w/metal bail handle, green 32
Ice bucket, w/metal bail handle, pink 61
Ice tub, tab handles, clear 16
Ice tub, tab handles, green 60
Ice tub, tab handles, pink 86
Mug, green 35
Pitcher, 7 5/8" h., 54 oz., bulbous, green 82
Pitcher, 7 5/8" h., 54 oz., bulbous, pink 495
Pitcher, 8" h., 80 oz., clear 37
Pitcher, 8" h., 80 oz., green 100
Pitcher, 8 1/2" h., 54 oz., clear 15
Pitcher, 8 1/2" h., 54 oz., green 60
Pitcher, 8 1/2" h., 54 oz., pink 38
Plate, 6" d., sherbet, clear 1
Plate, 6" d., sherbet, green 4
Plate, 6" d., sherbet, pink 5
Plate, 6" d., sherbet, yellow 5
Plate, 8" d., luncheon, clear 2
Plate, 8" d., luncheon, green 6
Plate, 8" d., luncheon, pink 8
Plate, 8" d., luncheon, yellow 8
Plate, 9" d., dinner, clear 4
Plate, 9" d., dinner, green 28
Plate, 9" d., dinner, pink 25
Plate, 9" d., dinner, yellow 40
Plate, 9" d., grill, clear 5
Plate, 9" d., grill, green 75
Plate, 9" d., grill, pink 85
Plate, 9" d., grill, yellow 75
Plate, 10 1/4" d., sandwich, clear 6
Plate, 10 1/4" d., sandwich, green 25
Plate, 10 1/4" d., sandwich, pink 28
Salt & pepper shakers, footed, clear, pr. 24
Salt & pepper shakers, footed, green, pr. 50
Salt & pepper shakers, footed, pink, pr. 85
Salt & pepper shakers, footed, yellow, pr. 95
Salt & pepper shakers, squatty, green, pr. 125

Sandwich server w/center handle, green 70
Sandwich server w/center handle, pink 75
Saucer, green, 5 3/4" d. 8
Saucer, pink, 5 3/4" d. 10
Saucer, green, 6 1/8" d. 8
Saucer, pink, 6 1/8" d. 10
Saucer, yellow, 6 1/8" d. 8
Sherbet, cone-shaped, footed, green
    (ILLUS. second from left with other piec-
    es, previous page) 6
Sherbet, stemmed, clear, 3 1/4" h., 5 1/2
    oz. 3
Sherbet, stemmed, green, 3 1/4" h., 5 1/2
    oz. 6
Sherbet, stemmed, pink, 3 1/4" h., 5 1/2 oz. 8
Sherbet, stemmed, yellow, 3 1/4" h., 5 1/2
    oz. 10
Sherbet, stemmed, clear, 4 3/4" h., 6 oz. 6
Sherbet, stemmed, green, 4 3/4" h., 6 oz. 18
Sherbet, stemmed, pink, 4 3/4" h., 6 oz. 20
Sherbet, stemmed, yellow, 4 3/4" h., 6 oz. 22
Sugar bowl, open, various styles, clear 5
Sugar bowl, open, various styles, green
    (ILLUS. second from right with other
    pieces, previous page) 12
Sugar bowl, open, various styles, pink 14
Sugar bowl, open, various styles, yellow 16
Tumble-up bottle, green 20
Tumble-up set: bottle & 3" h. tumbler:
    green, 2 pcs. 125
Tumbler, whiskey, pink, 1 5/8" h., 1 oz. 45
Tumbler, whiskey, clear, 2 1/4" h., 2 oz. 12
Tumbler, whiskey, green, 2 1/4" h., 2 oz. 32
Tumbler, whiskey, pink, 2 1/4" h., 2 oz. 38
Tumbler, footed, green, 2 5/8" h., 3 oz. 36
Tumbler, footed, pink, 2 5/8" h., 3 oz. 36
Tumbler, juice, clear, 3 1/2" h., 5 oz. 5
Tumbler, juice, green, 3 1/2" h., 5 oz. 28
Tumbler, juice, pink, 3 1/2" h., 5 oz. 32
Tumbler, footed, clear, 9 oz. 6
Tumbler, footed, green, 9 oz. 20
Tumbler, footed, pink, 9 oz. 18
Tumbler, footed, yellow, 9 oz. 26
Tumbler, clear, 3 7/8" h., 9 1/2 oz. 6
Tumbler, green, 3 7/8" h., 9 1/2 oz. 16
Tumbler, pink, 3 7/8" h., 9 1/2 oz. 18
Tumbler, iced tea, footed, green, 6" h., 10 oz. 32
Tumbler, iced tea, footed, clear, 6" h., 10
    oz. 8
Tumbler, iced tea, footed, pink, 6" h., 10 oz. 35
Tumbler, green, 5" h., 10 to 11 oz. 26
Tumbler, pink, 5" h., 10 to 11 oz. 24
Tumbler, green, 4 7/8" h., 12 oz. 28
Tumbler, pink, 4 7/8" h., 12 oz. 30
Tumbler, green, 5 1/4" h., 15 oz. 46
Tumbler, pink, 5 1/4" h., 15 oz. 45
Vase, 5 3/4" h., green 345

Cameo or Ballerina or Dancing Girl, Hocking Glass Co., 1930-34 (Process-etched)

Bowl, 4 1/4" d., sauce, clear 10
Bowl, 4 3/4" d., cream soup, green 165
Bowl, 5 1/2" d., cereal, clear 6
Bowl, 5 1/2" d., cereal, green 35
Bowl, 5 1/2" d., cereal, yellow 30
Bowl, 7 1/4" d., salad, green 70
Bowl, 8 1/4" d., large berry, green 48
Bowl, 8 1/4" d., large berry, pink 160
Bowl, 9" d., soup w/flange rim, green 85

Bowl, 10" oval vegetable, green 40
Bowl, 10" oval vegetable, yellow 45
Butter dish, cov., green 245
Butter dish, cov., yellow **1,600**
Cake plate, three-footed, green, 10" d. 35
Candlesticks, green, 4" h., pr........................ 145
Candy jar, cov., green, 4" h. 95
Candy jar, cov., pink, 4" h. 525
Candy jar, cov., yellow, 4" h........................... 115
Candy jar, cov., green, 6 1/2" h.......................... 195
Compote, mayonnaise, 5" d., 4" h., cone-shaped, green 48
Compote, mayonnaise, 5" d., 4" h., cone-shaped, pink 215
Console bowl, three-footed, green, 11" d. 85
Console bowl, three-footed, pink, 11" d. 75
Console bowl, three-footed, yellow, 11" d. 115
Cookie jar, cov., green 65
Creamer, green, 3 1/4" h. 24
Creamer, yellow, 3 1/4" h. 24
Creamer, green, 4 1/4" h. 28
Creamer, pink, 4 1/4" h. 145
Cup, clear 5
Cup, green 15
Cup, pink 85
Cup, yellow 10
Decanter, no stopper, green 50
Decanter w/stopper, clear, 10" h...................... 175
Decanter w/stopper, green, 10" h..................... 195
Decanter w/stopper, green frosted, 10" h. 45
Domino tray, clear, no indent, 7" d. 125
Domino tray, green, w/indent, 7" d.................... 185
Domino tray, pink, no indent, 7" d. 300
Goblet, wine, green, 3 1/2" h........................ 1,100
Goblet, wine, green, 4" h. 85
Goblet, wine, pink, 4" h. 245
Goblet, water, green, 6" h................................ 65
Goblet, water, pink, 6" h................................ 185
Ice bowl, tab handles, clear, 5 1/2" d., 3 1/2" h.. 275
Ice bowl, tab handles, green, 5 1/2" d., 3 1/2" h.. 225
Ice bowl, tab handles, pink, 5 1/2" d., 3 1/2" h.. 795
Jam jar, cov., closed handles, clear, 2" 165
Jam jar, cov., closed handles, green, 2" 225
Pitcher, syrup or milk, 5 3/4" h., 20 oz., green 295
Pitcher, syrup or milk, 5 3/4" h., 20 oz., yellow 2,200
Pitcher, juice, 6" h., 36 oz., green 75
Pitcher, water, 8 1/2" h., 56 oz., jug-type, clear 495
Pitcher, water, 8 1/2" h., 56 oz., jug-type, green 75
Pitcher, water, 8 1/2" h., 56 oz., jug-type, pink 1,250
Plate, 6" d., sherbet (or ringless saucer), clear 2
Plate, 6" d., sherbet (or ringless saucer), green 6
Plate, 6" d., sherbet (or ringless saucer), pink 85
Plate, 6" d., sherbet (or ringless saucer), yellow 5
Plate, 7" d., salad, clear................................... 4
Plate, 8" d., luncheon, clear 4
Plate, 8" d., luncheon, green 15
Plate, 8" d., luncheon, pink 32

Plate, 8" d., luncheon, yellow 12
Plate, 8 1/2" sq., green.................................... 65
Plate, 8 1/2" sq., yellow................................. 275
Plate, 9 1/2" d., dinner, green 24
Plate, 9 1/2" d., dinner, pink 95
Plate, 9 1/2" d., dinner, yellow 14
Plate, 10" d., sandwich, green 18
Plate, 10" d., sandwich, pink 54
Plate, 10 1/2" d., closed handles, green............. 16
Plate, 10 1/2" d., closed handles, yellow 14
Plate, 10 1/2" d., dinner, rimmed, green............ 115
Plate, 10 1/2" d., dinner, rimmed, pink.............. 225
Plate, 10 1/2" d., grill, green 16
Plate, 10 1/2" d., grill, pink 50
Plate, 10 1/2" d., grill, yellow 12
Plate, 10 1/2" d., grill, closed handles, green 75
Plate, 10 1/2" d., grill, closed handles, yellow 8
Platter, 12", closed handles, green.................... 28
Platter, 12", closed handles, yellow 42
Relish, footed, three-part, green, 7 1/2" 34
Salt & pepper shakers, green, pr. 85
Salt & pepper shakers, pink, pr. 950
Sandwich server w/center handle, green .. 6,200
Saucer w/cup ring, green................................ 185
Sherbet, green, 3 1/8" h. 16
Sherbet, pink, 3 1/8" h.................................... 75
Sherbet, yellow, 3 1/8" h.................................. 38
Sherbet, thin, high stem, green, 4 7/8" h. 18
Sherbet, thin, high stem, pink, 4 7/8" h. 75
Sugar bowl, open, green, 3 1/4" h...................... 24
Sugar bowl, open, yellow, 3 1/4" h..................... 24
Sugar bowl, open, green, 4 1/4" h...................... 28
Sugar bowl, open, pink, 4 1/4" h...................... 145
Tumbler, juice, footed, green, 3 oz..................... 70
Tumbler, juice, footed, pink, 3 oz..................... 145
Tumbler, juice, green, 3 3/4" h., 5 oz. 45
Tumbler, juice, pink, 3 3/4" h., 5 oz. 85
Tumbler, water, clear, 4" h., 9 oz....................... 8
Tumbler, water, green, 4" h., 9 oz...................... 38
Tumbler, water, pink, 4" h., 9 oz....................... 75
Tumbler, footed, green, 5" h., 9 oz. 35
Tumbler, footed, pink, 5" h., 9 oz. 115
Tumbler, footed, yellow, 5" h., 9 oz. 18
Tumbler, green, 4 3/4" h., 10 oz........................ 35
Tumbler, pink, 4 3/4" h., 10 oz......................... 95
Tumbler, green, 5" h., 11 oz............................. 38
Tumbler, pink, 5" h., 11 oz.............................. 95
Tumbler, yellow, 5" h., 11 oz............................ 60
Tumbler, footed, green, 5 3/4" h., 11 oz. 75
Tumbler, footed, pink, 5 3/4" h., 11 oz. 135
Tumbler, green, 5 1/4" h., 15 oz. 85
Tumbler, pink, 5 1/4" h., 15 oz. 135
Tumbler, footed, green, 6 3/8" h., 15 oz. 600
Vase, 5 3/4" h., green 300
Vase, 8" h., green.. 60
Water bottle, dark green "White House Vinegar" base, 8 1/2" h................................... 24

Colonial or Knife & Fork (Press-mold)

Bowl, 3 3/4" d., berry, pink 60
Bowl, 4 1/2" d., berry, clear................................ 5
Bowl, 4 1/2" d., berry, green 20
Bowl, 4 1/2" d., berry, pink 18
Bowl, 4 1/2" d., cream soup, clear 35
Bowl, 4 1/2" d., cream soup, green...................... 75
Bowl, 4 1/2" d., cream soup, pink........................ 70
Bowl, 5 1/2" d., cereal, clear............................. 24
Bowl, 5 1/2" d., cereal, green............................ 100

Bowl, 7" d., soup, clear 15
Bowl, 7" d., soup, green 65
Bowl, 7" d., soup, pink 60
Bowl, 9" d., clear 18
Bowl, 9" d., green 35
Bowl, 10" oval vegetable, clear 18
Bowl, 10" oval vegetable, green 40
Bowl, 10" oval vegetable, pink 35
Butter dish, cov., clear 44
Butter dish, cov., green 53
Butter dish, cov., pink 675
Celery or spooner, clear 135
Celery or spooner, green 114
Cheese dish, wooden base w/green dome
   cover 420
Creamer or milk pitcher, clear, 5" h., 16
   oz. 22
Creamer or milk pitcher, green, 5" h., 16
   oz. 16
Creamer or milk pitcher, pink, 5" h., 16 oz. 15
Cup, clear 5
Cup, green 10
Cup, milk white 5
Cup, pink 10
Cup & saucer, clear 10
Cup & saucer, green 18
Cup & saucer, pink 18
Goblet, cordial, clear, 3 3/4" h., 1 oz. 17
Goblet, cordial, green, 3 3/4" h., 1 oz. 30
Goblet, wine, clear, 4 1/2" h., 2 1/2 oz. 15
Goblet, wine, green, 4 1/2" h., 2 1/2 oz. 28
Goblet, cocktail, clear, 4" h., 3 oz. 10
Goblet, cocktail, green, 4" h., 3 oz. 27
Goblet, claret, clear, 5 1/4" h., 4 oz. 16
Goblet, claret, green, 5 1/4" h., 4 oz. 25
Goblet, water, clear, 5 3/4" h., 8 1/2 oz. 21
Goblet, water, green, 5 3/4" h., 8 1/2 oz. 33
Goblet, water, pink, 5 3/4" h., 8 1/2 oz. 17
Mug, green, 4 1/2" h., 12 oz. 750
Pitcher, ice lip or plain, 7" h., 54 oz., clear 33
Pitcher, ice lip or plain, 7" h., 54 oz., green 54
Pitcher, ice lip or plain, 7" h., 54 oz., pink 56
Pitcher, ice lip or plain, 7 3/4" h., 68 oz.,
   clear 30
Pitcher, ice lip or plain, 7 3/4" h., 68 oz.,
   green 66
Pitcher, ice lip or plain, 7 3/4" h., 68 oz.,
   pink 58
Plate, 6" d., sherbet, clear 4
Plate, 6" d., sherbet, green 9
Plate, 6" d., sherbet, pink 7
Plate, 8 1/2" d., luncheon, clear 6
Plate, 8 1/2" d., luncheon, green 10
Plate, 8 1/2" d., luncheon, pink 10
Plate, 10" d., dinner, clear 26
Plate, 10" d., dinner, green 63
Plate, 10" d., dinner, pink 67
Plate, 10" d., grill, clear 19
Plate, 10" d., grill, green 25
Plate, 10" d., grill, pink 26
Platter, 12" oval, clear 14
Platter, 12" oval, green 25
Platter, 12" oval, pink 33
Salt & pepper shakers, clear, pr. 72
Salt & pepper shakers, green, pr. 145
Salt & pepper shakers, pink, pr. 112
Saucer, green 6
Saucer, pink 6
Sherbet, pink, 3" h. 17

Sherbet, clear, 3 3/8" h. 7
Sherbet, green, 3 3/8" h. 10
Sherbet, pink, 3 3/8" h. 8
Sugar bowl, cov., clear 23
Sugar bowl, cov., green 26
Sugar bowl, cov., pink 60
Tumbler, whiskey, clear, 2 1/2" h., 1 1/2 oz. 12
Tumbler, whiskey, green, 2 1/2" h., 1 1/2
   oz. 14
Tumbler, whiskey, pink, 2 1/2" h., 1 1/2 oz. 12
Tumbler, cordial, footed, clear, 3 1/4" h., 3
   oz. 13
Tumbler, cordial, footed, green, 3 1/4" h., 3
   oz. 24
Tumbler, footed, pink, 3 1/4" h., 3 oz. 17
Tumbler, juice, clear, 3" h., 5 oz. 4
Tumbler, juice, green, 3" h., 5 oz. 25
Tumbler, juice, pink, 3" h., 5 oz. 24
Tumbler, footed, clear, 4" h., 5 oz. 14
Tumbler, footed, green, 4" h., 5 oz. 43
Tumbler, footed, pink, 4" h., 5 oz. 31
Tumbler, water, clear, 4" h., 9 oz. 14
Tumbler, water, green, 4" h., 9 oz. 42
Tumbler, water, pink, 4" h., 9 oz. 22
Tumbler, footed, clear, 5 1/4" h., 10 oz. 21
Tumbler, footed, green, 5 1/4" h., 10 oz. 44
Tumbler, footed, pink, 5 1/4" h., 10 oz. 46
Tumbler, clear, 5 1/8" h., 11 oz. 19
Tumbler, green, 5 1/8" h., 11 oz. 42
Tumbler, pink, 5 1/8" h., 11 oz. 38
Tumbler, iced tea, clear, 12 oz. 15
Tumbler, iced tea, green, 12 oz. 32
Tumbler, iced tea, pink, 12 oz. 45
Tumbler, lemonade, clear, 15 oz. 11
Tumbler, lemonade, green, 15 oz. 73
Tumbler, lemonade, pink, 15 oz. 60

Cube or Cubist, Jeannette Glass Co., 1929-33 (Press-mold)

Bowl, 4 1/2" d., deep, pink 10
Bowl, 4 1/2" d., deep, ultramarine 45
Bowl, 4 1/2" d., dessert, clear 4
Bowl, 4 1/2" d., dessert, green 10
Bowl, 4 1/2" d., dessert, pink 12
Bowl, 6 1/2" d. green 8
Bowl, 6 1/2" d., salad, green 18
Bowl, 6 1/2" d., salad, pink 11
Coaster, green, 3 1/4" d. 10
Coaster, pink, 3 1/4" d. 8
Creamer, amber, 2 5/8" h. 2
Creamer, clear, 2 5/8" h. 1
Creamer, clear, 3 1/2" h. 1
Creamer, pink, 3 1/2" h. 6
Pitcher, 8 3/4" h., 45 oz., green 245
Pitcher, 8 3/4" h., 45 oz., pink 230
Plate, 6" d., sherbet, clear 2
Plate, 6" d., sherbet, green 6
Plate, 6" d., sherbet, pink 5
Powder jar, cov., pink 32
Powder jar, cov., three-footed, clear 15
Salt & pepper shakers, green, pr. 45
Salt & pepper shakers, pink, pr. 40
Sherbet, footed, green 10
Sherbet, footed, pink 8
Sugar bowl, cov., green, 3" h. 24
Sugar bowl, cov., pink, 3" h. 20
Sugar bowl, open, green, 2 3/8" h. 8
Sugar bowl, open, pink, 2 3/8" h. 5
Tumbler, green, 4" h., 9 oz. 80
Tumbler, pink, 4" h., 9 oz. 75

Diamond Quilted or Flat Diamond, Imperial Glass Company, late 1920s-early 1930s (Press-mold)

Bowl, 4 3/4" d., cream soup, blue 20
Bowl, 4 3/4" d., cream soup, clear 8
Bowl, 4 3/4" d., cream soup, green 15
Bowl, 4 3/4" d., cream soup, pink 15
Bowl, 5" d., cereal, black 16
Bowl, 5" d., cereal, clear 4
Bowl, 5" d., cereal, green 8
Bowl, 5" d., cereal, pink 8
Bowl, 5 1/2" d., single handle, black 20
Bowl, 5 1/2" d., single handle, blue 20
Bowl, 5 1/2" d., single handle, clear 5
Bowl, 5 1/2" d., single handle, pink 10
Bowl, 7" d., crimped rim, black 21
Bowl, 7" d., crimped rim, clear 5
Bowl, 7" d., crimped rim, green 10
Bowl, 7" d., crimped rim, pink 10
Bowl, 7" d., crimped rim, red 20

Doric, Jeannette Glass Co., 1935-48 (Press-mold)

Bowl, 4 1/2" d., berry, Delphite 48
Bowl, 4 1/2" d., berry, green 12
Bowl, 4 1/2" d., berry, pink 12
Bowl, 5" d., cream soup, green 475
Bowl, 5 1/2" d., cereal, green 95
Bowl, 5 1/2" d., cereal, pink 85
Bowl, 8 1/4" d., large berry, Delphite 145
Bowl, 8 1/4" d., large berry, green 34
Bowl, 8 1/4" d., large berry, pink 32
Bowl, 9" d., two-handled, green 24
Bowl, 9" d., two-handled, pink 22
Bowl, 9" oval vegetable, green 45
Bowl, 9" oval vegetable, pink 42
Butter dish, cov., green 95
Butter dish, cov., pink 85
Cake plate, three-footed, green, 10" d. 32
Cake plate, three-footed, pink, 10" d. 30
Candy dish, three-section, Delphite, 6" 18
Candy dish, three-section, green, 6" 14
Candy dish, three-section, pink, 6" 14
Candy jar, cov., green, 8" h. 45
Candy jar, cov., pink, 8" h. 42
Coaster, green, 3" d. 20
Coaster, pink, 3" d. 18
Creamer, green, 4" h. 16
Creamer, pink, 4" h. 16
Cup, green 12
Cup, pink 11
Pitcher, 5 1/2" h., 32 oz., Delphite 1,300
Pitcher, 5 1/2" h., 32 oz., green 60
Pitcher, 5 1/2" h., 32 oz., pink 55
Pitcher, 7 1/2" h., 48 oz., footed, green 1,250
Pitcher, 7 1/2" h., 48 oz., footed, pink 725
Pitcher, 7 1/2" h., 48 oz., footed, yellow 1,850
Plate, 6" d., sherbet, green 6
Plate, 6" d., sherbet, pink 5
Plate, 7" d., salad, green 26
Plate, 7" d., salad, pink 24
Plate, 9" d., dinner, green 24
Plate, 9" d., dinner, pink 22
Plate, 9", grill, green 26
Plate, 9", grill, pink 24
Platter, 12" oval, green 34
Platter, 12" oval, pink 32
Relish or serving tray, green, 8" x 8" 35
Relish or serving tray, pink, 8" x 8" 30
Relish tray, green, 4" x 4" 14

Relish tray, pink, 4" x 4" 12
Relish tray, green, 4" x 8" 18
Relish tray, pink, 4" x 8" 16
Salt & pepper shakers, green, pr. 45
Salt & pepper shakers, pink, pr. 40
Sandwich tray, handled, green, 10" d. 24
Sandwich tray, handled, pink, 10" d. 22
Saucer, green 4
Saucer, pink 3
Sherbet, footed, Delphite 8
Sherbet, footed, green 16
Sherbet, footed, pink 14
Sugar bowl, cov., green 48
Sugar bowl, cov., pink 42
Tumbler, green, 4 1/2" h., 9 oz. 98
Tumbler, pink, 4 1/2" h., 9 oz. 85
Tumbler, footed, green, 4" h., 10 oz. 90
Tumbler, footed, pink, 4" h., 10 oz. 75
Tumbler, footed, green, 5" h., 12 oz. 135
Tumbler, footed, pink, 5" h., 12 oz. 90

Doric & Pansy, Jeannette Glass Co., 1937-38 (Press-mold)

Bowl, 4 1/2" d., berry, clear 7
Bowl, 4 1/2" d., berry, pink 14
Bowl, 4 1/2" d., berry, ultramarine 24
Bowl, 8" d., large berry, clear 28
Bowl, 8" d., large berry, pink 32
Bowl, 8" d., large berry, ultramarine 92
Bowl, 9" d., handled, clear 18
Bowl, 9" d., handled, pink 24
Bowl, 9" d., handled, ultramarine 40
Butter dish, cov., ultramarine 500
Creamer, clear 50
Creamer, ultramarine 120
Cup, clear 8
Cup, pink 12
Cup, ultramarine 18
Plate, 6" d., sherbet, clear 6
Plate, 6" d., sherbet, pink 10
Plate, 6" d., sherbet, ultramarine 16
Plate, 7" d., salad, ultramarine 45
Plate, 9" d., dinner, clear 12
Plate, 9" d., dinner, pink 15
Plate, 9" d. dinner, ultramarine 38
Salt & pepper shakers, ultramarine, pr. 395
Saucer, clear 2
Saucer, pink 4
Saucer, ultramarine 6
Sugar bowl, open, clear 50
Sugar bowl, open, pink 75
Sugar bowl, open, ultramarine 120
Tray, handled, ultramarine, 10" 38
Tumbler, ultramarine, 4 1/2" h., 9 oz. 120

Pretty Polly Party Dishes Creamer, pink 45
Pretty Polly Party Dishes Creamer, ultramarine 55
Pretty Polly Party Dishes Cup, pink 38
Pretty Polly Party Dishes Cup, ultramarine 45
Pretty Polly Party Dishes Plate, pink 12
Pretty Polly Party Dishes Plate, ultramarine 16
Pretty Polly Party Dishes Saucer, pink 8
Pretty Polly Party Dishes Saucer, ultramarine 10
Pretty Polly Party Dishes Sugar bowl, pink 45
wPretty Polly Party Dishes Sugar bowl, ultramarine 55

English Hobnail, Westmoreland Glass Co., 1920s-40s (Handmade - not true Depression)

Ashtray, clear, various shapes 10
Ashtray, green, various shapes........................... 24
Ashtray, pink, various shapes 24
Ashtray, turquoise, various shapes 26
Basket, handled, clear, 5" h. 25
Bowl, 4 1/2" d., nappy, amber............................ 10
Bowl, 4 1/2" d., nappy, clear 8
Bowl, 4 1/2" d., nappy, green............................ 14
Bowl, 4 1/2" d., nappy, ice blue 28
Bowl, 4 1/2" d., nappy, pink............................... 14
Bowl, 4 1/2" d., nappy, turquoise...................... 26
Bowl, 4 1/2" sq., nappy, clear 8
Bowl, 4 1/2" sq., nappy, green............................ 16
Bowl, 4 1/2" sq., nappy, pink.............................. 16
Bowl, 4 1/2" sq., nappy, turquoise...................... 32
Bowl, 4 3/4" d., cream soup, clear..................... 10
Bowl, 6" d., amber.. 10
Bowl, 6" d., clear... 8
Bowl, 6" d., pink... 16
Bowl, 6" sq., nappy, clear 8
Bowl, 6" sq., nappy, green................................. 16
Bowl, 6" sq., nappy, pink 16
Bowl, 6 1/2" d., grapefruit, clear....................... 12
Bowl, 8" d., fruit, two-handled, footed, amber... 40
Bowl, 8" d., fruit, two-handled, footed, clear....... 45
Bowl, 8" d., fruit, two-handled, footed, cobalt blue 165
Bowl, 8" d., fruit, two-handled, footed, green.. 85
Bowl, 8" d., fruit, two-handled, footed, ice blue 125
Bowl, 8" d., fruit, two-handled, footed, pink 85
Bowl, 8" d., fruit, two-handled, footed, turquoise.. 125
Bowl, 8" d., nappy, amber................................. 26
Bowl, 8" d., nappy, clear 24
Bowl, 8" d., nappy, green.................................. 48
Bowl, 8" d., nappy, pink.................................... 48
Bowl, 11" d., nappy, ice blue............................ 85
Bowl, 12" d., canted sides, clear 25
Bowl, 12" d., canted sides, green...................... 60
Bowl, 12" d., canted sides, pink........................ 60
Bowl, 12" d., flared, clear.................................. 30
Candlesticks, amber, 3 1/2" h., pr.................... 24
Candlesticks, clear, 3 1/2" h., pr...................... 20
Candlesticks, green, 3 1/2" h., pr. 30
Candlesticks, ice blue, 3 1/2" h., pr. 42
Candlesticks, pink, 3 1/2" h., pr........................ 30
Candlesticks, turquoise, 3 1/2" h., pr................ 42
Candlesticks, clear, 9" h., pr. 40
Candlesticks, green, 9" h., pr............................ 65
Candlesticks, ice blue, 9" h., pr. 125
Candlesticks, pink, 9" h., pr.............................. 65
Candlesticks, turquoise, 9" h., pr. 125
Candy dish, cov., three-footed, amber, 6" 30
Candy dish, cov., three-footed, clear, 6" 25
Candy dish, cov., three-footed, green............... 60
Candy dish, cov., three-footed, pink................. 60
Candy dish, cov., cone-shaped, amber, 1/2 lb.. 35
Candy dish, cov., cone-shaped, clear, 1/2 lb.. 30
Candy dish, cov., cone-shaped, cobalt blue, 1/2 lb. 195

Candy dish, cov., cone-shaped, green, 1/2 lb. 60
Candy dish, cov., cone-shaped, pink, 1/2 lb. 6,043
Candy dish, cov., urn-shaped, green, 15" h. 395
Celery tray, clear, 9" l..................................... 18
Celery tray, green, 9" l.................................... 32
Celery tray, pink, 9" l...................................... 34
Celery tray, clear, 12" l................................... 20
Celery tray, green, 12" l.................................. 40
Celery tray, pink, 12" l.................................... 42
Cigarette box, cov., clear............................... 15
Cigarette box, cov., green.............................. 35
Cigarette box, cov., ice blue.......................... 68
Cigarette box, cov., pink................................ 25
Cigarette box, cov., turquoise........................ 68
Cologne bottle, amber 18
Cologne bottle, clear...................................... 15
Cologne bottle, green 30
Cologne bottle, ice blue 60
Cologne bottle, pink....................................... 30
Cologne bottle, turquoise 60
Creamer, flat or footed, amber 18
Creamer, flat or footed, clear......................... 15
Creamer, flat or footed, green........................ 40
Creamer, flat or footed, ice blue 48
Creamer, flat or footed, pink.......................... 40
Creamer, flat or footed, turquoise 48
Cup, demitasse, clear..................................... 20
Cup, demitasse, pink...................................... 58
Cup, clear 8
Cup, green 18
Cup, ice blue 28
Cup, pink 18
Cup, turquoise 28
Decanter w/stopper, clear, 20 oz.................... 95
Egg cup, clear 18
Egg cup, green.. 26
Egg cup, pink.. 30
Goblet, cordial, round foot, clear, 1 oz. 12
Goblet, wine, round foot, clear, 2 oz................ 14
Goblet, wine, round foot, green, 2 oz. 28
Goblet, wine, round foot, pink, 2 oz. 28
Goblet, cocktail, round foot, amber, 3 oz.......... 24
Goblet, cocktail, round foot, clear, 3 oz............ 20
Goblet, cocktail, round foot, green, 3 oz. 28
Goblet, cocktail, round foot, ice blue, 3 oz. 48
Goblet, cocktail, round foot, pink, 3 oz. 28
Goblet, cocktail, round foot, turquoise, 3 oz...... 48
Goblet, claret, round foot, clear, 5 oz. 12
Goblet, sherbet, round foot, amber, 6 1/4 oz... 8
Goblet, sherbet, round foot, clear, 6 1/4 oz.......... 8
Goblet, sherbet, round foot, cobalt blue, 6 1/4 oz. 36
Goblet, sherbet, round foot, green, 6 1/4 oz........ 14
Goblet, sherbet, round foot, ice blue, 6 1/4 oz... 18
Goblet, sherbet, round foot, pink, 6 1/4 oz. 14
Goblet, sherbet, round foot, turquoise, 6 1/4 oz... 12
Goblet, water, clear, 8 oz. 12
Goblet, water, green, 8 oz................................ 30
Goblet, water, ice blue, 8 oz. 50
Hat, high, clear.. 16
Ice tub, clear... 50
Lamp, electric, clear, 6 1/4" h. 35
Lamp, electric, green, 6 1/4" h......................... 75

Lamp, electric, pink, 6 1/4" h. 75
Lamp, electric, amber, 9 1/4" h. 75
Lamp, electric, clear, 9 1/4" h. 70
Lamp, electric, green, 9 1/4" h. 145
Lamp, electric, pink, 9 1/4" h. 145
Lamp, turquoise, 9 1/4" h. 195
Lamp shade, clear, 17" d. 195
Marmalade jar, cov., clear 25
Marmalade jar, cov., green 55
Marmalade jar, cov., pink 55
Marmalade jar, cov., turquoise 80
Oil bottle, clear, 2 oz. 20
Parfait, footed, round, clear 14
Pitcher, 23 oz., clear 70
Pitcher, 23 oz., green 160
Pitcher, 23 oz., pink 160
Pitcher, 38 oz., clear 85
Pitcher, 38 oz., green 260
Pitcher, 38 oz., pink 260
Pitcher, 60 oz., clear 95
Pitcher, 60 oz., green 325
Pitcher, 60 oz., pink 325
Pitcher, 1/2 gal., straight sides, amber 175
Pitcher, 1/2 gal., straight sides, clear 150
Pitcher, 1/2 gal., straight sides, green 350
Plate, 5 1/2" or 6 1/2" d., sherbet, clear 5
Plate, 5 1/2" or 6 1/2" d., sherbet, green 10
Plate, 5 1/2" or 6 1/2" d., sherbet, pink 10
Plate, 8" round or square, luncheon, clear 7
Plate, 8" round or square, luncheon, green 15
Plate, 8" round or square, luncheon, ice
  blue 30
Plate, 8" round or square, luncheon, pink 15
Plate, 8" round or square, luncheon, tur-
  quoise 30
Plate, 10" d., dinner, amber 22
Plate, 10" d., dinner, clear 20
Plate, 10" d., dinner, green 45
Plate, 10" d., dinner, ice blue 75
Plate, 10" d., dinner, pink 45
Puff box, cov., clear 24
Puff box, cov., green 48
Puff box, cov., ice blue 85
Puff box, cov., pink 48
Puff box, cov., turquoise 85
Relish dish, amber, 8" oval 20
Relish dish, clear, 8" oval, three-part 18
Relish dish, green, 8" oval 30
Relish dish, ice blue, 8" oval 36
Relish dish, pink, 8" oval 30
Relish dish, turquoise, 8" oval 36
Relish dish, amber, 9" oval 18
Relish dish, clear, 9" oval 15
Relish dish, green, 9" oval 34
Relish dish, ice blue, 9" oval 36
Relish dish, pink, 9" oval 34
Relish dish, turquoise, 9" oval 36
Relish dish, amber, 12" oval 20
Relish dish, clear, 12" oval 18
Relish dish, green, 12" oval 36
Relish dish, ice blue, 12" oval 45
Relish dish, pink, 12" oval 36
Relish dish, turquoise, 12" oval 45
Rose bowl, clear, 4" 20
Rose bowl, green, 4" 48
Rose bowl, pink, 4" 48
Rose bowl, clear, 6" 20
Rose bowl, green, 6" 48
Rose bowl, pink, 6" 48

Salt dip, footed, amber, 2" 10
Salt dip, footed, clear, 2" 8
Salt dip, footed, green, 2" 16
Salt dip, footed, pink, 2" 16
Salt & pepper shakers, flat, amber, pr. 75
Salt & pepper shakers, flat, clear, pr. 70
Salt & pepper shakers, flat, green, pr. 160
Salt & pepper shakers, flat, pink, pr. 160
Salt & pepper shakers, flat, turquoise, pr. 250
Saucer, demitasse, clear 8
Saucer, round, clear 1
Saucer, round, green 4
Saucer, round, ice blue 6
Sherbet, footed, amber 6
Sherbet, footed, clear 5
Sherbet, footed, green 12
Sherbet, footed, ice blue 16
Sherbet, footed, pink 12
Sugar bowl, open, footed or flat, clear 15
Sugar bowl, open, footed, or flat, green 40
Sugar bowl, open, footed or flat, ice blue 48
Sugar bowl, open, footed or flat, pink 40
Sugar bowl, open, footed, or flat, turquoise 48
Tumbler, whiskey, clear, 1 1/2 oz. 12
Tumbler, whiskey, clear, 3 oz. 10
Tumbler, clear, 3 3/4" h., 5 oz. 10
Tumbler, green, 3 3/4" h., 5 oz. 18
Tumbler, pink, 3 3/4" h., 5 oz. 18
Tumbler, footed, clear, 7 oz. 10
Tumbler, footed, clear, 9 oz. 10
Tumbler, amber, 3 3/4" h., 9 oz. 10
Tumbler, iced tea, clear, 4" h., 10 oz. 14
Tumbler, iced tea, green, 4" h., 10 oz. 30
Tumbler, iced tea, pink, 4" h., 10 oz. 30
Tumbler, iced tea, clear, 5" h., 12 oz. 12
Tumbler, iced tea, green, 5" h., 12 oz. 34
Tumbler, iced tea, pink, 5" h., 12 oz. 34
Tumbler, footed, clear, 12 1/2 oz. 10
Vase, 6 1/2" h., clear 28
Vase, 7 1/2" h., amber 55
Vase, 7 1/2" h., clear 45
Vase, 7 1/2" h., green 95

Florentine No. 1 (Old) or Poppy No. 1, Hazel Atlas Glass Co., 1932-35 (Process-etched)

Bowl, berry, 5" d., clear 8
Bowl, cereal, 6" d., clear 20
Bowl, cereal, 6" d., green 38
Bowl, cereal, 6" d., yellow 45
Butter dish, cov., clear 85
Butter dish, cov., green 145
Butter dish, cov., yellow 148
Coaster-ashtray, clear, 3 3/4" d. 15
Coaster-ashtray, green, 3 3/4" d. 18
Coaster-ashtray, pink, 3 3/4" d. 30
Creamer, plain rim, clear 8
Creamer, plain rim, green 12
Creamer, plain rim, yellow 14
Cup, green 13
Cup & saucer, clear 3
Cup & saucer, yellow 14
Pitcher, 7 1/2" h., 48 oz., pink 150
Plate, sherbet, 6" d., clear 4
Plate, sherbet, 6" d., green 6
Plate, sherbet, 6" d., yellow 8
Plate, salad, 8 1/2" d., clear 8
Plate, salad, 8 1/2" d., pink 10
Plate, salad, 8 1/2" d., yellow 10
Platter, 11 1/2" oval, green 24

Salt & pepper shakers, footed, clear, pr. 39
Sugar bowl, cov., clear 18
Sugar bowl, cov., yellow 40
Sugar bowl, open, clear 8
Sugar bowl, open, green 38
Sugar bowl, open, yellow 11
Tumbler 10
Tumbler, footed, yellow, 3 1/4" h., 4 oz. 20

Florentine No. 2 or Poppy No. 2, Hazel Atlas Glass Co., 1932-35 (Process-etched)

Bowl, 4 1/2" d., berry, clear 12
Bowl, 4 1/2" d., berry, green 18
Bowl, 4 1/2" d., berry, pink 20
Bowl, 4 1/2" d., berry, yellow 25
Bowl, 4 3/4" d., cream soup, plain rim, clear 13
Bowl, 4 3/4" d., cream soup, plain rim, green 18
Bowl, 4 3/4" d., cream soup, plain rim, pink 18
Bowl, 4 3/4" d., cream soup, plain rim, yellow 26
Bowl, 5 1/2" d., clear 20
Bowl, 5 1/2" d., green 38
Bowl, 5 1/2" d., yellow 45
Bowl, 6" d., cereal, clear 20
Bowl, 6" d., cereal, green 38
Bowl, 6" d., cereal, yellow 45
Bowl, 7 1/2" d., shallow, yellow 110
Bowl, 8" d., clear 20
Bowl, 8" d., green 32
Bowl, 8" d., pink 40
Bowl, 8" d., yellow 42
Bowl, 9" oval, cov., vegetable, clear 45
Bowl, 9" oval, cov., vegetable, green 85
Bowl, 9" oval, cov., vegetable, yellow 98
Bowl, 9" d., flat, clear 18
Bowl, 9" d., flat, green 30
Bowl, 9" oval vegetable, clear 25
Bowl, 9" oval vegetable, green 40
Bowl, 9" oval vegetable, yellow 55
Butter dish, cov., clear 85
Butter dish, cov., green 145
Butter dish, cov., yellow 175
Candlesticks, clear, 2 3/4" h., pr. 35
Candlesticks, green, 2 3/4" h., pr. 60
Candlesticks, yellow, 2 3/4" h., pr. 75
Candy dish, cov., clear 95
Candy dish, cov., green 125
Candy dish, cov., pink 160
Candy dish, cov., yellow 195
Coaster, pink, 3 1/4" d. 18
Coaster, clear, 3 1/4" d. 12
Coaster, green, 3 1/4" d. 15
Coaster, yellow, 3 1/4" d. 24
Coaster-ashtray, clear, 3 3/4" d. 15
Coaster-ashtray, green, 3 3/4" d. 18
Coaster-ashtray, yellow, 3 3/4" d. 30
Coaster-ashtray, clear, 5 1/2" d. 18
Coaster-ashtray, green, 5 1/2" d. 20
Coaster-ashtray, yellow, 5 1/2" d. 38
Compote, 3 1/2", ruffled, clear 15
Compote, 3 1/2", ruffled, cobalt blue 75
Compote, 3 1/2", ruffled, green 48
Compote, 3 1/2", ruffled, pink 28
Creamer, clear 8
Creamer, green 12

Yellow Florentine No. 2 Pieces

Creamer, yellow (ILLUS. left with sugar & tumbler) 14
Cup, clear 6
Cup, green 10
Cup, yellow 10
Custard cup, clear 45
Custard cup, green 75
Custard cup, yellow 95
Gravy boat, yellow 75
Gravy boat w/platter, yellow, 11 1/2" oval 120
Pitcher, 6 1/4" h., 24 oz., cone-shaped, yellow 200
Pitcher, 7 1/2" h., 28 oz., cone-shaped, clear 22
Pitcher, 7 1/2" h., 28 oz., cone-shaped, green 40
Pitcher, 7 1/2" h., 28 oz., cone-shaped, ice blue 600
Pitcher, 7 1/2" h., 28 oz., cone-shaped, yellow 45
Pitcher, 7 1/2" h., 48 oz., straight sides, clear 65
Pitcher, 7 1/2" h., 48 oz., straight sides, green 80
Pitcher, 7 1/2" h., 48 oz., straight sides, pink 150
Pitcher, 8 1/4" h., 76 oz., clear 95
Pitcher, 8 1/4" h., 76 oz., green 120
Pitcher, 8 1/4" h., 76 oz., pink 245
Pitcher, 8 1/4" h., 76 oz., yellow 475
Plate, 6" d., sherbet, clear 4
Plate, 6" d., sherbet, green 6
Plate, 6" d., sherbet, yellow 8
Plate, 6 1/4" d., w/indentation, clear 15
Plate, 6 1/4" d., w/indentation, green 25
Plate, 6 1/4" d., w/indentation, yellow 38
Plate, 8 1/2" d., salad, clear 8
Plate, 8 1/2" d., salad, green 12
Plate, 8 1/2" d., salad, yellow 10
Plate, 10" d., dinner, clear 12
Plate, 10" d., dinner, green 20
Plate, 10" d., dinner, yellow 22
Plate, 10 1/4" d., grill, clear 8
Plate, 10 1/4" d., grill, green 16
Plate, 10 1/4" d., grill, yellow 18
Plate, 10 1/4" d., w/cup ring, grill, green 48
Platter, 11" oval, clear 12
Platter, 11" oval, green 24
Platter, 11" oval, pink 30
Platter, 11" oval, yellow 28
Platter, 11 1/2", for gravy boat, yellow 60
Relish dish, three-part or plain, clear, 10" 18
Relish dish, three-part or plain, green, 10" 26
Relish dish, three-part or plain, pink, 10" 34
Relish dish, three-part or plain, yellow, 10" 36
Salt & pepper shakers, clear, pr. 39
Salt & pepper shakers, green, pr. 45
Salt & pepper shakers, yellow, pr. 60

Iris or Iris & Herringbone, Jeannette Glass Co., 1928-32 (Press-mold)

Iris & Herringbone Pieces

Sherbet, footed, clear, 4" h............................... 28
Sugar bowl, cov., footed, amber iridescent........ 35
Sugar bowl, cov., footed, clear............................ 28
Sugar bowl, open, footed, amber iridescent...... 12
Sugar bowl, open, footed, clear.......................... 15
Tumbler, clear, 4" h. 150
Tumbler, footed, amber iridescent, 6" h.............. 20
Tumbler, footed, clear, 6" h................................. 24
Tumbler, footed, clear, 6 1/2" h. 38
Vase, 9" h., amber iridescent.............................. 26
Vase, 9" h., clear... 30
Vase, 9" h., green... 185
Vase, 9" h., pink.. 185

Mayfair or Open Rose, Hocking Glass Co., 1931-37 (Process-etched)

Bowl, 5", cream soup, pink.................................. 60
Bowl, 5", cream soup, pink frosted..................... 30
Bowl, 5 1/2", cereal, blue.................................... 60
Bowl, 5 1/2", cereal, green.................................. 95
Bowl, 5 1/2", cereal, pink.................................... 30
Bowl, 5 1/2", cereal, pink frosted....................... 15
Bowl, 5 1/2", cereal, yellow................................. 95

Blue Mayfair 7" Vegetable Bowl

Bowl, 7", vegetable, blue (ILLUS.) 62
Bowl, 7", vegetable, green................................... 145
Bowl, 7", vegetable, pink 38
Bowl, 7", vegetable, pink frosted........................ 18
Bowl, 7", vegetable, yellow................................. 160
Bowl, 9" d., 3 1/8" h., three-footed console, green.. 5,800
Bowl, 9" d., 3 1/8" h., three-footed console, pink... 5,950
Bowl, 9 1/2" oval vegetable, blue 80
Bowl, 9 1/2" oval vegetable, green...................... 135
Bowl, 9 1/2" oval vegetable, pink 38
Bowl, 9 1/2" oval vegetable, yellow..................... 148
Bowl, 10", cov. vegetable, blue........................... 175
Bowl, 10", cov. vegetable, pink........................... 140
Bowl, 10", cov. vegetable, yellow....................... 1,100
Bowl, 10", open vegetable, blue 85
Bowl, 10", open vegetable, pink.......................... 38
Bowl, 10", open vegetable, pink frosted............. 19
Bowl, 10", open vegetable, yellow 148
Bowl, 11 3/4" d., low, blue 95
Bowl, 11 3/4" d., low, green................................. 60
Bowl, 11 3/4" d., low, pink................................... 65
Bowl, 11 3/4" d., low, yellow............................... 260
Bowl, 12" d., fruit, deep, scalloped, blue........... 125
Bowl, 12" d., fruit, deep, scalloped, green.......... 65
Bowl, 12" d., fruit, deep, scalloped, pink 75
Bowl, 12" d., fruit, deep, scalloped, pink frosted... 38

Bowl, 12" d., fruit, deep, scalloped, yellow 275
Butter dish, cov., blue 345
Butter dish, cov., green....................................... 1,450
Butter dish, cov., pink.. 95
Butter dish, cov., pink frosted............................. 48
Butter dish, cov., yellow...................................... 1,450
Cake plate, footed, blue, 10"............................... 75
Cake plate, footed, green, 10"............................. 195
Cake plate, footed, pink, 10"............................... 40
Cake plate, handled, blue, 12" 85
Cake plate, handled, green, 12".......................... 65
Cake plate, handled, pink, 12"............................ 60
Cake plate, handled, pink frosted, 12" 30
Candy jar, cov., blue 345
Candy jar, cov., green.. 650
Candy jar, cov., pink 65
Candy jar, cov., pink frosted............................... 35
Candy jar, cov., yellow... 550
Celery dish, green, 10" l...................................... 150
Celery dish, blue, 10" l. 75
Celery dish, pink, 10" l. 55
Celery dish, yellow, 10" l. 150
Celery dish, two-part, green, 9" l......................... 225
Celery dish, two-part, yellow, 9" l. 225
Celery dish, two-part, blue, 10" l......................... 80
Celery dish, two-part, clear, 10" l. 65
Celery dish, two-part, pink, 10" l. 275
Cookie jar, cov., blue 325
Cookie jar, cov., green 650
Cookie jar, cov., pink 65
Cookie jar, cov., pink frosted.............................. 35
Cookie jar, cov., yellow.. 950
Creamer, footed, blue 95
Creamer, footed, green 240
Creamer, footed, pink.. 40
Creamer, footed, pink frosted 20
Creamer, footed, yellow 245
Cup, blue 60
Cup, green.. 165
Cup, pink 24
Cup, yellow 175
Decanter, no stopper, pink, 10" h., 32 oz. 95
Decanter w/stopper, pink, 10" h., 32 oz. 235
Goblet, cordial, green, 3 3/4" h., 1 oz................. 1,000
Goblet, cordial, pink, 3 3/4" h., 1 oz............... 1,250
Goblet, pink, 4" h., 2 1/2 oz................................ 95
Goblet, cocktail, green, 4" h., 3 oz..................... 425
Goblet, cocktail, pink, 4" h., 3 oz........................ 125
Goblet, wine, green, 4 1/2" h., 3 oz..................... 450
Goblet, wine, pink, 4 1/2" h., 3 oz. 125
Goblet, claret, green, 5 1/4" h., 4 1/2 oz. 1,100
Goblet, claret, pink, 5 1/4" h., 4 1/2 oz. 1,200
Goblet, water, green, 5 3/4" h., 9 oz................... 500
Goblet, water, pink, 5 3/4" h., 9 oz...................... 85
Goblet, water, thin, blue, 7 1/4" h., 9 oz............. 245
Goblet, water, thin, pink, 7 1/4" h., 9 oz............. 275
Pitcher, juice, 6" h., 37 oz., blue......................... 175
Pitcher, juice, 6" h., 37 oz., clear 20
Pitcher, juice, 6" h., 37 oz., green....................... 575
Pitcher, juice, 6" h., 37 oz., pink......................... 70
Pitcher, juice, 6" h., 37 oz., yellow...................... 600
Pitcher, 8" h., 60 oz., jug-type, blue................... 215
Pitcher, 8" h., 60 oz., jug-type, green................. 575
Pitcher, 8" h., 60 oz., jug-type, pink................... 80
Pitcher, 8" h., 60 oz., jug-type, yellow................ 575
Pitcher, 8 1/2" h., 80 oz., jug-type, blue............. 295
Pitcher, 8 1/2" h., 80 oz., jug-type, green........... 775
Pitcher, 8 1/2" h., 80 oz., jug-type, pink............. 125
Pitcher, 8 1/2" h., 80 oz., jug-type, yellow 775

Plate (or saucer), 5 3/4", blue.............................. 24
Plate (or saucer), 5 3/4", green........................... 95
Plate (or saucer), 5 3/4", pink............................. 25
Plate (or saucer), 5 3/4", yellow.......................... 95
Plate, 6 1/2" d., sherbet, off-center indenta-
tion, blue... 45
Plate, 6 1/2" d., sherbet, off-center indenta-
tion, green... 145
Plate, 6 1/2" d., sherbet, off-center indenta-
tion, pink.. 35
Plate, 6 1/2" d., sherbet, pink............................. 18
Plate, 8 1/2", luncheon, blue............................... 60
Plate, 8 1/2", luncheon, green............................. 95
Plate, 8 1/2", luncheon, pink............................... 35
Plate, 8 1/2", luncheon, yellow............................ 95
Plate, 9 1/2", dinner, blue.................................... 95
Plate, 9 1/2", dinner, green................................ 175
Plate, 9 1/2", dinner, pink.................................... 65
Plate, 9 1/2", dinner, yellow............................... 175
Plate, 9 1/2", grill, blue.. 65
Plate, 9 1/2", grill, green...................................... 95
Plate, 9 1/2", grill, pink... 48
Plate, 9 1/2", grill, yellow...................................... 95
Plate, 11 1/2", grill, handled, yellow.................. 125
Platter, 12" oval, open handles, blue.................. 80
Platter, 12" oval, open handles, clear................. 18
Platter, 12" oval, open handles, green............. 185
Platter, 12" oval, open handles, pink.................. 40
Platter, 12" oval, open handles, yellow............ 185
Platter, 12 1/2" oval, closed handles,
green.. 275
Platter, 12 1/2" oval, closed handles, yellow..... 275
Relish, green, 8 3/8"... 350
Relish, pink, 8 3/8".. 275
Relish, yellow, 8 3/8".. 350
Relish, four-part, blue, 8 3/8".............................. 80
Relish, four-part, green, 8 3/8".......................... 185
Relish, four-part, pink, 8 3/8".............................. 40
Relish, four-part, pink frosted, 8 3/8"................. 20
Relish, four-part, yellow, 8 3/8".......................... 185
Salt & pepper shakers, flat, blue, pr............... 345
Salt & pepper shakers, flat, green, pr.......... 1,200
Salt & pepper shakers, flat, pink frosted,
pr... 38
Salt & pepper shakers, flat, pink, pr................. 75
Salt & pepper shakers, flat, yellow, pr........... 950
Salt & pepper shakers, footed, pink, pr....... 9,500
Sandwich server w/center handle, blue,
12"... 95
Sandwich server w/center handle, green,
12"... 60
Sandwich server w/center handle, pink,
12"... 65
Sandwich server w/center handle, pink
frosted, 12"... 35
Sandwich server w/center handle, yellow,
12"... 120
Saucer w/cup ring, pink...................................... 35
Saucer w/cup ring, yellow................................. 145
Sherbet, flat, blue, 2 1/4" h............................... 175
Sherbet, flat, pink, 2 1/4" h............................... 200
Sherbet, footed, pink, 3" h.................................. 24
Sherbet, footed, blue, 4 3/4" h............................ 95
Sherbet, footed, green, 4 3/4" h....................... 175
Sherbet, footed, pink, 4 3/4" h............................ 95
Sherbet, footed, yellow, 4 3/4" h....................... 185
Sugar bowl, cov., footed, green..................... 1,600
Sugar bowl, cov., footed, pink....................... 1,850
Sugar bowl, cov., footed, yellow................... 1,450
Sugar bowl, open, footed, blue........................... 95
Sugar bowl, open, footed, green...................... 240
Sugar bowl, open, footed, pink........................... 40

Sugar bowl, open, footed, pink frosted.............. 20
Sugar bowl, open, footed, yellow..................... 245
Tumbler, whiskey, pink, 2 1/4" h., 1 1/2 oz......... 85
Tumbler, juice, footed, pink, 3 1/4" h., 3 oz........ 95
Tumbler, juice, blue, 3 1/2" h., 5 oz.................. 145
Tumbler, juice, pink, 3 1/2" h., 5 oz................... 60
Tumbler, water, blue, 4 1/4" h., 9 oz................. 135
Tumbler, water, pink, 4 1/4" h., 9 oz................... 50
Tumbler, footed, blue, 5 1/4" h., 10 oz............. 150
Tumbler, footed, pink, 5 1/4" h., 10 oz............... 48
Tumbler, footed, yellow, 5 1/4"h., 10 oz........... 185
Tumbler, water, blue, 4 3/4" h., 11 oz.............. 165
Tumbler, water, green, 4 3/4" h., 11 oz............ 235
Tumbler, water, pink, 4 3/4" h., 11 oz.............. 230
Tumbler, water, yellow, 4 3/4" h., 11 oz........... 245
Tumbler, iced tea, blue, 5 1/4" h., 13 1/2 oz.... 250
Tumbler, iced tea, pink, 5 1/4" h., 13 1/2 oz...... 75
Tumbler, iced tea, footed, blue 6 1/2" h., 15
oz.. 300
Tumbler, iced tea, footed, green, 6 1/2" h.,
15 oz... 260
Tumbler, iced tea, footed, pink, 6 1/2" h., 15
oz.. 60
Vase, 5 1/2" x 8 1/2", sweet pea, hat-
shaped, blue... 160
Vase, 5 1/2" x 8 1/2", sweet pea, hat-
shaped, green... 400
Vase, 5 1/2" x 8 1/2", sweet pea, hat-
shaped, pink... 195

Miss America, Hocking Glass Co., 1935-38 (Press-mold)

Bowl, 4 1/2" d., berry, green................................ 16
Bowl, 6 1/4" d., berry, clear................................. 12
Bowl, 6 1/4" d., berry, green................................ 24
Bowl, 6 1/4" d., berry, pink................................. 35
Bowl, 8" d., fruit, curved in at top, clear.............. 50
Bowl, 8" d., fruit, curved in at top, pink.............. 125
Bowl, 8" d., fruit, curved in at top, red............... 545
Bowl, 8 3/4" d., fruit, deep, clear......................... 45
Bowl, 8 3/4" d., fruit, deep, pink.......................... 95
Bowl, 10" oval vegetable, clear........................... 16
Bowl, 10" oval vegetable, pink............................ 60
Butter dish, cov., clear...................................... 250
Butter dish, cov., pink....................................... 600
Cake plate, footed, clear, 12" d.......................... 35
Cake plate, footed, pink, 12" d........................... 75
Candy jar, cov., clear, 11 1/2" h.......................... 85
Candy jar, cov., pink, 11 1/2" h......................... 185
Celery tray, clear, 10 1/2" oblong....................... 18
Celery tray, pink, 10 1/2" oblong........................ 48
Coaster, clear, 5 3/4" d....................................... 18
Coaster, pink, 5 3/4" d.. 45
Compote, 5" d., clear.. 18
Compote 5" d., pink.. 48
Creamer, footed, clear.. 12
Creamer, footed, pink... 28
Creamer, footed, red... 250
Cup, clear.. 12
Cup, green... 18
Cup, pink... 35
Goblet, wine, clear, 3 3/4" h., 3 oz...................... 26
Goblet, wine, pink, 3 3/4" h., 3 oz..................... 130
Goblet, wine, red, 3 3/4" h., 3 oz....................... 350
Goblet, juice, clear, 4 3/4" h., 5 oz..................... 28
Goblet, juice, pink, 4 3/4" h., 5 oz..................... 135
Goblet, juice, red, 4 3/4" h., 5 oz....................... 350
Goblet, water, clear, 5 1/2" h., 10 oz.................. 24

Goblet, water, pink, 5 1/2" h., 10 oz................... 75
Goblet, water, red, 5 1/2" h., 10 oz. 325
Pitcher, 8" h., 65 oz., clear 75
Pitcher, 8" h., 65 oz., pink 195
Pitcher w/ice lip, 8 1/2" h., 65 oz., clear............ 85
Pitcher w/ice lip, 8 1/2" h., 65 oz., pink 275
Plate, 5 3/4" d., sherbet, clear............................. 8
Plate, 5 3/4" d., sherbet, ice blue..................... 48
Plate, 5 3/4" d., sherbet, pink 24
Plate, 6 3/4" d., green 12
Plate, 8 1/2" d., salad, clear............................. 10
Plate, 8 1/2" d., salad, green 12
Plate, 8 1/2" d., salad, pink 40
Plate, 8 1/2" d., salad, red 195
Plate, 10 1/4" d., dinner, clear........................... 18
Plate, 10 1/4" d., dinner, ice blue 150
Plate, 10 1/4" d., dinner, pink 48
Plate, 10 1/4" d., grill, clear............................. 12
Plate, 10 1/4" d., grill, pink 38
Platter, 12 1/4" oval, clear............................... 18
Platter, 12 1/4" oval, pink................................ 75
Relish, four-part, clear, 8 3/4" d. 14
Relish, four-part, pink, 8 3/4" d. 50
Relish, divided, clear, 11 3/4" d. 40
Relish, divided, pink, 11 3/4" d. 4,800
Salt & pepper shakers, clear, pr. 38
Salt & pepper shakers, green, pr...................... 450
Salt & pepper shakers, pink, pr......................... 85
Saucer, clear... 5
Saucer, pink... 12
Sherbet, clear... 10
Sherbet, ice blue 48
Sherbet, pink.. 30
Sugar bowl, open, footed, clear 12
Sugar bowl, open, footed, pink 28
Sugar bowl, open, footed, red 250
Tumbler, juice, clear, 4" h., 5 oz....................... 24
Tumbler, juice, ice blue, 4" h., 5 oz.................. 145
Tumbler, juice, pink, 4" h., 5 oz........................ 55
Tumbler, water, clear, 4 1/2" h., 10 oz. 18
Tumbler, water, green, 4 1/2" h., 10 oz............... 28
Tumbler, water, pink, 4 1/2" h., 10 oz................. 75
Tumbler, iced tea, clear, 6 3/4" h., 14 oz. 35
Tumbler, iced tea, pink, 6 3/4" h., 14 oz. 145

Moonstone, Anchor Hocking Glass Corp., 1941-46 (Press-mold)

Berry set, master bowl & 4 sauce dishes, 5
  pcs.. 28
Berry set, master bowl & 6 sauce dishes, 7
  pcs.. 38
Bonbon, heart-shaped, w/handle, 6 1/2" w. 11
Bowl, 5 1/2" d., berry 15
Cigarette box, cov., rectangular....................... 24
Creamer, footed 8
Cup 8
Cup & saucer 14
Goblet, 10 oz. 20
Puff box, cov., 4 3/4" d 28
Relish bowl, divided, 7 3/4" d............................ 12
Sugar bowl, footed 8

Moroccan Amethyst, Hazel Ware, Division of Continental Can, 1960s (Early 1960s - not true Depression)

Ashtray, 3 3/4" triangle 8

Ashtray, 5"... 10
Ashtray, 6" triangle... 12
Ashtray, 6 7/8" triangle.................................... 12
Ashtray, 6 7/8" triangle w/metal base 18
Ashtray, 8" sq.. 12
Bowl, 4 3/4" w., octagonal, fruit........................ 18
Bowl, 5 3/4" sq., cereal, deep 18
Bowl, 6" d.. 16
Bowl, 6" d., w/metal center handle..................... 24
Bowl, 6" sq., w/metal center handle................... 24
Bowl, 7 3/4" oval 28
Bowl, 7 3/4" oval w/center handle...................... 30
Bowl, 7 3/4" rectangle 18
Bowl, 9 1/2" oval, low 18
Bowl, 9 1/2" oval, w/metal center handle............ 20
Bowl, 10 3/4" 32
Candy jar, cov., short....................................... 35
Candy jar, cov., tall... 40
Celery dish, 9 1/2".. 14
Chip & dip set, w/metal holder (5 3/4" &
  10 3/4" bowls) 65
Cocktail set: cocktail stirrer w/pouring lip,
  stirring rod & two 2 1/2" h. 4 oz. tumblers;
  w/original box, the set................................... 37
Cocktail shaker w/chrome lid, 32 oz................. 60
Cocktail stirrer, w/pouring lip, 6 1/4" h., 16
  oz. 25
Compote 20
Creamer 6
Cup 6
Cup & saucer 8
Goblet, wine, 4" h., 4 1/2 oz. 8
Goblet, juice, 4 3/8" h., 5 1/2 oz. 10
Goblet, water, 5 1/2" h., 10 oz. 14
Ice bucket 40
Plate, 5 3/4" w., octagonal 8
Plate, 7 1/4" w., salad 12
Plate, 12" w., sandwich 20
Relish, 8".. 9
Relish, 9 1/2" 10
Sandwich server, w/metal center handle,
  12"... 24
Saucer 3
Sherbet, footed, 4 1/4" h.................................. 10
Snack set, four seashell-shaped plates,
  w/box.. 48
Tidbit server, two-tier 24
Tidbit server, three-tier.................................... 38
Tumbler, juice, 2 1/2" h., 4 oz. 10
Tumbler, Old Fashioned, 3 1/4" h., 8 oz............. 12
Tumbler, water, crinkled bottom, 4 1/4" h.,
  11 oz.. 12
Tumbler, water, 4 5/8" h., 11 oz. 12
Tumbler, iced tea, 6 1/2" h., 16 oz. 14
Vase, 8 1/2" h., ruffled..................................... 42

Number 612 or Horseshoe, Indiana Glass Co., 1930-33 (Process-etched)

Bowl, 4 1/2" d., berry, green 28
Bowl, 4 1/2" d., berry, yellow............................ 26
Bowl, 6 1/2" d., cereal, green............................ 32
Bowl, 6 1/2" d., cereal, yellow........................... 34
Bowl, 7 1/2" d., salad, green 28
Bowl, 7 1/2" d., salad, yellow............................ 28
Bowl, 8 1/2" d., vegetable, green 38
Bowl, 8 1/2" d., vegetable, yellow...................... 38
Bowl, 9 1/2" d., large berry, green 48

Bowl, 9 1/2" d., large berry, yellow...................... 48
Bowl, 10 1/2" oval vegetable, green 35
Bowl, 10 1/2" oval vegetable, yellow 35
Butter dish, cov., green...................................... 850
Candy in metal holder, motif on lid, green 250
Candy in metal holder, motif on lid, pink 175
Cup, green... 12
Cup, yellow.. 14
Cup & saucer, green... 13
Cup & saucer, yellow 14
Pitcher, 8 1/2" h., 64 oz., green 350
Pitcher, 8 1/2" h., 64 oz., yellow 395
Plate, 6" d., sherbet, green 10
Plate, 6" d., sherbet, yellow 10
Plate, 8 3/8" d., salad, green 14
Plate, 8 3/8" d., salad, yellow 14
Plate, 9 3/8" d., luncheon, green........................ 15
Plate, 9 3/8" d., luncheon, yellow....................... 16
Plate, 10 3/8" d., dinner, green........................... 19
Plate, 10 3/8" d., dinner, yellow.......................... 18
Plate, 10 3/8" d., grill, green 125
Plate, 10 3/8" d., grill, yellow............................ 160
Plate, 11 1/2" d., sandwich, green...................... 25
Plate, 11 1/2" d., sandwich, yellow 30
Platter, 10 3/4" oval, green................................. 32
Platter, 10 3/4" oval, yellow................................ 38
Relish, three-part, footed, green......................... 40
Saucer, green 6
Saucer, yellow 8
Sherbet, green.. 18
Sherbet, yellow... 18
Sugar bowl, open, footed, green......................... 20
Sugar bowl, open, footed, yellow........................ 24
Tumbler, footed, yellow, 9 oz............................... 38
Tumbler, green, 4 1/4" h., 9 oz............................. 32
Tumbler, footed, green, 12 oz. 185
Tumbler, footed, yellow, 12 oz. 195
Tumbler, green, 4 3/4" h., 12 oz........................ 185

Royal Lace, Hazel Atlas Glass Co., 1934-41 (Process-etched)

Bowl, 4 3/4" d., cream soup, blue...................... 48
Bowl, 4 3/4" d., cream soup, clear...................... 14
Bowl, 4 3/4" d., cream soup, green..................... 38
Bowl, 4 3/4" d., cream soup, pink....................... 28
Bowl, 5" d., berry, blue.. 85
Bowl, 5" d., berry, clear....................................... 28
Bowl, 5" d., berry, green 65
Bowl, 5" d., berry, pink... 45
Bowl, 10" d., berry, blue....................................... 85
Bowl, 10" d., berry, clear...................................... 24
Bowl, 10" d., berry, green 48
Bowl, 10" d., berry, pink.. 42
Bowl, 10" d., three-footed, rolled edge, blue..... 850
Bowl, 10" d., three-footed, rolled edge,
clear 295
Bowl, 10" d., three-footed, rolled edge,
green.. 350
Bowl, 10" d., three-footed, rolled edge, pink..... 195
Bowl, 10" d., three-footed, ruffled edge,
blue 950
Bowl, 10" d., three-footed, ruffled edge,
clear 85
Bowl, 10" d., three-footed, ruffled edge,
green.. 225
Bowl, 10" d., three-footed, ruffled edge,
pink.. 195
Bowl, 10" d., three-footed, straight edge,
blue 85

Bowl, 10" d., three-footed, straight edge,
clear.. 35
Bowl, 10" d., three-footed, straight edge,
green... 75
Bowl, 10" d., three-footed, straight edge,
pink... 60
Bowl, 11" oval vegetable, blue 85
Bowl, 11" oval vegetable, clear 35
Bowl, 11" oval vegetable, green........................... 75
Bowl, 11" oval vegetable, pink............................. 60
Butter dish, cov., blue 750
Butter dish, cov., clear 95
Butter dish, cov., green...................................... 350
Butter dish, cov., pink... 195
Candlesticks, rolled edge, blue, pr. 550
Candlesticks, rolled edge, clear, pr. 95
Candlesticks, rolled edge, green, pr. 195
Candlesticks, rolled edge, pink, pr.................... 175
Candlesticks, ruffled edge, blue, pr. 550
Candlesticks, ruffled edge, clear, pr. 85
Candlesticks, ruffled edge, green, pr. 165
Candlesticks, ruffled edge, pink, pr. 145
Candlesticks, straight edge, blue, pr. 175
Candlesticks, straight edge, clear, pr. 75
Candlesticks, straight edge, green, pr. 95
Candlesticks, straight edge, pink, pr. 85
Cookie jar, cov., amethyst 100
Cookie jar, cov., blue 395
Cookie jar, cov., clear 38
Cookie jar, cov., green 110
Cookie jar, cov., pink 75
Creamer, footed, blue 60
Creamer, footed, clear 14
Creamer, footed, green... 35
Creamer, footed, pink.. 24
Cup, blue 40
Cup, clear 8
Cup, green... 28
Cup, pink 20
Nut bowl, blue 1,450
Nut bowl, clear 195
Nut bowl, green 395
Nut bowl, pink 350
Pitcher, 48 oz., straight sides, blue................... 195
Pitcher, 48 oz., straight sides, clear 85
Pitcher, 48 oz., straight sides, green................. 135
Pitcher, 48 oz., straight sides, pink................... 110
Pitcher, 8" h., 64 oz., without ice lip, blue......... 295
Pitcher, 8" h., 64 oz., without ice lip, clear.......... 65
Pitcher, 8" h., 64 oz., without ice lip, green....... 165
Pitcher, 8" h., 64 oz., without ice lip, pink......... 125
Pitcher, 8" h., 68 oz., w/ice lip, blue................. 350
Pitcher, 8" h., 68 oz., w/ice lip, clear 85
Pitcher, 8" h., 68 oz., w/ice lip, pink................. 120
Pitcher, 8" h., 86 oz., without ice lip, clear.......... 85
Pitcher, 8" h., 86 oz., without ice lip, green....... 250
Pitcher, 8" h., 86 oz., without ice lip, pink......... 165
Pitcher, 8 1/2" h., 96 oz., w/ice lip, blue........... 525
Pitcher, 8 1/2" h., 96 oz., w/ice lip, clear............ 95
Pitcher, 8 1/2" h., 96 oz., w/ice lip, green 195
Pitcher, 8 1/2" h., 96 oz., w/ice lip, pink 175
Plate, 6" d., sherbet, blue 16
Plate, 6" d., sherbet, clear 6
Plate, 6" d., sherbet, green.................................. 14
Plate, 6" d., sherbet, pink.................................... 10
Plate, 8 1/2" d., luncheon, blue 45

Plate, 8 1/2" d., luncheon, clear 12

Green Royal Lace Luncheon Plate

Plate, 8 1/2" d., luncheon, green (ILLUS.) 24
Plate, 8 1/2" d., luncheon, pink 28
Plate, 9 7/8" d., dinner, blue 45
Plate, 9 7/8" d., dinner, clear 18
Plate, 9 7/8" d., dinner, green.............................. 32
Plate, 9 7/8" d., dinner, pink................................. 32
Plate, 9 7/8" d., grill, blue 38
Plate, 9 7/8" d., grill, clear 14
Plate, 9 7/8" d., grill, green.................................. 28
Plate, 9 7/8" d., grill, pink..................................... 24
Platter, 13" oval, blue 65
Platter, 13" oval, clear 22
Platter, 13" oval, green... 48
Platter, 13" oval, pink.. 45
Salt & pepper shakers, blue, pr. 320
Salt & pepper shakers, clear, pr. 60
Salt & pepper shakers, green, pr...................... 145
Salt & pepper shakers, pink, pr......................... 95
Saucer, blue.. 14
Saucer, clear.. 5
Saucer, green.. 10
Saucer, pink.. 8
Sherbet, footed, blue 54
Sherbet, footed, clear 16
Sherbet, footed, green 35
Sherbet, footed, pink 24
Sherbet in metal holder, amethyst 48
Sherbet in metal holder, blue.............................. 38
Sherbet in metal holder, clear............................... 5
Sugar bowl, cov., blue 240
Sugar bowl, cov., clear 35
Sugar bowl, cov., green 110
Sugar bowl, cov., pink 85
Sugar bowl, open, blue.. 60
Sugar bowl, open, clear 14

Sugar bowl, open, green.. 35
Sugar bowl, open, pink... 24
Toddy or cider set: cookie jar w/metal lid, 6
   roly-poly tumblers & metal tray; ame-
   thyst, 8 pcs. 350
Toddy or cider set: cookie jar w/metal lid, 8
   roly-poly tumblers, metal tray & ladle;
   blue, 11 pcs. 395
Tumbler, blue, 3 1/2" h., 5 oz. 62
Tumbler, clear, 3 1/2" h., 5 oz. 20
Tumbler, green, 3 1/2" h., 5 oz. 42
Tumbler, pink, 3 1/2" h., 5 oz............................... 40
Tumbler, blue, 4 1/8" h., 9 oz. 50
Tumbler, clear, 4 1/8" h., 9 oz. 16
Tumbler, green, 4 1/8" h., 9 oz. 38
Tumbler, pink, 4 1/8" h., 9 oz. 32
Tumbler, blue, 4 7/8" h., 10 oz. 195
Tumbler, clear, 4 7/8" h., 10 oz. 45
Tumbler, green, 4 7/8" h., 10 oz. 120
Tumbler, pink, 4 7/8" h., 10 oz. 110
Tumbler, blue, 5 3/8" h., 12 oz. 145
Tumbler, clear, 5 3/8" h., 12 oz. 45
Tumbler, green, 5 3/8" h., 12 oz. 85
Tumbler, pink, 5 3/8" h., 12 oz. 95

Sierra or Pinwheel, Jeannette Glass Co., 1931-33 (Press-mold)

Bowl, 5 1/2" d., cereal, green................................ 22
Bowl, 5 1/2" d., cereal, pink.................................. 18
Bowl, 8 1/2" d., berry, green 38
Bowl, 8 1/2" d., berry, pink 36
Bowl, 9 1/4" oval vegetable, green 160
Bowl, 9 1/4" oval vegetable, pink 75
Butter dish, cov., green (ILLUS. left with
   cup and saucer, bottom of page)..................... 85
Butter dish, cov., pink 75
Creamer, green 24
Creamer, pink 22
Cup, green... 14
Cup, pink (ILLUS. with butter dish) 12
Pitcher, 6 1/2" h., 32 oz., green.......................... 145
Pitcher, 6 1/2" h., 32 oz., pink............................ 118
Plate, 9" d., dinner, green 28
Plate, 9" d., dinner, pink 26
Platter, 11" oval, pink 55
Platter, 11" oval, green 65
Salt & pepper shakers, green, pr. 60
Salt & pepper shakers, pink, pr. 60
Salt & Pepper shakers, green, pr. 60

Sierra Butter Dish & Cup & Saucer

Saucer, green 9
Saucer, pink (ILLUS. with butter dish) 8
Serving tray, two-handled, green 24
Serving tray, two-handled, pink 22
Sugar bowl, cov., green 48
Sugar bowl, cov., pink 42
Tumbler, footed, green, 4 1/2" h., 9 oz 88
Tumbler, footed, pink, 4 1/2" h., 9 oz. 68

Windsor Diamond or Windsor, Jeannette Glass Co., 1936-46 (Press-mold)

Ashtray, clear, 5 3/4" d. 12
Ashtray, Delphite, 5 3/4" d. 55
Ashtray, green, 5 3/4" d. 45
Ashtray, pink, 5 3/4" d. 40
Ashtray w/patterned rim, pink.......................... 325
Bowl, 4 3/4" d., berry, clear 4
Bowl, 4 3/4" d., berry, green............................... 12
Bowl, 4 3/4" d., berry, pink.................................. 13
Bowl, 5" d., cream soup, clear 6
Bowl, 5" d., cream soup, green............................ 30
Bowl, 5" d., cream soup, pink.............................. 26
Bowl, 5" d., pointed edge, clear............................ 5
Bowl, 5" d., pointed edge, pink 40
Bowl, 5 1/8" or 5 3/8" d., cereal, clear 8
Bowl, 5 1/8" or 5 3/8" d., cereal, green................ 35
Bowl, 5 1/8" or 5 3/8" d., cereal, pink.................. 30
Bowl, 7" d., three-footed, clear........................... 10
Bowl, 7" d., three-footed, pink............................ 38
Bowl, 8" d., pointed edge, clear.......................... 16
Bowl, 8" d., pointed edge, pink 95
Bowl, 8" d., two-handled, clear 8
Bowl, 8" d., two-handled, green........................... 25
Bowl, 8" d., two-handled, pink............................. 22
Bowl, 8 1/2" d., berry, clear 8
Bowl, 8 1/2" d., berry, green................................ 26
Bowl, 8 1/2" d., berry, pink.................................. 24
Bowl, 9 1/2" oval vegetable, clear 8
Bowl, 9 1/2" oval vegetable, green....................... 30
Bowl, 9 1/2" oval vegetable, pink 26
Bowl, 10 1/2" d., pointed edge, clear.................. 30
Bowl, 10 1/2" d., pointed edge, pink 195
Bowl, 10 1/2" d., salad, clear.............................. 18
Bowl, 7 x 11 3/4" boat shape, clear 20
Bowl, 7 x 11 3/4" boat shape, green.................... 45
Bowl, 7 x 11 3/4" boat shape, pink...................... 42
Bowl, 12 1/2" d., fruit, clear................................ 28
Bowl, 12 1/2" d., fruit, pink............................... 125
Butter dish, cov., clear 30
Butter dish, cov., green...................................... 98
Butter dish, cov., pink... 65
Cake plate, footed, clear, 10 3/4" d.................... 10
Cake plate, footed, green, 10 3/4" d. 30
Cake plate, footed, pink, 10 3/4" d...................... 28
Candlesticks, clear, 3" h., pr. 24
Candlesticks, pink, 3" h., pr............................... 95
Candy jar, cov., clear 28
Coaster, clear, 3 1/4" d. 5
Coaster, green, 3 1/4" d.. 20
Coaster, pink, 3 1/4" d... 18
Creamer, flat, blue 65
Creamer, flat, clear 6
Creamer, flat, green.. 16
Creamer, flat, pink.. 14
Creamer, footed, clear.. 8
Cup, clear 4
Cup, green.. 12
Cup, pink... 10
Pitcher, 4 1/2" h., 16 oz., clear 26
Pitcher, 4 1/2" h., 16 oz., pink........................... 145

Pitcher, 6 3/4" h., 52 oz., clear 18
Pitcher, 6 3/4" h., 52 oz., green.......................... 75
Pitcher, 6 3/4" h., 52 oz., pink............................ 35
Pitcher, 6 3/4" h., 52 oz., red........................... 475
Plate, 6" d., sherbet, clear 3
Plate, 6" d., sherbet, green 8
Plate, 6" d., sherbet, pink..................................... 6
Plate, 7" d., salad, clear....................................... 4
Plate, 7" d., salad, green...................................... 24
Plate, 7" d., salad, pink.. 20
Plate, 9" d., dinner, blue...................................... 75
Plate, 9" d., dinner, clear....................................... 8
Plate, 9" d., dinner, green.................................... 35
Plate, 9" d., dinner, pink....................................... 30
Plate, 10 1/4", sandwich, handled, clear 8
Plate, 10 1/4", sandwich, handled, green............. 20
Plate, 10 1/4", sandwich, handled, pink............... 18
Plate, 13 5/8" d., chop, clear 14
Plate, 13 5/8" d., chop, green.............................. 42
Plate, 13 5/8" d., chop, pink................................ 40
Platter, 11 1/2" oval, clear 10
Platter, 11 1/2" oval, green.................................. 30
Platter, 11 1/2" oval, pink.................................... 26
Powder jar, cov., clear... 24
Powder jar, cov., pink.. 295
Relish, divided, clear, 11 1/2" 15
Relish, divided, pink, 11 1/2"............................. 325
Salt & pepper shakers, clear, pr. 18
Salt & pepper shakers, green, pr. 60
Salt & pepper shakers, pink, pr. 50
Saucer, clear... 2
Saucer, green.. 8
Saucer, pink.. 6
Sherbet, footed, clear... 4
Sherbet, footed, green 18
Sherbet, footed, pink... 16
Sugar bowl, cov., flat, clear 12
Sugar bowl, cov., flat, green............................... 45
Sugar bowl, cov., flat, pink.................................. 40
Sugar bowl, cov., footed, clear 14
Sugar bowl, cov., no lip, pink 145
Sugar bowl, open, clear.. 6
Sugar bowl, open, green...................................... 16
Sugar bowl, open, pink.. 14
Tray, pink, 8 1/2 x 9 3/4", without handles........... 98
Tray, clear, 4" sq., w/handles 5
Tray, clear, 4" sq., without handles 10
Tray, green, 4" sq., w/handles 12
Tray, pink, 4" sq., w/handles 10
Tray, pink, 4" sq., without handles 50
Tray, clear, 4 1/8 x 9", w/handles 4
Tray, clear, 4 1/8 x 9", without handles 12
Tray, green, 4 1/8 x 9", w/handles....................... 16
Tray, pink, 4 1/8 x 9", w/handles.......................... 14
Tray, pink, 4 1/8 x 9", without handles 60
Tray, clear, 8 1/2 x 9 3/4", w/handles.................... 8
Tray, clear, 8 1/2 x 9 3/4", without handles......... 14
Tray, green, 8 1/2 x 9 3/4", w/handles................. 36
Tray, pink, 8 1/2 x 9 3/4", w/handles................... 28
Tumbler, clear, 3 1/4" h., 5 oz............................. 10
Tumbler, green, 3 1/4" h., 5 oz............................ 34
Tumbler, pink, 3 1/4" h., 5 oz.............................. 32
Tumbler, clear, 4" h., 9 oz................................... 10
Tumbler, green, 4" h., 9 oz.................................. 32
Tumbler, pink, 4" h., 9 oz. 20
Tumbler, clear, 5" h., 12 oz................................. 10
Tumbler, green, 5" h., 12 oz................................ 55
Tumbler, pink, 5" h., 12 oz.................................. 38
Tumbler, footed, clear, 4" h., 9 oz....................... 10

Tumbler, footed, clear, 5" h., 11 oz...................... **12**
Tumbler, footed, clear, 7 1/4" h. **18**

deVez & Degué

The Saint-Hilaire, Touvier, de Varreaux and Company of Pantin, France used the name de Vez on their cameo glass early in the 20th century. Some of their examples were marked "Degué" after one of their master glassmakers. Officially the company was named "Cristallerie de Pantin."

DeVez and Degué Marks

Cameo vase, 5 1/2" h., flared foot tapering to a flaring body w/a low wide flaring rim, citron yellow overlaid in crimson & maroon & etched w/a continuous desert landscape w/palm trees in the foreground & a Moroccan temple in the background, signed in cameo "Degué," ca. 1910 (ILLUS. bottom row, far left, bottom of page) **$575**

Cameo vase, 6 1/2" h., bottle-form body w/squatty base, pale mottled yellow & pink overlaid in royal blue & etched w/a continuous exotic landscape w/palm trees around a lake, signed in cameo "deVez," ca. 1910 (ILLUS. bottom row, second from right with other vases, bottom of page) **431**

Cameo vase, 7" h., 3" d., tall tapering cylindrical shape w/a flared rim, shaded pale pink to white to yellow ground overlaid in dark green & cameo cut w/flower vines around the top above a harbor scene w/sailboats & mountains in the distance, signed "deVez" **625-725**

Cameo vase, 7 3/4" h., bottle-form w/swelled neck & cupped small mouth, pale pink overlaid in royal blue & etched w/large leafy thistles on the front & sailing ships on the back, signed in cameo "deVez," ca. 1910 (ILLUS. bottom row, second from left with other vases, bottom of page) **489**

DeVez Landscape Cameo Vase

Cameo vase, 8" h., cushion foot supporting a trumpet-form body, pastel pink overlaid w/dark maroon & etched w/a continuous lakeside scene w/a rowboat, large trees in the foreground & mountains in the distance, signed in cameo "deVez," early 20th c. (ILLUS.)... **1,265**

Cameo vase, 8" h., flared foot & tall flaring cylindrical body w/a flattened shoulder to the small flaring neck, mottled pink & grey overlaid in dark blue & etched w/a continuous Athenian landscape w/a sailboat on a lake, leafy trees in the foreground, mountains in the distance, signed in cameo "deVez," ca. 1910 (ILLUS. bottom row, far right with other vases, bottom of page).................................... **805**

Grouping of deVez Cameo Vases

Cameo vase, 8" h., footed wide tapering cylindrical body w/flat rim, light blue overlaid in amethyst & etched w/a continuous waterside landscape w/a sailing ship, large trees in the foreground & mountains in the distance, signed in cameo "deVez," ca. 1910 (ILLUS. top row, far left with other vases, bottom previous page).. **489**

Cameo vase, 8" h., swelled cylindrical form w/flat rim, grey overlaid w/dark red & crimson & etched w/a continuous lakeside landscape w/large trees in the foreground & mountains in the distance, signed in cameo "deVez," ca. 1910 (ILLUS. top row, far right with other vases, bottom of previous page).. **805**

Cameo vase, 8" h., 3 1/2" d., squatty base tapering to a tall cylindrical body w/flared rim, dark maroon & red overlaid on a shaded deep red to pale yellow to red ground & cameo cut w/a Venetian canal scene, signed "deVez" **725-825**

Cameo vase, 8 1/4" h., a cushion base below the tall trumpet-form body, mottled pink & yellow overlaid in royal blue & etched w/a continuous Venetian harbor scene w/ships, signed in cameo "deVez," ca. 1910 (ILLUS. top row, second from left with other vases, bottom of previous page) **633**

Degué Landscape Cameo Vase

Cameo vase, 8 3/4" h., footed bulbous ovoid body tapering to a short cylindrical neck w/a deeply ruffled rim, frosted butterscotch overlaid in cobalt blue & etched w/a continuous landscape w/a water buffalo standing in a rippling body of water, large leafy trees in the foreground & mountains in the distance, signed in cameo "Degué," early 20th c. (ILLUS.)................ **920**

Cameo vase, 9 3/4" h., slightly swelled cylindrical form w/a flat mouth, amber overlaid in green & cranberry & etched w/a landscape of tall trees silhouetted against a lake shore w/mountains in the distance, signed in cameo "deVez," ca. 1910.. **690**

Cameo vase, 10 1/2" h., flat-bottomed ovoid body tapering to a slender neck w/bulbed rim, pale pink overlaid in orange & royal blue & etched w/a continuous lakeside landscape w/cascading wisteria in the foreground & mountains in the distance, signed in cameo "deVez," ca. 1910 (ILLUS. previous page, top row, second from right with other vases) **978**

Cameo vase, 19 1/2" h., cushion foot supporting the tall baluster-form body, green & blue overlaid w/various shades of purple & etched w/a tall oak tree w/squirrel in the foreground & a lake & mountains in the background, signed in cameo "deVez," ca. 1910 .... **1,725**

Duncan & Miller

Duncan & Miller Glass Company, a successor firm to George A. Duncan & Sons Company, produced a wide range of pressed wares and novelty pieces during the late 19th century and into the early 20th century. During the Depression era and after, they continued making a wide variety of more modern patterns, including mold-blown types, and also introduced a number of etched and engraved patterns. Many colors, including opalescent hues, were produced during this era, and especially popular today are the graceful swan dishes they produced in the Pall Mall and Sylvan patterns.

The numbers after the pattern name indicate the original factory pattern number. The Duncan factory was closed in 1955. Also see ANIMALS.

Almond dish, Early American Sandwich patt. (No. 41), clear, 2 1/2" d. **$15**

Ashtray, Canterbury patt. (No. 115), clear, 3".. **12**

Ashtray, First Love etching, rectangular, clear, 6 1/2" **28**

Ashtray, model of a duck, clear, 4"...................... **16**

Ashtray, model of a duck, clear, 7"...................... **45**

Ashtray, model of a duck, ruby, 7"...................... **275**

Banana boat, Early American Sandwich patt. (No. 41), milk white, w/label, 9 1/2" l. **125**

Basket, handled, Hobnail patt. (No. 118), clear, 7" h.. **30**

Basket, Early American Sandwich patt., clear, 12".. **250**

Bonbon, Diamond patt. (No. 75), round, two-part, two-handled, amber, 6 1/2" l........... **20**

Bowl, bouillon, Spiral Flutes patt., pink **16**

Bowl, 5" d., Canterbury patt. (No. 115), fruit, clear **8**

Bowl, 5" d., Early American Sandwich patt., clear **15**

Bowl, 6 3/4" d., Spiral Flutes patt., grapefruit, green **8**

Bowl, 9" d., Canterbury patt., crimped, clear....... **30**

Bowl, 9" d., Caribbean patt., tab-handled, clear **40**

Bowl, 10" d., etched First Love patt., flared, clear.. **85**

Bowl, 10 1/2" d., 5" h., etched First Love patt., crimped rim, clear **85**

Bowl, 12" d., etched First Love patt. (No. 6), flared, flower, clear.............................. **95**

Bowl, 13", Canterbury patt., flared oval, clear **45**

Bowl, 13", etched First Love patt., oval, flared, clear.. **100**

Butter, cov., Sandwich patt., clear, 8" d............ **145**

Candlesticks, one-light, Caribbean patt.,
w/prisms, blue, 8" h., pr. **425**
Candlesticks, three-light, Early American
Sandwich patt., clear, 5" h., pr. **125**
Candlesticks, Canterbury patt., pink opal-
escent, 3" h., pr. **85**
Candy dish, cov., Canterbury patt. (No.
115), clear, 7" h. **40**
Candy dish, cov., Canterbury patt., three-
part, clear, 8" d. **33**
Candy dish, cov., Canterbury patt., three-
part, ruby, 8" d. **165**
Candy dish, cov., Early American Sand-
wich patt., three-part, clear, 7" sq. **425**
Candy jar, cov., etched First Love patt. (No.
25), footed, three-part, clear, 4 1/2" h. **135**

Ruby Dover Goblet & Champagne

Champagne, Dover patt., ruby bowl w/clear
stem (ILLUS. right w/water goblet) **20**
Champagne, etched First Love patt., clear **22**
Cigarette box, cov., Early American Sand-
wich patt., rectangular, clear, 4" l. **55**
Cigarette box, cov., rectangular, Canter-
bury patt., clear, 4 1/2" **30**
Cigarette jar, cov., Nautical patt., blue opal-
escent **695**
Claret, Canterbury patt., clear, 5" h. **20**
Coaster, Early American Sandwich patt.,
clear, 5" d. **11**
Cocktail, Early American Sandwich patt.,
clear, 3 oz. **14**
Cocktail, Teardrop patt., clear, 4 1/2" h.,
3 1/2 oz. **12**
Cocktail shaker, Caribbean patt., blue
w/chrome lid, 9" h. **300**
Compote, 5" h., 7" w., Puritan patt., green **40**
Console bowl, Caribbean patt., flared,
blue, 12" d. **120**
Cordial, Teardrop patt., clear, 4" h., 1 oz. **40**
Creamer, Teardrop patt., clear **10**
Creamer & cov. sugar bowl on tray, Fes-
tive patt. (No. 155), aqua, 3 pcs. **85**
Creamer & sugar bowl, individual-size,
Early American Sandwich patt., clear, pr. **35**
Cruet w/original stopper, Hobnail patt.,
clear **35**
Cup & saucer, Canterbury patt., clear **15**
Cup & saucer, Caribbean patt., blue, pr. **68**
Cup & saucer, First Love etching, clear, pr. **35**
Cup & saucer, demitasse, Puritan patt.,
pink **25**

Hobnail Decanter & Tumblers

Decanter w/stopper, Hobnail patt., clear,
12 oz. (ILLUS. w/four tumblers) **60**
Deviled egg plate, First Love etching, clear,
12 1/2" d. **175**
Deviled egg plate, Early American Sand-
wich patt., clear, 12" d. **85**
Finger bowl & liner, Spiral Flutes patt., am-
ber, 2 pcs. **18**
Goblet, blown Canterbury patt., water,
clear, 7 1/4" h. **20**
Goblet, Caribbean patt., water, blue, 8 oz.,
5 3/4" h. **50**
Goblet, Dover patt., water, ruby bowl w/clear
stem (ILLUS. left w/champagne) **35**
Goblet, etched First Love patt., water, clear,
6 3/4" h., 10 oz. **35**
Goblet, Spiral Flutes patt., water, green **17**
Ice bucket, Nautical patt., blue **150**
Ice tub, Spiral Flutes patt., handled, pink **90**
Lamp, oil-type, Mardi Gras patt. (No. 42),
clear **225**
Mayonnaise set: bowl, liner & ladle; Early
American Sandwich patt., the set **55**
Model of a swan, Pall Mall patt. (No. 30),
clear, 5" l. **15**
Model of a swan, Sylvan patt. (No. 122),
pink opalescent, 5 1/2" l. **95**
Model of a swan, Pall Mall patt. (No.
30 1/2), clear, 7" l. **15**
Model of a swan, Pall Mall patt. (No. 30),
cranberry stained, 8" l. **55**
Model of a swan, Pall Mall patt. (No.
30 1/2), clear, 10" l. **40**
Model of a swan, Pall Mall patt. (No. 30),
ruby red, 12" l. **125**
Nut bowl, Early American Sandwich patt.,
cupped, clear, 11" **65**
Nut cup, Spiral Flutes patt., amber **12**
Oyster cocktail, Early American Sandwich
patt., clear **16**
Parfait, Spiral Flutes patt., amber **17**
Pitcher, Mardi Gras patt., clear **195**
Pitcher, Caribbean patt., blue, 16 oz.,
4 3/4" h. **275**
Pitcher, 8" h., Hobnail patt., clear **75**
Pitcher w/ice lip, Canterbury patt., martini,
clear, 32 oz. **75**
Pitcher w/ice lip, Canterbury patt., water,
clear, 64 oz. **150**
Plate, 6" d., Early American Sandwich patt.,
bread & butter, clear **9**

Plate, 6" sq., Terrace patt., cobalt blue............... 38
Plate, 7" d., Puritan patt., green........................... 10
Plate, 7" d., Spiral Flutes patt., pink 9
Plate, 7 1/2" d., Canterbury patt., clear............... 10
Plate, 7 1/2" d., Hobnail patt., clear..................... 12
Plate, 7 1/2" w., etched First Love patt., sal-
ad, clear...... 25
Plate, 8" d., Early American Sandwich patt.,
salad, green...... 18
Plate, 8 1/4" d., Canterbury patt. (No. 115)
w/Lily of the Valley cutting............................. 25
Plate, 8 1/2" d., etched First Love patt., sal-
ad, clear...... 24
Plate, 8 1/2" d., Sanibel patt., pink opales-
cent 45
Plate, 9 1/2" d., Early American Sandwich
patt., dinner, clear...... 55
Plate, 10" d., Nautical patt., blue....................... 120
Plate, 10 1/2" d., Caribbean patt., dinner,
blue 165
Plate, 11" d., Canterbury patt., two-handled
sandwich, clear 22
Plate, 11" d., Caribbean patt., cracker w/in-
dent, blue 60
Plate, 12" d., Early American Sandwich
patt., clear...... 45
Plate, 13" d., Early American Sandwich
patt., cracker, clear...... 40
Plate, 13" d., Terrace patt., torte, clear............... 45
Plate, 14" d., Canterbury patt., torte, clear......... 30
Plate, 14" d., Teardrop patt., torte, clear 35
Plate, 16" d., Early American Sandwich
patt., clear 105
Plate, 18" d., Teardrop patt., Lazy Susan-
type, w/leaf cutting, clear...... 80
Punch bowl, Caribbean patt., clear, 1 1/2
gal. 90
Punch bowl & ladle, Festive patt., clear, 2
pcs...... 60
Punch ladle, Hobnail patt., yellow opales-
cent 120
Relish dish, Canterbury patt., three-part,
three-handled, chartreuse, 8"........................ 30
Relish dish, Caribbean patt., five-part,
clear, 12 3/4" d...... 40
Relish dish, Early American Sandwich
patt., four-part, two-handled, clear, 10" l. 45
Relish dish, Early American Sandwich
patt., two-part, round, ring-handle, clear,
6" d. 20
Relish dish, etched First Love patt., three-
part, clear, 6 x 10 1/2"...... 60
Relish dish, etched Language of Flowers
patt. (No. 115), three-part, three-handled, clear, 9" l. 35
Relish dish, Hobnail patt., oval, two-handled, clear, 12" l. 30
Relish dish, Sanibel patt., two-part, pink
opalescent, 9" l. 75
Relish dish, Teardrop patt., square, four-
part, four-handled, clear, 12" d. 45
Relish dish, Terrace patt. (No. 111), five-
part, round, clear...... 40
Relish dish, Canterbury patt., three-part,
handled, clear, 9" d. 22

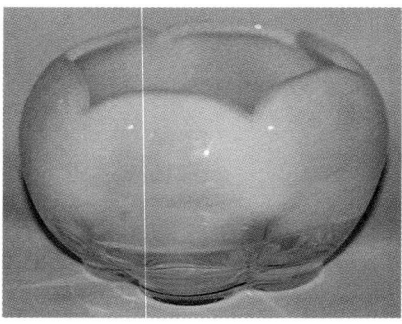

Canterbury Rose Bowl

Rose bowl, Canterbury patt., Jasmine, yel-
low opalescent (ILLUS.) 110
Salt dip, Early American Sandwich patt.,
clear, 2 1/2" d...... 15
Salt & pepper shakers, etched First Love
patt., clear, pr...... 65
Salt & pepper shakers, Hobnail patt., clear,
3" h., pr...... 35
Sauce ladle, Festive patt., aqua...... 35
Sherbet, Early American Sandwich patt.,
clear, 5 oz. 14
Soup plate w/flanged rim, Puritan patt.,
pink, 8" d...... 35
Sugar bowl, cov., Terrace patt., ruby............... 100
Sugar bowl, Early American Sandwich
patt., clear, 5 oz. 15
Tray, mint, Sanibel patt. (No. 130), blue
opalescent, 7" l. 45
Tumbler, Canterbury patt., flat, blue opales-
cent, 6 1/4" h...... 75
Tumbler, Canterbury patt., flat, clear,
6 1/4" h...... 18
Tumbler, Canterbury patt., luncheon, foot-
ed, clear, 9 oz. 16
Tumbler, Early American Sandwich patt.,
juice, clear, 5 oz...... 12
Tumbler, Early American Sandwich patt.,
water, footed, clear, 4 3/4" h., 9 oz. 16
Tumbler, Hobnail patt., flat, clear, 2 oz.,
each (ILLUS. previous page, of four
w/Hobnail decanter)...... 18
Tumbler, Nautical patt., water, blue, 9 oz........... 32
Tumbler, Plaza patt., iced tea, flat, ruby........... 22
Tumbler, Puritan patt., iced tea, flat, pink........... 28
Tumbler, Spiral Flutes patt., footed, green,
2 1/2 oz. 8
Tumbler, Spiral Flutes patt., iced tea, flat,
green 75
Tumbler, Teardrop patt., juice, footed,
clear, 5 oz. 9
Tumbler, Canterbury patt., juice, footed,
clear, 4 1/4" h...... 10
Tumbler, Early American Sandwich patt.,
iced tea, footed, clear, 12 oz. 18
Urn, cov., Terrace patt., 5111 1/2, Royal
Blue...... 325
Vase, bud, First Love etching, cylindrical,
footed, clear...... 120
Vase, 3" h., Canterbury patt., violet-type,
clear 15
Vase, 4 1/2" h., Canterbury patt., oval, clear........ 20

Vase, 5" h., Early American Sandwich patt., crimped rim, footed, clear **45**

Sanibel Blue Opalescent Vase

Vase, 5 1/2" h., Sanibel patt., footed, blue opalescent (ILLUS.).. **325**

Vase, 6 1/2" h., Caribbean patt., cylindrical, blue **85**

Vase, 8" h., Three Feathers patt. (No. 117), footed cornucopia shape, pink opalescent **135**

Vase, 8 3/4" h., Spiral Flutes patt., green........... **35**

Vase, 9" h., Caribbean patt., ruffled rim, footed, blue... **195**

Vase, 15" h., Two Ply Swirl patt., amber **165**

Vase/flower arranger, 10 1/2" h., Canterbury patt., clear **55**

Vase/ice bucket, 6" h., Canterbury patt. (No. 115), clear **35**

Vegetable bowl, Spiral Flutes patt., handled, green, 10" oval **45**

Wine, Caribbean patt., blue, 3 oz. **75**

Wine, etched First Love patt., clear, 5 1/4" h., 3 oz. **50**

Wine, blown Canterbury patt., clear, 3 1/2 oz., 6" h. **20**

Wine, Early American Sandwich patt., clear....... **16**

Durand

Fine decorative glass similar to that made by Tiffany and other outstanding glasshouses of its day was made by the Vineland Flint Glass Works Co. in Vineland, New Jersey, first headed by Victor Durand Sr. and subsequently by his son, Victor Durand Jr., in the 1920s.

Compote, 7" d., 5 1/4" h., Optic Ribbed patt., gently fluted plate on baluster stem & disk foot, polished pontil, amethyst, w/signature & "744" **$130**

Lamp, table model, the footed spherical optic ribbed body in clear w/iridescent silver, blue, red & green swirled banding, fitted on a round pad-footed gilt-brass base, electric fittings in the top, body 7" h., overall 17 1/2" h. (ILLUS., top next column).. **1,668**

Unusual Durand Table Lamp

Unusual Luminaire with Durand Shade

Luminaire, table model, a flaring cylindrical shade in an iridescent crackled orangish brown on yellow, fitted on an ornamental pierced brass base w/figural dolphin feet, early 20th c., shade 4" d. at top, overall 6 1/8" h. (ILLUS.).. **546**

Vase, 4" h., footed spherical body w/a closed rim, amber w/overall golden iridescence, signed in silver "V Durand 1002-4," ca. 1925 .... **891**

Small Engraved Durand Vase

Vase, 6" h., a wide disk foot below the gently flaring cylindrical body w/a widely flaring flat rim, bright iridescent yellow w/an engraved band of stylized leaves & flowers around the middle, early 20th c. (ILLUS., previous page) **230**

Small Durand King Tut Vase

Vase, 6" h., footed wide squatty body below the tall widely flaring trumpet neck, gold iridescence w/green King Tut decoration, signed on the bottom "Durand 1990," early 20th c. (ILLUS.) **1,035**

Fine Durand Green King Tut Vase

Vase, 8 1/2" h., slender ovoid body w/a short flaring neck, green ground decorated overall in silvery iridescent King Tut design, bright orange iridescent interior, signed on the base "Durand 1812," early 20th c. (ILLUS.) **2,300**

Dark Blue Durand King Tut Vase

Vase, 9" h., gently swelled cylindrical body tapering to a wide trumpet neck, dark blue iridescence w/orange & cream swirled King Tut decoration, small chip on lip, early 20th c. (ILLUS.) **920**

Vase, 9 1/2" h., baluster-form body w/a flaring trumpet neck, opal w/an overall pulled & coiled iridescent blue decoration, unsigned, ca. 1920 .... **633**

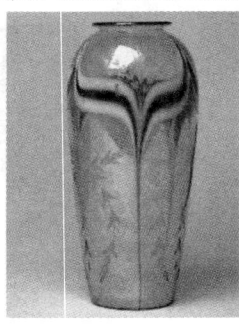

Pulled-Feather Engraved Durand Vase

Vase, 9 3/4" h., simple ovoid body w/a small flattened flared mouth, citron yellow iridescent ground w/opalescent white & blue pulled-feather designs forming three panels up the sides, each panel engraved w/stylized flowers & leaves, worn signature on the base, early 20th c. (ILLUS.) **780**

Gold & White Durand King Tut Vase

Vase, 10" h., baluster-form body w/closed rim, gold iridescent ground w/overall white King Tut decoration, signed on the pontil "Durand 1937-10," early 20th c. (ILLUS.) **1,610**

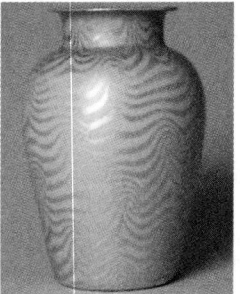

Durand King Tut Vase in Green & Gold

Vase, 11" h., simple ovoid body w/a short cylindrical neck & flattened rim, lime green ground w/overall silvery gold iridescent King Tut decoration, interior in orange iridescence, signed in pontil "Durand," early 20th c. (ILLUS., previous page)... **1,080**

Nice Threaded Durand Vase

Vase, 11 1/2" h., disk foot on a tall gently flaring trumpet-form body, white iridized ground w/stylized leaves in half green & half gold, overall random gold threading, iridescent gold foot, signed on the base "V Durand 20120-12," early 20th c. (ILLUS.) **575**

Fenton

Fenton Art Glass Company began producing glass at Williamstown, West Virginia, in January 1907. Organized by Frank L. and John W. Fenton, the company began operations in a newly built glass factory with an experienced master glass craftsman, Jacob Rosenthal, as their factory manager. Fenton has produced a wide variety of collectible glassware through the years, including Carnival. Still in production today, its current productions may be found at finer gift shops across the country.

William Heacock's three-volume set on Fenton, published by Antique Publications, is the standard reference in this field.

Fenton Mark

Ashtray, w/pressed flower on back, Mongolian Green **$48**
Basket, Emerald Crest, handled, 5".................... **95**
Basket, No. 203, Diamond Optic, Mulberry w/clear applied handle (ILLUS., top next column).. **150**
Basket, Spanish Lace Silver Crest, handled, 10" **125**
Basket, Hobnail patt., cranberry opalescent, 4 1/2" h. **75**
Bonbon, Hobnail patt., crimped rim, cranberry opalescent, 6" h. **35**
Bowl, Silver Crest, fruit, pedestal-footed, square **80**

No. 203 Diamond Optic Basket

Bowl, 5" d., Lincoln Inn patt., fruit, jade............... **24**
Bowl, 6" d., cupped, ruby stretch glass.............. **195**
Bowl, 7" d., Hobnail patt., double crimp, topaz opalescent.. **48**
Bowl, 9 3/4" d., fruit, Mandarin Red on black glass stand, No. 846, 2 pcs. **135**
Bowl, 10", Silver Crest, No. 7221, yellow jonquil decoration w/gold trim on crest edge... **50**
Bowl, 10 1/2" d., Lincoln Inn patt., fruit, flared, cobalt blue **125**
Bowl, 13" d., Peach Crest, rolled rim.................. **135**
Bowl, 13" d., Silver Crest...................................... **75**
"Boxtle," cov. powder jar base w/lid in the form of stoppered perfume bottle, blue opalescent, 3 pcs. **265**
Butter, cov., Hobnail patt., oblong 1/4 lb. size, milk glass.. **28**
Cake plate, Silver Crest, high-footed, 13" d. **45**

No. 318 Candleholders

Candleholder, one-light, No. 318, Cameo Opalescent, 3" h. (ILLUS. top w/three other colors) **28**
Candleholder, one-light, No. 318, Diamond Optic, green, 3" h. (ILLUS. left w/three other colors) **24**
Candleholder, one-light, No. 318, Mandarin Red, 3" h. (ILLUS. right w/three other colors)... **60**
Candleholder, one-light, No. 318, Velva Rose stretch glass, 3" h. (ILLUS. bottom w/three other colors) **75**

Candy dish, cov., Florentine Green stretch glass, dolphin handles 150
Champagne, Lincoln Inn patt., aquamarine, 6 oz. 25
Cocktail glass, Historic America patt., clear 22
Compote, Lincoln Inn patt., pink, 4 1/2" w., 3 3/4" h. 24

No. 950 Console Set in Rose

Console set: bowl & two cornucopia candleholders; No. 950 w/Ming etchings, rose, the set (ILLUS.)..................................... 165
Cookie jar, cov., Big Cookies patt., black, handled, 7" h. 150
Cruet w/original stopper, Coin Dot patt., No. 208, cranberry opalescent 175
Cruet w/original stopper, Fern patt., No. 815, Persian blue opalescent 125
Cruet w/original stopper, Rose Burmese 100
Cup & saucer, Hobnail patt., square shape, blue opalescent, pr. 48

Epergne, Rose Burmese, one-lily, No. 7202...... 125
Goblet, Historic America patt., clear................... 30
Guest set: pitcher & tumbler; Topaz iridescent, the pitcher w/cobalt blue handle, the set.. 450
Ice bucket, Diamond Optic patt., aquamarine w/metal handle, 6 1/2" h........................... 70
Lamp, Gone-with-the-Wind type, Poppy patt., custard, 24" h.. 295
Mug, Georgian patt., ruby, 10 oz. 35
Nymph figure w/flower block, September Morn, Chinese Yellow...................................... 345
Pitcher, Hobnail patt., footed spherical form, cranberry opalescent, applied clear handle 115
Pitcher, Hobnail patt., milk white, 70 oz............. 75
Pitcher, 7 1/2" h., Lincoln Inn patt., ruby........... 700
Pitcher w/indented ice lip, Coin Dot patt. No. 1353, cranberry opalescent 275
Plate, 8" square, No. 1639, etched, cobalt blue 30
Plate, 8 1/2" d., Silver Crest 18
Plate, 10" d., Lincoln Inn patt., dinner, cobalt blue... 65
Plate, 12" d., Silver Crest 35

French Blue Reamer

Reamer, French blue, two-piece, 6 3/8" h. (ILLUS.).. **3,000-3,500**
Rose bowl, No. 857, Periwinkle blue 48
Salt & pepper shakers w/original lids, Hobnail patt., flat, cranberry opalescent, pr. 100
Tumbler, Hobnail patt., juice, blue opalescent, 5 oz. 20

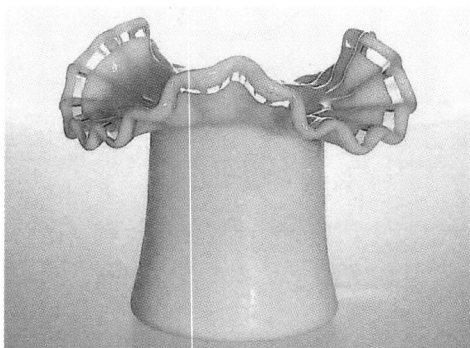

Crystal Crest 4" Hat-shaped Vase

Decanter with Pressed Floral Stopper
Decanter w/stopper, No. 1934, w/pressed floral stopper, ruby (ILLUS.)............................ 185

Vase, 4" h., Crystal Crest, hat-shaped, double crimped rim (ILLUS., previous page) **45**
Vase, 4 1/2" h., Hobnail patt., double crimp, cranberry opalescent **40**
Vase, 6 1/2" h., No. 1923, Aqua Crest, waisted cylindrical body w/a four-lobed flattened crimped rim **45**
Vase, 8" h., Hanging Heart patt., ovoid body w/flaring trumpet neck, custard iris, Robert Barber Collection, etched "Fenton 1976" **225**
Vase, 8" h., Hobnail patt., No. 3958, double crimped rim, milk glass **25**
Vase, 8" h., Sheffield patt., flared, aquamarine **38**
Vase, 11" h., Hanging Heart patt., ovoid body tapering to a long flared neck, turquoise iris, Robert Barber Collection, etched "Fenton 351/600DGS" **220**
Vase, 14" h., No. 1532, Tangerine stretch glass.. **245**

Fostoria

Fostoria Glass company, founded in 1887, produced numerous types of fine glassware over the years. Its factory in Moundsville, West Virginia, closed in 1986.

Fostoria

Fostoria Label

Almond dish, American patt., clear, 3 3/4" **$24**
Almond dish, footed, Colony patt., clear, 2 1/4" d. **24**
Ashtray, American patt., clear, 5" sq. **100**
Ashtray, individual, Century patt., clear, 2 3/4"... **12**
Basket, American patt., w/reeded handle, clear, 7 x 9" **100**
Beer mug, American patt., clear, 12 oz., 4 1/2" h. **88**
Bonbon, American patt., three short feet, Canary, 7 1/2" d. (ILLUS., bottom of page)... **225**

Bonbon, Baroque patt., three-toed, clear, 7 3/8" **24**
Bottle w/original stopper, American patt., cordial, clear, 9 oz., 7 1/4" h. **85**
Bowl, American patt., toddler's, flared, No. 150, clear... **45**
Bowl, cream soup, Colony patt., clear................. **77**
Bowl, 4 1/2" d., Jamestown patt., dessert, No. 421, amber **15**
Bowl, 5" d., Coronet patt., fruit, clear.................. **15**
Bowl, 5" d., Lafayette patt., fruit, Wisteria **30**
Bowl, 8" d., American patt., footed, two-handled (Trophy), clear **115**
Bowl, 8 1/2" d., Chintz etching, two-handled, flared, clear... **75**
Bowl, 9" oval, Coin patt., ruby............................. **55**
Bowl, 9 3/8" w., 4" h., Colony patt., deep cupped shape, clear.. **65**
Bowl, 10" d., Seascape patt., salad, pink opalescent **65**
Bowl, 10 1/2" d., 3 3/8" h., Navarre etching, flared, handled, four feet, No. 2496, clear **95**
Bowl, 11" d., Myriad patt., fruit, flared, clear....... **38**
Bowl, 11" w., American patt., tri-cornered, three footed, clear **40**

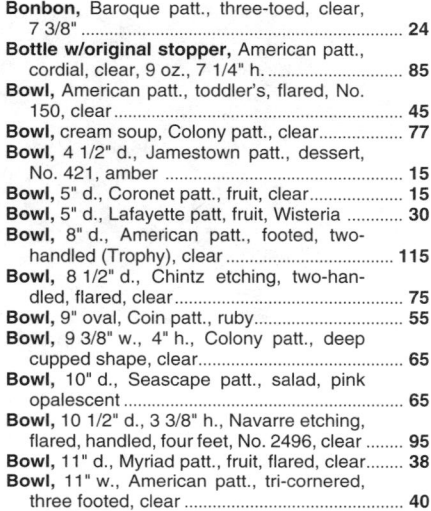

Bowl with Brocade Grape Etching

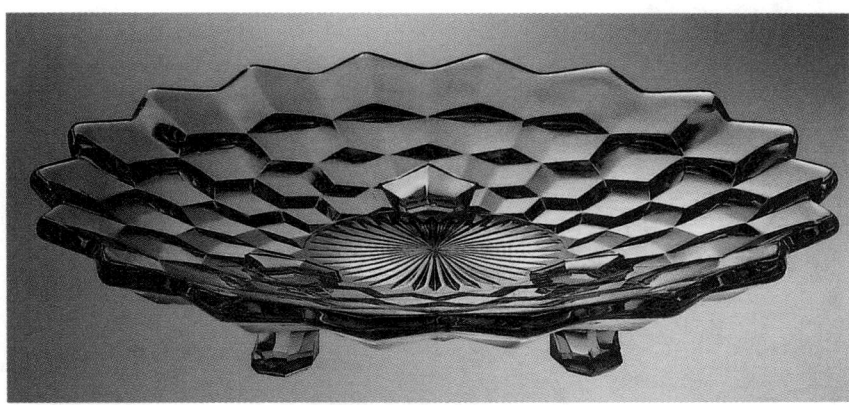

American Pattern Bonbon

Candlesticks with Mayflower Etching

Bowl, 12" d., No. 2362, Brocade Grape etching, flared, green (ILLUS., previous page)... 85

Butter dish, cov., American patt., round, clear.. 135

Butter dish, cov., Colony patt., No. 2412, clear, 1/4 lb. 60

Cake plate, Colony patt., handled, clear, 10" d... 45

Cake salver, Colony patt., clear, 12" d. 75

Cake stand, American patt., clear, 10" sq. 250

Candleholders, one-light, No. 2394, socket on a three-footed base w/six scallops, cobalt blue, ca. 1928, pr. 90

Candlestick, one-light, Coin patt., ruby, 4 1/2" h... 30

Candlestick, one-light, Coronet patt., clear, 4 1/2" h... 20

Candlestick, one-light, Mayflower etching, clear, 4" h. (ILLUS. right w/two-light candlestick, top of page)......................... 36

Candlestick, three-light, Romance etching, clear... 75

Candlestick, two-light, American patt., clear, 4 3/8" h..................................... 45

Candlestick, two-light, Flame patt., clear 95

Candlestick, two-light, Mayflower etching, clear, 5 1/8" h. (ILLUS. left w/one-light candlestick, top of page) 67

Candlestick, two-light, Mayflower etching, Line 2496, clear, 8" w., 4 1/2" h. 75

Candlesticks, one-light, Brocade Cupid etching, Ebony, 4" h., pr. 325

Candlesticks, one-light, Century patt., clear, 4 1/2" h., pr. 34

Candlesticks, one-light, Flame patt., Azure blue, 2" h., pr.................................... 48

Candlesticks, one-light, June etching, Topaz, 2" h., pr. 50

Baroque Blank Pieces with Navarre Etching

Candlesticks, one-light, Navarre etching, Baroque blank, No. 2496, clear, 4" h., pr. (ILLUS. of one, left w/compote & champagne, bottom previous page).......................... 65
Candy box, cov., Meadow Rose etching, three-part, clear... 95
Candy dish, cov., American patt., wedding bowl-type, milk glass, 8" h.............................. 125
Candy dish, cov., Coin patt., ruby, 6" 65
Candy dish, cov., Royal etching, three-part, amber.. 70
Celery dish, Chintz etching, clear....................... 40
Celery tray, American patt., clear, 10" l. 25
Chambersticks w/finger hold, American patt., clear, pr. 70
Champagne, No. 6016 w/Navarre etching, clear (ILLUS. right w/candlestick & compote, bottom, previous page)........................ 23
Champagne, Romance etching, clear, 7" h........ 24
Cheese compote, American patt., clear............. 24
Cigarette box, cov., Myriad patt., oblong, clear.. 65
Cigarette box, cov., Oriental etching, rectangular, clear... 70
Claret, American Lady patt., clear, 3 1/2 oz., 4 5/8" h. 18
Claret, American patt., clear, 4 7/8" h., 7 oz. 50
Coaster, Hermitage patt., green 12
Cocktail, American Lady patt., clear, 3 1/2 oz., 4" h. 14
Cocktail, American patt., footed, clear, 3 oz. 12
Cologne bottle w/original stopper, American patt., clear.. 100
Compote, open, 4 1/2" h., Navarre etching, Baroque blank, clear (ILLUS. center w/candlestick & champagne, previous page).. 48
Compote, 4 3/4" d., Baroque patt., clear, ... 30
Compote, 6"d., June etching, clear 65
Compote, 6" h., No. 2433 "Tripod," Wisteria bowl w/clear base & stem.............................. 125
Compote, 6 1/2" d., cov., Colony patt., jelly, clear.. 45
Condiment tray, cloverleaf-shaped, American patt., clear.. 200
Console bowl, Baroque patt., Topaz, 12" d. 55

Oak Leaf Brocade Console Set

Console set: rolled edge bowl & two low candlesticks; Oak Leaf Brocade etching, No. 2375 1/2, clear, the set (ILLUS.)............. 175
Cordial, Colonial Dame patt., clear, 3 1/2" h.. 42
Cordial, Colonial Dame patt., green bowl, clear foot & stem, 3 1/2" h............................. 46
Cordial, Mayflower etching, clear, 3 3/4" h......... 55
Cordial, Navarre etching, clear, 1 oz., 3 7/8" h... 65
Cracker jar, cov., American patt., clear 275
Creamer, American patt., clear, 4 1/4" h., 9 1/2 oz. 18
Creamer, individual, Colony patt., clear, 3 1/4" h., 4 oz. 12
Creamer & open sugar bowl, Chintz etching, individual, clear, pr.................................. 40
Creamer & open sugar bowl, Romance etching, clear, pr.. 38
Creamer & open sugar bowl, Seascape patt., pink opalescent, pr.............................. 75
Creamer, open sugar bowl & undertray, individual, American patt., clear, the set......... 45
Cruet w/original stopper, American patt., clear, 5 oz. 35
Cruet w/original stopper, Coin patt., clear, 6" h... 45
Crushed fruit jar, cov., American patt., clear, 10" h. (chip on lid)............................. 1,600
Cup, American patt., clear, 7 oz. 8
Cup & saucer, American patt., flared, clear....... 12
Cup & saucer, Baroque patt., blue 35
Cup & saucer, Century patt., clear..................... 12
Cup & saucer, Lafayette patt., Wisteria 28
Decanter set: three bottles w/original stoppers, marked "Scotch," "Rye" & "Gin" in metal frame w/lock; American patt., clear, the set.. 500
Decanter w/original stopper, Coin patt., clear... 110
Decanter w/stopper, Hermitage patt., Azure blue... 120
Figure of Madonna, clear, 10" h......................... 95
Finger bowl, Colony patt., clear 22
Fruit stand, American patt., flat, on pedestal base, clear, 16" d. 150
Goblet, American Lady patt., clear, 10 oz., 6 1/8" h. 24
Goblet, Chintz etching, No. 6026, tall stem, clear, 7 5/8" h., 9 oz. 34
Goblet, Colonial Dame patt., green bowl, clear stem & foot, 6 1/2" h.............................. 26
Goblet, Holly cutting, clear, 10 oz, 8 3/8" h. 25
Goblet, Jamestown patt., clear............................ 15
Goblet, Jamestown patt., green, 6" h................... 22
Goblet, June etching, pink, 8 1/4" h..................... 70
Goblet, Navarre etching, blue, 10 oz. 85
Goblet, Vesper etching, No. 5093, amber 35
Gravy boat w/undertray, Chintz etching, clear, 2 pcs... 100
Hurricane lamp, American patt., clear, 8 1/2" h.. 500
Ice bucket, Brocade Oakwood etching, iridescent w/gold trim, Azure blue w/metal handle.. 225
Ice bucket, Chintz etching, clear........................ 140
Ice dish w/juice tumbler, Hermitage patt., Topaz... 45

Ice tub w/liner, American patt., clear,
5 5/8" d., 3 3/4" h. 98
Jelly jar, cov., American patt., clear.................... 45
Marmalade, cover & spoon, American
patt., clear, the set 120
Mayonnaise bowl, underplate & spoon,
Century patt., clear, 3 pcs. 55
Mayonnaise set: blue opalescent bowl &
liner, clear ladle; Seascape patt., the set....... 95
Muffin tray, American patt., clear, 10" l............. 36
Mug, Bicentennial, No. 2493/705, clear, 15
oz.. 24
Mustard jar, cover & spoon, Century patt.,
clear, 3 pcs. 60
Napkin ring, American patt., clear, 2" 35
Nappy, American patt., deep, clear, 8" d. 50
Nappy, American patt., handled, clear,
4 1/2" d. 15
Novelty, model of a top hat, American patt.,
clear, 2 1/2" h. 25
Onion soup, cov., Sunray patt., tab han-
dles, clear... 62
Oyster cocktail, Colony patt., clear,
3 3/8" h., 4 oz. 20
Party plate, Century patt., clear, 8" d. 28
Pickle dish, American patt., clear, 8" l. 22
Pin tray, oval, American patt., clear,
4 1/2 x 5 1/2" 300
Pitcher, 6 1/2" h., American patt., clear, 3
pt. 85
Pitcher, cov., 7" h., Rogene etching, clear 275
Pitcher, 7 3/4" h., Colony patt., No. 2412,
clear 150
Pitcher, Century patt., clear, 16 oz. 75
Pitcher w/ice lip, 7 1/2" h., Sunray patt.,
frosted clear, 2 qt. 75
Pitcher w/ice lip, 8 1/2" h., Colony patt.,
clear, 3 pt. 225
Plate, 6" d., American patt., bread & butter,
clear 10
Plate, 6" d., Pioneer patt., bread & butter.,
Topaz... 3
Plate, 7" d., Baroque patt., salad, Azure 18
Plate, 7" d., Fairfax patt., salad, Orchid.............. 12
Plate, 7 1/2" d., June etching, Rose 18
Plate, 7 1/2" d., June etching, Topaz 15
Plate, 7 1/2" d., Mayflower etching, Rose 15
Plate, 7 1/2" d., Navarre patt., clear 18
Plate, 8 1/4" d., Jamestown patt., amber............ 15
Plate, 8 1/4" d., Jamestown patt., ruby 30
Plate, 8 1/2" d., Holly cutting, clear.................... 15
Plate, 9 1/2" d., Century patt., dinner, clear 25
Plate, 9 1/2" d., Navarre etching, dinner,
clear 65
Plate, 9 1/2" d., Pioneer patt., dinner, Topaz....... 10
Plate, torte, 14" d., American patt., clear............ 45
Plate, torte, 14" d., Century patt., clear.............. 45
Plate, torte, 14" d., Holly cutting, clear.............. 45
Platter, 10 1/2" l., American patt., clear.............. 55
Platter, 15" l., Royal etching, blue 95
Pomade or rouge box, cov., American
patt., clear, 2" sq... 550
Puff box, cov., American patt., clear, 3" sq. 225
Punch bowl, Tom & Jerry-type, pedestal
footed, American patt., clear, 12" d. 235
Punch cup, American patt., clear.......................... 8
Relish dish, American patt., boat-shaped,
clear, 8 1/2" l... 22

Relish dish, Baroque patt., three-part,
clear, 10" l. 24
Relish dish, Baroque patt., three-part, To-
paz, 10" l. 35
Relish dish, Colony patt., three-part, han-
dled, clear, 10 1/2" l. 30
Relish dish, Fairfax patt., two-part, green,
8 1/2" l. 15
Relish dish, Mayfair patt., five-part, Topaz 38
Relish dish, Navarre etching, five-part,
clear, 13 1/4" l. 100
Relish dish, Romance etching, three-part,
clear, 10" l.. 55
Rose bowl, American patt., clear, 5" d.............. 35

Victoria Pattern Rose Bowl

Rose bowl, Victoria patt., clear w/satin fin-
ish (ILLUS.).. 200
Salt dip, American patt., clear, 2 1/2" d. 12
Salt & pepper shakers, Baroque patt., To-
paz, 2 3/4" h., pr. 150
Salt & pepper shakers, Coin patt., ruby, pr........ 70
Salt shakers w/tray, individual, American
patt., clear, 3" h., set 45
Sandwich server w/center handle, Colony
patt., clear 45
Sauceboat & underplate, Fairfax patt., To-
paz, 2 pcs. 75
Sherbet, American Lady patt., burgundy
bowl w/clear stem, 5 1/2 oz., 4 1/8" h. 35
Sherbet, American patt., low, flared, clear, 5
oz., 3 1/4" h. 11
Sherbet, Baroque patt., clear, 5 oz....................... 10
Sherbet, Coin patt., clear, 5 1/8" h....................... 26
Sherbet, Jamestown patt., green, 7 oz. 12
Sherbet, Lido etching, clear, 6 oz. 15
Sherbet, Versailles etching, tall foot, Rose,
12 oz. 35
Shrimp bowl, American patt., clear, 12 1/4"..... 395
Sugar bowl, Baroque patt., individual, clear........ 12
Sugar bowl, Colony patt., individual, clear 15
Sugar shaker, American patt., clear, tall 125
Sweetmeat dish, cov., Baroque patt.,
Azure blue... 295
Syrup pitcher w/original glass top & un-
derplate, American patt., clear, 10 oz., 3
pcs. 150
Tidbit tray, Colony patt., three-toed, clear,
7 1/2" 22
Tumbler, American Lady patt., juice, footed,
cobalt blue, 5 oz., 4 1/8" h. 65

Vegetable Bowl with June Etching

American Pattern Iced Tea Tumbler

Tumbler, American patt., iced tea, clear, 12 oz., 5 3/4" h. (ILLUS.)..................................... 22
Tumbler, Cameo patt., opaque white w/multicolor decoration..................................... 45
Tumbler, Coin patt., ruby, 9 oz., 4 1/4" h. 45
Tumbler, Colony patt., flat, clear, 9 oz., 4" h. 22
Tumbler, Jamestown patt., juice, footed, ruby, 4 3/4" h. 22
Tumbler, June etching, iced tea, Topaz 58
Tumbler, Kashmir etching, footed, green, 5" h.. 30
Tumbler, Mayflower etching, juice, footed, clear, 4 7/8" h. 19
Urn, cov., Colony patt., clear w/patterned base 125
Vase, sweet pea, 4 1/2" h., American patt., clear 75
Vase, 6" d., Colony patt., bud, clear.................... 20
Vase, 6" h., American patt., aqua 120

Vase, 7 1/2" h., Century patt., handled, clear... 95
Vase, 7 1/2" h., Colony patt., flared, clear........... 55
Vase, 8" h., Brocade Oakwood etching, flip-type, iridescent w/gold trim, Rose................. 265
Vase, 9 1/2" h., American patt., flared rim, clear... 175
Vase, 10" h., American patt., cupped-in top, clear... 135
Vase, 10" h., Flame patt., footed, Azure blue... 98
Vase, 14" h., Colony patt., clear 250
Vase, bud, Coin patt., ruby 55
Vegetable bowl, June etching, oblong, Rose, 9 1/2" l. (ILLUS., top of page) 145
Water bottle, American patt., clear, 9 1/4" h., 44 oz.. 800
Wedding bowl, American patt., clear, large.. 1,000
Whipped cream pail, Brocade Grape etching, green w/metal handle............................... 65
Wine, American Lady patt., clear, 2 1/2 oz......... 28
Wine, Century patt., clear, 3 1/2 oz., 4 1/2" h. 20
Wine, Jamestown patt., green, 4 5/16" h., 4 oz. 22
Wine, June etching, Topaz 55
Wine, Romance etching, clear, 3 oz. 35

Fry

Numerous types of glass were made by the H.C. Fry Company of Rochester, Pennsylvania. One of its art lines was called Foval and was blown in 1926-27. Cheaper was its milky-opalescent oven-ware (Pearl Oven Ware), made for utilitarian purposes but also now being collected. The company also made fine cut glass.

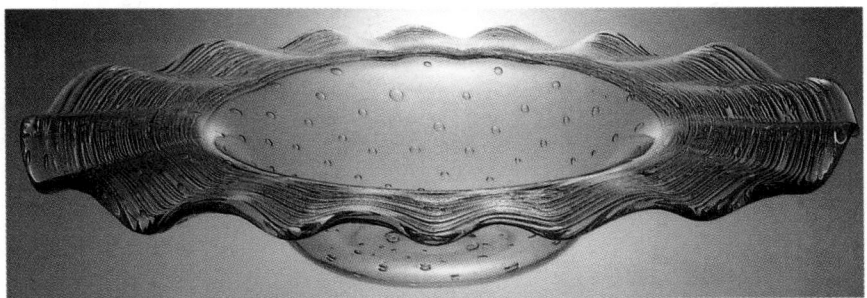

Fry Bowl with Bubbles & Threading

Fry Foval Creamer & Open Sugar

Collectors of Fry glass will be interested in the recent publication of a good reference book, The Collector's Encyclopedia of Fry Glassware, by The H.C. Fry Glass Society (Collector Books, 1990).

Bowl, 14" l., oval shape, light blue w/controlled bubbles in bowl & blue threading in wavy rim, polished pontil (ILLUS., bottom previous page).. **$245**
Candlestick, seven-socket, low black base w/clear swirl connector **95**
Candlesticks, Foval, opalescent wide disk foot w/a blue connector to the tall slender cylindrical white shaft wrapped w/a thin thread of blue below a translucent blue bobeche supporting the pearl white cylindrical socket w/gently flared rim, ca. 1926, one w/faint Fry Shield acid stamp, 10 3/8" h., pr. **950**
Champagne, pink w/"Cactus" stem..................... **75**
Compote, open, 8 1/2" d., 5" h., white opalescent w/royal blue baluster-form stem & foot **275**
Cookie jar, cov., Sunnybrook patt., black w/wicker handle **275**
Creamer & open sugar bowl, Foval, creamy opalescent body w/applied dark blue handles, pr. (ILLUS., top of page) . **350-450**
Cruet w/original stopper, Foval, milky white w/a Delft blue stopper & applied handle, 9 3/4" h. **375**

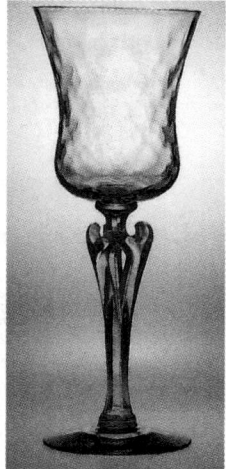

Fry Goblet with "Cactus" Stem

Goblet, water, pink bowl & foot, green "Cactus" stem (ILLUS.) **175**

Fry Foval Lemonade Set

Lemonade set: cov. pitcher & six tall handled glasses; Foval, bulbous pitcher w/applied green handle & cover w/applied green knob finial, six cylindrical glasses w/applied green handles, teapot 5 1/4" h., glasses 9 1/2" h., the set (ILLUS.).. **720**
Pitcher, cov., 11" h., water, Foval, milky white w/Delft blue finial & applied handle, early 20th c. **550**

Fry Platter in Chrome Holder

Platter in chrome holder, 12 1/2" l., Pearl Oven Ware, oval, engraved leaf & floral design, 2 pcs. (ILLUS.)...................................... **95**
Trivet, three-footed, Pearl Oven Ware, 8" d........ **35**
Vase, 8 1/2" h., Foval, tall waisted cylindrical body w/flared & ruffled rim, on an applied foot w/a blue applied squared knop **325**
Vase, 12" h., cylindrical, Pearl art line, pulled loopings, pink **550**

Gallé

Gallé glass was made in Nancy, France, by Emile Gallé, a founder of the Nancy School and a leader in the Art Nouveau movement in France. Much of his glass, both enameled and cameo, is decorated with naturalistic motifs. The finest pieces were made in the last two decades of the 19th century and the opening years of the 20th.

Pieces marked with a star preceding the name were made between 1904, the year of Gallé's death, and 1914.

Various Gallé Marks

Gallé Cameo Box with Flowers

Cameo box, cov., low slightly flaring cylindrical base w/low domed cover, internally decorated amber overlaid w/wine red & etched w/stylized flowers & leaves, signed in cameo, 5" d., 3" h. (ILLUS.) **$690**

Cameo box, cov., squatty round body w/fitted low cover, grey internally decorated w/pink & overlaid in green & etched in a thistle design, signed in cameo, ca. 1900, 4 1/2" d., 1 3/4" h. **431**

Rare Miniature Gallé Cameo Vase

Cameo vase, 3" h., 3 1/2" d., miniature, squatty bulbous body w/a wide short cylindrical neck, mottled clear & red ground, overlaid in deep red, deep blue & green & wheel-carved w/stylized leaves & a large grasshopper, signed on the base "Gallé Cristallerie Décor Déposé - Nancy," late 19th c. (ILLUS.) **6,325**

Three Decorative Gallé Vases

Cameo vase, 6 1/4" h., tapering cylindrical body w/trumpet-form mouth, lavender base shading to pale yellow sides cased in deep purple & cameo blue w/crocus-like blossoms on slender leafy stems, signed (ILLUS. right with other vases) **400**

Cameo vase, 6 1/2" h., ovoid body tapering to a short flattened flaring neck, pink opal overlaid in various shades of crimson & decorated w/mold-blown & cameo-carved flowers & leaves, signed in cameo, ca. 1900 .... **4,485**

Cameo vase, 7 1/2" h., cushion footed & short pedestal supporting the tall ovoid body w/a wide flat mouth, rose & frosted ground overlaid in dark green & etched w/a forested lake scene, signed in cameo, ca. 1900 .... **1,265**

Cameo vase, 8 3/4" h., wide flattened round body tapering to a short neck w/long cupped rim, amber overlaid in various shades of blue & green etched w/tall pine trees silhouetted against a continuous rocky mountain range, signed in cameo, ca. 1900 .... **4,600**

Gallé Cameo Vase with Lake Landscape

Cameo vase, 9 1/2" h., slender swelled cylindrical shape, shaded apricot overlaid in deep maroon & etched w/a continuous waterside landscape w/large trees in the foreground, signed (ILLUS.)......................... **2,013**

Rare Large Gallé Cameo Vase

Cameo vase, 10 1/2" h., stepped cushion foot below the spherical body w/a flaring cylindrical neck, dark green shaded to dark pink overlaid w/bubble gum pink & etched w/large stylized lily blossoms, signed on base "Cristallerie E. Gallé - Nancy - Modele Leion Déposé" (ILLUS.).. **12,650**

Cameo vase, 10 3/4" h., tall slightly tapering cylindrical body, deep purple shaded to cream & light orange cased in deep purple & cameo cut w/a continuous landscape of tall fir trees w/mountains in the distance, signed (ILLUS. center with other vases, previous page) **1,000**

Tall Gallé Cameo Vase with Landscape

Cameo vase, 12" h., swelled tapering cylindrical body w/a flared rim, shaded pale yellow to blue ground overlaid w/deep amethyst & etched w/a continuous

mountain landscape w/fir trees in the foreground & lake & mountains in the distance, signed in cameo (ILLUS.)................ **1,955**

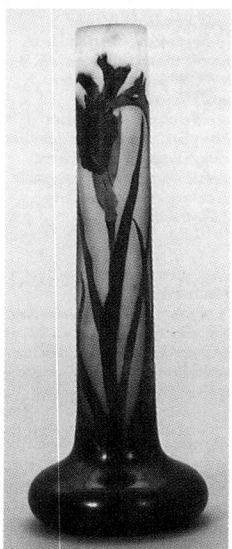

Tall Iris-cut Gallé Cameo Vase

Cameo vase, 13 1/2" h., a wide cushion base tapering to the tall cylindrical neck, deep lavender cut to frosted white in an iris & leaves decoration, signed in script on the neck (ILLUS.).................................... **1,380**

Two Tall Gallé Cameo Vases

Cameo vase, 13 1/2" h., a wide flaring foot tapering to a slender ovoid body, mottled grey & pink overlaid in lavender & green & etched w/a large stem of blossoms up the sides, signed in cameo, drilled (ILLUS. right with other cameo vase)............. **748**

Cameo vase, 14 1/2" h., swelled cylindrical form w/a flat rim, mottled pink & light blue overlaid in amethyst & etched w/cascading wisteria vines, signed in cameo, ca. 1900 (ILLUS. left with other cameo vase, previous page)................................... 1,610

Cameo vase, 20" h., tall tapering rounded cylindrical body w/a flaring rim, amber overlaid in deep crimson & etched w/stemmed leafy tiger lilies, signed in cameo, ca. 1900 4,255

Silver-mounted Gallé Ewer

Ewer w/silver plate cover, neck, handle & foot, the ovoid body w/a clear chipped ice finish enameled w/white blossoms on tall green & blue leafy stems, signed on the base "Modele et Decore Déposé - Cristallerie Emile Gallé - Nancy," late 19th c., 10" h. (ILLUS.) 1,668

Finely Decorated Gallé Tray

Tray, rounded ruffled dish w/two sides curled up & inward, crystal finely enameled w/stylized flowers, stems & leaves in russet, brown & royal blue, highlighted by a detailed dragonfly, gilt borders, base signed "E. Gallé - Nancy," late 19th c., 7 3/4 x 10 1/2" (ILLUS.) 1,179

Rare Gallé Fish Vase

Vase, 5 3/4" h., modeled as a pair of entwined stylized upright fish, light amber w/transparent violet iridescent heads, enameled black & white cabochon eyes, signed on the bottom in gold "E. Gallé - Nancy" (ILLUS.)... 1,323

Rare Etched & Foil-backed Gallé Vase

Vase, 7 1/2" h., footed bulbous ovoid body w/a small flared neck, seafoam green ground mottled w/dark brown & cased in clear, etched w/brown leaves & clear flowers backed in the interior w/foil, impressed signature on the side & marked on the bottom "Ges. Gesch." (ILLUS.) 3,450

Vase, 10" h., pale amber ovoid & optic ribbed body, engraved & enameled up the sides w/large thistle blossoms & leafy stems in deep purple & yellow, signed "Gallé Déposé," early period (ILLUS. left with other vases, page 613)........................ 1,100

Heisey

Numerous types of fine glass were made by A.H. Heisey & Co., Newark, Ohio, from 1895. The company's trademark, an H enclosed within a diamond, has become known to most glass collectors. The company's name and molds were acquired by Imperial Glass Co., Bellaire, Ohio, in 1958, and some pieces have been reissued. The glass listed below consists of miscellaneous pieces and types. Also see ANIMALS and CUSTARD GLASS.

Heisey Empress Bowl in Sahara

Heisey Diamond "H" Mark

Ashtray, Crystolite patt., clear, 3" sq. $12
Basket, Lariat patt., footed, clear, 10" 325
Beer mug, Old Sandwich patt., Moongleam
(light green), 12 oz. 350
Berry set: master bowl & six sauce dishes;
Prison Stripe patt., No. 357, clear
w/some worn gold trim, marked, 7 pcs. 75
Bowl, cream soup, two-handled, Yeoman
patt., Sahara (light yellow) 30
Bowl, 4 1/2" d., Pleat & Panel patt.,
Moongleam 15
Bowl, 6" d., mint, footed, Chintz etching,
Sahara 34
Bowl, 8" d., Lodestar patt., Dawn (light
grey) 75
Bowl, 9" d., Twist patt., floral-type,
Moongleam 69
Bowl, 10" d., Orchid etching, Queen Ann
blank, crimped rim, clear 110
Bowl, 11" d., Empress patt., flared shape,
dolphin feet, Sahara ILLUS, top of page) 125
Bowl, 11" d., Lariat patt., two-handled,
clear 30
Bowl, 11" d., Minuet etching, floral-type,
clear 125
Bowl, 11 1/2" d., Ridgeleigh patt., oval, flo-
ral-type, clear 65
Bowl, 13" d., Rose etching, Waverly blank,
floral-type, shallow, clear 100
Bowl, 13" l., Ipswich patt., oval, floral-type,
clear 36
Butter dish, cov., Orchid etching, square,
clear 165
Butter dish, cov., Rose etching, clear, Cab-
ochon blank, 1/4 lb. 375
Cake stand, Orchid etching, Waverly blank,
footed, clear, 13" d. 295

Candlesticks, one-light, Grape Cluster
patt., No. 1445, ca. 1935, clear, 5 3/4" d.,
10 1/2" h., pr. 325
Candlesticks, two-light, Ridgeleigh patt.,
w/bobeches & prisms, scalloped base,
clear, pr. 155
Candlesticks, one-light, Pluto patt., No.
114, Moongleam, 3 1/2" h., pr. 60
Candlesticks, one-light, Colony patt., flared
socket on a swelled six-paneled stem on
a ground hexagonal foot, clear, 9" h., pr. 85
Candlesticks, two-light, Lariat patt., clear,
pr. 80
Candlesticks, two-light, Orchid etching,
Waverly blank, clear, pr. 150
Candlesticks, three-light, Lariat patt., clear,
pr. 95
Candlesticks, three-light, Rose etching,
clear, pr. 300
Candy box, cov., Stanhope patt., round,
clear w/black knob stem on round foot 130
Candy dish, cov., Plantation patt., clear,
5" h. 165
Catsup bottle w/stopper, Old Sandwich
patt., clear 70
Celery dish, Plantation patt., clear, 13" l. 50
Celery tray, New Era patt., clear, 13" l. 40
Champagne, Albermarle patt., saucer-type,
clear 25
Champagne, Lariat patt., clear 22
Champagne, Old Dominion patt., Empress
etching, saucer-type, clear stem w/Mari-
gold (dark yellow) bowl 30
Champagne, Orchid etching, saucer-type,
clear, 6 oz. 45
Champagne, Pied Piper etching, saucer-
type, clear 35
Cheese & cracker set: 10 1/2" tray & com-
pote; Pleat & Panel patt., Flamingo
(pink), the set 85
Cigarette box, cov., Lariat patt., clear 55
Cigarette holder, Ridgeleigh patt. 15
Claret, Rose etching, clear, 4 oz. 130
Coaster, Lariat patt., clear 12
Cocktail, Carcassone patt., clear stem
w/Sahara bowl, 3 oz. 35
Cocktail, figural rooster stem, clear 75
Cocktail, figural sea horse stem, clear 175

Cocktail, Lariat patt. w/Moonglo cutting, clear 32

Cocktail, Minuet etching, No. 5010, clear, 3 1/2 oz. 30

Cocktail, Old Dominion patt., Empress etching, saucer-type, clear stem w/Marigold bowl 25

Cocktail, Rosalie etching, Kenilworth (No. 4092) blank, clear, 3 oz. 18

Cocktail icer w/insert, Orchid etching, clear 275

Cocktail shaker, cov., Orchid etching, No. 4225, clear, 1 pt. 195

Compote, 6" d., Old Sandwich patt., open, No. 1404, Moongleam 85

Compote, 6" h., Orchid etching, Waverly blank, clear 50

Compote, 7" h., Empress patt., oval, Sahara 110

Compote, 7" h., Rose etching, Waverly blank, oval, clear 175

Compote, 7" h., Twist patt., Flamingo 85

Compote, Charter Oak etching, Flamingo 65

Cordial, New Era patt., clear, 1 oz. 75

Cornucopia-vase, Warwick patt., cobalt blue, 9" h. 350

Creamer, Empress patt., dolphin-footed, Sahara 55

Creamer, Ridgeleigh patt., individual, clear 25

Creamer, Sawtooth Band patt., miniature, floral etching, ca. 1900 55

Creamer & open sugar bowl, Empress patt., individual, oval, Sahara, pr. 90

Creamer & open sugar bowl, Provincial patt., Limelight (pale green), pr. 200

Creamer & open sugar bowl, Rose etching, Waverly blank, clear, pr. 90

Creamer & open sugar bowl, Rose etching, individual, clear, pr. 75

Cruet w/original stopper, Crystolite patt., clear, 3 oz. 36

Cruet w/original stopper, Orchid etching, footed, clear, 3 oz. 200

Cruet w/original stopper, Rose etching, Waverly blank, clear, 3 oz. 225

Cruet w/original stopper, Twist patt., Flamingo 175

Cruet w/original stopper, Victorian patt., clear, 3 oz. 75

Zircon Cruet with Clear Stopper

Cruet w/stopper, Saturn patt., Zircon (blue green) w/clear stopper (ILLUS.) 650

Cruets w/original stoppers, Lariat patt., oil, clear, 6 oz., pr. 225

Cup, Old Sandwich patt., pink 45

Cup & saucer, Chintz etching, clear, pr. 18

Cup & saucer, Empress patt., Sahara 48

Cup & saucer, New Era patt., clear 20

Cup & saucer, Orchid etching, footed, clear 60

Cup & saucer, Waverly patt., clear 20

Ridgeleigh Decanter with Stopper

Decanter w/stopper, Ridgeleigh patt., clear, 1 pt. (ILLUS.) 250

Goblet, Albemarle patt., clear 30

Goblet, Chintz etching, clear, 9 oz. 24

Goblet, Graceful patt., No. 5022, clear 25

Goblet, Lariat patt., blown, clear, 10 oz. 25

Goblet, Old Dominion patt., Marigold, 8 3/4" h. 55

Goblet, Orchid etching, clear, tall, 10 oz. 55

Goblet, Rose etching, clear, 9 oz. 60

Goblet, Saturn patt., Zircon, 10 oz. 125

Goblet, Spanish patt., water, cobalt blue, 10 oz. 130

Goblet, Victorian patt., two-ball stem, clear 26

Ice bucket, Chintz etching, footed, w/metal handle, Sahara 150

Ice bucket, Minuet etching, Queen Ann blank, dolphin-footed, clear 200

Ice bucket, Twist patt., w/metal handle, Moongleam 195

Jelly dish, Plantation patt., Ivy etching, two-handled, 6 1/2" h. 45

Lemon dish, cov., Yeoman patt., round, Moongleam, 5" d. 45

Mayonnaise set, Rose etching, clear, 3 pcs. 135

Mustard jar, cov., Twist patt., Flamingo 125

Mustard jar, cover & spoon, Empress patt., Sahara, 3 pcs. 140

Nut dish, Empress patt., footed, Sahara 35

Nut dish or ashtray, New Era patt., individual size, clear 60

Oil & vinegar bottle w/original stopper, Provincial patt., clear 75

Oyster cocktail, Ipswich patt., footed, clear 12

Parfait, Yeoman patt., clear 9
Pilsner glass, New Era patt., clear, 12 oz. 60
Pitcher, Charter Oak patt., Flamingo 175
Pitcher, Old Colony etching, Empress blank, Sahara, 73 oz. 395
Pitcher, Orchid etching, Donna blank (No. 3484), clear, 1/2 gal. 625
Pitcher, Rose etching, Waverly blank, clear, 76 oz. 660
Pitcher, Orchid etching, ice tankard, clear, 64 oz. 625
Pitcher w/ice lip, Plantation patt., blown, clear, 1/2 gal. 450
Pitcher w/ice lip, Pleat & Panel patt., Moongleam, 3 pt. 165
Plate, 4 3/4" d., Colonial patt., clear 5
Plate, 6" d., Empress patt., Sahara 15
Plate, 7" d., Crystolite patt., salad, clear 15
Plate, 7" d., Crystolite patt., two-handled, clear 20
Plate, 7" d., Empress patt., Moongleam 18
Plate, 7" d., Empress patt., Sahara 18
Plate, 7" d., Orchid etching, salad, clear 25
Plate, 7" d., Rose etching, Waverly blank, salad 25
Plate, 7 1/2" d., Empress patt., Alexandrite (lavender) 90
Plate, 8" d., Empress patt., salad, Sahara 20
Plate, 8" d., Minuet etching, luncheon, clear 26
Plate, 8 1/2" d., Saturn patt., Zircon 75
Plate, 10 1/2" d., Charter Oak patt., dinner, Flamingo 52
Plate, 10 1/2" d., Lariat patt., dinner, clear 130
Plate, 10 1/2" d., Orchid etching, dinner, clear 200
Plate, 12" d., Orchid etching, Queen Ann blank, center handle 200
Plate, 14" d., Orchid etching, Waverly blank, torte, clear 95
Plate, 14" d., Plantation patt., sandwich, clear 95
Plate, 15" oval, Lariat patt, deviled egg, clear 250
Platter, 14" l., oval, Chintz etching, Sahara 95
Punch bowl, Crystolite patt., clear, 7 1/2 qt. 120
Punch bowl & base, Greek Key patt., clear, 14 1/2" d., 15" h., 2 pcs. 375
Punch cup, Crystolite patt., clear 10
Punch cup, Lariat patt., clear 10
Punch cup, Locket & Chain patt., ca. 1900, clear 45
Punch set: 14" d. punch bowl, 21" d. under-plate & eight punch cups; Lariat patt., original hooks, clear, 10 pcs. 325
Punch set: 9 qt. Dr. Johnson punch bowl, six cups & ladle; Plantation patt., clear, 8 pcs. 1,100
Relish dish, Crystolite patt., three-part, clear, 9 1/2" 29
Relish dish, Lariat patt., three-part, clear, 10 1/2" 35
Relish dish, New Era patt., three-part, clear, 13" l. 40
Relish dish, Plantation patt., four-part, clear, 8" l. 95
Relish dish, Plantation patt., three-part, clear, 11" l. 85
Relish dish, Provincial patt., four-part, Limelight 175

Relish dish, Rose etching, Waverly blank, oval, three-part, clear, 11" l. 80
Relish tray, Crystolite patt., three-part, clear, 12" l. 38
Rose bowl, Mermaid etching, clear, 5" d. 500
Rose bowl, Pillows patt. (No. 325), pedestal foot, clear 275
Salt dip, Fandango patt., No. 1201, clear 22
Salt & pepper shakers w/original tops, Orchid etching, clear, pr. 100
Salt & pepper shakers w/original tops, Rose etching, Waverly blank, clear, pr. 120
Sandwich server, Rose etching, Waverly blank, center-handled, clear, 14" d. 240
Sherbet, Carcassone patt., clear stem w/Sahara bowl, 6 oz. 30
Sherbet, Colonial patt., clear 10
Sherbet, Lariat patt. w/Moonglo cutting, clear 20
Sherbet, Old Dominion patt., Empress etching, low, clear stem w/Marigold bowl 24
Sherbet, Pied Piper etching, clear 25
Sherbet, Victorian patt., two-ball stem, clear 15
Sherry, Orchid etching, clear, 2 oz. 175
Spooner, Greek Key patt., large, clear 110
Straw jar, cov., Greek Key patt., clear 450
Sugar bowl, Empress patt., open, dolphin-footed, three-handled, Sahara 40
Syrup bottle w/top, Plantation patt., clear 200
Toothpick holder, Continental patt., clear 135
Toothpick holder, Fancy Loop patt., clear, late 1890s 85
Tray, Ridgeleigh patt., oval, clear, 10 1/2" l. 65
Tumbler, Arch patt., cobalt blue 180
Tumbler, Carcassone patt., juice, clear stem w/Sahara bowl, 5 oz. 25
Tumbler, Greek Key patt., flat, clear, 10 oz. 99
Tumbler, Ipswich patt., soda, clear, 5 oz. 25
Tumbler, Lariat patt., Moonglo cutting, iced tea, footed, clear, 12 oz. 32
Tumbler, Minuet etching, iced tea, Symphone blank No. 5010, 12 oz. 60
Tumbler, Old Dominion patt., footed, Sahara, 5 oz. 25
Tumbler, Old Sandwich patt., toddy, clear, 6 1/2 oz. 18
Tumbler, Orchid etching, iced tea, clear, 12 oz. 64
Tumbler, Provincial patt., footed, clear, 8 oz. 24
Tumbler, Twentieth Century patt., iced tea, Dawn (light grey) 60
Tumbler, Twist patt., juice, footed, Flamingo, 5 oz. 45
Vase, 4" h., No. 4224, ivy-type, clear 125
Vase, 7" h., Orchid etching, fan-shaped, footed, clear 150
Vase, 7" h., Warwick patt., Sahara 250
Vase, 9" h., Empress patt., dolphin-footed, Sahara 155
Wine, Albermarle patt., clear, 2 1/2 oz. 25
Wine, Lariat patt., pressed, clear, 3 1/2 oz. 20
Wine, Orchid etching, No. 5025, clear, 3 oz. 95

Hobbs, Brockunier & Co.

The Hobbs Company originated about 1845 in Wheeling, West Virginia, with the founding of Hobbs, Barnes & Co. by John L. Hobbs and James B. Barnes, both former employees of the

Ruby Satin Hobbs Bowl with Canary Rim

New England Glass Company. Their sons eventually joined the firm and in 1863 the company became Hobbs, Brockunier & Co. when John L. and John H. Hobbs and Charles Brockunier took over. That year they hired William Leighton Sr., former superintendent of the New England Glass Company. Leighton took charge of production and in 1864 he revolutionized the American glass industry by devising a formula for soda lime glass, a cheaper method of producing clear glass that didn't require lead oxide. By the 1880s Hobbs was producing a number of decorative glassware lines including Peach Blow, Spangled, pressed Amberina and various opalescent patterns. The plant closed in the 1890s. Also see PEACH BLOW and OPALESCENT GLASS.

Bowl, 8 1/2" d., 3 1/2" h., wide flat bottom w/straight sides below the crimped & flared rim, ruby w/satin finish & applied opal canary applied rim band, ca. 1880s (ILLUS., top of page).............................. **$375-450**
Butter dish, cov., sapphire blue, Hobnail (323 Dew Drop) patt., polished pontil, 5" d. (several flakes under lid) **35**

Pressed Amberina Butter Pat

Butter pat, pressed Amberina in the Daisy & Button patt., notched corners, ca. 1884, 2 3/4" w. (ILLUS.) **125-150**
Celery vase, canary opalescent, Hobnail (323 Dew Drop) patt., applied hobnail prunt under base, 6 1/2" h. **210**
Celery vase, cranberry opalescent, Hobnail (323 Dew Drop) patt., polished pontil, 6 1/2" h. **230**

Rare Ruby & Blue Cheese Dish

Cheese dish, cov., mold-blown domed cover in the Inverted Thumbprint patt., shaded ruby to sapphire blue w/applied clear knob finial, on a round pressed sapphire blue Daisy & Button base, ca. 1880s, 7" d., 8" h. (ILLUS.) **575-700**
Child's water set: No. 0 jug-type 4" h. pitcher, four 2 1/2" h. tumblers, round tray; amber, Hobnail (323 Dew Drop) patt., 6 pcs. (several minor hob flakes).......... **400**
Child's water set: No. 0 jug-type 4" h. pitcher, four 2 1/2" h. tumblers, round tray; clear w/Frances decoration, Hobnail (323 Dew Drop) patt., 6 pcs. (one tumbler w/amethyst tint)... **475**
Child's water set: No. 1 jug-type 4 1/4" h. pitcher, four 2 1/2" h. tumblers, round

tray; blue, Hobnail (323 Dew Drop) patt., 6 pcs. (several minor hob flakes) **325**

Cobalt Blue & Amber Spangled Creamer

Creamer, bulbous squared body w/a wide flaring neck w/molded rings & a shaped rim, spangle glass in cobalt blue cased in amber, large overall mica flecks, applied amber handle w/mica flecks, ca. 1883, 5" h. (ILLUS.) **275-325**

Wheeling Peach Blow Dark Cruet

Cruet w/original amber facet cut stopper, Wheeling Peach Blow, unusually deep color, applied handle, ca. 1886, 6 3/4" h. (ILLUS.) **1,000-1,100**

Lamp, tapering cylindrical hobnail shade in Hobbs Hobnail (No. 323 Dew Drop) patt. w/Frances decoration, w/ovoid brass font marked "The Rochester" & "Columbia" central draft burner, 4" fitter **275**

Pitcher, No. 0 jug type, 3 7/8" h., cranberry opalescent, Hobnail (323 Dew Drop) patt., applied clear handle, polished pontil (chipping to several base hobs) **160**

Pitcher, No. 0 jug type, 4" h., blue plated, Hobnail (323 Dew Drop) patt., blue applied handle, polished pontil **110**

Pitcher, No. 0 jug type, 4" h., canary light opalescent, Hobnail (323 Dew Drop)

patt., applied vaseline handle, polished pontil (one hob chipped) **180**

Pitcher, No. 0 jug type, 4" h., rubina verde light opalescent, Hobnail (323 Dew Drop) patt., applied vaseline handle, polished pontil **500**

Pitcher, No. 1 jug type, 4 1/2" h., blue, Hobnail (323 Dew Drop) patt., blue applied handle, polished pontil (chipping to several base hobs) **200**

Pitcher, No. 1 jug type, 4 1/2" h., Hobnail (323 Dew Drop) patt., canary satin, applied canary handle, polished pontil **220**

Pitcher, No. 1 jug type, 4 1/2" h., Hobnail (323 Dew Drop) patt., vaseline plated, applied vaseline handle, polished pontil **220**

Pitcher, No. 2 or 3 jug type, 5 1/2" h., vaseline plated, Hobnail (323 Dew Drop) patt., applied canary handle, polished pontil **170**

Pitcher, No. 3 jug type, 5 3/4" h., Hobnail (323 Dew Drop) patt., Frances decoration, applied handle, polished pontil (flake & bruise to several base hobs) **200**

Pitcher, No. 4 jug type, 6 3/4" h., Hobnail (323 Dew Drop) patt., crystal opalescent, applied clear handle, polished pontil **90**

Pitcher, No. 4 jug type, 7" h., Hobnail (323 Dew Drop) patt., frosted, polished pontil (several hobs chipped) **50**

Pitcher, water, 7 1/2" h., Polka Dot patt., rubina verde, applied vaseline handle, polished pontil **475**

Hobbs Neapolitan Pink Pitcher

Pitcher, 7 3/4" h., Neapolitan line, spherical cased pink satin body w/molded ribbing, tapering to the flaring neck w/wide spout, applied frosted ribbed clear handle, 1/2 gal., ca. 1887 (ILLUS.) **475-525**

Pitcher, No. 5 jug type, 7 3/4" h., cranberry opalescent, Hobnail (323 Dew Drop) patt., clear applied handle, polished pontil **600**

Pitcher, No. 5 jug type, 7 3/4" h., rubina verde opalescent, Hobnail (323 Dew Drop) patt., applied vaseline handle, polished pontil (chip on one hob) **700**

Pitcher, No. 5 jug type, 8" h., Hobnail (323 Dew Drop) patt., Frances decoration, applied handle, polished pontil (one hob off & frosted over, several hob flakes) **170**

Hobbs Venetian Line Pitcher

Pitcher, 9 1/2" h., Venetian line, footed spherical body below the tall cylindrical neck w/a pinched spout, clear w/opal Nailsea-style loopings, fine cranberry threading around the neck, applied clear handle, ca. 1883 (ILLUS.) **625-675**

Wheeling Peach Blow Salt Shaker

Salt shaker w/original metal lid, Wheeling Peach Blow, footed spherical body shading from deep ruby to pale yellow, ca. 1886, 2 3/4" h. (ILLUS.) **400-450**
Tumbler, cranberry opalescent, Hobnail (323 Dew Drop) patt., polished pontil **70**
Tumbler, Hobnail (323 Dew Drop) patt., sapphire blue opalescent, polished pontil **70**

Imperial

From 1902 until 1984 Imperial Glass of Bellaire, Ohio, produced hand made glass. Early pressed glass production often imitated cut glass and may bear the raised "NUCUT" mark in the interior center. In the second decade of the 1900s Imperial was one of the dominant manufacturers

of iridescent or Carnival glass. When glass collecting gained popularity in the 1970s, Imperial again produced Carnival and a line of multicolored slag glass. Imperial purchased molds from closing glass houses and continued many lines popularized by others including Central, Heisey and Cambridge. These reissues may cause confusion but they were often marked.

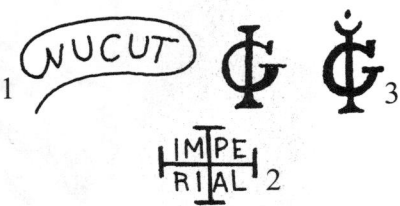

Imperial Marks; 1-Imperial Nucut; Mark 2- Early Imperial Cross; Mark 3. Later Imperial Marks

Candlewick
Ashtray, clear, No. 400/133, 5" d **$8**
Ashtray, w/embossed eagle center, No. 1776/1, clear, 6 1/2" **70**
Ashtray, No. 400/118, clear, no match holder **12**
Ashtray w/match holder, No. 400/118, clear **85**
Baked apple dish, No. 400/53X, clear, 6 1/2" **25**
Basket, No. 400/273, beaded handle, clear, 5 1/2" **320**
Basket, No. 400/40/0, clear w/gold beads, 6 1/2" h. **60**
Basket, No. 400/73/0, clear, 11" **255**
Bell, No. 400/108, clear, 5" h. **85**
Bitters bottle, No. 400/117, clear **85**
Bonbon bowl, heart-shaped, handled, No. 400/51H, clear, 6" **32**
Bonbon bowl, heart-shaped, No. 400/174, clear, 6 1/2" **22**
Bowl, 7" d., No. 400/5F, blue **65**
Bowl, 5", heart-shaped, No. 400/49H, clear **20**
Bowl, 5" sq., No. 400/231, clear **150**
Bowl, 5 1/2", heart-shaped, No. 400/53H, clear **25**
Bowl, 6" d., clear, No. 400/3F **12**
Bowl, 6" d., divided jelly, two-handled, clear **26**
Bowl, 6" h., No. 400/183, three-toed, clear **73**
Bowl, 6 1/2" d., No. 400/84, divided, clear **38**
Bowl, 8-8 1/2" d., No. 400/74B, four-toed, ribbed, clear **110**
Bowl, 8 1/2" d., handled, No. 400/72B, clear **39**
Bowl, 8 1/2" l., caramel slag, a long oval flaring bowl w/beaded rim, tapering to a three-toed base, No. 400/182 (ILLUS., top of next page) **425-475**
Bowl, 9" sq., No. 400/74SC, four-toed, crimped, ribbed, black w/flower **550**
Bowl, 10" d., fruit, footed, pedestal base, ruffled rim, No. 400/103C, clear **265**
Bowl, 10" d., salad, No. 400/75B, clear **50**
Bowl, 10-11", No. 400/75F, float-type, clear **45**
Bowl, 10 1/2" d., bell-shaped, No. 400/63B, clear **55**

Rare Candlewick Caramel Slag Bowl

Bowl w/underplate, 8" d., two-handled w/10" underplate, bowl No. 400/4272B, underplate No. 400/4272D, clear, the set **85**

Butter dish, cov., No. 400/144, clear, 5 1/2" d. **35**

Butter dish, cov., short oblong shape, No. 400/276, beads on lid, clear **140**

Cake plate, No. 400/160, clear w/swirl center, 72 candle holes in rim, 13-14" d. **575**

Cake stand, No. 400/103D, high-footed, three-bead stem, 11" d., clear **90**

Candleholder, three-way, No. 400/115, three-light block, clear **200**

Candleholder/vase, No. 400/40CV, clear **125**

Candleholders, No. 400/100, two-light, clear, pr. **55**

Candleholders, No. 400/147, three-light, clear, pr. **72**

Candleholders, No. 400/207, 4 1/2" h., clear, pr. **260**

Candleholders, No. 400/79R, clear, pr. **35**

Candleholders, No. 400/86, clear, pr. **84**

Candlesticks, No. 400/40C, flower form, crimped, clear, 5" h., pr. (ILLUS. of one, bottom right w/other Candlewick pieces, bottom of page) **85**

Candy box, cov., No. 400/59, two-bead finial, clear, 5 1/2-6 1/2" **55**

Imperial Candlewick Pieces

Candy box, cov., deep shape, No. 400/260, clear, 7" **225**

Candy dish, cov., divided, No. 400/65, clear..... **250**

Celery tray, oval, handled, No. 400/105, clear, 13 1/2" l. **35**

Center bowl, No. 400/13B, Viennese Blue, 11" d... **150**

Champagne/sherbet, No. 3400, saucer-type, clear, 6 oz... **17**

Cigarette box, cov., No. 400/134, clear, 3" **45**

Coaster, 10-ray, No. 400/78, clear, 4" d............. **10**

Cocktail, No. 3400, clear, 4 oz. **16**

Compote, oval, No. 400/137, footed, clear.... **3,300**

Compote, 5" h., No. 400/220, beaded tri-stem, clear **165**

Compote, 5 1/2" h., No. 400/66B, two-bead stem, clear **30**

Compote, flared shape, four-beaded stem, No. 400/45, clear, 5 1/2" tall............................ **32**

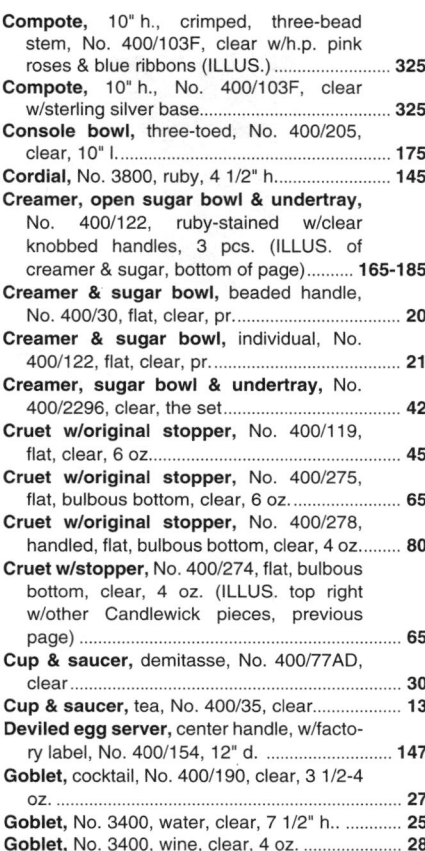

Rose-decorated Candlewick Compote

Compote, 10" h., crimped, three-bead stem, No. 400/103F, clear w/h.p. pink roses & blue ribbons (ILLUS.) **325**

Compote, 10" h., No. 400/103F, clear w/sterling silver base....................................... **325**

Console bowl, three-toed, No. 400/205, clear, 10" l.. **175**

Cordial, No. 3800, ruby, 4 1/2" h....................... **145**

Creamer, open sugar bowl & undertray, No. 400/122, ruby-stained w/clear knobbed handles, 3 pcs. (ILLUS. of creamer & sugar, bottom of page)......... **165-185**

Creamer & sugar bowl, beaded handle, No. 400/30, flat, clear, pr...................................... **20**

Creamer & sugar bowl, individual, No. 400/122, flat, clear, pr....................................... **21**

Creamer, sugar bowl & undertray, No. 400/2296, clear, the set................................... **42**

Cruet w/original stopper, No. 400/119, flat, clear, 6 oz... **45**

Cruet w/original stopper, No. 400/275, flat, bulbous bottom, clear, 6 oz. **65**

Cruet w/original stopper, No. 400/278, handled, flat, bulbous bottom, clear, 4 oz........ **80**

Cruet w/stopper, No. 400/274, flat, bulbous bottom, clear, 4 oz. (ILLUS. top right w/other Candlewick pieces, previous page) **65**

Cup & saucer, demitasse, No. 400/77AD, clear.. **30**

Cup & saucer, tea, No. 400/35, clear.................. **13**

Deviled egg server, center handle, w/facto-ry label, No. 400/154, 12" d. **147**

Goblet, cocktail, No. 400/190, clear, 3 1/2-4 oz. **27**

Goblet, No. 3400, water, clear, 7 1/2" h. **25**

Goblet, No. 3400, wine, clear, 4 oz. **28**

Ruby Candlewick Creamer & Sugar

Candlewick Goblet with Ruby Bowl

Goblet, tall bell-form deep ruby bowl on a clear knopped stem, No. 3400 (ILLUS.) **150-175**

Gravy boat, No. 400/169, clear 120

Hurricane candle lamp, No. 400/79, clear, 2 pcs. 165

Icer, No. 400/53C, clear, 6" 75

Jam set: oval tray w/two cov. marmalade jars w/ladles; No. 400/1589, clear, 5 pcs. 125

Jar tower, three sections w/cover, No. 400/655, Verde Green **1,000**

Jelly dish/ashtray, No. 400/33, blue, 4" d......... 35

Knife, butter cutter, No. 4000, clear 550

Marmalade set, No. 400/8918, beaded, domed base, clear, 3 pcs. 110

Mayonnaise bowl, ladle & underplate, No. 400/23, clear, 3 pcs. (ILLUS. bottom left w/other Candlewick pieces, page 622) 48

Mayonnaise set: divided bowl & underplate; No. 400/84, clear, 2 pcs. 80

Mint bowl, ring-handled, No. 400/51F, clear, 6" 28

Muddler, No. 400/19, clear, 4 1/2" l. 35

Nappy, fruit, No. 400/1F, blue, 5" 45

Party set: round plate & cup; overall etched Rose of Sharon patt. in gilt, No. 400/98D & 98E, 2 pcs. (ILLUS., bottom of page).. **450-500**

Pastry tray, center heart-shaped handle, ruby red, 11 1/2" d.................................... **650**

Pickle/celery dish, No. 400/57, clear, 7 1/2" 32

Pitcher, juice/cocktail, No. 400/19, clear, 40 oz. 250

Pitcher, bead-footed, No. 400/18, clear, 80 oz. 310

Plate, 4 1/2" d., No. 400/34, clear......................... 12

Plate, 6" d., bread & butter, two-handled, No. 400/1D, clear.. 12

Plate, 7" d., No. 400/52E, two-handled, black 375

Plate, 7" d., strawberry, small indent, No. 400/83D, clear..................................... 85

Plate, 9" d., luncheon, No. 400/7D, clear 15

Plate, 11" d., No. 400/145D, two-handled, clear 35

Plate, 13", torte, No. 400/75V, rolled edge, clear 58

Plate, 14" d., No. 400/113D, two handled, clear... 75

Plate, 14" d., No. 400/92D, clear 35

Plate, 17" d., torte, cupped edge, No. 400/20V, clear...................................... 72

Platter, 16" l., oval, two-handled, No. 400/131D, clear **234**

Punch set: punch bowl, underplate, 12 cups & ladle; No. 400/20, bowl & cups w/cut Mallard patt., 15 pcs. 650

Relish dish, No. 400/213, oblong, handled, no dividers, clear, 10" l. **1,000**

Relish dish, two-part, No. 400/234, clear, 7" sq.. 140

Relish dish, two-part, oval, No. 400/268, clear, 8" l. 31

Relish dish, cov., three-part, rectangular, No. 400/216, clear, 10" l.............................. 850

Relish dish, four-part, No.400/112, clear, 10 1/2" l. 33

Relish tray, three-part, handled, No. 400/213, clear, 10" l. 74

Relish tray, five-part, five-handled, No. 400/56, clear, 10 1/2" l.............................. 55

Relish tray, five-part, No. 400/102, clear, 13" 95

Salad serving set, fork & spoon, No. 475, clear, 9 1/2" l., the set................................. 46

Salt & pepper shakers, individual, No. 400/109, clear w/chrome lids, pr..................... 20

Salt & pepper shakers w/chrome tops, individual, No. 400/190, footed, clear, pr.......... 65

Gilt Party Set in Rose of Sharon Etching

Seafood cocktail, No. 400/190, clear,
3 1/2-4 oz. 89
Tidbit server, two-tier, cupped, No.
400/2701, clear 95
Tray, No. 400/72C, two-handled, crimped,
clear, 10" 45
Tray, oval, No. 400/159, clear, 9" l. 29
Tray, No. 400/52E, turned-up sides, 7" 65
Tumbler, No. 400/15, footed beaded base,
clear, 10 oz. 235
Tumbler, water, No. 3400, clear, 10 oz. 20
Tumbler, iced tea, No. 3400, clear, 6 1/2" h. 28
Tumbler, water, No. 400/19, clear, 10 oz. 15
Vase, bud, 5 3/4" h., No. 400/107, base
beads, clear (ILLUS. w/other Candlewick
pieces, page 622) 65
Vase, 8" h., fan-shaped w/beaded handles,
No. 400/87F, blue 175
Vase, 8" h., fluted rim w/beaded handles,
No. 400/87C, clear 44
Vegetable bowl, No. 400/69B, clear w/cut-
ting, 8 1/2" d. 55
Wine, No. 400/19, footed, clear 40

Cape Cod

Baked apple dish, clear, 5 3/4" 12
Basket, footed, clear, 11" h. 120
Bowl, 4 1/2" d., spider, handled, No.
160/180, clear 25
Bowl, 8 1/2" d., low, cupped, clear 34
Bowl, 14" d., shallow float, No. 92F, clear 50
Butter dish, cov., clear, 1/4 lb. 75
Cake plate, flat, w/72 birthday candle holes,
clear, 13" d. 425
Cake stand, No. 160/103D, plain top, clear,
11" d. 115
Candlestick, single light, clear, 3" h. 22
Center bowl, No. 160/75L, ruffled edge,
clear 65
Cigarette lighter, stemmed, purple slag 40
Coaster, No. 160/78, clear, 4" d. 15
Cocktail, No. 1602, clear, 3 1/2 oz. 10
Cookie jar, cov., clear w/wicker handle,
9" h. 250
Cordial, No. 1602, clear, 3 3/4" h. 16
Creamer, clear, 3" sq. 45
Creamer & open sugar bowl, No. 160/30,
six-sided base, clear, pr. 24
Cruet w/original stopper, spherical, No.
160/119, Verde green, 4 oz. 45
Cruet w/original stopper, No. 160/241,
clear, 6 oz. 55
Cup & saucer, tea, clear 12
Decanter w/original stopper, clear, 30 oz.,
9 3/4" h. 89
Decanter w/original stopper, clear, 13" h. 180
Goblet, No. 1602, ball stem, clear, 11 oz. 15
Goblet, water, No. 160, wafer stem, ruby, 9
oz. 35
Goblet, magnum, No. 160, clear, 14 oz. 45
Gravy boat w/liner, clear 95
Lamp, hurricane-type, clear, 12" h. 96
Muddler, clear 30
Mustard jar, cover & spoon, clear, 3 pcs. 45
Oyster cocktail, No. 1602, clear 9
Pitcher, No. 160/24, clear, 2 qt. 95
Pitcher, milk, No. 160/240, clear, 16 oz. 50
Plate, 8 1/2" d., amber 12
Plate, 9" d., clear 26

Punch bowl & base, clear, 1 gal., 2 pcs. 75
Relish dish, three-part, No. 160/1602,
clear, 11 1/4" 90
Salt dip, footed, clear, 2 1/4" d. 21
Salt & pepper shakers, footed, ball stem,
clear, 5" h., pr. 50
Salt & pepper shakers w/original tops, in-
dividual, original factory label, No.
160/251, clear, pr. 25
Sherbet, tall, No. 1602, Verde green, 6 oz. 15
Sugar bowl, wafer stem, footed, clear,
4 1/4" h. 10
Tray, for creamer & sugar, oval, No. 160/29,
clear, 7" l. 20
Tumbler, iced tea, flat, clear, 5 1/2" h. 18
Tumbler, iced tea, clear, 6" h. 16
Tumbler, juice, footed, No. 1602, clear, 6
oz. 12
Tumbler, juice, No. 1600, clear, 5 1/4" h., 6
oz. 12
Tumbler, water, footed, No. 1602, clear, 10
oz. 10
Vegetable bowl, 11" oval, clear 90
Vegetable bowl, divided, oval, clear, 11" l. 85

Free-Hand Ware

Candlestick, slender baluster-form stem
w/cushion foot in clear w/white heart &
vine decoration, a tall cylindrical iridescent dark blue socket, original paper label, 10" h. 440
Vase, 6 1/2" h., wide ovoid body w/a short
trumpet neck, overall marigold iridescence on interior & exterior 195

Imperial Free-Hand Vase

Vase, 7" h., ovoid body tapering to a short
rolled neck, green iridescent ground decorated w/trailing burgundy hearts &
vines, cobalt blue rim band (ILLUS.) 460
Vase, 8" h., small swelled base below the
tall slightly flaring cylindrical body w/a
widely flaring flattened & deeply ruffled
rim, iridescent metallic hues of purple,
green & blue in a wavy random design 220
Vase, 8 1/2" h., decorated w/a dark blue
drapery design on a marigold iridescent
ground 325

Vase, 8 3/4" h., green heart & vine decoration on opaque white body w/iridescent lustre overall 690

Vase, 10" h., bulbous ovoid bottom below a tall trumpet neck, exterior in a mottled taffeta w/amber shoulder band, slate blue interior 325

Navy Blue Over Orange Imperial Vase

Vase, 10" h., squatty bulbous base tapering to a tall trumpet-form neck, dark navy blue cased on a bright iridescent orange (ILLUS.) 300

Vase, 10" h., tall slender form, iridescent orange exterior w/deep orange throat.............. 210

Vase, 10 1/2" h., tall body w/flared rim, a white swagged design on an iridescent ground, stretched multihued design at the rim... 550

Vase, 11" h., slender swelled cylindrical body w/short rolled neck, overall orange lustre over a milk glass body, ground pontil 190

Miscellaneous Patterns & Lines

Animal covered dish, Atterbury lion, purple slag 185

Basket, Twisted Optic patt., canary, 10" h........ 120

Basket, Twisted Optic patt., canary, 10" h........ 120

Book end, Cathay line, Lu-tung/Mandarin, No. 5030, jade... 85

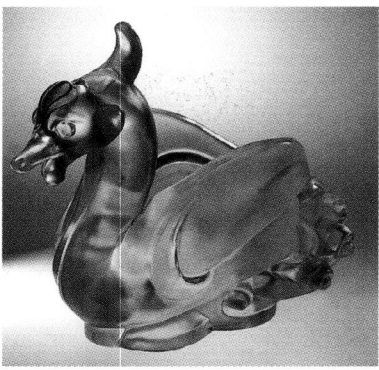

Imperial Phoenix Bowl

Bowl, Cathay Line, figural Phoenix, No. 5026, clear satin, marked "Virginia B Evans" in script (ILLUS.) 295

Box, cov., model of duck on nest, jade green slag.. 75

Candlestick, single-light, Packard patt. No. 320, vaseline, 8 1/2" h. 75

Candy box, cov., Zodiac patt., No. 619, Azure blue, carnival.. 78

Compote, No. 3297, shell bowl w/dolphin stem, black w/gold decoration...................... 140

Imperial Milk Glass Console Set

Console set: compote & two candlesticks; all w/figural elf stems, satin milk glass, the set (ILLUS, bottom previous page.) **195**
Creamer & open sugar, No. 760, "Hazen," ruby, pr. **68**
Ivy ball, Hobnail patt., No. 742, black **35**
Plate, 8" d., Spun patt., reeded, red **30**
Powder box, cov., Hobnail patt., green opalescent **48**

Molly Rose Bowl with Silver Deposit

Rose bowl, Molly line, black w/silver deposit floral decoration, 5" h. (ILLUS.) **75**
Tumbler, Hobnail patt., No. 742, clear **10**

Imperial Fu Wedding Vase

Vase, Fu Wedding, No. 5016 Cathay Line, octagonal body w/embossed design, clear satin, marked "Virginia B Evans" in script (ILLUS.) **275**
Vase, bud, 5" h., Spun patt., reeded, amber **28**
Wine, Old Williamsburg patt., amber **10**

Jack-in-the-Pulpit Vases

Glass vases in varying sizes and resembling in appearance the flower of this name have been popular with collectors since the 19th century.

They were produced in various solid colors and in shaded wares.

Pink Cased Jack-in-the-Pulpit Vase

Cased, deep pink interior cased in white w/clear applied band on the ruffled edge, the interior enameled w/a pair of small blossoms, the exterior enameled w/multicolored florals, 5 1/2" d., 7 1/2" h. (ILLUS.) **$175-225**

Hobbs Cranberry Jack-in-the-Pulpit

Cranberry, round clear foot supporting the tall trumpet-form cranberry body w/a widely rolled & crimped top w/an applied white rim band, Hobbs, Brockunier & Co., 8 1/2" h. (ILLUS.) **500-600**

Three Rare Lacy Glass Pieces

Gold Iridescent Jack-in-the-Pulpit Vase

Iridescent, disk foot on a very slender slightly flaring body w/a widely flaring ruffled top, overall gold iridescence w/green, purple & blue tones, fake Tiffany signature on base, 17 1/2" h. (ILLUS.)..... **460**

Lacy

Lacy Glass is a general term developed by collectors many years ago to cover the earliest type of pressed glass produced in this country. "Lacy" refers to the fact that most of these early patterns consisted of scrolls and geometric designs against a finely stippled background that gives the glass the look of fine lace. Formerly this glass was often referred to as "Sandwich" for the Boston & Sandwich Glass Company of Sandwich, Massachusetts, which produced a great deal of this ware. Today, however, collectors realize that many other factories on the East Coast and in the Pittsburgh, Pennsylvania, and Wheeling, West Virginia, areas also made lacy glass from the 1820s into the 1840s. All pieces listed are clear unless otherwise noted. Numbers after salt dips refer to listings in Pressed Glass Salt Dishes of the Lacy Period, 1825-1850, by Logan W. and Dorothy B. Neal. Also see CUP PLATES and SANDWICH GLASS.

Bowl, 12" d., round w/lightly scalloped rim, shallow rounded sides, central Peacock Feather Medallion patt., cartouches & peacock feather border, ca. 1835-45 (large chips, roughness to rim)................... **$470**

Six Colored Lacy Dishes & Nappies

Pair of Lacy Dishes & a Large Nappy

Compote, open, 6 7/8" d., 5 1/2" h., the round bowl in an Eagle patt., raised on an ornately scrolling triangular pedestal base ending in hairy paw feet, Boston & Sandwich Glass Co., ca. 1835-40 (rim chips) **7,638**

Compote, open, 10 1/2" d., 6" h., deep widely flaring bowl in the Gothic Arch patt. w/Heart & Leaf border, on a twisted rib knob stem above the round domed diamond design foot, rim & base chips (ILLUS. center with sugar bowl & sweetmeat, top of previous page) ....

Dish, round, Daisy & Peacock Eye patt., Boston & Sandwich Glass Co., ca. 1830-45, cobalt blue, chips & roughness, 6 1/4" d. (ILLUS. bottom row, center with other dishes & nappies, bottom previous page)................................... **353**

Dish, round, Roman Rosette patt., Boston & Sandwich Glass Co., ca. 1838-50, fiery opalescent, edge chips, 7 1/2" d. (ILLUS. top row, far left with dishes and nappies, bottom of previous page)................................ **118**

Dish, round, Roman Rosette patt., Boston & Sandwich Glass Co., ca. 1838-50, fiery opalescent, edge chips, roughness, 6" d. (ILLUS. top row, center with dishes & nappies, bottom of previous page) **118**

Dish, shell-shaped w/open loop end handle, Peacock Eye design, Boston & Sandwich Glass Co., ca. 1830-40, 7 3/4 x 9 1/2" (minor edge chips).. **5,581**

Dishes, octagonal, Beehive & Thistle patt., Boston & Sandwich Glass Co., ca. 1835-50, clear, edge roughness, 9 1/4" w., pr. (ILLUS. left & right with Trefoil & Circular Medallion nappy, top of page).......................... **176**

Nappy, round, Stippled Bull's-eye patt., Boston & Sandwich Glass Co., ca. 1838-50, fiery opalescent, rim chips, 6 3/4" d. (ILLUS. top row, far right with dishes and napples, bottom previous page)..................... **176**

Nappy, round, Tulip & Acanthus Leaf patt., Boston & Sandwich Glass Co., ca. 1830-45, cobalt blue, small edge chips, 6 1/4" d. (ILLUS. bottom row, far left with dishes and nappies, bottom previous page) **382**

Nappy, round, Tulip & Acanthus Leaf patt., Boston & Sandwich Glass Co. ca. 1835-50, small rim chips, cobalt blue, 6 1/4" d. (ILLUS. bottom row, far right with other dishes & nappies, bottom previous page)...... **499**

Nappy, round w/gently scalloped rim, Rose & Thistle patt., Boston & Sandwich Glass Co., ca. 1835-45, 8 1/4" d. (edge roughness).. **176**

Nappy, round w/small scallops on rim, quatrefoil in center bottom, Trefoil and Circular Medallion Border patt., Boston & Sandwich Glass Co., ca. 1830-45, clear, two edge cracks, 11" d., 2 1/8" h. (ILLUS. center with pair of Beehive & Thistle dishes, top of page).. **441**

Plate, 8" d., round w/tiny rim scallops, central Peacock Feather Eye & Thistle patt., bull's-eye border band, ca. 1835-45 (minor edge roughness).. **118**

Group of Rare Colored Lacy Salt Dips

Rare Lacy Tray & Window Pane

Salt dip, model of a boat, starburst stern, opalescent purplish blue, rim roughness, BT 9, 2 x 3 7/8", 1 1/2" h. (ILLUS. top row, far left with other salt dips, bottom previous page) **999**

Salt dip, model of sidewheel steamboat, "Lafayet" on the paddle wheel, Boston & Sandwich Glass Co., dark opalescent blue, BT 4d, small chips on keel, rim & scroll, 2 x 3 1/2", 1 1/2" h. (ILLUS. top row, far right with other salt dips, bottom previous page) **2,468**

Salt dip, model of sidewheel steamboat, "Lafayet" on the paddle wheel, Boston & Sandwich Glass Co., dark opalescent blue, BT 8, edge chips, 2 x 3 1/2", 1 1/2" h. (ILLUS. bottom row center, with other salt dips, bottom previous page) **2,703**

Salt dip, oblong, deep sides in the Beaded Strawberry Diamond patt., opaque purplish blue with light mottling, OL 15, tiny rim chips & base edge roughness, 2 3/8 x 3 1/2", 1 5/8" h. (ILLUS. bottom row, far right with other salt dips, bottom previous page) **940**

Salt dip, sleigh bed-shaped, Beaded Scroll & Basket of Flowers patt., light emerald green, very tiny rim nicks & machined to remove chips, tiny chips on feet, BS 2, 2 x 3 1/4", 1 3/4" h. (ILLUS. top row, center with other salt dips, bottom previous page) **558**

Salt dip, sleigh bed-shaped, Lyre patt., cornucopias at the rim, opaque dark blue, LE 3, very minor flakes to rim, scrolls & feet, 2 x 3", 1 3/4" h. (ILLUS. bottom row, far left with other salt dips, bottom previous page) **2,468**

Sugar bowl, cov., Gothic Arch patt., alternating finely ribbed & diamond lattice arches, Boston & Sandwich Glass Co., ca. 1840-50, sapphire blue, 5 1/2" h. (edge roughness on cover & bowl edge)... **1,880**

Sugar bowl, cov., Gothic Arch patt., alternating finely ribbed & diamond lattice arches, Boston & Sandwich Glass Co., ca. 1840-50, deep amethyst,

5 1/2" h. (chips to base of finial, cover rim & bowl edge) **3,819**

Sugar bowls, cov., Gothic Arch patt., alternating finely ribbed & diamond lattice arched panels, Boston & Sandwich Glass Co., ca. 1840-50, chips to cover edges, rim roughness on bowls, 5 1/2" h., pr. (ILLUS. of one, right, with two other pieces, top page 628) **235**

Sweetmeat dish, cov., a round domed foot on the deep flaring Peacock Eye patt. bowl w/grapevine border, matching domed cover w/florette finial, Boston & Sandwich Glass Co., ca. 1830-45, edge chips to cover & base, 6 1/4" d., 5" h. (ILLUS. far left with other pieces, page 628) **1,293**

Tray, rectangular, U.S.F. Constitution under sail in the center w/the name above, heart border, Boston & Sandwich Glass Co., ca. 1833-45, small rim chips, very rare, 4 5/8 x 7" (ILLUS. left with window pane, top of page) **7,344**

Tray, rectangular w/beveled corners, Lyre & Leaf border patt., diamond centered by small scrolls in the bottom, 6 1/2 x 9" (edge chips, roughness) **411**

Window pane, rectangular, a small center rectangular plaque w/a scene of an early steamboat w/the name "J & C Ritchie," a thistle & cornucopias below & vases of flowers & flowering vines up the sides & across the top, Pittsburgh, 1830s, extremely rare, very minor edge roughness, 5 x 7" (ILLUS. right with Constitution tray, top of page) **12,925**

Lalique

Fine glass, which includes numerous extraordinary molded articles, has been made by the glasshouse established by René Lalique early in the 20th century in France. The firm was carried on by his son, Marc, until his death in 1977 and is now headed by Marc's daughter, Marie-Claude. All Lalique glass is marked, usually on or near the bottom, with either an engraved or molded signature. Unless otherwise noted, we list only those pieces marked "R. Lalique," produced before the death of René Lalique in 1945.

Lalique Marks

Lalique Amber "Cleones" Box

Box, cov., "Cleones," low cylindrical round base w/slightly domed cover, amber, the cover molded w/beetles among fern leaves, signed in block letters "R. Lalique France," two small chips on cover rim (ILLUS.) **$1,093**

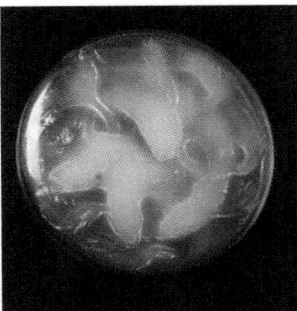

Rare Lalique "Grande Cyprins" Box

Box, cov., "Grande Cyprins," low cylindrical base w/slightly domed cover, opalescent, the cover molded w/swirling fish, signed in block letters "R. Lalique France," 10" d., 2" h. (ILLUS.) **3,163**

Center bowl & underplate, "Annecy," a widely flaring flat-sided bowl in frosted clear molded w/wavy zippered bands around the sides, on a matching wide flattened underplate, introduced in 1935, signed "R. Lalique," underplate 13" d., bowl 9 1/2" d., 2 pcs. **575**

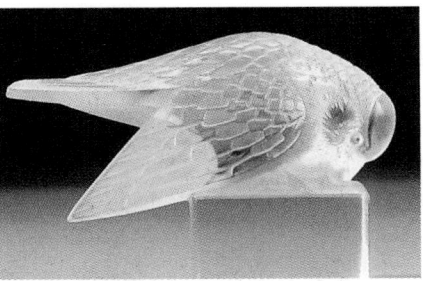

Lalique Figural Bird Paperweight

Paperweight, figural, "Moineau sur Socle, Ailes Overtes" (Sparrow on base, open wings), frosted clear model of a bird, introduced in 1929, inscribed "R. Lalique," 4" h. (ILLUS.) **374**

Vase, 6 3/4" h., "Bagatelle," clear frosted ovoid body molded in relief w/large fruits among leaves, clear footring & short neck, introduced in 1939, signed "R. Lalique France" **575**

Lovely Blue Lalique Fern Vase

Vase, 7" h., spherical body tapering to a small neck, dark blue molded overall w/fern leaves, signed "R. Lalique France No. 996" (ILLUS.) **2,875**

Blue-Stained Lalique "Orsin" Vase

Vase, 7 1/4" h., "Orsin," spherical body w/short flaring rim, clear stained overall in light blue, molded w/overall knobs resembling a sea urchin, signed in block letters "R. Lalique, France" (ILLUS.) **1,560**

Lalique "Coquilles" Vase

Vase, 7 1/2" h., "Coquilles," footed swelled cylindrical body w/a small cylindrical neck, frosted clear w/an overall light blue stain, molded overall w/overlapping seashells, signed in block letters "R. Lalique" (ILLUS.) **1,495**

Fine Lalique "Monnaie du Pape" Vase

Vase, 9 1/2" h., "Monnaie du Pape," footed wide ovoid body w/a short cylindrical neck, deep reddish amber molded overall w/silver dollar plant, introduced in 1914, embossed mark "R. Lalique" (ILLUS.) **4,600**

Vase, 10 1/4" h., "Archers," wide ovoid body in frosted clear, molded in relief w/archers shooting at flying birds, short clear neck, introduced in 1921, marked "R. Lalique" (minor roughness inside rim, very minor bruise on one figure) **3,335**

Vase, 10 1/2" h., "Archers," wide ovoid body w/a short cylindrical neck, frosted amber molded overall w/archers shooting at large flying birds, signed in block letters & script "R. Lalique" (ILLUS., top of column) **11,500**

Rare Version of Lalique Archers Vase

Le Verre Francais

Glassware carrying this marking was produced at the French glass factory founded by Charles Schneider in 1908. A great deal of cameo glass was exported to the United States early in the 20th century and much of it was marketed through Ovingtons in New York City.

Various Le Verre Francais Marks

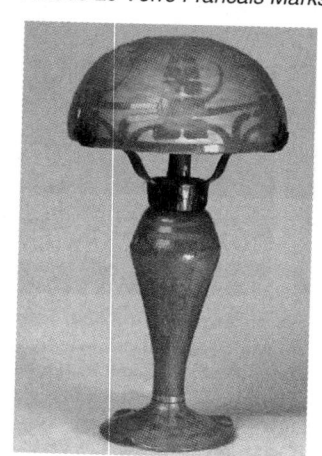

Fine Le Verre Francais Cameo Lamp

Cameo lamp, table model, the baluster-form base w/a wide disk foot, fitted w/a matching domical shade, pink ground overlaid in mottled orange & green, both etched w/stylized Art Deco vines & bands of leaves, signed on the foot, ca. 1930, shaded 7 3/4" d., overall 15" h. (ILLUS., previous page) **$4,888**

Small Le Verre Francais Cameo Vase

Cameo vase, 6 1/2" h., bulbous ovoid body tapering to a cupped rim, mottled pink & yellow ground overlaid in mottled dark brown & orange & etched w/dark brown leaves & stems around the top suspending large orange blossoms, signed on the side in cameo "Charder," engraved on the base "Le Verre Francais" & "France" (ILLUS.) **1,380**

Lavender-blue Le Verre Francais Vase

Cameo vase, 11 1/4" h., a cushion foot & knop stem supporting the tall trumpet-form body, mottled frosted white, pink & clear ground overlaid in mottled lavender & blue & etched w/a stylized Art Deco floral design, signed in cameo on the side "Charder," etched on the foot "Le Verre Francais," early 20th c. (ILLUS.) **1,783**

Le Verre Francais Stylized Floral Vase

Cameo vase, 12 1/8" h., a cushion foot & knop stem supporting a large inverted bell-form body, mottled deep rose overlaid in mottled amethyst & deep burgundy & etched w/large stylized blossoms on leafy stems, signed in cameo on the side "Charder," base signed "Le Verre Francais" & "France," early 20th c. (ILLUS.) **863**

Fine Le Verre Francais Vase with Geese

Cameo vase, 13 3/4" h., a cushion foot below the tall ovoid body tapering to a flattened flaring rim, mottled yellow ground overlaid in mottled brown & blue & etched around the top w/flying geese & around the base w/marsh grass, applied small brown loop handles, signed on the foot "Le Verre Francais" & on the bottom "France," ca. 1930 (ILLUS.) **3,450**

Colorful Le Verre Francais Cameo Vase

Cameo vase, 15 1/2" h., ovoid shouldered body w/a short cylindrical neck flanked by small applied amethyst loop handles, mottled red, blue & amethyst overlaid w/mottled orange & amethyst & etched w/a bold design of large fuchsia blossoms & leaves above a band of large leaves around the base, engraved "Le Verre Francais - France," ca. 1930 (ILLUS.) **3,220**

Legras

Cameo and enameled glass somewhat similar to that made by Gallé, Daum Nancy and other factories of the period was made at the Legras works in Saint Denis, France, late in the 19th century and until the outbreak of World War I.

Legras 8

Typical Legras Mark

Cameo vase, 9 1/2" h., very wide flattened ovoid body tapering to a wide flat mouth, grey w/amethyst overtones overlaid & etched in various shades of green w/tall trees silhouetted against a forested lake, signed in cameo, ca. 1900 .... **$2,415**
Cameo vase, 21" h., rounded tapering cylindrical body w/a short flaring neck, amber overlaid w/peach & etched & enameled w/tall aquatic plants in green, crimson & yellow, signed in cameo, ca. 1900 (ILLUS. left with other cameo vase, top of next column) **978**
Cameo vase, 22" h., tall slender tapering ovoid body w/a small cupped mouth, amber overlaid in peach & etched & enameled w/long aquatic plants in crimson &

Tall Legras Cameo Vases

green, signed in cameo (ILLUS. right with other cameo vase) **805**

Finely Decorated Legras Table Lamp

Lamp, table model, a baluster-form base in yellow enameled w/large flowers in red & yellow on brown leafy stems, supporting a wide domed mushroom-shaped matching shade, both base & shade signed, some minor chipping to edge of shade, shade 21" d., overall 31" h. (ILLUS.) **1,380**

Legras Vase Decorated with Ribbons

Vase, 12 1/2" h., ovoid body tapering to a flaring neck, frosted clear chipped ice exterior etched & enameled in maroon w/angular looping ribbons, signed in cameo (ILLUS., bottom previous page) **316**

Vase, 15 3/4" h., tall slender square waisted body, frosted orange etched & enameled w/a continuous winter landscape in shades of brown, white & black, signed (ILLUS.).. **403**

Libbey

In 1878, William L. Libbey obtained a lease on the New England Glass Company of Cambridge, Massachusetts, changing the name to the New England Glass Works, W.L. Libbey and Son, Proprietors. After his death in 1883, his son, Edward D. Libbey, continued to operate the company at Cambridge until 1888 when the factory was closed. Edward Libbey moved to Toledo, Ohio, and set up the company subsequently known as Libbey Glass Co. During the 1880s, the firm's master technician, Joseph Locke, developed the now much desired colored art glass lines of Agata, Amberina, Peach Blow and Pomona. Renowned for its Cut Glass of the Brilliant Period (see CUT GLASS), the company continues in operation today as Libbey Glassware, a division of Owens-Illinois, Inc.

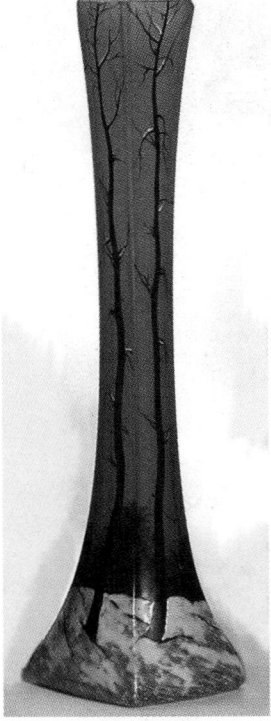

Tall Legras Vase with Winter Landscape

Partial Set of "Patrician" Champagnes

Champagnes, a wide flaring bowl on a slender tapering stem & round foot, wheel-cut & polished crystal in the "Patrician" patt., each w/Libbey mark, early 20th c., 6" h., set of eight (ILLUS. of part).................. **$300-500**

Set of Libbey Silhouette Pattern Cocktails

Loetz Bowl, Compote & Vases

Cocktails, Silhouette patt., clear bowl on a moonstone figural kangaroo stem, ca. 1930s, one w/very slight rim chip, 6" h., set of four (ILLUS., bottom previous page).. **288**

Loetz

Iridescent glass, some of it somewhat resembling that of Tiffany and other contemporary glasshouses, was produced by the Bohemian firm of J. Loetz Witwe of Klostermule and is referred to as Loetz. Some cameo pieces were also made. Not all pieces are marked.

Loetz Mark

Bowl, 3 3/4" d., a low cylindrical form in orange w/iridescent silvery green "Titania" finish decorated w/ornately undulating floral & vine silver overlay, ca. 1905 (ILLUS. front row, center with compote & vases, top of page).................................... **$1,035**

Compote, open, 7" h., a flaring funnel foot supporting a widely flaring bell-form bowl, yellow bowl w/the lower half decorated w/an iridescent blue "Phanonem" finish that continues down over the foot, ca. 1925 (ILLUS. back row, left with bowl & vases, top of page)........................... **1,150**

Fine Loetz Art Nouveau Ewer in Frame

Ewer, squatty bulbous base tapering to a tall cylindrical neck w/upright pointed spout, gold iridescent oil spot finish, fitted in an Art Nouveau style gilt-metal four-footed frame w/a grotesque masque up the front & an ornate arched high handle at the back, 11" h. (ILLUS.)......................... **1,800**

Loetz "Titania" Paperweight-type Lamp

Lamp base, paperweight style w/"Titania" finish, bulbous tapering gourd-form, internally decorated w/random silver in the upper half & emerald green around the lower half, w/electric fittings, 8" h. (ILLUS.).. **460**

Shell-shaped and Other Small Loetz Vases

Vase, 4 1/4" h., tapering bulbous base w/a wide shoulder tapering to a cylindrical neck, green w/overall blue iridescent oil spot finish, ca. 1920 (ILLUS. left with conch shell vase, top of page)...................... **374**

Vase, 4 1/2" h., "Marmorierte" type, bulbous spherical body w/a rounded shoulder & low cylindrical neck, mottled dark reddish orange & yellow agate-style body enameled around the base & neck w/spearpoints in dark purple trimmed in blue & tiny white beading, ca. 1900 (ILLUS. front row, far right with bowl & compote, previous page) **460**

Vase, 4 3/4" h., bulbous tapering ovoid body w/deeply indented sides & a flaring flat rim, cobalt blue w/overall bright iridescent blue "Papillon" finish, ca. 1920 (ILLUS. at right with conch shell vase, above)... **431**

Vase, 5" h., flat-bottomed tapering cylindrical form w/a widely flaring ruffled rim, orange decorated w/an iridescent green & silver "Titania" finish, ca. 1905 (ILLUS. front row, left with bowl & compote, previous page) **2,070**

A Short & Tall Loetz Vase

Vase, 6 1/2" h., a thin cushion foot & swelled stem supporting an upper body w/a wide compressed center tapering to a rolled rim, dark amber w/overall swirled purple iridescence (ILLUS. left with tall signed vase)... **1,265**

Fine "Federzeichnung" Satin Vase

Vase, 6 3/4" h., footed ovoid body tapering to a short cylindrical neck, satin mother-of-pearl "Federzeichnung" design in dark brown w/lighter swirls, enameled w/fine gold tracery & gilt trim, late 19th c. (ILLUS.).. **1,668**

Vase, 7" h., a model of a large conch shell reclining on a pinched & pulled rounded base, green w/an overall light iridescent blue "Papillon" finish, ca. 1900 (ILLUS. center with two small vases, top of page).. **3,335**

Very Fine Iridescent Loetz Vase

Vase, 7 1/4" h., slightly flaring cylindrical body w/pinched-in sides & a pinched & ruffled rim, bronze ground decorated overall w/swirling silvery blue iridescent bands, signed on the pontil "Loetz Austria" (ILLUS., previous page) **2,530**

Squared Iridescent Loetz Vase

Vase, 7 1/2" h., squared tapering bulbous body w/a flat rim, clear w/overall bright gold oil spot iridescence, signed on the base "Loetz Austria" (ILLUS.) **575**

Vase, 8" h., a bulbous lower body below a wide cylindrical neck w/a flaring rim, mounted on a stepped silver socle base, in blue w/an overall iridescent blue "Papillon" finish, ca. 1925 (ILLUS. back row, right with bowl & compote, page 636) **719**

Fine Loetz Silver Overlay Vase

Vase, 8" h., bulbous ovoid body tapering to a swelled cylindrical neck w/a pinched-in mouth, light iridescent blue ground decorated w/ornate Art Nouveau style silver overlay in the form of large flowers, vines & ribbons, some minor scuff marks (ILLUS.) **2,280**

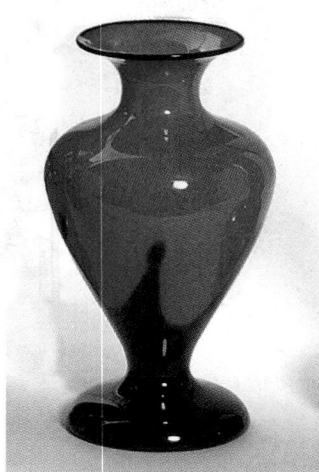

Loetz "Tango" Vase

Vase, 8 1/2" h., "Tango" type, wide cushion foot below the wide ovoid body w/a flaring trumpet neck, tangerine orange above pulled amethyst bands around the lower section, signed on the base "Czechoslovakia," ca. 1920s (ILLUS.) **288**

Rare Loetz Vase with Applied Shells

Vase, 9 1/2" h., wide cylindrical body w/a narrow angled shoulder & wide flat mouth, overall textured green ground w/blue iridescent oil spot decoration & seven applied gold iridescent figural seashell prunts, ca. 1909 (ILLUS.) **3,910**

Loetz Tall "Neptun" Iridescent Vase

Vase, 11 1/4" h., Neptun (sic) line, bulbous ovoid base tapering to a ruffled cupped rim, molded w/slender vertical vining, dark blue w/green iridescence, ca. 1906 (ILLUS.) **425-525**

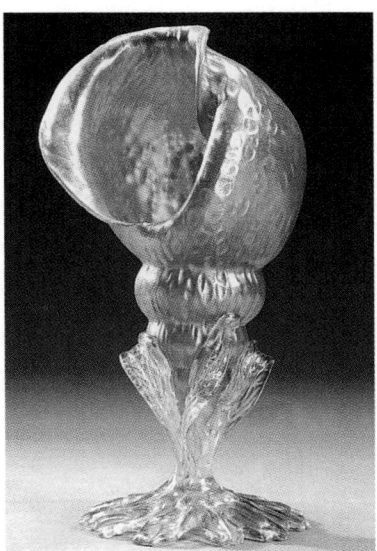

Rare Loetz Shell-shaped Iridescent Vase

Vase, 11 1/2" h., modeled as a large upright seashell supported on leaves of seaweed continuing to a foot composed of leaves, iridescent gold "Candia Diaspora Silveriris" finish on the shell, the leaves in clear w/an iridescent finish, ca. 1898 (ILLUS.) **3,450**

Vase, 12" h., a tall stylized bulbed flower form in cobalt blue w/a blue iridized finish

Rare Stylized Floral Loetz Vase

supported by swirled gold iridescent leaves & round foot, ca. 1910 (ILLUS.)...... **3,795**

Vase, 14" h., a thin cushion foot supporting the tall double-swelled ovoid body w/a short flared rim, clear w/overall heavy iridescent loopings in shades of purple, green, blue & gold, signed in script "Loetz - Austria" (ILLUS. right with small vase, page 637) **748**

Lustres

Lustres were Victorian glass vase-like decorative objects often hung around the rim with prisms. They were generally sold as matched pairs to be displayed on fireplace mantels. A wide range of colored glasswares were used in producing lustres and pieces were often highlighted with colored enameled decoration.

Cased clear, round domed foot overlaid in white & cut w/large leaves, tapering to a ring at the base of the slender panel-cut body slightly flaring to the wide rolled scallop-cut white-cased rim, the rim w/round gold-bordered roundels decorated w/alternating color designs of busts of children & floral bouquets, the rim hung w/long triangular facet-cut spearpoint prisms, overall gilt trim, Bohemia, late 19th c., 14 1/4" h., pr.................. **$1,840**

Cased ruby, round panel-cut foot tapering to a tall panel-cut & slightly flaring body below the wide rolled rim overlaid in white & cut w/a band of oval plaques w/enameled floral decoration, hung w/long triangular facet-cut prisms, France, late 19th c., 12" h., pr. **2,645**

Pair of Cut Glass Lustres

Cut, trumpet shape, w/serrated top & bottom borders, prisms of two lengths & two designs, originals probably 6 1/2", replacements probably 7 1/2", overall 10" h., lacking three prisms, pr. (ILLUS.)...... **495**

Decorated Ruby Glass Lustres

Ruby, a cushion foot below the baluster-form stem supporting the wide bulbous ovoid bowl w/a flaring scalloped crown-form rim, enameled w/white floral branches & blossoms w/gold trim & gold shoulder band, hung w/triangular cut spearpoint prisms, Bohemia, early 20th c., 15" h., pr. (ILLUS.) **550-600**

Very Fine Decorated Ruby Lustres

Ruby, a domed foot tapering to a ringed pedestal supporting a bowl w/a ringed bottom below a wide cylindrical shouldered bowl w/a scallop-cut crown-style rim, enameled overall w/delicate blossoms & leaves, the bowl suspending two tiers of long triangular facet-cut spearpoint prisms, Bohemia, late 19th c., 14 1/4" h., pr. (ILLUS.)................................. **1,323**

Ruby, round cushion foot supporting a baluster-form standard below the deep rounded bowl w/a sawtooth cut rim, the bowl enameled w/colorful floral garlands w/additional enameled trim on the standard & foot, hung w/long triangular spearpoint prisms, probably Bohemia, late 19th c., 13 3/4" h., pr. (slight imperfections)... **660**

Mary Gregory

Glass enameled in white with silhouette-type figures, primarily of children, is now termed "Mary Gregory" and was attributed to the Boston and Sandwich Glass Company. However, recent research has proven conclusively that this was not decorated by Mary Gregory, nor was it made at the Sandwich plant. Miss Gregory was employed by Boston and Sandwich Glass Company as a decorator; however, records show her assignment was the painting of naturalistic landscape scenes on larger items such as lamps and shades, but never the charming children for which her name has become synonymous. Further, in the inspection of fragments from the factory site, no paintings of children were found.

It is now known that all wares collectors call "Mary Gregory" originated in Bohemia beginning in the late 19th century and were extensively exported to England and the United States well into this century.

For further information, see The Glass Industry in Sandwich, Volume #4 by Raymond E. Barlow and Joan E. Kaiser, and the book Mary Gregory Glassware, 1880-1900 by R. & D. Truitt.

Creamer, slightly tapering cylindrical form w/an applied clear handle, emerald green enameled in white w/the figure of a Victorian girl in a garden, ca. 1900, 4" h........ **$86**

Patch box w/hinged cover, thin disk-form w/brass fitting on the rim & hinged cover, cobalt blue, the cover enameled in white w/the figure of a little girl, the base enameled w/a band of tiny white dots, Bohemia, ca. 1900, 2 1/2" d. **259**

Tumble-up set: footed bulbous carafe w/cylindrical neck fitted w/an inverted cylindrical tumbler, both in cranberry, the carafe enameled in white w/the figure of a Victorian lady seated by a column, the tumbler enameled w/a Victorian lady standing by a column, Muhlhaus factory, Bohemia, ca. 1895, tumbler 3 3/4" h., carafe 7 1/2" h., the set.. **575**

Vase, 12" h., ringed domed foot supporting a tall ovoid body tapering to a trumpet neck, light blue opaline enameled in

white w/the figure of a Victorian girl standing in a garden, Bohemia, ca. 1900 ..... **115**
Vases, 6 1/4" h., simple cylindrical form, blue opaline, one enameled in white w/the figure of a small boy playing a drum, the other enameled w/the figure of a small boy dancing & holding a tambourine, Muhlhaus factory, Bohemia, ca. 1900, facing pr. **230**

Facing Pair of Mary Gregory Vases

Vases, 8" h., cylindrical ring-type, mottled white & clear cased in light blue, white enameled figure of a Victorian girl in a garden, Muhlhaus factory, Bohemia, late 19th c., facing pr. (ILLUS.) **431**
Vases, 9 1/2" h., ovoid body tapering to a tall slender trumpet neck, cranberry enameled in white on one w/the figure of a Victorian boy blowing a bubble pipe & on the other w/a Victorian girl holding a small flag, Bohemia, ca. 1900, facing pr. **403**
Vases, 11" h., footed ovoid body tapering to a slender trumpet neck, cranberry decorated w/a white enamel figure of a boy in a garden on one & a girl in a garden on the other, Bohemian, ca. 1900, facing pr. **518**

McKee

The McKee name has been associated with glass production since 1834, first producing window glass and later bottles. In the 1850s a new factory was established in Pittsburgh, Pennsylvania, for production of flint and pressed glass. The plant was relocated in Jeanette, Pennsylvania, in 1888 and operated there as an independent company almost continuously until 1951, when it sold

out to Thatcher Glass Manufacturing Company. Many types of collectible glass were produced by McKee through the years including Depression, Pattern, Milk Glass and a variety of utility kitchenwares. See these categories for additional listings.

McKee

PRESCUT

McKee Marks

Kitchenwares

Bowl, 8" d., Red Polka Dots patt. **$35**
Butter dish, cov., Red Ships patt. on white opal, 1 lb. **60**
Canister, cov., French Ivory, 40 oz. **45**
Egg beater bowl w/spout, French Ivory **35**
Egg cup, Red Ships patt. **45**
Flour shaker w/original metal lid, Red Ships patt. **42**
Measuring cup, handled, two spouts, Chalaine Blue, 1 cup **1,250**
Mixing bowl, black, 7 3/8" d. **50**
Pepper shaker w/original metal top, Roman Arch patt., Chalaine blue **145**

McKee Glass Reamer

Reamer, butterscotch, embossed "SUNK-IST," marked "Pat. No. 18764 Made in USA," 6" d. (ILLUS.) **850**
Reamer, embossed "Sunkist," Chalaine Blue **285**

McKee Saucer-type Reamer

Reamer, lemon-type, saucer-shaped, Skokie Green on base, loop handle, 5 1/2" d. (ILLUS.) **50-60**

McKee Red Ships Refrigerator Dish

Refrigerator dish, cov., rectangular, Red
Ships patt. on white opal, 4 x 8" (ILLUS.) **45**
Rolling pin, Chalaine Blue **2,500**
Sugar shaker w/original metal lid, Roman
Arch style, French Ivory, 4 1/4" h. **45**
Towel bar, Chalaine Blue, 17" l. **55**

Rock Crystal

Bowl, 8 1/2" d., center handle, cupped,
plain edge, ruby **195**
Candlesticks, clear, 8 1/2" h., pr. **45**
Cup & saucer, scalloped edge on saucer,
ruby, pr. (ILLUS. w/plate, top of column) **90**
Pitcher, tankard-type, cobalt blue **850**
Plate, 8 1/2" d., plain edge, ruby (ILLUS.
w/ruby Rock Crystal cup & saucer) **35**
Tumbler, flat, clear, 13 oz. **32**
Vase, 12" h., square top, clear **80**
Wine, ruby, 3 oz. **65**

Miscellaneous Patterns & Pieces

Bowl, berry, 4 3/4" d., Laurel patt., French
Ivory **10**
Bowl, soup, 7 3/4" d., Laurel patt., Skokie
Green **45**
Candy dish, cov., triangular shape w/de-
sign of nude figures, Skokie Green,
7 1/2" h. **695**
Creamer & open sugar, child's, Laurel
patt., Skokie Green w/Scottie decoration,
pr. **325**

Ruby Rock Crystal Pieces

Creamer & sugar, child's, French Ivory,
Laurel patt. (ILLUS., bottom of page) **45-55**
Cup & saucer, child's, Laurel patt., Skokie
Green w/Scottie decoration, pr. **250**
Plate, grill, 9 1/4" d., Laurel patt., French
Ivory **14**

Laurel Child's Creamer & Sugar

Clico Pattern Sherbet

Sherbet, Clico patt., green bowl on square
black base (ILLUS.)... **38**

Art Deco Skokie Green Vase

Vase, 8" h., Art Deco-style triangular "Art
Nude" design, Skokie Green (ILLUS.)........... **375**
Vegetable bowl, Laurel patt., oval, Poudre
Blue, 9 3/4" l. **95**
Whiskey tumbler & base, Bottoms-Up
patt., Skokie Green, satin finish, 2 pcs. **350**

Milk Glass

*Opaque white glass, or "opal," has been called
"milk-white glass" perhaps to distinguish it from
transparent or "clear-white glass." Resembling
fine white porcelain, it was viewed as an inexpensive substitute. Opacity is obtained by adding
bone ash or oxide of tin to clear molten glass. By
the addition of various coloring agents, the
opaque mixture can be turned into blue milk
glass, or pink, yellow, green, caramel, even black
milk glass. Collectors of milk glass now accept not
only the white variety but virtually any opaque
color and color mixtures, including slag or marbled glass. It has been made in numerous forms
and shapes in this country and abroad from
about the first quarter of the 19th century. Many
of the items listed here were also made in colored
opaque glass, which collectors call blue or green
or black "milk glass." It is still being produced,
and there are many reproductions of earlier
pieces. Pieces here are all-white unless otherwise
noted.*

Chicks in Rectangular Basket Dish

Animal covered dish, Chicks in basket,
four large chicks in a rectangular woven
basket w/arched center handle, unknown
maker (ILLUS.).. **$400**

Dog on Rug on Flowered Base Dish

Animal covered dish, Dog on diamond-lattice rug, molded flowers on tapered oblong base, the dog trimmed in brown reclining on a gold-painted rug, flowers on
base trimmed in red, Portieux, France
(ILLUS.).. **175-200**

Hen on Basketweave Base Dish

Animal covered dish, Hen on basketweave base, red painted comb & eyes, Fostoria (also comes in pink & aqua), 7 1/8" (ILLUS.) **120**
Animal covered dish, Hen w/amethyst head, lacy base, Atterbury **200-225**
Animal covered dish, Horse on split-ribbed base, McKee... **275-300**

Blue & White Lamb Covered Dish

Animal covered dish, Lamb on picket base, blue body & white head, Westmoreland Specialty Co., 5 1/2" l. (ILLUS.) **120**
Animal covered dish, Lion, Majestic Lion, molded bird & foliage base, 6 3/4" h........... **2,600**

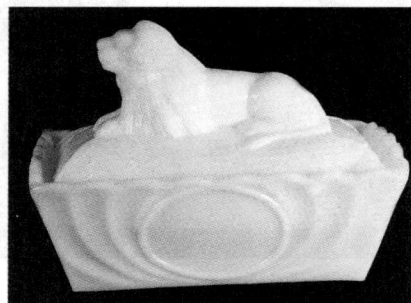

Lion on Scroll Base Dish

Animal covered dish, Lion on scroll base, 5 3/4" l. (ILLUS.) **75**

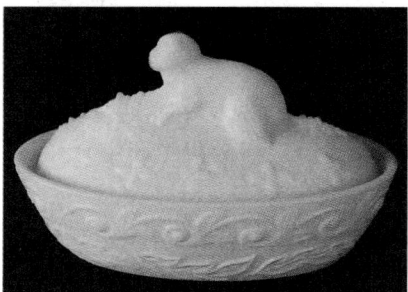

Rare Monkey On Grass Mound Dish

Animal covered dish, Monkey on Grass Mound w/leaf & scroll patt. base, 6 1/4" l. (ILLUS.) **1,800-2,000**

Animal covered dish, Owl Head on split-ribbed base, McKee **800-1,000**

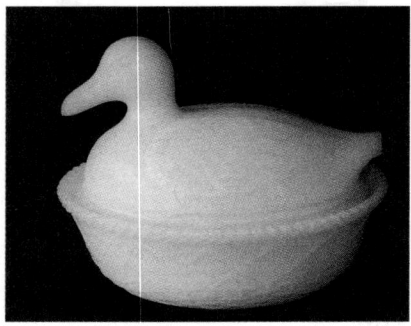

Pintail Duck Covered Dish

Animal covered dish, Pintail Duck on basketweave base, Westmoreland Specialty Co., 5 1/4" l. (ILLUS.).. **90**
Animal covered dish, Rabbit, Flat-Eared Rabbit on split-ribbed base, McKee, 5 1/2" l. **300**

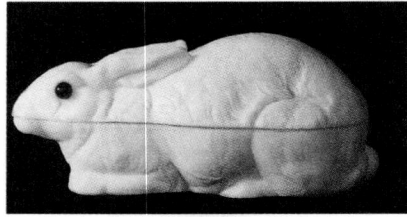

Atterbury Rabbit Dish

Animal covered dish, Rabbit, original red glass eyes, patent date stamped on bottom, Atterbury, 9" l. (ILLUS.)................... **250-275**
Animal covered dish, Robin on pedestal nest, signed "Vallerysthal"....................... **200-225**
Animal covered dish, Rooster on wide ribbed base, Westmoreland Specialty Company, 5 1/2" l. **45**

McKee Squirrel on Split-Ribbed Base

Animal covered dish, Squirrel on split-ribbed base, McKee, excellent, 5 1/2" l. (ILLUS.).. **300**
Animal covered dish, Swan w/raised wings & glass eyes on lacy-edged base, Atterbury, 9 1/2" l..................................... **150-175**

Animal covered dish, Turkey on ribbed base, McKee, 5 1/2" l. **85**

Animal covered dish, Turkey on split-ribbed base, McKee **250-275**

Animal covered dish, Turtle on two-handled oblong base, Westmoreland Specialty Co., overall 7 1/2" l. **225-250**

Basket, chick emerging from egg on cover, two-handled **75**

Bowl, 7" d., 5" h., Chain & Petal Edge patt. **35**

Bowl, 8" d., footed Wide Weave Basket design, Atterbury, open **60**

Bowl, 8 3/4" d., 3 1/2" h., Crinkled Lacy Edge patt. **38**

Rectangular Open Edge Bowl

Bowl, 8 3/4 x 9 1/4", rectangular w/open edge loop border (ILLUS.) **55-60**

Bowl, 10" d., 4 1/2" h., Acanthus Leaf patt. **75**

Bowl, 10" l., 5 3/4" h., oblong, Shell patt., two ribbed & two petal feet **55**

Box, cov., heart-shaped, embossed floral design highlighted w/touches of blue & gold, McKee **35**

Rabbit in Egg Covered Box

Box, cov., in the form of an egg, w/the head of a brown painted rabbit breaking out of the shell forming the handle of the lid, some floral & clover decoration also on lid, Gillinder, 3 3/4" h. (ILLUS.) **135**

"Three Kittens" Covered Box

Box, cov., rectangular, w/scroll & bead decoration around rim, raised oval in center of lid featuring embossed "Three Kittens" design, traces of paint, hairline crack in lid, 5 1/2" (ILLUS.) **55**

Bread tray, Basketweave patt., Atterbury, patent-dated 1874, 9 3/4 x 12" **65**

Bust of Admiral Dewey

Bust, Admiral Dewey, satin finish, 5 1/2" h. (ILLUS.) **175**

Butter dish, cov., Blackberry patt. **75**

Butter dish, cov., Daisy & Tree of Life patt. **175**

Cake stand, Lacy Edge patt., Atterbury, 12" d., 2 3/4" h. **55**

Challinor, Taylor "Scroll" Compote

Compote, 8" h., round, "Scroll," on stepped base, Challinor, Taylor (ILLUS.)................... **210**

Miniature Oil Lamp

Lamp, figural miniature, oil-type, "Reclining Elephant" base, original shade, some paint, 7 3/4" h. (ILLUS.) **750-800**

Indian Head Match Holder

Match holder, Indian Head, in feathered headdress, satin finish, Challinor, Taylor, 4 3/4" h. (ILLUS.).. **95**

Match holder, model of bulldog head w/striker on back of head, possibly McKee, 2 1/4" h. **125-150**

Match holder, pierced for hanging, basket-shaped w/scrolls & relief-molded painted rabbit & chick, attributed to Eagle Glass Co. **125**

Mug, Swan & Cattails patt. **45**

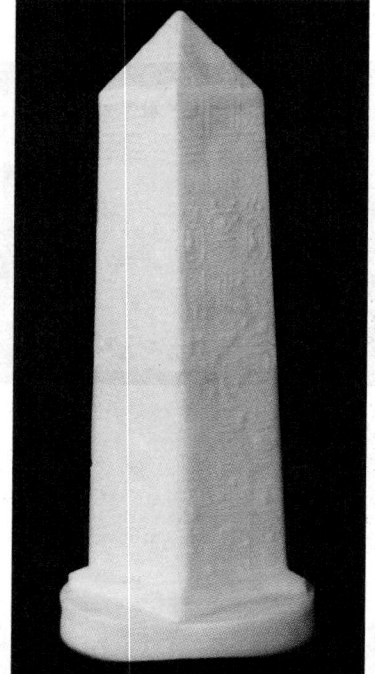

Cleopatra's Needle Obelisk

Obelisk, in the form of Cleopatra's Needle, unknown maker, possibly English, 8 1/2" h. (ILLUS.).. **120**

Pickle dish, model of a fish, Atterbury, 5 1/4 x 8"... **32**

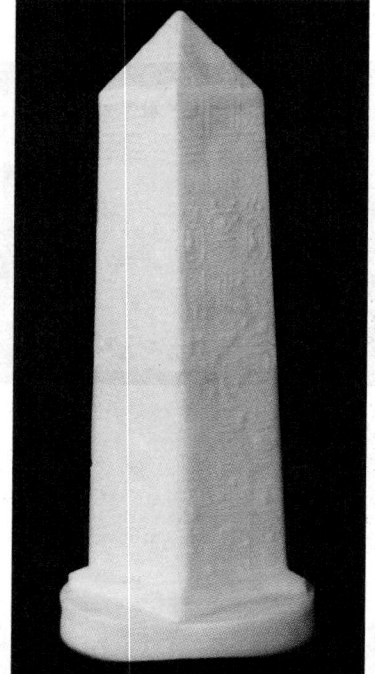

Challinor, Taylor Fish Pickle Dish

Pickle dish, model of a fish on base, waffle pattern on sides, glass or molded eyes, Challinor, Taylor & Company, 9" l., 3" h. (ILLUS.)... **125**

"Birds on Branch" Pitcher

Pitcher, 5 3/4" h., "Birds on Branch," paint on embossed elements, maker unknown (ILLUS.) **145**

Nicely Decorated "Woof Woof" Plate

Plate, 6" d., "Woof Woof" by Westmoreland, realistic dog face in center, arched open loop border, w/finely decorated blue eyes & brown fur (ILLUS.) .... **75+**

Mont Joye

Cameo and enameled glass bearing this mark was made in Pantin, France, by the same works that produced pieces signed de Vez.

Mont Joye Cameo Vase

Cameo vase, 6 7/8" h., cylindrical, pale green textured ground overlaid in cranberry red & cut w/leafy plant stalks & melons, gold enamel trim, early 20th c. (ILLUS.) **$403**

Rose bowl, spherical w/a six-crimp rim, textured frosted body cameo-etched & enameled w/a large purple flower & gold leaves, signed on the base, 3 1/2" h. **431**

Vase, 3" h., miniature, double-gourd form w/widely flaring trumpet neck, textured translucent ground decorated w/enameled purple iris on cameo-cut & leafy stems, unsigned, ca. 1920 .... **288**

Vase, 12" h., a tall slightly tapering cylindrical form w/a bold molded twist in the body up the sides, shaded Rubena enameled overall w/large yellow & rose red flowers on green leafy stems, ca. 1900 .... **518**

Morgantown (Old Morgantown)

Morgantown, West Virginia, was the site where a glass firm named the Morgantown Glass Works began in the late 19th century, but the company reorganized in 1903 to become the Economy Tumbler Company, a name it retained until 1929. By the 1920s the firm was producing a wider range of better quality and colorful glass tablewares; to reflect this fact, it resumed its earlier name, Morgantown Glass Works, in 1929. Today its many quality wares of the Depression era are growing in collector demand.

Basket, No. 20 Jennie, Ebony w/clear twist applied handle, 4 1/2" d. **$550**

Bowl, Crinkle patt., dessert, yellow **15**

Bowl, 5" d., Crinkle patt., moss green **12**

Bowl, 13" d., Janice patt. No. 4355, Ritz Blue w/plain rim **195**

Candlestick, No. 7640 Art Moderne, one-light, clear stem & foot, Ritz Blue socket, 4 1/4" h. **195**

Candy dish, cov., No. 1212 Michael, flat, Ritz Blue w/clear golf ball finial, 7" **600**

Champagne, Churchill patt., saucer-type, No. 7692 .... **50**

Champagne, Golf Ball patt., ruby bowl w/clear golf ball stem, large **35**

Morgantown Goblet & Champagne

Champagne, No. 7634 Tiburon, Aquamarine stem & foot, clear iridescent optic bowl, 6 oz. (ILLUS. previous page, right w/Brilliant goblet) 48

Champagne, Plantation patt., No 8445, cobalt blue.. 50

Champagne, Sunrise Medallion (Dancing Girl) etching, No. 7664, clear 37

Champagne, Yale patt., No. 7684, ruby red 85

Claret, Golf Ball patt., ruby bowl w/clear golf ball stem... 55

Cocktail, aka Mai Tai, amber stem 45

Cocktail, amethyst, w/Farber chrome holder.. 15

Cocktail, Crinkle patt., flat, ruby red 20

Cocktail, Golf Ball patt., ruby bowl w/clear golf ball stem... 35

Cocktail, Plantation patt., No. 8445, cobalt blue 35

No. 7801 Cumberland Compote

Compote, cov., 4 7/8" h., No. 7801 Cumberland, Ebony w/green foot & finial (ILLUS.) 475

Cordial, Golf Ball patt., Stiegel green bowl w/clear golf ball stem........................... 50

Cordial, Plantation patt., No. 8445, cobalt blue 125

Decanter w/stopper, No. 1 Little King, Ebony w/silver overlay..................................... 365

Finger bowl, Queen Louise silk screen decoration, footed, clear 250

Goblet, American Beauty etching, No. 7668 45

Goblet, Golf Ball patt., water, cobalt blue bowl w/clear golf ball stem............................. 55

Goblet, Golf Ball patt., water, smoke bowl w/clear golf ball stem................................. 45

Goblet, No. 7617 Brilliant, water, green stem & foot, pink bowl, 10 oz. (ILLUS. previous page, left w/Tiburon champagne) 85

Goblet, Old English patt., water, No. 7678, ruby red 55

Goblet, Sunrise Medallion (Dancing Girl) etching, No. 7630, Azure blue 135

Goblet, Golf Ball patt., juice, Ritz Blue bowl w/clear golf ball stem, 5" h. 45

Guest set: bottle & tumbler; No. 24 Trudy, opaque Baby Blue, 2 pcs. 95

Ivy ball vase, Golf Ball patt., ruby w/clear golf ball stem 95

Muddler, reeded handle, clear w/Spanish Red filament 48

Crackle & Meadow Green Pieces

Pitcher, cov., No. 37 Barry, clear Crackle w/Meadow Green foot, handle & finial (ILLUS. right w/tumbler) 425

Sherbet, Golf Ball patt., amber bowl w/clear golf ball stem 30

Sherbet, Golf Ball patt., cobalt blue bowl w/clear golf ball stem 35

Sherbet, Golf Ball patt., topaz bowl w/clear golf ball stem 30

Sherbet, Golf Ball patt., No. 7643, Stiegel green bowl w/clear golf ball stem, 7 oz........... 30

Tumbler, Crinkle patt., iced tea, footed, Moss green...................................... 18

Tumbler in Stiegel Green

Tumbler, footed iced tea, No. 7682 Ramona, Stiegel Green (ILLUS., bottom previous page) 45
Tumbler, Golf Ball patt., iced tea, Stiegel green bowl w/clear golf ball stem 48
Tumbler, Mayfair patt., water.............................. 20
Tumbler, No. 9074 Belton, clear Crackle w/Meadow Green foot & handle (ILLUS. left w/pitcher, previous page).......................... 55
Tumbler, Crinkle patt., footed, amethyst, 10 oz... 15
Tumbler, Crinkle patt., amethyst, 14 oz. 20
Vase, 6" h., Palm Optic patt., No. 59, squat, aquamarine 85
Vase, 12" h., No. 35 1/2 Naples, crimped rim, Ritz Blue w/clear Italian base.................. 975
Wine, Golf Ball patt., cobalt blue bowl w/clear golf ball stem.. 50
Wine, Golf Club patt., low, ruby bowl w/clear golf ball stem 45
Wine, Plantation patt., No.8445, cobalt blue....... 85
Wine, Sunrise Medallion patt., crystal, 2 1/2 oz... 65
Wine, Russel Wright, smoke, 4 oz. 30

Moser

Ludwig Moser opened his first glass shop in 1857 in Karlsbad, Bohemia (now Karlovy Vary, in the former Czechoslovakia). Here he engraved and decorated fine glasswares especially to appeal to rich visitors to the local health spa. Later other shops were opened in various cities. Throughout the 19th and early 20th century lovely, colorful glasswares, many beautifully enameled, were produced by Moser's shops and reached a wide market in Europe and America. Moser died in 1916 and the firm continued under his sons. They were forced to merge with the Meyer's Nephews glass factory after World War I. The glassworks were sold out of the Moser family in 1933.

Cruet w/original blue facet-cut stopper, squatty bulbous blue body tapering to a cylindrical neck w/arched spout, applied blue handle, enamel-decorated overall w/white lily-of-the-valley w/gold leaves **$358**
Cruet w/original gilt ball stopper, miniature, cranberry, footed spherical body w/a slender neck & pinched rim spout, applied gilt handle from rim to shoulder, heavy gilt band around top of neck & the shoulder w/overall ornate gilt scrolling & dainty flowers 440
Cruet w/original teardrop stopper, blue, pedestal base w/stepped foot supporting a flattened spherical body tapering to a tall cylindrical neck w/arched spout, applied blue handle, tall stopper, neck & shoulder decorated w/wide gold bands w/jewels & gold stylized flowers 1,210
Cup & saucer, cranberry, tall cylindrical cup w/rounded base, heavy wide gilt band around the rim & applied gilt handle, overall ornate gilt flowers & vines, on a matching saucer w/a light scalloped rim, decorated w/a wide undulating gilt rim band & dainty gilt flowers in the center 385
Mug, cylindrical, cranberry w/applied amber handle, the sides ornately enameled

overall w/raised acorns & multicolored leaves 495
Tumbler, juice, cranberry, polychrome enamel & gilt floral decoration w/butterfly, signed & numbered in gold 180

Fine Facet-cut Moser Covered Urn

Urn, cov., wide baluster-form panel-cut body w/a matching domed cover w/pointed finial, the shoulder, neck & cover border decorated w/acid-etched gold bands of Greek warriors, signed "Moser Karlsbad," ca. 1925, 14" h. (ILLUS.) 920

Decorated Cranberry Glass Moser Vase

Vase, 5 1/4" h., slightly tapering cylindrical body in cranberry applied w/three clear handles, decorated w/heavy scrolling gold top band w/spearpoints around the base, trimmed overall w/small multicolored blossoms, signed on the side, some gold wear on lip, late 19th c. (ILLUS.).. 300-500
Vase, 5 1/2" h., a footring below the wide squatty bulbous body centered by a tall trumpet neck w/an angled rim & long dripping icicles down the neck, cranberry decorated overall w/delicate gilt scrolls & colorfully enameled stylized flowers & insects, the rim & icicles w/heavy gold enameling, ca. 1900, original paper label...... 374

Gilt-decorated Blue Moser Vase

Vase, 6" h., a spherical cobalt blue body w/a short flared & scalloped neck, overall delicate gilt-decorated wheel-carved flowers & leaves, three applied amber rigaree bands down the side, raised on three amber scroll feet, etched signature, late 19th c. (ILLUS.).. **259**

Vase, 9 3/4" h., "Florentine Cameo" line, a round domed foot & short stem supporting a large bulbous ovoid body tapering to a trumpet neck flanked by arched applied handles, deep Prussian blue w/a satin finish enameled in white w/a large, detailed figure of an 18th c. woman seated on a rock holding a small book in one hand, signed "Moser 594," ca. 1895.............. **690**

Cobalt Blue & Gold Moser Vase

Vase, 11" h., footed flaring cylindrical body w/a wide waisted neck, deep cobalt blue decorated around the lower body & neck w/gold-outlined panels, the upper body w/a gold band of Grecian figures, signed on the bottom "Moser Carlsbad," some minor enamel wear, late 19th c. (ILLUS.).. **259**

Beautiful Moser Portrait Vase

Vase, 12" h., a domed flaring pedestal base supporting a large urn-form body, emerald green very ornately enameled w/delicate gold florals & leafy scrolls centered by a large oval medallion enameled in color w/a bust portrait of a beautiful woman, unmarked, base reattached w/a metal fixture, ca. 1900 (ILLUS.)`........................... **546**

Mt. Washington

A wide diversity of glass was made by the Mt. Washington Glass Company of New Bedford, Massachusetts, between 1869 and 1900. It was succeeded in 1900 by the Pairpoint Corporation. Miscellaneous types are listed below.

Mt. Washington Miniature Lamp

Lamp, miniature, "Dresden" ware, squatty bulbous paneled base tapering sharply to the brass fitted w/burner, shade ring & matching paneled ball shade, milk white h.p. w/colorful delicate flowers (ILLUS.)... **$750-1,000**

Mt. Washington Cockle Shell Shaker

Salt shaker w/original metal cap, cockle shell-shaped, pale pink ground h.p. w/lavender, green & tan leaves & tiny white blossoms, scarce form (ILLUS.) .. **750-850**

Large Egg-shaped Sugar Shaker

Sugar shaker w/original metal lid, egg-shaped, painted dark pink to yellow Burmese-like background decorated w/yellow & brown daisies & green leaves, 7" h. (ILLUS.) **350-500**

Sugar shaker w/original top, egg-shaped, opaque white, glossy to satin, w/floral decoration, 4 1/4" h. (wear to decoration, some damage to top) **80**

Sugar shaker w/original top, egg-shaped, satin opaque shaded pink to white, polychrome pansy decoration, 4 1/4" h. **500**

Rare Mt. Washington Lava Vase

Vase, 6" h., "Lava" glass, ovoid body tapering to a widely flaring neck, black ground w/dark pink, green, blue & white inclusions, ca. 1878 (ILLUS.)............ **2,000-2,500**

Mt. Washington Satin Glass Vase

Vase, 6 1/2" h., ovoid body tapering to a ring below the fan-shaped rolled & crimped neck, shaded dark blue mother-of-pearl satin glass in the Diamond Quilted patt. (ILLUS.)... **225-275**

Muller Freres

The Muller Brothers made acid-etched cameo and other fine glass at Luneville, France, starting in 1910 and until the outbreak of World War II in Europe.

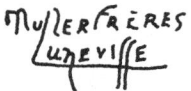

Muller Freres Mark

Muller Fres. Cameo Vase with Poppies

Three Fine Muller Freres Cameo Vases

Cameo vase, 6 1/4" h., wide ovoid body tapering to a wide flat mouth, mottled clear & yellow frosted ground overlaid in mottled teal blue, crimson & burgundy & etched w/large poppy flowers above stems & large leaves, signed on the body (ILLUS., previous page)............................. **$1,380**

Cameo vase, 9" h., ovoid body tapering to a short flaring rim, mottled white & amber overlaid & etched in deep crimson in a forested lake scene, signed in cameo, ca. 1900 .... **1,380**

Cameo vase, 10" h., simple ovoid body w/a flat mouth, mottled grey & pale yellow ground overlaid in deep blue, yellow & brown & etched w/a continuous mountain lake landscape w/tall fir trees in the foreground, known as the "Broken Pine" design, signed in cameo "Muller Fres Luneville," ca. 1910 (ILLUS. right with other vases, top of page)............................ **3,220**

Cameo vase, 10 1/2" h., ovoid body tapering to a short flared rim, citron yellow mottled w/blue & yellow, overlaid in dark blue & cranberry & etched w/large red poppies on dark blue leafy stems, signed in cameo "Muller Fres Luneville," ca. 1910 (ILLUS. left with other vases, top of page)........................... **4,370**

Cameo vase, 11" h., bulbous ovoid body tapering to a short cylindrical neck, grey mottled w/dark yellow ground, overlaid in crimson & dark red & etched w/large reddish orange lilies on dark leafy stems, signed in cameo "Muller Fres Luneville," ca. 1910 (ILLUS. center with other vases, top of page)............................ **3,220**

Cameo vase, 11" h., tall angular ovoid body tapering to a low flared rim, peach ground overlaid w/mottled red, yellow & dark brown & etched w/large roses on dark leafy stems, signed in cameo "Muller Fres. Luneville" (ILLUS., top of next column)........................... **3,105**

Muller Fres. Cameo Vase with Roses

Fine Muller Freres Chandelier

Chandelier, five-light, a large inverted mushroom-shaped central shade in mottled dark blue, red & yellow suspended in a wrought-iron framework of scrolled grapevines & gilt grape clusters, the frame w/a scrolled arm at each corner suspending a socket holding a matching glass trumpet-form shade, signed "Muller Fres. Luneville," early 20th c., 31" d., overall 34" h. (ILLUS., bottom, previous page).. **4,715**

Vase, 7 1/4" h., flugravure cameo-type, ovoid body tapering to a cylindrical neck w/closed rim, pink & amethyst vitrified w/various browns, greens & white & engraved in a scenic design of a birch tree-laden shoreline, molded & cameo-signed "Muller Fres Luneville," France, ca. 1910... **3,910**

Vase, 5 3/4" h., ovoid body tapering to a short flattened & flared rim, grey etched w/a lakeshore scene & enameled in shades of green, brown & amethyst, signed in enamel, ca. 1900 .... **690**

Vase, 10 1/4" h., tall waisted cylindrical form, grey w/yellow, blue & brown mottling overlaid w/vitrified powders in blues, greys & reds & etched & enameled w/ribbons & butterflies, signed in black enamel, ca. 1900 .... **3,220**

New Martinsville

The New Martinsville Glass Mfg. Co. opened in New Martinsville, West Virginia, in 1901 and during its first period of production came out with a number of colored opaque pressed glass patterns. Also developed was an art glass line named "Muranese," which collectors refer to as "New Martinsville Peach Blow." The factory burned in 1907 but reopened later that year and began focusing on production of various clear pressed glass patterns, many of which were then decorated with gold or ruby staining or enameled decoration. After going through receivership in 1937, the factory again changed the focus of its production to more contemporary glass lines and figural animals. The firm was purchased in 1944 by The Viking Glass Company (later Dalzell-Viking).

Covered Batter Jug

Batter jug, cov., dark green (ILLUS.) **$130**
Bonbon, Radiance patt. (No. 42 Line), footed, red, 6".. **32**

Book end, "Nautilus," clear, 6" h. **35**
Bowl, Moondrops patt., cream soup, amber........ **30**
Bowl, 8" d., Moondrops patt., three-footed, amber **26**

No. 18 Crystal Eagle Bowl

Bowl, 15" oval, Crystal Eagle patt. No. 18, amber (ILLUS.) **90-100**
Bride's basket, Muranese line, vivid gold iridescence in ornate silver-plated holder, 9" d.. **400**
Butter dish, cov., Carnation patt. (No. 88 Line), clear w/ruby-stain & gold decoration **275**

No. 10/4 Candleholders

Candleholder, No. 10/4, blue (ILLUS. left)......... **20**
Candleholder, No. 10/4, jade green (ILLUS. right) **45**
Candleholder, No. 10/4, light green (ILLUS. center) **15**

Modernistic Candleholders

Candleholders, Modernistic patt. (No. 33 Line), light green w/cut decoration, pr. (ILLUS.)... **125**
Celery dish, Janice patt., No. 4521-1SJ, oval, swan handle, red, 11" l. **85**
Cocktail shaker, cov., Prelude etching, clear w/chrome lid **200**
Comport, No. 35 (Fancy Squares), jade green, small... **50**
Creamer & sugar bowl, Modernistic patt. (No. 33 Line), green satin finish, pr. **125**

Silver Overlay Creamer & Sugar Bowl

Creamer & sugar bowl, Modernistic patt.
(No. 33 Line), opaque jade green w/Call
of the Wild silver overlay, pr. (ILLUS.).......... 250
Cruet set: oil & vinegar cruets w/original
tops & tray; Janice patt (No. 45 Line),
light blue, the set... 220
Cup & saucer, Janice patt., blue........................ 28

No. 35 Cup & Saucer

Cup & saucer, No. 35 (Fancy Squares),
jade green, pr. (ILLUS.)..................................... 35
Flower bowl, Janice patt. (No. 45 Line),
crimped rim, light blue, 5 1/2" 95

Moondrops Mug

Mug, handled, Moondrops patt. (No. 37
Line), amber, large (ILLUS.) 35
Plate, 8" d., Janice patt., blue.............................. 18
Plate, 14" d., No. 42 w/Meadow Wreath
etching, clear 48
Punch bowl w/underplate & ladle, Radi-
ance patt. (No. 42 Line), ruby, the set.......... 485
Salt & Pepper shakers w/original tops,
Radiance patt. (No. 42 Line), ruby, pr. 100
Sandwich tray, No. 34 (Addie), handled,
black.. 45
Sherbet, Janice patt., blue.................................... 24

Spooner, Carnation patt. (No. 88 Line),
clear w/ruby-stain & gold decoration.............. 125
Sugar bowl, Moondrops patt., individual,
red... 18
Swan dish, Janice patt., crystal body, co-
balt blue head, 12" l. 95
Tumbler, Janice patt., footed, blue 35

Cobalt Blue Old Fashioned Tumbler

Tumbler, No. 38 Hostmaster patt., Old
Fashion, cobalt blue (ILLUS.)............................ 24
Tumbler, Moondrops patt., handled, green,
9 oz.. 18
Vase, 8" h., Janice patt. (No. 45 Line), flared
rim, light blue.. 150
Vase, Modernistic patt. (No. 33 Line), blue
satin finish... 125
Vase, Modernistic patt. (No. 33 Line), pink,
satin finish 125
Vase, 9 1/4" h., "Rocket" style, Moondrops
patt., cobalt blue 280

Opaline

*Also called opal glass (once a name applied to
milk-white glass), opaline is a fairly opaque glass
with a color resembling the opal; however, pieces
in such colors as blue, pink, green and others also
are referred to now as opaline glass. Many of the
objects were decorated.*

Goblet, opaque pink bowl w/applied fiery
opalescent stem & foot, 7" h........................ **$100**

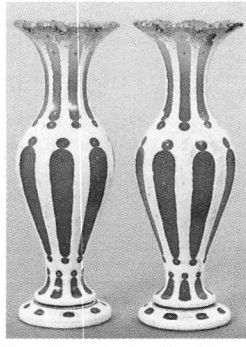

Fine French Opaline Vases

Vases, 13 1/2" h., cut-overlay, baluster-form, white cut to blue opaline in long lancet panels decorated w/gilt stars, the white w/lattimo elements w/traces of gilt vermicelli, the flaring scalloped rim in the Van Dyck cut, France, late 19th c., pr. (ILLUS., previous page)................................... 633

Orrefors

This Swedish glasshouse, founded in 1898 for production of tablewares, has made decorative wares as well since 1915. By 1925, Orrefors had achieved an international reputation for its Graal glass, an engraved art glass developed by master glassblower Knut Berquist and artist-designers Simon Gate and Edward Hald. Ariel glass, recognized by a design of controlled air traps and the heavy Ravenna glass, usually tinted, were both developed in the 1930s. While all Orrefors glass is collectible, pieces signed by early designers and artists are now bringing high prices.

Orrefors

Orrefors Mark

Engraved Smoky Orrefors Bowl

Bowl, 8 x 9 1/2", 3" h., elongated six-panel form, smoky color finely engraved in each panel w/partially clad women in various dancing positions, trimmed w/carved & frosted arches & lines, the bottom carved w/a cartouche & rays, signed on the bottom "Orrefors P. Gabe 937.1927 R. Bayer," first half 20th c. (ILLUS.) **$489**

Engraved Crystal Orrefors Bowl

Bowl, 10 3/4" l., 6" h., elongated oval form w/flattened slightly flaring sides, crystal engraved w/a kneeling woman wearing a filmy gown & two flying birds, signed on the base "Orrefors Palmquist 2327 R B 5," one interior scratch, mid-20th c. (ILLUS.) 240

Vase, 5 5/8" h., 4 3/4" d., "Ariel," heavy walled cylindrical form internally decorated w/rows of geometric transparent trapped bubbles, w/cobalt blue layer within colorless glass, base inscribed "Orrefors Ariel N.V. 174 N Ingeborg Lundin," designed by Ingeborg Lundin, later 20th c. (minor scratches)................................ 863

Simple Engraved Crystal Orrefors Vase

Vase, 5" h., simple ovoid form w/a closed rim, crystal intaglio-carved w/a stylized nude woman, signed on the bottom "Orrefors S. Gate 191 ASRR," first half 20th c. (ILLUS.) 633

Overshot

Popular since the mid-19th century, Overshot glass was produced by rolling a gather of molten glass in finely crushed glass to produce a rough exterior finish. The piece was then blown to the desired size and shape. The finished piece has a frosted or iced finish and is sometimes referred to as "ice glass." Early producers referred to this glass as "Craquelle" and, although Overshot is sometimes lumped together with what glass collectors now call "crackle," that type was produced using a totally different technique.

Bowl, 11" d., a small footring below the widely flaring ruffled & crimped sides, cranberry w/clear overshot exterior, ca. 1900 .... **$75-125**

Compote with Shaded Cranberry Bowl

Compote, open, 6 1/4" h., 8 1/2" d., the shallow cranberry shaded to clear bowl w/deeply crimped & ruffled rim & overshot decoration, raised on an ornate silver plate pedestal base w/scrolled edges & raised floral decoration, late 19th c. (ILLUS., previous page).......................... **175-225**

Paden City

The Paden City Glass Manufacturing Company began operations in Paden City, West Virginia, in 1916, primarily as a supplier of blanks to other companies. All wares were handmade, that is, either hand-pressed or mold-blown. The early products were not particularly noteworthy, but by the early 1930s the quality had improved considerably. The firm continued to turn out high quality glassware in a variety of beautiful colors until financial difficulties necessitated its closing in 1951. Over the years the firm produced, in addition to tablewares, items for hotel and restaurant use, light shades, shaving mugs, perfume bottles and lamps.

Bowl, 9" l. oval, Crow's Foot (No. 412) line, red **$70**
Bowl, 9" d., Peacock & Rose etching, footed, flared, pink.................................... **175**
Bowl, 11" d., Ardith etching, Mrs. "B" line No. 411, footed, yellow **95**
Bowl, 11" d., Cupid etching, rolled edge, pink.. **350**

Maya Pattern Oval Bowl

Bowl, 12" l., Maya patt., oval, handled, light blue (ILLUS.) **65**
Bowl, 13 1/4" d., Black Forest etching, rolled edge, green.. **225**
Cake plate, Peacock & Rose etching, footed, tall stem, pink, 9" d. **155**
Candlesticks, one-light, Black Forest etching, mushroom, green, 5", pr. **175**
Candy dish, cov., Crow's Foot line, three-part, cobalt blue, 7" d. **195**
Candy dish, cov., Nora Bird etching, flat, pink **270**
Cheese plate, Peacock & Rose etching, pink, 10 1/2" d. **95**
Compote, 6" sq., 4" h., Gothic Garden etching, yellow **55**
Compote, open, 7" d., Peacock & Rose etching, rolled edge, tall stem, green **165**
Console bowl, Peacock & Rose etching, rolled edge, green, 14" l. **250**
Creamer & open sugar, Largo patt., footed, ruby, pr. **95**
Cup & saucer, Black Forest etching, black, pr. **150**

Cup & saucer, Cupid etching, pink.................. **165**
Ice tub, Black Forest etching, pink **200**
Ice tub, Peacock & Rose etching, green........... **215**
Mayonnaise set, Ardith etching, ruby, 3 pcs. **225**
Plate, Ardith etching, two-handled, pink.............. **95**
Plate, 9" d., Gadroon patt., dinner, red **30**
Server, Black Forest etching, center-handled, green... **125**
Tray, Cupid etching, oval, center handle, pink **290**
Tumbler, Regina (No. 210) line, clear, 5 oz. **5**
Vase, 8" h., Peacock & Rose etching, elliptical, green **245**

Ebony Vase with Lela Bird Etching

Vase, 8" h., etched Lela Bird patt., ovoid, ebony (ILLUS.).. **175**
Vase, 10" h., Peacock & Rose etching, ebony **225**

Pairpoint

Originally organized in New Bedford, Massachusetts, in 1880 as the Pairpoint Manufacturing Company on land adjacent to the famed Mount Washington Glass Company, this company first manufactured silver and plated wares. In 1894, the two famous factories merged as the Pairpoint Corporation and enjoyed great success for more than forty years. The company was sold in 1939 to a group of local businessmen and eventually bought out by one of the group who turned the management over to Robert M. Gundersen. Subsequently, it operated as the Gundersen Glass Works until 1952 when, after Gundersen's death, the name was changed to Gundersen-Pairpoint. The factory closed in 1956. Subsequently, Robert Bryden took charge of this glassworks, at first producing glass for Pairpoint abroad and eventu-

ally, in 1970, beginning glass production in Saga-
more, Massachusetts. Today the Pairpoint
Crystal Glass Company is owned by Robert and
June Bancroft. They continue to manufacture fine
quality blown and pressed glass.

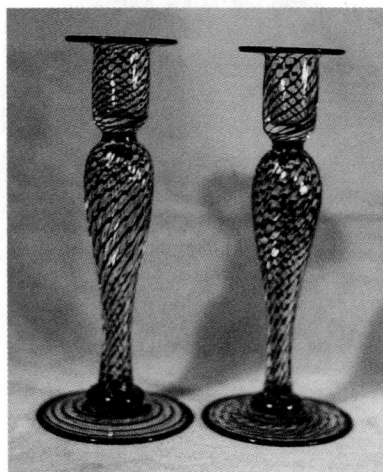

Blue Swirl Pairpoint Candlesticks

Candlesticks, tall blown baluster-form w/a
cylindrical socket & flattened rim, clear
optic ribbed design w/dark blue swirls,
12" h., pr. (ILLUS.).......................... **$1,200-1,800**
Comport, cut-decorated, clear, shape #Un-
known 22, cut w/Unknown "D" patt., pol-
ished pontil, 4 7/8" d., 4 1/2" h.......................... 60

Cut Lincoln Pattern Compote

Compote, open, 6" d., cut overlay, Lincoln
patt., a shallow wide round bowl in cobalt
blue cut to clear, on a tapering facet-cut
stem & star-cut round foot (ILLUS.)....... **650-750**

Pairpoint Fine Arts Line Tazza

Tazza, Fine Arts line, a rib-cut cylindrical
flaring amber glass bowl mounted in a
swag-cast brass-plated metal holder
supported by a figural putto standing on a
square onyx platform w/a cast brass-plated border, signed, ca. 1920s, 10" h.
(ILLUS.).. **500-750**

Cobalt Blue Blown Pairpoint Vase

Vase, 12" h., blown chalice-form, the cobalt
blue ovoid body w/a flaring rim supported
by a clear controlled bubble connector to
the cobalt blue foot (ILLUS.)................... **450-650**

Rare Crown Pairpoint Ware Vase

Vase, 12 1/2" h., Crown Pairpoint Ware, painted overall w/dark earthtone colors w/a large realistic owl on the front, signed, ca. 1895, rare (ILLUS.) **3,500-5,000**

Two Fine Pairpoint Purple Vases

Vases, 12" h., tall blown purple urn-form flaring bowl raised on a clear swirled ball connector over the clear round foot, ca. 1940s, each (ILLUS. of two) **375-450**

Pate de Verre

Pate de Verre, or "paste of glass," was molded by very few artisans. In the pate de verre technique, powdered glass is mixed with a liquid to make a paste which is then placed in a mold and baked at a high temperature. These articles have a finely pitted or matte finish and are easily distinguished from blown glass. Duplicate pieces are possible with this technique.

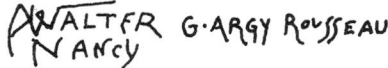

Pate De Verre Marks

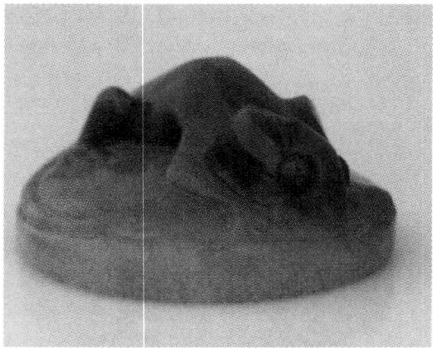

Pate de Verre Figural Paperweight

Paperweight, figural, round, molded w/a green rodent w/large blue eyes, resting on a mottled pink base, impressed round mark "DeCorchemont," ca. 1920s, 4" d. (ILLUS.) **$2,280**

Tray, rectangular w/beveled corners, mottled yellow & citron decorated along the long edges w/raised bands of crimson roses, engraved "A. Walter" & "M. Corrette," ca. 1920, 6 1/4 x 6 1/2".............. **1,380**

Tray, rounded medallion form, amber decorated w/a blue & red butterfly, engraved signature "A Walter Nancy" & "Berge SC," ca. 1920, 6" w. **1,035**

Pate de Verre Vase with Scrolls

Vase, 6" h., slightly swelled cylindrical body molded around the top w/geometric scrolls, mottled purple, red, brown & peach, signed on the side "G. Argy-Rousseau," ca. 1920s (ILLUS.).................. **6,038**

Fine Argy-Rousseau Vase with Figures

Vase, 9 1/2" h., simple ovoid form w/a wide flat mouth, molded w/a continuous scene of women walking & picking up apples below arching apple trees, in shades of orange, mottled yellow, green & brown, signed on the side "G. Argy-Rousseau," ca. 1920s (ILLUS.) **9,488**

Pattern

Though it has never been ascertained whether glass was first pressed in the United States or abroad, the development of the glass pressing machine revolutionized the glass industry in the United States, and this country receives the credit for improving the method to make this process feasible. The first wares pressed were probably small flat plates of the type now referred to as "lacy," the intricacy of the design concealing flaws.

In 1827, both the New England Glass Co., Cambridge, Mass., and Bakewell & Co., Pittsburgh, took out patents for pressing glass furniture knobs; soon other pieces followed. This early pressed glass contained red lead, which made it clear and resonant when tapped (flint.) Made primarily in clear, it is rarer in blue, amethyst, olive green and yellow.

By the 1840s, early simple patterns such as Ashburton, Argus and Excelsior appeared. Ribbed Bellflower seems to have been one of the earliest patterns to have had complete sets. By the 1860s, a wide range of patterns was available.

In 1864, William Leighton of Hobbs, Brockunier & Co., Wheeling, West Virginia, developed a formula for "soda lime" glass that did not require the expensive red lead for clarity. Although "soda lime" glass did not have the brilliance of the earlier flint glass, the formula came into widespread use because glass could be produced cheaply.

An asterisk (*) indicates a piece which has been reproduced.

Ashburton

Ale glass, flint, 6 1/2" h. **$75**
Bitters bottle w/original pewter lid **65**

Celery vase, plain rim, flint **85**
Celery vase, scalloped rim, canary yellow, flint **775**
Celery vase, scalloped rim, clear, flint **125**
Champagne, barrel-shaped, flint **75**
Claret, flint, 5 1/4" h. **75**
Cordial, non-flint **85**
Creamer, applied handle, flint **175**
Decanter, bar lip & facet-cut neck, clear, flint, qt. **110**
Decanter, bar lip w/patent pewter stopper, canary yellow, flint **1,600**
Decanter, bar lip w/patent pewter stopper, clear, flint **185**
Decanter w/original stopper, clear, flint, qt. **135**
Egg cup, clambroth, flint **155**
Egg cup, clear, flint **30**
Egg cup, clear, non-flint **20**
Egg cup, double **95**
Goblet, flared, flint, clear w/gold, 6" h. **58**
Goblet, barrel-shaped, flint **58**
Goblet, flared, flint, clear **58**
Goblet, non-flint **58**
Goblet, short, flint **58**
Honey dish, 3 1/2" d. **15**
Mug, applied handle, 4 3/4" h. **88**
Pitcher, water, applied hollow handle, flint **425**
Sauce dish, flint **8**
Sugar bowl, cov., fiery opalescent, flint **1,650**
Sugar bowl, cov., flint **165**
Tumbler, water, flint **65**
Tumbler, water, footed **75**
Tumbler, whiskey, applied handle, flint **115**
Tumbler, whiskey (small), flint **75**
Vase, 10 1/2" h., flint **250**
Wine, clear, flint **55**
Wine, clear, knob stem **85**
Wine, non-flint **25**

Atlanta (Lion or Square Lion's Head)

Bowl, 4 3/4 x 6 7/8" oblong, flat **60**
Bowl, 6" sq. **65**
Bowl, 6 x 8 3/4" oblong, flat **75**
Bowl, 7" sq. **80**
Bowl, 5 x 8" oblong, flat **68**
Butter dish, cov. **125**
Cake stand **145**
Celery vase **90**
Compote, cov., 5" sq., 6" h. **145**
Compote, cov., 6" sq., low stand **185**
Compote, cov., 7" sq., high stand **188**
Compote, cov., 7" sq., low stand **200**
Compote, open, jelly, 4 1/4" sq., 4" h. **55**
Compote, open, 5" sq. **85**
Compote, open, 6" sq., 7 1/2" h. **85**
Compote, open, 7" sq., high stand **120**
Compote, open, 8" sq., high stand **130**
Creamer **100**
Cruet w/original stopper **175**
Egg cup **95**
*Goblet **175**
Lamp, kerosene type, mini **300**
Marmalade jar, cov., w/lion's head finial **150**
Mustard jar, cov. **750**
Relish, boat-shaped, 5 x 7 3/4" **75**
Salt dip, individual size **100**

Salt dip, master size 75
Sauce dish 30
Spooner 80
Sugar bowl, cov., engraved 160
Sugar bowl, cov., plain 135
Syrup pitcher w/original top, rare 190
Toothpick holder, clear & frosted satin milk
    glass 65
Tumbler, plain 40
Tumbler, ruby-stained 80

Bleeding Heart

Bowl, cov., 7" d., 5" h. 110
Bowl, cov., flat, 8" d. 125
Bowl, cov., 9 1/2" d. 140
Bowl, cov., 7 1/4" oval 35
Butter dish, cov. 80
Cake stand, 9 1/2" to 11" d. 90
Compote, cov., 7" d., w/Bleeding Heart fini-
    al 135
Compote, cov., 8" d., high stand w/Bleed-
    ing Heart finial 150
Compote, cov., 8 1/2" d., high stand 150
Compote, cov., 8 1/2" d., low stand 150
Compote, cov., 9" d., 12" h., w/Bleeding
    Heart finial 165
Creamer, applied handle 60
Creamer, molded handle 35
Egg cup 45
Goblet, knob stem 60
Honey dish 20
Mug, 3" h. 40
Pickle dish, pear-shaped w/scalloped rim,
    8 3/4" l., 5" w. 35
Pitcher, water 195
Relish, 3 5/8" x 5 1/8" oval 45
Salt dip, master size, flat, oval 85
Salt dip, master size, footed 95
Sauce dish, flat 24
Spooner 45
Sugar bowl, cov. 70
Tumbler, flat 110
Tumbler, footed 150
Wine, plain stem 150

Compact - see Snail Pattern

Daisy in Panel - see Two Panel Pattern

Dakota (Baby Thumbprint)

Basket, cake w/metal handle, 10" l., 2" h.,
    engraved, flat 265
Basket, cake w/metal handle, 10" l., 2" h.,
    engraved, footed 265
Butter dish, cov., engraved, floral edge on
    base 250
Butter dish, cov., hotel, engraved 75
Butter dish, cov., hotel, plain 70
Butter dish, cov., table, engraved 75
Butter dish, cov., table, plain 60
Cake stand, 8" d., engraved 95
Cake stand, 8" d., plain 70
Cake stand, 9 1/2" d., engraved 115
Cake stand, 9 1/2" d., plain 80
Cake stand, 10 1/2" d., engraved 125
Cake stand, 10 1/2" d., plain 90
Cake stand, w/high domed cover 700-900

Castor set: salt shaker, oil & vinegar cruets,
    w/salt/pepper shakers, w/original stop-
    pers & tray, 4 pcs. 450
Celery vase, flat base, clear, engraved 75
Celery vase, flat base, clear, plain 65
Celery vase, flat base, clear, ruby-stained 145
Celery vase, pedestal base, engraved 90
Celery vase, pedestal base, plain 80
Celery vase, pedestal base, ruby-stained 165
Cologne bottle w/original stopper, 7" h. 150
Compote, cov., jelly, 5" d., 5" h., engraved 50
Compote, cov., jelly, 5" d., 5" h., plain 30
Compote, cov., 6" d., high stand, engraved 50
Compote, cov., 6" d., high stand, plain 40
Compote, cov., 7" d., high stand, engraved 70
Compote, cov., 7" d., high stand, plain 60
Compote, cov., 8" d., high stand, engraved 80
Compote, cov., 8" d., high stand, plain 70
Compote, cov., 9" d., high stand, engraved 145
Compote, cov., 9" d., high stand, plain 145
Compote, cov., 12" d., high stand, en-
    graved 250
Compote, open, jelly, 5" d., 5 1/2" h., en-
    graved 40
Compote, open, 6" d., plain 40
Compote, open, 7" d., engraved 60
Compote, open, 7" d., plain 50
Compote, open, 8" d., engraved 70
Compote, open, 8" d., plain 60
Compote, open, 9" d., high stand, engraved 40
Compote, open, 10" d., high stand, en-
    graved 90
Creamer, hotel 70
Creamer, table, engraved 50
Creamer, table, plain 40
Cruet w/original stopper, engraved 150
Cruet w/original stopper, plain 125
Dish, ice cream, flat 16
Finger bowl 45
Goblet, clear, engraved 45
Goblet, clear, plain 25
Goblet, ruby-stained, engraved 95
Goblet, ruby-stained, plain 95
Honey dish 25
Lamp, kerosene-type, footed finger 65
Lamp, kerosene-type, high standard 145
Mug, etched 75
Mug, plain 65
Mug, ruby-stained, 3 1/2" h. 85
Pitcher, milk, jug-type, engraved, pt. 120
Pitcher, milk, tankard, clear, plain, pt. 95
Pitcher, milk, tankard, engraved, pt. 120
Pitcher, milk, tankard, engraved, qt. 145
Pitcher, milk, tankard, ruby-stained, pt. 165
*Pitcher, water, tankard, engraved
    leaves, 1/2 gal. 140
*Pitcher, water, tankard, engraved
    leaves, 1/2 gal. 165
Pitcher, water, tankard, ruby-stained, 1/2
    gal. 275
Plate or water tray, 10" d. 90
Plate or water tray, 10 1/2" d., ruffled 120
Salt shaker w/original top, plain 50
Salt shaker w/original top, ruby-stained 85
Sauce dish, flat, clear, engraved, each 40
Sauce dish, flat, clear, plain, each 30
Sauce dish, flat or footed, ruby-stained,
    each 40
Sauce dish, footed, clear, engraved, each 25

Sauce dish, footed, clear, plain, each 20
Sauce dish, footed, cobalt blue, each 40
Shaker bottle w/original top, 5" h. 110
Shaker bottle w/original top, hotel size,
    6 1/2" h. 85
Spooner, engraved 45
Spooner, hotel 65
Spooner, plain 35
Sugar bowl, cov., engraved 60
Sugar bowl, open, covered, hotel size 80
Tumbler, clear, engraved 55
Tumbler, ruby-stained 65

Ruby-stained Dakota Tumbler

Tumbler, ruby-stained, souvenir (ILLUS.) 55
Waste bowl, engraved 103
Waste bowl, plain 65
Water tray, 12 1/2" d., piecrust rim, en-
    graved 225
Water tray, 12 1/2" d., piecrust rim, plain 145
Water tray, 13" d., piecrust rim, plain 145
Wine, clear, engraved 35
Wine, clear, plain 20
Wine, ruby-stained 50
Wine tray, 10 1/2" d., engraved 165
Wine tray, 10 1/2" d., piecrust rim 125
Wine tray, 10 1/2" d., plain 125

Deer & Pine Tree

Bowl, 5 1/2 x 7 1/4" 55
Bowl, 5 1/2 x 8" 55
Bowl, 5 1/2 x 9" 65
Bread tray, amber, 8 x 13" 95
Bread tray, apple green, 8 x 13" 145
Bread tray, blue, 8 x 13" 125
Bread tray, canary yellow, 8 x 13" 185
Bread tray, clear, 8 x 13" 55
Butter dish, cov. 110
Cake stand clear 125
Cake stand in color, depending on size &
    color 150-185
Celery vase 110
Compote, cov., 8" sq., high stand, clear 185
Compote, open, 7 x 9", high stand 215
Creamer 63
*Goblet 52
Honey dish 30
Marmalade jar, cov. 188
Mug, child's, amber 55

Mug, child's, apple green 43
Mug, child's, blue 60
Mug, child's, canary yellow 80
Mug, child's, clear 40
Mug, large, amber 75
Mug, large, apple green 80
Mug, large, blue 60
Mug, large, canary yellow 100
Mug, large, clear 50
Mug, medium, amber 65
Mug, medium, apple green 70
Mug, medium, canary yellow 90
Mug, medium, clear 45
Pickle castor w/metal frame 225
Pickle dish 4 1/2" x 7" 75
Pitcher, milk 225
Pitcher, water 200
Sauce dish, any color, flat or footed,
    each 45-55
Sauce dish, clear, flat or footed, each 25-35
Spooner 85
Sugar bowl, cov. 165
Tray, bread, w/handles, amber, 11 x 15" 120
Tray, bread, w/handles, apple green,
    11 x 15" 160
Tray, bread, w/handles, canary yellow,
    11 x 15" 150
Tray, bread, w/handles, clear, 11 x 15" 250
Waste bowl 95

Egyptian

Bowl, 7 1/4" d. 60
Bowl, 8 1/2" d. 65
Bowl, cov., 8" d., low stand, sphinx base 45
Bowl, open, 6" d., low stand 50
Bread platter, Cleopatra center, 9 x 12" 65
*Bread platter, Salt Lake Temple
    center 375-400
Butter dish, cov. 125
Celery vase 120
Compote, cov., 5" d., sphinx base 125
Compote, cov., 6" d., 6" h., sphinx base 185
Compote, cov., 7" d., high stand, sphinx
    base 225
Compote, cov., 8" d., high stand, sphinx
    base 260
Creamer 65
Goblet 60
Honey dish 20
Pickle dish 25
Pitcher, water 255
Plate, 12" d., handled 125
Relish, 5 1/2 x 8 1/2" 30
Sauce dish, flat, 3 1/2", 4 1/2", 5" 25-35
Sauce dish, footed, 3 1/2", 4 1/2", 5" 25-35
Spooner 35-45
Sugar bowl, cov. 100

Eyewinker

Banana boat, flat, 8 1/2" l. 110
Banana stand 285
Bowl, 6 1/2" d., true open 140
Bowl, 7 1/2" d., true open 160
Bowl, cov., 6 1/2" d. 200
Bowl, cov., 7 1/2" d. 200
Bowl, 8" d., 3 5/8" h., true open 185
Bowl, cov., 8" d., 3 5/8" h. 245
Bowl, cov., master berry or fruit, 9" d.,
    4 1/2" h. 260

Bowl, master berry or fruit, 9" d., 4 1/2" h.,
  true open 200
*Butter dish, cov. 185
Cake stand, 8" d. 125
Cake stand, 9 1/2" d. 160
Celery vase, 6 1/2" h. 175
Compote, cov., 6" d., high stand 245
Compote, open, 4" d., 5" h., scalloped rim 45
Compote, open, 6" d., scalloped rim 80
Compote, open, 6 1/2" sq., high stand 70
*Compote, open, 7 1/2" d., high stand,
  flared rim 145
Compote, cov., 4" d. 85
Compote, cov., 8 1/2" d., high stand 245
Compote, open, 9 1/2" d., high stand 165
Compote, open, 10" d., high stand 250
Creamer 115
Cruet w/original stopper 225
*Goblet (Cannon ball) 95
*Honey dish, cov. 90
Lamp, kerosene-type, w/original burner,
  8 1/2"-9 1/2" h. 225-275
Plate, 7" sq., 1 1/2" h., turned-up sides 40
Plate, 8 1/2" d., turned-up sides 45
Plate, 9" sq., 2" h., turned-up sides 65
Plate, 10" sq., 2" h., turned-up sides 85
Salt shaker w/original top 85
*Sauce dish, round 30
Sauce dish, square 30
Spooner 90
*Sugar bowl, cov. 100
Syrup pitcher w/silver plate top 135
Tumbler 60

Feather (Doric, Indiana Swirl or Finecut & Feather)

Banana boat, footed, clear 150
Bowl, 5 1/2" d., flat round 25
Bowl, 5 1/2" d., footed round 30
Bowl, 6 1/2" d., flat round 35
Bowl, 6 1/2" d., footed round 40
Bowl, 7 1/2" d., flat round 45
Bowl, 7 1/2" d., footed round 50
Bowl, 7 1/2" square (rare) 145
Bowl, 7 1/4" oval 30
Bowl, 8 1/2" d., flat round 55
Bowl, 8 1/2" d., footed round 60
Bowl, 8 1/2" oval 35
Bowl, 9 1/4" oval 40
Butter dish, cov., clear 65
Butter dish, cov., green 210
Cake stand, 8 1/2" d. 75
Cake stand, clear, 9 1/2" h. 85
Cake stand, green, 9 1/2" h. 195
Cake stand, amber-stained, 11" d. 650
Cake stand, clear, 10" d. 100
Cake stand, clear, 11" d. 125
Celery vase, clear 85
Celery vase, green 195
Compote, cov., 7 1/2 " d., open, high stand 65
Compote, cov., 7" d., high stand 140
Compote, cov., 8" d., high stand, green 550
Compote, cov., 8 1/2" d., high stand 155
Compote, open, jelly, 5" d., 4 3/4" h., am-
  ber-stained 200
Compote, open, jelly, 5" d., 4 3/4" h., clear 35
Compote, open, 8" d., high stand 75
Cordial 175
Creamer, amber-stained 175
Creamer, clear 50

Cruet w/original stopper, clear 95
Cruet w/original stopper, green 450
Goblet, amber-stained 395
Goblet, clear 75
Honey dish, 3 1/2" d. 20
Marmalade jar, cov. 150
Pitcher, milk, clear 95
Pitcher, water, amber-stained, 1/2 gal. 385
Pitcher, water, clear 95
Pitcher, water, green 285
Plate, 10" d., clear 60
Relish, 8 1/4" oval, amber-stained 125
Relish, 8 1/4" oval, clear 30
Salt shaker w/original top, clear, blown
  short 100
Salt shaker w/original top, clear, pressed
  tall 60
Sauce dish, clear, flat or footed, each 25
Sauce dish, square flat (rose) 45
Spooner, amber-stained 150
Spooner, clear 40
Spooner, green 120
Sugar bowl, cov., clear 60
Sugar bowl, cov., green 175
Syrup pitcher w/original top, clear 285
Syrup pitcher w/original top, green 495
Toothpick holder, clear 150
Toothpick holder, green 350
Tumbler, clear 80
Tumbler, green 125
Wine, amber-stained 225
*Wine, clear 40
Wine, green 150
Wine, pink-stained (1950s reproduction) 15

Festoon

Bowl, 4 1/2 x 7" rectangle 30
Bowl, berry, 5 1/2 x 9" rectangle 40
Bowl, 7" d. 30
Bowl, 7" d. 40
Butter dish, cov. 65
Cake stand, high pedestal, 9" d. 65
Cake stand, high pedestal, 10" d. 75
Compote, open, 9" d., high stand 75
Creamer 40
Mug, handled 58
Pitcher, water 65
Plate, 7 1/2" d. 36
Plate, 8" d. 42
Plate, 9" d. 46
Relish, 4 x 7" 20
Relish, 5 1/2 x 9" 30
Sauce dish 15
Spooner 45
Sugar bowl, cov. 65
Tray, water, 10" d. 45
Tumbler 35
Waste bowl 55

Florida Palm

Cake stand, 9 1/2" d. 65
Celery vase 35
Compote, cov., 7" d., high stand 95
Compote, open, 9" d. 45
Creamer 35
Goblet 45
Plate, 9" d. 30
Relish 18
Spooner 35
Sugar bowl, cov. 45

Tumbler, footed 25
Wine 30

Frosted Circle

Bowl, 6" d. 20
Bowl, 7" d., 3" h. 25
Bowl, 8" d., 3 1/4" h. 30
Butter dish, cov. 75
Cake stand, 9 1/2" d. 78
Celery tray 48
Champagne 48
Claret 48
Compote, cov., 5" d., 9" h. 65
Compote, open, 5 3/4" d., 5 1/8" h. 35
Compote, cov., 7" d., high stand 85
Compote, open, 9" d., 6" h. 65
Compote, open, 9" d., 8 1/2" h. 75
Compote, open, 10" d., high stand, scal-
  loped rim 85
Creamer 58
Cruet w/original stopper 75
*Goblet 48
Pitcher, water, tankard 145
Plate, 7" d. 23
Plate, 9" d. 45
Punch cup 15
Relish, 4 1/2 x 8" 25
Salt shaker w/original top 35
Sauce dish, flat or footed 18
Spooner 45
Sugar bowl, cov. 70
Sugar shaker w/original top 48
Syrup pitcher w/original top 145
Tumbler 45
Waste bowl 36
Wine 36

Frosted Leaf

Butter dish, cov. 175
Celery vase 165
Champagne 225
Creamer 450
Egg cup 125
Goblet 175
Goblet, buttermilk 85
Goblet, lady's 130
Goblet, small, 5 3/4" h. 77
Salt dip, individual 65
Salt dip, master size 145
Sauce dish 30
Spooner 165
Spooner, rim w/12 scallops, short octago-
  nal stem & circular foot, 5 1/4" h.,
  3 1/2" d. 50
Sugar bowl, cov. 225
Tumbler, flat 145
Tumbler, footed 195
Wine 195

Frosted Lion (Rampant Lion)

Bread tray, oval, lion handles, frosted or
  non-frosted, 10" l. 145
Bread tray, blue, rope edge, closed han-
  dles, 10 1/2" d. **(Richards & Hartley) 200
Bread tray, canary, rope edge, closed handles, 10 1/2" d. **(Richards & Hartley) 200
Bread tray, clear, rope edge, closed handles, 10 1/2" d. **(Richards & Hartley) 100
Butter dish, cov., crouched lion finial 165

Butter dish, cov., child's 150
*Celery vase 125
Cheese dish, cov., rampant lion finial 850
Cologne bottle w/stopper 1,000-1,200
Compote, cov., 6" d., high stem, lion head
  finial 150
Compote, cov., 6" d., high stem, rampant
  lion finial 200
Compote, cov., 3 7/8 x 6 7/8" oval, collared
  base, crouched lion finial 150
Compote, cov., 7" d. high stand, rampant
  lion finial 225
Compote, cov., 7" d., high stem, lion head
  finial 170
Compote, cov., 7" d., round collared base,
  rampant lion finial 250
Compote, cov., 4 5/8 x 7 3/4" oval, collared
  base, crouched lion finial 175
Compote, cov., 8" d., high stand, rampant
  lion finial 200
Compote, cov., 8" d., round collared base,
  rampant lion finial 250
*Compote, cov., 8 1/4" d., high stand, ram-
  pant lion finial 250
Compote, cov., 5 5/8 x 8 3/4" oval, collared
  base, crouched lion finial 200
Compote, cov., 9" d., high stand, lion head
  finial 300
Compote, cov., 9" d., high stand, rampant
  lion finial 350
Compote, cov., 6 3/8 x 9 7/8" oval, collared
  base, crouched lion finial 250
Creamer, child's, clear & frosted 125
Creamer, full size 110
Creamer & cov. sugar bowl, hotel-style,
  plain base, pr. 175
Creamer & cov. sugar bowl, child's, clear
  & frosted, pr. 225
Cup & saucer, child's, blue opaque (very
  rare) 125
Cup & saucer, child's, clear frosted 125
*Egg cup 175
*Goblet 95
Inkwell 900
Lamp, urn-shaped, two lion heads on sides 900
Marmalade jar, cov., crouched lion finial 175
Marmalade jar, cov., lion's head finial 200
Paperweight, oval, embossed "Gillinder &
  Sons, Centennial" 300
Paperweight, round, lion's head 195
Pitcher, milk (very rare) 2,500
*Pitcher, water 700
Powder jar, cov. (very rare) 1,500-1,750
Relish 95
Salt dip, master, collared base, oval 350
*Sauce dish, 4" & 5" d., each 30-40
*Spooner 80
Sugar bowl, cov., crouched lion finial 125
Syrup pitcher w/original dated top (three
  sizes) 500-700
Wine, 4 1/8" h. 900

Galloway (Mirror)

Basket, twisted handle, 5 x 8 1/2 x 10" 95
Bowl, 5 1/2" d. 20
Bowl, 6 1/2" d. 25
Bowl, 7 1/4" d., 3 1/2" h. 35
Bowl, 8 1/2" d. 55
Bowl, 8 1/2" oval, flared rim 55
Bowl, 9 1/2" d., flat 65
Bowl, ice cream, 11" d., 3 1/2" h. 75

Bowl, ice cream, 12" d., 3 1/2" h. 75
Butter dish, cov., clear 85
Butter dish, cov., rose-stained 170
Cake stand, 8 1/2" d., 6" h. 125
Carafe 90
Celery vase, clear 45
Celery vase, rose-stained 90
Compote, open, 5 1/2" d. 25
Compote, open, 6 1/4" d., 7 1/2" h. 30
Compote, open, 7 1/2" d. 40
Compote, open, 8 1/2" d., 7" h. 60
Compote, open, 8 3/4" d., flared, rose-
   stained 120
Compote, open, 10" d., 8" h., scalloped rim 90
Cracker jar, cov. 175
Creamer, clear, full size 55
Creamer, rose-stained, full size 110
Creamer, individual size, oval, clear 25
Creamer, individual size, oval, rose-stained 50
Cruet w/stopper 40
Goblet, rose-stained 160
Mint dish, footed 30-35
Mug, 4 1/2" d. 40
Nappy, handled, gold rim, 5" d. 30
Nappy, handled, tricornered, 5 3/4" w. 30
Olive dish, 4 x 6" 22
Olive dish, rose-stained, 4 x 6" 44
Pickle castor w/silver plate lid & frame 225
Pitcher, child's, clear 24
Pitcher, child's, rose-stained 48
Pitcher, milk 85
Pitcher, water, clear 90
Pitcher, water, rose-stained 180
Plate, 6 1/2" d. 30
Plate, 8" d. 45
Punch bowl, 14" d. 135
Punch cup 12
Punch cup, rose stain 24
Punch set w/underplate, 14" d. bowl & 12
   cups, 14 pcs. 335
Relish, 8 1/4" l. 38
Relish, ruby-stained 76
Salt dip, master size, scalloped rim, 2" d. 55
Salt dip, oval, individual 45
Salt shaker w/original top 45
Sauce dish, flat or footed, each.......................... 15
Sherbet, footed, 3 1/4" h., 4 1/4" d. 27
Spooner, amber-stained 35
Spooner, clear 40
Spooner, rose-stained 80
Sugar bowl, cov., clear 49
Sugar bowl, cov., rose-stained 120
Sugar bowl, open, oval, individual size.............. 25
Sugar shaker w/original top 75
Syrup pitcher w/metal spring top, clear.......... 95
Syrup pitcher w/metal spring top, rose-
   stained 200
*Toothpick holder, clear 25
*Toothpick holder, green 50
Tray, flat, 8" d. 195
Tumbler, clear 30
Tumbler, rose-stained 60
Vase, bud, pressed, 6" h. 30
Vase, 7" h., flared rim.. 19
Vase, 8" h. 25
Vase, 9" h., green... 30
Vase, 11" h. 45
Waste bowl 65
Wine 38

Garfield Drape

Bowl, 6" d. 40
Bread plate, "We Mourn Our Nation's
   Loss," 11 1/2" d. 75
Butter dish, cov. 85
Cake stand, 9 1/2" d. 125
Celery vase, pedestal base 75
Compote, cov., 6" d., low stand 105
Compote, cov., 7" d., 9 1/2" h. 125
Compote, cov., 8" d., 12 1/2" h. 145
Creamer 55
Goblet, lady's.. 60
Goblet, regular 45
Honey dish, 3 1/2" d. 15
Lamp, kerosene-type, cobalt blue, 9" h. 150
Pickle dish, 7 1/4" oval....................................... 25
Pitcher, milk.. 245
Pitcher, water 135
Plate, 10" d., star center..................................... 45
Sauce dish, flat or footed, each 15
Spooner 40
Sugar bowl, cov. 80
Tumbler, flat 45

Harp

Bowl, 6" d. 47
Butter dish, cov. 275
Goblet, 6 3/8" h. 3,300
Goblet, flared sides 2,000
Lamp, kerosene, hand-type w/applied fin-
   ger grip.. 250
Lamp, kerosene, hexagonal font, shaped
   base, brass collar, flint, 9 1/2" h. 300
Salt dip, master size.. 75
Spillholder 95

Horseshoe (Good Luck or Prayer Rug)

Bowl, open, 5 x 8" oval, flat................................ 50
Bowl, open, 5 x 8" oval, flat, w/lid..................... 110
Bowl, open, 6 x 9" oval, flat................................ 55
Bowl, open, 6 x 9" oval, flat w/lid...................... 125
Bowl, cov., 6 1/2 x 10" oval............................... 145
Bowl, cov., 6" round, footed 65
Bowl, cov., 7" round, footed, w/lid 90
Bowl, cov., 8" round, footed.............................. 110
Bowl, open, 6 1/2 x 10" oval 65
Bowl, open, 6 1/2 x 10" round, footed 30
Bowl, open, 7" round, footed............................... 40
Bowl, open, 8" round, footed............................... 48
*Bread tray, single horseshoe handles............... 50
Butter dish, cov. 140
Cake stand, 7" d. 100
Cake stand, 8" d., 6 1/2" h. 100
Cake stand, 9" d., 6 1/2" h. 110
Cake stand, 10" d. 125
Cake stand, 10 3/4" d. 130
Celery vase 95
Cheese dish, cov., w/woman churning but-
   ter in base 285
Compote, cov., 6" d., 10 1/2" h. 125
Compote, cov., 7" d., high stand 150
Compote, cov., 8" d., high stand 175
Compote, cov., 7" d., low stand 95
Compote, cov., 8" d., low stand 125
Compote, 9" h., 9 1/4" d., true open (bent
   rim), high stand 275
Compote, open, 7" d., 7" h., footed 75
Compote, open, 8" d., 7 3/4" h., footed.............. 85
Creamer 40

Goblet, knob stem 55
Goblet, plain stem 40
Marmalade jar, cov. 225
Pitcher, milk 215
Pitcher, water 175
Plate, 7" d. 50
Plate, 8" d. 60
Plate, 10" d. 70
Relish, 5 x 7" 25
Salt dip, master size, horseshoe shape 195
Sauce dish, flat or footed, each 22
Spooner 40
Sugar bowl, cov. 85
Waste bowl, 4" d., 2 1/2" h. 185
Water tray, double horseshoe handles 93
Wine 295

Hummingbird (Flying Robin or Bird & Fern)

Bowl, 6" d., amber 35
Butter dish, cov., amber 150
Butter dish, cov., blue 150
Butter dish, cov., clear 85
Celery vase, amber 130
Celery vase, blue 130
Celery vase, clear 75
Compote, cov., 7" d., clear 110
Compote, cov., 7" d., high stand, blue 245
Creamer, amber 95
Creamer, blue 95
Creamer, clear 70
Goblet, amber 90
Goblet, blue 90
Goblet, clear 60
Pitcher, milk, amber 175
Pitcher, milk, blue 175
Pitcher, milk, clear 95
Pitcher, water, amber 225
Pitcher, water, blue 225
Pitcher, water, clear 120
Sauce dish, small & large 20-25
Spooner, amber 120
Spooner, blue 120
Spooner, clear 60
Sugar bowl, cov., amber 125
Sugar bowl, cov., blue 125
Sugar bowl, cov., clear 85
Tray, water, amber 265
Tray, water, blue 265
Tray, water, clear 100
Tumbler, amber 85
Tumbler, blue 85
Tumbler, clear 50
Waste bowl, blue 125
Waste bowl, clear 55

Illinois

Basket, 12" l. 155
Basket, 7 1/2" l. 125
Basket, 8 1/2" l. 135
Basket, applied handle, 7 x 7" 95
Basket, applied reeded handle, 7 x 11 1/2" 140-145
Bowl, 6" sq. 30
Bowl, 8" sq. 45
*Butter dish, cov., 7" sq. 80
Candlestick, each 125
Celery tray, 10 1/2" l. 45
*Celery vase 45
Compote, open, 5" sq. 40

Compote, open, 9" sq. 90
Creamer, small 25
Creamer, large 45
Creamer & open sugar bowl, small, pr. 35-45
Cruet w/original stopper 145
Lamp, banquet-style 1,200
Marmalade jar in silver plate frame w/spoon, 3 pcs. 175
Pitcher, milk 85
Pitcher, water, tankard 100
Pitcher, water, tankard, silver plate rim, clear 130
Pitcher, water, tankard, silver plate rim, green 260
Plate, 7" sq. 35

Illinois Boat-shaped Relish

Relish, long boat-shaped, 3 x 8 1/2", clear (ILLUS.) 30
Relish, long boat-shaped, 3 x 8 1/2", green 55
Salt dip, individual size 30
Salt shaker w/original top, each 40
Sauce dish 20
Soda fountain (straw-holder) jar, cov., clear, 12 1/2" h. 300
Soda fountain (straw-holder) jar, cov., green, 12 1/2" h. 450
Spooner 40
Sugar bowl, cov. 50
Sugar shaker w/original pewter top 95
Syrup pitcher w/original pewter top 125
Toothpick holder (common) 35
Tumbler 50
Vase, 6" h. 40
Vase, 9" h., 4" d., scalloped top, clear 95
Vase, 9" h., 4" d., scalloped top, green 145

Jacob's Ladder (Maltese)

Bowl, 5" d. 20
Bowl, 6 3/4" d., 4 3/4" h., footed 30
Bowl, 7 1/4" d., footed 35
Bowl, 6 x 8 3/4" oval, flat 30
Bowl, 9" d., flat 45
Bowl, 10" d., flat 65
Bowl, 7 1/2 x 10 3/4" oval 35
Butter dish, cov., Maltese Cross finial 95
Cake stand, 8" d. 65
Cake stand, 9" d. 75
Cake stand, 11" d. 95
Cake stand, 12" d. 110
Castor set, cruet w/original Maltese Cross stopper, salt & pepper shakers & mustard jar w/original tops & pewter frame, 5 pcs. 200
Celery vase 65
Cologne bottle w/original Maltese Cross stopper, footed 175
Compote, cov., 6 1/2" d., 10 1/4" h. 65
Compote, cov., 8 1/4" d., high stand 135
Compote, cov., 9 1/2" d., high stand 165
Compote, open, 6" d., high stand 30
Compote, open, 7" d., high stand 35

Compote, open, 8" d., high stand........................ 50
Compote, open, 9 1/2" d., high stand................. 70
Compote, open, 10" d., high stand.................... 80
*Creamer 65
Cruet w/original stopper, footed..................... 155
Goblet 75
Honey dish, open 12
Marmalade jar, cov.. 135
Pickle castor, complete w/stand............... 175-200
Pickle dish, Maltese Cross handle,
　　amber.. 55
Pitcher, water, applied handle 213
Plate, 6" d., amber.. 105
Plate, 6" d., clear.. 35
Plate, 6" d., purple.. 110
Platter, 8 3/4" oval.. 35
Platter, 9 3/4" oval.. 40
Sauce dish, clear, flat or footed, each............... 20
Spooner 52
Sugar bowl, cov.. 95
*Sugar bowl, open.. 26
Syrup jug w/metal top 105
Tumbler, bar 85
Wine 35

Jumbo and Jumbo & Barnum

Butter dish & cover w/frosted elephant
　　finial, oblong 900
Butter dish & cover w/frosted elephant
　　finial, round... 750
Castor set, w/four original bottles & metal
　　tops, clear 750
Compote, cov., 7 7/8" d. 900
Compote, cov., 12" h., frosted elephant fin-
　　ial.. 1,400
Creamer, square 450
Creamer, w/Barnum head at handle................. 300
Goblet 1,200
Marmalade jar, cov., w/Barnum head han-
　　dles & cover w/frosted elephant finial........... 750
Match holder 85
Mug, water, large, w/elephant in base 1,200
Spoon rack, clear 1,200
Spooner, square 200
Spooner, w/Barnum head at handles................ 250
Sugar bowl, cov., square 500
Sugar bowl, w/Barnum head handles &
　　cover w/frosted elephant finial...................... 475
Toothpick holder, "Baby Mine"........................ 125

Kentucky

Bowl, 7" d. 25
Bowl, 8" d.. 35
Cake stand, 9 1/2" d.. 85
Cake stand, 10 1/2" d. 100
Celery tray 30
Compote, cov., 5" d... 50
Compote, cov., 6" d... 60
Compote, cov., 7" d... 70
Compote, cov., 8" d... 80
Cruet w/original stopper 60
Nappy, handled, clear 20
Nappy, handled, green... 30
Pitcher, water 95
Plate, 7" sq. 30
Punch cup, clear... 15
Punch cup, green 24

Salt & pepper shakers w/original tops, pr........ 60

Blue Kentucky Footed Sauce Dish

Sauce dish, blue w/gold trim, footed
　　(ILLUS.).. 32
Sauce dish, clear, footed 18
Sauce dish, green, footed..................................... 20
Spooner 40
Sugar bowl, cov.. 65
Toothpick holder, clear 45
Toothpick holder, green....................................... 45
Toothpick holder, green w/gold 75
Toothpick holder, ruby-stained......................... 150
Tumbler, clear.. 30
Tumbler, green.. 45
Wine, clear 40
Wine, green 55

Lily-Of-The-Valley

Bowl, 5 1/2 x 8" oval... 33
Butter dish, cov., plain base.............................. 95
Butter dish, cov., three-footed 125
Celery vase 125
Champagne 450
Compote, cov., 8" d., low stand 165
Compote, cov., 8 1/2" d., high stand 195
Compote, open, 7" d., low stand........................ 56
Creamer, plain base, applied handle.................. 85
Creamer, three-footed, molded handle 100
Cruet w/original stopper 250
Egg cup 80
Goblet, buttermilk.. 65
Goblet, plain 95
Honey dish 20
Pickle dish, scoop-shaped.................................. 24
Pitcher, milk, applied handle.............................. 285
Pitcher, water, bulbous, applied handle 225
Relish, 4 1/2 x 7"... 23
Relish, 5 1/2 x 8".. 28
Salt dip, cov., master size, three-footed 145
Salt dip, true open, master size, three-foot-
　　ed 85
Sauce dish 16
Spooner, plain base 55
Spooner, three-footed... 75
Sugar bowl, cov., pedestal base........................ 78
Sugar bowl, cov., three-footed........................... 110
Tumbler, bar (rare)... 125
Tumbler, footed (rare)... 145
Wine 225

Lincoln Drape & Lincoln Drape with Tassel

Butter dish, cov. 175
Celery vase 145

Compote, cov., 6" d., high stand (sweet-
meat)... 375
Compote, open, 6" d. 150
Compote, open, 6 3/4" d., 5 1/4" h.................. 170
Compote, open, 7 1/8" d., 5" h. 185
Compote, open, 7 1/2" d., 3 1/2" h.................. 185
Compote, open, 8" d., medium stand.............. 225
Compote, open, 8 1/4" d., 5 1/8" h., domed
foot... 225
Compote, open, 9" d. 245
Egg cup 70
Goblet without tassel...................................... 200
Goblet w/tassel 450
Salt dip, master size 70
Salt dip, master size, w/tassel 125
Sauce dish, 4" d.. 25
Spooner 95
Sugar bowl, cov... 195
Syrup pitcher w/original pewter top, clear..... 225
Syrup pitcher w/original top, opaque
white.. 600
Tumbler, flat... 145
Wine (rare)... 210

Log Cabin

Bowl, cov., 5 1/4 x 3 5/8", w/door in base,
clear.. 375
Butter dish, cov., no door in base, clear.......... 425
Compote, cov., 6", high stand......................... 500
Compote, cov., 7" l. 625
Compote, cov., 8" l. 750
*Creamer, 4 1/4" h. 155
Marmalade jar, cov., 6 3/4" h......................... 425
Pitcher, water 550
Sauce dish, flat oblong 85
Sauce dish, footed... 95
*Spooner, clear 145
Spooner, sapphire blue.................................... 700
*Sugar bowl, cov., 8" h., clear 300
Sugar bowl, cov., canary................................ 1,000

Mascotte

Apothecary jar, cov., various shapes & siz-
es.. 100-300
Bowl, open, flared rim 45-70
Bowl, 6", 7", 8" or 9" d., flat, open 45-60
Bowl, cov., 6", 7", 8" or 9" d......................... 65-80
Butter dish, cov. 85
Butter dish, cov., horseshoe-shaped,
"Maude S.".. 150+
Butter dish, cov., plain...................................... 38
Butter pat 25
Cake basket w/handle 90
Cake stand, 8", 9" or 10" d......................... 75-100
Celery vase 50
Cheese dish, cov. 135
Compote, open, flared rim........................... 55-75
Compote, open, jelly 45
Compote, cov., 5" d... 60
Compote, cov., 6" d... 70
Compote, cov., 7" d... 80
Compote, cov., 8" d., high stand....................... 95
Compote, cov., 9" d., high stand..................... 125
Creamer, clear 36
Goblet 45
Jar, cov., globe-type, embossed patent
date, milk white 265
Pitcher, water 120
Salt dip, individual size 25

Salt dip, master.. 35
Salt shaker w/original top 30
Sauce dish, flat 15
Sauce dish, footed 20
Spooner, canary 135
Spooner, clear, engraved................................. 38
Spooner, clear, plain 30
Tray, water, clear, engraved............................. 65
Tray, water, clear, plain.................................... 59
Tray, wine 45
Tumbler, clear, engraved 45
Tumbler, clear, plain 25
Wine, clear, engraved 35
Wine, clear, plain... 26

Palmette

Bowl, 6" d., flat 30
Bowl, 8" d., flat 35
Bowl, 9" d., flat 40
Bowl, three sizes, oval, flat......................... 30-35
Butter dish, cov., round.................................... 65
Butter dish, two-handled................................ 100
Butter pat 45
Cake stand 195
Castor set, three-bottle, complete 75
Castor set, five-bottle, complete 125
Celery vase 75
Champagne 250
Compote, cov., 7", 8" or 9" d., high stand.... 85-100
Compote, cov., 8" d., low stand 75
Compote, open, 7" d., low stand, scalloped
rim 45
Compote, open, 8" d., low stand, scalloped
rim 50
Compote, open, 9" d., low stand...................... 55
Creamer, applied handle 70
Cruet w/original stopper 150
Egg cup 35
Goblet 45
Lamp, kerosene-type, table model w/iron &
marble base.. 100
Lamp, kerosene-type, table model w/stem,
several sizes, clear.................................. 125-175
Pickle dish, scoop-shaped................................ 30
Pitcher, milk, applied handle........................... 200
Pitcher, water, applied handle......................... 250
Relish 25
Salt dip, flat, round 125
Salt dip, master size, footed 35-40
Salt & pepper shakers w/original tops,
5 1/2" h., pr. 55
Salt shaker w/original top, large, hotel-
style 85
Sauce dish, flat 15
Spooner 40
Sugar bowl, cov.. 75
Syrup pitcher w/original top, applied han-
dle 155
Tumbler, water, flat 75
Tumbler, water, footed...................................... 55
Wine 125

Post (Square Panes)

Berry set, 7 1/2" d. master bowl & 3 sauce
dishes, 4 pcs. 48
Bowl, cov., 6 3/4" d., footed 45
Bowl, 8" sq., footed 30
Bowl, cov., 8" sq., engraved, footed 65
Bread tray, rectangular, Bible handles............. 65
Butter dish, cov. 68
Cake stand, 9 1/2" d. 70

Celery vase 65
Compote, cov., 6" d., high stand 57
Compote, cov., 7 1/2" d., high stand 70
Compote, cov., 8" d., high stand 85
Creamer 50
Goblet, engraved 50
Goblet, plain 35
Honey dish, rectangular, sunflower finial
    w/bee 150
Lamp, kerosene-type, collared, no engrav-
    ing, 8 1/2" h. 145
Lamp, kerosene-type, collared, w/original
    floral insert in stem, 7 1/2" h. 225
Lamp, kerosene-type, collared, w/original
    floral insert in stem, 8 1/2" h. 225
Lamp, kerosene-type, collared, 7 1/2" h. 155
Lamp, kerosene-type, collared, engraved,
    8 1/2" h. 195
Lamp, kerosene-type, 9 1/2" h. 155
Lamp, kerosene-type, 10 1/2" h. 165
Lamp, kerosene-type, 11 1/2" h. 165
Marmalade jar w/original cover 95
Pitcher, water, engraved 90
Pitcher, water, plain 70
Relish, flat, 4 3/4 x 7 1/4" 12
Salt dip, master size 10
Salt dips, individual size, set of 6 60
Spooner 45
Sugar bowl, cov. 60

Shell & Jewel (Victor)

Banana stand 250
Bowl, 8" d. 65
Butter dish, cov. 100
Cake stand, 10" d., 5" h. 175
Creamer 45
Pitcher, water, amber 150
Pitcher, water, blue 150
Pitcher, water, clear 45
Pitcher, water, green 150
Relish, oblong 45
Sauce dish, amber 45
Sauce dish, clear 25
Spooner 48
Sugar bowl, cov. 85
Tumbler, amber 38
Tumbler, blue 38
Tumbler, clear 25
Tumbler, green 38
Water tray, clear (rare) 250

Snail (Compact)

Bowl, 5 1/4 x 8" oval 35
Butter dish, cov. 125
Cake stand, 10" d. 125-150
Celery vase 50-60
Compote, cov., 7" d., high stand 90-110
Compote, open, 10" d., 7" h. 145
Cracker jar, cov., 8" d., 9" h. 295
Creamer 58
Goblet 125
Pitcher, milk, bulbous, applied handle,
    large 195-215
Pitcher, water, tankard 125-150
Salt & pepper shakers w/original tops, pr. 110
Spooner 45
Syrup jug w/original brass top 145-165

Sprig

Bowl, 7" oval 25

Bowl, 8" oval 40
Bowl, 9" oval 50
Bowl, 10" oval 65
Bowl, cov., 7" round 45
Bowl, cov., 8" round 60
Bowl, cov., 9" round 70
Bowl, cov., 10" round 85
Bowl, 7" round, open 25
Bowl, 8" round, open 40
Bowl, 9" round, open 50
Bowl, 10" round, open 65
Bread platter, 11" oval 60
Butter dish, cov. 85
Cake stand 95
Celery vase 55
Compote, cov., 6" d., high stand 90
Compote, cov., 7" d., high stand 110
Compote, cov., 8" d., high stand 125
Creamer 40
Goblet 30
Honey dish, cov., diamond shape, flat 250
Marmalade jar w/glass lid 95
Pitcher, water 75
Relish, ... 25
Salt dip, individual 25
Salt dip, master size 50
Sauce dish, flat or footed, each 20
Spooner 40
Sugar bowl, cov. 65
Wine 45

Three Face

*Butter dish, cov., engraved 200-225
*Butter dish, cov., plain 190
*Cake stand, 8" to 10 1/2" d. 175-250
*Celery vase 100-125
*Champagne 325
*Compote, cov., 4 1/2" d., 6 1/2" h. 100
*Compote, cov., 6" d., high stand 150-175
*Cracker jar, cov. 1,700
Creamer 85-90
*Creamer w/mask spout 150
*Goblet, engraved 100-125
*Goblet, plain 50
Pitcher, water 575
*Sauce dish, 4" d. 35
*Spooner, engraved 120-125
*Spooner, plain 70
*Sugar bowl, cov. 125-150
*Wine 200-225

Two Panel (Daisy in Panel)

Bowl, cov., 7" oval, canary 75
Bowl, 5 1/2 x 7" oval, blue 25
Bowl, 7 1/2 x 9" oval, amber 35
Bowl, 7 1/2 x 9" oval, canary 26
Bowl, 7 1/2 x 9" oval, clear 15
Bread tray, apple green 39
Bread tray, blue 45
Bread tray, clear 30
Butter dish, cov., blue 85
Celery vase, amber 30
Celery vase, blue 50
Compote, cov., 6 1/2 x 8", 11" h., canary 85
Compote, cov., high standard, canary,
    7 1/2 x 9 1/8", 12 3/4" h. (chip on interior
    of lid flange) 170
Compote, open, 9" oval, 4" h., apple green 60
Creamer, amber 36

Creamer, apple green 45
*Goblet, amber 34
*Goblet, apple green 32
*Goblet, blue 41
*Goblet, canary.. 42
*Goblet, clear... 25
Salt dip, individual size, apple green 24
Sauce dish, amber, flat or footed, each 10
Sauce dish, blue, flat or footed, each............. 14-18
Spooner, amber 36
Spooner, blue.. 40-45
Sugar bowl, cov., apple green........................... 55
Sugar bowl, cov., canary................................... 54
Tray, water, apple green, 10 x 15" oval 65-70
Tray, water, blue, 10 x 15" oval................. 100-125
Tumbler, amber.. 25
Tumbler, blue 33
Tumbler, canary 40
*Wine, amber 35
*Wine, apple green... 35
*Wine, blue 38
*Wine, canary 35-45
*Wine, clear.. 29

Washington (State)

Bowl, berry, 8" d., w/color stenciled floral
 band.. 45
Bowl, berry, 8" d., plain 30
Cake stand, 10" d. 50-60

Decorated Washington Creamer

Creamer, miniature, w/floral enamel deco-
 ration (ILLUS.)... 30
Creamer, table size, plain 40
Creamer, table size, w/colored enameling......... 45
Jelly compote, 3 1/2" d. 35
Pitcher, milk, ruby-stained........................ 150-175
Pitcher, tankard, half-gallon 75
Relish dish, rectangular w/scalloped rim,............. 8
Salt dip, individual, 1 7/8" d............................... 35
Sauce dish, 4" d., w/color stenciled floral
 band.. 18
Sauce dish, 4" d., plain.. 8
Spooner, w/stenciled floral band decoration .. 45-55
Sugar bowl, cov., plain 45-50
Sugar bowl, cov., w/stenciled floral band
 decoration 55-65

Toothpick holder, w/enameled floral deco-
 ration.. 30
Tumbler 25

Willow Oak

Bowl, cov., 7" d., flat... 49
Bread plate, amber, 9" d. 40-50
Bread plate, blue, 11" d.................................. 45-55
Butter dish, cov., amber................................ 65-75
Butter dish, cov., blue 70-80
Cake stand, amber, 11" d., 5 1/4" h. 40
Cake stand, blue, 8" to 10" d. 65
Celery vase, amber 45
Compote, cov., 6" h., clear................................ 95
Creamer, amber.. 35-40
Creamer, blue.. 65
Creamer, canary 65-75
Creamer, clear.. 25-35
Goblet, amber... 40-45
Goblet, blue 65
Goblet, clear 30
Mug, blue.. 40-45
Mug, clear.. 27
Pitcher, milk, amber 85
Pitcher, milk, clear... 30-40
Pitcher, water, amber 65-75
Pitcher, water, blue 75-85
Plate, 7" d., amber 35
Salt & pepper shakers w/original tops,
 clear, pr. 65
Salt shaker w/original top, amber..................... 40
Salt shaker w/original top, blue........................ 66
Sauce dish, blue, flat or footed, each............ 20-30
Sauce dish, clear, flat or footed, each 15
Spooner, amber 35
Spooner, blue.. 50
Sugar bowl, cov., amber 65-75
Sugar bowl, cov., blue 75-85
Tray, water, amber, 10 1/2" d....................... 75-85
Tray, water, blue, 10 1/2" d. 80-90
Tray, water, clear, 10 1/2" d. 35-40
Tumbler, amber... 35-45
Tumbler, blue 45-55
Tumbler, clear 25-30

Peach Blow

*Several types of glass lumped together by col-
lectors as Peach Blow were produced by half a
dozen glasshouses. Hobbs, Brockunier & Co.,
Wheeling, West Virginia, made Peach Blow as a
plated ware that shaded from red at the top to yellow at the bottom and is referred to as Wheeling
Peach Blow. Mt. Washington Glass Works produced an homogeneous Peach Blow shading from
a rose color at the top to pale blue in the lower
portion. The New England Glass Works' Peach
Blow, called Wild Rose, shaded from rose at the
top to white. Gundersen-Pairpoint Co. also reproduced some of the Mt. Washington Peach Blow in
the early 1950s and some glass of a somewhat
similar type was made by Steuben Glass Works,
Thomas Webb & Sons and Stevens & Williams of
England. New England Peach Blow is one-lay-
ered glass and the English is two-layered.*

*Another single-layered shaded art glass was
produced early in the 20th century by the New
Martinsville Glass Mfg. Co. Originally called
"Muranese," collectors today refer to it as "New
Martinsville Peach Blow."*

A Large Group of Peach Blow Pieces

Gunderson

Decanter w/original stopper, footed tapering ovoid body w/a flattened rim, ovoid bulbous stopper, shades deep pink to soft cream, first half 20th c. (ILLUS. top row, right, with other Peach Blow pieces).. **$403**

Vase, 9" h., lily-type, tall slender flaring body w/undulating rim, soft pink shading to opal on a tinted round foot, first half 20th c., each (ILLUS. of two, bottom row, far right & center row, far left, with other Peach Blow pieces).. **230**

Vase, 9 1/4" h., jack-in-the-pulpit style, tall slender flaring body w/a ruffled upturned rim, shading soft pink to opal, first half 20th c. (ILLUS. bottom row, second from right with other Peach Blow pieces).............. **173**

Mt. Washington

Toothpick holder, cylindrical w/a tricorner rolled-in rim, satin finish, ca. 1885 (ILLUS. left, below)............................ **3,000-4,000**

Toothpick holder, squatty bulbous base tapering to a squared neck, satin finish (ILLUS. right, below) **2,500-3,000**

Two Mt. Washington Peach Blow Toothpick Holders

New England

New England Peach Blow Cruet

Cruet w/original stopper, squatty bulbous
body tapering to a cylindrical neck w/tri-
corner rim, applied pink handle, white
hollow ball stopper, deep color w/glossy
finish (ILLUS.)..................................... **1,200-1,500**
Darner, ball-shaped w/handle, deep rose
pink shaded to white, glossy finish,
2 1/4" d., 6" l. **135-160**
Model of a pear, deep pink shaded to white,
glossy finish, 3" d., 5" l. **135**
Sauce dish, wide low round form, deep
fuchsia pink shading to cream, late 19th
c., 4" d. (ILLUS. bottom row center with
other Peach Blow pieces, page 670)............ **144**
Tumbler, cylindrical, deep pink shading to
cream, glossy finish, 3 3/4" h. (ILLUS.
bottom row, second from left w/other
Peach Blow pieces, page 670)...................... **173**
Tumbler, satin finish, polished pontil,
3 1/2" h. **100-130**
Vase, 5 1/2" h., lily-type, fuchsia pink shad-
ing to opal (ILLUS. middle row, second
from right w/other Peach Blow pieces,
page 670).. **431**

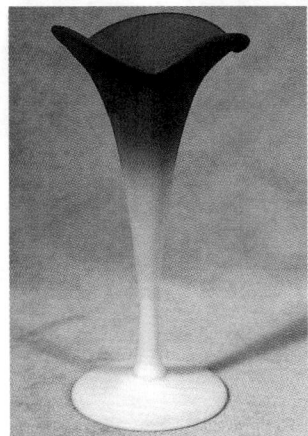

New England Peach Blow Lily Vase

Vase, 6" h., lily-type, deep rose shading to
white (ILLUS.).. **600-750**

Vase, 6" h., lily-type, deep rose shading to
white (ILLUS. middle row, second from
left w/other Peach Blow pieces, page
670).. **748**
Vase, 6 3/4" h., jack-in-the-pulpit style, slen-
der flaring body w/ruffled upturned rim,
deep salmon pink shading to opal, glossy
finish (ILLUS. bottom row, far left with
other Peach Blow pieces, page 670) **863**
Vase, 9" h., lily-type, deep rose shading to
opal (ILLUS. middle row, far right with
other Peach Blow pieces, page 670) **748**
Vase, 12" h., lily-type, deep fuchsia pink
shading to opal (ILLUS. top row, left
w/other Peach Blow pieces, page 670) **633**

Wheeling

Wheeling Peach Blow Conical Cruet

**Cruet w/original facet-cut amber ball
stopper,** sharply tapering conical body
w/a cylindrical neck & tricorner rim, applied amber handle (ILLUS.)............ **1,250-1,750**
**Cruet w/original facet-cut amber ball
stopper,** spherical w/a short neck &
spout, applied amber handle & facet-cut
stopper, glossy finish, 7" h. **1,725**

Wheeling Peach Blow Morgan Vase

Morgan Vase, 8" h., Wheeling Peach Blow, ovoid body w/tall slender ringed neck, deep ruby to yellow w/satin finish, ca. 1886 (ILLUS., previous page).......... **1,200-1,500**

Pitcher, 5" h., wide ovoid body w/a flared quatreform neck, applied amber handle, glossy finish, late 19th c. **805**

Wheeling Peach Blow Water Pitcher

Pitcher, 8" h., water-type, bulbous ovoid body tapering to a squared rolled neck, applied amber handle, glossy finish (ILLUS.)... **1,500-2,200**

Tumbler, cylindrical, glossy finish, 3 3/4" h....... **288**

Tumbler, glossy, polished pontil, 3 5/8" h. **400**

Tumbler, cylindrical, satin finish, good even color, 3 3/4" h. **375**

Wheeling Peach Blow Small Vase

Vase, 3 1/2" h., Wheeling Peach Blow, bulbous ovoid body w/a short cylindrical neck, deep ruby shading to yellow, ca. 1886 (ILLUS.).. **325-375**

Wheeling Peach Blow Bottle Vase

Vase, 7" h., bottle-form, bulbous base tapering to a tall stick neck w/an applied band of amber rigaree around the lower neck, glossy finish (ILLUS.) **900-1,200**

Two Wheeling Peach Blow Vases

Vase, 9" h., bottle-form, bulbous base tapering to a tall stick neck, satin finish (ILLUS. left with other vase) **750-950**

Vase, 9" h., teardrop-shaped body tapering to a tall stick neck, dark coloring, glossy finish (ILLUS. right with other vase) **650-900**

Pillar Molded Compote & Celery Vases

Ovoid Wheeling Peach Blow Vase

Vase, 10" h., ovoid body tapering to a short trumpet neck, satin finish (ILLUS.)... **1,500-2,200**

Vase, 10 1/4" h., a footed wide squatty bulbous lower body tapering to a tall stick neck, shading from very dark red to dark yellow, glossy finish... **978**

Pillar-Molded

This heavily ribbed glassware was produced by blowing glass into full-sized ribbed molds and then finishing it by hand. The technique evolved from earlier "pattern moulding" used on glass since ancient times, but in pillar-molded glass the ribs are very heavy and prominent. Most examples found in this country were produced in the Pittsburgh, Pennsylvania, area from around 1850 to 1870, but similar English-made wares made before and after this period are also available. Most American items were made from clear flint glass, and colored examples or pieces with colored strands in the ribs are rare and highly prized. Some collectors refer to this as "steamboat" glass, believing it was made to be used on American riverboats, but most likely it was used anywhere that a sturdy, relatively inexpensive glassware was needed, such as taverns and hotels.

Celery vase, eight-rib, tall tulip-form bowl w/a flared rim, applied baluster-form stem on a thick disk foot, clear, 9 1/2" h. (ILLUS. center with compote).............. **$150-200**

Celery vase, eight-rib, tall tulip-form bowl w/a flared rim, applied baluster-form stem on a thick disk foot, clear, 11 1/2" h. (ILLUS. right with compote) **200-225**

Celery vase, eight-rib, tall waisted tulip-form bowl w/a widely flaring ruffled rim, each panel cut w/three notches, on a cylindrical stem & disk foot, clear, 10 3/4" h....... **300**

Celery vase, six-rib, deep tulip-form bowl w/a ruffled rim, the vertical ribs alternating w/panels of molded cascading drapes, hollow baluster-form stem on a disk foot, clear, 9 3/4" h. **650**

Compote, open, 11" d., 6 1/2" h., eight-rib, very wide shallow bowl raised on a baluster-form stem & heavy disk foot, clear, some light scratching (ILLUS. left with vases, top of page)... **440**

Decanter w/bar lip, eight-rib, bulbous ovoid body tapering to an applied shoulder ring & tapering neck w/bar lip, pt., 9 1/4" h. **375**

Decanter w/bar lip, eight-rib, tapering triangular form w/neck ring, clear, qt., 11" h. **99**

Decanters w/original stopper, eight-rib, bell-form body tapering to a knob at the base of the cylindrical neck w/flared rim, hollow ribbed inverted pear-shaped stopper, clear, pt., 11 5/8" h., pr. **220**

Quezal

In 1901, Martin Bach and Thomas Johnson, who had worked for Louis Tiffany, opened a competing glassworks in Brooklyn, New York. The Quezal Art Glass and Decorating Co. produced wares closely resembling those of Tiffany until the plant's closing in 1925.

Quezal

Quezal Mark

Quezal Bowl with Pulled-Feather Design

Bowl, 6" d., squatty bulbous tapering sides w/a wide low rolled rim, golden brown iridescent ground w/silvery blue iridescent pulled-feather decoration, light blue iridescent interior, signed on the pontil "Quezal N.Y." (ILLUS.) **$2,300**

Master salt dip, wide squatty sharply tapering ribbed body w/a very wide rolled rim, amber w/overall gold iridescence, signed, ca. 1920, 3 3/4" d.............................. **230**

Gold Iridescent Quezal Scent Bottle

Scent bottle w/disc stopper, tapering cylindrical form w/four ribs spaced around the sides, overall golden iridescence w/green highlights, hexagon stopper, signed on the bottom, tiny fleabite on edge of stopper, early 20th c., 7 1/2" h. (ILLUS.) **690**

Small Nicely Decorated Quezal Vase

Vase, 4 1/4" h., 3 3/4" d., flattened squatty round bottom centered by a tall trumpet neck, the bottom on opal decorated w/golden iridescent lappets & green & gold triple-hooked designs, the neck in golden iridescence, signed on pontil (ILLUS.) **3,450**

Green, Gold & White Quezal Vase

Vase, 6" h., footed squatty bulbous body tapering to a large trumpet neck, opal ground decorated w/green, white & gold pulled feathers alternating down from the rim & up from the base, orange iridescent interior, signed on the pontil (ILLUS.)......... **1,380**

Vase, 8 3/4" h., flora-form, round gold iridescent domed foot supporting a knopped stem below the tall trumpet-form bowl w/deeply ruffled rim, opal w/a stretched gold iridescent interior, the exterior w/five gold-outlined pulled green feathers, polished pontil signed "Quezal 3" **3,450**

Quezal Vase with Blue & Green Swirls

Vase, 10" h., a disk foot below the bulbous lower body tapering to a tall swelled upper body, golden iridescence w/green & blue swirling designs, signed on the base (ILLUS.)... **1,550**

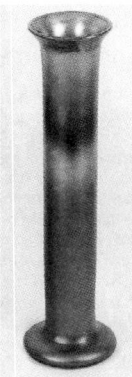

Blue Quezal Stick Vase

Vase, 10" h., stick-form w/flared rim, overall dark blue iridescence, signed (ILLUS., previous page) **800**

Rare Quezal Jack-in-the-Pulpit Vase

Vase, 13" h., jack-in-the-pulpit style, a wide cushion foot below the tall slender stem issuing a widely flaring ruffled & upturned rim, overall amber iridescence w/rings of pink & green, signed on the bottom "Quezal G562" (ILLUS.) **9,200**

Vase, 15" h., jack-in-the-pulpit form w/cushion foot, slender cylindrical body & widely flaring gently ruffled rim, the exterior decorated w/green & gold pulled-feather decoration, iridescent gold interior, signed **5,500**

Rose Bowls

These decorative small bowls were widely popular in the late 19th and early 20th centuries. Produced in various types of glass, they are most common in satin glass or spatter glass. They are generally a spherical shape with an incurved crimped rim, but ovoid or egg-shaped examples were also popular.

Their name derives from their reported use, to hold dried rose petal potpourri or small fresh-cut roses.

Cabbage Rose Pink Satin Rose Bowl

Cased satin, eight-crimp rim, "Cabbage Rose" form, pink shaded to white w/molded petals, 4" h. (ILLUS.) **$125-175**

Swirled Pink Satin Rose Bowl

Cased satin, eight-crimp rim, shaded pink to white, molded swirled lobe design, enameled w/delicate sprigs of blue & white blossoms on gold stems, 5" h. (ILLUS.) **100-175**

Blue Mother-of-Pearl Satin Rose Bowl

Cased satin, six-crimp rim, blue mother-of-pearl Ribbon patt., ovoid body w/pinched-in sides, 3" d., 3 5/8" h. (ILLUS.) **150-200**

Shaded Pink Satin Rose Bowl

Cased satin, six-crimp rim, lightly molded swirled ribs, pink shaded to white enameled w/delicate gold leaf & blossoms clusters, 3 1/2" h. (ILLUS.) **100-150**

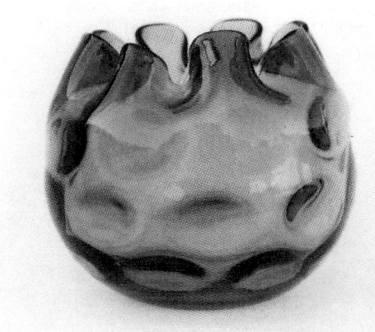

Modern Cranberry Rose Bowl

Cranberry, eight-crimp rim, Inverted Thumbprint patt., made in Japan, ca. 1980s, 4 1/2" d., 4" h. (ILLUS.)............. **45-55**

Royal Flemish

This ware, made by Mt. Washington Glass Co., is characterized by very heavy enameled gold lines dividing the surface into separate areas or sections. The body, with a matte finish, is variously decorated.

Rare Royal Flemish Decorated Cologne

Cologne bottle w/original stopper, squatty bulbous body tapering to a short cylindrical neck w/a small domed cap w/knob finial, a clear frosted ground enameled w/gold-outlined flowers w/lavender-washed centers & three butterflies enameled in gold, turquoise & blue, neck & stopper decorated in a rich purple wash & trimmed w/raised gold filigree, very minor wear, 4 1/2" d., 5 1/2" h. (ILLUS.) **$6,038**

Fancy Royal Flemish Vase

Vase, 9 1/2" h., bulbous body tapering to a small neck w/a deep cupped rim, applied gold shoulder handles, gold-outlined panels w/stylized flowerheads & leaves in shades of tan, beige, maroon & green, the shoulder w/scrolling black leafy floral vines, the cupped rim w/a brown dragon against a black ground (ILLUS.) **4,500-5,500**

Griffin-decorated Royal Flemish Vase

Vase, 10" h., bulbous body w/a small slightly flaring cylindrical neck, a background of pale mauve & tan geometric panels framed in raised gold & also decorated w/a large winged griffin in heavy gold on the front & a gold dragon on the back, the neck w/gold-outlined florals on a mauve ground, bottom resting on a gold beaded foot (ILLUS.) **4,140**

Royal Flemish Roman Coin Vase

Vase, 10 1/2" h., a wide squatty bulbous body w/a tiny neck supporting the wide tri-lobed cupped rim, the body w/gold-outlined panels in tan, brown & maroon w/Roman coin decoration, the cupped rim w/gold-trimmed lavender scrolling florals (ILLUS.) **4,500-6,000**

Rubina

This glass, sometimes spelled "Rubena," is a flashed ware, shading from ruby to clear. Some pieces are decorated, others are plain.

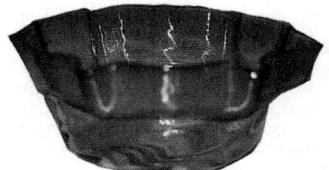

Threaded Rubina Finger Bowl

Finger bowl, round w/widely flaring ruffled upright rim, threading around exterior, 4 1/2" d., 2" h. (ILLUS.) **$85-95**
Pitcher, 7 1/2" h., Hobnail patt., spherical body w/flaring squared neck, shaded deep pink to clear w/a frosted finish, applied frosted clear handle, attributed to Hobbs, Brockunier & Co., ca. 1880s **259**
Pitcher, water, 8" h., bulbous base tapering to flaring ruffled rim, clear applied handle, concentric diamonds patt. **275**

Tall Rose-decorated Rubina Pitcher

Pitcher, 13" h., 4 1/2" d., tankard-type, tall baluster-form body w/a wide arched spout, applied clear handle, frosted body enameled w/large pink rose buds on leafy stems, gold band on rim (ILLUS.) **275-325**

Rubina Verde

This decorative glass, popular in the late 19th and early 20th centuries, shades from ruby or deep cranberry to green or greenish-yellow.

Cheese dish, cov., domed blown Rubina Verde Inverted Thumbprint patt. cover w/applied greenish knob finial, on a round pressed Daisy & Button patt. greenish underplate, Hobbs, Brockunier & Co., ca. 1880s, underplate 7" d., cover 5 1/2" d., 4 1/2" h. **$431**

Fine Rubina Verde Decanter

Decanter w/original stopper, a disk foot & knob stem below the bulbous inverted pear-shaped body tapering to a tall slender stick neck w/flared rim, a swirled & pointed green stopper, the optic ribbed body decorated w/fine colorful stylized flowers, late 19th c., 13 1/2" h. (ILLUS.) **661**
Pitcher, 7 3/4" h., bulbous ovoid Inverted Thumbprint body tapering to a flaring squared neck, applied green transparent handle, Hobbs, Brockunier & Co., ca. 1880s **431**

Fine Bohemian Rubina Verde Vase

Vase, 10" h., a cushion foot & slender stem supporting the bulbous Inverted Thumbprint patt. bowl w/an inwardly rolled rim pulled into three crimped points, light iridescent finish, Rindskopf factory, Bohemia, late 19th c. (ILLUS.) **633**

Sandwich

Numerous types of glass were produced at The Boston & Sandwich Glass Works in Sandwich, Massachusetts, on Cape Cod, from 1826 to 1888. Those listed here represent a sampling. Also see BLOWN THREE MOLD, PATTERN GLASS *and* LACY.

All pieces are pressed glass unless otherwise noted. Numbers after salt dips refer to listings in Pressed Glass Salt Dishes of the Lacy Period, 1825-1850, *by Logan W. and Dorothy B. Neal.*

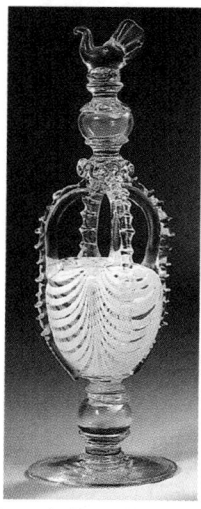

Extremely Rare Blown Bank

Bank, free-blown, a clear disk base & hollow knob stem supporting the blown ovoid body w/a center opening in clear w/white loopings, applied w/four arching rigaree ribs joined above the body & topped w/a rigaree band supporting a hollow knob applied w/a stylized rooster on a disk in clear, the base & top hollow knob each containing an 1833 American half-dime coin, extremely rare, w/a matching dug fragment, overall 11" h. (ILLUS.) **$19,975**

Beautiful Dolphin Candlesticks

Candlesticks, pressed flint glass, figural dolphin stem w/a petal socket, on a single-step square base, ca. 1845-70, dark blue, minor base roughness, 10 1/4" h., pr. (ILLUS.) **9,988**

Candlesticks, pressed flint glass, hexagonal flaring socket on a Loop patt. base, ca. 1840-60, cobalt blue, 6 1/2" h., pr. (one w/minor chips to base) **6,463**

Cologne bottle w/original stopper, pressed flint glass, Star & Punty patt., paneled sides & tall paneled stopper, ca. 1841-70, apple green, 7 1/4" h. (few tiny nicks to stopper) **823**

Decanter w/bar lip, pressed flint glass, Ashburton patt., pewter stopper, ca. 1840-60, canary yellow, small chip on neck ring, light scratches, 11 5/8" h. (ILLUS. center with lamps & vase, top next page) **1,410**

Inkstand, pressed flint glass, a squatty round melon-ribbed inkwell w/metal rim & cap & matching sand shaker, each set on a raised platform on a long rectangular stand w/round peg feet, silvery mottled opaque blue, several edge nicks & small cracks on stand, ca. 1835-55, extremely rare, 6 1/3" l., bottles 2" h., the set (ILLUS., middle, next page) **32,900**

Lamp, fluid-type, pressed flint glass, Loop patt. font on several wafers above the swelled octagonal standard & square base, cobalt blue, few small chips on loops, minor base edge nicks, 8 1/2" h. (ILLUS. far right with decanter, lamps & vase, top next page) **1,880**

Sandwich Decanter, Lamps & Vase

Extremely Rare Opaque Blue Glass Sandwich Inkstand

Lamp, whale oil-type, an inverted pressed lacy clear cup plate foot supporting a widely flaring trumpet-form mold-blown twisted rib font in cobalt blue, the angled shoulder centered by an opening fitted w/a two-spout tin whale oil burner, ca. 1828-35, extremely rare, 6 1/2" h. (chips to base edge) **22,325**

Lamp, whale oil-type, pressed flint glass, flaring octagonal font on a waisted paneled stem & square base, fitted w/a tin two-spout whale oil burner, ca. 1840-60, dark green, 10" h. (minor nick & scratch to font, two base corners chipped) **1,880**

Lamps, whale oil-type, pressed flint glass, mold-blown bulbous waisted hexagonal fonts w/whale oil burners attached to a pressed flaring hexagonal base, ca. 1840-55, deep amethyst, few minor base edge & corner chips, 8 1/2" h., pr. (ILLUS. left & right of decanter in group photo, top of page) **4,994**

Pomade jar, figural, pressed flint glass, model of a seated bear, head forms cover, ca. 1850-87, black, marked in gilt under bottom "Niagara Falls 1895," 4 1/2" h. (two chips to front & back of collar, two chips on neck) **499**

Smoke bell, blown flint glass, milk glass flaring flora-form body w/a ruffled rim applied w/a blue rim band, ca. 1870-87, 6" h. **153**

Vase, 9" h., 5" d., Twisted Loop patt., pressed flint glass, gauffered rim, hexagonal standard on round foot, ca. 1840-60, amethyst (very minor base edge nicks) **2,703**

Three Colored Sandwich Vases

Vase, 9 1/2" h., 5" d., pressed flint glass, Twisted Loop patt. top w/flaring ruffled rim, on wafers above the waisted & paneled standard & round foot, amethyst, ca. 1850, tiny rim nick, very small rough spot on foot rim, some interior residue (ILLUS. right with other two vases, above) **1,760**

Vase, 9 5/8" h., 5 1/2" d., pressed flint glass, Loop-Leaf patt., the top w/seven large loops widely flaring at the top, a wafer & knop stem above the pressed flaring hexagonal base, dark deep violet blue, near proof, ca. 1850 (ILLUS. left with other two vases, above) **8,525**

Vase, 10 1/8" h., pressed flint glass, tall Loop patt. bowl w/flaring rim, hexagonal baluster-form standard on a round foot, ca. 1840-60, canary, few chips below wafer in standard (ILLUS. far left with decanter & lamps, top previous page) **823**

Vase, 11 3/4" h., 4 1/2" d., pressed flint glass, Four-Printie Block patt., tall slender paneled top w/a flaring ruffled rim, knob & wafer stem above the flaring pressed hexagonal base, ca. 1850, deep emerald green, shallow chip on base edge, small corner base chip & minor flakes (ILLUS. center with other two vases, above) **2,310**

Vases, 11 3/4" h., pressed flint glass, Four Printie Block patt., ruffled rim, knobbed pedestal & octagonal flaring base, ca. 1840-60, cobalt blue, pr. (one w/minor nick, minor base edge nicks on both) **5,581**

Satin

Satin glass was a popular decorative glass developed in the late 19th century. Most pieces were composed of two layers of glass with the exterior layer usually in a shaded pastel color. The name derives from the soft matte finish, caused by exposure to acid fumes, which gave the surface a "satiny" feel. Mother-of-pearl satin glass was a specialized variety wherein air trapped between the layers of glass provided subtle surface patterns such as Herringbone and Diamond Quilted. A majority of satin glass was produced in England, Bohemia and America, but collectors should be aware that reproductions have been made for many years.

Group of Satin Glass Pieces

Bowl, 6 1/2" d., wide squatty rounded form w/an eight-crimp rim, shaded deep pink to white mother-of-pearl Peacock Feather patt., late 19th c. (ILLUS. bottom row, far right with other satin pieces, bottom previous page) **$633**

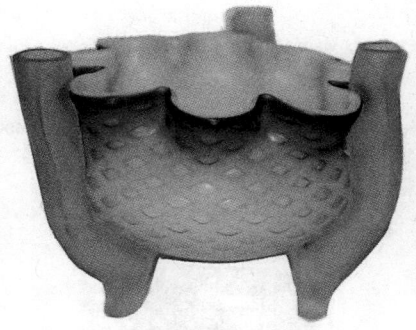

Unusual Mother-of-Pearl Satin Bowl

Bowl, 6 1/2" d., 4 7/8" h., deep rounded form w/deeply ruffled rim, shaded dark blue to white mother-of-pearl Diamond Quilted patt., framed by three heavy clear frosted branch legs, white lining (ILLUS.) **325-375**

Two Rainbow Mother-of-Pearl Satin Ewers

Ewer, footed bulbous body tapering to a slender neck w/a rolled & ruffled rim, applied frosted clear handle, Rainbow mother-of-pearl in the Herringbone patt., 6 3/4" h. (ILLUS. right with other ewer) **1,093**

Ewer, squatty bulbous body centered by a tall slender cylindrical neck w/a rolled & crimped rim, applied clear frosted handle, Rainbow mother-of-pearl Herringbone patt., 8 1/4" h. (ILLUS. left with other ewer) **748**

Tumbler, yellow mother-of-pearl Diamond

Satin Ewers and a Vase

Ewers, a cushion foot below the ovoid shouldered body w/a tall cylindrical neck w/a crimped & rolled rim, frosted clear applied thorn handle, shaded pink mother-of-pearl Diamond Quilted patt., mid-20th c., 12 1/2" h. (ILLUS. left & right with vase) **431**

Fairy lamp, the open-topped domed shade w/molded swirled ribs & a pink satin mother-of-pearl Swirled Stripe patt., on a shaded mother-of-pearl Diamond Quilted patt. cup base, late 19th c., 4 1/2" h. (ILLUS. front row, far left with satin bowl and vases, previous page).............................. **431**

Pitcher, water, 7 1/4" h., tapering ovoid body, flared ruffled rim, yellow mother-of-pearl Diamond Quilted patt., applied frosted clear reeded handle, ground pontil.. **375**

Decorated Satin Glass Tumbler

Tumbler, cylindrical, shaded dark blue mother-of-pearl Diamond Quilted patt., colorful enameled pink flowers on leafy stems, 3 7/8" h. (ILLUS.) **375-450**
Quilted patt., polished pontil **120**

Vase, 5 1/2" h., mother-of-pearl "Federze-ichnung" patt., pearl trailings on a deep yellow ground w/overall fine gold trailings, bulbous form tapering to a short ruffled flaring neck, signed "Pat. 9159" **978**

Vase, 6" h., a bulbous ovoid body w/shoulder indentations & a tri-lobed cupped neck, deep pink mother-of-pearl Flower & Acorn patt., late 19th c. (ILLUS. bottom row, second from right with satin bowl & other pieces, page 680)................. **891**

Vase, 7" h., bulbous base tapering to short neck w/ringed rim, two applied rustic handles, yellow mother-of-pearl Diamond Quilted patt. (tiny star crack in one diamond)................. **90**

Vase, 7" h., ovoid body tapering to a slender trumpet neck, shaded pink mother-of-pearl Diamond Quilted patt., ca. 1900 (ILLUS. bottom row, second from left w/satin bowl & other pieces, page 680) **173**

Vase, 9" h., bulbous body tapering to a tall stick neck w/a cupped rim, shaded deep pink mother-of-pearl Diamond Quilted patt., late 19th c. (ILLUS. center with pair of ewers, previous page) **144**

Large Fan-shaped Satin Vase

Vase, 10" h., fan-shaped, widely arched sides w/crimped rim, shaded blue mother-of-pearl Diamond Quilted patt., on applied frosted clear peg feet (ILLUS.)...... **650-850**

Vases, 5 1/2" h., footed squatty bulbous body tapering to a short neck w/a rolled four-lobe rim, three frosted clear applied thorn handles, shaded pink mother-of-pearl Herringbone patt., early 20th c., rough pontil marks, pr. (ILLUS. of two top row, far right with satin bowl & other pieces, page 680) **431**

Vases, 7" h., ovoid body w/a short cylindrical neck w/a four-lobed ruffled & rolled rim, shaded deep peach mother-of-pearl Diamond Quilted patt., early 20th c., pr. (ILLUS. of two top row, left with satin bowl & other pieces, page 680)..................... **201**

Schneider

This ware is made in France at Cristallerie Schneider, established in 1913 near Paris by Ernest and Charles Schneider. Some pieces of cameo were marked "Le Verre Francais" and others were signed "Charder."

Schneider Mark

Pitcher, water, 7 1/4" h., spherical base w/cylindrical neck & flat rim w/pinched spout, slightly mottled orange w/applied black amethyst handle, polished base w/acid signature... **$400**

Vase, 3 7/8" h., squatty bulbous form tapering from the shoulder to a wide molded flat mouth, pale pink w/an etched textured surface w/stylized rays & arched designs, etched signature, early 20th c........ **115**

Small Red Decorated Schneider Vase

Vase, 5 1/2" h., a cushion foot tapering to a flaring bell-form body w/incurved rim, deep red decorated w/splashes of blue & brick red, signed on the foot "Schneider France," ca. 1920s (ILLUS.) **420**

Large Glass & Iron Schneider Vase

Vase, 15 3/4" h. glass & iron, a multicolored blown glass body in green, orange, dark blue & mustard yellow blown into an iron lattice framework so as to form lobed sides, signed on the bottom w/an etched circle in three sections, each w/an initial "F - B - S," "France" below the circle, ca. 1920s (ILLUS.)... **2,760**

Silver Deposit - Silver Overlay

Silver Deposit and Silver Overlay have been made commercially since the last quarter of the 19th century. Silver is deposited on the glass by various means, most commonly by utilizing an electric current. The glass was very popular during the first three decades of this century, and some pieces are still being produced. During the late 1970s, silver commanded exceptionally high prices and this was reflected in a surge of interest in silver overlay glass, especially in pieces marked "Sterling" or "925" on the heavy silver overlay.

Rare Steuben Red Overlaid Basket

Basket, flaring foot tapering up to widely flaring fan-shaped ruffled sides, Selenium Red ground decorated w/an ornate silver overlay lattice design w/vines & flowers, the arched handle covered w/silver, silver marked "999/1000 Fine 607," Steuben Glassworks Model No. 455, early 20th c., 14 1/2" h. (ILLUS.)..................... **$3,565**

Decanter w/original ball stopper, footed spherical body tapering to a tall cylindrical neck w/a wide arched spout, applied long arched silver-encased handle, crystal ornately decorated w/silver overlay foliate & scroll designs w/a cartouche at the front, the foot, rim & stopper also encased in silver, American-made, early 20th c., 11 1/2" h. **1,955**

Lovely Green Silver Overlaid Decanter

Decanter w/original stopper, flat-bottomed cylindrical form w/a rounded shoulder tapering to a cylindrical neck fitted w/a cylindrical stopper, applied loop handle, dark green w/ornate silver overlay looping vines, flowers & leaves, silver-covered clear stopper & handle, silver faintly marked w/the Gorham trademark & "D M Z 999/1000 Fine," some staining on interior, late 19th - early 20th c., 10 3/4" h. (ILLUS.) **863**

Tapering Green Silver Overlay Decanter

Decanter w/original stopper, widely flaring body tapering sharply to a cylindrical neck w/flattened rim, dark green decorated w/overall silver overlay swirling flowering vines w/an engraved central cartouche, the green ball stopper w/further silver overlay, base of stopper repaired, late 19th - early 20th c., 12 3/4" h. (ILLUS.).. **1,208**

Silver Overlay Perfume Bottle

Perfume bottle w/original stopper, clear squatty tapering lobed form w/a short cylindrical neck & flattened rim, tall pointed & lobed stopper, decorated overall w/silver overlay scrolling design w/inscription dated 1913, 4 3/4" h. (ILLUS.)................ **300-350**

Three Silver Overlay Vases

Fine Overlay Presentation Pitcher

Pitcher, 9 1/4" h., tankard-type w/a flaring base & pulled rim spout, applied loop handle, ruby red decorated overall w/silver deposit grapevines w/grape clusters, a central cartouche engraved "City of Boston 4th of July 1899 1st Prize 25ft. Cabin Yacht Won By Eleanor," two tiny fleabites under bottom (ILLUS.) **1,840**

Vase, 5 3/8" h., bulbous lower body tapering to a swelled neck w/flared rim, green iridized finish w/geometric banded sterling silver overlay, probably Loetz, Austria (ILLUS. center with other vases, top of page) **325**

Vase, 6 1/2" h., round footring below the wide compressed base below the baluster-form body w/a flared rim, deep purple w/red spatter & overall heavy green iridescence, pierced serpentine loop Art Nouveau-style sterling silver overlay bands descending from the rim, probably Loetz, Austria (ILLUS. left with other vases, top of page) **625**

Vase, 7 1/2" h., ovoid body w/wide flared rim, emerald green diamond quilted design w/satin finish, decorated w/sterling silver flower & vine overlay marked by the La Pierre Mfg. Co., the rim monogrammed & dated 1909 .... **748**

Vase, 8" h., slightly tapering cylindrical optic-ribbed pale amethyst body w/a flaring mouth, long ornate panels of sterling silver overlay flowers down both sides, ground pontil (ILLUS. right with other vases, top of page).................................... **225-250**

Large Vase with Silver Overlay Tulips

Vase, 8 1/2" h., simple ovoid body w/closed rim, shaded deep amethyst to yellow body decorated w/iridescent silver looping & applied w/sterling silver overlay tulips & leaves, probably Loetz, Austria (ILLUS.)... **1,250**

Vase, 10" h., slender baluster-form body in emerald green w/relief-blown oval sections through the ornate pierced sterling silver lattice design of lilies, leaves & vines, silver marked "G3223 - 925 fine" **825**

Ornate Silver Deposit Vase

Vase, 12 1/2" h., squatty wide base w/a wide shoulder centered by a gently flaring cylindrical body w/a bulbed shoulder below the short cylindrical neck, clear w/smoky iridescence & an overall silver deposit design of scrolling leafy stems & carnation blossoms, ca. 1920s (ILLUS.)................ **700-800**

Vase, 12 3/4" h., cushion foot below the tall swelled slender cylindrical body, pale green satin finish decorated w/angular Secessionist-style sterling silver overlay, Austria, late 19th - early 20th c. (minor wear).. **518**

Smith Brothers

Originally established as a decorating department of the Mt. Washington Glass Company in the 1870s, the firm later was an independent business in New Bedford, Massachusetts. Beautifully decorated opal white glass was its hallmark, but it also did glass cutting. Some examples carry its lion-in-the-shield mark.

Smith Brothers Mark

Lovely Smith Brothers Flower-decorated Bowl

Bowl, 10" d., wide squatty melon-ribbed body w/a silver plate rim band, creamy ground h.p. w/large pink & white flowers on green leafy vines, signed (ILLUS.). **$750-950**

Small Smith Brothers Vase with Daisies

Vase, 4" h., 4 1/4" d., small spherical body w/small cylindrical neck, shaded dark yellow to pale yellow satin enameled w/scattered white daisy blossoms (ILLUS.).. **200-250**

Bird-decorated Pink Ring Vase

Vase, 6" h., 2 1/2" d., ring-type, pale pink ground & gold-trimmed white rings, enameled w/a scene of a white bird landing on a stem w/blue & green leaves (ILLUS.).. **200-225**

Canteen-shaped Smith Bros. Vase

Vase, 8" h., footed flattened canteen-shape w/a small cylindrical neck, creamy ground h.p. w/large gold-trimmed brown & green stalks of wheat, signed, rare (ILLUS., previous page).................... **1,500-2,000**

Smith Brothers Vase with Clematis

Vase, 11" h., flattened pillow-type, satin white ground h.p. w/large pink & blue clematis flowers on green leafy vines, signed (ILLUS.) **1,000-1,500**

Spangled

Spangled glass incorporated particles of mica or metallic flakes and variegated colored glass particles embedded in the transparent glass. Usually made of two layers, it might have either an opaque or transparent casing. The Vasa Murrhina Glass Company of Sandwich, Massachusetts, first patented the process for producing Spangled glass in 1884, and this factory is known to have produced great quantities of this ware. It was, however, also produced by numerous other American and English glasshouses. This type, along with Spatter, is often erroneously called "End of the Day."

A related decorative glass, Aventurine, features a fine speckled pattern resembling gold dust on a solid color ground. Also, see ART GLASS BASKETS and ROSE BOWLS.

Spangled Art Glass Basket

Basket, cased, the interior w/blue & brown spatter w/silver mica flecks, exterior in white, applied clear reeded & pointed handle, 8" d., overall 11 1/2" h. (ILLUS.) **$250-275**

Pitcher, 5" h., ring neck form, w/pinched body, applied amber handle, polished pontil, amber plated deep cobalt w/mica flakes, Hobbs, Brockunier & Co. **350**

Pitcher, 5" h., ring neck form, w/pinched body, applied clear handle, polished pontil, clear w/opal plated interior & mica flakes, Hobbs, Brockunier & Co. **100**

Pitcher, 5 1/4" h., tapering ovoid body w/slightly ruffled rim, applied amber reeded handle, amber w/overall gold Aventurine, polished pontil **600**

Pitcher, water, 8 1/2" h., spherical base w/cylindrical neck flaring out to tricorner rim, cranberry cased light amber, blood red & opal w/mica flakes, applied clear reeded handle, ground pontil **250**

Spangled Jack-in-the-Pulpit Vase

Vase, 5" h., 3 1/4" d., jack-in-the-pulpit-style, cased w/dark pink interior & dark gold spangled exterior, the crimped rim w/applied clear border (ILLUS.) **115-130**

Fine Rainbow Striped Spangled Vase

Vase, 10 1/4" h., footed ovoid body tapering to a flaring crimped rim, Rainbow vertical striped ground in deep pink, blue & yellow cased in clear w/mica flecks, late 19th c. (ILLUS.) **661**

Spatter

This variegated-color ware is similar to Spangled glass but does not contain metallic flakes. The various colors are applied on a clear, opaque white or colored body. Much of it was made in Europe and England. It is sometimes called "End Of Day."

Syrup pitcher w/reproduction lid, Royal Ivy patt. in pink & white, clear applied handle, 6 1/4" h. (crack in upper handle).... **$325**
Toothpick holder, Ribbed Pillar patt., cranberry & opal spatter, satin finish (bruise on exterior of rim) **50**
Tumbler, overshot ruby & opal, Hobbs, Brockunier & Co. **100**

Steuben

Most of the Steuben glass listed below was made at the Steuben Glass Works, now a division of Corning Glass, between 1903 and about 1933. The factory was organized by T.G. Hawkes, noted glass designer Frederick Carder, and others. Mr. Carder devised many types of glass and revived many old techniques.

Steuben Marks

Acid Cut-Back

Lamp, ovoid body in Jade Yellow cased in black & acid-cut w/an Art Deco style scene of Pegasus, applied gold Aurene drips around the top, silvered metal fittings & pierced scrolling footed base, Shape No. 8496, glass base 14" h. (minor bubble burst) **$4,000-4,500**

Acid Cut-Back Floral Lamp Base

Lamp, table model, the baluster-form glass body w/a rolled rim in Green Jade cutback to Alabaster in an overall flowering vine design, mounted on a bronzed metal swag-cast base on scroll feet, early 20th c., body 12" h., overall 28" h. (ILLUS.) **863**

Rosaline Acid Cut-back Bulbous Vase

Vase 7" h., nearly spherical body w/a wide flat mouth, Rosaline cut-back to Alabaster w/an overall flowering vine design, unsigned (ILLUS.) **1,150**

Rare Acid Cut-Back Bird Pattern Vase

Vase 12" h., a funnel foot supporting the trumpet-form body, light amethyst cutback to Alabaster in the Birds #2 patt., Shape No. 6034, ca. 1924 (ILLUS.) **8,626**

Vase, 12" h., Rosaline trumpet form body acid-cut overall w/flowers on leafy vines, applied flaring Alabaster foot, rough pontil (burst in Alabaster foot) **1,000-1,100**

Alabaster Figure & Flower Frog

Rare Acid Cut-Back Tropic Design Vase

Vase 12 1/2" h., wide ovoid body tapering to a flattened rim, Mirror Black cut-back to Green Jade in the Tropic patt., Shape No. 7097, ca. 1928 (ILLUS.) **9,925**

Alabaster

Figure & flower frog, a Quan Yin figure, Shape No. 7133, standing on a matching flower frog, Shape No. 7064, frog 4 1/2" d., 2" h., figure 7 1/2" h., the set (ILLUS., top next column).............................. **949**

Aurene

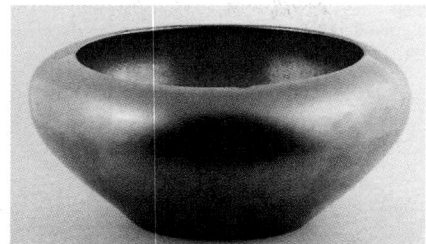

Gold Aurene Steuben Bowl

Varied Group of Steuben Pieces

Bowl, 8" d., 3 3/4" h., wide squatty tapering round form w/closed rim, overall golden iridescence, signed (ILLUS., center previous page) **375-450**

Bowl, 9" d., 2 1/2" h., wide shallow flat-bottomed form w/incurved sides raised on three applied prunt feet, overall blue iridescence, Shade No. 2586, signed on the pontil (ILLUS. bottom row, second from left with other Steuben pieces, bottom previous page) **690**

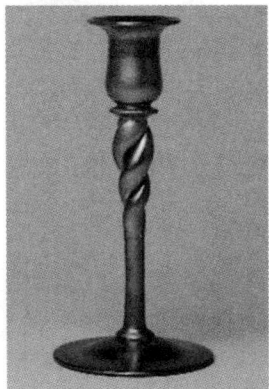

Blue Aurene Candlestick

Candlestick, a thin round foot below the slender twisted stem & cylindrical flaring socket, all in iridescent blue, signed on the base, Shape No. 686, 8" h. (ILLUS.) **920**

Etched Blue Aurene & Calcite Compote

Compote, 8" d., 3 1/2" h., a round foot & pedestal in Calcite supporting a widely flaring shallow bowl in Calcite lined w/blue Aurene intaglio etched in a stylized violet design, Shape No. 3234 (ILLUS. of top interior) **1,380**

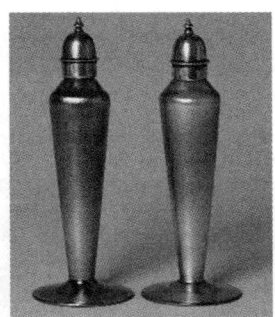

Gold Aurene Salt & Pepper Shakers

Salt & pepper shakers w/original brass tops, a thin round foot below the flaring cylindrical body in overall gold Aurene, unsigned, 6 3/4" h., pr. (ILLUS.) **949**

Gold Aurene Triple Stump Vase

Vase, 6" h., triple stump-form, overall gold Aurene iridescence, Shape No. 1744, signed (ILLUS.) **780**

Extremely Rare Decorated Aurene Vase

Vase, 7 1/2" h., bulbous nearly spherical body w/a wide short trumpet neck, overall blue Aurene iridescence decorated w/random threading of leaves & vines in silvery blue, the neck in gold iridescence w/zigzag intarsia bands in white & blue, opal white interior, signed on the base (ILLUS.) **25,875**

Vase, 7 3/4" h., footed swelled tapering cylindrical body w/a flaring rim, amber w/overall golden iridescence, unsigned, ca. 1910 .... **920**

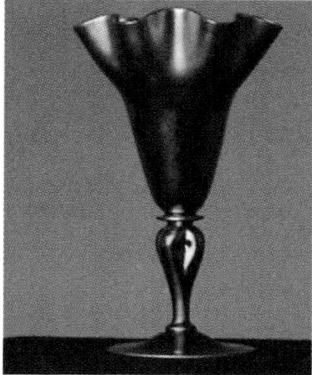

Fine Blue Aurene Ruffled Vase

Vase, 8 1/2" h., flora-form, a thin round foot & tapering ovoid lobed stem below the trumpet-form bowl w/a deeply ruffled flaring top, overall blue iridescence, Shape No. 2708, signed on base "Steuben Aurene 2708" (ILLUS.) **3,680**

Fine Bulbous Blue Aurene Vase

Vase, 10 3/4" h., bulbous ovoid body w/a short flaring neck, overall blue Aurene iridescence, Shape No. 1683, signed on the bottom (ILLUS.) **1,800**

Calcite

Compote, 6" d., 3" h., the wide round foot & exterior of the widely flaring rounded bowl in white, gold iridescent interior, ca. 1920 .... **316**

Compote, 10" d., 4 1/2" h., a Calcite disk foot & stem supporting a widely flaring shallow bowl in Calcite lined w/gold iridescent Aurene, Shape No. 3234 (ILLUS. middle row, center with other Steuben pieces, page 688) **431**

Calcite & Aurene Sherbet & Underplate

Sherbet & underplate, a Calcite stem & exterior on the bell-form sherbet lined w/gold Aurene iridescence, the underplate w/a Calcite exterior & gold Aurene interior, underplate 6" d., sherbet 4" h., the set (ILLUS.) **288**

Celeste Blue

Celeste Blue Goblet

Goblet, a blue round foot & swelled clear stem below the flaring optic ribbed bell-form Celeste Blue bowl, signed on the base "F. Carder Steuben," 6" h. (ILLUS.) **180**

Vases, 4" h., lily-type, round foot on the widely flaring optic ribbed bowl, Shape No. 346, pr. (ILLUS. of two bottom far left with other Steuben pieces, page 688) **431**

Cintra

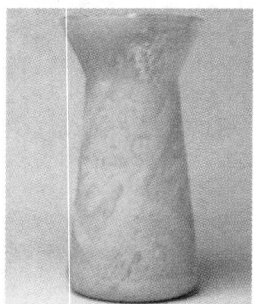

Rare Cintra Acid Cut-Back Vase

Vase, 12" h., tall slightly tapering cylindrical body w/a flat flaring neck, green Cintra acid cut-back w/a design of stylized flowers & trellis (ILLUS., previous page).......... **4,025**

Cluthra

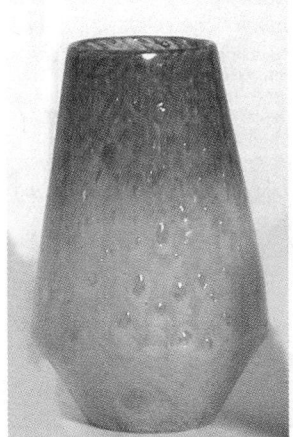

Gold, Ruby & White Cluthra Vase

Vase, 8 1/4" h., angular tapering cylindrical form w/a flat mouth, mottled gold, ruby & white, unsigned, Shape No. 6882 (ILLUS.).. **1,035**

Grotesque

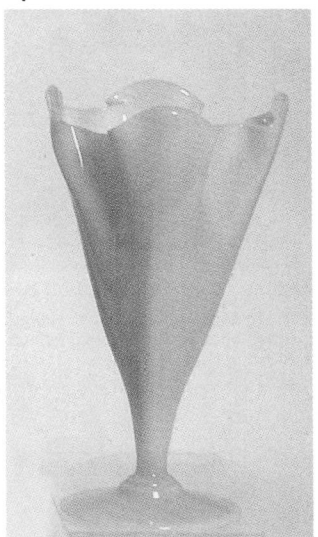

Grotesque Ivrene Vase No. 7090

Vase, 9" h., Ivrene glass in a widely flaring trumpet form w/a deeply ruffled & pulled rim, Shape No. 7090 (ILLUS.) **460**

Grotesque Ivrene Vase

Vase, 9 1/4" h., Ivrene glass in a trumpet form w/a pulled & ruffled top w/four pinched corners, silver paper Steuben label (ILLUS.) **403**

Jade

Green Jade Short Candlesticks

Candlesticks, Green Jade, a wide flaring round foot supporting a short stem w/four applied Alabaster prunts below the cylindrical socket w/a deeply rolled rim, signed w/the Steuben fleur-de-lis mark, 4" h., pr. (ILLUS.)... **575**

Center bowl, Green Jade, a disk foot below the deep & widely flaring bowl, Shape No. 3200, 15" d., 5 3/4" h. (ILLUS. top row, center with other Steuben pieces, page 688)... **805**

Unusual Green Jade Donut Holder

Donut holder, Green Jade, a wide low domed foot centered by a baluster-form upright w/twisted knob finial, a scratch at the rim & one open bubble, 9" d., 5 1/2" h. (ILLUS.)... **460**

Green Jade Small Ovoid Vase

Vase, 6 1/4" h., Green Jade, wide ovoid shouldered body w/a short cylindrical neck, swirled optic ribbing, Steuben fleur-de-lis mark (ILLUS.) **230**

Vase, 7" h., Yellow Jade, footed squatty bulbous lower body below the tall trumpet neck, small loop handles w/rings at the shoulder, ca. 1925, Shape No. 5007 (minor inclusions) **2,000-2,500**

Vase, 7 1/8" h., 8" d., Green Jade, bulbous ovoid shape w/a closed rim, acid cutback in the "Carved" patt., Shape No. 6078 (ILLUS. top row, far left with other Steuben pieces, page 688) **1,150**

Moss Agate

Cologne bottle w/original stopper, paperweight-type, heavy cylindrical crystal body internally decorated w/silver flecks, pale green Cintra & trapped bubbles, the exterior deeply engraved w/crosshatching & alternating facets & arched recesses, pointed facet-cut stopper, ca. 1930, Shape No. 6917, marked, 7 1/4" h. (few nicks, minor staining at top) **4,500-4,800**

Oriental Poppy

Goblet, a slender Pomona green foot & stem supporting the pink pastel striped bell-form bowl, Shape No. 6522, 8 1/4" h. (ILLUS. top row, far right with other Steuben pieces, page 688) **661**

Goblet, the deep round bowl w/flaring rim in pink striped opalescent raised on a slender clear opalescent stem, ca. 1910, 8" h. **403**

Wine, a small rounded flaring pink bowl w/white opalescent stripes, raised on a slender clear opalescent stem, ca. 1910, 6" h. **403**

Pomona Green

Candlestick, a Topaz domed swirled optic ribbed foot supporting the Pomona Green knobbed slender optic ribbed stem & Topaz bulbous candle socket w/a widely rolled rim, Shape No. 6110 (ILLUS. bottom row, second from right with other Steuben pieces, page 688) **316**

Pomona Green Oblong Center Bowl

Center bowl, footed oblong shaped shallow Pomona Green bowl w/applied Topaz loop end handles, signed w/Steuben fleur-de-lis mark, 8 1/4 x 15 3/4", 4 1/2" h. (ILLUS.) **403**

Pomona Green & Clear Compote

Compote, 8" d., 7" h., a flaring domed swirled optic rib Pomona Green foot supporting a knobbed clear stem supporting the shallow widely flaring swirled optic rib bowl shading from Pomona Green to clear, signed w/the Steuben block letter signature (ILLUS.) **288**

Pomona Green Optic Ribbed Vase

Vase, 7" h., footed wide cylindrical swirled optic ribbed body w/a flaring rim, signed w/the Steuben fleur-de-lis mark (ILLUS.) **100-200**

Selenium Red

Selenium Red Finger Bowl & Plate

Finger bowl & underplate, a deep rounded flaring bowl on a flattened underplate, each intaglio etched w/a grapevine design, underplate signed, underplate 6" d., finger bowl 4 1/4" d., 2 1/2" h., 2 pcs. (ILLUS., previous page) **230**

Topaz

Topaz Swirled Optic Ribbed Vase

Vase, 7" h., footed wide cylindrical swirled optic ribbed body w/a flared rim, signed w/Steuben fleur-de-lis mark (ILLUS.) **230**

Vase, 9" h., fan-type, a Pomona disk foot & knopped stem supporting the flattened optic ribbed fan-shaped Topaz vase (ILLUS. bottom row, far right with other Steuben pieces, page 688) **259**

Verre de Soie

Candlesticks, Venetian-style, delicately blown w/a wide round domed foot below the stem w/a baluster-form section below two knops below the ovoid candle socket w/a flattened rim, unsigned, 12" h., pr. **374**

Steuben Verre de Soie Perfume Bottle

Perfume bottle w/original stopper, squatty bulbous tapering melon lobed body w/a short neck & flared rim, pointed

blown hollow stopper, Shape No. 1455, 2 3/4" d., 4 1/2" h. (ILLUS.) **431**

Vase, 11 1/2" h., flora-form, a thin round foot & slender stem supporting the upright flaring bowl w/ruffled rim, the bowl decorated near the top w/a band of pulled & swirled green, variation of Shape No. 676 .... **2,200-2,300**

Miscellaneous Wares

Bowl, 10 7/8" d., 6 7/8" h., a wide flaring plain colorless crystal bowl raised on a cylindrical hollow body base w/applied wave designs, signed **489**

Candelabra, two-light, Scroll design, cylindrical sockets supported atop pairs of scroll arms centered by a large knob, signed, 7 1/4" w., 4 3/4" h., pr. **489**

Dessert set: eight goblets, eight finger bowls & eight 8 1/4" d. dessert plates; crystal, all in simple plain rounded forms, mid-20th c., in original fitted box, the set **1,000-1,200**

Model of a dinosaur, colorless crystal stylized elongated brontosaur, signed, 12 3/4" l. (base wear) **1,840**

Model of a donkey, colorless crystal standing stylized & elongated animal w/upright ears, signed, 10 1/2" h. (base scratches) **978**

Model of a frog, colorless crystal seated frog, signed, 4 1/4" l. (minor base wear) **230**

Stevens & Williams

This long-established English glasshouse has turned out a wide variety of artistic glasswares through the years. Fine satin glass pieces and items with applied decoration (sometimes referred to as "Matsu-No-Ke") are especially sought after today. The following represents a cross-section of its wares.

Fine Stevens & Williams Center Bowl

Center bowl, a squatty bulbous optic ribbed aqua bowl w/a small short neck decorated w/fancy applied decoration including two lifelike amber pears w/deep purple bloom spots & also applied amber stems & green leaves, applied amber branches forming the footed base, 9" d., 7 3/4" h. (ILLUS.) **$1,495**

Rare Stevens & Williams Cut Decanter

Decanter w/original stopper, upright oblong hexagonal form, clear cased in green & cut in each panel w/stylized flowers & leaves, cased & cut stopper & applied clear shoulder handle, overall 10" h. (ILLUS.) **2,530**

Stevens & Williams Fancy Satin Vase

Vase, 7" h., 6" d., a squatty bulbous melonribbed body tapering to a short ribbed trefoil neck, shaded dark brown mother-ofpearl Zippered Ribbon patt. satin further decorated w/tiny enameled white flowers, raised on three applied clear frosted feet, small flake on one foot (ILLUS.) **748**

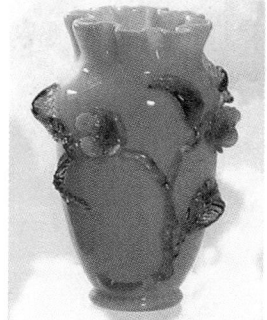

Stevens & Williams Floral-applied Vase

Vase, 7 1/4" h., footed ovoid body w/a wide upright ruffled rim, shaded deep lemon

yellow to pearl white, decorated w/applied opal flowers tinged w/pink & green & red-tinted leaves on amber branches, ca. 1890 (ILLUS.) **345**

Unusual Brass-mounted Vase

Vase, 14 1/4" h., a bulbous lower body tapering to a tall cylindrical neck, moldblown optic diamond quilted body w/a slightly opalescent color & swirled red & blue rainbow colors around the neck, mounted on a domed & pierced cast brass base w/grotesque mask feet, the neck topped by a crown-form brass rim flanked by fancy S-scroll handles, signed on the bottom of the glass "S & W Artglass," late 19th c. (ILLUS.) **661**

Tiffany

This glassware, covering a wide diversity of types, was produced in glasshouses operated by Louis Comfort Tiffany, America's outstanding glass designer of the Art Nouveau period, from the last quarter of the 19th century until the early 1930s. Tiffany revived early techniques and devised many new ones.

Various Tiffany Marks & Labels

Bowl, 3 1/2" h., a swelled flaring & ribbed lower body below a widely flaring rim, overall iridescent gold intaglio cut w/grape leaf design, signed "5 - L.C. Tiffany - Favrile," ca. 1900 .... **$863**

A Grouping of Four Tiffany Pieces

Bowl, 5 1/4" d., 2" h., round upright sides below the flattened widely flaring rim, molded ribbing in the pastel body w/iridescent opalescent green, signed "LCT Favrile," ca. 1900 .... **690**

Bowl, 6 1/4" d., 2 1/4" h., footed wide shallow lightly ribbed form w/a flattened flaring & lightly scalloped rim, overall gold iridescence, signed "LCT," ca. 1900 (ILLUS. bottom right with other pieces, top of page)... **460**

Gold Tiffany Favrile Bowl

Bowl, 7 1/4" d., 3 1/2" h., squatty ribbed form w/incurved scalloped rim, overall gold iridescence, signed on the base "L.C.T. Favrile," ca. 1900 (ILLUS.)................ **460**

Center bowl, a deep rounded bowl on four small applied peg feet, a widely flaring upturned & ruffled rim, overall gold iridescence w/red highlights, signed "1952 C LC Tiffany - Favrile," ca. 1908, 8" d., 4" h. (ILLUS. top row center with bowl & pieces, top of page) **978**

Center bowl, a shallow round center w/a wide flattened & gently undulating rim, iridescent gold decorated w/an intaglio-cut leaf border, signed "5-1406 LC Tiffany - Inc. - Favrile," ca. 1900, 3" h........................ **1,093**

Decanter w/original stopper, ovoid double-gourd form tapering to a cylindrical neck, iridescent pale green applied w/tadpole prunts around the sides, bulbous acorn stopper, signed "LCT 03668," slight loss to one prunt & slight wear, ca. 1900, 11 1/2" h. (ILLUS. bottom left with Tiffany bowl & pieces, top of page) **633**

Dish, shallow round form, overall gold iridescence, inscribed "L.C.T." & paper label, 5 7/8" d. **201**

Finger bowl & underplate, the bowl w/deeply ruffled flaring sides, in a matching ruffled plate, overall gold iridescence w/good onion skin edge finish, both signed "L.C.T.," ca. 1900, plate 7" d., bowl 3" h., the set... **633**

Tiffany Pastel Goblet

Goblet, pastel type w/an optic ribbed opalescent domed foot & slender stem supporting a stepped & flaring bell-form optic ribbed bowl shading from pearly opalescent to aqua to yellow, signed on the foot "L.C.T. Favrile," 7 1/2" h. (ILLUS.)................ **518**

Rare Blue Decorated Tiffany Inkwell

Inkwell w/hinged bronze neck & cap, footed squatty round waisted well in iridescent blue w/silver & blue iridescent pulled-feather decoration, signed on bottom "L.C.T. H205," 5 1/2" h. (ILLUS.) **6,038**

Gold Leaf-decorated Tiffany Loving Cup

Loving cup, swelling wide cylindrical body w/three applied long loop handles, overall gold iridescence decorated w/green leaf & vine decoration, signed on base "LC Tiffany - Favrile 5127C" & w/original Tiffany paper label, 7 1/4" h. (ILLUS.) **2,588**

Parfait, amber foot & knop stem below the cylindrical waisted & ribbed bowl w/a pink opalescent flaring rim, signed "LCT," ca. 1910, 5" h. **431**

Tiffany Aqua Pastel Parfait

Parfait, pastel, a disk foot & tall optic ribbed slightly flaring cylindrical bowl, aqua w/opalescent vertical bands, signed "L.C. Tiffany - Favrile" & original Tiffany paper label, 6 1/4" h. (ILLUS.) **604**

Tall Tiffany Gold Favrile Pitcher

Pitcher, 12" h., tall waisted cylindrical shape w/a pinched rim & applied loop handle, overall gold iridescence, signed "Louis C. Tiffany - Favrile" (ILLUS.)... **2,000 - 2,500**

Salt dips, small squatty bulbous form w/impressed stylized floriform & zigzag band around the sides, overall gold iridescence, signed "L.C.T. Favrile," 2 3/8" d., pr. **920**

Urn, a wide flat mouth above a sharply tapering body ending in a bronze round foot, the body in opal w/iridescent gold & green draped loop decoration, the bronze foot stamped "Louis C. Tiffany Furnaces Inc. 525" w/monogram, ca. 1900, 8 1/4" h... **1,093**

Vase, 3" h., miniature, footed bulbous ovoid melon-lobed body tapering to a flared cupped rim, amber w/overall gold iridescence, signed "1019 4034 LCT Tiffany - Favrile," ca. 1917 (ILLUS. far left with other miniature vases, top of next page) **690**

Vase, 4" h., bulbous nearly spherical form w/pinched-in sides, amber w/overall gold iridescence, engraved "NLEA 1901- 1911," ca. 1911... **431**

Vase, 4 1/2" h., miniature, footed ovoid body tapering to a trumpet neck, cobalt blue w/overall deep blue iridescence decorated w/iridescent gold hooked feather design, signed "D865 Louis C. Tiffany," ca. 1895 (ILLUS. second from left with other miniature vases, next page) **1,840**

Vase, 4 1/2" h., miniature, lightly ribbed ovoid body tapering to a flaring & lightly ruffled neck, amber w/overall gold iridescence, signed "LCT Favrile - W4867," ca. 1905 (ILLUS. far right with other miniature vases, top next page) **575**

Group of Four Miniature Tiffany Vases

Vase, 4 1/2" h., miniature, slender baluster form tapering to a short swelled neck, dark amethyst w/an overall iridescent blue zipper design, signed "LCT," ca. 1900 (ILLUS. second from right with other miniature vases, above)............................ **575**

Vase, 7 1/4" h., slender tall tapering cylindrical body w/a rounded shoulder & tall slightly flaring stick neck, amber w/overall gold iridescence, unsigned, ca. 1900 (ILLUS. top row, right with bowl & other pieces, top page 695) **890**

Rare Green Iridescent Tiffany Vase

Vase, 8" h., wide baluster form body w/a cupped round neck, dark green iridescent body, the neck in bronze iridescence w/intertwined zigzag lines in lime green &

blue, signed on the base "8745M LC Tiffany Inc. Favrile" (ILLUS.)........................... **7,763**

Fine Tiffany Floriform Vase

Vase, 12" h., floriform, a round domed foot w/a green & white pulled-feather design below the pale green slender stem continuing into the bulbous ovoid body tapering to a flared rim, the body in pale iridescent green w/a green & blue pulled-feather design issuing from the stem, cream iridescent lining, signed "L.C.T. Q2073," late 19th c. (ILLUS.)...................... **6,900**

Vase, 12 1/2" h., floriform, a round slightly domed foot supporting the tall slender stem swelling into the bulbed top tapering to a low flared rim, cobalt blue w/a rich iridescent blue finish, decorated w/a multitude of green & white hearts on random elongated stems, signed "2321 M L.C. Tiffany - Favrile," ca. 1918 .... **4,888**

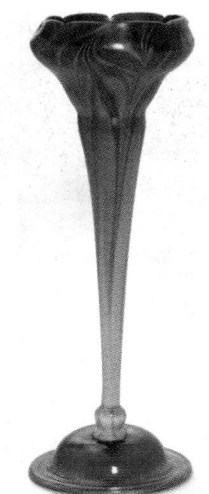

Early Tiffany Floriform Vase

Vase, 15" h., floriform, an amber domed
foot w/opalescent edge supports a slender knopped stem continuing into the tall
slender bowl w/a widely flaring cupped
tulip-form top w/scalloped rim decorated
in striated green & amber iridescent
feathering, early Corona factory
example, ca. 1892 (ILLUS.) **5,060**

Vase, 15 1/2" h., tall slender swelled cylindrical body w/slightly flared mouth, overall golden iridescent pulled Peacock
Feather design **18,500-19,000**

Wine, round foot & baluster-form stem supporting the flaring cupped bowl, aquamarine w/strong opalescence, signed "5 -
LCT Favrile," ca. 1900, 4" h. **374**

Tiffin

*A wide variety of fine glasswares were pro-
duced by the Tiffin Glass Company of Tiffin,
Ohio. Beginning as a part of the large U.S. Glass
Company early in the 20th century, the Tiffin factory continued making a wide range of wares
until its final closing in 1984. One popular line is
now called "Black Satin" and included various
vases with raised floral designs. Many other acid-
etched and hand-cut patterns were also produced
over the years and are very collectible today. The
three "Tiffin Glassmasters" books by Fred Bicken-
heuser are the standard references for Tiffin collectors.*

Tiffin Glass Label

Carafe, etched Roses patt., clear **$80**

Champagne, etched Flanders patt., pink............ 42
Champagne, etched June Night patt., clear,
6 oz. 40
Cocktail, etched Cordelia patt. 20
Compote, 7 1/2", twist stem, No. 315, vase-
line satin 20
Console set: 13" d. bowl w/deep everted
rim & pair of candleholders; Fontaine
etching, bowl No. 8153, candleholders
No. 9758, Twilite, 3 pcs. 400
Creamer & sugar bowl, etched Fuchsia
patt., clear, pr. 70
Creamer & sugar bowl, etched June Night
patt., clear, pr. 80
Flower bowl, cut Twilight patt., No. 9153-
108, clear, 10" d. 180
Goblet, Diamond Optic patt., all Rose-Pink,
10 oz. 25
Goblet, etched Classic patt., clear 35
Goblet, etched Flanders patt., pink...................... 60
Goblet, etched Fuchsia patt., water, clear
7 5/8" h. 45
Goblet, etched Persian Pheasant patt.,
clear 38

Etched Coronet Oyster Cocktail

Oyster cocktail, etched Coronet patt.,
clear, 3 3/8" h. (ILLUS.) 13
Plate, 8 1/8" d., etched Fuchsia patt., clear 20
Plate, 8" d., etched Flanders patt., yellow........... 17
Rose bowl w/three ball feet, Copen blue,
medium 70
Sherbet, etched Fuchsia patt., clear.................... 20
Tumbler, etched Fuchsia patt., iced tea,
footed, clear.. 35
Tumbler, etched June Night patt., footed,
clear, 10 1/2 oz. 38
Tumbler, etched Persian Pheasant patt.,
juice, footed, clear, 5 oz. 25
Vase, 5" h., etched Poppy patt., black ame-
thyst.. 75
Vase, 6 1/2" h., Black Satin ground w/alter-
nating glossy stripes 65
Vase, 6" h., cut Twilight patt., four-footed,
clear.. 185
Vase, bud, 10" h., etched Cherokee Rose
patt., clear.. 70
Wine, etched June Night patt., clear 50

No. 606 Etching on No. 1117 Wine

Wine, No. 606 etching, No. 1117 (ILLUS.)......... **18**

Venetian

Venetian glass has been made for six centuries on the island of Murano, where it continues to be produced. The skilled glass artisans developed numerous techniques, subsequently imitated elsewhere.

Large Venetian Centerpiece with Fish

Centerpiece, a wide shallow bowl base centered by two large upright leaping salmon, the fish in gold Sommerso glass w/Bullicante under a paperweight finish, the base in amber Bullicante glass, mid-20th c., 17" d. (ILLUS.) **$748**

Figures, a man & a woman standing & dancing in stylized costumes, in shades of greenish blue, blue & white w/gold trim, mid-20th c., 8" h., pr. (ILLUS. front row, center w/other figures, below)......... **300-500**

Figures, a standing man & woman each dressed in 18th c. costume, in variegated colors & Latticinio glass w/gilt trim, mid-20th c., 8 1/2" h., pr. (ILLUS. back row, center w/other figures, below) **300-500**

Large Grouping of Venetian Figurals

Figures, a stylized standing man & woman dressed in Victorian costumes, in mottled pink w/applied white glass features & gilt accents, 11 1/2" h., pr. (ILLUS. front row, left w/other figures, previous page)........ **600-900**

Model of a chicken, highly stylized bulbous blown hollow bird, blue w/three bands at base alternating blue & green, peaked top representing the beak w/an applied eye nearby, lower side peak representing the tail, raised on stick metal legs & feet, attributed to Vistosi, designed by Alessandro Pianon, ca. 1960, 9 3/4" h. (several minor abrasions)............................ **1,725**

Models of fish, large leaping fish in clear enclosing canes of blue, pink, white & yellow, applied fins & swirled pedestal base w/gilt fleck inclusions, mid-20th c., 10 3/4" h., pr. (ILLUS. of two far right with other figures, previous page)......................... **201**

Venetian Models of Roosters

Models of roosters, each stylized bird w/a very long tapering pointed tail, in various colors of Sommerso glass, mounted on swirled domed bases, mid-20th c., 19 1/2" h., pr. (ILLUS.)................................... **403**

Vase, 11" h., swelled cylindrical body w/a wide flat rim, red decorated w/a grid of white & rust lines, large polished pontil, attributed to Archimede Seguso, original foil label, mid-20th c. **1,400-1,500**

Verlys

Verlys originated in France in the mid-1930s and was produced by the French Holoplane Co. A branch, Verlys in America, soon was opened in Newark, Ohio, and produced wares similar to the French examples but less expensive. Various Art Deco designs, some resembling Lalique glass, were blown or molded in clear, frosted clear and colors. Between 1955-57 the Heisey Company used some Verlys molds.

A Verlys France

French Verlys Mark

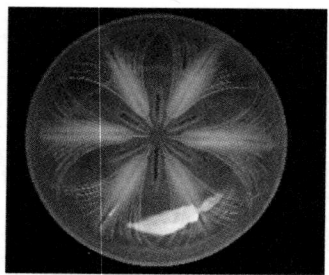

Large Shallow Verlys Bowl

Bowl, 11 3/4" d., wide shallow form in frosted clear w/opalescent rib feet, molded w/a starburst design, signed, mid-20th c. (ILLUS.).. **$288**

Frosted & Clear Small Verlys Vase

Vase, 6 1/2" h., footed flaring body w/the frosted ground molded w/small leaves & stems surrounding large clear knob-form blossoms, etched signature on the bottom, ca. 1930s (ILLUS.)............................ **288**

Vase, 10 1/4" h., clear & frosted, gently flaring cylindrical form, the lower half frosted & molded in bold relief w/mermaids & dolphins, the top half in plain clear, engraved mark **330**

Victorian Colored Glass

There are, of course, many types of colored glassware of the Victorian era, and we cover a great variety of these in our various glass categories. However, there are some pieces of pressed, mold-blown and free-blown Victorian colored glass which don't fit well into other specific listings, so we have chosen to include a selection of them here.

Sapphire Blue Enameled Compote

Glass - Victorian Colored Glass

Compote, open, 7 1/8" h., 5 3/4" d., a deep slightly flaring sapphire blue optic ribbed bowl raised on a blown baluster-form stem on a disk foot, the bowl enameled w/delicate yellow & white flowers on gold leafy branches (ILLUS., previous page).. **$150-175**

Cobalt Blue Decorated Creamer

Creamer, footed squatty bulbous body w/a wide neck & arched spout, cobalt blue body decorated w/large gold enameled floral scrolls, applied clear handle, 3" d., 3 1/2" h. (ILLUS.) **150-175**

Creamer, peach opalescent to clear, Diamond Quilted design, applied clear handle, polished pontil, 4 1/2" h............................ **140**

Tall Lobed & Decorated Decanter

Decanter w/original stopper, ovoid four-lobed sapphire blue body tapering to a tall cylindrical neck w/a flared rim, two panels enameled w/large white & grey flowers & green leaves w/gold trim & border beading, on an applied clear foot, clear facet-cut stopper, 4 1/8" d., 14 1/2" h. (ILLUS.)................................... **175-225**

Ruby Jar with Gold Filigree Decoration

Jar, cov., cylindrical deep ruby base w/a domed cover w/pointed knob finial, the base enclosed by delicate gold filigree w/further filigree on the cover, raised on small gold ball feet, 3" d., 5 1/4" h. (ILLUS.).. **150-175**

Sapphire Blue Pitcher with Metal Lid

Pitcher, cov., wide ovoid sapphire blue optic ribbed body w/a wide short cylindrical neck fitted w/a flat hinged metal top w/thumb rest attached to the applied sapphire blue handle, the sides decorated w/a band of gold arches enclosing scrolls below clusters of white blossoms & gold leaves, further decorated w/a French inscription in gold script, late 19th c., 4" d., 6" h. (ILLUS.).. **150-175**

Pitcher, water, 8" h., Diamond Quilted design, overall light yellow opalescent, applied clear handle, polished pontil................... **275**

Tumblers, lemonade, blown, six various opalescent & six various transparent colors in Polka Dot patt., all w/applied reeded handles, original box & lid w/end label, "No. 269 Lemonade Tumblers, No. 1 Assortment," 2 1/2" h., box is 10 x 11 1/2" **3,100**

Decorated Blue Vase on Stand

Vase, 9 1/2" h., 8" d., a wide bulbous ovoid cobalt blue body tapering to a low notched & scalloped upright rim, the sides heavily enameled w/orange thorny branches w/orange leaves & white blossoms, raised on a pierced & footed silver plate stand, late 19th c., stand resilvered (ILLUS.) **350-400**

Wall Pocket Vases

Amber, satin finish, style No. 16258 by Tiffin Glass Co., 3 7/8 x 9 1/4" (ILLUS. top left, w/Tiffin wall pockets, next column) **$95-125**

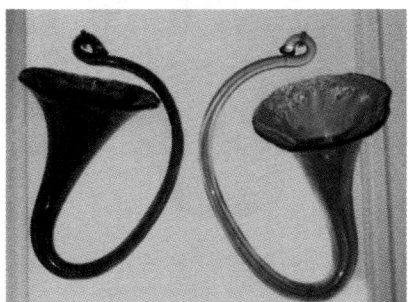

Morning Glory-shaped Wall Pockets

Amethyst, morning glory shape, 7 3/4" l. (ILLUS. left).. **50-75**

Black, satin finish, Kimberley decoration, No. 320, Tiffin Glass Company, 3 3/8" w., 9 1/8" l. (ILLUS. lower left, top of next column).. **75-95**

Black, satin finish, No. 320, Tiffin Glass Company, 3 3/8" w., 9 1/8" l. (ILLUS. upper right w/Tiffin wall pockets, top of next column)... **75-95**

Black, satin finish, No. 320, Tiffin Glass Company, Echec's decoration w/gold trim, 3 3/8" w., 9 1/8" l. (ILLUS. lower right w/Tiffin wall pockets, top of next column)... **75-95**

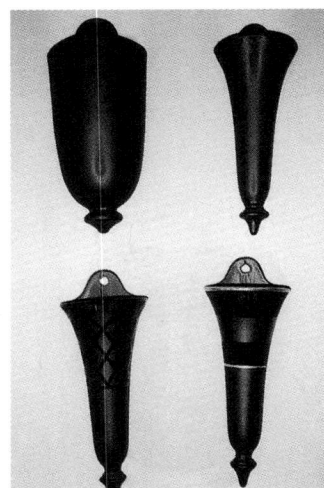

Tiffin Wall Pocket Vases

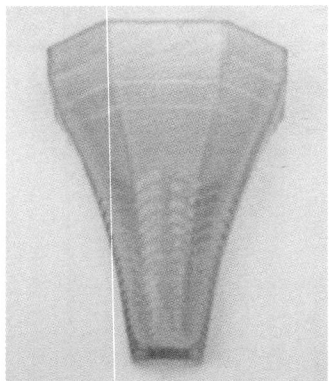

Czechoslovakian Wall Pocket Vase

Green, paneled conical form w/ribbed top, flat base w/scalloped design, Czechoslovakia, 5 1/4 x 6 1/2" (ILLUS.).................. **100-125**

Carnival Wall Pocket Vase

Marigold carnival, conical form, raised leaf & grape pattern & bird, 7 x 7 3/4" (ILLUS., bottom, previous page) **65-85**

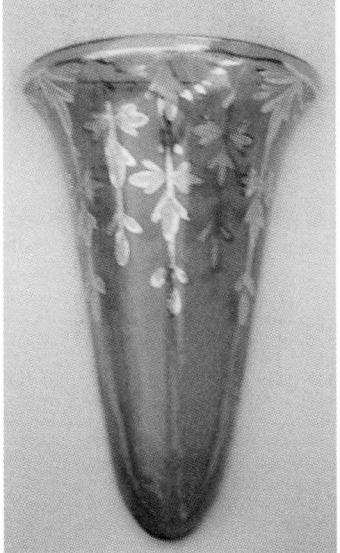

Peacock Blue Wall Pocket Vase

Peacock blue, conical form w/applied gold trim, 4 x 6 1/2" (ILLUS.) **135-175**
Peacock blue, morning glory shape, 7 3/4" l. (ILLUS. right, w/morning glory-shaped wall pockets, previous page) **50-75**
Red, brilliant finish, slender conical form w/pointed end finial, Style No. 320 by Tiffin Glass Co., 3 3/8 x 9 1/8" **150-185**

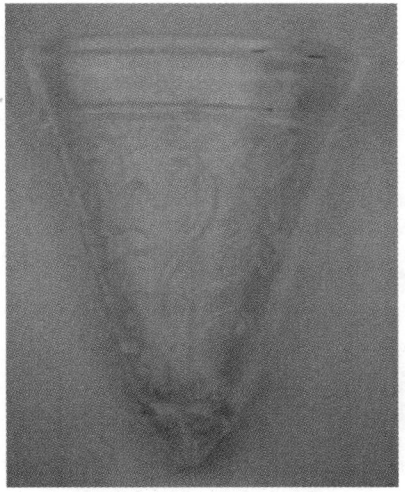

U.S. Glass Wall Pocket Vase

Vaseline, conical form w/molded scroll design, pointed end finial, U.S. Glass Co., 5 x 6" (ILLUS.) **65-85**

Westmoreland Glass Wall Pocket Vase

White milk glass, wide conical shape w/pointed end finial & scalloped rim, Panelled Grape patt., Westmoreland Glass Co., 5 x 8" (ILLUS.) **150-200**

Wave Crest

Now much sought after, Wave Crest was produced by the C.F. Monroe Co., Meriden, Connecticut, in the late 19th and early 20th centuries from opaque white glass blown into molds.

It was then hand-decorated in enamels and metal trim was often added. Boudoir accessories such as jewel boxes, hair receivers, etc., were predominant.

WAVE CREST WARE

Wave Crest Mark

Box w/hinged lid, Pansy blown-out mold, dark green low flaring box & domed cover molded w/a large pink & amethyst pansy blossom, original metal fittings, signed on base, 4" w., 2 3/8" h. **$863**

Helmschmeid Swirl Box with Lilacs

Box w/hinged lid, Helmschmeid Swirl mold, decorated w/white & purple lilacs w/pale pink leaves, original metal fittings, unsigned, 6" d., 4 1/2" h. (ILLUS.) **575**

Rare Holly Decorated Wave Crest Box

Box w/hinged lid, Helmschmeid Swirl mold, satin crystal h.p. overall w/green holly branches w/red berries, 7" d., 4" h. (ILLUS.) **1,150**

Wave Crest Box with Floral Panels

Box w/hinged lid, round w/molded border bands of delicate scrolls, the sides & top h.p. w/floral panels in deep pink, purple, green & gold, original metal fittings, marked w/red banner mark, 7 1/4" d., 6" h. (ILLUS.) **460**

Cracker jar, cov., a waisted cylindrical body molded around the top & bottom w/scrolls & flowers, transfer-printed color florals on the sides, silver plate rim, swing bail handle & cover, 7 1/2" h. (ILLUS. far right with other cracker jars, bottom of page) **196**

Cracker jar, cov., barrel-shaped opal body w/molded bands, decorated w/colorful transfer-printed florals, silver plate rim, swing bail handle & domed cover, 8 1/2" h. (ILLUS. second from right with other cracker jars, bottom of page) **173**

Rare Long Rectangular Wave Crest Box

Box w/hinged lid, long rectangular form molded w/borders of scrolls, pistachio green ground around gilt scroll-bordered white reserves decorated w/delicate daisies, original metal fittings, signed w/red banner mark, 4 x 7", 5" h. (ILLUS.) **1,438**

Cracker jar, cov., slightly flaring cylindrical body w/four molded ribs, opal ground decorated w/delicate transfer-printed florals, silver plated rim, swing bail handle & domed swirled cover, 7 1/2" h. (ILLUS. far left with other cracker jars, below) **173**

Cracker jar, cov., squared opal body w/delicate molded scrolls, decorated w/colorful transfer-printed florals on each side, brass-plated rim, swing bail handle & low domed cover, 9" h. (ILLUS. second from left with other cracker jars, below) **156**

A Group of Four Wave Crest Cracker Jars

Wave Crest Creamer & Sugar Set

Creamer & cov. sugar bowl, Helmschmeid
Swirl mold, each decorated w/delicate
painted floral sprigs, each fitted w/silver
plate rims, handles & cover, unsigned,
creamer overall 4 1/2" w., sugar overall
6" w., pr. (ILLUS.) **288**

Rare Daisy-decorated Glove Box

Glove box w/hinged lid, long rectangular
form, the border of the cover w/molded
white & yellow daisies w/further molded
daisies on the base, a cobalt blue background, the top center h.p. w/pink & white
daisies, on a gilt-brass footed base &
w/original brass hinge, w/original key,

signed w/red banner mark, 4 1/4 x 9 3/4",
5 1/2" h. (ILLUS.) **2,588**

Wave Crest Decorated Humidor

Humidor w/hinged cover, barrel-shaped,
molded w/bands of delicate scrolls, pale
blue ground decorated on the cover
w/pink & maroon flowers, the side panel
painted in large letters w/"Cigars" framed
w/delicate florals, 9 1/2" h.
(ILLUS.) **1,200-,750**

Salt & pepper shakers, Helmschmeid Swirl
patt., one w/alternating white & pink panels, the other w/white & shaded yellow
panels, each w/blossom & leaf decoration in the white panels, ca. 1900,
2 1/4" h., pr. (ILLUS., bottom of
page) **200-250**

Syrup w/original hinged top, shiny
opaque white, squatty bulbous base
w/polychrome floral decoration, ribbed
neck, lid w/attached handle, 5 3/4" h. **140**

Wave Crest Helmschmied Swirl Salt & Pepper Shakers

Small Decorated Wave Crest Vase

Vase, 5 1/2" h., cylindrical w/large molded leafy scrolls around the bottom, raised on a pierced gilt brass footed base, white ground decorated w/yellow, brown & white daisies & leafy stems (ILLUS.)..... **450-550**

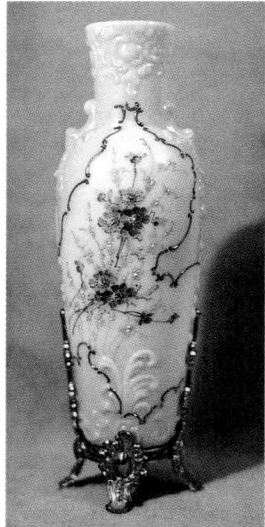

Tall Wave Crest Vase in Stand

Vase, 10 1/2" h., tall cylindrical body tapering slightly to a cylindrical neck, molded overall w/scrolls & floral clusters, an asymmetrical white panel outlined in gold decorated w/purple & blue blossoms on pale leafy stems, the background in pale pink, resting in a gilt-brass scroll-cast footed base, signed (ILLUS.).................. **750-950**

Webb

This glass is made by Thomas Webb & Sons of Stourbridge, one of England's most prolific glasshouses. Numerous types of glass, including cameo, have been produced by this firm through the years. The company also produced various types of novelty and "art" glass during the late Victorian period. Also see BURMESE, ROSE BOWLS, and SATIN & MOTHER-OF-PEARL.

Extremely Rare Webb Cameo Rose Jar

Cameo rose jar, cov., bulbous ovoid body w/a citron yellow mother-of-pearl ground cased in crimson & finely etched w/large apple blossoms & leaves trimmed in gold, gilt-metal filigree collar & domed cover, 8 3/4" h. (ILLUS.)......................... **$22,425**

Unusual Ivory Webb Cameo Vase

Cameo vase, 6" h., 6" d., footed low wide cushion-form body tapering to a trumpet neck flanked by two carved elephant head handles, ivory cased in white & etched w/an overall delicate flower & scroll design outlined in heavy gold, signed on the base "Thomas Webb & Sons Limited" (ILLUS.) **2,243**

Three-layer Webb Gem Cameo Vase

Cameo vase, 7 1/2" h., three-color type, citron yellow cased in red & white & etched w/large roses on leafy branches, signed "Tiffany & Co. Paris Exposition 1889 Thomas Webb & Sons Gem Cameo" (ILLUS.) **3,278**

Nice Blue & White Webb Cameo Vase

Cameo vase, 8 1/4" h., footed ovoid body tapering to a low widely flaring flattened neck, dark blue overlaid in white & etched w/large daisy-like flowers on leafy stems, the reverse w/two cameo-etched bees & a butterfly, signed on the bottom "Thomas Webb & Sons Gem Cameo" (ILLUS.) **1,438**

Extraordinary Webb Cameo Vase

Cameo vase, 8" h., a round foot supporting the bulbous ovoid body w/a short neck & wide cupped rim, Prussian blue overlaid in white & etched w/an elaborate Passion flower decoration, leaf & spearpoint etched bands around the foot & leaf & lappet w/fleur-de-lis bands around the neck, signed "Thomas Webb & Sons" (ILLUS.) **10,063**

Large Rare Webb Gem Cameo Vase

Cameo vase, 11 1/2" h., bulbous double-gourd form body, deep rose to grey ground overlaid in white & etched w/large Passion flowers on leafy stems, stippled floral band at the top, Gem Cameo (ILLUS.) **10,350**

Ferner, squatty oval swirled rib body, cased rainbow w/gilt rim & white enamel scroll decoration, polished base, 5 x 9", 4 3/4" h. **425**

Lovely Webb Cameo Scent Bottle

Scent bottle, cameo glass, deep red cased in white & etched w/a lily-of-the-valley design, signed on the base "Thomas Webb & Sons," original silver neck & cap, 5 1/4" h. (ILLUS.) **3,738**

Westmoreland

In 1890 Westmoreland opened in Grapeville, Pennsylvania, and as early as the 1920s was producing colorwares in great variety. Cutting and decorations were many and are generally under appreciated and undervalued. Westmoreland was a leading producer of milk glass in "the antique style." The company closed in 1984 but some of their molds continued in use by others.

Early Westmoreland Label & Mark

Animal covered dish, Camel, amber satin, Humphrey **$48**
Animal covered dish, Cat on a lacy base, glass eyes, purple slag, copied from the Atterbury original **150**
Animal covered dish, Duck, ruby carnival **65**
Animal covered dish, Hen on Nest, looking left, milk white, red decoration **38**
Animal covered dish, Mother Eagle w/chicks, milk white **85**
Animal covered dish, Rooster, wide rib base, opaque blue body, milk glass head **100**
Ashtray, Beaded Grape patt., milk white **10**
Banana bowl, bell-footed, Paneled Grape patt., No. 47, milk white, 12" **150**
Basket, American Hobnail patt., oval, lilac opalescent, small **32**
Basket, Della Robbia patt., handled, clear w/ruby stain, 12" d. **165**
Basket, Paneled Grape patt., footed, scalloped, milk white, 10 1/2" **125**
Basket, Woolworth patt., handled, green, 5 1/2" **35**

Bell, No. 1902, blue satin w/Mary Gregory decoration **28**
Bonbon, Waterford patt., heart-shaped, handled, No. 36, clear w/ruby stain, 8" **69**
Bowl, 4 1/2" d., English Hobnail patt., Ice Blue **35**
Bowl, 6" d., Old Quilt patt., footed, milk white **18**
Bowl, 8" d., Della Robbia patt., clear w/ruby stain **75**
Bowl, 9" d., 6" h., Paneled Grape patt., skirted base, milk white **95**
Bowl, 11" oval, Paneled Grape patt., footed, milk white **125**
Bowl, Paneled Grape patt., sherbet, low foot, milk white **16**
Box, cov., figural rabbit on eggs, milk white w/painted eggs, 7" **55**
Butter dish, cov., American Hobnail patt., milk white **38**
Butter dish, cov., Paneled Grape patt., milk white, 1/4 lb. **30**
Cake salver, Waterford patt., clear w/ruby stain **100**
Cake stand, Beaded Grape patt., footed, milk white, 11" sq. **108**
Cake stand, Blue Moonstone, flat squared top w/scalloped ring & petal border raised on a ringed pedestal & domed base w/a flat squared foot, 11" d. **99**
Candle lamp, two-part, milk white stemmed base, blue satin shade w/Mary Gregory decoration **55**
Candlestick, single-light, Beaded Grape patt., milk white, 4" h. **16**
Candlestick, single-light, Lotus patt., green, 9" h. **40**
Candlestick, three-light, Lotus patt., green satin **56**
Candlesticks, one-light, Beaded Grape patt., milk white, 4" sq., pr. **30**
Candlesticks, one-light, Old Quilt patt., milk white, 4" h., pr. **30**
Candy container, novelty, model of clock, green **20**
Candy dish, cov., English Hobnail patt., green, 8" h. **65**
Candy dish, cov., Old Quilt patt., square, milk white, 6 1/2" h. **27**
Celery vase, Paneled Grape patt., footed, milk white, 6" h. **39**
Champagne, Princess Feather patt., pink **18**
Cheese dish, cov., Paneled Grape patt., milk white, 7" d. **60**
Cigarette box, cov., Beaded Grape patt., milk white, 4 x 6" **25**
Cocktail, English Hobnail patt., round footed, clear, 3 oz. **8**
Cologne w/stopper, English Hobnail patt., Ice Blue, 5 oz. **75**
Compote, 5" d., 6" h., Colonial patt., handled, Dark Blue Mist **30**
Compote, 4 1/2" d., 6" h., Paneled Grape patt., ruffled rim, milk white w/pansy decoration No. 34 .... **30**
Compote, 6" d., Della Robbia patt., clear w/ruby staining **50**
Compote, 9" d., Paneled Grape patt., crimped & ruffled rim, stem-footed, milk white **75**
Compote, 11" d., dolphin stem, hexagonal foot, amber **145**

Condiment set: two 2 oz. handled oil bottles w/stoppers on oval tray; Colonial patt., green, the set 120

Paneled Console Bowl in Pink

Console bowl, paneled body w/elephant head handles that double as candle sockets, pink, 8" d. (ILLUS.) 175
Console set: bowl & pr. of candlesticks; Thousand Eye patt., clear, 3 pcs. 75
Cordial, Waterford patt., footed, No. 5, clear w/ruby stain, 1 oz. 65
Creamer & open sugar bowl, American Hobnail patt., milk white, pr. 26
Creamer & open sugar bowl, Della Robbia patt., milk white, pr. 20
Creamer & open sugar bowl, Paneled Grape patt., individual, milk white, pr. 25
Creamer & open sugar bowl, Woolworth patt., green, pr. 48
Creamer & sugar cube tray, No. 1721, handled Domino sugar cube tray w/indent for creamer, pink, the set 72
Cruet w/original stopper, Paneled Grape patt., milk white 28
Cup & saucer, American Hobnail patt., milk white 12
Cup & saucer, Beaded Edge patt., milk white 12
Cup & saucer, Paneled Grape patt., milk white 25
Decanter w/stopper, American Hobnail patt., milk white 42
Dish, Della Robbia patt., heart-shaped, handled, clear w/colored staining, 8" l. 95
Dresser tray, Paneled Grape patt., milk white 100
Epergne, Paneled Grape patt., milk white, 12" lip bowl & 8 1/2" vase, ... 235
Finger bowl, Della Robbia, clear w/ruby stain, 5" d. 35
Flowerpot, Paneled Grape patt., milk white, 4 1/4" h. 48
Goblet, American Hobnail patt., clear, 6" h. 16
Goblet, Beaded Grape patt., round, footed, clear, 8 oz. 15
Goblet, English Hobnail patt., round base, clear, 6" h. 14
Goblet, Paneled Grape patt., clear, 6" h. 15
Goblet, Paneled Grape patt., water, No. 14, milk white, 8 oz. 12
Goblet, Waterford patt., water, clear w/ruby stain 50
Gravy boat & undertray, Paneled Grape patt., No. 8, milk white, 2 pcs. 65
Honey, cov., Beaded Grape patt., Roses & Bows decoration, milk white, 5" d. 50
Ivy ball vase, Paneled Grape patt., footed, cupped rim, milk white 45
Jardiniere, Paneled Grape patt., cupped, milk white, 6 1/2" h. 35

Marmalade jar, cover & ladle, English Hobnail patt., milk white, 5 1/2", 3 pcs. 30
Mayonnaise set: bowl, liner & ladle; Lotus patt., light blue, the set 78
Model of butterfly, No. 2, green satin, small 18
Model of owl w/glass eyes, dark blue, 5 1/2" h. 35
Model of Pouter Pigeon, clear, 2 1/2" h. 25
Model of slipper, grandma's, blue satin w/white decoration 18
Nappy, Paneled Grape patt., round, milk white, 4 1/2" d. 9
Novelty, model of a straw hat, milk white w/decoration, 4 1/2" 38
Nut dish/place card holder, English Hobnail patt., oval, footed, green 38
Pitcher, 7 1/4" h., American Hobnail, milk white 68
Pitcher, 8 1/2" h., Old Quilt patt., water, milk white 38
Pitcher, Paneled Grape patt., milk, milk white, 16 oz. 48
Pitcher, Rocker patt., cov., No. 101, clear 80
Planter, Paneled Grape patt., rectangular, milk white, 5" x 9" 45
Plate, lattice border, black w/white enamel Mary Gregory decoration 38
Plate, Three Owls patt., milk white 48
Plate, 7" d., Beaded Edge patt., milk white 7
Plate, 8" d., English Hobnail patt., green............ 18
Plate, 8" d., Woolworth patt., scalloped edge, green 25
Plate, 8 1/2" d., Paneled Grape patt., salad, milk white 25
Plate, 10 1/2" d., Beaded Edge patt., dinner, milk glass w/red trim 28
Plate, 10 1/2 d., Paneled Grape patt., dinner, milk white 46
Plate, torte,14" d., Thousand Eye patt., clear w/ruby stain 75
Punch bowl & base, Princess Feather patt., bell-shaped, clear 280
Punch bowl, base & underplate, Colonial Paneled patt., black, 3 pcs. 340
Punch set: punch bowl, large underplate, ladle & 12 punch cups; Della Robbia patt., clear w/ruby stain, 15 pcs. 750
Relish dish, Beaded Grape patt., three-part, milk white, 9 1/2" d. 58
Salt & pepper shakers w/original tops, Della Robbia patt., footed, clear w/ruby stain, pr. 75
Salt & pepper shakers w/original tops, Lotus patt., footed, pink, pr. 95
Salt & pepper shakers w/original tops, Paneled Grape patt., footed, milk white, 4 1/4" h., pr. 25
Sherbet, American Hobnail patt., milk white, 3 3/4" 10
Sugar bowl, Beaded Grape patt., open, milk white 15
Sweetmeat, cov., Old Quilt patt., high-footed, milk white, 6 1/2" h. 35
Tidbit tray, two-tier, Paneled Grape patt., center-handled, milk white 55
Tumbler, Della Robbia patt., iced tea, stained ruby, 6" h. 50
Tumbler, Old Quilt patt., iced tea, milk white, 5 1/4" h., 11 oz. 12
Tumbler, Old Quilt patt., water, footed, milk white, 8 oz. 10
Tumbler, Paneled Grape patt., juice, clear, 4 3/4" h. 12

Urn, cov., Waterford patt., clear w/ruby
stain, 12 1/2" h. 95
Vase, miniature, jack-in-the-pulpit shape,
pink satin w/white "snow flower" decora-
tion 22
Vase, 9" h., Old Quilt patt., bell-rimmed,
footed, milk white 45
Vase, 11 1/2" h., Paneled Grape patt., bell-
rimmed, footed, milk white 45
Vase, 15" h., Paneled Grape patt., milk
white... 50
Wine, Della Robbia patt., milk white,
4 3/4" h. 16
Wine, Paneled Grape patt., milk white............... 16
Wine, Paneled Grape patt., ruby, 4" h. 29

HALLOWEEN
COLLECTIBLES

*Although Halloween is an American tradition
and holiday, we must credit the Scottish for
bringing it to the United States. The earliest symbols of Halloween appeared around the turn of
the 20th century. During Victorian times, Halloween parties became popular in the United States.
Decorations were seasonal products, such as
pumpkins, cornstalks, vegetables, etc. Many early
decorations were imported from Germany, only to
be followed by increased demand in the United
States during World War I, when German
imports ceased.*

*Today Halloween collectibles are second only
to Christmas collectibles. Remembering the excite-
ment one felt as a child dressing up in costume,
going treat or treating, carving pumpkins, bobbing for apples, etc., the colors of orange and
black trigger nostalgia for our youth for many of
us.*

*The variety of Halloween collectibles is
immense. Whether it be noisemakers, jack o' lanterns, candy containers, paper or plastic goods,
candy molds or costumes, with the availability,
the choice is yours.*

*Remember to buy the best, be it the very old or
not so old. Search antiques shops, flea markets
and house sales.*

Hat-shaped Candy Container

Candy container, cardboard hat shape
covered w/black crepe paper, orange
band of crepe paper above brim, orange
jack-o'-lantern decoration, ca. 1940s-50s
(ILLUS.) **$50**

Composition Pumpkin Man Candy Container

Candy container, composition figure
w/pumpkin head, dressed in yellow, yellow hat, black shoes, standing round
cardboard container, Germany, ca. 1920
(ILLUS.).. **175**
Candy container, composition jack-o'-lan-
tern stein w/excellent painted details,
marked "Germany".. **660**
Candy container, glass w/reverse painting,
figure of bespectacled witch w/pumpkin
head, raised triangular nose & sunken
painted mouth, wearing black pointed hat
& green cape w/red bow, carrying embossed broom, indentation on either side
of head for missing bail handle, tin screw-
on closure, ca. 1920, 4 3/4" h......................... **600**

Pumpkin-head Policeman Candy Container

Candy container, glass w/reverse painting,
figure of policeman w/pumpkin head
wearing spectacles, w/raised triangular
nose & sunken painted mouth, dressed in
grey overcoat & black hat, indentation on
either side of head for bail handle, goldtone screw-on closure, ca. 1920,
4 1/4" h. (ILLUS.) **1,150**

Candy container, hard plastic, figural pumpkin carriage w/four green wheels & a cat & a witch, Kokomold, Inc., Indiana....... **550**

Candy container, jack-o'-lantern head, 3 1/2" h. **297**

Witch on Pumpkin Candy Container

Candy container, papier-mâché, figure of witch dressed in black & sitting on top of orange pumpkin, America, ca. 1940s-50s (ILLUS.) **250**

German Pumpkin Man on Candy Container

Candy container, papier-mâché, gingerbread man-type figure w/pumpkin head on round cardboard container w/plaid decoration, Germany, ca. 1930s (ILLUS.) **250**

Jack-O'-Lantern Man Candy Container

Candy container, papier-mâché, orange figure w/jack-o'-lantern head, yellow mouth, nose & eyes, black shoes & tie, America, ca. 1940s-50s (ILLUS.).................. **525**

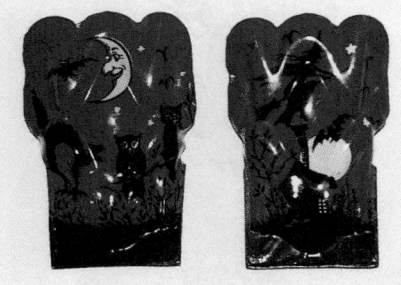

Lithographed Tin Clickers

Clickers, lithographed tin, black & orange Halloween scenes, ca. 1950s, each (ILLUS. of two) **25**

Die-cut Jack-O'-Lantern with Scarf

Decoration, die-cut cardboard, jack-o'-lantern w/scarf, America, ca. 1930s, 10" h. (ILLUS., previous page)............................... **20-30**

Large Die-cut Embossed Pumpkin

Decoration, die-cut cardboard, large embossed pumpkin, Luhrs, early 1940s, 9 1/2" h. (ILLUS.) **25-45**

Die-cut Cat with Checkered Pants

Decoration, die-cut cardboard, large jointed cat w/checkered pants, Japan, ca. 1940s (ILLUS.) **44-65**

Dennison Die-Cut Owl

Decoration, die-cut cardboard, owl, orange & black, Dennison, ca. 1940s, 9" h. (ILLUS.).. **15-25**

Die-cut Cardboard Owl with Moon

Decoration, die-cut cardboard, owl w/moon, ca. 1960s, 16" h. (ILLUS.)............. **5-10**

Die-cut Cardboard Scarecrow

Decoration, die-cut cardboard, scarecrow, America, ca. 1930s, 10" h. (ILLUS.)........... **20-30**

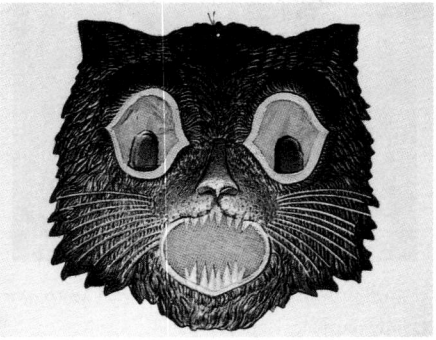

Die-cut Cat

Die-cut, black cat, w/tissue inserts at eyes & mouth, unmarked (ILLUS.)................................. **75**

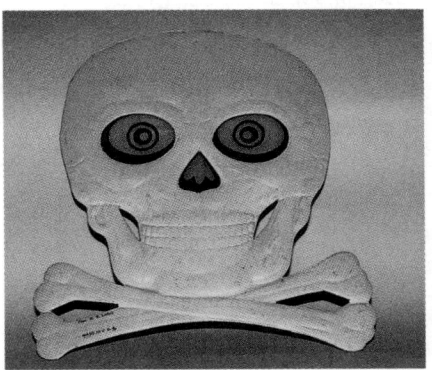

Skull & Crossbones Die-cut

Die-cut, skull & crossbones w/tissue inserts for nose & eyes, by H.L. Luhrs, ca. 1935, 10" h. (ILLUS.).. **50**

Figure, hard plastic witch riding a motorcycle w/jack-o'-lantern...................................... **495**

Figure, "Squash Body Bird Man" w/jack-o'-lantern head & top hat.................................... **248**

Jack-o'-lantern, painted tin, two molded rotating half-spheres on a heavy wire central shaft w/wooden knob at the top, wound at the bottom to hold a pole, cut-out features w/black trim, 19th c., 6 1/2" d., 9 1/4" h. (scattered paint wear).. **2,530**

Jack-o'-lantern, papier-mâché, bulbous tapering molded form w/smiling cut-out mouth & eyes w/a paper insert w/rows of teeth & side-glancing eyes, orange w/green lower section, early 20th c., 6 1/2" w., 5" h. (minor wear)........................... **195**

Jack-o'-lantern, pressed, formed paperboard w/tissue insert, 5" **385**

German Cardboard Jack-O'-Lantern

Lantern, cardboard, orange, black, red & green jack-o'-lantern w/paper inserts for eyes, nose & mouth, Germany, ca. 1920s (ILLUS.)... **225**

Glass & Tin Jack-O'-Lantern

Lantern, glass & tin, jack-o'-lantern, orange & black, battery-operated, made in Hong Kong, ca. 1960, 6" h. (ILLUS.) **65**

Orange Cat Lantern

Lantern, papier-mâché, orange cat w/green paper eye inserts, red paper mouth insert w/sharp white teeth, America, 1940s-50s (ILLUS.).. **275**

Jack-O'-Lantern with Stem

Lantern, papier-mâché, orange & green jack-o'-lantern w/closed top & stem, blue, white, yellow & red paper inserts, America, ca. 1940s (ILLUS., previous page).. **250**

Papier-mâché Jack-O'-Lantern

Lantern, papier-mâché, orange jack-o'-lantern w/paper inserts, America (ILLUS.)......... **175**

Pair of Owls on Branch

Models of owl, crepe paper, grey & black w/feather detail, perched on branch, pr. (ILLUS.).. **65**

German Nodder Figure

Nodder, papier-mâché, figure of man in blue, green & yellow w/green cap on orange head, Germany, ca. 1920s (ILLUS.).. **195**

Nodder, papier-mâché, gentleman w/jack-o'-lantern head w/black top hat, spring-mounted on wax body, felt tie & shoes, Germany **413**

Noisemaker, cardboard horn w/wooden mouthpiece, pipe-shaped, covered w/Halloween motif paper, Germany, ca. 1920 (ILLUS., bottom of page)..................... **165**

Noisemaker, composition figure of a goblin.. **220**

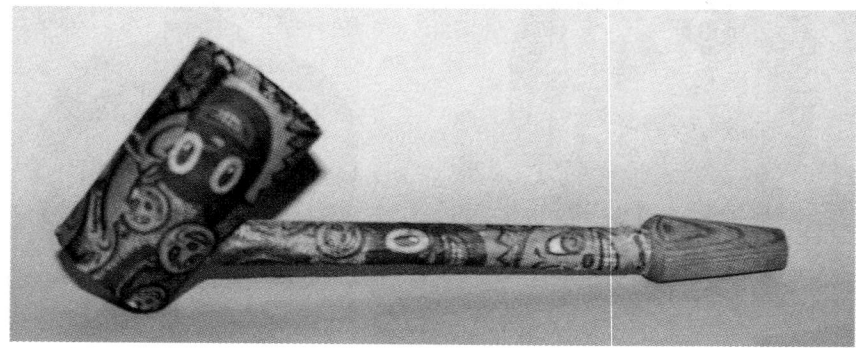

Pipe-shaped Horn Noisemaker

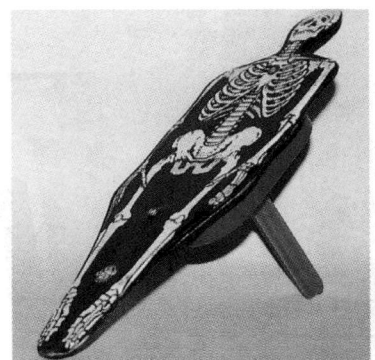

Skeleton Noisemaker

Noisemaker, metal, wood & plastic, skeleton, rare, unmarked, America, ca. 1950s (ILLUS.) **95**

Winking Owl Tin Noisemaker

Noisemaker, tin lithographed winking owl w/plastic handle, US Metal Toy, ca. 1950s, 4 3/4" h. (ILLUS.) **20-40**

Halloween Nut Cup

Nut cup, cardboard & crepe paper, w/orange & black twisted overhead handle, orange w/black bow around middle section, ca. 1950s (ILLUS.) **15**

Paper plate, cat bobbing for apples w/pumpkin people, ca. 1950s, 9" l. **12-20**

Paper Plate with Trick-Or-Treating Children

Paper plate, children trick-or-treating, ca. 1950s, 9" l. (ILLUS.) **12-20**

Party Hat

Party hat, cardboard, orange & black w/cat decoration, 1950s (ILLUS.) **15**

Tambourine with Witch

Tambourine, tin w/lithograph of witch's head w/long hair, hoop earrings, large hat w/small broom trim, orange, black & yellow, T. Cohn, America, ca. 1950s (ILLUS., previous page) **95**

Tea Bag Can with Halloween Decoration

Tea bag container, cov., metal, round, black decorated on lid w/scene of young girl wearing mask, a yellow dress & long green ruffled cape & pointed hat holding a broom w/jack-o'-lantern on top, ca. 1940s (ILLUS.) **95**

HAWAIIANA

Hawaiiana is a blossoming collectibles arena, one which holds many surprises for the newcomer. For starters, some of the best Hawaiiana was not made in Hawaii, and some of the most valuable pieces are brand new. Tiki mugs comprise one of the most active categories of Hawaiiana collectibles, and many of the priciest mugs are those of recent vintage designed by artists Shag and Munktiki. Hawaiiana covers a broad range of items, from vintage rayon shirts to surfboards to rattan furnishings and original artwork from the likes of Witco, Frank MacIntosh and Frank Oda (Hale Pua). With the current popularity of vintage tropical and tiki lounge decor, this is one collector area that is fun for everyone.

United Airlines Advertising Display

Advertising display, plastic, United Airlines Menehune figures of man & woman, 28", pr. (ILLUS.) **$400-500**

Bamboo Bar with Stools

Bar with stools, bamboo, Tropical Sun Co., Pasadena, ca. 1938, 57" l., the set, (ILLUS.) **1,400-1,700**

Wooden Pineapple-shaped Coasters

Coasters, wooden, pineapple-shaped w/cork inserts in carrier, 1940-1950s, 6" l., set (ILLUS.) **20-30**

Brass Figural Pineapple Container

Container, brass, figural pineapple, India, 8" (ILLUS., previous page)............................ **9-15**

Whimsical "Hula Maid" Sock Doll

Doll, cloth, whimsical "hula maid" doll made from sock, ca. 1950s, 5" h., (ILLUS.)............ **8-15**

Ceramic Male Dancer Figurine

Figurine, ceramic male dancer, brown w/white crackle glaze, Treasure Craft, ca. 1950s, 11" h. (ILLUS.) **20-30**

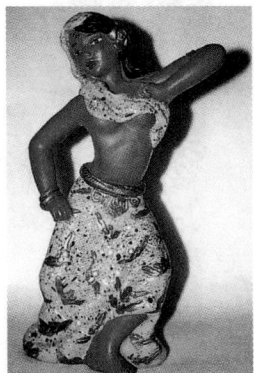

Figural Chalkware Dancer

Figurine, chalkware dancer, Universal Statuary, ca. 1940s, 10" h. (ILLUS.).......... **20-35**

Hawaiian Scene Handbag/Tote

Handbag/tote, canvas & vinyl, decorated w/graphics of surfer, hula girl & tikis, Taiwan, ca. 1970s, 14 x 15 1/2" (ILLUS.).. **12-18**

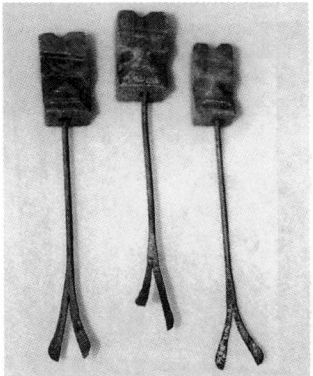

Onyx Carved Hors d'ouvres Picks

Hors d'ouvres picks, green onyx carved tiki heads w/metal forks, set of 8 (ILLUS.).. **35-50**
Lamp, motion lamp, figural bronze-tone Hula dancer w/grass skirt, ca. 1940s, 19" l... **600-1,200**

Pair of Hula Girl and Boy Lamps

Lamps, plaster, hula girl & boy, brown painted plaster w/drizzle pattern shades, ca. 1950s, pr. (ILLUS., previous page)........ **100-150**

Tiki Mask Wood Carving

Mask, carved wood, Tiki mask on leopard backer, Witco, ca. 1950s-1960s, 12 x 23" h. (ILLUS.)................................ **175-250**

Menu Cover by Frank MacIntosh

Menu cover, artwork by Frank Macintosh for Master Cruise Lines, 9 x 12" (ILLUS.).. **60-75**

"Mahalo" Green Ceramic Tiki Mug

Mug, ceramic Tiki mug, green, "Mahalo," Tiki Ceramics Inc., ca. 1964, 5" l. (ILLUS.).. **20-30**

Tiki Mug, Kon Tiki, Sheraton

Mug, ceramic Tiki mug w/brown glaze, Kon Tiki, Sheraton, Steve Crane Associates, ca. 1950s-60s, 7" h. (ILLUS.).. **15-25**

Monkey Pod Wood Tiki Mug

Mug, monkey pod wood Tiki mug, carved, 5" l. (ILLUS.).. **8-12**

Cream and Brown Tiki Mug

Mug, Tiki mug, cream & brown, Otagiri of Japan, ca. 1950-60s, 7" l. (ILLUS., previous page) **10-15**

Figural Hula Girl Music Box

Music box, vinyl & plastic, figural hula girl spins, plays "You Light Up My Life," ca. 1970s (ILLUS.) **15-20**

Paint-by-Number Hawaiian Scene

Paint-by-number picture, Hawaiian seashore landscape w/palms & huts, ca. 1950s, 12 x 16" h. (ILLUS.) **20-35**
Painting, original floral by Frank Oda (Hale Pua), ca. 1940s **250-500**

Pebble Art of Island Native

Pebble art, island native w/big leaf, ca. 1950s-1960s, 6 x 12" h. (ILLUS.) **10-15**

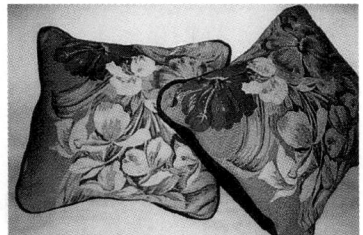

Vintage Tropical Flower Print Pillows

Pillows, vintage barkcloth w/tropical flower print, 14 x 14", each (ILLUS.) **15-20**

Tropical Flower Planter

Planter, ceramic, green, tropical flower, Royal Haeger, R1294, 5 x 10" (ILLUS.) **25-35**

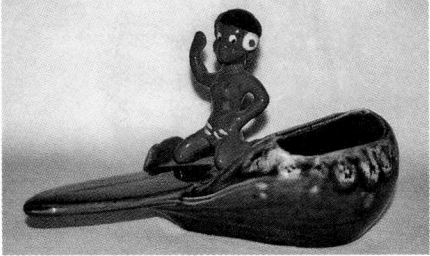

Surfboard Hula Girl Planter

Planter, ceramic, topless hula girl on green surfboard, Tiki Ceramics, ca. 1952, 7" h. (ILLUS.) **30-50**

Figural Pineapple Salt & Pepper Shakers

Salt and pepper shakers, ceramic, figural pineapples, "Aloha Hawaii," Japan, 2 3/4" h., pr. (ILLUS., previous page).......... **8-12**

Ceramic Tiki Head Salt and Pepper Shakers

Salt and pepper shakers, ceramic, tiki heads, OMC Japan, 4" h. pr. (ILLUS.) **18-26**

"The Bird of Paradise" Sheet Music

Sheet music, "The Bird of Paradise," photo/art cover, ca. 1914 (ILLUS.) **20-30**

Pineapple-shaped Serving Dish

Serving dish, wooden, pineapple-shaped divided bowl, 10 1/2" (ILLUS.) **6-12**

Shelves of Woven Bamboo & Glass

Shelves, woven bamboo w/rattan border & glass shelves, round, ca. 1940s-1950s, 25 1/2" d. (ILLUS.)....................................... **50-80**

Bamboo & Glass Serving Tray

Serving tray, bamboo & textured glass, round, ca. 1940s-1950s, 20" d. (ILLUS.) ... **30-40**

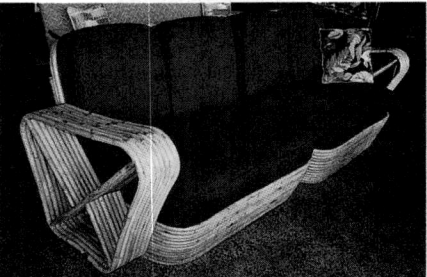

Rattan "Square Pretzel" Design Sofa

Sofa, rattan, 8-banded "square pretzel" sectional style, by Paul Frankl, ca. 1940s, 50" sections (ILLUS.) **1,000-1,500**

"Aloha Hawaii" Souvenir Spoon

Spoon, souvenir, "Aloha Hawaii" w/hula girls on handle, 4 3/4" l. (ILLUS.) **8-12**

"Hawaii - United Air Lines" Travel Poster

Travel poster, "Hawaii - United Air Lines," w/hula girl graphic, ca. 1950s-1960s, 25 x 40" (ILLUS.) **300-400**

SiestaWare Glasses with Caddy

Tumblers with caddy, colored glass w/mahogany bands & Hawaiian scenes, SiestaWare, set (ILLUS.) **50-70**

Mahogany Wall Carving

Wall carving, mahogany, island native w/palms & hut, ca. 1950s-1960s (ILLUS.).. **25-45**

HEINTZ ART METAL SHOP WARES

Otto Heintz (Buffalo, N.Y., 1877-1918) changed the name of his Art Crafts Shop to Heintz Art Metal Shop in 1906 as he shifted his focus from copper to machine-formed bronze bodies and from colored enamels to sterling silver overlays as decoration. A patent for the solderless application of the overlays was awarded in 1912 and the diamond mark enclosing the conjoined letters "HAMS" came into use. A series of sophisticated chemical patinas and plated finishes was developed for a line of vases, bowls and book ends. Otto died suddenly in 1918, but the company struggled through the Depression until the end came on Feb. 11, 1930. Values are a function of form, rarity, overlay and originality of patina.

Lamp, boudoir-type, flaring conical bronze shade w/panels of cutout Art Nouveau flowers & leafy vines, on a squatty bulbous bronze base w/a similar silver overlay design, paper label, shade 8 1/2" d., 9 1/4" h. (two dents) **$1,265**

Heintz Art Metal Desk Lamp

Lamp, desk-type, the domed helmet shade decorated w/silver overlay berries & leaves, adjusting in a scrolled harp above the trumpet-form base w/matching silver overlay, marked, shade 7 3/4" d., overall 11" h. (ILLUS., previous page) **748**

Heintz Art Metal Bowling Trophy

Trophy, the gilded deep round bowl flanked by flattened scroll handles & raised on a trumpet-form base, the bowl w/sterling silver overlay of a bowler framed by chain swags, original dark patina, marked, minor interior wear, few scratches, 7 1/4" w., 7 1/2" h. (ILLUS.) **403**

Short Heintz Art Metal Vase with Rose

Vase, squatty ovoid body w/a short widely flaring neck, dark verdigris ground decorated w/a large sterling silver overlay rose on leafy branch, marked, 5" d., 5" h. (ILLUS.) **546**

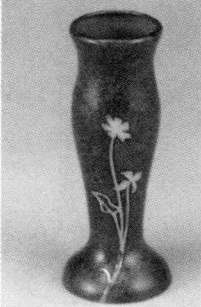

Heintz Art Metal Vase with Violets

Vase, baluster-form, original verdigris patina decorated w/a sterling silver overlay of violets on leafy stems, marked, 2 1/2" d., 6" h. (ILLUS.).. **431**

Heintz Art Metal Tall Vase with Poppies

Vase, slightly tapering cylindrical form, original verdigris patina decorated w/a sterling silver overlay of long stems of poppies, marked, few minor base dents, 5" d., 11" h. (ILLUS.)....................................... **759**

Unusual Heintz Vase with Enameling

Vase, slightly tapering cylindrical form, original verdigris patina, decorated w/an overlay of poppies cold-painted in shades of orange on green stems w/sterling silver leaves, some enamel flakes, few shallow scuffs & scratches, marked, 5" d., 11" h. (ILLUS.)....................................... **863**

Vase, tall slender amphora-form w/long angled handles, original dark patina, decorated w/sterling silver overlay delicate garlands near the rim, marked, 5" d., 13" h. (ILLUS., top next page)........................ **546**

Heintz Art Metal Amphora-form Vase

HOLIDAY COLLECTIBLES

Hallmark Merry Miniatures

Hallmark has often concentrated on seasonal items, and Merry Miniatures are just that. They are miniature plastic figures that can represent every day but usually focus on special days and times of the year such as Christmas and Easter, Valentines Day and Halloween. Most of these cute little decorative pieces can be bought at auction for less than $20. There are some, however, that are quite hard to find; when they show up, prices climb. While some of the very early pieces are unmarked, most will say "Hallmark" somewhere.

Betsey Clark, 1976.................................. $75
Betsey Clark, 1983................................... 15
Christmas calico mouse, 1977......................... 35
Christmas "JOY" elf, 1978 40
Christmas penguin, 1981............................. 32

Christmas Redbird Merry Miniature

Christmas redbird throwing snowball,
   1981 (ILLUS.)...................................... 10
Christmas reindeer on snow base, 1980......... 40
Christmas Santa, 1983............................... 15
Christmas Santa, dated "1988" 25
Christmas Santa holding kitten, 1976............. 12
Christmas Santa holding peppermint
   stick, 1975 50
Christmas Santa on peppermint, 1974 145
Christmas Sebastian, 1986.......................... 35
Christmas sitting reindeer, 1974.................. 275
Christmas waving snowman, mint in
   package, 1974 65

Christmas Mouse Merry Miniature

Christmas white mouse, 1979 (ILLUS.)............ 45
Easter Barnaby Bunny, 1977........................ 40
Easter Bunny w/carrot, 1975 250
Easter chick, 1974................................. 235
Easter child, 1974................................. 185
Easter duck, 1979.................................. 12
Easter sleeping bunny, 1987........................ 40
Halloween cute witch w/frog on hat, 1982...... 125

Halloween Devil Merry Miniature

Halloween devil, mint in plastic, 1975
(ILLUS.) 185
Halloween flocked kitten, 1982 35
Halloween flocked kitten in green hat,
1978 10
Halloween ghost coming out of pumpkin,
1981 230
Halloween Jack-o'-Lantern, 1974 18
Halloween Jack-o'-Lantern tipping top,
1984 12

Halloween Owl Merry Miniature

Halloween owl on pumpkin, in plastic,
1976 (ILLUS.) 70
Halloween raccoon witch, 1987 11
Halloween scarecrow, 1974 220
Halloween ugly witch, mint in package,
1977 50
Halloween witch w/striped legs, 1986 40
Raggedy Andy, mint on card, 1974 65
Raggedy Ann, mint on card, 1974 80
St. Patrick's Day tumbling leprechaun,
1981 18
Thanksgiving Indian, 1975 45
Thanksgiving Pilgrim boy or girl, 1978 12
Thanksgiving Pilgrims, 1974 95
Thanksgiving turkey, 1974 125
Thanksgiving turkey, 1976 85

Thanksgiving Turkey Merry Miniature

Thanksgiving turkey, 1978 (ILLUS.) 40
Thanksgiving turkey, 1987 15

Valentine Cupid Merry Miniature

Valentine Cupid on cloud, dated "1983" on
heart held by Cupid (ILLUS.) 225
Valentine Kermit on heart, 1982 55

Valentine Kitten Merry Miniature

Valentine kitten on pillow, 1983 (ILLUS.) 30

Valentine Miss Piggy Merry Miniature

Valentine Miss Piggy Queen of Hearts,
1982 (ILLUS.) 40

Valentine penguin w/heart, 1984 .... **10**
Valentine pink giraffe, 1987 .... **45**
Valentine turtle, 1980 .... **22**
Valentine Woodlook "LOVE," 1979.................. **55**

HORSE COLLECTIBLES

Reproduction Pony Bank

Bank, cast iron, tan & white pinto pony, reproduction, 4 3/4" (ILLUS.)........................ **$10-15**

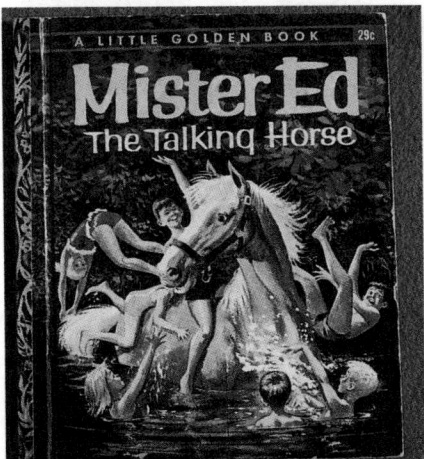

"Mister Ed" Little Golden Book

Book, "Mister Ed The Talking Horse" Little
Golden Book, w/color picture on cover of
Mister Ed in pond amid group of frolicking
children, 1962 (ILLUS.)............................... **12-20**

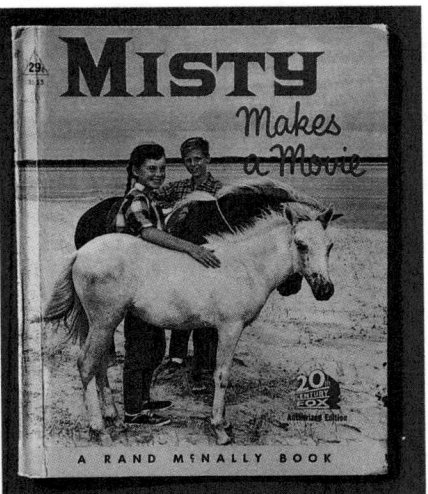

"Misty Makes a Movie" Book

Book, "Misty Makes a Movie," cover w/color
illustration of two children w/pony & foal,
inside w/photos from movie, Rand Mc-
Nally Book, 1961 (ILLUS.) **12-18**

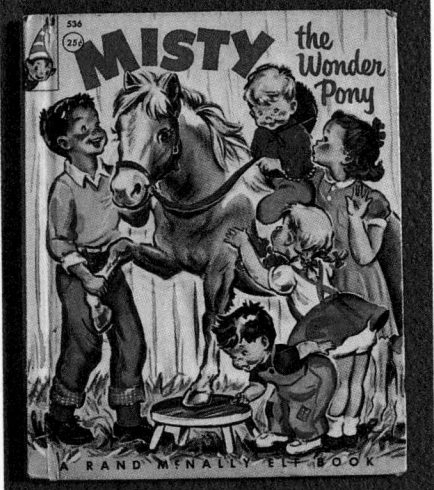

"Misty the Wonder Pony" Book

Book, "Misty the Wonder Pony," cover
w/color illustration of Misty of Chincoteague & group of children, Rand McNally
Tip Top Elf Book, copyright 1960
(ILLUS.)... **10-15**

"Champion" Comic Book

Comic book, "Gene Autry's Champion," painted cover of Champion scrambling up rocky terrain w/mountain in background, Dell #12, 1954 (ILLUS.) **10-25**

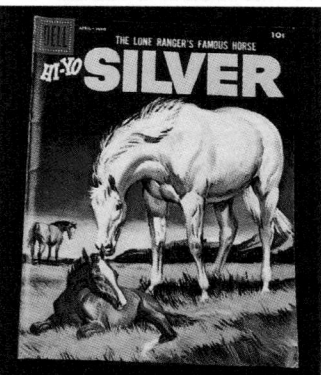

"Hi-Yo Silver" Comic Book

Comic book, "Hi-Yo Silver," Dell #26, cover w/color illustration of Silver standing over brown foal, another horse in the distance, 1958 (ILLUS.) **12-20**

"Roy Rogers and Trigger" Comic Book

Comic book, "Roy Rogers and Trigger," Dell #128, cover w/color photo of Roy standing by Trigger w/gun drawn, beneath "TREACHERY marks the trail of 'THE DRIFTER'" in yellow, 1958 (ILLUS.).. **10-20**

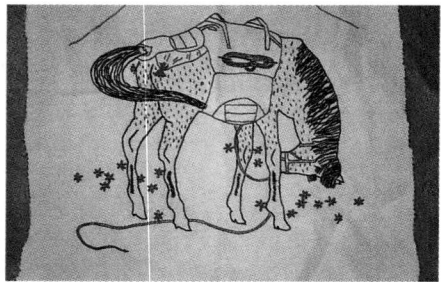

Cross-stitch Picture of Horse

Cross-stitch picture, image of saddled horse w/head down, in black, brown & red thread on white fabric, 1940s, 18 x 20" (ILLUS.) **25-35**

Ceramic Mare & Foal Figurines

Figural group, ceramic, brown mare & foal w/white stockings, mare w/head turned to side, foal w/head down, grazing, base painted to simulate grass, Japan, 5" (ILLUS.) **15-25**

Pony Express Souvenir

Figural group, metal, molded image of Pony Express rider whipping galloping horse, gold tone, souvenir of Pony Express Station, Gothenburg, Nebraska, 1980s, 3 1/2" (ILLUS., previous page) **20-30**

QuickDraw McGraw TV Tinykin

Figure of QuickDraw McGraw, plastic, TV Tinykin, figure based on cartoon character stands on one foot & shoots guns into air, white w/black tail, blue neckerchief & guns, reddish belt, holsters & hat, Marx, early 1960s, 2" (ILLUS.) **35-45**

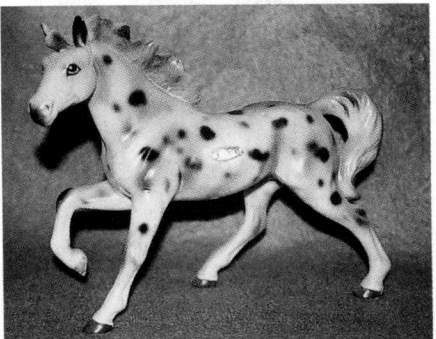

Breyer Arabian Stallion Figurine

Figurine, Arabian Family Stallion, glossy finish palomino, Breyer, 1960s, 9" (ILLUS.) **40-65**

Olimco Ceramic Appaloosa Figurine

Figurine, ceramic, appaloosa w/leopard spot pattern, Olimco, Japan, 7 x 8" (ILLUS.) **25-35**

Ceramic Clydesdale Figurine

Figurine, ceramic, Art Deco-style Clydesdale draft horse, rust/brown w/black mane & tail & four white socks, 1930s, 4" (ILLUS.) **18-24**

Figurine, ceramic, foal, brown w/white blaze & socks, Beswick, England, 4 1/2"... **20-35**

Ceramic Foal Figurine

Figurine, ceramic, foal w/front legs straddled, marbleized tan & white paint, 2 1/2" (ILLUS.) **8-12**

Norleans Grey Horse Figurine

Figurine, ceramic, grey w/darker grey mane & tail, white socks, Norleans, Japan, 4 1/2" (ILLUS., previous page) **6-12**

Ceramic Horse in Mod Style

Figurine, ceramic, mod-stylized horse w/gold glaze, flower decorations, Japan, late 1960s, 9" (ILLUS.)................................. **10-15**

Breyer Phantom Wings Figurine

Figurine, Phantom Wings bay foal from Misty series, Breyer, 1980s, 5 1/2" (ILLUS.) **12-20**

Breyer Shetland Pony

Figurine, Shetland pony, bay, matte finish, Breyer, 6" (ILLUS.) **10-15**
Figurine, Stablemates, Breyer, early 1970s molds, 3" **15-20**

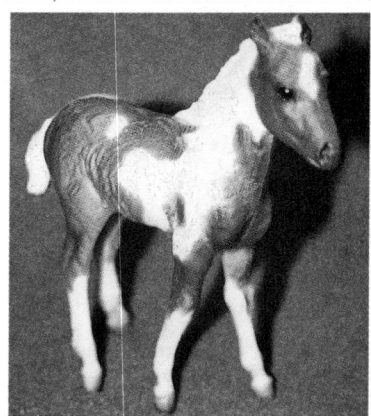

Breyer's Stormy Figurine

Figurine, Stormy (foal of Misty of Chincoteague), tan & white pinto, Breyer, 5 1/2" (ILLUS.)... **15-25**
Figurine, Western pony w/saddle & chain reins, glossy finish, Breyer, some unmarked, 1956-63 .... **45-75**
Figurine, wood grain mustang, Breyer, 1960s, 10" (price dependent on wood grain quality)... **100-500**
Game, Mister Ed board game, Parker Brothers, 1962... **60-85**

Roy Rogers & Trigger Lamp Base

Lamp base, ceramic, Roy Rogers on rearing Trigger, base reads "Happy Trails

Roy Rogers [star] Trigger," 8 1/2"
(ILLUS.) **150-250**

Trigger Lunch Box

Lunch box, steel, w/illustration of Trigger
without saddle or bridle half rearing in
meadow, American Thermos, 1956
(ILLUS.) **150-250**

Pewter Model of Foal with Butterfly

Model of foal, pewter, foal stands w/head
turned back toward yellow-painted but-
terfly on tail, 1970s, 1 1/2" (ILLUS.) **12-20**

Bronzed Metal Standing Horse

Model of horse, bronzed metal, w/molded
ornate saddle, bridle & reins, 2 1/2"
(ILLUS.) **15-20**

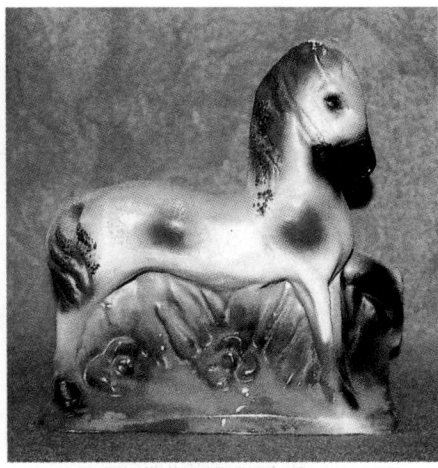

Carnival Chalkware Pinto

Model of horse, Carnival chalkware brown
& white pinto, w/glitter accents on mane
& tail, the base simulating meadow
grasses, 1950s, 6 1/2" (ILLUS.) **20-30**

Folk Art Carved Wooden Horse

Model of horse, folk art carved wooden
horse w/straw tail, sequin eye & visible
teeth, early 1900s, 3 1/4" (ILLUS.) **25-40**

Ivory Miniature Carving of Horse

Model of horse, ivory, miniature horse
carving, Kenya, early 1970s, 3/4"
(ILLUS.) **30-40**

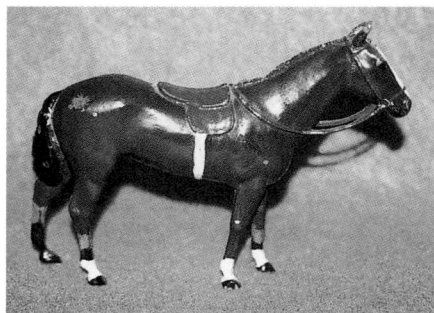

Britains Lead Horse

Model of horse, lead, painted brown w/black tail, white blaze & three white socks, molded red English saddle, bridle & reins, Britains, Ltd., England, 4" (ILLUS.) **15-20**

Metal Horse with Chain Reins

Model of horse, metal, w/molded saddle & bridle & chain reins, painted tan w/white main & tail, 1960s, 2 3/4" (ILLUS.) **10-15**

Durham Industries Walking Horse

Model of horse, metal, walking horse painted yellow/orange, Durham Industries, 1977, 3 1/4" (ILLUS.) **10-15**

Plastic Rearing Horse

Model of horse, plastic, rearing pose, light brown w/black mane & tail, white stockings, Hong Kong, 1960s, 5" version (ILLUS.) **5-10**

"Thundercolt" by Marx

Model of horse, plastic, "Thundercolt" from "Best of the West" series, dark brown bay, Marx, 1960s, 9 3/4" (ILLUS.) **10-20**

Tinymite Tennessee Walker

Model of horse, plastic, Tinymite Tennessee Walker, white w/black mane, tail & stockings, Hartland Plastics, 1960s-70s, 2 3/4 x 3" (ILLUS., previous page)............... **7-12**

Hartland Plastics Rearing Mustang

Model of horse, plastic w/cherry wood grain finish, rearing mustang, Hartland Plastics, 1964-66, 9 1/4" (ILLUS.).............. **15-30**

Nuzzling Horses of Glazed Chalkware

Model of horses, glazed chalkware, brown horses nuzzling each other on yellow oval stepped base, 1930s, 5 1/2 x 7 1/2" (ILLUS.)... **30-45**

Pot Metal Model of Jockey on Horse

Model of jockey on horse, coated pot metal, the jockey w/painted red shirt, white pants & black cap, Japan, 2 1/2 x 2 3/4" (ILLUS.) **15-20**

Lone Ranger on Rearing Silver

Model of Lone Ranger on rearing Silver, plastic, white horse w/black saddle, bridle & reins, figure of Lone Ranger in blue w/red neckerchief, white hat, black mask & boots, w/box, one of three poses issued by Hartland Plastics, 1954, 9 1/2" (ILLUS.).. **200-300**

Small Version of Trigger & Roy

Model of Trigger & Roy Rogers, plastic, all tan Trigger w/molded black saddle, bridle & reins, Roy in white w/red neckerchief, black belt w/holster & boots, no hat, Hartland Plastics, small version, 4 1/2" (ILLUS.)... **65-85**

Hartland Plastics Arabian Horses

Models of horses, plastic, mare & foal from Arabian Family series (5 in series), white w/black manes, tails & stockings, Hartland Plastics, 1960s, pr. (ILLUS.) **10-16**

Lobby Card for "The Black Stallion"

Movie lobby card, for movie "The Black Stallion," w/scene of black horse cantering through surf above "The Black Stallion" in stylized black lettering, a stylized silhouette of a horse head in the lower left corner, 1979, 11 x 14" (ILLUS.)................... **8-15**

Paint-by-numbers Picture of Horse

Paint-by-numbers picture, image of horse head in white, framed, 1950s (ILLUS.) **15-20**

Pebble Art Picture of Foal

Picture, pebble art depiction of foal & rabbit, 1960s (ILLUS.)... **10-15**

Planter, ceramic, draft horse, 1930s-40s, 5 1/4" **12-20**

Ceramic Horse & Cart Planter

Planter, ceramic, whimsical tan & white horse w/black mane & tail, w/tan cart that holds plant, "Made in Occupied Japan," 3 x 4" (ILLUS.)... **15-20**

Mister Ed Talking Hand Puppet

Puppet, Mister Ed talking hand puppet, plastic head & plush neck w/yarn mane, in working condition, Mattel, 1962, 11 1/2" (ILLUS., previous page) **150-300**

Mounted Knight Radio

Radio, rectangular plastic base topped w/figure of knight in armor on rearing steed, Peter, Japan, 1970s, 8 3/4" (ILLUS.) **30-40**

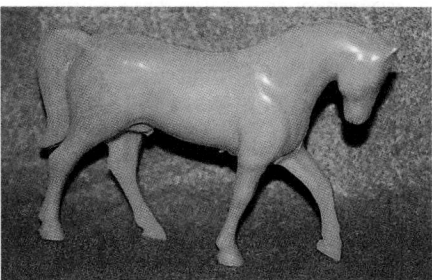

Horse Rattle

Rattle, plastic, model of horse, yellow, HavAtoy, 1950s, 3 1/2 x 4 1/5" (ILLUS.) **6-10**

Rearing Horse Salt & Pepper Shakers

Salt & pepper shakers, rearing horses, one black w/white blaze & one palomino, Japan, 1950s, 4 1/2" (ILLUS.) **15-20**
Sticker set, Chincoteague Pony Farm set, image of Stormy on card top, sealed, 1980s... **20-30**

Horse & Coach Toothpick Holder

Toothpick holder, ceramic, brown horse pulling green, white & yellow coach that holds toothpicks, Japan, 1936, 2 1/2" (ILLUS.).. **10-15**

Talking Stallion Toy in Box

Toy, Grand Champions Talking Stallion, model of pinto w/saddle, in box reading "Try Me! Press my saddle and hear me 'Whinny' and 'Gallop,'" Empire, 1994 (ILLUS.)... **30-45**
Toy, My Little Pony, Baby Bonnet School of Dance, Hasbro, 1980s................................ **20-40**
Toy, My Little Pony, Ballerina Ponies w/molded leotards, Hasbro, 1980s................. **3-8**
Toy, My Little Pony, Twice-As-Fancy Ponies, w/more patterns on bodies, Hasbro, 1980s... **8-12**
Toy, My Little Pony, Winged Ponies, not flutter-wing style, Hasbro, 1980s................. **12-25**

Pokey Toy

Toy, Pokey, Gumby's horse, bendable rubber figure w/wire support, orange & black, 1980s-90s (ILLUS.) **5-10**

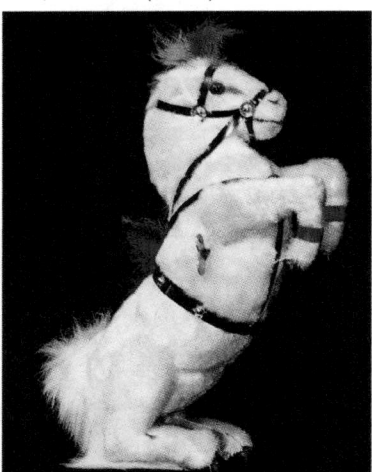

Circus Horse Wind-up Toy

Wind-up toy, rearing circus horse w/fur tail & feather decorations, West Germany, 9" (ILLUS.) **100-150**

Prancing Ponies by Tomy

Wind-up toys, plastic, jointed horses, Prancing Ponies by Tomy, 1980s, 3", each (ILLUS. of chestnut & pinto) **15-20**

INDIAN ART & ARTIFACTS

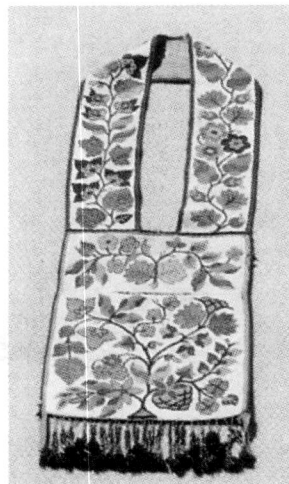

Chippewa Beadwork Bandolier

Bandolier, Chippewa, fine beadwork in floral vining design in shades of pink, blue, turquoise, green & yellow against white beaded background, the back lined w/cotton & edged w/red wool braid, fringes of tubular glass beads & yarn pompoms suspended along bottom, 14 1/4 x 17 3/4", 41" h. (ILLUS.) **$1,725**

Navaho Blanket in Red, Brown & Tan

Blanket, Navajo, hand-loomed chief's blanket decorated w/diamonds & stripes in shades of red, brown & tan, small damages in center & along edge, 4'4" x 7'4" (ILLUS.) **4,370**

Hopi "Citulilu" Kachina

Kachina, Hopi, "Citulilu," deriving from Zuni word for rattlesnake, wearing yellow case mask w/rattlesnake painted on forehead, w/long black snout, red tongue & fan-shaped crest of turkey tail feathers, 7 5/8" h. (ILLUS.) **780**

Hopi "Sio Heimis Ta Amu" Kachina

Kachina, Hopi, "Sio Heimis Ta Amu," "Zuni Kachina's Uncle," wearing green squash-shaped case mask w/black band painted across eyes, tubular mouth, 9 3/4" h. (ILLUS.) **920**

Hopi "Tungwup" Kachina

Kachina, Hopi, "Tungwup," "The Whipper," wearing black case mask w/protruding eyes, large curved horns & long beard & carrying yucca whip in right hand, repair to horns, 7 1/8" h. (ILLUS.) **780**

Southern Plains Child's Moccasins

Crow Parfleche Case

Moccasins, Southern Plains, child-size, natural leather decorated w/bands of turquoise, black, pink & red beads, several areas missing bead strings, 8 1/2" l., pr. (ILLUS., previous page) **403**

Acoma Pottery Olla

Olla, Acoma, pottery w/bulbous shape & short rimless neck, short foot, decorated w/black & off-white geometric designs w/red accents to upper neck, base & inside of neck, 12" d. at widest point, 11" h. (ILLUS.) **4,600**

Parfleche case, Crow, natural ground w/polychrome geometric designs in mustard yellow, sky blue, red & deep green in symmetrical pattern, 19th c., some areas of repolychroming, 14 x 27" closed (ILLUS., bottom previous page) **635**

Pipe Bag with American Flag Motif

Pipe bag, leather, turquoise trim decorated w/red, white & blue opposing American flags & other similarly colored designs, 9" end fringe w/tin cone beginnings, overall 4 1/2 x 23" (ILLUS.) **403**

Pouch, moose calf hide & remnants of colored silk-like fabric trim, worked w/silk-like thread in style of work introduced to Indians by French nuns in 18th c. Canada, embroidered w/red flowers & green leaves on front, flap embroidered w/images of lions, rare, mounted in contemporary matted 17 x 23" shadowbox,

Rare 18th Century Embroidered Hide Pouch

some loss of material & decoration, slight deterioration of moose hide, pouch 9 x 15 1/4" (ILLUS.) **1,438**

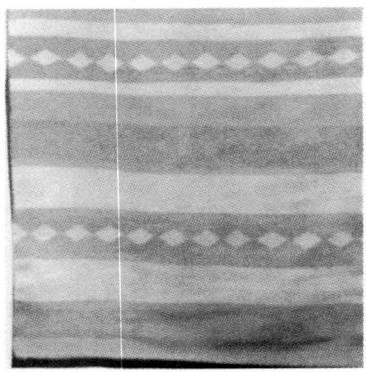

Navajo Chinle Rug

Rug, Navajo, Chinle-style, wool, decorated w/wide stripes & rows of diamonds in shades of cream, mustard & taupe in vegetal dyes, 1930s, 39 1/2 x 64 1/2" (ILLUS. of part) **460**

Navajo Crystal/Ganado Rug

Rug, Navajo, Crystal/Ganado-style, decorated w/pattern of repeating diamonds within diamonds in natural dark brown, cream, deep red & dark camel on natural grey ground w/dark brown & dark camel borders, 20th c., minor unraveling to edges, 37 x 62" (ILLUS. of part, previous page).. **863**

Navajo Ganado Rug

Rug, Navajo, Ganado-style, decorated w/pattern of serrated diamonds in red, natural cream, greys & browns on natural grey ground w/red border, early 20th c., 55 x 81" (ILLUS. of part)................................... **690**

Rug, Navajo, Ganado-style, decorated w/pattern of serrated & stepped figures in red, charcoal & natural cream, on grey ground w/two borders of natural cream & brown, 1930s, 33 x 34 1/4" (ILLUS., top of next column)... **1,150**

Rug, Navajo, Ganado-style, handwoven wool, three-band border in shades of brown & beige, center panel a deep red

Navajo Rug from 1930s

w/design in same colors as border radiating from red & black "X" in center, ca. 1930, small early repair, some soiling, 57 x 81" (ILLUS., bottom of page)............. **1,955**

Bright Navajo Rug with Diamond Design

Rug, Navajo, red ground decorated w/jagged-edged multicolored diamonds

Navajo Ganado Rug

w/central smaller diamonds, border comprised of stripes in blue, green, orange, black, white & red, one small area of pulled weave in center, 61 x 85" (ILLUS., previous page) **2,645**

Navajo Transitional Period Rug

Rug, Navajo, Transitional Period-style, decorated w/interlocking serrated diamonds in browns, red & charcoal grey on natural white ground within red border, 20th c., minor stains, 50 1/2 x 75" (ILLUS. of part).. **1,840**

Two Gray Hills-type Navaho Rug

Rug, Navajo, Two Gray Hills-type, black, grey & white, the center section w/stepped design & interior diamond w/swastika, light stain on one end, 59 x 91" (ILLUS.) **690**

Navajo Rug in Natural Colors

Rug, Navajo, Two Gray Hills-type, wool, natural shades of cream, brown & over-

dyed black w/black border, ca. 1930s, 24 1/4 x 35" (ILLUS. of part).......................... **920**

Small Rug with Zigzag Design

Rug, Navajo, rectangular, central tan field containing serrated zigzags & diamonds in brown, tan, red & black, surrounded by orange border w/dental-type designs in red, green & white on black backing, 38 1/2 x 59" (ILLUS.) **920**

Woodland Indian Shoulder Pouch

Shoulder pouch, Woodland Indian, black fabric backing decorated w/floral decoration in green, blue, mustard, clear, gold, pink & red beads, the shoulder strap w/similarly colored beads in flower & leaf motif, top section w/area of backing loss, 24" l. (ILLUS.).. **288**

JEWELRY

Antique (1800-1920)

Bracelet, gold, 14k, bangle-type, hinged bangle w/four-leaf clover mount & seed pearl stem over an interlocking loop design, three green stone accents, Edwardian **$264**

Brooch, cat's-eye chrysoberyl, memorial-type, bezel-set w/oval cabochon w/14k gold ropetwist frame, verso w/locket containing hair **382**

Brooch, diamond, sapphire & 14k gold, gem-set model of insect, wings & body collet & bead-set w/twenty-nine rose, old mine & old European-cut diamonds & twenty oval & circular-cut sapphires, ruby eye, rose gold legs & antennae, detachable silver-topped rose, gold mount **3,525**

Enamel & Diamond Butterfly Brooch

Brooch, enamel & diamond, model of butterfly, red, yellow, blue & black basse taille enamel wings & old mine-cut diamond body, ruby eyes, rose-cut diamond accents, silver-topped 14k gold mount, Austro-Hungarian hallmarks (ILLUS.) **6,463**

Brooch, gold (14k) & diamond, stickpin-type bar w/ribbon swags suspended by five antique & Art Nouveau full-cut diamond-set stickpin heads, diamond flowerhead surmount, stickpins w/hallmarks for "Carter, Howe & Co. and Dieges & Clust." **646**

Edwardian Opal & Diamond Brooch

Brooch, opal & diamond, oval opal framed by seed pearls & old European-cut diamonds, 14k gold mount, Edwardian, hallmark for Krementz & Co., w/original Tiffany & Co. box (ILLUS.) **1,293**

Brooch, platinum & diamond, bead & prong-set throughout w/seventy-six rose,

single, and full-cut diamonds, approx. total wt. 1.70 cts., French hallmark, Edwardian **2,000**

Cross pendant, sapphires & 14k gold, gem-set cross w/circular-cut sapphires, cross suspended on gold chain w/five square step-cut sapphires, bloomed gold mount, signed "Tiffany & Co.," 32" l. **3,819**

Earpendants, gold (14k) & turquoise cabochon, hemisphere & sphere design, bow & hanging tassel suspended, bezel & gypsy-set throughout w/turquoise cabochons, applied wirework accents, 10.5 dwt., Victorian (evidence of solder, small dents, missing elements) **104**

Necklace, diamond, graduating geometric scroll design links bead-set w/rose-cut diamonds, silver-topped 18k gold mount, 15 1/4" l. **7,050**

Necklace, gold (14k), composed of oval wirework links w/floret & flattened bead accents, 18 1/4" l. **705**

Necklace, gold (18k), diamond & enamel, Art Nouveau-style, delicate trace link chain w/figure of woman in blue enamel dress suspended, framed by curving branches w/pink & blue plique-a-jour enamel leaves, bezel-set w/seven old European-cut diamonds & bead-set w/rose-cut diamond highlights, freshwater pearl terminal, 18" l. **4,935**

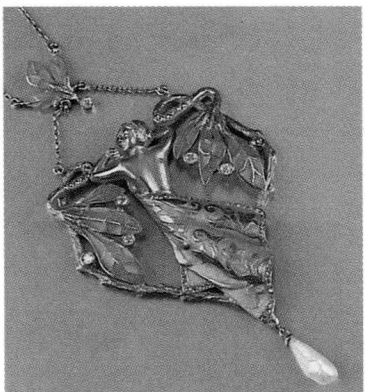

Art Nouveau Gold, Diamond & Enamel Necklace

Necklace, gold, diamond & enamel, Art Nouveau style, delicate trace link chain, suspended figure of woman in blue enamel dress, framed by curving branches w/pink & blue plique-a-jour enamel leaves, bezel-set w/seven old European-cut diamonds & bead-set w/rose-cut diamond highlights, freshwater pearl terminal, 18" l. (ILLUS.) **4,935**

Necklace, pearl, cultured, 101 white pearls graduated in size from 3.75-7.01 mm, completed by openwork 18k white gold barrel clasp w/diamond accents, Continental hallmark, 22" l. **382**

Necklace, pearl, cultured, composed of 46 white pearls w/rose overtones measuring approx. 8.05-8.20 mm, completed by 18k gold X-form clasp, signed "T & Co." for Tiffany & Co., w/original suede pouch, 16 1/4" l. **2,233**

Pendant, black onyx & rose gold, mourning-type, inscribed "Charles Lord Southampton, obt 22 March 1797" & "George Lord Southampton, obt 24 June 1810," centering a glass compartment containing locks of hair, enameled crown design bail, early 19th c. **259**

Pendant, gold (14k), opal & enamel, Art Nouveau-style, oval opal framed by a pink guilloché enamel lotus design, two diamond accents, suspended by a 14k gold trace link chain, hallmark for Krementz & Co. (crack to opal) **705**

Pendant, silver, ivory & coral, designed as cluster of silver leaves & scrolling tendrils w/two fluted ivory bellflowers suspended, accented by three coral beads, probably designed by Dagobert Peche, Wiener Werkstatte, Austria, early 20th c. **3,525**

Pendant-brooch, bloodstone, rose-cut diamond, ruby & 18k gold, the oval bloodstone surmounted by a rose-cut diamond & cabochon ruby floral design within an 18k gold pierced, chased & engraved floral & foliate frame set w/rose-cut diamonds & rubies, French import stamp, Victorian **489**

Pendant-brooch, chalcedony, ruby & enamel, oval chalcedony carved w/four intaglio classical figures within a Holbeinesque polychrome floral enamel frame set w/three circular cut rubies, 18k gold mount **1,840**

Pendant-brooch, diamond & 14k gold, starburst pendant/brooch set w/fifty old mine-cut diamonds, 14k gold mount, hallmark for Krementz & Co., ca. 1900 ...... **2,990**

Tiffany Starburst Pendant/Brooch

Pendant-brooch, diamond & 18k gold, starburst design, set w/fifty-five old European-cut diamonds, 18k gold mount, signed "Tiffany & Co." (ILLUS.) **7,168**

Pendant-brooch, diamond, bow design w/five loops, each set w/nine old mine-cut diamonds & centered by an old European-cut diamond, 18k gold mount, ca. 1895 ...... **1,955**

Pendant-brooch, diamond & demantoid garnet, model of a leaf bead-set w/circular-cut demantoid garnets within a gold ring decorated w/nine bezel-set old mine-cut diamonds, platinum-topped 18k gold mount **3,055**

Pendant-brooch, diamond & gold, oval frame containing portraits of young girls painted front & back, silver-topped 18k gold mount designed as a bow set w/old mine-cut diamonds, Edwardian, England .. **1,410**

Diamond and Sapphire Pendant-Brooch

Pendant-brooch, diamond & sapphire, centered by oval sapphire measuring approximately 10.10 x 7.85 x 5.05 mm, surrounded by fifty-eight old mine, old European, & single-cut diamonds, approx. total wt. 5.56 cts., silver-topped 14k gold mount (ILLUS.) **8,225**

Black Opal and Diamond Necklace

Pendant-necklace, black opal & diamond, delicate trace link chain suspending a pendant w/two bezel-set harlequin black opals & thirty-one bead & bezel-set single-cut diamonds, millegrain accents and pierced gallery, platinum-topped 18k gold mount, platinum chain, 16 1/2" l. (ILLUS.) **3,525**

Pendant-necklace, gold (14k bi-color) & enamel, reeded trace link chain suspended by three foxtail tassel pendants & medallion w/enamel cherubs, all joined by swags, black tracery enamel accents, Victorian, 16 1/2" l. **764**

Pendant-necklace, sterling silver & enamel, Art Nouveau style, tripartite abstract-form pendant decorated en plein w/blue & green enamel, suspended from a baton-link chain, hallmarks for Chester, date letter for 1911, maker "C.H.," England **323**

Pendant-necklace, sterling silver & green agate, shaped pendant centered by an oval green agate, suspended from a silver paper clip chain, pendant stamped on reverse "TF (for Theodor Fahrner) - 935 - Déposé," 21" l. **1,528**

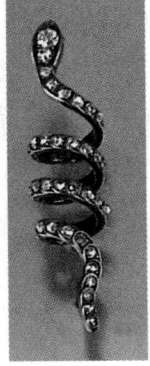

Rose-cut Diamond Serpent Pin

Pin, diamond & ruby, designed as coiled rose-cut diamond serpent w/ruby eyes, silver-topped, 14k gold mount, Austro-Hungarian hallmarks (ILLUS.) **1,058**

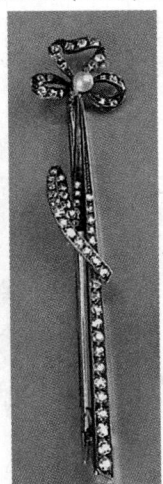

Diamond & Seed Pearl Pin

Pin, diamond & seed pearl, designed as a diamond baton tied w/ribbon, bead-set w/fifty-nine old mine-cut diamonds, seed

pearl & millegrain accents, silver-topped 18k gold mount, (ILLUS.) **646**

Pin, enamel & diamond, flying mallard w/basse taille enamel head, body & wings bead-set w/old mine, rose & single-cut diamonds, silver-topped 18k gold mount, w/fitted Asprey box **1,880**

Pin, gold (18k) & diamond, Art Nouveau-style, designed as griffin clutching an old European-cut diamond, rose-cut diamond accents, marker's mark "GC" (ILLUS.) **2,350**

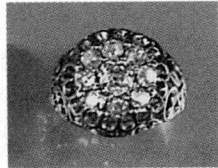

Diamond Ring

Ring, diamond, floret composed of nine old mine-cut diamonds weighing approx. 0.89 cts., scrolling openwork white metal & 18k yellow gold mount, English karat stamp, size 2, shank indistinctly inscribed (ILLUS.) **764**

Ring, ruby & diamond, Art Nouveau style, bezel-set w/faceted cushion-shaped ruby measuring approx. 6.05 x 5.55 x 4.06 mm, flanked by old European-cut diamonds, approx. total wt. 1 ct., scrolling foliate 18k gold mount, size 7 1/4.................. **4,406**

Sets

Brooch & earpendants, enamel, diamond, gem-set demi-parure, brooch w/flexible plaques decorated w/golden basse taille enamel & bezel-set w/five circular-cut citrines & ten old European-cut diamonds, pear-shape faceted citrine terminal, 18k gold mount, signed "Marcus & Co.," the set **9,400**

Necklace plaques, gold (18k), diamond & turquoise "Placque de Cou," Art Nouveau design, largest 2 x 7" rectangular curved openwork plaque centered w/carved turquoise woman's head w/chased flowing gold hair highlighted by old European-cut diamond blossoms, signed "Lalique," similar 2" square plaque also w/carved turquoise head & signed "Lalique," also a pair of smaller openwork plaques set

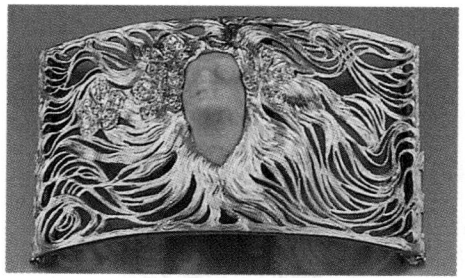

18k Gold "Placque de Cou"

w/diamond blossoms, accompanied by 18k gold flattened baton link chain, 20 1/2" l., two gold satin ribbons, one gold satin cord, & two screwdrivers, may be worn as chokers or necklaces, one plaque w/brooch fitting, the set (ILLUS. of largest plaque) **49,938**

Costume

Bar pin, cloisonné on copper, design of blue flowers, ca. 1920, 2 3/4" w. **45-65**
Bar pin, glass, oval shape, black, rectangular facets, Czechoslovakia, 7/8 x 1 7/8" **30-45**
Bracelet, Bakelite, bangle-type, carnelian orange, w/carved leaves & flowers, 5/8" w. **80-100**
Bracelet, Bakelite, bangle-type, chartreuse green/yellow marbled, no carving, 1/2" w. **35-50**
Bracelet, Bakelite, bangle-type, yellow, no carving, 7/8" w. **55-75**
Bracelet, brass, link-type, w/six large figural brass rose charms, ca. 1900 .... **45-65**
Bracelet, gold plate, bangle-type, hinged, top set w/clear rhinestones, 1" w. **50-70**
Bracelet, gold plate, bangle-type, ribbed design, signed "Ciner," 3/4" w. **50-75**
Bracelet, gold plate, link-type, set w/individual multicolored carved glass scarabs, 1/2" w. **55-70**
Bracelet, gold plate, linked chain w/ten varied charms decorated w/blue, green & turquoise enamel **40-60**
Bracelet, gold-filled, link-type, hinged, five links w/oval shell cameos on scalloped center pieces, each link w/borders of cylinders & twisted metal, signed "Sammartino Bros. Providence," ca. 1910, 1" w. **375-400**
Bracelet, Lucite, bangle-type, double row of applied black cone-shaped designs around entire bracelet, ca. 1965, 2" w. **40-60**
Bracelet, rhinestone & metal, expansion-style, white metal bracelet completely covered w/large emerald-cut clear rhinestones, 1/2" w. **85-100**
Bracelet, rhinestone & white metal, link-type, decorated w/clear stones & large marquise-shaped center stones, 5/8" w..... **50-70**
Bracelet, sterling, bangle-type, hinged w/safety chain, no decoration, Mexico, 1" w. **65-80**
Bracelet, sterling, link-type, w/connected curved ribbed leaves, signed "Jewelart," 1/2" w. **55-75**

Bracelet, sterling, link-type, w/enamel on sterling Pekinese dog charm, 1930s **55-75**
Bracelet, sterling, link-type, w/matching sterling cat charm, 1950s, 1/4" w. **45-65**

Sterling Bracelet with Rhinestones

Bracelet, sterling silver & rhinestone, late Retro style, openwork design of ribbons/scrolls in rectangular panels linked together, entirely set w/clear rhinestones, signed "Unicraft Sterling," 1 3/8" w. (ILLUS.).. **175-195**
Bracelet, turquoise & metal, assorted real turquoise nuggets strung on elastic w/white metal textured spacer beads, 1/2" w. **70-90**
Clip, dress-type, 935 grade sterling & rhinestone, large clear baguettes & marquise stones in center, openwork sides set w/small clear rhinestones, 1 3/4" h.......... **90-120**
Clip, dress-type, antiqued gold plate, leaf shape w/openwork flowers in center, each flower set w/blue, white or turquoise center, signed "NE," 1 7/8 x 2 1/2"............. **40-50**
Clip, dress-type, antiqued gold plate & rhinestone, curved ribbon shape, openwork metal decorated w/four center handset large oval red rhinestones in graduated sizes, from large on top to small on bottom, each surrounded by clear rhinestone trim, 1 1/4 x 3 1/4"......... **85-110**
Clip, dress-type, copper-finish metal & glass, ornate filigree & etched design decorated w/large pink art glass oval stone on top, 2 x 2 1/2"............................... **50-75**

Amber Flower Dress Pin

Clip, dress-type, gold plate, glass & rhinestone, large spray of three gold bell-shaped flowers w/large center amber crystal centers & pavé clear rhinestone petals & stem, 2 x 3 1/2" (ILLUS.)........... **75-100**

Dress Clip of Multicolored Rhinestones

Clip, dress-type, goldtone metal, openwork kite-shaped design studded w/large purple, pink, aqua, yellow, green & clear rhinestones, 1 3/4 x 2 1/4" (ILLUS.)........... **55-75**

Multicolored Cabochon Dress Clip

Clip, dress-type, goldtone metal, oval openwork design w/large oval red cabochon stone in center surrounded by panel w/leaf decoration & four smaller round multicolored cabochon stones in rope-twist border, an outer panel decorated w/fleur-de-lis & 12 oval multicolored cabochon stones, 2 1/4 x 2 1/2" (ILLUS.) **70-90**

Clip, dress-type, rhinestone, floral motif set w/large blue, red, green & yellow marquise stones around green domed center, 1 3/4" d. **35-50**

Clip, dress-type, rhinestone, green crackle glass center stone inside frame of pink cabochons, upper bottom rows of pink,

green, yellow & blue rhinestones, lower bottom row of five ribbon-style designs set w/tiny blue, red & purple cabochons, three hanging blue glass cone shapes, 2 1/2 x 2 3/4" **65-85**

Clip, dress-type, rhinestone, inverted triangle shape, large pink oval rhinestones in openwork design w/matching channel-set square rhinestone borders & accents, 1 5/8 x 2 3/4" **65-85**

Clip, dress-type, rhinestone, openwork metal completely set w/clear rhinestones in Art Deco design, center large oval marquise stone w/red, emerald green & blue etched glass leaves above & below, small black enamel accents, 1 1/2 x 2" **70-95**

Black & Clear Rhinestone Dress Pin

Clip, dress-type, rhinestone, three vertically stacked large round black stones framed by slightly smaller clear oval & marquise rhinestones, signed "Doctor Dress," 2 x 2 1/2" (ILLUS.)..................................... **75-100**

Clip, dress-type, white metal & glass, openwork design completely set w/pale blue faux moonstones, clear rhinestone trim between stones, 1 3/4 x 2 1/4" **70-90**

Clip, dress-type, white metal & rhinestone, ornate openwork rococo design w/double swag chains & large oval clear & pink rhinestones in center, signed "Doctor Dress," 2 1/4 x 3"..................................... **75-100**

Clip, fur-type, gold plate, glass, enamel & pearl, floral spray design w/pink, green, blue & purple glass squares forming flowers, a single side spray of graduated pearls, a light pink enameled bow at bottom, 2 1/4 x 3 3/4" **100-120**

Clip, fur-type, gold plate, glass & enamel, spray design of three flowers w/large amber rhinestone centers, small clear rhinestone trim, navy blue enamel ribbon at top, signed "Trifari," 2 5/8" h. **125-150**

Clip, fur-type, gold plate, sword design w/filigree hilt set w/large red cabochon on top, smaller red, green & blue cabochons on border & at center, signed "Monet," 2 x 3"... **125-150**

Clip, fur-type, rhinestone, spray design of pink etched glass leaves w/turquoise, pink & lavender oval rhinestone flowers w/blue-green enameled stems & pavé rhinestones, 1 1/2 x 2 1/4"........................ **80-100**

Clip, sweater-type, gold plate & pearl, chain of pearls hanging between gold-plated leaves **25-35**

Clip, sweater-type, sterling, two circles connected by 3" chain, signed "Tiffany & Co." **75-100**

Earrings, glass, hanging teardrop style, green Peking glass, screwback-type, ca. 1925, 2 1/4" l., pr. **65-85**

Gold Plate & Cabochon Earrings

Earrings, gold plate & cabochon, hoop top w/double circle drop w/blue oval cabochon set stones, drop can be removed so hoop top can be worn alone, signed "Agatha," 2" l., pr. (ILLUS.).............................. **45-60**

Earrings, gold plate, three-dimensional flower motif w/striped gold finish, signed "Jomaz," 1 1/2" d., pr.................................... **50-70**

Earrings, pearl, large 1/2" d. cultured pearl ball drops, clip-on type, signed "Richelieu," 1" l., pr. **45-65**

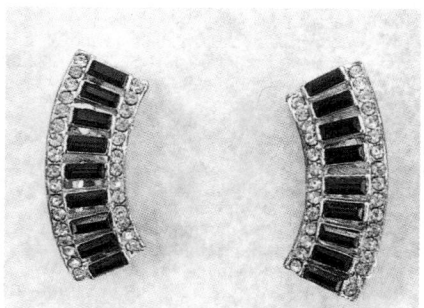

Red & Clear Rhinestone Earrings

Earrings, rhinestone, slightly curved design w/horizontal rows of red baguette stones inside bordering clear round rhinestones, clip-on style, 1" l., pr. (ILLUS.)..................... **40-55**

Earrings, sterling & enamel, fan design in blue & green enamel, signed "Siam," 1 1/4" w., pr.. **50-70**

Multicolored Glass Bead Necklace

Necklace, glass, beads of various colors & shapes accented w/long cylindrical art glass beads, 38" l. (ILLUS.) **65-85**

Necklace, glass, bright multicolored beads w/large flat bright orange accents, 39" l. .. **50-65**

Necklace, gold plate, glass & pearl, multiple chains w/large 6 1/2" pendant & pink, fuchsia & moss-green rhinestones around pink/blue center cabochon, w/hanging clusters of pearl teardrops, the pearl clusters repeated along chains, signed "Florenza," about 17" l. **175-190**

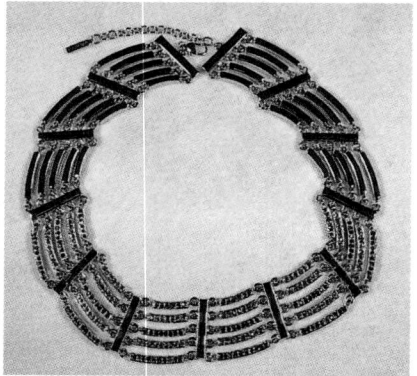

Necklace of Gold Plate & Rhinestones

Necklace, gold plate & rhinestone, collarstyle, six front panels, each made up of five horizontal rows of pink & red rhinestones, the panels separated by vertical bars of pink & red baguettes; six back panels, each w/six horizontal gold plate bars separated by vertical gold plate bars, all without rhinestones, signed "Napier," 14" adjusts to 16 1/2" (ILLUS.) **75-100**

Necklace, gold plate & rhinestone, three graduated chains w/large links decorated w/large gold-plated beads cabochon set w/large blue, red & green marquise rhinestones, the center chain w/large medallion-style star pendant, unsigned, 27" l. **75-95**

Necklace, green malachite beads in graduated sizes w/green bead spacers, 23" l. . **85-100**

Necklace, pale blue agate beads w/silver metal spacers, 23" l. **30-45**

Necklace, plastic & rhinestone, amber-colored beads marbled to look genuine, set w/black rhinestones, black faceted glass spacers, 12" adjusts to 15"........................... **35-50**

Necklace, sterling & amethyst, sterling chain decorated w/center flower design of pear-shaped amethysts w/matching drop, three pear-shaped amethysts on either side, 18" l. **140-165**

Pendant, carnelian, heart-shaped, 1" (no chain).. **35-50**

Kitten Pendant in Gold Plate

Pendant, gold plate & rhinestone, three dimensional model of kitten w/green rhinestones eyes sitting in rope-twist circle hanging from 24" chain, 2" d. (ILLUS.)....... **55-75**

Pendant, gold plate, sterling & shell cameo, oval shape w/Three Graces motif, 1 1/8" (no chain) **125-150**

Pendant, jade, pale green 2 1/4" d. pendant w/embossed Chinese characters on black cord w/slide adjuster, ca. 1925, 32" l... **95-120**

Pendant, sterling, 1 1/2" pendant of 1920s-style girl wearing locket, 16" l. **125-145**

Pendant, sterling & garnet, birds in nest pendant w/single garnet accent, 21" l. **50-70**

Pendant, sterling, openwork 1" pendant w/heart motif & leaf & vine design, 16" l. ... **45-65**

Pin, enamel & rhinestone, contemporary design of parrot in flight, its wings & tail of red, blue & green enamel, its body & wings trimmed w/clear pave rhinestones, unsigned, 5 x 5 1/4".............................. **125-150**

Pin, enamel & rhinestone, dragonfly design w/black & turquoise enamel body w/blue rhinestones set in head, signed "Hattie Carnegie," 2 1/4 x 3" **85-110**

Pin, gold plate & enamel, circle design w/iridescent green Christmas tree w/white enamel star attached, 1 3/8" d. **30-45**

Pin, gold plate, enamel & pearl, elephant w/red & green enamel saddle, a large cultured pearl on trunk, signed "Monet," 1 3/4 x 3".. **60-80**

Pin, gold plate, enamel & plastic, large & small white daisies w/raised yellow plastic centers, green leaf, signed "Weiss," 2 3/4" h. **50-75**

Pin, gold plate & glass, large elongated trapezoid-shaped olive green glass stones arranged in flower style, separated by citrine-colored stones, a hexagon-shaped yellow/green center stone, unsigned, 2 1/4" d. **75-100**

Pin, gold plate & glass, snail design w/ribbed jade green glass body, pavé rhinestone trim, signed "Panetta," 1 1/2" ... **55-75**

Pin, gold plate & rhinestone, Christmas tree set w/red, green, blue & clear rhinestones, 2".. **40-60**

Pin, gold plate, rhinestone & enamel, bird w/long tail on branch, red, blue & green enamel feathers, two rows of tiny clear rhinestones between wing & tail feathers, green rhinestone eye, 2" **40-60**

Sunburst Pin with Rhinestones

Pin, gold plate & rhinestone, medal-style, three-dimensional sunburst design w/four pear-shaped amber stones & four smaller pear-shaped black stones radiating from large amber center stone framed by eight smaller clear rhinestones, signed "Joan Rivers," 2 1/2" d. (ILLUS.)... **125-150**

Pin, gold plate, rhinestone, pearl & enamel, bird on branch w/iridescent blue & green enamel head & tail feathers, blue, green & red wings, the body set w/clear pavé rhinestones, green rhinestone eye, pearls & green enamel leaves on branch, signed "DJV Taiwan," 2"............................... **35-50**

Pin, gold plate & rhinestone, three-dimensional flower w/brushed gold petals & center rhinestones, in original box, signed "Coro" in block letters, ca. 1970, 2 1/4" d. **65-80**

Garnet-colored Rhinestone Pin

Pin, rhinestone, garnet colored marquise stones set in snowflake-style design, unsigned, 1 1/2 x 2" (ILLUS.) **60-85**

Pin, rhinestone, large handset Aurora Borealis stones in emerald, square & kite shapes w/large amber rhinestones in round, marquise & emerald cuts, Austria, 1 1/2 x 2 5/8" **75-100**

Pin in the Form of a Snake

Pin, white metal & glass, in the form of a snake, large oval purple stones & smaller round light blue stones set as flexible body of snake, fasteners w/antique finish forming its head & tail, unsigned, 7 3/4" l. (ILLUS.) **95-120**

Pin, white metal, marcasite & hematite, swirled design w/large hematite oval stone, smaller matching black rhinestones & two marcasite set swirls, West Germany, 1 x 1 1/2" **40-55**

Pin, white metal & rhinestone, center emerald-cut purple stone in frame of clear rhinestones w/side trim of pear-shaped purple stones, clear rhinestone accents, signed "McClelland Barclay," 1 1/4 x 2 1/2" **200-225**

Pin, white metal, rhinestone & opaline stones, floral spray set w/white opaline pear-shaped stones, trimmed w/round clear rhinestones, signed "Kramer," 2 1/2" **65-85**

Pin, white metal & rhinestone, snowflake design set w/large emerald green marquise stones in small clear round rhinestone borders, signed "Weiss," 2 1/2" d.. **80-110**

Sets

Cabochon & Marcasite Necklace & Earring Set

Necklace & earrings, French iridescent glass, marcasite & gold plate, the 16 1/2" necklace made of nine green oval mold-formed cabochons, each w/pontil mark on back, in ornate gold-plated settings filling front half of necklace, the back half of necklace a link chain w/18 large marcasites in cup settings; the matching 2 1/8" l. drop earrings each made of two green oval cabochons in ornate settings connected by gold-plated links, the set (ILLUS.) **250-275**

Necklace & earrings, rhinestone, 16" l. necklace w/three-dimensional squares set w/clear, citrine & grey rhinestones & clear baguette centers, 5/8" each, grey rhinestone chain; matching 3/4" sq. earrings, all signed "Hobé," the set **150-175**

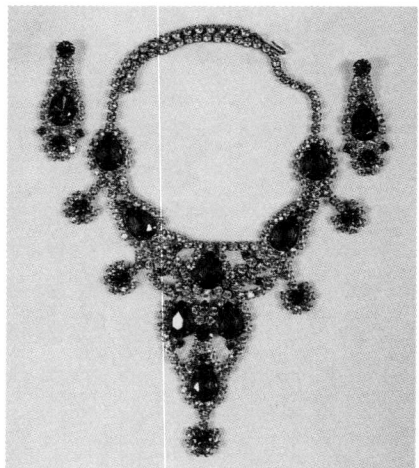

Dramatic Bib-style Necklace & Earrings

Necklace & earrings, rhinestone, the 16" bib-style necklace w/eight large 3/4" royal blue crystal pear-shaped stones in descending design w/clear floral accents w/matching blue centers, all on chain made of clear rhinestones; the matching 2 1/4" l. drop earrings w/blue pear-shaped & smaller blue round stones set in frame of clear rhinestones, unsigned, the set (ILLUS.)... **325-350**

Venetian Necklace & Earring Set

Necklace & earrings, Venetian art glass, the 17" necklace made of 13 large flat red circular beads w/gold flecks & much smaller cylindrical matching spacers; simple matching 1" d. earrings, the set (ILLUS.)... **75-100**

Pin & earrings, rhinestone, the 3" d. pin w/large round red crystal center stone surrounded by/row of smaller red rhinestones, a third row made up of blue ba-

guettes radiating from center w/red pear-shaped stones at ends, resembling candles; the matching 1 1/4" d. earrings w/blue center stones & alternating blue & red baguettes radiating from center, the set (ILLUS., bottom of page) **125-150**

Chatelaine-style Pin & Earring Set

Pin & earrings, white metal, faux turquoise, the 5" l. chatelaine-style pin w/two chains ending in white metal blackamoor heads w/filigree trim & round turquoise stones;

Red & Blue Pin & Earring Set

the matching 1" d. earrings in floral design w/turquoise stone centers, the set (ILLUS.) **65-85**

Pin & necklace, enamel on gold plate, the 2 5/8 x 3" pin w/three open iridescent purple & gold flowers w/clear rhinestone trim on petals in three-dimensional design; the 16" l. necklace w/single row of conforming flowers, chain ends, 1 1/4" w., unsigned, the set **145-170**

Modern (1920-1960s)

Platinum, Sapphire and Diamond Bar Pin

Bar pin, platinum, sapphire & diamond, Art Deco bezel, bead-set throughout w/sixty-six old European, French, baguette & single-cut diamonds, approx. total wt. 1.98 cts., rectangular and triangular-cut sapphire accents, millegrain accents & pierced gallery (ILLUS.) **3,055**

Bracelet, gold (14k), Retro-style, yellow gold oval links connected by domed half links alternating w/gadrooned pink gold links, European hallmark, 8 1/4" l. **489**

Bracelet, gold (18k bi-color) & diamond, Retro-style interlocking hexagonal links, clasp w/radiating elements, bead-set w/single-cut diamond highlights, 33.0 dwt., 7" l. **705**

Bracelet, gold (18k), gem-set, composed of flexible circular-cut emerald, sapphire, & full-cut diamond flore, signature & hallmarks for Van Cleef & Arpels France, ap-

prox. total diamond wt. 8.64 cts., 7" l., w/original box & receipt (ILLUS., bottom of page, top) **18,500**

Bracelet, gold (18k) & sapphire, rectangular links each w/gypsy-set oval-shaped pink sapphire, signed "RR" for Robin Rotenier, retailed by Bergdorf Goodman, 26.6 dwt., 6 3/4" l. **2,115**

Bracelet, platinum & diamond, Art Deco style composed of articulated geometric-form plaques set w/three marquise, four half-moon, ninety baguette, & 394 full & single-cut diamonds, approx. total wt. 11 cts., 7 1/4" l. (ILLUS., bottom of page, center) **22,913**

Bracelet, platinum, sapphire, & diamond, Art Deco style, articulated links w/channel-set calibre & square step-cut sapphires & bead-set old European, rose, & single-cut diamonds, approx. total wt. 3.34 cts., 7 1/4" l. (ILLUS., bottom of page, bottom) **11,163**

Brooch, diamond & gem-set, cascade of flexibly set cabochon ruby, faceted emerald, sapphire, aquamarine & old mine-cut diamond & champagne diamond blossoms, approx. total wt. 3.05 cts., interspersed w/engraved vines & leaves, 18k gold & platinum mount, made by Anna Bachelli **14,100**

Diamond and Sapphire Bow Brooch

Gold and Gem-set Bracelet

Platinum and Diamond Bracelet

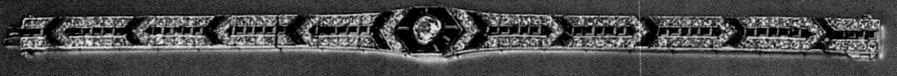

Art Deco Platinum & Diamond Bracelet

Brooch, diamond & sapphire, Art Deco-style bow, bead-set w/seventy-two old European & old single-cut diamonds weighing approx. 1.60 cts., edged by channel-set rectangular step-cut and calibre-cut sapphires, millegrain accents, platinum mount (ILLUS., previous page)... **6,463**

Gem-set and Enamel Bird Brooch

Brooch, gem-set & enamel, calibré-cut buff-top sapphire, emerald & ruby exotic bird & flowers mounted on meandering black enamel branch within circular frame bead-set w/seventy-six old European-cut diamonds weighing approx. 1.33 cts., platinum & gold mount, signed "E. Besson," ca. 1920s (ILLUS.)...................... **16,450**

Brooch, gold (18k), lapis & diamond, spray of three carved lapis flowers, each centering full-cut diamond melee clusters **1,763**

Art Deco Brooch

Brooch, platinum, diamond & onyx, bow-shaped Art Deco-style, bead-set w/110 old European & single-cut diamonds, channel-set French-cut onyx & millegrain accents, pierced gallery (ILLUS.)............... **4,230**

Pink Diamond and Ruby Dress Clip

Dress clip, pink diamond & ruby dress clip, Art Deco design, centered w/emerald-cut pink diamond weighing 1.90 cts. framed by square step-cut rubies, further enhanced by bead-set single-cut diamonds & two diamond baguettes weighing approx. 2.26 cts., square step-cut ruby accents, platinum mount, ca. 1930 (ILLUS.) **35,250**

Ruby & Diamond Dress Clips

Dress clips, platinum, ruby & diamond, five prong-set circular-cut rubies & sixty-one full-cut and baguette diamonds, approx. total wt. 4.48 cts., w/14k gold brooch attachment (ILLUS.) **5,875**

Art Deco Sapphire and Diamond Dress Clips

Dress clips, sapphire & diamond, Art Deco-style, bead-set w/seventy-two full & single-cut diamonds, channel-set, square, step & calibre-cut highlights, millegrain accents, platinum mount, w/brooch conversion, pr. (ILLUS.).................................... **3,173**

Earpendants, platinum, ruby & diamond, chandelier designed as cascade of flexibly set circular-cut rubies & full, marquise & pear-cut diamonds, platinum mount, signed "HW" for Harry Winston, pendants detachable **11,750**

Earrings, gold (14k bi-color) & gem-set earrings, designed as a cluster of yellow & rose gold blossoms, full-cut diamond & garnet accents, 7.4 dwt., pr. **558**

Locket, gold (14k), diamond & enamel, Art Deco-style, centered exotic bird in flight w/bead-set single-cut diamond body & ruby eye, black enamel background w/delicate white enamel border, opening to reveal two interior compartments, platinum bail.. **2,350**

Carnelian & Enamel Necklace

Necklace, carnelian & enamel, Art Deco design, five graduating floral carved & pierced carnelian plaques joined by bowform celadon green & black enamel links, seed pearl accents, 14k gold mount, partially obliterated hallmark for "Carter Howe & Gough," 16 1/2" l. (ILLUS., above).. **4,700**

Necklace, gold (18k) & diamond, open abstract-form links, each bezel-set w/full-cut diamonds, signed "C. Deneuve" for Catherine Deneuve, approx. total wt. 0.82 cts., 15" l. **1,410**

Pendant, silver & enamel, Art Deco-style, square plaque w/clipped corners surmounted by an urn & flower design on a green & black enamel ground, hallmark for David **1,725**

Pendant-brooch, platinum & diamond, Art Deco-style, oblong openwork form beadset w/fifty-seven old European & full-cut diamonds, total wt. 2.20 cts., detachable bail.. **2,468**

Pendant-brooch, platinum, diamond & emerald, Art Deco-style, openwork plaque set w/twenty-three old European- & single-cut diamonds & eighteen emerald & green stone accents, millegrain accents, deployant bail... **2,938**

Pendant-locket, platinum, diamond & faux green jade enamel, Art Deco-style oval locket w/millegrain platinum mount set w/three circular-cut diamonds, faux green jade "en plein" enamel surface **920**

Pendant-necklace diamond & platinum, Art Deco-style, detachable pendant centering a flexibly set faceted pear-shaped yellow diamond weighing approx. 9 cts., frame, bail & necklace further bezel & bead-set w/one marquise & 164 old mine & old European-cut diamonds weighing approx. 5.25 cts., millegrain accents, platinum mount, 16" l. (ILLUS.).............. **193,000**

Pendant-necklace, sterling silver, marcasite & glass baguettes, Art Deco-style, pierced rectangular pendant set w/carved blue & pink flowerheads over a row of clear glass baguettes, set throughout w/marcasites, completed by a baton-link chain, one marcasite missing, chain not silver, 32" l. **489**

Pin, jadeite & enamel, Art Deco-style, black, green & yellow enamel pagoda framing a pierced jadeite plaque depicting a bird among flowers, 14k gold mount, hallmark for Sloan & Co. **3,055**

Art Deco Sapphire and Diamond Pin

Pin, sapphire & diamond, Art Deco-style, bezel-set w/one faceted oval & two cushion-cut sapphires, w/forty-six old European & old mine-cut diamonds, approx. total wt. 1.88 cts., millegrain accents, platinum mount, French hallmark & guarantee stamps (ILLUS.)................................. **4,700**

Ring, diamond, Art Deco-style, box-set w/three old European-cut diamonds, gallery & shoulders pierced in a scroll design, platinum mount, size 6 .... **8,338**

Ring, diamond, Art Deco-style, set w/a pear-shaped solitaire diamond weighing approx. 2.35 cts. further set w/six straight baguettes, nine single- & six transitional-cut diamonds, platinum mount signed "Shreve & Co., no. B9550," size 8 .... **17,625**

Ring, diamond, Art Deco-style, set w/three old European-cut diamonds, approx. to-

Art Deco Diamond & Platinum Pendant

tal wt. .60 cts., within a pierced & engraved platinum mount set w/four single-cut diamonds, millegrain accents, size 6 3/4 .... **881**

Ring, diamond, Art Deco-style, transitional-cut solitaire diamond weighing approx. .94 cts. framed by 12 circular-cut diamonds, shoulders set w/six circular-cut diamonds, millegrain accents, incised shank, size 5 1/4 .... **2,350**

Ring, diamond & gold, Art Deco-style, 14k white gold filigree mount w/one marquise diamond, ca. 1920 .... **11,200**

Ring, diamond & onyx, Art Deco-style, navette-shaped onyx tablet bezel-set w/old European-cut diamond weighing approx. 2.89 cts., platinum & 18k gold mount, size 1 1/2 (evidence of solder) **6,169**

Ring, diamond & platinum, Art Deco-style, bezel-set cushion-shaped old mine-cut diamond weighing approx. .81 cts., framed by 18 old mine-cut diamonds, platinum openwork mount w/millegrain accents, size 5 3/4 .... **1,528**

Ring, diamond, yellow radiant-cut solitaire diamond weighing 1.64 cts. framed by ten faceted half-moon shaped diamonds weighing 2.13 cts., shoulders pavé-set w/twenty full-cut diamond melée weighing 0.31 cts., custom-made 18k white gold mount, size 7 1/2 .... **9,106**

Ring, emerald & diamond, Art Deco-style, 18k yellow gold silver washed crown holding center oval cabochon emerald surrounded by two rows of round diamonds flanked on each side by round diamonds, ca. 1930 .... **896**

Ring, gold (18k), diamond & platinum, Retro-style, two old European-cut & six single-cut diamonds vertically set in platinum tiered shoulders, size 6 .... **294**

Ring, platinum & diamond, centered w/European-cut diamond weighing approx. 1.19 cts., w/single-cut diamond highlights, millegrain accents, pierced gallery, size 6 1/2 .... **2,585**

Ring, sapphire & diamond, Art Deco-style, openwork pierced platinum mount w/millegrain accents centered by a collet-set circular-cut sapphire, framed by eight old mine-cut diamonds, size 6 1/2 .... **863**

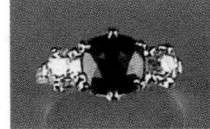

Sapphire & Diamond Ring

Ring, sapphire, diamond & platinum, prong-set w/cushion-cut sapphire weighing 3.01 cts. flanked by old mine-cut diamonds, approx. total diamond wt. 1 ct., open gallery, size 5 (ILLUS.) **4,406**

Ring, white gold (18k), sapphire & diamond, bezel-set w/sapphire cabochon flanked by swirls of pavé-set diamonds interspersed w/shaped lilac chalcedony plaques, approx. 12.48 x 9.65 x 5.90 mm, size 6, French hallmarks, marked "Van Cleef & Arpels, NY63876" **5,581**

Sets

Necklace & bracelet, gold (18 k), "Connections" necklace & bracelet designed as interlocking circles, signed "Paloma Picasso & Tiffany & Co.," w/original suede sleeve, necklace 16 1/2" l., bracelet 7 1/2" l., the set **2,233**

JUKE BOXES

Introduced in the late 1920s, juke boxes helped to put the "roar" into this era's end. Found mostly in bars and honky tonks, the bulky nickel-play device began mass production by the 1930s. Companies such as Wurlitzer, Seeburg, Rock-Ola and AMI competed in design, sound and bright lights.

By the 1940s and 1950s, juke boxes had transformed to more streamlined models and were now found in almost every soda shop & diner in the country.

With the coming of the stereo, fast-food establishments and urban renewal during the 1960s, juke box popularity began to decline. Today, the sounds of days-gone-by may still be heard in some cafes, bars and "50s" restaurants.

AMI Model 500, plays 78s, 1950s, 64" h. **$750**

Gabel Automatic Entertainer, upright paneled oak case, holds twenty 78 rpm records, 1930s, 36" h. **900**

Ristaucrat table model, simple design w/domed glass top, 5¢ play for 45 rpms, white plastic case w/a spinning record & music chords on the front, 1951 .... **700**

Seeburg diner console model, made to fit in diner booths, single play was 10¢, entire album was 25¢, aluminum cases, fairly common, 1950s **225**

Seeburg Model 100C, 100-selection, unrestored, working, 1952 .... **1,500**

Seeburg Model 148, "trash can" style, working, unrestored, 1948 .... **800**

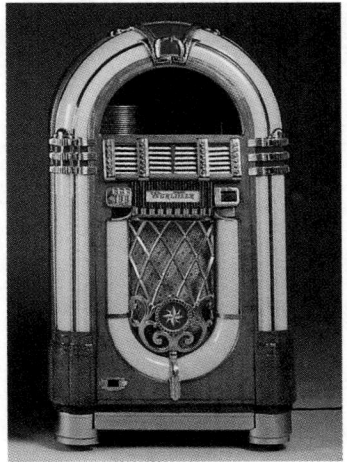

Wurlitzer Model 1015

Wurlitzer Model 1015, 24-selection, unrestored, working, 1946-1947
(ILLUS., previous page)................. **2,500 - 4,500**
Wurlitzer Model 61, table model, burl
wood, metal & red & white plastic.............. **1,900**

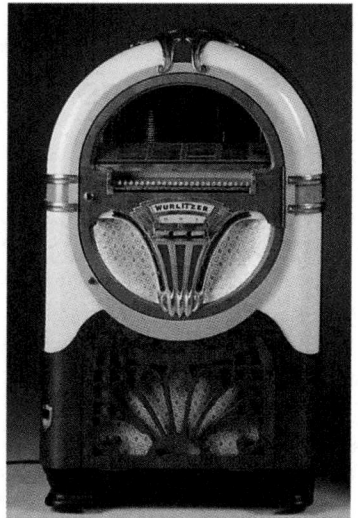

Wurlitzer Model 750

Wurlitzer Model 750, 24-selection, unrestored, working, 1941 (ILLUS.)................... **5,200**
Wurlitzer Model 800, 24-selection, unre-
stored, working, 1940 .... **6,500**
Wurlitzer Model 950, white tubing up sides,
colored arched light-up tubing at top
w/faun playing pipes, panels of leaping
gazelles flanking the cloth-covered
speaker panel, restored top condition,
1942 .... **29,000**

KITCHENWARES
Coffee Mills

Coffee mills, commonly called grinders, are perfectly collectible for many people. They are appealing to the eye and are frequently coveted by interior decorators and today's coffee-consuming homeowners. Compact, intricate, unique, ornate, and rooted in early Americana, coffee mills are intriguing to everyone and are rich and colorful.

Coffee milling devices have been available for hundreds of years. The Greeks and Romans used rotating millstones for grinding coffee and grain. Turkish coffee mills with their familiar cylindrical brass shells appeared in the 15th century, and perhaps a century or two later came the earliest spice and coffee mills in Europe. Primitive mills were handmade in this country by blacksmiths and carpenters in the late 1700s and the first half of the 19th century. These were followed by a host of commercially produced mills, which included wood-backed side mills and numerous kinds of box mills, many with machined dovetails or finger joints. Characterized by the birth of upright cast-iron coffee mills, so beautiful with their mag-

nificent colors and fly wheels, the period of coffee mill proliferation began around 1870. The next 50 years saw a staggering number of large and small manufacturers struggling to corner the popular home market for box and canister-type coffee mills. After that, the advent of electricity and other major advances in coffee grinding and packaging technology hastened the decline in popularity of small coffee mills.

Value-added features to look for when purchasing old coffee grinders include:
* *good working order and no missing, broken, or obviously replaced parts*
* *original paint*
* *attractive identifying markings, label or brass emblem*
* *uncommon mill, rarely seen, or appealing unique characteristics*
* *high quality restoration, if not original.*
—Mike White

Box Mills

Parker National Box Mill

Box mill, iron cover w/gear opening & crank
& sunken hopper, on wooden box w/pull-
out drawer in front, Parker National
(ILLUS.)... **$120**

*Logan & Strobridge Brighton No. 1180
Box Mill*

Box mill, iron crank & side handle on wood-
en box w/pull-out drawer in front, 1 lb. capacity, Logan & Strobridge Brighton No.
1180 (ILLUS.).. **180**

Decorative Moravian Box Mill

Box mill, raised brass hopper & crank, Moravian base & inlaid drawer, signed by maker (ILLUS.)... **250**

Norton Painted Tin Box Mill

Box mill, raised iron hopper & crank on tin canister w/picture of woman painted on front, drawer in back, patented Norton (ILLUS.) **600**

Arcade Favorite No. 357 Box Mill

Box mill, raised iron hopper w/patented partial cover design & crank on wooden box w/pull-out front drawer, Arcade Favorite No. 357 (ILLUS.)..................................... **100**

Side Mills

Kenrick Patented Side Mill

Side mill, iron, sliding cover, Kenrick patented, England (ILLUS.).................................. **120**

Peck Smith Mfg. Side Coffee Mill

Side mill, tin hopper on wood backing, brass emblem reads "Peck Smith Mfg." (ILLUS.).. **120**

Upright Mills

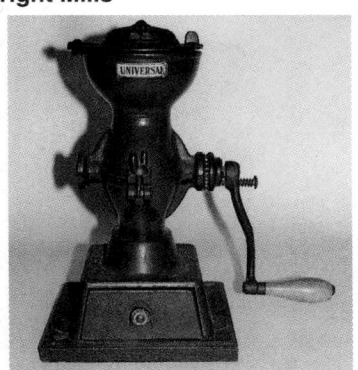

L.F. & C. Universal Coffee Mill

Upright mill, cast iron, L.F. & C. New Britain, Conn. Universal, overall green paint w/gold highlights, hand crank w/wooden grip, slide-out base drawer, mounted on wooden board, all-original & like new, late 19th c., 11 1/2" h. (ILLUS., previous page).. **440**

Miniature Upright Coffee Mill

Upright mill, cast iron, miniature model for children, two 2"-h. wheels, Arcade No. 7, rare, overall about 2 1/2" h. (ILLUS.)............. **350**

Coles No. 4 Upright Coffee Mill

Upright mill, cast iron, pivoting lid on hopper, two 12"-h. wheels, Coles No. 4 (ILLUS.).. **1,000**

Clawson & Clark No. 1 Upright Mill

Upright mill, cast iron, single wheel, cup, patented Clawson & Clark No. 1 model (ILLUS.)... **1,050**

Enterprise No. 7 Upright Coffee Mill

Upright mill, cast iron, w/17" wheels, pivoting cover on hopper, original red paint, decals & pin striping, 1898 patent date marked on grinding burrs, Enterprise #7 (ILLUS.).. **1,400**

Enterprise No. 4 Upright Coffee Mill

Upright mill, cast iron, w/nickel-plated brass hopper, 10 3/4" wheels, Enterprise No. 4 (ILLUS.).. **1,600**

Wall Canister Mills

One-of-a-Kind Wall Mill

Wall canister mill, cast iron, decorative design based on Ami Clark's 1833 patent, w/adjusting thumbscrew in back & two-sided grinding burr, only known example (ILLUS., previous page) **1,500**

Children's Ceramic Wall Canister Mill

Wall canister mill, ceramic, children's model, glass measure, "Cafe" on front, Europe, about 6" h. (ILLUS.) **450**

Douwe-Egberts Koffie Wall Mill

Wall canister mill, ceramic w/glass measure, marked on front "Douwe-Egberts Koffie," Europe (ILLUS.) **150**

Red Iron Clamp-on Wall Mill

Wall canister mill, iron, clamp-on type, w/pivoting lid, red, rare National Specialty No. 0 (ILLUS.) **28**

L.F. & C. Universal No. 24 Wall Mill

Wall canister mill, iron & glass, w/2-qt. jar, L.F. & C. Universal No. 24 (ILLUS.) **200**

Bronson-Walton Holland Beauty Wall Mill

Wall canister mill, litho-printed tin, decorated w/picture of woman in period clothing, Bronson-Walton Holland Beauty (ILLUS.) 550

Rare Hollis Telephone Wall Mill

Wall canister mill, wood, w/side crank, rare patented Hollis Telephone model (ILLUS.) 1,200

Egg Timers

A little glass tube filled with sand and attached to a figural base measuring between 3" and 5" in height was once a commonplace kitchen item. Although egg timers were originally used to time a 3-minute egg, some were used to limit the length of a telephone call as a cost saving measure.

Many beautiful timers were produced in Germany in the 1920s and later in Japan, reaching their heyday in the 1940s. These small egg timers were commonly made in a variety of shapes in bisque, china, chalkware, cast iron, tin, brass, wood or plastic.

Egg timers had long been considered an essential kitchen tool until, in the 1920s and 1930s, a German pottery company, W. Goebel, introduced figural egg timers. Goebel crafted miniature china figurines with attached glass vials. After the Great Depression, Japanese companies introduced less detailed timers. The Goebel figural egg timers are set apart by their trademark, delicate painting and distinctive clothes. It is best to purchase egg timers with their original tube, but the condition of the figure is most important in setting prices.

Black chef, ceramic, sitting w/arm up holding timer, variety of sizes, Germany **$85**

Black Chef with Fish Egg Timer

Black chef, ceramic, standing w/large fish, timer in fish's mouth, Germany, 4 3/4" h. (ILLUS.).. 125
Boy, ceramic, skiing pose, marked "Germany," 3" h... 50
Cat, ceramic, standing by base of grandfather clock, Germany, 4 1/2" h. 40
Chef, ceramic, winking, white w/black shoes & trim, turning figure on its head activates sand, 4" h... 40
Chick with cap, ceramic, Josef Originals............ 40
Chimney sweep, ceramic, Goebel, Germany 50

Chimney Sweep Egg Timer

Chimney sweep, ceramic, carrying ladder, Germany, 3 1/4" h. (ILLUS.) 50

Colonial lady with bonnet, ceramic, variety of dresses & colors, Germany, 3 3/4" h., each 50

Dog, ceramic, lustre ware, white w/brown ears & tail, Japan 75

Goebel Dutch Boy & Girl Egg Timer

Dutch boy & girl, ceramic, double-type, unknown modeler, timer marked w/3-, 4- & 5-minute intervals, Goebel, Germany, 1953 (ILLUS.) 95

Elephant, ceramic, white, sitting w/timer in upraised trunk, marked "Germany" 50

Elf by Well Egg Timer

Elf by well, ceramic, Manorware, England (ILLUS.) 35

Friar Tuck, ceramic, single, Goebel, Germany, 4" h. 50

Golliwog Egg Timer

Golliwog, bisque, England, 4 1/2" h., minimum value (ILLUS.) 150

Gollywog, ceramic, character-type, marked "FOREIGN" 125-150

Grandfather clock, composition, Manorware, England 45-55

House with clock face, ceramic, yellow & gold, Japan 40

Huckleberry Finn Egg Timer

Huckleberry Finn, ceramic, sitting in front of post, Japan (ILLUS.) 95-125

Leprechaun, glazed chalkware, sitting on wishing well, "Porkush" on front base, marked "Manorware," England 35

Leprechaun, shamrock on base, brass, Ireland, 3 1/4" h. 35

Little Girl On Phone Egg Timer

Little girl on phone, ceramic, Germany (ILLUS.) 95

Goebel Little Girl & Chick Egg Timer

Little girl with chick on her toes, ceramic, Goebel, Germany (ILLUS., previous page).. **100**
Newspaper boy, ceramic, Japan, 3 1/4" h. **50**

Rooster Egg Timer

Rooster, painted cut-out wood, w/sequins (ILLUS.).. **35**
Roosters, ceramic, double-type, modeled by Horst Ashermann, timer marked w/3-, 4- & 5-minute intervals, Goebel, Germany, 1953.. **85-100**
Sailboat, ceramic, lustre ware, tan boat w/white sails, Germany **75**
Sailor, ceramic, blue, Germany **50**
Santa Claus, ceramic, sitting, unmarked **50-75**
Santa Claus w/present, ceramic, Sonsco, Japan, 5 1/2" h.. **85**

Swami Egg Timer

Swami, ceramic, standing wearing turban, Germany (ILLUS.)... **110**

Windmill & Dog Egg Timer

Windmill, ceramic, w/dog on base, Japan, 3 3/4" h. (ILLUS.).. **75**
Woman in cap, composition, Josef Originals **25-45**

Kitchen Utensils

Apple peeler, cast iron, "Baldwin".................. **$125**
Apple peeler, cast iron, "F.W. Hudson Improved - Pat. Dec. 2, 1862"............................. **150**
Apple peeler, cast iron, marked only "Reading, PA" on turntable **200**
Apple peeler, cast iron, "Wiggin Pat. Aug. 4, 1868" (ILLUS., bottom of page)............. **1,000**
Butter churn, table model, all-tin, marked only "FRIES".. **85**
Butter churn, table model, cast iron frame w/tin container, "1 Gal. - Patented 130B Dazey Churn & Mfg. Co. St. Louis MO" cast in top of frame.. **650**
Butter churn, table model, cast iron & tin top w/glass jar, "Dazey No. 20 - Patented Feb 14, 22 - Dazey Churn & Mg. Co., St. Louis, MO Made in U.S.A."............................. **250**
Can opener, cast iron, marked "OK Pat 90 EWR," 7" l. **45**

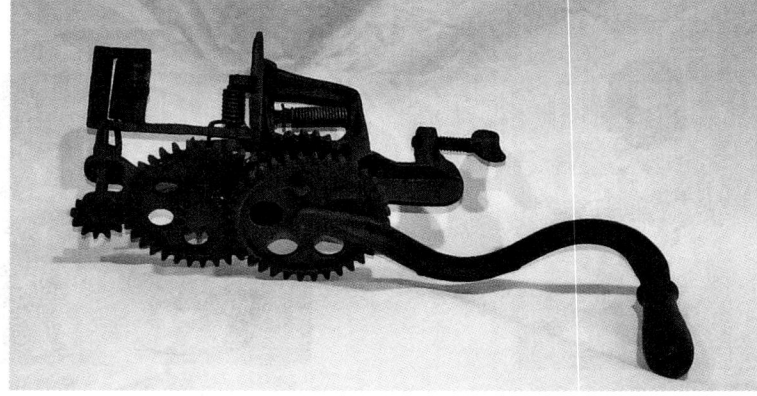

Rare Wiggin Apple Peeler

Can opener, cast-iron w/steel blade, figural bull's head, 7" l. 25

Can opener, cast-iron w/steel blade, marked "Pat Apl. 2 90," 5" l. 25

Cherry pitter, cast iron, standing on four legs, "Electric Cherry Seeder" 125

Cherry pitter, cast iron, standing on three legs, "Pat'd Nov 17, 1863". 200

Cherry pitter, nickel-plated cast iron, "New Standard Corp. Mt. Joy, PA. Pat. Pend. No. 50" in all caps. 35

Cookie cutter, early tin w/strap handle, double overlapping hearts, 2 1/2 x 4". 225

Cookie cutter, tin, w/advertising reading "Garland Stoves and Ranges - The World's Best," 2 3/4 x 3 3/4" 175

Egg beater, cast-iron top w/wire dashers & glass base, marked "New Keystone Beater No. 20 - North Bros. Pat Dec 15 '85" 350

Patented "Dover" Egg Beater

Egg beater, cast-iron w/tin dashers, cut-out letters "D-O-V-E-R" spelled out on the rotary wheel, also marked "Patented Feb. 9, 1904 - New Style" (ILLUS.). 175

Egg beater, cast-iron w/tin dashers, marked "Peerless Egg Beater - Patent Applied For". 1,000

Egg beater, cast-iron w/tin dashers, marked "Triumph Sept 26, 1876". 750

Egg beater, cast-iron w/tin dashers & stand, marked "Dover Egg Beater - Patd May 6th 1873 Apr. 3d 1888 Nov. 24th 1891". 200

Egg beater, metal w/vertical wooden handle, marked "Merry Whirl - Pat. 11-28-16 Other Pat. Pend." 20

Egg beater, water-powered, painted tin top w/decal reading "The World Beater Mfrd by the World Novelty Co. Elgin, Ill." 125

Egg beater on glass jar base, tin top w/slightly green glass jar, marked "Jiffy Cream Whip - Patented Dec. 12, 1922 - Kohler Die & Sp'lty Co. DeKalb, Ill U.S.A." 150

Egg scale, tin & aluminum, marked "Acme Egg Grading Scale Pat. June 24, 1924 - The Specialty Mfg. Co. St. Paul, Minnesota," 9 3/4" h. 30

Egg scale, tin, marked "H.L. Piper Montreal," four egg holes. 100

Egg separator, tin, advertising-type, "Compliments of Mothers Oats" 30

Egg separator, tin, advertising-type, "Use Big Jo Flour - Best in The World" 15

Flour sifter, tin w/wire handle, advertising-type, "Snow King Powder - 30 Years of Success," 3 1/2" d. plus handle. 50

Ice cream freezer, tin w/advertising, "Champion Triple Action - Brooklyn, NY," 8" d., 13" h. 200

Jar lid reformer, cast-aluminum w/wooden handle, round, marked "Miller Pattern Co. Toledo, Ohio," 3" d. 45

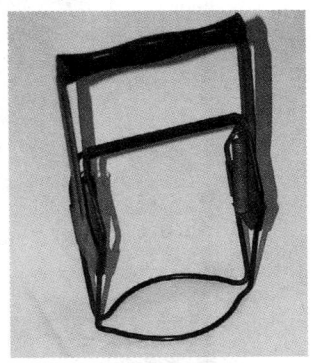

Tin & Wood Jar Lifter

Jar lifter, tin w/red wood handle, spring-operated, marked "Pat. Pend," 8 1/2" l. (ILLUS.). 25

Patented Iron Jar Opener

Jar opener, cast iron, very unusual screw clamp mechanism, marked "Pat June 18, 1888," 8 3/4" l. (ILLUS.). 150

Jar opener, steel w/tin strap, scissors-type, marked "Pat Feb 11, 1902," 7 3/4" l. 10

Jar opener, wood & steel w/spring-operated mechanism, marked "Ken Standard Corp. Evansville, Ind Jar Wrench Pat Pend," 6" d. 50

Jar opener, wood, tin & wire, marked "Off-On Jar Cap Remover - Detroit, Michigan

- Patented In Canada, Patent Pending in USA," 4" d. **75**
Knife sharpener, steel, combination can opener, marked "Lightning Sharpener," 5 1/2" l. **30**

Sammis Patented Lemon Reamer

Lemon reamer, cast iron, marked "EM Sammis - Pat Sept 21, 1876," 14" l. (ILLUS.) **500**
Lemon reamer, cast iron, marked "Pat Nov 21, 1885," 9 1/2" l. **25**

English Tin Acme Nut Grater

Nut grater, tin, half-round w/hanging hole at top, stamped "Acme Nut Grater Rd 114671," English (ILLUS.) **40**
Nutmeg grater, tin & wood, marked "Dec 25, 1877," 6 1/2" l. **125**

Rare Sterling Nutmeg Grater

Nutmeg grinder, sterling silver oval cylindrical case w/engine-turned design & hinged cover holding the grater, touch marks for Thomas Hall, Exeter, England, 1855-56, 1 1/4" w., 3" l. (ILLUS.) **275**
Pie crimper, brass w/a design on the handle, 6" l. **75**
Pie lifter, wire w/a red wood handle, paper label reads "Manufactured by W.M. Streets Wickenburg, Arizona," 14 3/4" l. **30**
Pie lifter, wire w/long turned black wood handle, an unusual wire lever top opening the wire grips, 12 1/2" l. (ILLUS., bottom of page) **75**
Pot scraper, grey graniteware, in the shape of a loaf of bread, advertising-type, marked "American Maid Bread" **250**
Raisin seeder, cast iron, marked "Enterprise Mfg. Co. Philadelphia, PA USA - Pat. Apr. 2, Aug. 20, 95 - Pat Apl'd For - Wet The Raisins - No. 36" **45**
Raisin seeder, cast iron, marked "Magic Factory Antrum NH - Patd Feb 13th 1894" **1,250**

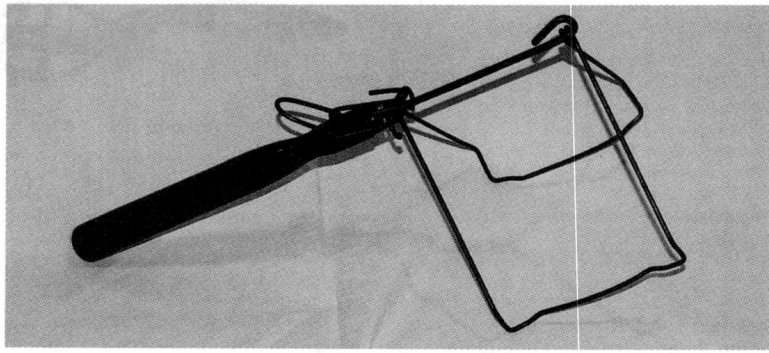

Unusual Wire & Wood Pie Lifter

Wooden Springerle Rolling Pin

Rolling pin, stoneware w/wooden handle, white w/three rust-colored bands at each end, 8" l. 250

Rolling pin, wooden, turned wood handles, the cylinder carved w/20 springerle designs in rows of blocks, early, overall 17" l. (ILLUS., top of page) 350

Rolling pin, yellowware pottery w/wooden handles, 8" l. 550

Tea strainer, tin, advertising-type, marked "Daniel Webster Flour - Better Than The Best" 20

Napkin Dolls

Until the 1990s, napkin dolls were a rather obscure collectible, coveted by only a few savvy individuals who appreciated their charm and beauty. Today, however, these late 1940s and 1950s icons of postwar America are hot commodities.

Ranging from the individualistic pieces made in ceramics classes to jeweled Japanese models and the wide variety of wooden examples, these figures are no longer mistaken as planters or miniature dress forms. Of course, as their popularity has risen, so have prices, putting smiles on the faces of collectors who got in on the ground floor and stretching the pocketbooks of those looking to start their own collections.

Bobbie Zucker Bryson is co-author, with Deborah Gillham and Ellen Bercovici, of the pictorial price guide Collectibles For The Kitchen, Bath & Beyond - Second Edition, published by Krause Publications. It covers a broad range of collectibles including napkin dolls, stringholders, pie birds, figural egg timers, razor blade banks, whimsical whistle milk cups and laundry sprinkler bottles. Bryson can be contacted via e-mail at Napkindoll aol.com.

Ceramic, figure of "Daisy," girl w/long brown braids wearing green dress, marked "Holland Mold," 7" h. **$75-100**

Ceramic, figure of girl w/red hair standing w/hands on hips wearing yellow dress & white bow in hair, Holland Mold H-730, 5" h. (ILLUS., top next column) **65-85**

Ceramic, figure of girl w/reddish brown hair wearing white dress w/large bow at waist & ruffled hem, neckline & cuffs, holding pink roses, bending over slightly so that back of full skirt holds napkins, 8" h. (ILLUS., bottom next column) **75-95**

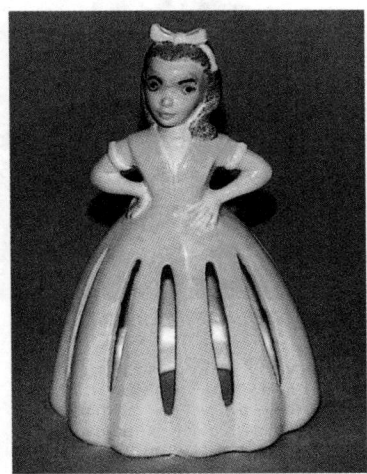

Holland Mold H-730 Napkin Doll

Girl with Roses Napkin Doll

Ceramic, figure of Santa Claus, wearing red & white suit & hat, white beard, slits in rear for napkins, holes in hat for toothpicks, marked "Japan," 6 3/4" h. **100-150**

Holt Howard "Sunbonnet Miss"
Napkin Holder

Ceramic, figure of "Sunbonnet Miss," girl wearing yellow dress w/white ruffled neckline & yellow picture hat trimmed w/pink rose, the hat serving as candle-holder, marked "Holt Howard 1958," 5" h. (ILLUS.) **125-150**

Napkin Doll from Puerto Rico

Ceramic, figure of woman w/black hair standing w/hands folded in front, wearing white dress w/pink bodice & hem, elbow-length gloves, front of skirt marked in gold "Arecibo Puerto Rico 1990," 12 1/2" h. (ILLUS.).. **45-65**

Napkin Doll on Leafy Base

Ceramic, figure of woman w/black braids wearing light blue knee-length skirt & white top w/molded stays & blue cuffs, standing on leaf-covered base, one hand on hip, the other raised to head, 15" h. (ILLUS.) **125-150**

Woman with Umbrella Napkin Doll

Ceramic, figure of woman w/black hair wearing lavender skirt & purple blouse w/gilt buttons & collar, purple hat, holding green unfurled umbrella behind back, slits in skirt for napkins, 10 3/4" h. (ILLUS.) **90-110**

Ceramic, figure of woman w/brown hair in colonial style, wearing yellow dress trimmed in white & decorated in gold fur-like trim, w/matching hat forming candle-holder, gold-gloved hands in matching white & gold muff, marked "Kreiss and Company," 10 1/4" h. **95-110**

Woman with Bowl Napkin Holder

Ceramic, figure of woman w/brown hair in pigtails wearing white dress w/blue flowers at hem, pink lace trim at neckline & cuffs, black bodice, standing w/one hand on hip, the other holding large bowl, 9" h. (ILLUS.) **75-85**

Red & White Napkin Doll

Ceramic, figure of woman w/brown hair wearing vivid red full-skirted coat w/white fur-like trim, hat & muff, white gloves, 11" h. (ILLUS.) **80-95**

Pink Ceramic Napkin Doll

Ceramic, figure of woman w/colonial-style hairdo, wearing period dress & holding large picture hat at side, all pink, marked "USA" on bottom, 12" h. (ILLUS.) **50-60**

Colonial Woman Napkin Doll

Ceramic, figure of woman w/colonial-style yellow hair, dressed in pink, white & yellow period dress trimmed in gold w/bell sleeves, ink mark reads "Japan," 9" h. (ILLUS.) **75-85**

Napkin Doll Holding Bowl on Head

Ceramic, figure of woman w/short brown hair, wearing blue dress w/short puffy sleeves & black trim & decorated w/flowers on skirt, both hands raised to hold large bowl on head, marked "Japan," 9 1/4" h. (ILLUS.) **50-65**

Napkin Doll/Toothpick Holder

Ceramic, figure of woman wearing pink dress & black & pink wide-brimmed hat,

holding white toothpick holder at each side, marked "4059," 9 1/2" h. (ILLUS.) **60-75**

Ceramic, figure of woman wearing white dress w/green decoration & gold necklace, a gold shoe peeking out from under skirt, 9 1/2" h. **95-125**

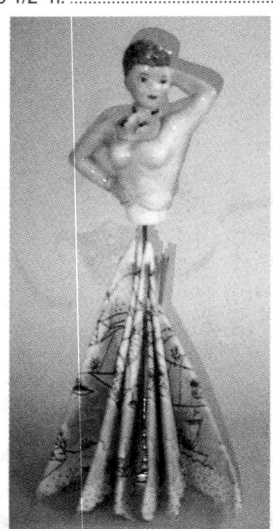

German Half-doll Napkin Holder

Ceramic, half-doll type, figure of woman w/red ponytail wearing pale shirt & yellow polka-dot scarf at neck, posing w/one hand at waist, the other behind head, on metal stand w/wires to hold napkins, Germany, 9 1/4" h. (ILLUS.) **150-175**

Umbrella-form Napkin Holder

Chrome, umbrella, wire holder forms umbrella when napkins are placed in it, on metallic red disk base, comes w/red, white & blue napkins, 9" h. (ILLUS., previous page) **15-35**

Metal Umbrella Napkin Holder

Metal, umbrella, wire holder forms umbrella when napkins are placed in it, comes w/original red napkins & box that reads "Porte Serviettes" & "Napkin Holder," Canada, 9 1/2" h. (ILLUS.) **30-40**

Metal & Plastic Napkin Holder

Metal & plastic, umbrella, red & white holder on silver-tone circular base w/white-dotted red plastic pouches near bottom that hold napkins to form umbrella, 11" h. (ILLUS.) **15-20**

Wood, figure of woman on wooden base, red, w/jointed arms, wearing picture hat & holding yellow wooden bucket, marked "G. Fried, Peplerhandlig Newer Market, Ges. Gesch.," 11 1/5" h. **50-60**

Green Painted Wood Napkin Doll

Wood, figure of woman w/disproportionately short jointed arms wearing dark green dress w/narrow skirt & white vest, dark green brimmed hat, 10 1/2" h. (ILLUS.)..... **40-50**

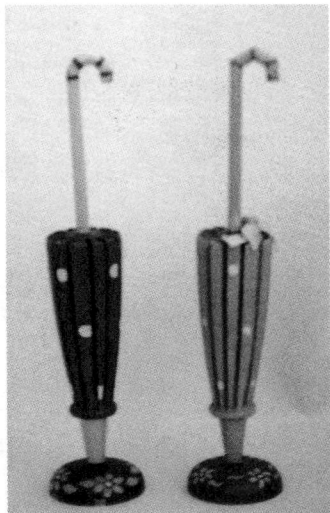

Umbrella Napkin Holders

Wood, model of umbrella, blue w/polka dots, tan cane-form handle, on circular base w/floral decoration, 8 1/2" h. (ILLUS. right w/red umbrella)...................... **25-35**

Wood, model of umbrella, red w/polka dots, tan cane-form handle, on circular base w/floral decoration, 8 1/2" h. (ILLUS. left w/blue umbrella, previous page) 25-35

Wooden Dutch Girl Napkin Holder

Wood, two-dimensional half-figure of woman w/yellow braids in white Dutch-style hat, wearing red shirt w/white sleeves & yellow waist, on red & yellow circular base, 9 3/4" h. (ILLUS.) 20-25

Pie Birds

A pie bird can be described as a small, hollow device, usually between 3-1/2" to 6" long, glazed inside and vented from the top. Its function is to raise the crust of a pie to allow steam to escape, thus preventing juices from bubbling over onto the oven floor while providing a flaky, dry crust.

Originally, in the 1880s, pie birds were funnel-shaped vents used by the English for their meat pies. Not until the turn of the 20th century did figurals appear, first in the form of birds, followed by elephants, chefs, etc. By the 1930s, many shapes were found in America.

Today the market is flooded with many reproductions and newly created pie birds, usually in many whimsical shapes and subjects. It is best to purchase from knowledgeable dealers and fellow collectors.

Advertising, "Kirkbrights China Stores Stockton on Tees," ceramic, white, England $75
Advertising, "Lightning Pie Funnel England," ceramic, white, England 75-120
Advertising, "Paulden's Crockery Department Stretford Road," ceramic, white, England 70
Advertising, "Roe's Patent Rosebud," ceramic, England, 1910-30 55-65
Advertising, "Rowland's Hygienic Patent," ceramic, England, 1910-30 55-65
Advertising, "Sequel...Porcelain," ceramic, white, England 50

Advertising, "The Gourmet Crust Holder & Vent, Challis' Patent," ceramic, white, England 100
Advertising, "The Grimmage Purfection Pie Funnel," ceramic, England, 1910-30 ... 55-65
Bird, ceramic, black on white base, yellow feet & beak, Nutbrown, England 50

Bird on Log Pie Bird

Bird, ceramic, black, perched on log, England (ILLUS.) 50
Bird, ceramic, Camark Pottery, Camden, Ark., ca. 1950s-60s, 6 1/2" h. 195

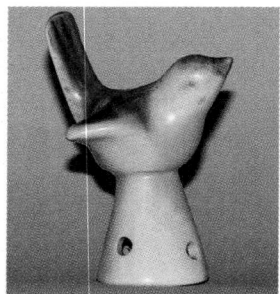

Half-doll Style Pie Bird

Bird, ceramic, half-doll style, blue & yellow on conical base, USA (ILLUS.) 275
Bird, ceramic, "Midwinter," black, England.... 50-60

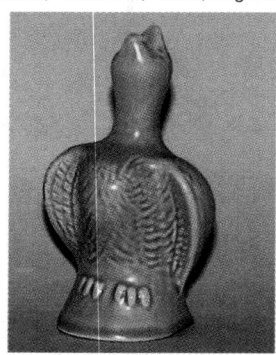

Sunglow Pie Bird

Bird, ceramic, Sunglow, tan glaze, England (ILLUS., previous page) **95**
Bird, ceramic, w/flowers, Chic Pottery, ca. 1930s-60s, hard to find **195**
Bird, pottery, "Scipio Creek Pottery, Hannibal, MO" **25**

Bird on Nest Pie Bird

Bird on nest w/babies, ceramic, Artisian Galleries, Fort Dodge, Iowa (ILLUS.) .... **500+**
Black chef, ceramic, full-figured, green smock, "Pie-Aire," USA **185**

Jackie Sammond Pie Bird & Owl

Blackbird, ceramic, 3" h., Jackie Sammond, early 1970s (ILLUS. right with owl) **150**
Blackbird, ceramic, England **20-30**
Blackbird, ceramic, for child's pie, 2 3/4" **150**

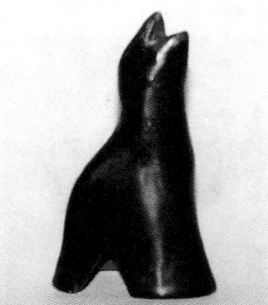

Stylized English Blackbird

Blackbird, ceramic, simple stylized shape w/brown beak, ca. 1930s-40s, English (ILLUS.) **125**

Very Large Black Pie Bird

Blackbird, ceramic, very large, 2 1/2" w x 5" h., English (ILLUS.) **150**
Blackbird, ceramic, w/yellow trim on brown base **85**

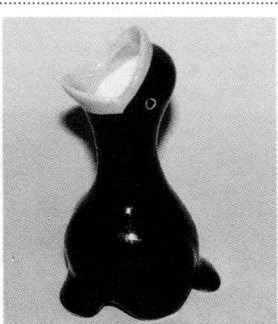

Wide-Mouth Blackbird

Blackbird, ceramic, wide mouth, yellow beak, fat, English (ILLUS.) **235**
Blackbird, clay w/black & yellow glaze, ca. 1960s-70s **65-75**
Blackbird, red clay w/black glaze, ca. 1930s-40s **75-85**
Bluebird, ceramic, Japan, post-1960 .... **50**
Chef, ceramic, "A Lorrie Design, Japan," Josef Originals, 1980s **125**

"Benny the Baker" Pie Bird

Chef, ceramic, "Benny the Baker," w/tools & box, Cardinal China Co., USA (ILLUS., previous page) **175**
Chef, ceramic, half-figure, all-white, England **90**

"Pie-Aire" Chefs

Chef, ceramic, "Pie-Aire," solid color, green, red or yellow, each (ILLUS.) **175**
Chef, ceramic, "Servex Oven China, Bohemia, Guaranteed Heatproof, RD 17494 Aus., RD 4098 N.Z.," Australia, 4 5/8" h. **150**
Cherry, apple & peach, ceramic, ca. 1950s, in original box, set of three **500-600**

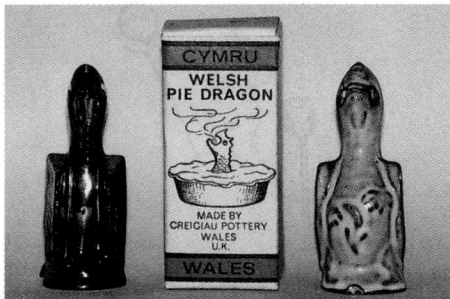

Chick with Dust Cap

Chick, ceramic, w/dust cap, Josef Originals (ILLUS.) **95**
Chick, ceramic, yellow w/pink lips, Josef Originals **55**

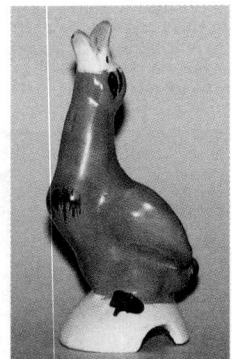

Brown English Duck Pie Bird

Duck, ceramic, brown w/white & yellow beak, black trim, white base, England (ILLUS.) **100**
Duck, ceramic, pink, blue or yellow, full-bodied, USA, each **75**
Duck head, ceramic, pink, England **125**

Dutch Girl Multipurpose Pie Bird

Dutch girl, ceramic, doubles as pie vent, measuring spoon holder and/or receptacles for scouring pads & soap, Cardinal China, rare (ILLUS.) **125-150**
Dwarf Dopey, ceramic, Disney **500**

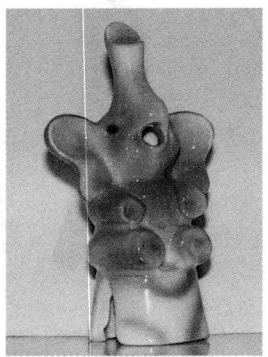

Welsh Dragon Pie Birds

Dragon, ceramic, Creiciau Pottery, Wales, United Kingdom, each (ILLUS.) **195**

Elephant Pie Bird

Elephant, ceramic, grey & pink w/swirled pink base, Cardinal China Co., USA (ILLUS., previous page)................................. **250**
Elephant, ceramic, white, ca. 1930s **200**

Granny Pie Baker

Granny, ceramic, "Pie Baker," figure of woman holding bowl, Josef Originals (ILLUS.) **95**

Luzianne Mammy Pie Baker

Luzianne Mammy, ceramic, black woman dressed in yellow shirt & green skirt, carrying a red tray w/coffee service, white turban on head (ILLUS.) **150**
Mammy, ceramic, doubles as pie vent, measuring spoon holder, and/or receptacles for scouring pads & soap **85-100**
Mammy, ceramic, outstretched arms, USA **95**

Josef Originals Owl

Owl, ceramic, "A Lorrie Design, Japan," Josef Originals, 1980s (ILLUS.) .... **300+**
Owl, ceramic, Jackie Sammond, USA. ca. 1970s (ILLUS. left with blackbird, page 767)... **150**

Peasant Woman Pie Baker

Peasant woman, ceramic, brown glaze, 1960s-70s (ILLUS.) **125**

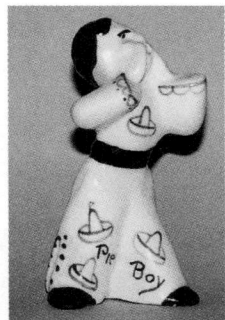

Rare Pie Boy Pie Bird

"Pie Boy," ceramic, Squire Pottery of California, USA, rare (ILLUS.) .... **500+**
"Pie Chef," ceramic, Josef Originals **95**
"Pie-Chic," ceramic, given as premium in Pillsbury Flour, USA **55**
Rooster, ceramic, white & black w/red comb, brown base, Marion Drake.............. **65-85**
Rooster, ceramic, white w/tan trim, Pearl China, USA **150-250**

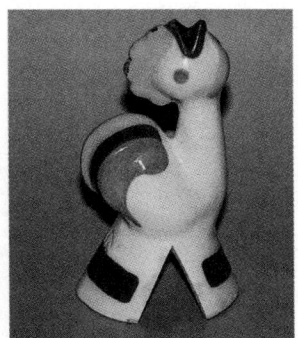

"Patrick" Pie Bird

Rooster "Patrick," ceramic, many color variations, California Cleminson, USA, each (ILLUS., previous page).................... **50-75**

Songbird

Songbird, ceramic, beige, blue & pink variations, USA, each (ILLUS.)............................ **50**

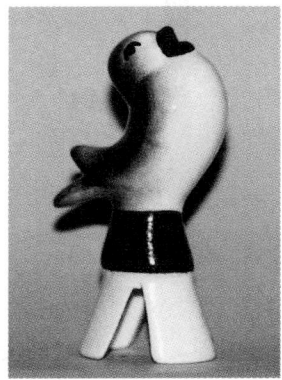

Puff-chested Pie Bird

Songbird, ceramic, lavender & brown trim, puff-chested, ca. 1940s (ILLUS.) **275**
Unusual pie vent, ceramic, "The Bleriot Pie Divider," white, 1910-20.............................. **300+**
Yankee pie bird, ceramic, Millford, New Hampshire, ca. 1960s................................. **40-50**

Reamers

Reamers are a European invention dating back to the 18th century. Devised to extract citrus juice as a remedy for scurvy, by the 1920s they became a must in every well-equipped American kitchen. Although you can still purchase inexpensive glass, wood, metal and plastic squeezers in today's kitchen and variety stores, it is the pre-1950s models that are so highly sought after today. Whether it's a primitive wood example from the late 1800s or a whimsical figural piece from post-World War II Japan, the reamer is one of the hottest kitchen collectibles in today's marketplace - Bobbie Zucker Bryson

Boat-shaped Ceramic Reamer

Ceramic, boat-shaped, white w/gilt line trim, decorated w/rust-colored leaves & navy blue, small loop handle, 3 1/2" h. (ILLUS.).. **$65-85**

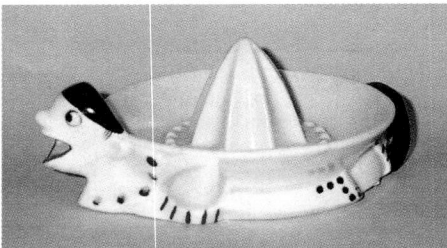

Prone Clown Reamer

Ceramic, figure of clown lying supine, the open mouth forming the spout, white w/yellow, red, blue & black trim, incised "6358," 4" d. (ILLUS.) **150-185**

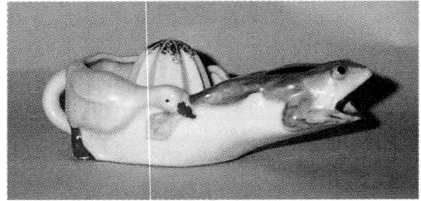

Goose Chasing Frog Reamer

Ceramic, model of green frog chased by white goose, the open-mouthed frog forming the spout, the goose forming the side of the saucer, embossed "Made in Japan," 1 3/4" h. (ILLUS.) **150-175**

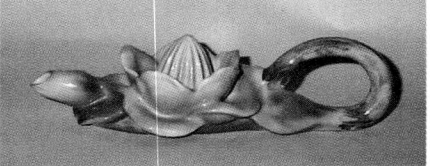

Reamer in the Form of a Rose

Ceramic, model of rose, pink flower on green leaves, stem forming handle, a rosebud forming the spout, marked "Erphila Germany," 1 3/4" h. (ILLUS.) **200-250**

Leaf-form Reamer

Ceramic, saucer shape, in the form of a green leaf holding the yellow cone, 4" d. (ILLUS.) **30-35**

Pink Ceramic Teapot-style Reamer

Ceramic, teapot-style, pink, marked "Jiffy Juicer, US Pat. 2,130,755, Sept. 2, 1938," 5 1/4" h. (ILLUS.) **85-100**

Bucket-style Reamer

Ceramic, two-piece, bucket-style, tan w/embossed cherub, flowers & decorative panels, green trim, rattan handle, marked "Made In Japan, Pat. 49541," 7 3/4" h. (ILLUS.) **75-95**

Reamer in the Form of Amish Man

Ceramic, three-piece, figural Amish man, black pants, green shirt, yellow cone top & hat, marked "JCC, NRCA, PA-1996," 5 1/2" h. (ILLUS.) **40-50**

Ceramic, three-piece, figural elephant w/trunk raised, large ears w/yellow, green & brown design, cane handle, 7" h. **250-300**

Figural Cat Ceramic Reamer

Ceramic, two-piece, figural cat w/stylized blue & white face, pink bow tie, yellow & white top, handle w/finger grips, 5 1/4" h. (ILLUS.) **65-85**

Ceramic, two-piece, figural chef lying on his back, white w/blue, black shoes, yellow pants, white cone, turquoise & black trim, 2 1/2" h. **275-350**

Green & White Clown Reamer

Ceramic, two-piece, figural clown, green body w/green & white cone hat, small loop handle, marked "Made in Japan," 4 1/2" h. (ILLUS.) **50-65**

Ceramic, two-piece, figural clown, white pitcher bottom w/black & orange stripes, orange collar, orange & black cone hat, 6 1/2" h. **85-95**

Ceramic, two-piece, figural clown, white w/green polka-dot body, green & black collar, black feet, brown hands, blue & white cone hat, loop handle, marked "Made In Japan," 7" h. **85-95**

Ceramic Mouse Reamer

Ceramic, two-piece, model of mouse, grey body w/pink ears & stylized smiling face, cone hat in dark blue & white, limited edition, 4 1/2" h. (ILLUS.) **45-55**

Ceramic Snail Reamer

Ceramic, two-piece, model of snail, beige shell w/rust-colored dots, green body & cone, open-mouthed head forms spout, 4 1/2" h. (ILLUS.) **50-65**

Ceramic Two-piece Pitcher Reamer

Ceramic, two-piece, pitcher-style, light pink w/green trim & multicolored flowers, marked "Pantry BAK-IN by Ware, Crooksville," 8 1/4" h. (ILLUS.) **100-135**

LaVerne Hemmers Reamer

Ceramic, two-piece, teapot-style, decorated w/lavender & purple flowers on pink ground, marked "1990 LaVerne Hemmers," 5" h. (ILLUS.) **20-30**

Ceramic Floral-decorated Reamer

Ceramic, two-piece, teapot-style, decorated w/pink, blue & orange flowers & black leaves on white ground, deep orange lustre rim band & handle, black line trim, orange lustre & white top, marked "Japan," 4 3/4" h. (ILLUS., previous page) **60-70**

Blue & Yellow Clown Reamer

Ceramic, two-piece, teapot-style, figural clown, white body w/blue vest & cone dotted w/yellow, yellow ruffled collar, 7 3/4" h. (ILLUS.) **65-85**

Fenton Blue Milk Glass Reamer

Glass, blue milk glass, ovoid shape w/tiny spout, loop handle & disk base, Fenton Art Glass Co., 6 3/8" h. (ILLUS.) **3,000-3,800**

Glass Reamer on Pedestal Base

Glass, boat-shaped, clear, long spout, C-form handle, on short pedestal base, 3 1/4" h. (ILLUS.) **50-55**

Saunders Black Glass Reamer

Glass, round shape w/pointed cone, black, angled handle, marked "Saunders Reamer Pat. Appl'd For," 6 1/8" d. (ILLUS.)... **1,750-2,000**

Green Hazel Atlas Glass Reamer

Glass, saucer-style, green, crisscross line pattern, Hazel Atlas Glass Co., 6 1/8" d. (ILLUS.).. **25-35**

Pink Glass Reamer

Glass, saucer-style, pink, w/star & heart design, tab handle, 4 7/8" d. (ILLUS.) **60-75**
Metal, handheld model, Foley, 8 1/4" l. **2-4**

Meriden Silver Plate Reamer

Silver plate, two-piece, teapot-style, marked "Meriden S.P. Co. International S. Co.," 5 1/8" h. (ILLUS., previous page).. **100-125**

Silver plate, two-piece, teapot-style, marked "T&T - Hand Hammered," 4" h... **125-150**

Stainless Steel Lemon Slice Squeezer

Stainless steel, hinged lemon slice squeezer type, 5" l. (ILLUS.).. **6-8**

Gorham Sterling Silver Reamer

Sterling silver, saucer shape, open tab handle, marked "Black Starr - Gorham Sterling 908," 4 1/4" d. (ILLUS.)............ **225-275**

String Holders

String holders were standard equipment for general stores, bakeries and homes before the use of paper bags, tape and staples became prevalent. Decorative string holders, mostly chalkware, first became popular during the late 1930s and 1940s. They were mass-produced and sold in five-and-dime stores like Woolworth's and Kresge's. Ceramic string holders became available in the late 1940s through the 1950s. It is much more difficult to find a chalkware string holder in excellent condition, while the sturdier ceramics maintain a higher quality over time.

Betty Boop, chalkware, original **$250**
Bird in birdcage, chalkware **95**

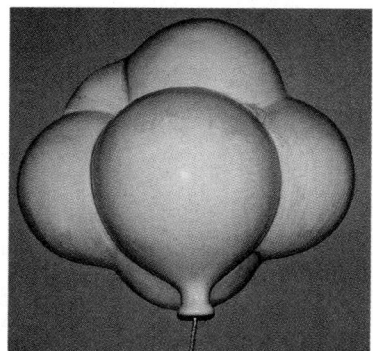

Bunch of Balloons String Holder

Bunch of balloons, ceramic, green, pink & blue, ca. 1983, Fitz & Floyd (ILLUS.) **50**

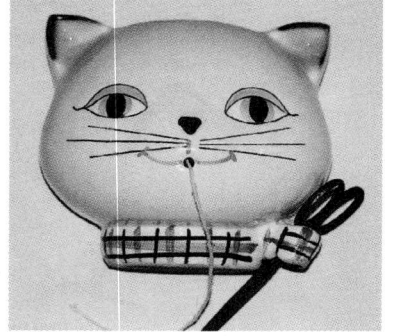

Holt Howard Cat String Holder

Cat, ceramic, head w/scissors held in plaid neck ribbon, Holt Howard (ILLUS.).................. **40**

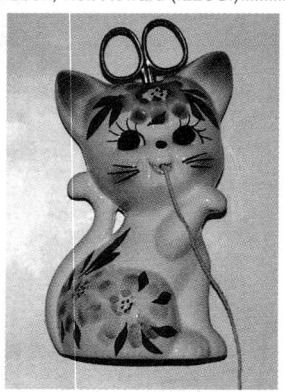

Cat with Flowers String Holder

Cat w/flowers, ceramic, scissors in head (ILLUS.).. **45**
Chef, chalkware, black face, white hat **200**
Chef, chalkware, chubby-faced, "By Bello, 1949," rare **350**
Chef, chalkware, common **60**
Chef, chalkware, "Little Chef," Miller Studio....... **150**
Chef, chalkware, unusual version of chef w/bushy eyebrows **85**

Bunch of Cherries String Holder

Cherries, chalkware, bunch on leafy stem
(ILLUS., previous page)................................... **95**
Chicken, ceramic, unmarked **40-50**
Chicken, ceramic, yellow & green w/red
trim, scissors in tail, France **95-125**
Chipmunk, ceramic **35-45**

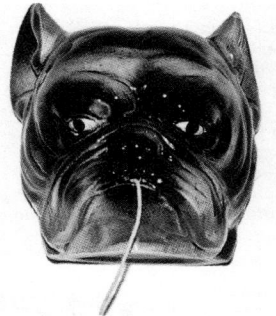

Ceramic Boxer String Holder

Dog, ceramic, Boxer (ILLUS.) **95**
Dog, ceramic, Collie, "Royal Trico," Japan.......... **95**

Shaggy Dog String Holder

Dog, ceramic, full-figured Shaggy Dog,
w/scissors as glasses, marked "Babba-
combe Pottery, England" (ILLUS.).................. **35**
Dog, ceramic, German Shepherd, "Royal
Trico, Japan"... **95**

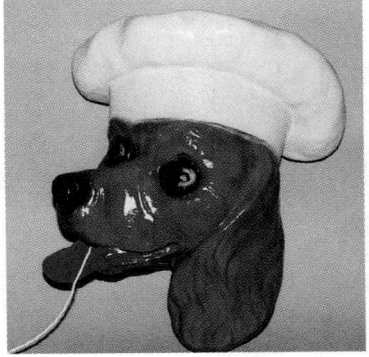

Dog with Chef's Hat

Dog, chalkware, w/chef's hat, "Conovers
Original" (ILLUS.).. **175**
Dog, chalkware, Westie, bow at neck **200**
Dove, ceramic, Japan.. **35**
Dutch Girl, chalkware, face only, common **60**
Dutch Girl, chalkware, head only, w/large
hat... **65-95**
Elephant, ceramic, "Hoffritz, England" **50**
Elephant, ceramic, marked "Babbacombe
Pottery, England," scissors as glasses **35**
Funnel-shaped, w/thistle or cat & ball, ce-
ramic... **85**
Ladybug, chalkware.. **95**
Lovebirds, ceramic, Morton Pottery **65**
Maid, ceramic, Sarsaparilla, 1984 .... **85**

Full-figure Mammy String Holder

Mammy, ceramic, full-figured, plaid & polka
dot dress, Japan (ILLUS.) **125-175**
Mammy, chalkware, head only, w/polka-dot
bandana, marked "Genuine Rockalite,"
made in Canada **250**
Man, chalkware, head only, marked across
collar "Just a Gigolo" **85**

Common Mexican Man Holder

Mexican man, chalkware, head only, com-
mon (ILLUS.).. **60**

Monkey on Ball of String Holder

Monkey, chalkware, sitting on ball of string, found in various colors (ILLUS.) **165**

Mouse, ceramic, countertop-type, Josef Originals sticker **55-75**

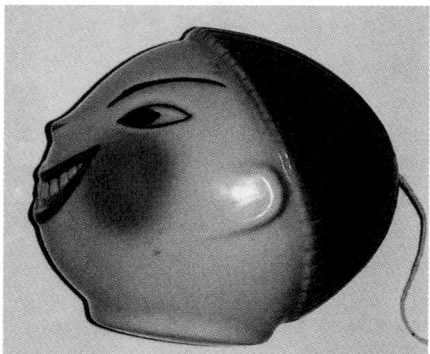

Oriental Man String Holder

Oriental man, ceramic, w/coolie hat, Abingdon Pottery (ILLUS.) **400**

Pear, chalkware **55**

Soldier, chalkware, head only, w/hat **75**

Teapot, ceramic, w/parakeet, Japan **75**

Teddy Bear String Holder

Teddy bear, ceramic, brown, hole for scissors in bow at neck, marked "Babbacombe Pottery, England" (ILLUS.) **35**

Tomato chef, ceramic, eyes closed, "Japan" **95**

Young black girl, ceramic, w/surprised look, Japan **175**

Tea Serving Accessories

People around the world have been drinking tea for centuries, and the brewing of the perfect cup has long been considered an art form. Tea balls, or infusers as they're sometimes called, were used to hold loose tea and hung into the pot or cup to properly steep. Most of the pieces came with a bottom or tray to catch the residual drips of water and tea. When tea bags came into common use and the potential of tea stains persisted, the decorative tea strainer was put into service as an acceptable receptacle even at the most elegant tables.

Tea Strainer with Roses & Heavy Gold

Ceramic, two-part tea strainer, white w/large deep rose red & pink h.p. roses & green leaves w/heavy bands of gold trim, 5" l., 1 1/2" h. (ILLUS.) **$40-55**

Tea Strainer with Blue Flowers

Ceramic, two-part tea strainer, white w/small dark blue flowers & blue border, 5" l., 1 1/2" h. (ILLUS.) **25-30**

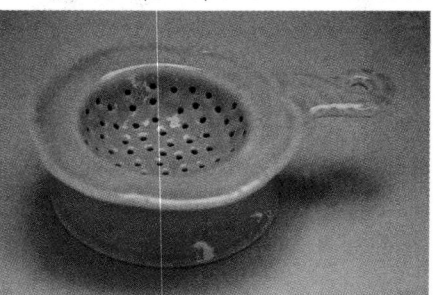

Celadon Green Tea Strainer

Ceramic, two-piece tea strainer, celadon green glaze, marked "Made in Japan," 6" l., 1 1/2" h. (ILLUS., previous page)....... 40-50

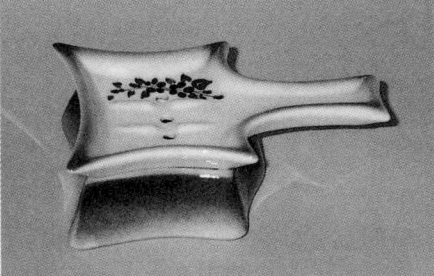

California-made Painted Tea Strainer

Ceramic, two-piece tea strainer, the squared top w/pointed corners & a rectangular tab handle resting on a conforming flaring base, dark blue trim, small h.p. red blossoms & green leaves on the top, marked "Decora Ceramics Handpainted California," 4" l., 1 1/2" h. (ILLUS.).............. 15-20

Pansy-shaped Ceramic Tea Strainer

Ceramic, two-piece tea strainer, the top molded as a pansy blossom in purple, yellow & pink w/a green leaf handle, white base, marked "Made in Japan," 4" l., 1 1/4" h. (ILLUS.) 15-20

Cobalt-trimmed Tea Strainer

Ceramic, two-piece tea strainer, white w/cobalt blue scalloped border trim & h.p. small blue flowers & green leaves, marked "Made in Japan," 6 1/8" l., 2" h. (ILLUS.) 40-55

Made in Japan Painted Tea Strainer

Ceramic, two-piece tea strainer, white w/h.p. purple & pink flowers & green leaves w/gold trim, marked "Made in Japan," 5 7/8" l., 1 1/2" h. (ILLUS.)................ 35-45

Rose-decorated Tea Strainer

Ceramic, two-piece tea strainer, white w/printed dark pink roses & green leaves, gold trim, marked "T-103," 3 5/8" l., 1 1/4" h. (ILLUS.)... 15-20

Nippon Two-piece Tea Strainer

Porcelain, two-piece tea strainer, deep yellow & dark brown h.p. decoration of red trees & gold trim, marked "Hand Painted Nippon," early 20th c., 4 7/8" l., 1 1/4" h. (ILLUS.).. 25-35

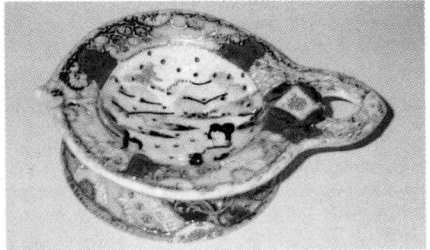

Geisha Girl Porcelain Tea Strainer

Porcelain, two-piece tea strainer, Geisha Girl porcelain decorated w/a central landscape w/Geishas, trimmed w/panels of dark red w/green, pink & blue highlights & ornate gold trim, ca. 1920s, 6" l., 1 1/2" h. (ILLUS., previous page)............................. **95-125**

Fancy Painted Nippon Tea Strainer

Porcelain, two-piece tea strainer, pale green, pink & yellow ground w/ornate overlaid gold flowers & beading, marked "Nippon Hand Painted," 6" l., 1 5/8" h. (ILLUS.) **95-125**

LAUNDRY ROOM ITEMS

Irons

Very few people intentionally set out to become "iron collectors." For most it just seems to happen - perhaps they first acquire one to use as a doorstop or a pair to use as book ends. Soon, a collection begins to form.

The incredible diversity of the irons that have been produced and manufactured over the last few centuries is staggering, and it is that diversity that fuels the interest in adding to one's collection. From early primitive or blacksmith-made irons to interesting patented special purpose irons to unusual ironing devices that look more like works of art than functional tools for accomplishing mundane household chores, the variety of different irons to be found is seemingly endless.

The field of iron collecting has evolved over the years. Just a few decades ago it was common to find irons in every antique store and at every show. As more and more collectors came into the field, the supply began to diminish and prices shot up. The knowledge base among collectors has increased and large collections that were amassed over the last few decades have come up for sale recently. Market prices have fluctuated widely. As is the case with many areas of antiques and collectibles, when these large iron collections come up for sale, the rarest pieces bring previously unheard of prices. The more common pieces, on the other hand, seem to sell reasonably, at similar prices to what they have been bringing for many years. Meanwhile, the middle of the market has actually softened a bit, with prices falling off somewhat for mid-range examples. All in all, it's a great time - perhaps the best time in years - to begin an iron collection!

The prices listed here are based on recent auction results of a large and longtime iron collection.

Carole Meeker

Kenrick Billiard Table Iron

Billiard table iron, Kenrick, rectangular shape w/metal handle & trivet (ILLUS.) **$140**

Box Iron Inscribed "1711"

Box iron, brass, swing gate, top highly decorated w/leaf & swirl pattern covering top from rear post & continuing around front post, the design somewhat resembling a heart, turned wooden grip, inscribed date of 1711 (ILLUS.) **95**

Decorated Box Iron

Box iron, brass, swing gate w/lock, wooden handle carved in leaf & vine motif, top of iron decorated w/pierced floral design, outside perimeter w/pierced dot border (ILLUS.) **110**

Box Iron with Decorative Details

Box iron, brass, teardrop shape, wooden handle on turned supports, decorative finials on lift gate, Denmark (ILLUS.)............. **225**

Early Box Iron with Wooden Grip

Box iron, early model, w/unusual stirrup posts supporting wood grip handle & spring latch operating rear door (ILLUS.).. **1,350**

Decorative Box Iron from Denmark

Box iron, iron, teardrop shape, w/lift gate, heating slug, turned wooden grip on decorative iron standards, Denmark (ILLUS.)...... **275**

Cast-iron Charcoal Iron from Japan

Charcoal iron, cast iron, highly polished, w/removable chimney, front latch, wooden grip, heat shield w/gold paint, Japan (ILLUS.).. **200**

Serpent-headed Charcoal Iron

Combination Flatiron & Fluter

Charcoal iron, nickel-plated iron, w/decorative scallop & bead design, ornate scroll & serpent-head latch & handle w/arched grip (ILLUS., previous page) **95**

"The Queen" Charcoal Iron

Charcoal iron, "The Queen," w/unique release mechanism & front venting system, wooden grip, marked "patent applied for," Los Angeles, California (ILLUS.) **400**

Charcoal Tailor Iron

Charcoal tailor iron, front smoke stack, wooden grip, top embossed "The Boss

Imp'd No. 18 1890 N.W. Stove Repair Co. Chicago," 11" l., 11" h. (ILLUS.) **575**

Combination iron, flatiron/fluter, charcoal heated, side fluter plate, rocker handle, hinged trivet holds iron on its side for fluting, Pease (ILLUS., top of page) **95**

Combination Flatiron & Polisher

Combination iron, flatiron/polisher, round-front polishing iron embossed w/star on top, auxiliary clamp-on spade-shaped flat bottom base (ILLUS.) **385**

Round Doily Iron

Doily iron, round w/angular handle, round trivet, 4 1/2" d. (ILLUS., previous page) **180**

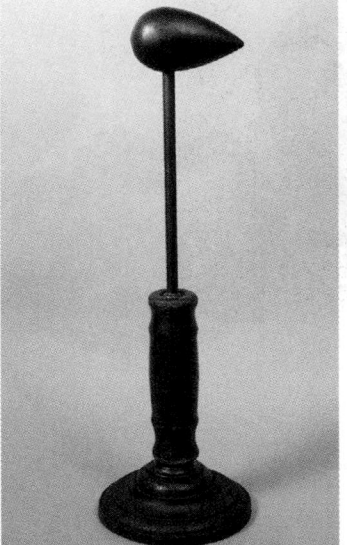

Egg Iron on Stand

Egg iron, cast-iron stand w/circular molded base & wooden grip near base for steadying or carrying, teardrop-shaped egg, 14" h. (ILLUS.) **60**

"Cordlessmatic" Electric Iron

Electric iron, "Cordlessmatic," red spun aluminum w/plastic handle, streamline design, gauge window in top (ILLUS.) **75**

Early Pelouze Electric Iron

Electric iron, early model, wooden grip, standard decorated in honeycomb-like design, porcelain plug, Pelouze (ILLUS.) **25**

Diminutive Primitive Flatiron

Flatiron, primitive style w/simple elongated teardrop shape, forge-welded sweeping handle w/decorative curlicue at end, diminutive size, 2 1/2" h. x 5 1/2" l. (ILLUS.) **100**

Flatiron with Ribbon Candy Design

Flatiron, simple design w/wooden grip on unusual handle standards designed to resemble ribbon candy, the matching horseshoe-shaped trivet w/matching ribbon candy design, Warren, Pennsylvania, ca. 1910 (ILLUS.) **1,800**

Flatiron with Horseshoe Logo

Daisy-form Flower Iron

Flatiron, spade-shaped, horseshoe logo w/"3" inside inscribed on top, rolled metal strap handle applied w/screws (ILLUS., previous page) **35**

Flower iron, embossed daisy form, for shaping silk flowers, one half bronze, the other half iron, 4" daisy (ILLUS.. top of page) **75**

"Howell's Wave Fluter" Iron

Fluter, "Howell's Wave Fluter," cast-iron base w/built-in slug, wavy brass plates, patented Aug. 21, 1866 (ILLUS.) **330**

"Star" Machine Fluter

Fluter, machine-type, cast-iron body w/brass rollers, decorated w/red & gold pinstriping, "Star" & image of star embossed on base (ILLUS.) **275**

Manville Machine Fluter

Fluter, Manville, machine-type, round fluted base & body, brass rollers (ILLUS.) **900**

Fluter, rocker-type, "JBK" embossed on top (ILLUS., top next page) **165**

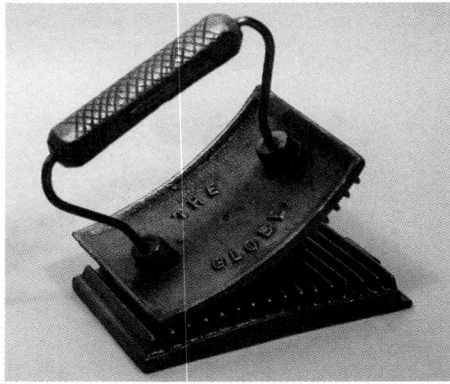

"The Globe" Fluter

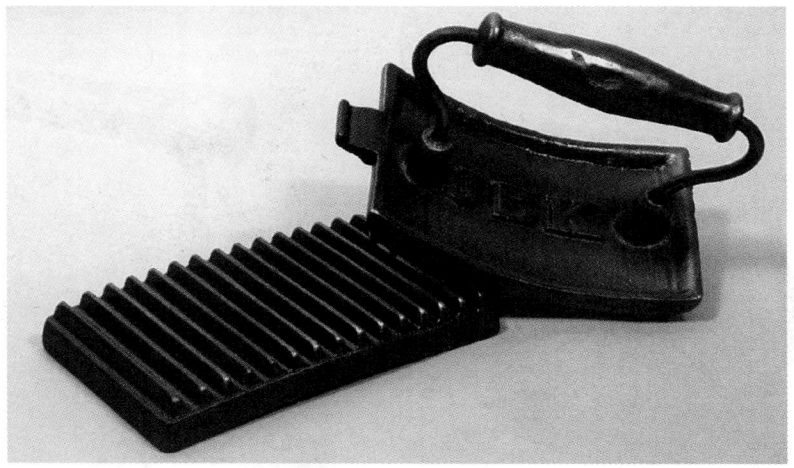

Simple "JBK" Rocker-type Fluter

Fluter, "The Globe," rocker-type, grip w/crisscross design, marked "R. Young & Gordon, Geneva, OH - Pat. Applied For" (ILLUS., bottom previous page) **115**

Fluting Iron with Dutch Bonnet Roller

Fluter, wooden, w/7" Dutch bonnet roller, base 3 1/4 x 3 3/4" (ILLUS.).......................... **225**

Acorn Brass Mfg. Co. Gas Iron

Gas iron, Acorn Brass Mfg. Co., black enamel body, the cylindrical fuel tank sitting atop handle, patented May 13, 1913 (ILLUS.).. **1,250**

"Grand Jewel" Gas Iron

Gas iron, "Grand Jewel," cast-iron top embossed w/name in ornate type, offset fuel tank at rear (ILLUS.) **165**

"J. Gross" Gas Iron

Gas iron, rear mount fitting, wooden grip, "J. Gross, No. 3, Patd May 3, 1898" embossed on side of base (ILLUS., previous page) **165**

"Sultana Toilet Iron"

Gas jet-heated iron, "Sultana Toilet Iron," heated by inverting over gas jet, patent date of July 4, 1893 (ILLUS.) **330**

Two-barrel Goffering Iron

Goffering iron, cast-iron octagonal base w/leaf & scroll embossed decoration, highly turned standard holding two steel

barrels, plugs, France, 15 1/2" h. (ILLUS.) **750**

Single-barrel Goffering Iron

Goffering iron, single-barrel type, quatrefoil stepped base w/shell-decorated corners, turned standard holding short, fat barrel, 9" h. (ILLUS.) **110**

European Wrought-iron Goffering Iron

Goffering iron, wrought iron, "rat tail" type, two opposing barrels on tripod base w/three curlicue decorations, Europe, 10" h. (ILLUS.) **2,100**

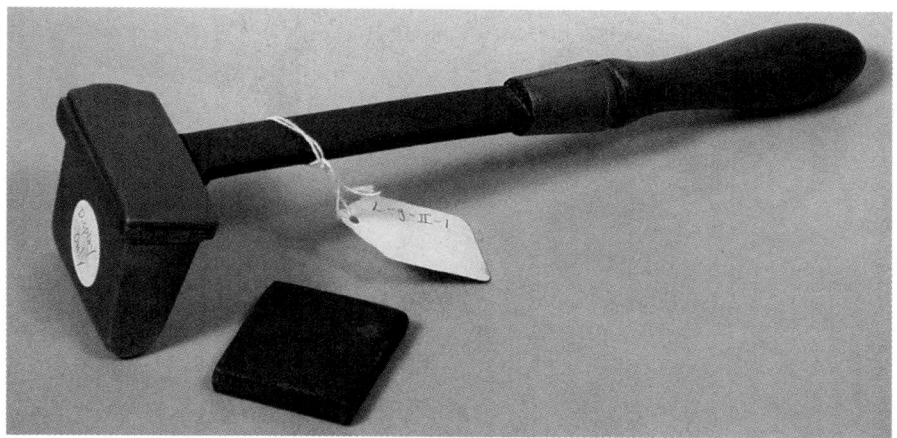

Brass Hat Iron

Hat iron, brass, long handle, w/slug, 1 x 2 x 2" box, used to finish women's caps, 11" l. (ILLUS., top of page) **90**

McCoy's Hat Iron

Hat iron, iron, oblong shape w/arched cutout in bottom, metal handle embossed "McCoy's," 4 3/4" l. (ILLUS.) **65**

"Centennial" Iron Heater

Iron heater, "Centennial," stovetop sadiron type, round, two-piece mechanical hinged lid, opens as the iron is taken out (ILLUS.) **360**

A & W Iron Heater

Iron heater, stovetop-type, rectangular shape w/slightly scalloped rim, inscribed "Pat'd Feb 13 83 - No. 3 - Sad Iron Heater - A & W. M'F'G Co - Chicago" (ILLUS.) **195**

Oval Cap Iron with Embossed Design

Little cap iron, oval, top embossed w/wreath surrounding crown & "S," metal strap handle, 3 3/4" l. (ILLUS.) **45**

Little Cap Iron

Little cap iron, teardrop shape, top embossed w/"DC" in circle, metal strap handle, 4" l. (ILLUS.)... **85**

Child-size Little Iron

Little iron, child-size, double-pointed shape, end-mount base, removable handle w/lift latch & wooden grip, marked "G.H. Ober - Cha Falls O - Pat 1896," 4" l. (ILLUS.)... **300**

"Enterprise" 2 1/2" Iron

Little iron, "Enterprise Mfg. Co., Phila, Pat Iron" embossed on top, double-pointed shape, ventilation holes in curved metal handle, 2 1/2" l. (ILLUS.)................................. **110**

Little Sleeve Iron

Little sleeve iron, child-size, w/detachable center-mount handle w/wooden grip, patented by Frederick Myers, 4 1/4" l. (ILLUS.)... **450**

Otto Natural Gas Iron

Natural gas iron, Otto, double pointed, w/side mount natural gas fitting, heat shield, wooden grip (ILLUS.)........................... **105**

"Brevete SGDG" Polisher

Polisher, "Brevete SGDG," rectangular shape w/arched nose, deep diamond patterned sole, marked w/anchor & "CF," France (ILLUS., previous page) **10**

"Mrs. Streeter's No. 2 Gem Polisher"

Polisher, iron, solid body w/angled base, removable handle w/wooden grip, marked "Mrs. Streeter's No. 2, Gem Polisher - Pat Sept. 6th 1887," 5 1/4" l. (ILLUS.) **295**

Sweeney Polishing Iron

Polisher, unusual long shape, metal grip w/diamond design & embossed "No. 4," top marked "Nov 17 [18]98 - Pat Pending - Sweeney Iron" patented by Mary Sweeney, manufactured by Baird & Co., Pittsburgh, Pennsylvania, 7" l. (ILLUS.)........ **115**

Sleeve Iron with Removable Handle

Sleeve iron, elongated "big toe" shape, removable arched wooden handle, embossed w/patent date of June 15, 1897, 10" l. (ILLUS.)... **200**

Press for Straw Hats

Straw hat press, gas heated, hinged top, four movable plates to adjust size, T-handle screw to tighten, marked "H. Maillard - Paris - Patent 405952," France, 14 x 18", 9" h. (ILLUS.).................................... **280**

Tailor Iron for Pressing Seams

Tailor iron, forged iron, primitive style, long narrow shape for ironing seams, twist handle attached at one end, 1 1/2 w. x 11" l. (ILLUS.) **25**

Tailor Iron with Unique Handle Mechanism

Tailor iron, iron, elongated shape w/unique handle release mechanism, marked "Nahmaschinenversandhaus Strauss Wien VII Siebensterngasse 13," Austria (ILLUS.)... **95**

Group of Beaded Swirl & Other Miniature Lamps

LIGHTING DEVICES

Miniature Lamps

Our listings are generally arranged numeri-cally according to the numbers assigned to the various miniature lamps pictured in Frank R. & Ruth E. Smith's book Miniature Lamps, now referred to as Smith's Book I, and Ruth Smith's sequel, Miniature Lamps II. All references are to Smith's Book I unless otherwise noted. Lamps are glass unless otherwise noted.

Blue, Daisy with Large Bull's-eye patt., oc-tagonal stem, no chimney or shade, 4 3/4" h., No. 112 (ILLUS. second from right with Beaded Swirl & other lamps, top of page).. **$143**

Green, Daisy with Large Bull's-eye patt., oc-tagonal stem, no chimney or shade, 4 3/4" h., No. 112 (ILLUS. far right with Beaded Swirl & other lamps, above)............ **165**

Green, Floral Embossed patt., stand-type, paneled font w/molded flowers, brass collar & burner, clear chimney, 5 1/2" h., No. 114 (ILLUS. center with Famous and Fishscale lamps, bottom next page)............. **132**

Blue, Fishscale patt., stand type, brass col-lar & burner, clear chimney, foot flakes, 5" h., No. 116 (ILLUS. second from left with Fishscale & Famous lamp, bottom next page).. **99**

Green, Greek Key patt., paneled rounded font w/band of design on a paneled stem & square foot w/further design, brass col-lar & burner, clear chimney, 3 1/2" h., No. 167 (ILLUS. second from right with Fa-mous and Fishscale lamps, bottom next page)... **330**

Pink, Greek Key patt., paneled rounded font w/band of design on a paneled stem & square foot w/further design, brass collar & burner, clear chimney, small loss to burner, 3 1/2" h., No. 167 (ILLUS. far right with Famous and Fishscale lamps, bottom next page).. **275**

Milk glass w/pink decoration, Chrysan-themum patt., squatty bulbous milk glass font molded w/swirled ribs & blossom-heads decorated in pink w/yellow trim, non-matching open-topped domed ribbed pink cased shade, brass collar, burner, three-arm spider & clear chim-ney, base flake on shade, 3 1/4" h., No. 213 (ILLUS. center with Beaded Swirl & other lamps, top of page) **275**

Cranberry, Beaded Swirl patt., brass #1 collar w/slip burner & matching shade, minor rim flakes, 3 1/2" h., No. 369 (ILLUS. far left with other lamps, top of page) **660**

Frosted rubina, Royal Ivy patt., brass collar & burner, clear chimney, rim flakes to shade, chimney base chipped, burner dents, 2 3/4" h., No. 431 (ILLUS. far right with cranberry opalescent Reverse Swirl lamp, top page 790) **385**

Amethyst, Twinkle patt., squatty bulbous font & matching open-topped ball shade, brass collar & burner, large chip on base of shade, 3" h., No. 432 (ILLUS. second from right with Spanish Lace and Swan lamps, top next page) **121**

Blue, Twinkle patt., squatty bulbous font & matching open-topped ball shade, brass collar & burner, minute base flake on shade, 3" h., No. 432 (ILLUS. far right with Spanish Lace and Swan lamps, top next page)... **187**

Cranberry opalescent, Spanish Lace patt., base only w/brass collar, burner & clear chimney, 3 3/4" h., No. 470 (ILLUS. far left with Swan and other lamps, top next page) **440**

Blue Carlisle patt., stand lamp w/swirled de-sign in pedestal, brass collar, burner & glass chimney, 6" h., Smith II, No. 472 (ILLUS. second from left with Beaded Swirl & other lamps, top of page)..................... **77**

Clear w/gold paint trim, stand-type, Fa-mous patt., brass collar, burner & match-ing glass shade, some paint flaking, 5 1/4" h., No. 478 (ILLUS. far left with Fishscale & famous lamps, bottom next page) **303**

Spanish Lace, Swan & Other Lamps

Famous, Fishscale & Other Miniature Lamps

Amber, Ribbed Swirl patt., stand-type, squatty bulbous swirled rib font & pedestal base, brass collar & burner, clear chimney, 4 3/4" h., No. 479 (ILLUS. second from right with cranberry opalescent Reverse and other lamps, top next page)....... **77**

Blue, Ribbed Swirl patt., stand-type, squatty bulbous swirled rib font & pedestal base, brass collar & burner, clear chimney, 4 3/4" h., No. 479 (ILLUS. center with cranberry opalescent Reverse Swirl & other lamps, top next page) **154**

Blue opaque, Swan patt., model of a swimming swan, base only w/a brass collar, burner & clear chimney, 4" h., No. 499 (ILLUS. second from left with Spanish Lace & other lamps, top of page)................... **198**

Cranberry opalescent, Swirl patt., stand-type, w/a brass collar & burner w/matching petticoat shade on the molded clear chimney, two collar splits, 4 1/4" h., No. 503 (ILLUS. center with Spanish Lace and Swan lamps, top of page)................... **2,530**

Cranberry Opalescent Reverse Swirl & Other Lamps

Cranberry opalescent, Reverse Swirl patt., stand-type, pear-shaped glass font on a flaring ribbed brass-colored tin base, brass collar & burner, clear chimney, 4 3/4" h., No. 509 (ILLUS. far left with other lamps, above)...................................... **413**

Cranberry, Ribbed Swirl with Medallion, squared font raised on applied clear leaf feet, brass collar & turner w/blown cranberry optic ribbed ball shade w/ornate clear applied petals, base flakes on shade, 4 1/2" h., 547 (ILLUS. second from left with cranberry opalescent Reverse Swirl & other lamps, above)................ **825**

Handel Lamps

The Handel Company of Meriden, Connecticut (1885-1936), began as a glass and lamp shade decorating company. Following World War I it became a major producer of decorative lamps that have become very collectible today.

Handel Boudoir with Windmill

Boudoir lamp, 6 3/4" d. domical shade, reverse-painted w/a windmill & waterway landscape in shades of dark brown, orange & yellow, on a simple bronzed metal base w/a medium brown patina, overall 13 3/4" h. (ILLUS.)..................................... **$2,587**

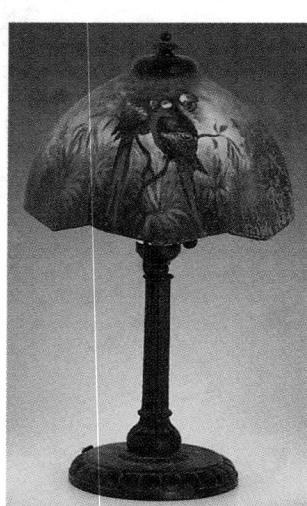

Handel Jungle Bird Boudoir Lamp

Boudoir lamp, 7" d. domical shade w/zigzag rim, reverse-painted in the Jungle Bird patt., a pair of large red & blue macaws perched together on branches w/green tropical foliage in the background on a mottled green, yellow & red ground, on a bronzed metal base w/a slender ribbed stem on a disk foot w/a gadrooned edge, shade signed "Handel," overall 14" h. (ILLUS.) **7,475**

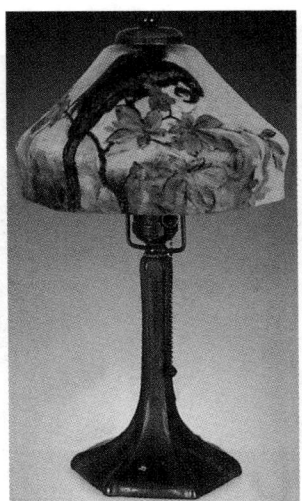

Handel Boudoir Lamp with Parrot

Boudoir lamp, 7" w. hexagonal domed shade, reverse-painted w/a large blue parrot perched on a leafy branch w/pink flowers, shaded bright yellow to clear background, shade signed "Handel," on a bronzed metal base w/a slender paneled stem & a flaring hexagonal base, overall 14" h. (ILLUS.) **4,312**

Desk lamp, a 5 1/2" w. hexagonal paneled shade w/caramel slag panels each overlaid w/a pierced lattice border & grape leaf border panel trimmed in red & green, supported by a high arched & curved harp on a simple ribbed stem & lobed disk foot, overall 18" h. **1,955**

Desk lamp, a half-round cylindrical leaded glass shade composed of a brick design in striated brown glass, adjusting on a long harp suspended on a slender arched stem on a round dished foot **1,725**

Desk lamp, a half-round cylindrical shade in caramel slag glass overlaid w/a pierced metal design of vines & leaves, adjusting on a long harp suspended from a slender arched arm adjusting above the round foot, shade 4" d., 10" l., overall 13" h. **2,012**

Floor lamp, 24" d. domical octagonal paneled yellow glass shade, each panel ornately decorated w/leafy bamboo stems, raised on a tall sender bamboo-shaped standard on a round leaf-molded foot, overall 61" h. (ILLUS., top next column) **7,475**

Hall globe, 10" d. spherical ball shade reverse-painted in the Jungle Bird patt., two large colorful macaws among jungle foliage in shades of red, blue, orange & pink, original hanging hardware including bottom tassel **7,475**

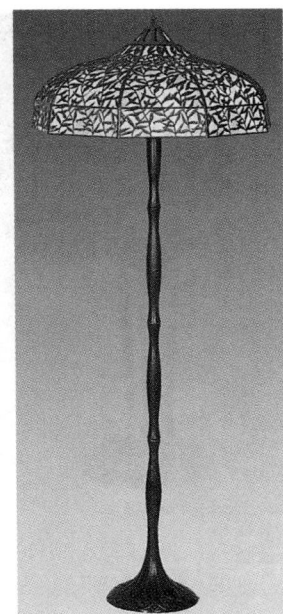

Handel Lamp with Bamboo Shade

Unusual Yellow & Black Handel Lamp

Table lamp, 15" d. domical glass shade, reverse painted in bright yellow w/a black border band decorated w/red roses & white blossoms on green leafy vines, on a black-finished pedestal base w/gold incised-line decoration around the bottom, overall 21" h. (ILLUS.) **2,300**

Rare Handel with Parrots Shade

Table lamp, 18" d. domical glass shade, reverse-painted in the Parrot patt., a large dark blue parrot & a colorful red, yellow & dark blue parrot perched amid colorful blossoms & a striated background in dark blue & purple, signed "Handel 7128," on a bronzed metal base w/a shallow urn raised on three slender legs & a central post above the round foot w/a lappet border band, signed on the collar "Handel Lamps Pat'd No. 979664," overall 23 1/2" h. (ILLUS.) **20,700**

Handel Lamp & Autumn Scene Shade

Table lamp, 18" d. domical glass shade, reverse-painted w/a continuos landscape w/stately trees & shrubs along a waterway, in autumnal shades of orange, brown, green, yellow & blue, signed "Handel 7111," on a simple slender

bronzed metal base signed "Handel," overall 23 1/2" h. (ILLUS.) **5,462**

Handel with Stormy Scene Shade

Table lamp, 18" d. domical glass shade, reverse-painted w/a continuous landscape of tall trees, meadows & hills under a dark stormy sky in shades of brown, chipped ice exterior, shade signed "Handel 6432 - HB," on a bronzed metal ovoid base w/four open loops at the top & cross-form feet, base rewired & probably repatinated, overall 23 1/2" h. (ILLUS.)...... **6,038**

Fine Handel & Rookwood Lamp

Table lamp, 18" d. domical glass shade, reverse painted overall w/large bouquets of red & yellow roses & green leaves against a shaded brown to yellow ground, signed "Handel 6741," on a cylindrical paneled Rookwood pottery base w/a flaring round foot & lightly embossed w/small blossoms & a warm yellow glaze, overall 24" h. (ILLUS.) **20,125**

Table lamp, 18" d. domical glass shade, reverse-painted w/overall wild rose blossoms & leaves in shades of pinks, reds & greens, chipped ice exterior, signed "Handel 6688," on a bronzed metal base w/three S-shaped leaf-trimmed legs & a central post on a stepped round foot, overall 24" h.. **12,650**

Outstanding Exotic Birds Handel Lamp

Table lamp, 18" d. domical glass shade, reverse-painted in the Exotic Birds patt., the fancy birds in red, yellow & dark blue flying among dark blue leaves & clusters of large round, green & yellow blossoms, signed "Handel 7125 Palme," raised on a bronzed metal base w/a shallow urn supported on three slender legs & a center post above the round foot w/a lappet border band, three orange glass teardrops hanging from the top of the base w/a matching finial above the shade, overall 26 1/2" h. (ILLUS.)...................................... **25,875**

Unusual Art Deco Handel Table Lamp

Table lamp, 18" d. domical glass shade, the textured citrine yellow ground enameled w/stripes of Art Deco swirls & scrolls in maroon & teal blue, signed "Handel 7499," on a cast-meal & onyx columnar standard w/a squared, stepped base w/scroll feet, overall 26 1/2" h. (ILLUS.) **3,450**

Bent-panel Handel Shade & Lamp Base

Table lamp, 18 1/2" d. octagonal bent caramel slag shade w/wide shaped border panels in green slag overlaid w/a pierced oak leaf design, raised on a simple ribbed bronzed metal base w/an octagonal foot, panel strips re-soldered at the crown, rewired, overall 23" h. (ILLUS.)...................... **2,588**

Fine Sunset Overlay Handel Lamp

Table lamp, 24" w. domical octagonal bent-panel shade, mottled orange & red slag panels overlaid w/metal filigree pine trees above a narrow yellow slag border panel overlaid w/pine needles, overall 30" h. (ILLUS.) **9,775**

Rare Rose Filigree Handel Lamp

Table lamps, 18" w. domical octagonal bent-panel shade, ribbed white glass panels overlaid w/delicate rose vine filigree trimmed in yellow & green, simple bronzed metal base w/lobed foot, shade signed "Handel 924457," base signed "Handel," overall 23" h., pr. (ILLUS. of one) **10,350**

Pairpoint Lamps

Well known as a producer of fine Victorian art glass and silver plate wares between 1907 and 1929, the Pairpoint Corporation of New Bedford, Massachusetts, also produced a wide range of decorative lamps.

Pairpoint "Puffy" Rose Boudoir Lamp

Boudoir lamp, 6 1/2" d. "Puffy" shade in the Rose patt., large molded rose blossoms in pink, red, yellow & orange against a dark blue, green & brown ground, on a silvered cast metal tree trunk base, base signed w/Pairpoint logo & "B3079," overall 6 1/2" h. (ILLUS.) **$4,025**

Fine "Puffy" Pairpoint Grape Lamp

Table lamp, 12" d. "Puffy" shade in the Grape patt., reverse-painted in deep purple, dark & light green, orange & red, raised on a cast-metal base w/molded grapes & leaves up the standard & around the foot, shade signed "Pat. Applied For," base signed w/Pairpoint logo & "B3010," overall 19" h. (ILLUS.) **14,560**

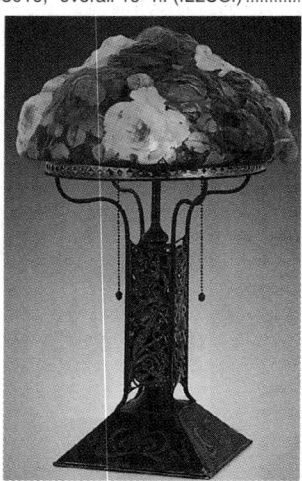

Pairpoint "Puffy" Rose Bouquet Lamp

Table lamp, 12 3/4" d. "Puffy" shade in the Rose Bouquet patt., the large molded rose blossoms reverse-painted in dark red & yellow against dark green leaves, on an unusual square cast- and pierced-metal base w/whiplash vines & flowers on the standard above the pyramidal scroll-decorated foot, base signed "Pairpoint 3054," overall 21" h. (ILLUS.) **17,825**

Hummingbird & Roses Pairpoint Lamp

Table lamp, 13" d. "Puffy" shade in the "Devonshire" shape, Hummingbird & Roses patt., reverse-painted in greens, yellows, reds & orange against a frosted ground, on a gold-washed cast-metal base w/a slender paneled & floral-cast standard on a square paneled foot, overall 21 1/2" h. (ILLUS.) **9,200**

Rare "Puffy" Lilac Tree Pairpoint Lamp

Table lamp, 14" d. "Puffy" shade in the Lilac Tree patt., reverse-painted w/pink &

white blossoms against dark green leaves w/two yellow & red butterflies, gilt cast-metal baluster-form base w/floral garlands & leaf bands, shade signed "Pairpoint Corp.," base signed w/Pairpoint logo & "73," overall 22" h. (ILLUS.). **21,840**

Chesterfield Shade with Harbor Scene

Table lamp, 16" d. "Puffy" shade in the "Chesterfield" shape, painted in vibrant sunset colors w/a Venetian harbor scene, the bronzed metal base w/a slender panel & floral-cast standard on a square paneled foot, base signed w/the Pairpoint logo & "B320," overall 22" h. (ILLUS.).. **7,475**

Very Rare Begonia Pairpoint Lamp

Table lamp, 16" d. "Puffy" shade in the Begonia patt., large molded leaves reverse-painted in green, white, yellow & orange against a deep red ground, four pink flowers w/yellow centers at the top center, bronzed metal tree trunk base w/a dark green & black matte patina, shade signed "The Pairpoint Corp. Patented July 9, 1901," base signed w/the Pairpoint logo & " 3092," overall 25" h. (ILLUS.) **46,000**

"Puffy" Milano Harbor Scene Lamp

Table lamp, 18" w. "Puffy" shade in the "Milano" shape, reverse-painted w/a Venetian harbor scene w/a painted square tasseled cloth across the top, on a gilded cast-metal base w/a paneled standard above the four-lobed foot, shade signed "The Pairpoint Mfg. Co. B3040" & the Pairpoint logo, overall 19 1/2" h. (ILLUS.).. **8,400**

Tiffany Lamps

Desk lamp, counterbalance type, a 7" d. domical green Damascene shade w/bluish green ribbon decoration, held on an S-scroll arm w/weighted ball end adjusting on a slender pedestal w/a domed base, shade signed "L.C.T. Favrile," base signed "Tiffany Studios - New York 417," overall 14" h. **$10,080**

Tiffany Desk Lamp in Zodiac Pattern

Desk lamp, 7" d. domical shade w/a gold iridescent damascene exterior, supported in the arched harp of a bronze Zodiac patt. base, shade signed "LCT Favrile," base marked "Tiffany Studios - New York 661," two minor fitter rim shade chips, overall 13 1/2" h. (ILLUS.).......................... **6,900**

Floor lamp, 22" d. domical leaded glass shade in a geometric design composed of graduated blocks of mottled green & yellow glass, signed "Tiffany Studios - New York," on a tall slender bronze standard w/a round cushion base w/small scroll tab feet, base also signed, overall 5' 6" h. **34,500**

Floor lamp, "Dogwood," the domical leaded glass shade w/an irregular border of blossoms composed of pale pink & light blue segments w/an upper block design in yellowish green mottled glass, original pierced cap, signed "Tiffany Studios - New York," on a tall slender bronze standard w/a domed cushion base w/scroll tab feet **89,500**

Tiffany Daffodil Table Lamp

Table lamp, "Daffodil," 16" d. domical leaded glass shade composed of segments forming long-stemmed yellow daffodils & long green & yellow stems & leaves against a white shaded to green background, on a bronze base w/a ribbon-wrapped standard above the scroll and lobe-decorated domed base on scroll tab feet, base signed "Tiffany Studios - New York 28615" & w/the TGD Co. monogram, overall 21" h. (ILLUS.) **25,200**

Table lamp, "Greek Key," 16" d. domical leaded glass shade composed of mottled green panels above a wide Greek key border band in bright green & yellow bordered w/amber, shade signed "Tiffany Studios - New York," on a bronze base

Rare Tiffany Greek Key Table Lamp

w/a long ovoid stem supported on three arms above the rectangular foot, base marked "Tiffany Studios - New York 444," overall 23 1/2" h. (ILLUS.) **27,600**

Rare Tiffany Kerosene Table Lamp

Table lamp, kerosene-type, 18" d. conical shade composed of 48 narrow panels of caramel slag glass terminating in a saw-tooth border, decorated w/a jewelry-type wirework crown at the open top above an overall wirework lattice overlay, twisted wire beaded hangings around the rim, raised on a specially made base w/an ornate pierced bronze shoulder collar on the spherical blown amber glass font raised on scrolled bronze feet, each foot fitted w/an amber glass turtleback scroll, base signed & numbered, overall 23" h. (ILLUS.) **46,000**

Fine Seven-Arm Tiffany Lily Lamp

Table lamp, "Lily," seven-light, a bronze lily pad base issuing seven slender upright arching stems each supporting a long flora-form golden iridescent shade, shades signed "LCT," base signed "Tiffany Studios- New York 385," overall 20" h. (ILLUS.) **17,250**

Unusual Tiffany "Linenfold" Lamp

Table lamp, "Linenfold," 19" w. twelve-paneled domical shade w/a pierced top plate, each panel w/emerald green linenfold glass trimmed at the top & bottom w/clear frosted panels, on a gilt-bronze base w/a slender reeded standard above a round lobed foot, shaded marked "Tiffany Studios - New York 1927 Pat. Apl'd For," base signed "Tiffany Studios - New York 26847," overall 23" h. (ILLUS.) **24,150**

Unusual Tiffany Mushroom Lamp

Table lamp, mushroom-style, a 6 1/2" d. domical blown mushroom-shaped bluish green shaded to gold shade & cylindrical stem on a domed green & gold iridescent wide round base on a bronze plate w/small knob feet, bronze base impressed "Tiffany Studios - New York" w/the Tiffany Glass & Decorating logo & the number "23693" that is scratched out w/the number "23639" impressed below, rewired, ca. 1900, overall 12" h. (ILLUS.).. **6,613**

Rare Tiffany Poppy Table Lamp

Table lamp, "Poppy," 20" d. conical leaded glass shade composed of red, fuchsia &

purple striated blossoms & green mottled leaves against a striated yellow & orange ground, two narrow border bands in apple green & one in orangish yellow, on a slender simple bronze standard on a ribbed & dished base on tab feet, shade signed "Tiffany 8805," base signed "Tiffany Studios - New York, " overall 25" h. (ILLUS.)... **89,500**

Table lamp, "Woodbine," 16" d. domical leaded glass shade decorated w/colorful leaves in yellow, red, streaked purple & confetti glass, on a slender ribbed & scroll-trimmed standard w/a wide bumpy cushion base on four scroll tab feet......... **30,240**

One of Two Tiffany Wall Sconces

Wall sconces, a bronze wall mount w/a dark brown patina & a drop finial & arched arm ending in a leaf-cast socket, fitted w/a bell-shaped shade decorated in a gold & green pulled-feather design on a yellow ground, shades unsigned but numbered "09463" & "09472," mounts extend 10", shade 4 3/4" h., pr. (ILLUS. of one) **8,338**

Lamps, Miscellaneous

Early Non-Electric

Banquet lamp, kerosene-type, a blown squatty bulbous font in green glass w/an oil spot finish & decorated w/random brown threading, on a ringed brass connector to the matching cylindrical glass standard on a stepped square metal base, brass collar & burner marked w/the Star of David & Freya Brenner Patent, glass by Pallme-Konig, Bohemia, ca. 1890, overall 20" h. **$1,093**

Banquet lamp, kerosene-type, a bulbous milk glass font decorated w/transfer-printed red roses on a shaded green ground, raised on an ornate polished brass pedestal base, a matching milk glass ball shade decorated w/cherries, ca. 1890s, electrified, overall 27" h. (ILLUS., top next page)........................ **115**

Late Victorian Banquet Lamp

Longwy Pottery & Bronze Lamp

Banquet lamp, kerosene-type, a cylindrical decorated Longwy Pottery central body in blue decorated exotic birds & foliage in red, yellow, black, white & green, fitted w/a pierced cylindrical upper body & raised on a cylindrical bronze footed base w/a cut-out design of stylized leaves & flowers, fitted w/a brass burner & clear frosted ball shade acid-etched w/bands of urns, bands & scrolls, marked "H.G. Moehring," ca. 1880s, overall 23 1/2" h. (ILLUS.)... **748**

Fine Pairpoint-Limoges Banquet Lamp

Banquet lamp, kerosene-type, an onion-shaped porcelain font decorated w/a painted blue Dutch windmill scene, raised on a tall swelled cylindrical matching pedestal on a fancy pierced brass foot, the stamped brass shoulder supporting a brass burner & ring for the

Cut-overlay Banquet & Table Lamps

Banquet & Dolphin-based Lamps

matching decorated ball shade, clear chimney, Pairpoint-Limoges, ca. 1890, overall 35" h. (ILLUS.)..................................... **633**

Banquet lamp, kerosene-type, cut-overlay, opaque white cut to deep green inverted pear-shaped font on a brass connector attached to the bronzed spelter figural standard on a square black soapstone base, brass #2 fine line collar, minor scratching to white on font, some bronze finish wear, ca. 1880, overall 18 3/4" h. (ILLUS. left with ruby cut-overlay banquet & cut-overlay table lamp, bottom previous page) **1,870**

Banquet lamp, kerosene-type, cut-overlay, opaque white cut to ruby font w/a peg fitted in a brass connector on the heavy cast-brass base decorated w/scrolls & cartouches, brass #2 fine line collar, base attributed to Henry N. Hooper & Co., ca. 1880, overall 19 3/4" h. (ILLUS. right with other cut-overlay banquet lamp & cut-overlay table lamp, bottom previous page)... **440**

Banquet lamp, kerosene-type, cut-overlay, the inverted bell-form font in ruby cut to clear w/a punty design, on a brass connector to the matching cut waisted stem on a stepped gilt-bronze & marble base, w/a brass collar, burner & ring supporting a tulip-form frosted clear & floral- and leaf-engraved shade, wear to gilt on base, edge & corner chips on marble, attributed to the Boston & Sandwich Glass Company, ca.

1860-1880, base 17 1/2" h., overall 25" h. (ILLUS. center with dolphin-based candle lamps, above) **5,875**

Banquet lamp, kerosene-type, mold-blown melon-lobed shaded cranberry mother-of-pearl satin glass font holder in the Diamond Quilted patt., raised on a brass stem & pierced cast-brass foot, fitted w/a wide brass collar & burner supporting the tulip-shaped ribbed matching shade w/a ruffled & crimped rim, late 19th c., electrified, overall 16" h. **1,208**

Tall Cut Glass & Marble Banquet Lamp

Banquet lamp, kerosene-type, the clear flute-cut onion-form font raised on a ringed brass connector atop a black marble standard & brass ring on a square stepped black marble base, electrified burner, Anglo-American, late 19th c., 31" h. (ILLUS., bottom previous page) **345**

Candle lamps, pressed flint glass three-dolphin stem on a round base in milky clambroth, supporting a gilt-metal collar w/a candle socket fitted w/a tall cylindrical clear chimney etched w/stylized leafy vines & blossoms, Boston & Sandwich Glass Co., ca. 1850-60, base 6 1/2" h., overall 11", pr. (ILLUS. with cut-overlay banquet lamp, top previous page) **16,450**

Gone-with-the-Wind Cherub Lamp

Gone-with-the-wind table lamp, kerosene-type, frosted clear inverted pear-shaped blown-molded font holding base decorated w/cherub heads & scrolls raised on a domed pierced bronzed-metal foot, a wide brass collar & burner support the matching ball shade & chimney, ca. 1900, overall 25" h. (ILLUS.) **403**

Hanging Lamp with Cranberry Shade

Hanging parlor lamp, kerosene-type, a 14" d. open-topped domical Hobnail patt. cranberry glass shade on a pierced-brass ring hung w/facet-cut prisms, a brass frame supporting a clear pressed glass font, suspended by three adjustable chains joined by an upper ring, electrified, ca. 1900 (ILLUS.) **518**

Unusual Quezal Boudoir Lamps

Quezal boudoir lamps, kerosene-type, a bulbous ovoid font base resting on a stamped & pierced brass foot, fitted w/a brass collar & burner supporting the matching bulbous ovoid open-topped shade, all glass in opal iridescence decorated w/a gold band of hooked & pulled design, both signed on fitters, 12" h., the pair (ILLUS.) **2,185**

Student lamp, brass, double-type, a round disk foot supporting a thin rod continuing through a large adjustable urn-form body & terminating w/a ring grip at the top, center urn issuing two straight arms ending in large acorn-shaped kerosene fonts supporting burners & a shade ring, a tall straight bar atop the center urn ending in a ring grip, each shade ring supporting a domed green cased glass shade, wick knobs marked "Apollo Duplex E.M. & Co.," late 19th - early 20th c., 24 1/2" h. (minor flakes on shades) **990**

Student lamp, brass, single-font, a disk foot centered by a tall slender rod w/a top ring, fitted w/an adjustable ring w/a cylindrical kerosene font on one side & the other side w/a projecting slender arm ending in a slender cylindrical tube holding the burner & shade ring, burner marked "Manhattan Brass Co., NY Pat'd May 27-76," fitted w/a domed milk glass shade & clear glass chimney marked "Macbeth Pearl Glass," late 19th c., electrified, 22 3/4" h. **330**

A Cut-overlay, Onion and Ripley Table Lamp

Table lamp, cut-overlay, cylindrical whale oil/fluid font in ruby cut to clear, attached w/a wafer to the pressed hexagonal clear base, brass #1 fine line collar, attributed to the New England Glass Co. or the Boston & Sandwich Glass Co., ca. 1850, font w/few minor abrasions & tiny flakes, 10 1/2" h. (ILLUS. center with Onion and Ripley Wedding lamps, above)................... **1,870**

Figural Cast-metal & Glass Table Lamp

Table lamp, kerosene-type, a squatty frosted clear engraved font raised on a cast white metal figural pedestal & square metal foot, fitted w/a burner & flaring cylindrical cranberry glass shade, some restoration, ca. 1870, 19" h. (ILLUS.)............ **173**

Table lamp, kerosene-type, an alabaster inverted pear-shaped font cut w/two bands of ribbing, the upper band curved & surrounding spaced quatrefoils, a brass connector to the pressed mint green Baroque lobed base, brass #1 collar, ca. 1860-70, 10" h. (ILLUS. left with two other green-based lamps, bottom of page)........ **770**

Table lamp, kerosene-type, blown clear squatty round font w/a frosted shoulder & cut w/quatrefoil & punty band, a brass connector to the pressed translucent lime green Baroque base, brass #2 fine line collar, ca. 1870, 10 1/2" h. (ILLUS. center with other green-based table lamps, bottom of page)... **165**

Table lamp, kerosene-type, blown milk glass onion-shaped font on a brass connector to the pressed dark bluish-green #40 base, brass #1 fine line collar, ca. 1870, 9 3/8" h. (ILLUS. right with other two green-based table lamps, bottom of page) **330**

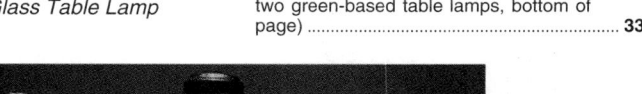

Three Green-based Early Kerosene Lamps

Table lamp, kerosene-type, cut-overlay, opalescent white cut to clear inverted pear-shaped font w/worn gilt trim on a brass connector on the opaque white Gem-type base, w/a Plume & Atwood lip burner w/adjuster wheel marked "P&A Pat. Aug. 11 1885," period 4" d. brass shade ring w/clear chimney & milk glass ball shade, minor base flakes, overall 12 1/2" h. (ILLUS. center with two cut-overlay banquet lamps, bottom page 799) **715**

Table lamp, kerosene-type, Onion (or Eaton) patt., mottled opaque robin's egg blue blown-molded squatty ribbed font on a brass connector above the tall pressed ribbed matching base, #2 brass fine line collar, Boston & Sandwich Glass Co., ca. 1870-80, overall 13 1/4" h. (ILLUS. left with cut-overlay and Ripley Wedding table lamps, top previous page) **2,530**

Table lamp, kerosene-type, Ripley Wedding lamp, pressed clambroth bulbous fonts flanking the translucent blue pressed match holder center section on a brass connector to the matching blue flattened standard & round base, match holder section indicating the patent date of September 20, 1870, #1 brass collars, no match holder cover, overall excellent condition, overall 12 1/2" h. (ILLUS. right with cut-overlay & Onion table lamps, top previous page) **1,870**

Rare Pair of Blue Flint Fluid Lamps

Table lamps, fluid-type, pressed cobalt blue flint glass, tapering ovoid hexagonal paneled font joined by a wafer to the stepped hexagonal base, minor base edge & corner chips, ca. 1850-60, 10 1/2" h., pr. (ILLUS.) **2,468**

Electric

Figural Alabaster Table Lamp

Alabaster figural table lamp, the alabaster base carved as a seated figure of a young lady holding a tambourine, a cylindrical shaft w/a flaring cupped top supporting the electric socket, missing the shade, early 20th c., 14" h. (ILLUS.) **$173**

Lovely Duffner & Kimberly Lamp

Duffner & Kimberly table lamp, 19" d. domical leaded glass shade, the upper shade w/graduated blocks of purplish brown slag glass above a wide border band of green fleur-de-lis & ribbons w/yellow ground, on a Duffner & Kimberly cast-metal base w/a tall reeded standard & a round foot cast w/oak leaves & acorns, overall 21 3/4" h. (ILLUS.) **6,613**

Emeralite Electric Desk Lamp

Emeralite desk lamp, 9 1/2" d. domical green cased in white shade supported on a simple flaring copper pedestal base marked "Bussmann Mfg. Co.," shade marked "Emeralite Trademark Austria," early 20th c., overall 13" h. (ILLUS.)........... **2,243**

Quality Gallé Cameo Table Lamp

Gallé cameo table lamp, 8" d. domical mushroom cameo shade in dark purple cut to mottled light blue, lavender & yellow w/a flower cluster & leaf design, on a matching baluster-form base, base & shade both signed in cameo, overall 17 1/2" h. (ILLUS.)... **6,900**

Le Verre Francais cameo table lamp, 8 1/2" d. domical cameo-cut shade in mottled orangish red cut to mottled yellow w/a continuous design of Art Deco blossoms & stems, raised on a three-arm metal spider above the matching ovoid glass standard on an applied maroon glass disk foot, signed on the foot, ca. 1920s, overall 15" h. (ILLUS., top next column).. **6,325**

Fine Le Verre Francais Cameo Lamp

Fine Moe Bridges Table Lamp

Moe Bridges table lamp, 18" d. domical reverse-painted shade decorated w/a landscape of autumn trees near a small lake, on a paneled tapering bronzed metal base (ILLUS.)..................................... **3,000-3,500**

Dutch Windmill Novelty Lamp

Novelty table lamp, a cast-spelter base w/a bronze finish modeled as a Dutch windmill, supporting a pressed mushroom-shaped tinted orange & frosted clear closed-top shade, ca. 1930, overall 14" h. (ILLUS., previous page) **115**

Reverse-painted Pittsburgh Table Lamp

Pittsburgh table lamp, 16" d. domical shade, reverse-painted w/a white border of red & yellow roses against a green lattice background, the upper shaped w/bands of rose leaves & vertical lines, on a simple bronzed metal pedestal base w/leaf & stem designs, two replaced sockets, overall 21 1/2" h. (ILLUS.) **2,875**

Fine Quezal "Lily" Table Lamp

Quezal "Lily" table lamp, a round bronzed metal bulbous-waisted base issuing six upright arched arms each ending in a socket & a ruffled trumpet-form ribbed shade in iridescent white w/four gold iridescent wavy bands, gold iridescent interiors, each shade signed, shade 4 3/4" l., overall 15" h. (ILLUS.) **6,325**

Domed Bent-panel Slag Table Lamp

Slag glass bent-panel table lamp, domical bent-panel hexagonal shade w/bronzed metal banding, raised on a bronze metal baluster-form base w/flaring foot, ca. 1920, overall 21" h. (ILLUS.) **431**

Slag Bent-panel Electric Table Lamp

Slag glass bent-panel table lamp, wide hexagonal umbrella-form shade w/bent caramel & green mottled slag panels above vertical deep ruby glass border panels, a painted green framework w/border filigree, on a simple ribbed matching green cast-metal base, ca. 1920, overall 21" h. (ILLUS.) **604**

Ornate Slag Lamp with Lighted Base

Slag glass table lamp, 18" d. octagonal umbrella-form caramel slag paneled shade w/the upper tapering panels decorated w/lattice filigree & the wide border panels decorated w/scroll & loop filigree, supported above a lighted octagonal base w/tapering rectangular caramel slag side panels decorated w/filigree bands above the loop-cast shaped base, ca. 1920, overall 25" h. (ILLUS., previous page) **1,150**

Hexagonal Simple Slag Glass Lamp

Slag glass table lamp, pyramidal caramel slag hexagonal shade w/swag & pierced filigree trim on each panel, on a simple bronzed metal base, some losses, ca. 1920, overall 20" h. (ILLUS.)........................... **259**

Simple Slag & Filigree Table Lamp

Slag glass table lamp, pyramidal caramel slag shade w/small flared panels around the open top, each side decorated w/scenic metal filigree, on a simple bronzed metal base w/a square foot, ca. 1920, minor losses, overall 21" h. (ILLUS.) **403**

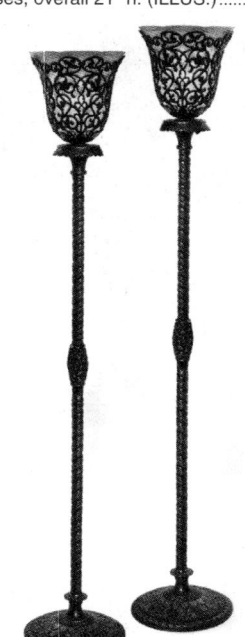

Fancy Art Nouveau Torchieres

Torchieres, Art Nouveau-style, round acanthus-leaf cast base supporting a tall slender spiral-turned standard below an inverted bell-shaped scroll-pierced frame enclosing a blown iridescent glass shade, ca. 1900, overall 63" h., pr. (ILLUS.)... **7,763**

Other Lighting Devices

Chandeliers

Antler, five-light, composed of two entwined deer antlers drilled for five fixtures, Europe, late 19th c., 31" d., 26" h. (ILLUS., below).. **$288**

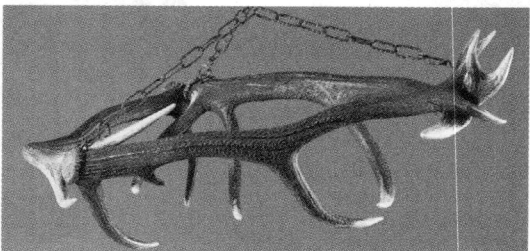

Five-light Antler Chandelier

Fine French Art Deco Chandelier

Art Deco, one-light, frosted clear glass & nickel-plated bronze, a six-lobed frosted glass shade molded w/large stylized flower blossoms suspended in a framework of six curved button-cast scroll arms joined to six long & slender C-scroll arms suspended from the paneled ceiling plate, attributed to Genet-Michon, France, ca. 1930, 25" d., 39" h. (ILLUS.)... **1,955**

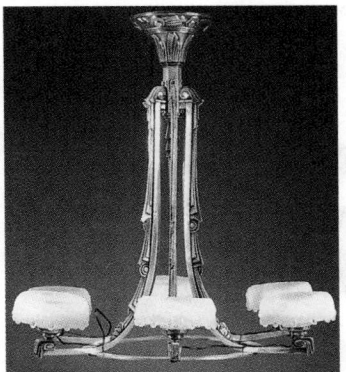

French Art Deco Six-Light Chandelier

Art Deco, six-light, the tall center nickel-plated bronze framework w/six square drapery-cast arms curving out at the bottom to each support an opalescent glass shade w/a molded drop decoration, ca. 1930, 28" d., overall 29" h. (ILLUS.).......... **2,530**

Louis XVI-Style French Chandelier

Cut glass & gilt-brass, ten-light, Louis XVI-Style, the brass scroll arms elaborately dressed w/glass fleurettes, jewel-cut beaded chains & faceted drops & cut palmette-like leaves, France, late 19th c., 25 1/2" d., 28" h. (ILLUS.) **1,610**

Handel, 24" d. domical octagonal slag glass shade, the large tapering upper bent panels in deep mottled reds & oranges above a border panel in mottled yellow & green, the upper panels decorated w/a delicate tropical palm tree metal filigree overlay, the border panels overlaid w/whiplash scroll filigree (ILLUS., below)...................... **6,325**

Muller Freres, three-light, a wide bowl-shaped central glass shade in mottled blue, pink, yellow & white supported by three chains w/scrolled gilt-iron rim brackets, each bracket supporting a socket w/a flaring cylindrical matching glass shade, ca. 1920, 22" d., overall 23" h. (ILLUS., top next page)................... **1,495**

Fine Handel Slag & Filigree Chandelier

Colorful Muller Freres Chandelier

Quezal, four-light, a brass central fixture w/a long shaft suspending a wide round deep disk suspending a central metal tassel & fitted around the rim w/squared scrolls each suspending a metal socket fitted w/a signed ribbed flora-form golden iridescent Quezal shade, shades 6" h., overall 31" h. (ILLUS., top next column) **2,300**

Four-light Quezal Chandelier

Steuben, four-light, a long brass ceiling shaft suspending a round center disk w/a tapering center drop finial, the rim fitted w/four sockets each fitted w/a signed Steuben bell-form shade in ivory iridescent decorated w/gold iridescent heart-shaped leaves & random threading, shade Shape No. 904, each shade 4 3/4" h., overall 18" d. (ILLUS., below)..... **1,265**

Brass Chandelier with Steuben Shades

Mistletoe-form Art Nouveau Chandelier

Wrought iron & opaline glass, three-light, modeled as an ornate cluster of mistletoe in the Art Nouveau taste, green-painted leaves & small opaline glass berries, the cluster concealing three bulb sockets, France, early 20th c., 13" d., 11" h. (ILLUS.) **1,380**

Lanterns

Arts & Crafts Electric Lanterns

Arts & Crafts, electric, cylindrical metal cage frame w/conical top enclosing amber glass shades, verdigris patina, early 20th c., for exterior use, 5 3/4" d., 11" h., set of 4 (ILLUS.)... **$546**

Barn lantern, painted wood & glass, a square upright wooden frame w/corner posts mortised through the top & base, arched tin vent cover on top, three side panes of glass & glass door w/wire staple hinges w/wire latch, interior candle socket, wire bail handle on top, frame w/old red stain, interior charred from use, 19th c., 7" sq., 12 3/4" h. (top split) **688**

Barn lantern, wood & glass, upright square form w/reeded wooden corner posts mortised through the top & bottom & held w/iron nails, two glass sides & door w/wire staple hinges, wire bail handle in top, 19th c., 6 1/2" h. (one glass pane gone, interior charred from use)..................... **578**

Candle lantern, tin & glass, spherical onion-form globe fitted w/a pierced cylindrical vent cap w/conical top & large ring handle, cylindrical low tin base w/pierced stars centering the candle socket, traces of black paint, 19th c., 8 1/4" h. plus handle **578**

Candle lantern, tin & glass, upright tin hexagonal frame w/one side forming door, removable panes of glass on each side fitted w/wire guards, peaked top pierced w/holes & fitted w/large ring handle, interior candle socket, 19th c., 11" h. plus handle (minor rust, few edge chips on glass) **275**

Shades

Durand-attributed, tall domed shape in white opal cased in iridescent gold & swirled red, blue & gold decorated, 5" h. (ILLUS. bottom row, third from left, bottom of page) **489**

Durand & Various Other Decorative Shades

Jefferson Reverse-painted Shade

Jefferson-signed, hexagonal tapering shape, each panel reverse-painted w/an Art Deco design in dark orange & green chevrons, signed on metal fitter rim, ca. 1920s, 14" w., 9" h. (ILLUS.) **863**

Lily, modern blown trumpet-form w/overall gold iridescent finish on amber glass, 4 1/2" h., set of 3 (ILLUS. of set bottom row, far right with Durand & other shades, bottom previous page) **374**

Fine Lustre Art Shade

Lustre Art-signed, trumpet-form w/swelled band at the top below the connector flange, overall golden orange iridescence w/green hanging leaf design & decorated w/fine gold threading, early 20th c., 5 1/2" h. (ILLUS.) **275-325**

Opalescent swirl, large trumpet-form blown form w/translucent greenish hues, 8" h. (ILLUS. top row, second from left with Durand & other shades, bottom previous page) **115**

Quezal-signed, ribbed tall floral-form in opal decorated w/a green pulled-feather decoration outlined in gold, 5" h., pr. (ILLUS. of pair top row, right with Durand & other shades, bottom previous page) **460**

Fancy Signed Quezal Shade

Quezal-signed, ribbed trumpet-form, opal decorated w/overall golden iridescent ribbons, gold iridescent interior, 5" h. (ILLUS.) **552**

Quezal-signed, waisted tulip-form w/scalloped rim, iridescent white decorated w/green hearts & overall random gold threading, 5" h. (ILLUS. bottom row, second from left with Durand & other shades, bottom previous page) **230**

Slag glass, blossom-form, six outer panels of bent & pointed green slag separated w/decorated leaf-cast bands, enclosing six pink slag pointed panels, four metal mounts missing, probably by Handel, 6" h., pr. (ILLUS. of pair far left with Durand & other shades, bottom previous page) **201**

Large Slag Bent-Panel Shade

Slag glass bent-panel, umbrella-shaped eight-paneled style, each panel in mottled red & green w/pointed crown panels at the top center, a drop border w/ruby panels decorated w/fancy pierced metal filigree, ca. 1925, 22" d. (ILLUS.) **230**

Blue Aurene Steuben Shade

Steuben-signed, ribbed trumpet-form, blue iridescent Aurene, 5 1/2" h. (ILLUS.) **633**

Green Alabaster Steuben Shade

Steuben-signed, ribbed trumpet-form, green Alabaster, 5 3/4" h. (ILLUS., previous page) **518**

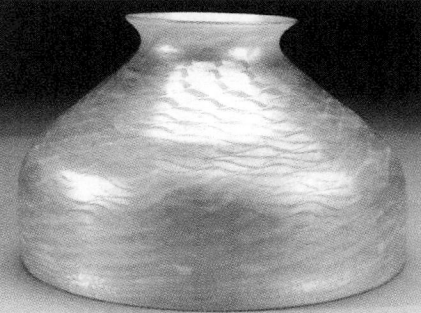

Large Green Damascene Tiffany Shade

Tiffany-signed, domical open-topped shape in green w/overall iridescent gold damascene decoration, numbered "56837," ca. 1900, large (ILLUS.) **3,450**

Fine Tiffany Gold Damascene Shade

Tiffany-signed, domical open-topped shape in ribbed opal decorated overall w/a gold damascene decoration, signed, ca. 1900, 10" d. (ILLUS.) **8,740**

Silver & Green Tiffany King Tut Shade

Tiffany-signed, domical open-topped shape, silver iridescent ground decorated overall w/a green King Tut design,

cased in white, signed, two small chips to outside top rim, 10" d. (ILLUS.) **7,475**

Silvery Green Tiffany Damascene Shade

Tiffany-signed, domical open-topped shape, silver w/overall green iridescent damascene decoration, cased in white, 12" d. (ILLUS.) **8,050**

MATCHCOVERS & MATCH BOXES

The history of matchcovers and match boxes can be traced back to 1895 when the Mendelson Opera Company purchased 100 blank boxes from the Diamond Match Company. Members of the opera company pasted photos and advertisements about their company on each box for public distribution. In 1896 Pabst Beer was also advertised on similar boxes, and by the early 1900s Wrigley's Chewing Gum distributed millions of special boxes for advertising.

Today all types of smoking-related items are becoming increasingly collectible as smoking declines in popularity. Since cheap lighters have pretty much replaced the giveaway matchbook covers and boxes, collector demand is likely to continue to grow.

Match Box with Cowboy Scene

Match box, color cover scene of a cowboy on a bucking bronco, made for Ohio Blue Tip matches, 1940s, 1 1/2 x 2 1/4" (ILLUS.) **$5**

Ted Williams on Match Box Cover

Match box, color drawing of Ted Williams in batting pose, made exclusively for Ohio Blue Tip, 1940s, 1 1/2 x 2 1/4", in top condition (ILLUS. in poor condition) 25

Match box, "National State Bank of Elizabeth, New Jersey," silver & blue featuring a square-rigged sailing ship, matches made in Sweden, 1950s, 1 x 1 3/4" 2

Typical BOAC Advertising Matchcover

Matchcover, "BOAC - the worldwide airline," various advertising covers promoting travel to Africa, Australia & other locales w/various scenes, the cover interior showing a stewardess w/an aircraft on a runway, by Bryant and Mays, 1950s, each (ILLUS. of one) 10

Matchcover for British & Irish SP Co.

Matchcover, British and Irish SP Co., Ltd., front reads "Nightly Express Passenger Service - Sunday Excepted," connections from Liverpool to Dublin, back cover w/color scene of an ocean liner, Novaco Match Company, Sweden, 1950s, in top condition (ILLUS. in fair condition) 5

Matchcover, "Carstairs White Seal Blended Whiskey," blue, gold & red cover w/a seal balancing a ball, 1940, 3 1/2 x 4 1/2" 4

Matchcover, Coca-Cola, advertising for the 1964-65 New York World's Fair w/slogan "Peace through Understanding," 1964 10

Matchcover, Coca-Cola, cover features a Haddon Sundblom Santa Claus w/"Seasons Greetings," shows Santa sitting drinking a bottle of Coca-Cola, 1958 13

Matchcover, Coca-Cola, "Delicious and Refreshing" on the front, back w/a picture of a young woman wearing a large white feathered hat, ca. 1910 1,100

Matchcover, Coca-Cola, "Drink Coca-Cola - Delicious and Refreshing," back shows a young woman drinking a bottle of Coca-Cola, ca. 1913 650

Matchcover, Coca-Cola, front reads "Enjoy Coca-Cola at home - carton or 12 bottles - 50 cents - Delivered cold by your local iceman," back w/an ad for a local ice company, 1930s 45

Matchcover, Coca-Cola, made in the shape of a Cola-Cola store dispenser, released by Westinghouse, 1960s 25

Matchcover, Coca-Cola, white w/red wording "Things Go Better with Coke," 1960s........ 10

Matchcover, Creamsicles advertising, ad on front, back w/ad promoting the Buck Rogers radio show & note to "Save Creamsicle bags for free gifts," 1930s 50

Matchcover, Diamond Match USA National Hockey League series cover, a total of 60 different players in the set, first series w/a silver finish w/green & black stripes running vertically on the left, player's portrait on the front, their resume on the back, 1933-1935, Red Dutton, US Americans, open 1 1/16 x 4 1/2", each 50

Matchcover, Diamond Match USA National Hockey League series cover, a total of 60 different players in the set, first series w/a silver finish w/green & black stripes running vertically on the left, player's portrait on the front, their resume on the back, 1933-1935, Tiny Thomson, Goalie, Boston Bruins, open 1 1/16 x 4 1/2", each............ 60

Matchcover, Diamond Match USA National Hockey League series cover, part of a series of sets produced between 1936-1939, each series featured various players & had design variations, Type 1, Lorne Chabot, Goalie, Chicago Black Hawks, each.. 40

Matchcover, Diamond Match USA National Hockey League series cover, series of sets produced between 1936-1939, each series featured various players & had design variations, Type 3 , common players, each 20

Matchcover, Diamond Match USA National Hockey League series cover, series of sets produced between 1936-1939, each series featured various players & had design variations, Type 3 , Howie Morenz, Chicago Black Hawks **350**

Matchcover, Diamond Match USA National Hockey League series covers, series of sets produced between 1936-1939, each series featured various players & had design variations, Type 2, Bill Cook, New York Rangers **50**

Matchcover for Manchester Lines, Ltd.

Matchcover, "Manchester Lines Limited," black ground w/red lettering & red & white flag logo, lists company agents in Canada, England & the U.S., Eddy Match Company, ca. 1950s (ILLUS.) **4**

Matchcover Advertising Manger Hotels

Matchcover, "Manger Hotels," black ground w/brown & white advertising, lists locales in various American cities, late 1950s, Match Corp. of America (ILLUS.) **4**

Matchcover, Mayglen Butter, green cover w/advertising on the front & back, Bryant and Mays Matches Co., ca. 1950 .... **3**

Matchcover, New York Central Railroad, cover shows a cowboy on a rearing horse watching an early train steam by, "The New Southwestern Limited," ca. 1920 .... **7**

Matchcover, New York Central Railroad, cover shows a new diesel engine, "The New Ohio State Limited," ca. 1940 .... **7**

Matchcover, New York Central Railroad, cover shows an Art Deco style locomotive, "Empire State Express," ca. 1940.............. **8**

Matchcover, New York Central Railroad, cover shows an early steam engine & "Water Level Route," ca. 1920 .... **7**

Early Olympic Park Matchcover

Matchcover, "Olympic Park," large New Jersey amusement park, yellow, red, black & white printing, Lion Match Company, 1930s, open 1 1/4 x 3 3/4" (ILLUS.)... **25**

Matchcover, "P and O Shipping Lines," dated 1837-1937, commemorates the 100th anniversary of the company.............................. **10**

Matchcover, part of a large series w/various flora & fauna illustrated on the cover, includes flowers, exotic fish, birds, animals & butterflies, Ohio Blue Tip matches, 1957, each cover **3**

Matchcover for Powers Restaurant

Matchcover, "Powers Restaurant, Inc.," brown, tan & white cover w/a large steer, for a restaurant in Tulsa, Oklahoma, Universal Match Company, Kansas City, Missouri, 1950s (ILLUS.)................................... **2**

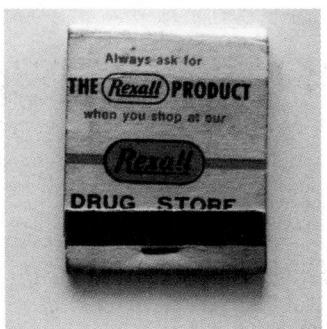

Rexall Drug Store Matchcover

Matchcover, "Rexall Drug Store," white ground w/dark blue & orange advertising, D.D. Bean and Sons Matches, ca. 1960 (ILLUS., previous page)....................................... 2

Matchcover, Sheraton Hotels, red front & back w/a select list of hotel locations, D.D. Bean & Sons Matches, 1950s................... 2

Matchcover, souvenir of 1939 New York World's Fair featuring a scene of the Trylon & Perisphere 15

Matchcover, Superior Match Company "Girlie" cover, various models drawn by Petty, 1950s, 2" l., each book.......................... 18

Matchcover, Sylvania Fluorescent Lamps, "More Light Per Watt - More Light Per Dollar - Look Up to Sylvania - for Leadership in Lighting," ca. 1960s............................. 2

Matchcover, "The Balsam House - An Elegant Inn - Chestertown, New York," green front & back w/advertising, Universal Match Corp., Albany, New York, 1970s, 1 1/2 x 2" 2

Matchcover, World War II patriotic cover, shows Uncle Sam standing in the United States looking across the ocean, "United We Stand," ca. 1942 50

Matchcover, World War II patriotic cover, slogan "V for Victory" on front & back as well as the name of a store or organization, early 1940s.. 8

Matchcover, World War II patriotic cover, "Strike 'Em Dead - Remember Pearl Harbor," ca. 1942................................... 50

Matchcover set, Diamond Match USA National Hockey League series covers, a total of 60 different players in the set, first series w/a silver finish w/green & black stripes running vertically on the left, player's portrait on the front, their resume on the back, 1933-1935, complete set............ 2,000

Matchcover set, Diamond Match USA National Hockey League series covers, series of sets produced between 1936-1939, each series featured various players & had design variations, Type 4, same as Type 3 but only 15 in the set, the set... 235

Matchcover set, Diamond Match USA National Hockey League series covers, series of sets produced between 1936-1939, each series featured various players & had design variations, Type 5, same as Type 3 but only 14 in the set, the set... 235

Matchcover set, Diamond Match USA National Hockey League series covers, series of sets produced between 1936-1939, each series featured various players & had design variations, Type 3 , front imprint in two lines, reads "Made in the USA - Diamond Match Co.," set of 60........ 1,400

Matchcover set, Diamond Match USA National Hockey League series covers, series of sets produced between 1936-1939, each series featured various players & had design variations, Type 1, tan front w/a picture of the player on the front, his resume on the back, set of 70.............. 1,500

Matchcover set, Diamond Match USA National Hockey League series covers, series of sets produced between 1936-1939, each series featured various players & had design variations, Type 2, same as Type 1 except team name and position of the player removed from the player resume on the back, set of 65........ 1,500

METALS

Aluminum

Hammered Aluminum Coaster Set

Coaster set, hammered, four coasters w/stamped bamboo motif, the rectangular holder w/four short feet, fluted rim & indents for coasters, Everlast, 4 x 6 3/4", the set (ILLUS.)... $13

Coasters, embossed tulip motif, in caddy w/decorative ribbon & flower design handle, Rodney Kent, the set............................... 30

Coasters, hammered, rose decoration, in caddy w/curled handle, Everlast, set of 6.. 16-20

Cocktail shaker, cov., double looped finial on cover, Buenilum, 9 1/2" h. 85-95

Condiment server, hammered, apple blossom design on undertray & slotted cover on glass jar, Wendell August #592, the set 35-50

Condiment server, hammered, Ferriswheel style, three "baskets" holding dishes, Continental 55

Cast Aluminum Turtle Corkscrew

Corkscrew, cast, model of a turtle w/a corkscrew tail, original worn paint, 2 1/4 x 4 1/4" (ILLUS.) 95

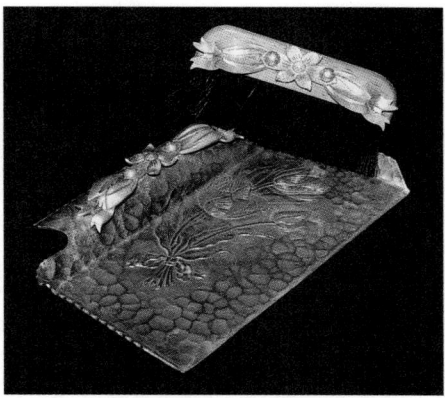

Crumber Set with Tulips

Crumber set: brush & rectangular tray; the tray w/a rolled handle w/applied blossoms & leaf spring & an engraved tulip cluster in tray, the brush w/a wooden handle applied w/a blossom & leaf sprig, Rodney Kent #444, tray 3 1/4 x 8 1/2", 2 pcs. (ILLUS.)... **25-35**

Crumber set: scraper & tray; hammered, scalloped edges, grape decoration on each piece, Everlast, the set............................ **35**

Crumber set: tray & scoop; the two pieces forming a disk, the larger tray section w/a tight curl handle, stamped wild rose sprig decoration, the scoop w/a long curved bar handle, Continental #725, 2 pcs.......... **18-25**

Dresser set: two covered glass dishes on a tray; hammered, covers w/tulip finials, ribbon & flower design caddy handles extend to form feet, Rodney Kent #403, tray 6 x 12", the set **45**

Drink mixer, hammered, one-piece construction, large hole for long-handled stirring spoon, Everlast, 7" h. **50-60**

Gravy boat on attached undertray, hammered, w/ladle, looped handles, Buenilum **35**

Ice Bucket with Chrysanthemums

Ice bucket, open, hammered, chrysanthemum decoration, loop strap handles above figural leaves at the sides, Continental #504 (ILLUS.).. **55**

Jewelry, bracelet, hammered, zinnia link design, Wendell August..................................... **55**

Jewelry, bracelet, stamped w/Western motif on each section, unmarked **25-30**

Pie server, round w/stepped flared sides & flanged rim w/embossed stylized leaf & fruit decoration, geometric beaded handles, glass pie plate fits inside, Everlast **18**

Punch set: bowl, cups, tray & bottle opener; spun aluminum, bamboo rail on tray, Russel Wright design, bowl 11 1/2" d., 6 1/4" h., the set.. **1,250**

Punch set: bowl, ladle & glass cups; hammered, pedestal base, hammered cup hooks, Everlast, the set........................... **175-225**

Relish server, round w/the wide dimpled outer rim embossed w/fruit & flowers, the center shallow well w/further fruits & flowers & fitted w/a three-part clear glass insert, Cromwell **27-32**

Carousel Server with Baskets

Server, carousel-type w/four baskets suspended on chains, disk foot, original came w/four 10 oz. Fire King glass inserts w/scalloped edges, Everlast, 13 1/2 w., 10 1/2 h. (ILLUS.)...................... **45-55**

Serving utensil, gravy ladle, polished, double looped handle, unmarked Buenilum **15**

Serving utensil, pie or cake server, hammered, twisted double looped handle, unmarked Buenilum **35**

Silent butler, round, hammered, apple blossoms decoration, thick handle, notched edge, Wendell August #95, 7" d... **45-55**

Silent butler, round, hammered, tulip decoration, Rodney Kent, 7 1/2" d. **18-20**

Silent butler, round, hammered, wooden handle, Corduroy patt., Continental #1505, 8" d. **20**

Silent butler, round, polished, intaglio design of roses, World, 6 1/4" d. **10**

Smoking set: hammered undertray, ashtrays & cov. cigarette box; blue pottery box, bittersweet decoration on metal, Wendell August #75, the set........................... **195**

Hammered Aluminum Tray with Wild Rose

Smoking stand, hammered, ducks pattern on ashtray, "bubble" protrusions on domed base, twisted stand & ring around top, Wendell August #926, 22 1/4" h............. **275**

Tray, hammered, w/rolled handle, serrated rim, stamped wild rose decoration, style 1071, Continental Silver Co., 6 1/4 x 13 1/2" (ILLUS., top of page)............. **12**

Tray, hammered, tab handles, tropical fish decoration, Everlast, 9 x 14"............. **45**

Tray, hammered, tab handles, Bittersweet patt., Wendell August, 9 1/2 x 14"............. **55**

Tray, spun, raffia-wrapped handle grips, Russel Wright design, 14 1/2" d............. **65**

Tray, hammered, looped handles, lake scene w/dock, fluted edge, Cromwell, 12 1/2 x 14 1/2"............. **18-20**

Tray, anodized highly polished compass design in brass, Kensington, 15" d............. **20-25**

Tray, hammered, looped handle w/leaf decoration, fruits decoration, Cromwell, 15 1/2" d............. **20-25**

Everlast Apple Wastebasket

Wastebasket, hammered, oval w/ruffled rim, embossed Apple (hawthorn) patt., Everlast (ILLUS.)............. **75**

Wastebasket, hammered, wildflowers decoration, Everlast............. **65**

Brass

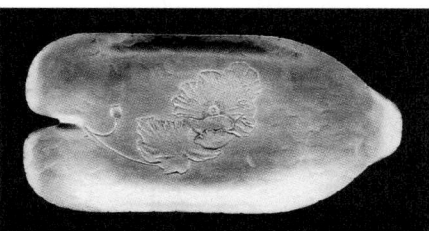

Tray with Poppy Decoration

Tray, flattened bullet-form w/slightly curved rim, notched at one end, embossed w/a large poppy blossom, Wendell August Forge #523, 8 1/2 x 18" (ILLUS.)............. **75-85**

Tray, hammered, handled, chrysanthemum decoration, handles w/decorative leaves, Continental #524, 11 x 22"............. **45**

Brass Art Deco Candlestick

Candlestick, Art Deco style, four-bobeche type, figural Pierrot stands on one foot on lobed base, arms & other leg outstretched, the bobeches balanced on extended foot, two hands & head, stamped w/"GRG" figural mark & "Germany," 9 x 10" (ILLUS., previous page) **$173**

Arts & Craft Brass Coal Hamper

Coal hamper, English Arts & Crafts style, hammered brass w/stylized répoussé design to side panels, riveted corners & handles, inset lid, zinc liner, 14" sq., 16" h. (ILLUS.)... **460**

Glasgow School of Art Brass Tray

Tray, Scottish Arts & Crafts style, oval shape, embossed w/images of stylized pods, by Ms. T. Muir-Wood, Glasgow School of Art, stamped "MTW," 15 x 18 1/2" (ILLUS.)...................................... **403**

Brass Arts & Crafts Tray

Tray, Scottish Arts & Crafts style, rectangular shape w/cutout handles, decorated w/embossed dragonflies & Glasgow roses, unmarked M. Gilmour, 8 x 24 1/4" (ILLUS.) **633**

Brass Wine Bucket

Wine bucket, cov., cylindrical shape w/angular turned mahogany side handles & finial lid, decorated w/vertical & horizontal bands of stamped fruit, Austria or Germany, 13 x 14" (ILLUS.) **230**

Decorated Brass Wood Box

Wood box, rectangular w/slant lid, two ladies head columns in front, & front paw feet, large lion head handles at sides, decorated w/embossed images of rampant lions & eagles, 18 x 30", 21" h. (ILLUS.) **403**

Bronze

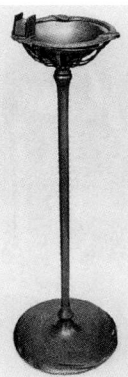

Tiffany Studios Bronze Ashtray

Ashtray, floor model, gold finish, flared base supporting long shaft holding bowl-shaped tray w/hinged top & match holder, marked on base "Tiffany Studios, New York, No. 1649," 9 x 28" (ILLUS., previous page) .... $3,000+

Bronzed Baby Shoes

Baby shoes, high-button, worn-looking, 2 1/2 x 4", 6 1/2" l., the pr. (ILLUS.) 35

Cast Bronze Book End

Book ends, cast, copper finish, flat base merging into upright embossed w/heads of Abraham Lincoln & George Washington in profile, 4" h., the pr. (ILLUS. of one)..... 195

Knight Book End

Book ends, cast, silver finish, stepped base, arched open Moorish-style upright w/figure of knight in armor holding a shield standing between pillars w/background of embossed vining leaves, marked on reverse "Travelers Convention, Palm Beach, Florida, 1931 - patent pending," 3 x 4 1/2", 8" h., the pr. (ILLUS. of one) 250

Tiffany & Co. Bronze Jewel Casket

Jewel casket, eight-sided shape on beveled base, adorned on sides & lid w/Wedgwood blue & white jasper medallions, inside lined w/possibly original purple velvet, inside of lid marked "Tiffany & Co. New York," back edge of base marked "G. Betjemann & Sons Makers London," 6 3/4 x 10", 6 1/2" h. (ILLUS.)..... 2,185

Medallion Honoring Labor

Medallion, commemorative, honoring labor, rectangular, w/embossed scene of classically garbed woman w/arm around boy & pointing to distant industrial scene and the word "Labor" radiating from it, 2 x 2 1/4" (ILLUS.) 75

Medallion, commemorative, w/embossed profile of 21st president of United States in center surrounded by "Chester A. Arthur," dated Sept. 20, 1881, 3" d................ 135

Medallion, memorial for Graf Ferdinand Zeppelin, w/embossed profile of him on front surrounded by "Graf Ferdinand V. Zeppelin [star] 8 Juli 1838 - 8 Marz 1917" around rim, reverse shows figure of Mercury holding zeppelin, 2 5/8" d. 35

Japanese Bronze Vase with Flowers

Vase, wide baluster-form body w/a wide rolled gadroon-cast rim, scrolled foliate handles & raised on a foliate scroll base, the sides cast w/chrysanthemums in relief, good dark patina, Japan, early 20th c., 15" h. (ILLUS.) **201**

Copper

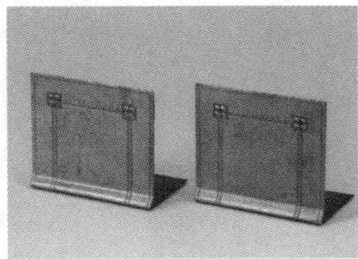

Roycroft Floral Motif Book Ends

Book ends, hammered copper w/brass wash, upright form decorated w/stylized floral motif, marked w/orb & cross, Roycroft, 4 1/2 x 5", pr. (ILLUS.) **$201**

Roycroft Copper Book Ends

Book ends, hammered copper w/brass wash, upright form w/curled & riveted straps, marked w/orb & cross, Roycroft, 2 3/4 x 5", pr. (ILLUS.) **201**

Roycroft Owl Book Ends

Book ends, ovoid upright shapes w/embossed owl motifs & riveted decoration to bases, orb & cross mark, Roycroft, 5 x 5 1/2", pr. (ILLUS.) **431**

Roycroft Copper Card Tray

Card tray, round w/raised rim, hammered copper, orb & cross mark in center, Roycroft, 8" d. (ILLUS.) **518**

Arts & Crafts Copper Coal Scuttle

Coal scuttle, Arts & Crafts style, tapering cylindrical shape, hammered copper w/répoussé floral decoration, riveted seams & rolled scalloped rim, some dents & replaced rivets, new patina, 12 x 15" (ILLUS.) **633**

Ice bucket, cov., cylindrical shape, w/brass riveted side handles, lid handle & foot-ring, the lower body pressed w/ham-mered design, complete w/liner, 12 x 15" (ILLUS.) **201**

Hammered Copper Hanging Mirror

Mirror, English Arts & Crafts style, hanging type, oval shape, frame of hammered texture w/répoussé vine motif inset w/ce-ramic cabochon at top, 23 x 28" (ILLUS.) .. **2,070**

Dirk Van Erp Copper Dish

Dish, round shape w/scalloped rim, ham-mered texture, new interior patina, open box mark, Dirk Van Erp, 7 1/2" d., 1 1/2" h. (ILLUS.) **633**

Cape Cod Shop Copper Firestarter

Firestarter, hinged can, stone rod & footed square tray, the can embossed w/image of fish, stamped "Cape Cod Shop, Pat. 1916," can 6 1/2" (ILLUS.)............................ **288**

Karl Kipp Hammered Copper Plate

Plate, 9 3/4" d., hammered copper, the raised rim w/stylized quatrefoil designs & rolled borders, die-stamped mark, Karl Kipp (ILLUS.).. **460**

Pressed Copper & Brass Ice Bucket

Arts & Crafts Copper Tray

Tray, hand-hammered, Arts & Crafts style, rectangular w/low flared rim, narrow angled end handles, each corner incised w/peacocks in blue-patinated squares, in the manner of the Roycrofters, unmarked, original patina w/normal wear, early 20th c., 11 3/4 x 16 1/2" (ILLUS.)........ **345**

Hammered Copper Oval Tray

Tray, oval shape, hammered copper w/riveted wrought end handles, orb & cross mark, Roycroft, some ring stains to enhanced patina, 10 x 20" (ILLUS.).................. **374**

Copper Tray with Rolled Handles

Tray, rectangular shape w/riveted rolled handles, stamped, Drumgold, 12 x 18" (ILLUS.)... **46**

Stickley Brothers Lobed Rim Tray

Tray, rounded shape w/raised lobed rim embossed w/center dots, no patina, stamped "36," Stickley Brothers, 13 1/2" d. (ILLUS.)... **805**

Copper & Brass Jugenstil Vases

Vases, 11" h., Jugenstil tapering cylindrical forms w/brass bases, rims & buttressed cutout side handles, polished finish, unmarked, Europe, early 20th c., pr. (ILLUS.)... **115**

Arts & Crafts Spherical Vessel

Vessel, Arts & Crafts style, spherical shape w/very short neck, rolled rim & base, 16 1/4" d., 21 1/4" h. (ILLUS.) **2,070**

Iron

Cast-iron African-American Pieces

Andirons, cast, figure of African-American man standing w/hands on bent knees, early paint w/white shirt, red pants, black skin & painted facial features, ca. 1870, paint imperfections, minor corrosion, 12 1/2 x 16 1/2", 19 1/2" h., pr. (ILLUS. left & right with hitching post finial) **$1,380**

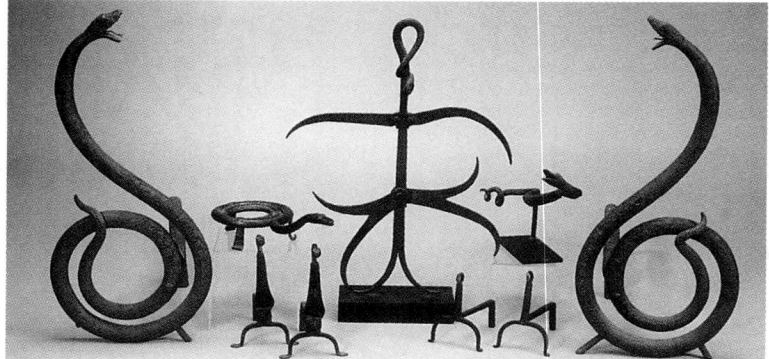

Various Wrought-iron Pieces

Andirons, hand-wrought, miniature, gilded forward looped finial on a simple square shaft above curved front legs w/penny feet, American, early 19th c., 3 1/2" w., 5" h., pr. (ILLUS. second from right, front row with various iron pieces, top of page).. 460

Andirons, hand-wrought, miniature, knife blade-style, polyhedron finial on shaft, arched legs on penny feet, worn black paint, American, late 18th - early 19th c., 4" w., 6 3/4" h., pr. (ILLUS. second from left, front row with various iron pieces, above).. 58

Andirons, hand-wrought, modeled as an upright coiled serpent, the head w/open mouth & projecting tongue, S-form body ending in a coiled tail, bolted to a log support, found in New York state, 19th c., surface rust, 19 3/4" h., pr. (ILLUS. far left & right with various iron pieces, top of page).. 5,463

Calipers, hand-wrought, the handle in the form of a coiled snake continuing to a shaft w/four bifurcating riveted arms, w/stand, possibly Boston Foundry, late 18th c., surface corrosion, 12 3/4" w., 17" h. (ILLUS. center, back row with various iron pieces, top of page)..................... 2,875

Candle or Whale Oil Lantern

Candle or whale oil lantern, hand-forged, w/tapering vents & pierced top, wire ring handle, bull's-eye glass panes, French, ca. 1710, 8 1/2 x 8 1/2", 13 1/2" h. (ILLUS.)................................... **500-600**

Sheet Iron Christmas Light

Christmas light, soldered sheet iron, star-shaped, w/opaque white glass inserts (one missing) & hole in hinged back for bulb, ca. 1930, 4 1/2 x 12 1/4 x 12 1/2" (ILLUS.)... **150-200**

Door handle, hand-wrought, modeled as a snake, the head w/open mouth & teeth continuing to a curving body & coiled tail, w/stand, late 19th - early 20th c., surface corrosion, 12 1/4" l., 3 1/2" h. (ILLUS. right, back row with various iron pieces, top of page) **1,150**

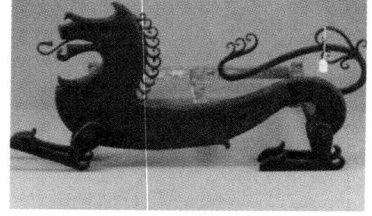

E. Brandt Wrought-iron Firebox

Firebox, wrought-iron cutout stylized figure of rampant lion or mythical beast w/curlicue embellishments to mane & whiplash tail, marked E. Brandt, 14 x 30" (ILLUS., bottom previous page) 805

Hitching post finial, cast, stylized head of African-American man holding a ring & chain in his mouth, 19th c., w/later stand, 5 1/2 x 6", 9 1/2" h. (ILLUS. center with figural andirons, page 821) 2,300

Hitching posts, cast, model of a human clenched fist w/articulated knuckles & fingernails holding a chain & ring, cast in the round, on tall cylindrical posts, modern base, American, late 19th c., 5 x 5", 43" h., pr. 7,638

Hitching posts, cast, the top w/a horse head cast in the round w/a detailed mane, eyes, nostrils & mouth above a ring & oval leaf-cast capital above the faceted column w/acanthus leaves around the bottom on a waisted cylindrical base, modern foot, attributed to J.W. Fiske & Co., New York, New York, late 19th c., 48" h., pr. 4,465

State seal, cast, a scrolled cartouche featuring the State Seal of Massachusetts, cast in the half-round w/a raised arm w/sword at the top enclosing a standing figure of a Native American w/bow & arrow, all above a banner w/legend in Latin, America, late 19th - early 20th c., 13 x 13 1/2" 588

Stove, cast, narrow upright rectangular six-plate type raised on tall cabriole legs w/paw feet, a wide oblong front shelf below the two-part end door, finely cast foliage panels w/wrought-iron levers, raised cast signature of the Zoar Furnace, Zoar, Ohio, ca. 1830-1850, together w/related book on Zoar, stove front shelf pan 18 3/4 x 31", body 12 1/4" w., 25" h. 3,190

Sugar nippers, hand-wrought, scissor-form w/slender gently arched handles & hinged heavy incurved tips ending in small curved blades, stamped star & scallop design & inscribed "J. Nibb," 19th c., 9 1/4" l. 358

Iron & Glass Claw & Ball Feet

Table or stool feet, cast, a large iron talon grasping a clear glass ball, original black paint, light rust, late 19th - early 20th c., 5" h., set of 4 (ILLUS.) 70

Toy, cast, 1920s era model coupe w/fold-out rumble seat, vulcanized rubber wheels, original worn blue paint, 2 1/4 x 2 1/2", 6 1/2" l. 495

Toy, cast, stock truck w/plank-sided bed, in original red paint, possibly by Williams, 1 3/4 x 4 3/4", 2 3/8" h. 225

Trivet, hand-wrought, model of a coiled snake, on three short scroll legs, incised underside, found in Pennsylvania, 19th c., minor surface corrosion, 4 3/4 x 10 1/2", 3 1/4" h. (ILLUS. left, back row with various iron pieces, previous page) 978

Pewter

Candlesticks, round foot tapering to a baluster-form standard w/a top ring below the tall cylindrical socket w/a flatted wide rim, touch mark of Flagg & Homan, Cincinnati, Ohio, ca. 1850, 9 7/8" h., pr. (surface wear) $633

Charger, round w/wide flanged rim w/molded edge, partial crowned rose touch mark & stamped initials "IWE," 14 3/4" d. (surface wear, shallow pitting) 578

Dish, deep round form w/flat flanged rim, touch mark of Thomas Danforth III, Philadelphia, 1777-1818, 13" d. (pitting, knife scratches) 605

Flagon, cov., slightly tapering cylindrical body w/flared base, hinged stepped domed cover w/thumbrest, small curved rim spout, double-scroll metal handle, lion touch mark of Thomas D. Boardman, Hartford, Connecticut, ca. 1830-60, 11 1/8" h. (minor dents) 1,210

Ladle, touch mark of Josiah Danforth, Middletown, Connecticut, 1825-1837, 12 1/2" l. (repair w/short split where bowl & handle meet) 303

Lamp, thin saucer base centering a knopped stem below a flaring cylindrical font w/a domed top centering a whale oil burner, unmarked, 19th c., 7" h. (minor base damage) 193

Four-egg Pewter Chocolate Mold

Mold, chocolate, in the shape of four Easter eggs decorated w/lambs, rabbits & chicks, hinged down middle of mold, closed measures 3 x 8 1/4", 10 1/2" h. (ILLUS.) 395

Pitcher, footed ovoid body tapering to a gently flaring rim w/arched rim spout, angled scroll pewter handle, touch mark of Rufus Dunham, Westbrook, Maine, 1837-1861, 6 3/4" h. (small dents, surface wear) 495

Porringer, round bowl w/heart & crescent-design handle, worn bottom inscription "Plymouth," possibly Roswell Gleason or Richard Lee, Jr., Massachusetts, early 19th c., 3 1/2" d. (minor battering) 248

Porringer, round bowl w/pierced crown-style handle, unidentified "IG" touch mark, New England, ca. 1800, 4 1/4" d. (minor dents) 275

Porringer, round bowl w/pierced floral scroll handle, touch mark of William Billings, Providence, Rhode island, 1791-1806, 5" d. (small split & roughness on handle) .. 1,100

Teapot, cov., footed squatty spherical body w/widely flared rim, hinged domed cover w/disc finial, swan's-neck spout & angled scroll metal handle, touch mark of Israel Trask, Beverly, Massachusetts, 1807-1856, 6 3/4" h. (minor dents, slightly out of round, small repair) 413

Teapot, cov., footed tall tapering ovoid body w/a flared rim & hinged domed cover w/wooden wafer finial, double-scroll metal handle w/black paint, touch mark of John Palethorp & John Connell, Philadelphia, ca. 1820-40, 10 3/4" h. (finial glued, minor dents, cover hinge w/some resoldering) 523

Teapot, cov., individual size, pear-shaped w/hinged domed cover w/finial post, short shaped spout & scrolled wooden handle, crowned touch mark for S. Ellis, England, 19th c., 5 1/2" h. (some dents, slightly out of shape, repair in base) 605

Teapot, cov., pear-shaped body w/hinged domed cover w/finial, paneled spout & arched metal scroll handle w/worn black paint, unmarked, 7 1/4" h. 633

Sheffield Plate

Fine Boulton Sheffield Candlesticks

Candlesticks, an inverted tapering stem gadrooned on the lower half & connected by a gadrooned knop to a circular ogee-domed foot w/gadrooned banding, the top w/a thistle-form gadrooned socket w/gadrooned bobeche, some rosing, Matthew Boulton, ca. 1810, 12 1/4" h., pr. (ILLUS.) **$1,610**

Fine Sheffield Plate Hot Water Urn

Hot water urn, cov., large spherical bee-hive-form body raised on four flat columnar legs & scroll feet on a concave square & serpentine-edged base on four ball feet, a spigot w/loop handle at the bottom front, ring handles at the sides, small cover w/knob finial, the base w/a spherical beehive-form covered burner, possibly Roberts, Cadmen & Company, England, ca. 1800, 9" d., 19" h. (ILLUS.)....... 920

Silver

American (Sterling & Coin)

Fine Tiffany Sterling Bowl

Bowl, round w/deep rounded sides w/a flat rim & a thin footring, embossed w/spiral gadrooning separated by a matte band from the milled & applied shell-and-scroll border band, Tiffany & Company, New York, ca. 1884, 8 1/2" d., 3 1/2" h. (ILLUS.)... **$2,185**

Large Unger Brothers Bread Tray

Bread tray, Art Nouveau style, shallow rounded navette form, the wide everted rim decorated w/deep répoussé irises on a matte ground, the center monogrammed, Unger Brothers, New York, ca. 1895, 7 1/2 x 12 1/2" (ILLUS.) **403**

Francis I Pattern Bread Tray

Bread tray, oval w/wide rolled & scalloped rim, Francis I patt., Reed & Barton, dated 1949, 7 1/2 x 12" (ILLUS.) **690**

Cann, coin, cylindrical keg-shaped w/stave design, stamped mark of Robert & William Wilson, Philadelphia, ca. 1825-46, inscribed "Carrie," 3" h. (minor dents & some resoldering) **248**

Rare Colonial Boston Caster

Caster, coin, slender baluster-form w/molded banding, raised on an ogee-domed foot, the cap w/pierced & engraved panels, molded banding & baluster-form finial, marked on the base w/initials of Zachariah Bridgon of Boston, & a set of wedding initials of a couple, ca. 1760, 1 3/4" d., 5 1/2" h. (ILLUS.) **3,738**

Engraved Coin Silver Creamer

Creamer, bulbous shape w/scroll handle & three trifid feet, the front w/crest & "Rand R M 1758," inscription on one side reading "E.S. & S. Rand to Caroline M. Fitch July 4th, 1828" & on other side "Caroline M. Fitch to Mary F. Jenks April 1st, 1882," square hallmark "T.S.," Thomas Barton Simpkins, 3 3/4" h. (ILLUS.) **6,900**

American Sterling Pitcher & Platter

Pitcher, Neoclassical style, large urn-form body decorated w/milled swag banding & engraved acanthus scrolls, raised on an ogee-domed foot, a waisted neck w/integral spout, angled loop handle w/scroll finial, monogrammed body, Frank M. Whiting, ca. 1920, 10 1/2" h. (ILLUS. left with platter) **863**

Platter, rounded w/four-lobed edge w/ogee-shaped rim threaded & chased w/vases & swags, a milled laurel & ribbed edge, a monogram in the center, Coleman E. Adler, New Orleans, ca. 1920, 12 1/2" d. (ILLUS. right with Whiting pitcher) **345**

Coin Silver Porringer

Porringer, round shape, 2 1/2" l. pierced handle, engraved "MR to MF," w/"Simpkins" touch mark, William Simpkins, Boston, 18th c., 5 1/4" d. (ILLUS.) **2,875**

Sugar tongs, coin, shaped arched handle embossed w/baskets of flowers, shell-form tips, stamped mark of Aime Mathey, New York, New York, ca. 1824-35, 6 1/2" l. **165**

Tea & coffee service: cov. teapot, cov. coffeepot, creamer, cov. sugar bowl, waste bowl & kettle on lamp stand; the upper parts of the fluted bodies cast w/roses & foliage on matted grounds framed by scrollwork, flower basket finials, marked on bases w/presentation inscription, Whiting Mfg. Co., New York, New York, retailed by H. Murh's Sons, ca. 1905, kettle on stand overall 13" h., the set **6,900**

Tea service: cov. teapot, cov. sugar urn & creamer; each of classical form, the teapot oval w/beaded border at foot & rim & the hinged cover w/urn finial, straight spout, wooden loop handle, the creamer & sugar of vase form on a square base, each engraved w/a monogram within a mantle, teapot 12 3/4" l., John Vernon, New York, New York, ca. 1792, the set **8,365**

Vase, trumpet-form body on a round, domed foot, decorated overall in the traditional Baltimore manner w/répoussé flowers on a matte ground, weighted base, A.G. Shultz & Co., Baltimore, Maryland, ca. 1925, 10 1/2" h......................... **345**

English & Other

English Silver Bowl

Bowl, round, w/elaborate raised design of scrolls, flowers & leaves along flaring sides, marked "WC" & hallmarks for London, England, 4 3/4" d. (ILLUS.) **$155**

Bowls, two deep rounded bowls on a plain foot ring, embossed around the sides w/prunus branches on a textured ground, presentation inscriptions around the foot ring, Wang Hing, Hong Kong, China, w/a lobed reticulated bowl w/the sides embossed & engraved w/dragon & cloud reserves, supported by three cast dragon feet, w/a blown cranberry glass insert, Wan Nam & Co., Hong Kong, late 19th - early 20th c., 5 1/2" d., the group **1,380**

Candlesticks, hexagonal shaft & wide base, the tapered candle socket w/removable bobeches, the shafts applied w/dragons, panels engraved w/presentation inscription dated 1934, weighted foot w/applied dragons, marked "Y.C. Co.," China, 8 1/4" h., pr. **1,380**

Compote, open, the wide shallow flaring bowl w/a scalloped reticulated edge & engraved w/prunus blossoms, raised on a three-part stem formed as three flowering trees, offset by small applied cranes, on a squat, lobed pear-form base engraved w/scrolling florals & a shaped rim applied w/similar scrolls, Wang Hing, Canton/Hong Kong, China, late 19th - early 20th c., 7" h.. **1,093**

Russian Carte-de-Visite Frame

Frame, for carte-de-visite picture, Art Nouveau style, hallmarked "84," Imperial-era Russia, 3 1/4 x 5 5/8" (ILLUS.)....................... **295**

Server with Frederick the Great Figure

Serving spoon, figural relief handle w/a standing figure of Frederick the Great of Prussia, royal emblems at base of handle, chased scrolls in the wide shovel-form bowl, Europe, early 20th c., 11" l. (ILLUS.) 595

Mary, Queen of Scots on Silver Server

Serving spoon, figural relief handle w/a standing figure of Mary, Queen of Scots, engraved initials in the wreath & swag-trimmed wide shovel-form bowl, back marked "800," Europe, early 20th c., 10 1/2" l. (ILLUS.) 645

Silver Server with Napoleon Handle

Serving spoon, figural relief handle w/a standing figure of Napoleon I above his imperial emblem & his initial & swags in the large shovel-form bowl, Europe, early 20th c., 10 1/2" l. (ILLUS.) 550

Large Server with Lady on Handle

Serving spoon, figural relief handle w/a standing lady in Victorian dress, above a section of pierced entwined branches, chased musical instruments & sheet music in the wide oblong handle, marked "800," Europe, early 20th c., 11 1/4" l. (ILLUS.) 595

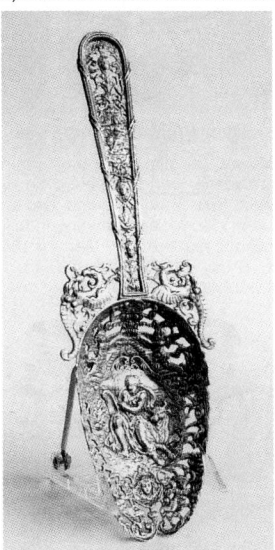

Ornate Pierced Serving Spoon

Serving spoon, the long oval bowl chased & pierced, a central figure of Moses & cherubs, a classical head below, the long flat handle w/pierced scrolls & masks & pierced griffins at the base, Europe, late 19th - early 20th c., 12" l. (ILLUS.) 750

English Sterling Silver Tray

Tray, footed shell-shaped tray w/elaborate scrollwork & engraved but indistinct initials, England, 9 1/2 x 16" (ILLUS.)............... **995**

Silver Plate (Hollowware)

Candelabra, three-light, of typical form, the central waisted sconce w/cast flame finial above a floral-embossed drip tray, w/two reeded scroll arms supporting a candle socket, the floral knopped stem above a stepped square base w/embossed floral bands & shaped rims, England, early 20th c., 17 1/2" h., pr................. **$230**

Silver Plate Candleholder

Candleholders, a slightly domed round base w/a leaftip band centering an upright short leaf & bud issuing two upturned long slender arms ending in tulipform sockets, marked "Her Majesty 1847 Rogers Bros. 009056 I.S.," 20th c., 10 7/8" w., 6 3/4" h., pr. (ILLUS. of one) **200**

Silver Plate Card Tray

Card tray, four-lobed squared-shape tray decorated w/engraved flowers & insects, attached to round base by three legs &

two applied leaf & flower supports, maker's name indistinct, 5 7/8 x 6 1/4" (ILLUS.)... **175**

Art Nouveau Girl with Clock

Clock, figural, figure of an Art Nouveau bonneted girl holding folds of cloak open, w/clock set in folds on one side, 2 1/2 x 7 x 7" (ILLUS.) **795**

Basket-form Condiment Holder

Condiment holder, in the form of a woven basket containing three egg-shaped holders for salt & pepper shakers & mustard cup, w/spread-winged baby bird perched on rim, English, indistinct maker's mark on bottom, 5 1/2" h. (ILLUS.) **1,295**

Silver Plate Handled Cup

Cup, cylinder shape on flared base, repeating panels w/stylized floral design around rim & base, made by Rockford Silver Co., style number 288, 3 x 4 x 4 1/4" (ILLUS., previous page) **45**

Silver Plate Palm Tree Epergne

Epergne, model of a palm tree w/sinuous trunk and six palm fronds, w/a fox running at the circular, ringed base, topped w/a cranberry glass trumpet-shaped flower, 6 1/2" h. (ILLUS.) **1,495**

Art Nouveau Hairbrush

Hairbrush, Art Nouveau style, decorated at one end w/the head & shoulders of a woman in profile w/long flowing hair, heavily embossed w/floral & whiplash design, 1 3/4 x 2 1/4 x 7 1/4" (ILLUS.) **21**

Hot water urn, Neoclassical style, the large ovoid body w/reeded band & concave top w/a domed cover & vasiform finial, the sides w/ringed lion-mask handles, raised on four flat reeded columnar legs ending in paw feet connected by a concave square base centered by a bowl-shaped burner, the whole w/four flattened bun feet, plain downturned spout w/pineapple spigot, England, ca. 1890, 10 1/2" d., overall 20 1/2" h. **863**

Art Nouveau-style Covered Box

Jewelry box, cov., Art Nouveau style, footed, decorated w/roses, marked on bottom "92 DL," possibly a hair receiver, 2 3/4 x 2 3/4 x 3 1/2" (ILLUS.) **165**

Oaken Bucket Match Holder

Match holder, model of old oaken bucket w/two branch handles on sides, sitting on raised base ribbed for striking matches, 4" l. (ILLUS.) **325**

Cockatoo Napkin Ring

Napkin ring, domed stepped circular base holding cockatoo perched on stylized branch, ring resting atop tail, marked "738," 4" h. (ILLUS.) **595**

Lion Napkin Ring

Napkin ring, stepped base holding reclining lion figure, ring resting on lion's back and engraved with "HEP" and floral motifs, 1 1/4 x 2 1/4 x 2 1/2" (ILLUS.) **475**

Triangular Napkin Ring

Napkin ring, triangular shape on claw-and-ball feet, w/pierced floral rims and crossed wishbones forming a border around engraved leaf frond decoration & "Best Wishes," made by Meriden, style number 630, 1 7/8 x 2 3/8 x 3" (ILLUS.) **175**

Figural Owl Smoking Accessory

Smoking accessory, consisting of model of owl on branch attached to three hollow tree stumps w/removable inserts for holding cigarettes, matches & ashes, 5 x 7 x 7 1/2" (ILLUS.) **750**

Monkey Toothpick Holder

Toothpick holder, figural, round stepped base holding figure of monkey holding staff & carrying on its back a basket w/basketweave decoration & rope twist rim, Meriden, 3 1/3" h. (ILLUS.) **550**

Billy Goat Toothpick Holder

Toothpick holder, model of a billy goat next to a large sack w/flared rim, Meriden, 2 1/4 x 2 3/4 x 3" (ILLUS.) **375**

Wine coasters, low cylindrical reticulated sides decorated w/Oriental-style arabesques, wavy gadrooned rim, turned wooden base w/inset round silver plaque, unidentified maker's mark, England, late 19th c., 5 1/2" d., 3" h., pr. **173**

Spelter

Spelter Horse Head Book End

Book ends, image of turned horse head w/flaring nostrils & open mouth, on stepped base, gold finish, 4 1/2 x 4 1/2 x 6", pr. (ILLUS. of one, previous page)............ **95**

Sulgrave Manor Book End

Book ends, in image of Sulgrave Manor, North Hamptonshire, George Washington's family home in England, base forms lawn, marked "JB 22386," 2 x 4 x 5", each (ILLUS. of one).. **75**

Souvenir Calendar Holder

Calendar holder, souvenir in the form of a galleon in full sail attached to a shield embossed w/"The Wrigley Building - Chicago" and image of the building, which holds complete paper date cards for calendar, 1 3/4 x 2 3/8 x 4" (ILLUS.).................... **95**

Silver-finish Eiffel Tower Inkstand

Inkstand, square lidded inkwell in front of image of Eiffel Tower on stepped base, w/pen rest between the two parts, marked "LL 10" on bottom, silver finish, 4 x 4 1/8 x 5 1/2" (ILLUS.).............................. **135**

Whippet Spelter Inkwell

Inkwell, in the form of the head of a whippet w/glass eyes, bronzed finish, head forms lid, neck is well for ink, 3 1/2 x 3 3/4 x 5 1/2" (ILLUS.)........................ **295**

Spelter Basket-shaped Music Box

Music box, model of small woven wicker basket w/swing handle, enclosing music box works & lined w/red velvet, 2 1/2 x 2 3/4", 2" h. (ILLUS.).............................. **12**

Spelter Advertising Paperweight

Paperweight, rectangular base w/"Upper Mississippi Towing Corporation" on side of base, topped w/image of towboat "Harriet Ann" in choppy water decoration, bronzed finish, 5 1/2" l. (ILLUS.)...................... **95**

Caricature Pencil Sharpener

Pencil sharpener, caricature of a black man's face, traces of original red & white paint, 1/2 x 1 1/8 x 1 1/2" (ILLUS.)................ 145

Spelter Shoe Pincushion

Pincushion, model of woman's high-heeled shoe, copper finish w/ornate cast scroll & lattice decoration, fabric lining, marked on base "JB - 1248," 7 3/4" l., 3 1/2" h. (ILLUS.).. 59

Spelter Toy Stock Truck

Toy, stock truck w/worn original red paint, rubber wheels, marked on bottom "Hubley Kiddie Toy - Lancaster, Pa." & on inside of cab top w/"2," 6 5/8" l. (ILLUS.).......... 85

Tin & Tole

Apple tray, tole, rectangular w/low flared sides & flaring rounded ends, interior sides decorated w/white bands w/feathered tulips & leaves in red, yellow & olive green, the bottom w/a crystalized band, slate blue border & a worn center w/trac-

es of yellow, worn exterior japanning, early 19th c., 7 3/4 x 12 5/8", 2 3/4" h........ **$660**

Colorful Toleware Box

Box, cov., rectangular shape, the lid w/clasp & ring handle, the front panel w/colorful mustard & red fruit & flowers w/green leaves, the edge w/vine border, all on black ground, 4 3/4 x 8 3/4", 5 1/2" h. (ILLUS.).. 1,438

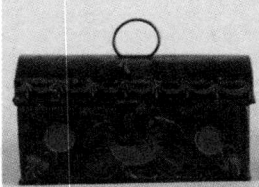

Toleware Dome-lidded Box

Box, cov., rectangular shape w/domed lid, the lid w/ring handle & hasp, decorated w/red fruit & green & mustard leaves & feather design on copper lustre-type ground, a red swag border on the lid, 3 x 6 1/2", 3 1/2" h. (ILLUS.)...................... 1,035

Coffeepot, cov., punched tin, tall pigeon-breasted body on a flaring footring, small domed hinged cover, strap handle, finely worked design of tulips in a flowerpot w/a heart, three bands of wavy intersecting lines & "Samuel and Lida Leidy," handle stamped "M.U.," attributed to M. Uebele of Berks County, Pennsylvania, first half 19th c., 10 3/4" h. (few areas of resoldering, spout w/minor damage) 4,125

Coffeepot, cov., tole, tall slighting tapering cylindrical body w/flaring base band, hinged low domed cover, strap handle, angled gooseneck spout, worn dark japanned background w/bold fruit & floral designs in unusual blue, red, yellow, olive green & tan w/white circular backgrounds, early 19th c., 10 3/4" h. (wear w/minor resoldering) 963

Toleware Dipper

Dipper, cylindrical bowl w/tapering strap handle, the bowl decorated w/red & mustard decorative band on black ground, the handle w/mustard & red leaf decoration, bowl 3 1/2" d., 2 1/4" h., 8" w/handle (ILLUS.) **480**

Toleware Document Box

Document box, cov., rectangular w/domed lid, the lid w/ring handle, the lid & sides decorated w/crisscross decoration in mustard yellow, the front w/brightly colored large round red flowers, green leaves & yellow sprigs, all on black japanned ground, 19th c., 5 x 9", 4" h. (ILLUS.)... **403**

Doll head, tin, unpainted except teeth, inset glass eyes, marked on front "Minerva," marked on back "Germany - 7," 6 1/4" h. **75**

Match holder, tole, hanging-type, rounded scalloped crest w/hanging hole, w/starburst & flourishes on the pocket in shades of blue, yellow & red on a black ground, 19th c., 7 1/2" h. (minor wear)......... **660**

Tea caddy, cov., tole, cylindrical w/a flattened shoulder centered by a short neck w/fitted cap cover, dark brown japanned ground decorated w/a band of red, yellow & green fruit, 19th c., 4 1/8" h. (some wear, mainly on the cover)............................. **523**

Tea caddy, cov., tole, footed casket-form, rectangular w/flaring curved sides & a flat-sided stepped & domed cover w/embossed pull finial, on small paw feet, golden japanning w/yellow bands, white stripes & black leopard spots, painted heart escutcheon, early 19th c., 3 1/4 x 4 1/2", 4 3/8" h. (minor wear, two short seam splits).. **1,100**

Toleware Teapot

Teapot, cov., oval form w/angled front spout & shaped hinged lid, strap handle, decorative finial, back & front decorated w/two-part rose w/leaves, the lid w/blue/green leaf design, 5 3/4" h. (ILLUS.)... **1,840**

Tole Tray with Apple Decoration

Tray, tole, four-lobed shape, the rim decorated w/band of red apples & green leaves, the center w/leaf & line highlights on brownish-copper ground, 12 1/2" d., 2 1/2" h. (ILLUS.)... **300**

Scenic Tray with Tole Decorated Rim

Tray, tole, rectangular shape w/rounded corners & raised rim, the rim decorated w/stenciled gold leaves & black & red highlights on black ground, the interior w/painted landscape w/woman tending goats & cows in pastoral wooded setting, first half 19th c., 16 1/2 x 21 3/4" (ILLUS.)...... **403**

Tray, tole, rectangular w/angled corners, black ground decorated w/yellow swags & a bold flower in red, orange, yellow & green repaint, first half 19th c., 8 3/4 x 12 1/2" (wear)....................................... **220**

MILITARIA & WARTIME MEMORABILIA

Since the early 19th century, every war that America has fought has been commemorated with a variety of war-related memorabilia, often in the form of propaganda items produced during the conflict or as memorial pieces made after the war ended. These materials are today quite collectible and increasingly important for the historic insights they provide. Most common are items dating from World War I and II.

Civil War

Ambrotype, cased portrait of a young Union Infantry sergeant in almost full gear wearing his frock coat w/cartridge box, cap box & kepi, a musket w/bayonet at his side, good clear image w/overall light tinting, case taped at hinge, 3 1/4 x 4 1/4" **$495**

Bayonet w/scabbard, Union 1861 Collins model, bright blade & worn plating on brass handle, leather scabbard w/brass ends, 28 1/2" l. (old splits on sides of the ring)... **275**

Carte-de-visite, portrait of General Doubleday, w/Brady Studio mark on front & back (bend near bottom).. **55**

Cutlass, Union Naval model, brass hilt & pommel, 25 1/2" l. blade, unsigned, w/old nickel plating, leather wrapping remains on handle but wire missing, overall 31" l. **330**

Saber, scabbard & hanger, Union Cavalry Model 1860, 34 1/2" l. blade stamped "Ames Mfg., Chicopee, U.S. 1865," overall dark patina on sword & scabbard, leather hanger w/original gilding on the ends, the set **1,100**

Sword, Confederate artillery model, cast brass handle w/star pommel & crude relief letters "C.D." on the guard, 19" l. blade pitted & appears to be dug, overall 24 1/2" l. **1,540**

Confederate Sword Belt Plate

Sword belt plate, Confederate, tongue-in-wreath type, Haiman style, metal w/dark brown patina, round center w/relief letters "CS" in decorative embossed border, 3 3/4" w. (ILLUS.) **4,888**

Sword & scabbard, Union officer's, brass hilt w/traces of original gilding & openwork floral details, 30" l. blade etched w/"U.S. - Ames Mfg. Co., Chicopee, Mass." & scrolled vining, worn sharkskin grip retains wire wrapping, leather scabbard w/brass bands & taped break, overall 36" l., the set **1,320**

Sword & scabbard, Union presentation-grade officer's model, the blade w/engraved signature "W.H. Horstmann & Sons, Philadelphia," & relief etching w/an eagle & "U.S." w/gold detailing, cast brass hilt w/openwork detail w/original gilding, engraved nickel silver handle, worn sharkskin covering on the scabbard w/cast & gilded brass bands & drag, 38" l. (areas of surface pitting on blade).. **2,750**

Tintype, cased portrait of Union cavalryman w/bugle standing in front of painted studio backdrop w/camp scene, wearing Colt pistol stuck in his U.S. belt & holding a cavalry saber, slightly dark, 2 3/4 x 3 1/4" **1,073**

Tintype, fine gutta percha case holding two images within a gilt liner of the same Union soldier w/a pillar, one shot close-up, the other further back, in both he holds a musket & wears a belt w/cap box & cartridge box w/cross belt, molded patriotic case shows crossed cannons, eagles & shields, 4 1/4 x 5 1/2" (liner damage)... **990**

MINIATURES (REPLICAS)

Lithograph-decorated Blanket Chest

Blanket chest, mahogany, dovetail construction, brass hinges, molded base, the front & sides decorated w/applied lithographs of sailing ships, missing feet, finish alligatored, 6 1/4 x 11 3/4", 7 1/2" h. (ILLUS.)... **$220**

Blanket chest, pine, rectangular top opening to a deep well w/till, the dovetailed case fitted w/a brass batwing keyhole escutcheon, a long dovetailed drawer at the base, molded base on bracket feet, old dark stain, T-head nail construction, late 18th - early 19th c., 7 1/2 x 12 1/2", 10 1/2" h. (replaced staple hinges & wooden pull, wear, some repairs)................. **578**

Rare Painted Tole Mini Sconces

Candle sconces, red-painted tole, the round crimped top above the rectangular backplate & narrow projecting base w/a cylindrical socket, 2" w., 7" h., pr. (ILLUS.) **1,380**

Chest of drawers, country-style, painted pine, a nearly square top above an upright case w/three drawers w/turned wood pulls, applied & carved decorations on the front corners w/molded edging along the flat base, old red over black grained decoration & black line detail, 19th c., 9 1/2 x 10 1/2", 13" h. (old edge split) **1,155**

Miniature Empire Chest of Drawers

Chest of drawers, Empire style, mahogany & mahogany veneer, top w/two small drawers above four graduated drawers w/fancy crotch-figure veneer, tapered columns w/scrolled feet, back feet turned, pencil inscription under full top drawer reads "Wife Ellen P.T(?)uttle by her father when a baby. Made at Bath, Maine, 1842 by Robert Tuttle. Took first premium at Bath fair," losses to veneer, chips & separations, top missing piece of molding, 11 x 19", 21" h. (ILLUS.) **1,540**

Chest of drawers, Federal style, mahogany veneer over pine, a rectangular top above a case w/four beaded graduated long dovetailed drawers w/wooden knob pulls, simple bracket feet, silver inset heart & letter "B" on the top, constructed w/T-head nails, inside drawer fronts & undersides stained, early 19th c., 7 7/8 x 10 1/4", 10 1/2" h. (minor veneer splits) **2,860**

Rare Miniature Victorian Safe

Safe, cast iron, upright black case on rollers, gold band trim, the door painted w/small oval landscape w/bears, the door w/gold letters reading "Deposit Vault," w/key, 19th c., 8 1/2 x 9 1/2", 14 1/4" h. (ILLUS.) **1,380**

Table, oak, draw-leaf style, turned box-stretcher base, w/two draw leaves, probably 19th c. in the 18th c. style, scattered worm damage, 18 x 24" (opens to 41"), 18" h. (ILLUS., below) **550**

Miniature Oak Draw-leaf Table

MOVIE MEMORABILIA

*Also see: ADVERTISING ITEMS; CAT COL-
LECTIBLES;   DOLLS;   HORSE COLLECTI-
BLES;   POP   CULTURE   MEMORABILIA;
SHEET MUSIC and VIEW-MASTER & TRU-
VUE VIEWERS & REELS.*

Costumes

"Ghostbusters" Ghost Costume Head

Ghost head, "Ghostbusters," latex, pink,
widely grinning ghost head worn in the
movie, signed by Dan Aykroyd, 1989
(ILLUS.) **$345**

*Oompa Loompa Costume from Willy Wonka
& The Chocolate Factory*

Oompa Loompa, "Willy Wonka & The
Chocolate Factory," 1971, off-white
bibbed trousers, chocolate brown top
w/striped stand-up collar & cuffs & shoes,
comes w/green wig (ILLUS.)...................... **5,284**

Lobby Cards

"Gone With the Wind," 1939, full-color de-
pictions of cast members, one devoted to
each of the four leads, three group shots,
& the title card, each 11 x 14", comes
w/original   9 x 12"   20-page   program
booklet, all mounted on rag board in maroon slipcase album w/gold leaf spinal
lettering, the set **4,333**

"The Great Dictator" Lobby Card Set

"Great Dictator (The)," 1940, full-color
cards w/scenes from movie, each w/yel-
low rectangular panel in lower corner
containing info about movie/scene, plus
title card w/yellow ground reading "Charlie Chaplin - The Great Dictator - He
Talks..." w/caricature of Chaplin in the title role & rectangular red panel containing other film info, each 11 x 14", the set
(ILLUS.)... **1,121**

Posters

"Breakfast at Tiffany's," Paramount,
1961, full length color illustration of Au-
drey Hepburn in elegant long black dress
slit to knee & long black gloves, w/ex-
tremely long cigarette holder in her
mouth & cat on her shoulder, white background w/black & red lettering, linen-
backed, one-sheet, 27 x 41"..................... **2,717**

*One-sheet Movie Poster for "Frankenstein
Meets the Wolf Man"*

"Frankenstein Meets the Wolf Man," 20th Century-Fox Film Corporation/Terry-Toon Cartoons, 1938, linen-backed one-sheet featuring monochromatic illustration of the two characters grappling w/each other beneath the words "Fiend of Fury vs. Night-born Killer!" & at bottom a black & white photo of woman half-reclining & looking up, seemingly at action taking place in top of poster, the title in red-bordered white block letters across the center, cast info in black in bottom right, all within red border, 27 x 41" (ILLUS., previous page)............................... **1,150**

Three-sheet Poster for "Willy Wonka" Movie

"Willy Wonka & The Chocolate Factory," Paramount, 1971, three-sheet, white ground w/color illustrations of Gene Wilder as Willy Wonka w/arms outstretched, other characters arranged along his arms & in the background, above the title in red & chocolate brown lettering, general info at bottom, never used, 41 x 81" (ILLUS.) **1,321**

Miscellaneous

Caricature, lithograph, line drawings of four characters from "The Godfather," by Al Hirschfeld, limited edition numbered "93/175" & signed by Hirschfeld in pencil, 21 x 25" **1,497**

Certificate of nomination, "Taxi Driver" for Best Picture of 1976 by the Academy of Motion Picture Arts & Sciences, mounted-to-wood "perma-plaque," 12 x 13 1/2".. **2,087**

Contract, Charlie Chaplin signed contract w/Associated First National Pictures, dated January 8, 1923, four-page carbon copy signed by Chaplin in black ink............ **3,580**

Marx Brothers Folk Art Figures

Figures of Marx Brothers, wood, folk art-style, hand-painted, two-dimensional figures w/caricature faces capturing the comic personalities of Harpo, Chico, Groucho & Zeppo, each initialed by artist, one dated 1931, on square bases, 6 1/2" h., the set (ILLUS.)............................ **1,598**

Letter, signed by Greta Garbo, dated July 30, 1941, typed business letter to Loew's Incorporated of Culver City, California, signed in blue fountain pen, rare............... **1,201**

Photograph, Douglas Fairbanks & Mary Pickford, matte-finish sepia studio photo of Fairbanks in three-quarters pose & Pickford in profile, inscribed & autographed in blue fountain pen "Very Sincerely - Douglas Fairbanks - 1928" & "Sincerely Yours - Mary Pickford - 1929," 7 7/8 x 9 3/4" **345**

Autographed James Dean Photo

Photograph, James Dean, black & white, high-angle shot of Dean wearing jacket similar to the one he wore in "Rebel without a Cause," signed in black "To Karen, With my best wishes, James Dean," 8 x 10" (ILLUS.) **4,333**

Signed Marilyn Monroe Photo

Photograph, Marilyn Monroe, black & white, shot of Monroe lying back on satin pillow wearing off-the-shoulder dress & glittering necklace & earrings, smiling seductively at viewer, signed "To Ronnie, Love & Kisses, Marilyn Monroe," 8 1/2 x 12 1/2" matted & framed (ILLUS.) **6,346**

Realty Sign Prop from "The Amityville Horror"

Realty sign prop, "The Amityville Horror," rectangular, yellow & white on black ground, reading "For Sale - Amityville Realty - 666-1818 - Agent Clifford Sanders" w/icon of house, few minor chips, 1979, 18 x 24" (ILLUS.) **380**

Script, "Dr. Jekyll and Mr. Hyde," Paramount, original copy of finished script, each page permanently mounted on high quality rag pages & covered in leather binding w/gold leaf labeling, 1931 .... **991**

MUSICAL INSTRUMENTS

Grand piano, Victorian Rococo style rosewood case w/scalloped apron & ebonized trim, supported by cabriole legs w/fruit-carved cartouches at knees, the case & works labeled "Weber N.Y.," in playing condition, mid-19th c., 43 x 83", 38 1/2" h. (ILLUS., bottom of page).......... **$2,070**

Victorian Rosewood Weber Grand Piano

Decorative Early Hurdy Gurdy

Hurdy gurdy, 23-key organ w/31 violin & flute pipes in front & bottom, front of case w/decorative inlay & marquetry w/mother-of-pearl & an embossed image of a Victorian lady, seven-tune pinned cylinder, original paper label listing tunes, hardwood case w/beveled brass corners, in playing condition, Muzzio Organ Works, Glen Rock, New Jersey, ca. 1920s, replaced leather straps & wooden bottom frame, 15 1/2 x 17", 18" h. (ILLUS.) **4,600**

Rococo Revival Melodian

Melodian, rosewood, Rococo Revival, the fold-over top opening to reveal scroll-sawn music rack, the keys retaining their period ivory, on tapering octagonal legs, w/gilt-stenciled label of "Austin C. Chase, Syracuse, New York," in playing condition, mid-19th c., 26 x 49", 33" h. (ILLUS.) **863**

Victorian Hand-cranked Melodista

Melodista, hand-operated tabletop reed organ w/five 14-note paper rolls, wooden case w/original finish w/gold stenciling, side crank handle, made by G. H. W. Bates, Boston, ca. 1880s, all-original & unrestored, original instruction decals on the bottom, needs bellows work, 9 1/2 x 14", 9" h. (ILLUS.) **420**

"Rolmonica" Mouth Organ

Mouth organ, "Rolmonica," metal case w/end crank handles, plays paper rolls by blowing through them, w/eight rolls, ca. 1928, 5" l. (ILLUS.) **259**

Late Federal Mahogany Piano Forte

Piano forte, Federal style, inlaid mahogany, the long rectangular case w/banded veneer & line inlay, the fold-up top opening to the keyboard below two lattice-covered sound panels, the lower case w/a pair of drawers flanking a long concave central drawer, all w/early pressed glass knobs, on heavy ring- and spiral-turned legs on casters, possibly Boston or Philadelphia, original finish, ca. 1825, 34" h. (ILLUS.) **1,000-1,200**

Fine Victorian Walnut Pump Organ

Pump organ, walnut, the high superstructure w/a central arched sawtooth crest above a raised burl panel over three small open shelves & flanked by half-round sunburst panels w/rosettes flanked by downswept shaped sides, a cloth-line sounding board w/three panels of ornate wood lattice above the sliding top over the keyboard above two more cloth-lined sounding panels, paneled lower section w/incised-line decoration flanked by turned columns at the front, made by J. Estep & Co., Brattleboro, Vermont, ca. 1880, w/an organ stool w/squared needlepoint top adjusting on a turned pedestal over a tripod base w/carved cabriole legs valued at $40, the organ alone (ILLUS. of organ & stool) **1,600**

"Chautauqua" Model Roller Organ

Roller organ, "Chautauqua" model, oak case w/original stencil on top, crank handle below opening for the 6 1/2" l. pinned cylinder player, hinged glass door on top, in playing condition, late 19th - early 20th c., 18" sq., 12 1/2" h. (ILLUS.) **633**

NUTTING (WALLACE) COLLECTIBLES

In 1898, Wallace Nutting published his first hand-tinted pictures, which remained popular for more than 20 years. An "assembly line" subsequently colored and placed a signature and (sometimes) a title on the mat of these copyrighted photographs. Interior scenes featuring Early American furniture are considered the most collectible of these photographs. Nutting's photographically illustrated travel books and early editions of his antiques reference books are also highly collectible.

The items listed here were compiled by noted Nutting authority and auctioneer Michael Ivankovich of Doylestown, Pennsylvania. For more information on Wallace Nutting check out his Web site at www.wnutting.com.

Books

"Connecticut Beautiful," second edition $35
"England Beautiful," second edition 55
"Furniture of the Pilgrim Century," first edition 100
"Ireland Beautiful," first edition 50
"Maine Beautiful," second edition 35
"Massachusetts Beautiful," second edition 40
"New Hampshire Beautiful," second edition 45
"New York Beautiful" second edition 50
"Pennsylvania Beautiful," second edition 40
"Photographic Art Secrets" 200
"The Clock Book," first edition 75
"Vermont Beautiful," first edition 45
"Virginia Beautiful," second edition 50
"Wallace Nutting Biography" 100

Furniture

Armchair, child's, No. 211 .... **2,700**
Armchair, Windsor comb-back, No. 415 .... **1,500**
Armchair, Windsor continuous-arm, No. 401 .... **550**
Armchair, Windsor tenon-type, No. 422 .... **1,500**

Nutting Writing-arm Windsor

Armchair, Windsor writing-arm, No. 430 (ILLUS.) **6,600**

Bed, mahogany, No. 823-B 2,600
Candlestand, three-legged, No. 17 1,125
Chair, rocking, Windsor-Style, No. 477 700
Chair, side, Windsor-Style fan-back, No.
310 750
Chair, side, Windsor-Style, No. 301 525
Chair, side, Windsor-Style, No. 326 660
Mirror, wall-type, three-feather decoration,
No. 761 625
Settle, winged-style, pine, No. 416 3,700
Stand, four-legged, No. 653 500
Stool, four-legged, Windsor-Style, No. 145 150
Stool, Jacobean-Style, No. 171 750
Table, butterfly-type, maple, No. 623 1,900

Nutting Queen Anne Card Table

Table, card-type, Queen Anne-Style, wal-
nut, No. 697 (ILLUS.) 6,600
Table, trestle-type, pine top, No. 614 550

Prints

A Barre Brook, 11 x 14" 120
A Berkshire Brook, 10 x 16" 115
A Call for More, 10 X 13" 375
A Canopied Road, 14 x 17" 100
A Catskill Bank 170
A Chair for John, 12 x 16" 150

A Cluster of Zinnias

A Cluster of Zinnias, 13 x 16" (ILLUS.) 715
A Dahlia Jar, 13 x 16" 450
A Delicate Stitch, 8 x 11" 200
A Fleck of Sunshine, 11 x 17" 175
A Fruit Luncheon, 9 x 12" 130
A Garden of Larkspur, 13 x 16" 120
A Gettysburg Crossing, 14 x 17" 275
A Gran'pa and Gran'ma Bed 300
A Leaf Strewn Brook, 12 x 16" 100
A Little Rose of Ireland 1,900
A Maryland Porch 1,450

Rare A Masque Pitcher Print

A Masque Pitcher, 16 x 20" (ILLUS.) 1,815
A May Countryside 145
A May Drive 60
A Memory of Childhood, 10 x 12" 160
A New England Road in May 160
A New Hampshire Bridge 150
A Nova Scotia Idyl 160
A Nuttinghame Nook, 13 x 16" 210
A Part of Milan's Towers 950
A Perkiomen October, 9 x 11" 255
A Rangeley Shore 80
A Romance of the Revolution 140
A Rug Pattern, 13 x 16" 255
A Scottish Stronghold 3,700
A Stately Tea Pouring 160
A Stitch in Time, 11 x 14" 125
A Tap at the Squire's Door 110
A True D.A.R. 100
A Walpole Road 75
A Warm Spring Day, 11 x 17" 220
A Washington Spring 140
A Wilkes-Barre Brook, 13 x 16" 290
Affectionately Yours, 14 x 17" 190
An Afternoon Tea, 10 x 14" 90
An Annapolis Garden 1,250
An Elaborate Dinner, 14 x 17" 140
An Eventful Journey, 13 x 16" 1,300
An Old Time Romance, 13 x 16" 120
At the Fender, 14 x 16" 190
At the Hilltop 90
Autumn Grotto, 14 x 17" 115
Below the Arches 160

Mary's Little Lamb

Braiding a Rag Rug, 11 x 14" 120
Cathedral Brook, 9 x 11" 80
Charles River Elm 150
Dandelion and Buttercup 1,500
Decked as a Bride, 13 x 16" 100
Dream and Reality, 10 x 16" 75
Dykeside Blossoms, 11 x 17" 110
Evangeline Lane, 13 x 16"............................... 220
Flowering Time, 11 x 14"..................................... 85
Garden of Poe Shrine 1,500
Good Night! 140
Gorgeous May, 11 x 14"...................................... 70
Grace, 16 x 20" 110
Happy Valley Road, 11 x 17" 70
Hollyhock Cottage, 12 x 14" 110
Hollyhocks 1,100
Honeymoon Blossoms 70
Honeymoon Cottage, 11 x 17" 60
Honeymoon Drive, 13 x 16" 85
Honeymoon Stroll, 10 x 12"................................ 80
Honeymoon Windings, 10 x 16" 75
Hope, 16 x 20"... 115
In Tenderleaf, 10 x 16" 80
Ivy and Rose Cloister, 13 x 16" 250
Ivy Pruning 275
Joy Path, 13 x 16".. 90
Justifiable Vanity 150
La Jolla, 11 x17" (ILLUS., next column)........... 250
Larkspur, 13 x 15" 110
Litchfield Minster, 14 x 17" 135
Litchfield Minster, 10 x 12" 160
Little Washerwomen, Amalfi 1,500
Mammy's Darling 5,250
Many Happy Returns, 13 x 16" 70
Mary's Little Lamb, 13 x 16" (ILLUS., top
  of page)... 350
Maryland, My Maryland 525
Nethercote, 8 x 10" 110
Orchard Heights, 16 x 20" 85
Returning from a Walk, 11 x 17" 140
Sea Ledges, 13 x 16".. 230
Slack Water, 9 x 14" 90
Tea in Yorktown Parlor, 13 x 15"..................... 160
The "Chateau" on Lake Mohonk 1,300
The Coming Out of Rosa, 11 x 14" 170

La Jolla Seascape

The Eames House 1,250
The Fair Vale 180
The Footbridge by the Ford, 16 x 20" 350
The Goose Chase Quilt, 7 x 11"....................... 260
The Great Wayside Oak, 14 x 17" 180
The Guardian Mother, 11 x 17" 3,080
The Life of the Golden Age, 10 x 15" 275
The Maple Sugar Cupboard, 11 x 16"............. 120
The Meeting of the Ways, 11 x 14" 100
The Nest, 14 x 17".. 165
The Northern Hudson 150
The Old Homestead 230
The Pasture of Muckross, 9 x 16" 140
The Pasture Pool 140
The Pergola Amalfi, 13 x 15"............................ 250

PERFUME, SCENT & COLOGNE BOTTLES

Decorative accessories from milady's boudoir have always been highly collectible, and in recent years there has been an especially strong surge of interest in perfume bottles. Our listings also include related containers such as pocket bottles and vials, tabletop containers & atomizers. Most readily available are examples from the 19th through the mid-20th century, but earlier examples do surface occasionally. The myriad varieties have now been documented in several recent reference books, which should further popularize this collecting specialty.

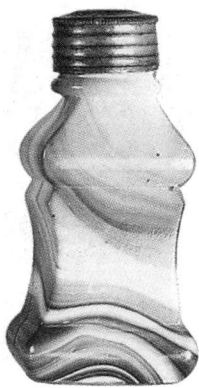

Blue & White Swirled Glass Scent Bottle

Blue & white swirled glass, four-sided slightly waisted form w/bulging shoulder tapering to rough sheared & ground lip w/original screw-on metal cap, marbled decoration in shades of blue on white, America, ca. 1860-90, two minor chips off edge of lip, possibly from time of manufacture, 2 1/8" h. (ILLUS.) **$364**

Cameo glass, figural engraved duck head in overlay colors of white over yellow, original silver cap marked underneath, England, 8 3/4" l. (ILLUS, bottom of page.) **4,600**

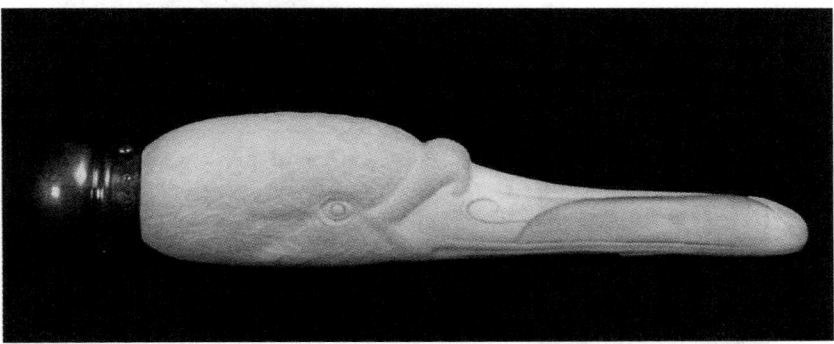

Duck Head Scent Container

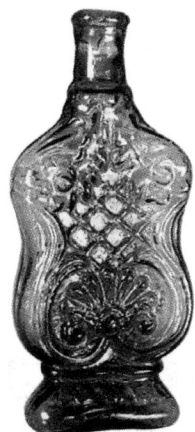

Cobalt Blue Glass Scent Bottle

Cobalt blue glass, waisted form on flaring base, ringed neck w/inward rolled lip, the body decorated w/diamonds, scrolls & fans, medium color in center shading to light at sides, open pontil, America, ca. 1835-55, 5 5/8" h. (ILLUS.) **2,128**

Enameled Egg-shaped Scent Bottle

Enameled brass, egg form w/decorative brass collar about a third of the way from the top, the top decorated w/delicate enameled flowers, the lower section w/enameled winged cherub & more flowers, all on deep brown, near-black ground, missing interior stopper, 3/4 x 1 1/4" (ILLUS.) **805**

Enameled Scent Bottle

Enameled white metal, cylindrical form decorated w/scene of woman sitting in garden reading letter, trees & garden gate filling the rest of the pink enamel ground, decorative white metal collar & foot, top of flaring hinged lid enameled w/images of scythe, basket & sheaf of wheat, lid opening to reveal small glass stopper, 2 1/2" h. (ILLUS.) **1,323**

Teardrop Cologne Bottle

Glass, teardrop form, clear glass decorated w/alternating blue, white & pink vertical stripes, tooled mouth, pontil, America, ca. 1840-70, 4 3/4" h. (ILLUS.)....... **147**

Round Lalique Perfume Bottle

Matte blue glass, round shape decorated w/randomly spaced & sized cameo stars on matte blue ground, matching stopper, bottle signed on bottom "R. Lalique," stopper held in place w/original metallic rope ties, each w/paper label reading "Worth, Paris" on one side & "Dans La Nuit" on other, in original box, wear to labels, box w/some wear & looseness to hinge, 3" h. (ILLUS.) **403**

*Opalescent Milk Glass Monument
Scent Bottle*

Milk glass, monument form on rectangular base, w/short cylindrical neck & rolled lip, in fiery opalescent color, pontil, rare, America, 1835-55, 4 1/2" h. (ILLUS.) **2,688**

*Porcelain Scent Bottle of
Fashionable Woman*

Porcelain, figure of woman wearing white dress in the style of the 18th century & decorated w/h.p. flowers & leaves, maroon trim, head removes at neck & holds brass dauber, 4 1/2" h. (ILLUS.).................... **403**

Loop-decorated Satin Glass Scent Bottle

Satin glass & silver, bulbous form w/long slender neck, an engraved & hallmarked silver band at base of neck w/silver chain extending from it to embossed silver floral cap, w/overall pink & cream loop decoration, 6 1/2" h. (ILLUS.) **575**

Hourglass Cologne Bottle

Teal blue glass, eight-sided hourglass form w/long slender neck, tooled lip, smooth base, America, ca. 1850-80, 4 5/8" h. (ILLUS.)... **840**

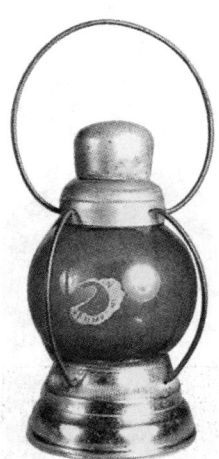

Figural Lantern Scent Bottle

Teal glass & metal, figural lantern, center glass globe in metal cage w/stepped base, screw top & loop handle, original label on base reading "Use Tappan's Famous Sweet Bye & Bye Perfume, it is Fine Sold Everywhere," America, ca. 1890-1910, 3 3/8" h. (ILLUS.)........................... **90**

PINBALL GAMES

Pinball games take on many forms, from the tiny prizes issued over the years in Crackerjack boxes to tabletop children's games to large floor models.

The children's games, also called "bagatelle," used marbles of various colors but generally white or black. In general the black marble doubled any score where it landed.

The larger floor models are of two types: one meant for home use in a recreation room and the second a commercial type, played for money, and often found in bars, bowling alleys and other recreational facilities.

"Airway," floor model, first mechanical scoring pinball game, featuring airplanes of various types of the period, Bally, 1933... **$900**

Marx "Baseball" Pinball Game

"Baseball," baseball diamond-shaped lithographed metal base w/clear plastic cover showing various players on the field, w/six white marbles, various indentations indicating baseball play, Louis Marx & Co., ca. 1950 (ILLUS.) **100**

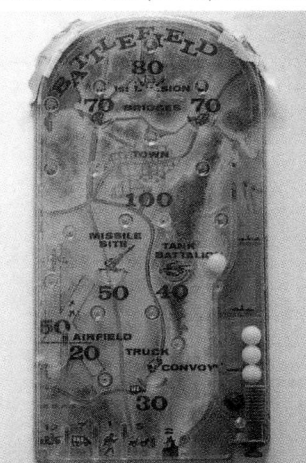

Marx "Battlefield" Pinball Game

"Battlefield," rounded lithographed tin background w/clear plastic cover, printed w/an aerial view of a battlefield w/ships off the coast, various areas of the field featuring different point values, corner lever for shooting white or black marble, Louis Marx & Co., ca. 1960, 12 1/4" l. (ILLUS.).............. **60**

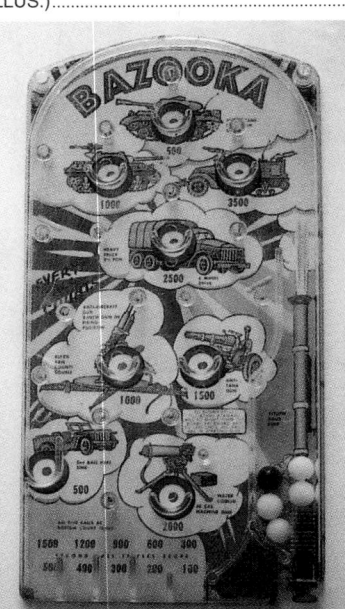

Marx "Bazooka" Pinball Game

"Bazooka," lithographed tin background w/clear plastic cover, illustrated w/various military vehicles & weapons worth various points, pull lever in lower corner for shooting white or black marbles, Louis Marx & Co., New York, New York, ca. 1950s, 12 1/4" l. (ILLUS.)................................ **125**

"Big Game Safari," lithographed tin background w/plastic cover, showing various African big game animals, each worth different points, Reliable Toy Company, Toronto, Canada, 1950s..................................... **35**

"Big Parade" exhibit pinball game, floor model, colorful patriotic images & Art Deco designs, 1941 .... **400**

"Coney Island," floor model, coin-operated, upright glass backboard w/Coney Island scenes & classic bathing beauties, two metal side buttons controlling the flippers, 1950s.. **800**

Crackerjack premium, various miniature types given away in the packages, one of the most graphic depicting a World War I airplane dogfight, w/tiny metal ball, ca. 1950s, 2 1/4 x 3 1/4", each **12**

"Funny Andy - Hoop-O-Loop," colorfully lithographed metal angled board showing four big game hunters, the lower end w/a gun w/a spring mechanism to shoot

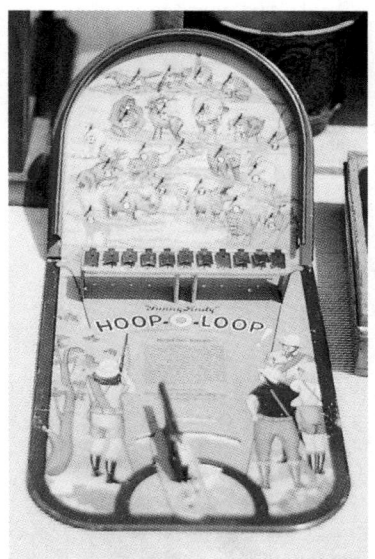

"Funny Andy Hoop-O-Loop" Game

balls up at the various African & North American game animals shown on the angled end, manufactured in Pennsylvania, early 20th c. (ILLUS.)................................ **125**

Horse race, floor model on four legs, coin-operated, w/miniature models of horses moving around the enclosed track, Germany, ca. 1935...................................... **2,000**

"Ice Hockey Game" by Gotham

"Ice Hockey Game," lithographed tin board showing players on the ice, raised angled grandstands in each corner, a standing metal figure at each end of the board acting as marble shooter & goalie, deep blue sides, Gotham Game Company, ca. 1920s (ILLUS.)................................ **225**

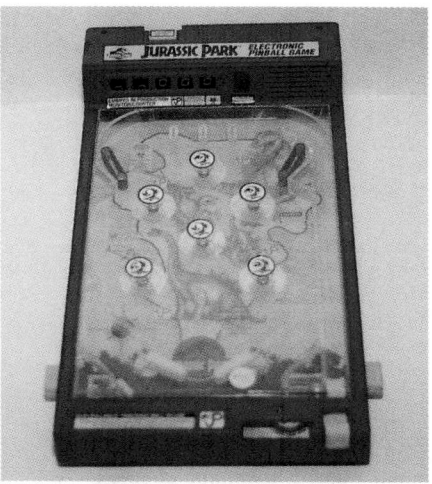

"Jurassic Park Electronic Pinball Game"

"Jurassic Park Electronic Pinball Game," red rectangular plastic board w/clear plastic cover & images of various dinosaurs worth different points, the dinosaurs roaring when hit, two side controls for interior paddles, battery-operated, 1993, 9 1/4 x 17" (ILLUS.)................................ **50**

"Lite-A-Line," first floor model game w/a lighted backboard, Pacific Amusement, 1934.. **600**

"Lucky Clown," child's game w/colorful graphics, 1950s, 6 1/2" l.................... **30**

"Moon Base," lithographed tin base w/clear plastic cover showing various scenes of space exploration w/satellites, a moon base, spaceman, rocket ship, etc., each worth various points, corner lever for shooting marbles, Louis Marx & Co., ca. 1960s... **70**

Niagara Falls Souvenir Game

"**Niagara Falls, Canada,**" souvenir toy, arched color printed background w/Canadian scenes & emblems under a clear plastic cover, sealed in original bag, ca. 1970 (ILLUS., previous page).............................. 7

"Poosh-M-Up Lucky 7" Pinball Game

"**Poosh-M-Up Lucky 7,**" flat round-topped metal background w/colorfully printed circus scenes & animals, red pull handle for shooting marbles, ca. 1930s, 12 1/4" l. (ILLUS.).. **100**

"**Sparkplug,**" tabletop model, coin-operated 5¢ play, horse race game w/wooden case & metal framing, small metal horses moving around the track in the box compartment, Bally, 1930s, 11 x 14 x 16"......... **2,500**

"**The Man from U.N.C.L.E.,**" based on the TV show, Ideal, 1966 .... **200**

Early Wooden Tray Pinball Game

Wooden tray-type, square frame w/floating inner wooden tray that can be tipped to roll the silver ball past the 55 trap holes, two control knobs, ca. 1940 (ILLUS.) **125**

PLANT WATERERS

For more than 50 years, these handy household helpers have kept plants moist even when left unattended. Generally made of plastic or a ceramic material, an open hole in the top received the water and the porous stem allowed it to slowly seep into the soil, watering the plant as necessary. Both decorative and functional, these often-whimsical objects are often confused, priced and sold as the more expensive collectible pie birds. For the most part, plant waterers are still affordable, but as their popularity rises, it's only a matter of time before market prices start to climb.- Bobby Zucker Bryson

Ceramic, figure of elf, green w/rust beard, 4 1/2" h.. **$15-20**

Ceramic, figure of girl in blue dress, pink bow in hair, holding a pink flower, 5 1/4" h.. **18-20**

Ceramic, figure of girl wearing yellow dress & matching hat, holding gold watering can, Josef Originals, 6" h. **55-75**

Gnome Plant Waterer

Ceramic, figure of gnome, green suit & hat, black shoes, white beard, sitting w/feet crossed & holding brown pipe, 6 1/2" h. (ILLUS.).. **15-20**

Ceramic, figure of man in flowing robes, dark green, marked "©INARCO Cleve - Ohio, E-192," 6" h....................................... **18-24**

Ceramic, figure of pixie holding green watering can, 6" h... **65-85**

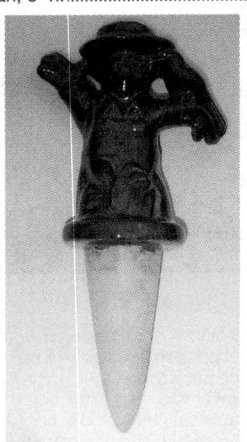

Ceramic Scarecrow Plant Waterer

Ceramic, figure of scarecrow w/one arm raised, the other extended at side & holding crow, all brown, 6" h. (ILLUS., previous page) **12-15**

Ceramic, model of bumblebee, yellow & black, wearing blue tie & red shoes, sitting on lavender flower, 7" h. **8-12**

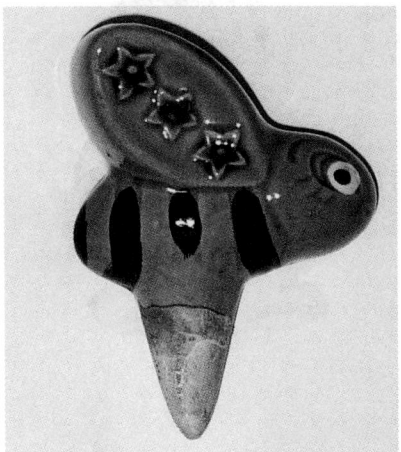

Ceramic Bumblebee Plant Waterer

Ceramic, model of bumblebee, yellow w/black stripes, raised wings decorated w/red & green star-shaped flowers, 4" h. (ILLUS.) **6-8**

Butterfly Plant Waterer

Ceramic, model of butterfly, yellow, decorated w/pink flowers, 4 1/2" h. (ILLUS.)........ **8-12**

Ceramic, model of cat, white, 4 3/4" h............. **8-15**

Ceramic, model of chick hatching from egg, yellow, 4-1/2" h... **15-25**

Ceramic, model of chick peeking out of egg shell, white & yellow, 4 1/2" h. **15-20**

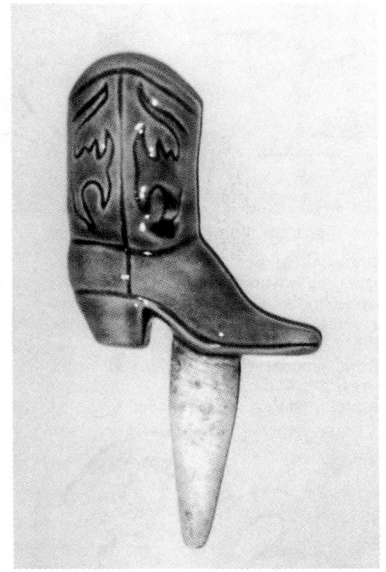

Cowboy Boot Plant Waterer

Ceramic, model of cowboy boot, brown, 5 3/8" h. (ILLUS.)... **15-25**

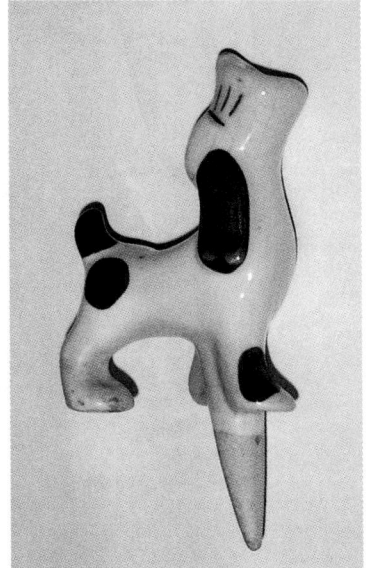

Ceramic Howling Dog Plant Waterer

Ceramic, model of dog w/head back & mouth open as if howling, white w/brown patches & ears, black tail, 6" h. (ILLUS.)... **35-45**

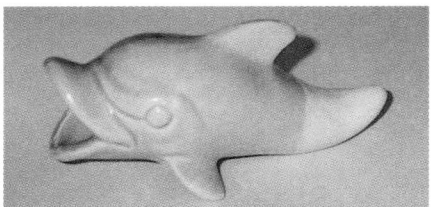

Ceramic Dolphin Plant Waterer

Ceramic, model of dolphin w/mouth open, pale grey w/white tail, 4 1/2" l. (ILLUS.) **18-22**

Ceramic, model of fish w/curled tail, yellow & white, black eye, Shawnee Pottery, 5" h. **35-50**

Ceramic, model of fish w/curved head, green, 6 1/4" h. **6-8**

Ceramic, model of flamingo, pink, 5 1/2" h. ... **25-30**

Flamingo Plant Waterer

Ceramic, model of flamingo, pink, 6" h. (ILLUS.) **20-30**

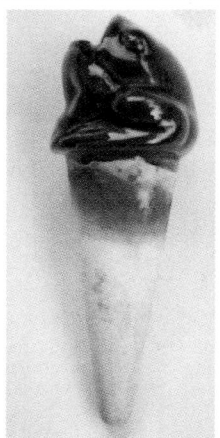

Sitting Frog Plant Waterer

Ceramic, model of frog, sitting w/mouth open, green w/brown highlights, 4 1/2" h. (ILLUS.) **6-8**

Yellow & Green Frog Waterer

Ceramic, model of frog w/detachable head, sitting up on hind legs, gold w/yellow & green splotches, 4 1/2" h. (ILLUS.) **25-35**

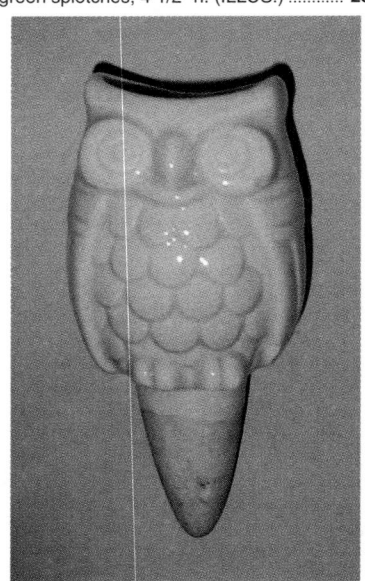

Ceramic Owl Plant Waterer

Ceramic, model of owl on perch, molded feathers, pale yellow, 4 1/4" h. (ILLUS.) **8-10**

Pig Plant Waterer

Ceramic, model of pig, blue, 4 1/2" h.
(ILLUS.).. **35-45**

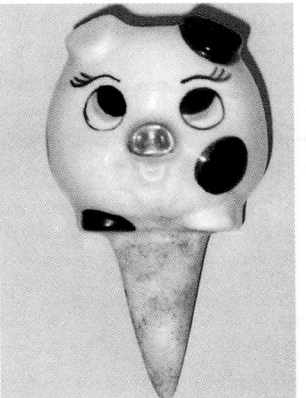

Stylized Pig Plant Waterer

Ceramic, model of pig, white w/one black
ear, cheek & foot, pink nose, oversize
blue & black eyes, 6 1/4" h. (ILLUS.).......... **45-55**

Ceramic Toucan Plant Waterer

Ceramic, model of toucan, white w/black &
gold head & beak, molded feathers, 5" h.
(ILLUS.).. **18-25**
Ceramic, model of tulip, blue & white Delft
patt., 6" h... **18-25**
Ceramic, model of tulip, yellow, 4 1/4" h........ **15-20**
Ceramic, model of turtle, green, 3 1/2" h. **6-10**

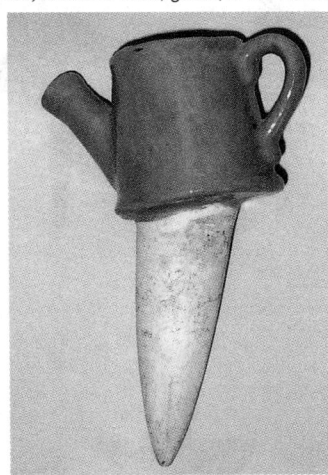

Plant Waterer in Form of Watering Can

Ceramic, model of watering can, green,
5" h. (ILLUS.).. **6-8**

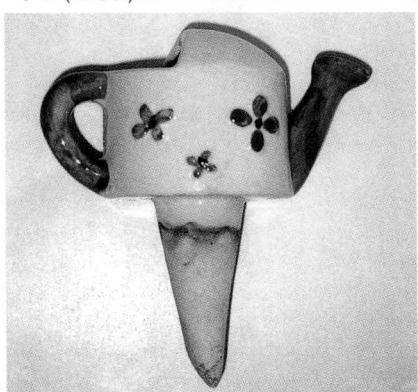

Watering Can Plant Waterer

Ceramic, model of watering can, white
w/blue handle & spout, maroon flowers
decorating sides, 4 1/2" h. (ILLUS.)............ **12-18**

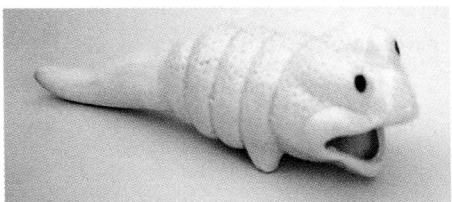

Worm Plant Waterer

Ceramic, model of worm w/open mouth & bulging eyes, yellow, newer vintage, 6 1/2" l. (ILLUS., previous page) **6-10**
Plastic, model of alligator, 4" h. **5-8**
Plastic, model of bird, blue, 4" h. **5-8**

Flying Birds Plant Waterers

Plastic, model of bird in flight, mouth open, blue w/black trim, 4" h. (ILLUS. left w/red flying bird) **8-12**
Plastic, model of bird in flight, mouth open, red w/black trim, 4" h. (ILLUS. right w/blue flying bird) **8-12**

Red Plastic Pig Waterer

Plastic, model of pig, red, 4" h. (ILLUS.).......... **8-12**
Plastic, model of poodle, white, 4" h................ **8-12**

POCKET KNIVES

ALSO SEE: Character Collectibles & Western Character Collectibles.

Advertising, Coca-Cola Bottling Company, banner-stamped brass handle w/company name, one blade, marked "Kaster & Company - Made in Germany," ca. 1905-15 .... **$400**
Advertising, Coca-Cola Bottling Company, fantasy item, brass nickel-plated handle in the shape of an early Coca-Cola bottle w/logo, blade marked "Remington U.M.C.," no early counterpart, ca. 1970 .... **15**

Advertising, Coca-Cola Bottling Company, white celluloid handle printed "Delicious and Refreshing," marked by Camco USA, many variations, 1930-50 .... **90**
Advertising, Coca-Cola Bottling Company, white celluloid handles printed "Drink Coca-Cola in Bottles" on one side & image of a bottle on the other, two blades, blade marked "Remington," ca. 1935............. **125**
Advertising, Coca-Cola Bottling Company, wide mother-of-pearl handle printed w/logo, a swing-out corkscrew on one side & single blade on the other, blade marked "Colonial Prov. R.I.," ca. 1935............. **75**
Advertising, Coca-Cola Bottling Company, wide mother-of-pearl handle w/two small window openings reading "Serve - Coca-Cola," when opened reads "Be Smart," single blade & nail file, blade marked "Solingen, Germany," ca. 1940 .... **215**
Advertising, "Edwards Hats" marked on both sides of the hat-shaped handle, small blade marked "Made in Germany," ca. 1930 .... **125**

Bullet-shaped Imperial Pocket Knife

American-made, bullet-shaped w/mother-of-pearl handles w/silver shield emblem, two blades, Imperial Knife Company, Providence, Rhode Island, 1940s, overall 3 1/4" l. (ILLUS.) **50**
American-made, Colonial Cutlery Co., Providence, Rhode Island, models, various photos in the handles, some of nudes, ca. 1940s, each **50**
American-made, model of an early commercial airliner w/props, generic design, unknown maker, ca. 1950s, 4" l. **140**

Serpentine Imperial Pocket Knife

American-made, serpentine shape w/mother-of-pearl handles w/silver shield emblem, two blades, Imperial Knife Company, Providence, Rhode Island, 1940s, overall 3 1/4" l. (ILLUS.) **50**

American-made Red-handled Knife

American-made, serpentine shape w/red plastic handles, one-blade, marked

"Made in the USA," 1940s, 3 1/4" l.
(ILLUS.) **25**
Bakelite, tortoiseshell-designed handles
w/a single blade & a delicate fold-out
plastic blade & grooming pick, ca. 1930s,
2" l. **50**
Boy Scout, official model w/black plastic
wood bark handles, five blades, by Impe-
rial Knife Company, ca. 1950s......................... **40**
Character, Babe Ruth, steel model of a
baseball bat, one side inscribed w/his
name, the other w/a baseball scene,
1930s **140**
Character, Buck Rogers, give-away from
Cream of Wheat, sponsor of the radio
show, handle shows Buck Rogers &
space scene, two blades colored red,
green or blue, Camillus Cutlery Compa-
ny, New York, New York, 1935 .... **1,550**
Character, Buck Rogers, Solar Scouts promotional item, found w/handles in red,
blue or green, handle w/image of Buck
sitting at the controls of his spaceship, his
name at the narrow end, by A. Kastor &
Bros., New York, New York, 1930s, each **800**
Character, Davy Crockett, steel blade &
black handle w/key chain, handle printed
"Davy Crockett's Own Frontier Knife,"
Barlow, 1955, 3 1/2" l.................................... **110**
Character, Dick Tracy & B.O. Plenty, similar
to Tracy & Junior pen knife, includes
blade, whistle & magnifying glass, glows
in the dark, ca. 1950...................................... **85**
Character, Dick Tracy & Junior, shows Dick
Tracy on the left & Junior on the right,
built-in whistle & magnifying glass, Cam-
co, 1930s, 3 1/4" l.. **140**
Character, Dick Tracy, white celluloid han-
dle w/full image of Tracy holding a gun &
printed "Dick Tracy Detective," single
blade, Imperial Knife Company, 1930s **130**
Character, Frank Buck, premium from Ivory
Soap, sponsor of the radio program, han-
dle printed w/Buck facsimile signature &
"Bring Em Back Alive," offered in con-
junction w/the 1939-40 New York World's
Fair.. **180**
Character, Hopalong Cassidy, silvered
metal w/black plastic handles w/a black &
white image of Hoppy & Topper, Imperial
Knife Company, 1950s, 3 1/2" l..................... **110**
Character, Jimmie Allen, tie-in for "Jimmie
Allen's Air Adventure" radio show, bone-
handled w/two blades & a silvered metal
club symbol, 1930s... **170**
Character, Jimmie Allen, tie-in for "Jimmie
Allen's Air Adventure" radio show, bone-
handled, inscribed "Official Jimmie Allen
Outing Knife," w/sheaf, rarer version,
1930s **325**
Character, Lone Ranger, pearl-style handle
grip w/a picture of the Lone Ranger & Silver on one side & a silver bullet on the
other, regular knife blade & bottle opener
blade, 1940s.. **95**
Character, Marilyn Monroe, clear plastic
handle w/color photo of Marilyn, 1950s **70**
Character, Moon Mullins, image and name
on the handle as well as images of Little

Egypt & other comic strip characters, advertising imprint of local sponsor, 1930s **160**
Character, Red Ryder, plastic handles
w/his picture on one side & name on the
other, Camco USA, ca. 1940s........................ **260**
Character, Skyriders Club, early group fo-
cused on aviation & developing the interest of youngsters, similar to the Boy
Scout knife, handle w/the club name,
rare, 1930s **160**
Character, Tom Mix "Straight Shooters"
model, premium from the Ralston Purina
Company, name of radio show in center
flanked by the red checkerboard Ralston
logo design at the ends, 1939, 3 1/4" l.......... **100**
English-made, mother-of-pearl handles,
fruit knife blade & a button hook, ca.
1890, 2 1/4" l. **60**
English-made, pen knife w/heavy metal
handle in the form of a shield w/a crest,
one small blade & a button hook, ca.
1880, 1" sq. **80**
English-made, pen knife w/sterling silver
handle decorated w/flowers & leaves,
marked, ca. 1880s, 3" l................................... **170**
Figural, pen knife in the shape of a rabbit or
cat, brass painted black, early 20th c.,
2 1/2" l., each **45**
Souvenir, New York World's Fair 1964-65,
one side of handle in red, the other in
blue, one side printed w/an image of the
Unisphere, the other printed w/"New
York World's Fair," single blade, Imperial
Knife Company **25**
United States Army, utility knife w/blade,
bottle opener & other implements, Camil-
lus Cutlery Company, ca. 1940s.................... **100**

POLITICAL & CAMPAIGN ITEMS

Campaign Items

Advertising Tray Promoting Republican Candidates of 1900

Advertising ashtray or pin tray, 1900
campaign of William McKinley & Theodore Roosevelt, aluminum, rectangular
w/wavy edges, the center w/color flag illustrations & round jugate portraits under
spread-winged eagle, a banner at top
reading "Philip Rosenbaum," another
banner at the bottom reading "Clothier -
7th & Penn Sts. Reading, PA.,"
3 1/8 x 4 3/4" (ILLUS.) **$335**
Belt, 1896 campaign of William McKinley &
Garret A. Hobart, cloth w/metal buckle,
yellow, white & gold banded design read-

ing "Gold - McKinley & Hobart - Gold," the rectangular buckle w/raised "McK & H," rare, 2 x 36" **665**

William Henry Harrison 1841 Campaign Brooch

Brooch, 1840 campaign of William Henry Harrison, sulfide, rectangular, gold tone metallic scroll-decorated frame holds image of log cabin w/"Harrison" above & "& Reform" below, all in white on lime green ground, rare vertical orientation, w/original pinback clasp, 7/8 x 1" (ILLUS.)............ **1,794**

Button, 1860 campaign of Abraham Lincoln & Hannibal Hamlin, ferrotype w/jugate portraits, captioned "Lincoln and Hamlin," w/metal border accented w/beading, re-attached vintage pin on reverse, 7/8" d. **4,333**

Button, 1868 campaign of Ulysses S. Grant & Schuyler Colfax, ferrotype jugate pin w/rounded rectangular portraits of candidates in brass border, 1 1/4" d. **1,091**

1896 Campaign Clock

Clock, 1896 campaign of William McKinley, mantel type, bronze-plated metal, rectangular central panel w/4" d. clock face w/Roman numerals, the date "1896" & Republican slogan "Sound Money," below which is a rectangular plaque reading "Protection - Prosperity," the central panel flanked by images of sailing ship on one side & factory machinery on the other, a 5" h. bust of McKinley topping all, molding at top & bottom, on rectangular wooden base, rare, about 15" h. (ILLUS.) .. **1,497**

1872 Campaign Goblet

Goblet, 1872 campaign of Ulysses S. Grant & Henry Wilson, blown glass, clear, w/incised bust portraits of the two candidates, one on either side, 3 1/2" d. bowl, short knobbed stem, 6" h. (ILLUS.) **991**

1961 "Inaugural Spectacle"

Magazine Inaugural souvenir edition, 1961, "Inaugural Spectacle" published by Life Magazine, packed w/photos & text recounting first hours of John F. Kennedy's presidency, w/ink inscription on front "To Mrs. Frank W. Burke, with very best wishes, John Kennedy" (ILLUS.).. **984**

Al Smith 1928 Hanging Pin

Pin, 1928 campaign of Al Smith, 2 1/2"-d. celluloid pin w/sepia portrait of Smith & encircling caption reading "For President - Alfred E. Smith" suspended on textured flag replica anchored by brass pinback bar & tucked into button's collet, the rear reading "The Whitehead & Hoag Co. - Newark, N.J. - Buttons, Badges, Novelties and Signs," overall 4" l. (ILLUS. front & back, previous page).. **604**

Rare 1896 Pinback Button

Pinback button, 1896 presidential campaign between William McKinley & William Jennings Bryan, round pinback type w/color caricature of McKinley wearing blue dress, short lacy pantalettes & Napoleonic hat & riding a hobby horse, the words "My 'Hobby'" in arch over illustration & "A Winner" beneath, rare, some moisture staining, minor surface blemishes, faint discoloration on reverse rim, 2 1/4" d. (ILLUS.) **3,618**

Pinback button, 1904 campaign of Alton Parker & Henry Davis, sepia jugate button w/round portraits side by side under spread-winged eagle, w/images of waving flags at bottom, the reverse inscribed "St. Louis Button Co., - St. Louis," 1 1/4" d. **830**

Teddy Roosevelt Campaign Pin for 1904

Pinback button, 1904 campaign of Theodore Roosevelt, color illustration of saluting Roosevelt in Rough Rider regalia astride horse, a large flag planted on distant hill labeled "San Juan" in background, encircling caption reading "Theodore Roosevelt - For President 1904,"

marked w/copyright of Charles K. Cohn of Detroit, 1 1/4" d. (ILLUS.) **685**

Pinback Button from 1908 Taft Campaign

Pinback button, 1908 campaign of William Howard Taft, celluloid, center sepia portrait of Taft encircled by red & dark blue border w/gold scroll & bead decoration & gold shield w/flag center, 2 1/4" d. (ILLUS.)... **455**

1908 Campaign Pin for William Jennings Bryan

Pinback button, 1908 campaign of William Jennings Bryan, 2 1/2" d. button w/portrait of candidate in center, "For President - Wm. J. Bryan" around rim, w/flag ribbon suspended below, the original back paper insert stamped w/its maker, J.H. Shaw of Philadelphia, overall 5" l. (ILLUS.).. **498**

Pinback button, 1912 campaign of William Howard Taft & James Sherman, black & white jugate portraits in shield under spread-winged eagle against background of red & white & blue flag motif, by The Meek Company of Coshocton, Ohio, rare, 7/8" d... **1,236**

Pinback button, 1920 campaign of Channing H. Cox for governor of Massachusetts, trigate black & white portrait of Cox placed between those of presidential candidates Warren Harding & Calvin Coolidge, rare trigate coattail button, 1 1/4" d. **2,958**

Pinback from 1924 Coolidge Campaign

Pinback button, 1924 campaign of Calvin Coolidge, black & white photo of Coolidge in center, a gold-trimmed red, white & blue border bearing words "Support the Coolidge Administration," 1 3/4" d. (ILLUS.) **818**

Pinback button, 1940 campaign of Wendell Willkie, blue & white color illustration of smiling candidate within red & blue border reading "Willkie - For President," the collet marked "Midwest Badge and Novelty Co.," 2 3/4" d. **373**

Teddy Roosevelt "Bull Moose" Pin

Pinback button w/hanger, 1912 campaign of Theodore Roosevelt, 2 1/4" d. button w/color portrait of Roosevelt flanked by words "Bull" & "Moose," "Theodore Roosevelt" at bottom, a brown composi-

tion moose, the symbol of Roosevelt's Progressive Party, hanging from a ribbon attached to the pin, rare, overall 5" l. (ILLUS.) **3,850**

1840 Campaign Pitcher

Pitcher, 1840 campaign of William Henry Harrison, ceramic, decorated on one side w/mulberry-colored illustration of candidate flanked by draped flags under words "The Country's Hope" & over "Harrison & Reform," the other side w/illustration of Harrison's campaign symbol, the log cabin, w/plaque hanging from front door reading "To let in 1841," below the shell-form spout a spread-winged eagle holding in its beak a banner reading "Union for the sake of Union," C-form applied handle, gold trim, 11" spout to handle, about 8" h. (ILLUS.) **8,210**

1840 Campaign Plate

Plate, 1840 campaign of William Henry Harrison, ceramic, w/log cabin & cider barrel trademarks of the campaign in the center, the scalloped rim ornately decorated w/basketweave design & floral garlands w/three oval bust portraits of Harrison in profile w/his name spelled out around the edges alternating w/three cartouches holding urns of flowers, the reverse w/logo inscription log cabin, repaired edge crack on back of rim, 6" d. (ILLUS.)...... **613**

McKinley/Roosevelt Campaign Poster

1900 "Octopus" Campaign Poster

Poster, 1900 campaign of William Jennings Bryan, full color litho "Octopus" poster, a 9 x 12" oval portrait of McKinley in center w/scroll & laurel leaf border under banner reading "No Crown of Thorns - W.J. Bryan - No Cross of Gold" & flanked by American flags, the top reading "The Issue - 1900 - Liberty - Justice - Humanity" in bold yellow/orange lettering, the bottom reading "Equal Rights to All - Special Privileges to None" in red, w/many images & symbols scattered throughout including gold Liberty Bell reading "1776," silver Liberty Bell reading "1900 - No Imperialism," crowing rooster, plowshare, Statue of Liberty, blindfolded Justice, a silver coin reading "Dollar of the Daddies," a smaller gold coin, uniformed men waving flags, robed female figure raising ax above image of octopus whose tenta-

cles entwine various businesses, copyright 1900 by Neville Williams of Columbus, Ohio, lithographed by Strobridge of Cincinnati, Ohio, w/applied linen backing, 19 1/2 x 29 1/2" (ILLUS.).............................. **5,670**

Poster, 1900 campaign of William McKinley & Theodore Roosevelt, full color litho, jugate portraits in oval scroll borders flanking figure of Liberty holding American flag standing over scene of bustling commerce, bold white lettering reading "PROSPERITY" in red panel at top, "MCKINLEY and ROOSEVELT" in red panel at bottom, 28 x 40" (ILLUS., top of page) **7,225**

Poster, 1900 campaign of William McKinley & Theodore Roosevelt, jugate full-length charcoal-type illustrations of candidates, McKinley holding poster from 1896 headed "The Real Issue" & including McKinley quote "I do not know what you think about it but I believe it is a good deal better to open up the mills of the United States to the labor of America than to open up the mints of the United States to the silver of the world," the figures backed by a large waving American flag & standing on a stage emblazoned "Prosperity at Home, Prestige Abroad, Sound Money" in front of masses of supporters, "McKinley Was Right" in bold lettering at top, "1896 - Poverty - Depression" in upper left corner, "One Country - One Flag" across flag, "1900 - Prosperity" at center, credit line identifies artistry of Edwards-Deutsch-Heitmann & attributes publication to Chicago Republican National Committee, linen backed, 38 x 45".......................... **7,046**

Ribbon, 1844 campaign of Henry Clay & Theodore Frelinghuysen, white silk/satin jugate ribbon w/black & white likenesses of candidates in ornately scrolled oval borders, vertically aligned one above the other & each topped by spread-winged eagle, the top eagle holding banner in its beak reading "For President - Henry Clay," the bottom portrait w/caption reading "For Vice President Theodore Frelinghuysen," 3 x 8 1/2" (minor spotting & soiling, one tiny hole) **506**

1860 Campaign Ribbon for Lincoln/Hamlin

Ribbon, 1860 campaign of Abraham Lincoln & Hannibal Hamlin, pink, w/fringed edge, reads "Prairie City - REPUBLICAN CLUB" over illustration of two hands clasped in unity under spread-winged eagle holding banner in its beak reading "United we stand - Divided we fall," bottom reading "For President - ABRAHAM LINCOLN - For Vice President - HANNIBAL HAMLIN!" 2 5/16 x 4 3/8" (ILLUS.) **3,581**

1860 Campaign Ribbon for Stephen Douglas

Ribbon, 1860 campaign of Stephen Douglas, white w/delicately scalloped edges

on sides & original selvage across top & bottom edges, central black & white illustration of Douglas, "DOUGLAS" in arch over illustration & "INVINCIBLES" below, hint of water toning, 3 1/4 x 5 5/8" (ILLUS.) **2,018**

1916 Campaign Stickpin

Stickpin, 1916 campaign of Charles Evans Hughes, celluloid, flag-shaped, w/black & white oval portrait of candidate alongside colored shield reading "For President," a red, white & blue flag & green laurel branch in the background, 7/8 x 1 1/8" flag on 2 3/8"-l. ball-topped stickpin (ILLUS.) **498**

Non-Campaign

U.S. Grant Glass Bowl

Bowl, glass, clear, round shape w/bottom decorated w/frosted image of bust of U.S. Grant in profile, the sides reading "The Patriot and Soldier - Gen. Ulysses S. Grant," scalloped rim, 9 1/4" d. (ILLUS.) **45-65**

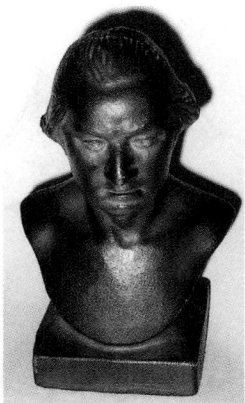

Brass Bust of George Washington

Bust, brass, figure of George Washington, marked "Bicentennial 1732-1932," 6 1/2" h. (ILLUS.) **15-20**

Bronze Bust of Abraham Lincoln

Bust, bronze, figure of Abraham Lincoln, marked "Geo. E. Bisell Gorham Co. Founders 046, Copyrighted SC," 16 7/8" h. (ILLUS.) **500**

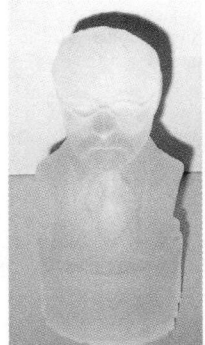

Satin Glass Bust of Theodore Roosevelt

Bust, glass, figure of Theodore Roosevelt, clear w/satin finish, 4" h. (ILLUS.) **35-45**

U.S. Grant Glass Dish

Dish, glass, clear, square shape w/squared corners, the bottom decorated w/frosted image of bust of U.S. Grant in profile surrounded by "The Patriot and Soldier - Gen. Ulysses S. Grant," 9 1/2" sq. (ILLUS.) **45-65**

George Washington Flag Holder

Flag holder, ceramic, cone-shaped, red w/color bust of George Washington in oval framed w/words "George Washington Bi-Centennial 1732-1932," 3" h. (ILLUS.) **20-25**

Macerated Money "Lincoln Family" Portrait

Framed illustration, macerated money, image of Abraham Lincoln, his wife and two sons above title "Lincoln Family," sepia tone, 3 3/4 x 4 3/4" (ILLUS., previous page) **50-75**

Framed "Washington's Prayer"

Framed prayer, "Washington's Prayer for our Country," the words of the prayer flowing around an illustration of George Washington on bended knee w/hands clasped as if in prayer, ca. 1970, 8 3/4 x 10 3/8" (ILLUS.) **10-12**

Washington Bar Pin with Ribbon

Pin w/ribbon, metal bar pin w/bust of George Washington in color in center, from which depends canvas ribbon w/color images of crossed American flags, spread-winged eagle & five-pointed star, gold fringe at bottom, 5 3/4" l. (ILLUS.) **12-15**

Sesquicentennial Plaque

Plaque, metal w/bronze-colored finish, model of Liberty Bell under bust of Thomas Jefferson & crossed flags & reading "1776 - 1926 - Sesquicentennial," 6 1/2" h. (ILLUS.) **20-25**

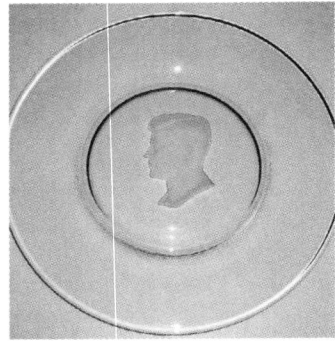

John F. Kennedy Decorative Plate

Plate, glass, clear, round shape w/bottom decorated w/frosted image of bust of John F. Kennedy, 8" d. (ILLUS.) **45-50**

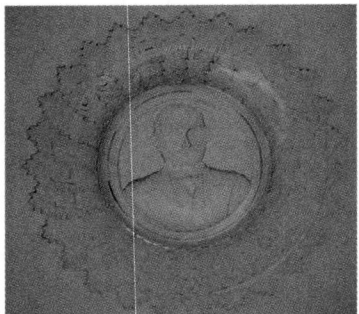

Green Glass U.S. Grant Plate

Plate, glass, green, round shape w/serrate leaf sides, the bottom decorated w/image of bust of U.S. Grant surrounded by words "Let Us Have Peace - U.S. Grant," 10 1/2" d. (ILLUS., previous page)............. **45-65**

Portrait pendant, round pewter rim portrait of James Monroe w/mirror reverse, attached to delicate mourning ribbon w/ornate gilded loop at top, very rare, ca. 1831, 1 3/8" d. **10,189**

"1732 - Washington - 1799" Ribbon

Ribbon, paper, red, white & blue stars & stripes design w/bust of George Washington in oval at top, "1732 - Washington - 1799" at bottom, back reads "Fold back this flap and use for pinning to coat," 4" l. (ILLUS.) **40-50**

POP CULTURE COLLECTIBLES

Women Singers - Pre-1950s

Female vocalists? Chanteuses? Divas? Whatever you may call them, women singers have been around almost as long as music, certainly as long as recorded music. In fact, when we think of famous singers, we almost always think of the women who have captured our hearts and souls with their voices.

Female singers made their appearance as stars in the world of opera in the 1800s. By the early 1900s, the music hall, musical "theater" and vaudeville provided other venues for female vocal talent. But with the arrival of recorded sound, the female "pop" singer emerged in all her glory. Jazz and popular recordings in the 1920s and '30s gave us the bluesy Bessie Smith and Ethel Waters while the "torch" singers like Ruth Etting and Helen Morgan held up the ballads and sentimental side. In the 1930s, Hollywood introduced singers like Judy Garland and Alice Faye. By the

1940s, big bands were adding female vocalists like Doris Day and Peggy Lee to "front" their songs. Many of these songbirds would go on to successful solo careers in the 1950s and beyond. Broadway musicals also arrived in the '40s, providing yet another arena for talented singers like Mary Martin and Ethel Merman.

The listings here are for pre-1950s memorabilia. Collectors and fans search not only for recordings by singers, but sheet music, autographs, photos, and other printed ephemera.

Alice Faye Photo

Alice Faye, photo, signed & inscribed, 5 x 7" (ILLUS.)... **$25-30**

Alice Faye Postcard

Alice Faye, postcard, color, shows Beverly Hills residence, ca. 1930s (ILLUS.) **4-8**

Alice Faye, publicity photo, ca. 1930s, 8 x 10" **5-10**

"You're A Sweetheart" Sheet Music

Alice Faye, sheet music, "You're A Sweetheart" from the film of the same name,
copyright 1937, Robbins Music Corp.
(ILLUS.) 5-10

Andrew Sisters Album Set

Andrews Sisters, 78 rpm album set, 10
songs, Decca Records, the set (ILLUS.) ... 10-25
Andrews Sisters, sheet music, "Sabre
Dance," copyright 1946, Leeds Music
Corp. 5-10
Andrews Sisters, song folio, "Army, Navy &
Marines," 60 songs, Leeds Music Corp.,
1942 10-20
Aunt Jemima (Tess Gardella), 78 rpm,
#1304D, "Can't Help Lovin' Dat Man,"
Columbia Records, ca. 1929 10-15
Bessie Smith, 78 rpm, #2476, "St. Louis
Blues/Reckless Blues," w/Louis Arm-
strong 20-30
Bessie Smith, 78 rpm, #2480, "Yellow Dog
Blues/Trombone Cholly," Parlophone
Records 10-20
Bessie Smith, 78 rpm, "Cold in Hand
Blues/You've Been a Good Old Wagon,"
Columbia Records 10-20
Betty Hutton, sheet music, "Arthur Murray
Taught Me Dancing in a Hurry," from the
film The Fleet's In, copyright 1942, Fa-
mous Music Corp. 5-10
Blossom Seeley, 78 rpm, #386D, "Yes Sir,
That's My Baby," Columbia Records, ca.
1925 5-10

"Hawaiian Butterfly" Sheet Music

Blossom Seeley, sheet music, "Hawaiian
Butterfly," copyright 1917, Leo Feist Inc.
(ILLUS.) 10-20

The Boswell Sisters 78 rpm Record

Boswell Sisters, 78 rpm, #4495, "St. Louis
Blues/Travelin' All Alone," Vocalion Label
Corporation (ILLUS.) 4-8
Boswell Sisters, 78 rpm, "Rock and
Roll/The Object of My Affection," Colum-
bia Records 5-10
Deanna Durbin, book, "Deanna Durbin and
the Feather of Flame," copyright 1941,
Whitman Publishing Co. 5-10

Deanna Durbin Magazine Cover

Deanna Durbin, magazine cover, Pho-
toplay, May 1940, 102 pgs. (ILLUS.) 15-20
Deanna Durbin, publicity photo, 4" x 6",
signed & inscribed, "To Dennis Best
Wishes" 5-10
Deanna Durbin, sheet music, "Spring Will
Be a Little Late This Year," copyright
1944, Saunders Publications, California 5-10
Deanna Durbin, song folio, "Deanna Durbin
Sings," 11 songs, Leo Feist Inc., 1940 10-15
Dinah Shore, 78 rpm, "Buttons and
Bows/Daddy-O," Columbia Records, ca.
1950 4-6
Dinah Shore, sheet music, "I'm Confessin',"
copyright 1930, Bourne Music Publishing .. 10-12

"Yes, My Darling Daughter" Music

Dinah Shore, sheet music, "Yes, My Darling Daughter," copyright 1940, Leo Feist Inc. (ILLUS.) **5-10**

Dorothy Shay 10" Record

Dorothy Shay, 10" record, 8 songs by the "Park Avenue Hillbillie," Capitol Records (ILLUS.) **5-10**

Edith Piaf 10" Record

Edith Piaf, 10" record, Edith Piaf Sings, 8 songs, copyright 1950, Columbia Records (ILLUS.) **10-15**

Edith Piaf, programme, L'Etoile, 1947-48, 4 1/2" x 6" **10-20**

Ethel Merman, 78 rpm, album set, 6 records with booklet, "Annie Get Your Gun," Decca Records **10-20**

Ethel Merman Signed Magazine Photo

Ethel Merman, magazine photo, color, 8" x 12", signed (ILLUS.) **30-40**

Ethel Merman, program, The Playbill magazine, December 15, 1947, Broadway production of "Annie Get Your Gun," 6 1/2" x 9", 42 pgs. **4-8**

Ethel Merman, sheet music, "Let's Be Buddies," from Panama Hattie, copyright 1940, Chappell & Co. **5-10**

Ethel Waters, 78 rpm, #1837D, "Am I Blue," Columbia Records, ca. 1929 .... **10-20**

Ethel Waters, 78 rpm, #2183D, "What Did I Do To Be So Black and Blue?," Columbia Records, ca. 1930 .... **10-20**

Gay White, sheet music, "There's a Silver Moon on the Golden Gate," copyright 1936, Irving Berlin Inc. **5-10**

"I Can't Get Started" Sheet Music

Ginny Simms, sheet music, "I Can't Get Started," copyright 1935, Chappell & Co. (ILLUS.) **5-10**

Ginny Simms, sheet music, "With the Wind and the Rain in Your Hair," copyright 1940, Paramount Music Corp. **5-10**

"Harry Holmes Ballads ... " Song Book

Ginny Simms, song book, "Harry Holmes Ballads for Broadcasting - No. 1" (ILLUS.) **5-10**

Helen Forrest, sheet music, "He's My Guy," copyright 1942, Leeds Music Co. **5-10**

Latest Hit Songs Magazine Cover

Helen O'Connell, magazine, Latest Hit Songs, October-November 1943, photo on cover (ILLUS.) **10-20**

Hildegard, sheet music, "Lili Marlene," copyright 1943, Chappell & Co. **10-15**

Irene Bordoni, sheet music, "Can't You Hear Me Say I Love You," copyright 1928, J.W. Jenkins Sons **5-10**

Jeannette MacDonald (w/Nelson Eddy), sheet music, "Italian Street Song," from "Naughty Marietta," copyright 1931, M. Witmark & Sons **5-10**

Joan Davis (w/Jane Grazee & Judy Clarke), sheet music, "Shoo-Shoo Baby," from the film "Beautiful But Broke," copyright 1943, Leeds Music Corp. **5-10**

Judy Garland, magazine cover, Life Magazine, 12/11/44 .... **10-25**

Judy Garland, movie poster, one sheet linen, "The Harvey Girls," copyright 1946 .... **300-400**

Judy Garland, sheet music, "Nine Pins in the Sky," copyright 1938, Sun Music Publishing Co. **10-20**

Judy Garland, song folio, "Judy Garland Sings," 15 songs, 1940, Leo Feist Inc. **10-20**

Kate Smith, 78 rpm, "God Bless America/The Star Spangled Banner," copyright 1939, Victor Records **5-10**

Kate Smith, 78 rpm, "Moanin' Low/Waiting at the End of the Rainbow," Diva Records.. **10-12**

Kate Smith, magazine ad, color, for Jell-O, 1942, 9 1/4" x 12 1/2" **3-6**

Kate Smith, recipe booklet, "Kate Smith's Favorite Recipes," copyright 1940, Swans Down Flour & Calumet Baking Powder, 47 pgs. **5-10**

Kate Smith, sheet music, "Last Time I Saw Paris," copyright 1940, Chappell & Sons **4-8**

Le Brun Sisters, sheet music, "The Starlit Hour," copyright 1939, Robbins Music Corp. **5-10**

Lee Morse, 78 rpm, #11592, "What A Girl/I Love You So," Perfect Records **10-20**

Lee Morse, 78 rpm, #11618, "A Little Love/Lonesome and Sorry," Perfect Records **10-20**

Margaret Whiting, magazine ad, "The Barry Wood Show," black & white, 1946 .... **5-10**

Margaret Whiting, sheet music, "That's Where I Came In," copyright 1946 .... **4-8**

Marlene Dietrich, magazine cover, Pelicula Magazine, 1932 .... **10-20**

Marlene Dietrich, postcard, black & white, ca. 1930s, 4" x 6" **4-8**

Mary Martin, 10" record, soundtrack to the musical "The Bandwagon," Columbia Records **5-10**

Mary Martin & Ethel Merman, 10" record, 4 recordings, from the Ford 50th Anniversary Television Show, Decca Records **10-1**

Mildred Bailey, sheet music, "Something Tells Me," copyright 1938, M. Witmark & Sons **5-10**

Nancy Walker, sheet music, "Milkman Keep Those Bottles Quiet," from Broadway Rhythm, copyright 1944, Leo Feist Inc. **5-10**

Rae Samuels, sheet music, "I Want a Daddy to Cuddle Me," copyright 1927, J.W. Jenkins Sons Music Co. **10-15**

Ruth Etting, 78 rpm, "If I Didn't Have You/Let Me Call You Sweetheart," Conqueror Records **8-12**

Ruth Etting, 78 rpm, "Love Me or Leave Me/I'm Bringing a Red Red Rose," Columbia D Disc Records **10-15**

Ruth Etting, autograph, inscribed "To Howard - Every Good Wish" **10-15**

Ruth Etting, sheet music, "Till To-Morrow," copyright 1932, Connelly, Robbins Music.... **5-10**

Sophie Tucker, 78 rpm, #23982, "My Yiddish Momme (sung in English)/My Yiddish Momme (sung in Yiddish)," Decca Personality Records **10-25**

Sophie Tucker, 78 rpm, #29913, "I'm Doing What I'm Doing for Love/I'm Feathering a Nest," Victor Records **5-10**

Sophie Tucker, promo advertisement, Billboard Magazine, copyright 1946 .... **10-15**

Sophie Tucker, sheet music, "Daddy I Love You More and More Each Day," copyright 1914, Jerome H. Remich Co. **10-20**

Sophie Tucker, sheet music, "My Heart Belongs to Daddy," copyright 1938, from the stage musical Leave it to Me, Chappell & Co. **5-10**

Sophie Tucker, wax cylinder record, #10449, "Reuben Rag," Edison Molded Records **30-50**

Vaughn De Leath, sheet music, "Cheerie-Beerie-Be," copyright 1927, Leo Feist Inc. **5-10**

POSTERS

Also see: CAT COLLECTIBLES; HAWAIIANA; MOVIE MEMORABILIA; POLITICAL & CAMPAIGN ITEMS; STEAMSHIP MEMORABILIA & WESTERN CHARACTER COLLECTIBLES.

1970s Aretha Franklin Poster

Concert, "Aretha Franklin," cardboard w/yellow background print in black w/a large half-length photo of the star, early 1970s concert in Palo Alto, California, staple holes & corner wear, 11 x 17" (ILLUS.) **$575**

Early Beach Boys Concert Poster

Concert, "Beach Boys Show," cardboard printed in red, yellow & black on a white ground, three photos of the group, 1968 concert in Lincoln, Nebraska, near mint, 14 x 22" (ILLUS.) **2,070**

Diana Ross & The Supremes Poster

Concert, "Diana Ross & the Supremes," cardboard w/a shaded yellow to orange to blue background, photo of the group & wording in black, 1960s concert in San Diego, 13 1/2 x 22" (ILLUS.) **3,031**

Pink Floyd Rock Concert Poster

Concert, "Pink Floyd - Atom Heart Mother Earth Tour," long narrow rectangular form printed in pink & red on white, photos of the band at the top & bottom, 1970 performance in Salt Lake City, 7 x 29" (ILLUS.) **1,150**

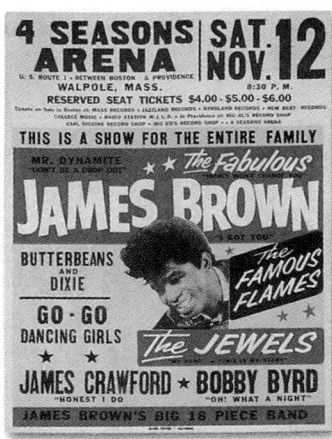

Colorful Early James Brown Poster

Concert, "The Fabulous James Brown," cardboard printed in orange, yellow, white, blue & black, James Brown head photo, 1966 concert in Providence, Rhode Island, 22 x 28" (ILLUS.) **3,699**

Early Ithaca Guns Color Poster

Firearms, "Ithaca Guns," large color picture by artist Louis Agassiz Fuertes of passenger pigeons w/red wording above "Extinct Passenger Pigeon," advertising below the picture reads "Ithaca Guns - Out Shoot Them All - Authorized Agent," ca. 1910, bands at top & bottom, excellent condition, 16 1/2 x 27 3/4" (ILLUS.) **1,540**

Original Woodstock Festival Poster

Music festival, "Woodstock Music & Art Fair - An Aquarian Exposition in White Lake, N.Y. - 3 Days of Peace & Music," cardboard w/a red background printed in white, blue, green & black, August 1969, excellent condition, 24 x 36" (ILLUS.) **993**

Rare Parrish Ferry's Seeds Poster

Seeds, "Ferry's Seeds," color lithograph w/artwork by Maxfield Parrish of a young girl seated beside a watering can, advertising below reads "Mary Mary quite contrary - How does your garden grow? - Plant Ferry's Seeds," framed, two horizontal creases w/two softer vertical folds, ca. 1920, 19 1/2 x 27" (ILLUS.) **5,520**

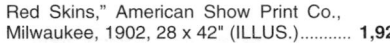

"Bunco In Arizona" Stage Play Poster

Stage play, "Bunco in Arizona," colorfully lithographed design of a cowboy on a bucking bronco, advertising across the top reads "J.L. Veronee Amusement Company's Original Co. in the Queen Bee of All Comedy Drama - Bunco in Arizona," wording at bottom of the scene reads "Billy Craver and His Bucking Pony 'Chub,'" American Show Print Co., Milwaukee, Wisconsin, 1902, minor edge tears, 28 x 42" (ILLUS.) **1,485**

Early Stage Play Color Poster

Stage play, "Bunco in Arizona," colorfully lithographed design w/a large oval central portrait of a pretty young woman framed by portraits of four Indian chiefs, reads "The Original Company - in The Queen Bee of All Comedy Dramas - Bunco in Arizona - Nae St. Clair Among The

Red Skins," American Show Print Co., Milwaukee, 1902, 28 x 42" (ILLUS.)........... **1,925**

Early French Threatre Poster

Theatre, "La Yetta," long narrow color lithograph showing a full-length portrait of an exotic belly dancer in Mideastern attire, by F. Garric, Paris, France, ca. 1900, excellent condition, 22 x 61" (ILLUS.) **690**

Early Red Star Line Travel Poster

Travel, "Red Star Line - Antwerpen - New York," lovely color scene of a mother & her young daughter looking out at an arriving ocean liner, artwork by H. Lassiers, printed in Belgium, ca. 1900, near mint, matted & framed, poster 24 x 34" (ILLUS.)... **1,150**

James M. Flagg World War I Poster

World War I, "Boys and Girls! You can help your Uncle Sam Win the War - Save your Quarters - Buy War Savings Stamps," colorful James Montgomery Flagg image of Uncle Sam w/a young girl & boy, minor creasing, tiny corner chips, 20 x 30" (ILLUS.) 288

1917 Liberty Loan Poster

World War I, "Remember Your First Thrill of American Liberty - Your Duty - Buy United States Government Bonds - 2nd Liberty Loan of 1917," the upper half w/a large color scene of immigrants arriving by ship w/the State of Liberty in the distance, slight border staining, 22 1/2 x 33" (ILLUS.) 173

PRINT ARTISTS - EARLY 20TH CENTURY

Since the late 19th century colorful lithographed prints have been a part of American interior decoration. During the first half of the 20th century an even wider variety of color prints became available. Favorite themes included children, landscapes and flowers. Many artists active during those decades also worked as commercial illustrators, producing magazine covers and advertising illustrations. Names like Maxfield Parrish, Bessie Pease Gutmann and Jessie Willcox Smith are well known to collectors today, but below we will also include works by various lesser known artists. The prints are arranged alphabetically by the FIRST name of the artist.

This material is based on recent sales and was compiled by Michael Ivankovich of The Michael Ivankovich Antiques & Auction Company, Doylestown, Pennsylvania. Mr. Ivankovich is a well known author and auctioneer in this field, including the works of Wallace Nutting. Further information may be found at his Web site, www.wnutting.com.

Adelaide Hiede

Be It Ever So Humble	$10
Indian Maiden magazine cover	30
Magazine covers, pr.	50

Bessie Pease Gutmann

A Brown Study, original artwork	**1,000**
A Chip off the Old Block	170
A Little Bit of Heaven	60
Awakening	90
Baby's First Christmas	360
Chums	325
Falling Out	70
Feeling	190
Goldilocks	30
Good Morning	120
Harmony	100
Hearing	250
I Love To Be Loved By A Baby	375
In Disgrace	90
In Slumberland	30
Just A Little Bit Independent	220
Love is Blind	150
Love's Blossom	80
Making Up	310
Miss Flirt	70
My Darling	120
On Dreamland's Border	65
On the Up and Up	140
Seeing	150
Sonny Boy	60
Sun Kissed	70
Sunbeam	260
Television	70
Thank You God!	170
The Anxious Mother	325
The Butterfly	110

Wait Your Turn Print

The Message of the Roses Print

The Message of the Roses (ILLUS.) 145
The New Love 100
The Reward 100
To Love And To Cherish 180

Boris O'Klein

Down with the Peeping Toms 110
Naughty Dog print 80
Naughty Dogs 90
Wait Your Turn (ILLUS., top of page) 77

Buzza Motto

"A Friend" verse 10
Friendship's Road 10
"If" by Rudyard Kipling 30
"If" For Girls 30
Mother 30
My Friend 40
Old Friends 15
Sweetheart of Mine 40

The Making of Friends 40
Trees 60

Gene Pressler

A Fair Equestrienne 100
Pirate Girl 40

Harrison Fisher

A Picnic on the Beach 30
Graduates 10
If You Want A Kiss 25
Pals (or Diana) 30
Shirley 40
Six Stages of a Girl's Life postcard se-
ries, the set 80
The Husbands of Edith 30
The Serenade 15
The Six Senses 70
Welcome Home 20
Well Protected 30

Haskell Coffin

Advertising fan 25

Howard Pyle

Book of Pirates 100

Hy Hintermeister

1932 calendar 50
Grandma Show Em How 30
Grandma Shows calendar 30

Ida Waugh

Baby in White Hat 30
Smiling Baby 30

Jessie Willcox Smith

Beauty and the Beast 60
Billy Boy 50
Checkers 10
Goldilocks & The Three Bears 170
O-O-Oh It's Cold! 80

The Garden of Allah Parrish Print

Maxfield Parrish

A Musician in the Palace 30
A Perfect Day 200
Air Castles 140
Altas bookplate print 25
Bellerophon bookplate print 20
Book, "Poems of Childhood" 80
Calendar of Cheer, 1924 40
Centaur bookplate print 70
Chancellor Informs Violette, from Knave
of Hearts 70
Christmas card, "Evening" 50
Christmas card, "Twilight" 45
Circe's Palace 70
Daybreak, 10 x 18" 240
Daybreak jigsaw puzzle 40
Djer-Kiss magazine advertisement 110
Dream Garden 130
Dreaming 440
Edison Mazda advertising pencil 10
Errant Pan 70
Evening 100
Ferry Seed advertising piece 50

Fisherman and the Genie bookplate print 40
Fisk Tire advertisement 30
Garden of Allah (The), 15 x 30" (ILLUS.,
top of page) 330
Harvest bookplate print 30
Jell-O recipe book, 1920s 30
King Enters in Full Regalia, from Knave of
Hearts 70
Magazine cover, Collier's, December 11,
1909 100
Magazine cover, Collier's, November 20,
1909 40
Magazine cover, Yankee Magazine, 1970s 20
Morning 250
Old King Cole (ILLUS., bottom of page) 700
Pierrot's Serenade 75
Royal Gorge of the Colorado 200
Scribner's Magazine cover, framed 20
Sea Nymphs 180
Stars 310
The Clown 460
The Dinkey Bird 160
The Knave 70
The Lantern Bearers 100
The Lute Players, 10 x 18" 350

Large Old King Cole Parrish Print

Grimball Pies That Mother Used To Make Print

Philip Boileau

R. Atkinson Fox

Wild Geese Maxfield Parrish Print

Meta Grimball

Chandler Landscape with a Rustic Church

R. H. Palenske

Greyhound - World's Champ 10
Print & blotter grouping 10

William Henry Chandler Pastels

William Chandler is one of the best known of the pastel artists working in the early 20th century. His signed landscapes have been increasing in demand and value in recent years. The various scenes listed here will vary in value depending on their size and detail.

Calendar landscape print, 1928 40
Campfire scene - Evening 120
Campfire scene - Evening 225
Campfire scene - Evening 275
Campfire scene - Evening 500
Camping - Daytime 120

Camping scene - Daytime 275
Chromolithograph, Winter landscape................ 70
Lakeside landscape - Evening 80
Lakeside landscape - Evening 260
Landscape - Evening 250
Landscape - Evening scene, rustic church
  by a rutted road, stormy skies (ILLUS.,
  top of page) 410
Landscape - Lake & Mountains 150
Landscape - Lake & Mountains 250
Landscape - Lake & Mountains 400
Landscape - Lake & Mountains 725
Landscape - Lake & Mountains (ILLUS.,
  bottom of page).. 190
Landscape - Winter scene 190
Landscape with stream 110
Landscape with stream 260
Seascape - Shoreline view 115
Seascape - Shoreline view 675

Chandler Lake & Mountains Landscape Pastel

Chandler Seascape with Rocky Coastline

Seascape - Waves & Rocky Shoreline
(ILLUS., top of page)..................................... 275
Seascape with sailboat 500
Still life - Bird & Fruit 185
Still life - Hanging Game 130
Still life - Hanging Game 160

Zula Kenyon

End of a Perfect Day 40

RADIO & TELEVISION MEMORABILIA

Not long after the dawning of the radio age in the 1920s, new programs were being aired for the entertainment of the national listening audience. Many of these programs issued premiums and advertising promotional pieces that are highly collectible today.

With the arrival of the TV age in the late 1940s, the tradition of promotional items continued. In addition to advertising materials, many toys and novelty items have been produced that tie in to popular shows.

Below we list alphabetically a wide range of items relating to classic radio and television. Some of the characters originated in the comics or on the radio and then found new and wider exposure through television. We include them here because they are best known to today's collectors because of television exposure. ALSO SEE: Cat Collectibles, Horse Collectibles and Western Character Collectibles.

The A-Team Game

A-Team (The) game, in original box w/color illustration of Mr. T in close-up w/other characters escaping explosion in background, simulated bullet holes running across the "A" of "The A-Team" in bold red letters above "B.A. Lends a Hand in the Race for the Formula" in black at the bottom, "Color Photo of B.A. Inside!" in red in upper corner, 1984 (ILLUS.)................ **$12**
Addams Family (The) coloring book, #4331, Artcraft 50
Addams Family (The) game, Ideal, 1964.......... 70
Alfred Hitchcock Why Mystery game, Bradley, 1958... 15

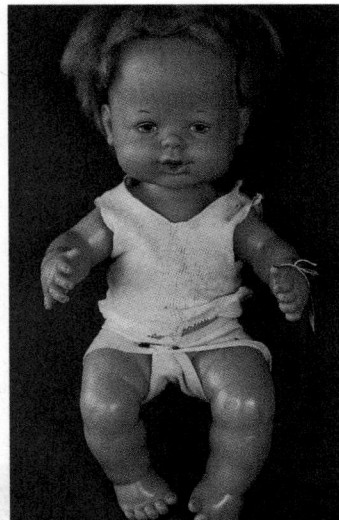

Archie Bunker's Grandson Doll

All in the Family doll, Archie Bunker's grandson, Ideal, 1976 (ILLUS.)........................ 25
Andy Griffith coloring book, 1963.................... 15
Art Linkletter's House Party game, Whitman, 1968.. 25
Baretta game, Bradley, 1976............................... 20
Barney Miller game, Parker Brothers, 1977........ 15

Ben Casey Doctor Outfit

Ben Casey Doctor Outfit, w/medicine bag & various instruments, in original box, 1960s (ILLUS.) 55

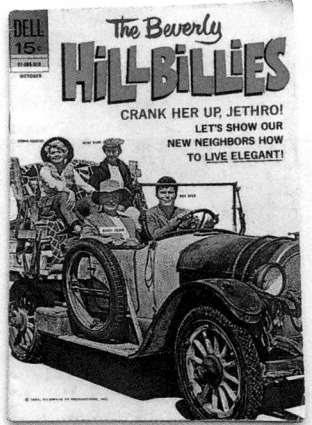

Beverly Hillbillies Comic Book

Beverly Hillbillies (The) comic book, Dell #01-065-010, Filmways TV Productions, back cover w/advertisement for Daisy BB guns w/Buffalo Bill's grandson as spokesman, 1963 (ILLUS.) 5

The Beverly Hillbillies Game

Beverly Hillbillies (The) game, in original box w/black & white head shots of four stars on colorful stylized cartoon bodies on bright red ground, "The Beverly Hillbillies" in bold white lettering & "if you like the TV show - you'll love the game" in black script below, "As seen on [CBS eye icon] the CBS television network" in panel at side, Toykraft, 1963 (ILLUS.) 65
Beverly Hillbillies (The) paper doll, Ellie May, Strathmore, 1963 60
Beverly Hillbillies (The) paper doll, Whitman, 1964 25
Bewitched doll, Samantha, Ideal, 1965 45
Candid Camera game, Lowell, 1963 40
Captain Kangaroo doll, Bob Keeshan as the Captain, late 1950s 75
Captain Kangaroo game, Bradley, 1956 30

Captain Windy Scuttlebutt Marionette

Captain Windy Scuttlebutt marionette, character from Howdy Doody show, wearing red & white striped shirt, navy blue coat, white trousers, & captain's cap sporting red anchor, constructed by Rufus & Margo Rose, ca. 1953 (ILLUS.) 20,069
Car 54 Where Are You? coloring book, Whitman 22
Car 54 Where Are You? game, Allison Toys, 1961 100

Charlie McCarthy in Buggy

Charlie McCarthy toy, tin, figure of top hatted Charlie McCarthy driving black benzine buggy w/whoopee action, white accents, red steering wheel, "Charlie McCarthy" in script on rumble seat, copyright Edgar Bergen, 7 1/2" l. (ILLUS.) 300

Charlie McCarthy Ventriloquist Doll

Charlie McCarthy ventriloquist doll, composition figure wearing off-white linen suit & cap, w/painted features & monocle, 34" h. (ILLUS.).. **230**

Charlie's Angels doll, Farrah Fawcett, Mego, 1977.. **42**

Clarabell's Horn with Box

Clarabell's horn, bicycle type, red & black, in original bright yellow & black box without lid reading "ton-air" in bold red lettering & "horn" in black script w/ascender of "h" forming treble clef, Sound Devices, Inc., 1950s (ILLUS.) **611**

Dark Shadows game, Barnabas Collins Dark Shadows, Bradley, 1969........................ **75**

Dennis the Menace game, Toykraft, 1960 .... **40**

Dennis the Menace Tiddley Winks **15**

Deputy Dawg game, Bradley, 1960 .... **45**

Dick Van Dyke game, Toykraft, 1965................. **55**

Dilly Dally Marionette from Howdy Doody Show

Dilly Dally marionette, character from Howdy Doody show, animated eyes, mouth & ears, wearing original costume of striped trousers, red wool turtleneck letter sweater, baseball hat w/upturned brim, & wire-rimmed glasses, constructed by Scott Brinker, comes w/initialed storage case, ca. 1949 (ILLUS.) **47,316**

Donny & Marie Colorforms Set

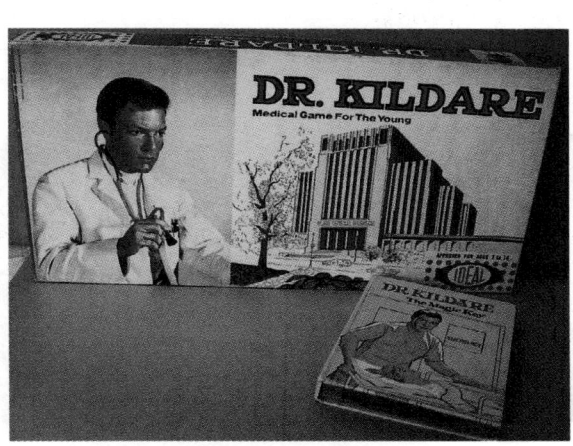

Dr. Kildare Game & Book

Donny & Marie Osmond Colorforms Dress-up Set, in original box w/brightly colored illustration of Donny & Marie performing, 1977 (ILLUS., previous page) 15

Dr. Kildare book, "Dr. Kildare - The Magic Key," cover w/color illustration of star w/patient on gurney, hard bound, Whitman, 1964 (ILLUS. w/Dr. Kildare game, bottom previous page) 10

Dr. Kildare game, in original box w/color photo of star on one side of lid & on other a color drawing of hospital beneath "Dr. Kildare - Medical Game For The Young" in red & black, Ideal, 1962 (ILLUS. w/Dr. Kildare book, bottom previous page) 40

Dream House game, Dream House TV Home Game, Bradley, 1968 20

Family Affair doll, Buffy, talking rag doll, 25" 40

Family Affair game, Whitman, 1971 25

Family Affair paper doll, Whitman, 1968 45

Family Feud game, 2nd Edition, Bradley, 1978 10

Flintstones doll, Pebbles, Ideal 30

Flintstones game, Flintstones Hoppy the Hopparoo, Transogram, 1966 65

Flintstones Play Set

Flintstones play set, brightly colored structure w/sign reading "Elementary School" & yellow handle inscribed "Bedrock School," four main characters & Dino, various playthings including swing set, peddle cars, etc., 1980s (ILLUS.) 20

Flub-A-Dub from Howdy Doody Show

Flub-A-Dub marionette, character from Howdy Doody show comprising duck's bill, cat's whiskers, cocker spaniel's ears, giraffe's neck, dachshund's body, seal's flippers & pig's tail, w/animated mouth, eyes & Persian wool ears, the tongue, whiskers & flippers made from inner-tube rubber, constructed by Scott Brinker, head was repainted from blue to red when show went to color & evidence of old paint is peeking through age cracks on back of head, ca. 1948 (ILLUS.) **58,685**

Flying Nun (The) game, Bradley, 1968 35

Flying Nun (The) paper doll, Artcraft, 1972 25

Fugitive (The) game, Ideal, 1966 130

Get Smart coloring book, Saalfield 20

Gilligan's Island book, Whitman, 1966 18

Gilligan's Island game, Game Gems, 1965 100

Gomer Pyle game, Transogram, 1960s 45

Green Acres game, Toykraft, 1960s 65

Happy Days game, Parker Brothers, 1976 15

The Hardy Boys Comic Book

Hardy Boys (The) comic book, "The Hardy Boys on the Beat!," Gold Key #10254-101, by Filmation Associates, 1970 (ILLUS.) 3

Hawaii Five-O game, Remco, 1968 45

Hee Haw coloring book 10

Hogan's Heroes game, Transogram, 1966 85

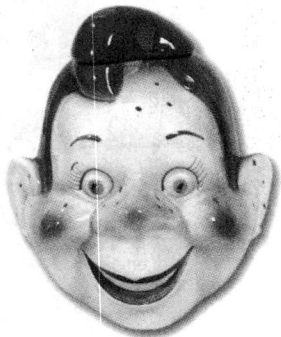

Howdy Doody Cookie Jar

Howdy Doody Board Game

Howdy Doody cookie jar, cov., figural head of Howdy, Purinton, 1950s (ILLUS., previous page) **863**

Howdy Doody Doll

Howdy Doody doll, Ideal, 1953 (ILLUS.) **125**

Howdy Doody game, Howdy Doody's 3-Ring Circus, Harett-Gilmar, 1950 .... **75**

Howdy Doody game, in original box w/color illustration of Howdy Doody & red banner reading "Howdy Doody's Electric Carnival Game" in yellow & white, all on blue ground, Harett-Gilmar, 1950s (ILLUS., top of page) **100**

Back-up Howdy Doody Marionette

Howdy Doody marionette, made as back-up to puppet used on show, wearing trademark plaid shirt, jeans, red bandana & cowboy boots of wood, suede & leather, constructed by Rufus & Margo Rose, 1950s (ILLUS.)... **35,166**

Howdy Doody marionette, made for Canadian version of show, wearing plaid shirt, jeans, red bandana & cowboy boots of wood, suede & leather, constructed by Rufus & Margo Rose.................................. **39,701**

Howdy Doody Promotional Bag

Howdy Doody promotional bag, rectangular w/cut-out handle, decorated w/color illustration of Howdy amid blue five-pointed stars, "HOWDY DOODY" in bold red letters arching over image, "Welcome to the 1955 Toy Fair" in blue at bottom, all on white ground, hole at one side used for hanging, copyrighted Kagran, 11 3/4 x 14" (ILLUS.)...................................... 348

Huckleberry Hound game, Huckleberry Hound & Yogi Bear Bumps, Transogram, 1961 50

I Dream of Jeannie game, Bradley, 1965 50

I Love Lucy coloring book, 1955 30

I Love Lucy doll, Little Ricky, American Character, 1953 50

I've Got a Secret game, I'm Garry Moore...and I've Got a Secret, Lowell, 1956 40

Incredible Hulk (The) game, Bradley, 1978 25

Jackie Gleason's and Awa-a-a-a-y We Go! game, Transogram, 1956 125

Jeopardy game, Bradley, 1964 10

Lassie book, "Lassie and the Secret of the Summer," Whitman, 1958 12

Lassie game, Adventures of Lassie, 1955 25

Lassie game, Game Gems, 1965 50

Laugh-In game, Laugh-In's Squeeze Your Bippy, Hasbro, 1968 100

Laverne & Shirley Board Game

Laverne & Shirley game, in original box w/color photo of two stars in character, Parker Brothers, 1977 (ILLUS.) 15

Leave It to Beaver game, Leave It to Beaver Money Maker, Hasbro, 1959 100

Leave It to Beaver game, Leave It to Beaver Rocket to the Moon, Hasbro, 1959 100

Lieutenant (The) game, Transogram, 1963 70

Looney Tunes game, Bradley, 1968 40

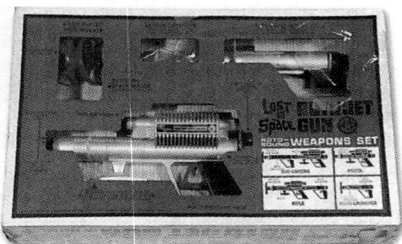

Lost In Space Weapons Set in Box

Lost in Space weapons set, includes items showing through cutouts in lid labeled "2 Safe Plastic Roto Missiles," "Launch Cartridge," "Roto Launcher," "Shrieking Space-Tracer" & "Pistol," the red lid top reading "Lost in Space - Roto Jet Gun" in black & "Roto-Sound Weapons Set" in white above white panels w/black & white labeled drawings of weapons, flip side of window display features painting on heavy foil paper of Robinson family fighting off Cyclops monsters w/roto-jet components, in original partially sealed box (ILLUS.)... 7,737

Lucy Show (The) game, Transogram, 1962 85

*M*A*S*H Signed Cast Photo*

M*A*S*H cast photo, black & white glossy photo of cast members in costume, caption at bottom identifying actors, signed in various inks by Larry Linville, Loretta Swit, Alan Alda, McLean Stevenson, Wayne Rogers, Bill Christopher, Gary Burghoff & Jamie Farr, 8 x 10 (ILLUS.) 902

Magilla Gorilla game, Ideal, 1964 55

Man From U.N.C.L.E. (The) book, Whitman, 1967 12

Man From U.N.C.L.E. (The) target game, Marx, 1966 275

Margie game, The Game of Whoopie, Bradley, 1961 25

Match Game home game, Bradley, 1963 25

McHale's Navy game, Transogram, 1962 50

Mighty Mouse game, Mighty Mouse Rescue Game, Harett-Gilmar, 1960s 60

Mission: Impossible game, Ideal, 1967 100

Monkeemobile Die-cast Toy

Monkees Monkeemobile, die-cast red vehicle manned by cartoon alter egos of Monkees, in original yellow & blue cutaway cellophaned box w/red, black & white lettering, "The Monkees Monkeemobile" at top, "Corgitoys - Monkeemobile" at bottom w/Corgi logo & stylized guitar illustration, the end w/red illustration of car, Playcraft Toys, Great Britain, cellophane is ripped, 1967 (ILLUS.) **348**

Mork & Mindy Board Game

Mork & Mindy game, in original box illustrated w/two stars in scene from show, Parker Brothers, 1978 (ILLUS.) **25**
Mr. Ed coloring book **20**
Mr. Ed game, Parker Brothers, 1962 .... **40**
Mrs. Beasley doll in box, Mattel, marked "© 1967 Family Affair Company - © 1966 Mattel, Inc./ Hawthorne, Calif./Printed in U.S.A." from TV's "Family Affair," large vinyl head, oversize painted blue eyes, single-stroke brows, exaggerated smile, blonde rooted hair, blue & white polka dot print for clothing w/removable collar & skirt trimmed w/bright yellow rickrack, large yellow flannel feet, vinyl hands, original glasses, pull ring for talking mechanism at left hip, in original pink cardboard box illustrated w/picture of Buffy character from show holding doll, 20" (talking mechanism not working, part of cellophane has been removed from box) **230**
Munsters (The) book, "The Last Resort," Whitman, 1966 .... **25**
Munsters (The) game, Munsters Drag Race, Hasbro, 1965 .... **125**
Munsters (The) game, Munsters Masquerade Party, Hasbro, 1964 .... **125**

The Munsters Paper Dolls

Munsters (The) paper dolls, five dolls, Whitman, 1966 (ILLUS.) **50**
My Favorite Martian game, Transogram, 1963 .... **60**

My Little Margie Paper Doll

My Little Margie paper doll, Saalfield, 1954 (ILLUS.) **50**
Nanny and the Professor paper doll, Artcraft, ca. 1970 .... **25**
Newlywed Game (The) home game, Hasbro, 1967 .... **7**
No Time for Sergeants game, Ideal, 1964 .... **40**
Ozzie and Harriet coloring book, Saalfield **28**
Partridge Family (The) game, Bradley, 1971 .... **20**
Perry Mason game, Perry Mason, Case of the Missing Suspect, Transogram, 1959 .... **30**
Petticoat Junction game, Toykraft, 1963 .... **40**
Rat Patrol game, Transogram, 1966 .... **55**
Road Runner game, Bradley, 1968 .... **30**
Route 66 game, Transogram, 1960 .... **125**

Ruff & Reddy Board Game

Ruff & Reddy game, in original box w/color illustration of various cartoon characters, Transogram, 1962 (ILLUS.) 50

"TV Guide" with Superman Cover

Superman "TV Guide" cover, full color photos of George Reeves as bespectacled Clark Kent & as flying caped Superman w/caption reading "George Reeves - Man and Superman," headline at top reads "Can Sportscasters Spot a Curve? - Viewing Guide to World Series," for last week of September 1953 (ILLUS.) 316
Taxi game, Selchow & Righter, 1960 30
Terrytoons Hide 'n' Seek game, Transogram, 1960 75
That Girl paper doll, Saalfield, 1967 40
Top Cat game, Transogram, 1962 95
Truth or Consequences game, Lowell, 1962 28
Untouchables (The) game, Elliot Ness & The Untouchables, Transogram, 1961 75
Waltons (The) doll, Grandpa Zeb, Mego, 1975 65
Welcome Back Kotter paper doll, Toy Factory 7
You Bet Your Life game, Groucho's You Bet Your Life, Lowell, 1955 100

RAGGEDY ANN & ANDY COLLECTIBLES

Say the names Raggedy Ann and Andy and visions of red yarn hair, floppy striped legs, and friendly smiling faces come to mind. Without a doubt, they are the most famous rag dolls of all time. Books that feature the famous duo and dolls number high in this collectible field. Other Rag-

gedy Ann and Andy items have always been out there, but not in the numbers that appeared in the early 1970s when there was a newfound interest in these lovable characters.

Ball, musical roly-poly, 1974 .... **$55**
Bank, Raggedy Ann, vinyl, 1972, 11" **12-22**
Bedspread/curtains, 1970s 50

"Beloved Belindy" Book

Book, "Beloved Belindy," 1926, Volland edition (ILLUS.) 160
Book, "Raggedy Ann and Andy and the Camel with the Wrinkled Knees," 1924, Donohue 85
Book, "Raggedy Ann and Fido," 1969, Little Golden Book.. 7
Book, "Raggedy Ann and Marcella's First Day at School," 1952, Wonder Book 25
Book, "Raggedy Ann Helps Grandpa Hoppergrass," 1943, McLoughlin, "Westfield Classic" 40
Book, "Raggedy Ann Stories," 1918, Volland edition .... 150+
Book, "Raggedy Ann's Friendly Fairies," 1919, Donohue 60

Raggedy Ann & Andy Clock

Clock, talking alarm, w/figures of Ann, Andy & Arthur, 1972 (ILLUS.) 60

Volland Raggedy Ann Doll

Doll, Ann or Andy, original clothes, good condition, marked "Patented Sept. 7, 1915," Volland, 23-24", each (ILLUS. of Ann) **2,500**
Doll, Ann or Andy, talking, Knickerbocker, 1974, 12", each 50
Finger puppets, Hallmark, 1974, ea. 28
Game, candle craft kit, 1974 65

"A Happy Thought" Greeting Card

Greeting card, "A Happy Thought," large Raggedy Andy, Hallmark, 15 x 18" (ILLUS.) 15
Hand puppet, mint in package, 1973 45

Lunch box, metal w/thermos, unused, Aladdin, 1973 90
Magnets, Magnetics, 1978, 4", ea. 2
Music box, Schmidt, Japan, 1971 75
Music box, w/stuffed felt figures, 1972 55
Nightlight, figural Ann, Bobbs Merrill, 1976 65
Ornament, Christmas, handcrafted Ann or Andy, Hallmark, 1975, each.................... **300-350**
Paper dolls, Raggedy Ann & Andy, boxed set, 1975 .... **7-10**
Paper dolls, Raggedy Ann & Andy, circus, Whitman, 1974.. **10-15**
Paper dolls, Raggedy Ann & Andy, Ethel Hays Simms, uncut, Saalfield, 1945 65

Raggedy Ann Paper Napkins

Paper napkins, Bobbs Merrill, 1974 (ILLUS.)... 5
Pattern, Awake/Asleep doll, McCalls, 1941........ 25
Pillow, heart-shaped 45
Pin, plastic, Ann & Andy w/flowers, Hallmark, early 1970s... 35

Raggedy Ann Ceramic Planter

Planter, ceramic, #4185, 1976, 6" h. (ILLUS.) 30

Raggedy Ann Postalettes

Postalettes, Hallmark, in box, 1972, each (ILLUS.) 12

Raggedy Ann Postcard

Postcard, Raggedy Ann from postal series of 1997 (ILLUS.) 5

Pull toy, Ann & Andy play drum when pulled, Fisher-Price, 1941, 12" l. 700

Raggedy Ann Puzzle

Puzzle, Raggedy Andy & camel w/wrinkled knees, frame tray, Milton Bradley, 1980s (ILLUS.) 7

Puzzle, Raggedy Ann & Andy, frame-tray, Milton Bradley, 1955, complete 20

Quilt, single bed, 1970s 37

Radio, transistor, in box 65

Record, Raggedy Ann, 1977 20

Raggedy Ann Record with Pop-Up Book

Record, w/pop-up book, Hallmark, 1974 (ILLUS.) 25

Record player, heart-shaped 90

Sand pail, metal, 1940s 70

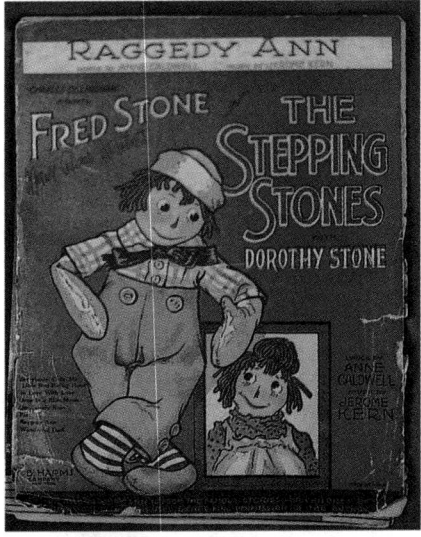

Raggedy Ann Sheet Music

Sheet music, large format, 1923 (ILLUS.) 25

Stationery, kiddie, boxed, 1960s 20

Toy house, furniture & miniature Ann & Andy, 1970s 45

Tray, metal, features Ann & Andy, 1970s 15

RIBBON DOLLS

The craft of making ribbon dolls dates to a time when a woman's worth was measured by her skill with a needle. Young and old alike practiced their skills on crewel, embroidery, ribbon dolls and other home arts. Some of these framed ladies were completely homemade projects, from the actual design of the paper figure to all the lace, ribbon and trim that went into her ensemble. Others were purchased in kit form, complete with paper doll, ribbon supplies and the actual frame. One could also purchase a paper pattern for a mere ten cents and add the necessary decorative materials. Today collectors are particularly interested in ladies in unusual poses, pictured in unique settings or the hard-to-find male examples.- Bobbie Zucker Bryson

Ballerina, black hair, wearing pink & white feather skirt w/multicolored ribbons around waist & wrist, holding pink feather pompom, 10 3/4 x 13" **$125-175**

Bride Wearing Veil Trimmed with Pearls

Bride, off-white ribbon dress & veil, holding bouquet w/ribbon streamers, headpiece & veil trimmed w/pearls, 9" w. x 11" h. (ILLUS.) **115-135**
Colonial man, green ribbon pantalettes & dark pink waistcoat w/ruffled ribbon cuffs & collar, 8 1/2" h. (companion to Colonial woman) **50-65**

Colonial Ribbon Doll with Bouquet

Colonial woman, blonde wearing pale blue velvet ribbon dress, lace petticoat showing on bottom, smelling a ribbon flower bouquet, 11 1/4" h. (ILLUS.) **65-85**
Colonial woman, dark pink ribbon dress & hat w/green ribbon sash & trim, holding multicolored ribbon bouquet, 8 1/2" h. (companion to Colonial man) **50-65**

"The Proposal" Ribbon Doll

Couple, a man on bended knee gazes up at woman wearing pink petal dress decorated w/black marquisette beading, a full moon & trees in background, "The Proposal" in panel underneath, 9 x 11" (ILLUS.) **50-60**

Dutch Girl Ribbon Doll

Dutch girl, beige dress w/large bow in back, white apron & cap w/lace trim & wooden clogs, carrying a red & yellow bouquet of flowers, 10 1/2" h. (ILLUS.) **55-65**

Ribbon Doll in Pink Dress

Faceless Ribbon Doll

Girl, faceless form in profile, head bowed, wearing pink dress & holding gold-circled bouquet & matching cap, 9 3/4 x 12 3/4" (ILLUS.) **25-35**

Girl, wearing green ribbon dress trimmed in lace & a lace bonnet, holding a coordinating nosegay, 6" h. **35-55**

Girl, wearing pink ribbon dress w/lace hem, large pink ribbon hat w/flower trim hiding face, holding a flower-encircled bouquet, 7" h. (ILLUS.) **40-50**

Lady, blonde bobbed hair, elongated neck, long-lashed eyes cast downward, yellow velvet dress trimmed in lace & ribbon, holding ribbon & lace bouquet **100-135**

Little Girl Ribbon Doll In White

Girl, wearing off-white ruffled ribbon dress trimmed in lace, lace pantalettes, matching cloche cap, black ballet slippers, mounted on black velvet w/pink flowers & white birds painted on it, 6 3/4 x 8" (ILLUS.) **50-60**

Ribbon Doll in Pink Dress & Bonnet

Lady, faceless, pink ribbon & white lace, trimmed w/pink & blue ribbon flowers, large pink ribbon hat, carrying a bouquet of ribbon flowers, 7" h. (ILLUS.) **50-65**

Lady, made completely of green ribbon, trimmed in pink ruffled ribbon & decorated w/needlepoint designs & flowers, holding matching bouquet, 7 1/2" h. **45-65**

Lady, on tiptoe, pink satin ribbon & lace dress, holding a string of ribbon flowers, 10" h. **65-85**

Lady, rosy-cheeked, standing on toes, wearing light blue ribbon dress w/large lace collar & Colonial style hat, carrying an umbrella, 9 1/4" h. **60-75**

Ribbon Doll in Pink Dress w/Bouquet

Lady, w/blonde, curly bobbed hair, lace around the neck w/spread-out pink ribbon skirt, holding a multicolored bouquet, 12" h. (ILLUS.) **100-135**

Ribbon Doll with Real Hair

Lady, w/real light brown hair, wearing a pink ribbon layered dress, trimmed in pink lace, carrying a multicolored bouquet encircled in lace, 12 1/2" h. (ILLUS.) **45-65**

Lace-trimmed Ribbon Doll

Lady, w/red curls, square-topped hat, wearing a pale pink ribbon dress w/ecru lace trim & carrying a pastel ribbon flower bouquet, 11" h. (ILLUS.)............................. **50-65**

Lady, wearing a pale gold lace dress w/black velvet bows & chiffon cuffs & bodice, 18" h. **40-60**

Paper Patterns for Ribbon Dolls

Paper pattern, lady w/black curly hair & bonnet, ruffled skirt w/lace on shoulder, hem & pantalettes, high heels, holding circle for bouquet, packed in cellophane envelope w/sticker reading "Salem Chemical Mfg. Co." (ILLUS. without envelope, left, w/other pattern) **8-12**

Paper pattern, lady w/red hair in colonial style, standing on tiptoe w/toes peeking out from hoop skirt, holding circle for bouquet, packed in cellophane envelope w/sticker reading "Salem Chemical Mfg. Co." (ILLUS. without envelope, right, w/other pattern)... **8-12**

Ribbon Doll Pattern

Pattern, woman, black & white, ca. 1951 (ILLUS.) **3-6**
Set: busts of Colonial man & woman; the man wearing top hat, lace cuffs & cravat, the blonde woman wearing bonnet, lace-trimmed bodice & black sash, pr. 4 3/4" h. **85-100**

Silhouette of Black Felt

Silhouette of girl, black felt w/white stitched trim, wearing dress w/trimmed sleeves, three-tiered skirt over pantalettes, & large bonnet w/streamers, carrying purse in one hand & parasol over other shoulder, 7 3/4 x 9 3/4" (ILLUS.) **25-35**
Southern Belle, w/beauty mark on cheek & three long curls of blonde hair, wearing a beige lace dress decorated w/ribbon flowers, large brimmed bonnet w/ribbon

trim & bows, long black net gloves on hands, holding ribbon flower bouquet encircled by lace, 7 3/4" h. **45-50**

Spanish Dancer Ribbon Doll

Spanish dancer, black-haired woman wearing dress of silver-trimmed white ribbon w/matching ribbon sash, beige lace petticoat, yellow beads over one shoulder, holding large lace fan behind head, other hand at hip, 9 x 11" (ILLUS.) **110-150**

Ribbon Doll in Green

Woman, black hair, wearing green ribbon dress & cap trimmed in ivory lace, coordinating lace pantalettes, holding multicolored rose bouquet, matching ribbon roses on cap & shoulders, 9 1/2 x 11 1/2" (ILLUS.) **40-50**
Woman, blonde hair piled high on head, wearing yellow ribbon dress, holding a

multicolored ribbon bouquet in out-
stretched hand, 10" h. **35-50**

Ribbon Doll in Peach Dress

Woman, blonde hair, wearing peach ribbon
dress w/white lace overlay, blue ribbon
flowers on hat, pastel ribbon bouquet, in
oval frame, 8 3/4 x 10 3/4" (ILLUS.) **60-70**

Woman Walking Dog Ribbon Doll

Woman, brown hair, wearing pink ribbon
dress w/white ribbon ruffles on skirt &
shoulders, holding matching parasol &
walking a dog on a leash, matted on
black background decorated w/scene of
house & walkway, 6 3/4 x 8 1/2"
(ILLUS.)... **35-50**
Woman, "Colonial Dame," white hair, wear-
ing pink ribbon dress w/lace trim, holding
a red feather, Bucilla, ca. 1930s-40s,
8 3/4" h.. **75-95**
Woman, flapper w/real hair, wearing sheer
pajamas, reclining on a divan w/pillows,
smoking a cigarette, 13"............................. **35-50**
Woman, full-face w/blonde curls, wearing
pink ribbon peplum w/lace undercoat,
pink streamers, matching lace & ribbon
bonnet, holding parasol, 10 x 12" **100-125**

Blonde Ribbon Doll in Pink

Woman, blonde hair, wearing pink ruffled
ribbon dress trimmed in ivory lace, w/ivo-
ry lace pantalettes & hat trimmed in ruffled moss green ribbon & maroon flowers, holding ivory lace fan w/pastel
streamers, 10 3/4 x 13" (ILLUS.)................ **40-50**

Ribbon Doll in Pink Ruffles

Woman, long white curls, wearing pink ruffled dress w/full skirt w/white underside,
pink & green flowers at bodice neckline &
on matching pink cap, gold high-heeled
shoes, skirt raised to expose legs from
knees down, 11 1/4 x 13 1/4" (ILLUS.) **75-95**

Ribbon Doll in Green Dress

Woman, red curls, wearing a light green ribbon dress, carrying a lace bouquet, 11" h. (ILLUS.).. **45-55**

Ribbon Doll Trimmed in Lace

Woman, red curly hair, wearing pale pink ribbon dress accented w/pink, yellow & green ribbon roses, large ribbon sash, brim of matching square-topped hat & hem of skirt trimmed in ivory lace, one hand held up toward mouth, 9 x 11" (ILLUS.)... **40-50**

Woman, red hair, wearing a ruffled yellow & gold ribbon dress, holding a garland of multicolored ribbon flowers in outstretched arms, 10" h. (ILLUS., next column)... **65-85**

Ribbon Doll in Ruffled Yellow Dress

Red-haired Ribbon Doll

Woman, red hair, wearing green ribbon dress w/pink streamers, ribbon rose & ivory lace cap, ivory lace pantalettes, holding pink & white ribbon roses in lace encircled bouquet, framed w/black textured mat, 9 1/2 x 11 1/2" (ILLUS.)............. **40-55**

Ribbon Doll & Velvet Flower Bouquet

Woman, silk thread blonde wearing bright yellow ribbon dress w/gold threads, sash tied into large bow, lace pantalettes, holding a lace & velvet bouquet, 11 1/2" h. (ILLUS., previous page)............. **60-75**

Woman, wearing black lace dress w/white petticoat, matching black lace hat w/yellow feather, holding yellow bouquet, 8 x 10"... **25-35**

Ribbon Doll in Print Dress

Woman, wearing floral print dress w/pink ribbon bow at waist, large pink hat & carrying a painted bouquet, 12 3/8" h. (ILLUS.).. **35-45**

Ribbon Doll in Pale Blue Dress

Woman, wearing pale blue ribbon & ecru lace dress, lace pantalettes & a bonnet, carrying a flower & lace bouquet w/pink ribbon streamers, 10 1/2" h. (ILLUS.)......... **40-55**

Woman, wearing peach-colored flared dress w/light green ribbon trim, holding finger up to her mouth, eyes downcast, 10" h... **65-85**

Ribbon Doll with Watering Can

Woman, white pompadour hairstyle, wearing peach dress w/black bodice, holding green watering can, 5 1/2 x 7" (ILLUS.)..... **55-75**

RUGS - HOOKED & OTHER

Hooked

Black Dogs Hooked Rug

Dogs, hand-hooked image of two black dogs w/spaniel-type ears, long bodies & short legs, one standing, one reclining in front of white picket fence w/red flowers, in the background a distant cottage & trees, red line border within broader black border, mounted on cloth & wood stretcher frame, ca. early 20th c., 23 x 43" (ILLUS.).. **$690**

Large Floral Hooked Rug

Hooked Rug with Robin & Dog

Floral, rectangular, central medallion of colorful flowers w/smaller bouquets of flowers arranged around it, all within wide border of leaves, all on light mauve ground, by Mildred Callahan, Stockton Springs, Maine, 1st half 20th c., 7'8" x 10'7" (ILLUS., previous page)............. **920**

Hooked Rug with Lion & Cub

Lions, oblong, central image of large recumbent lion with cub surrounded by flowers, foliage & palm trees, in shades of brown, red, green & black, a border of diagonal stripes in red & purple, Wal-

doboro, some repair & small holes, 30 x 62 1/2" (ILLUS.) **900**

Robin & dog, wool & cotton, a red-breasted bird perching on leafy maple tree branch filling foreground at one side, a dog looking up at the bird from the lower opposite side, against background of green w/blue sky above, all in primitive scroll border in yellows & reds on black ground, mounted on wood frame, America, 19th c., several small repairs, 25 1/4 x 38 1/2" (ILLUS., top of page) **1,293**

Robins, wool & cotton, brown rectangular central panel containing cream-colored cartouche w/two red-breasted birds perching on either side of flower pot that holds plant w/shoots bearing red flowers growing to either side & arching over each bird, surrounded by border of red, green & cream-colored diamonds on brown ground, mounted on wooden frame, several losses & minor repairs, America, 19th c., 23 3/4 x 36" (ILLUS., below)... **1,528**

Hooked Rug with Robins

Seascape Hooked Rug

Sailing ships at sea, rectangular, seascape showing two-masted schooner in blue water against pink & yellow sunset, two other ships & birds in the distance, mounted on black fabric on stretcher in mottled frame, Grenfell label attached to back, 26 x 39" (ILLUS.)............................... **3,450**

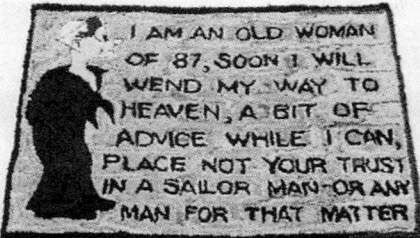

Sailor & Verse Hooked Rug

Sailor & verse, rectangular, folk art style, caricature of sailor stands on one side, the rest of the area filled w/verse reading "I am an old woman of 87, soon I will wend my way to heaven, a bit of advice while I can, place not your trust in a sailor man - or any man for that matter," in black on multicolored ground, black border, appears to have initials "JEB" & date of 1946, 34 x 43" (ILLUS.) **4,313**

Valentine Folk Art Rug

Valentine, rectangular, folk art style, the central area w/large flowering vine surrounded by frame of red hearts & blue crosses or Xs, "RWH" at top & "MBH" at bottom of frame, all in border w/corner bow ties, small hearts & arrows, "his Valentine" at top, "Feb 14" in one upper corner & "1941" in the other, "their rug" at bottom, two bites in bottom edge, 40 x 64" (ILLUS.) **920**

Hooked & Braided Welcome Rug

Welcome, rectangular, a semicircular panel w/large red flowers in center & flowering vines w/smaller red flowers arching over the word "Welcome" inscribed at bottom, all on natural ground within braided black border, 32 x 44" (ILLUS.) **230**

Winter landscape, rectangular, a figure wearing parka & boots walking w/dog through snow-covered hilly landscape w/evergreen trees toward cabin in distance w/smoking chimney, a crescent moon overhead, worked in unraveled burlap in shades of blue, green, red, tan & brown, w/tan line border within wider black border, woven maker's label on reverse, Grenfell Labrador Industries, Newfoundland & Labrador, early 20th c., 24 1/2 x 37 3/4" (ILLUS., top next page) **1,645**

Grenfell Winter Scene Hooked Rug

Winter scene, rectangular, sampler type w/images of sailing ship, compass, fish house on stilts, canoe, evergreen trees, snowshoes, birds & dogs near body of water, & two hooded figures, one in skirt, red, blue, white & green on fawn-colored ground, mounted to linen backing w/stretcher frame, Grenfell label attached to back, 20 x 25 1/2" (ILLUS.) **3,163**

Winter Landscape Hooked Rug

Other

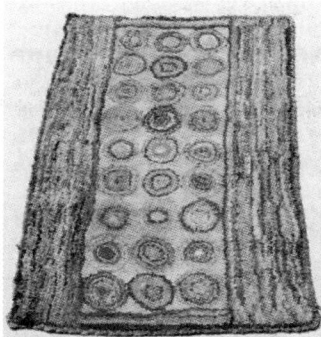

Folk Art-style Rag Runner

Rag runner, folk art style, composed of wide striped border around central area consisting of nine rows of three concentric circles in various colors, 39 x 64" (ILLUS.) **863**

SCOTTISH TARTANWARE

Tartanware is a name we recognize today as describing plaid-covered souvenir items from Scotland. These tartan objects first appeared in the form of snuff boxes around the turn of the 19th century. About fifty years later many household and decorative tartanware items appeared throughout England and Scotland.

The principal company that produced tartanware was owned by the Smith brothers of Mauchline, Ayrshire in Scotland, who used sycamore wood to make their decorative goods. Known as Mauchlineware, these items were deco-

rated with transfers, photographs and tartan paper. Many items were beautiful examples of applying tartan paper stamped in gold with the name of the Scottish family clan. Objects made include purely decorative cubes as well as sewing, desk and kitchen items and even jewelry and furniture.

The popularity of collecting tartanware has grown. Consequently, prices can be quite high, especially for the rare and unusual items.

Tartanware Dome-shaped Box

Box, dome-shaped rectangular form (ILLUS.) **$275**

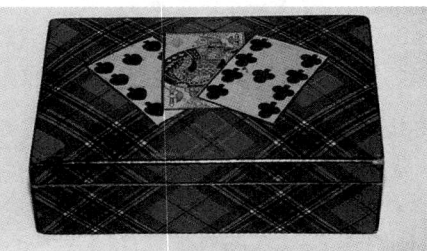

Box For Playing Cards

Box, rectangular, for holding playing cards, scene of cards on cover (ILLUS.) **250**

Tartanware Calling Card Case

Calling card case, picture of Robert Burns
on the front (ILLUS.).. **265**

Game Score Board

Game score board, rows of numbers
w/small holes for pegs (ILLUS.)...................... **150**

Egg Cup & Original Cloth Cozy

Egg cup & original cloth cozy (ILLUS.).......... **325**

Tartanware Glasses Case

Glasses case, oblong w/hinged end open-
ing (ILLUS.) **350**
Ink dip pen, tartan-handled (ILLUS. w/ink-
stand, below)... **125**

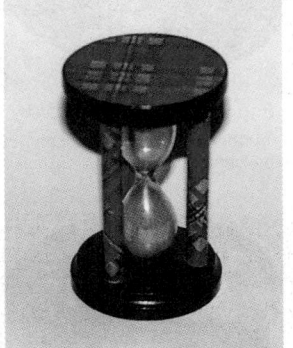

Tartanware Egg Timer

Egg timer, original glass timer (ILLUS.)............ **185**

Inkwell & Ink Dip Pen

Inkstand, horseshoe-shaped w/jockey hat
lid for inkwell, opening for tartan-handle
pen, rare, inkstand only (ILLUS. w/pen) **850**

Tartanware Inkwell

Inkwell, clear, domed glass well w/Tartanware lid (ILLUS.) **150**

Tartanware Napkin Ring

Napkin ring (ILLUS.) **50**

Heart-shaped Pincushion

Pincushion, heart-shaped w/cloth cushion around the sides (ILLUS.) **185**

Tartanware Pincushion on Box

Pincushion on lid of square box (ILLUS.) **195**

Tartanware Round Stamp Box

Stamp box, low round form w/stamp on lid (ILLUS.) **250**

Tape Measure, Pincushion & Waxer

Tape measure-pincushion-thread waxer, upright cylindrical form w/pincushion on top, tape measure in center and waxer around bottom, ca. 1820 (ILLUS.) **800**

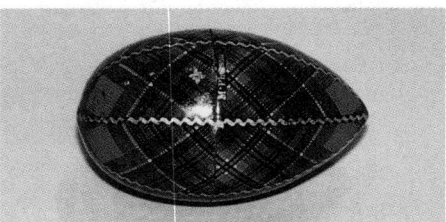

Egg-shaped Thimble Holder

Thimble holder, egg-shaped, can be opened at center (ILLUS.) **200**

Tartanware Thread Holder

Thread holder, round box w/tiny holes for thread around the base, real photo on lid (ILLUS.) **225**

SCRIMSHAW

Scrimshaw is a folk art byproduct of the 19th century American whaling industry. Intricately carved and engraved pieces of whalebone, whale's teeth and walrus tusks were produced by whalers during their spare time at sea. In recent years numerous fine grade hard plastic reproductions have appeared on the market, so the novice collector must use caution to distinguish these from the rare originals.

Cribbage board, walrus tusk, carved in relief w/images of various fish & sea life of the Northwest, polychrome decorated, America, late-19th c., 11" l. **$353**

Cribbage board, walrus tusk, carved on both sides, one side w/floral decorated panel flanked by scenes of animals & fish of the Northwest, the reverse depicting scenes of life in the Northwest, America, late-19th c., minor age splits, 23" l. **470**

Whale's tooth, engraved & polychrome scene of a woman wearing a green dress surrounded by a leafy vine entwined at the top forming a heart, indistinct inscription on the reverse, America, 19th c., 6 3/8" h. (small age cracks)........................... **920**

Whale's tooth, engraved portrait of a lady wearing a hat w/feathers, red polychrome accents, America, 19th c., 4 1/2" h. (cracks) **978**

SHEET MUSIC

"Alexander's Ragtime Band" Sheet Music

"Alexander's Ragtime Band," by Irving Berlin, ABC Music Corp, Alice Faye version, 1938 (ILLUS.) **$3**

"Anchors Aweigh" Sheet Music

"Anchors Aweigh," Chas. A. Zimmermann, Navy emblem in red, white & blue on the cover, Robbins Music Corp., 1943 (ILLUS.) **32**

World War I Era Patriotic Sheet Music

"Joan of Arc They Are Calling You," by Jack Wells, Alfred Bryan & Willie Weston, World War I era, silhouetted image of Joan of Arc on cover (ILLUS.) **5**

"Semper Paratus" Sheet Music

"Semper Paratus (Always Ready)," Official Coast Guard Marching Song, by Capt. Francis S. Van Boskerck, photos of large airplane, ship & life saving boat w/Coast Guard emblem on the cover, 1928 (ILLUS.) **9**

"The Rose of No Man's Land," Music

"The Rose of No Man's Land," by James A. Brennan & Jack Caddigan, published by Leo Feiss, Inc., World War I era, dedicated to Red Cross Nurses w/photo of nurse on the cover, 1917 (ILLUS.) **8**

"The Alcoholic Blues" Sheet Music

"The Alcoholic Blues (Some Blues)," by Albert Vontilzer & Edward Laska, 1919 (ILLUS.) **7**

Shirley Temple Movie Sheet Music

"When I'm With You," from "The Poor Little Rich Girl" movie starring Shirley Temple, Alice Faye & Jack Haley, photo of Shirley, Alice & Jack on the cover, 1936 (ILLUS.) **10-20**

SIGNS & SIGNBOARDS

Roll-down Sign for Angostura Bitters

Angostura Bitters, roll-down banner type, color illustration of young woman w/flowing blonde hair wearing draped gown leaning on ornamental pedestal & being served bitters by two cherubs, "Presented by Dr. J.C.B. Siegert & Sons, Sole manufacturers of the Celebrated Angostura Bitters" at lower right, w/original metal bands at top & bottom, one of four known examples, very minor edge damage, 12 1/2 x 29" w/frame (ILLUS.) **$2,645**

Trade Sign in Form of Pretzel

Bakery, wood & tin, wood carved in shape of pretzel & gilt painted, a figural gilt tin crown sitting atop it, original alligatored surface, 16 x 17 1/4" (ILLUS.) **805**

Sign for Dr. Russell's Pepsin Calisaya Bitters"

Bitters, paper, rectangular, chromolithograph of scene of clouds in the middle of which a woman w/long flowing hair & wearing a pink gown holds a cornucopia out of which seems to spill the words "Dr. Russell's" in red lettering, "Pepsin Calisaya Bitters" directly underneath & flowing around illustration of two globes of the world w/bottle of product set between them draped in American flag, for the Dr. Russell Medicine Company of Chicago, ca. 1880-90, 15 x 21" (ILLUS. framed).. **8,970**

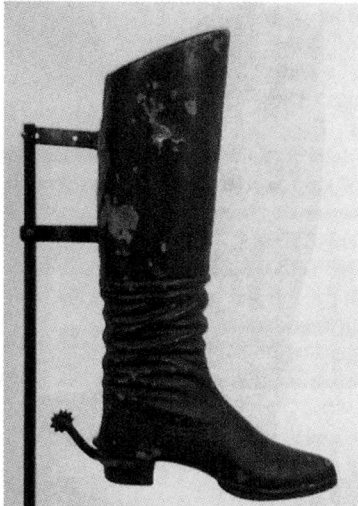

Figural Metal Boot Trade Sign

Boots, metal, full-bodied figural boot w/spur, w/old coat of red paint, the metal & some original gilt showing through worn spots, 19th c., 21" h. (ILLUS.)............ **4,083**

Chromolithograph Sign for Woonsocket Boots

Boots, paper, rectangular, chromolithograph of man & woman fishing at stream, both wearing black waders, "Wear - WOONSOCKET - Rubber Boots and Shoes" below, by American Lithographic Co., New York, ca. 1880s-90s, 17 x 25" (ILLUS.) **3,853**

Early Carved Wooden Boot Trade Sign

Boots, wood, carved full-bodied figural boot w/metal hanger at top, painted black, one side reading "Boots," the other "Repairing," in stencil-type lettering, 25" h. (ILLUS.) **1,955**

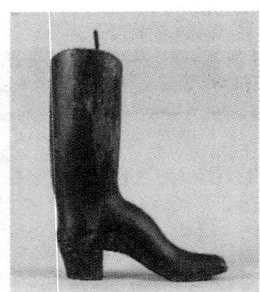

Hanging Boot Trade Sign

Boots, wood, full-bodied carved figural boot w/steel hanging hardware, patinated original gilt & painted surface, 19" h. (ILLUS.) **1,495**

Paper Sign Advertising Farm Machinery

Farm machinery, paper, rectangular, chromolithograph of woman holding scythe & bundle of wheat amid circular insets showing scenes of farm machinery harvesting wheat, "Adriance Buckeye Harvesting Machinery" at top, "Adriance, Platt & Co. - Poughkeepsie, New York USA" at bottom, ca. 1890s, 20 x 26" (ILLUS. in old original frame) **1,323**

Polychromed Wood Fish Trade Sign

Fish, wood, figural fish w/polychrome decoration, original metal hangers at top, scratches to polychrome side, 11 x 35" (ILLUS.) **489**

Tin Sign for Bludwine Grape Drink

Grape drink, tin, rectangular, double-sided wall hanging type, chromolithograph of glass labeled bottle w/contents in white panel at right, left w/diagonal orange panel reading "Bludwine - For Your Health's Sake" in white, dividing the top black section reading "ICE COLD" in white & the bottom dark green section w/"5¢" in red lettering in white circle, illustration of a grape-laden vine curling around bottle into text panels, 9 1/2 x 12 3/4" (ILLUS.) **518**

Large Hardware Dealer Sign

Hardware store, porcelain, square w/red border & four-lobed store logo in red, white, dark blue & gold in center reading "Belknap Inc. - Trade Mark - Extra Quality Blue Grass - Independent Dealer," ca. 1930s, near mint, 4' sq. (ILLUS.) **209**

Embossed Tin Sign for Stafford's Ink

Ink, embossed tin, rectangular, chromolithograph of desk top w/short gallery, a bottle of "Stafford's Ink" standing upon it near partial view of hands writing on piece of paper, by Sentenne & Green, New York City, 12 x 16" (ILLUS. framed) .. **1,035**

Earliest Known Dated Ink Sign

Ink, paper, rectangular, "Davids & Blacks" hand colored in yellow arching above illustration of pen nib reading "Steel Pen" on its side above "INK" in bold black lettering, "SOLD HERE" in hand colored red lettering at very top of sign, product information covering bottom third of sign below drawing of spread-winged eagle holding banner, earliest known dated sign, one of only two known to exist, 1847, light staining, soiling & wrinkling, 12 3/4 x 16" (ILLUS. framed) **2,875**

Insurance Company Tin Sign

Long Three-piece Livery Sign

Insurance, embossed tin, rectangular, self-framed, black ground, a center oval w/colorful illustration of Lady Liberty standing on a mountaintop before a rising sun holding an American flag in one hand, a spread-winged bald eagle at her feet, her other hand supporting a shield illustrated w/image of stag standing against backdrop of trees & mountains, orange/red lettering reading "National Fire" above oval & "of Hartford" below it, by Meek Co., Coshocton, Ohio, some very light white paint overstray, some surface scuffs, 20 x 24" (ILLUS., previous page) **1,800**

Chromolithograph for Becker Leather Co.

Leather goods, paper, rectangular, chromolithograph of man fishing in marsh, standing in oversized shoe w/"Becker's Fishermen's Grain" in white lettering on its side, the shoelace acting as stringer, caption below reading "Compliments of THE WM. BECKER LEATHER CO., Milwaukee, Wis.," by The Milwaukee Litho. Co., ca. 1880-90, 20 1/2 x 26" (ILLUS. framed) **3,278**

Livery, three-piece sign painted black w/gold lettering reading "B.R. Cobb - Stable. - Hack and Boarding. - Erected 1888," a hand painted bust of horse framed in gilt in the center, 40" h., 20' l. (ILLUS., top of page).................... **5,750**

Locksmith Trade Sign

Locksmith, two-sided scroll bracketed sign w/cutout of skeleton key at side, wording illegible, traces of original paint, 34 x 37" (ILLUS.)... **316**

Porcelain Sign for Massanutten Caverns

Massanutten Caverns, porcelain, rectangular w/cut-out corners, cobalt ground w/orange border & orange lettering reading "____ Miles - to - MASSANUTTEN - CAVERNS - Gem of - The Shenandoah Valley - Harrisonburg - Va.," w/space left at beginning for varying number, stamped "Made by Baltimore Enamel 200 5th Ave New York," 17 x 20" (ILLUS.).. **403**

Embossed Tin Sign for Squire's Meat

Meat, embossed tin, rectangular, center black oval w/color illustration of sitting pig mascot wearing medallion around neck that reads "John P. Squire & Company - 27 - Boston," the oval framed w/corn stalks & ears of corn, "Squire's - Arlington," in black lettering at top & "Hams -

Indian & Henderson Motorcycles Sign

Bacon - Sausage" at bottom, 20 1/4 x 24 1/4" (ILLUS.) **2,760**

Rare Oval Tin Sign for Lion Brand Meats

Meat, tin, oval, chromolithograph of maned lion lying w/package of labeled meat between front paws, "Lion Brand Meats" in banner at top, "The Geo. Zehler Provision Co." in banner at bottom, artist signed by R. Fraundart, chromolithographed by Mayer & Lavenson, New York, rare, believed to be unique, some chipping, slight edge denting, 14 1/2 x 17 1/4" (ILLUS.) **1,725**

Motorcycles, galvanized sheet metal, rectangular, two sections seamed horizontally across the middle, hand painted illustration of man in cap driving motorcycle w/woman dressed in skirt & sailor-style top riding behind, right side of sign reading "INDIAN and HENDERSON MOTORCYCLES - BICYCLES," bottom reading "H.R. HENNEBERGER - 73 Lincoln Way, West, at the Bridge, Chambersburg," top reading "Supplies - Repairs," by the Ithaca Sign Works of Ithaca, New York, in original frame surrounded by new stabilizing frame, ca. 1920, overall surface scuffs & scrapes, 48 x 72" (ILLUS., top of page) **11,788**

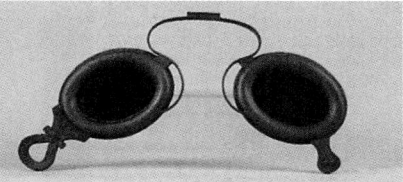

Optometrist Trade Sign

Optometrist, metal & glass, figural spectacles, hollow-bodied gilt metal rims set w/blue stained glass lenses, some oxidation, 12 1/2 x 25" (ILLUS.) **2,990**

Optometrist Figural Trade Sign

Optometrist, metal & glass, figural spectacles, hollow-bodied metal rims set w/one red & one blue stained glass lens, original wrought-iron mounting bracket, one seam at nose piece needs re-soldering, 12 x 35" (ILLUS.) **3,220**

Trade Sign in the Form of Eyeglass Frames

Optometrist, sheet metal, figural spectacles w/traces of original red paint, no lenses, some metal loss at former mounting bracket areas, 16 x 46" (ILLUS.) **978**

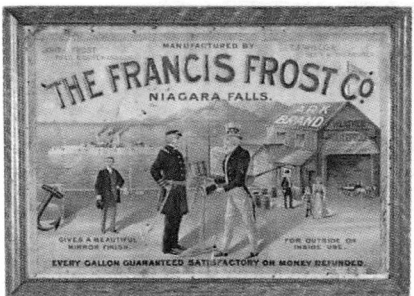

Embossed Tin Sign for Frost Paint

Paint, embossed tin, rectangular, color illustration of Uncle Sam & admiral standing
against backdrop of a harbor w/battleship
anchored offshore, a waterfront ware-
house w/"Ark Brand" in white lettering on
sloping roof & horse-drawn delivery wagon, Victorian family & wooden barrels of
paint in front of it, all against a mountain-
ous horizon, Uncle Sam pouring red/or-
ange paint out of a can onto the ground
before the admiral, "Manufactured by
THE FRANCIS FROST CO.," - Niagara
Falls" at top, "Every Gallon Guaranteed
Satisfactory or Money Refunded" at bottom, "Gives a Beautiful Mirror Finish" at
lower left, "For Outside or Inside Use" at
lower right, by Tuscarora Advertising Co.
of Cochocton, Ohio, ca. 1889-99, nail
holes, some dents & paint loss, scratches
& scuffs, light flaking, soiling & foxing,
19 1/2 x 27 1/4" (ILLUS.) **2,300**

Sign for "Dr. McMunn's" Medicines

Patent medicine, cardboard, rectangular,
top reads "Dr. McMunn's" in red lettering,
"Kinate of QUININE and Cinchonine" in
yellow arching over color illustration of
woman at bedside of sick person, the
bedside table holding bottles of the two

advertised products plus Opium Elixir, by
Thomas & Eno., ca. 1860s,
9 1/2 x 13 3/4" (ILLUS. framed) **1,093**

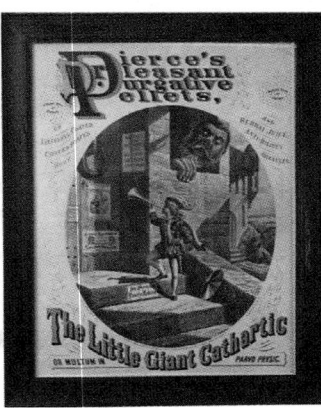

Early Paper Patent Medicine Sign

Patent medicine, paper, rectangular, chromolithographed oval illustration in red-
dish-orange & black on white of a mean-
looking giant looking out the window of
his castle at a young Jack blowing his
horn at the front door, top of sign reading
"Dr. Pierce's Pleasant Purgative Pellets"
(one capitol "P" for all four words) in or-
ange-shadowed black lettering, "The Little Giant Cathartic" in black-shadowed
orange at the bottom, stamped "Entered
in accordance to the Act of Congress in
the year 1872 by R.B. Pierce MD in the
Office of the Library of Congress at
Washington Printed by Clay Cosack &
Co., Buffalo, NY," one of only two known
to exist, 27 x 32" (ILLUS.) **3,680**

Varnished Cardboard Sign for Eagle Pencils

Pencils, varnished cardboard, rectangular,
"Eagle Pencils" in bold lettering w/small
color illustrations of bald eagle crouching
as if about to take flight, boxes of pencils,
groups of loose pencils, & small drawing
of factory, by Wemple & Co., New
York, ca. 1870s, 16 x 23" (ILLUS. framed
& matted) **1,323**

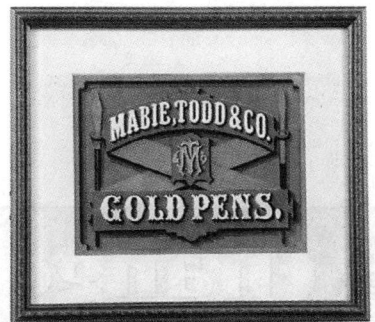

Sign for Mable, Todd & Co. Gold Pens

Pens, cardboard, rectangular, color wood-block graphics of red banners crisscrossing between two fountain pens, reading "Mable, Todd & Co. Gold Pens" in white lettering, the company logo in shield in the center, ca. 1860s, rare early sign, 7 1/4 x 10" (ILLUS. framed & matted) **690**

Rare RCA Victor Porcelain Sign

RCA Victor, porcelain, rectangular, black ground w/tan, gold & white illustration of seated Nipper looking pensively into horn of record player, the caption at bottom reading "His Master's Voice," 18 x 24" (ILLUS.) **1,035**

Early Double-sided Wooden Trade Sign

Shoe maker, wood, double-sided, figural boot, its top painted red & reading "Shoe Maker" in white, the foot painted black w/the outline of a pointing hand in white (these may have been added later), 19th c., some cracks & minor wood loss, 38 1/2" h. (ILLUS.) **2,645**

Simple Early Shoe Repair Sign

Shoe repair, wood, rectangular, double-sided, black silhouette of boot at left & shoe at right flanking "and" over the word "REPAIRED" in stencil-type lettering in black at the bottom, black border, 19th c., one side soiled, some paint loss, a couple screw holes, 16 x 24" (ILLUS.) **1,093**

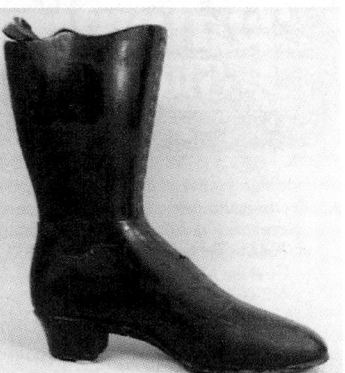

Carved Wood Shoe Trade Sign

Shoemaker, laminated wood, full-bodied carved figural shoe w/carved lacing on top of shoe, mid-19th c., repainted, minor wood loss, 36" h. (ILLUS.) **4,140**

American Girl Shoes Sign

Shoes, die-cut tin, two-sided hanging type w/jagged side edges, each side featuring a background of simulated quarter-sawn oak w/steel battens, decorated chromolithograph bust portrait of smiling pretty young brunette woman w/pink hair decoration & frilly white dress, "American Girl" in red above, "'A Shoe as Good as it's [sic] Name'" in red below, "Always" & "$2.50" in black flanking portrait, by Meek & Beach Co., Coshocton, Ohio, ca. 1901-05, 10 x 13 3/4" (ILLUS. w/replacement bracket, previous page) **3,680**

Colorful Tin Sign for Patriot Shoes

Shoes, tin, rectangular, colorful circular center panel w/illustration of Prescott at the Battle of Bunker Hill standing amid attacking Colonial militia & approaching British infantry w/warships & cannon fire on the horizon, "Men's" in light blue over panel, "Patriot Shoe" below, simulated wood grain border reading "Star Brand Shoes are Better" at top & "Roberts, Johnson & Rand Shoe Co. - St. Louis, U.S.A." at bottom, white circles w/star logo in red at upper left & price of $3.50 in red at lower right, self framed, lithographed by Meek Co., Coshocton, Ohio, some margin bends, small surface blemishes, 18 x 26" (ILLUS.).............................. **3,105**

Trolley Card Sign with Gold Dust Twins

Soap, rectangular trolley card sign, color illustration of the Gold Dust twins, wearing orange/red skirts reading "Gold Dust," in white carrying box of soap & cleaning paraphernalia & walking toward a house w/a woman standing in front of it, trees & lawns in the background, "Gold Dust" in yellow at upper right, "For Spring Housecleaning" in light blue at lower left, rare, 14 1/2 x 25" (ILLUS.) **1,208**

Large Outdoor Porcelain Orange-Crush Sign

Soft drink, porcelain, rectangular, bright orange ground w/"Drink" in black & "Orange-Crush" in white block letters, a color illustration of a labeled bottle of Orange-Crush on the left, raised rim, marked "Beach, Coshocton Ohio," extremely rare, some perimeter chips, 35 1/2 x 59 1/2" (ILLUS.)............................. **3,450**

Penn Esther Cardboard Sign

Stoves, cardboard, self-framed, rectangular, decorative red & grey embossed border w/scroll corners framing embossed illustration of stove in center, "We Sell the" in red lettering above, "PENN ESTHER - The Best and Finest Kitchen Stove - Made by - Mt. Penn Stove Works - Reading, Pa." below in red or black lettering, hanging hole at top, by Ketterlinus, Philadelphia, ca. 1890-1900, 18 x 22" (ILLUS.)... **1,380**

Ingersoll Watches Figural Sign

Watches, hollow-bodied 3D figural pocket watch w/embossed faces on either side reading "The Ingersoll Watches," bezels w/older repaint, faces w/more recent repaint, 25 x 34" (ILLUS.) **540**

Tin Self-framed Sign for Springfield Watches

Watches, tin over cardboard, self-framed, rectangular, chromolithograph of train conductor holding oil can in one hand, a pocket watch in the other, on black ground, caption below reading "Always on Time," "Illinois - Springfield - Watches" at top, white lettering, ca. 1900-10, small dents along beveled edge, 13 x 19" (ILLUS.) **1,323**

Watches, tin, rectangular, color illustration of Columbia holding shield reading "Always Right," "Springfield Illinois" at top, "WATCHES" at bottom, banner below figure reading "Key & Stem Winders - of all sizes," by Wells & Hope, some chipping, light scratching, major ding in "A" of "WATCHES," 8 x 19 1/2" (ILLUS. framed, top next column)............................ **1,150**

Tin Sign for Springfield Watches

Pocket Watch Trade Sign

Watchmaker, cast iron, double-sided figural pocket watch, Roman numerals, subsidiary seconds dial, reads 2:47, original paint, 22" h. (ILLUS.) **770**

Buffalo Club Rye Whiskey Sign

Whiskey, rectangular, illustration of buffalo head looking out of circular red frame

reading "BUFFALO CLUB - RYE WHIS-
KEY" in white, "C. Person's Sons" at top
of sign, "Importers and Distillers - Buffalo,
N.Y." at bottom, all on pale blue ground,
by Chas. W. Shonk Co., Chicago, scattered surface scratches & blemishes,
23 1/2 x 33 1/2" (ILLUS.) 960

STATUARY - BRONZE, MARBLE & OTHER

Bronze

Small Barye Bronze of a Wolfhound

Barye, Antoine Louis, seated Wolfhound,
front leg raised, signed on the round
base, mounted on a square black marble
base, France, late 19th c., 6" h. (ILLUS.) ... **$900**

Contemporary Bronze of Bighorn Sheep

Bronson, Clark E., "A Lofty View," group of
Bighorn sheep on a rocky crag, on an ob-
long wooden base, a 1974 limited edition
signed "Clark Bronson NSS, NAWA,
SAA," w/certificate, overall 14" h.
(ILLUS.) **2,588**

Bronze Bust of Marshall Foch

Davidson, Joseph, bust of Marshall Foch
wearing his military uniform, signed & dated November 1918, C. Valsuani foundry,
Paris, France, 9 1/2" h. (ILLUS.) **1,323**

Fine Russian Bronze of a Bear

Liberich, Nicholai Ivanovitch, standing
bear, realistic detail w/open mouth &
fierce expression, mounted on a white
onyx oval base w/a bronze plaque reading "Nicholai Liberich 1868," Russia, late
19th c., overall 20 1/2" h. (ILLUS.) **5,750**

Contemporary Figural Bronze

Mignery, Herb, "Blizzard of 88," shows a
woman bundled up on horseback w/a
man in deep snow beside her, based on
images from the Blizzard of 1888, signed
& dated "1994 - 12/50," mounted on an
oblong wooden base, America, overall
16" h. (ILLUS.) **863**

Vienna Bronze of a Boy & Donkey

Vienna bronze, miniature group of an Arab boy standing beside his donkey, painted in red, blue, gold & silver, good detail, Austria, late 19th - early 20th c., 3" l., 3" h. (ILLUS., previous page) **173**

Other

Terra Cotta Model of "The Dying Gaul"

Terra cotta, stone-painted model of "The Dying Gaul," after the Antique, France, late 19th c., 20" l., 11" h. (ILLUS.)................. **431**

STEAMSHIP MEMORABILIA

The dawning of the age of worldwide airline travel brought about the decline of the luxury steamship liner for long-distance travel. Few large liners are still operating, but mementos and souvenirs from their glamorous heyday are much sought-after today.

Advertisement, Cunard Line, shows an unnamed liner passing through the Panama Canal Zone, ca. 1930, 15" l. **$250**

Advertisement, magazine-type, half-page black & white ad for the Cunard Line, large image of one of its liners, early 1950s (ILLUS., bottom of page) **10**

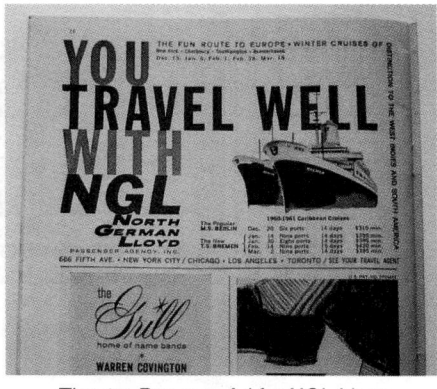

Theatre Program Ad for NGL Lines

Advertisement, "North German Lloyd Lines - You Travel Well With NGL," half-page ad that ran in Broadway theatre programs, 1950s (ILLUS.) **5**

Advertisement, travel agency sign for the Italian liner S.S. Rex, 1936, 29 x 40", ... **800**

Azimuth circle, illuminated device used for taking compass bearings while at sea, 1940s, 12" d. **180**

Badge, brass enameled in red, white & blue w/the company crest, from the French liner Normandie, 1930s **35**

Banner, from the gangway of the S.S. United States in New York harbor, canvas w/blue wording "United States Lines," red border band, 1950s...................................... **1,950**

Book, "Rigby's Book of Model Ships," features a picture of the S.S. United States on the cover, includes a three-foot paper punch-out model of the S.S. United States to assemble, sold in stores & the ship's gift shop, complete & intact, 1953... **100**

1950s Cunard Lines Magazine Advertisement

Book Shelf from the Moro Castle

Book shelf, wood & metal, from the liner Moro Castle, which caught fire off the coast of New Jersey on September 8, 1934 & was beached at Asbury Park, New Jersey, 23" l., front metal rail 2" h., backboard 6 1/4" h. (ILLUS.) 125

Booklet, premium from the Seth Parker Show on radio sponsored by Frigidaire, 1929-1933, Parker being a sailor on an old sailing ship, the booklet illustrating & describing interior & exterior of an early sailing ship, 1934 18

Booklet, premium from the Seth Parker Show on radio sponsored by Frigidaire, 1929-1933, Parker being a sailor on an old sailing ship, the booklet illustrating & describing his ship & other cruise liners, 1930s 35

Booklet, "Souvenir View Book of Prince Edward Island, Canada - A Dominion Series View Book," brown leatherette cover w/oval cut-out, filled w/photos of steamships used for travel to & from Prince Edward Island, by the Canadian Railway News Company, Ltd., ca. 1920s (ILLUS., bottom of page) 20

Booklet, "The Steamer - Reliance to the West Indies," Hamburg American Line, 42 pp., 1927, 6 x 9" 15

Bridge score pad, Elmer Dempster Lines, featuring a picture of ship at sea w/the company logo & flags, ca. 1920s, 8" l. 25

Calendar, 1912, White Star Line, featuring advertisements for its various ships including the Olympic & Titanic, illustrations by Montague B. Black, rare, 11 3/4 x 19 3/4" 6,000

Candy tin, cov., Benson's Candy, sold in the gift shop of the H.M.S. Queen Mary, w/colorful scene of the liner & tugs on the cover, 1930s 25

Cigarette card set, "History and Evolution of the Steamship," set of 50 cards issued by Duncan & Company, Ltd., Glasgow, Scotland, front of cards show picture of ship w/ship's statistics on reverse, 1920s, complete set of 50 100

Commemorative, sinking of R.M.S. Titanic, tissue paper, showing the Titanic & reading "Dedicated to the Captain, Crews and Passengers of the Ill-fated Ship," 1913, 14 x 15" 550

Creamer, china, R.M. S. P. Danube, marked "The Royal Mail Steam Packet Company," ca. 1880s, 3" h. 90

Creamer, white china w/tan & light grey striping & the logo of the Cunard White Star Lines, 1930s, 3" h. 60

Early Prince Edward Island Booklet

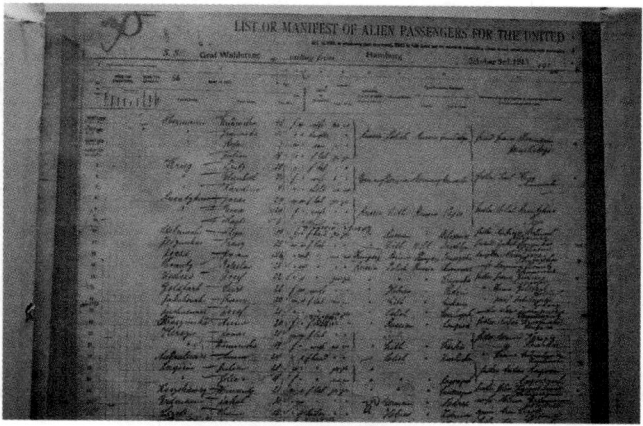

List or Manifest of Alien Passengers

Deck plan, for the S.S. Manhattan, showing the entire deck plan for the ship, 10 pp., 1936, 9 x 28" **55**

Figural souvenir, model of a mermaid sitting on a colored base & cradling the liner S.S. France, 1960s, 1 3/4" h. **650**

Key, metal, for a first class stateroom on the French liner Normandie, 1935, 4 x 6".............. **10**

Letter opener, silvered metal w/an enameled ship logo embossed on the handle, from the H.M.S. Liverpool, 1921 .... **80**

Life preserver, white canvas, no ship marking, 1920s, 22" d.. **90**

Map, Korea & Japan, issued by the United States Department of the Army, featuring Military Sea Transport Service (MSTS) w/steamships & cargo ships in military service in the Far East, front w/a photo of a Liberty ship, the back page featuring a history of the Military Sea Transport Service, 1949, 4 1/4 x 6".. **12**

Matchbook cover, "P and O Shipping Lines - 100th Anniversary," 1837-1937...................... **10**

Menu, Christmas dinner on the S.S. Oakwood Export Lines, titled "Voyage to the Pacific Islands," 1939...................................... **10**

Menu, dinner menu from the R.M.S. Queen Mary, 1948... **18**

Menu, for the German Homes Lines, cover art featuring Viking long ships w/striped sails, 1956.. **5**

Menu, luncheon menu from the Alaska Steamship Company, 1941............................ **12**

Menu, Thanksgiving dinner at the Naval Repair base, San Diego, California, titled "Commodore's Thanksgiving Dinner," cover showing two sailors carrying a platter holding a large turkey, 1945...................... **12**

Newspaper, The London Daily News, headline reporting the sinking of the R.M.S. Titanic but incorrectly stating "All Lives Are Safe," April 1912... **250**

Passenger manifest, "List or Manifest of Alien Passengers for the United States from Hamburg, Germany," from the S.S.

Graf Waldersee, indicating a landing at Ellis Island & including background on each passenger, dated October 3, 1913 (ILLUS., top of page)...................................... **200**

Buffalo Pottery Pitcher for a Ship

Pitcher, jug-type, heavy china, ovoid body tapering to a wide arched spout, dark blue shield mark on the side above "USSB," Buffalo Pottery mark on bottom, ca. 1928, 6" h. (ILLUS.)........................ **90**

Postcard, color illustration of the R.M.S. Titanic sailing on smooth seas, printed by Tuck of England, commemorative piece sold after the sinking of the liner, 1912......... **225**

Postcard, color scene of the "Steamer St. Louis on the Mississippi River," 1917................ **6**

Postcard, Cunard Lines view of the R.M.S. Berengaria, 1930s... **7**

Postcard, "Greetings from San Francisco," showing a harbor scene of steamships, sailing ships & ferries, 1921............................... **5**

Postcard, "M.S. Chi-Cheemaun by Cove Island Light, Ontario, Canada," glossy color card showing a Great Lakes liner, 1960s, 4 x 5 3/4" (ILLUS., top next page)......... **2**

1960s Postcard of a Great Lakes Liner

Swedish American Lines Postcard

Postcard, Swedish American Lines, color photo of the M.S. Gripsholm sailing into New York Harbor, 1950s, printed in Sweden, 3 1/2 x 5 1/4" (ILLUS.).............................. 10

Poster, launching of the S.S. France, illustrated w/images of champagne & confetti in front of large night-lit bow of the ship, 1961, 30 x 46" 475

Poster, S.S. Michelangelo & S.S. Raffaello, showing detailed cut-away views of the Italian liners, used in travel agency offices, 1964, 22 x 54"............................ 400

Record player, portable/travel type, RCA model, crank-operated, interior section for holding 78 rpm records & needles, brown or black leatherette carrying case, used by troops during World War II, ca. 1940 100

Sheet music, "The Wreck of the Titanic," published by the Steuffen Publishing Company, 1912.. 150

Ship's bell, brass, from the M.V. Cambria, engraved w/the statistics of the ship & dated 1949, 12" h. 500

U.S. Navy Ship's Clock

Ship's clock, U.S. Navy model, black metal case w/brass wind key, serial number 78558E, manufactured by the Chelsea

Clock Company, Boston, Massachusetts, ca. 1940, 7 1/2" d. (ILLUS.) .... **50 - 100**

Sugar bowl, cov., silver plate, marked for the Union Castle Passenger Lines, ca. 1930, 4" h. **150**

Telegraph message form, from the R.M.S. Queen Mary, 1930, 8 1/2 x 9 1/2" **10**

Tile, souvenir, china, from the Holland American Line, w/company logo & the ship K. Sola 90 Va - Waneburg, 1950s, 14" w. **50**

Vendor sheet for newspaper, The London Daily Mirror, sheet used at newsstands, reading "Hymn Played While the Titanic Sank," a portion of the hymn printed on the sheet, rare, dated April 20, 1912 .... **1,200**

STEIFF TOYS & DOLLS

From a felt pincushion in the shape of an elephant, a world-famous toy company emerged. Margarete Steiff (1847-1909), a polio victim as a child and confined to a wheelchair, planned a career as a seamstress and opened a shop in the family home. Her plans were dramatically changed, however, when she made the first stuffed elephant in 1880. By 1886 she was producing stuffed felt monkeys, donkeys, horses and other animal forms. In 1893 an agent sold her toys at the Leipzig Fair. This venture was so successful that a catalog was printed and a salesman hired. Margarete's nephews and nieces became involved in the business, assisting in its management and the design of new items.

Through the years, the Steiff Company has produced a varied line including felt or plush animals, Teddy Bears, gnomes, elves, felt dolls with celluloid heads, Kewpie dolls and even radiator caps with animals or dolls attached as decoration. Descendants of the original family members continue to be active in the management of the company, still adhering to Margarete's motto, "For our children, the best is just good enough."

Giraffe, mohair tail, brightly colored spots, Steiff tag in ear, some mohair loss on tip of tail, moth damage in mouth, 24" l., 24" h. **$300**

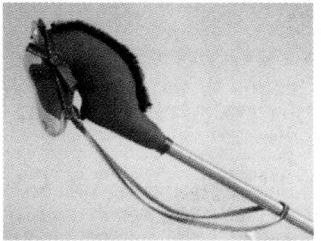

Steiff Hobby Horse

Hobby horse, brown felt, white on face, short black mane, long reins, w/button in ear, ca. 1940s, 40" l. (ILLUS.) **58**

Steiff Curly Mohair Lamb

Lamb, curly white mohair, green glass eyes, embroidered nose & mouth, wearing blue neck ribbon w/bell, ca. 1920s, 7" h. (ILLUS.) **588**

Teddy bear, blond mohair, glass eyes, embroidered nose, mouth & claws, excelsior-stuffed fully jointed body, script ear button, mid-20th c., 30" (felt feet pads w/moth holes, break at sides) **1,955**

Steiff 10" Teddy Bear

Teddy bear, blond mohair, jointed limbs, hump back, glass eyes, foot pads, button in ear, replaced foot pads, 10" (ILLUS.) **660**

Teddy bear, blonde mohair, glass eyes, embroidered nose & mouth, no-pad style, wearing a pink print dress w/pink checked collar, yellow knit overalls, green corduroy jacket, red scarf, black felt hat & bell around the neck, ca. 1930, 5 1/2" **345**

Teddy bear, golden mohair, embroidered nose & claws, black shoe button eyes, squeaker, fully jointed body, excelsior stuffing, ear button, original felt pads, ca. 1905, 14" (mouth embroidery missing, thin small fabric tear on right front arm joint, very minor fur loss, overall soil) **1,955**

Teddy bear, light apricot, shoe button eyes, embroidered nose, mouth & claws, fully jointed body w/excelsior stuffing, felt pads, ear button, ca. 1905, 12 1/2" (fur loss, slight moth damage on pads) **1,610**

Teddy bear, light brown mohair, shoe button eyes, jointed arms & legs, swivel head, ca. 1910, 14" **450**

Teddy bear, light golden mohair, black shoe button eyes, center seam, black embroidered nose, mouth & claws, fully jointed body, felt pads, underscored ear button, ca. 1905, 17" (holes in paw pads) .. **4,888**

Teddy bear, miniature, honey blond mohair, black bead eyes, embroidered nose &

mouth, fully jointed body, padless style, ca. 1950s, 3 1/2"....................................... **98**

Teddy bear, miniature, rattle-type, blond mohair, black shoe button eyes, embroidered nose & mouth, fully jointed body, working rattle, excelsior stuffing, no-pad style, no ear button, ca. 1910, 5" (overall wear, stains & rip on arm) **403**

Teddy bear, "Zotty," long curly beige mohair, apricot chest, fully jointed body, glass eyes, airbrushed mouth, embroidered nose, peach felt pads, 1950s-60s, 21".. **173**

Teddy bear, caramel mohair plush swivel head, brown glass eyes, brown floss nose & mouth, five-piece body w/non-working squeaker in tummy, gold felt pads on paws & feet, four brown floss claws on each, silver "Steiff" button in left ear, 11".. **230**

White 12" Steiff Bear

Teddy bear, white, long limbs, felt pads, minor fur loss to nose, 12" (ILLUS.)................ **3,910**

16" Honey-colored Steiff Bear

Teddy bear, w/hump, long arms & legs, felt pads, honey-colored, w/original Steiff button in ear, ca. 1910, some moth holes to pads, fur matted, 16" (ILLUS.) **3,565**

1950s Gold-colored 20" Bear

Teddy bear, gold-colored mohair, jointed, glass eyes, embroidered nose, felt pads, working growler, 1950s, thinning snout, wear to pads, 20" (ILLUS.)............................... **600**

Steiff Teddy Roosevelt on Horse

Teddy Roosevelt on horse, figure of Roosevelt w/composition painted head & wearing Rough Rider uniform complete w/gloves & boots, w/original white Steiff tag on pocket, mounted on mohair covered rearing appaloosa horse w/glass eyes, outfitted w/old saddle blanket, original leather saddle & leather bridle, on rectangular base, rare, spots on horse faded, Roosevelt missing hat, horse about 38" l., Roosevelt about 27" h. (ILLUS.) **6,900**

TEDDY BEAR COLLECTIBLES

Theodore (Teddy) Roosevelt became a national hero during the Spanish-American War by leading his "Rough Riders" to victory at San Juan Hill in 1898. He became the 26th president of the United States in 1901 when President McKinley was assassinated. The gregarious Roosevelt was fond of the outdoors and hunting. Legend has it that while on a hunting trip soon after becoming president he refused to shoot a bear cub because it was so small and helpless. The story was picked up by a political cartoonist who depicted President Roosevelt, attired in hunting garb, turning away and refusing to shoot a small bear cub. Shortly thereafter, toy plush bears began appearing in department stores labeled "Teddy's Bear" and they became an immediate success. Books on the adventures of "The Roosevelt Bears" were written by Seymour Eaton and first published in newspapers under the pseudonym of Paul Piper. The four stories were then published in book form with Seymour Eaton noted as the author. The four books used four different illustrators for the artwork.

Teddy bear, beige mohair, jointed limbs, glass eyes, velvet pads, mild back hump, Germany, early 20th c., some fur loss, pads showing wear, 15" h. (ILLUS.) **213**

Early White Mohair Teddy Bear

Teddy bear, white mohair, black button eyes, jointed limbs, woven cloth paw, large back hump, some fur loss, minor discoloration spot, early 20th c., 16" h. (ILLUS.) **300**

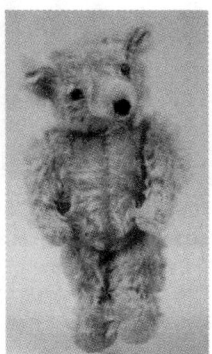

Yellow Fleecy Teddy Bear

Teddy bear, blond fleecy mohair, shaved pointed black-embroidered snout, glass eyes, back hump, felt pads, some soil & hair loss, growler not working, early 20th c., 14" h. (ILLUS.) **$155**

Early "Yes/No" Teddy Bear

Teddy bear, beige fleecy mohair, "Yes/No" type, glass eyes, black-embroidered snout, felt pads, wear at mechanism, which is loose in body, early 20th c., 17" h. (ILLUS.) **300**

Early German Teddy Bear

Light Brown Mohair Teddy Bear

Centennial U.S. Flag

Teddy bear, light brown mohair, jointed limbs, brown button eyes, stubby ears, felt pads, some leg repair, some fur loss, early 20th c., 22" h. (ILLUS., previous page) **144**

Large Brown Mohair Teddy Bear

Teddy bear, brown mohair, jointed limbs, glass eyes, flat back, heavy fur loss on back, repair to leg & back, one eye reattached, 20th c., 25" h. (ILLUS.) **98**

Ca. 1830-60 Handstitched U.S. Flag

Thirteen star U.S. flag, woven wool & cotton, entirely handstitched w/twelve stars appliquéd in circle around center star on navy blue canton, the reverse w/blue cut away within the stitches of each star, the canvas hoist w/handwritten inscription "G.W. Chatfield Elm St." in ink, ca. 1830-60, repairs, losses, stains, approximately 70 x 95" (ILLUS.) **8,225**

TEXTILES

Bedspreads

Toile cotton, red w/classical print depicting Cupid & other allegorical figures in scenes of love, handsewn, pieced & quilted in diamond pattern, backed w/white homespun fabric, constructed w/extended center panel, two pillow gussets & side drops, w/scalloped border on three sides & white binding, New England, late 18 - early 19th c., center panel 52 1/2 x 109 1/2" l., side drops 31 1/2" l. . **$1,293**

Flags

Centennial U.S. flag, printed fabric, the blue star field w/near concentric circle pattern of stars, metal grommets, ca. 1876, corner repair, 34 x 57" (ILLUS., top of page) **720**

Twenty-two Star U.S. Flag

Twenty-two star U.S. flag, woven wool & cotton, handstitched w/arrangement of stars appliquéd in five staggered rows on either side of flag to the canton, canvas heading securing a rope w/wooden toggle at top & a running eye at bottom, ink inscription on heading reads "Presented to Capt. C.H. Beckshafft by W.H. Ball," ca. 1819, approximately 42 x 97" (ILLUS.) **2,468**

Linens & Needlework

Embroidered Linen Pillow Cover

Pillow cover, Arts & Crafts-style, rectangular, embroidered w/stylized flowers in blue, yellow & green on oatmeal linen ground, 14 1/4 x 17 1/2" (ILLUS.) **431**

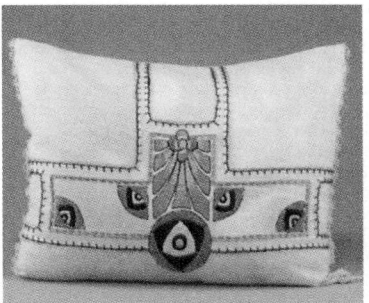

Arts & Crafts-style Pillow Cover

Pillow cover, Arts & Crafts-style, rectangular, embroidered w/stylized flowers in black, gold & celadon green on ivory ground, some soiling (ILLUS.) **546**

Embroidered Fabric Pouch

Pouch, Arts & Crafts-style, rectangular, embroidered w/stylized geometric designs in green, blue, brown & rose & monogrammed on natural ground, 9 1/2 x 12 1/2" (ILLUS.) **144**

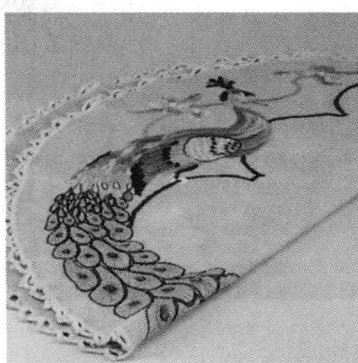

Arts & Crafts-style Table Linen

Tablecloth, Arts & Crafts-style, circular, embroidered w/large blue & gold peacock & coral & green floral border on natural linen ground, crocheted edge, 36" d. (ILLUS.) **345**

Needlework Pictures

Moses in the Bulrushes Needlework Picture

Biblical scene, silk, chenille, watercolor & pencil, rectangular w/oval panel depicting the story of finding Moses in the bulrushes, a classically dressed woman standing over a basket containing the baby against a background of the river, trees, rolling landscape & blue sky, watercolor used for the woman's features, water & sky, unfinished, America, ca. 1806, 15 3/4 x 17 3/4" (ILLUS.) **1,410**

Silk Needlework Coat of Arms

Coat of arms, rectangular, silk, gold & silver metallic thread, gold metallic cord & ink on silk, raised-work spread-winged eagle at top holding swagged floral garland in beak, over raised-work fish crest directly above the center green velvet shield showing raised-work rampant lion, the shield partly surrounded by crossed palm fronds w/encircling banner reading "REGARD - WILLIAMS - THE END" in ink above script initials "NGW," another swagged floral garland at the bottom, framed, America, ca. 1800-1810, tears, minor stains, 12 5/8 x 15 3/4" (ILLUS.) .. **18,800**

Silk-on-Silk Metallic Work Coat of Arms

Coat of arms, square, silk, gold & silver metallic thread & cord on silk, small figure of a lion at top standing over elaborate scroll, chains looping from the ends of the scroll & flanking a center shield decorated w/panels of roses, fleur-de-lis & crosses, scrolling leaves & a banner below reading "By The Name of Howard," signed "Lucy Howard" in lower right, w/related documents, America, 1806, 23 1/4" sq. (ILLUS.) **23,500**

Silk Needlework Memorial Picture

Memorial picture, silk, rectangular, depicting a willow tree overhanging two monuments, one reading "Sacred to the Memory of Mrs. Margery Clark who died Nov. 26th 1808 in the 39th year of her age," the other "Sacred to the Memory of Mr. John Clark who died March 19th 1814 in the 69th year of his age," each monument topped w/arching willow branch, spread-winged bird & the word "Hope," each base w/"MEMENTO MORI," a church, pine tree & flowers in gold, red & green at the sides, a crescent moon & stars in the sky above, "Wrought by Sarah Goodridge aged fourteen Years" at the bottom of the picture, America, early 19th c., 18 7/8 x 22" framed (ILLUS.)......... **3,055**

Memorial picture, silk, rectangular w/oval panel showing young woman leaning against urn-topped monument on which is written in ink "To the memory of Mrs. Rebecca Bacon, wife of Ebenezer Bacon Esq. & two of their children...," a church & gravestones in the background & large weeping willow at side whose branches arch over the scene, facial features & sky done in watercolor, in eglomise mat, New England, early 19th c., 15 1/2 x 17 1/4" framed (light stains, insignificant tears) **2,233**

Patriotic Needlework Picture

Patriotic, square, depicting gold & white eagle flying w/draped tasseled American flag against a sunburst, all on white silk ground, Oriental export, grain painted frame, some brown spots to background, 19 1/2" sq. (ILLUS., previous page)............... **259**

Needlework Picture of Romantic Couple

Romantic couple, silk thread on silk ground, rectangular w/oval panel depicting woman wearing an empire-waist dress & man wearing top hat & cutaway coat in pastoral setting, the couple holding a flowering vine & wreath, a small dog at the woman's feet, painted facial features & sky, indistinct inscription in lower left corner, in molded & gilded frame, America, 1806, 16 1/2 x 19 1/2" (ILLUS.) **5,288**

Needlework Picture of Pastoral Scene

Shepherdess & young man, solid stitches on silk ground, rectangular, depicting a young woman dressed in white & pale yellow & holding shepherd's crook standing next to man wearing cutaway coat & playing flute, the couple flanked by two trees, five sheep in the background, painted facial features & sky, in molded & gilded frame, America, early 19th c., 13 1/4 x 14 1/2" (ILLUS.) **5,288**

Quilts

Silk & Velvet Crazy Quilt

Crazy quilt, embroidered silk & velvet, multicolored design embellished w/variety of embroidery stitched & painted motifs, black satin border, stitched date of "1885," America, 64" sq. (ILLUS.).............. **1,293**

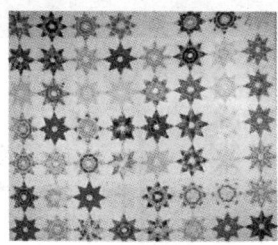

Friendship Quilt with Starbursts

Friendship quilt, handstitched, each square w/multiple starburst pattern & each centered w/a name & place, mid-19th c., 80 x 88" (ILLUS.)............................... **600**

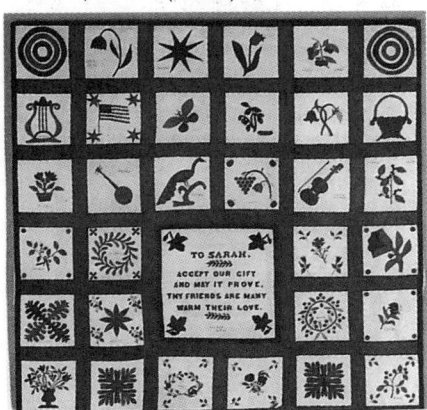

Friendship Quilt Top with Inscription

Friendship quilt top, appliquéd cotton, forty-eight blocks of red, blue & green fabrics appliquéd to white ground & separated by red cotton grid, decorated w/naturalistic, patriotic, geometric & musical instrument designs including flowers, fruit, butterfly, peacock, flag, violin, circles & stars, the large central square w/appliquéd lettering reading "To Sarah - Accept our gift - and may it prove - thy friends are many - warm their love," & embroidered signature of "Amanda Birdsell Apr 20th, 1858," many squares w/embroidered & pen & ink signatures, mounted on wooden frame, 65 1/2 x 86" (ILLUS., previous page)............................... **4,113**

w/three figural vignettes based on illustrations from popular publications of the day w/captions & facial features inscribed in ink, panels on either side w/figures of two dogs, a cat & a cow, each corner w/a cornucopia issuing budding flowers, all worked in calico printed cotton in shades of red, green, pink & brown, green calico border, all appliquéd to a white woven cotton ground quilted w/leaf & diagonal line stitching, mounted & enclosed in Plexiglas frame, comes w/copy of book Small Endearments: Nineteenth-century Quilts For Children and Dolls, in which it appears, America, last quarter 19th c., 35 x 37" (ILLUS.).......................... **30,550**

Pictorial Quilt of Ship "Mary Edson"

Pictorial quilt, pieced cotton, center image of three-masted ship "Mary Edson" constructed of pieced rose pink calico segments on brown calico ground w/applied & embroidered silk American flag, silk magenta pennant reading "Mary Edson," blue silk flag w/thirty stars, & white silk flag embroidered "8215," the corners decorated w/hexagonal rose-pink calico rosettes, the whole bordered in same rose calico fabric, white cotton backing, made by Hope Atkins Howes, America, third quarter 19th c., 72 x 90" (ILLUS.) **1,528**

Red, White & Blue Union Quilt

Union quilt, appliquéd & pieced cotton, central thirteen-star flag w/spread-winged eagles in each corner, all in red, white & blue cotton fabric on white field, all enclosed in red, white & blue striped border, white cotton binding & backing, overlapping circle, rosette & diagonal line quilt stitching, probably Pennsylvania, ca. 1915, 68 x 75" (ILLUS.) **9,988**

Samplers

"Scenes of Childhood" Quilt

"Scenes of Childhood" quilt, embroidered & appliquéd cotton, a center panel

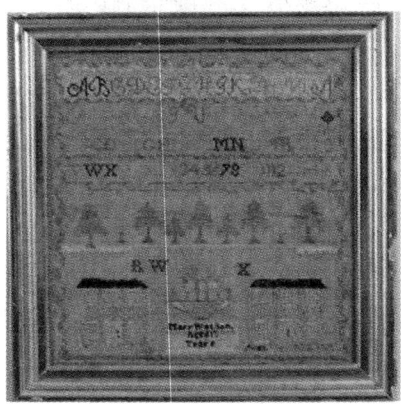

Needlework Alphabet Sampler

Alphabets & numerals, two alphabet rows & one numeric row, w/central row of trees of various sizes, bottom w/central basket of fruit or flowers over rectangular box w/"Mary Watson aged 16 years," flanked by colonial houses w/black roofs, double chimneys, five twelve-pane windows & front doors w/iron latches, strawberry-type vine border, presently mounted on fine linen affixed to light cardboard in lemon gold molded frame, probably Connecticut, 15 x 16" (ILLUS., previous page)... **3,738**

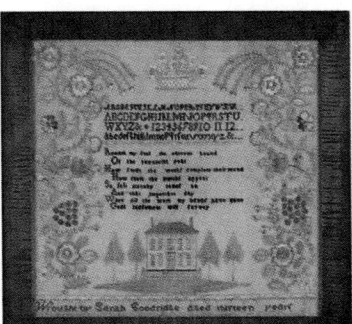

"Sarah Goodridge" Sampler

Alphabets & pious verse, silk thread on linen, alphabet panels at top under central basket of flowers & over verse reading "Remark my soul the narrow bound - Of the revolving year - How swift the weeks complete their round - How short the months appear - So fast eternity comes on - And that important day - When all the work my hands have done - Gods judgment will survey," "Wrought by Sarah Goodridge aged thirteen years" at bottom under depiction of two-story house w/double chimneys & flanked by pine trees, elaborate floral vine borders on each side, comes w/several items pertaining to Sarah Goodridge, New Hampshire, 1818, 18 7/8 x 19" framed (ILLUS.).. **3,173**

Alphabets & Pious Verse Sampler

Alphabets & pious verse, silk & wool blue, white, yellow & green thread on linen, alphabet panels in upper half over verse reading "My youth is but a summer's day - Then like the bee and ant, I'll lay - A stove of learning by - And though from flower to flower I rove - My stock of wisdom I'll improve - Not be a butterfly" & "Wrought by Mahala S. Hamblen Aged 11 years Wareham Sept th 1st 1836," surrounded by floral border, framed, 17 5/8 x 21" (ILLUS.) **8,813**

Pictorial Pious Verse Sampler

Pictorial pious verse, silk thread on linen, the needlework centered by a house w/a fence & two trees & surrounded by various birds, flowers, butterflies, two verses, the signature "Susanna Stanley born October 24th __23," her parents' names, William & Rebecca Stanley, & the probable date the sampler was completed, "October 12, 1832," all enclosed in geometric floral border, probably Pennsylvania, thread losses, toning, staining, 15 3/4 x 22" (ILLUS.) **2,233**

Sampler with Two Pious Verses

Pious verse, multicolored silk thread on linen ground, two pious verses at top & center, the bottom w/central tree w/birds flanked by two small pine trees, deer, butterflies & two houses & surrounded by various potted flowers, baskets of fruit, birds & the figure of a man, all enclosed in geometric floral border, signed "Elizabeth Viner October The 13 1790," framed, probably England, 12 x 14 1/2" (ILLUS.)... **1,763**

TOBACCIANA

Although the smoking of cigarettes, cigars & pipes is controversial today, the artifacts of smoking related items - pipes, cigar & tobacco humidors, and cigar & cigarette lighters - and, of course, the huge range of advertising materials are much sought after. Unusual examples, especially fine Victorian pieces, can bring high prices. Below we list a cross section of Tobacciana pieces.

Also see: CANS & CONTAINERS and Antique Trader Advertising Price Guide.

Pious Verse Sampler from 1839

Pious verse & building, silk thread on linen ground, a central two-story brick house surrounded by fruit trees, birds, potted flowers, crowns & eight-pointed stars, over a pious verse & various potted flowers, trees, dogs, deer & birds, all enclosed by chain border & geometric strawberry vine, signed by "Charlotte Mussell 1839," framed, England, 15 1/2 x 12 7/8" (ILLUS.) **1,645**

Porcelain Ashtray-Match Holder

Ashtray-match holder, "Abdulla Pure Virginia Superb Cigarettes," porcelain, the rectangular ashtray base w/rounded corners decorated w/printed black border & advertising, opening in top to insert a small box of matches, a box included, early 20th c., 4 x 5", 3" h. (ILLUS.) **$99**

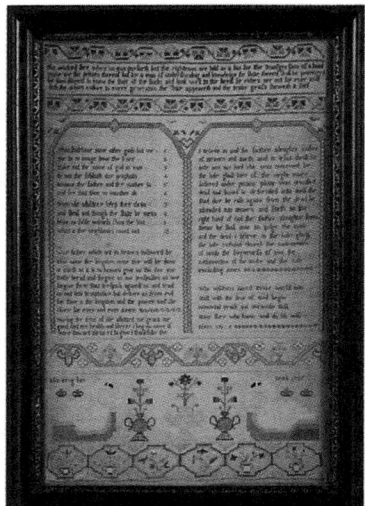

Sampler with Pious Verse & Prayers

Pious verse & prayers, multicolored silk thread on linen, a pious verse over panels listing the Ten Commandments, the Lord's Prayer, the Apostle's Creed & a Psalm, floral & geometric borders accented w/birds, hearts, swans, urns w/flowers, & crowns, signed "Eliz Berg her work 1735," 10 1/2 x 16 1/2" framed (ILLUS.) **1,645**

Possum Cigar Can with Contents

Can, "Possum Cigars," cylindrical red can w/a color scene on the front of a white possum, complete w/contents & interior label sheet, early 20th c., excellent condition, 5 1/4" d., 5 1/4" h. (ILLUS.) **330**

U.S. Marine Cut Plug Tobacco Lunch Box

Can, "U.S. Marine Cut Plug Tobacco," tin lunch box-style, bail handle, porthole illustrations of sailor holding package of product, the end panels w/lithos of White Fleet battleships, 4 1/2 x 7 1/2", 5" h. (ILLUS.) **210**

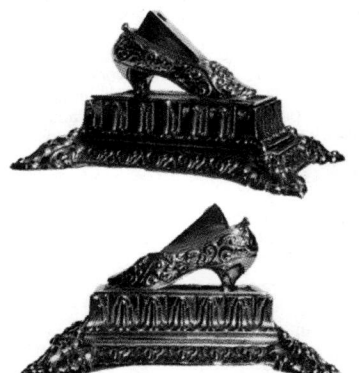

Unusual Cigar Cutter-Humidor

Cigar cutter-humidor, nickel-plated bronze, a model of a lady's slipper forming the cigar cutter on the lid of a rectangular humidor w/a flaring base w/long gargoyle face feet, late 19th - early 20th c., 4 1/2 x 8", 5 1/2" h. (ILLUS. of two views) **385**

Rare Victorian Figural Cigar Lighter

Cigar lighter, black marble & bronze w/green patina, a thick rectangular black marble platform base supporting the bronze figure of a large reclining Sphinx w/the lighter tube in her mouth, plumbed w/original gas hookup, late 19th c., base 4 1/4 x 8 3/4", 2" h., figure 3 1/4 x 7 1/4", 5 1/2" h. (ILLUS.) **1,018**

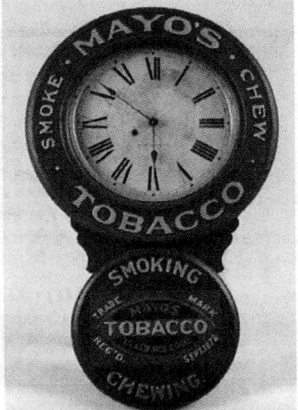

Baird Clock for Mayo's Tobacco

Clock, "Mayo's Tobacco," figure-8 style, Roman numerals, "Mayo's - Tobacco - Smoke - Chew" around clock face, "Smoking - Chewing - Mayo's - Tobacco - is always good" in papier-mâché door of bottom section, along w/"Trade Mark Rec'd. Sept. 1878," Baird Clock Co., Plattsburg, New York, ca. 1893, 18 1/2" w., 30 1/2" h. (ILLUS.) **1,898**

Clock, "Mayo's Tobacco," figure-8 style, Roman numerals, papier-mâché bezels, "Mayo's - Tobacco - Smoke - Chew" around clock face, "Smoking - Chewing - Mayo's - Tobacco - is best" in bottom section, Baird Clock Co., Plattsburg, New York, 4 1/2 x 18", 30 1/2" h. (original advertising relief on bezels is gone, both bezels & body of clock repainted & re-lettered) **633**

Unused Cigarette Display

Counter display, "Old North State Cigarettes," cardboard, w/color cutout bust illustration of flapper-type woman
w/bobbed hair holding cigarette in holder
alongside package of "Old North State
Superfine Ready Rolled Cigarettes," on
black ground, never unfolded for use,
1920s, 10 1/2 x 12" assembled (ILLUS.,
previous page) 72

Old Player's Navy Cut Tobacco Mirror

Mirror, "Old Player's Navy Cut Tobacco,"
glass reverse-painted w/"Tobacco and
Cigarettes," applied paper lifesaver-
shaped label w/"Player's Navy Cut"
around central bust image of old-time
sailor, some silvering loss & light flaking
to reverse silvering, 18" w., 22" h.
(ILLUS.) 460

Herald Tobacco Store Container

Store container, "Herald Tobacco," cylindrical bentwood container w/fitted cover,
large paper label depicting a trumpeter
heralding the arrival of tobacco from the
Scotten, Lovett & Co. Hiawatha Tobacco
Works factory, late 19th c., 14" d.,
14 3/4" h. (ILLUS.) 375

TOOLS

*Also see: ANTIQUE TRADER TOOLS PRICE
GUIDE (Krause Publications, 2003)*

Braces & Bits

Auger bit, cast iron, huge size, 4 1/4" wide
at base, good condition.................................. $83

Auger bits, cast iron, marked "Russell Jennings," set of 13 in tiered wooden case,
very good condition, the set............................ 85
Bit brace, cast iron, Stanley No. 945-10
Inch, new in original box, fine condition......... 105

Tillotson & Co. Brace

Brace, beech & plated metal, marked "Tillotson & Co.," slide chuck as most often
found on Ultimatums, good condition,
chip on edge of pad (ILLUS.).......................... 176
Brace, brass & steel w/rosewood head,
marked "D.W. Goodell. Northampton,
Mass. Patent No. 28, 1865.," brass &
steel chuck w/locking jaws inside close
as outside ring is turned, mark weak &
not readable, unusual brace, good condi-
tion 210
Gang mortiser, cast iron, unmarked, five
bits cut a 3/4 x 4" lock pocket mortise,
unusual, good condition 127

Drills

Beam drill, wooden frame, marked "Star,"
fully adjustable front or back, hold-up &
rack removal, one 2" auger, good condi-
tion 160
Bow drill, brass w/rosewood knob handle &
iron spindle, good condition, 9" h................... 110
Breast drill, cast iron w/50% finishes,
marked "Winchester No. 8733," two
speeds achieved by moving gear & crank
up or down a notch, level built into body,
good condition.. 85

Brass and Ivory Frame Drill

Frame drill, brass & ivory, all-brass except
for chuck & ivory handle , open 6-spoke
wheel, mushroom pad, very showy, fine
condition, 10" l. (ILLUS.) 193
Hand drill, cast iron, marked "Jellinghaus &
Co.," w/crank set at 45 degree angle, per-

haps designed for drilling next to vertical surfaces, turned wood handle, unique design, good condition.................................... 310

Pipe auger, cast iron w/wooden "T" handle, 1 1/4" diameter, 11 1/2' l. fixed shaft, good condition.. 75

Push drill, cast iron w/ivory forward hand grip, marked "A.H. Reid. Phil'ada. Pat. Dec. 12, 1882.," traditional Reid design, front grip old & appears to be original, unusual & unique, good condition 380

Edged Tools

Adz, cooper's-type, wrought iron head, white bone handle, good condition, head 7" wide, overall 8" l. 220

Adz, wrought-iron pole-type, marked "IR" w/decorative stamp, old wood handle, good condition.. 50

Ax, cast iron, marked "Fulton Special Extra Quality Fully Warranted," w/stars, leaves & designs, deep embossing, nearly new, leather blade edge protector, good wooden handle, fine condition.............................. 248

Ax, early iron goosewing-style, old wooden handle, marked "IK," long slipper edge, German, head 6" deep, edge 16" w. 358

Ax, wrought iron, goosewing-style, large left-handed type, applied edge, old wooden handle, good condition (some pitting & crack at one end, wormholes in handle)... 220

Ax, wrought iron, goosewing-style, unmarked, decorated in line & dot motif, applied edge, old handle, good condition, head 7 1/4" deep, edge 16" w. 450

Classic American Design Ax

Ax, wrought iron, goosewing-type, marked "G.Sener.," classic American design, old handle, Lancaster, Pennsylvania, very good condition, edge 13 1/2", 8 1/2" l. (ILLUS.)... 413

Ax, wrought iron, marked "Philip His.," goosewing-style, distinctive ogee at the back edge, marked w/weak name stamp & letters "I+P," Berks County, Pennsylvania, very good condition, head 8" deep, edge 14" w.. 1,375

Bark spud, early hand-wrought iron, spade-type, old wood handle, very good condition 61

Battle ax, wrought iron, ornately scroll-cut sides & cut-out trefoil in the center of the head, overall etching on both sides of head, surfaces fine w/minimal pitting,

wood handle, early & important, good condition... 260

Broad ax, wrought iron, "J.P. Billings. Clinton, Maine," early applied edge, strong mark, ca. 1830, good condition (handle new but great handmade example)................. 50

Chisel, cast iron, marked "T.H. Witherby," slick-type, wooden handle w/much original finish, fine condition, 3" 286

Cooper's shave, cast iron w/55% japanning, Stanley No. 56 1/2, 4" marked blade, hard to find, good condition 160

Draw shave, hand-wrought iron, curved blade w/vine & dot decoration along top, original handles, fine condition...................... 105

Hand saw, steel blade w/carved rosewood handle, marked "The Simonds Saw. No. 7A.," 4 1/2-point, w/handle protector, clean & near mint.. 220

Hand saw, steel, marked "Geo. H. Bishop & Co. 7," applewood handle, eight points, very clean, very good condition......................... 66

Hatchet, cast iron, marked "American Beauty" embossed logo w/full stem rose, original handle, rare mark, fine condition, head 7" deep, edge 3 1/2" w. 85

Hatchet, cast iron, marked "Winchester," w/nail puller, original handle, good condition, head 5" deep, edge 3" w. 45

Spoke shave, cast iron w/worn japanning, marked "L. Bailey. Boston," hollow face, good condition.. 37

Hammers

Ball peen hammer, beryllium copper w/95% green accent paint, Stanley No. B4, extremely rare marked Stanley beryllium tool, fine condition 525

Claw hammer, cast iron, Selsor Patent-type, double polls, face rounded, old but probably not original wood handle, good condition... 36

Claw hammer & wrench combination, cast iron, marked "Anchor Plumb," head in fine condition w/old wooden handle, overall good condition.................................... 130

Rare Double-face Hammer

Double face hammer, cast iron & hardwood, marked "D. Maydole," hits on both forward & backward stoke, mark strong & clear, old & possible original handle, rare, very good condition (ILLUS.) 600

Hammer, cast iron, marked "A.T. Nelson Pat'd July 28, 1908. Wilton, Iowa.," patented cutting edge on front of head acts

Pinwheel Open Filigree Work Level

as scraping tool, very uncommon hammer, old handle, fine condition....................... 105

Levels

Bench level, hardwood w/nearly perfect gold pinstriping & black japanning, marked "Queen & Co. Phil'a.," brass edges, complete w/original wooden case, fine condition, 8" l. 1,265

Rare Corner Level

Corner level, cast iron w/98% japanning, marked "Millers Falls Co. No. 20," 4" sides w/90 degree corner, can read plumb & level w/one vial, rare due to limited sales, fine condition (ILLUS.) 1,760

Inclinometer, cast iron w/85% japanning, marked "Davis Level & Tool Co.," ornate pierced scrolling design, very good condition, 18" l., 2 7/8" h. 165

Inclinometer, cast iron w/95% gold leafing, marked "L.L. Davis' Adjustable Spirit Level," ornate pierced scrolling design, top & bottom retain most original finish markings, fine condition, 12" l. 1,155

Level, aluminum & brass, marked "The Chapin-Stephens Co.," Vogel patent, good condition, 24" l. 65

Level, brassbound mahogany, marked "Goodell-Pratt Company," w/traces of original finish, decal label, good condition, 2 1/4" h., 30" l. 45

Level, brassbound mahogany, Stanley No. 95, w/full decal, ca. 1925, unused condition, 24" l. 440

Level, brassbound mahogany, Stanley No. 98, first Sweet Hart trademark, very hard-to-find trademark, near mint, 12" l. (brass polished) 300

Level, brassbound rosewood, marked "Stratton Brothers No. 10," rare type w/porthole plumb vial, very good condition, 8" l. 330

Level, cast iron, marked "American Level Co. Detroit Mich.," nonadjustable frame, vials set in gold-painted holders, fine condition.. 50

Level, cast iron, marked "Davis & Cook," pinwheel open filigree design, sometimes called pretzel level because of pinwheel shape, needs cleaning, very good condition (ILLUS., top of page) 1,045

Level, cast iron w/100% plating, marked "Athol Machine Co.," fine condition, 12" l........ 65

Pitch level, cast iron w/100% japanning, marked "L.S. Starrett No. 133 B," adjustable level vial set pitch, 15" l. 66

Machinery

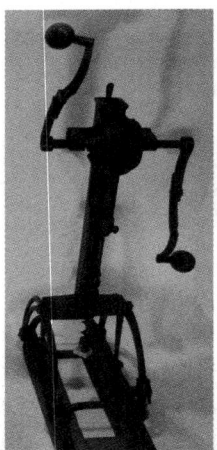

Early R. Ball Beam Boring Machine

Beam boring machine, cast iron, marked "R. Ball & Co. Worcester, Mass. Patented July 2, 1868.," wooden base w/metal column for drill, 180-degree vertical adjustment, rack & pinion adjusting, geared advance & retract, traces of red paint, rare, good condition (ILLUS.)................................... 660

Dowel maker, cast iron w/95% japanning, Stanley No. 77, complete w/nine cutter heads, great walnut display & storage stand, rare complete set, very good condition 880

Jigsaw, iron, treadle-type, marked "Empire. Seneca Falls Mfg. Co. Seneca Falls, N.Y.," professional model, completely restored w/black, red & gold paint & refinished wood trim, large-sized, 19th c. 605

Lathe, oak frame w/sliding tailstock, 13" centers, 6" swing, very well made w/beaded edge decorations, very good condition 220

Planes & Scrapers

Beader, cast iron, Stanley No. 66, Type 1, w/tall screw, w/cutters & both stops, in original green box & copy of the 1886 pocket catalog, very good condition (box & catalog well worn, box end label missing) 143

Beading plane, cast iron, Stanley No. 69, single hand-type, very light use, original box w/good label, fine condition 743

Bench plane, cast iron, marked "Millers Falls No. 10," extra heavy, two-piece lever cap, near new 50

Birdsill Holly Bench Plane

Bench plane, cast iron & rosewood, marked "Birdsill Holly Bench," Dwights & French iron, 2" w. cutter, smooth sole, rosewood tote dovetailed to body, Seneca Falls, 1850, rare size, fine condition, 9" l. (ILLUS.) **2,860**

Bench plane, cast iron, Stanley No. 2, in original box w/script label, fine condition (light storage stain on plane) 605

Bench plane, cast iron, Stanley No. 8C, tool new & mint, corrugated bottom, in original box w/full label, fine condition 275

Bench plane, cast iron w/85% japanning, Stanley Bed Rock No. 603, Type 4, wooden handle, good condition 176

H.B. Price Bench Plane

Bench plane, cast iron w/cast-brass cap, marked "H.B. Price Patent June 17, 1879," frog seat w/stair-stepped incline that changes the frog pitch as frog moves up ramp, frog adjustable by sliding the seat, four cutter pitches possible, laminated wood handles, very good condition (ILLUS.) **3,960**

Bench rabbet plane, carriage maker's, cast iron w/80% japanning, Stanley No. 10, 5/8" cutter, wooden handle & knob grip, ca. 1910, good condition 143

Block plane, aluminum w/98% plating, Stanley No. A18, Sweet Hart logo, bright & clean, name on both sides, good condition 83

Block plane, cabinetmaker's, cast iron w/90% japanning, Stanley No. 9, w/hot dog side handle, finishes fine, ca. 1900, very good condition (ILLUS., bottom of page) **1,430**

Block plane, cast iron, marked "Victor No. 0 1/2 Block.," adjustable, 1 3/4" blade, rejapanned, otherwise OK w/proper parts, good condition 220

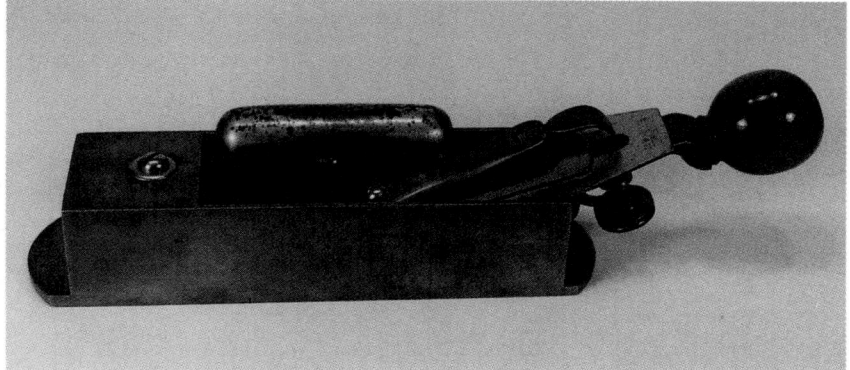

Stanley No. 9 Cabinetmaker's Block Plane

Block plane, cast iron, Stanley No. 95, unused in original box, fine condition.............. 226

Block plane, cast iron w/45% japanning, marked "Defiance Model B Block," adjustable, all proper parts, front wood knob original but chipped, good condition, 7 1/2" l. 495

Block plane, cast iron w/45% japanning, Stanley No. 103, wooden front knob, first type, proper blade, good condition 110

Block plane, cast iron w/50% japanning, Stanley No. 120, star cap-type, proper front wood knob 39

Block plane, cast iron w/70% japanning, marked "L. Bailey No. 0 1/2 Block," adjustable, no breaks, good Victor cap, good condition... 330

Block plane, cast iron w/about 99% finishes, Stanley No. 18 1/4, rare version w/nonadjustable mouth, ca. 1950 83

Stanley No. 72 1/2 Chamfer Plane

Chamfer plane, cast iron, Stanley No. 72 1/2, w/beading & molding attachments, beading attachment in separate orange box w/earlier green box label, also includes bullnose attachment, tools near new, main box w/picture label, fine condition, the set (ILLUS.)........................... 3,850

Chisel plane, cast iron w/92% japanning, Stanley No. 97, Sweet Hart logo, good corners on nose of body, wooden knob handle, ca. 1920s, very good condition 358

Circular plane, cast iron w/90% japanning, Stanley No. 113, Type 2, wooden handle & hand grip knob, clean, good condition...... 132

Combination plane, cast iron w/80% japanning, Stanley No. 45 Type 1, 18 cutters, two depth stops, short & long rods, early design box w/some carved decoration, in custom case, good condition 250

Crown molding plane, hardwood, marked "H. Hills. Springfield, Mass.," original applied fence & pull stick, very clean, excellent condition, 3 1/2" iron, overall 4 5/8" l...... 850

Dado plane, cast iron, Stanley No. 39 7/8, improved-type, Sweet Hart logo vintage,

in original box w/picture label, unused tool, fine condition 248

Floor plane, cast iron w/70% japanning, Stanley No. 74, original handle w/the proper parts, rare w/handle, ca. 1900, good condition..................................... 880

Infill panel plane, cast iron w/rosewood infill, marked "Spiers Ayr Panel," dovetailed construction, Mathieson cap iron, very good condition, 13 3/4" l. 358

Infill plane, cast iron, marked "Mathieson & Son," coffin-shaped smoother-type, dovetailed, rosewood infill, gunmetal lever cap, small size, very good condition, iron 2 1/8" w., 7 1/4" l....................................... 385

Jack plane, cast iron, Stanley No. 5 1/2 Heavy Jack Plane, tool mint & probably unused, original box w/full label w/factory stick-on "Heavy" sticker, fine condition (box worn w/one bad corner)..................... 2,860

Jack plane, cast iron, Stanley No. 5 1/4 Junior Jack, ca. 1930s, in original box w/Sweet Hart label, fine condition................. 275

Jointer Plane

Jointer plane, annealed steel w/gunmetal cap, 97% original finish, marked "Norris" blade, postwar model w/adjustment, appears to be an A-1 but isn't dovetailed, fine condition, 22 1/2" l. (ILLUS.) 2,970

Match plane, cast iron/plating near 100%, Stanley No. 48, hardwood handle w/original finish, very fine condition......................... 160

Mitre plane, gunmetal w/beech wedge cut out to straddle the crossbar, good condition, 8" l. 61

Mitre plane, pattern maker's, cast brass w/rosewood wedge, very good condition, 9" l. 50

Molding plane, birch, marked "Jo. Fuller. Providence.," astragal-type, relieved wedge, fine details, very good condition, 1 1/4" w., 10" l. 193

Molding plane, cast iron & hardwood, marked "Multiform Moulding Plane Co. Boston," wood bottom w/iron frame, bolt from rear of plane holds cutter in place, wooden tote overhangs tail of plane nearly 2", wooden knob grip, very good condition 310

Molding plane, cast iron w/98% plating, Stanley No. 143, Miller's Patent-type, Sweet Hart logo, last production run w/number cast into side, wooden handle w/much original finish, fine condition............. 660

Molding plane, hardwood, marked "L. Kenney.," A mark, astragal & cove-type, very uncommon maker, fine condition, 1/2 size.. 240

Panel raiser plane, hardwood, marked "John Bell," adjustable fence & stop, dark patina, very good condition, 4" w. **165**

Pattern maker's plane, gunmetal, marked "A.F. White.," mahogany infill, three interchangeable soles, soles held in place by tapered dovetails at ends, one cutter, very good condition, 6" l. **100**

Rare Chapin Solon Rust Patent Plane

Plow plane, applewood, marked "Chapin Solon Rust Patent Mar. 31, 1868," second model w/screw to hold adjuster arm from side of body & brass fence rods, marked w/Union Factory stamp & patent date on nose, one of only three Rust patent types to surface, good condition, fence replaced (ILLUS.) **1,980**

Plow plane, applewood, marked "Isaac Field - Providence," A mark, slide arm, wood stop, strong mark, very good condition **138**

Plow plane, beech & cast iron, marked "D. Kimberley Patent," handled, three-arm w/steel center adjusting screw, original key, good condition **297**

Plow plane, beech, marked "I. Teal," A mark, wedge arm, brass depth stop, near mint **77**

Very Rare Israel White Plow Plane

Plow plane, beech, marked "Israel White - No. 106," handled three-arm style w/ivory tips & scales, brass & steel fence rollers, ebony slide arms, one of two known, professionally restored, couple of light burn marks, very good condition (ILLUS.) **21,450**

Plow plane, beech, marked "J.H. Lamb. New Bedford.," handled, screw arm, box-

wood arms, nuts & washers, little used, fine condition **330**

Plow plane, boxwood w/good tiger stripe, marked "Edward Carter Troy - NY," unhandled, good condition (a few chips) **143**

Plow plane, hardwood, marked "Collins - Hartford," friction-fit arms w/screw locks, ca. 1800, very good condition **220**

Plow plane, rosewood w/boxwood arms, nuts, washers & fence boxing, marked "J.E. Boker & Co. Boston.," handled, very striking, arm threads near perfect, fine condition **600**

Rabbet block plane, cast iron, Stanley No. 140, mint & unused, in original unusual grey craft-color box w/perfect Sweet Hart label, mint & boxed, ca. 1920s **468**

Rabbet plane, cabinet maker's, cast iron w/100% plating, Stanley No. 93, like-new **132**

Router plane, cast iron w/85% plating, Stanley No. 71 Patent Router Plane, S casting, in original wooden box w/full green label, tool fine condition **350**

Sash molding plane, hardwood, marked "E.W. Carpenter. Lancaster.," screw adjusts, good condition **110**

Scraper, cast iron w/85% japanning & wood, Stanley No. 112, good condition **190**

Scraper, cast iron w/93% japanning, Stanley No. 12 1/4, rosewood handles, very good condition.. **220**

Smoothing plane, cast iron, Stanley Bed Rock No. 603, Type 5, in original box, fine condition (light tool use, box faded) **935**

Smoothing plane, cast iron w/90% japanning, marked "Birmingham Plane Mfg. Co. - Mosher Patent Dec. 16, 1884," adjustable, very good condition, 9" l. w/2" iron **440**

Rules & Gauges

Architect's rule, ivory, Stanley No. 86 1/2, fourfold, good condition, 2' l. (tobacco yellow color, pins missing) **250**

Randel & Stickney Bench Gauge

Bench gauge, cast iron w/98% japanning & most of gold highlights, marked "Randel

& Stickney. Waltham, Mass.," adjustable table & lever action dial indicator, fine condition, 12" h. (ILLUS.) 116

Bevel square, brass & rosewood, marked "F.E. Witter. Patent US Feb. 22, 87. Canada Aug. 13, 87," double blades w/much original plating, uncommon, very good condition....................... 440

Board rule, hardwood & brass, marked "C.T. Younglove, Fitchburg, Mass.," calculates board feet in boards to 20 feet long, brass pointer spins to keep tally as boards are measured, brass tips, fine condition................................ 250

Builder's square, iron w/60% finishes, marked "Starrett," used, very good condition 185

Caliper, burlwood, good form & grain pattern, very good condition, 16" l...................... 176

Caliper, hand wrought iron, legs worked into round section, opens to 25 1/2", unusual tool, good condition, 21" h. 80

Carpenter's rule, boxwood, marked "Standard Rule Co. Unionville, CT. No. 2.," twofold, brass arch joint, good condition, 2' l....................... 65

Carpenter's rule, boxwood, Stanley No. 4, twofold, extra thin, drafting scales, brass arch joints, rare, very good condition, 2' l...... 330

Center finder, cast iron, marked "Darling, Brown & Sharpe," Ames Patent model, very good condition, 8" l. 70

Combination square, cast iron w/nearly 100% japanning, marked "P.L. Fox. Pat. Oct. 2, 88.," try square w/adjustable bevel & mitre, blade bright & shiny, fine condition 413

Desk rule, boxwood, marked "Stephens & Co. Riverton, CT.," straight & unjointed, w/Gunter's slide, beveled edge, rare rule, very good condition, 12" l. (chip one end of slide groove)...................... 120

Engineer's rule, boxwood & brass, marked "Routledge Engineer Improved Rule.," two-fold, calculating rule w/many tables, Gunther's slide, extra wide to allow tables, steel tips, brass arch joint, mint condition, 2' l....................... 475

Gauge, cast iron w/80% japanning, Stanley No. 60, Traut's patent-type, polished surfaces, very good condition 110

Log caliper, mahogany beam w/maple jaws, marked "M.E. Hatheway 1881," scales unusual & may not be for logs, fine condition, beam 41" l...................... 180

Marking gauge, cast iron w/97% original finish, Stanley No. 165, clearly marked w/"165," Sweet Hart vintage, circular fence plate, fine condition.................... 100

Measuring tape, steel w/nearly 100% plating, marked "Stevens by K.&E. Pat. Mar. 23, 86, and June 15, 02," wooden handle, fine condition, 50'............................... 248

Rope caliper, boxwood & brass, marked "Rabone No. 1207," tables & scales, very good condition, 6" l. 61

Rule, bone, graduated w/lines only, good condition, 12" l. (light yellowing) 85

Rule, boxwood, A. Stanley & Co. No. 76, fourfold, bound, early & rare, great color, very good condition, 24" l.............................. 935

Sterns Boxwood Rule

Rule, boxwood, marked "E.A. Sterns & Co. - Makers - Brattleboro, Vt - Warranted Box Wood" and "No. 5," two-fold w/arch joint, slide w/scales & tables, fine condition, 24" l. (ILLUS.)............................ 468

Rule, boxwood, marked "Hatter's," slide & tables, very clean, fine condition, 5" l............. 50

Rule, boxwood, Stanley No. 3, fourfold caliper, traces of original finish, very good condition, 112" l. 193

Rule, boxwood, Stanley No. 78 1/2, fourfold, bound, arch joint, much original finish, fine condition, 24" l.......................... 220

Rule, German silver-bound ivory, marked "E.A. Stearns & Co. No. 53B," fourfold, fine condition, 12" l........................... 385

Slide rule, German silver, marked "Kerr & Co. Aarau.," unusual scales, all-metal cursor, w/original case, like new, fine condition........................ 375

Square, cast iron w/brass-fitted rosewood handle, Stanley No. 24, handle marked, good condition, 9" l........................... 99

Square, iron w/rosewood-infilled handle, Stanley No. 10, very clean, very good condition, 12" l. 100

Tape measure, steel, Stanley No. 7886, round red case, mint 160

Tape measure, steel w/brushed satin finish, Stanley No. 1166 Four Square model, round case, mint.............................. 210

Saws

Backsaw, brass-backed steel w/mahogany handle, marked "Cortlandt-Wood. NYC, NY," carcass-type, near perfect condition, blade 10" l. 75

Backsaw, steel blade, marked "Disston No. 4," wooden handle, in original box, fine condition........................ 138

Boxwood & Ebony Bow Saw

Bow saw, steel blade in boxwood frame w/ebony handles & tensioner, marked "Heanshaw Bros. & Nurse - London," England, showy, very good condition (ILLUS., previous page)............................. **743**

Frame saw, wooden frame & ram's-horn nut for blade tightening, flat chamfered stretchers, found in Pennsylvania, 18th c., fine condition, 37" h. **77**

Hand rip saw, steel blade, marked "Winchester No. 10," carved applewood handle, brass saw nuts, six point, good condition **80**

Hand saw, cast steel w/applewood handle, marked "Our Saw. Warranted Cast Steel," extra small panel saw w/six points, Disston-made, clear etching on blade, very good condition **150**

Hand saw, steel blade & ornate wood handle, marked "Henry Disston No. 43" in early stamped arched mark, combination-type w/saw, rule, square, level & scribe, very good condition (blade cleaned, chip off both handle tangs).......... **1,815**

Woodrough & McParlin Handsaw

Hand saw, steel blade w/wooden handle, marked "Woodrough & McParlin," ink stamped patent date "Jnr'y 13, 1880" on handle, logo w/panther on blade, handle decorated w/carved panther head on each side, Cincinnati, Ohio, very good condition (ILLUS.)................................ **3,300**

Hand saw, steel w/hardwood handle, marked "Lame & McNiece Saw Works. Philada.," split nuts, strong stamps on both blade & saw nut, early Philadelphia maker, very good condition **190**

Hand saw, steel w/rosewood handle, marked "Disston D-15 Victory," logo good, very good condition **55**

Stair saw, steel blade w/applewood handle, marked "Geo. H. Bishop.," adjustable depth of cut, uncommon Bishop saw, good condition.............................. **250**

Surgeon's bone saw, cast iron & ebony, cast & hand finished, ebony handle, very fancy w/lots of detail, rare, good condition, 19" l. (handle w/age check) **775**

Special Use & Miscellaneous Tools

Anvil, cast iron, miniature, marked "Amos Seamans. Nov. 1899.," anvil w/one har-

dy, very well made, fine condition, 3 1/2" h., 9 1/2" l. **325**

Balance scales, wrought-iron base w/copper pans, 18th c., good condition, beam 18" l., overall 21" h. **193**

Brace wrench, cast iron, marked "P. Lowentraut," Schultz 55, all the proper parts including the crank & screwdriver bit, good condition............................... **70**

Cabinetmaker's Bench

Cabinet maker's bench, cast iron w/laminated top, marked "Emmert's," w/small pattern maker's adjustable vise at one end, a 3 1/2" bench vise on other end, six drawers in base, fine condition, top 22 x 57" l. (ILLUS.).. **770**

Compass, brass case w/engraved & silvered dial, level vial set into dial, unmarked but heavy & high quality, 3 1/4" l. needle, very good condition, 4" d. **135**

Corn sheller, cast iron & wood, marked "Little Giant," double-jaw type w/wooden handle, finishes fine, shows little use, very good condition.......................... **248**

Glass cutters, diamond points & rosewood handles, marked "Bush & Chipper. Makers," stored in fitted box w/inlaid diamond design on top, good condition, pr..................... **72**

Monkey wrench, cast iron, marked "Winchester No. 1007," adjustable, rare, fine condition, 21" l. (small chips) **110**

Patent model, mahogany, marked "H.R. Packard. Machine for Affixing Caps to Nails and Tacks. Patented Apl. 5, 1881.," very complex, two parts w/small broken sections, good condition................................. **385**

Carriage Hinge Patent Model

Patent model, wood, brass & steel, marked "George A. Royce. Carriage Hinge. Patented Oct. 1st. 1889.," fancy working model w/swing-down & swing-out hinge for carriage, original papers, fine condition (ILLUS.) 495

Pipe & nut wrench, cast iron, marked only "1869," lever lock & screw adjusts, clean & working, very good condition, 15" l. 210

Plumb bob, brass, needle-type, 1/2" diameter, 8" l. 165

Plumb bob, brass, Stanley No. 1, reel-type, fine condition (a few nicks) 253

Plumb bob, cast iron, Stanley No. 1, early unmarked version, good condition (some nicks & bangs) 130

Screwdriver, iron, marked "Yankee No. 90-10" - North Bros.," in original box, tool like new, box w/edge wear but good label 44

Screwdriver, steel, marked "Mann's Hold-fast Screw Driver," in original box w/full picture label, fine condition (slight tool use, box worn) 55

Thatcher's comb, wood, early wooden tool for laying thatch roofs, clean & rare, very good condition 94

Vise, cast iron, marked "Stephen's Patent," quick action type for jeweler or pattern maker, pressure applied to work via lever arm, good condition, jaws 2" w., overall 5" l. 85

Wagon jack, wood & iron, Conestoga wagon-type, decorated wood post w/iron crank, carved date unclear, ca. 1871, very good condition 121

Wagon wrench, iron, marked "Joy's Wagon Wrench No. 3," old long wood handle, working, large, 20" l. 80

Wrench, cast iron, marked "Bay State Tool Co. Pat. June 7, 1904," Schultz 476, quick adjusts w/the flip of a lever, works well, good condition 130

Wrench, cast iron, marked "Hande," quick-adjust-type, slide adjusts work well, very good condition, 10" l. 41

Wrench, cast iron, quick adjuster, as handle rotates jaws tighten on nut, good condition, 12" l. 95

Tool Chests

Tool chest, milk-painted wood, dovetailed inside & out, rope handles, four sliding tills inside painted red & w/cockbead edges, outside painted soldier blue, ca. 1800, very good condition 300

Pattern Maker's Tool Chest

Tool chest, pattern maker's, wooden, marked "G. Ralphs," wide rectangular hinged top overhanging & opening to a rectangular base w/two drawers, flat base, includes full complement of tools including plane sets, brace w/bit, gouges & chisels, w/key, very good condition, chest 17 x 31", 16" h., the set (ILLUS.)...... 2,420

Tool chest, wood, signed "J.C. Hockenbury," w/lift-out tray, name painted on top w/pinstripe decoration, fine condition, 11 x 23", 8" h. 110

TOYS

Also see: Advertising Items; Black Americana; Cat Collectibles; Character Collectibles; Disney Collectibles; Horse Collectibles; Metals; Radio & Television Memorabilia; Raggedy Ann & Andy Collectibles; Steiff Toys & Bears; Teddy Bear Collectibles and Antique Trader Toys Price Guide.

Red 1930s Cast-iron Sedan

Automobile, cast iron, red sedan w/black running boards, white rubber tires, top can be removed from frame, original paint, marked "Patent Pending - 12," ca. 1930s, 4 1/4" l. (ILLUS.) **$225**

Long Red Limousine

Automobile, cast metal, long stylized limousine in bright red w/white rubber tires, ca. 1930s, 5 1/2" l. (ILLUS.).................. 175

Tootsie Toy Orange Touring Car

Studebaker Commander 1950s Auto

Automobile, cast spelter, early touring car, orange body & silver metal wheels, Tootsietoy, ca. 1930s, 2 3/4" l. (ILLUS., previous page) **125**

Tootsie Toy Blue Sedan

Automobile, cast spelter, four-door sedan, dark blue paint, rubber wheels, separate metal front grill w/letter "K," Tootsietoy, Model 746, original paint, ca. 1950, 6" l. (ILLUS.) **85**

Tootsie Toy Blue Coupe

Automobile, cast spelter, vintage coupe model, original dark blue paint & silver metal wheels, Tootsietoy, marked inside, ca. 1930s, 3" l. (ILLUS.) **95**

Small Green Coupe by Tootsie Toy

Automobile, cast spelter, vintage coupe w/worn original green paint & black metal tires, Tootsietoy, ca. 1930s, 2 1/4" l. (ILLUS.) **55**

Stylized Art Deco Pressed Steel Auto

Automobile, pressed steel, friction-operated, stylized Art Deco style bubble-form body in red w/applied metal green, side exhaust pipes & windshield, original worn paint, windshield missing, possibly by Wyandotte, 9" d. (ILLUS.) **135**

Automobile, stamped metal, friction-operated, Studebaker Commander model, dark red & cream body, includes driver, black rubber wheels, marked on rear "Made in Western Germany," ca. 1950s, windshield missing, 15 3/4" l. (ILLUS., top of page) **70**

Marx Airport Transportation Bus

Bus, stamped metal, friction-operation, Airport Transportation Service in red on the side, dark blue & silver w/black rubber wheels, by Marx, ca. 1950s-60s, 6 1/2" l. (ILLUS.) **145**

Made in Japan Greyhound Bus Toy

Bus, stamped metal, friction-powered, Greyhound Scenicruiser, no raised roofline, dark blue, white & yellow, rubber tires, made in Japan, ca. 1950s, 7" l. (ILLUS.) **125**

Greyhound Friction-powered Bus

Wyandotte Steel Coal Truck

Cowboys and Indians Cast Lead Set

Bus, stamped steel, friction-powered, Greyhound Scenicruiser w/luggage rack on top, rubber wheels, marked "HTC," Japan, ca. 1950s, 11 1/2" l. (ILLUS., top of page) **225**

Cowboys & Indians set, cast lead, miniature action figures painted in bright colors, Set No. 20 by Lincoln Logs, Chicago, Illinois, in original box, ca. 1950s, each 2" h., set of 7 (ILLUS., above) **85**

Old Toy Cast-iron Cannon

Cannon, cast iron, flattened model of military canon, ca. 1930s, 3 1/2" l. (ILLUS.) **10**

Coal truck, pressed steel, red cab & yellow box w/red lettering, metal wheels, Wyandotte, ca. 1930s, very good condition, 11 1/4" l. (ILLUS., middle of page) **195**

Rare Milk & Cream Delivery Truck

Delivery truck, cast iron, closed cab, orange body cast on the side "Milk -

Cream," white rubber tires, ca. 1930s, 3 1/2" l. (ILLUS.) **550**

Tootsie Toy Truck with Wrigley Decal

Delivery truck, cast spelter, closed cab & open back, overall dark red w/decal on the side for Wrigley's Spearmint Gum, white rubber tires, Tootsietoy, Model 1010, ca. 1930s, 4 1/2" l. (ILLUS.)................ **125**

Wyandotte Railway Express Truck

Delivery truck, pressed steel, dark blue cab w/rare compartment printed in red, green, yellow, white & red, reads "Wyandotte Toys - Railway Express Agency," black rubber wheels, ca. 1930s, some overall wear, 6 1/2" l. (ILLUS.).......................... **65**

Steel Candy Delivery Truck

Delivery truck, pressed steel, friction-operated, white cab & white rear compartment w/red sides reading "Fanny Farmer Candies for Boys and Girls," black rubber tires, ca. 1950s, 8 1/4" l. (ILLUS.)................. **145**

Hubley Fire Ladder Truck

Fire ladder truck, cast metal, long red truck mounted w/removable steel ladders, black rubber tires, Hubley, marked "Made in USA," worn paint, ca. 1930s, 8 3/4" l. (ILLUS.) **85**

Hubley Fire Water Cannon Truck

Fire water cannon truck, cast metal, long red body mounted in the back w/a silver water cannon & search light, a silver wooden globe on the hood, black rubber tires, Hubley, ca. 1930s, 7 1/2" l. **125**

Small Vilmer Cast Flatbed Truck

Flatbed truck, die-cast spelter, yellow cab & red flatbed, black tires w/spare tire on roof turning front wheels, by Vilmer of Denmark, w/original box, ca. 1950s, 3 7/8" l. (ILLUS.) **125**

Pressed Steel Marx Garbage Truck

Garbage truck, pressed steel, white background w/red & black wording reading "Help Keep Your City Clean - City Sanitation Dept.," by Marx, ca. 1930s, original paint w/some wear, 13" l. (ILLUS.)................. **150**

Unusual Girl on Motorcycle Toy

Girl on motorcycle, stamped metal, friction-powered, girl w/vinyl head w/synthetic hair in ponytail seated on red motorcycle, marked "Haji," made in Japan, ca. 1950s, 8" l. (ILLUS.) 325

Early Cast-iron Hand Pump

Hand pump, cast iron, upright working pump w/attached basin, original red paint, early 20th c., 4 1/2 x 7", 8 1/2" h. (ILLUS.) 180

Marx Army Jeep & Antiaircraft Gun

Jeep, pressed steel, Army model w/two soldiers in seats & one in the rear aiming the large antiaircraft gun, dark green w/white trim, black tires, by Marx, ca. 1950s, 7 1/2" l. (ILLUS.) 375

Tootsie Toy Milk Truck

Milk truck, cast metal, green body cast w/the word "Milk," white metal wheels, Tootsietoy, ca. 1930s, 3" l. (ILLUS.).............. 145

Model kit, Daddy the Way-out Suburbanite, Hawk, Weird-ohs, designed by Bill Campbell, 1963... 40-90

Model kit, Dimetrodon, 1/10 scale, Pyro, plastic kit, late 1950s - late 1960s.............. 20-40

Model kit, dinosaurs, 1/13 scale, reissues from Aurora Prehistoric Scenes, Revell/Monogram, plastic kit, 1992-93, each... 12-30

Model kit, Elasmosaurus, 1/30 scale, Horizon, vinyl kit, 1980s-90s............................. 35-45

Model kit, Freddy Kreuger, 1/6 scale, reissue of Kaiyodo mold, Screamin' Productions, large vinyl kit, 1980s-90s.................. 45-65

Model kit, Sail Back Reptile (Dimetrodon), No.745, 1/13 scale, copper & green, Aurora, 1971 50-75

Model kit, Satan's Crate, Lindberg, plastic kit, Lindy Loonys, "The Hep Model in the 'Square' Box," 1965...................................... 35-80

Model kit, Scuttle Bucket, Lindberg, plastic kit, Lindy Loonys, "The Hep Model in the 'Square' Box," 1965...................................... 35-80

Model kit, Scuz-Fink, Revell, plastic kit, Custom Monsters Series, designed by Ed "Big Daddy" Roth, 1964...................... 165-300

Model kit, Thunder Lizard, Brontosaurus, 1/72 scale, Pyro, plastic kit, late 1950s - late 1960s, 11" h.. 20-40

Motorcycle Racer Friction Toy

Motorcycle racer, stamped metal, friction-powered, a man in a red suit posed on a silver & blue racing cycle w/two rubber wheels, made in Japan, ca. 1950s, 4 1/2" l. (ILLUS.) **125**

Motorcycle Stunt Driver Toy

Motorcycle stunt driver, stamped metal, friction-operated, colorfully printed, rubber wheels & a flip bar at the side, marked "ALPS," made in Japan, ca. 1950s, 5 1/2" l. (ILLUS.) **210**

Cast-iron Toy Parlor Stove

Parlor heating stove, cast iron, lobed ovoid body w/lift-off top, raised on squared base on scroll legs, painted black, early 20th c., 5" h. (ILLUS.).. **49**

Tootsie Toy Red Pickup Truck

Pickup truck, cast spelter, red cab & open rear compartment, on white rubber wheels, Tootsietoy, ca. 1930s, 5 3/4" l. (ILLUS.)... **95**

Mego Wizard of Oz Playset

Play set, "Wizard of Oz and the Emerald City," Mego, copyright by Metro-Goldwyn-Mayer, 1974, complete in original box, the set (ILLUS.)... **130**

Modern Horse Pull Toy

Pull toy, horse on wheeled platform, papier-mâché horse w/dappled grey & white paint & red cloth saddle, on a narrow red board platform on rubber-rimmed metal wheels, modern copy of early toy, ca. 1980s, 21" l., 20" h. (ILLUS.).......................... **225**

Cast-aluminum Red Race car

Long Stamped Metal 1930s Race car

Race car, cast aluminum, red body w/single silver side exhaust pipe, black rubber wheels, marked on the inside "Thimbledrome Special L.M. Cox Mfg. Co., Santa Ana, Calif.," worn paint, ca. 1950s, 8 3/4" l. (ILLUS., previous page) **120**

"Speed King" Race car

Race car, friction-operated, "Speed King" racer w/red & green body w/large black rubber wheels, marked "San - Made in Japan," ca. 1950s, 4 3/4" l. (ILLUS.) **175**

Race car, stamped metal, long body in bright yellow & red, head of driver at top, large black & red metal wheels, ca. 1930s, slightly worn & rusted, 12 3/4" l. (ILLUS., top of page) **160**

Sled, child's size, painted wood, long board platform w/iron band handrails & incurved at the front & rounded at the back, raised on board runners w/upturned fronts & fitted w/iron runners, solid braces under top attached w/iron brackets, original dark red paint w/black & goldenrod scrolls, one runner painted w/"L" & the other w/"Khedive," underside w/several branded labels including "Canonious" (?), late 19th c., 16 3/4" w., 49 3/4" l. (age cracks, minor wear) **385**

Soldier on Motorcycle Friction Toy

Soldier on motorcycle, stamped metal, friction-powered, seated soldier w/machine gun, colorfully printed, made in Japan, ca. 1950s, 2 x 5 1/2", 3 3/4" h. (ILLUS.).. **375**

Arcade Cast-iron Stake Truck

Stake truck, cast iron, worn green back & stack bed on vulcanized white rubber tires w/red hubs, Arcade, style No. 2217, ca. 1930s, 5 1/4" l. (ILLUS.)................. **145**

Danish Die-cast Stake Truck

Stake truck, die-cast metal, dark green cab w/yellow flatbed, black tires w/yellow hubcaps, spare tire on roof of cab turns front wheels, made in Denmark by Vilmer, ca. 1950s, 3 7/8" l. (ILLUS.) **95**

Cast Spelter Small Tanker Truck

Tanker truck, cast spelter, original dark green paint, vulcanized white rubber tires, American-made, style No. 78, ca. 1930s, 3 3/4" l. (ILLUS., previous page) ....

Toy Soldier with Field Radio

Toy soldier, cast lead, kneeling soldier operating field radio, wearing a separate steel helmet, worn brown paint, ca. 1930s, 2 1/4" h. (ILLUS.) 35

Parachuting Toy Soldier

Toy soldier, cast lead, parachuting & holding rifle, brown w/silver trim, marked "M" in a circle & "Made in USA - 102," ca. 1930s, 3 1/2" h. (ILLUS.) 60

Toy Soldier with Machine Gun

Toy soldier, cast lead, reclining soldier w/machine gun, brown & silver, marked "Made in USA - 728," ca. 1930s, 4 3/8" l. (ILLUS.) 29

Toy Soldier with Search Light

Toy soldier, cast lead, soldier pointing a searchlight, brown w/silver trim, marked "Made in USA," ca. 1930s, 2 1/2" h. (ILLUS.) 36

Toy Soldier Blowing Bugle

Toy soldier, cast lead, standing soldier blowing bugle, brown w/silver trim, green base, ca. 1930s, 3" h. (ILLUS.) 22

Toy Soldier Leading a Charge

Toy soldier, cast lead, standing soldier leading a charge, separate steel helmet, worn brown paint, ca. 1930s, 3 1/2" h. (ILLUS.) 23

Britains Cavalry Soldiers Boxed Set

Cast-iron Artillery Soldiers & Cannon

Toy soldiers, Britains mounted cavalry set, brown horses w/riders wearing red uniforms, in original box, first half 20th c., each figure 3" h., the set (ILLUS., top of page)... 285

Toy soldiers, Britains, Set No. 2108, Drums & Fifes of the Welsh Guards, marching in review order w/five fifers, three side drummers, tenor drummer, bass drummer, cymbalist & drum major, issued only 1956-1960, plastic drums, ca. 1960, original box, rare, chips, drum decals are replacements, set of 12...................................... 700

Toy soldiers, Britains, Set No. 212, The Royal Scots, marching at the slope in review order w/piper, original box, set of 5 (dirt stains on box lid, tie-in card not original) 110

Toy soldiers, Britains, Set No. 38, South African Mounted Infantry, mounted at the gallop w/rifles & officer holding pistol, ca. 1920, in earlier printer's box, marked "Dr. Jameson and the African Mounted Infantry," rare, set of 5, some chips, small tears in box lid & fraying 1,300

Toy soldiers, Britains, Set No. 47, Skinner's Horse, mounted at the gallop in review order w/trumpeter, original box, set of 5 (some chips noticeable on legs of three horses, glue repairs to tears in box lid & tray) 100

Toy soldiers, Britains, Set No. 76, The Middlesex Regiment/Duke of Cambridge's Own, marching at the slope in review order w/officer, ca. 1945, original Whisstock box, set of 8.. 140

Toy soldiers, Britains, Set No. 77, The Gordon Highlanders, marching at the slope in review order w/piper, original box, set of 6 (one feather missing from piper's Glengarry cap) 130

Toy soldiers, Britains, Set No. 92, Spanish Infantry, marching at the slope in review order, ca. 1935 set, original "Types of the Spanish Army" printer's box, set of 8, a few chips, some fraying & small crease on box lid... 425

Toy soldiers, Built Rite, cardboard, soldiers, 1930s, each...................................... **10-20**

Toy soldiers, cast iron, a line of artillery soldiers on horses pulling a four-wheeled cannon, ca. 1930s, 6 3/4" l. (ILLUS., above) 18

Toy soldiers, Mignot, Boy Scouts, marching w/poles, w/scout bugler, original box, set of 12, a few chips, end label missing on box.. 325

Toy soldiers, Mignot, French Alpine Chasseurs, 1890-1914, in action in summer white uniforms, standing, kneeling, lying firing & charging w/officer firing pistol, original box, set of 12...................................... 275

Toy soldiers, Mignot, French Army Bicycle Dispatch Riders, 1915, standing w/bikes in horizon blue uniforms & steel helmets, original box, set of 6 (a few chips).................. 150

Small Cast Spelter Toy Tractor

Tractor, cast spelter, stylized red body & driver, white rubber tires, marked "Made in USA," some paint wear, ca. 1930s, 2 3/4" l. (ILLUS., bottom previous page)......... **65**

Train accessory, barrel loader, grey & yellow, brown plastic fence, Lionel No. 362, 1952-57 .... **145**

Train accessory, billboard set in original box, Lionel No. 310, scarce, 1950-68............. **90**

Lionel No. 97 Coal Elevator

Train accessory, coal elevator, O-gauge, grey & yellow w/red roof, operating, Lionel No. 97, 1941 (ILLUS.)................................. **275**

Train accessory, coal loader, diesel operating, O-gauge, grey base, red tray & blue motor cover, no yard light, Lionel No. 397, 1948-57 .... **185**

Train accessory, floodlight tower, yellow base & tower, Lionel No. 395, 1949-56......... **170**

Lionel No. 352 Icing Station

Train accessory, icing station, white & red on brown base, Lionel No. 352, 1955-57 (ILLUS.).. **250**

Train accessory, oil derrick, operating, red base, green tower, orange diesel engine, Sunoco sign, Lionel No. 455, 1950-54.......... **225**

Train accessory, passenger station, O-gauge, green & white, Lionel No. 133, 1957-66 .... **80**

Train accessory, ZW transformer, 275 watt, black, Lionel, 1950-53...................... **395**

Train car, AEC security car, O-gauge, red, black & grey w/white lettering, Lionel No. 3535, 1960-61 .... **125**

Train car, boxcar, "Hobo Rest," red & blue w/blue frame, Marx Joy Line No. 355, very rare, 1927-30.. **75**

Train car, boxcar, Johnny Cash, silver & black, Lionel No. 9780, scarce, 1976.............. **45**

Ives No. 1712 Caboose

Train car, caboose, O-gauge, orange, maroon, yellow & black w/brass journals, Ives No. 1712, 1932 (ILLUS.)........................... **90**

Train car, cattle car, standard gauge, olive green & orange, Lionel No. 513, 1927-38...... **140**

Train car, coal dump car, O-gauge, black w/white lettering, operating, Lionel 3469, 1949-55.. **60**

Train car, crane car, O-gauge, "New York Central," orange, red & black, Marx No. 550, 1950.. **35**

Train car, crane, S-gauge, black w/white lettering, American Flyer No. 944, 1952-56 .... **75**

Train car, crane, standard gauge, peacock green w/red boom & brass trim, Lionel No. 219, 1926.. **245**

Train car, flat car, standard gauge, black, Lionel No. 211, 1926-40 .... **140**

Train car, flat service car, S-gauge, brown, silver & yellow, American Flyer No. 948, 1953-56 .... **42**

Lionel O-gauge Gang Car

Train car, gang car, die cast, O-gauge, orange & black w/blue bumpers, three men on car, Lionel No. 50, 1954-64 (ILLUS., bottom of previous page) 75

Train car, gondola, O-gauge, brown, tan & black w/brass journals, Ives No. 1707, 1932 40

Train car, gondola, O-gauge, red & black w/white lettering, Lionel No. 1677, 1933-42 50

Train car, gondola, standard gauge, green & black, Lionel No. 512, 1927-39 50

Train car, hopper car, O-gauge, "General Coal Co.," red, yellow & black, Marx No. 554, 1938 20

Train car, hopper, O-gauge, Canadian National, red w/white lettering, Lionel No. 9013, 1972-76 15

Train car, hopper, O-gauge, green & black w/white lettering, Lionel No. 803, 1923-28 45

Train car, livestock car, O-gauge, yellow & black w/red roof, brass journals, Ives No. 65, 1929-30 45

Train car, loader, O-gauge, Evans Auto , red & black, w/four premium cars, Lionel No. 6414, 1955-56 125

Train car, passenger car, S-gauge, red, yellow & black, American Flyer No. 1306, 1926 55

Train car, Pullman car, S-gauge, New Haven, green & black, American Flyer No. 650, 1946-53 80

Train car, Pullman parlor car, O-gauge, red & black w/brass trim, Ives No. 141, 1926-30 80

Train locomotive, diesel engine, O-gauge, Santa Fe, also double A units, silver, red & black, Lionel No. 212, 1964-66 165

Train locomotive, diesel engine, S-gauge, Union Pacific, yellow, grey & red, American Flyer No. 372, 1955-57 265

Train locomotive, engine, F-3, "Texas Special" ABA units, w/portholes, red & white, Lionel No. 2245, very rare, 1954-55 (ILLUS., top next page) 800

Train locomotive, engine, O-gauge, F-3, Wabash AB units, blue, grey & white w/"Wabash" in yellow lettering, Lionel No. 2240, rare, 1956 (ILLUS., second from top, next page) 1,165

Train locomotive, engine, O-gauge, GG1, 4-6-6-4, tuscan, gold "Pennsylvania" on side, Lionel No. 2340, scarce, 1955 (ILLUS., third from top, next page) 1,350

Train locomotive, engine, switcher & caboose, blue w/"Alaska Railroad" in yellow lettering, Lionel No. 614 (engine) & 6027 (caboose), 1959-60 (ILLUS., bottom on next page)... 425

Train locomotive, Hiawatha engine & tender, S-gauge, orange, grey, yellow, black & maroon, American Flyer No. 1742, 1937 95

Train locomotive, keywind, 0-4-0, yellow, black, red & blue, Marx Joy Line No. 350, very rare, 1927-30 415

Train locomotive, steam engine, O-gauge, dull black, Marx No. 666, 1955 45

Train locomotive, steam engine, S-gauge, 0-6-0, American Flyer No. 429, 1953 80

Train locomotive, steam engine, S-gauge, die cast, New York Central, 4-6-4, American Flyer No. 322, 1946-50 165

Train locomotive, steam engine & switcher/slant-back tender, O-gauge, die cast, 0-4-0, black w/"Lionel Lines" in white on side, without backup light, Lionel No. 1615, 1955-57 (ILLUS., below, top) 195

Lionel No. 1615 Engine & Tender

Lionel No. 671 Steam Engine & Tender

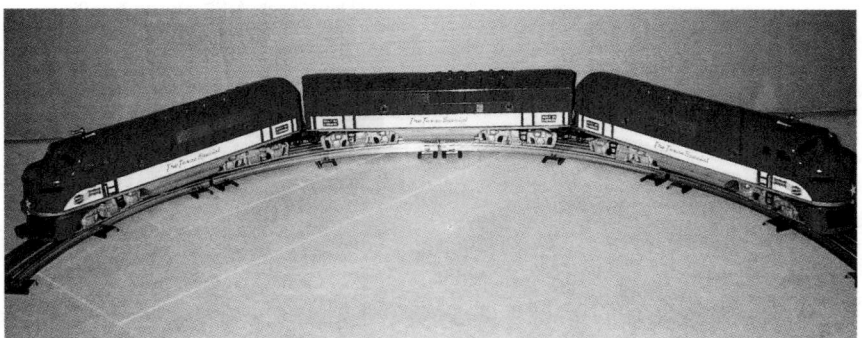

Lionel No. 2245 Engine

Lionel No. 2240 Engine

Lionel No. 2340 Engine

Lionel No. 614 Engine & 6027 Caboose

Train locomotive, steam engine & tender, 6-8-6, Turbine, black w/"Lionel Lines" in white lettering, Lionel No. 671, 1946-49 (ILLUS., bottom page 940) 300

Train locomotive, steam engine & tender, 6-8-6, Turbine, Lionel No. 681, 1950-53 300

Train locomotive, steam engine & tender, 6-8-6, Turbine, scarce, Lionel No. 671RR, 1952 400

Train locomotive, steam engine & tender, O-gauge, die cast, 4-6-4, Lionel No. 2056, 1952 215

Train locomotive, steam engine & tender, O-gauge, die cast, Lionel No. 224E, 1938-42 230

Train set: electric engine & tender, 0-4-0, Pullman club car, observation car; standard gauge, Ives No. 3235 engine & tender, No. 184 Pullman club car, No. 186 observation car, 1926-30, the set (ILLUS., top next page) 460

Train set: engine & tender, baggage car, Pullman car, observation car; O-gauge, "The Blue Comet," light & dark blue, Lionel No. 263E engine & tender, No. 615 baggage car, No. 613 Pullman car, No. 614 observation car, rare, 1936-39, the set 2,225

Train set: engine, two Pullman cars, observation car; O-gauge, "Macy Special," maroon, Lionel No. 252 engine, No. 607 Pullman cars, No. 608 observation car, rare, 1926-27, the set 1,050

Train set: steam engine, combination car, vista dome car, observation car; S-gauge, black engine & tender, cars all silver, American Flyer No. 322 engine, No. 660 combination car, No. 662 vista dome car, No. 663 observation car, 1950-52, the set (ILLUS., second from top next page) 420

Train set: steam engine & tender, 0-4-0, two "New York Central" passenger cars; O-gauge, Ives No. 1116 engine & tender, No. 210 passenger cars, 1916-22, the set (ILLUS., third from top on next page) 245

Train set: "The General #3" engine & tender, "W.&A.R.R." baggage car, "W.&A.R.R." passenger car, "W.&A.R.R." flat car w/horses; O-gauge, Lionel No. 8701 engine & tender, No. 9551 baggage

car, No. 9552 passenger car, No. 9553 flat car w/horses, 1978-80, the set (ILLUS., bottom next page) **275**

Early Cast-iron Stake Truck

Truck, cast iron, stake-type, closed cab, overall worn original green paint, solid metal wheels, ca. 1930s, 4 5/8" l. (ILLUS.) **195**

Old Cast-iron Yellow Stake Truck

Truck, cast iron, stake-type w/closed cab & rails in the back, worn yellow paint, white vulcanized rubber tires, comes apart w/wire connections for chassis & frame, ca. 1930s, 3 3/8" l. (ILLUS.) **150**

Marx Steel Lumber Truck

Rocket-carrying Truck and Original Box

Ives Train Set

American Flyer Train Set

Ives "New York Central" Train Set

Lionel Train Set with Horses

Truck, pressed steel, flatbed-type, red cab w/low-sided yellow stake back, black rubber tires, sign on cab door reading "Tri-State Lumber Co.," by Marx, made in Japan, ca. 1950s, 5" l. (ILLUS., previous page).. **95**

Truck, pressed steel, friction-operated, flatbed rocket-carrying truck, black body w/rubber tires, mounted w/a red & white rocket marked "X-18," Cragston, Japan, w/original box, ca. 1950s, 9 1/2" l. (ILLUS., bottom previous page)..................... **250**

Rare Tootsietoy Truck Set in Box

Truck set, cast spelter, open-cab orange truck w/three detachable back beds in various colors, in original colorfully printed box w/label reading "Tootsietoy Truck Set," ca. 1930s, box 3 x 3 5/8", the set (ILLUS., top of page).. **700**

Small Cast Trucker with Car Hauler

Truck with car hauler, cast spelter & steel, the red cab w/black rubber tires, steel hauler trailer w/five removable cars, by Manoil, ca. 1930s, 4 1/2" l. (ILLUS.)................ **95**

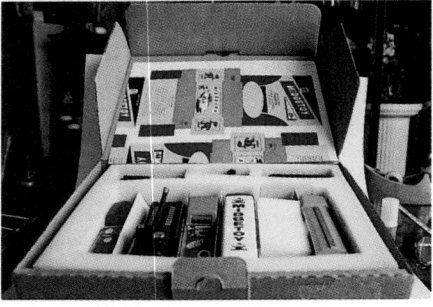

New Boxed Midgetoy Vehicle Set

Vehicle set, cast metal, includes tanker truck, convertible car, delivery truck, fire truck & three different tanks & cannon, new in original box, Midgetoy, ca. 1950s, box 10 1/2 x 14", 4 1/2" h., the set (ILLUS.)... **275**

Early Cast-iron Horse-drawn Stake Wagon

Wagon, cast iron, horse-drawn stake wagon w/driver, red wagon on black metal spoked wheels, pulled by a white & black horse, early 20th c., 10 1/4" l. (ILLUS., bottom previous page) **395**

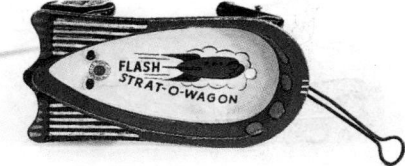

Toy Flash Strat-O-Wagon

Wagon, stamped metal, streamlined bullet-shaped body printed in red, white & blue, the interior showing spaceship & reading "Flash Strat-O-Wagon," black wheels, wire bail pull handle, Wyandotte, ca. 1930s, 9 1/2" l. (ILLUS.) **115**

Mint Windup Tin Ford Touring Car

Windup tin 1915 Ford Touring Car, dark grey exterior & red interior, black metal wheels, by Banda Baby, Japan, 1950s, mint in original box, car 7" l. (ILLUS.) **425**

Windup tin beetle pulling oak leaf, a large red stag beetle pulling a large yellow oak leaf steered by a monkey, w/two squirrels on the leaf, marked "TPS - Made in Japan," ca. 1950s, 11 1/2" l. (ILLUS., bottom of page) **275**

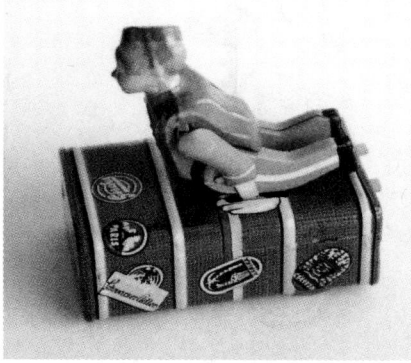

Windup Tin Bellhop on Trunk Toy

Windup tin bellhop on steamer trunk, brown trunk w/white bands, bellhop in blue outfit, bellhop first pushes then jumps on the trunk when wound, marked "Gescha. 667474 - 57-1 - Made in U.S. Zone Germany," 3" l., 2 3/4" h. (ILLUS.)........ **295**

Rare Windup Tin Boy on Sled Toy

Windup tin boy on sled, large white sled w/blue top, a body dressed in a red snowsuit at the back, marked "Gescha. 57/3 - Made in U.S. Zone Germany," 1950s, 4 1/2" l. (ILLUS.) **395**

Beetle & Oak Leaf Windup Tin Toy

Scarce Windup Tin Circus Car Toy

Windup tin circus car, red vintage auto printed w/figures inside including a clown, musicians & ringmaster, black & red metal wheels, stack on roof goes up & down when wound, marked "KO Made in Japan," 1950s, near mint in original box, 5" l. (ILLUS.) **365**

Rare Marx "Drummer Boy" Windup Toy

Windup tin "Drummer Boy," a drummer boy wearing a red suit, white hat & blue & white striped pants pushing a large drum printed in dark yellow, red & blue w/black lettering reading "Let the Drummer Boy Play While You Swing and Sway," Marx, ca. 1930s, 8 1/2" l. (ILLUS.) **995**

Windup Tin Fighting Roosters

Windup tin fighting roosters, two facing birds mounted on small platforms raised on pairs of wheels & joined by a central flexible metal rod, made in Japan, ca. 1950s, 6" l. (ILLUS.) **145**

Windup Tin Fire Chief's Car

Windup tin fire chief's car, red & white sedan w/yellow lettering, black rubber wheels, ca. 1950, 6" l. (ILLUS.) **95**

Windup Tin Fire Ladder Truck

Windup tin fire ladder truck, red body w/open yellow back, black hard rubber tires, a Walt Reach Toy by Courtland, ca. 1950s, 8 3/4" l. (ILLUS.) **225**

G.I. Joe & K-9 Pups Windup Toy

Windup tin "G.I. Joe & the K-9 Pups," light green w/red & yellow trim, Unique Art Mfg. Co., ca. 1930s, 9" h. (ILLUS.) **265**

Rare Arnold Indian in Canoe Windup

Windup tin Indian in canoe, a large white canoe w/black rim holds a dark brown Indian figure operating yellow oars, Arnold, ca. 1930s, w/original box, 8 1/2" l. (ILLUS.) **1,495**

Windup Tin Action Jalopy

Windup tin jalopy, a green jalopy w/driver, large metal rear wheels & tiny front wheels, careens & backs up when wound, ca. 1930s, 5 1/2" l. (ILLUS.).............. **170**

Windup Tin Jumpin Jeep Toy

Windup tin "Jumpin Jeep," four riders dressed in yellow in a green & yellow jeep w/oversized rear wheels & small front wheels, Marx, ca. 1940s, fine condition, 5 1/2" l. (ILLUS.)...................................... **245**

Windup tin speedboat, long tapering red body w/wood-grained top, windup key at top rear, Ohio Art, ca. 1950s, 14 1/4" l. (ILLUS., bottom of page) **75**

Early Windup Tin Steam Engine

Windup tin steam engine, large model of an early steam engine in red & green, large metal wheels, probably made in Germany, early 20th c., smokestack missing, 6 1/2" l., 4 1/2" h. (ILLUS.) **75**

Marx "Toytown Dairy" Wagon

Windup tin "Toytown Dairy" wagon, horse-drawn wagon, wagon in white, red & yellow w/silver metal wheels, pulled by a black horse, Marx, ca. 1930s, slight wear, 10" l. (ILLUS.)... **265**

Ohio Art Windup Tin Speedboat

Unusual Windup Waterwheel & Squirrel Toy

Windup tin waterwheel & squirrel, long base w/lobed ends centered by a large red waterwheel, figure of a squirrel rolling around the track & through the wheel, marked "K," made in Japan, w/original box, 1950s, overall 20" l., 6 1/2" h. (ILLUS., top of page)....................................... **265**

Cap Guns, Pistols & BB Guns

1947 Daisy Air Rifle Advertisement

Advertisement, full-page color ad for Daisy Air Rifle, from the back of the December-January 1947 "Calling All Boys" comic book, tie-in w/Red Ryder comics (ILLUS.) **15**

Advertisement, full-page color ad for Daisy Air Rifles, from the back page of the January 1966 "Laughs" comic book, various models shown (ILLUS., top next column).......... **5**

1966 Daisy Air Rifles Advertisement

1944 Color Ad for Daisy Air Rifles

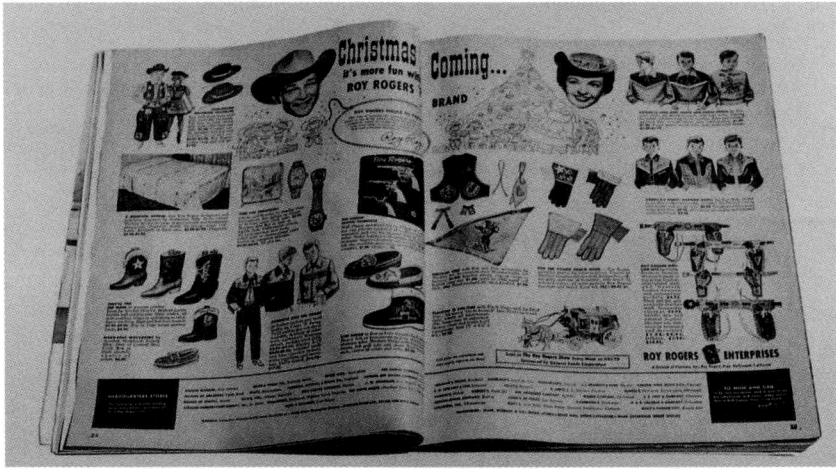

1954 Two-page Advertisement Featuring Roy Rogers & Dale Evans - 2 column

Advertisement, full-page color ad for Daisy Air Rifles, from the back page of a 1944 "Superman" comic, drawing of a boy holding an air rifle, also mentions Buck Roger pistol & holster set (ILLUS., previous page) **70**

Evans promoting clothing & toys for the Christmas season (ILLUS., top of page) **20**

Badge, Air Rifle Safety Badge, metal, given out w/the purchase of a Daisy Red Ryder air rifle, late 1930s - early 1940s **35**

Catalog, Daisy Air Rifles for 1940, featuring the famous Red Ryder BB carbine w/compass in the stock, made famous in the 1983 movie "A Christmas Story," Red Ryder & Little Beaver illustrated **260**

Handbook, "Daisy Handbook #2," characters including Red Ryder & Captain Marvel on the cover, 1948 .... **285**

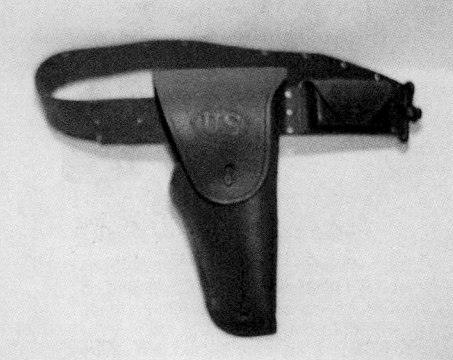

Holster for the Marx Army 45 Cap Pistol

1975 Daisy Air Rifle Advertisement

Advertisement, full-page color ad for Daisy air rifles, from the first issue of "Manhunter" comic from D.C. Comics, August 1975, two models shown (ILLUS.) **5**

Advertisement, two-page black & white spread from 1954 "Saturday Evening Post," featuring Roy Rogers & Dale

Holster, plastic holster made for the Marx Army 45 pistol, flap stamped w/"US," includes small pouch for extra caps, originally part of a set, 1950s (ILLUS.) **90**

Holster set, "Dale Evans Holster Set," yellow & brown leather w/white fringe, decorated w/butterflies & "DE" initials, no pistols, by Classy, early 1950s **175**

Pistol, Atomic Disintegrator Gun, die-cast heavy metal w/bright red plastic handles, w/various space dials, pulling on front drops down the loading mechanism for caps, 1954, w/original box, pistol 8" l. **700**

Pistol, Billy the Kid model, cast-iron cap gun, Stevens Company, 1938, 6 3/4" l. **180**

Pistol, Bobby Benson cap pistol, tie-in w/"Bobby Benson Adventures" radio show, his initials on the gun, 1934, pistol 7" l. **160**

1950s Cap Pistol with Western Designs

Pistol, cast-metal w/white plastic grip, embossed w/designs of cactus & other Western motifs, pushing down release lever opens cap compartment, unknown maker, 1950s (ILLUS.)..................... **40**

Pistol, Daisy No. 50 Golden Eagle model, copper-plated finish w/black painted stock, w/50th Anniversary logo of Daisy & the dates "1886 - 1936" **140**

Pistol, "Daniel Boone Wilderness Scout Derringer," Louis Marx, late 1950s **75**

Ideal 1960s Detective Pistol

Pistol, detective pistol, cast-metal body w/brown plastic handle, front release on barrel opens cap compartment, Ideal, 1960s (ILLUS.)..................... **20**

Pistol, Gene Autry model, cast iron, Autry appears on the metal frame, ornate cast designs, by Kenton Hardware Co., 1939, 6 1/2" l. **200**

Pistol, "Jack Dan Space Gun," black, red or blue-painted die-cast metal, character's name imprinted on the trigger, made in Spain by the Metamol Company, 1959, 7 1/2" l. **300**

Pistol, Marshal Matt Dillon cap pistol, based on the TV show "Gunsmoke," front release in the trigger to drop the cap compartment, Leslie-Henry Company, 1950s, 10" l..................... **180**

Pistol, Red Ryder, Jr. cap gun, silvered metal w/white plastic handle grips, Wyandotte, 1950s **135**

Pistol, "Roy Rogers Tuck-A-Way Gun," attached to original card reading "The Smallest Cap Firing Pistol in the World - only 2 inches," Roy shown on the card, 1950.................. **200**

Pistol, "Scout" model, cast iron, Stevens Company, ca. 1890, 7" l................. **100**

Pistol, "Texan Gold Plated Deluxe Pistol," original box featuring two Longhorn cattle, pistol w/white grip w/star logo, Hubley, 1950, 9" l. **350**

Pistol, "The Lone Ranger 45 Flasher Frontier Pistol," name on barrel, his horse Silver on the hand grip, Marx, w/original box w/an image of the Lone Ranger & Silver on the top, ca. 1950 .... **275**

Pistol, Wild Bill Hickok cap pistol, based on the TV show, similar to the Matt Dillon model, front release in the trigger drops the cap compartment, Leslie-Henry Company, 1950s, 10" l. **245**

Pistol outfit, "Lone Ranger Official Cowboy Outfit," w/pistol & holster, each w/image of the Lone Ranger, w/original box showing the Lone Ranger & Silver on the top, tie-in w/the early radio show, ca. 1938.......... **250**

Pistol outfit, "The Roy Rogers Official Flash Draw Holster Outfit," genuine leather holster w/swivel-hip firing-action pistol, Roy shown on the butt of the handle of the gun, in original box, Classy Company, 1948 .... **800**

Pistol set, Bat Masterson outfit, TV show tie-in, w/pistol, holster, cane & vest, picture of Gene Barry, star of the show, on the cover of the original box, Carnell, 1958...................... **350**

Pistol set, "Have Gun Will Travel Holster Set," early TV program tie-in, w/holsters, guns, business cards for Paladin, a small cap-firing derringer & 12 bullets, w/original box, Artists Service Enterprise, 1958...................... **150**

Miniature Marx Army 45 Pistol

Pistol set, miniature Army 45 pistol, Marx, New York, New York, 1950s, 2 1/4 x 3 1/2", other models in the series include a Civil War era pistol, a Western Plains era saddle rifle & a Tommy gun, each set in original package (ILLUS. of Army 45 pistol)................................. **125**

Small "Apache" Cap Rifle

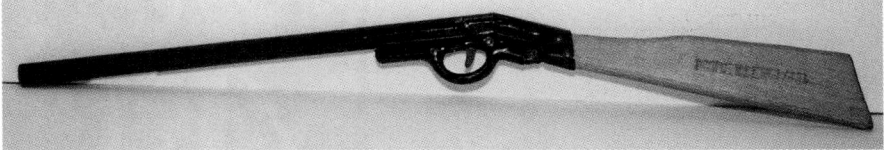

Early English-made BB Rifle

Small Cap Pistol & Holster Set

Pistol set, pistol & black plastic belt & holster, small size, maker unknown, 7" l. (ILLUS.) **5**

Russell Cowboy Holster Set

Pistol set, "Russell Cowboy Holster Set," pair of cast silvered metal pistols w/white plastic grips & double black leather holsters w/metal studs, metal belt buckle, ca. 1950, complete set in original box (ILLUS.) **350**

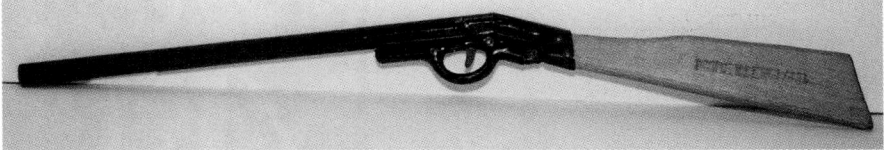

1980s Tootsietoy Wild West Pistol Set

Pistol set, "Tootsietoy Wild West" set, diecast metal cap pistol w/a single black holster printed w/a red & white scene of a cowboy on a rearing horse, sealed in original bubble pack, 1980s, holster 9" l. (ILLUS.).. **25**

Rifle, "Apache" cap rifle, small size, metal body w/plastic handle grip, made to resemble a Winchester repeating rifle, side of body embossed w/the word "Apache" & a bust portrait of a Native American chief, the handle molded w/images of cattle & horse, 1950s, 10 1/2" l. (ILLUS., top of page, top)... **7**

Rifle, BB rifle, black metal barrel & wooden stock stamped "Made in England," ca. 1940, overall 23 1/2" l. (ILLUS., top of page, bottom) **30**

Rifle, "Buck Jones Special - Daisy Air Rifle - No. 107," special store item sold by Daisy in Plymouth, Michigan, stock of rifle w/compass & sundial, 1936 .... **300**

Rifle, Lone Ranger carbine-rifle, gray plastic repeating cap rifle, cap magazine dropping down for inserting roll of caps, character's name on the stock, Louis Marx, 1950s, 26" l. **225**

Rifle, Roy Rogers carbine-rifle, gray plastic repeating cap rifle, cap magazine dropping down for inserting roll of caps, character's name on the stock, Louis Marx, 1950s, 26" l. **225**

GI Joe

Nobody can doubt the fact that the GI Joe 12" action figure (or doll) of the 1960s and 1970s is a highly sought after collectible today. Many price guides have been published concerning their values. The listings here reflect actual prices realized during 2003-2004.- Kerra Davis

Action figures

Action Girl Series nurse, No. 8060, mint in box, 1976 .... **$4,000**

Action Marine, dressed, painted hair, 1964 (stress knee cracks) **71**

Action Pilot, w/two tagged outfits **70**

Action Sailor, dressed, painted hair (stress knee cracks) **3**

Adventure Team soldier, w/Kung Fu grip, some gear **42**

Air Adventurer, w/lifelike body, No. 7282, mint in box, 1976 .... **160**

Black Action Soldier, w/tagged outfit **225**

Black Adventurer, No. 7283, in box, 1976 (minor shelf wear) **180**

Black soldier, nude, painted hair, mint **170**

Eagle Eye Man of Action, w/moving eyes, No. 7277, mint in package, 1976 (ILLUS.) **180**

German Soldier of the World (stress cracks at knees, some bleached out spots on torso) **69**

Japanese Imperial Soldier, dressed (cracked knee & forearm).............................. **123**

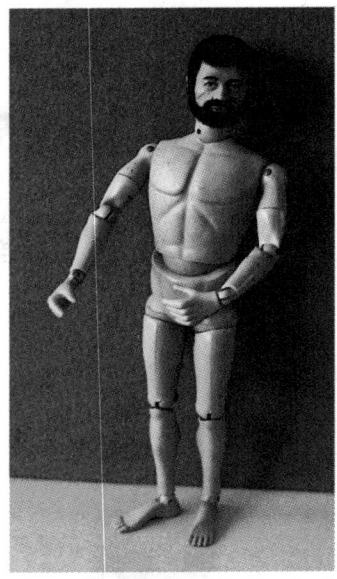

GI Joe Action Figure Without Outfit

Jointed model, nude, w/lifelike hair & beard, crack in knee (ILLUS.)........................... **42**

GI Joe Land Adventurer in Box

Land Adventurer, w/Kung Fu grip, No. 7280, in box, 1974, box damaged (ILLUS.)... **148**

Eagle Eye GI Joe in Package

GI Joe Man of Action in Box

Talking Man of Action GI Joe

Clothing & accessories

Desert Explorer Outfit in Package

Loose Miscellaneous GI Joe Clothing

GI Joe Marine Demolition Set

Marine Demolition accessory set, w/mine detector, No. 7730, mint in package, 1966 (ILLUS.) **260**
Marine Dress Parade, No. 7710, mint in box, 1964 .... **499**
Marine Medic accessory set, No. 7719, mint in package, 1964 (ILLUS., top of next column) **366**
Navy Attack workshirt **12**
Navy Basics set **25**
Paratrooper Camouflage set, complete **18**
Scramble vest & parachute **20**
SCUBA diver jacket, pants, hood, orange, soft condition **71**
Tank commander helmet, mint **160**
Tank commander jacket **14**

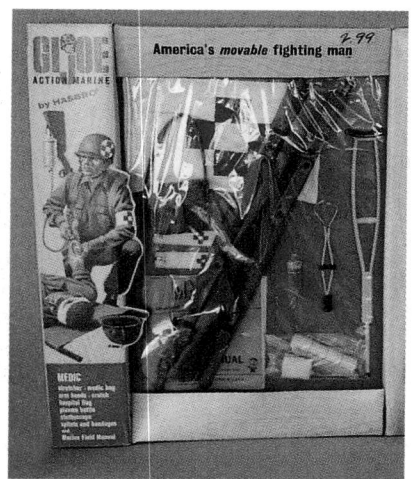

GI Joe Marine Medic Set

Miscellaneous

Action Sailor box, uniform & paperwork, mint (no figure) **154**
Amphicat vehicle, 1973 .... **35**
Capture Copter, No. 7481, mint in box, 1976 .... **295**
Colorforms, in box, 1973, several pieces missing (ILLUS., bottom of page) **10**
Foot locker, metal (damaged) **5**

GI Joe Colorforms

GI Joe Foot Locker

Foot locker, wood w/cardboard sleeve, hinged lid featuring name, rank & serial number in stencil-style type, strap handle on either side, 1964 (ILLUS., above)............ 202

GI Joe Club membership extras: identification card, membership certificate, catalog, iron-on transfer, dog tag, The Command Post News, complete 32

GI Joe Combat Infantry Game, mint in box, 1964... 75

GI Joe Navy Frogman Game, mint in box, 1964... 100

Hands for GI Joe action figure, hard plastic, pr... 25

Kid-size Joe flare gun flashlight 20

Lite Brite, w/GI Joe refill, Hasbro 12

Marine Manual, 1964 8

Motorcycle & sidecar, No. 5651, in box, Irwin, 1967.. 175

Premium ring, marked "Hasbro" 8

Sea sled, "Sears Exclusive" (damage) 25

Shovel, featuring GI Joe 7

Signal All Terrain Vehicle, 1973....................... 60

Toy compass 5

Viewmaster reel, mint in package 12

Walkie Talkie, working, 2 parts 9

TRAMP ART

Tramp art flourished in the United States from about 1875 into the 1930s. These chip-carved woodenwares, mostly in the form of boxes or other useful items, were made mainly from old cigar boxes, although fruit and vegetable crates were also used. The wood is predominantly edge-carved and subsequently layered to create a unique effect. Completed items were given an overall stained finish, which was sometimes further enhanced with painted highlights. Though there seems to be no written record of the artists, many of whom were itinerants, there is a growing interest in collecting this ware.

Birdcage, two tiers w/cupola, doors decorated w/carved starbursts, peak decorated w/carved birds, white w/red & green accents, two drawers for cleaning, 8 3/4 x 14 1/2", 29 3/4" h. (edge damage)... **$1,430**

Birdhouse, dark varnished finish, three mesh-covered windows & two openings, door on one end, w/articulated figure of Native American, hatchet in one hand, knife in the other, standing next to two hands w/first fingers raised, 20" l., 19" h. (edge damage)... 1,430

Box, cov., rectangular shape, w/stepped rectangular & square designs, lid w/center panel decoration of carved hearts & teardrops, canted feet, walnut & maple colored varnish, 7 x 10 1/2", 7" h. 165

Frame, rectangular, molded edge w/two interior bands of diamond designs, molded liner, warm brown finish, fitted w/mirror, 25" w., 29" h. 770

Frame, rectangular, stepped designs, w/hearts in corners, dark varnished finish, fitted w/mirror, 19 1/2" w., 24" h. 440

Jewelry box, cov., stepped rectangular design, canted feet, divided interior, brown varnish, 7 1/4 x 10", 5 1/2" h. (minor wear)... 303

Mirror, three-part dresser-top type, w/arched panels, each holding rectangular mirror w/smaller square mirror in arch, frame decorated w/carved hearts, diamonds & rosettes, chip carved base, multicolor varnishes, light to dark, 15 1/2" w., 12" h. 275

Sewing box, cov., stepped design w/opaque white ball finials & feet, heart pincushion on lid, center panel w/"Felicie," interior lined w/purple velvet, brown varnish, 10 x 13", 6 1/2" h. (minor damage/wear).. 330

Wall pocket, a large pierced & stepped latticework backing w/rosettes above & below the projecting pocket w/an angled front, the pocket sides w/bird cut-outs & a three-part mirror at the front, dry red paint w/some alligatoring, late 19th - early 20th c., 10 x 17", 38" h. (replaced mirror, wear at top from hanging)... 440

Window planter, arched gateway flanked by gabled trellises, picket fencing, old creamy white paint, 6 1/2 x 20", 16 1/2" h. (paint wear, minor damage) **138**

TRAYS - SERVING & CHANGE

Both serving and change trays, once used in taverns, cafes and the like and usually bearing advertising for a beverage maker, are now being widely collected. All trays listed are heavy tin serving trays, unless otherwise noted.

Also see: Antique Trader Advertising Price Guide.

Fairy Soap Change Tray

Change, "Fairy Soap," round, red shading to yellow background w/little girl in red coat & frilly black hat sitting on white oval bar of soap marked "Fairy," black border marked w/yellow letters reading "Fairy Soap - 'Have you a little Fairy in your home?,'" N.K. Fairbank Co., Chicago, Illinois, litho by Passaic Metalware Co., Passaic, New Jersey, ca. 1910, 4 1/2" d. (ILLUS.) **$100-175**

Liberty Beer Change Tray

Change, "Liberty Beer - American Brew. Co. - Rochester, N.Y. - In Bottles Only," round w/central bust portrait of an Indian maiden in a feathered headdress, arrows & peace pipes framing central circle, minor edge scuffs, 4 1/2" d. (ILLUS.) **259**

Resinol Soap Change Tray

Change, "Resinol Soap and Ointment," round, metal, center bust portrait of beautiful woman w/long brown hair, low cut dress w/red flower decoration, red flowers in hair, black border w/gold lettering reading "Resinol Soap and Ointment - For All Skin Diseases - At All Drug Stores," 4 1/4" d. (ILLUS.) **125-150**

Rockford Watches Change Tray

Change, "Rockford High-Grade Watches," rectangular w/flared sides & crimped corners, center color scene of seated pretty young maiden w/flowers, near mint, early 20th c., 3 x 4 5/8" (ILLUS.).............................. **209**

Swan Vestas Glass Change Tray

Change, "Swan Vestas - the Smoker's match," glass, square, bright red label pasted on the bottom w/logo & wording in gold, black, white & red, England, 6" sq., 1 3/4" h. (ILLUS.) **143**

The Prefect Havana Cigar Change Tray

Change, "The Prefect Havana Cigar," round, central color full-length portrait of man in 17th c. attire, made in Germany, early 20th c., minor scratch & edge scuffs, 4 1/4" d. (ILLUS.) **77**

Edelweiss Beer Serving Tray

Serving, "Edelweiss Beer," center color bust portrait of a pretty young red-headed girl wearing a white & red shawl against a black ground, the border band w/edelweiss blossoms, dated 1913, excellent condition, 13" d. (ILLUS.) **176**

Hopsburger Beer Serving Tray

Serving, "Hopsburger - the Golden Beer," round, color bust portrait of a lovely young woman wearing an off-the-shoulder gown against a black background, ca. 1910, very light surface wear, 13" d. (ILLUS.) **308**

Hauser & Co. Fine Shoes Tray

Serving, "John H. Hauser & Co. - Fine Shoes," oval, a large colorful central scene of patriotic allegorical figures among clouds, Liberty standing in the center, early 20th c., spot at bottom left inpainted, few tiny chips, 13 x 16" (ILLUS.).. **374**

Polar Ginger Ale Serving Tray

Serving, "Serve Polar Ginger Ale," round, a large white polar bear against a green ground, wording in white & green, ca. 1930s, 13" d. (ILLUS., previous page) **62**

Serving Tray with Maple Sugaring Scene

Serving, "W.T.B. McDonald, Granby, Que. - Mfg. of The McDonald Patent Sap Spout," oval, large colorful winter maple sugaring scene & an oval reserve showing the sap spout, nail hole in top border, wear to Greek key border design, early 20th c., 15 1/2 x 18 1/2" (ILLUS.) **230**

Walter Baker Chocolate Serving Tray

Serving, "Walter Baker Chocolate," oval, color images of various projects in the center on a black background, yellow & red border band, ca. 1905, excellent condition, 13 3/4 x 16 1/2" (ILLUS.) **288**

White Rock Beer Serving Tray

Serving, "White Rock Beer - Akron Brewing Company," round, large beautiful color center scene of an exotic beauty lounging against the head of a large tiger, 1912, very good condition, 13 1/2" d. (ILLUS.) **690**

TRUMP INDICATORS

 A trump indicator is a device that was placed on the table during card games such as Whist and its successor, Bridge. They were to remind the players what the trump suit was. The earlier trump indicators from the 19th century, used in the game of Whist, had only the four suits of hearts, spades, diamonds and clubs. Later, in the game of Bridge, "No Trump" was added.

 These gadgets are difficult to find and appear in many forms: people, animals, buildings, useful objects, etc. Some are made of beautiful porcelain while others are crudely made from metal and wood. The ones made from celluloid can be dated from the first half of the 20th century. One thing trump indicators all have in common is their movable pointer or spinner displaying what card suit is trump.

 As with so many items from the past, their usefulness has become outdated. In the modern game of Bridge, a player would probably be reminded "If you can't remember what the trump is, you shouldn't be playing Bridge." But, as gaming collectibles increase in popularity, the desirability of trump indicators will continue to score high.

Globe Trump Indicator

Brass, model of a globe map, ring w/card suits around center (ILLUS.) **$50**

Harp with Celluloid Flip Cards

Brass, ornate scrolling harp-form holder on domed base, celluloid flip cards w/suits (ILLUS., previous page)..................................... **50**

Trump Indicator with Enameled Base

Brass, serpentine metal uprights suspending the suit flip cards, rectangular black enameled base (ILLUS.)................................... **40**

Lady Bather Trump Indicator

Celluloid, figural lady bather w/jointed arms pointing to suits in arch above (ILLUS.).......... **85**

Black Cat Trump Indicator

Celluloid, model of a black cat, arched back & tail as pointer, green base (ILLUS.)............. **85**

Die Cube Trump Indicator

Celluloid, model of a die cube, suit on each side, w/a built-in tape measure (ILLUS.)....... **150**

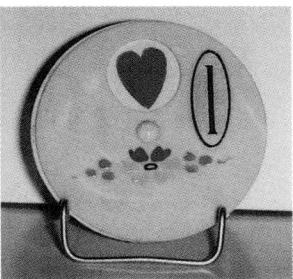

Celluloid Disk Trump Indicator

Celluloid, model of a disk, turning ring indicates suit, h.p. floral trim (ILLUS.) **35**

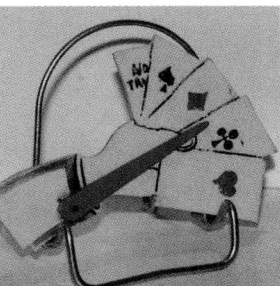

Hand with Cards Trump Indicator

Celluloid, model of a hand holding cards, red pointer indicating suits (ILLUS.) **85**

Playing Card Trump Indicator

Celluloid, model of a playing card, disks indicating suits & numbers, h.p. floral trim (ILLUS.).. **50**

Double Celluloid Wheels

Celluloid, rounded & flattened frame w/scalloped top & rectangular foot, holding two small turn wheels for indicating trump (ILLUS., previous page) **40**

Clown On Ashtray

Ceramic, ashtray, figural clown on back rim beside upright disk w/suits (ILLUS.) **125**

Japanese Clown Ashtray

Ceramic, ashtray, figural clown standing on back rim holding disk w/suits, iridized orange base, Japan (ILLUS.) **175**

Wade Ashtray Trump Indicator

Ceramic, ashtray, round w/upright metal frame w/flip suit cards, an enameled shield w/early ship at base of frame, blue glaze, Wade, England (ILLUS.) **135**

Gnome Trump Indicator

Ceramic, figural, gnome standing beside square block w/an opening to show suits, Germany (ILLUS.) **175**

Copper Souvenir Trump Indicator

Copper, souvenir-type, low domed shape w/stamped souvenir scene at front & opening to show suit at rear (ILLUS.).............. **75**

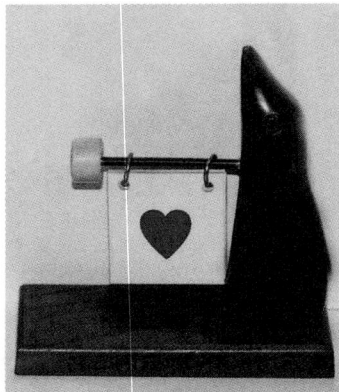

Seal Trump Indicator

Horn & wood, rectangular wood base w/upright horn carved as a seal w/a projecting base holding flip suit cards (ILLUS.)................ **85**
Wooden, barrel-shaped, pencil holders at top, w/ring of suits marked around the base **60**

"Don't Forget The Kitty"

Wooden, box-form, low rectangular form w/pull-out suit indicators, painted in inside "Don't forget the Kitty" w/black cat (ILLUS.) **65**

Inlaid Woods with Flip Cards

Wooden, finely inlaid domed base w/upright metal frame for suit flip cards (ILLUS.) **50**

Twig & Fence Trump Indicator

Wooden, souvenir-type, twig base w/opening painted w/name, fence-form upright support for suit flip cards (ILLUS.) **75**

VALENTINES

Paper Lace over Tissue Paper Card

Card, gold embossed paper lace & lace relief over purple tissue-like paper, embossed "Lang's pat. Process Berlin & Jones Manfrs. N.Y.," 1860s (ILLUS.) .... **$60+**
Card, paper hinges, gold embossed lace & scraps, handwritten date of 1896, 5 x 7" **25**
Card, paper hinges, wafers, scraps, ribbon & paper lace, paste-in verse, marked w/George Whitney's red "W," 1870s, 5 x 6" .... **50+**
Pinpricked paper, round, extensive pinprick designs of multiple hearts surrounded by flowers & foliage colored in w/watercolors in red, blue, yellow, green & orange, hearts are filled w/German verse & "December 1837," back has inked initials, sandwiched between two pieces of glass, Pennsylvania German, minor wear & stains, 14" d. **3,025**

Children's

The lacy frills and layered look of antique valentines had become a thing of the past by the 1920s. Larger and larger numbers of valentines were being printed expressly for children. Big eyes, cute kiddies and animals became the illustrated favorites. The Valentine box appeared in every grammar school room across the land. Children's valentines had become big business!

Beatnik, U.S.A., 1960s, 2 x 8" **1-4**
Big band & radio broadcasting, USA, 1940s, 6 x 7 1/2" **15**
Booklet, Mary Had a Little Lamb, 1940s **15**
Boy in barrel, "Campbell Kid" look, 1930s, 4 x 7" **20**
Boy painting girl's portrait, USA, 1930s, 4 x 6" **4**

Boy & Teddy bear walking, w/movable
eyes, Germany, 3 x 5" **2-6**
Card, gift-giving card w/lollipop, 1930s,
5 x 5" **25**
Cat w/fishing pole, w/movable ears, Ger-
many, 3 x 6" **10**
Charlie Chaplin, caricature, feet turn into
easel base, 4 1/2 x 6" **50**
Chocolate soldier, USA, 1950s, 3 x 8" **8**

Disney Valentine

Clarabell Cow, Disney, 1938, 2 x 6"
(ILLUS.) **75**
Cowboy stick person, USA, 1940s,
4 1/2 x 5 1/2" **10**
Dimensional, Collie & doghouse/chain,
USA, 6 x 6" **40**

Doubl-Glo Valentines

Doubl-Glo, make your own valentine book,
complete w/envelopes, 1940s, 100 pcs.,
makes 50 valentines (ILLUS.) **10-20**
Flat, Bull Terrier, USA, 1940s, 4 1/4 x 9 1/2" **35**

Girl Fold-out Valentine

Fold-out type, big-eyed girl w/honeycomb
tissue skirt, 1930s, Germany, 8" (ILLUS.).. **15-25**
Fold-out type, w/honeycomb tissue, boy &
girl exchanging valentines, 1930s, 3 x 4" **15**

Cat Fold-out Valentine

Fold-out type, w/honeycomb tissue, cat
looking in fish bowl, Germany, 1930s,
6 x 10" (ILLUS.) **35-45**
Fold-out type, w/honeycomb tissue, chil-
dren on phone, 1930s, Germany, 6 x 8" **25**
Fold-out type, w/honeycomb tissue, sailor,
World War II, USA, 1940s, 4 x 5" **30**
Fold-out type, w/honeycomb tissue, two
girls in heart-shaped frame of flowers ride
in auto w/pink hearts where headlights
would be, pale pink daisy-type flowers
w/heart-shaped deep pink centers in
background, 1920s, 5 x 8" (ILLUS., top of
next page).. **22**
Folded paper, African American girl in bub-
ble, USA, 1940s, 2 1/2 x 3 1/2" **15**

Girls in Auto Fold-out Valentine

Folded paper, die-cut, boy w/valentine, bashful girl, Raphael Tuck Co., 1920, 4 x 5 1/2" **20**

Duck Folded Paper Valentine

Folded paper, for "teacher," duck standing at easel painting the valentine with brush, 1940s, 3 x 4" (ILLUS.)..................................... **3-5**

Folded paper, freestanding, bespectacled woman sitting at desk w/quill pen in hand, a blackboard behind her, front of desk reads "To my Valentine - I love my Teacher," box below reads "O.K. kid you may stay after school," 1930s, 3 x 3" (ILLUS.,top of column)...................................... **4-6**

"I love my Teacher" Valentine

For Teacher Folded Paper Valentine

Folded paper, freestanding, girl & boy w/school books, "For My Teacher," USA, 1940s, 4 x 5" (ILLUS.) **2-3**

Girl & Desk Paper Valentine

Folded paper, little girl by desk & blackboard, for teacher, freestanding, 1930s, 3 x 3" (ILLUS.)... **4-6**

Girl with Flowers Valentine

Folded paper, thin paper, tied w/ribbon, young girl w/arms full of flowers, USA, 3 x 5" (ILLUS.)... **3**

Little Girl with Wooden Duck Valentine

Little girl w/wooden duck, possibly an unsigned Charles Twelvetrees design, Germany, 1930s, 3 x 4" (ILLUS.)............................ **12**
Love-Line bus, unsigned Charles Twelvetrees, USA, 1920s, 1 3/4 x 8" **15**
Mechanical, boy & girl on motorcycle, printed in Germany, 1930s, 6 1/2 x 7"..................... **12**

Boy in Car Mechanical Valentine

Mechanical, boy in car, opens up to reveal message, USA, 1930s, 3 x 5" (ILLUS.)........... **12**
Mechanical, boy playing piano, girl on piano, 1950s, 8 x 10" **10**
Mechanical, Boy Scout, USA, 1940s, 4 x 6"........ **25**
Mechanical, boy w/three legs that simulate running, 1930s, 3 x 4"..................................... **7**

Bumble Bee Boy Mechanical Valentine

Mechanical, bumble bee boy inserted in heart, moves from side to side, 1930s, 8 x 10" (ILLUS.) **15**
Mechanical, child w/barrel that slides up & down on body, 1930s, 4 x 5" **7**
Mechanical, clown on dog, rocks back & forth revealing message, 1930s, Germany, 5 x 7"... **35**

Child with Lute Mechanical Valentine

Mechanical, die-cut, folded, freestanding, child playing lute & singing to girl who swings back & forth w/tab, USA, 1930s, 4 x 6" (ILLUS.)... **15-20**
Mechanical, girl looking in mirror, Carrington Co., 1940s, 4 x 6".................................. **9**
Mechanical, girl w/valentine that moves in & out of envelope, USA, 1940s, 4 x 6"............ **10**

Boy with Trombone Mechanical Valentine

Mechanical, little boy playing trombone, trombone moves up & down, USA, 4 x 8" (ILLUS.) **15**

Mechanical, little boy riding scooter, when wheel is turned message is revealed, Germany, 1930s, 3 1/2 x 5 1/2" **8**

Girl with Buggy Mechanical Valentine

Mechanical, little girl pushing dog in baby buggy, printed in Germany, 4 x 5" (ILLUS.) **25**

Mechanical, little girl skating w/puppy at her heels, 1950s, 8 x 10" **7-9**

Mechanical, little girl stirring kettle, 1930s, 4 x 6" **7**

Mechanical, little girl under umbrella, message shown between movable slats, Germany, 1930s, 3 x 4 1/2" **10**

Girl with Heart Valentine

Mechanical, little girl w/heart message hidden behind flowers, printed in Germany, 3 x 6" (ILLUS.) **12**

Girls with Movable Legs Valentine

Mechanical, little girls w/movable legs that go up in the air, playing w/dogs, Germany, 3 x 4", each, (ILLUS.) **7-10**

Magician Mechanical Valentine

Mechanical, magician pulling rabbit out of hat, die-cut, 1940s, 4 x 5" (ILLUS.) **6**

Mechanical, monkey w/lobster, 1940s, 5 x 7"... 35
Mechanical, Skippy, USA, 1930s, 6 1/2 x 7"... 25
Mechanical, soldier looking at his sweetheart, printed in USA, 1940s, 8 1/2 x 9"......... 50

Ambulance Mechanical Valentine

Mechanical, World War II ambulance, 1940s, 4 x 5" (ILLUS.)................................... 15-18
Mechanical, young man presenting a pot of flowers, 1920s, 2 1/2 x 5 1/2" 15

Chicken Novelty Valentine

Novelty, chicken cracking egg, front attached to back by spring causing a wiggle effect, USA, late 1940s - early 1950s, 4 x 6" (ILLUS.).. 10

*Valentine with Punch-out
Paper Doll & Outfit*

Paper doll, punch-out type, little girl w/Dutch outfit & wooden shoes, message reads "Wooden-Shoe like to be my Valentine?" (ILLUS.) 6-8
Pink Panther, sheet of valentines, Orange-Crush giveaway, 12 per sheet.......................... 20
Policeman, Carrington Co., 1930s, 5 x 7" 25
Pop-up type, pilot flies up to meet his lady love when opened, 1920s, 4 x 5".............. 20-25
Pop-up type, ship w/boy & girl, 1920s, Germany, 12".. 207
"Punch & Judy," puppet theater, 1920s, 2 x 5"... 35
Stand-up type, Little Lulu & Tubby, 8"................ 20
Strawberry Shortcake, American Greeting, 1980s, 8 x 10"... 5

VENDING & GAMBLING DEVICES

"Beast" Electric Arcade Machine

Arcade, "Beast - From Which Are You Descended?," electric, upright wood cabinet w/a reverse-painted glass front decorated in color w/various jungle beasts, inserting penny & squeezing handle determines which beast is your ancestor, Exhibit Supply Co., Chicago, copyrighted 1947, good working condition, 10 x 11 1/2", 28" h. (ILLUS.)....................... **$719**

Rare Early Olympic Strength Tester

Arcade, Caille Bros. "Olympic Puncher," cast-iron strength tester, upright pedestal on square base, inserting coin & punching the padded leather disk records the force of the punch on the dial above, red paint on base, nickel-plated cast-iron dial bezel & marquee, oak & cast-iron wall mounting bracket, restored w/reproduction paper dial face, ca. 1906, 69 1/2" h. (ILLUS., previous page) **12,938**

"Disposition Register" Arcade Machine

Arcade, "Disposition Register - How Do You Impress People?," upright wooden case w/glass front, inserting penny & squeezing handle indicates how you impress people, Exhibit Supply Co., Chicago, ca. 1934, very good condition, 10 x 11", 23 1/2" h. (ILLUS.) **578**

Rare Early Crane Digger Machine

Arcade, "Electric Traveling Crane" digger machine, oak cabinet w/glass & aluminum front, interior aluminum castings of the Empire State Building flank a background scene of ironworkers erecting steel girders, includes two bags of prizes & capsules, Art Deco graphics, Mutoscope Reel Company, New York, New York, patented 1932, very good condition, 20 x 23", 41 1/2" h. (ILLUS.) **2,128**

Early "Electricity Is Life" Coin-Op

Arcade, "Electricity Is Life," upright steel cabinet on oak base, one-cent operation, cranking side handles produces mild electric shock, early 20th c., Standard Advertising Company, light restoration, 10 x 16 1/2", 19 1/2" h. (ILLUS.) **4,025**

Early "Lift-O-Graph" Strength Tester

Arcade, "Lift-O-Graph" strength tester, electrified, tall upright oak cabinet on a heavy cast-iron base, one-cent operation allowing player to pull up on the large steel handle to measure strength, colored lights & a bell at the top, International Mutoscope Reel Co., early 20th c., older cabinet repaint, 23 x 36", 98" h. (ILLUS.) **4,600**

Early Mill's "Autostereoscope"

Arcade, "Mill's Autostereoscope," tall upright serpentine-front quarter-sawn oak cabinet w/raised panel sides & door at the front, raised on cast-iron cabriole legs w/claw & glass ball feet, all-original decorated cast-iron parts including coin feed slot & viewer, top w/upright oak-framed marquee w/original cardboard insert sign reading "The French Doll," w/a photo of a scantily clad woman, appears to be original & untouched, working condition, early 20th c., 16 x 20", 73" h. (ILLUS.)............ **3,450**

Model DL Mutoscope for Silent Movie

Arcade, Model DL mutoscope, early electrified cast-metal "clamshell" style body

w/"iron horse" base, upright serpentine marquee frame at top w/cardboard insert card for silent screen star Ted Wells in the Western "Desert Dust," refinished in two-tone blue & white w/gilt trim, ca. 1920s, overall 75" h. (ILLUS.) **3,220**

Mutoscope with Risqué Views

Arcade, mutoscope, upright oak cabinet w/cabriole legs ending in cast-metal claw & glass ball feet, a lower door w/a rectangular beveled glass mirror, the top w/an upright oak-framed risqué title card reading "Pretty and Peppy - Very Pretty" w/a picture of a scantily clad woman, E.S. Company, New York, dated 1926, complete w/key, old original electric cord, plank & original cards, some wear but overall very good, 17 x 17 1/2", 70" h. (ILLUS.).. **3,105**

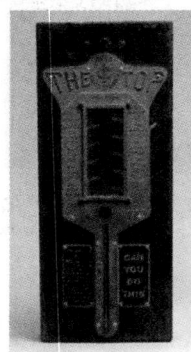

"Over The Top" Arcade Skill Game

Arcade, "Over The Top" skill game, upright steel case w/aluminum & glass front, the object being to move a coin through the aluminum & glass maze, Boyce Coin Machine Co., Tuckahoe, New York, ca. 1926, some corrosion to steel box, 2 x 8 1/2", 20 1/2" h. (ILLUS.) **804**

Early "Swami" Fortune Teller Machine

Arcade, "Swami" fortune teller w/stand, floor-model, cast-aluminum top figure of a turbaned swami peering into a crystal ball, one-cent operation w/handle turning clockwork mechanism, activating internal filmstrip of fortunes & light bulb w/large dry cell battery, fortunes projected up into the crystal ball, Future Products Co., Chicago, Illinois, ca. 1920s, cast-metal crystal ball w/a few cracks, some metal loss to its base, battery dead, good all-original paint, 48" h. (ILLUS.) **3,048**

Early Zeno Collar Button Vendor

Collar button vendor, "Zeno," upright square glass-sided case w/six interior columns & tin top w/coin slots, on a square cast-iron base, 10-cent operation, early 20th c., small chip to side of one glass panel, 5 1/2" sq., 10 1/2" h. (ILLUS.) **518**

Duchess Doubl-Jack Fortune Teller

Fortune vendor, Jennings "Duchess Doubl-Jack" fortune telling machine, "bull's-eye" version, cast-aluminum front w/oak case retaining original "Fortune Teller" reel strips, glass viewing window, ca. 1933, repainted casting, w/keys, 14 x 16", 19" h. (ILLUS.) **1,323**

Bally "777" Slot Machine

Gambling, Bally "777" tabletop slot machine, electro-mechanical cast metal & plastic case, 10-cent play w/five coin multiplier, late 1960s - early 1970s, few burn marks on top of plastic cabinet, good working condition, 16 x 18 1/2", 33 1/2" h. (ILLUS.) **1,080**

Buckley "Bones" Slot Machine

Gambling, Buckley "Bones" (dice) tabletop slot machine, cast-metal case w/oak base, coin-op crap game w/25-cent play, ca. 1936, very good original condition w/key & operating instructions, 11 1/2 x 16", 12 1/2" h. (ILLUS., previous page) **1,825**

Early "Automatic Dice Machine" Copy

Gambling, Clawson "Automatic Dice Machine," floor-model, Gorsky reproduction of the ca. 1890s dice machine, 5-cent play, machine picking up dice, shaking & tossing them via a clockwork mechanism, professionally restored, w/key, 9 3/4 x 10", case 26 1/2" h., stand 30" h. (ILLUS.) **3,680**

Mills "Bell-O-Matic" Slot Machine

Gambling, Mills "Bell-O-Matic" tabletop slot machine, cast-metal classic "hightop" triple-7 machine w/Art Deco styling, ca. 1949, some light paint wear, replaced coin view window, w/key not working, 15 x 16", 26 1/2" h. (ILLUS.) **1,323**

Mills "Brown Front Bell" Slot Machine

Gambling, Mills "Brown Front Bell" tabletop slot machine, cast-aluminum front & original stenciled oak case, front w/variant of "Bursting Cherry" design, 10-cent play, ca. 1938, cracked glass coin window, original working condition w/keys, 15 x 16", 26" h. (ILLUS.) **1,725**

Gambling, Mills "Hi-Top" tabletop slot machine, cast-aluminum front w/oak case, 50-cent play, Art Deco design, few shrinkage cracks in oak case, w/key, ca. 1930s, 15 1/2 x 16", 26 1/2" h. **1,323**

Rare Mills "Liberty Bell" Slot Machine

Gambling, Mills "Liberty Bell Gum-Fruit" tabletop slot machine, early cast-iron footed case w/three reels showing playing card symbols, 5-cent play, original marquee showing various playing card payouts in trade, unique horizontal coin mechanism & side panel castings w/the Statue of Liberty & the New York skyline, ca. 1914, appears all-original, original worn paint, rear door w/small vertical crack, working condition, no key, 13 x 13", 20 1/2" h. (ILLUS.) **8,050**

Mills "Operator Bell" on Oak Stand

Gambling, Mills "Operator Bell" slot machine on oak stand, cast-aluminum front w/oak record cabinet base, w/classic Mills owl designs, 25-cent play, hinged door in base opens to two pull-out drawers, slot w/replacement rear door, lock, coin drawer, coin chute & payout card, original reels, working condition w/key, ca. 1921, slot machine 15 x 16", 24" h., cabinet 18" sq., 35" h. (ILLUS.)....... **1,668**

Mills "Q.T." Slot Machine on Stand

Gambling, Mills "Q.T." slot machine on stand, cast-aluminum case w/Art Deco designs, introduced in 1934 w/a one-cent play, this later version w/5-cent play, on original sheet metal Q.T. customer stand, front repainted, replacement jackpot card, good working order w/original front & rear locks w/key, slot machine 12 1/2 x 13", 18" h. (ILLUS.)...................... **1,610**

Mills Miniature Boxed Roulette Wheel

Gambling, Mills roulette wheel, portable miniature version in a wooden case, featuring a paper numbers face on a wooden wheel fastened to a cast-iron bearing assembly, interior box lid showing the gaming number layout for placing nickel bets w/cigar payoffs, stamped-brass decorative cartouches applied inside & outside, early 20th c., overall paint wear to box, moisture staining on paper, some chips to inside of paper roulette wheel face, 13" sq., 4 1/2" h. (ILLUS.)...................... **900**

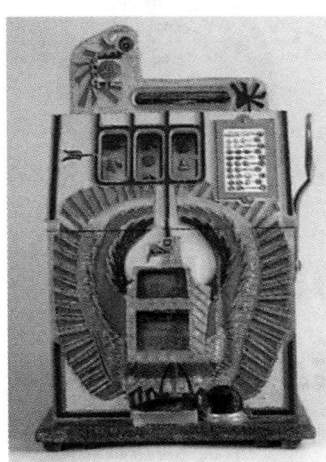

Mills "War Eagle" Slot Machine

Gambling, Mills "War Eagle" tabletop slot machine, cast-aluminum front w/eagle motif on oak case, 25-cent play, original excellent decals, front casting repainted w/new jackpot card, working condition w/keys, ca. 1930s, 15 x 16", 26" h. (ILLUS.).. **1,955**

Evans-type Glass Roulette Wheel

Gambling, roulette wheel, Evans reverse-painted glass type, wheel w/nickel-plated pins & framework, reverse decoration on glass appears to represent dice, center reverse-painted star, signed "Arthur Popper, New York" inside the hub, original cast-iron tripod base & wood post & indicator, slight damages, flaps replaced or repaired, some rust on foot, some bent pins, early 20th c., wheel 53" d., overall 7' h. (ILLUS.) **1,725**

Early Painted Wood Roulette Wheel

Gambling, roulette wheel on base, colorfully painted wooden wheel on a cross-form base, good patina & paint, ca. 1900, wheel 25" d., overall 34" h. (ILLUS.)............. **978**

Early French-made Roulette Wheel

Gambling, roulette wheel, wooden board mounted w/colorful six-panel lithographed paper wheel illustrating various animals in each panel, made in France, early 20th c., 9 1/2" d. (ILLUS.)...................... **150**

Early Evans Wooden Roulette Wheel

Gambling, roulette wheel, wooden wheel decorated w/elaborate nickel-plated ornaments, on its original cast-iron tripod base, by the H.C. Evans Co., Chicago, Illinois, ca. 1900, working condition, wheel 33" d., overall 47" h. (ILLUS.) **1,955**

Watling "Rol-A-Top" Slot Machine

Gambling, Watling "Rol-A-Top" tabletop slot machine, classic cast-metal front w/cornucopia & gold coins, twin jackpot model w/5-cent play, ca. 1930s, professionally repainted, cracked wired glass jackpot window, working condition w/keys, 15 x 16", 26 1/2" h. (ILLUS.) **2,645**

Rare Early Adams Gum Vendor

Gum vendor, "Adams' Pepsin Tutti-Frutti Gum," upright wood cabinet w/white porcelain front & side porcelain panels, two-column style, one-cent operation, ca. 1898, old red wood finish, some wood loss on rear panel, small chip on one side panel, 5 x 11 1/2", 29 1/2" h. (ILLUS.)........ **6,038**

Pulver Chewing Gum Vendor

Gum vendor, "Pulver Chewing Gum," upright red porcelain case w/glass front showing rare cop & robber characters inside, one-cent operation, a few paint chips, w/key, ca. 1930s, 4 1/2 x 9", 20 1/2" h. (ILLUS.)....................................... **1,553**

1950s "Topper" Gumball Vendor

Gumball vendor, "Topper," stepped metal top on the squared glass jar above the cast-metal base, Victor Vending Corp., some paint loss & corrosion to base, w/key, ca. 1950s, 16" h. (ILLUS.) **90**

Early "Van-Lite" Lighter Fluid Vendor

Lighter fluid vendor, "Van-Lite," cast-metal figural countertop gas pump for refilling pocket lighters, by Arthur Kauf, Lockport, New York, ca. 1933, good condition, 19" h. (ILLUS.) **540**

Northwestern Model 33 Peanut Vendor

Peanut vendor, Northwestern Model 33, red porcelain lid on the cylindrical glass container on a red metal base, one-cent operation, concealed chip to glass globe rim, w/key, ca. 1930s, 15 1/2" h. (ILLUS.)...... **345**

Rare "Smilin' Sam" Peanut Vendor

Peanut vendor, "Smilin' Sam From Alabam' - The Salted Peanut Man," figural cast-aluminum in the shape of a bald man, one-cent operation, pull tongue to get peanuts,original red paint, minor paint loss & salt wear, very good original condition, w/key, ca. 1931, 13 1/2" h. (ILLUS.).... **4,370**

Orange & Green "Five Jacks" Machine

Trade stimulator, Rock-Ola "Five Jacks" tabletop coin drop machine, cast-aluminum front panel on a dovetailed quartersawn oak case w/5-cent play mechanism, orange & green enameled trim, player inserts nickel & launches it w/finger, Rock-Ola Mfg. Co., Chicago, Illinois, ca. 1930, working condition w/key, 10 x 17 3/4", 20" h. (ILLUS.)............ **1,035**

Pink & Green "Five Jacks" Machine

Trade stimulator, Rock-Ola "Five Jacks" tabletop coin drop machine, cast-aluminum front panel on a dovetailed quartersawn oak case w/5-cent play mechanism, pink & green repainted enameled trim, player inserts nickel & launches it w/finger, Rock-Ola Mfg. Co., Chicago, Illinois, ca. 1930, working condition w/key, 10 x 17 3/4", 20" h. (ILLUS.) **1,560**

VIEW-MASTER & TRU-VUE VIEWERS & REELS

View-Master, manufactured by Sawyer, Inc. of Portland, Oregon, was first marketed at the 1939-40 New York World's Fair. Several of its earliest reels feature buildings at the Fair. At the same time, on the West Coast, it marketed reels of the Golden Gate International Exposition. During World War II the company shifted from entertainment reels to materials for military use.

After the war a new competitor appeared on the market. The Tru-Vue viewer was produced in Beaverton, Oregon, and was sold through various dimestores.

The two companies sold similar viewers, but the design of their slides differed. View-Master reels were disk-shaped and featured seven scenes, while Tru-View slides were long and rectangular but also featured seven scenes.

Eventually View-Master bought out Tru-Vue and with the purchase also obtained the rights to Disney-licensed views.

Each View-Master three-reel pack came with a story pamphlet. Today the rarest View-Master reels are those made in the 1950s that were issued with motion picture previews. Some of these can sell for hundreds of dollars in top condition. The View-Master reels are listed here by their year of introduction.

Tru-Vue

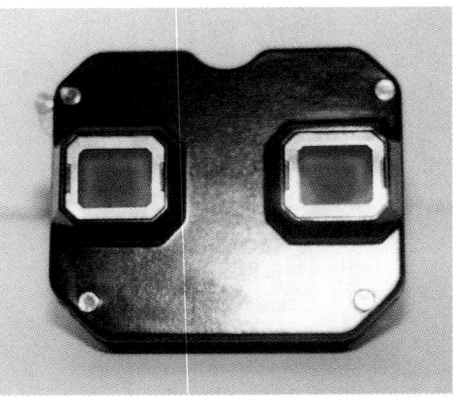

1950 Tru-Vue Viewer

Early viewer, a Tru-Vue handheld viewer, black plastic, ca. 1950 (ILLUS.) **$25**

Early View-Master Reel List

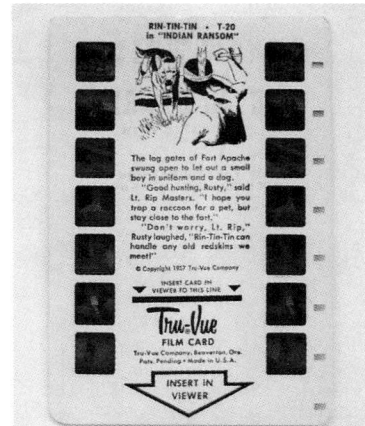

Tru-Vue Rin-Tin-Tin View Card

View card, Tru-Vue No. T20 w/a Rin-Tin-Tin story, w/packet, original sleeve (ILLUS.) **15**

Tru-Vue View Packet with View Card

View packet w/sleeve, Tru-Vue sleeve & reel for No. T20 - Rin-Tin-Tin in "Indian Ransom," 1950s (ILLUS.) **15**

View-Master

Junior Projector in original box, metal cased tabletop electric projector for use w/View-Master reels, various plastic parts, for use w/30 watt bulb, 1950s, 5 1/2 x 7 x 8", the set **75**
Model C viewer, Bakelite handles, ca. 1950........ **25**
Pamphlet, "View-Master Reel List," triple-fold, color-printed paper w/scenes of families using the View-Master, lists various reels & other accessories, ca. 1950, closed 10 x 12 3/4" (ILLUS. open, top of page) **15**
Reel - 1939-40, views of The New York World's Fair, four different reels offered, each.. **30**
Reel - 1940, Golden Gate International Exposition, four different reels w/scenes of the fair on Treasure Island, San Francisco, each... **30**

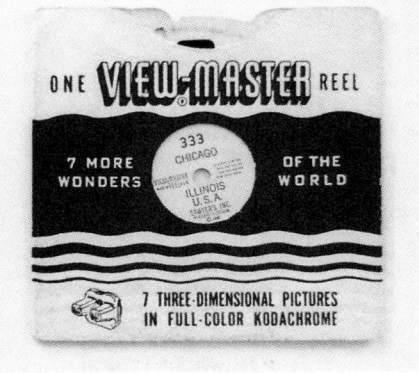

View-Master Reel No. 333 - Chicago

Reel - 1948, Chicago, Illinois, No. 333, seven views of sites around the city (ILLUS.)........ **10**

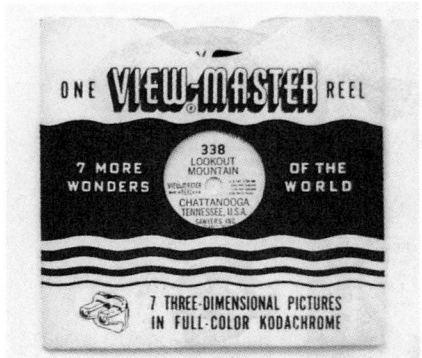

Reel No. 338 - Lookout Mountain

Reel - 1948, Lookout Mountain, Chattanooga, Tennessee, No. 338 (ILLUS.) 10

1950 "Adventures of Sam Sawyer" Reel

Reel - 1950, "Adventures of Sam Sawyer - Sam Flies to the Moon" (ILLUS.) 20

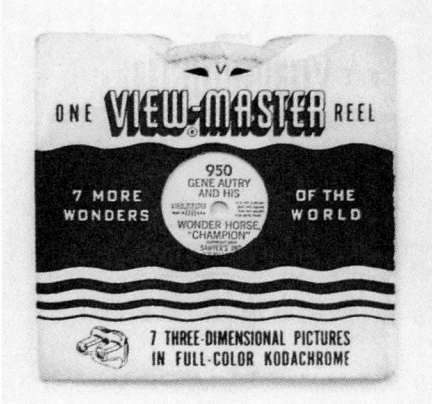

Early Gene Autry View-Master Reel

Reel - 1950, "Gene Autry and His Wonder Horse, Champion," No. 950 (ILLUS.) 7
Reel - 1950, "Roy Rogers - King of the Cowboys & 'Trigger,'" No. 945 10
Reel - 1950, "Rudolph the Red-Nosed Reindeer," based on the 1939 Robert L. May story, No. FT-25 15
Reel - 1950s, "A Day at the Circus - The Ringling Brothers and Barnum & Bailey Circus," No. 701 15
Reel - 1950s, "Homes of the Movie Stars," No. 220, includes homes of Loretta Young, Jack Benny, Cary Grant, Ida Lupino, Robert Taylor & Barbara Stanwyck, Robert Montgomery, & Ray Milland 20

Booklet for "Snow White" Reel

Reel - 1950s, "Snow White and the Seven Dwarfs," non-Walt Disney story in a single reel, No. FT4, reel & booklet (ILLUS. of booklet)... 6
Reel - 1950s, "Tarzan Rescues Cheetah," No. 975, reel & booklet.. 8

"Wild Birds in Natural Habitat" Reel

Reel - 1950s, "Wild Birds in Natural Habitat," No. 895A-C (ILLUS.).................................. 10

"Fire Fighters in Action" Reel & Booklet

Reel - 1951, "Life with the Cowboys - Cattle
Roundup & Branding," No. 942 .... **25**
Reel - 1951, "Tom and Jerry in The Cat
Trapper," No. 810 .... **8**

Reel - 1953, "It Came From Outer Space,"
preview reel for movie starring Richard
Carlson & Barbara Rush, rare **250**
Reel - 1953, "The House of Wax," preview
reel for Warner Bros. 3D movie starring
Vincent Price & Frank Lovejoy, rare.............. **260**

"Aircraft Carrier in Action" Reels

Reel - 1952, "Aircraft Carrier in Action at
Sea," No. 760A-C (ILLUS.) **40**
Reel - 1953, "Fire Fighters in Action," No.
710 (ILLUS. of sleeve, reel & booklet, top
of page) **18**

Early Tom Corbett, Space Cadet Reel

Reel - 1954, "Tom Corbett - Space Cadet -
The Mystery of the Asteroids," based on
the early television show, No. 970A-C,
set of 3 (ILLUS. of one) **35**

1955 Boy Scout Jamboree Reel Set

Reel - 1955, "Eighth World Boy Scout Jamboree," held at Niagara-on-the-Lake, Canada, scenes of the Jamboree, No. 435A-C (ILLUS. with original booklet, bottom previous page) **45**

Reel - 1956-1959, Disneyland series of six reels, No. 175 - Main Street USA, No. 176 - Frontierland, No. 177 - Adventureland, No. 178 - Fantasyland, No. 179 - Tomorrowland, and No. 180 - New Orleans Square, each reel.................................... **22**

Reel - 1960, "Little League World Series on ABC Television's Wide World of Sports," No. B940 .... **60**

Reel - 1960s, "ABC Television's Wide World of Sports - World Bobsled Championships," No. B949 .... **90**

Reel - 1960s, "Lost in Space," based on the television program, No. B482 .... **70**

"Santa's Workshop" Reel Set

Reel - 1970s, "Santa's Workshop - North Pole, New York," three reels (ILLUS.)............... **4**

American Bicentennial Reel Set

Reel - 1974, "America's Bicentennial Celebration - The 20th Century," set of three reels (ILLUS.) **8**

Reel - 1980s, "Alf," based on the television show about the furry alien, No. 4082.............. **10**

Fairy Castle & U-505 Submarine Set

Reel - 1983, "Colleen Moore's Fairy Castle and the U-505," featuring two exhibits at the Chicago Museum of Science and Industry, the Fairy Castle & a German submarine, three reels w/booklet (ILLUS.) **4**

WEATHERVANES

Arrow Weathervane

Arrow, zinc, rotating arrow on ball & pedestal base w/pineapple finial & four flower stems coming off ball, seam splits, repair at front half of arrow, surface rust, base 11" sq., overall 43" h. (ILLUS.).................... **$360**

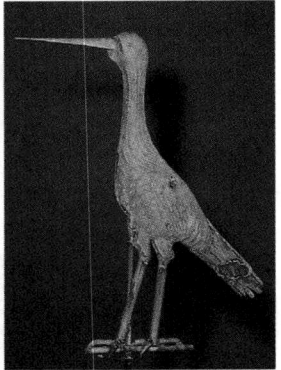

Molded Copper Heron Weathervane

Heron, molded copper, flattened full body, verdigris surface w/traces of old yellow polychrome, mounted on rod & metal plate attached to wood base, America, late 19th c., 36" l., 49" h. (ILLUS., previous page) **39,950**

Prancing Horse Weathervane

Horse, copper, prancing stance, full body mounted on original rod support, verdigris patina over areas of gilt, America, 19th c., 25" l., 22" h. (ILLUS.) **10,350**

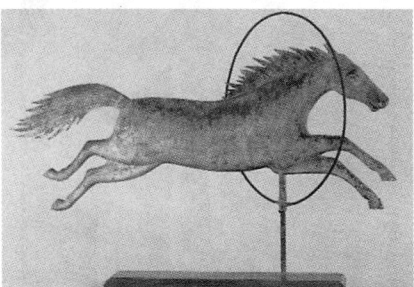

Jumping Horse Weathervane

Horse, gilt copper & cast metal, horse w/copper body, flame-style mane, stamped tail & cast-metal head jumping through iron hoop, set in custom wood stand w/metal rod, A.L. Jewell & Co., America, one old tiny split to front hoof, 30" l., 15 1/4" h. from top of hoop to bottom of hoop (ILLUS.) **16,100**

Walking Horse Weathervane

Horse, molded copper, walking stance, verdigris surface w/traces of paint & gilt, includes black metal stand, America, 19th c., dents, seam separations, 26 3/4" l., 24 1/4" h. (ILLUS.)....................................... **2,585**

Running Horse Weathervane

Horse, molded copper & zinc, running stance, flattened full body w/zinc ears, vestiges of putty-colored paint & verdigris surfaces, no stand, America, 19th c., seam separations, dents, 32" l., 19" h. (ILLUS.).. **2,233**

Horse & Jockey on Stand

Horse & jockey, the horse composed of molded sheet copper w/cast-iron head, the jockey having zinc head w/copper visor on his hat, verdigris patina w/traces of gilt, includes black metal stand, America, 19th c., dents, minor seam separations, 34" l., 19 1/4" h. (ILLUS.) **8,813**

Molded Copper Rooster Weathervane

Rooster, molded copper, Hamburg rooster w/flattened full body, verdigris patina w/traces of gilt, attributed to L.W. Cushing & Sons, Waltham, Massachusetts, late 19th c., repairs, bullet holes, dents, 29" l., 28" h. (ILLUS., previous page) **25,850**

Rooster, molded copper, Hamburg rooster w/flattened full body, verdigris patina w/traces of gilt, w/iron pole, copper sphere & parts of cast-iron directionals, attributed to L.W. Cushing & Sons, Waltham, Massachusetts, late 19th c., minor dents, 29 1/4" l., 28 1/2" h. **41,125**

Red-painted Tin Rooster Weathervane

Rooster, tin, narrow full body w/sheet cutout tail, a round hollow rod at center of body extending through leg, painted red, crimped & soldered edge, 19th c., rusted hole to bottom edge, some repair to beak & some loss to comb & tail tip, 28 3/4" h. (ILLUS.) **2,300**

Handmade Whale Weathervane

Whale, copper, handmade body dovetailed at seams, w/applied fin & tail, old verdigris & oxidized finish, some dents & scuffs, about 33" l. (ILLUS.) **2,300**

WEDDING MEMORABILIA

Once considered valuable only to the persons who owned them, wedding cake toppers have become increasingly sought after collectibles. Sugar confections in European bakeries in the early 1800s started the true "icing on the cake" idea. By the late 1800s, American bakeries were copying from their European counterparts, using marzipan, gum paste, wood, plaster of Paris and even crystal beads. Porcelain, celluloid, composition, saltware, plastic and china would all be used over the years in the construction of ever more sophisticated toppers.

The majority have no identifying marks with which to accurately date them, although a few produced in the 1940s bear dates and manufacturers' names. Toppers are mostly dated by materials used, clothing styles of bride and groom, and other characteristics such as age-related patina.

Related memorabilia is a wonderful enhancement to a wedding topper collection. Included would be announcement cards for bridal showers and weddings, favors, old marriage licenses, bridal books and an assortment of unique handcrafted and commercially produced items.

Old wedding mementos, especially cake toppers, are very fragile and irreplaceable. Handle them with care. Prices reflect items in good to fine condition with no serious flaws or missing parts.

Cake Toppers

1900-1920

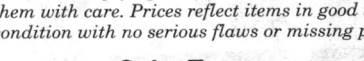

Gum Paste Wedding Cake Topper

Gum paste, bride & groom, the bride wearing long gown w/high-necked collar, full-length sleeves, net veil, the groom in black tuxedo w/long overcoat, standing under bower of dogwood & lily of the valley arrangement, on round base w/latticework pedestal, 6" h. (ILLUS.) **$100**

Gum paste, bride & groom, the bride wearing long layered, draped gown, arms folded to one side, the groom wearing black tuxedo w/tails, standing in arch of dogwood & lilies of the valley & two green & white pussy willow spikes, on round base w/filigreed pedestal, 8" h. **100**

Plaster of Paris Cake Topper

Plaster of Paris, bride & groom, the bride wearing gown w/tiered skirt & net veil, standing in front of spray of white leaves & flowers w/clear bell in center, on cylindrical base & footed pedestal w/leaf design, the pedestal feet half circles bearing intricate carvings, 7" (ILLUS.) **100**

1920s

Bisque Kewpie Wedding Cake Topper

Bisque, bride & groom Kewpies standing together under arch of lilies of the valley & big plastic bell, the bride w/net veil, on pedestal base w/pierced design, 10" h. (ILLUS.) **150**

Gum paste, bride & groom, the bride in short skirt, the groom in black tuxedo, w/sprig of flowers & silver glass bell, on pedestal base, 7" h. **75**

1930s

Bisque, bride & groom atop oval base & pedestal that conceals music box, decorated w/flower arbor of lilies of the valley, dogwood & satin ribbon, 11" h. **150**

Bisque, bride & groom "googlies" w/jointed arms, dressed in crepe paper, standing on cardboard steps under four-poster bower w/paper fringe, crepe paper bell & satin ribbon trim, 6" h. **75**

Bisque set: bride, groom, preacher, maid of honor & best man "googlies," 5 1/2" h., w/jointed arms, 2 1/2" h. celluloid flower girl & ring bearer, all dressed in crepe paper, also satin kneeling pillow, wood & satin kneeler, crepe paper-covered wooden stepped flower bower, 10 pcs. **250**

Celluloid, bride, groom, best man, maid of honor & preacher, the bride in gown of taffeta & netting, groom & best man in black coats, dove grey trousers & top hats, preacher in black frock coat, maid of honor in dress of pale blue netting, 8 1/2" h., 5 pcs. **125**

Chalkware, bride & groom under domed roof supported by four round columns on round base & pedestal, 10" h. **50**

Art Deco Bride & Groom Cake Topper

Composition, bride & groom, Art Deco-style, the skirt of the bride's form-fitting gown swirling to form the scroll-decorated pedestal base, the figures standing under arbor of flowers & Bakelite bell, 5" h. (ILLUS.).. **75**

Composition, bride & groom on three-tiered base resembling wedding cake, under arbor of white velvet leaves & flowers w/Bakelite bell, 7" h. **35**

Crepe Paper Wedding Cake Toppers

Crepe paper, bride & groom, separate figures on cardboard disk bases, each w/stylized drawn features, the bride w/blonde hair, a net veil & carrying a bouquet, 6" h., pr. (ILLUS.)..................................... **30**

Plastic & crepe paper, bride, groom & preacher, each w/hard plastic head, the bride wearing netting over crepe paper grown, the groom wearing crepe paper cutaway, the preacher in cassock & surplice, wearing glasses & holding Bible, 6" h., 3 pcs. **125**

1940s

Bisque, bride & groom, World War II-era, the groom in crepe paper blue Navy uniform & white cap, the bride in crepe paper & net wedding gown, 4" h........................ **175**

Chalkware, bride & groom under bower wrapped in netting & clear cellophane held in place by faux pearls & center paper bell, on cardboard base & pedestal, the pedestal wrapped w/pleated ribbon, 7 1/2" h. **65**

Chalkware, bride & groom, World War II-era, the groom a sailor wearing blue uniform, the couple flanked by two 48-star American flags, flower spikes behind each flag, 4 1/2" h... **100**

Composition 1940s Cake Topper

Composition, bridal & groom, single mold on base decorated to look like wedding cake, under bell-shaped arbor of satin flowers & netting, Cake Novelty Co., Los Angeles, California, 9" h. (ILLUS.).................... **50**

Soldier & Bride Cake Topper

Composition, bride & groom, World War II-era Army officer in khaki dress uniform & bride standing together under arch trimmed w/white lilies of the valley & centered by 48-star American paper flag, 4 1/2" h. (ILLUS.).. **100**

Electric, bride, groom, five bridesmaids, five groomsmen & flower girl, approximately 12" h., 13 pcs..................................... **100**

Plastic, bride & groom standing in cathedral window at top of three steps flanked by flower-filled urns, 8" h. **65**

Saltware, bride & groom, World War II-era, single mold, the groom in two-tone blue coat & trousers w/white belt & white & blue uniform hat, 3 1/2" h. **125**

1950s

Bisque, children in dress-up wedding costumes, marked "Made in Japan," 4" h. **40**

Glazed Ceramic Bride & Groom Cake Toppers

Ceramic, bride & groom, separate figures, the groom in morning coat & striped trousers holding gloves in right hand, the bride wearing gown w/starched beige net overskirt & veil, holding flowers in right hand & looking at ring on left hand, glazed decoration, 5 3/4" h., pr. (ILLUS.) **40**

Chalkware, 25th anniversary, bride & groom encircled by stubby pillars connected w/silver chain, a silver flaked numeral "25" serving as backdrop, two silver bells decorating front, 7 1/2" h. **75**

Chalkware, bride & groom under double bower of flowers & leaves & filigreed bell, on plastic base & filigreed pedestal, 6" h. **35**

Plastic, bride & groom flanked by two large bells turned on sides & filled w/flowers, the couple dwarfed by two white swans in front of bells, 4 1/2" h. **35**

1960s

Bisque, bride & groom, the groom in Army dress uniform, 4" h. **75**

Bisque, bride & groom, the groom in Marine dress uniform, 4" h. **75**

Gum paste, 50th wedding anniversary, gold foil leaves & flowers, a gold die-cut paper wreath in center commemorating the year, 9" h. **50**

Plastic, 50th wedding anniversary, grey-haired bride & groom, the bride wearing gold gown, under archway of lattice hearts threaded w/gold ribbon, 7 1/2" h. **40**

Plastic, bride & groom, the groom in generic uniform & bride w/Jackie Kennedy look, 4 1/2" h. **25**

Plastic, bride & groom, two doves holding wedding rings, plastic daisies w/bright green leaves decorating bower, 6" h. **25**

1970s

Plastic, bride & groom, the bride in lace overskirt, the groom in white dinner jacket, under bower of lilies of the valley, roses & center bell w/pearl bead swags, 9" h. **20**

1970s Plastic Cake Topper

Plastic, bride & groom, the bride in taffeta overskirt, standing under half-arch of white cabbage roses & lilies of the valley, on domed pedestal w/cut-out decoration, 7" h. (ILLUS.)... **25**

Plastic, white doves of spun cotton nesting on round plastic base decorated w/netting, lilies of the valley, silver bells & faux wedding rings, 4" h... **45**

1980s

Bisque, ethnic bride & groom under porcelain archway w/white doves perching in porcelain flower swag, 5" h. **40**

Black Bride & Groom Cake Toppers

Plastic, black bride & groom gazing at each other, the bride wearing satin overskirt, under arch of white flowers, leaves & ribbons, on domed pedestal w/hearts & swags design, 7" h. (ILLUS.) 35

1990s
Cast resin, pastel-hued bride & groom w/intricately detailed clothing, under arch of roses, ribbons, leaves & bells, 7" h 20
Ceramic, bride & groom in very pale pastel colors, glazed finish, 7 1/2" h. 25

2000+
Bisque, bride & groom holding hands, the bride wearing lace veil, 2000, 5" h. 20
Ceramic, bride & groom dancing, the bride wearing gown w/intricate detail, all white glaze, 2000, 6" h. 20

Miscellaneous

1900-1920
Booklet, "Cupid's Game of Hearts," hard cover, string binding, six full-color lithographed pages, copyright by Hayes Lithographing Co., Buffalo, N.Y., 1911, 6 x 8" 5
Marriage certificate, full color illustration of biblical scene of man, woman & child in field near pond, a spray of flowers decorating one edge, a ribbon banner at base reading "Whither thou goest, I will go and where thou lodgest, I will lodge, thy people shall be my people and thy God my God," Concordia Publishing House, St. Louis, Missouri, 14 x 18" (ILLUS., top of next column) 20
Postcard, wedding, full color illustration of bride, groom & preacher w/caption "Tying the Knot," copyright by Julies Bien & Co., New York, 1907 2

1907 Marriage Certificate

1920s
Announcement of engagement, paper card w/full-color illustration of engagement ring & Cupid holding message that opens to reveal name of engaged 3

Bride & Groom Cut-outs

Cut-outs, thick cardboard, figures of elegantly clad bride & groom, the bride in short dress w/long train & full veil, the groom in cutaway, w/tabs in back allowing figures to stand alone, "copyright Newman Pub & Art Co, NY," 1921, 4 3/4" h. (ILLUS.) 20
Greeting card for wedding, single-thickness heavy cardboard, color floral illustration on one border, 3 x 4" 5
Placecard for shower, paper, full-color engagement ring & profile of bride, the name tag attached to ring w/pink silk ribbon, 1 x 3", 7 1/2" h. 20

1930s

Bride's book, heavy paper cover reading "Our Wedding Day," inside color pages w/poems & sentimental sayings, entry pages for recording names, guests, etc., copyright Abington Press, 1936, 6 x 8" 5

Greeting card for wedding, heavy cardboard, showing bride in profile holding bouquet of flowers, "Created by Paramount" on back, 4 x 5" 1

Salt & peppers, cast iron, figural bride & groom, w/enamel paint decoration, the groom in black tux, the bride carrying pink flowers, 3 1/2", pr. 25

1940s

1942 Bride's Book

Bride's book, padded satin cover w/color illustration of bride & groom & "For Your Wedding Day" in fancy script, the binding tied w/white silken cord, 1942, 4 x 5" (ILLUS.) 5

Bridal Shower Favor

Favor for bridal shower, bride's face w/painted features & net veil topping candy-filled cylindrical base wrapped in clear cellophane & tied w/ribbon, 3 1/2" h. (ILLUS.) 5

Crepe Paper Floral Bouquet

Floral bouquet, crepe paper, five handmade long-stemmed roses in cream & pale pink, w/wire stems wrapped in green crepe paper, each about 10" l., the set (ILLUS.) 5

Wedding Bell Shower Placecards

Placecard for wedding shower, paper, in the shape of two overlapping silver bells decorated w/silhouette of man's bust in profile on one, a woman's on the other, outline of bows at top, the bells opening to display name & seating arrangement (ILLUS.) 2

1950s

Miniature Bride's Basket

Bride's basket, ceramic, miniature glazed form w/tiny bride & groom seated on rim, color accents & gold trim, marked "Japan" on bottom, 2 1/2" (ILLUS., previous page)... 5

Favor for wedding, china, miniature cup & saucer, the cup filled w/nuts & candy, enclosed in netting & tied w/ribbon, white w/gold trim, marked "Made in Japan," 1 1/4" h. 3

Napkins, paper, for bridal shower & wedding reception, w/full-color illustrations, 12" sq., pr. 6

Plate for wedding cake, ceramic, center w/images of bride & groom in relief, scalloped rim, glazed finish, 10" d. 20

Talcum powder container, bisque, figural bridal couple, sprinkler holes in bouquet, headpiece & back of figurine, made for the Coty Company, 4 1/2" h. 5

1960s

Bride & Groom Candle Climbers

Candle climbers, ceramic, bride & groom, glazed paint decoration, the bride w/blonde hair & carrying pink, yellow & green bouquet w/pink ribbon trim & pink headband, the groom in grey, black & white formal attire, holding top hat, marked "Napco," 3 1/4" h., pr. (ILLUS.) 20

Covered Container Wedding Favor

Favor for wedding, plastic, cov., white cylindrical container w/figures of bride & groom standing on lid, Hong Kong, 3 1/2" h. (ILLUS.)... 2

Ceramic Convertible with Bride & Groom

Model of automobile, ceramic convertible w/large floral decoration applied to hood, plastic figures of bride & groom in front seat, glazed color decoration w/gold trim, stamped "Japan" on bottom, 5 1/2" l. (ILLUS.)... 5

1970s

50th Anniversary Bell

Bell, china, pair of lovebirds perched on top, front of bell reading "50th Golden Anniversary" in gold lettering, marked "Georgian - fine bone china," 2 1/4" h. (ILLUS.)......... 5

WESTERN CHARACTER COLLECTIBLES

Since the closing of the Western frontier in the late 19th century, the myth of the American cowboy has loomed large in popular fiction. With the growth of the motion picture industry early in this century, cowboy heroes became a mainstay of the entertainment industry. By the 1920s major Western heroes were a big draw at the box office, this popularity continuing with the dawning of the TV

age in the 1950s. We list here a variety of collectibles relating to all American Western personalities popular this century. ALSO SEE: Horse
Collectibles.

Annie Oakley book, "Annie Oakley in Dan-
ger at Diablo," Whitman, 1955...................... **$15**
Annie Oakley game, Bradley, 1950s **50**
Bat Masterson book, Whitman, 1960............... **12**
Bonanza game, Bonanza Michigan Rum-
my, Parker Brothers, 1964 .... **35**
Cisco Kid coloring book, 1950 .... **18**

Dale Evans Red Felt Hat

Dale Evans hat, blocked red felt w/white
ribbon trim & white stitching & neck cord
w/natural wooden chin slide, w/rare color
photo tag attached w/original string
w/picture of Roy Rogers & Dale Evans &
Trigger above words "Best Western
Brand" w/"Roy Rogers' Pledge to parents" on back of tag w/company name, in
original mailer box, Miller Brothers Hat
Company, slight water marks on interior
of crown, size "Small" (ILLUS.) **276**
Gunsmoke book, "Showdown on Front
Street," Whitman, 1969 (ILLUS. right
w/holster set) **14**
Gunsmoke game, Lowell, 1958 .... **75**

Gunsmoke Holster Set & Book

Gunsmoke two-gun holster set, leather,
buff w/dark trim & "GUNSMOKE" on belt,
"Marshal Matt Dillon" on holsters (ILLUS.
left w/book) **40**

"Have Gun, Will Travel" Book

Have Gun, Will Travel book, hard bound,
cover w/color illustration of Paladin in saloon holding gun, another character
peering over saloon doors at him, "Have
Gun, Will Travel" in bold red lettering,
"featuring PALADIN of the CBS Television Program" in small black print below,
Whitman, 1959 (ILLUS.)................................ **22**
Have Gun, Will Travel game, Parker Broth-
ers, 1959 .... **80**
Hopalong Cassidy game, Official Hopal-
ong Cassidy Lasso Game, Transogram,
1950... **100**
Lone Ranger game, Lone Ranger and Ton-
to Spin Game, Pressman, 1967...................... **25**
Lone Ranger (The) coloring book, 1951 .... **30**

The Lone Ranger Mounted Scarf

Lone Ranger (The) scarf, silk, black,
mounted on photo on foam core, the bust
portrait of Clayton Moore as the Lone
Ranger in foreground, the head of Silver
in the background, the screen-worn scarf
mounted on photo at character's neck as
if part of the photo, "The Lone Ranger" &
"The Personal Property of Clayton
Moore" printed in upper right of photo,
24" sq. (ILLUS.) **560**
Rifleman (The) book, Whitman, 1959 .... **20**

Rin Tin Tin Coloring Book

Rin Tin Tin coloring book, 1959 (ILLUS.)........ **20**
Roy Rogers book, "Roy Rogers and The
Enchanted Canyon" Whitman, 1954.............. **25**

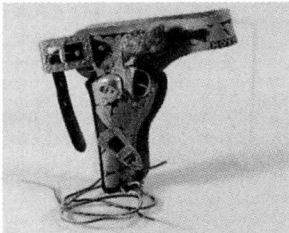

Roy Rogers Gun & Holster Set

Roy Rogers gun & holster set, two-gun
set w/studded, jeweled, heavily embossed black & buff leather belt & holsters w/"RR" badges & buckles, & nickel-
plated die-cast Roy Rogers Kilgore 9" l.
guns w/plastic grips, grips have been replaced, bullets missing from belt (ILLUS.) **345**

Poster Featuring Tom Mix

Tom Mix poster, rectangular, full color oval
bust portrait of white-hatted Mix under

"TOM MIX CIRCUS" in dark bold letters,
oval at bottom containing facsimile Tom
Mix signature over "Entertainment Insur-
ance - Plus Courtesy, Honesty - and Ap-
preciation," all on textured gold/orange
ground, 28 x 42" (ILLUS.) **605**
Tonto coloring book, 1957 .... **15**
Virginian (The) game, Transogram, 1962 .... **80**
Wagon Train game, Bradley, 1960 .... **40**
Zorro coloring book, 1958................................. **28**
Zorro game, Parker Brothers, 1966 .... **75**

WOOD SCULPTURES

*American folk sculpture is an important part
of the American art scene today. Skilled wood
carvers turned out ships' figureheads, cigar store
figures, plaques and carousel animals of stylized
beauty and great appeal. The wooden shipbuild-
ing industry, which had originally nourished this
folk art, declined after the Civil War, and the talented carvers then turned to producing figures for
tobacconists' shops, carousel animals and show
figures for circuses. These figures and other early
ornamental carvings that have survived the elements and years are eagerly sought.*

Larger-than-life Carnival Figures

Carnival figure, hollow-bodied woman
w/detachable arms w/bayonet-type
mounts to hold flag or banner, brown
hair, wearing polychrome yellow classical Greco-Roman gathered & draping
garment, on rectangular base, ca. 1880-
1900, mild age cracks to upper body,
wood chips, rubs & wear to paint, 96" h.
(ILLUS. left w/other carnival figure) **$7,763**
Carnival figure, hollow-bodied woman
w/detachable arms w/bayonet-type
mounts to hold flag or banner, fair-haired,
wearing polychrome green classical Greco-Roman gathered & draping garment,
on rectangular base, ca. 1880-1900, mild
age cracks to upper body, wood chips,
rubs & wear to paint, 96" h. (ILLUS. right
w/other carnival figure) **8,625**

Carved Pine Cat with Traces of Paint

Cat, pine, minimalist style carving of feline lying in relaxed crouch position, carved in full relief, mounted on pine board, vestiges of white paint, America, 19th c., 15 x 31 5/8", 10 3/8" h. including base (ILLUS., top of page)................................... **10,575**

Double-headed Eagle

Eagle, double-headed eagle w/spread wings, carved in the style of John H. Bellamy, w/heads pointed to either side, sharply hooked beaks w/red tongues, deeply carved eyes, feathers & talons, front view w/triangle shape in breast, probably Masonic symbol, 30" w., 30 1/2" h. (ILLUS.).. **5,750**

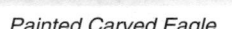

Painted Carved Eagle

Eagle, pine, carved in the style of John H. Bellamy, w/head pointed to side, squared beak w/red tongue, spread wings w/paint-enhanced feathers, greenish/white patina w/some gilt remaining, 26" l. (ILLUS.)... **1,840**

Eagle with banner, pine, carved bird w/head pointed to side, sharply hooked beak w/red tongue, red eye, spread wings w/paint-enhanced feathers & red & blue line decoration at tail, attached to pole w/red-bordered banner reading "Don't Give Up The Ship!" in blue & red on white, a carved white five-pointed star on blue at one end, by John H. Bellamy, Kittery Point, Maine, repaired break where banner meets pole, 26" l. (ILLUS., bottom of page) **24,150**

Carved Eagle with Banner

Figures of Seated Man & Woman

Figures of seated couple, carved figures in traditional costume seated on bench, the woman wearing red skirt w/white apron & fringed shawl w/pink rose, green brimmed hat, the man wearing shorts w/suspenders w/design resembling embroidery, knee socks & green Alpine hat, holding a lute in one hand, his other arm around the shoulders of the woman, life-size, original paint worn in many places, 36" w., about 53" h. (ILLUS.) **3,450**

Folk Art Perched Owl

Owl, folk art-style carving of bird on perch, off-white w/faint black feather highlights, inset carved eyes painted gold & black, sculpted beak, feet, ears & tail feathers, mounted on dowel w/brass fitting, one ear repaired, minor chips to tail feathers, 16" h. (ILLUS.)... **4,025**

Painted Carved Folk Art Owl

Owl, minimalist folk art style, w/attached legs, simple black dash paint strokes indicating feathers, painted black beak, perched on rectangular base, 14 1/2" h. (ILLUS.) **1,380**

Carved Wooden Soldier Whirligig

Whirligig, carved & painted soldier wearing faded red jacket w/black belt, tin cap, carved & paint-enhanced facial features, two-tone wooden knife-blade arms, 33" h. (ILLUS.) **2,013**

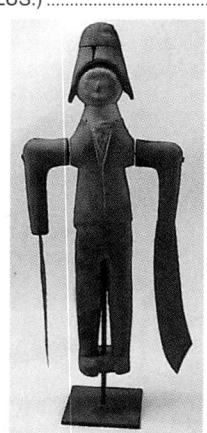

Folk Art Hessian Soldier Whirligig

Whirligig, folk art Hessian-style soldier wearing blue pants, red coat & white shirt, red, black & blue hat, the coat w/tuxedo-type tail made of separate piece of wood screwed onto rear, eyes & mouth indicated by minimal carving, the protruding nose nailed to face, arms extending to 8" shaped metal knife blades, 7 3/4" w. at shoulders, 17 3/4" h. (ILLUS., previous page).............................. **5,750**

WOODENWARES

Bowl, cov., mahogany w/old red, pumpkin orange & black painted line decoration, small turned foot below the wide half-round bowl w/a fitted domed cover w/button finial, found in Indiana, 19th c., 7 3/4" d., 5 3/4" h. **$550**

Bowl, turned burl, low turned foot below the rounded flaring sides w/a turned rim, good figure & dark patina, 19th c., 9" d., 2 1/2" h. **1,380**

Fine Large Turned Burl Bowl

Bowl, burl, heavy deep turned sides w/carved lines on base & rim, fine figure, interior crack, 19th c., 12 1/4" d., 4 3/4" h. (ILLUS.)... **345**

Bowl, turned ash burl, very wide & deep sides w/incised decorative line below the rim, good nut brown color & tight figure, large size, 19th c., 18 1/2" d., 6 1/2" h. (short rim age crack) **3,080**

Bowl, hand-hewn walnut, unusual shallow leaf shape, mellow brown finish, 8 3/8 x 21", 4 1/2" h. (minor rim chip) **86**

Bowl, hand-turned w/turned foot, widely flaring fairly shallow form, dark brown finish, raised rim band, 23 1/4" d., 6 3/8" h. (age split) **201**

Bucket, stave construction w/two steel bands, slightly tapering cylindrical form w/wire bail handle, old light brown over tan paint, illegible writing on the bottom, 19th c., 6 3/8" h. plus handle **83**

Cake board, double-sided, rectangular, one side carved w/a full-length figure of a man in 18th c. costume, the other side carved w/a matching figure of a woman, some worm holes, early, 10" w., 33" l. (ILLUS. of both sides, top next column) **575**

Cookie board, rectangular flat board w/small rectangular integral handle at one end, chip-carved in the center w/a large compass star framed by geometric carved corners, good patina, 19th c., 6 3/4" w., overall 12 3/4" l. **468**

Early Figure-carved Cake Board

Jar, cov., burl, wide urn-shaped turned body on a wide disk foot, fitted domed cover w/raised button finial, good patina & good figure, traces of dark red color, 19th c., 6" h. **7,700**

Jar, cov., slightly tapering cylindrical shape w/base & rim molding, deep cranberry red stain, stamped label "Berea Souvenir 1909," attributed to Pease of Ohio, 5 1/8" d., 6 5/8" h. (minor edge wear) **330**

Jar, cov., turned hardwood, squatty bulbous body on a narrow flared round foot, fitted low domed cover w/urn-shaped finial, old varnish finish w/good patina, attributed to Pease of Ohio, 19th c., 6 1/2" d. 6 3/4" h. (age crack).. **660**

Jar, cov., turned poplar w/worn original vinegar decoration in reddish brown over green over the mustard yellow base coat, wide flat bottom w/low curved sides, fitted domed cover w/large button finial, found in Indiana, 19th c., 8" d., 6 3/4" h. (edge chip on cover, age split in base) **770**

Jar, cov., turned squatty bulbous body on a small round foot, fitted round cover w/knob finial, wire bail handle, soft, shiny varnish finish, attributed to Pease of Ohio, 7 1/4" d., 7 1/2" h. (age crack in cover, glued split) **605**

Jar, cov., barrel-shaped w/ring-turned base & rim band, fitted slightly domed cover w/small button knob, overall fan-shaped vinegar sponge decoration in red over mustard yellow, good color, 19th c., 8 3/4" d., 9" h. (glued repair, damage on cover flange & age crack) **1,210**

Kraut cutter, pine w/good patina & traces of old red, rectangular board w/screwed-on side rail, angled blade, a heart-shaped cut-out crest w/hanging hole, 19th c., 7 3/4" w., 19" l. (wear, some old splits).......... **110**

Kraut cutter, two-tier style, hickory or ash w/old brown surface, steel blade & brass fittings in the top level, the two levels supported between pierced scroll-cut sides, 19th c., 7 x 13", 7 1/4" h. (age splits, one scallop missing) 86

Kraut cutter, walnut, rectangular board w/screwed side rails, angled blade, round crest w/hanging hole, old patina, 7 1/2 x 24 1/2" 83

Mangle or smoothing board, poplar, long heavy rectangular board w/integral turned handle projecting from one end, chip-carved edges, incised overall w/folk art designs of flowering tulips, double hearts, compass stars & dated "1798," old refinishing, 29 1/2" l. 385

Mortar & pestle, turned burl w/flame graining, a thick ringed foot below the wide cylindrical bowl, pestle of darker wood, probably lignum vitae, 19th c., overall 7" h., the set (age splits)................................. 374

Rare Early Hanging Pipe Box

Pipe box, hanging-type, red-stained, upright nearly square form constructed w/rose-head nails, serpentine-cut sloping top rims w/a round backboard top w/a hanging hole, a small dovetailed drawer w/ring handle at the base, early, 4 1/2 x 5 1/2", 18" h. (ILLUS.) **4,313**

Spoon rack, hanging-type, butternut or walnut w/old faint bluish green graining on a black ground, red bird's claw decoration, three racks mounted on a vertical board w/incurved sides between each rack, arched & pierce-cut crest & triangular cut-out scallops along the bottom edge, 19th c., 10" w., 20" h. (nailed splits, one scallop repaired) 288

Spoon rack, painted pine, a narrow shelf w/narrow scroll-cut apron & fifteen cutouts for spoons mortised into narrow scalloped end supports, rosehead nails, old black paint, early, 5 x 13", 13 1/4" h. (some regluing at joints, age splits & chip on top edge) 413

Old Painted Sugar Bucket

Sugar bucket, cov., stave construction w/three finger lappets w/copper tacks, swing bentwood hickory bail handle, old mustard yellow paint, 19th c., minor wear & edge chips, 13 3/4" h. (ILLUS.) **460**

Sugar bucket, cov., stave construction w/three finger lappets w/copper tacks, old bluish grey paint over earlier colors, bottom painted green, arched bentwood swing handle, 19th c., 21" h. (old chips on the lid) 489

Tape loom, floor model, a heavy cross-form base centered by a ring-turned wormy maple post supporting the pegged-in wide upright squared finely slatted loom top, 19th c., 39 1/2" h. (one base bar replaced, one side of loom a replacement)....... **110**

WRITING ACCESSORIES

Inkstands & Inkwells

Arts & Crafts Decorated Copper Well

Copper well, Arts & Crafts style, a rectangular metal case w/sloping sides & outswept scroll feet, the hinged flattened rectangular cover opening to original double inserts, decorated w/stylized flowers in red, green & blue, stamped mark of the Buffalo Art Craft Shop, Buffalo, New York, early 20th c., original dark patina, 3 x 7 1/2" (ILLUS.).. **$403**

French Louis XV-Style Inkstand

Gilt-bronze stand, Louis XV-style, an ornate oblong scroll-cast stand fitted at one end w/a covered cylindrical holder for a blown glass inkwell, underside touch-marked "EG" in block letters, w/a later rose gold-mounted & inlaid carved ivory nib pen, France, late 19th c., stand 4 x 7 1/4", 3 1/4" h. (ILLUS., previous page)... **460**

Empire Style Marble & Bronze Inkstand

Red marble & bronze stand, First Empire taste, the rectangular red marble base fitted w/patinated bronze covered center ink vase flanked by a pens vase & short vase, trimmed in gilt-bronze & on gilt-bronze feet, France, late 19th c., 6 x 13 1/4", 7 1/2" h. (ILLUS.)........................ **690**

Staffordshire pottery well, figural, model of a bird & hatchlings in a sanded nest, white w/blue wings, babies in yellow, nest in yellow & pink, gilt trim, mid-19th c., 2 5/8" h... **165**

Staffordshire pottery well, figural, model of a seated Spaniel in white w/red spots, on a cobalt blue pillow, traces of gilt trim, 19th c., 3 3/4" h. (worn black on muzzle) **275**

Staffordshire pottery well, figural, model of a swan in white w/pink wings & gilt trim, lying on a coleslaw nest in pink, yellow & orange, mid-19th c., 3 1/4" h. **204**

Lap Desks & Writing Boxes

Mahogany & mahogany veneer, rectangular form w/hinged fold-over top section opening to a divided interior w/worn green felt, interior pencil inscription reads "Property of Hon. Parker Tuck of Bucksport, Maine, Judge of probate. Hancock county for forty years. (1840-1880)," includes several sheets of stationery for the State of Maine Senate from the 1890s, old finish, 11 x 22", 8 3/4" h. (age split in top) **385**

Index

Carlton Persian Vase with Landscape,
$350-$400

also see ABC Plates; Advertising Items; Barberiana; Cat Collectibles; Disney Collectibles; Hawaiiana; Horse Collectibles; Kitchenwares; Plant Waterers; Writing Accessories

Chairs - see Furniture

Chandeliers - see Lighting Devices

Character Collectibles.........................303
also see Banks; Candy Containers; Cat Collectibles; Ceramics; Christmas Collectibles; Disney Collectibles; Dolls; Kitchenwares; Matchcovers & Match Boxes; Movie Memorabilia; Pinball Games; Pocket Knives; Radio & Television Memorabilia; Valentines; View-Master & Tru-Vue Viewers & Reels; Wedding Memorabilia

Charlie Chaplin - see Movie Memorabilia; Valentines

Charley McCarthy - see Radio & Television Memorabilia

Chests & Chests of Drawers - see Furniture

Christmas Collectibles 309
also see Advertising Items; Banks; Candy Containers; Cat Collectibles; Ceramics; Holiday Collectibles; Jewelry; Kitchenwares; Print Artists; Raggedy Ann & Andy Collectibles; Steamship Memorabilia; Toys; View-Master & Tru-Vue Viewers & Reels

Civil War - see Militaria & Wartime Memorabilia

Clocks..315
also see Advertising Items; Breweriana; Ceramics; Coca-Cola; Disney Collectibles; Metals; Political & Campaign Items; Raggedy Ann & Andy Collectibles; Steamship Memorabilia; Tobacciana
Coat Racks - see Furniture (Hall Racks & Trees)

Coca-Cola Items 328
also see Bottles; Matchcovers & Match Boxes; Pocket Knives

Coffee Mills - see Kitchenwares

Cologne Bottles - see Perfume, Scent & Cologne Bottles

Compacts & Vanity Cases 334

Copper - see Metals

Cupboards - see Furniture

Cranberry Rose Bowl with Applique, $125-$150

Rare Handel with Parrots Shade, $20,700

Shirley Temple Movie Sheet Music, $10-$20

FURNITURE DATING CHART

AMERICAN FURNITURE
Pilgrim Century – 1620-1700
William & Mary – 1685-1720
Queen Anne – 1720-50
Chippendale – 1750-85
Federal – 1785-1820
Hepplewhite – 1785-1800
Sheraton – 1800-20
Classical (American Empire) – 1815-40
Victorian – 1840-1900
Early Victorian – 1840-50
Gothic Revival – 1840-90
Rococo (Louis XV) – 1845-70
Renaissance Revival – 1860-85
Louis XVI – 1865-75
Eastlake – 1870-95
Jacobean & Turkish Revival – 1870-90
Aesthetic Movement – 1880-1900
Art Nouveau – 1895-1918
Turn-of-the Century
    (Early 20th Century) – 1895-1910
Mission-style
    (Arts & Crafts movement) – 1900-15
Colonial Revival – 1890-1930
Art Deco – 1925-40
Modernist or Mid-Century – 1945-70

ENGLISH FURNITURE
Jacobean – Mid-17th Century
William & Mary – 1689-1702
Queen Anne – 1702-14
George I – 1714-27
George II – 1727-60
George III – 1760-1820
Regency – 1811-20
George IV – 1820-30
William IV – 1830-37
Victorian – 1837-1901
Edwardian – 1901-10

FRENCH FURNITURE
Louis XV – 1715-74
Louis XVI – 1774-93
Empire – 1804-15
Louis Philippe – 1830-48
Napoleon III
    (Second Empire) – 1848-70
Art Nouveau – 1895-1910
Art Deco – 1925-35

Germanic Furniture
Since the country of Germany did not exist before 1870, furniture from the various Germanic states and the Austro-Hungarian Empire is generally termed simply "Germanic." From the 17th century onward furniture from these regions tended to follow the stylistic trends established in France and England. General terms are used for such early furniture usually classifying it as "Baroque," "Rococo" or a similar broad stylistic term. Germanic furniture dating from the first half of the 19th century is today usually referred to as Biedermeier, a style closely related to French Empire and English Regency.

AMERICAN FURNITURE TERMS

CHAIRS

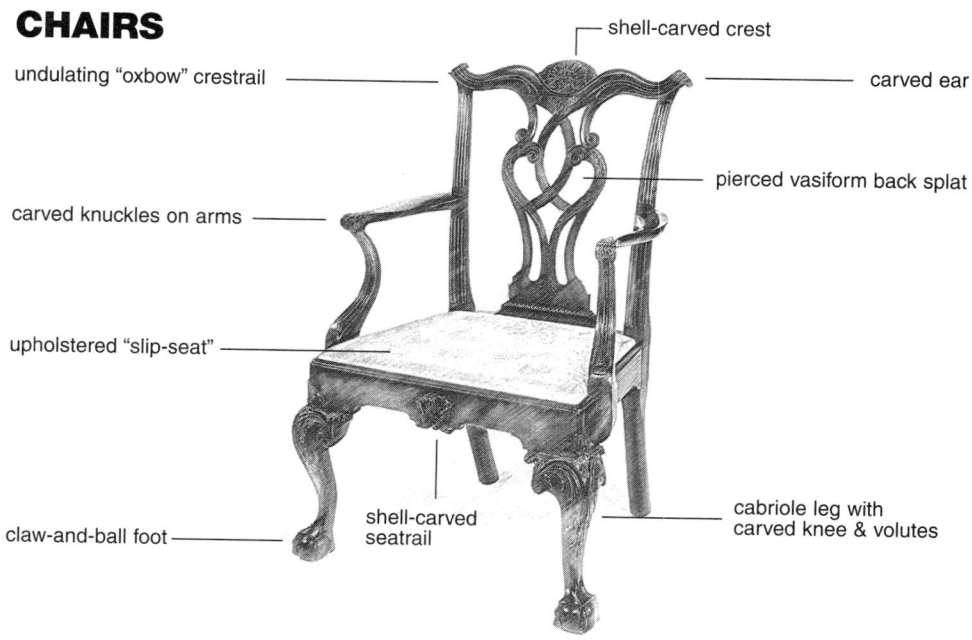

shell-carved crest

undulating "oxbow" crestrail

carved ear

pierced vasiform back splat

carved knuckles on arms

upholstered "slip-seat"

claw-and-ball foot

shell-carved seatrail

cabriole leg with carved knee & volutes

Chippendale Armchair

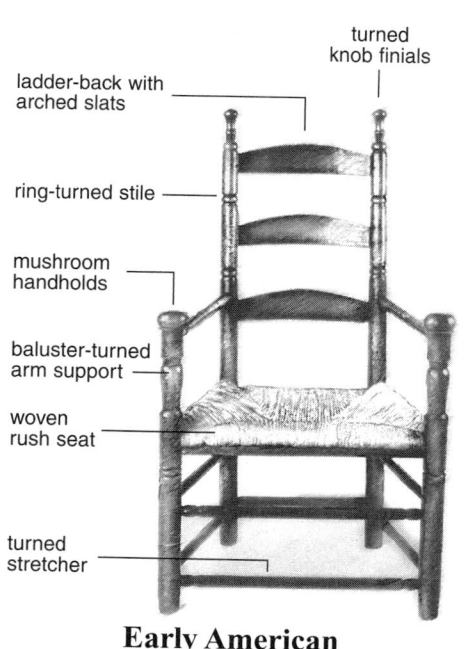

ladder-back with arched slats

turned knob finials

ring-turned stile

mushroom handholds

baluster-turned arm support

woven rush seat

turned stretcher

Early American "Ladder-back" Armchair

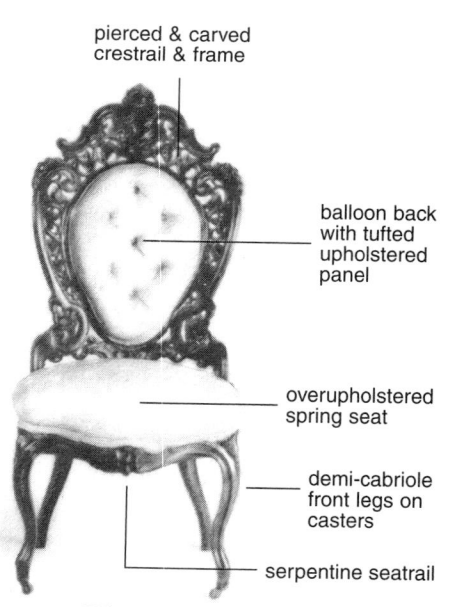

pierced & carved crestrail & frame

balloon back with tufted upholstered panel

overupholstered spring seat

demi-cabriole front legs on casters

serpentine seatrail

Victorian Roccoco Side Chair

CHESTS & TABLES

pierced brass pull

graduated drawers

straight bracket feet

shaped molded edge

pierced brass keyhole escutcheon

beaded drawer dividers & stiles

serpentine front

Chippendale Chest of Drawers

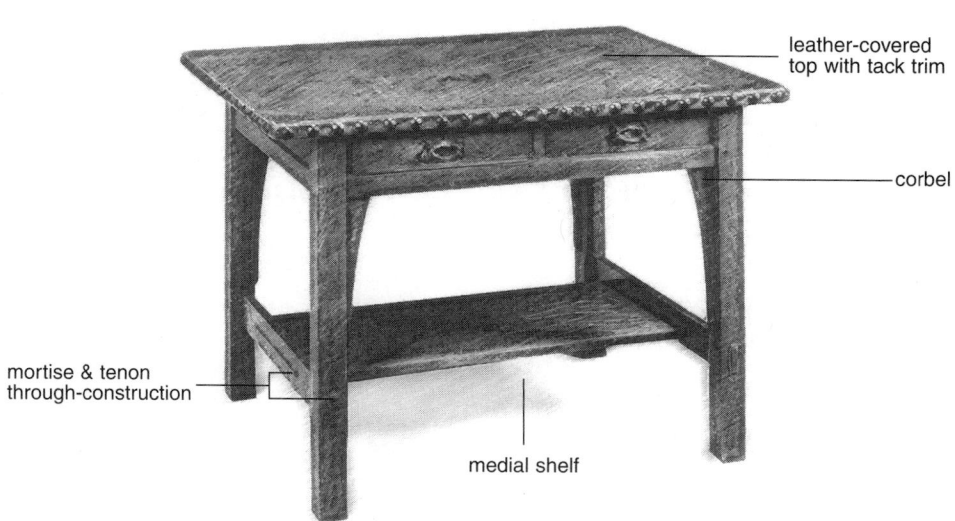

leather-covered top with tack trim

corbel

mortise & tenon through-construction

medial shelf

Mission Oak Library Table

FURNITURE PEDIMENTS & SKIRTS

Classic Pediment

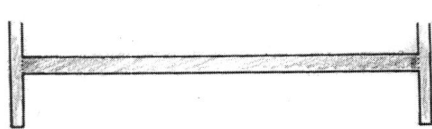

Plain Skirt

Broken Arch Pediment

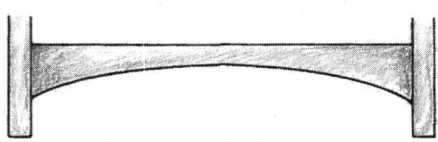

Arched Skirt

**Bonnet Top with
Urn & Flame Finial**

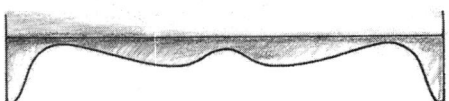

Valanced Skirt

**Bonnet Top with Rosettes &
Three Urn & Flame Finials**

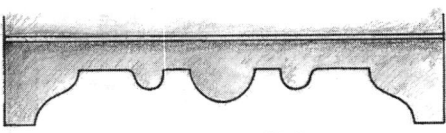

Scalloped Skirt

FURNITURE FEET

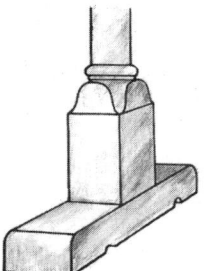

Trestle Foot

Pad Foot

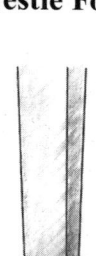

Block Foot

Slipper Foot

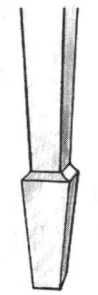

Spade Foot

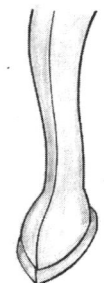

Snake Foot

Tapered or Plain Foot

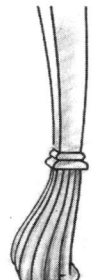

Spanish Foot

FURNITURE FEET

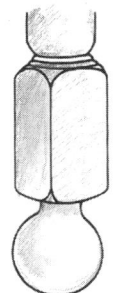

Ball Foot

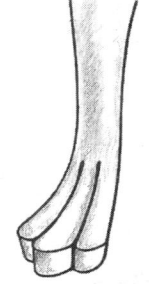

Trifid Foot

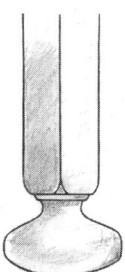

Bun Foot

Hoof Foot

Turnip Foot

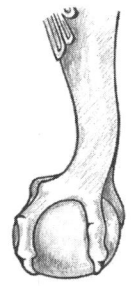

Claw-and-Ball Foot

Arrow or Peg Foot

Paw Foot